Handbook of Research on Entrepreneurship Development and Opportunities in Circular Economy

Neeta Baporikar
Namibia University of Science and Technology, Namibia & University of Pune, India

IGI Global
PUBLISHER of TIMELY KNOWLEDGE

A volume in the Advances in Business Strategy and Competitive Advantage (ABSCA) Book Series

Published in the United States of America by
IGI Global
Business Science Reference (an imprint of IGI Global)
701 E. Chocolate Avenue
Hershey PA, USA 17033
Tel: 717-533-8845
Fax: 717-533-8661
E-mail: cust@igi-global.com
Web site: http://www.igi-global.com

Copyright © 2020 by IGI Global. All rights reserved. No part of this publication may be reproduced, stored or distributed in any form or by any means, electronic or mechanical, including photocopying, without written permission from the publisher. Product or company names used in this set are for identification purposes only. Inclusion of the names of the products or companies does not indicate a claim of ownership by IGI Global of the trademark or registered trademark.

Library of Congress Cataloging-in-Publication Data

Names: Baporikar, Neeta, editor.
Title: Handbook of research on entrepreneurship development and opportunities in circular economy / Neeta Baporikar.
Description: Hershey : Business Science Reference, 2020. | Includes bibliographical references and index. | Summary: "This book advances the understanding of entrepreneurship development, identifies the opportunities, and manages the entrepreneurship development, policies, and programs in order to further a circular economy. In addition to entrepreneurship development and entrepreneurial opportunities, the book will cover and discuss a number of other factors necessary for a successful transformation, such as entrepreneurship and innovation, entrepreneurship and change, and entrepreneurship education"-- Provided by publisher.
Identifiers: LCCN 2020002716 (print) | LCCN 2020002717 (ebook) | ISBN 9781799851165 (hardback) | ISBN 9781799851172 (ebook)
Subjects: LCSH: Entrepreneurship. | Recycling industry. | Organizational change.
Classification: LCC HB615 .H265968 2020 (print) | LCC HB615 (ebook) | DDC 338/.04--dc23
LC record available at https://lccn.loc.gov/2020002716
LC ebook record available at https://lccn.loc.gov/2020002717

This book is published in the IGI Global book series Advances in Business Strategy and Competitive Advantage (ABSCA) (ISSN: 2327-3429; eISSN: 2327-3437)

British Cataloguing in Publication Data
A Cataloguing in Publication record for this book is available from the British Library.

All work contributed to this book is new, previously-unpublished material. The views expressed in this book are those of the authors, but not necessarily of the publisher.

For electronic access to this publication, please contact: eresources@igi-global.com.

Advances in Business Strategy and Competitive Advantage (ABSCA) Book Series

Patricia Ordóñez de Pablos
Universidad de Oviedo, Spain

ISSN:2327-3429
EISSN:2327-3437

Mission

Business entities are constantly seeking new ways through which to gain advantage over their competitors and strengthen their position within the business environment. With competition at an all-time high due to technological advancements allowing for competition on a global scale, firms continue to seek new ways through which to improve and strengthen their business processes, procedures, and profitability.

The **Advances in Business Strategy and Competitive Advantage (ABSCA) Book Series** is a timely series responding to the high demand for state-of-the-art research on how business strategies are created, implemented and re-designed to meet the demands of globalized competitive markets. With a focus on local and global challenges, business opportunities and the needs of society, the **ABSCA** encourages scientific discourse on doing business and managing information technologies for the creation of sustainable competitive advantage.

Coverage

- Economies of Scale
- Strategy Performance Management
- Cost Leadership Strategy
- Business Models
- Strategic alliances
- Co-operative Strategies
- Tacit Knowledge
- Small and Medium Enterprises
- Entrepreneurship & Innovation
- Innovation Strategy

IGI Global is currently accepting manuscripts for publication within this series. To submit a proposal for a volume in this series, please contact our Acquisition Editors at Acquisitions@igi-global.com or visit: http://www.igi-global.com/publish/.

The Advances in Business Strategy and Competitive Advantage (ABSCA) Book Series (ISSN 2327-3429) is published by IGI Global, 701 E. Chocolate Avenue, Hershey, PA 17033-1240, USA, www.igi-global.com. This series is composed of titles available for purchase individually; each title is edited to be contextually exclusive from any other title within the series. For pricing and ordering information please visit http://www.igi-global.com/book-series/advances-business-strategy-competitive-advantage/73672. Postmaster: Send all address changes to above address. Copyright © 2020 IGI Global. All rights, including translation in other languages reserved by the publisher. No part of this series may be reproduced or used in any form or by any means – graphics, electronic, or mechanical, including photocopying, recording, taping, or information and retrieval systems – without written permission from the publisher, except for non commercial, educational use, including classroom teaching purposes. The views expressed in this series are those of the authors, but not necessarily of IGI Global.

Titles in this Series

For a list of additional titles in this series, please visit:
http://www.igi-global.com/book-series/advances-business-strategy-competitive-advantage/73672

Principles and Practices of Small-Scale Sport Event Management
Anestis Fotiadis (Zayed University, UAE) and Chris Vassiliadis (University of Macedonia, Greece)
Business Science Reference • © 2020 • 335pp • H/C (ISBN: 9781799847571) • US $215.00

Entrepreneurial Innovation for Securing Long-Term Growth in a Short-Term Economy
Jorge Gamez-Gutierrez (Universitaria Agustiniana, Colombia) and Jose Manuel Saiz-Alvarez (Tecnologico de Monterrey, Spain)
Business Science Reference • © 2020 • 300pp • H/C (ISBN: 9781799835684) • US $215.00

Handbook of Research on Transmedia Storytelling, Audience Engagement, and Business Strategies
Víctor Hernández-Santaolalla (University of Seville, Spain) and Mónica Barrientos-Bueno (University of Seville, Spain)
Business Science Reference • © 2020 • 457pp • H/C (ISBN: 9781799831198) • US $265.00

Developing Creative Economy Through Disruptive Leadership Emerging Research and Opportunities
Kristin Joyce Tardif (University of Arkansas – Fort Smith, USA)
Business Science Reference • © 2020 • 226pp • H/C (ISBN: 9781799834168) • US $185.00

Knowledge Management, Innovation, and Entrepreneurship in a Changing World
Murray Eugene Jennex (San Diego State University, USA)
Business Science Reference • © 2020 • 463pp • H/C (ISBN: 9781799823551) • US $215.00

Developing Entrepreneurial Competencies for Start-Ups and Small Business
Jarmila Šebestová (Silesian University in Opava, Czech Republic)
Business Science Reference • © 2020 • 316pp • H/C (ISBN: 9781799827146) • US $225.00

Leadership and Followership in an Organizational Change Context
Sajjad Nawaz Khan (University Malaysia Sarawak, Malaysia) and Abdul Halim Busari (University Malaysia Sarawak, Malaysia)
Business Science Reference • © 2020 • 300pp • H/C (ISBN: 9781799828075) • US $225.00

Digital Marketing Strategies and Models for Competitive Business
Filipe Mota Pinto (Polytechnic Institute of Leiria, Portugal) and Teresa Guarda (Universidad Peninsula de Santa Elena (UPSE), Ecuador)
Business Science Reference • © 2020 • 240pp • H/C (ISBN: 9781799829638) • US $225.00

IGI Global
PUBLISHER of TIMELY KNOWLEDGE

701 East Chocolate Avenue, Hershey, PA 17033, USA
Tel: 717-533-8845 x100 • Fax: 717-533-8661
E-Mail: cust@igi-global.com • www.igi-global.com

Editorial Advisory Board

Elena Burdenko, *Plekhanov Russian University of Economics, Russia*
Mukund Deshpande, *Independent Researcher, India*
Teresa Dieguez, *ICPA, Portugal*
Vannie Naidoo, *University of KwaZulu-Natal, South Africa*
Ninel Nesheva-Kiosseva, *New Bulgarian University, Bulgaria*
Rafael Pérez-Uribe, *EAN University, Colombia*
Damini Saini, *Indian Institute of Management, Raipur, India*
Jose Manuel Saiz-Alvarez, *EGADE Business School, Tecnologico de Monterrey, Mexico*
Michael Torres Franco, *EAN University, Colombia*
José Vargas-Hernández, *University of Guadalajara, Mexico*

List of Reviewers

Wilfred Isak April, *University of Namibia, Namibia*
Sulaiman Atiku, *Namibia University of Science and Technology, Namibia*
Dileep Baragde, *G. S. Moze College, India*
Peterson Dewah, *National University of Science and Technology, Zimbabwe*
Mufaro Dzingirai, *Midlands State University, Zimbabwe*
Idahosa Igbinakhase, *University of KwaZulu-Natal, South Africa*
Gordana Jukic, *The University of Belgrade, Serbia*
Nyanjige Mbembela Mayala, *Moshi Co-Operative University, Tanzania*
Takaruza Munyanyiwa, *Apollos University, USA*
K.S. Sastry Musti, *Namibia University of Science and Technology, Namibia*
Harold Andrew Patrick, *Jain University (Deemed), India*
Yanamandra Ramakrishna, *Skyline University College, UAE*
Colin Reddy, *University of Johannesburg, South Africa*
Sigried Shikokola, *Ministry of Safety and Security, Namibia*
Booysen Tubulingane, *Namibia University of Science and Technology, Namibia*
Hylton Villet, *Namibia University of Science and Technology, Namibia*

List of Contributors

Table of Contents

Detailed Table of Contents

Humankind wastes resources in a way that is unsustainable over time, which makes it necessary and desirable to implement waste recycling policies that benefit all of humanity. The arrival of the circular economy is strengthening the environmental awareness of the population as well as more efficient use of scarce resources on the planet. In addition to the circular economy, this chapter briefly analyzes the different models that currently exist to combat the deterioration of the environment, since it is the responsibility of current generations to leave a better world for future generations.

The purpose of this chapter is to analyze the green and circular economy (GCE) model from the point of view of the resources and capacities of the organization. How is the application of the circular economy model related to strategic management? At first glance, it seems that the CE is operating within an operational level with a social impact. However, it also has implications that allow us to think that it can be used as an internal resource of the company that, if applied in the right way, can become a competitive advantage. In other words, the application of the CE is related to strategic management through the point of view based on resources and capabilities. Therefore, the present investigation has a descriptive-correlational nature, which was analyzed through Peng's VRIO framework.

The arguments for growth, inequality and persistent poverty, climate change, and finite resources call for stronger sustainable development policies, from both developed and developing countries. Situations of more or less (un)sustainability that encourage the idea of finding reasonable ways out of humanity's desire for progress can be conceived. The economy is nowadays mainly based on the called linear economy, which demands a paradigm shift within public administration, companies, and citizens must be committed. The present study has the main goal to understand how entrepreneurship and business have shaped the sustainability and the circular economy model requirements. It also aims to review important concepts like circular economy, sustainable development, sustainable entrepreneurship, servitization, and product-service system. A hypothetical conceptual model for the operationalization of the circular economy model is proposed. Finally, some discussion is done, future research is suggested, and conclusions are presented.

The reflections of linear and circular economy models, which are completely separated from each other in the ways of evaluating resources and wastes, also differ completely in the production and consumption processes. The linear economy, which consists of production and consumption mechanisms, converts resources into waste after using one time and is supported by planned obsolescence practices and causes economic and environmental damages. The scarcity of resources and the pressure of environmental pollution have led to an industrial transformation in which production and consumption forms redesigned in a way that does not create waste. Because of this transformation, the circular economy model emerged, and its application direction evolved to cradle-to-cradle practices. In this study, firstly, the linear economy model and planned obsolescence are discussed, and then circular economy and cradle-to-cradle applications are explained with examples.

Circular economy and innovation are creating a new scenario for companies. There are many frameworks in the market, which allow a company to manage risks. In this chapter, some of these frameworks are analyzed to try to determine how helpful they are in an enterprise to succeed in managing risks. The authors have been working with one of the existing risks frameworks of risk management, but digital transformation and circular economy have introduced new variables and factors that have to be taken into account. New features need to be defined into a new risk management framework, having in mind the velocity of change of information technologies. Success factors are also considered to complete this perspective.

The aim of this chapter is to present the state of the art of academic research in the intersection between circular economy and tourism, trying to identify the approaches used by authors when studying the application of circular economy principles and initiatives in the tourism industry. For this purpose, a systematic search in ISI Web of Science and Scopus databases was performed. The characterization of research carried out in this field, with both a bibliometric and bibliographic analysis, is offered, presenting a detailed picture of the content of the research carried out in the abovementioned intersection, synthesizing what has been done so far. To conclude, a research agenda is proposed to develop this still understudied domain.

The main characteristic of pension systems is financial stability. The authors will present some models of the pension system, economics models such as the theory of income uncertainty, overlapping generations' model. The authors will present the interrelation of employment, population, and circular economy, trying to improve the existing pension system in Serbia. The circular economy is a response to the growing needs of humanity. It is referred to as sustainable development in all the spheres of human life. The circular economies can also refer to the sustainability of the pension system, which is linked to the quality of life. The quality of life is part of sustainable development as its social component. The chapter provides an overview of the sustainability of the pension system by reducing the costs with employment increasing. As an example of good practice, the authors present Australia and Chile in a small analysis that indicates pension fund sustainability. This practice can serve as an example of the improvement of the pension system in Serbia and similar smaller countries.

New forms of production and consumption seek greater respect for the environment and the environment in which economic agents are. This has led to circular business practices becoming more important and generating benefits in the final product. This chapter will show the relationship between this practice and SMEs, the problems faced by these companies, and the benefits that this practice can generate for the growth and competitiveness of organizations. The chapter will show in its first part the evolution of the circular economy, and then explain the relationship between it and the SMEs, highlighting the problems and obstacles faced by these companies to implement best practices in production. Finally, recommendations are given to facilitate the implementation of this practice in companies.

The chapter focuses on the historical aspect of economic development stages. It identifies agriculture-based, industrial, and post-industrial economies' characteristics. It is demonstrable that the problem of limited resources, the use of waste from consumption, and production has always existed. However, these problems were solved differently in different historical periods. The accumulated problems can be solved by the transition to a circular economy model. When studying the Russian experience in the transition to a circular economy model, the focus remains on Russian legislation. The example of Russian industrial enterprises shows the practical application of the circular economy principles. The research covers such enterprises as PJSC NK ROSNEFT (which includes PJSC ANK Bashneft, Bashneft-Ufaneftekhim, JSC Novokuibyshevsky Oil Refinery, and JSC Rospan International), PJSC TATNEFT, PJSC MMC Norilsk Nickel, PJSC Magnitogorsk Iron and Steel Works. The presentation is on strategies, policies, and programs aimed at ensuring industrial safety, labor protections, and the environment.

The purpose of this chapter is to explore some of the problems of the transformation necessary to the business model of water and wastewater utility companies into a circular economy. This goal is accomplished by extending the understanding of the business model beyond the conventional understanding "within the framework of the corporation." This expansion of the scope of the water and wastewater utility companies' business model is justified by the fact that water, the source of their business, is a vital natural capital, and along with its economic value, water is a recognized human right. The study elaborates on the part of the business model related to the issues of fair treatment of society in its relations with business. The authors also explore the issue of value creation for stakeholders not only within a business but also through cooperation between water businesses and stakeholders.

The circular economy (CE) model has become highly relevant in recent years, with the electronics industry being one of the divisions that have thought about its application. Regardless of just a constrained measure of writing being accessible on waste electric and electronic equipment (e-waste), electronic waste or e-waste is a developing and quickly developing test for waste administration in the world. E-waste is a term for electronic items that have turned out to be undesirable, non-working, or outdated, and have basically come to the 'part of the arrangement', inside only a couple of brief years, given the quick innovative advances inside the business. E-waste is created from anything electronic —PCs, TVs, screens, PDAs, PDAs, VCRs, CD players, fax machines, printers, and coolers— and is commonly broken into two classes, information technology (IT) and consumer electronics (CE), on account of divergent systems and technologies required for recycling these products.

Entrepreneurship plays a significant role in national economies around the world, including the Republic of Zimbabwe, which has largely focused on the socio-economic devolution program. The necessity for entrepreneurship and policymakers around the world currently is to advance the quality of the entrepreneurship outcomes rather than just increase the number of entrepreneurs. To strengthen the context of entrepreneurship and innovation, the authors suggested that governments need to move to what is called an entrepreneurial ecosystem approach. Isenberg's model for the entrepreneurial ecosystem is applied as a catalyst for building a robust entrepreneurial ecosystem under circular economies.

This chapter acknowledges the undeniable fact that the manufacturing sector plays a key role in the growth of any economy, and it is from this sector that Tanzania can catch up with the rest of the world. The stagnant contribution share of the manufacturing sector is linked with implementation lags on ambitious, uncoordinated plans and slow transforming economic structure, which is dominated by agriculture and competition from low priced manufactured import from Asian economies. Shifting the labor force from agriculture to manufacturing remains the best option for the country to enhance efforts towards industrialization, thus increasing the overall productivity. On the other hand, entrepreneurship and policies have a multifaceted nature and linkages with other areas, such as education and skills development, technology and innovation, finance and capacity building. Multiple new types of financial instruments can contribute to diversifying the financial solutions available to Tanzanian entrepreneurs in the process of industrialization.

In this chapter, some key factors of the companies were analyzed, which during the development of their activities marked positively or negatively their passage through different growth scenarios for the transition from a medium to a large company in a circular economy in Colombia. The methodology that served as the basis of analysis aimed at compiling the information in secondary sources of the growth data in the last five years (2014-2018) of 100 medium and large Colombians with more operational income. Focus explicitly was one those working with the concept of a circular economy, registered in public sources in Colombia, such as the superintendence of companies (Supersocieties) and EMIS database. After this analysis, the findings, conclusions, and steps of the analysis model were identified so that the transition between the different scenarios proposed would produce the expected results to the companies. The working hypothesis was that there are some key factors that allow a medium-sized company to become

Preface

Entrepreneurship is the capacity and willingness to develop, organize and manage a business venture along with any of its risks to make a profit. Thus, entrepreneurship comprises both "enterprising individuals" and "entrepreneurial opportunities" (Baporikar, 2018b; 2014). The knowledge economy has already paved the way to a different breed of entrepreneurs and enterprises (Baporikar, 2016). The shift has been from mortar to mental models and brick to e platforms. Hence the need to study not only the nature of the individuals who identify opportunities when others do not but also the opportunities themselves and the nexus between individuals, opportunities and prevalent economic systems.

Over the last decade, the concept of the circular economy has regained attention, especially related to efforts to achieve a more sustainable society (Reike, Vermeulen & Witjes, 2018). Further, many multinational companies and small and medium-sized enterprises are becoming aware of the potential benefits and are beginning to explore the options of circular economy business models (Schroeder, Anggraeni & Weber, 2019). Switching from the current linear model of the economy to a circular one has recently attracted increased attention from major global companies e.g., Google, Unilever, Renault, and policymakers attending the World Economic Forum as there are likely to be huge financial, social and environmental benefits (Lewandowski, 2016). However, the global shift from one model of the economy to another also concerns entrepreneurs and smaller companies on a micro-level and their sustainability (Baporikar, 2018a). Thus, comprehensive research and knowledge on designing circular business models are needed to stimulate and foster the implementation of the circular economy.

With the need for sustainability, what is emerging is a focus on developing an economic system, which aims at minimizing waste and commonly referred to as "circular economy" based on the concept of "circularity". The circular economy makes both environmental and business sense. In the circular economy, growth no longer requires an increasing extraction and consumption of resources, energy, water, and primary raw materials. There is no waste and products and resources maintain their value in the economy for as long as possible (European Commission, 2017). A circular economy is an economic system aimed at minimizing waste and making the most of resources. To eliminate waste and ensure the sustainability world over there is a refocus on economic systems and herein is the pitch of the Circular Economy (CE). The circular economy and studies related to it have gained worldwide attention, as it seems to be an effective alternative economic system. That means there is likely to be a shift in how entrepreneurship development and entrepreneurial opportunities will be perceived, developed and resourced. Hence, the focus of this book will be to examine entrepreneurship development and the emerging opportunities in the circular economy.

Further, the book is dedicated to "entrepreneurship" with a special emphasis on entrepreneurs in a circular economy. It provides discussion and the exchange of information on principles, strategies, models, techniques, methodologies, and applications of entrepreneurship in the circular economy in the field of public and private organizations. It aims to communicate the latest developments and thinking on the entrepreneurship subject worldwide. Drawing on the latest developments, ideas, research, and best practice, this book intends to examine the implications of the changes taking place due to circularity focus and how this affect entrepreneurship and motivation of entrepreneurs belonging to this economic paradigm, It is important to know what is happening on both national and international fronts to be able to understand and develop effective responses to meet these new demands.

Entrepreneurs and entrepreneurship have always been the key to prosperity but in today's circular economies who are these entrepreneurs and what does entrepreneurship include? What are the developments sweeping over economies? As entrepreneurship becomes increasingly intertwined with the global economy, investment continues to be done in entrepreneurship development. Especially in knowledge-based circular economies; entrepreneurship development is not a unidirectional effort of a region that follows from developed world economies, but also in a complex pattern that involves investment at the regional or individual economy level which means it is more multi-perspective. A multidimensional approach to entrepreneurship, especially in the circular economy, is having an important influence on the state of business and government, especially when considering the effects of technological development, innovation, glocalization and nationalization policies which are being adopted for inclusive sustainable regional growth utilization for enhanced and efficient resources.

The circular economy has high economic potential; it is a driver for a modernized economy with high environmental relevance while contributing to the SDGs (European Commission, 2017). This needs to be underpinned by strong research and innovation to ensure apt solutions to transform its potential into reality. To achieve a circular economy, there is a need for incremental and ground-breaking innovations. Further, companies and organizations are increasingly aware of the importance of people and their knowledge for dealing with economic scenarios as complex as those we are seeing today, and of individuals with a capacity for long-term vision and leadership. How these knowledge interplays in developing entrepreneurship in the circular economy is the core of this book.

The subject area is a combination of entrepreneurship, circular economy, growth, and development. The goal of this book is to be an international platform to bring together academics, researchers, decision-makers, policymakers, and practitioners for sharing new theories, research findings, and case studies to enhance understanding and collaboration in issues of entrepreneurship development and opportunities in the circular economy.

OBJECTIVE OF THE BOOK

This book explores the need to advance the understanding of entrepreneurship development, identify the opportunities, and manage entrepreneurship development, policies, and programs to further a circular economy. In addition to entrepreneurship development and entrepreneurial opportunities, the book will cover and discuss several other factors necessary for a successful transformation, such as entrepreneurship and innovation, entrepreneurship and change and entrepreneurship education. Addressing the different challenges of the circular economy envisioned it outlines strategies, policies, and models needed to gain momentum for entrepreneurship development in different and emerging sectors.

TARGET AUDIENCE

The primary intended audience is scholar-practitioners who require qualified Reference material regarding the subject matter of the proposed publication as outlined above. The secondary intended audience is managers, organization development specialists, consultants, educationalists, policymakers and undergraduate/graduate business students who require the same Reference material. At the same time, while having academic rigor, the writing of the book will be in a way such that non-academics and non-specialists can understand it; it will be appealing to the public.

TOPICS OF INTEREST

The book includes, among others, the following topics of interest for academics and practitioners:

- Evolution of Economics Systems;
- Entrepreneurship Ecosystem, Opportunities, and Education;
- Opportunities and Challenges in Circular Economy;
- Creativity and Innovation in Circular Economy;
- Knowledge Management in Circular Economy;
- SMEs in Circular Economy;
- Management and Leadership in Circular Economy;
- Principles of Circular Economy;
- Practices in Circular Economy;
- Case studies and Sector Applications.

This book presents a collection of 30 chapters contributed by academicians, researchers, practitioners, and managers, who are experts in the field and each chapter address a key topic. For better readability and lucidity the book is divided into three sections: Principles and Practices of Circular Economy, Entrepreneurship and Economic Development in Circular Economy and Managing Circular Economy. A brief outline of 30 chapters is given below:

Chapter 1: "Circular Economy: An Emerging Paradigm - Concept, Principles, and Characteristics," discusses on circular economy and analyzes the different models that currently exist to combat the deterioration of the environment.

Chapter 2: "Circular Green Economy: Resources and Capabilities - Theory-Based Analysis," analyzes the Green and Circular Economy (GCE) model from the resources and capacities of the organization.

Chapter 3: "Operationalization of Circular Economy: A Conceptual Model," aims to understand how entrepreneurship and business have shaped the sustainability and the circular economy model requirements and proposes a hypothetical conceptual model for the operationalization of the circular economy model.

Chapter 4: "Linear Economy to Circular Economy: Planned Obsolescence to Cradle-to-Cradle Products Perspective," discusses first the linear economy model and planned obsolescence and explains with examples a circular economy to cradle-to-cradle applications.

Chapter 5: "Circular Economy and Risk Management Synergies in Disruptive Environment," deliberates on frameworks to manage risks in the circular economy. The author also considers the new features which need to be defined into a new risk management framework, due to the velocity of change of information technologies and also identify the success factors.

Chapter 6: "Opportunities and Challenges of Circular Economy for the Tourism Industry," present the state of the art of academic research in the intersection between circular economy and tourism.

Chapter 7: "Sustainability of Mandatory Pension Insurance in Circular Economy: A Comparative Analysis," presents models of the pension system and economics. The chapter provides an overview of the sustainability of the pension system and also present good practices of Australia and Chile that indicate pension fund sustainability.

Chapter 8: "Implementation of Circular Practices in Small and Medium Enterprises in Developing Countries," shows the relationship between circular practice and SMEs. Problems faced by SMEs, benefits of circular practices to generate growth and competitiveness with the implementation methods of best practices in production are the coverage.

Chapter 9: "Circular Economy Experience: A Russian Perspective," focuses on the historical aspect of economic development stages in the context of Russian experience transition to a circular economy model.

Chapter 10: "Sustainability and Justness for Transforming the Water Utility Companies' Business Model in the Circular Economy," explore the problems of the transformation necessary to the business model of water and wastewater utility companies into a circular economy.

Chapter 11: "Circular Economy Model for E-Waste Management Sector," presents the importance of circular economy model for the E-waste management sector where e-waste is created from anything electronic: PCs, TVs, screens, PDAs, PDAs, VCRs, CD players, fax machines, printers, etc.

Chapter 12: "Development of Supply Chain Framework for Circular Economy," highlights the significance of circular economy by developing a supply chain framework (SCM) to reduce the imbalance and wastage created due to rapid pace at which technology has contributed technological products and gadgets to create a surplus in some areas and deficiencies in some areas of the modern world.

Chapter 13: "Circular Economy in Energizing Smart Cities," focuses on opportunities and challenges of adopting circular economy principles in the energy sector specifically in managing futuristic smart cities and a novel, industry 4.0 based information system for monitoring various energy-related processes in a smart city with the conceptual dashboard to visualize key indicators; is proposed.

Chapter 14: "Entrepreneurial Motivation to Participate in Circular Economy," develops an academic argument using expectancy theory to understand an entrepreneur's motivation to participate in the circular economy which is critical for entrepreneurial development in this alternative economy.

Chapter 15: "Application of Isenberg Model for Entrepreneurial Ecosystem as Blueprint for Zimbabwe Socio-Economic Devolution," deliberates on the application of Isenberg's model for the development of the entrepreneurial ecosystem as a catalyst for building a robust entrepreneurial ecosystem under circular economies in the context of the Republic of Zimbabwe that has largely focused on the Socio-Economic Devolution Program.

Chapter 16: "Industrialization in Tanzania: A Window of Entrepreneurial Opportunity," critically reviews the role of the manufacturing sector in Tanzania for economic growth as a window of opportunity for entrepreneurship development in a circular economy.

Chapter 17: "Transitioning From Medium to Large Companies in Circular Economy: Key Factors for Colombian Companies," analyzes some key factors of the companies in Colombia, which during the development of their activities marked positively or negatively their passage through different growth scenarios for the transition from medium to a large company in the circular economy.

Chapter 18: "Youth Entrepreneurship in the Circular Economy," is a critical analysis of youth entrepreneurship in a circular economy. Challenges experienced by youth entrepreneurs and key solutions to these challenges faced by youth entrepreneurs form the core of the discussion.

Chapter 19: "Women's Power as Employees and Entrepreneurs in Circular Economy: A Comparative Analysis," measures optimism in terms of success factors and lack of success factors through a study of the personality and optimism level of women employees and women entrepreneurs in the circular economy.

Chapter 20: "Viability of Entrepreneurship Education for Employability to Meet Industry 4.0 Challenges in Circular Economy: A Namibian Case," analyses the viability of the current state of entrepreneurial education in Namibian higher education institutions, as a case study and in the process also identifies the educational benefits and challenges in implementing circular entrepreneurial education.

Chapter 21: "Design Thinking Perspective in Entrepreneurship Education," captures in detail the worldwide practices and controversies associated with entrepreneurship education from a design thinking standpoint.

Chapter 22: "Critical Review of Entrepreneurship Development in Namibia," is a critical review of entrepreneurship development in Namibia to suggest the way forward regarding entrepreneurship development for youth and entrepreneurs to fight poverty and unemployment.

Chapter 23: "Entrepreneurship Development Interventions as a Pragmatic Approach to Political and Economic Restructuring in Nigeria," discusses the imperative of entrepreneurship development interventions as pragmatic responses to political and economic restructuring in Nigeria.

Chapter 24: "Inclusive Markets and Enterprises' Growth Through Public-Private Partnerships for Local Economic Development," explores the rationale of inclusive markets and enterprises' growth through PPPs for local economic development to identify suitable recommendations for improvement.

Chapter 25: "Knowledge Management for Entrepreneurship Development in Circular Economy," looks at the ability of knowledge management to revamp the economy and reduce the awful environmental impact. The chapter reveals a three-prong approach based on economics, regulations, and technology dimensions as important to the development of entrepreneurship in a circular economy.

Chapter 26: "Sustainable Entrepreneurship and Management Skills at Crossroad in Circular Economy," explores the relationship between entrepreneurship and management skills within a circular economy and also examines problems and solutions to developing sustainable entrepreneurship.

Chapter 27: "Knowledge Management for Circular Economy," presents the importance of knowledge management in ensuring effective transition into a circular economy by developing a circular business model as an alternative to the conventional linear economic model.

Chapter 28: "Creativity and Innovation for Entrepreneurs' in Circular Economy," deliberates on the role of creativity and innovation for SMEs if they are to uplift a country's economic wellbeing by creating jobs and alleviating poverty.

Chapter 29: "Leadership to Cultivate the Circular Economy," discusses the valuable role of leadership to ensure sustainable development within a business so that it can create value for customers, investors, and the environment. The purpose of this chapter is to highlight in which ways leadership can be helpful to cultivate and promote the circular economy.

Chapter 30: "Measuring Infopreneurial Intentions of Library and Information Science Graduating Students," aims to measure the extent to which the graduating students from the Department of Library and Information Science intend to venture into infopreneurship in Zimbabwe.

In short, this book includes a wide variety of approaches, problems, and discussions in the field of entrepreneurship development and opportunities in a circular economy. It provides color and fresh look at some difficult concepts and a field that is difficult to unify. The expertise provided herein comes from all over the world, and although there are common themes among the chapters, each provides a unique viewpoint that results from cultural and geographic differences. I believe that such diversity of thought is a necessary component in the advancement of the body of knowledge, regardless of the discipline of inquiry. I hope that you agree and enjoy the contributions of our authors. Alongside the established theories and concepts, the reader will encounter several issues for discussion promoted and defended by different contributors from many countries. This book is aimed at a wide audience of potential readers, including students, teachers, researchers, entrepreneurs, managers, and policymakers. I trust that the book will provide an opportunity to learn about new ideas and methods of entrepreneurship in a circular economy based on a cross-cultural context. The book also focuses on expanding and improving entrepreneurship teaching and knowledge-transfer activities, for policymakers to appropriate support initiatives and frameworks apart from enhanced understanding to stimulate additional research in this area.

The transformation from a linear to a circular economy is ambitious. But together, we can make the circular economy a reality for a better world for all and in sum, *Handbook of Research on Entrepreneurship Development and Opportunities in Circular Economy* is a step in that direction by presenting an inclusive analysis and blends of the research streams on entrepreneurship development and opportunities in the circular economy. It provides an understanding of this complex and multi-faceted process. It is useful in guiding future research as it presents comprehensive knowledge relating to entrepreneurship in the circular economy. It is the first book that gives systematic information about entrepreneurship development, opportunities, global implications, entrepreneurship education with some interesting sectored applications, practices and case studies in circular economies.

On a final note, we expect the readers and users to cherish the contents as much as we enjoyed putting them together and hope that this book will further the cause of quality higher education for entrepreneurship development, which is crucial in the emergent knowledge economy.

Neeta Baporikar
Namibia University of Science and Technology, Namibia & University of Pune, India

REFERENCES

Baporikar, N. (2014). *Entrepreneurial Education (Process of Creating Entrepreneurs)*. Mumbai, India: Himalaya Publishing House.

Baporikar, N. (2016). *Handbook of Research on Entrepreneurship in the Contemporary Knowledge-Based Global Economy*. Hershey, PA: IGI Global. doi:10.4018/978-1-4666-8798-1

Baporikar, N. (2018a). *Knowledge Integration Strategies for Entrepreneurship and Sustainability*. Hershey, PA: IGI Global; doi:10.4018/978-1-5225-5115-7

Baporikar, N. (2018b). *Entrepreneurship Development & Project Management (Text and Cases)*. Mumbai, India: Himalaya Publishing House.

European Commission, Directorate-General for Research and Innovation. (2017). *Circular Economy Research and Innovation: Connecting Economic & Environmental Gains*. Publications Office of the European Union.

Lewandowski, M. (2016). Designing the business models for circular economy—Towards the conceptual framework. *Sustainability*, *8*(1), 43. doi:10.3390u8010043

Reike, D., Vermeulen, W. J., & Witjes, S. (2018). The circular economy: New or refurbished as CE 3.0?—exploring controversies in the conceptualization of the circular economy through a focus on history and resource value retention options. *Resources, Conservation and Recycling*, *135*, 246–264. doi:10.1016/j.resconrec.2017.08.027

Schroeder, P., Anggraeni, K., & Weber, U. (2019). The relevance of circular economy practices to sustainable development goals. *Journal of Industrial Ecology*, *23*(1), 77–95. doi:10.1111/jiec.12732

Acknowledgment

I thank the editorial staff at IGI Global for providing the opportunity to create this handbook.

It was indeed an interesting and joyful experience for me, due to their smooth and supportive process. In addition, the contributors and the reviewers of the chapters provided the opportunity to create a resource that I think will benefit researchers, practitioners and global community. Hence, I would like to express my heartfelt thanks to all the authors for their high-quality contributions and reviewers for their effort in providing constructive comments and useful suggestions. The successful completion of this book has been the result of cooperation of many people, including the editorial advisory board. I express my thanks and gratitude to all of them.

I am indebted to my husband Jayant and daughter Neha. Their continued support in my writing and research journey enables me to see the value of discovering and applying new-fangled knowledge with a hope, that fresh opportunities open up for one and all.

Neeta Baporikar
Namibia University of Science and Technology, Namibia & University of Pune, India

Section 1

Principles and Practice of the Circular Economy

Chapter 1
Circular Economy:
An Emerging Paradigm – Concept, Principles, and Characteristics

José Manuel Saiz-Alvarez
https://orcid.org/0000-0001-6435-9600
The Enzo Faletto Center for Studies and Research, University of Santiago de Chile and the Mexican Academy of Sciences, Mexico

ABSTRACT

Humankind wastes resources in a way that is unsustainable over time, which makes it necessary and desirable to implement waste recycling policies that benefit all of humanity. The arrival of the circular economy is strengthening the environmental awareness of the population as well as more efficient use of scarce resources on the planet. In addition to the circular economy, this chapter briefly analyzes the different models that currently exist to combat the deterioration of the environment, since it is the responsibility of current generations to leave a better world for future generations.

INTRODUCTION

According to the World Bank (2012), each year, 1.3 billion tons of garbage are produced by 3 billion urban residents, which uses 54 percent of the world's delivered energy, especially in energy-intensive industries such as petrochemicals, cement, metals, and paper (United States of America Energy Information Administration, 2016). Besides, each year, 322 million tons of plastic, 240 million tons of paper and 59 million tons of aluminum are produced in the world (FAO, 2017; World Aluminum, 2016), much of which goes to export markets and is not recycled (Plastics Europe, 2016).

This strong waste of resources is unsustainable over time, which makes it necessary and desirable to implement waste recycling policies, which benefits all of humanity. In this sense, the arrival of the circular economy is strengthening the environmental awareness of the population, as well as the more efficient use of scarce resources.

As a result, circular models could help nations raise with resources already available in their regions. This may imply a decrease in global trade, yet the 140 million people joining the middle class each year

DOI: 10.4018/978-1-7998-5116-5.ch001

Copyright © 2020, IGI Global. Copying or distributing in print or electronic forms without written permission of IGI Global is prohibited.

promise progress in trade (Kharas, 2017). The circular economy is a reply to the aspiration for sustainable growth in the context of the growing pressure of production, mass distribution, and consumption on the limited planet's scarce economic resources. Until now, the economy has mainly operated on a 'take-make-dispose' model – a linear model where every product is bound to reach its 'end of life' (European Commission, 2014), to be rejected and thrown away after it.

With the final scope of designing product circularity, business is in the driver's seat in the changeover to a circular economy. Short product lifetimes have been a key tactic for many companies in the past, promoting frequent advancements to adapt the cleanest technologies in the market. Now, a business can hold opportunities to extend product lifetimes and create competitive and sustainable products that will last for a long time to benefit new generations.

The objective of this chapter is to analyze what is understood by the circular economy, as well as to compare it with other similar concepts that also seek environmental sustainability. All these facts will give us foot to analyze its principles and characteristics.

A NEW PARADIGM?

The circular economy is understood as "an economic system that represents a change of paradigm in the way that human society is interrelated with nature and aims to prevent the depletion of resources, close energy and materials loops, and facilitate sustainable development through its implementation at the micro(enterprises and consumers), meso (economic agents integrated in symbiosis) and macro (city, regions, and governments) levels. Attaining this circular model requires cyclical and regenerative environmental innovations in the way society legislates, produces, and consumes" (Prieto-Sandoval et al., 2018, p. 610). For the impact to be effective, it must be integral, with the union of the macro, meso, and micro aspects of the circularity. This triple union is driven by technology and by the social awareness of the need to recycle, which must be done since childhood.

From the definition of circular economy, six components emerge: a) the recirculation of resources and energy; b) the minimization of demand for resources; c) the recovery of value from waste, d) a multi-level approach, e) its importance as a path to achieve sustainable development, and f) its close relationship with the way society innovates (Prieto-Sandoval, Ormazabal, Jaca, and Viles, 2018). The first component is entropy as an extensive property of a thermodynamic system, and more specifically, the second principle of thermodynamics so that the system is in equilibrium that is achieved with the transformation of energy as it is recycled following a circular economy scheme. Hence, it is so important to achieve the recovery of value from waste by following a multi-level approach to achieve sustainable development through innovation. This process of innovation allows the use of new recycling systems that are more efficient in the use of resources to have a lower environmental deterioration where the supply chain has a key role to play.

A multi-loop supply chain system complements the second principle of thermodynamics. In fact, Multi-loop supply chain system activities broaden the economic benefits achieved by the society and rarely link the activities to economic benefits, especially mostly dealt with optimization of resource use by minimizing waste, emissions, energy leakage, and resource input (Tseng et al., 2020). To avoid energy leakage is key to have sustainable and highly effective production systems to benefit both economies and societies. This loss of energy, especially in transport, is at least partially mitigated using superconductors in the transmission of energy, as well as by the reduction of distances from the origin to the final consumer, be it a company or a natural person.

The circular economy is a paradigm that aims to generate economic prosperity by protecting the environment and preventing pollution (Prieto-Sandoval et al., 2018; Prieto-Sandoval, Jaca, and Ormazabal, 2016). Within this paradigm, resources are taken from nature, transformed into products, distributed in the marketplace, consumed, and then recovered through biological and technical cycles (McDonough and Braungart, 2002). In the circular economy, the results are so effective that they lead to the generation of an imitation effect by other countries, regions, municipalities, and companies. When the application of the circular economy is part of a comprehensive strategy, it is when its effects on society are maximized, which benefits future generations.

The good results of the circular economy make it increasingly popular. According to Google Trends (as of 27 June 2019), the term "circular economy" is the strongest in Scandinavian countries, South America, and South Africa, and the concept of "sharing economy" is strongest in Russia, the USA, the core of the EU, and Australia (Tóth, 2019). By using Google Trends, the author has done the same research six months later to test if results have varied. The results are shown in Table 1.

Table 1. Top-10 most interested countries on the term "circular economy"

Ranking	Nation	Interest
1	Luxembourg	100
2	St Helena (UK)	93
3	Finland	66
4	Belgium	66
5	Zimbabwe	56
6	Singapore	54
7	Netherlands	48
8	Ethiopia	47
9	South Africa	45
10	Switzerland	44

Source: Adapted from Google Trends (December 21st, 2019)

It is interesting to note that of the ten countries most aware of the circular economy, five are European and enjoy the highest standards of living in Europe. Luxembourg stands out, which since 2014 is integrally applying the circular economy in its territory, which has allowed its companies to achieve an annual saving of 650 million euros on average and the creation of 2,200 jobs. A feature of the circular economy programs in the Grand Duchy of Luxembourg is that students participate since training in principles of the circular economy is inserted in higher education subjects in architecture and design, to achieve sustainable buildings. Besides, the circular economy projects will be carried out together with an important initiative whose objective is to convert old industrial areas into land adapted to homes, where a new residential complex of 26 hectares has been built.

Another notable case is the island of St Helena, which, being located halfway between Africa and America, makes environmental sustainability vital for the island to remain habitable. Its isolation makes the circular economy necessary to preserve the environment and to create economic value within this remote island inhabited only by 4,500 people.

The circular economy is related to a multitude of economic concepts, as seen in Table 2. Among these concepts highlights its relationship with the term "productivity," which indicates that it is a concept that especially interests companies, as well as with the terms "stakeholder" and "goal setting." Being related to the concept of "productivity" with circular economy shows a greater environmental awareness of companies by wishing to increase productivity with the use of more environmentally friendly methods, techniques, and strategies to reduce the environmental impact. Therefore, when productivity increases, taking into account the environmental impact, this means that productive resources are used more efficiently and cleanly. Therefore, the company has a fundamental role to play in achieving the implementation of a circular economy. In other words, the company is the main economic agent in this process of environmental change and improvement.

Table 2. Interest on the circular economy and related terms

Ranking	Related Term	Interest
1	Productivity	+400%
2	Disposable Product	+350%
3	Stakeholder	+300%
4	Goal setting	+180%
5	Theory	+180%
6	Green Economy	+170%
7	Conference	+140%
8	Economic Value	+140%
9	Packaging	+130%
10	Supply Chain	+120%

Source: Adapted from Google Trends (December 21st, 2019)

Innovation adoption and diffusion by firms are key pillars for the EU strategy on resource efficiency and the development of a circular economy (Cainelli, D'Amato, and Mazzanti, 2020). Eco-innovation is defined as any directed/oriented innovation aiming at reducing environmental impacts. Eco-innovation is not only a technology change; it also embraces organizational, social, and system innovations (Vence and Pereira, 2019). As a result, "eco-innovation is the production, assimilation or exploitation of a product, production process, service or management or business method that is novel to the organization (developing or adopting it) and which results, throughout its life cycle, in a reduction of environmental risk, pollution and other negative impacts of resources use (including energy use) compared to relevant alternatives" (Kemp and Pearson 2007, p. 7).

Altvater (2012), cited by Vence and Pereira (2019), "identifies three different revolutions towards a new renewable energy-based society: a) the *efficiency revolution*, which extends Capitalism and the fossil regime; b) the *sufficiency revolution*, based on the use-value rather than on exchange value; and iii) the *consistency revolution*, where a new alliance among economy, ecology, society, production, consumption, and nature is achieved. The latter implies to set limits to production and consumption, hence, to block the coherence of capitalist society, fossil energies, and the industrial rationale that dominates the world" (p. 3).

Despite this Altvater's limitation to capitalism, environmental deterioration also occurs in non-capitalist countries, as is the case in sub-Saharan Africa where environmental deterioration is very strong without any environmental protection to reduce it. In this sense, ecological dumping is largely guilty of this environmental damage due to the non-use of filters or safety systems in the production process. Ecological dumping used when the State does not dispose of an adequate supervision system or when there are high levels of political, social, and economic corruption.

Once at this point, we could ask ourselves what the principles of the circular economy are. This is what we will analyze in the next section.

PRINCIPLES OF THE CIRCULAR ECONOMY

According to the 7th Environment Action Program, approved by the European Union, the "economic prosperity and healthy environment stem from an innovative, circular economy where nothing is wasted and where natural resources are managed sustainably, and biodiversity is protected, valued and restored in ways that enhance our society's resilience." (p. 3). In addition to the traditional types of capital existing in the economy (human capital, relational capital, structural capital, and monetary capital), the concept of natural capital has recently been introduced to value the environment. Economic prosperity and a healthy environment based on five principles, as follows.

Cooperation

Greater cooperation within and across supply chains can cut costs, waste, and environmental harm. Growing cooperation that can be external between companies, NGOs (non-governmental organizations), state and universities to form 4-helix entrepreneurial systems, as internally (intra-cooperation) that allows to optimize the use of resources, improve the value chain of the company and eliminate inefficiencies. For this reason, the introduction and implementation of strategic policies based on cooperation improve the use of resources, tend to avoid wasting resources, and increases productivity by having better human resources in key positions, a process that can be rotated in a collaborative environment.

Eco-Innovation

Advances in eco-innovation provide new products, processes, technologies, and organizational structure to organizations. Eco-innovation promises a double gain (economic and environmental benefits), it may support increased productive efficiency, augmented production and diffusion, as well as enlarged diversity in new products and services (Vence and Pereira, 2019). As a result, organizational strategies based on eco-innovation foster productivity, and permit achieving first-order competitive advantages (R&D and eco-innovation) to benefit stakeholders, especially shareholders and human resources.

Maintenance and repair based on eco-innovation are considered important enablers to attain more sustainable consumption practices by re-using, re-manufacturing, and recycling products in the market with the use of eco-friendly technologies and key partnerships to create networks that support the business model execution by providing some resources and performing eco-friendly business activities.

Eco-Friendly Business Models

Organizations develop eco-friendly business models when they are based on leasing, sharing, repairing, upgrading, or recycling individual components of the firm's value chain. Leasing and lease-back business strategies offer new opportunities for allocating limited economic resources more efficiently, and when they are focused on being eco-friendly, these strategies also benefit stakeholders, especially final consumers.

The sharing economy is an emerging type of eco-friendly business model, as it optimizes the use of economic resources. During the last years, ICTs (information and communication technologies) have enabled the rise of the so-called "collaborative consumption" – a form of consumption where people share goods and services online. As Hamari, Sjöklint, and Ukonnen (2016) affirm, collaborative consumption has been expected to alleviate societal problems such as hyper-consumption, pollution, and poverty by lowering the cost of economic coordination within communities. This type of consumption is especially useful for expatriates who do not wish to be outside their home country for many years. Thus, through the sharing economy, they can solve their transportation (Uber, Didi, Cabify) and accommodation (Airbnb) problems without the need for an expensive investment that would even lead to a waste of resources.

Eco-friendly business models offer product access and retain ownership to internalize the benefits of circular resource productivity. Especially in emerging countries, growing middle-class spending has a positive impact on carbon emissions, but the size depends on governmental environmental-friendly policies. If cities are properly planned with energy-efficient buildings and sustainable transport, and if environmental campaigns are used to provide universal (and cost-free) secondary education, then the carbon footprint of this global middle-class expansion can be reduced considerably (Kharas, 2017).

Design on Circularity

Business strategies conceived on circularity can be designed with durability, reuse, repair, remanufacturing, and recycling in mind. That is why the entire recycling process begins even in the design and in what materials are going to be used for the construction of the product that will be offered in the market. That is why the type of materials to be used, and their assembly is so important (if necessary).

Eco-friendly well-designed products having recycling in mind can be recycled indefinitely, which favors the conservation of the environment and circularity through a correct selective treatment of waste. In this sense, it is possible to achieve circularity when there is a process of public-private collaboration, as in small towns where it is easier for this type of collaboration to occur.

To optimize the design process, the HEI (higher educational institutions) should have an active role in the product design process with the incorporation of products manufactured with easily recyclable materials. This cooperation is essential in products built and assembled with hundreds (and thousands) of parts, as in the automobile industry and the aerospace industry, among others.

This design process must be continuous overtime following a kaizen model (better continuous). For this, it can be very useful to listen to the voice of the final client, who can answer online questionnaires to know how to express his opinion and, incidentally, help the company improve.

New Sustainable-Based Thinking on Consumers

As the consumer has a growing role, companies have moved from a traditional one-way relationship to a two-way connection where customers feel heard. As a result, business thinking has changed from 'consumer' to 'user' or from 'owner' to 'sharer' to create more demand for services linked to renting, sharing, swapping, repairing, and remanufacturing products.

While renting is highly developed, swapping is less used because of differences in ownership between the two parties they exchange. Therefore, it is easier for the swap to take place between companies, which have greater ease of exchanging products, than among individuals who generally have more limited resources.

The rest of the strategies used (renting, sharing, repairing, and remanufacturing) are easier to use and are much more common in practice. The final goal is to reach sustainability to preserve the natural environment. Today's generations have a very strong moral responsibility towards future generations, who see the sustainability of the planet in danger. As a result, some business sustainability movements have appeared, and they will be described briefly in the next section.

BUSINESS SUSTAINABILITY MOVEMENTS AND THE CIRCULAR ECONOMY

Combined with other business sustainability movements (Table 3), the circular economy promotes system innovations that aim to design out waste, increase resource efficiency, and achieve a better balance between economy, environment, and society, as this balance directly affects the quality of living. Currently, there are three levels of indicators for measuring circular economy: macro (global, national, regional, city, and village), meso (industrial symbiosis, and eco-friendly industrial parks), and micro (single firm, product, and service). How to measure and document this progress towards a circular economy is lacking, especially on a micro-level. This fact is a barrier both for producers to provide circular products and services and for consumers who want to compare products and services received from firms (Kristensen and Mosgaard, 2020).

As seen in Table 3, there is a well-nurtured number of business sustainability movements that have the same scope of achieving sustainability. It is remarkable to note that the first scientific mentions mainly come from the US and the European Union. Asia, Africa, and Latin America seem to be almost absent in this debate that is crucial for humankind.

The Triple Bottom Line (3P) is formed by three 'P' (People, to achieve social equity; Planet, to preserve the environment, and Profit, to adequate production for not damaging the environment), and when the 3P links to Social Corporate Responsibility, the social effects achieved are more sustainable over time. Therefore, environmental preservation must be done gradually following the 3P, by impacting the planet through people and firms.

Related to the Circular Economy, the 'Blue Economy' encourages better stewardship of oceans, seas, and lakes, also known as 'blue' natural resources that create economic value through the exploitation of maritime and marine resources – for example through shipping, commercial fishing, and the oil, gas, minerals, and mining industries. As a result, environmental damage tends to be very strong in many cases and are almost irreversible.

In the face of these active strategies and policies in the fight against environmental deterioration, the Zero Growth theory has been dismissed in practice, mainly harming emerging and developing countries

Table 3. Business sustainability movements

Business Sustainability Movement	First Scientific Mention	Date
Recycling	Plato	4th Century B.C.
Waste minimization	Taylor	1974
Cleaner Production	UNEP-UNIDO	1992
Zero Emission	US Senate	1970
Zero Growth	Meadows *et al.*	1972
Green Economy	Pearce	1989
Triple Bottom Line (3P)	Elkington	1994
Life Cycle Assessment	Vigon	1994
Sustainable Consumption	Oslo Symposium	1994
Corporate Social Responsibility	Goodpaster-Matth	1982
Blue Economy	Pauli	2010
Creating Sharing Value	Porter	2011
Eco-friendly Industrial Economy	Frosch and Gallopoulos	1989
Sharing Economy	Benkler	2002
Circular Economy	Boulding	1965

Source: Adapted from Tóth (2019)

in their economic growth strategies. All the nations of the world must grow economically to offer their citizens higher standards of living and greater socioeconomic well-being. In this way, greater local and regional development would improve the preservation of the environment by increasing the educational level reached by the population, which would be aware of the importance of preserving the environment and applying sustainable strategies over time.

The growing environmental damage that is being done on the planet is causing a growing awareness to preserve the environment. A conscience that is being given all over the planet and, especially, in the countries that are suffering the most from pollution diseases, both from the air, soil, and water. In the preservation of the environment lies the future of the planet. Hence it is a problem that must be solved urgently.

On the other hand, barriers to circular business model innovation are found at all socio-technical levels, and, overall, most barriers are encountered by companies at the organizational level, followed by adaptation problems in the value chain, employees, markets, and institutions (Guldmann and Huulgaard, 2020). Hence, the circular economy is necessary to improve waste treatment and, thus, improve the environment.

Smart enabling technologies can aid in a transformation of waste management toward a circular economy, but three casual barriers persist the lack of regulatory pressures, a generally weak environmental education and culture of environmental protection, and feeble market pressures and clients' demand (Zhang et al., 2019). These weaknesses indeed vary between countries, and there are exceptions. For example, in the European Union, the environmental sensitivity is very high in the Nordic countries (Finland, Sweden, Norway, Denmark, and Iceland), Baltic nations (Estonia, Latvia, and Lithuania), and Mediterranean countries, especially Spain. The main reason for this achievement is because the European environment policy has the scope by 2050 to protect, conserve and enhance the European Union's natural capital to safeguard EU citizens from environment-related pressures and risks to health and wellbeing and to turn the EU into a resource-efficient, green, and competitive low-carbon economy.

To achieve this ambitious goal, some instruments to achieve circularity can be used, as shown in Table 4. All these instruments have been applied in the European Union, and as a result, according to the official website of the European Union, citizens from the European Union benefit from some of the highest environmental standards in the world.

Table 4. Instruments for promoting circularity

Command and Control	Economic	Public-Private
Waste disposal and trade standards	Landfill and/or incineration taxes	Improved logistics and infrastructure
Minimum recycling requirements	Different taxation levels for reused or recycled products	Circularity certification and labeling schemes
Deposit refund systems, for example, for plastic bottles	Reduced value-added taxes for repair and reuse services	Extended producer responsibility schemes
Circular public procurement	Increased taxes on non-reparable products	Discounts for efficiency
Waste disposal and trade standards	Landfill and/or incineration taxes	Improved logistics and infrastructure
Extended legal warranties	Tax shifts from labor to consumption	Products designed for recycling
Streamlined regulations for leasing and sharing businesses	Incentives for access over ownership	Virtual platforms for asset sharing

Source: Adapted from Wellesley, Preston, and Lehne (2019) and UNCTAD (2018)

Concerning the economic instruments focused on promoting circularity, it is striking that many of them are related to the implementation of taxes. The reason for this is given because taxes serve to cover the expenses incurred in achieving the preservation of the environment. Therefore, taxes offset the negative externalities created after environmental deterioration, which is positive for the whole society.

One interesting point to have in mind is the growing role that China, as the future strongest economic power, is playing in the world. Aware of being one of the most polluting countries on the planet as a result of its rapid industrialization, the implementation of the "Siberian Force" plan, Russia will send natural gas to China in a trade agreement that will arrive initially until 2030. A trade union between Russia and China that began on June 15, 2001, through the economically powerful Shanghai Cooperation Organization, where Europe has a fundamental role to play. As a result, the increasingly stronger link between the European Union and China is fostering sustainable consumption facilitating the circular economy in China to strengthen "cradle-to-cradle" practices (Shao, 2019), also known as regenerative designs. Based on Nature, "cradle-to-cradle" practices suggest that industry must protect and enrich ecosystems and nature's biological metabolism by producing eco-friendly products with no conservatives, preservatives, and base chemical products, to be eco-friendly sold in the market.

This strategy has a direct and positive impact on health, as "cradle-to-cradle" practices create "passive positive" lists, formed by three lists of materials categorized according to their safety level, and is defined by a) the G (gray) list, formed by problematic substances that are not so urgently in need of phasing out; b) the P (positive) list, defined by safe substances for use, and c) the X (negative) list, demarcated by substances that must be phased out, such as carcinogenic, mutagenic, and teratogenic chemical substances to avoid. Despite the existence of list X, there are still companies that use health-damaging products, which mainly provoke type 2 diabetes and cholesterol, especially in very popular products belonging to the food and soft drinks industry. Hence, it is necessary and desirable for the consumer to become aware of this fact, as well as to discourage their consumption so as not to impact the health of consumers negatively. As a result, Table 5 shows how the circular economy can be implemented in firms to increase citizen's quality of living by slowing down (and ideally stopping) environmental deterioration.

Public administrations have traditionally given the implementation of the circular economy in the company. The reason for this is because public administrations have the objective of preserving the general interest so that the circular economy benefits the entire society, especially future generations. For this reason, the impact of the circular economy must be holistic; that is, it must have a global impact so that its effects are lasting over time. Also, the circular economy determines, to a large extent, the quality of life of a society, so its implementation creates positive externalities in the environment.

Related to the impact of the circular economy to be lasting over time, it must occur successively in five fields of action:

1. **Take:** Either a) through the selection of biodegradable (water and crystal bottles, six-pack rings, cutlery, polymers, among others) or easily recirculated materials (used clothes, batteries, furniture, phones, and semiconductors) in different value chains to prepare them for recycling, the search for an environmental efficiency of production processes to reduce resource use and emissions, and achieve new and clean-oriented sustainable energy sources for production, mainly solar, wind, tidal, biomass and geothermal energy;
2. **Make:** By applying environmental innovation in the design of pretotypes and prototypes made of sustainable products and services to extend their lifecycles and facilitate future recovery. A second possibility is through recovering second-hand materials (e.g., automobile industry) to apply eco-friendly resources in the internal production process of the firm. Given the growing environmental awareness of the population, only socially responsible companies with the environment will be able to survive in the medium and long term;
3. **Distribute:** With the development of a sustainable, eco-friendly logistics system with the use of natural gas and electric vehicles in the distribution process;
4. **Use:** With the development of business models, where the final consumer is not the owner of the goods. In this sense, shared consumption is increasingly popular among consumers, not only in the transport sector (e.g., Uber, Didi, Cabify, and Beat), but also in the hotel industry (e.g., Airbnb, HomeAway, Couchsurfing, Onefinestay, Wimdu, and Flipkey). A second business strategy is to offer services that extend the life of the products or services with the use of new technologies. According to the European Parliament (2006), a minimal increase of 1% of value added by economic activities related to a longer lifetime for products would have an aggregated effect of 7.9 billion EUR per year across the European economy. Finally, a third eco-friendly business strategy is defined by designing products that work with sustainable energies;
5. **Recover:** Defined by two complementary strategies, defined by a) public and private channels of communication with customers and producers to retrieve products no longer used or wanted to renew, and b) recovery and industrial recirculation of materials from products that consumers do not use any more. This two-fold process of recovery assures economic benefits to the firm, and transform it into a smart firm by increasing value-added in the products and services offered in the market, achieving a necessary trade balance, creating jobs in the labor market, and offering social

Table 5. Circular economy's implementation in firms

Category		Element	References
Circular Economy - Fields of action	Take	Selection of biodegradable or easily recirculated materials in different value chains	McDonough and Braungart (2002), Stahel (2016)
		Environmental efficiency of production processes to reduce resource use and emissions	Lieder and Rashid (2016)
		Sustainable energy sources for production	Park, et al. (2010)
	Make	Environmental innovation in the design of sustainable products and services to extend their lifecycles and facilitate future recovery	Carrillo-Hermosilla, Del Río, & Könnölä (2010); Del Río, Carrillo-Hermosilla, Könnölä, and Bleda (2016); McDonough and Braungart (2002)
		The recovery of raw material and resources in the internal process of the company	Park et al. (2010)
	Distribute	The development of a sustainable logistics system	Lieder and Rashid (2016); Van der Wiel et al. (2012)
	Use	The development of business models where the final consumer is not the owner of the goods	Antikainen and Valkokari (2016); Stahel (1998); Tukker (2015)
		The offer of services that extend the life of the products or services	Graedel (2000); Kortmann and Piller (2016)
		Design of products that work with sustainable energies	McDonough, Braungart, Anastas, and Zimmerman (2003)
	Recover	Channels of communication with customers to retrieve products that they no longer use or that they want to renew	Lewandowski (2016); Lieder and Rashid (2016)
		Recovery and industrial recirculation of materials from products that consumers do not use any more	Antikainen and Valkokari (2016); Park et al. (2010); Sihvonen and Ritola (2015); Stahel (2016)
Industrial symbiosis		Belonging to an industrial association, cluster or related organization	Daddi, Nucci, and Iraldo (2017); Daddi and Iraldo (2015); Deutz and Gibbs (2008); Short, Bocken, Barlow, and Chertow (2014)
		Sharing infrastructure or services with industrial neighbors	Chertow (2007)
		Valuing the "waste" of some companies as resources for others	Chertow (2007); Kortmann and Piller (2016); Tibbs (2006)
		Creating joint value between companies	Chertow (2007); Cohen-Rosenthal (2000); Park et al. (2010); Sihvonen and Ritola (2015)
		Managing aspects such as trust and transparency among potential partners in the industry	Baas (2011); Chertow (2007)
		Government and public institution intervention	Gibbs and Deutz (2007); Rizos et al. (2016); Yu, Davis, and Dijkema (2014)
Certifications		Certifications of environmental management systems for a company	AENOR (2016); BSI Group (2017); EU Commission (2017a)
		Certifications of the product or service	EU Commission (2017b)

Source: Prieto-Sandoval, Ormazabal, Jaca, and Viles (2018)

benefits and an attractive distribution of skills (social capital) to enable inclusive business growth and competitive advantages.

Complementary to these fields of action, belonging to an industrial association, cluster, or related organization is a must for achieving business success. This drastic opinion is based on that circular economy must be implemented by following a shared business strategy where cooperation is fundamental. Especially in business organizations, the objectives are achieved as a team, so when they are complex and difficult to achieve, a growing inter-company collaboration (internationally, if needed) becomes necessary on many occasions.

Finally, obtaining certifications of environmental management systems for a company and certifications of the product or service is necessary to apply the circular economy successfully. In this sense, the European Union is very advanced in the application of the circular economy with the implementation of some certificates whose compliance facilitates its implementation. Of all existing legislation, the following should be noted, related to producer support and regulation (Directive on Waste of Electrical and Electronic Equipment (also known as WEEE), Integrated Product Policy, EU Eco-design Directive 2009/125/EC, Eco-innovation Action Plan (EIAP), Directive on batteries and accumulators 2006/66, Regulation (EC) No 595/2009 on type-approval of motor vehicles and engines, EU action plan for the circular economy (COM 2015: 614)), or focused on consumer protection (The Consumer Sales Directive (1999/44/EC), EU Consumer Rights Directive (2011/83/EC), Green Paper on consumer rights preceding the CRD (COM 1993), and the European Ecolabel initiative, based on accurate, non-deceptive, and scientific, environmental information).

The only negative side of this strong environmental regulation put in place by public administrations is the generation of a strong bureaucratic process that slows down decision making and, above all, generates a cost for the company. Therefore, small and medium-sized enterprises are far behind in meeting these regulations are directed towards large producers., To them, being the most deteriorate the environment if they did not comply with the regulations. Against this, one of the great advantages of this excessive regulation is given by the practical impossibility of carrying out ecological dumping, whose realization damages the environment in developing countries.

SOLUTIONS AND RECOMMENDATIONS

The appearance of a strong civil society is of great importance to control, from the McClelland's N-effect to companies that carry out ecological dumping in their territory. However, and contrary to what happens in the most developed nations of the planet, the civil society is very fragmented and, in general, is very weak in developing countries. This fact means that companies, especially if they are large companies, can campaign freely to make an environmental deterioration whose damage can be very important and whose environmental recovery can last for several generations.

Being the role of civil society more active in first world countries, the introduction and implementation of public policies based on the circular economy are stronger than in third world nations. One of the keys to this difference is given by education, even from primary education, since the importance of environmental education is already instilled in younger citizens. Therefore, it is essential to introduce this environmental awareness in the primary education educational plans of the third world educational systems.

Besides, the circular economy does not work if it does not include an active recycling policy from home. One of the keys to the success of the circular economy comes from the installation of various recycling containers in household kitchens to separate organic (including used oil) and inorganic (paper, plastic and metal) waste from the source). Recycling costs are thus reduced, which makes recycling efficient and economically viable.

It is essential that, for a structural transformation process of the economy from the circular economy to be successful, it is important to achieve an effective public-private collaboration process. This collaboration is especially intense and effective when the State is free from corruption, and there is a transparent behavior of State actions and accountability towards its citizens. Therefore, the less corruption in the public administration, the greater the effectiveness in the implementation of a circular economy, the lower the levels of tax evasion.

Complementary to this fight against corruption, the entire process of implementing the circular economy is accelerated when there is electronic administration (eGovernment), which facilitates decision-making and impact measurement. Both the monitoring and implementation processes are essential to increase the impact and credibility in the circular economy by citizens, where both the imitation and the success effect between different administrations determine, at least in part, their generalization of use between different public administrations.

The development of eco-friendly business models is necessary to combat global warming. This fight must be done collectively and in a coordinated manner so that it has sustainable positive effects over time. Hence, it is essential to achieve good coordination between different levels of public administrations, especially in those countries with different levels (supranational, national, regional and local) related to each other, as is the case of nations integrated into processes of regional integration, as is the case, for example, of the European Union.

Complementary to the circular economy, the blue economy is a cornerstone of this environmental improvement of the planet. More than 70 percent of our planet are oceans, seas and lakes, and plastics and all types of waste increasingly damage them. This situation is unsustainable, especially for future generations. Maritime pollution is so important that even microplastics are entering the food chain, which is leading to an even harmful situation towards the human species. We have to clean the world's oceans, and in this sense, the initiatives led by the Dutch of Croatian origin, Boyan Slat with his "The Ocean Cleanup" or the cleaning initiatives led by the Spanish multinational Iberdrola, are improvement initiatives that can change the planet for the better.

FUTURE RESEARCH DIRECTIONS

As future research directions, we can cite the following ones:

1. Circular Economy and Frugal Innovation;
2. Impact of the Circular Economy on Sustainable Regional Growth;
3. The Circular Economy in the Public Administration;
4. Eco-friendly Entrepreneurship and the Circular Economy;
5. Public Expenditure and Social Efficiency in the Circular Economy.

CONCLUSION

Since the beginning of the 21st century, economies of industrialized countries are characterized by their populations account for only 20% of the world population, but they account for 80% of world resource consumption; their markets for traditional goods, such are automobiles, are saturated; the stock of goods remains fairly constant, and 90% of sales are replacement sales (Stahel, 1998). This situation has worsened in the 21st century as globalization has expanded in emerging countries, leading to the need for achieving a growing circular economy.

To achieve environmental improvement, there must be a close collaboration between the public initiative and the private company, no matter its size. This public-private collaboration creates positive externalities throughout the environment, which favors the preservation of the environment from the implementation of mechanisms and strategies based on the circular economy.

One of the bases of the circular economy is the eco-friendly innovation that aims to find the most effective and sustainable recycling systems in time. Innovation processes that generate value in the recycling chain, so that its impact is greater. Therefore, in the creation and implementation of the circular economy, public-private collaboration is of decisive importance, and its effects are even better when public administrations support with proper regulation and with the granting of minimum economic resources to start everything the recycling process, while the private initiative is the one who supports with its 7-K (know-how, know-when, know-why, know-who, know-what, know-whose, and know-where) (Saiz-Alvarez, 2019) all the development of the circular economy so that it has a sustainable socioeconomic impact over time.

Within the innovation, the so-called frugal innovation stands out because it is often associated with (ecological and social) sustainability because it is characterized by minimizing the use of resources (raw material, production resources, energy, fuel, water, waste, financial resources), it is more affordable, and better accessible than conventional innovations (Albert, 2019). As frugal innovation is defined by non-affluent customers' opportunities to consume affordable products and services suited to their needs, these products and services tend to be more ecologically sustainable, being its products less industrially transformed.

In this respect, Kumar and Puranam (2012) identify six principles of frugal innovation (robustness, portability, de-featuring, leapfrog technology, mega-scale production, and service ecosystems). Thanks to robustness and portability, products and services can be more easily distributed to benefit consumers, as both economies of scale and economies of scope can be achieved through techniques focused on achieving mega-scale production.

Leapfrog technology determines the positions of leadership within the industrial sectors, by obtaining companies that enjoy this disruptive technology, competitive advantages of the first order that is sustainable, generally, over a long period. As a result, a feedback effect can be given, so that leapfrog technologies are happening over time.

Besides, a sustainable economy could be helped by an appropriate business structure, characterized by the regionalization of jobs and skills (mini-mills for materials recycling, re-manufacturing workshops for products, decentralized production of services such as insurance), supplemented by centralized design, research, and management centers (Stahel, 1998). This regionalization of jobs and skills links to new technologies and innovation inserted into a 4-helix entrepreneurial eco-friendly model formed by the combination of eco-friendly firms, Public Administrations with social and ecological consciousness, environmentally aware HEI (Higher Education Institutions), and eco-friendly NGOs (Non-Governmental

Organizations). In many cases, the greatest impact is achieved with regional and local eco-friendly related business measures, as they focus on the final consumer.

Given the accelerated process of environmental deterioration of the planet due to excessive industrialization, in some cases, and others caused by an excessive massification of the population, schemes of production and distribution of resources based on the circular economy must be applied. The implementation of a circular economy allows to optimize the use of resources, contributes to increasing the quality of life of citizens and generates sustainable value chains over time. In this way, and thanks to the circular economy, the main beneficiaries will be future generations who have the right to receive a cleaner and more eco-friendly world from current generations. It is our responsibility to achieve this so that the world is ecologically more fair and supportive, both towards the present and future generations. And to achieve this goal, the circular economy has an important role to play, as is currently the case in some of the most developed (and more eco-friendly) countries on the planet.

REFERENCES

AENOR. (2016). Hacia el residuo cero [Towards the Zero Waste]. In Revista La Norma y la Certificación. AENOR.

Albert, M. (2019). Sustainable frugal innovation - The connection between frugal innovation and sustainability. *Journal of Cleaner Production*, *237*, 117747. doi:10.1016/j.jclepro.2019.117747

Antikainen, M., & Valkokari, K. (2016). A Framework for Sustainable Circular Business Model Innovation, *Technology Innovation. Management Review*, *5*, 1–8.

Baas, L. (2011). Planning and Uncovering Industrial Symbiosis: Comparing the Rotterdam and Östergötland Regions. *Business Strategy and the Environment*, *20*(7), 428–440. doi:10.1002/bse.735

Benkler, Y. (2002). Coase's Penguin, or, Linux and "The Nature of the Firm,". *The Yale Law Journal*, *112*(3), 369–446. doi:10.2307/1562247

Boulding, K. E. (1965). *The Economies of the Coming Spaceship Earth*. Boulder, CO: The University of Colorado at Boulder Libraries.

Cainelli, G., D'Amato, A., & Mazzanti, M. (2020). Resource-efficient eco-innovations for a circular economy: Evidence from EU firms. *Research Policy*, *49*(1), 103827. doi:10.1016/j.respol.2019.103827

Carrillo-Hermosilla, J., Del Río, P., & Könnölä, T. (2010). Diversity of Eco-innovations: Reflections from Selected Case Studies. *Journal of Cleaner Production*, *18*(10-11), 1073–1083. doi:10.1016/j.jclepro.2010.02.014

Chertow, M. R. (2007). "Uncovering" Industrial Symbiosis. *Journal of Industrial Ecology*, *11*(1), 11–30. doi:10.1162/jiec.2007.1110

Cohen-Rosenthal, E. (2000). A Walk of the Human Side of Industrial Ecology. *The American Behavioral Scientist*, *44*(2), 245–264. doi:10.1177/00027642000044002007

Daddi, T., & Iraldo, F. (2015). The Effectiveness of Cluster Approach to Improve Environmental Corporate Performance in an Industrial District of SMEs: A Case Study. *International Journal of Sustainable Development and World Ecology*, *23*, 1–11.

Daddi, T., Nucci, B., & Iraldo, F. (2017). Using Life Cycle Assessment (LCA) to measure the environmental benefits of industrial symbiosis in an industrial cluster of SMEs. *Journal of Cleaner Production*, *147*, 157–164. doi:10.1016/j.jclepro.2017.01.090

Del Río, P., Carrillo-Hermosilla, J., Könnölä, T., & Bleda, M. (2016). Resources, capabilities, and competences for eco-innovation. *Technological and Economic Development of Economy*, *22*(2), 274–292. doi:10.3846/20294913.2015.1070301

Deutz, P., & Gibbs, D. (2008). Industrial Ecology and Regional Development: Eco-Industrial Development as Cluster Policy. *Regional Studies*, *42*(10), 1313–1328. doi:10.1080/00343400802195121

Elkington, J. (1997). *Cannibals with Forks: The Triple Bottom Line of 21st Century Business*. Oxford, UK: Capstone.

EU Commission. (2017a). *History and idea behind the EMAS Awards*. Available at ec.europa.eu

EU Commission, . (2017b). *COM(2017) 355 Final Report*. Brussels, Belgium: EU Commission.

European Commission. (2014). *The Circular Economy. Connecting, creating, and conserving value*. Author.

European Parliament. (2006). *A Longer Lifetime for Products: Benefits for Consumers and Companies*. Brussels, Belgium: Directorate-General for Internal Policies.

FAO (Food and Agriculture Organization of the United Nations). (2017). Pulp and Paper Capacities. UN Publications.

Frosch, R. A., & Gallopoulos, N. E. (1989). Strategies for Manufacturing—Wastes from one industrial process can serve as the raw material for another, thereby reducing the impact on the environment. *Scientific American*, *261*(3), 144–152. doi:10.1038cientificamerican0989-144

Gibbs, D., & Deutz, P. (2007). Reflections on implementing industrial ecology through eco-industrial park development. *Journal of Cleaner Production*, *15*(17), 1683–1695. doi:10.1016/j.jclepro.2007.02.003

Goodpaster, K. E., & Matthews, J. B. Jr. (1982). Can a Corporation Have a Conscience? *Harvard Business Review*, *60*, 132–141.

Graedel, T. (2000). The Evolution of Industrial Ecology. *Environmental Science & Technology*, *34*(1), 28A–31A. doi:10.1021/es003039c PMID:21657590

BSI Group. (2017). *Resource Management and the Circular Economy*. Available at bsigroup.com

Guldmann, E., & Huulgaard, R. D. (2020). Barriers to circular business model innovation: A multiple-case study. *Journal of Cleaner Production*, *243*, 118160. doi:10.1016/j.jclepro.2019.118160

Hamari, J., Sjöklint, M., & Ukkonen, A. (2016). The Sharing Economy: Why People Participate in Collaborative Consumption. *Journal of the Association for Information Science and Technology*, *67*(9), 2047–2059. doi:10.1002/asi.23552

Kemp, R., & Pearson, P. (2007). *Final report MEI project about measuring eco-innovation*. UM-MERIT, United Nations University, and Maastricht University.

Kharas, K. (2017). *The unprecedented expansion of the global middle class: An update*. Global Economy and Development Working Paper, 100. Washington, DC: The Brookings Institution.

Kortmann, S., & Piller, F. T. (2016). Open Business Models and Closed-Loop Value Chains: Redefining the Firm-Consumer Relationship. *California Management Review*, *58*(3), 88–108. doi:10.1525/cmr.2016.58.3.88

Kristensen, H. S., & Mosgaard, M. A. (2020). A review of micro-level indicators for a circular economy – moving away from the three dimensions of sustainability? *Journal of Cleaner Production*, *243*, 118531. doi:10.1016/j.jclepro.2019.118531

Kumar, N., & Puranam, P. (2012). Frugal engineering: an emerging innovation paradigm. *Ivey Business Journal*, *76*(2). Retrieved from https://iveybusinessjournal.com/publication/frugal-engineering-an-emerging-innovation-paradigm/

Lewandowski, M. (2016). Designing the Business Models for Circular Economy-Towards the Conceptual Framework. *Sustainability*, *8*(1), 43. doi:10.3390u8010043

Lieder, M., & Rashid, A. (2016). Towards circular economy implementation: A comprehensive review in the context of the manufacturing industry. *Journal of Cleaner Production*, *115*, 36–51. doi:10.1016/j.jclepro.2015.12.042

McDonough, W., & Braungart, M. (2002). *Cradle to cradle. Remaking the way we make things*. New York: North Point Press.

McDonough, W., Braungart, M., Anastas, P. T., & Zimmerman, J. B. (2003). Peer-Reviewed: Applying the Principles of Green Engineering to Cradle-to-Cradle Design. *Environmental Science & Technology*, *37*(23), 434–441. doi:10.1021/es0326322

Meadows, D., Donatella Meadows, J., Randers, W., & Behrens, W. III. (1972). *The Limits to Growth—A Report for the Club of Rome's Project on the Predicament of Mankind*. Universe Books.

Norwegian Ministry of the Environment. (1994). *Oslo Roundtable on Sustainable Production and Consumption*. Oslo, Norway: Norwegian Ministry of the Environment.

Park, J., Sarkis, J., & Wu, Z. (2010). Creating an integrated business and environmental value within the context of China's circular economy and ecological modernization. *Journal of Cleaner Production*, *18*(15), 1494–1501. doi:10.1016/j.jclepro.2010.06.001

Pauli, G. (2010). *The Blue Economy—10 Years, 100 Innovations, 100 Million Jobs*. Brookline, MA: Paradigm Publications.

Pearce, D. W., Barbier, E. B., Markandya, A., & Barbier, E. (1989). *Blueprint for a Green Economy*. London, UK: Earthscan.

Plastics Europe. (2016). *World Plastics Production 1950–2015*. Available at https://committee.iso.org/files/live/sites/tc61/files/The%20Plastic%20Industry%20Berlin%20Aug%202016%20-%20Copy.pdf

Porter, M. E., & Kramer, M. R. (2011). How to reinvent capitalism and unleash a wave of innovation and growth? *Harvard Business Review*, *89*, 62–77.

Prieto-Sandoval, V., Jaca, C., Santos, J., Baumgartner, R. J., & Ormazabal, M. (2019). Key strategies, resources, and capabilities for implementing circular economy in industrial small and medium enterprises. *Corporate Social Responsibility and Environmental Management*, *26*(6), 1473–1484. doi:10.1002/csr.1761

Prieto-Sandoval, V., Jaca García, C., & Ormazabal Goenaga, M. (2016). Circular Economy: An economic and industrial model to achieve the sustainability of society. In *Proceedings of the 22nd Annual International Sustainable Development Research Society Conference. Rethinking Sustainability Models and Practices: Challenges for the New and Old World Contexts*. ISDRS.

Prieto-Sandoval, V., Ormazabal, M., Jaca, C., & Viles, E. (2018). Key elements in assessing circular economy implementation in small and medium-sized enterprises. *Business Strategy and the Environment*, *27*(8), 1525–1534. doi:10.1002/bse.2210

Rizos, V., Behrens, A., van der Gaast, W., Hofman, E., Ioannou, A., Kafyeke, T., ... Topi, C. (2016). Implementation of Circular Economy Business Models by Small and Medium-Sized Enterprises (SMEs): Barriers and Enablers. *Sustainability*, *8*(11), 1–18. doi:10.3390u8111212

Saiz-Álvarez, J. M. (Ed.). (2019). Handbook of Research on Digital Marketing Innovations in Social Entrepreneurship and Solidarity Economics. Hershey, PA: Information Science Reference (IGI Global). doi:10.4018/978-1-5225-8939-6

Shao, J. (2019). Sustainable consumption in China: New trends and research interests. *Business Strategy and the Environment*, *28*(8), 1507–1517. doi:10.1002/bse.2327

Short, S. W., Bocken, N. M. P., Barlow, C. Y., & Chertow, M. R. (2014). From Refining Sugar to Growing Tomatoes. Industrial Ecology and Business Model Evolution. *Journal of Industrial Ecology*, *18*(5), 603–618. doi:10.1111/jiec.12171

Sihvonen, S., & Ritola, T. (2015). Conceptualizing ReX for aggregating end-of-life strategies in product development. *Procedia CIRP*, *29*, 639–644. doi:10.1016/j.procir.2015.01.026

Stahel, W. R. (1998). From Products to Services. Selling Performance Instead of Goods. Geneva: Institute for Prospective Technological Studies (ITPS).

Stahel, W. R. (2016). Circular Economy. *Nature*, *531*(7595), 6–9. doi:10.1038/531435a PMID:27008952

Taylor, P. R. (1974). *The Kroll Institute for Extractive Metallurgy*. Golden, CO: KIEM.

Tibbs, H. (2006). The Value Loop – A New Framework for Business Thinking. In *The International Handbook on Environmental Technology Management*. Cheltenham, UK: Edward Elgar.

Tóth, G. (2019). Circular Economy and its Comparison with 14 Other Business Sustainability Movements. *Resources*, *8*, 159. doi:10.3390/resources8040159

Tseng, M.-L., Chiu, A. S. F., Liu, G., & Jantaralolica, T. (2020). The circular economy enables sustainable consumption and production in the multi-level supply chain system. *Resources, Conservation and Recycling*, *154*, 104601. doi:10.1016/j.resconrec.2019.104601

Tukker, A. (2015). Product services for a resource-efficient and circular economy – A review. *Journal of Cleaner Production*, *97*, 76–91. doi:10.1016/j.jclepro.2013.11.049

UNCTAD. (2018). *Policy Brief, 61*. Author.

UNEP-UNIDO. (1992). *Resource Efficient and Cleaner Production (RECP)*. Available online: https://www.unido.org/our-focus/safeguarding-environment/resource-efficient-and-low-carbonindustrial-production/resource-efficient-and-cleaner-production-recp

United States of America Energy Information Administration. (2016). *International Energy Outlook*. Washington, DC: Author.

US Senate. (1970). Federal Low-Emission Vehicle Procurement Act: Joint Hearings Before the Subcommittee on Energy, Natural Resources, and the Environment. *Proceedings of the Ninety-first Congress*.

Van der Wiel, A., Bossink, B., & Masurel, E. (2012). Reverse logistics for waste reduction in cradle-to-cradle oriented firms: Waste management strategies in the Dutch metal industry. *International Journal of Technology Management*, *60*(1/2), 96–113. doi:10.1504/IJTM.2012.049108

Vence, X., & Pereira, A. (2019). Eco-innovation and Circular Business Models as Drivers for a Circular Economy. *Contaduría y Administración, 64*(1), 1-19.

Vigon, B. W. (1994). *Life-Cycle Assessment: Inventory Guidelines and Principles*. Boca Raton, FL: CRC Press.

Wellesley, L., Preston, F., & Lehne, J. (2019). *An Inclusive Circular Economy: Priorities for Developing Countries*. London, UK: Chatham House. The Royal Institute for International Affairs.

World Aluminum. (2016). *Primary aluminum production database*. Author.

World Bank. (2012). *What A Waste: A Global Review of Solid Waste Management*. Washington, DC: Author.

Yu, C., Davis, C., & Dijkema, D. P. J. (2014). Understanding the Evolution of Industrial Symbiosis Research. *Journal of Industrial Ecology*, *18*(2), 280–293. doi:10.1111/jiec.12073

Zhang, A., Venkatesh, V. G., Liu, Y., Wan, M., Qu, T., & Huisingh, D. (2019). Barriers to smart waste management for a circular economy in China. *Journal of Cleaner Production*, *240*, 118198. doi:10.1016/j.jclepro.2019.118198

KEY TERMS AND DEFINITIONS

Biological Cycle: As part of a cradle to cradle (C2C) model, in this cycle, materials return to the biosphere in the form of compost or other nutrients, from which new materials emerge.

Blue Economy: It consists of the sustainable use of ocean and sea resources for economic growth, improves the quality of living, creates socioeconomic wealth while preserving the health of oceans and seas of the planet.

Circular Economy: It is an economic system aimed at eliminating waste and the continual use of resources. Based on a close-loop eco-friendly system, the circular economy aims at eliminating all waste (zero waste) and the continual use of economic resources by reusing, sharing, and recycling used products.

Cradle to Cradle: It is a design concept inspired by nature formed by a biological cycle, for products to consumption, and a technical cycle, for products for services.

Four-Helix Entrepreneurial Eco-Friendly Models: Formed by the combination of eco-friendly firms, Public Administrations with social and ecological consciousness, environmentally aware HEI (Higher Education Institutions), and eco-friendly NGOs (Non-Governmental Organizations), these models focus on achieving higher standards of living and nature preservation.

Frugal Innovation: Also known as frugal engineering, it consists of a group of functional solutions by minimizing the use of resources.

Industrial Symbiosis: A business situation formed by creating joint value between companies, managing aspects, such as trust and transparency among potential partners in the industry, belonging to an industrial association, cluster or related organization, and/or sharing infrastructure or services with industrial neighbors.

Technical Cycle: It is defined by eco-friendly materials reprocessed to be used in new products.

Chapter 2
Circular Green Economy:
Resources and Capabilities – Theory-Based Analysis

José G. Vargas-Hernández
https://orcid.org/0000-0003-0938-4197
University Center for Economic and Managerial Sciences, University of Guadalajara, Mexico

Marlene de Jesús Morales Medrano
University Center for Economic and Managerial Sciences, University of Guadalajara, Mexico

Jorge Armando López-Lemus
https://orcid.org/0000-0001-6989-1065
University of Guanajuato, Mexico

ABSTRACT

The purpose of this chapter is to analyze the green and circular economy (GCE) model from the point of view of the resources and capacities of the organization. How is the application of the circular economy model related to strategic management? At first glance, it seems that the CE is operating within an operational level with a social impact. However, it also has implications that allow us to think that it can be used as an internal resource of the company that, if applied in the right way, can become a competitive advantage. In other words, the application of the CE is related to strategic management through the point of view based on resources and capabilities. Therefore, the present investigation has a descriptive-correlational nature, which was analyzed through Peng's VRIO framework.

INTRODUCTION

In recent decades, the care of the planet has begun to appear on international political agendas as a matter of urgent concern, since we have begun to notice the consequences of the decisions taken by past generations to obtain economic benefits without worrying about the damage to the environment they

DOI: 10.4018/978-1-7998-5116-5.ch002

Copyright © 2020, IGI Global. Copying or distributing in print or electronic forms without written permission of IGI Global is prohibited.

caused. As such, it has been decided that it is time to worry and take measures to survive in a planet of limited resources with a population that does not stop growing.

Beyond the individual responsibility, those who can make a noticeable change and chain reaction are the companies that, regardless of size or classification, are important actors in the global scope since they have an active role in the degradation or preservation of its environment close to social, economic and environmental level. Then, it can be considered that it is of vital importance that companies begin to have the main goal of achieving sustainability.

That is why the Circular Economy (CE) represents an essential factor that arises from the reengineering of existing products or the creation of new products that are generated (Ünal, Urbinati, & Chiaroni, 2018). According to the Ellen MacArthur Foundation, an organization dedicated to the study and dissemination of the circular economy, the beginning of the concept as such has not been registered, but is the result of an evolution of several schools of thought such as Regenerative Design, economics of performance, industrial ecology, biomimetics, blue economy and natural capitalism.

In this sense, regenerative design it is a school of thought that focuses on the theory of systems oriented to design processes. That is, the theory emphasizes the fact that existing processes are modified to improve, eliminate or adhere new sources of energy and / or materials (Morlet, et al., 2016). Therefore, the regenerative design has a base derived from the ecology of the systems that is responsible for providing a biokinetics in the ecosystems (Ballie & Woods, 2018) with the aim of achieving an ecological economy system (Gleason Espíndola, Cordova, & Casiano Flores, 2018) that is viable and closed for any industry (Liakos, et al., 2019). It also seeks to ensure that the resulting system does not generate waste, which is completely effective, to achieve this it is necessary to redesign the culture of human habitats (Heaven Grown, s.f.)

According to the European Commission, the regenerative design will impact the processes at the social level through the generation of jobs, in economic competitiveness (Ecointeligencia, 2017), in the new distribution in the use of resources and waste. The CE promotes a performance economy in companies (Kumar, Sezersan, Garza-Reyes, Gonzalez, & AL-Shboul, 2019) through four main objectives to extend the useful life of existing products, generate new products that are considered durable from their design, think of campaigns or activities for the prevention of waste and reuse of these (Bocken, De Pauw, Bakker, & Van der Grinten, 2016; Ellen MacArthur Foundation, 2019). Therefore, the green circle economy is one of the essential sustainability factors in SMEs.

GREEN ECONOMY, GREEN GROWTH AND SUSTAINABLE DEVELOPMENT

The green economy concept is called the next oxymoron after sustainable development because they overlap each other (Green & McCann, 2011). Conference on Sustainable Development (Rio+20) in 2012 agreed that in the context of sustainable development, the concept of green economy should be promoted. The transition to a green economy has economic and social justifications for public and private actors to contribute offering opportunities for investments and green procurement by providing new market-based incentives and mechanisms (Shimova, 2019; Popkova, Bogoviz, & Ragulina, 2018).

It is because the green economy prioritizes well-being for the present and for future generations and the efficiency of improved technology is not necessarily sufficient. Likewise, a green economy is essential for sustainable development (Popkova, Bogoviz, & Ragulina, 2018; Shimova, 2019), improving social equity, human well-being, reducing ecological scarcity and environmental risks. Green economy supports sustainable development aimed to replace the social and environmental costs of the current economic model that is reaching limits in terms of greenhouse gas emissions, use of natural resources, water, land, forests (Barry, 2010).

Green economy (GE) transformation and inclusive greener growth strategy initiatives are needed to pursue the economic and social benefits of sustainable development (Zsolnai, 2002) while reducing negative environmental, inequality and poverty impacts, sustainable management of natural resources, reduce greenhouse gas emissions, climate change, resilience to natural disasters, improve public services (Barry, 2010; Jones & Wynn, 2019). Green economy and sustainable development strategies strengthen the resilience of communities and regions.

In this sense, the GE supports sustainable development aimed at replacing the social and environmental costs (Gliedt & Parker, 2007) of the current economic model that is reaching limits in terms of greenhouse gas emissions, use of natural resources, water, land, forests, etc. Initiatives are needed to pursue the economic and social benefits of sustainable development while reducing negative impacts on the environment, inequality and poverty, sustainable management of natural resources, greenhouse gas emissions, change climate, resistance to natural disasters, improvement of public services (Popkova, Bogoviz, & Ragulina, 2018). GE and sustainable development strategies strengthen the resilience of communities and regions such as SMEs (Bıçakcıoğlu, Theoharakis, & Tanyeri, 2019; Gliedt & Parker, 2007)

Green growth responds to critical emerging issues by facing the global challenge of environmental sustainability. However, the elements of the green economy concept are already integrated in strategic documents focused on achieving sustainable green growth, rather than merely achieving a green economy. Green growth is based upon the sustainable development strategies used to support the transition to green economy defined as the process of improving the economic, social and cultural and environmental well-being of future generations.

Likewise, the GE promotes economic growth and development, ensures the natural assets that provide environmental resources and services for the benefit of humanity's well-being, focusing on synergies and compensation between sustainable environmental and economic development. The interactions between society and the environment drive change and the transformation of the green economy as an opportunity to achieve sustainable development and human well-being. It is worth seeking the green economy as an opportunity to prioritize well-being and sustainable development for the present and for future generations.

According to Klingenberg and Kochanowski, (2015) GE is one of the tools used to achieve the sustainable (Shimova, 2019) development goals (SDGs) of eradicating poverty, hunger and food security, good health and wellness, education, gender equality and empowerment of women, water and sanitation, energy, economic growth, infrastructure, industrialization, inequality, cities, sustainable consumption and production, climate change, oceans, biodiversity, associations (Popkova, Bogoviz, & Ragulina, 2018).The socio-ecological and SDG indicators of the green economy described go beyond GDP as a transformative concept to measure wellness (Ferguson 2014; Fioramonti 2014; Stiglitz et al. 2009). The visions of the green economy are relevant to the legitimacy and the global green economy under the SDGs.

It should be noted that ecological sectors and industries (Shurrab, Hussain, & Khan, 2019) have the potential to become engines of ecological growth by reducing the use of fossil fuels as climate-resistant development. Some of the most relevant sectors for the green economy are agriculture (Sbicca, 2019), energy, water management, tourism, waste (Haldar, 2019). In this sense, green growth policies promote economic growth and environmental development by ensuring that natural resources provide environmental services for human wellness.

Green economy is acritical component of sustainable development which implies a greening change in the social construct of all the economy sectors. Details about the scale of the greening of specific sectors of the green economy development and implementation are required to be explicitly for absolute decoupling. Rural and urban development programs are a vehicle for enabling the transition from traditional rural and urban economy to a rural and urban green economy. Locally led development programs and group actions can often respond more effectively to local needs in the transition to the green economy. Urban green brands are already developing focusing more on green growth and low carbon economy which may be stronger and attract greater interest.

Green economy approaches offer economic opportunities of low carbon transitions under the framework of an agreement of a collective carbon finance goal (United Nations 2015). Resource and energy efficiency supports green products, services and low-carbon green economy as part of the transition to deliver economic, social and environmental benefits. Low carbon actions are part of a transition towards green economies can make the most of the resources available. The transition towards a green economy by investing and preserving the natural capital to generate growth, create jobs and eradicate poverty. A green job is defined as one that works with information, data, technologies, and materials, and requires specialized knowledge, training, skills, and experience for activities that minimize environmental impact.

The green economy concept is mutually complementary between different dimensions of sustainable development and poverty eradication to enhance convergence through different approaches, among which are the internalization of externalities, systemic economic structure, reconciling social goals, policies and objectives and the macroeconomic framework of development strategy (UNDESA 2010).

The design of green economy to contribute to sustainable development is away from the dysfunctionalities of traditional mainstream economy and results in human well-being and equitable access to opportunities safeguarding economic and environmental economic integrity. Green economy contributes to sustainable development with different forms of implementation for different countries. Resource efficiency is a green economy process is supported by environmental awareness and technological green innovation, although the increase in consumption may occur when efficiency gains are lost leading to the so called Jevons paradox, which may be addressed by specific policies on fiscal mechanisms and education.

GREEN ECONOMY PRINCIPLES

Guiding principles of a Green Economy helping practitioners in the application of the green economy concept are sustaining that it is a means for sustainable development, is equitable, just and fair, creating green jobs, protects biodiversity and ecosystem services, provide green resources and efficient green energy within the ecological limits, delivers well-being, access to essential services, poverty reduction, livelihoods, social protection. The principles of a green economy that according to GEC deliver a sustainable, inclusive and participative green economy are: sustainability, justice, dignity, healthy planet, inclusion, good governance and accountability, resilience, efficiency and sufficiency and generations.

The sustainable development and green economy strategies and policies is a model based on the core principles of economic efficiency, equity, social inclusion, environmental sufficiency and accountability which requires dialogue among all the involved stakeholders and participative policy design.

Also, these principles consider the measurement of green economy using appropriate metrics and indicators, internalizes externalities, improves governance and the rule of law being democratic, participatory, inclusive, transparent and accountable and more other principles. A good indicator of the relevance of green growth and economy for a specific society is to identify the number or share of population involved in any form, as employee, consumer, etc.

Equitable green economy is linked to sustainable development supported by principles and informed by policy and market decisions. Green economy principles must be integrated in sustainable development programs and initiatives such as in pollution prevention and sustainable production and consumption. Green economy principles aimed to develop a fair and inclusive economy to provide a better quality of life are the sustainability, justice, dignity, healthy planet, inclusion, good governance and accountability, resilience, efficiency and sufficiency and generations principles (Green Economy Coalition 2012).

Green economy principles can be applied to urban sustainable development by coordinating some deliverables with other organizations and donors relating to methodologies, platforms, best practices and tools that contribute to poverty eradication (UNCSD, 2012).

Green economy principles must be developed after engaging in discussion with the different stakeholders to meet the vision, priorities and needs of each sector. A set of green economy principles emerging from dialogue can serve as guidelines for making decisions which can be applied across sectors and institutions to operationalize a green economy. Social equity, ecological limits and community ownership are core principles for green economy.

TRANSFORMATIONAL TRANSITION OF GREEN ECONOMY

The transition towards green economy can solve the interconnected economic, social, and environmental crises. Green economy and transformation as enabling approaches are related to potentially create dynamic change (Pelling and Manuel Navarrete 2011; Pelling et al. 2014). Green economies integrate economic, social and environmental activities. The concept of green economy represents a transition for more environmentally friendly and resource-efficiency technologies to tackle environmental degradation by reducing carbon emissions and mitigating the effects of climate change (Jänicke 2012).

Transition to green economies require that green activities and investments in the interlinkages between rural-urban areas can contribute to green economic growth. Public and private funding of green economy has to be scaled up at all institutional levels and sectors supporting sustainable and responsible green investments in green business and companies, clean technology, green investments, etc. A green company is defined as a company that produces goods and services designed to reduce their environmental impact.

Green technologies should be developed with government financial support and subject to wider dissemination. Private investment flows in green technology should ensure that achieve full potential in spin-off benefits. Any percentage of global GDP invested to green economy sectors increase the growth, employment and reduce water, energy, etc. Public and private investments in green economy, promote revenue growth and employment from a rational use of natural and financial resources and energy efficiency that reduce carbon emissions and pollution and prevent loss of biodiversity and environmental services.

Development programs structured according priorities supports transition to the green economy in practice although the term may not be explicitly used, planning authorities may use different approaches and measures. Design and implementation of rural and urban and urban development programs support the transition of business activities to the green economy and the environmental performance. Development programs can provide financial support to support the transition towards a green economy with impact in long-term business opportunities. Business can foster practices that contribute to the green economy transition.

Equitable green economy is a transformation process in constant dynamic progression, although it has been questioned if green economy is equitable. One of the four green economy typologies is green transformation of economic growth through political interventions (Death 2015, 2216). Building on Ferguson's typologies based on weak/strong green economy, the UNEP's concept is more transformational providing enabling conditions for green economy transitions (UNEP 2011). Transformational green economy renders strong green economy and growth concepts deployed as organizing principles for climate change (Pelling et al. 2014).

The term green economy comprises the application of some economic instruments which requires social, institutional and political contexts to harness economic activities in support of sustainable development goals. Design of development plans can contribute to the transition to the green economy activities such as mitigation of climate warming, sustainable water and waste management, sustainable infrastructure, ecosystems services and buildings, investment in natural resources and capital, renewable energy feedstocks and energy efficiency, green research, green tourism and eco-innovation, agricultural and forest land management, forestry and fisheries (bio economics) green manufacturing and supply chain green public procurement, etc.

The transition to the green economy makes sure that agriculture and forestry are both economically and environmentally sustainable activities for the long-term. For example, the use of procurement policies for the greening of business. Green agriculture requires natural and physical capital assets, knowledge and financial investments and enhance the capacity building in efficient and sustainable management of soil fertility, water use, farm mechanization, crop and livestock diversification; etc. the analysis of investments measures benefits and costs of green economy and green energy policies taking into account capacity building, management, operation, research and development, expenditures in infrastructure, incentives, etc.

Measures for business and farm diversification can support transition activities to green economy. The sectors considered to have green potential are energy renewable, water, waste/recycling, sustainable farming and forestry, fisheries, public transport, green buildings, tourism, health care, education and training (Rosenberg, Lotz-Sisitka, & Ramsarup, 2018), green finances, etc.

Greening the fishery sector requires strengthening the fisheries management and financing fishing activities to maintain sustainable stocks within biological limits limit the environmental impact. Assessment of the impact on the dynamics of the fishing and marine ecosystem and biodiversity using quantitative indicators for socio-economic factors is required for a more effective exploitation of fisheries.

Greening the sector of forestry must be focused on reducing deforestation and increasing reforestation in accordance with economic and market mechanisms including payments for ecosystem services, certified benefit sharing and other schemes, community-based partnerships, sustainable forest management instruments aimed to carbon reduction, enhance protection of forests against fires and pollution, biodiversity and forest ecosystems, provision of environmental services, etc.

Greening the industry and manufacturing sector implies design to extend the useful life of goods and recycling them to support the use of by-products and alternatives for substitution to achieve a circular economy with a close-loop manufacturing in eco-industrial parks.

Greening the building sector requires a policy framework with instruments for development of sustainable building capacities and standards, cost-efficiency and incentives. Greening building requires investment and incentives for energy supply and renewable performance for sustainability of new and renovated buildings.

Greening transport policies intend to integrate land use and transportation planning for more environmentally efficient modes shifting to non-motorized transport and improving vehicle and fuel technology, avoiding or reducing trips and using water and rail transport for freight. All these policies are aimed to reduce the negative environmental and social effects. A greening transport policy framework to enhance sustainability though greener and efficient roads includes a strategy focused on the cost of transport in terms of environmental damage to society and reducing noise pollution.

Greening the tourism sector can be done by increasing the involvement of the local community in the tourism value chain and the interplay between internal factors and structural conditions.

Greening the waste management sector requires decoupling waste from economic growth and addressing the challenges of increasing the recycle rate of electrical and electronic equipment or e-waste, turning bio mass waste into recovered energy and other valuable resources, reducing food waste in the food chain, etc. The treatment of waste in the whole cycle from waste generation to waste disposal, should emphasize recovery for reuse and recycling of waste materials. Strategy for the prevention of industrial waste are based on industrial symbiosis resulting of collaboration to facilitate the exchange of by-products, water, energy and other materials.

Greening the water sector requires water management based on quality standards, to increase investments with better financial arrangements, to achieve a more efficient water supply, to improve the institutional arrangements and allocation systems, entitlements and use pf payments for ecosystem services.

Green economy transition is relevant to all economic sectors and requires a change in their economic activities perspective. Green economic transformation should be supported by new institutional forms for organization and decision making supported by participation and collaboration structures between public, private and community agents and actors for sharing resources and knowledge in green economic activities. One of these economic transformations into green economy is the circular economy.

CIRCULAR ECONOMY (CE)

Since its creation, the Circular Economy has been defined in different ways, in order to make it more understandable and easy to transmit for its application. Here are three ways to define this concept:

1. Claudia García Caicedo, in her publication Circular economy and its role in sustainable design and innovation, mentions that the Circular Economy aims to achieve product designs that reduce or completely eliminate waste, and also seeks to ensure that products are simple to dismantle-disassemble for reuse in new products. The CB is also responsible for defining business models that are exclusively dedicated to companies that apply the Circular Economy in their processes to achieve sustainable innovation and consequently feel economically motivated to recover their product after fulfilling its main function, use it again in manufacturing and repeating the cycle (Caceido García, 2017);
2. Catalina Balboa and Manuel Domínguez, in their work Circular economy as a framework for ecodesign: the ECO-3 model, define CS as a "philosophy of systems organization inspired by living beings, which pursued the change of an economy linear (produce, use and throw) increasingly difficult to implement due to the depletion of resources towards a circular and regenerative model,

as occurs in nature and which also represents a great opportunity in the business world "(Balboa & Domínguez Somonte, 2014). The interesting thing in the definition of Balboa and Dominguez is that they mention it as a way to try to solve the problem of scarcity of resources;

3. The Ellen MacArthur Foundation mentions that the Circular Economy usually has other names related to the schools of thought on which it is based, and that were already mentioned above, for example: economy of the cradle to the cradle or economy of closed loop (Ellen MacArthur Foundation (2), 2019). It is important to mention that this foundation declares that the defenders of the theory do not consider the Circular Economy as part of an ecological movement, but as a form of improvement of the design.

CONCEPTUAL BACKGROUND

Strategy

To define the strategy, the present work was based on the works of Michael Eugene Porter. This author defines the strategy as a differentiator that is created by making choices about several options that in the end would generate a unique value combination. Based on the conclusion by Porter, what really defines a strategy are the activities to which it specializes, that is, decision making is conditioned by the company's interest in differentiating itself from the competition. If the above is not respected, competitive advantage would not work as a differentiator but as an idea of marketing (Porter, 1996).

Porter talks about how a strategy can scale a company in the market, and become a strategic position. This position comes from three sources that sometimes work together:

1. Positioning based on the variety of products or services that exist in the area. The companies that use this positioning are usually those that have a better possibility of producing some good or service due to certain special characteristics that only they handle in the process;
2. Positioning based on needs, is one that is responsible for trying to meet the needs, or most of these, of a certain group of people. In a market there are many types of customers who request special products, which require certain characteristics in the good they want to buy, with different tastes or preferences, so they usually need guidance, support or very specific services;
3. Positioning by customer segmentation according to the way to access them or positioning based on access. Normally, this type of positioning is determined by the position or geographic location in which the client of interest is located. It can also be determined by the dimension or some specific situation that would hinder or hinder easy access to the client.

According to Porter, usually more threats come from sources outside the organization. When a strategy becomes part of a competitive advantage, it is likely to be threatened by changes in areas such as technology or the actions of competitors. It is mentioned that the event that can cause a certain strategy to fail is internal to the firm, and is mainly due to the underestimation of rival companies in the industry, poor planning, lack of information, or great ambition to grow without finalizing details.

Sustainability

The term Sustainability does not have a precise definition by itself, it is a rather ambiguous term that derives from the word sustainable, an adjective that implies "that can be maintained for a long time without exhausting resources or causing serious damage to the environment" (RAE, 2017, page sp). We can also find that Sustainability comes from Latin etymologies such as sustenance, sustenance, sustentare, sustentavi, sustentatum, which mean: sustain, maintain in good condition, care, conserve, support, favor (Ecología UNAM, 2015). In practice, we define Sustainability as a process that aims to ensure the satisfaction of the needs of the current and future generations.

Competitive Advantage

Competitive advantage can be defined as the essential aspect that demonstrates the performance of markets that are competitive, over the years the focus on competitive advantage has been lost to focus on the diversification and growth of organizations (Porter, 2015). Porter declares that the source or origin of the competitive advantage is the value that the firm generates in its products or services to satisfy the clientele, in other words, it is considered as a plus that manages to surpass the competition, even when the rivals try reach the company that has an advantage of this kind. In Porter's book "Competitive Strategy" he describes three general strategies for achieving competitive advantage: cost leadership, differentiation and concentration.

THEORETICAL BACKGROUND

The main objective of any firm is to generate high rates of return, in other words, obtain profits. Because of this, in the research work Sustainable Competitive Advantage: Combining Institutional and Resource-Based Views, Christine Oliver decided to create a hybrid model that would include the Approaches Based on Resources and Institutions, in this way the Model of the Advantage was born. Competitive Sustainable This author mentions that the reason why the resource-based approach is not only used is due to its limitations (Oliver, 1998):

1. Explain the heterogeneity of companies through the properties of resources and the markets of resources;
2. Does not worry about including the social context, which affects the decision making about the use of resources;
3. It does not talk about how the selection of resources is made.

By including the Institutional Approach, we seek to complete the spaces left, in the social sphere, by the Resource-based Approach, so that the Institutional will contribute (Oliver, 1998):

1. A study on how social influence affects decision making within a company;
2. It will show us the close relationship that exists between the selection of resources and sustainable competitive advantage in relation to decision making;
3. The importance of having an "institutional context" in the three levels of the company:

a. Individual level, are the normal and individual values;
b. Company level, are represented by the organizational culture and politics;
c. Inter-company level, as an example: public relations and its pressure on the market, regulations and standards faced by firms.

Oliver also inspected the general notions of the new hybrid approach of the Sustainable Competitive Advantage, which turned out to be the following:

1. The model divides decision making into three levels, as does the institutional one: Individual or managerial choice, company level, and inter-company;
2. Includes the way in which managers select resources and capacities, that is, the decision of which resources and capacities to implement;
3. Determines that in order to create and apply strategies, resources and institutional regulations must be taken into account;
4. It defines what is a capacity, resources and its idea of sustainability of an advantage that must be competitive;
5. Its analytical model consists of three determinants that assure us a sustainable competitive advantage, if it is integrated in the right way: those based on resources, such as managerial decisions; the selection of resources, the heterogeneity of the company; the institutional determinants: rational / individual regulation, institutional / business factors, and isomorphic pressure / between companies.

In relation to the selection of resources for its application, this new approach mentions that there are three cases in which it is more likely that a company is willing to acquire them or use the ones they have in reserve (Oliver, 1998):

1. When resources are acquired that are not major for the company, in this way we managers do not feel that they are risking their main activity;
2. Companies tend to be traditional, they are affected by their institutional part, so the acquisition of resources must belong to the same item that the company manages;
3. When a resource of the company is no longer considered productive, it is time to acquire new, since the organization does not feel so threatened by the change. The opportunity cost will have less impact;
4. The accumulated resources should be periodically monitored to know what we have and what we can use;
5. The training of the assets of the company helps them to know how to use potential resources;
6. From the moment of hiring, people with attitudes that have a notion of the use of resources for an optimal management should be chosen.

From the point of view of the Institutions approach, there are certain assumptions that would allow achieving a sustainable competitive advantage, in relation to the use of valuable resources (Oliver, 1998):

1. The acquisition of a valuable resource will be accepted by the company when it does not violate the regulations or the corporate culture;
2. The acquisition will be accepted if senior management gives it political support;

3. For reasons of power struggle, certain valuable resources will be acquired if with it the power of a decisive voter increases or strengthens its place in the company.

The creation of a model that unites the two approaches was necessary, since all approaches have deficiencies that tend to focus too much on production, resources or institutions and their regulations at different levels. This theory also shows concern for the factors that affect the individual as such and the impact that this would have on the decision-making process when selecting resources and applying them in the correct manner. The Focus of the Sustainable Competitive Advantage can be considered as an advance in the evolution of the strategies, since not only is oriented to obtain an objective, but also it is in charge of making known how to achieve it.

RESEARCH METHODS

Although the theoretical perspective that will be used in the present work is the theory of resources and capacities slightly influenced by the approach of the institutions, an analysis will be carried out through the VRIO Framework (Value, rarity, inimitability, and organization) to determine if The Circular Economy model could be considered as a viable resource as a competitive advantage that allows the company to achieve its objectives and position itself in the market, which would generate a competitive strategy.

ANALYSIS OF RESULTS

As already mentioned before, the tool that will be used to analyze the situation of the Circular Economy as a competitive resource within an organization, is through an internal analysis called Marco VRIO. First the analysis will be shown in the form of a table and after the explanation will be made by means of the answer to the four questions that this frame generates.

To obtain the results, the research work matrix was used as a base: ICT as a source of competitive advantage in SMEs (Moncada Niño & Oviedo Franco, 2013). The pertinent changes were made to be able to apply it in this specific case, as given below in Figure 1 and Figure 2 respectively.

Next, the explanation of the previous table, concept by concept, in addition to the specific interpretation to this particular case:

- **Valuable:** Answer the following question: is it a valuable resource to gain an advantage? According to Álvaro Fernando Moncada Niño and Martha Lucía Oviedo Franco in their work, valuable resources are considered those that can be used as a response to external threats, and in turn, help take advantage of opportunities. "The definition of the value of the resource or capacity is related to its possibility to exploit an opportunity or mitigate a threat in the market. If one of those two things is done, it can be considered as a strength of the company; otherwise, it is a weakness. When these are properly exploited, they generally lead to an increase in income or a decrease in costs or both "(Moncada Niño & Oviedo Franco, 2013, page 129).

Figure 1. VRIO analysis table

¿Valioso?	¿Raro?	¿Costoso de Imitar?	¿Explotado por la organización?	Fortaleza o debilidad	Implicación competitiva
No	-	-	No	Debilidad	Desvantaja competitiva
Si	No	-	-	Fortaleza	Paridad competitiva
Si	Si	No	-	Fortaleza	Ventaja competitiva temporal
Si	Si	Si	Si	Fortaleza	Ventaja competitividad sostenible

Source: Moncada Niño & Oviedo Franco, (2013)

Figure 2. VRIO analysis concept

Table 2 VRIO Analysis: The Circular Economy as a business resource	
Concept	**Answer**
Valuable: is it a valuable resource to achieve an advantage?	**Yes**
Rarity: is it being used by a small group of firms?	**Yes**
Inimitability: is it expensive to imitate?	**Yes**
Organization: Is the organization prepared in its policies and procedures to use this resource?	**NO**
Strength or weakness: is it considered a strength or a weakness	Strength
Competitive implication: results.	**Temporary Competitive Advantage**

Source: Own elaboration

Due to the above, the Circular economy can be considered a valuable asset, by exploiting the opportunity to reduce costs and reduce the waste generated by the company through a reengineering of processes and design.

The VRIO framework considers that resources must be rare, limited or unique, that is, very few companies are using it in their activities, otherwise the resource would not serve as a competitive advantage. If the rarity remains, and few companies manage to acquire it this would mean that the resource would remain scarce, which would give it the characteristic of sustainable competitive advantage (Moncada Niño & Oviedo Franco, 2013). The Circular Economy is a scarce resource that has not been applied in a large number of companies due to its complexity, but it is very likely that this rarity is not held too long, because of the changes in the policies related to sustainability and its derivatives, so it is considered as a temporary competitive advantage.

- **Inimitability:** Is it expensive to imitate? "... resources are inimitable when the possibility for competitors to analyze and duplicate them makes their acquisition or acquisition costly or takes too long to replicate" (Moncada Niño & Oviedo Franco, 2013, page 129). This characteristic of the VRIO Framework is usually related to the previous two, since the cost of use or application directly affects the rarity and its value. The CE is considered an inimitable resource, because when applied it would be considered quite expensive, since the generation of totally new designs thinking about the reduction of waste is expensive at the beginning, not any company can achieve it.

- **Organization:** Is the organization prepared in its policies and procedures to use this resource? "Relating to the fact that the company has certain organizational aspects, such as the organizational structure, processes and systems, as well as the business culture itself, to exploit the full competitive potential of its resources and capabilities. Therefore, the resources and capacities have to be exploited efficiently by the company "(Moncada Niño & Oviedo Franco, 2013, page 130).

When referring to this characteristic, it is deduced that the companies are not prepared, in their great majority, to install and use the Circular Economy, due to the great complexity changes and improvements necessary for an optimal operation.

CONCLUSION AND RECOMMENDATIONS

At the beginning, it was mentioned that this document aims to determine if the Circular Economy is a resource with the aim of becoming a competitive advantage that will impact on the focus of resources and capabilities. In this specific case, it turns out that, if it has the majority of the features of the VRIO Framework that allow it to be a competitive advantage, but of a temporary nature, because in the Rarity it is considered that in the coming years the business political demands will change, forcing companies to look for ways to include this type of model, regardless of the cost.

As a recommendation, it can be highlighted that organizations that wish to implement this model in their activities will need to have a good economic position. The initial costs of application are usually very high as a result of the changes that must be made from the root of the product: the design of this.

According to the results obtained in the present investigation, the EC is considered as one of the main factors that SMEs should consider carrying out re-engineering in the products they develop as in those that they generate through the innovation they generate. In this sense, the results are focused on those proposed by Ünal, Urbinati and Chiaroni, 2018.

Likewise, for the business sector, the EC turns out to be a competitive advantage that can be used for SMEs to develop a green economy through the EC, being a strategy that can position not only in national markets but also international markets. In conclusion, it was proved that the Circular Economy can be considered as a competitive advantage, but of a temporary nature according to the characteristics of the VRIO Framework.

REFERENCES

Alvial Muñoz, A. (2015). *Economía Azul: Una revisión en el marco de nuevas tendencias en Economía.* Obtenido de Bioeconomía Argentina: http://www.bioeconomia.mincyt.gob.ar/wp-content/uploads/2014/12/1.-Econom%C3%ADa-azul-A.-Alvial.pdf

Balboa, C. H., & Domínguez Somonte, M. (2014). *Economía circular como marco para el ecodiseño: el modelo ECO-3.* Obtenido de Universidad Nacional de Educación a Distancia: https://www2.uned.es/egi/publicaciones/articulos/Economia_circular_como_marco_para_el_ecodiseno_el_modelo_ECO-3.pdf

Ballie, J., & Woods, M. (2018). Circular by Design: A Model for Engaging Fashion/Textile SMEs with Strategies for Designed Reuse. In Unmaking Waste in Production and Consumption: Towards the Circular Economy, (pp. 103-121). Emerald Publishing Limited. Doi:10.1108/978-1-78714-619-820181010

Barry, J. (2010). Towards a model of green political economy: From ecological modernisation to economic security. In Global Ecological Politics (Advances in Ecopolitics, Vol. 5) (pp. 109-128). Emerald. Doi:10.1108/S2041-806X(2010)0000005010

Bıçakcıoğlu, N., Theoharakis, V., & Tanyeri, M. (2019). Green business strategy and export performance: An examination of boundary conditions from an emerging economy. *International Marketing Review*, *37*(1), 56–75. doi:10.1108/IMR-11-2018-0317

Bocken, N., De Pauw, I., Bakker, C., & Van der Grinten, B. (2016). Product design and business model strategies for a circular economy. *Journal of Industrial and Production Engineering*, *33*(5), 308–320. doi:10.1080/21681015.2016.1172124

Brundtland, G. H. (1987). *Our Common Future.* Obtenido de UN: http://www.un-documents.net/our-common-future.pdf

Caceido García, C. L. (2017). *Economía circular y su papel en el diseño e innovación sustentable.* Obtenido de Libros Editorial UNIMAR: http://ojseditorialumariana.com/index.php/libroseditorialunimar/article/view/1154

Cezarino, L., Liboni, L., Oliveira Stefanelli, N., Oliveira, B., & Stocco, L. (2019). Diving into emerging economies bottleneck: Industry 4.0 and implications for circular economy. *Management Decision*, MD-10-2018-1084. doi:10.1108/MD-10-2018-1084

Ecointeligencia. (2017). *¿En qué consiste la Economía del Rendimiento?* Recuperado el Mayo de 2019, de Ecointeligencia: https://www.ecointeligencia.com/2017/01/economia-rendimiento/

Ecología, U. N. A. M. (2015). *Fundación UNAM*. Obtenido de UNAM: http://www.fundacionunam.org.mx/ecologia/sostenibilidad-vs-sustentabilidad/

Ellen MacArthur Foundation. (2019a). *Economía Circular: Concepto*. Recuperado el 10 de Mayo de 2019, de Ellen MacArthur Foundation: https://www.ellenmacarthurfoundation.org/es/economia-circular/concepto

Ellen MacArthur Foundation. (2019b). *Economía Circular: Escuelas de pensamiento*. Recuperado el 16 de Mayo de 2019, de Ellen MacArthur Foundation: https://www.ellenmacarthurfoundation.org/es/economia-circular/escuelas-de-pensamiento

Gleason Espíndola, J., Cordova, F., & Casiano Flores, C. (2018). The importance of urban rainwater harvesting in circular economy: The case of Guadalajara city. *Management Research Review*, *41*(5), 533–553. doi:10.1108/MRR-02-2018-0064

Gliedt, T., & Parker, P. (2007). Green community entrepreneurship: Creative destruction in the social economy. *International Journal of Social Economics*, *34*(8), 538–553. doi:10.1108/03068290710763053

Green, D., & McCann, J. (2011). Benchmarking a leadership model for the green economy. *Benchmarking: An International Journal*, *18*(3), 445–465. doi:10.1108/14635771111137804

Gro Harlem Brundtland. (1987). *Our Common Future*. Obtenido de UN Documents: http://www.un-documents.net/our-common-future.pdf

Grown, H. (n.d.). *Diseño Regenerativo*. Recuperado el Mayo de 2019, de Heaven Grown: http://heavengrown.com/arquitectura-regenerativa/

Haldar, S. (2019). Green entrepreneurship in the renewable energy sector – a case study of Gujarat. *Journal of Science and Technology Policy Management*, *10*(1), 234–250. doi:10.1108/JSTPM-12-2017-0070

Hawken, P., Lovins, A., & Lovins, L. (2000). *Natural Capitalism: Creating the Next Industrial Revolution*. Obtenido de Research Gate: https://www.researchgate.net/publication/265074221_Natural_Capitalism

Jones, P., & Wynn, M. (2019). The circular economy, natural capital and resilience in tourism and hospitality. *International Journal of Contemporary Hospitality Management*, *31*(6), 2544–2563. doi:10.1108/IJCHM-05-2018-0370

Kavinski, H., De Souza-Lima, J. E., Maciel-Lima, S. M., & Floriani, D. (2010). La apropiación del discurso de la sustentabilidad por las organizaciones empresariales brasileñas. *Cultura y Representaciones Sociales*, *4*(8), 34–69.

Klingenberg, B., & Kochanowski, S. (2015). Hiring for the green economy: Employer perspectives on sustainability in the business curriculum. *Journal of Management Development*, *34*(8), 987–1003. doi:10.1108/JMD-06-2014-0058

Kumar, V., Sezersan, I., Garza-Reyes, J., Gonzalez, E., & AL-Shboul, M. A. (2019). Circular economy in the manufacturing sector: Benefits, opportunities and barriers. *Management Decision*, *57*(4), 1067–1086. doi:10.1108/MD-09-2018-1070

Liakos, N., Kumar, V., Pongsakornrungsilp, S., Garza-Reyes, J., Gupta, B., & Pongsakornrungsilp, P. (2019). Understanding circular economy awareness and practices in manufacturing firms. *Journal of Enterprise Information Management*, *32*(4), 563–584. doi:10.1108/JEIM-02-2019-0058

McDonough, W., Braungart, M., & Bollinger, A. (2007). *Cradle-to-cradle design: creating healthy emissions – a strategy for eco-effective product and system design*. Obtenido de Science Direct: https://www.sciencedirect.com/science/article/pii/S0959652606002587

Mejía Dugand, S. (2010). *La Ecología Industrial*. Obtenido de El Colombiano: https://www.elcolombiano.com/historico/la_ecologia_industrial-HEEC_101107

Missé, A., Moreno, J. A., Vázquez Oteo, O., Escorsa, P., & Casado Cañeque, F. (2015). *Responsabilidad Social de la Empresa: ¿RSE o RIP?* Obtenido de jstor: http://www.jstor.org/stable/26360524

Moncada Niño, Á. F., & Oviedo Franco, M. L. (2013). Las TIC como fuente de ventaja competitiva en las PYMES. *Sotavento M.B.A.*, *21*, 126-134. Recuperado el Mayo de 2019, de Universidad Externado de Colombia: https://revistas.uexternado.edu.co/index.php/sotavento/article/view/3441/3128

Morlet, A., Blériot, J., Opsomer, R., Linder, M., Henggeler, A., Bluhm, A., & Carrera, A. (2016). *Intelligent Assets: Unlocking the Circular Economy Potential*. Ellen MacArthur Foundation.

Oliver, C. (1998). *Sustainable Competitive Advantage: Combining Institutional and Resource-Based Views.* Recuperado el Mayo de 2019, de Strategic Management Journal: http://www.jstor.org/stable/3088134

Popkova, E., Bogoviz, A., & Ragulina, J. (2018). Technological Parks, "Green Economy," and Sustainable Development in Russia. In Exploring the Future of Russia's Economy and Markets (pp. 143-159). Emerald. Doi:10.1108/978-1-78769-397-520181008

Porter, M. (1996). *¿Qué es la estrategia?* Recuperado el Mayo de 2019, de Harvard Business Review: https://s3.amazonaws.com/academia.edu.documents/37851742/4_Que_es_Estrategia.pdf?AWSAccessKeyId=AKIAIWOWYYGZ2Y53UL3A&Expires=1558381861&Signature=132Q27yedrcb1MADZWvjsnckcC8%3D&response-content-disposition=inline%3B%20filename%3DQue_es_la_estrategia.pdf

Porter, M. (2015). *Ventaja Competitiva: Creación y sostenimiento de un desempeño superior.* Recuperado el Mayo de 2019, de Grupo Editorial Patria: https://books.google.com.mx/books?hl=es&lr=&id=wV4JDAAAQBAJ&oi=fnd&pg=PT3&dq=que+es+ventaja+competitiva&ots=mwvClbT58A&sig=O2eioD4ADfMxwU5PBfOy20qH-SA#v=onepage&q=que%20es%20ventaja%20competitiva&f=false

Puentes-Poyatos, R., Yebra-Rodríguez, Á., & Guerrero, F. (2016). *Responsabilidad Social Corporativa: El compromiso de la Universidad con los ciudadanos.* Obtenido de Revista de Antropología Experimental: http://revistaselectronicas.ujaen.es/index.php/rae

RAE. (2017). *Real Academia Española.* Obtenido de DLE: http://dle.rae.es/?w=diccionario

Rosenberg, E., Lotz-Sisitka, H., & Ramsarup, P. (2018). The green economy learning assessment South Africa: Lessons for higher education, skills and work-based learning. *Higher Education. Skills and Work-Based Learning*, *8*(3), 243–258. doi:10.1108/HESWBL-03-2018-0041

Saavedra García, M. L., & Saavedra García, M. E. (2014). La PYME como generadora de empleo en México. *Revista Clío América*, 153-172.

Sbicca, J. (2019). Urban Agriculture, Revalorization, and Green Gentrification in Denver, Colorado. *The Politics of Land*, 149-170. Doi:10.1108/S0895-993520190000026011

Secretaria Internacional de la Carta de la Tierra. (2019). *La Carta de la Tierra.* Obtenido de http://cartadelatierra.org/descubra/la-carta-de-la-tierra/

Shimova, O. (2019). Belarus on the Way to Sustainable Development: Circular Economy and Green Technologies. In Modeling Economic Growth in Contemporary Belarus (Entrepreneurship and Global Economic Growth) (pp. 89-106). Emerald. Doi:10.1108/978-1-83867-695-720191007

Shurrab, J., Hussain, M., & Khan, M. (2019). Green and sustainable practices in the construction industry: A confirmatory factor analysis approach. *Engineering, Construction, and Architectural Management*, *26*(6), 1063–1086. doi:10.1108/ECAM-02-2018-0056

UANL. (2013). *El desarrollo sustentable en México.* Obtenido de Sustentabilidad: http://sds.uanl.mx/el-desarrollo-sustentable-en-mexico-3/

Ünal, E., Urbinati, A., & Chiaroni, D. (2018). Managerial practices for designing circular economy business models. *Journal of Manufacturing Technology Management.* doi:10.1108/JMTM-02-2018-0061

UNAM. (2015). *Ecología UNAM*. Obtenido de Fundación UNAM: http://www.fundacionunam.org.mx/ecologia/sostenibilidad-vs-sustentabilidad/

Zsolnai, L. (2002). Green business or community economy? *International Journal of Social Economics*, *29*(8), 652–662. doi:10.1108/03068290210434198

KEY TERMS AND DEFINITIONS

Circular Economy: The circular economy proposes an economic and productive model characterized by sustainability and saving of resources and energy sources in which goods are produced, consumed, recycled, produced and re-consumed, entering a life cycle.

Green Economy: That which leads to the improvement of human well-being and social equality, while environmental risks and ecological scarcity are significantly reduced.

Green Growth: The one that promote economic growth and development while ensuring that natural assets continue to provide the environmental resources and services on which our well-being depends.

Resources and Capabilities: The theory of resources and capabilities states that organizations are different from each other based on the resources and capabilities they have at a given time, as well as the different characteristics of the same and that these resources and capabilities are not available to all companies in the same.

Strategic Plan: It is a document integrated in the business plan that includes the planning at the economic-financial, strategic and organizational level with which a company or organization has to address its objectives and achieve its future mission.

Sustainable Development: Development that meets the needs of the present without compromising the ability of future generations to meet their own needs.

Transformation: The result of a process of change of form. It happens when one thing, fact or idea is converted into another.

Transition: A change from one form or type to another, or the process by which this happens.

VRIO Analysis: VRIO analysis is an internal business analysis tool that is included in the theory of resources and responds to the four basic characteristics that a resource must meet to give the company a competitive advantage.

Chapter 3
Operationalization of Circular Economy: A Conceptual Model

Teresa Dieguez
https://orcid.org/0000-0002-4886-1446
Polytechnic Institute of Cávado and Ave, Portugal

ABSTRACT

The arguments for growth, inequality and persistent poverty, climate change, and finite resources call for stronger sustainable development policies, from both developed and developing countries. Situations of more or less (un)sustainability that encourage the idea of finding reasonable ways out of humanity's desire for progress can be conceived. The economy is nowadays mainly based on the called linear economy, which demands a paradigm shift within public administration, companies, and citizens must be committed. The present study has the main goal to understand how entrepreneurship and business have shaped the sustainability and the circular economy model requirements. It also aims to review important concepts like circular economy, sustainable development, sustainable entrepreneurship, servitization, and product-service system. A hypothetical conceptual model for the operationalization of the circular economy model is proposed. Finally, some discussion is done, future research is suggested, and conclusions are presented.

INTRODUCTION

The arguments for growth, inequality and persistent poverty, climate change and finite resources call for stronger Sustainable Development policies, from both developed and developing countries. Situations of more or less (in) sustainability that encourage the idea of finding reasonable ways out of humanity's desire for progress can be conceived.

One of these, which have recently appeared, is "prosperity without growth" (Jackson, 2009). Based on the realization that doubting the dogma of growth is an act of lunatics, idealists or revolutionaries, Tim Jackson insists that growth must be questioned. "The idea of a non-growing economy may be an

DOI: 10.4018/978-1-7998-5116-5.ch003

Copyright © 2020, IGI Global. Copying or distributing in print or electronic forms without written permission of IGI Global is prohibited.

anathema to an economist. But the idea of a continually growing economy is an anathema to an ecologist" (Jackson, 2009: 14).

Tim Jackson (2009) takes up the line of thought launched by the Club of Rome in the 1970s, reaffirming the physical impossibility of our economy to expand infinitely on a finite planet for the simple reason that the economy is fuelled by physical resources. The dilemma will be between unsustainable growth and unstable growth.

Another possible alternative to the economic growth paradigm is "sustainable degrowth" (Schneider & Williams; 2011), based on the premise that economic growth is not synonymous with increased quality of life or justice, nor is it ecologically sustainable. It arises in this context of the inevitability of ecological collapse if nothing is done to stop the steamroller of economic growth (Romeiro, 2012).

However, sustainable growth must be an option (UNCTAD, 2018), a social choice of the individual to which it associates, leading to a profound transformation of values. The primacy of efficiency will be replaced by a focus on sufficiency (Research & Degrowth, 2012) and innovation will focus on new social and technological combinations that will allow for moderate living and co-living (Research & Degrowth, 2012).

The world economy at the beginning of the 21st century is mainly based on converting natural resources into waste via production: goods are manufactured and then discarded as waste, deteriorating the environment. It is the called Linear Economy (LE) and although recycling is fully developed in our society, and improving resource efficiency is encouraged, activities focused on achieving this efficiency fail to consider the finite nature of material stock (EMF, 2013).

These realities demand a paradigm shift where an effort is needed to replace the end-of-life concept with reducing, reusing, recycling and recovering (4Rs) materials and to slow down, close and narrow material and power loops. This concept is much discussed in the academic literature and it is known as Circular Economy (CE) (Garcés-Ayerbe, Rivera, Perales, & Leyva-de la Hizm, 2019). The transition from a linear system to a circular one will require commitment from three key social actors: public administration, companies and citizens (Moyano & Paniagua., 2018).

In fact, this concept must be clarified as it is incipient in the academic literature since the concept is novel (Ghisellini, Cialani & Ulgiati. 2016; Korhonen, Nuur, Feldmann, & Eshetu-Birkie, 2018). Based on the document presented by the Ellen MacArthur Foundation (2015), three principles are the support of CE: (1) defending and enhancing natural capital by controlling finite stocks and balancing renewable resource flows; (2) optimizing resource yields by circulating products, components and materials in use at the highest utility; (3) fostering system effectiveness by revealing and designing out negative externalities. The 4Rs the CE is based on - reduction, reuse, recycling and recovery - are extracted from these principles.

With limited resources, increasing demand and profitability, the circular economy is a promising model that is fit for the future. Due the problem of (un)sustainability that is invisible and silent the vision of a sustainable future calls for genuine entrepreneurship where the leaders and decision makers believes that in the long run only responsible entrepreneurship is profitable (Diacono, 2017)

The present study has a main goal to understand how entrepreneurship and business have shaped the sustainability and the Circular Economy model requirements. It also aims to review important concepts like Sustainable Development, Circular Economy, Sustainable Entrepreneurship, Servitization and Product-Service System. A Hypothetical Conceptual Model for the Operationalization of the Circular Economy Model is proposed. Finally some discussion is done, future research is pointed out and conclusions are presented.

LITERATURE REVIEW

The Economic Linear Model 'Leaving Out the Word' Unsustainable

The contemporary socioeconomic system is based on a linear economy: firms make products and the consumers use and dispose them (Michelini, Moraes, Cunha, Costa & Ometto, 2017). This linear production model incurs unnecessary resource losses in several ways: production chain and end-of-life waste, excessive energy use and erosion of ecosystems (EMF, 2013). A new economic model is required (EMF, 2015) and the European Union has chosen resource-efficiency as one of the flagships of its Europe 2020 strategy (Tukker, 2015). The big challenge relies on the possibility or not to combine the current paradigm with a prosperous future, since natural resources are finite and natural resources' regeneration impossible or too slow in time.

The United Nations (2017), through its Department for Economic and Social Affairs, provided some data on demographic trends and future prospects with the aim of driving economic and social policies towards more sustainable development. As can be show on Figure 1, there are currently in the world 7.6 billion people. Even as the number of annual births declines, the UN predicts the continual population increase, which will mean that, within 13 years, the world's population should reach about 8.7 billion. By 2050 this number is expected to increase to about 9.8 million people and by 2100 it is expected to reach a mark of over 11 billion.

Figure 1. Estimates for population growth in the world, ranging from 1950 to 2100
Source: United Nation, 2017

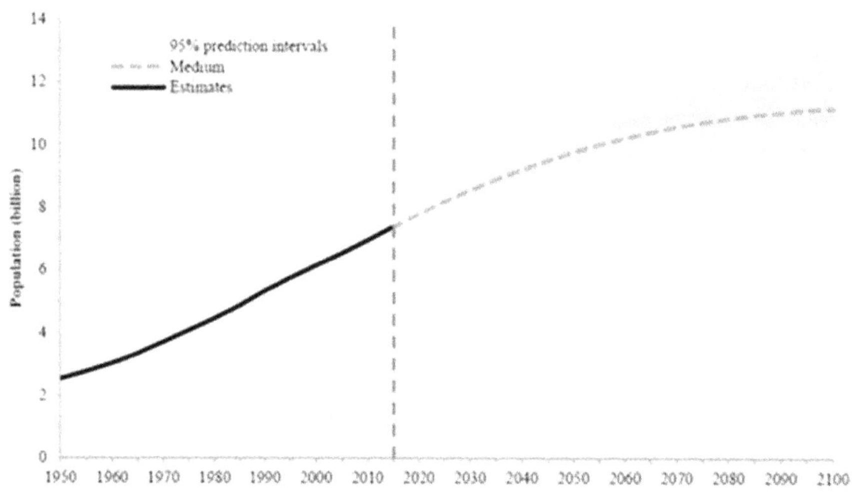

This projection reveals that Planet Earth faces unprecedented levels of growth and some researchers, like Weterings, Bastein, Tukker, Rademaker & de Ridder (2013) even mention that humanity, in order to satisfy its consumption needs, already needs more than the equivalent of the productive capacity of a Planet Earth.

In our current economic model, manufactured capital, human capital and natural capital all add to human welfare by supporting "the production of goods and services in the economic process, where natural capital - the world's stock of natural resources (provided by nature before their extraction or processing by humans) - is typically used for material and energy inputs into production and acts as a "sink' for waste from the economic process" (Brears, 2018, p. 2). It is fundamentally a matter of a linear model in which resource consumption follows a 'take-make-consume-dispose' pattern where natural resources are consumed for the manufacturing of products, which are then disposed of after consumption. In terms of volume, around 65 billion tonnes of raw materials entered the economic system in 2010 and this figure is expected to increase to around 82 billion tonnes in 2020 (EMF, 2013).

This model is considered truly unsustainable (Constanza et al., 2012) and unable to satisfy growth in a sustainable way (UNEP, 2015) due to a growing shortage of materials, increased levels of pollution, increased material demand, and a growing demand for responsible products by consumers (Brears, 2018). In contrast, the circular economy aims resources in use for as long as possible, extract value from them while in use, and recover and regenerate products and materials at the end of each service life (WRAP, 2019).

To counteract and prevent the trend of the linear economic model, the circular economy arises as an industrial system that is restorative or regenerative by intention and design (Hobson, 2015), which principles are three (EMF, 2015): preserve and enhance natural capital, optimize resource yields and foster system effectiveness. The circular economy brings the idea of restoration and circularity in order to replace the traditional concept of end-of-life, shifting towards the use of renewable energy, eliminating the use of toxic chemicals, and aims for the elimination of waste through the superior design of material, products, systems and business models (Michelini et al., 2017). Some key differences between the linear and circular economies are summarised in Table 1.

The Sustainable Development and the Circular Economy

In the 80's of the twentieth century, the problems associated with the relationship "society *versus* environment" occupied a relevant place on the world agenda (Dieguez, 2018). The World Commission on Environment and Development has promoted a report on these issues referred to as "Our Common Future" (WCED, 1987) - also known as the "Brundtland Report" – a document which is still a reference for everybody who is interested in exploring the concept of Sustainable Development.

Published in 1987, this Report offers what is considered the first definition of Sustainable Development, stating that "the concept of sustainable development provides a framework for the integration of environment policies and development strategies" and that the word "development" specifically refers to all "processes of economic and social change…" where "integration of environment and development is required in all countries, rich and poor". Moreover, and according to the same report, "the pursuit of sustainable development requires changes in the domestic and international policies of every nation." Perhaps the most mediated phrase in this report will be that it considers that "sustainable development seeks to meet the needs and aspirations of the present without compromising the ability to meet those of the future". A brief review of the available scientific literature makes it easy to gather other definitions of the concept of sustainable development: a controversial concept (Dieguez, 2018).

Governments, investors, companies and the civil society more and more are interested on sustainability and circular economy topics. Sustainability envisions a balanced integration of economic performance, social inclusiveness, and environmental resilience, to the benefit of current and future genera-

Table 1. Innovative circular economy approaches

Circular Economy Approaches	Description
Light-weighting	Reducing the quantity of materials required to deliver a service
Durability	Lengthening a product's useful life
Efficiency	Reducing the use of energy and materials in production and use phases
Substitution	Reducing the use of materials that are hazardous or difficult to recycle in products and production processes
Recyclates	Creating markets for secondary raw materials
Eco-design	Designing products that are easier to maintain, repair, upgrade, remanufacture, or recycle
Maintenance/ repair services	Developing the necessary services for consumers to have products maintained or repaired
Waste reduction	Incentivising and supporting waste reduction and high-quality separation by consumers
Waste separation	Incentivising separation and collection systems that minimise the costs of recycling and reuse
Industrial symbiosis	Facilitating the clustering of activities to prevent by-products from becoming wastes
Consumer options	Encouraging wider and better consumer choice through renting, lending, or sharing services as alternatives to owning products, while safeguarding consumer interests (in terms of costs, protection, information, contract terms, insurance aspects, etc.)

Source: Brears (2018)

tions (Geissdoerfer et al., 2017). Circular economy provides a positive, coherent, innovation challenge through which young people see the relevance and opportunity of these subjects in terms of rethinking and redesigning their future (EMF, 2013).

Being sustainable development based on three dimensions of well-being, namely economic, social and environmental, within its dimensions occurs complex synergies and mutual influence relationships (Cornesc &Adam, 2014). In this sense, Indicators become an important and broadly used tool to evaluate progress towards a more sustainable development (Gerlach, Richter & Richter, 2016). These indicators are needed in order to assist decision-makers and policy-makers at all levels and to increase focus on sustainable development (Čiegis & Štreimikienė, 2005). As a new paradigm for economic development, the circular economy has significant environmental, economic and social benefits at the global scale and promotes circularity to accomplish sustainable development. It also has links to many of the 17 Sustainable Development Goals (SDGs) approved by the United Nations in 2015 (SITRA, 2018).

Being circular economy emerged as an umbrella concept in the 2010's (Blomsma & Brennan, 2017), it perspectives the attainment of a more resource effective and efficient economic system by intentionally narrowing, slowing and closing materials and energy flows (Bocken, de Pauw, Bakker & van der Grinten, 2016; EMF, 2015). It is often seen as a way to attaining sustainability, but with a narrower focus on the economic and environmental dimensions (Geissdoerfer, Savaget, Bocken & Hultink, 2017). However, not all systems (e.g. businesses, value chains) incorporating circular principles are intrinsically more sustainable (Geissdoerfer, Vladimirova & Evans (2018). In business model literature, circular economy has been recently emerged, proposing feasible ways to business innovation linked to sustainability concerns (Annarelli, Battistella & Nonino, 2016).

Circular Economy model is a design restorative and regenerative industrial model that aims to promote the transition to the use of renewable energy, eliminate the use of toxic chemicals and, above all, eliminate waste generation through better material projection, products, systems and business models. It is a model that also ensures the satisfaction of demand and consumption needs of the population in a sustainable way. The term further encompasses the transition from "consumer" to "user". Interestingly, the concept of Circular Economics is inspired by the study of nonlinear systems such as living systems, where the notion of optimization predominates (EMF, 2013). In the Appendix a scheme of the Circular Economy Model that falls into five essential principles, namely: i) Design out waste; ii) Build resilience through diversity: iii) Rely on energy from renewable sources; iv) Think in systems and v) Waste is food, is presented.

In addition to the Ellen MacArthur Foundation (EMF), other entities such as the World Economic Forum, McKinsey & Company, WCDE or the UN, among others, have been extremely proactive in spreading the concept of circular economy and its urgency of be really implemented, whether through periodic reporting, either through raising global awareness or international congresses.

Sustainable Entrepreneurship

Entrepreneurship is a research field with many concepts and theories, but without theoretical consensus (Palma & Cunha, 2006). It is a phenomenon which manifests itself across the economy in many ways, but results are not always related to the creation of financial resources (Dieguez, 2017). It contributes to social and economic development (Conceição, Dieguez & Duarte, 2019), being not only a driving force for job creation, competitiveness, growth and productivity enhancements, but also for personal fulfilment and social objective achievement (Flash Eurobarometer, 2010; Wiklund, Nikolaev, Shir & Bradley, 2019). It is a way of thinking, reasoning and acting that is obsessed in opportunity, holistic in approach and where leadership is related to purpose of creating and retaining value (Timmons & Spinelli, 2009). It is a buzz word and as there is no universal definition for its concept, but can be defined as a mind-set that constantly seeks to do new things, in an innovative way. It is a process that involves identifying a business opportunity and making every effort to materialize it into a new business product or service that people want or need.

In turn, the concept of "Sustainability" is a multidimensional concept that encompasses a set of objectives, namely: environmental protection, economic development and social equality (Choi & Gray, 2008). According to Weidinger, Fischler and Schmidpeter (2013), entrepreneurs or companies whose core businesses are directed towards sustainable development may be considered Sustainable entrepreneurs. The identified business opportunities by nearly all sustainable entrepreneurs emerge from public concern about environmental imbalances. These types of entrepreneurs seek to give a satisfactory answer without forgetting the lucrative aspect of the business. Following what has been written, the concept of Sustainable Entrepreneurship is the given designation to an integrated view of business, society and the environment that links the concepts of Entrepreneurship and Sustainable Development (Schaltegger & Wagner, 2011). Some authors have shown that even if entrepreneurship is a complex phenomenon, sustainable entrepreneurship is perhaps more so, given the presence of commercially viable ventures that pursue economic, social and environmental outcomes concurrently (Munoz & Dimov, 2015; Godelnik &van der Meer, 2019).

In other words, Sustainable Entrepreneurship is a business strategy focused on increasing value for society, the environment and the company or business. It "contributes to: i) solving societal and environmental problems through the realization of a successful business, ii) creating sustainable development through entrepreneurial corporate activities; iii) means and ends; iv) Core element of integrated end to contribute to sustainable development; v) from small contribution to large contribution to sustainable development" (Schaltegger & Wagner, 2011, p. 224).

Shepherd & Patzelt (2011) argue, therefore, that sustainable entrepreneurship "brings into existence future products, processes, and services for gain, where gain is broadly built to include economic and non-economic gains to individuals, the economy, and society". In turn, for Weidinger et al (2013) sustainable entrepreneurship "is a progressive management approach to generate new products and services, management systems, markets and organizational processes that increase the social as well as the environmental value of business activities". Sustainable entrepreneurship is characterized by some fundamental aspects of entrepreneurial activities which are less oriented towards management systems or technical procedures, and focus more on the personal initiative and skills of the entrepreneurial person or team to realize large-scale market success and societal change with environmental or societal innovations (Schaltegger & Wagner, 2011).

As a distinction to many views of conventional entrepreneurship, sustainable entrepreneurship furthermore extends the goal of corporate influence beyond market success to initiating societal change and changing market conditions and regulations. The ambition to achieve societal goals by means of entrepreneurship and business approaches has been dealt with under the term of social entrepreneurship (Prahalad & Hammond, 2002; Bull, 2008). Social enterprises constitute a heterogeneous business movement, which is oriented towards the equitable distribution and not accumulation of social and economic capital (Ridley-Duff, 2008). Defined more widely, sustainable entrepreneurship can thus be described as an innovative, market-oriented and personality driven form of creating economic and societal value by means of break-through environmentally or socially beneficial market or institutional innovations (Schaltegger & Wagner, 2011). This wide definition of sustainable entrepreneurship takes into account intrapreneurs (Pinchot, 1988; Gapp & Fisher, 2007) as an important subgroup of sustainable entrepreneurs; they represent actors inside an organization who substantially change and shape the environmental and business growth development of the company (Jorna, 2006; Zhao, 2005).

Servitization and Product-Service System

For mature industrial companies who have products with small differentiation from their competitors or if they are commodities, it is very difficult to maintain competitive advantages based solely on these same products. To circumvent this obstacle, entrepreneurs and industries in developed countries increasingly realize the urgency of moving downstream in their value chain, competing with a focus on the added value of products and services delivered to the customer, ie, through differentiation rather than a lower price (Walters, 2009). The value of services is increasingly and better understood by industrial companies and many are already seeking to include them in their offerings.

Servitization is the latest trend in business models; in servitization, manufacturing companies retain ownership of assets throughout their lifetime (Estarrona, Seneviratne, Villarejo & Galar, 2019). It is a challenge for industrial companies who are unaccustomed to designing services and who have traditionally relied on sales for their revenue. With servitization, assets are owned and maintained by asset manufacturers during the product's lifecycle. This change must be accommodated by companies if they wish to remain competitive (Schüritz, Seebacher, Satzger & Schwarz, 2017). In fact, "the innovation of an organization's capabilities and processes to shift from selling products to selling integrated products and services that deliver value in use" (Baines, Lightfoot, Benedettini, et al. 2009, p. 555) - has attracted fairly broad academic coverage and closely related topics include product-service-systems (PSS), service transition, and service transformation (Baines, Lightfoot, Benedettini, et al. 2009). Next table (Table 2) shows some of the main definitions that can be found in the literature review.

Table 2. Definition of servitization

Authors	Definition of Servitization
Vandermerwe & Rada (1988)	Market packages or 'bundles' of customer-focussed combinations of goods, services, support, self-service and knowledge".
Desmet, Van Dierdonck & Van Looy (2003)	A trend in which manufacturing firms adopt more and more services components in their offerings
Lewis, Portioli Staudacher & Slack (2004).	Any strategy that seeks to change the way in which product functionality is delivered to its markets.
Slack (2005)	Servitization is the generic (if somewhat unattractive) term that has come to mean any strategy that seeks to change the way in which product functionality is delivered to its markets.
Åhlström & Nordin (2006)	A "servitization" strategy attempting to establish service supply relationships to deliver product services to augment their physical products. This strategy achieved dominance during recent decades over, for instance, the goods-oriented strategy where cost minimisation is in focus
Neely (2008)	Manufacturing firms (...) move beyond manufacturing and offer services and solutions, often delivered through their products, or at least in association with them.
Baines *et al* (2009)	Servitization is the innovation of an organisation's capabilities and processes to shift from selling products to selling integrated products and services that deliver value in use
Schmenner (2009)	The term "servitization" was coined to capture the innovative services that have been bundled (integrated) with goods by firms that had previously been known strictly as manufacturers. Servitization extends the reach of the manufacturer ever closer to the customer and the customer's underlying needs.
Bascavusoglu-Moreau & Tether (2010)	A strategy whereby the offering is a customer focused package in order to add value to core corporate offerings is a way to flourish
Gebauer, Gustafsson & Vittel (2011)	Manufacturing companies are redirecting their efforts towards customer centricity and innovativeness, but also from goods to services. Instead of only innovation products, companies are investing in services differentiation. Consequently, instead of services being add-ons to the product, theu become the center of the total offering, with products as add-ons to the services.
Kinnusen & Turunen (2012)	(the) phenomenon of manufacturers adding services to their offering.
Ahamed, Inohara & Kamoshida (2013)	A transition process to the stage where organizations continuously innovate new services and add value with its coreproduct, which in the end signifies a firm as a value provider
Baines & Lightfoot (2013)	Manufactures themselves can base their competitors strategies on services, and the process through which this is achieved is commonly known as servitization.
Avlonitis, Frandsen, Hsuan & Karlsson (2014)	Competing through value propositions that integrate services with product offerings
Parida Sjödin, Wincent & Kohtamäki (2014)	Manufacturing companies have increasingly shifted from manufacturing products to adding industrial product-services.
Lütjen, Tietze & Schultz (2017)	Servitization is commonly taken to be a transition or transformation which is largely characterised as a linear and gradual move along a product continuum from less to more sophisticated services.

Source: Adapted from literature review

The Manufacturing Sector

Servitization is happening in almost all industries on a global scale and has reached almost every business and continent (Neely, 2008). Swept up by the forces of deregulation, technology, globalization and competitive pressure, both service companies and manufacturers are moving more dramatically into services (Parida, Sjödin, Wincent & Kohtamäki (2014). Servitization is therefore a phenomenon that is observed when manufacturing companies adopt strategies to broaden their position in the value chain in order to generate gains from the combination of Products and Services. However, when companies servitize in a basic, manner offering common services, they have little potential for differentiation. Enterprises need to identify other ways to offer unique value propositions and to stay competitive. In this context, the integration of technology is becoming a crucial element for organizations to develop, integrate and deliver novel services, and advancing the original limits of servitization (Dinges, Urmetzer, Martinez, Zaki, & Neely, 2015). Data analytics is expected to drive the next wave of servitization (Opresnik & Taisch, 2015) and, therefore, has the potential to become a new source of competitive advantage (Lavalle, Lesser, Shockley, Hopkins & Kruschwitz, 2011).

In turn, the concept of Product-Service System emerged during the 1990s and one of the first definitions given by Goedkoop et al, 1999) as a marketable set of products and services, with a combined capacity, satisfy a customer's need. A Product-Service System provider is intimately qualified with an industrial ecology and aims to reduce raw material consumption and promote sustainability (Goedkoop et al, 1999). Within well-established defined industrial enterprises, the implementation of the Product-Service System focuses on increasing strategy, increasing business wealth and reducing environmental impact. Baines et al (2007) are considered authors who officially have established a relationship between Servitization and Product-Service Systems. The concept of Product-Service System is one of the most widely used service strategies for industries wishing to have more profitable and sustainable businesses.

Michellini et al (2017) state that the PSS-Product-Service System may play a major role in promoting the transition from a Linear Model to a Circular Model. Basically, they consider that the PSS is an important aid in building the Circular Economy model, as its philosophy seeks to make waste a thing of the past.

The potential sustainability of a PSS relies on the integrated design of all the elements in the system to fulfil a function (Mont, 2001). Due to this integration, it is possible that the economic interests of the stakeholders, as partners in the development of the systems, converge thereby encouraging the optimisation of the whole system (Manzini &Vezzoli, 2003). It is from this optimisation that environmental and social benefits arise because one function can be fulfilled with many different system configurations (Goedkoop et al, 1999). It is that level of freedom that allows the stakeholders in the system to find efficient, innovative and sustainable solutions (Manzini & Vezzoli, 2003; Zeeuw van der Laan & Aurisicchio, 2019). However, this argument implies that not all PSSs may have the potential to be sustainable solutions (Hernandez, 2019).

CASE STUDY

Methodology

As the Operationalization of the Circular Economy is a complex theme, a multiple case study approach was used. First a literature review on sustainable PSS and business models was performed to conceptually frame how PSS performance and business models are related and can be integrated. Then it was chosen two big companies for conducting this study: big companies (henceforth referred to C1 and C2) that introduced sustainable PSS into the marketplace. One company (C1) is a huge supplier of telecommunication infrastructure, presented in more than 180 countries and employing more than 116.000 people. Another large company (C2), presented in 120 countries, direct employing more than 13.000 employees and manufacturing heavy machinery. Both companies felt big challenges while introducing PSS offerings, especially because they had global costumers. But they also got revenues from it and developed PSS business models. Company C1 cares about operations, migration and upgrading offers of their service communication delivery, for customers do not have to worry about it. Company C2 guarantees equipment to assure the levels of availability to their customers and offers it based on contracts of their construction equipment in global markets. Four interviews were conducted, between May and July 2018. The interviewed (2 from each organization) were executives in charge for their strategic business units and directly engaged in providing sustainable PSS. The interviews were recorded and transcribed for data treatment and analysis.

The main conclusion seemed to be linked with the value creation and value delivery. Both companies adopted good practices to solve changing problems and new market requirements. For value creation, companies took over responsibilities that customers previously handled, by providing complete lifecycle solutions to them: from the beginning (installation) right through its entire life period. Operational activities are controlled by the companies which see risks diminishing. Also, products and/or physical assets are managed by them, in an integrative way, which rely on fewer resources, more long-life assets and more opportunities to supply toward sustainable PSS provision. Efficiency can be improved by suppliers themselves or by agreements with other companies, if other companies are more efficient in special part(s) and are better equipped to do so. Also, value creation is reached through improvement of utilization's resource in minimizing downtime of the product, implying less service costs, materials and replacements. Remanufacturing and recycling products can re-enter on life cycle and this contributes to sustainability efforts. For customers, they must only focus on their personnel and product operations management, allowing suppliers to add value. In providing sustainable PSS, the intensity and quality of interaction with customers are critical, as companies must know customers' processes and closely interact with them in order to positively contribute to their operations: by understanding their needs and businesses, working closer facilitates solution findings, more customized and efficient.

For value delivery, companies need to establish real networks with external entities, sometimes from providing individual products or services and other times through integrated PSS. Even there are lots of possible partners with technical and product related knowledge; it looks like as if that they do not have enough knowledge about service and customer interaction skills. Also, it seems that they don´t have enough know-how about eco-system and delivering sustainable PSS from consumption until the end of the life cycle. These constraints, as understandable, require special careful when choosing which partners to have. Also, proximity of customers is needed, as qualified personnel and the availability of spare parts or other solutions related components are critical. Digital interface platforms are excellent tools to manage inputs, outputs, detect errors, etc, and those are reasons that surely justify its required development, as supplier companies need to surpass with the success all the changing renovations. As what concerns to networks inside the studied companies more than organized by functional units, companies need to work together, combining and coordinating skills across the product, services, support, and customer interfacing. Regional units are close to the customer's need to perform diverse and critical tasks to ensure value delivery in PSS. They participate in new activities and have more responsibilities. More developed routines are needed, more various components of the PSS must be designed and work closely with each other, if even they do not have to be integrated.

Discussion and Results

Many companies are already developing good sustainability practices, although the economic issue appears as the most relevant within the three-pillar conception of (social, economic and environmental) sustainability (Dieguez, 2012). The operationalization of the Circular Economy is a complex theme and demands a new paradigm. Companies that introduce sustainable PSS into the marketplace are aware of their impact and have especially to main strategies to develop their business and preserve the desired sustainability: through value creation and value delivery. Companies are experiencing a major renovation from a product centric business purpose in to one that focuses on the delivery of service (Erkoyuncu et al, 2009). More and new responsibilities, more control on operational activities, products and physical assets are required. Innovation is needed, especially for presenting solutions that are able to minimize downtime of the product, costs, materials and replacements. Companies must work close to their customers and in cooperation find customized and efficient solutions for them. Innovations are a key source of a competitive advantage that determines the economic success of each organisation (Sivam et al, 2019) and this means that a specific innovation can no longer be seen as the result of predefined and isolated innovation activities but rather as the outcome of a complex co-creation process, involving knowledge flows across the entire economic and social environment (Sivam et al, 2019). In this sense, opening up the innovation process to all active players is the central basis of open innovation: knowledge can circulate more freely and be transformed into products and services that create new markets, fostering a stronger culture of entrepreneurship (European Commission, 2016).

Companies also seem to understand that the establishment of networks with external entities are critical. Nevertheless, it is not easy to find informed and committed external partners to work with sustainable delivering PSS from consumption until the end of the life cycle. Similar constraints happen within the companies themselves: more than organized by functional units, companies need to work together, combining and coordinating skills across the product, services, support, and customer interfacing, as well regions and customers. Customers are the reason why companies exist and companies must know them well in order to fulfil their requirements. More qualified people, more proximity to them and availability of spare parts or other solutions related components are critical.

PPS demands competitive and innovative customer solutions and involves identifying actors, roles and scenarios that define the flow of material, energy (or work) and information. Understand the trends and form new relationships and partnerships with customers and between other businesses, leverage companies to collaborate in delivering ''product-service packages'. These packages are delivered according to preproduction, production, distribution, use and end-of-life phases or straight down the line according to service and product needs (Durugbo et al, 2010). PSS delivery involves one or more customers and some solution providers (companies). The customer could be an individual consumer or a company, but all the players (providers and customers) must collaborate to jointly design and deliver the PSS which is known as value co-creation. While production considers product characteristics such as dimensions and mechanical phenomena, incorporating services requires considerations for new characteristics such as time and interaction. PPS must be modelled as a 'social construct' or an organisation so as to deliver competitive and innovative customer solutions (Morelli, 2006).

Conceptual Model Guide

The contribution of the company to a promising future should come from the increased positive impact of the business in society and this could be achieved only if it becomes sustainable. In order to assume such a challenge, more and more companies should fully integrate the sustainability in their strategies and operations (Danciu, 2013). But the sustainability is not easy to achieve, as it must become an integral part of the business strategy and operations. Only if the company overpasses the different challenges at each stage of the process for sustainability and develop new capabilities to tackle these challenges may be able to achieve it (Nidumolu, Pralahad & Rangaswami, 2009; Willard, 2012). However, the companies which choose sustainable strategies and practices will be in the position to drive value by growing revenues through new products and services, reducing costs through eco-efficiency, managing operational and regulatory risks more effectively and building intangible assets such as brand, reputation and collaborative networks with customers, competitors and suppliers (Danciu, 2013).

The analysed literature review pointed three major strategies that allow companies to implement the principles of the Circular Economy model, namely: i) innovation, ii) recycling and iii) servitization and product-service system. The recent literature introducing the concept of sustainable entrepreneurship has integrated the social and environmental aspects (Kuckertz & Wagner, 2010; Cohen, 2006), simultaneously linking the entrepreneurial process to the concept of opportunity recognition, which is in many ways closely related to innovativeness (Wagner, 2010). Entrepreneurship and innovation are the keys to achieving lasting economic growth in the long run, being innovation essential for sustained corporate success (Bărbulescu & Constantin, 2019). In terms of employment and sales, innovative businesses grow twice as fast as those failing to innovate. A visible trend in recent years has been the increasing movement towards open innovation and, especially, collaboration with startups. This is particularly noticeable in high technology industries, where innovation rates are rapid and where knowledge is shared between several organizations, making it more difficult for a single entity to innovate without collaborating (Choi & Gray, 2008). Sustainable innovations are defined as the creation of new market space, products and services, or processes driven by social, environmental, or sustainability issues (ADL Group, 2015). It consists of introducing new or improved products or services, processes or organizational methods, aligned with the principles of Circular Economy (Mattos & Albuquerque, 2018).

The second strategy is Recycling and consists in the recovery of used and end-of-life materials and products and their reintroduction into the production cycle through a closed-loop recycling system. This is commonly referred to as the 3R (reduce, reuse, and recycle) approach, being a key aspect of this approach that materials, which have accumulated in the circular economy, constitute important man-made stocks that can be exploited through recycling to gain secondary raw materials and reused and remanufactured to keep products in the commercial life cycle (OECD, 2015). In fact, circular economy provides a new economic model that intends to eliminate waste by introducing assembly, use, and disassembly and re-use cycles that minimize recycling and disposal (Spring & Araújo, 2017). It suggests that industry can profit from investment in resource productivity by adopting circular business models (Bocken, Short,

Rana & Evans, 2014; Linder & Williander, 2015). These are business models where the conceptual logic for value creation is based on utilizing economic value retained in products after they are used in the production of new offerings (Linder & Williander, 2015). One of the staples of these business modes is that they focus on providing product functionality instead of ownership (Linder & Williander, 2015).

The third and last strategy is Servitization and Product-Service System (SPSS). It is a strategy to qualify how industrial profile companies can increase their position in the value chain, seeking to generate the gains associated with combining their main products with used services - Product-Service System. Instead of paying for the product, it is intended that the customer pays for its use and maintenance, promoting sustainable product management. Initial studies on PSS recognized the sustainability and environmental implications were fundamental, and the PSS concept was defined around these aims (Mont, 2002; Goedkoop et al, 1999). Over the years, however, sustainability was treated more as an inherited result of PSS, and the focus shifted to achieving economic benefits and customer satisfaction (Baines et al, 2007). In recent years, however, the emphasis has shifted to achieving sustainable benefits by recognizing the need to work actively to realize the full sustainability potential of PSS (Tukker, 2015). Sustainability in PSS can be reached mainly through improved resource utilization or innovations that change operations such that they are more beneficial for the environment (Reim, Parida & Örtqvist, 2015). To capture value, it is important to design sustainable PSS such that customers are willing to pay for the added value (Mont, 2002). At the same time, costs need to be handled efficiently. In addition, the profitability of PSS is difficult to show because cash flows are uncertain and quantifying savings is difficult (Gebauer, Fleisch & Friedli, 2005). Pricing and absorbing risks are significant problems that manufacturers need to address when capturing value from sustainable PSS (Baines et al, 2007; Reim et al, 2016). As such, significant opportunity exists to use the business models concept to align functions and activities in the firm toward a common strategic goal, to use the concept as a coordination device, and to reach internal and external fit in the transition toward providing PSS that could positively affect the firms' performance (Ferreira, Proença, Spencer & Cova, 2013). Thus, the possibilities to exploit the full potential of sustainable PSS increase significantly, and the economic, social, and environmental benefits can be fully captured (Reim et al, 2017).

In view of the above and based on the done literature review throughout this investigation, a conceptual model (Figure 2) is proposed with the aim of guide the operationalization of a Circular Economy model.

CONCLUSION

Providing sustainable PSS demands, among others, network, strategy, proactivity, critical thinking and education for sustainable development. Companies should fully integrate the sustainability in their strategies and operations for having better positioning in the market and building intangible assets. Innovation to find solutions and entrepreneurship to proactively act and recognise opportunities are fundamental pieces. A visible trend in recent years has been the increasing movement towards open innovation and, especially, collaboration with start-ups. Sustainable innovations consist of introducing new or improved products or services, processes or organizational methods, aligned with the principles of Circular Economy: eliminate waste by introducing assembly, use, and disassembly and re-use cycles that minimize recycling and disposal. Adopting this business model, the conceptual logic for value creation is based on focus on providing product functionality instead of ownership, where customers pay for the use and maintenance, promoting sustainable product management. Servitization and Product-Service System

Figure 2. Conceptual model guide for the operationalization of a circular economy
Source: Own elaboration

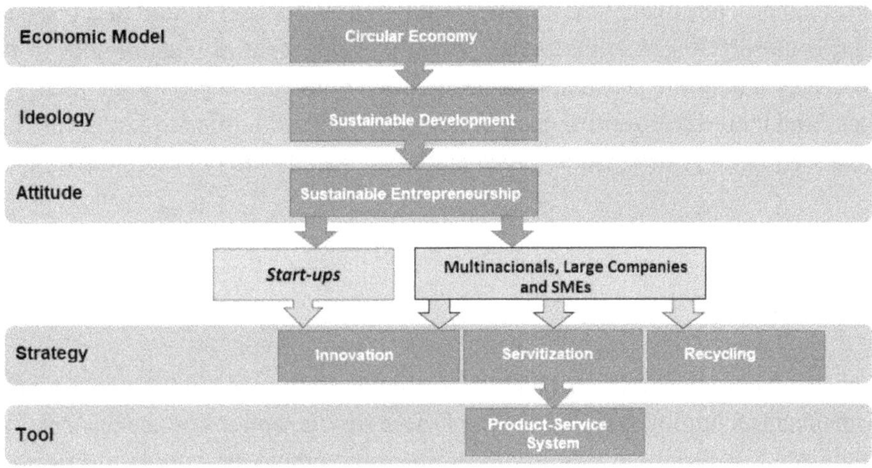

(SPSS) appears as a strategy to qualify how industrial profile companies can increase their position in the value chain, seeking to generate the associated gains with combining their main products with used services - Product-Service System.

The potential sustainability of a PSS relies on the integrated design of all the elements in the system to fulfil a function. Due to this integration, it is possible that the economic interests of the stakeholders, as partners in the development of the systems, converge thereby encouraging the optimisation of the whole system. It is from this optimisation that environmental and social benefits arise because one function can be fulfilled with many different system configurations. It is that level of freedom that allows the stakeholders in the system to find efficient, innovative and sustainable solutions.

However, not all PSSs may have the potential to be sustainable solutions and that is the reason why in this study is proposed a conceptual model for guide the operationalization of a Circular Economy, with an ideology of Sustainable Development and with an attitude of Sustainable Entrepreneurship. Whatever is the size or age of the company the major strategies that allow companies to implement the principles of the Circular Economy model are innovation, recycling and Servitization, having as a tool Product-Service System.

Sustainable Development provides a framework for the integration of environment policies and development strategies. Sustainable Entrepreneurship is a business strategy focused on increasing value for society, the environment and the company or business. Sustainable innovation consists of introducing new or improved products or services, processes or organizational methods, aligned with the principles of Circular Economy. Recycling consists in the recovery of used and end-of-life materials and products and their reintroduction into the production cycle through a closed-loop recycling system. Industry can profit from investment in resource productivity by adopting circular business models and the conceptual logic for value creation is based on utilizing economic value retained in products after they are used in the production of new offerings. Sustainability in PSS can be reached mainly through improved resource utilization or innovations that change operations such that they are more beneficial for the environment and is required a sustainable PSS such that customers are willing to pay for the added value.

Sustainability in PSS can be reached mainly through improved resource utilization or innovations that change operations such that they are more beneficial for the environment and customers are willing to pay for the added value. The concept may be a coordination device and should be a common strategic goal. Servitization is closely linked to the inclusion and development of technologies in the products underlying the services. The more sensors, processing power, and connectivity included in a product, the greater the potential there is for servitizing the product. The possibilities to exploit the full potential of sustainable PSS significantly increase and the economic, social, and environmental benefits can be fully captured.

FUTURE RESEARCH

For future research, it is recommended to further explore the studied topics, studying servitization together with the developments in technology and the effect of these service options on the business model of the companies. In addition, it is proposed to study the shift of the employed population from the primary to the secondary and tertiary sectors, a very common phenomenon in developed economies. As a way of proving this tertiarization (increasing importance of the services sector in GDP - Gross Domestic Product - developed countries), it would be interesting to consult the respective data on the evolution of the weight of the services sector in the GDP of several developed countries, including Portugal. The main sources of information for assessing these developments could be the analysis of data provided by The World Bank and, at national level, by the National Institute of Statistics.

REFERENCES

Ahamed, Z., Inohara, T., & Kamoshida, A. (2013). The servitization of manufacturing: An empirical case study of IBM corporation. *International Journal of Business Administration*, *4*(2), 18. doi:10.5430/ijba.v4n2p18

Åhlström, P., & Nordin, F. (2006). Problems of establishing service supply relationships: Evidence from a high-tech manufacturing company. *Journal of Purchasing and Supply Management, 12*(2), 75–89. doi:10.1016/j.pursup.2006.05.002

Annarelli, A., Battistella, C., & Nonino, F. (2016). Product service system: A conceptual framework from a systematic review. *Journal of Cleaner Production, 139*, 1011–1032. doi:10.1016/j.jclepro.2016.08.061

Arthur D. Little (ADL) Group. (2015). *How Leading Companies Are Using Sustainability-Driven Innovation to Win Tomorrow's Customers?* Innovation High Ground Report.

Avlonitis, V., Frandsen, T., Hsuan, J., & Karlsson, C. (2014). Driving competitiveness through servitization. A guide for practitioners. Academic Press.

Baines, T., & Lightfoot, H. (2013). *Made to Serve. How manufacturers can compete through servitization and product-service systems*. New York, NY: Jhon Wiley & Sons.

Baines, T., Lightfoot, H., Steve, E., Neely, A., Greenough, R., Peppard, J., ... Walton, I. (2007). State-of-the-art in product service-systems. Journal of Engineering Manufacture. *Proceedings of the Institution of Mechanical Engineers. Part B, Journal of Engineering Manufacture*, *221*(10), 1543–1553. doi:10.1243/09544054JEM858

Baines, T. S., Lightfoot, H. W., Benedettini, O., & Kay, J. M. (2009). The servitization of manufacturing: A review of literature and reflection on future challenges. *Journal of Manufacturing Technology Management*, *20*(5), 547–567. doi:10.1108/17410380910960984

Bărbulescu, O., & Constantin, P. S. (2019). Sustainable Growth Approaches: Quadruple Helix Approach for Turning Brasov into a Startup City. *Sustainability*, *11*(21), 6154. doi:10.3390u11216154

Bascavusoglu-Moreau, E., & Tether, B. (2010). *Servitization, Survival and productivity*. Paper presented at the DRUID conference. Copenhagen Business School.

Blomsma, F., & Brennan, G. (2017). The Emergence of Circular Economy: A New Framing Around Prolonging Resource Productivity. *Journal of Industrial Ecology*, *21*(3), 603–614. doi:10.1111/jiec.12603

Bocken, N. M. P., de Pauw, I., Bakker, C., & van der Grinten, B. (2016). Product design and business model strategies for a circular economy. *J. Ind. Prod. Eng.*, *33*(5), 308–320. doi:10.1080/21681015.2016.1172124

Bocken, N. M. P., Short, S. W., Rana, P., & Evan, S. (2014). A literature and practice review to develop sustainable business model archetypes. *Journal of Cleaner Production*, *65*, 42–56. doi:10.1016/j.jclepro.2013.11.039

Brears, R. C. (2018). *Natural Resource Management and the Circular Economy*. London, UK: Palgrave Macmillan. doi:10.1007/978-3-319-71888-0

Bull, M. (2008). Challenging tensions: Critical, theoretical and empirical perspectives on social enterprise. *International Journal of Entrepreneurial Behaviour & Research*, *14*(5), 268–275. doi:10.1108/13552550810897641

Choi, D. Y., & Gray, E. R. (2008). The venture development processes of "sustainable" entrepreneurs. *Management Research News*, *31*(8), 558–569. doi:10.1108/01409170810892127

Čiegis, R., & Štreimikienė, D. (2005). Integration of Sustainable Development Indicators into Sustainable Development Programmes. *The Engineering Economist*, *2*(42), 7–13.

Cohen, B. (2006). Sustainable valley entrepreneurial ecosystems. *Business Strategy and the Environment*, *15*(1), 1–14. doi:10.1002/bse.428

Conceição, O., Dieguez, T., & Duarte, M. (2019). A Multivariate Approach to Entrepreneurial Intentions. In J. Machado, F. Soares, & G. Veiga (Eds.), *Innovation, Engineering and Entrepreneurship. HELIX 2018. Lecture Notes in Electrical Engineering* (Vol. 505). Cham: Springer.

Constanza, R., Alperovitz, G., Daly, H. E., Farley, J. Franco, C., Jackson, T., … Victor, P. (2012). Building a Sustainable and Desirable Economy-in-Nature. New York: United Nations Division for Sustainable Development.

Cornescu, V., & Adam, R. (2013). Considerations regarding the role of indicators used in the analysis and assessment of sustainable development in the E.U. *Procedia Economics and Finance*, *8*, 10–16. doi:10.1016/S2212-5671(14)00056-2

Danciu, V. (2013). The sustainable company: New challenges and strategies for more sustainability. *Theoretical and Applied Economics*, *9*(586), 7–26.

Desmet, S., Van Dierdonck, R., & Van Looy, B. (2003). Servitization: or why services management is relevant for manufacturing environments. In B. Van Looy, P. Gemmel, & R. Van Dierdonck (Eds.), *Services Management: An Integrated Approach* (pp. 40–51). Harlow: Pearson Education.

Diacono, S. (2017). *Navigating the circular economy for entrepreneurial opportunities* (Master Dissertation). L'Universitàta Malta. Accessed on 18 September 2019. https://www.um.edu.mt/library/oar/handle/123456789/27819

Dieguez, T. (2017). Empowering Hub. In N. Baporikar (Ed.), Handbook of Knowledge Integration Strategies for Entrepreneurship and Sustainability (pp. 256–284). Academic Press.

Dieguez, T. (2018). Sustainable Development: A controversial concept. *International Journal of Modern Research in Engineering & Management*, *1*(7), 15–21.

Dieguez, T., Porfirio, J. A., & Amador, F. (2012). Institutions and the Emerging Challenges of Sustainable Development: The Case of Automotive Suppliers Industry. *ICERI2012 Proceedings*.

Dinges, V., Urmetzer, F., Martinez, V., Zaki, M., & Neely, A. (2015). *The future of servitization: Technologies that will make a difference*. Working Paper. Cambridge University.

Durugbo, C., Bankole, O., Erkoyuncu, J. A., Tiwari, A., Alcock, J. R., Roy, R., & Shehab, E. (2010). Product-Service Systems across Industry Sectors: Future Research Needs and Challenges. *CIRP IPS2 Conference 2010*.

Elgin, D. (1993). Voluntary Simplicity. In Sustainable Development or collapse, regeneration and transformation? From Noha's Ark to the Titanic and Back Again. Palacky University.

Ellen Macarthur Foundation (EMF). (2013). *Towards the Circular Economy: Economic and business rationale for an accelerated transition*. Cowes, UK: Ellen Macarthur Foundation.

Ellen Macarthur Foundation (EMF). (2015). *Towards the Circular Economy: Business Rationale for an Accelerated Transition*. Cowes, UK: Ellen Macarthur Foundation.

Erkoyuncu, J. A., Roy, R., Shehab, E., & Wardle, P. (2009). Uncertainty challenges in service cost estimation for products-service systems in the aerospace and defence industries. *Proceedings of the 1st CIRP IPS2 Conference*, 200-206.

Estarrona, U. M., Seneviratne, D., Villarejo, R. and Galar, D. (2019). The New Asset Management: Implications of Servitization in Circular Economy. *Journal of Industrial Engineering and Management Science*, 109-120.

European Commission. (2016). *Open Innovation, Open Science, Open to the World: A vision for Europe*. Directorate-General for Research and Innovation.

Ferreira, F. N. H., Proença, J. F., Spencer, R., & Cova, B. (2013). The transition from products to solutions: External business model fit and dynamics. *Industrial Marketing Management*, *42*(7), 1093–1101. doi:10.1016/j.indmarman.2013.07.010

Flash Eurobarometer. (2010). *Entrepreneurship in the EU and beyond 2010*. The Gallup Organization.

Gapp, R., & Fisher, R. (2007). Developing an intrapreneur-led three-phase model of innovation. *International Journal of Entrepreneurial Behaviour & Research*, *13*(6), 330–348. doi:10.1108/13552550710829151

Garcés-Ayerbe, C., Rivera-Torres, P., Suárez-Perales, I., & Leyva-de la Hiz, D. (2019). Is It Possible to Change from a Linear to a Circular Economy? An Overview of Opportunities and Barriers for European Small and Medium-Sized Enterprise Companies. *International Journal of Environmental Research and Public Health*, *16*(5), 85. doi:10.3390/ijerph16050851 PMID:30857193

Gebauer, H., Fleisch, E., & Friedli, T. (2005). Overcoming the service paradox in manufacturing companies. *European Management Journal*, *23*(1), 14–26. doi:10.1016/j.emj.2004.12.006

Gebauer, H., Gustafsson, A., & Vittel, L. (2011). Competitive advantage through service differentiation by manufacturing companies. *Journal of Business Research*, *64*(12), 1270–1280. doi:10.1016/j.jbusres.2011.01.015

Geissdoerfer, M., Savaget, P., Bocken, N. M. P., & Hultink, E. J. (2017a). The Circular Economy - A new sustainability paradigm? *Journal of Cleaner Production*, *143*, 757–768. doi:10.1016/j.jclepro.2016.12.048

Geissdoerfer, M., Vladimirova, D., & Evans, S. (2018). Sustainable business model innovation: A review. *Journal of Cleaner Production*, *198*, 401–416. doi:10.1016/j.jclepro.2018.06.240

GEM. (2017). *Women's entrepreneurship report*. Global Entrepreneurship Monitor.

Gerlach, J., Richter, N., & Richter, U. J. (2016). Mobility indicators put to test – German strategy for sustainable development needs to be revised. *Transportation Research Procedia*, *14*, 973–982. doi:10.1016/j.trpro.2016.05.077

Ghisellini, P., Cialani, C., & Ulgiati, S. (2016). A review on circular economy: The expected transition to a balanced interplay of environmental and economic systems. *Journal of Cleaner Production*, *114*, 11–32. doi:10.1016/j.jclepro.2015.09.007

Godelnik, R., & van der Meer, J. (2019). Sustainable Business Models in an Entrepreneurial Environment. In A. Aagaard (Ed.), *Sustainable Business Models* (pp. 239–276). Cham, Germany: Palgrave Macmillan. doi:10.1007/978-3-319-93275-0_9

Goedkoop, M. J., van Halen, C. J. G., te Riele, H. R. M., & Rommens, P. J. M. (1999). *Product Service System, Ecological and Economic Basic*. The Report No. 1999/36 Submitted to Ministerje van Volkshuisvesting, Ruimtelijke Ordening en Milieubeheer, Hague.

Hernandez, R. J. (2019). Sustainable Product-Service Systems and Circular Economies. *Sustainability*, *11*(19), 5383. doi:10.3390u11195383

Hobson, K. (2015). Closing the loop or squaring the circle? Locating generative spaces for the circular economy. *Progress in Human Geography*, 40.

Jackson, T. (2009). Prosperity without growth? The transition to a sustainable economy. Sustainable Development Commission.

Jorna, R. (2006). *Sustainable Innovation - the Organisational, Human and Knowledge Dimension.* Sheffield: Greenleaf.

Kinnunen, R., & Turunen, T. (2012). Identifying Servitization Capabilities of Manufacturers: A Conceptual Model. *The Journal of Applied Management and Entrepreneurship, 17*(3), 55–78.

Korhonen, J., Nuur, C., Feldmann, A., & Eshetu-Birkie, S. (2018). Circular economy as an essentially contested concept. *Journal of Cleaner Production, 2018*(175), 544–552. doi:10.1016/j.jclepro.2017.12.111

Kuckertz, A., & Wagner, M. (2010). The influence of sustainability orientation on entrepreneurial intentions - Investigating the role of business experience. *Journal of Business Venturing, 25*(5), 524–539. doi:10.1016/j.jbusvent.2009.09.001

Lavalle, S., Lesser, E., Shockley, R., Hopkins, M. S., & Kruschwitz, N. (2011). Big Data, Analytics and the Path From Insights to Value. *MIT Sloan Management Review, 52*(2), 21–32.

Lewis, M., Portioli Staudacher, A., & Slack, N. (2004). *Beyond products and services: Opportunities and threats in servitization.* Paper presented at IMS Intl. Forum, Italy.

Linder, M., & Williander, M. (2015). Circular Business Model Innovation: Inherent Uncertainties. *Business Strategy and the Environment, 26*(2), 182–196. doi:10.1002/bse.1906

Lütjen, H., Tietze, F., & Schultz, C. (2017). Service transitions of product-centric firms: An explorative study of service transition stages and barriers in Germany's energy market. *International Journal of Production Economics, 192*, 106–119. doi:10.1016/j.ijpe.2017.03.021

MacArthur, E. (2013). Towards the circular economy. *Journal of Industrial Ecology.*

Manzini, E., & Vezzoli, C. (2003). A strategic design approach to develop sustainable product service systems: Examples taken from the 'environmentally friendly innovation' Italian prize. *Journal of Cleaner Production, 11*(8), 851–857. doi:10.1016/S0959-6526(02)00153-1

Mattos, C. A., & Albuquerque, T. L. (2018). Enabling Factors and Strategies for the Transition Toward a Circular Economy (CE). *Sustainability, 10*(12), 4628. doi:10.3390u10124628

Michelini, G., Moraes, R. N., Cunha, R. N., Costa, J. M., & Ometto, A. R. (2017). From Linear to Circular Economy: PSS Conducting the Transition. *Procedia CIRP, 64*(C), 2–6. doi:10.1016/j.procir.2017.03.012

Mont, O. (2002). Clarifying the concept of product–service system. *Journal of Cleaner Production, 10*(3), 237–245. doi:10.1016/S0959-6526(01)00039-7

Morelli, N. (2006). Developing new product service systems (PSS): Methodologies and operational tools. *Journal of Cleaner Production, 14*(17), 1495–1501. doi:10.1016/j.jclepro.2006.01.023

Moyano, V., & Paniagua, S. (2018). Citizens and the Circular Economy, Current situation and prospects for the future. Creafutur. ESADE Business School. Cataluña.

Munoz, P., & Dimov, D. (2015). The call of the whole in understanding the development of sustainable ventures. *Journal of Business Venturing*, *30*(4), 632–654. doi:10.1016/j.jbusvent.2014.07.012

Neely, A. (2008). Exploring the Financial Consequences of the Servitization of Manufacturing. *Operations Management Research*, *1*(2), 1–50. doi:10.100712063-009-0015-5

Nidumolu,, R., Pralahad, K. C., & Rangaswami, M. R. (2009, Sept.). Why Sustainability Is Now the Key Driver of Innovation. *The Magazine*.

OECD. (2015). Material resources, productivity and the environment. *OECD Green Growth Studies*. Available: http://www.oecd.org/env/waste/material-resources-productivity-and-the-environment-9789264190504-en.htm

Opresnik, D., & Taisch, M. (2015). The value of Big Data in servitization. *International Journal of Production Economics*, *165*, 174–184. doi:10.1016/j.ijpe.2014.12.036

Palma, P. J., & Cunha, M. P. (2006). New challenges in entrepreneurship: Introduction to the special issue. *Comportamento Organizacional e Gestão*, *12*(1), 3–6.

Parida, V., Sjödin, D. R., Wincent, J., & Kohtamäki, M. (2014). Mastering the transition to product-service provision: Insights into business models, Learning activities, and capabilities. *Research Technology Management*, *57*, 44–52.

Pinchot, G. (1988). *Intrapreneuring*. Wiesbaden: Gabler. doi:10.1007/978-3-322-94468-9

Prahalad, C. K., & Hammond, A. (2002). Serving the world's poor, profitably. *Harvard Business Review*, *80*(9), 48–57. PMID:12227146

Reim, W., Parida, V., & Örtqvist, D. (2015). Product–Service Systems (PSS) business models and tactics–A systematic literature review. *Journal of Cleaner Production*, *97*, 61–75. doi:10.1016/j.jclepro.2014.07.003

Research and Degrowth. (2012). *Definition of degrowth. Research and Degrowth*. Available on https://degrowth.org/

Ridley-Duff, R. (2008). Social enterprise as a socially rational business. *International Journal of Entrepreneurial Behaviour & Research*, *14*(5), 291–312. doi:10.1108/13552550810897669

Romeiro, A. R. (2012). Sustainable development: An ecological economics perspective. *Estudos Avançados*, *26*, 74.

Schaltegger, S., & Wagner, M. (2011). Sustainable entrepreneurship and sustainability innovation: Categories and interactions. *Business Strategy and the Environment*, *20*(4), 222–237. doi:10.1002/bse.682

Schmenner, R. W. (2009). Manufacturing, service, and their integration: Some history and theory. *International Journal of Operations & Production Management*, *29*(5), 431–443. doi:10.1108/01443570910953577

Schneider, F., & Williams, C. C. (2013). The Shadow Economy. The Institute of Economic Affairs, IEA. doi:10.1017/CBO9781139542289

Schüritz, R. M., Seebacher, S., Satzger, G., & Schwarz, L. (2017). Datatization as the Next Frontier of Servitization - Understanding the Challenges for Transforming Organizations. *ICIS 2017 Proceedings*.

Shepherd, D. A., & Patzelt, H. (2011). The New Field of Sustainable Entrepreneurship: Studying Entrepreneurial Action Linking "What Is to Be Sustained" With "What Is to Be Developed". *Entrepreneurship Theory and Practice*, *35*(1), 137–163. doi:10.1111/j.1540-6520.2010.00426.x

SITRA. (2018). *Circular Economy for Sustainable Development*. Reports of the Finnish Environment Institute, 26/2018.

Sivam, A., Dieguez, T., Ferreira, L. P., & Silva, F. J. G. (2019). Key settings for successful Open Innovation Arena. *Journal of Computational Design and Engineering*, *6*(4), 507–515. doi:10.1016/j.jcde.2019.03.005

Slack, N. (2005). Operations strategy: Will it ever realize its potential? *Gestão & Produção*, *12*(3), 323–332. doi:10.1590/S0104-530X2005000300004

Spring, M., & Araujo, L. (2017). Product biographies in Servitization and the circular economy. *Industrial Marketing Management*, *60*, 126–137. doi:10.1016/j.indmarman.2016.07.001

Timmons, J., & Spinelli, S. (2009). *New Venture Creation: Entrepreneurship for the 21st Century* (8th ed.). McGraw-Hill.

Tukker, A. (2015). Product services for a resource-efficient and circular economy - A review. *Journal of Cleaner Production*, *97*, 76–91. doi:10.1016/j.jclepro.2013.11.049

UNCTAD. (2018). *Achieving the Sustainable Development Goals in the Least Developed Countries — A Compendium of Policy Options*. New York: United Nations.

United Nations. (2017). *World Population Prospects: The 2017 Revision, Key Findings and Advance Tables*. Working Paper No. ESA/P/WP/248. Department of Economic and Social Affairs - Population Division.

United Nations Environment Programme (UNEP). (2015). *Sustainable Consumption and Production Global edition*. UNEP.

Vandermerwe, S., & Rada, J. (1988). Servitization of business: Adding value by adding services. *European Management Journal*, *6*(4), 314–324. doi:10.1016/0263-2373(88)90033-3

Walters, D. (2009, Nov.). Understand the value chain network, understand te market, understand the industry and understand the customer. *Journal of Transport and Supply Chain Management*.

Weidinger, C., Fischler, F., & Schmidpeter, R. (2013). *Sustainable Entrepreneurship: Business Success through Sustainability*. Springer Berlin Heidelberg.

Weterings, R., Bastein, T., Tukker, A., Rademaker, M., & de Ridder, M. (2013). *Resources for our Future: Key issues and best practices in Resource Efficiency*. Amsterdam University Press.

Wiklund, J., Nikolaev, B., Shir, M., & Bradley, S. (2019). Conquering Relevance: *Entrepreneurship Research's Grand Challenge. Journal of Business Venturing*, *34*, 579–588. doi:10.1016/j.jbusvent.2019.01.002

Willard, B. (2012). *The new sustainability advantage: seven business case benefits of a triple bottom line*. New Society Publishers.

World Commission on Environment and Development. (1987). *Our common future*. Oxford University Press.

WRAP. (2019). *WRAP and the circular economy*. Available on http://www.wrap.org.uk/about-us/about/wrap-and-circular-economy

Zeeuw van der Laan, A., & Aurisicchio, M. (2009). Designing product-service systems to close resource loops: Circular design guidelines. *Procedia CIRP*, *2019*(80), 631–636.

Zhao, F. (2005). Exploring the synergy between entrepreneurship and innovation. *International Journal of Entrepreneurial Behaviour & Research*, *11*(1), 25–41. doi:10.1108/13552550510580825

KEY TERMS AND DEFINITIONS

Circular Economy: A circular economy is a systemic approach to economic development designed to benefit businesses, society, and the environment. It is regenerative by design and aims to gradually decouple growth from the consumption of finite resources. It follows the 3R approach: reduce, reuse and recycle. Resource use is minimized (reduce). Reuse of products and parts is maximized (reuse). And last but not least, raw materials are reused (recycled) to a high standard.

Linear Economy: A linear economy traditionally follows the "take-make-dispose" step-by-step plan. This means that raw materials are collected, and then transformed into products that are used until they are finally discarded as waste. Value is created in this economic system by producing and selling as many products as possible.

Product-Service System (PSS): A marketable set of products and services capable of jointly fulfilling a user's need. It is provided by either a single company or by an alliance of companies. It can enclose products (or just one) plus additional services.

Servitization: Servitization is commonly taken to be a transition or transformation which is largely characterised as a linear and gradual move along a product continuum from less to more sophisticated services.

Sustainable Development: Sustainable development is development that meets the needs of the present without compromising the ability of future generations to meet their own need.

Sustainable Entrepreneurship: Sustainable entrepreneurship is a business strategy focused on increasing value for society, the environment and the company or business.

APPENDIX

Figure 3. Representative scheme of the circular economy model
Source: Adapted from EMF (2013)

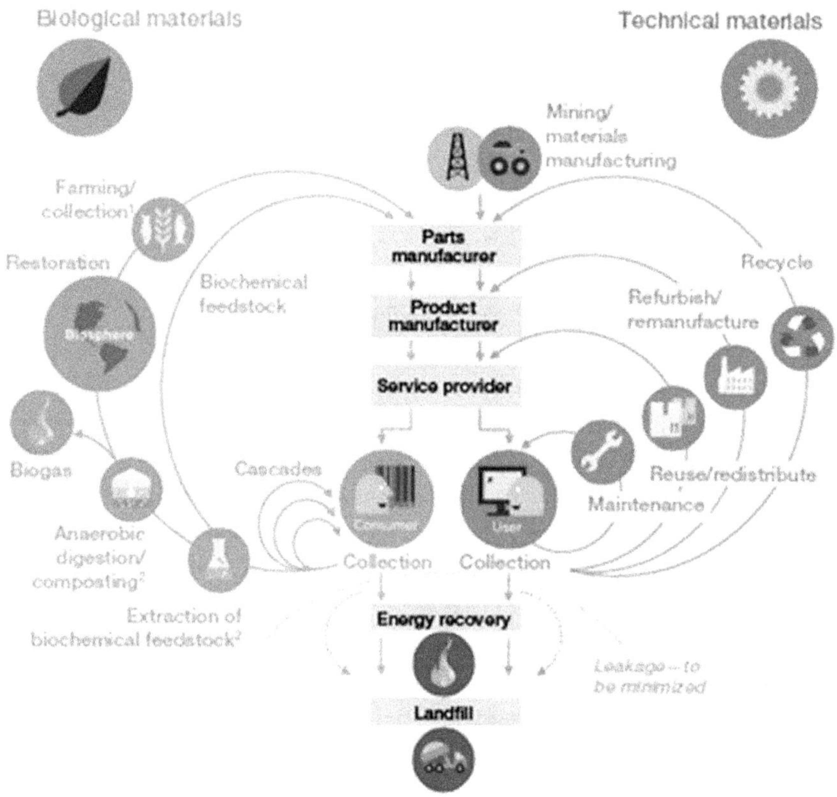

Chapter 4
Linear Economy to Circular Economy:
Planned Obsolescence to Cradle-to-Cradle Product Perspective

Pınar Özkan
Dokuz Eylül University, Turkey

Ezgi Karataş Yücel
https://orcid.org/0000-0001-5903-3091
Dokuz Eylül University, Turkey

ABSTRACT

The reflections of linear and circular economy models, which are completely separated from each other in the ways of evaluating resources and wastes, also differ completely in the production and consumption processes. The linear economy, which consists of production and consumption mechanisms, converts resources into waste after using one time and is supported by planned obsolescence practices and causes economic and environmental damages. The scarcity of resources and the pressure of environmental pollution have led to an industrial transformation in which production and consumption forms redesigned in a way that does not create waste. Because of this transformation, the circular economy model emerged, and its application direction evolved to cradle-to-cradle practices. In this study, firstly, the linear economy model and planned obsolescence are discussed, and then circular economy and cradle-to-cradle applications are explained with examples.

INTRODUCTION

In the economic systems consisting of consumption and production, the interaction between economy and environment takes place in terms of the use of resources, the way of disposal/utilization of wastes, the increase of population and consumption and the globalized consumption patterns. The management

DOI: 10.4018/978-1-7998-5116-5.ch004

Copyright © 2020, IGI Global. Copying or distributing in print or electronic forms without written permission of IGI Global is prohibited.

process and style of the economy change the environment, in return environmental characteristics steer the economy and lead it to success.

There are two different approaches in the economy that are completely separated from each other in the way they utilize resources and waste; *linear economy* and *circular economy*. Linear economic model starting with the industrial revolution consists of production and consumption mechanisms in which resources are returned into waste after a single-use. Those mechanisms ignore the environment and have to return processes. Due to the unidirectional flow and eventual depletion of resources, this structure has been considered to be linear. On the other hand, the circular economy model has realized the harm caused by the linear economy to the environment and refers to the mechanisms that focus on sustainability, redesigning the production processes and consumption patterns in a way that does not create waste and enables the continuous use of resources. In these models which have completely opposite points of view, this difference is clearly visible in the supply and production processes and strategies of the enterprises.

In the linear economy that continued throughout the 20th century, the operating activities in accordance with this economic model and, most especially, the marketing activities and practices caused economic, social and environmental devastation. This situation underlined the importance of business and marketing practices in achieving sustainability. Based on this fact, in this study firstly, "planned obsolescence strategy" which is among the marketing practices of the business manner imposed by the linear economic model and which is widely used product strategy, will be examined. Then, information about the circular economy model which aims to prevent ecocide and the product strategy, namely "cradle-to-cradle", applied by this model, will be given.

BACKGROUND

Linear Economy Model

Take-make-dispose consumption model and the global economy which started with the industrial revolution have operated in a structure that promotes the consumption constantly. This structure, in addition to expanding the companies, has provided income and development opportunities to individuals and macro-economies through creating income sources and employment power. The linear economy with this point of view has constituted an infrastructure supporting the increased quality of life.

The linear economy model, a unidirectional system in which natural resources are turned into waste by means of production, based on the assumption that natural resources are available, adequate, easily accessible and wasted, and that waste is cheap and trouble-free, this has resulted in exceeding the capacity of the planet in many areas (Steffen et al., 2015).

The first assumption on which the linear economic model is based is that the natural resources are unlimited; that is, there is continuity of the new resources to be used as long as industrial production continues. The second assumption is that the resources turning into waste after being used disappear. These two assumptions are based on the perception that resources are endless and that waste is harmless. This perception stems from the early periods of the industrial revolution and has accelerated the tendency of resource consumption and waste generation until today and has determined the development direction of production and consumption mechanisms (Ellen MacArthur Foundation, 2013; Barbier, 2003; World Economic Forum, 2016; Steffen et. al., 2015).

The natural resources in the mass production processes of the linear model, especially fossil fuels that have been formed within millions of years, are consumed in a short span of time compared to that it takes to regenerate. On the other hand, wastes are dissolved in nature generally in a much longer time than the life cycle of resources and products by damaging the environment. Besides the limited resources and the damage caused by the waste accumulation, the constant growth and productivity policies of the linear economy model also create various problems. The productivity of developing and modernizing industries has increased remarkably over time. In the modernization process of manufacturing methods, technologies and mechanisms that make possible the more efficient use of energy and raw materials continue to be developed. However, as the production mechanisms become more efficient; that is, less energy and resources per product, the total production volume and therefore the amount of energy and resources consumed are increasing each day (Ellen MacArthur Foundation, 2015a; 2015b).

Scientists, enterprises, and governments who realized these problems from the 1980s which have been created by the linear model made an effort to improve the model. Policies have been developed around fewer resources, more efficient production or recycling and reuse of waste. Despite the development of recycling technologies, most of the wastes today cannot be recycled due to the modes of production in which natural and synthetic raw materials cannot be separated from each other or they are collected in a landfill together with domestic wastes without reaching recycling centers. The efforts made without changing the intrinsic characteristic of the model are far from providing the expected benefits.

During the early 20th century abundance period that the model emerged, the strategies such as planned obsolescence triggered constant purchase and production and, at the same time created the culture of disposability. The abundance period from the beginning of industrial revolution to the Great Depression of 1929 and as of mid 1950's by the recovery of USA after the ending of Second World War, the planned obsolescence supported and developed the linear economy; the products became waste at the end of their lifetime within the "take-make-dispose" model. In the developed countries, while high income segment of the society throw away the stuffs that they disused, low income segment went to repair and reuse. During the Second World War between these two periods, because of the limited resources that are used in production processes; large segments of society resorted to reusing, repairing and recycling. With the end of the war, the understanding that the products become waste at the end of their lifetime returned. For the products which have an endless lifetime, the businesses have implemented strategies to shorten the product's economic life (Andrews, 2015; Satyro et al. quoting from Echegaray, 2017). Planned obsolescence which is mostly used among these strategies will be explained in the following section.

Planned Obsolescence

The businesses that make decisions at the conditions of global competition and linear economy and the insatiable consumers created by consumption culture are two poles and reasons for emergence of planned obsolescence strategy. The abundance of products provided by technological developments and the desire to consume created by the strategies of companies have changed the value judgments of society in time. According to Fromm (2004: 62-64), in the 19th century, saving was one of the most important virtues in life, but in the 20th century, consumption has started to be the meaning of life. Consumption has become the source of freedom and happiness for people. Times have changed to the ones in which consumption is glorified instead of saving.

The technological developments in production after the industrial revolution made it possible, for the first time from the beginning of humankind, to reach production quantities that caused the supply to exceed demand. At this point, the businesses whose existence depends on their sales volume have had to develop strategies in order to stimulate demand. One of the most widely used strategies in this period was *the planned obsolescence strategy* in which the products are planned and designed with an artificially limited useful life so that the consumers change their products frequently. Planned obsolescence encompasses all kinds of control over the products and consumers in order to increase the purchasing speed of the consumer. This strategy's reason for being is to establish a balance in the system as a means of providing high consumption rate against increased production as a result of technological developments.

Planned obsolescence describes a strategy of deliberately ensuring that the given products will become out of date or useless within a known time period in order to guarantee the product replacements in frequent intervals (Valant, 2006). That is; the time when a product will be out of date, unfashioned or useless, is determined before the product is designed and comes onto the market (Smeels & Stevels, 2003, Hindle, 2008). Bulow (1986: 729) says; planned obsolescence is the production of goods with uneconomically short useful lives so that customers will have to make repeat purchases. The important thing in planned obsolescence is to enable customers to make willing or compulse for replacement eventually in order to increase the profits. Companies have incentives to make durable goods faster obsolete in order to maintain the continuity of production (Nejedlá, 2011: 19).

Planned obsolescence does not only describe purchasing new products by consumers already having usable products. The important point is that there is a social and economic order that encourages the acquisition of goods and services in ever-increasing amounts. Consumers make decisions such as acts of purchase and consumption as a routine in their daily life (Maycroft, 2009: 4). For clarifying, the information about market conditions in which the concept has emerged will be given.

Historical Development of Planned Obsolescence

Henry Ford, who is the leader of the Fordism model stream, has realized that its model is unsustainable if it does not confront the mass consumption. He has noticed that his workers were also potential consumers and he has needed them to enlarge his market and he developed a strategy to forge a consumer class. Ford initiated a process to double the wages of his employees and reduce their working hours so that they had more time and money to consume. This helped to found mass consumption. Thus, in the five years from 1909 to 1914, Ford branded automobile sales increased by 21 times and the revenues by about 11 times (Koren, 2010:106; Leonard, 2010: 160). This system which makes it possible to produce standardized products at a mess level firstly has made it possible for people to gain money and then directed how to use this money (Saklı, 2007: 5-6). With that strategy, in addition to the speed-up generated by technological developments, Ford created a cycle; where as a result of technological developments, production and consumption are increased; increased production resulted with increased employment. When people are employed, their income was increased and by the way they started to consume more. When they consume more production was increased and that continued as a cyclical procedure.

In the same period, General Motors, another giant automotive company, has seen that it is enough to encourage its consumers by making new designs every year instead of offering standard models with mass production in order to increase sales. Through advertising activities, General Motors has achieved its product to turn into an attractive and fashionable status symbol (Nejedlá, 2011: 25; Slade, 2006: 4-5, Bauman, 2015). This design-based strategy has become very successful and has been implemented in other industries such as watch and radio industries (Slade, 2006: 4-5, Solczak, 2013: 24).

Thus, these two giant companies presented the first striking examples of the strategies that can be applied to increase consumption in two different aspects. In time, in order to increase consumption, there were different applications in different sectors in accordance with the nature of that sector. One of the most well-known is the meeting of lightbulb manufacturers, which resulted in the formation of the first known global cartel, "Phoebus Cartel" in 1924 in Genoa. Since the lifetimes of lightbulbs were 2500 hours, it would take a long time until the consumers buy them once again and so businesses could not sell as much as they wanted. In order to prevent this situation, global giants such as Osram, Philips, Compagnie and General Electric agreed to gradually reduce the lifetime of bulbs to 1000 hours and businesses that did not comply with it were punished by the board (Dannoritzer, 2010).

In 1939, the chemical giant DuPont started to produce fabrics from synthetic yarns (DuPont USA, 2018). The nylon socks produced by the company with using synthetic yarns were very durable and ladder-proof. However, if the firm continues to make socks with that durability, it will not be able to sell too many socks in a long time. Thereupon, the company began to work to produce less durable socks. And ultimately the ladder-proof socks had been removed from the market (Dannoritzer, 2010).

The Great Depression which began in the USA in 1929 and spread to the world was actually an economic crisis stemming from overproduction. In the process that began with the collapse of Wall Street, nearly 4.000 banks and thousands of companies declared bankruptcy and millions of people became unemployed in the United States. Unemployment rates have risen from 15% to 25% not only in the United States but also in other countries because of the crisis (Nejeala, 2011: 25). It is known that during this period when people starved and froze to death at the streets the warehouses were filled with goods to the brim. Even though new technologies provided an increase in supply, sufficient and cyclical demand did not come in sight; accordingly wealth distribution and insufficient money circulation became the main reasons that triggered the crisis (Solczak, 2013: 4). As a result of their increased production capacity by mass production, the producers obtained a large stock. However, because there was not sufficient demand, they could not deplete this stock. Consumers could not keep up with the producers. Businesses began to make a loss and the employees were laid off. But increasing unemployment caused shrinking demand and the crisis was deepened. In 1933, a quarter of the US was unemployed (Dannoritzer, 2010; Suğur, 2015: 41).

The term "planned obsolescence" took part in literature for the first time in this crisis period with the Bernard London's study, "Ending the Depression Through Planned Obsolescence" published in 1932. In this study, London proposed planned obsolescence as a solution to the World Economic Depression of 1929. The term planned obsolescence was used to mean the lifetime of a predetermined product by the government as an external factor. London recommended that; the government assign a lease of life to the products after the allotted time had expired these things would be legally "dead" and would be controlled by the duly appointed governmental agency and destroyed. Although his proposal has never been accepted and implemented by the governmental authorities, his strategy is still frequently used by enterprises as one of the basic strategies of the linear economy.

Planned obsolescence, especially in the USA in the post-Second World War period, was widely used to balance increasing unemployment and to provide economic development in the belief that the sooner one product wears out and is replaced, the faster the economy grows (London, 1932). Shopping during this period was almost considered a civic duty. Many of products are re-introduced to the market by making minor changes in their design and many of them are being manufactured in such a way that they cannot be repaired or upgraded. Advertisements were used as the driving force of this process in order to encourage consumers to wear out their existing products and replace them with new ones (Cooper, 2004: 424; Packard, 1960; Solczak, 2013: 5).

Planned obsolescence was brought to the agenda again by Brooks Stevens, an American industrial designer, in the 1950s. Stevens defined the concept as "a little sooner than it is necessary" (Adamson, 2003; Satyro et al, 2017). Stevens compared American shopping habits with old European habits; he determined that the products in the European markets were as durable as possible, but in the context of American mass market, the main purpose was constant change and incessant newness, that is; making good products, inducing people to buy them and then deliberately introducing something that will make these products old fashioned, out of date and obsolete (Dannoritzer, 2010). In the 1960s, planned obsolescence term was included in the consumption dynamics of the society, instead of forcing the consumer to wear out the products and planned obsolescence, promoting consumer desire to own the products, a little sooner than is necessary became more important (Packard, 1960).

At the point today world came, obsolescence of innovations of consumer goods and changing of their consumption styles has reached a hysterical speed (Yanıklar, 2006:192). It is known that a new product is created every three minutes all over the world (Dannoritzer, 2010). At the planet in which the resources are finite, there is an endless production and consumption frenzy.

Types of Planned Obsolescence

Planned obsolescence is a multidimensional issue, having regarded to variables such as consumer demands, competition, micro and macro environmental factors (Nejedlá, 2011: 19). These variables have caused businesses to apply different types of obsolescence. It can be said that, these types which had emerged at different times and as nonlinear can be used by businesses in different combinations.

According to Packard (1960: 38) who has made first and generally accepted the classification of planned obsolescence, it is seen in three ways in the market. These are technical or functional obsolescence, systemic obsolescence and style obsolescence. If a literature review is conducted, it can be seen that different classifications have been made by different academicians. For example; Heiskanen (1996), like Packard, identified three categories of obsolescence to explain why people replace products; failure, dissatisfaction, a change in consumer needs. Smeels and Stevels (2003: 267- 268) in their studies have called the concept as product renewal and they have examined as renewal related with the product (enterprises) and renewal related with consumers. They stated that six types of performances can affect product renewal; technical, economic, schematic, appearance, technological and environmental.

As is seen from the literature review, a distinction can be drawn between various different types of obsolescence: planned obsolescence in the strictest sense (designing a product to have a shorter life or designing it in such a way that it functions for only a limited number of operations); indirect obsolescence (occurring because the component required for repair is unobtainable or because it is simply not practical or worthwhile repairing the product, i.e. it costs the same to repair as to replace); incompatibility obsolescence (e.g. the case of tablets and personal computers that cannot run efficiently after successive software updates of the operating system, encouraging consumers to replace the product rather than try the potentially more costly repair option); and style obsolescence (related to marketing campaigns that can for instance lead to the replacement of perfectly functional mobile phones, gadgets or clothes, etc.). Other classifications of obsolescence also exist (Valant, 2006: 2). When the literature is viewed it ca be seen that it is very difficult to distinguish these obsolescence types from each other.

FROM LINEAR ECONOMY TO CIRCULAR ECONOMY

Besides linear system is a system that has been going on for years also it has a structure that cannot be given up easily by the enterprises and there are many criteria under which companies cannot give up the linear system. Many factors make the linear system dominant such as the financial costs of the environmental and social consequences of the activities of the enterprises cannot be calculated exactly or the amounts calculated and explained do not reflect the truth, reflection of the negative consequences of production and consumption such as environmental pollution and global climate change to the business itself is ignored, the short-term perspective seems easier for businesses than making a long-term plan and the transition to the new system is costly in all respects and requires a significant change in all business units (Huthala, 2015: 7). Although many factors, such as mentioned, cause businesses to remain in the linear system, they are also confronted with various changes that entail them to change that system. These changes can be grouped under three main categories (Wilson & Rogero, 2015: 27). From the classical point of view, which assumes that the main purpose of businesses is to make a profit (Duska, 1997: 1402; Gupta, 2008: P1), it is not surprising that this category is considered as primary. The second category is the necessity of addressing public health issues by businesses. The last category can be considered as environmental protection with the increase of environmental awareness in recent years.

According to Brears (2018: 12 - 13) the increasing importance of this last category is due to the characteristics of natural capital, such as that natural capital in contrast to human and physical capital cannot be produced by human beings - as can be predicted - if depleted, and therefore cannot be found again, it has geographical differences in terms of accessibility and presence because it does not take place in the same shapes and amounts across the world, it is more difficult to set the price of than other capitals etc. unlike any other type of capital.

Even though it is mentioned that if natural capital is exhausted, it will be a serious problem because it is not man-made, living beings that are perfectly connected with each other in natural life and acting independently of each other in the same perfection constitute a system in which there is no waste and all kinds of waste are used for another purpose. This system is cyclical rather than a linear line and is highly sustainable unless there are disasters and human intervention so it is very hard to be extinct. (Erten, 2018: 20; Dijk et al., 2014: 22). While increasing environmental problems forced people to seek solutions, with the recognition of this perfect cyclicality, people turned their eyes to nature and began to be inspired by nature to compensate for the harm they caused in their production and consumption behaviors. Thus, the strategies applied within the linear economic structure were replaced by Nature Inspired Design Strategies. These strategies, which "base a significant proportion of their theory on 'learning from nature' and regard nature as the paradigm of sustainability", as a reflection of the cycle in nature, brings economic structure to a cyclical form (Özsoy, 2018: 24; de Pauw et al., 2010: 4). Based on this perspective, in this part of the study, firstly the circular economy and then the cradle to cradle products that are actively used in the operations of the circular economy will be discussed.

CIRCULAR ECONOMY

With the understanding of the importance of factors such as public health and environmental awareness, many branches of businesses have had to make studies in the field of environmental management either voluntarily or through government regulations. In these studies, questions about the negative effects on the environment during production and consumption of a product and how these effects can be mitigated have started to strain the minds. These questions, on the other hand, began to find answers through the concept of life cycle analyzes that began to appear in the literature in the late 1980s (Berkhout, 1996: 145 - 146). *Life Cycle Analysis* (LCA) is one of the most comprehensive analyses used in the field of environmental management and can be defined as a tool that tries to "attempt to record and assess all the environmental impacts of a whole product life cycle" (Schaltegger, 1997: 1). This concept is suitable for linear modeling that assumes products have a beginning and an end at their lives (Scientific Applications International Corporation (SAIC), 2006: 1). On the other hand, according to Özkan et al. (2018: 86), the sustainability that has been increasingly emphasized in recent years requires that the system be cyclic rather than linear, and real sustainability can only be achieved when the system is completely closed, that is when it captures the full cycle. Therefore, the opinion that the economy should also have a cyclical structure emerges.

Like every new concept entering literature, firstly circular economy has been tried to be defined and there are many common and different points in these definitions. According to Kircherr et al. (2017), who examined the definitions of the circular economy in the literature and analyzed the contents of 114 definitions, the circular economy can be defined as "an economic system that replaces the 'end-of-life' concept with reducing, alternatively reusing, recycling and recovering materials in production/distribution and consumption processes". According to Önder (2018: 199), unlike the complex definitions of the circular economy, the most simple and qualitative definition belongs to the European Commission and according to the commission at circular economy "the value of products and materials is maintained as long as possible, waste and resource use are minimized, and when a product reaches the end of its life, it is used again to create further value" (European Commission, 2015). Preserving and enhancing the natural capital, optimizing resource yields and fostering system resources are three basic principles of the circular economy and those three principles focus both to the problems of system and resources (Antikainen et al., 2018; Önder, 2018: 199). With all these definitions, when considered in financial terms, a circular economic structure is very advantageous for businesses, as it brings the use of a product to the endpoint as possible as made by the legal framework (Datschefski, 1999: 44).

In the light of the definitions made, the main concepts discussed also provide a basis for drawing a circular economic model. Figure 1 presents a model proposal prepared by the European Environment Agency (EEA) (2016: 10), which treats the circular economy as a three-layered structure. This model, which from outside to inside represents the general energy flow, the main activities in the circular economy and finally the approaches to perform these activities, is based on the fact that each layer must move in harmony with each other (Sapmaz Veral, 2019: 21).

As can be seen in Figure 1, the process ongoing with eco-design, production and distribution, consumption and stock and ending with waste generation; by the fact that the materials obtained by recycling take part in the process design, leaves its place in the circular economy in a form of cycle as production and distribution, consumption and stocking of a new product, and recycling of the wastes obtained from this new product. A wide variety of approaches can be mentioned in obtaining this cycle and reuse, repair, redistribute, refurbish and remanufacture can be listed as some of them. Through the cycle obtained through those approaches, extraction and import of natural resources at the beginning of the process and incineration and landfill operations at the end of the process are minimized as much as possible. Thus, the view that natural resources are not unlimited and should be used efficiently is reinforced.

It is possible to consider the circular economy, whose boundaries are drawn within the framework of legislation, as a process that needs to be handled in an organized way by governments, businesses,

Figure 1. A model of circular economy
Source: European Environment Agency (2016)

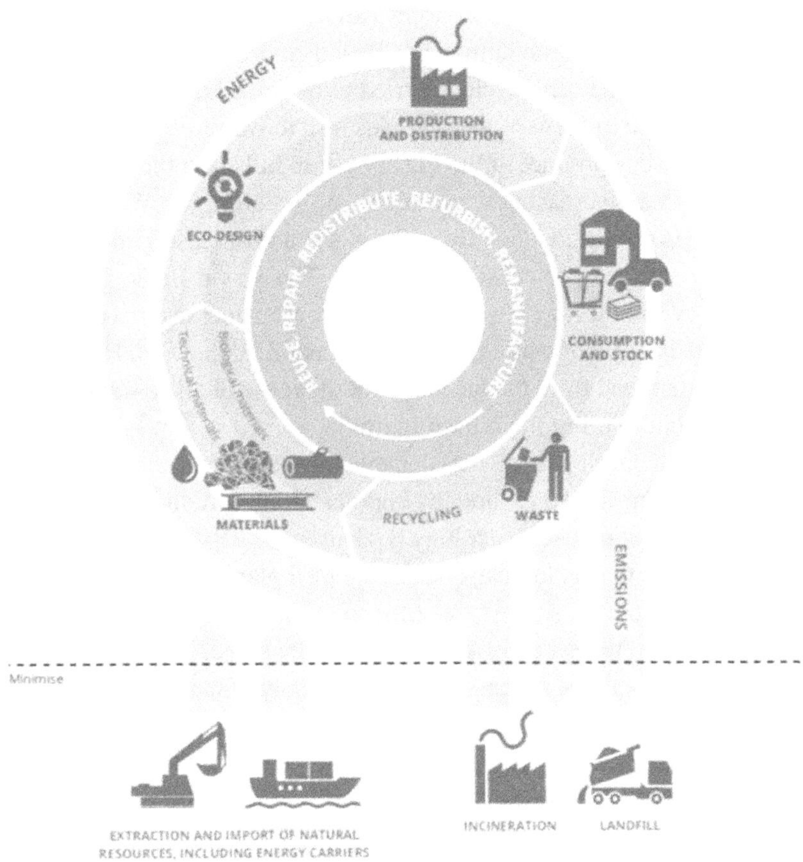

scientists, and citizens. Therefore, this perspective, which covers every layer of society, is very important in terms of bringing many benefits together such as efficient use of resources, less environmental damage, providing economic development and innovation, acquiring sustainable consumption behaviors, reshaping consumption habits, reducing costs, providing new jobs, creating new research areas etc. (European Environment Agency, 2016: 12 - 14; Huthala, 2015: 4; PAGEV, 2015: 5 – 6; Sapmaz Veral, 2018: 468 - 469; Türk Standardları Enstitüsü, 2018: 21 - 23). Besides, according to Brears (2018: 20 - 21), businesses willing to obtain these benefits in the transition to circular economy model should be sensitive to some issues as protecting and having information about natural resources, reviewing the life cycles of products and then identifying a cyclical life perspective, investigating, internalizing and implementing regulations correctly, achieving an ethical perspective and working with all stakeholders in doing so. This sensitivity brings many resources that will add value to the business as decreasing the costs by providing longer cycles, reduction in energy, material and labor utilization, diversification through the resale of recycled products as another product, and ensuring efficiency through flawless cycles (Sapmaz Veral, 2019: 22 - 23).

CRADLE TO CRADLE (C2C) PRODUCTS

Problems that occur in the flow of the linear economy can be listed as firstly what materials are made of and what are the effects of this content on human health and environment and secondly products cannot be used efficiently at the end of their life cycle are tried to be solved by means of the circular economy (Alston, 2008: 135). In response to these problems, eyes turn to waste. While consumption in the world continues at the last speed, every product in the linear system falls into the waste category without being converted and thus raises an increasing waste problem. According to World Bank data, an average of 2.5 billion tons of waste is produced annually in the world and at least 33 percent of these wastes are not in the environmentally safe category (Erten, 2018: 20; The World Bank, 2017). Although in many countries, especially after 1980s, the laws have determined how businesses will manage their waste; these regulations still govern the disposal of waste (Kumar & Putnam, 2008: 305). However, with the circular economy, it is not only the removal from the business but the reuse of all so-called waste. Therefore, the aim is not to kill products, but to bring them back to life.

This understanding, which develops with the idea that the waste (material or energy) of one business in the same industrial ecosystem is used as input by another and thus reducing environmental impacts in a cyclic system forms the basis of industrial ecology (Özkan et al., 2018: 85) and stating that the products have births and deaths just like the ecological system, the birthplace of them is the cradle and the death is called the grave (Paulsen, 2001: 3). At the same time, if all the life cycles of a product or service from the raw material supply (cradle) to waste disposal (grave) is analyzed, this situation is "cradle to grave" and if it is done in a way to cover all the processes from the supply of raw materials (cradle) to the factory (door), it is called as "cradle to door". If the life cycle analysis carried out from cradle to grave results in recovery of waste, which is the final stage of the cycle, it is referred to as cradle to cradle (Tangüler et al., 2015: 435). Cradle-to-cradle products, which are the major tools of the circular economic model, are also included in the literature as an extension of industrial ecology.

The main purpose of industrial ecology is to use ecological materials. Therefore, in the cradle-to-cradle design approach, all materials are divided into two groups and these categories are evaluated in terms of zero waste principle. The first group is technically originated materials produced by humans and without an organic property. Such materials (as plastic, metal, etc.) are insoluble in nature and can, therefore, be used repeatedly because their quality is not degraded. The second group consists of organic materials (wood, soil, etc.). When the materials in this group are released to nature, they dissolve and there is no waste (Koç & Ekşi Akbulut, 2017: 649; Niinimäki, 2013: 18), thus the closed-loop is completed (Yıldırım, 2017: 485). The "biological cycle" within the scope of the closed cycle, means that the products can be composted into the environment without harming the environment after use and the deals with the biological nutrients while the "technical cycle" emphasizes the technical nutrients by gaining insoluble products to the system again by recycling. According to these cycles, it is one of the basic researches to design the biodegradation of the products in nature or to try to reintroduce them to the industrial system. (Şahin & Odabaşı, 2018: 422).

While the technical and biological nutrients for the cradle-to-cradle approach are emphasized, the most important part that should be dealt with is the fact that a completely different structure from recycling is mentioned. While producing a new product from the products (reprocess) is intended for recycling, in the cradle-to-cradle approach reuse is aimed. All materials are considered as technical or biological nutrients to be re-evaluated. The goal is not to produce as little damage as possible, but to obtain completely reusable products so everything is useful rather than less harmful (Datschefski, 1999: 44; Zech,

2018). In cradle-to-cradle product applications, the right to use the products is sold to the consumer, not the right to ownership, and at the beginning of the purchasing process, consumers act with the knowledge that they will return the product at the end. In this way, the materials that will become waste are evaluated by the business with entering into a biological or technical cycle. For example, assuming that consumers want to buy a washing machine, instead of being sold to use until the washing machine is broken or dead, the right to use for 3,000 washes is purchased. Therefore, the parts that will become waste at the end of 3000 washings are replaced with new ones and the waste parts are taken back by the business, converted into raw materials through cycles and then reused (Doğa Sektörel Yayın Grubu, 2016; Karaca, 2018: 26; Zech, 2018).

Cradle to Cradle View

When waste management had not yet started to be discussed, hazardous practices were actually used indeed in terms of human and environmental health for the disposal of the remains of waste. For example, some of the wastes were directly poured into water sources such as sea, river, ocean; no specific area was determined for the wastes; some of the wastes were directly burned in public areas and caused toxic air to be inhaled and toxic contaminants were discharged into nature with uncontrolled conditions. As a result of increasing environmental awareness in the 1960s, regulations on waste management were needed and the first legal regulation in this respect was the Solid Waste Disposal Act adopted in 1965 at the American Congress (The Horinko Group, 2016: 1). In this embodiment, solid waste is defined in a very broad framework and is handled from a very broad perspective, which is being referred to as "solid, liquid, semisolid, or contained gaseous material resulting from industrial, commercial, mining, and agricultural operations and from community activities" (Public Law, 1965).

Although the first movement on waste management in the world was adopted in 1965, the first step in the transition from cradle to cradle dates back to 1976. The views of Walter Stahel, an architect, and his colleague Geneviève Reday – Mulvey, which are submitted as a report to the European Commission under the name "The Potential for Substituting Manpower for Energy" in 1976, and later published as a book in 1982, under the name "Jobs for Tomorrow, the Potential for Substituting Manpower for Energy", are considered the first starting point of their cradle-to-cradle practices (Devrim, 2014: 62). As mentioned earlier, according to the view starting out from the concept of the circular economy, similar to the cycle in nature, in contrast to only production-oriented views that disregard the outcome, a product should be separated into layers when its life expires and should include activities such as reuse what you can, recycle what cannot be reused, repair what is broken, remanufacture what cannot be repaired (Stahel, 2016) and thus, through the loops created, return products to useful lives (Lovins, 2008: 38)

William McDonough and Micheal Braungart were the pioneers of the studies in the field of products from cradle to cradle, and the authors have led to the emergence of the theoretical framework the concept in 2002 with their books Cradle to Cradle: Remaking the Way We Make Things. At the same time at Cradle to Cradle Products Innovation Institute which they established with the support of the fundamental ideas contained in the books in 2010, they are also guiding in theory and practice by certifying business products that comply with the Cradle to Cradle Certified Product Standards. In their book Cradle to Cradle: Remaking the Way We Make Things, they are also pioneers in their own standards and practice and the book is not made from the usual paper, but from material obtained from plastic resins and inorganic fillers, which can be recycled even in a simple plastic collection plant and washable ink.

Therefore, instead of cutting down the tree and damaging the nature, the book attracts attention with the opposite application (EPEA GmbH – Part of Drees & Sommer, 2002).

According to Mc Donough and Braungart (2002), three basic principles are required for a product to be included in the cradle to cradle category. The first principle of products from cradle to cradle is *waste equals food* approach. The work in this approach is not to dispose of the product after it is used, but to specialize in its transformation into waste during the course of its life, and how to evaluate it at the end of its life. Therefore, it is unthinkable that a correctly designed product can then be repeatedly studied and its transformation considered a problem. According to Braungart et al. (2007), what is needed is not only harm to nature, but also benefit to nature, people and economy. Therefore, all the concepts of environment, economy and equity mentioned in the three legged stool metaphor of sustainability will be supported and thus a balanced application will be achieved (Littig & Grießler, 2005: 66; Nijaki, 2014: 101; Warren, 2013: 29).

The second principle adopted in the cradle to cradle applications is *the use of renewable resources* such as solar energy and wind energy instead of energy-consuming and damaging to nature, such as the energy produced from fossil waste and atomic energy that has been going on throughout the historical process. Thus, instead of leaving a waste from the past to the future, a system that is produced instantaneously and which can be put into place by the environment by itself is unlimited, so that the principle of inspiration from nature will be fully implemented.

The last cradle to cradle principle can be called *respect diversity* (Bakker et al., 2010: 2). In order to establish a fully functioning cradle to cradle mechanism, it is necessary to first observe how a healthy functioning ecosystem functions. The most striking point in these observations is the encounter of a complex but perfectly functioning system established by millions of living organisms. Therefore, the last condition for a successful cradle to cradle design is to create structures that interact with each other by diversifying the design elements and making the organization of this diversification error-free (Kopnina, 2019).

R's of Cradle to Cradle

According to Cooper (1999: 11), contrary to the notion that increasing the life expectancy of the products and decreasing the frequency of purchasing will slow down the development of the economy in cases where the linear economy is the most preferred application of planned obsolescence, the focus of the circular economy is to constantly change the products in the cradle to cradle model. In contrast to the throwaway economy, a re-evaluation of the product is emphasized and thus an economy in which the service element comes to the fore.

When moving from a product-based approach to a service-based approach, the first starting point is actually the identification of the work done in the context of the service. According to Kirchherr et al. (2017: 223) those frameworks to pass from product base to service base can be called as *"how-to"s of cradle to cradle*. From theoretical perspective those *how-to's* are coded as R's – as all of the activities are started with letter "R". There is no generally accepted R's framework and each researcher took the activities from his own perspective. The simplest perspective is 3R framework and was the mostly used one from researchers as Reh (2013), Yong (2007), Tseng et al. (2018), Liu and Bai (2014) etc. and those R's can be listed as *recycle, reduce* and *reuse* and can be used at production, circulation, consumption and other processes sequentially. According to Yang (2014: 218) those R's can be defined as reducing the consumption of resources and the generation of wastes/pollutants in the process of production, circulation and consumption; reusing the discards as products directly or after repair, refurbishment or remanufacturing, or reusing them, wholly or partly, as parts of other products; and recycling waste as raw materials for direct use or regenerative use after waste recovery.

Also, the combinations of R's change according to the aim and the sample of researches. For example 4R's perspective was accepted in some researches as Kumar and Putman (2008); Garcés-Ayerbe et al. (2019); Rada et al. (2018). At their study on analyzing the definitions of circular economy Kirrcherr et. al (2017) found that nearly 35%–40% of definitions were using the 3R concept which include *recycle, reuse* and *reduce* as described above as a base and adds a fourth R to the list as recover (Kirchherr et al., 2017; Shao, 2019), *remanufacture* (Goh & Yoon - Chung, 2018), *restoration* (Amuda et al., 2014), *refuse* (Hadjichambis et al., 2015) etc.. Also there are other studies increasing the numbers of R's in literature as Halden (2010) with a 5R view that include *reduce, reuse, recycle, rethink* and *restrain*; Jawahir and Bradley (2016) who describe 6R's as *reduce, reuse, recover, redesign, remanufacture* and *recycle*; Kahriman-Öztürk et. al (2012) with 7R's *including reduce, reuse, respect, reflect, rethink, recycle* and *redistribute* and 9R's was classified by Potting et al. (2017) as *refuse, rethink, reduce, reuse, repair, refurbish, remanufacture, repurpose, recycle* and *recover*. Whether 3R or 9R the main point that should be in mind is the hierarchy which means the first R should be priority of second, second should be priority of third and so on. Also it should be noted that all those R's should be handled in accordance with the basic principles described by McDonough and Braungart (2002).

Negative Critiques for Cradle to Cradle

Of course it is not so easy for businesses to turn their product to cradle to cradle form and apply the R's. According to EEA (2016) as a beginning they need to collect and identify products and their materials, research all the ingredients of those they collect, list the potential risks to damage three stools of people, environment and economy and recommend and apply safe versions of those products. They need a radical change not just from design side but also the technology that used, the business models, the ways of using resources, the participants of supply chain, the rules and norms of work, the organizational structure and even the consumers and the behaviors of them should also be changed.

Producing cradle to cradle products is not always considered as a positive practice as it requires such a drastic change. For example Bjørn and Strandesen (2011) argued at their study that it is thermodynamically not practical to have a perfectly closed loop, it would create some trouble from the biological diversity view to add biological nutrients to environment and societies will experience diversity as a result of continuous economic growth therefore it cannot be said that C2C is always suitable for all products.

Also according to Kumlien (2010) cradle to cradle products are certified by McDonough and Braungart Design Chemistry who are the founders of the term so that the certification is kept in the hands of founders and this condition monopolizes the process. Businesses may produce a C2C product and serve it to market but to make it call as C2C they need to verify it from the organization. Also the information of ingredients and the classification of technical or biological waste of C2C is secretly kept in hand by organization so people do not know what is called as cradle to cradle is another criticism (Braungart, 2009).

In the cradle to cradle concept the starting point was nature inspired design as mentioned before *waste equals food* is the motto. But there defined no limit to the amount of waste. Reinjders (2008) for example suggests there is no enough capacity of environment to absorb all biological nutrients and all biological nutrients cannot be useful, some can damage the environment. In spite of those allegations it can be said that rather than classical production systems cradle to cradle forces businesses to organize and review all of their activities and at any point they start to regenerate and change.

Cradle to Cradle Products

According to Topoyan (2005) one of the basics of the science of economy can be described as limited natural resources opposite to the unlimited human needs. With this perspective, the perspectives that care about the environment and prevent environmental pollution, protect limited natural resources and transfer them to future generations are of increasing importance. So, cradle to cradle as a model that not just care about the environment but also equity and economy is being popular day by day.

Ellen MacArthur Foundation (2015a) as one of the leading organizations of circular economy and cradle to cradle products suggests that the businesses that are decisive for caring all those three stools need to adopt some actions which can be listed in six areas which are abbreviate as ReSOLVE. In this abbreviation "Re" corresponds to regenerate, "S" corresponds to share, "O" is for optimize, "L" is loop, "V" is virtualize and lastly "E" is for exchange. Some strategies for following those actions can be seen at Figure 2. The businesses can be successful at change if they obey as much as possible of those action plans.

Figure 2. The ReSOLVE framework
Source: Ellen Mac Arthur Foundation, 2015a

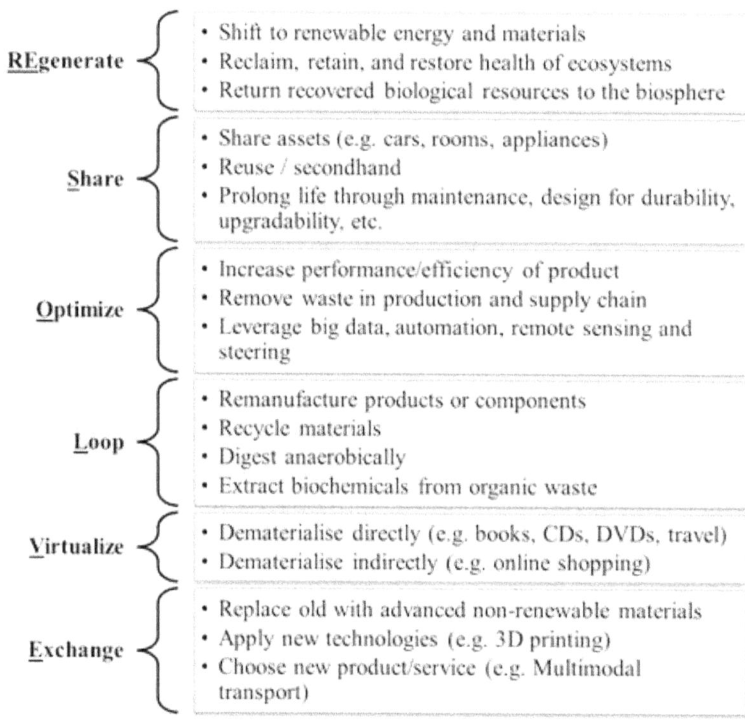

According to Cradle to Cradle Products Innovation Institute (2019), whether a business overhauls their actions and obeys an action plan, that does not mean they became cradle to cradle product producer. For a product to be called as C2C the business owners should consult to Cradle to Cradle Products Innovation Institute to be certified. Being certified is also a challenging process in itself as the product is tested for the degree of compliance into five categories defined as Cradle to Cradle Certified Product Standard where categories can be listed as material health, material reuse, renewable energy and carbon management, water stewardship, and social fairness. Products are evaluated for all five categories under 5 classifications and have a scorecard that includes *Basic, Bronze, Silver, Gold*, and *Platinum* degree for each category. As a last stage after all the categories are crossed with a degree, an overall degree is assigned for the product so that the product is called as Basic, Bronze, Silver, Gold, or Platinum category C2C certified product. Considering the current state of the institute, a total of 105 Gold; 186 Silver; 275 Bronze and 12 Basic products are C2C certified. In the Platinum category, there are no certified products yet. When the product categories are taken into consideration it is seen that the highest rates of certification is at first Interior Design & Furniture category with 216 products second Building Supply & Materials with 182; third Home & Office Supply with 70 continuing with Fashion + Textiles (41); Packaging & Paper (31); Health & Beauty (16); Basic Materials (14); Auto & Tires (4); Toys (3); Apparel, Shoes & Accessories (1); and Baby (1).

Of course the result that the first sector is building supply and materials is as expected as the founder of the concept McDonough is also an architect and the idea was emerged from the idea to build better for environment buildings. But in the list some examples stand out in relief as they are homomorphic with trends in consumer goods. For example the natural cosmetic market is growing remarkably since 2000's (Chen, 2009) and Kiehl's, which is one of the luxury group sub brands of L'Oréal and is a billionaire brand with double-digit sales growth (L'Oréal, 2018), by introducing its Silver C2C certified product which is called "Made For All" Gentle Body Wash in 2008 showed to both sellers and users of the market that it would be a determinative actor in natural products market. The product was %95 naturally-derived ingredients including Sustainably-Sourced Aloe Vera and Hand Harvested Soap Tree Extract and the packages of the product is produced totally from food and beverage containers retrieved from post-consumer products (Bresson and Gallon, 2008; Mann, 2008).

Another sector where the emphasis on nature has come to the forefront is toy sector. Again from 2000's toys made from sustainable sources, including renewable wood with water-based finishes, natural and organic-cotton plush toys, and toys colored with vegetable dyes instead of paint are among the latest toy trends (Consumer Reports News, 2008). In recent years the parents start to ignore buying nonecofriendly toys to their children and that rejection response forces the businesses to change their approach of production. For example LEGO, which is the world's most valuable toys brand (Brand Finance, 2017) has spent $150 million hiring scientists to test and develop alternatives to plastic and decided to convert to sustainable materials by 2030. In toys category Brandbase BV has two types of bronze cradle to cradle products which were certificated at 20 March 2019; first is Salt Water Super Cars and second is Sugar Cane Racetrack whom base material is a waste of sugar cane processing and called as Bagasse. Bagasse is perfectly dissolve in nature and can be converted to a package or another product. It is expected that with increasing demand and number of environment conscious consumer the number of C2C Certified toy number will also increase in near future.

Of course not all the C2C certified products are consumer products in fact the opposite is valid. The numbers of industrial products are higher than consumer products. One of the well-known İndustrial C2C examples is Climatex® which is a fabric that was produced by Gessner, a nearly 175 years old Swiss company led by Michael Braungart. It is very well known from both business friendly and consumer friendly sides (Sherburne, 2009). The producers use both biological cycle and technical cycle's structure as it should be and certificates are issued after the evaluation of all processes from the extraction and acquisition of the raw materials through packaging and processing to recycling. It is impossible to list all of 578 products in this part of course but it is expected that in near future the number of those certificated products will increase so rapidly with ongoing trend in environment consciousness.

CONCLUSION

The mass production model, which started with the industrial revolution, is characterized as linear due to the unidirectional flow it adopts in the use of resources and the loss of resources as waste. Throughout the 20th century, the economy has grown rapidly with business practices that require more consumption to produce more. The production model of this economical system, which proceeds linearly with the take-make-dispose perspective, is called planned obsolescence. Planned obsolescence, which aims to enable consumers to buy more new products in less time, has also caused excessive use of resources due to over consumption.

By the 1980s, it was understood that the world's natural resources were not unlimited, as assumed in the linear economy and as a result, problems such as oil crises, rise in raw material prices, increase in air pollution, and increasingly difficult access to clean water resources have begun to emerge. At this point, governments, businesses and consumers have simultaneously changed their strategies and behaviors to change this unsustainable situation. For a sustainable environment, states and supranational institutions, as regulators, have created a new economic and legal system, enterprises have changed their production and marketing approaches and consumers were directed to environmentally sensitive choices in all their consumption behaviors. The resulting new economic model is called circular economy. Although many different approaches to the circular economy are focused on different points in production and consumption processes; in line with the common elements encountered in these approaches, circular economy refers to a regenerative economic system in which waste is minimized and the maximum possible value is obtained from resources. This economic model is reflected in the field of business administration through Cradle to Cradle applications. Cradle to Cradle applications aims to achieve waste-free production by using wastes generated after consumption of one product as the raw material of another product.

According to Brears (2018), with the transformation of economic models from linear to circular; states, governments have made the necessary arrangements for the transition to environment-friendly production systems, focused on a more facilitating skilled workforce, ensured the formation of environmental policies to reduce risks in outsourcing jobs and assumed the necessary decisive roles in safety and health services. Businesses, that are creating extra value by adding technological innovations with social and business model changes, so as to reduce the amount of waste, have turned to product design that is more geared towards consumer needs and are committed to lowering operations costs where possible. Consumers, on the other hand, tried to give priority on local products, made more return to the enterprises and showed their needs and want more clearly, and collaborated with businesses to support the recycling processes after use. Thus, three legged stool metaphors of sustainability are supported.

Reike et al. (2018) suggests that while these changes are experienced in the field of application, there is a significant increase in the publications in this field, especially in terms of circular economy, in the following, waste management, recycling, etc. It has been observed that the number of publications in the

Scopus database on circular economy has increased by 50% in the last 10 years and that the concepts are increasingly being studied. These researches are of great importance both in terms of being inspirational in the field and creating awareness among stakeholders by attracting attention.

Research and observations on the health of the world ecosystem show that; despite this change in practice and theoretical perspectives and the awareness that has been created; there is still a long way to go in terms of sustainability. For example, according to The World Bank (2017) only 44% of worldwide waste is green products and food, and about 45% is made up of non-recyclable metals, plastic rubber and leather. Environmental pollution and surplus costs caused by not winning them in the transformation processes show that there is a long way to go.

Both the legal order and the social consciousness created by states and supranational institutions in the context of transformation are known to have the best rates for recycling in the EU member states. On the other hand, in the less developed countries, it can be seen that there is no public awareness about recycling and the state does not play a sufficient role either in legal regulations or in creating social awareness. Especially the fact that countries such as the USA and China, which are determinants of both the production and consumption aspects of the global economy, are in a position close to the linear line are among the factors that make it difficult to solve the problem at the global level. As the case of the European Union shows, the laws and system of states and supranational institutions are crucial to ensure change at the business and community level. With a legal basis and the public awareness movement, that will be created by taking the EU model as a basis the circular economy can be spread throughout the world.

States' support for enterprises that adopt critical circular economy elements such as waste management, environmentally sustainable production, reverse logistics and recycling, and the use of incentives such as tax exemptions and concessions can lead to a transformation in this direction for all enterprises. Circular waste management, reverse logistics and recycling are the three critical elements for achieving zero waste, one of the main objectives of the circular economy. In order to establish a healthy system in these dimensions, first of all, to present the current situation, to establish the necessary infrastructure and technology for the healthy operation of the recycling process and to provide incentives and investments in this regard, to train personnel on waste management and to raise awareness of the existing personnel, to reciprocate the methods and techniques used establishing an audit mechanism and communicating data to relevant stakeholders through various research and reports is extremely important

Governments also play a critical role in raising public awareness. Starting from the first stages of education, consumers will be informed about environmental awareness and will adopt circular patterns in their purchasing, consuming and post-purchasing processes. Businesses that can shape the economy with social responsibility activities, as well as production processes and waste management systems, can play an effective role in both consumers and stakeholders, especially in raising public awareness. Together with governments, they can raise awareness of the adoption of a sustainable consumption model. In all these contexts, the natural environment will be protected with the increase of studies and efforts on circular economy and related issues, economic value will be provided with more efficient use of resources and sustainable development principles will be implemented.

This study is important in terms of the comparative approach of linear economic model and circular economic model in terms of planned obsolescence and cradle to cradle. However, the subject matter can be analyzed in detail in terms of all functions of the business (production, management, financing etc.) and supported by financial and economic data. At the same time, this field is very suitable for multidisciplinary studies such as value engineering analysis, investment project analysis, multi-criteria decision making.

At the same time, as it is seen that in Turkey, which is below the world average in terms of waste production, but above the average in developed countries, the number of studies in this field is quite low and the studies are concentrated in non-business areas, it is aimed to pioneer developments in this field in the country where the researchers are located.

ACKNOWLEDGMENT

This research received no specific grant from any funding agency in the public, commercial, or not-for-profit sectors.

REFERENCES

Adamson, G. (2003). *Industrial strength design how brooks stevens shaped your world*. Cambridge: The MIT Press.

Alston, K. (2008). Cradle to Cradle design initiatives: Lessons and opportunities for prevention through design (PtD). *Journal of Safety Research*, *39*(2), 135–136. doi:10.1016/j.jsr.2008.02.017 PubMed

Amuda, O., Adebisi, S., Jimoda, L., & Alade, A. (2014). Challenges and possible panacea to the municipal solid wastes management in Nigeria. *Journal of Sustainable Development Studies*, *6*(1), 64–70.

Andrews, D. (2015). The circular economy, design thinking and education for sustainability. *Local Economy*, *30*(3), 305–315. doi:10.1177/0269094215578226

Antikainen, R., Lazarevic, D., & Seppälä, J. (2018). Circular economy: origins and future orientations. In H. Lehmann (Ed.), *Factor X: challenges, implementation strategies and examples for a sustainable use of natural resources* (pp. 115–129). Cham, Switzerland: Springer International Publishing; doi:10.1007/978-3-319-50079-9_7.

Bakker, C., Wever, R., Teoh, C., & De Clercq, S. (2010, March). Designing Cradle-to-Cradle products: A reality check. *International Journal of Sustainable Engineering*, *3*(1), 2–8. doi:10.1080/19397030903395166

Barbier, E. B. (2003). The role of natural resources in economic development. *Australian Economic Papers*, *42*(2), 253–272. doi:10.1111/1467-8454.00198

Bauman, Z. (2015). *Özgürlük*. İstanbul: Ayrıntı Yayınevi.

Berkhout, F. (1996). Life cycle assesment and innovation in large firms. *Business Strategy and the Environment*, *5*(3), 145–155. doi:10.1002/(SICI)1099-0836(199609)5:3<145::AID-BSE65>3.0.CO;2-P

Bjørn, A., & Strandesen, M. (2011). The Cradle to Cradle concept - is it always sustainable? Paper presented at the meeting of the The Life Cycle Management (LCM) conference: Towards Life Cycle Sustainability Management, Berlin, Germany.

Braungart, M. (2009). Criticism on Cradle to Cradle? Right on schedule. https://www.duurzaamgebouwd.nl/artikel/20090320-criticism-on-cradle-to-cradle-right-on-schedule-says-michael-braungart

Braungart, M., McDonough, W., & Bollinger, A. (2007). Cradle-to-Cradle design: Creating healthy emissions - a strategy for eco-effective product and system design. *Journal of Cleaner Production*, *15*(13-14), 1337–1348. doi:10.1016/j.jclepro.2006.08.003

Brears, R. (2018). *The circular economy. in: natural resource management and the circular economy*. Cham: Palgrave Studies in Natural Resource Management. Palgrave Macmillan; doi:10.1007/978-3-319-71888-0.

Bresson, M., & Gallon, V. (2008). Kiehl's Experiments New Green Cosmetic Concepts. Retrieved at 28.10.2019, from https://www.premiumbeautynews.com/en/Kiehl-s-experiments-new-green,367

Bulow, J. (1986). An economic theory of planned obsolescence. *The Quarterly Journal of Economics*, *101*(4), 729–749. doi:10.2307/1884176

Chen, Q. (2009, August). Evaluate the effectiveness of the natural cosmetic product compared to chemical-based products. *International Journal of Chemistry*, *1*(2), 57–59. doi:10.5539/ijc.v1n2p57

Consumer Reports News. (2008). Toy trend: organic and natural toys. Retrieved at 27.10.2019, from https://www.consumerreports.org/cro/news/2008/12/toy-trend-organic-and-natural-toys/index.htm

Cooper, T. (1999, January). Creating an economic infrastructure for sustainable product design. The Journal of Sustainable Product Design, (8), 7 - 17.

Cooper, T. (2004). Inadequate life? Evidence of consumer attitudes to product obsolescence. *Journal of Consumer Policy*, *27*(4), 421–449. doi:10.1007/s10603-004-2284-6

Cradle to Cradle Products Innovation Institute. (2019). What is Cradle to Cradle certified™? Retrieved at 28.10.2019, from https://www.c2ccertified.org/get-certified/product-certification

Dannoritzer, C. (Director) (2010). The light bulb conspiracy: The untold story of planned obsolescence (Documentary).

Datschefski, E. (1999, January). Cyclic, solar, safe - biodesign's solution requirements for sustainability. The Journal of Sustainable Product Design, 42 - 52.

De Pauw, I., Kandachar, P., Karana, E., Peck, D., & Wever, R. (2010). Nature inspired design: strategies towards sustainability. Paper presented at the meeting of the Knowledge Collaboration & Learning for Sustainable Innovation ERSCP-EMSU Conference, Delft, The Netherlands.

Devrim, Ö. (2014). Tarihsel süreç içinde C2C'nin izini sürmek. Retrieved at 28.10.2019, from https://trendyazilari.blogspot.com/2014/06/tarihsel-sureci-icinde-cradle-to-cradle.html

Dijk, S., Tenpierik, M., & den Dobbelsteen, A. (2014). Continuing the building's cycles: A literature review and analysis of current systems theories in comparison with the theory of Cradle to Cradle. *Resources, Conservation and Recycling*, (82): 21–34. doi:10.1016/j.resconrec.2013.10.007

Doğa Sektörel Yayın Grubu. (2016). 2. Sanayi devrimi: "beşikten beşiğe" tasarım. Retrieved at 08.10.2019, from https://www.termodinamik.info/guncel/2-sanayi-devrimi-besikten-besige-tasarim

DuPont, U. S. A. (2018). Innovation starts here. Retrieved at 05.03.2018 from Https://www.dupont.com/corporatefunctions/our-company/dupont-history.html

Duska, R. (1997). The Why's of business revisited. *Journal of Business Ethics*, *16*(12/13), 1401–1409. doi:10.1023/A:1005731008313

Ellen Mac Arthur Foundation. (2015a). *Delivering the circular economy: a toolkit for policymakers*. Author.

Ellen MacArthur Foundation. (2013). *Towards the circular economy. Economic and Business rationale for an accelerated transition*. Author.

Ellen MacArthur Foundation. (2015b). *Towards a circular economy: Business rationale for an accelerated transition*. Author.

EPEA GmbH – Part of Drees & Sommer. (2002). Cradle to Cradle: remaking the way we make things. Retrieved at 28.10.2019 from https://epea-hamburg.com/cradle-to-cradle-remaking-the-way-we-make-things/

Erten, D. (2018). Beşikten beşiğe atık. Yeşil Bina, (48), 20 - 23. Retrieved from http://www.yesilbinadergisi.com/edergi/21/48/index.html

European Commission. (2015). Circular economy. Retrieved at 19.08.2019 from https://ec.europa.eu/growth/industry/sustainability/circular-economy_en

European Environment Agency. (2016). *Circular economy in Europe: developing the knowledge base*. Luxembourg: Publications Office of the European Union.

Fromm, E. (2004). *Çağdaş Toplumların Geleceği*. İstanbul: Arıtan Yayınevi.

Garcés-Ayerbe, C., Rivera-Torres, P., Suárez-Perales, I., & Leyva-de la Hiz, D. (2019). Is it possible to change from a linear to a circular economy? An overview of opportunities and barriers for European small and medium-sized enterprise companies. *International Journal of Environmental Research and Public Health*, *16*(851), 1–15. doi:10.3390/ijerph16050851 PubMed

Goh, J., & Yoon-Chung, C. (2018). Towards a closed-loop system for the steel industry. *Asian Steel Watch*, *6*, 84–85.

Gupta, S. (2008). The purpose of business: profit maximization versus corporate citizens. *Proceedings of the Academy of Business Economics*, P1 - P2.

Hadjichambis, A., Paraskeva-Hadjichambi, D., Ioannou, H., Georgiou, Y., & Manoli, C. (2015). Integrating sustainable consumption into environmental education: A case study on environmental representations, decision making and intention to act. *International Journal of Environmental and Science Education*, *10*(1), 67–86. doi:10.12973/ijese.2015.231a

Halden, R. (2010, January). Plastics and health risks. *Annual Review of Public Health*, *31*(1), 179–194. doi:10.1146/annurev.publhealth.012809.103714 PubMed

Hindle, T. (2008). *Guide to management ideas and gurus*. Exmouth House.

Huthala, A. (2015, November). Circular economy: a commentary from the perspectives of the natural and social sciences. EASAC (European Academies Science Advisory Council), 1 - 18. Retrieved from https://www.easac.eu/fileadmin/PDF_s/reports_statements/EASAC_Circular_Economy_Web.pdf

Jawahir, I., & Bradley, R. (2016). Technological elements of circular economy and the principles of 6R-based closed-loop material flow in sustainable manufacturing. Procedia CIRP, 40, 103–108. doi:10.1016/j.procir.2016.01.067

Kahriman Öztürk, D., Olgan, R., & Güler, T. (2012, Autumn). Preschool children's ideas on sustainable development: How preschool children perceive three pillars of sustainability with the regard to 7R. *Educational Sciences: Theory and Practice*, 2987–2995.

Karaca, B. (2018). Sürüdürülebilir mobilya üretiminde tasarım bilinci üzerine bir araştırma (Unpublished Master's Thesis). Ankara: Başkent University Social Sciences Institute.

Kirchherr, J., Reike, D., & Hekkert, M. (2017). Conceptualizing the circular economy: An analysis of 114 definitions. *Resources, Conservation and Recycling*, *127*, 221–232. doi:10.1016/j.resconrec.2017.09.005

Koç, Z., & Ekşi Akbulut, D. (2017). Ekolojik tasarım kapsamında dünyada ve Türkiye'de toprak yapı standart ve yönetmeliklerinin değerlendirilmesi. *MEGARON*, *12*(4), 647–657. doi:10.5505/megaron.2017.48615

Kopnina, H. (2019). Green-washing or best case practices? Using circular economy and Cradle to Cradle case studies in business education. *Journal of Cleaner Production*, *219*, 613–621. doi:10.1016/j.jclepro.2019.02.005

Koren, Y. (2010). The global manufacturing revolution: product-process-business ıntegration and reconfigurable systems. Wiley. doi:10.1002/9780470618813

Kumar, S., & Putman, V. (2008). Cradle to Cradle: Reverse logistics strategies and opportunities across three industry sectors. *International Journal of Production Economics*, *115*(2), 305–315. doi:10.1016/j.ijpe.2007.11.015

Kumlien, S. (2010). From Here to Returnity - A Small Scale Effort for Big Scale Change. Design, 90 - 94.

L'Oréal. (2018). *L'Oréal Annual Report, 2018*. Author.

Leonard, A. (2010). *The story of stuff: How our obsession with stuff is trashing the planet, our communities, and our health - and a vision for change*. New York: Free Press.

Littig, B., & Grießler, E. (2005). Social sustainability: A catchword between political pragmatism and social theory. *International Journal of Sustainable Development*, *8*(1/2), 65–79. doi:10.1504/IJSD.2005.007375

Liu, Y., & Bai, Y. (2014). An exploration of firms' awareness and behavior of developing circular economy: An empirical research in China. *Resources, Conservation and Recycling*, *87*, 145–152. doi:10.1016/j.resconrec.2014.04.002

Lovins, L. H. (2008). Chapter three: rethinking production. in the world watch institute. In State of The World: Innovations for A Sustainable Economy (pp. 32–44). The Worldwatch Institute.

Mann, R. (2008). Kiehl's unveils new eco-effective body cleanser, created in partnership with Brad Pitt. Retrieved at 29.10.2019, from https://www.moodiedavittreport.com/kiehls-unveils-new-eco-effective-body-cleanser-created-in-partnership-with-brad-pitt-180908/

Maycroft, N. (2009). Consumption, planned obsolescence and waste. Working Paper. (Unpublished).

McDonough, W., & Braungart, M. (2002). *Cradle to Cradle: remaking the way we make things*. New York: North Point Press.

Nejeala, J. (2011). Planned obsolescence understanding the reality of durable goods obsolescence and consumers disposal behavior (Unpublished doctoral dissertation). University of Economics in Prague, Faculty of Business Administration International Business and Management, Czech Republic.

Niinimäki, K. (2013). *Sustainable fashion: new approaches*. Helsinki, Finland: Aalto University Publication Series.

Nijaki, L. (2014). Why sustainability is not a stool or pretzel, but a Mobius strip. *Open Citizenship*, *5*(1), 100–104.

Önder, H. (2018, July). Sürdürülebilir kalkınma anlayışında yeni bir kavram: döngüsel ekonomi. Dumlupınar Üniversitesi Sosyal Bilimler Dergisi, (57), 196 - 204.

Özkan, A., Günkaya, Z., Özdemir, A., & Banar, M. (2018). Sanayide temiz üretim ve döngüsel ekonomiye geçişte enüstriyel simbiyoz yaklaşımı: Bir değerlendirme. Anadolu Üniversitesi Bilim ve Teknoloji Dergisi B - Teorik Bilimler, 6(1), 84 - 97. doi:10.20290/aubtdb.332377

Özsoy, T. (2018). Endüstriyel ekolojiyi anlamak adına endüstriyel ortakyaşarlık örneklerinin incelenmesi. Artıbilim. *Adana Bilim ve Teknoloji Üniversitesi Sosyal Bilimler Dergisi, 1*(2), 22–34.

Packard, V. (1960). *The waste makers*. London: Penguin Books.

PAGEV. (2015). *Döngüsel ekonomi: Avrupa'da stratejik kaynak politikasının baş faktörü*. Türk Plastik Sanayicileri Araştırma, Geliştirme ve Eğitim Vakfı.

Paulsen, J. (2001, April). Life cycle assesment for building products: the significance of the usage phase (Unpublished doctoral dissertation). Kungliga Tekniska Höghskolan.

Potting, J., Hekkert, M., Worrell, E., & Hanemaaijer, A. (2017). *Circular economy: measuring innovation in the product chain*. The Hague: PBL Netherlands Environmental Assessment Agency.

Public Law. (1965). Solid waste disposal act. As Amended Through P.L. 115–232, Enacted August 13, 2018.

Rada, E., Ragazzi, M., Torretta, V., Castagna, G., Adami, L., & Cioca, L. (2018). Circular economy and waste to energy. Technologies and Materials for Renewable Energy, Environment and Sustainability, 1 - 6. doi:10.1063/1.5039237

Reh, L. (2013). Process engineering in circular economy: Invited review. *Particuology*, *11*(2), 119–133. doi:10.1016/j.partic.2012.11.001

Reijnders, L. (2008). Are emissions or wastes consisting of biological nutrients good or healthy? *Journal of Cleaner Production, 16*(10), 1138–1141. doi:10.1016/j.jclepro.2008.02.003

Reike, D., Vermeulen, W. J., & Witjes, S. (2018). The circular economy: New or refurbished as CE 3.0?—Exploring controversies in the conceptualization of the circular economy through a focus on history and resource value retention options. *Resources, Conservation and Recycling, 135*, 246–264. doi:10.1016/j.resconrec.2017.08.027

Şahin, Y., & Odabaşı, S. (2018). Sürdürülebilir kalkınmada moda tasarımcısının rolüne yönelik alanyazın incelemesi. *Uluslararası Yönetim İktisat ve İşletme Dergisi, 14*(2), 413–425. doi:10.17130/ijmeb.2018239940

Saklı, A. R. (2007). Kapitalist Gelişim Surecinde Fordizm ve Post - Fordizm. Retrieved at 15.11.2018 from http://2015.ses.org.tr/wp-content/uploads/fordizmpostfordizm.pdf

Sapmaz Veral, E. (2018). Döngüsel ekonomiye geçiş doğrultusunda yeni trendler ve AB üye ülkelerinin stratejileri. Ankara Avrupa Çalışmaları Dergisi, 17(2), 463–488. doi:10.32450/aacd.511998

Sapmaz Veral, E. (2019, March). An evaluation on the circular economy model and the loops design in the context of waste management. Avrupa Bilim ve Teknoloji Dergisi, (15), 18 - 27. doi:10.31590/ejosat.479333

Satyro, W. C. A., Sacomano, J. B. A., Contador, J. C. A., Cardoso, A. A., & Silva, E. P. (2017, May). Planned obsolescence and sustainability. Paper presented at the meeting of the 6th International Workshop Advances in Cleaner Production, Academic Work, São Paulo, Brazil.

Schaltegger, S. (1997). Economics of life cycle assessment: Inefficiency of present approach. *Business Strategy and the Environment, 6*(1), 1–8. doi:10.1002/(SICI)1099-0836(199702)6:1<1::AID-BSE84>3.0.CO;2-D

Scientific Applications International Corporation (SAIC). (2006). *Life-cycle assessment: principles and practice*. Cincinnati: National Risk Management Research Laboratory, Office of Research and Development, US Environmental Protection Agency.

Shao, J. (2019). Sustainable consumption in China: New trends and research. *Business Strategy and the Environment, 28*(8), 1–11. doi:10.1002/bse.2327

Sherburne, A. (2009). Achieving sustainable textiles: a designer's perspective. Sustainable Textiles, 3–32. doi:10.1533/9781845696948.1.3

Slade, G. (2006). *Make to break technology and obsolescence in America*. Harvard University Press.

Smeels, E., & Stevels, A. (2003). Influencing product lifetime through productdesign. Proceedings Of Ecodesign 2003.

Solczak, R. (2013). Planned obsolescence: A question of consumerism and production of waste. Centria University of Applied Aciences, Ylivieska Unit, Degree Programme.

Stahel, W. R. (2016, March 23). The circular economy. Retrieved at 26.10.2019, from https://www.nature.com/news/the-circular-economy-1.19594#b2

Steffen, W., Richardson, K., & Rockström, J., & Cornell. (2015). Planetary boundaries: Guiding human development on a changing planet. *Science, 347*(6223). doi:10.1126cience.1259855

Suğur, N. (2015). Endüstri Sosyolojisi. In V. Bozkurt & N. Suğur (Eds.), *Yeni Yönetim Metotları* (pp. 36–66). Eskişehir: Anadolu Üniversitesi Yayınları.

Tangüler, M., Gürsel, P., & Meral, Ç. (2015). Türkiye'de uçucu küllü betonlar için yaşam döngüsü analizi. Paper presented at the meeting of the 9. Ulusal Beton Kongresi, Antalya: TMMOB İnşaat Mühendisleri Odası.

The Horinko Group. (2016). *The future of RCRA — making the business case*. Washington, DC: The Horinko Group.

The World Bank. (2017). Trends in Solid Waste Management. Retrieved at 07.10.2019, from http://datatopics.worldbank.org/what-a-waste/trends_in_solid_waste_management.html

Topoyan, M. (2005). Yeniden üretim sistemleri için sürdürülebilir ürün tasarımlarının oluşturulması. Paper presented at the meeting of the V. Ulusal Üretim Araştırmaları Sempozyumu, İstanbul Ticaret Üniversitesi, İstanbul.

Tseng, M.-L., Tan, R., Chiu, A., Chien, C.-F., & Kuo, T. (2018). Circular economy meets industry 4.0: Can big data drive industrial symbiosis. *Resources, Conservation and Recycling, 131*, 146–147. doi:10.1016/j.resconrec.2017.12.028

Türk Standardları Enstitüsü. (2018). *Döngüsel ekonomi*. Ankara: TSE Basın Yayın Müdürlüğü.

Valant, J. (2006). Planned obsolescence: Exploring the issue. EPRS I European Parliamentary Research Service, PE 581.999.

Warren, L. W. (2013, August). Community economic shortcomings: The three legged stool of sustainability. Practicing Democracy, 29 - 31.

Wilson, D., & Rogero, A. (2015). Chapter 2: Background, definitions, concepts and indicators. In D. Wilson (Ed.), Global Waste Management Outlook (pp. 19 - 39). UNEP (United Nations Environment Programme).

World Economic Forum. (2016). From linear to circular – Accelerating a proven concept. Retrieved at Dec 21, 2016. from: http://reports.weforum.org/towardthe-circular-economy-accelerating-the-scale-up-across-global-supply-chains/fromlinear-to-circular-accelerating-a-proven-concept/

Yang, Q., Zhou, J., & Xu, K. (2014, April). A 3R implementation framework to enable circular consumption in community. *International Journal of Environmental Sciences and Development, 5*(2), 217–222. doi:10.7763/IJESD.2014.V5.481

Yanıklar, C. (2006). *Tüketimin Sosyolojisi*. İstanbul: Birey Yayıncılık.

Yıldırım, L. (2017, December). Geri dönüşüm/ileri dönüşüm/tekrar kullanım kapsamında ikinci el giysiler ve sürdürülebilirlik. *SDÜ ART-E Güzel Sanatlar Fakültesi Sanat Dergisi, 10*(20), 484–503. doi:10.21602duarte.305698

Yong, R. (2007). The circular economy in China. *Journal of Material Cycles and Waste Management*, *9*(2), 121–129. doi:10.1007/s10163-007-0183-z

Zech, T. (2018). Better than recycling. Retrieved at 07.10.2019, from https://www.deutschland.de/en/topic/environment/cradle-to-cradle-rather-than-recycling-these-are-the-advantages

ADDITIONAL READING

Brears, R. (2018). *The circular economy. in: natural resource management and the circular economy*. Cham: Palgrave Studies in Natural Resource Management. Palgrave Macmillan; doi:10.1007/978-3-319-71888-0.

Bulow, J. (1986). An economic theory of planned obsolescence. *The Quarterly Journal of Economics*, *101*(4), 729–749. doi:10.2307/1884176

Dannoritzer, C. (Director) (2010). The light bulb conspiracy: The untold story of planned obsolescence (Documentary).

Ellen Mac Arthur Foundation. (2015). Delivering the circular economy: a toolkit for policymakers.

European Environment Agency. (2016). *Circular economy in Europe: developing the knowledge base*. Luxembourg: Publications Office of the European Union.

McDonough, W., & Braungart, M. (2002). *Cradle to Cradle: remaking the way we make things*. New York: North Point Press.

Packard, V. (1960). *The waste makers*. London: Penguin Books.

Stahel, W. R. (2016, March 23). The circular economy. Retrieved at 26.10.2019, from https://www.nature.com/news/the-circular-economy-1.19594#b2

KEY TERMS AND DEFINITIONS

Circular Economy: An economic model in which every waste generated in a production system is re-evaluated so that the cost of raw materials is kept at minimum and resource efficiency and environmental benefits at maximum.

Cradle to Cradle: A business strategy based on the idea of using biodegradable parts of a finished product as biodegradable and using non-soluble as technical nutrient as raw material to produce the same product or another product, thus obtaining endless use.

Life Cycle Analysis: A concept used in environmental management and assumes that products have a beginning and end of life where the impacts of them on environment can be recorded.

Linear Economy Model: An economic model that can be defined taking resources from nature to make things, use them for a short time and when the end of the life cycle of a product is achieved, it is disposed and considered a waste that is without any concern to the pollution.

Planned Obsolescence: A business strategy that can be defined as planning or designing a product with an artificially limited useful life, so that instilling the desire in a buyer to own something a little better, a little sooner than is necessary in order to stimulate repetitive consumption.

R's of Cradle to Cradle: A framework consisting of abbreviations of fields of activities of cradle to cradle applications that are starting with the letter R and called as how-to's of Cradle to Cradle.

Take-Make-Dispose Model: A linear model of resource consumption that harvest and extract materials, use them to manufacture a product, and sell the product to a consumer, who then discards it as a waste.

Chapter 5
Circular Economy and Risk Management Synergies in Disruptive Environments

Beatriz Olalla-Caballero
https://orcid.org/0000-0002-1042-2675
Pontifical University of Salamanca, Spain

Montserrat Mata-Fernández
Deusto University, Spain

ABSTRACT

Circular economy and innovation are creating a new scenario for companies. There are many frameworks in the market, which allow a company to manage risks. In this chapter, some of these frameworks are analyzed to try to determine how helpful they are in an enterprise to succeed in managing risks. The authors have been working with one of the existing risks frameworks of risk management, but digital transformation and circular economy have introduced new variables and factors that have to be taken into account. New features need to be defined into a new risk management framework, having in mind the velocity of change of information technologies. Success factors are also considered to complete this perspective.

INTRODUCTION

Nowadays, globalization together with circular economy have an impact on strategic management, and there are new issues and features that may be considered. Companies have to try to afford new challenges and have new behaviors that make them survive in the market. They must be agile and do proper decision-making. Effectiveness and optimization of resources, processes and products is a key issue. Nowadays we work in a hyper connected environment and every company is influenced by external factors. For this reason, it is important to start working in new approaches regarding the management of a company, and obviously, related to Risk Management (RM), and the configuration of a team of CRO

DOI: 10.4018/978-1-7998-5116-5.ch005

Copyright © 2020, IGI Global. Copying or distributing in print or electronic forms without written permission of IGI Global is prohibited.

(Chief Risk Officer). It is needed to have a CRO as a leader of the group, but he has to hire a good team of CRO, each of them specialized in different items due to the new consideration of risks from a higher point of view, as we are going to describe. The sooner the team is created, the better for the company, because changes happen so quickly that the company needs to be prepared to face them quickly, maybe this will determine the life of the company. The capacity of the company to evaluate and lead with new risks and the leader's ability to improve resilience is determinant to succeed and to assure continuity of the business.

Risk management in companies sometimes is not considered a part of the strategy to succeed or to take the competitive advantage in the market. It is usually considered as an additional workload that does not add any value to the company. When a company is positioned in a disruptive environment, circular economy and continuously changing market, a traditional perspective relating to risk management does not work and gives no competitive advantage in the market. Risk management may help this project or service to succeed and to be efficiently completed on time and with the required quality.

It is a fact that risk management is one of the main areas of the Project Management Institute (PMI) Project Management Body of Knowledge (PMBOK), and it is featured in the Association for Project Management (APM) of the United Kingdom, that means that everyone is conscious about the value that risk management has for all project managers. It is necessary to spend more time doing an exercise of study and preparation from another point of view, the view of a CEO (Chief Executive Officer), without going down to the level of the problems and risks of each project, but focusing on a long-term point of view and considering the company as an organization with a mission in the society (Raz, Shenhar, & Dvir, 2002).

This study starts with the hypothesis that risk management may help a project to be successfully completed on time and with quality, and thus, this could be considered a discipline that might help a company to achieve its goals. So, in this chapter, an amount of more than 20 different projects developed in the European Union (EU) in the Information Technologies (IT) market is analyzed. The objective of this chapter is to understand how important risk management is in a company, studying some of the features, advantages and requirements of a risk management system or framework to make a company succeed in the market and in circular economy, gain the competitive advantage, and propose a proper risk management framework to cover these points. From the experience of managing these projects in the last 10 years, authors have detected good and bad practices when talking about risk management, so a risk management framework that includes these success issues is proposed and recommended at the end of the chapter, based upon this wide experience.

This chapter starts with a background analysis of circular economy and risk management process; after that, some existing risks, categories and risk frameworks are analyzed. The importance of a set of success factors and good practices are also analyzed and evaluated in this group of different completed projects to achieve benefits and value in a company, to understand how they help a company to obtain benefits when managing risks. After this analysis, a framework is recommended considering some important points and key issues to achieve the objectives of the organization.

CIRCULAR ECONOMY

The actual environment in which any company is moving, has led to new needs, among them it can be highlighted the concern about overexploitation of finite resources, since this entails a high impact and in some cases compromises security and balance environment. Until now the end of the process was the elimination of products and materials, but things changed and from some time, they began to think about recycling them, they started to think about how these products could be returned to the productive circuit. This is the reason why it was necessary to identify priorities and managers, bearing in mind that the context in which the company moves is characterized by innovation and change (Espaliat, 2017).

Several authors attribute the introduction of the concept "Circular Economy" to Pearce and Turner (1989) according to Geissdoerfer, Savaget, Bocken and Hultink (2017), as opposed to the linear and open-ended contemporary economic systems, that was being seen as unfeasible to contribute to the needs that society currently demanded. Obviating some divergences, the various schools of thought have the same starting point, the fact that the present industrial economy system is not sustainable, and a new model of circular economy has to be considered. Conceptually it is a "regenerative" model that encourages everything to maintain its value and utility permanently throughout the production cycle. It is therefore necessary to redirect the current economic model by banishing the identified deficits, proposing alternatives that offer a clear benefit and a higher competitive advantage. It has been said that in some areas the transition to this new model has taken place instinctively (Espaliat, 2017).

Another reason for the appearance of circular economy is the limit of the current economic model, the fact that it reduces economic dependence considerably and the possibility of regenerating new economic activities and new jobs. Its objectives may be regional development, zero waste and the concept of "cradle to cradle" (McDonough and Braungart, 2002) among others (Geissdoerfer et al., 2017). Obviously, the increasing pressure that companies are currently undergoing to be increasingly efficient in the use of resources and especially in the need to have less waste cannot be ignored (Bocken, De Pauw, Bakker, & Van der Grinten, 2016). Nowadays countries have taken measures to promote circular economy, and some have developed to some extent strategies compatible with circular activities while others have accepted the new model as a vital strategy to achieve a better development (George, Lin, & Chen, 2015).

All this change of economic model brings with the need to incorporate not only new technologies, processes and new business models but also new technical and professional profiles and a change through the whole organization involving also stakeholders (Ritzén, & Sandsröm, 2017). The new model, defined by Casadesus-Masanell and Zhu in 2013, will have to create and capture value for its stakeholders, the model will have to innovate to find new ways to generate better revenues and offer customers new valuable propositions (Dentchev et al., 2016). This optimization not only affects products but also resources and the way the return of investment can be optimized. Companies and organizations are aware that they have to implement this new model of circular economy, having in mind that this is something that has to be done with the commitment of the leader. This change is going to take place quickly than expected, due to the constant emergence of disruptive technologies in all fields.

The great schools of circular thought arose in the seventies, although it was not until the nineties when they began to take relevance. New options such as "renting" and "exchange of recoverable material" arise. Circular economy rests on these three principles (Espaliat, 2017):

1. Preserve and improve natural capital;
2. Optimize the performance of resources by distributing components and materials to achieve its maximum utility. This principle will involve designing to recycle or reuse components as much as possible;
3. Promote the effectiveness of the system by detecting and eliminating, as far as possible, external negative factors from the design.

It is relevant to consider these negative factors, because they will have an associated cost that has to be estimated. Even more, the lack of transparency about these costs will be an impediment to the balanced transition to a circular economy. It is obvious knowing all things that every company wants to know what and how they can adopt this new economic model, or what aspect of it can be incorporated into the company. Regarding this question, the Ellen MacArthur Foundation has identified six actions that can be adopted facing a transition to a circular economy. It has to be said that her definition of circular economy can be considered the most renowned, but other authors as Geng and Doberstein or Webster have proposed their own definitions (Geissdoerfer et al., 2017). These actions are Regenerate, Share, Optimize, Loop, Virtualize and Exchange, that applied in a combination way known as RESOLVE framework. To adopt this framework implies another task as Corporate Social Responsibility (CSR), the reorientation of the business model, the adoption of innovation procedures and substantial changes in the behavior of all those involved in the model.

All the things mentioned so far are encompassed in the so-called fourth industrial revolution. It uses AI (Artificial Intelligence) and real-time information to increase productivity and reduce costs. It is also characterized by the confluence of three major challenges: assimilating the technical advances developed by the Industry 4.0, assuming the change of the models from a linear one towards a circular economy and effectively facing climate change (Espaliat, 2017).

In December 2015, the European Commission estimated that the transition to a circular model in the EU could increase productivity by 30% in 2030, increasing Gross Domestic Product (GDP) by up to 1% and giving way to the creation of two million high quality jobs. The action plan to carry it out promotes cooperation between Member State, agencies and any interested party that participates in that circular economy, according to European Commission (2019). It is clear that circular economy is an irreversible and global trend and it is so important that in the Reflection Paper towards a Sustainable Europe by 2030 the circular economy should be made the backbone of the EU industrial strategy, making possible to enable circularity in new sectors and areas, according to European Commission (2019).

The application of the principles of a circular economy allows the following four sources of value to be promoted (Espaliat, 2017):

- Inner circle, the narrower the more valuable the strategy will be;
- Circulation for longer implies as cascade use;
- Job creation, new employment niches are being appearing as it is closely related to innovation and increases competitiveness;
- Innovation, thus seeing the need for greater and closer collaboration between companies and sectors, creating synergies that result in a highly effective and efficient result. The new model can be a driver for innovation, so it will facilitate the process of change to this model (Bocken et al., 2016).

As it has been seen so far, the adoption by a company of the circular economy or the incorporation of certain points of it should be almost innate given the disruptive and constantly changing environment. Hence, if the fundamental strategies for the implementation, development and consolidation of the circular economy are considered, it is worth highlighting the new models of business organization, some derived from legislative changes carried out by the demands of the actual society, in which highlights the need to be viable and profitable, being accompanied by considerable changes in organizational and work performance schemes, such as working for objectives, mobility, time flexibility and massive use of new technologies, called "Smart Working" (Espaliat, 2017). It is also very important to know the ability of the company to handle any disruptive change that can appear and to understand what difficulties or barriers they have to face (Ritzén, & Sandsröm, 2017).

Any company will consider this new model because according to Takacs, Frankenberger and Stechow (2020), nowadays companies are considered more than ever the engines of modern societies, their contribution brings technical innovation, creating value for society and developing solutions for burning issues. It is not merely a passing trend; there are several advantages to joining this model. Therefore, the following challenges or incentives have been identified (Espaliat, 2017):

- Research, promotion, information and dissemination;
- All the knowledge derived from the studies and implementation of the circular economy must be exposed and shared in an agile way, forgetting in these cases the concept of cascade design;
- Training and education;
- Economic and fiscal incentives, among which are agreements of the type "industrial symbiosis";
- CSR, this is a key point in the implementation of the circular economy;
- Multisectoral and cross-sectional projection;
- Governance or management styles must be adopted that make it possible to carry out the initiatives taken to achieve economic stability and integral sustainability;
- Indicators for the evaluation of results, the company must have the appropriate indicators to evaluate the results of the adoption of the circular model. Some organizations propose an indicator called the Material Circularity Indicator (MCI). It will be also interesting to compare the company with similar business in order to evaluate the results and have valid and extrapolated information that can be used for the incorporation of improvements of the eradication of possible defects.

RISK MANAGEMENT PROCESS IN CIRCULAR ECONOMY

No matter if, it is a new enterprise or a company already in the market, according to Stoneburner, Goguen and Feringa (2002), RM is the process that allows managers to balance the operational and economic costs of protective measures and protect the IT systems and data that support their organizations' missions. There are several roles involved in this process; one of the most important that have emerged partially due to the disruptive environment is the CRO, his commitment is to provide a voice that champions the protection of enterprise value at crucial decision-making moments when something in the company is exposed to an unacceptable risk.

The decision of when to start the process of analyzing risks is the responsibility of the CEO and CRO, as the lead of the risk team. For this purpose, CEOs need to choose a CRO, who has the task of forming a group of experts in risks. This CRO is the leader of risk management and he has to be aligned with the CEO and company mission. The main reason is that CEO awareness, commitment and responsibility with risk management are the keys to success in risk management. According to Paape and Speklè (2012), organizations with a CRO and audit committee have more mature Enterprise Risk Management (ERM) systems. More and more companies decide to adhere to better RM practices focusing for this reason on an ERM, especially in the European context where this study has been carried out. ERM will include methods and processes to manage risks and capture opportunities aligned with the company, leading to enhance information processing and communication contributing to increase company reputation and transparency (Malik, Zaman, & Buckby, 2020). At this point, it is very interesting to analyze the convenience of a CRO in a company. According to Nocco and Stulz (2006), to evaluate the job of a CRO, the board committee and the CEO must attempt to determine how well the company's risk is understood and managed. Sometimes, there may be a Risk Management Committee instead (Hoyt, & Liebenberg, 2011). Besides that, Kasperson et al. (1988) highlight one of the problems of risk analysis, and that is the psychological, sociological, and cultural perspectives of risk perception and risk related behavior.

CIOs must have the goal of the company clear in the long term and it is supposed they understand the capability of the company to adopt changes (Cearley, & Burke, 2018). The risk manager should be aware of the importance of the communication associated with risks and the regulatory systems. Both are areas where the state of the risk manager is empathized (Power, 2004). CEOs must think always in the next change, now it is not valid to think in a short period. Although the responsible must be the CEO, regarding risk it would be advisable to design an ownership of each risk area previously identified and defined. Although the risk team is a cross area, there would be a fluent and constant communication with other departments. There is also another issue to be considered when managing risks, and that is the governance applied to that process. According to Bannerman (2008), there could be two forms of effective project governance, being the most common the Project Steering Committee (PSC), chaired by a committed and involved senior business executive; and the other way could be through a no formal governance, where the PSC adopt a passive role.

There may be different stages considered in RM process depending on variations in the level of detail and on the assignment of activities to steps and phases (Raz, & Michael, 2001). Stoneburner et al. (2002) explain how risk management encompasses three processes: risk assessment, risk mitigation, and evaluation and assessment. Boehm (1991) identifies the following steps to cover the risk management related to software projects: identification, analysis, prioritization, management planning, resolution and monitoring. No matter the type of project, some key stages must be covered, defined and implemented. This series of steps will start with the identification of each risk:

- **Identification:** It is crucial to identify any risk in an early stage; what is more, before it the threat appears and before the competence has identified it. Risks have to be considered having in mind the evolution of the market in the country. The company has to anticipate the risks derived from the environment and the changing expectations of society;
- **Register:** After the identification of a risk, the register of this is required, to record all the information required related to a risk. This information involves for example, the category, the probability of the risk, the impact, and even the occurrence of it. Although according to PMI (2004) and Bannerman (2008) the risk may be usually defined as the probability-weighted impact of an event on a project, his risk level might be determined based on the values assigned to the probability, impact and occurrence term. Usually, a matrix is previously defined to do that, so that there is a risk level is calculated depending on the values assigned to those three features: probability, impact and occurrence term;
- **Analyze:** After registering the information related to the risk, there should be an analysis, to detect the causes and origin of it, and identify all the features related to that risk;
- **Manage:** The next step should be the management of the risk to implement the strategy defined regarding it. There is an important role at this stage: the owner of the risk. This role is in charge of the management of the activities, tasks and actions to afford regarding the risk. This strategy may be one of the following: avoid the risk, transfer, accept or mitigate it. According to Bannerman (2008), avoidance strategies aim to prevent a negative effect;

- **Follow-up:** Besides the management stage, there is another stage related to the control of the follow-up of it. Regarding circular economy is important to consider and control at any moment any external factor that may negatively effect on achieving the principles defined for circular economy, such as the optimization and effectiveness of any design and process in the company.

According to Tang and Musa (2011), companies are adopting globalization and outsourcing strategies due to cost pressure and competitive advantages. Alhawari, Karadsheh, Talet and Mansour (2012) consider that globalization introduces many challenges, and companies are required to become more innovative. Miller (1992) exposes how managing risks is one of the main objectives of firms operating internationally. Nowadays, organizations are exposed to frequent changes (Olalla, & Mata, 2016). According to Damodaran (2007), the most successful companies are good at finding particular risks that they are better at exploiting than their competitors find. Hoyt and Liebenberg (2011) explain how organizations with a wide range of investment opportunities are likely to benefit from being able to select investments based on a more accurate risk-adjusted rate. Taking into account these features, RM may help in decision-making based on proper information, which can be a competitive advantage for an organization. Sienou, Lamine and Pingaud (2008) explain that RM contributes to increase the level of confidence with regard to value preservation, management of uncertainties. According to Alhawari et al. (2012), the need to change is forcing enterprises to organize their projects and systems. Nocco and Stulz (2006) argue that when risk is well understood and managed, the company can command the resources required to invest in the valuable projects available.

Risks Types and Risk Categories

There are different types and categories of risks depending on several factors, such as the size of the company, the market share or the number of years the enterprise has been operating, so there is not a unique set of risks that may be extrapolated to other companies. According to Fatemi and Luft (2002), companies may face three sources of risks: business, strategic and financial. We have to consider that part of these risks can be controlled via management's internal operating decisions. Depending on the type of project that a company is developing, there may be different risks. For example, in software projects (Boehm, 1991), there may be some risks: unrealistic schedules and budgets, developing the user interface, continuing stream of requirements changes, etc. Attending a circular economy, issues related to effectiveness, optimization of resources, and recirculation should be considered when defining types and categories of risks in the company.

It is impossible to know all the threats that can affect a company, because some will appear throughout its life; but the more threats we identify the better response we will create. Thinking about the threats and consequences of the risks, the following ones have been identified:

- **Talent and KM (Knowledge Management):** Human factor is determinant (Olalla, San José, & Mata, 2012), and everyone has to be conscious of the importance of talent shortage in the risk analysis, something that influences the whole company and consequently on the staff, so the bad results will be for everyone working in this company. This fact has been detected specially in European companies analysed in this chapter, maybe it was due its idiosyncrasy, anyway the transcendence of human factor is becoming more and more relevant and critical to the success of the company;

- **Corporate responsibility:** Facts that can damage the image of the company but internally, without great repercussions outside, mostly caused by a lack or bad communication political. This risk is closely related to digital ethics and privacy;
- **Consequences of reputation risk:** It is a slightly new risk, the Economist called it in 2007 as "risk of risks" and Bonime-Blanc and Ponzi (2016) treated widely in their book, nowadays it has to be considered in every risk analysis. When this risk was to be analyzed, it has to be considered the importance and weight of stakeholders, although always have been considered as a growth lever, now its transcendence is higher (Bonime-Blanc, & Ponzi, 2016);
- **Environmental risks:** It can be considered as those derived from the political economic status of the country, of the relationship with other countries;
- **Economical, effectiveness, and optimization of resources consequences:** They are very important in circular economy;
- **Competitiveness and market share effects:** Related to market and other companies.

ANALYSIS OF FRAMEWORKS AND MODELS OF RISK MANAGEMENT AND PROPOSAL

Many frameworks in the market allow a company to manage risks. According to Alhawari et al. (2012), the objective of RM is to identify all applicable risks in a project, business or product, it requires analyzing their importance, frequency of occurrence and level of impact, and establishing the actions needed to control these risks. RM is one of the eight main areas of the PMBOK by the PMI (Raz, & Michael, 2001). It includes the processes concerned with risk management planning, identification, analysis, responses, monitoring and control in a project (Project Management Institute, 2004). There are frameworks for several kinds of risks, as for example risk governance, security risk, risk assessment, most of them focus on projects. Some of them have been used for a long time, but it can be said that all suffer from a lack of view from the point of view of the CEO (Hernández, Yelandy, & Cuza, 2013). Some of the existing risk management models are:

- **Boehm:** This framework identifies 8 management elements: objectives, restrictions, alternatives, risks, risk resolution, results, plans and commitment. It is called "espiral cycle" because each cycle is divided into four sectors: objectives definition, assessment and reduction of risks, development and validation and planning. One of the main disadvantages of this framework is that an expert in RM is required and is expensive in time and money, although it reduces risks and adds quality objects;
- **Magerit:** Its name refers to the acronym analysis methodology and risk management;
- **MoGeRi:** It suggests how to use several tools when making risk management.

There are also some causal models used to know the causes of some events and to discover how to predict its effects, for instance fuzzy cognitive models or Bayesian networks. Nowadays a radical turn in the management of the risks of a company is necessary (Hernández et al., 2013). Massingham (2010) proposes an intersection between two existing fields: RM and KM, explaining how knowledge can reduce risk leading to better risk management and defining the Hazard Risk Severity Score (HRSS), classified in terms of the level of risk to produce a Hazard Risk Index (HRI). Wieland and Marcus (2012) analyze and propose risk models and approaches for the supply chain market, and explain how it fosters improved agility and robustness and, hence, better performance. Paape and Speklè (2012) explain the COSO (COSO, 2004a) ERM framework that provides very broad guidance, suggesting key principles and concepts but leaving the specific details to the adopting organizations themselves (COSO, 2004b).

Anyway, some steps have to be executed; it is like a road map for the company to implement the framework. These are the basic steps (Alhawari, Karadsheh, Nehari Talet, & Mansour, 2011):

- **Scope establishment:** The starting point is the capture or identification of the possible risks that may appear, it is important to measure the effort of capture this kind of information and to provide it to the CEO or to the responsible in order to define the risk with the best possible information;
- **Risk identification:** To identify risks several tools can be used such as brainstorming, questionnaires, scenario analysis, lessons learned, etc. and although they are good, to identify new risks and also for the new changing environment, they are not enough. The source of the risk has to be identified and studied;
- **Risk analysis:** Members of the CRO's team have to decide how to deal with the risk, based on probability of occurrence, impact and extent of loss. The analysis has to consider firstly what is supposed to be the likelihood of events occurring, the details of the impact to be able to measure the severity of each risk, displays the effect of loss and finally the ability to react, the estimated time necessary to apply the defined action or actions for that risk;
- **Risk response planning:** At this moment, all risk information is translated into actions. There must exist a plan to prioritize not only risks but also action to be carried out for each risk. The objective of the plan is to minimize the probability of risk occurrence and its impact, the degree of the loss and obviously to improve the reaction time, the sooner the risk is treated the more probability to have a minor impact (Fabricius, & Büttgen, 2015);
- **Risk execution:** The way in which a risk can be treated has been profoundly studied and basically are: avoidance, which means that the company is not going to perform the action that carry the risk; transfer: it is merely to pass the risk to another department or person, is a way to get rid of the problem; reduction, not easy but the idea is to focus on the risk to try to reduce the impact and retention or acceptance of the risk, this is only advisable if the impact of it is low. When this step finishes a contingency plan needs to be defined or redefined;
- **Risk monitoring:** It is the continuous improvement of the risk framework. This step has the mission of keeping updated the treatment of risks guaranteeing its success or changing it to improve the action to execute.

Critical Success Factors and Practices to Avoid in Risk Management

How to manage risks in an enterprise should be one of the worries nowadays due to the impact that several risks may involve if they are not properly managed. Due to external factors it is relevant in European projects the way to deal with risks, every day is more important the way to manage and face risks, as it has been seen regarding all the companies analyzed. According to Raz and Michael (2001), risk management is one of the key project management processes in a company. Nocco and Stulz (2006) discuss how ERM creates value for shareholders. Stulz (1996) highlights how the worst consequence of an improper risk management and strategy of an organization may be becoming financially troubled.

There may be several Critical Success Factors (CSF) in risk management. RM practices may drive to a project success or might involve the project runs over budget or over time (Pimchangthong, & Boonjing, 2017), threatening the existence of the company. When to carry out a risk analysis also determines the success of a company managing risks, because besides the fact that an early analysis may obviously have more benefits, we also have to consider other factors that may affect the changing environment, the market trends or external and internal factors in the circular company.

Companies pursue opportunities in the face of uncertainty, constrained by capability and cost, being a challenge to find a position on each of these dimensions (Bannerman, 2008). Sometimes we might find bad practices of risk management in a company and we can understand that a risk must be properly managed to succeed. There are misunderstandings of the concept 'risk' and employees usually confuse many activities of risk management with others or just underestimate the importance of risk management. At this point, it is a very important issue: the involvement and compromise (Bannerman, 2008): risk-averse strategies may limit distinctive achievement and risk-embracing strategies might increase project losses. Another bad practice to be avoided is to consider RM as a minor theme when defining the strategy of the company; it is a critical point to be considered, analyzed and studied and not only extrapolated from the past. This practice has to be avoided because it can lead risk analyses to a wrong decision conditioned by experiences (Plummer et al., 2018). Some companies and professionals do not understand the meaning of the concept 'risk'. Employees sometimes misunderstand this concept with the cause of it. According to Wang, Lin and Huang (2010), it is very important to manage risks to improve project success rates. In some cases, there is another problem regarding the risk management practices in some companies, and that is that risk management strategies are not pursued and hence, the shareholder value is not enhanced (Fatemi, & Luft, 2002).

Boehm (1991) proposes an incremental implementation strategy, because it allows the company's culture to adjust gradually to risk-oriented management practices. This strategy may consist of identifying and establishing a top-10 risk process to do that and after, identifying an initial project in which to implement this plan. Obviously, it is not operative to try to initially define and implement a huge risk framework, system or process. It usually results in a too ambitious project that does not cover the important requirements and is never properly implemented. According to Paape and Speklè (2012), a large majority of organizations does not quantify risk tolerances, although this practice is contrary to COSO (COSO, 2004a), which require that quantification of risk tolerances is pretty much a compulsory condition for reliable risk management. This drives to a lack of ERM effectiveness. Besides that, although it depends on each company, some of the bad behaviors identified when managing risks are enumerated here because they are usually found and are relevant for any company:

- **The level of compromise of the CEO with RM sometimes is poor:** The commitment of the CEO cannot be limited to moral support, but also to an economic support designating an adequate amount of money, from the annual budget, to these tasks;
- **Level of risk they are willing to accept:** Until now this point was not considered, it was only referenced at first. However, as long as the company grows, the level of risk that it could accept is different. Therefore, the evaluation initially made of risks will lose its value, and it has to be done again;
- **Business goals and risk management:** CEOs needs to have clear the vision and mission of the company, and its requirement in the future. In recent years, it seemed that there was no relationship between business objectives and risk analysis;

- **List the possible risk:** It might seem a good idea to have a list with all the risks and every so often review and update the change in the probability of it happening, or in the way to treat each risk;
- **Some risks were not evaluated in the past:** In fact, some of those risks did not even exist. In addition, it would be advisable to share the list with some identified responsible in the company, not only in the IT department or financial one, but to all departments to have a good vision of what can be considered as a potential risk for the company.

There may be some difficulties in the risk management process. The following issues and factors should be considered:

- Frequency the risks are refreshed, risks are one of the tasks that have been done or reviewed periodically, it is something crucial to an evergreen view of the company risks;
- Identify what are the top risks of the company, these risks have to be identified from scratch and reviewed with an established periodicity by the responsible designated for this purpose;
- Decide who the owners of those identified risks are and what the communication plan are. The responsible need to have all the information required to make a decision about what to do with any risk. There must exist a risk report with the relevant information about the critical company risk, which has to be presented to executive management;
- Define the steps to be followed regarding risk appetite and risk tolerance to be considered;
- Take into account the resilience of the company since changes are continuously occurring that can influence the company and therefore affect some identified risk or become in a new one. It is important because versatility and adaptability are prized features to be considered in a fast-evolving and uncertain world, according to Ellen MacArthur Foundation (2013);
- Identify any possible organizational "blind spots" warranting attention. Themes as cultural issues can undermine the effectiveness of risk management or put at risk the policies and processes defined for this purpose;
- Analyze if the company is mature enough to understand what external factors can alter the key assumptions underlying its strategy and its competitive process;
- Study the capacity to collaborate with other companies; this has to be seen from the point of view of how parts influence another within a whole, and the relationship of the hole to these parts, according to Ellen MacArthur Foundation (2013);
- Consider the lack of engagement of stakeholders in the process of adoption of a circular economy, according to European Commission (2019);
- The treatment and the way to manage every risk have to be defined in a document and it will have to be reviewed and updated continuously. Besides that, the number of risk levels to be considered must be aligned to the volume of risk that are considered in a risk management system or framework.

To resolve these difficulties, there are some CSFs that must be considered in this new framework proposed, that may help a company to properly manage risk management process in a circular economy context (besides the name of the CSF, there is an identification of the stage -DIAMFC- of the new risk framework proposed in this section in which it is involved):

1. Guided analysis (Definition, D-Stage), through catalogues, matrix and procedures;

2. Risk quantification (Identification, I-Stage): economical and other types of impact, threats and consequences on the company;
3. Specific risk analysis (Analysis, A-Stage);
4. Root cause identification (Analysis, A-Stage);
5. Risk strategy (Management, M-Stage);
6. Strategy continuous follow-up (Follow-up, F-Stage);
7. Risks continuous follow-up (Control, C-Stage).

After studying and analyzing how every of these seven CSFs proposed may influence in benefits for a company, and considering 25 examples of completed projects of different duration, size, scope, number of people and stakeholders involved, and other features of a project, these are the results, trying to group the benefits for the company in the following categories (A to F). The effect of every CSF is explained in a three-level scale: high (H), medium (M) and low (L):

1. Teams ready and with enough capacity: 1(H), 2(H), 3(L), 4(M), 5(L), 6(L), and 7(L);
2. Cost savings: 1(H), 2(H), 3(L), 4(H), 5(M), 6(H), and 7(M);
3. Capitalization, social marketing and good reputation: 1(M), 2(L), 3(M), 4(L), 5(L), 6(M), 7(L);
4. Regulatory compliance: 1(M), 2(M), 3(M), 4(H), 5(L), 6(M), 7(H);
5. Technological pioneer: 1(M), 2(H), 3(H), 4(L), 5(H), 6(H), 7(L);
6. Increase market share and profit through effectiveness: 1(M), 2(M), 3(M), 4(L), 5(M), 6(H), and 7(L).

Considering the high impact of some of these CSFs on any of these benefits for a company, our risk management framework proposed must consider them to guarantee the success of the framework in a company. Taking these factors into account and the explained issues, a new framework could be defined. One has already been mentioned, as the necessity to know the ability of the company to react, but it is needed also to estimate the resilience of the company. In addition, this has to be done in the beginning. Other issues are related to effectiveness and optimization of resources. The points to highlight are detailed in each of these steps proposed for the new DIAMFC framework.

Prior to any stage, there should be a scope establishment stage, and there should be a committee for this task. It would be advisable to recruit someone expert on market analysis and trends. Those who are more involved with emerging technology and circular economy, those who know about political changes and laws added to the team that was destined for this purpose will obtain a better list of scope:

- **Definition update new stage (D):** This new stage proposed is identified to consider an updated catalogue of sources of risk, including and updating every new source of risk, especially those related to any external factors that may influence the effectiveness and optimization of our processes, products and resources;
- **Identification stage (I):** As the risks detected are, more or new this step needs to be expanded. Focus has to be on internal and external factors, both are equally important. Consequences of an internal risk can transcend out of the company and become a greater risk, it can be easily manageable just because it is internal but a comment in a social network and the result can be a great disaster. External factors are also important regarding circular economy. After this stage, we should consider the recording stage, when the risks are recorded in the risk system;

- **Analysis stage (A):** New decisions have to be considered. In addition, the biggest change here is the people that have to be aware of certain risks, being necessary in some cases to gather a committee to decide the best options for those risks. Luckily, this would be only required for some strategic risks, of low probability of occurrence but high impact;
- **Management stage (M):** New actions need to be defined, if has to be considered the time factor, a little difference can determine the results of the company regarding not only its economical result but also the image of it. The plan needs to consider also the interrelation among some risks, one can get worse other depending on the occurrence and it can happen that a risk causes another one that depends only on that cause. The idea is to have a matrix where all identified risk can be studied to get a visual image of possible consequences. The matrix once defined and approved will be a powerful tool to prevent and quantify the effect of one risk. At this point, it is also very important to consider the proper strategy to implement with the risk; for example: accept it, mitigate the risk, transfer it to another institution or part, or avoid it. If there is any other option, it must be also considered. It is necessary to highlight the communication plan, this task has to be a constant, what does not mean to tell everything to everybody, and the key here is to know who has to know what, who has the power to decide and who has enough information to be able to define a good contingency plan;
- **Follow-up stage (F):** Finally, the risk management have to be reviewed and improved constantly, that is, periodical meetings need to be defined, it is a good example of effectiveness to detect quickly the need to add a new risk or to modify for instance the questionnaire to identify a risk, and the company has to be faster than the competence;
- **Control new stage (C):** To be considered to gather all activities developed periodically to control the external factors and usual changing environment that involves a circular economy.

All companies need to know what new risks have to be considered having in mind all the threats that can appear, and what level of risk appetite the company can afford (Firstbrook et al., 2019). Regarding the risk appetite, the company is willing to accept, some aspects have to be considered (DeLoach, 2016):

- **Clarity and simplicity:** The definition of the risk can never be an unintelligible document written for certain experts. Each risk has to be detailed in a simple and clear way, all the staff needs to understand it;
- **Time and way of communication:** Risks have to be detected as soon as possible. Time has always been an important fact when giving information. Who and when need to know the existence of a risk is a sensitive issue that should be treated carefully. Since risks are being considered from a CEO point of view, some risks will only be known at first by CRO lead and CEO, they have to decide if it has to be communicated to other stakeholders;
- **Coherence and transparency:** The leader and the company has to follow a behavior line and maintain it through time, both the staff and the society should feel that it is a coherent company, and what is even more important, that it is transparent. But coherency has to exist also internally, it has to be a unique internal political known and followed by all the company, only if this exists the public image will be of coherence. Both aspects are closely linked to its reputational value. This issue is very relevant in circular economy to achieve the principles of this kind of economy;
- **Relevancy:** If the company wants not only to survive, but also to stay in time, it has to be relevant.

This new framework needs to consider new aspects; one has been already mentioned, as the necessity to know the ability to react, but it is needed also to estimate the resilience of the company and studying the risks derived from the adoption of a circular economy, a new model that adds new and important perspectives as understanding value to stakeholders and partners, evaluating the impact of circularity and recognizing trends and drivers at the ecosystem level (Antikainen, & Valkokari, 2016). It has alto to be highlighted that for this new model the EU has considered a framework presented by the Commission in 2018, which include 10, key indicators, although some Member States have developed additional indicators, according to European Commission (2019). Consequently, new issues have to be deeply analyzed and considered to evaluate the consequences that may influence the company. In the framework proposed, the following sources of risks have been identified to be considered in the Definition new stage (D):

- **Strategic decision-making:** Very important in this disruptive environment;
- **Technology adoption and innovation:** Nowadays the speed of change has accelerated due to overlapping and combinatorial technology concepts. CIOs must study predictions regarding new technologies that presumably will appear. For each new digital change, they will have to evaluate if the prediction is trending toward becoming true or not (Bonime-Blanc, & Ponzi, 2016). Once studied the prediction, the next step will be to position in the future market, knowing if the change can be in a short period or if on the contrary it is something that will change in the long term. The company needs to have the ability to reinvent itself, it needs to ensure and increase its competitiveness and persistence in time (Marmier, Gourc, & Laarz, 2013). Maybe it would also be possible to have different preventive strategies, more difficult to define, but easier to execute (Marmier et al., 2013);
- **External and internal factors:** Among all the factors, it can be also considered the human factor, as it has been said, the talent is something critical. But also those external factors that may have an effect on the effectiveness of circular economy and optimization of resources, products and processes of the company;
- **Policies of the firm:** Every company has a vision and mission, but the company is working in an environment and interact with it as a part of a whole;
- **Rules and trends that coexist in the market**;
- **Use of social networks by employees:** As it has been said, the most important thing is to have a good communication plan. Companies have to manage the compromise of all the staff in the prevention of risks, every single chain is important to achieve a robust enterprise;
- **Political changes:** Depending on the country and its political regime, companies will have to vary the course of their decisions;
- **The increasing necessity of being transparent:** Transparency has been gaining importance and is now taking place of importance in the detection of risks. In any case, transparency needs to be considered from an internal and from an external point of view (Auinger, Nedbal, & Hochmeier, 2013);
- **Capacity to adapt to new changes:** Agility is not a requirement it is a necessity. To be able to adapt is essential to be continuously updated;
- **Level of organizational resilience:** This point has to be part of the ERM program (Witty, & Jaggers, 2018). Gartner as "the ability of an organization to resist, absorb, recover and adapt to business disruption in an ever changing and increasingly complex environment to enable it to deliver its objectives, and rebound and prosper has defined organizational resilience". In addition,

resilience must be considered from different points of view but knowing that resilience is a benefit for the company, but also a cost (Perkins, Witty, Olyaei, Gregory, & Jaggers, 2018);

- **Security:** From the point of view of the risk derived from social media tampering. Someone, probably a team, has to use their time to follow this information and to investigate the source and veracity of it;
- **Culture and international projects:** These issues involve several legal requirements and different cultures;
- **Regulatory and privacy challenges**;
- **Contractual relationships:** It has to be considered the tendency to think projects of similar characteristics will have the same risks, this is not necessarily true, and every project has to be considered from scratch. The fact of having had other projects of similar characteristics will only be useful as experience in the process of identity risks.

CONCLUSION

Risk management is a very important part to be taken into account when talking about the strategy of a company and being competitive in the market and in a circular economy. There is no place in the market for enterprises that do not give importance or value to RM, especially when an organization is working in a changing environment and in a global and circular economy. After considering all this analysis, it can be concluded that certainly, it is impossible to know the evolution of the environment or what will happen in the future, but nowadays, with the amount of information available and the need for optimization of resources and processes, we need to build a scenario close to what reality could be in the future that allows us to properly manage risk. On the other hand, the role of the CEO and CRO has changed, and the leader needs to get in touch with reality and with his employees. It is important to know that their feedback is going to be positive to succeed. He has to become, as well as the company, people-centric (Scholtz, 2019). That was not a worry in recent years, because the leadership model was different, but now it is time to think more about people. However, to achieve that, the first step is to have a good team prepared, enthusiastic and committed with the company and its mission. It is relevant to note that the link among departments, people and risks is growing, and its importance is critical when talking about strategy and risks. Derived from this particular situation, it can be deduced that the vision of risk has changed, and a new analysis has to be done. Besides that, the focus has changed, and factors such as resilience have gained incredible relevance. The resilience of the company, the ability to react to an unexpected event, or the time it takes to give an answer or a solution to a risk, are things that have to be deeply considered and properly managed.

After the analysis explained in this chapter, it is concluded that there are some important issues and factors that may be considered in a RM process to succeed and they are explained and evaluated in this chapter, to understand how to focus a proper and advantageous risk management practices in a company, together with other proposals that may be considered in a company regarding risk management. A new framework is proposed to afford these challenges, considering all these issues.

This analysis and proposals may be completed in future research, in which complementary issues, key success factors, tools and considerations may be added to complete the present contents of this chapter, together with a set of indicators to control risk management, and a global completed framework may be defined gathering all these issues and concepts.

REFERENCES

Alhawari, S., Karadsheh, L, Nehari Talet, A., & Mansour, E. (2011). *Knowledge-Based Risk Management framework for Information Technology project*. Academic Press.

Alhawari, S., Karadsheh, L., Talet, A. N., & Mansour, E. (2012). Knowledge-based risk management framework for information technology project. *International Journal of Information Management, 32*(1), 50–65. doi:10.1016/j.ijinfomgt.2011.07.002

Antikainen, M., & Valkokari, K. (2016). A framework for sustainable circular business model innovation. *Technology Innovation Management Review, 6*(7).

Auinger, A., Nedbal, D., & Hochmeier, A. (2013). An Enterprise 2.0 project management approach to facilitate participation, transparency, and communication. *International Journal of Information Systems and Project Management, 1*(2), 43–60.

Bannerman, P. L. (2008). Risk and risk management in software projects: A reassessment. *Journal of Systems and Software, 81*(12), 2118–2133. doi:10.1016/j.jss.2008.03.059

Bocken, N. M. P., De Pauw, I., Bakker, C., & Van der Grinten, B. (2016). Product design and business model strategies for a circular economy. *Journal of Industrial and Production Engineering, 33*(5), 308–320. doi:10.1080/21681015.2016.1172124

Boehm, B. W. (1991). Software risk management: Principles and practices. *IEEE Software, 8*(1), 32–41. doi:10.1109/52.62930

Bonime-Blanc, A., & Ponzi, L. J. (2016). *Understanding Reputation Risk the Qualitative and Quantitative Imperative*. GEC Risk Advisory LLC & ReputationInc.

Cearley, D., & Burke, B. (2018). *Top 10 Strategic Technology Trends for 2019*. Gartner.

COSO. (2004a). *Enterprise risk management –integrated framework. Executive summary & framework*. Committee of Sponsoring Organizations of the Treadway Commission.

COSO. (2004b). *Enterprise risk management –integrated framework. Application techniques. Executive summary & framework*. Committee of Sponsoring Organizations of the Treadway Commission.

Damodaran, A. (2007). *Strategic risk taking: a framework for risk management*. Pearson Prentice Hall.

DeLoach, J. (2016). *Reimagining Risk*. Corporate Compliance Insights.

Dentchev, N., Baumgartner, R., Dieleman, H., Jóhannsdóttir, L., Jonker, J., Nyberg, T., ... Van Hoof, B. (2016). Embracing the variety of sustainable business models: Social entrepreneurship, corporate intrapreneurship, creativity, innovation, and other approaches to sustainability challenges. *Journal of Cleaner Production, 113*, 1–4. doi:10.1016/j.jclepro.2015.10.130

Ellen Macarthur Foundation (2013). Towards the circular economy. Economic and business rationale for an accelerated transition. *Rethink the Future, 1.*

Espaliat, M. (2017). *Economía circular y sostenibilidad: nuevos enfoques para la creación de valor*. CreateSpace Independent Publishing Platform.

European Commission. (2019). *Report from the Commission to the European Parliament, the Council, the European Economic and Social Committee and the Committee of the Regions on the implementation of the Circular Economy Action Plan.* Author.

Fabricius, G., & Büttgen, M. (2015). Project managers' overconfidence: How is risk reflected in anticipated project success? *Business Research*, *8*(2), 239–263. doi:10.100740685-015-0022-3

Fatemi, A., & Luft, C. (2002). Corporate risk management: Costs and benefits. *Global Finance Journal*, *13*(1), 29–38. doi:10.1016/S1044-0283(02)00037-6

Firstbrook, P., Reed, B., Olyaei, S., Sadowski, G., Mahdi, D., Bhajanka, P., Perkin, E. (2019). *Top Security and Risk Management Trends.* Gartner.

Geissdoerfer, M., Savaget, P., Bocken, N. M., & Hultink, E. J. (2017). The Circular Economy–A new sustainability paradigm? *Journal of Cleaner Production*, *143*, 757–768. doi:10.1016/j.jclepro.2016.12.048

George, D. A., Lin, B. C. A., & Chen, Y. (2015). A circular economy model of economic growth. *Environmental Modelling & Software*, *73*, 60–63. doi:10.1016/j.envsoft.2015.06.014

Hernández, N., Yelandy, M., & Cuza, L. (2013). Modelos causales para la Gestión de Riesgos. *Revista Cubana de Ciencias Informáticas*, *7*(4).

Hoyt, R. E., & Liebenberg, A. P. (2011). The value of enterprise risk management. *The Journal of Risk and Insurance*, *78*(4), 795–822. doi:10.1111/j.1539-6975.2011.01413.x

Kasperson, R. E., Renn, O., Slovic, P., Brown, H. S., Emel, J., Goble, R., ... Ratick, S. (1988). The social amplification of risk: A conceptual framework. *Risk Analysis*, *8*(2), 177–187. doi:10.1111/j.1539-6924.1988.tb01168.x

Malik, M. F., Zaman, M., & Buckby, S. (2020). Enterprise risk management and firm performance: Role of the risk committee. *Journal of Contemporary Accounting & Economics*, *16*(1), 100178. doi:10.1016/j.jcae.2019.100178

Marmier, F., Gourc, D., & Laarz, F. (2013). A risk oriented model to assess strategic decisions in new product development projects. *Decision Support Systems*, *56*, 74–82. doi:10.1016/j.dss.2013.05.002

Massingham, P. (2010). Knowledge risk management: A framework. *Journal of Knowledge Management*, *14*(3), 464–485. doi:10.1108/13673271011050166

McDonough, W., & Braungart, M. (2002). *Remaking the way we make things: Cradle to cradle*. New York: North Point Press.

Miller, K. D. (1992). A framework for integrated risk management in international business. *Journal of International Business Studies*, *23*(2), 311–331. doi:10.1057/palgrave.jibs.8490270

Nocco, B. W., & Stulz, R. M. (2006). Enterprise risk management: Theory and practice. *Journal of Applied Corporate Finance*, *18*(4), 8–20. doi:10.1111/j.1745-6622.2006.00106.x

Olalla, B., & Mata, M. (2016). *Value Creation in a Network Economy. In Handbook of Research on Social Entrepreneurship and Solidarity Economics* (pp. 93–110). IGI Global. https://www.igi-global.com/book/handbook-research-social-entrepreneurship-solidarity/142130

Olalla, B., San José, C., & Mata, M. (2012). Factor humano: un elemento clave en la búsqueda de la eficiencia de los proyectos. In *VII Congreso Nacional VISION12*. Madrid: itSMF Spain.

Paape, L., & Speklè, R. F. (2012). The adoption and design of enterprise risk management practices: An empirical study. *European Accounting Review*, *21*(3), 533–564. doi:10.1080/09638180.2012.661937

Pimchangthong, D., & Boonjing, V. (2017). Effects of Risk Management Practice on the Success of IT Project. *Procedia Engineering*, *182*, 579–586. doi:10.1016/j.proeng.2017.03.158

Plummer, D., Brethenoux, E., Lu, C. K., Andrews, W., Runyon, B., Lovelock, J. D., ... Tirosh, A. (2018). *Top Strategic Predictions for 2019 and Beyond: Practicality Exists Within Instability*. Gartner.

Project Management Institute. (2004). *A guide to the project management body of knowledge: PMBOK guide*. Project Management Institute.

Raz, T., & Michael, E. (2001). Use and benefits of tools for project risk management. *International Journal of Project Management*, *19*(1), 9–17. doi:10.1016/S0263-7863(99)00036-8

Raz, T., Shenhar, A. J., & Dvir, D. (2002). Risk management, project success, and technological uncertainty. *R & D Management*, *32*(2), 101–109. doi:10.1111/1467-9310.00243

Ritzén, S., & Sandström, G. Ö. (2017). Barriers to the Circular Economy–integration of perspectives and domains. *Procedia CIRP*, *64*, 7–12. doi:10.1016/j.procir.2017.03.005

Scholtz, T. (2019). *Shift From Managing Risk and Security to Enabling Value Creation: The SRM Leaders' New Imperative*. Gartner.

Sienou, A., Lamine, E., & Pingaud, H. (2008). A Method for Integrated Management of Process-risk. Université de Toulouse-Mines d'Albi, Centre de Génie Industriel Campus Jarlard Route de Teillet.

Stoneburner, G., Goguen, A. Y., & Feringa, A. (2002). *Risk management guide for information technology systems*. National Institute of Standards and Technology.

Stulz, R. M. (1996). Rethinking risk management. *Journal of Applied Corporate Finance*, *9*(3), 8–25. doi:10.1111/j.1745-6622.1996.tb00295.x

Takacs, F., Frankenberger, K., & Stechow, R. (2020). *Circular Ecosystems: Business Model Innovation for the Circular Economy*. Institute of Management & Strategy, University of St. Gallen.

Tang, O., & Musa, S. N. (2011). Identifying risk issues and research advancements in supply chain risk management. *International Journal of Production Economics*, *133*(1), 25–34. doi:10.1016/j.ijpe.2010.06.013

Wang, J., Lin, W., & Huang, Y. H. (2010). A performance-oriented risk management framework for innovative R&D projects. *Technovation*, *30*(11-12), 601–611. doi:10.1016/j.technovation.2010.07.003

Wieland, A., & Marcus, C. (2012). Dealing with supply chain risks: Linking risk management practices and strategies to performance. *International Journal of Physical Distribution & Logistics Management*, *42*(10), 887–905. doi:10.1108/09600031211281411

Witty, R., & Jaggers, M. (2018). *Organizational Resilience is More Than Just the Latest trend*. Gartner.

KEY TERMS AND DEFINITIONS

Critical Success Factors: Issues that are key to achieve an objective or goal, or to succeed.

Disruptive Environment: It is considered as such one, which the emergence of a new technology or working method directly influences the company.

External Factor: Any event that is beyond the control of the company and has to be considered for its possible effects.

Knowledge Management: Information and experience gathered by people in a company that should be properly managed so that they are kept in the company.

Linear Economy: The economy where the steps are always the same, collect materials, transform them and use them, without reusing anything.

Reputation Risk: The risk that influences the image that stakeholders and society have of the company.

Resilience: The ability that the company has to recover from complicated situations, returning to a normal operating state.

Risk Appetite: The capacity of a company to confront and successfully treat the risks that can appear.

Risk Averse: The way of behaving of a person or an entity that before an unknown situation prefers to remain immobile than assuming a risk.

Risk Tolerance: The amount of risk the company can afford without having serious consequences difficult to deal with.

Transparency: The company's ability to show not only its economic results but also its way of managing people and business.

Chapter 6
Opportunities and Challenges of Circular Economy for the Tourism Industry

Alfonso Vargas-Sánchez
https://orcid.org/0000-0003-0588-8654
University of Huelva, Spain

ABSTRACT

The aim of this chapter is to present the state of the art of academic research in the intersection between circular economy and tourism, trying to identify the approaches used by authors when studying the application of circular economy principles and initiatives in the tourism industry. For this purpose, a systematic search in ISI Web of Science and Scopus databases was performed. The characterization of research carried out in this field, with both a bibliometric and bibliographic analysis, is offered, presenting a detailed picture of the content of the research carried out in the abovementioned intersection, synthesizing what has been done so far. To conclude, a research agenda is proposed to develop this still understudied domain.

INTRODUCTION

The aim of this chapter is to present the state of the art of academic research in the intersection between Circular Economy (CE) and tourism, identifying contents and approaches used by researchers when studying the implementation of circular economy initiatives in the tourism industry. To this purpose, the databases of Web of Science and Scopus were utilized.

Thus, the main research question is to find out how the relationship between CE and tourism has been observed and addressed by authors, in the ongoing process of giving shape to this relatively new field of study.

Its relevance resides in the object of study (since the tourism industry, as one of the most impactful socio-economic activities at a global level, has a significant role to play in the undergoing model shift from a linear to a circular economy) and how it has been tackled. Thereby, it has been guided to system-

DOI: 10.4018/978-1-7998-5116-5.ch006

Copyright © 2020, IGI Global. Copying or distributing in print or electronic forms without written permission of IGI Global is prohibited.

atically present what has been done so far in academia and, on this foundation, to suggest new research developments and further knowledge generation efforts.

As a proof of this relevance, the prestigious hospitality education group 'Sommet Education', in its report on "Top Trends in Hospitality for 2019" includes "the shift towards a circular economy system" (Domenget, 2019), which "has the potential to transform the hospitality industry" (Imboden, 2019) into a system where resources are recycled and regenerated, rather than used once and disposed.

In this domain, the only previous work of this nature was recently published by Vargas-Sánchez (2018), which now is complemented with an updated bibliometric and bibliographic analysis in an extra step forward in the configuration of the academic research landscape in this emergent field of study.

Consequently, this document is organised as follows: firstly, a conceptual framework is provided on CE, as well as on its interrelation with the tourism industry; then the methodology used to achieve the proposed aim is presented, closing by providing the main results (from both a bibliometric and bibliographic perspective) and conclusions drawn from them, in terms of what has been done so far and the proposal of future research avenues.

CONCEPTUAL FRAMEWORK

Circular Economy is not a new concept. According to Hens at al. (2018), it dates back to late 1970s and has been shaped by a number of schools of thought such as "regenerative design", "industrial ecology" and "cradle to cradle". For these authors, it is a generic term for economic, technological and policy guidelines striving to (better) close material loops and to make the economy less resource-dependent.

It is important to note that Circular Economy, within the paradigm of sustainability, represents a model shift intended to replace the traditional Linear Economy (take-make-use-dispose), with deep repercussions at both production and consumption levels during this transition, that is, in how to use scarce resources in a smarter way. It is assumed that without circularity in the use of limited resources (in other words, without decoupling economic growth, resources consumption and environmental impact) a sustainable development cannot exist. Nonetheless, it is fair to recognize that the loops of materials cannot be closed indefinitely (always with zero losses or waste), which means that, in practice, this new model won't be totally circular, but it aims to be as close as possible to that desideratum.

Although a consensus within the scientific community doesn't exist yet with regard to its definition, the CE model is inspired by the cycles of ecological systems, trying to eliminate waste generation. In this line, in the Circular Economy Package Report issued in Brussels on 4 March 2019 by the European Commission, it is said that: "In a circular economy the value of products and materials is maintained for as long as possible; waste and resources use are minimised, and they are kept within the economy when a product has reached the end of its life, to be used again and again to create further value"[1]. In short, according to Ten Brink et al. (2017), the CE "is about keeping resources and their value in the economy and avoiding them becoming waste. This requires actions ranging from upstream product innovation to downstream waste and recycling infrastructure, as well as engagement by governments, businesses and citizens".

Thus, recycling, which usually is associated with CE, really is a second-level option in this model that is activated when it has not been possible to attain the main aim of waste eradication (the last, and the most negative, option is waste disposal in landfills). Therefore, recycling (waste management) represents a reactive approach within the CE model; the most genuine one is of proactive nature, trying to prevent waste generation via eco-design and eco-innovations (e.g. following the 'Cradle to Cradle' philosophy), industrial symbiosis[2], economy of functionality (sale of the use of a product rather than the product itself, or Product-as-a-Service business model), second-hand markets (favouring products or components reuse), etc. As stated by Pan et al. (2018): "To accelerate the transition to a circular economy, an economy that is restorative and regenerative by design should be developed for keeping resources at the highest use and value throughout their life cycle".

This model has evolved over time from a number of principles symbolized in the 3 R's (Reduce, Reuse, Recycle) to the so-called 10 R's, progressively advancing up the circularity ladder adding new elements (Recover -energy-, Redesign, Refurbish, Refuse, Remanufacture, Repair, Repurpose). However, as stated by Aragón-Correa (2019), "R principles" are at its base, but a circular economy goes beyond the implementation of each of them on its own. In fact: "A real circular economy requires greater collaboration between different companies to achieve more effective and efficient cycles", as "the circular economy is based on seeking productive processes that are as closed as possible, where nothing is thrown away and any possible surplus from a process can be used as the inputs for another process".

In this line, D'Amato et al. (2017) have identified the six main topics in CE: sustainable development in industrialization and urbanization; recycling in products life cycle for waste reduction; industrial symbiosis; efficiency evaluation techniques in logistic/supply chain management systems; carbon emission and energy in production plants; greening the supply chain.

Although originally applied to industrial activities, this approach to sustainability has gradually widened its scope, reaching also service sectors such as tourism (Hens et al., 2018).

To conclude this section, it is worth to underline the connection between CE and UN's Sustainable Development Goals in its Agenda 2030 (although CE is not explicitly mentioned, it relates particularly to number twelve goal: "Ensure sustainable consumption and production patterns"). Thereby, the potential of the tourism industry to contribute to the achievement of the UN's SDGs has been highlighted by Girardand & Nocca (2017), as well as to address threats associated with climate change.

METHODOLOGY

To identify the existing literature in the field under study, the databases of Web of Science (WoS) and Scopus were used, as platforms that include bibliographic references and citations of the main scientific publications in any academic discipline.

The search methodology is displayed in Table 1. Once the contents of the whole list of results produced by the searches were checked and duplications were eliminated, a total of 42 documents were considered for this study, most of them conference papers, a fact that anticipates the early stage in which the development of this body of knowledge still is.

Table 2 chronologically lists the 42 documents that make up this analysis.

It is relevant to note that almost 30% of the documents found have been published in the last year (2018).

Table 1. Search methodology in WoS and Scopus

Search Words	"circular economy" and touris*
Category	Title, Abstract and Keywords (designated as Topic in WoS)
Subject area	All
Document type	All
Period time	1900-2018
Language	All
Other Query Strings	"tourism circular economy"; circular tourism economy "; "circular tourism"
Search Date	May 2019

Source: own elaboration.

Table 2. Papers reviewed

Year	Papers	Nº	%
2008	(1) Fan, Y.	1	2.4
2009	(2) Yuan, Q. & Xue, X.	1	2.4
2010	(3) Han, L. et al.; (35) Fang, X. & Zhang, X.	2	4.8
2011	(4) Guo, P.; (5) Li, X. et al.; (6) Liu, L. & Liang, M.	3	7.1
2012	(7) Jia, Z. et al.; (8) Lu, Y.; (9) Xu, F.; (10) Zhou, R. et al.	4	9.5
2013	(11) Song, X.; (12) Zhu, Z. et al.; (34) Shi, C. & Zhang, G.	3	7.1
2014	(13) Cui, J.; (14) Liu, J.; (31) Zhang, Y. & Tian, L.; (32) Liu, F.L.; (33) Lu, Y. & Hu, X.X.; (42) Zhang, Y.	6	14.3
2015	(15) Zhao, P.	1	2.4
2016	(16) Ma, X. et al.; (17) Rakitovac, K.A.; (18) Scheepens, A.E. et al.; (19) Zhang, Q.; (20) Zhao, A.	5	11.9
2017	(21) D'Amato, D. et al.; (22) Girard, L.F. & Nocca, F.; (23) Giurea, R. et al.; (41) Patti, S.	4	9.5
2018	(24) Deselnicu, D.C. et al.; (25) Hens, L. et al.; (26) Immacolata, V.; (27) Pan, S.-Y. et al.; (28) Pamfilie, R. et al.; (29) Paulauskas, S.; (30) Vargas-Sánchez, A.; (36) Dong, S. et al.; (37) Bonanno, S. et al.; (38) Naydenov, K.; (39) Pagán, J.I. et al.; (40) Dong, Q.	12	28.6
Total		42	100.0

Source: own elaboration.

RESULTS

The characterization of research in this area, with both a bibliometric and bibliographic analysis, is offered in this section. More specifically, a detailed picture on the content of the research carried out in the abovementioned intersection is presented: evolution over time, most prolific authors, institutions and countries, conferences, journals and publishers that have paid more attention to this topic, type of research performed, objects of study, methodologies used, main contributions.

Bibliometric Analysis

Through the application of a series of indicators, the results of a descriptive-quantitative bibliometric analysis are presented in this subsection.

The subject areas in which the 42 documents under scrutiny have been categorized are quite diverse, but with a clear predominance of the following three in a fairly balanced way: Environmental Sciences/Ecology, Engineering, and Business/Economics; Social Sciences & other topics lag behind.

The breakdown of these documents by type, all of them in the English language, follows: meetings (conference papers), 28 (66.6%), articles (in journals and books), 12 (28.6%) and 2 reviews (4.8%). In short, two-thirds are papers presented in conferences and published in the corresponding proceedings; and the remaining one-third, papers published in the form of articles in journals or book chapters.

Chronologically, the first conference paper was authored by Fan in 2008, the first book chapter was published four years later (Zhou et al., 2012), the first article in a journal came out the following year (Shi & Zhang, 2013) and both reviews in the last year of the period under study (Pan et al., 2018; Vargas-Sánchez, 2018). In total, half of the documents have been published in the last three years (2016-2018), which is an evident sign of the growing interest for this topic by the academic community, in addition to its youth as a field of research.

Concerning the sources in which they have been published, the main outlet (with 7 papers) has been the Book Series "Advanced Materials Research" -ranked Q4 in Scopus in the category "Engineering (miscellaneous)"-, which collects papers from various scientific conferences under themes such as Architecture and Urban Development, Natural Resources and Sustainable Development, or Environmental Protection and Resources Exploitation. Next is the "Journal of Cleaner Production" (with 3), published by Elsevier, with an impact factor of 5.651 in 2017 and ranked as Q1 in the following JCR categories: "Engineering, Environmental", "Environmental Sciences" and "Green & Sustainable Science & Technology"[3]; this is, therefore, a well-established and reputed journal within the research domains of Science & Technology, Engineering, and Environmental Sciences & Ecology. Other sources, with 2 records each, are the Book Series "Energy Procedia" (an open-access collection of conference proceedings published by Elsevier, spanning the fields of energy science, technology and engineering) and the journal "Quality - Access to Success" (included in the Emerging Sources Citation Index and Q3 in Scopus in the categories "Business and International Management", "Management Information Systems" and "Strategy and Management"). Tourism specialized outlets are almost absent: only one paper published in the tourism journal "Worldwide Hospitality and Tourism Themes" in 2018 and four in conference proceedings.

The most prolific meeting title has been the 2010 International Conference on Energy, Environment and Development, which contributed with 2 papers on this topic. All the others have added one each.

The support of funding agencies is acknowledged in 6 papers only (14.3%). Going beyond national initiatives (in Finland, Taiwan, South Korea and China), EU Programs such as Interreg and the 7th Framework Programme for Research and Development (FP7) deserve to be underlined.

Trans Tech Publications has been the publisher that has accommodated the highest number of papers in this area (8, 19.0%), followed by Elsevier (6, 14.3%) and IEEE (3, 7.1%). As a consequence, among publishers' countries of origin, Switzerland leads, followed closely by the UK and USA.

The University Science & Technology Liaoning (China) and University of Catania (Italy) are the only institutions with more than one paper authored, three and two respectively. The University of Chinese Academy of Sciences is the institution with more authors (9), but all of as co-authors of the same paper.

The dominance of this country is overwhelming, with a total of 26 papers containing authors affiliated to institutions (28, very mostly universities) in the People's Republic of China (61.9% of total), and a total of 53 authors (47.3 of total). It is followed by Romania, with 12 authors (10.7%) involved in 3 papers (7.1%). Authors affiliated to Italian institutions are 11 (9.8%), with participation in 5 papers (11.9%).

With regard to authorships, most of the papers (45.2%) have one single author (mode = 1). Nevertheless, the dispersion is huge, ranging until nine co-authors in three of them (mean = 2.67 and standard deviation = 2.29). The median value is two co-authors, mostly affiliated to the same institution.

Among a total of 154 keywords allocated by authors, the most numerous ones are those related with sustainability issues (15, 9.7%), followed by eco[4] (10, 6.5%) and green (5, 3.2%) topics. Low carbon, renewable energy and development matters are next in quantitative importance. In addition, the application of the smart paradigm (smart cities/destinations and smart technologies, such as machine learning) is gaining momentum.

It is also interesting to highlight the tourism segments that have been targeted by this set of studies. They have been (in alphabetical order): agro-tourism (or agricultural tourism), coastal tourism, eco-tourism, farm tourism, forestry tourism, responsible tourism, rural tourism, tourism in world cultural heritage sites, water tourism/recreation.

In order to show the studies and authors with the most influence in this field (there is no author -among the 112 identified- with more than one paper of his/her authorship), Table 3 shows the five most referenced works, according to the number of citations obtained (dated at 24 July 2019). In Table 2 they are numbered as 18, 21, 25, 27 and 5, respectively.

In fact, the number of citations received by the whole set of papers in this area began to be significant only in 2017 (21), with a remarkable increase in 2018 (71), which demonstrates, once again, the youthfulness of this research field.

A particular reference to the five papers listed in Table 3 follows:

- The most cited paper is Scheepens et al. (2016), published in the Journal of Cleaner Production and aimed to propose a metric to assess new business models in the circular economy. Balancing the analysis of value and eco-burden, the proposed metric combines two Life Cycle Assessment based methods: Eco-efficient Value Creation (Eco-costs Value Ratio benchmarking) and the Circular Transition Framework (describing stakeholder activities which are required for the transition towards sustainable business models). To validate its usefulness, an application for the analysis, design and implementation of a business model for sustainable water recreation in Friesland (Netherlands) is presented, concluding that the approach of Eco-efficient Value Creation helps to avoid many pitfalls in the design of circular business models, at the same time that The Circular Transition Framework reveals pitfalls and opportunities in the implementation stage;
- With regard to D'Amato et al. (2016), in this work (also published in the Journal of Cleaner Production) a comparative analysis of the concepts of Circular Economy, Green Economy and Bioeconomy is carried out through a bibliometric review of almost two thousand scientific articles published within the last three decades. In spite of being joined by the common ideal to reconcile economic, environmental and social goals, authors argue for their clarification and reciprocal integration as key sustainability avenues. Irrespective of the generic scope of this paper, some specific references to tourism are established, as a topic linked to the social dimension of sustainability and within the 'umbrella' concept of Green Economy (eco-tourism, etc.);

Table 3. Most cited papers

Nº Citations	Authors (Year)	Organizations (Countries)	Titles
WoS: 51 Scopus: 56	Scheepens, A.E.; Vogtlander, J.G.; Brezet, J.C. (2016)	Delft Univ. of Technology (Netherlands)	Two life cycle assessment (LCA) based methods to analyse and design complex (regional) circular economy systems. Case: making water tourism more sustainable.
Wos: 43 Scopus: 49	D'Amato, D.; Droste, N.; Allen, B.; et al. (2017)	Univ. Helsinki (Finland); Helmholtz-Centre for Environmental Research (Germany); Institute for European Environmental Policy (UK); Univ. Vaasa (Finland); European Forest Institute (Finland); Dasos Capital (Finland)	Green, circular, bio-economy: A comparative analysis of sustainability avenues.
WoS: 19 Scopus: 19	Hens, L.; Block, C.; Cabello-Eras, J.J.; et al. (2018)	Flemish Institute for Technological Research, VITO (Belgium); 2C Ecosolutions (Belgium); Univ. de la Costa (Colombia); Univ. Cienfuegos (Cuba); Katholieke Univ. Leuven (Belgium)	On the evolution of "Cleaner Production" as a concept and a practice.
WoS: 8	Pan, S.-Y.; Gao, M.; Kim, H.; et al. (2018)	National Taiwan Univ. (Taiwan); Univ. Seoul (South Korea)	Advances and challenges in sustainable tourism toward a green economy.
WoS: 5 Scopus: 11	Li, X.; Deng, B.; Ye, H. (2011)	Huazhong Normal Univ. (China)	The Research Based on the 3-R Principle of Agro-circular Economy Model-The Erhai Lake Basin as an example.

Source: own elaboration.

- The third most cited paper also belongs to the same journal. In it, Hens at al. (2018) present the fundamental changes in the concept of 'Cleaner Production' (CP)[5] during the most recent quarter of a century, in relation to its scope, methods and application areas. The links between CP and green and circular economy are indicated, and CP for sustainable tourism is discussed as an example of its wider application in service sectors;
- Concerning the article by Pan et al. (2018) in the journal "Science of the Total Environment", authors propose six cross-disciplinary elements in sustainable tourism: green energy, green transportation, green buildings, green infrastructure, green agriculture and smart technologies. To overcome the challenges and barriers towards sustainability, strategies and the framework for a key

performance indicators system are provided. The Green Island, in Taiwan, is taken as a case study, in which transformative changes in tourism, such as water-energy-food nexus, are described;

- Finally, Li et al. (2011), in their conference paper published in "Energy Procedia", propose the implementation of an agro-circular economy development model in the Chinese Erhai Lake Basin, including an energy comprehensive utilization pattern, an ecological breeding pattern, an agriculture waste comprehensive utilization pattern, a pattern of agricultural eco-tourism, etc.

Bibliographic Analysis

In this subsection, the contents of the papers under analysis have been summarized in Table 4.

Recommendations: Future Research Lines

Further studies in the intersection between CE and tourism are clearly needed, as the development of this domain is still in an incipient phase. To promote them, new lines of research should be developed, among them those detailed in the following decalogue:

1. Beyond its environmental implications (research till now has been very focused on them), further studies are needed on the business implications of the transition to a CE in tourism;
2. In this line, as recognized by Scheepens et al. (2016), still a lot has to be learnt in practice about design and implementation of new circular business models in the Western free-market economy (the case of the Chinese State-controlled economy is totally different) and, therefore, about new entrepreneurial opportunities in the tourism industry under this unavoidable disruption (Vargas-Sánchez, 2018);
3. Taking the observation by Pan et al. (2018), "there is still a need for holistic planning, strict impact assessments, and effective management" of CE initiatives, with special emphasis, according to these authors, in water-energy-food nexus (particularly in regions of water scarcity);
4. Identification and dissemination of good practices in the tourism sector. An example could be the "Global Soap Project", for the recycling of hotels soaps[6];
5. The insertion of CE initiatives within the framework of CSR policies;
6. The creation of metrics for monitoring the progress of CE initiatives in tourism companies and destinations within a framework of smart tourism. This monitoring should include the tourism stakeholders' level of awareness on CE;
7. From a public policy perspective, the effectiveness analysis of the diverse instruments with the potential for stimulating the adoption of CE initiatives by tourism companies and destinations;
8. The interplay between Collaborative Economy (sharing of goods, collaborative consumption, the shift from product ownership to product usage) and CE in order to understand how this can affect the behaviour of tourism stakeholders;
9. A better understanding of the factors capable of facilitating (accelerators) and hindering (brakes) the implementation of CE strategies in hotels and other tourism operators;
10. To encourage research on unexplored segments until now, particularly on those with higher tourism density, impact on natural resources and problems of overtourism (such as sun & beach destinations, urban tourism, among others).

Table 4. Research lines

Paper	Content	Author Keywords
(1) Fan, Y. (2008)	The author argues that CE is the most realistic and inevitable choice to reach sustainable development of tourism in the Chinese province of Henan.	Henan Province; Tourism Circular Economy; Development; Research
(2) Yuan, Q. & Xue, X. (2009)	The construction of small towns in China under the principles of CE ("circular small towns") to promote its rural economic and social development. Within this framework, development based on "tour-driving mode" is considered, advocating for an ecological tourism development model. As an example of it, the combination of the tourism industry and agriculture can provide not only attractive tourism resources but also achieve efficient circle use of material, energy and money.	Small Town; Circular Economy; Eco-Industrial System
(3) Han, L. et al. (2010)	CE is proposed to address solutions relating to the construction and development of Hainan international tourism island (China).	Circular Economy; Tourism; International Tourist Island
(4) Guo, P. (2011)	To explore the state of Information Management Systems applied to tourism management in China in a period of circular economy implementation.	Information Systems; Supply Chain; Tourism Management; Policy Making
(5) Li, X. et al. (2011)	The pattern of the agro-circular economy as the agricultural sustainable development strategy for the Erhai Lake Basin in China based on the 3-R (Reduce, Reuse and Recycle) principles of CE. Within this pattern, the development of a model of agricultural eco-tourism is proposed.	3-R principle; Agro-Circular Economy; Erhai lake basin
(6) Liu, L. & Liang, M. (2011)	A reception model of low-carbon tourism in the Chinese rural area of Cuandixia Village is proposed, taking CE as a framework of reference in a way that every link of the tourism value chain (including catering, accommodation, transportation, sightseeing, shopping and entertainment) should be characterized by low-carbon emissions.	Rural Low-Carbon Tourism; Tourism Reception Model; Circular Economy; Cuandixia
(7) Jia, Z. et al. (2012)	The establishment of an overall development model for leisure agriculture tourism in Yi County (China) based on CE.	Tourism; Leisure Agriculture; Circular Economy; Sustainable Development
(8) Lu, Y. (2012)	The development of tourism in Lanzhou (China) based on a plan aligned with the principles of CE, including the establishment of a green performance evaluation system, the promotion of green consumption, the improvement of corporate social responsibility and environmental commitments, and the implementation of pollution control technologies.	Circular Economy; Lanzhou; Tourism Industry; Development Plan
(9) Xu, F. (2012)	The construction of an eco-industrial park in Fengcheng (China) under the new industrialization model of the CE, which is aimed to form a model zone where man and nature co-exist harmoniously and a demonstration which promotes industrial visiting and tourism.	The Regional Circle of Poyang Lake; Circular Economy; Industrial Park; Planning and Design
(10) Zhou, R. et al. (2012)	The configuration of a system to secure sustainable tourism development on the Chinese province of Shandong. That system is supported by the concept of CE, as a concept of environmental ethics, of new production forms based on the "3R's" (reduce, reuse, recycle) principle, and of new consumption pattern.	Circular Economy; Sustainable Development; Security System
(11) Song, X. (2013)	In the context of CE, the Chinese hotel industry has to strengthen its green marketing management, cultivating people's green consciousness and consumption spirit so as to achieve the common development of enterprise and society.	Circular Economy; Green Marketing; Marketing Management
(12) Zhu, Z. et al. (2013)	A new model of eco-agricultural tourism, for an eco-tourism resort in the Chinese city of Heyuan, is proposed based on the principles of CE.	Eco-Tourism; Eco-Agricultural Tourism; Circular Economy
(13) Cui, J. (2014)	How to tackle the problem of sustainable utilization of tourism resources in China and how to foster strengths and circumvent weaknesses to this respect through the concept of CE.	Circular Economy Concept; Tourism Resources; Sustainable Utilization
(14) Liu, J. (2014)	CE as the most effective way to solve the contradiction between tourism development and environmental protection, proposing specific measures for its implementation in scenic spots.	Circular Economy; Scenic Spot; Ecological Environment
(15) Zhao, P. (2015)	To determine the carbon footprint of the tourism sector and to put forward countermeasures to turn it into a more sustainable industry, limiting the CE scope to the so-called low carbon economy.	Low Carbon Economy; Low-Carbon Tourism; Environment
(16) Ma, X. et al. (2016)	The progress made towards a tourism CE in a scenic location from the perspective of the application of a renewable energy system.	Renewable Energy System; Tourism Circular Economy; PV System; Scenic Spot
(17) Rakitovac, K.A. (2016)	The role of the tourism industry in the transition from a linear to a circular economy. Within this framework, the importance to promote responsible tourism among its stakeholders is emphasized. With regard to the local community, the contribution of the local population in the environmental conservation of tourism destinations in the Istrian County of Croatia is empirically assessed.	Responsible Tourism; Tourism Destination; Local Inhabitants; Croatia; Istrian County
(18) Scheepens, A.E. et al. (2016)	The establishment of metrics to assess new business models in the circular economy based on combined analyses of value and eco-burden. Two life cycle assessment based methods are applied for sustainable water tourism in Friesland (a province in the Netherlands): the Eco-efficient Value Creation (Eco-costs Value Ratio benchmarking) and the Circular Transition Framework (describing stakeholder activities which are required for the transition towards sustainable business models).	Environment; Sustainability; Eco-Costs; Product-Service System; Eco-Efficient Value Creation; Circular Transition Framework
(19) Zhang, Q. (2016)	An application of CE to urban forestry tourism in the Chinese province of Heilongjiang, concluding that this kind of economic system has many advantages, such as low resources consumption, little environmental pollution and good economic returns.	Plateau Area; Development of Forestry Economy; Ecological Benefits; Efficient
(20) Zhao, A. (2016)	The application of CE theories to the development of rural tourism in Liaoning Province (China), in an attempt to set up a model based on harmonious interaction with the natural environment.	No keywords
(21) D'Amato, D. et al. (2017)	A comparative analysis (articulated around the environmental, social and economic pillars of sustainability) of the concepts of Circular Economy, Green Economy and Bioeconomy through a bibliometric review of the literature. Despite its generic scope, some specific references to tourism are made, particularly to its social dimension.	Bioeconomy; Circular Economy; Green Economy; Sustainability; Machine Learning; Latent Dirichlet Allocation
(22) Girard, L.F. & Nocca, F. (2017)	The potential of the tourism industry to contribute to the achievement of SDGs, as the third-largest socio-economic activity in the EU.	Circular Economy; Circular Processes; Circular Tourism; Climate Change
(23) Giurea, R. et al. (2017)	A comparison between the agro-tourism sectors in Italy (Trentino region) and Romania (Transilvania region), taking into account the main topics that can affect their sustainability and looking for the environmental optimization of this sector. The concept of CE is involved too.	Sustainability; Management; Circular Economy; Agro-Tourism
(24) Deselnicu, D.C. et al. (2018)	As waste management plays a central role in the CE, specific proposals to amend the EU's waste legislation are presented, seeking to improve waste management practices, stimulate recycling and innovation in materials management, and limit the use of landfilling. Smarter use of resources will create synergies for industries which most depend on it, such as tourism.	Circular Economy; Waste Management; Secondary Raw Materials; Recycling Materials

continued on following page

Table 4. Continued

Paper	Content	Author Keywords
(25) Hens, L. et al. (2018)	Beyond the 3R principles of the CE (reduce, reuse and recycle), it also includes the repurposing and rethinking of materials, and the repair, refurbishment and maintenance of products to be cycled back into supply chains, thereby closing the material loops. Tourism is analysed as an example of a service sector which might benefit from the experience of Cleaner Production methods in its struggle towards sustainability.	Cleaner Production; Corporate Social Responsibility; Renewable Energy; Sustainable Tourism; Smart City
(26) Immacolata, V. (2018)	To highlight the multifunctional character of agriculture, including its recreational and tourist function. In this line, it is argued that rural tourism, today, can only be an integrated and coordinated component within rural development models specific to each territory, able to ensure a balance between consumption and reproduction of rural collective resources through active participation, of all territorial stakeholders, in strategic choices in a new approach to the CE.	Tourism System; Circular Economy; Sustainable Tourism; Sustainability Indicators; Sustainability Paradigm; Circular Paradigm
(27) Pan, S.-Y. et al. (2018)	To provide an overview of the interrelationships between tourism and sustainability from a cross-disciplinary perspective. Sustainable materials management for a CE is a framework to be applied in the tourism sector to deal with waste management and other environmental issues such as water-energy-food consumption. The case study of Taiwanese Green Island is presented.	Renewable Energy; Green Building; Sustainable Transport; Green Infrastructure; Smart Technology; Water-Energy-Food Nexus
(28) Pamfilie, R. et al. (2018)	To study the influence of the implementation of integrated quality-environment-security systems (ISO 9001, ISO 14001 and OHSAS 18001) on the economic performance of hotel establishments in Romania from the perspective of industry managers, as a starting point for determining the applicability of the principles of circular economy in this sector.	Sustainable Development; Circular Economy; Circular Tourism; Integrated Management System; Economical Performance
(29) Paulauskas, S. (2018)	To frame Blue (maritime sector) growth, including coastal tourism, on the ground of the author's Circular Economy 3.0 methodology.	No keywords
(30) Vargas-Sánchez, A. (2018)	To present the state-of-the-art in the intersection of the CE and tourism in order to stimulate the discussion on the major challenges and opportunities in the transition process from the linear to the circular paradigm.	Circular Economy; Circular Tourism; Tourism Circular Economy; Tourism Management
(31) Zhang, Y. & Tian, L. (2014)	It is claimed that, in spite of their respective theories, practices and operations, ecological tourism, tourism circular economy and sustainable development of tourism are interconnected and shape current tourism development.	Ecological Tourism; Tourism Circular Economy; Tourism Sustainable Development
(32) Liu, F.L. (2014)	It advocates in favour of a circular economy approach (understood as the 3R principles of reduction, recycle and reuse) to carry out green management of tourist regions.	Circular Economy; Green Management; Tourist Attractions Region
(33) Lu, Y. & Hu. X.X. (2014)	Under the premise that the development model of CE has become the effective way to realize the sustainable development of tourism industry, the case of Shandong province, in China, is displayed, with the proposal of a development model and strategy for its tourism circular economy.	Path Study; Shandong Province; Tourism Circular Economy
(34) Shi, C. & Zhang, G. (2013)	As a model of economic development in harmony with the environment, CE is presented as the inevitable choice to realize the sustainable development of scenic spots. Through the analysis of environmental problems of tourism scenic spots, this article put forward construction measures and other suggestions to realize their sustainable development.	Circular Economy; Construction of Scenic Spots; Resources Saving
(35) Fang, X. & Zhang, X. (2010)	The implementation of CE theory as a new way to guide the long-term development of world cultural heritage sites in China through the practices of eco-designing, energy conservation, green services facilities providing, waste eco-disposing and green consuming.	Circular Economy; Environment Protection; World Heritage Sites
(36) Dong, S. et al. (2018)	This paper studies the current socio-economic and environmental situation of main regions along the China-Mongolia-Russia Economic Corridor. The main ecological risks are revealed and green development modes to achieve sustainable socio-ecological-economic development of the corridor are put forward. Prior actions to achieve its sustainable development are also proposed, including the establishment of a green, low-carbon, CE system, a low carbon eco-tourism pilot area etc.	No keywords
(37) Bonanno, S. et al. (2018)	This paper deals with a farm holiday company in the province of Enna, inland Sicily, which stands out thanks to the adoption of various techniques that make it a real closed-cycle business. The objective of this paper is to highlight how the analysed company applies different methods to achieve its sustainable goals under CE principles.	Circular Economy; Phyto-Depuration; Sustainable Tourism
(38) Naydenov, K. (2018)	Till now, the tourism sector has not been given much attention as a possible context for CE initiatives and analyses, but today is a trend and key priority in Europe, as a prerequisite for the sustainable development of this sector. Circular tourism follows the logic of the CE and it proposes a model in which each actor (traveller, host, tour operator, and supplier) adopts an eco-friendly approach.	Circular Economy; Circular Tourism; Eco-Innovations; Sustainable Development
(39) Pagán, J.I. et al. (2018)	In this work, the historical evolution of six beaches on the coast of Alicante (Spain) has been analysed. Both changes in land use associated with the process of urban development and the evolution of the shoreline have also been studied, concluding that to maintain their tourist attraction and defence function of the coast, alternatives to be implemented should be developed in a sustainable manner, following CE criteria.	Alicante; Beach Nourishment; GIS; Shoreline Evolution; Urban Growth
(40) Dong, Q. (2018)	A relevant aspect in the application of tourism circular economy is the use of renewable sources of energy, which can be widely used in tourist areas. For its promotion, government and technical support, together with other measures, are important. The usage of renewable energies in eco-tourism areas in China is explored in this article.	Development; Renewable Energy Technology; Situation; Strategy; Tourism Circular Economy
(41) Patti, S. (2017)	The paper focuses on attitude towards the circular economy and low-carbon tourism (CE and L-CT) by investigating the consumption behaviour of people who use sharing utilities. Different motivational factors affect tourists' behaviour in sharing goods and services, such as environmental protection, lower costs, research of a sustainable lifestyle, wellness and so on. The study examines how consumer behaviour can influence CE and L-CT attitude and how the former can be a determinant of the latter. It explores also motivations to share utilities and the knowledge and sensibility towards CE.	Circular Economy; Factor Analysis; Low-Carbon Tourism; Sharing Consumption
(42) Zhang, Y. (2014)	This paper studies the development of Eco-tourism Wanlu Lake Gathering Area, in the Chinese province of Guangdong, and the efforts to explore eco-tourism and environmental protection in a harmonious pathway with and industrial economy. CE analysis is part of it.	Circular Economy; Eco-Tourism; Gathering Area; Wanlu Lake

Source: own elaboration.

Table 5. Fields of application

Paper	Field of Application		Notes
	Tourism Scope	Geographical Scope	
(1) Fan, Y. (2008)	Sustainable development of tourism (recycling economic theory).	Province of Henan (China)	
(2) Yuan, Q. & Xue, X. (2009)	The combination of tourism and agriculture in an ecological tourism development model.	Small towns in China	
(3) Han, L. et al. (2010)	Sustainable tourism development in terms of a circular economy.	Hainan international tourism island (China)	
(4) Guo, P. (2011)	Information Management Systems applied to tourism management.	China	
(5) Li, X. et al. (2011)	Agricultural eco-tourism.	Erhai Lake Basin (China)	
(6) Liu, L. & Liang, M. (2011)	Low-carbon tourism.	The rural area of Cuandixia Village (China)	
(7) Jia, Z. et al. (2012)	Leisure agriculture tourism.	Yi County (China)	
(8) Lu, Y. (2012)	Green tourism.	Lanzhou (China)	
(9) Xu, F. (2012)	The construction of an eco-industrial park in which industrial visiting and tourism co-exist harmoniously.	Fengcheng (China)	
(10) Zhou, R. et al. (2012)	The configuration of a system to secure sustainable tourism development.	Province of Shandong (China)	
(11) Song, X. (2013)	Green hotels.	China	
(12) Zhu, Z. et al. (2013)	Eco-agricultural tourism for an eco-tourism resort.	City of Heyuan (China)	
(13) Cui, J. (2014)	The sustainable utilization of tourism resources.	China	
(14) Liu, J. (2014)	The eco-environmental protection of scenic spots.	China	
(15) Zhao, P. (2015)	Low-carbon tourism: carbon footprint and its countermeasures.		Theoretical paper
(16) Ma, X. et al. (2016)	The renewable energy systems used in tourism.	A scenic spot in China	
(17) Rakitovac, K.A. (2016)	Responsible tourism and the role of the local population in the environmental conservation of tourism destinations.	Istrian County (Croatia)	
(18) Scheepens, A.E. et al. (2016)	A metrics to assess new business models in the circular economy applied to sustainable water tourism.	Province of Friesland (The Netherlands)	
(19) Zhang, Q. (2016)	Urban forestry tourism.	Province of Heilongjiang (China)	
(20) Zhao, A. (2016)	Rural tourism.	Liaoning Province (China)	
(21) D'Amato, D. et al. (2017)	Comparative analysis of the concepts of Circular Economy, Green Economy and Bioeconomy.		A bibliometric review of the literature
(22) Girard, L.F. & Nocca, F. (2017)	Impacts produced by the tourism sector and its great potential in contributing to the achievement of SDGs.		Theoretical paper
(23) Giurea, R. et al. (2017)	Agro-tourism sector.	Italy (Trentino region) and Romania (Transilvania region)	
(24) Deselnicu, D.C. et al. (2018)	Waste management.	EU	
(25) Hens, L. et al. (2018)	Cleaner Production methods in the tourism sector.		Theoretical paper
(26) Immacolata, V. (2018)	Rural tourism.		Theoretical paper
(27) Pan, S.-Y. et al. (2018)	Ecotourism development.	Green Island (Taiwan)	It is also considered a review work
(28) Pamfilie, R. et al. (2018)	The applicability of the principles of the circular economy in the hotel sector	Romania	
(29) Paulauskas, S. (2018)	Coastal tourism and CE 3.0 as blue growth Methodology.	EU	
(30) Vargas-Sánchez, A. (2018)	CE and tourism.		Literature review (state of the art)
(31) Zhang, Y. & Tian, L. (2014)	The interplay among ecological tourism, tourism circular economy and sustainable development of tourism.	References to the situation in China	Theoretical paper
(32) Liu, F.L. (2014)	Green management of scenic areas following the 3 Rs of CE (reduction, recycle, reuse).	References to the situation in China	Theoretical paper
(33) Lu, Y. & Hu. X.X. (2014)	Proposal of a tourism circular economic development model.	Shandong Province (China)	

continued on following page

Table 5. Continued

Paper	Field of Application		Notes
	Tourism Scope	Geographical Scope	
(34) Shi, C. & Zhang, G. (2013)	CE as a model for the ecological construction of scenic spots.	References to the situation in China	Theoretical paper
(35) Fang, X. & Zhang, X. (2010)	Tourism circular economy and environmental protection in world cultural heritage sites.	China	
(36) Dong, S. et al. (2018)	Ecological environment risks and green development modes, including the four hierarchies of Chinese CE mode (enterprise, industry, region, society) and a low carbon eco-tourism pilot area.	China-Mongolia-Russia economic corridor	
(37) Bonanno, S. et al. (2018)	Case study of a farm holiday company where different methods have been applied to achieve sustainable goals under CE principles.	Province of Enna, Sicily (Italy)	
(38) Naydenov, K. (2018)	Concept and examples of circular tourism.		Theoretical paper
(39) Pagán, J.I. et al. (2018)	Tourism in coastal areas. CE criteria to maintain the coastal defence sites and their tourist attractiveness.	Province of Alicante (Spain)	
(40) Dong, Q. (2018)	The use of renewable energies in eco-tourism areas.	China	
(41) Patti, S. (2017)	Attitude towards CE and low-carbon tourism by users of (car, bike) sharing organizations.	Rome, Florence and Verona (Italy)	
(42) Zhang, Y. (2014)	Eco-tourism and environmental protection fostering a CE	Wanlu Lake, province of Guangdong (China)	

Source: own elaboration.

As a final comment, the bibliometric study has revealed that tourism-specific media are lagging very behind in this domain (very sharply in the case of journals). This fact shows us how much room for growth there should be in specialised tourism forums for CE matters.

CONCLUSION

What has Been Done so Far?

With regard to the question about how authors have addressed the relationship between CE and tourism, one of the characteristics of the pieces of research analysed is the applied character of the vast majority of them. The following Table 5 displays the theoretical or applied nature of each paper and the corresponding scope of application if this is the case.

Basically, the pursuit of sustainable utilization of tourism resources, contributing to solving the contradiction between tourism development and environmental protection, is the main conductive thread of what has been done, taking circular economy principles as an effective choice to reach that purpose. From this recognition, the exploration of the link between CE and tourism has been carried out with a heterogeneous scope, both geographically and with regard to tourist market segments.

There are not many conceptual and theoretical papers in this specific area, and from a chronological perspective, they haven't been the first to come out. In fact, and in spite of some not very elaborate previous references, they have been published in the last two years (D'Amato et al., 2017; Girard & Nocca, 2017; Hens et al., 2018; Vargas-Sánchez, 2018), which could be interpreted as the beginning of its consolidation process as a scientific field, with an articulated and multidisciplinary knowledge body that is taking shape in order to be able to give a more robust support when applied to particular problems in particular tourism segments and destinations.

With regard to the geographical scope of CE applications, the presence of China at different levels (provinces, towns, villages, islands…) is overwhelming, since the first work dated in 2008. As already explained by Vargas-Sánchez (2018), this fact relates to the decision of the Chinese government (in a law of 2008) to choose CE as its sustainable development strategy, promoted as a top-down national policy. By contrast, the EU elaborated its first Circular Economy Action Plan in December 2015, mainly focused in five priority sectors: plastics, food waste, critical raw materials, construction and demolition, biomass and bio-based products. Based on it, the first set of regulations entered into force in July 2018, conceding the member States a period of 24 months to incorporate the directives into national legislation. This fact explains, at least partially, why other countries or blocks (such as the EU) have still a minor presence in the academic literature (see Table 5).

Concerning the tourism, segments tackled, due to the weight of China, the combination of tourism and agriculture is predominant, referred in the literature under labels (in alphabetical order) such as agro-tourism, eco-agricultural tourism, eco-tourism, ecological tourism, leisure agriculture tourism, urban forestry tourism, rural tourism, etc. (including coastal tourism). Even the construction of eco-industrial parks intended to make compatible industrial visiting and tourism.

Other research lines identified follow, restricting the scope of CE to certain domains:

1. The application of a low-carbon approach in the whole tourism value chain (with countermeasures to compensate the carbon footprint), taking CE as a framework of reference (including the behaviour of sharing products);
2. The principles of CE as drivers of greener tourism (greener hotels, for instance), including the promotion of green performance evaluation systems, green consciousness and consumption, Corporate Social Responsibility (CSR) commitments (particularly of environmental nature), etc.;
3. CE as new environmental ethics, as new production forms based on the 3R's (and subsequent R's) and new consumption patterns intended to secure a sustainable tourism development via green management;
4. CE and renewable energies, waste management and cleaner production practices;
5. CE and the promotion of responsible tourism among the industry stakeholders, with particular attention to the contribution of the local population to environmental conservation of tourism destinations;
6. The establishment of new metrics for the evaluation and selection of new business models in a tourism circular economy;
7. The conceptual delimitation of CE in contrast to other interconnected concepts in sustainability research such as Green Economy (GE) and Bioeconomy (BE), all of them, therefore, joint by the common ideal to reconcile economic, environmental and social goals[7];
8. The connections between Circular Economy and UN's Sustainable Development Goals, as well as the role of the tourism industry to reach them;
9. The implementation of integrated quality-environment-security systems in hotels as a starting point for the applicability of CE principles;
10. CE and environmental protection in coastal areas, rural settings, and world cultural heritage sites.

REFERENCES

Aragón-Correa, J. A. (2019). *What is a Circular Economy: Why is industrial symbiosis the best approach to a circular economy?* Retrieved on 28th July 2019 from https://blogs.ugr.es/empresas-con-futuro/en/what-is-a-circular-economy-why-is-industrial-symbiosis-the-best-approach-to-a-circular-economy/

Bonanno, S., Amato, F., Silluzio, C., Trimarchi, E. G., Matarazzo, A., & Bentivegna, G. (2018). Smart and circular economy applied to a Sicilian company as a sewage treatment model. *Procedia Environmental Science. Engineering and Management*, *5*(1), 21–28.

Cui, J. (2014). Sustainable Utilization of Tourism Resources in the Concept of Circular Economy Analysis. *Proceedings of International Symposium - Management, Innovation & Development (MID2014)*, 73-76.

D'Amato, D., Droste, N., Allen, B., Kettunen, M., Laehtinen, K., Korhonen, J., ... Toppinen, A. (2017). Green, circular, bio-economy: A comparative analysis of sustainability avenues. *Journal of Cleaner Production*, *168*, 716–734. doi:10.1016/j.jclepro.2017.09.053

Deselnicu, D. C., Militaru, G., Deselnicu, V., Zainescu, G., & Albu, L. (2018). Towards a Circular Economy - A Zero Waste Programme for Europe. *Proceedings of the 7th International Conference on Advanced Materials and Systems*, 563-568. 10.24264/icams-2018.XI.4

Domenget, B.-E. (2019). *Top Trends in Hospitality for 2019*. Sommet Education. Retrieved on 28th July 2019 from http://www.sommet-education.com/wp-content/uploads/Sommet-Education-Top-Hospitality-Trends-2019.pdf

Dong, Q. (2018). Study on the development strategy of tourism circular economy based on renewable energy technology. *Journal of Advanced Oxidation Technologies*, *21*(2), 201809023.

Dong, S., Li, Y., Li, Z., Li, F., Cheng, H., Yang, Y., . . . Bazarzhapov, T. (2018). Ecological environment risks and green development modes of China-Mongolia-Russia economic corridor. *IOP Conference Series: Earth and Environmental Science*, *190*(1), art. no. 012053. 10.1088/1755-1315/190/1/012053

Fan, Y. (2008). Research on the development of tourism circular economy in Henan province. In H. Zhang, R. M. Zhao, & Z. Q. Xie (Eds.), Industry Cluster and Meta-Studies (pp. 550–554). Academic Press.

Fang, X., & Zhang, X. (2010). On tourism environment protection for world cultural heritage sites in China. *2010 International Conference on Management and Service Science (MASS 2010)*, art. no. 5578038. 10.1109/ICMSS.2010.5578038

Girard, L. F., & Nocca, F. (2017). From linear to circular tourism. *Aestimum (Firenze)*, *70*, 51–74.

Giurea, R., Ioan, A. M., Ragazzi, M., & Cioca, L.-I. (2017). Focusing agro-tourism structures for environmental optimization. *Quality - Access to Success*, *18*(1), 115–120.

Guo, P. (2011). Information Management System with the Application to Tourism Management in the Period of Circular Economy. *International Conference on Energy, Environment and Development (ICEED2010)*, *5*, 1525-1529.

Han, L., Pan, Z., & Yan, Q. (2010). Analysis of the Construction of Hainan International Tourism Island Based on Circular Economy. *Proceedings of 2010 International Symposium on Tourism Resources and Management*, 77-82.

Hens, L., Block, C., Cabello-Eras, J. J., Sagastume-Gutierez, A., Garcia-Lorenzo, D., Chamorro, C., ... Vandecasteele, C. (2018). On the evolution of Cleaner Production as a concept and a practice. *Journal of Cleaner Production*, *172*, 3323–3333. doi:10.1016/j.jclepro.2017.11.082

Imboden, A. (2019). *Top Trends in Hospitality for 2019*. Sommet Education. Retrieved on 28th July 2019 from http://www.sommet-education.com/wp-content/uploads/Sommet-Education-Top-Hospitality-Trends-2019.pdf

Immacolata, V. (2018). Agriculture, Rural Tourism and Circular Paradigm. *Quality - Access to Success*, *19*(1), 556–562.

Jia, Z., Qin, A., & Jia, H. (2012). Research on the Development of Leisure Agriculture Tourism in Yi County Based on Circular Economy. In M. Kuek, Z.Q. Xie, & R. Zhao (Eds.), *Proceedings of the Third International Symposium - Industrial Engineering and Management*, (pp. 125-129). Academic Press.

Li, X., Deng, B., & Ye, H. (2011). The Research Based on the 3-R Principle of Agro-circular Economy Model-The Erhai Lake Basin as an Example. *2010 International Conference on Energy, Environment and Development*, *5*, 1399-1404.

Liu, F. L. (2014). Green management of tourist attractions region under the background of circular economy. *Advanced Materials Research*, *989*(994), 989–994, 5592–5595. doi:10.4028/www.scientific.net/AMR.989-994.5592

Liu, J. (2014). Developing circular economy and protecting the ecological environment of scenic spot. *Manufacture Engineering and Environment Engineering, 84, 1369-1374.*

Liu, L., & Liang, M. (2011). A reception model of rural low-carbon tourism based on circular economy - Take Cuandixia Village as an example. *Proceedings of the Fifth International Symposium on Green Hospitality and Tourism Management*, 96-104.

Lu, Y. (2012). Study on the Development Plan of the Lanzhou Tourism Industry in Line with Circular Economy. *Proceedings of the 7th Euro-Asia Conference on Environment and CSR: Tourism, MICE, Hospitality Management and Education Session*, 100-105.

Lu, Y., & Hu, X. X. (2014). A path study on the tourism circular economic development of Shandong province. *Advanced Materials Research*, *962-965*, 2234–2239. doi:10.4028/www.scientific.net/AMR.962-965.2234

Ma, X., Li, S., Ai, Q., & Chen, K. (2016). Research on Renewable Energy Systems Used in Tourism Circular Economy. *Proceedings of the 28th Chinese Control and Decision Conference (2016 CCDC)*, 6203-6206. 10.1109/CCDC.2016.7532113

Naydenov, K. (2018). Circular tourism as a key for eco-innovations in circular economy based on sustainable development. *International Multidisciplinary Scientific GeoConference Surveying Geology and Mining Ecology Management*, *18*(5.3), 135-142.

Pagán, J. I., López, I., Tenza-Abril, A. J., Aragonés, L., & Villacampa, Y. (2018). Urban growth and beach nourishment: Experiences on the coast of Alicante, Spain. *WIT Transactions on the Built Environment, 179*, 93–102. doi:10.2495/UG180091

Pamfilie, R., Firoiu, D., Croitoru, A.-G., & Ionescu, G. H. I. (2018). Circular Economy - A New Direction for the Sustainability of the Hotel Industry in Romania? *Amfiteatru Economic, 20*(48), 388–404. doi:10.24818/EA/2018/48/388

Pan, S.-Y., Gao, M., Kim, H., Shah, K. J., Pei, S.-L., & Chiang, P.-C. (2018). Advances and challenges in sustainable tourism toward a green economy. *The Science of the Total Environment, 635*, 452–469. doi:10.1016/j.scitotenv.2018.04.134 PMID:29677671

Patti, S. (2017). Circular economy and sharing consumption: Attitudes towards low-carbon tourism. *Economics and Policy of Energy and the Environment, 2017*(1), 219–234. doi:10.3280/EFE2017-001011

Paulauskas, S. (2018). Blue Growth Circular Innovation. *Transnav-International Journal on Marine Navigation and Safety of Sea Transportation, 12*(4), 813–818. doi:10.12716/1001.12.04.21

Rakitovac, K. A. (2016). The Transition towards Responsible Tourism. *Political Sciences, Law, Finance, Economics and Tourism Conference Proceedings, 4*, 889-896.

Scheepens, A. E., Vogtlander, J. G., & Brezet, J. C. (2016). Two life cycle assessment (LCA) based methods to analyse and design complex (regional) circular economy systems. Case: Making water tourism more sustainable. *Journal of Cleaner Production, 114*, 257–268. doi:10.1016/j.jclepro.2015.05.075

Shi, C., & Zhang, G. (2013). The ecological construction of scenic spots. *BioTechnology: An Indian Journal, 8*(9), 1306–1310.

Song, X. (2013). Analysis of Green Hotel Marketing Management under the Background of Circular Economy. Advances in Energy Science and Technology, 291-294, 1478-1481. doi:10.4028/www.scientific.net/AMM.291-294.1478

Ten Brink, P., Kettunen, M., & Watkins, E. (2017). *Expert Group on Green and Circular Economy in the Outermost Regions: Final Report. For DG Regional and Urban Policy, European Commission.* Retrieved on 28th July 2019 from https://ec.europa.eu/regional_policy/sources/policy/themes/outermost-regions/pdf/green_circ_econ_report_en.pdf

Vargas-Sánchez, A. (2018). The unavoidable disruption of the circular economy in tourism. *Worldwide Hospitality and Tourism Themes, 10*(6), 652–661. doi:10.1108/WHATT-08-2018-0056

Xu, F. (2012). The Studies of the Concept Plan of the Fengcheng Industrial Park towards the Circular Economy. In Z. H. Zhang & Y. J. Li (Eds.), *Architecture and Urban Development* (Vol. 598, pp. 220–223). doi:10.4028/www.scientific.net/AMR.598.220

Yuan, Q., & Xue, X. (2009). The Eco-industrial System Study of Circular Small Town. *Proceedings of the 2009 IEEE 16th International Conference on Industrial Engineering and Engineering Management*, 1-2, 1636-1639. 10.1109/ICIEEM.2009.5344355

Zhang, Q. (2016). Discussion on Significance of Forestry Tourism Circular Economy's Development. *3rd International Conference on Management Innovation and Business Innovation (ICMIBI 2016)*, *58*, 358-361.

Zhang, Y. (2014). Circular economy perspective research Wanlu lake Eco-tourism Industry Gathering Area for innovation and development. *Advanced Materials Research*, *962-965*, 2301–2309. doi:10.4028/www.scientific.net/AMR.962-965.2301

Zhang, Y., & Tian, L. (2014). The sustainable development of circular economy under the perspective of ecological tourism. *Advanced Materials Research*, *1010-1012*, 2090–2093. doi:10.4028/www.scientific.net/AMR.1010-1012.2090

Zhao, A. (2016). Research on Circular Economy as Well as Energy Saving and Emission Reduction of Liaoning Rural Tourism. *International Conference on Material, Energy and Environment Engineering (ICM3E 2016)*, 129-133.

Zhao, P. (2015). Low Carbon Tourism and Strategies of Carbon Emission Reduction. *2nd International Symposium on Engineering Technology, Education and Management (ISETEM 2015)*, 391-399.

Zhou, R., Ai, H., & Shi, K. (2012). Security system of Sustainable Tourism Development in Shandong Province based on Circular Economy. Natural Resources and Sustainable Development II, 524-527, 3245. doi:10.4028/www.scientific.net/AMR.524-527.3245

Zhu, Z., Li, M., & Ma, C. (2013). Explore and analyse development model of eco-agricultural tourism based on circular economy. In Environmental Protection and Resources Exploitation, 807-809, 902. doi:10.4028/www.scientific.net/AMR.807-809.902

ADDITIONAL READING

Alonso-Almeida, M. D. M., Fernández-Robin, C., Celemín-Pedroche, M. S. C., & Santander-Astorga, P. (2017). Revisiting green practices in the hotel industry: A comparison between mature and emerging destinations. *Journal of Cleaner Production*, 140, 1415–1428. Retrieve on 15th November 2019 from https://www.sciencedirect.com/science/article/pii/S0959652616316080

Alonso-Almeida, M. D. M., Rocafort, A., & Borrajo, F. (2016). Shedding light on eco-innovation in tourism: A critical analysis. *Sustainability*, 8(12), 1262. Retrieve on 15th November 2019 from https://www.mdpi.com/2071-1050/8/12/1262

Fernández-Robin, C., Celemín-Pedroche, M. S., Santander-Astorga, P., & Alonso-Almeida, M. D. M. (2019). Green Practices in Hospitality: A Contingency Approach. *Sustainability*, 11(3), 3737. Retrieve on 15th November 2019 from https://www.mdpi.com/2071-1050/11/13/3737

Florido, C., Jacob, M., & Payeras, M. How to Carry out the Transition towards a More Circular Tourist Activity in the Hotel Sector (2019). The Role of Innovation. *Administrative Sciences*, 9(2), 47. Retrieve on 15th November 2019 from https://www.mdpi.com/2076-3387/9/2/47

Kennedy, C., & Burns, J. (2018). *Creating Canada's first circular food economy*. Retrieve on 15th November 2019 from https://guelph.ca/wp-content/uploads/SmartCities_Booklet.pdf

Manniche, J., Larsen, K. T., Broegaard, R. B., & Holland, E. (2017). *Destination: a circular tourism economy. A handbook for transitioning toward a circular economy within the tourism and hospitality sectors in the South Baltic region*. Nexoe, Denmark: Centre for Regional & Tourism Research. Retrieve on 15th November 2019 from https://circulareconomy.europa.eu/platform/sites/default/files/cirtoinno-handbook_eng-rev.-4.pdf

Nedyalkova, S. (2016). Applying circular economy principles to sustainable tourism development. In *Abstracts and Conference Proceedings of PM4SD European Summer School* (pp. 38-44). Akureyri, Iceland. Retrieve on 15th November 2019 from http://www.smartdestinationsworldconference.org/_files/_event/_19238/_editorFiles/file/24093_Nedyalkova_15_06%20Circular_tourism_Savina.pdf

Rodríguez-Antón, J. M., & Alonso-Almeida, M. D. M. (2019). The Circular Economy Strategy in Hospitality: A Multicase Approach. *Sustainability*, 11(20), 5665. Retrieve on 15th November 2019 from https://www.mdpi.com/2071-1050/11/20/5665

KEY TERMS AND DEFINITIONS

Bibliographic Analysis: A content analysis of the publications identified in a certain field of study.

Bibliometric Analysis: Analysis of a set of publications in a certain domain based on quantitative indicators such as its evolution over time, number of citations, most prolific authors, etc.

Circular Economy: Economic model oriented to eliminate waste generation, reuse/recycle products and materials, reduce as much as possible resources consumption as well as other actions to close material loops and, in sum, minimize the environmental impact.

Circular Economy Principles: Originally known as the 3R's (reduce, reuse, and recycle), others have been added over time, such as redesign, repair, refurbish, recover, and others.

Circular Tourism Economy (or Tourism Circular Economy): The application of circular economy principles to tourism companies and destinations.

Scopus: Multidisciplinary bibliographic database owned by Elsewier, one of the main international publishers of scientific journals; it also provides bibliometric analyses of publications.

Web of Science: A tool for scientific production evaluation based on citations; owned by Clarivate Analytics, this platform collects the main scientific publications in any knowledge discipline together with their references.

ENDNOTES

1. Available at: https://europa.eu/rapid/press-release_MEMO-19-1481_en.htm (accessed 28th July 2019).
2. Approach aiming to the creation of synergies between businesses/sectors so that waste of a company/sector become inputs of other companies/sectors. According to Aragón-Correa (2019), this is the best approach to a circular economy.

3 Also a Q1 journal in Scopus in the four categories in which it is indexed: "Environmental Science (miscellaneous)", "Industrial and Manufacturing Engineering", "Renewable Energy, Sustainability and the Environment" and "Strategy and Management". Available at: https://www.scimagojr.com/journalsearch.php?q=19167&tip=sid&clean=0 (accessed 28th July 2019).

4 Eco-agricultural tourism or Eco-tourism, Eco-costs, Eco-efficient value creation, Eco-industrial system, Eco-innovations, Ecological benefits/environment.

5 The United Nations Environmental Program developed in 1991 its often cited definition, in spite of the changes that have occurred later: "CP is the continuous application of an integrated preventive environmental strategy to processes, products, and services to increase efficiency and reduce risks to humans and the environment" (Hens et al., 2018).

6 https://www.livingcircular.veolia.com/en/eco-citizen/global-soap-project-redistributes-recycled-soap-those-need (accessed 28th July 2019).

7 Some conclusions gathered by D'Amato et al. (2017) have a singular interest to this respect: "The results show that the three concepts have different geographical distributions, with Chinese dominance in CE research, a strong European BE focus and a mostly global reach for GE. Content-wise, CE focuses on industrial urban processes for decoupling resource use and economic output; BE focuses on biological resource-based innovation and land use practices in the context of rural development; and GE envelops an umbrella perspective for a balanced social-environmental development with a global research area. We find that GE research is the most inclusive concept, including some ideas from both CE and BE. None of the concepts addresses degrowth topics and thus fail to deal with potential limits to growth".

Chapter 7
Sustainability of Mandatory Pension Insurance in the Circular Economy:
A Comparative Analysis

Biljana Stojan Ilic
https://orcid.org/0000-0001-6137-8478
Megatrend University of Belgrade, Serbia

Gordana P. Djukic
https://orcid.org/0000-0001-5419-0725
Faculty of Economics, The University of Belgrade, Serbia

Mladenka M. Balaban
Belgrade Banking Academy, Serbia

ABSTRACT

The main characteristic of pension systems is financial stability. The authors will present some models of the pension system, economics models such as the theory of income uncertainty, overlapping generations' model. The authors will present the interrelation of employment, population, and circular economy, trying to improve the existing pension system in Serbia. The circular economy is a response to the growing needs of humanity. It is referred to as sustainable development in all the spheres of human life. The circular economies can also refer to the sustainability of the pension system, which is linked to the quality of life. The quality of life is part of sustainable development as its social component. The chapter provides an overview of the sustainability of the pension system by reducing the costs with employment increasing. As an example of good practice, the authors present Australia and Chile in a small analysis that indicates pension fund sustainability. This practice can serve as an example of the improvement of the pension system in Serbia and similar smaller countries.

DOI: 10.4018/978-1-7998-5116-5.ch007

Copyright © 2020, IGI Global. Copying or distributing in print or electronic forms without written permission of IGI Global is prohibited.

INTRODUCTION

The subject of the chapter is to examine the sustainability of the pension system as a social category of sustainable development. Authors use descriptive and comparative methods with main objective- to find solutions for overcoming the unsustainability of the pension system in Serbia. Underdeveloped economy and fiscal system result lower standard of living, as well as a number of social problems in all categories of society, especially for retirees. Of course, the authors aware of the fact that it is not possible full implementation of the models that have been effective in developed countries. The labour market that is affected by an adequate circular economy policy, results employment, GDP increasing and higher income of the pension fund. This proves the connection of the pension system and the circular economy. However, the authors think that it is possible to modify the existing model of the pension system in Serbia that can be based on successful models of pension systems of development countries. Giving an overview of the relevant literature, controversy, and their own opinion of the pension sustainable system, authors present descriptive theoretical and mathematical models. It will be compared the pension systems of some development countries with Serbian (pension system), using composite Global Pension Grade Index. Finally, the concluding observations include the views of the authors as well as recommendations for a pension system sustainability model in Serbia. In many developed countries, besides the public pensions, the private pension system is becoming increasingly important. According to Bijlsma and colleagues: "Many countries encourage private funded pensions as a supplement to public pensions, which face increasing demographic pressure. It is likely that the role of institutional investors as pension funds and insurance companies in financial intermediation will increase in the future. This may positively affect economic growth as these institutional investors can be expected to be more committed to long term investments" (Bijlsma, M., Beonekamp. J., van Ewijk,C. & Haaijen, F. (2018). On the other hand, in many countries a public pension system are unique and originated within a specific demographic, political and economic conditions of states. Based on this context, the public system plan is well or poorly funded (Dustin, D. W., 2019). In the process of adopting new laws and reforms, it is very important to point out that pension reforms can lead to unfair distribution of earnings for employees doing the same job in state-owned and public enterprises. For this reason, and because of dissatisfaction with the level of wages, employees are looking for employment in the private sector, where they would have higher earnings and higher pension in the future. Also, by legal regulation, existing workers may have less legal protection than employees who had higher earnings before the law was passed. Dustin further explained that this kind of unfairness in benefits can have the effect of motivation reduce for work, lower employee morale and increasing of brain-draining. This is the situation in Serbia, where a large number of professional staff go abroad (for many years). Dustin presents that the pension system in each country is developing in a specific macroeconomic environment, that is, in a specific demographic economic and political context. The fact is that in some countries with a public pension system, political decision-makers increase pensions due to "political victories" instead of considering the long-term effects of the increase. According to Dustin, in cooperation with the state, unions play an important role in financing the pension fund. If public-sector unions are strong, pensions are usually increased. In contrast, weak unions do not contribute adequately to the pension fund, so pensions are not sufficiently increased, as is the case in Serbia. According to a European Commission report (2019) in the area of labor, employment and social policy, recommendation for Sebia is to implement a codex of equality and anti-discriminatory policy. In the area of social protection, in 2017, 7.2% of the population were in absolute poverty. In Serbia, about half a million people do not have the conditions to meet own basic living needs. There is highest unequal distribution of income in Serbia among all the European countries, based on the Living Standards Survey (SILC), equals 37.8% Gini coefficient in 2017. The risk-of-poverty rate is 25.7% - meaning that about 1.8 million of people are living in poverty (Serbia 2019 Report).

Adequate pension system provides sufficient funds i.e. retirement benefits for old age. The Adequate system is a global goal for all countries to prevent long-term poverty in old age (to pensioners). In that system, pensioners are provided with minimum living conditions, as well as sufficient amounts of pension benefits for the rest of their lives (Holzmann, 2005).The functional system makes financial resources available to the individual and at the same time,it has financial capacity at the national level to implies fiscal sustainability in the socio-economic sphere of society. According to Holzmann and based on the experience of manycountries, the World Bank indicates that a contribution rate that exceeds 20%, is detrimental to highly developed "high-income" countries, while the rate greater than 10% is not recommended for less-developed "low-income" countries. A financially sustainable pension system provides financial stability to pensioners who are regularly paid benefits, regardless of possible economic shocks in the financial market. A sustainable pension system has the financial capacity to support the financial costs of a pension fund in time. Efficient economic development eliminates the negative effects in unbalanced systems where there is high unemployment, underdeveloped financial markets, reduced national savings, and income deficits. Thus, pension schemes play an important role to maximize positive economic effects and sustainable economic growth. Economic growth through directing contributions helps in reducing labor market distortions, increasing individuals' and national savings, thereby creating conditions for the development of the financial market.

In each pension system, the main objective is the long-term functioning and sustainability of the pension system, which is achieved by maintaining the balance of the pension system in terms of reducing expenditures and increasing income. Applying public sector management in the mandatory public system, pension benefits are secured based onstatutory contributions. The funds for pension contributions depend on the earnings; the pension benefits depend on: replacement rates, risks (such as uncertain life expectancy), inadequate long-term planning, insufficient knowledge of risks in financial markets, etc. The public system has been emerging from 1945 to 1970. At that time, there was a favorable ratio between the number of employees and the number of beneficiaries of pension rights. Over the long decade, at the beginning of the twentieth century, because of the numerous factors such as demographic changes, aging population, declining birth rates, and fertility rates, the ratio of employees to the number of retirees, has become significantly less favorable.

In the process of globalization, privatization and transition, in many transition countries, there was a decrease in the number of employees i.e. fall in the gross domestic product, as well as decrease of income in pension funds. The sustainability of the pension system is based not only on the favorable ratio of employees and pensioners but also on high contribution rates, budgetary grants, and tax revenues. (Davis, 2004) considers to achieve balance in the mandatory pension system, it is necessary to consider direct and indirect impacts on economic growth for capital accumulation and pension system financing, such: (1) intensive adequate economic growth that provides sufficient capital and sufficient labor force in the labor market; intensification of investments, which directly affects economic growth (2) financial market i.e. financial capital and social/corporate responsibilities, which indirectly affects economic growth. A new and essential paradigm of development is "moving" from linear to circular growth for reducing and transforming waste, giving the new value to already existing forms (Descalzi, 2018).

BACKGROUND - PROBLEMS AND CONTROVERSIES

Financial stability of pension systems in the short term refers to the estimated value of funds allocated from GDP, to mitigate the financial crisis of pension systems and to mitigate financial shocks (Valdes-Prieto, 2006). The paper focuses on the financial risks rising in pension systems, that have caused shocks that lead to disruption of the pension system. Prieto explained that shocks can be: demographic, b) economic or changes in average tax revenue generated by employees, employee turnover, and c) financial shocks related to changes in share capital, changes in securities prices, shocks affecting principal capital accumulated in funded, in partly funded (and voluntarily funded) pension plans. In a situation when salaries and pension contributions are reduced, predefined pensions are also reduced. These changes cause shocks, which have an adverse financial impact on the liabilities of the pension fund, and therefore the aggregate financial costs. The impact of liabilities of the pension fund's have short-term character, while aggregate shocks have a long-term character. Prieto presents that the financial sustainability of the different pension systems can be considered in terms: a) differences in pension costs compared to different pension contributions, and b) differences in pension costs financed directly from the state budget (GDP). Height pension costs depend on the accumulated sums of public taxes. The percentage share of taxes in public pension expenditure depends on the type of pension scheme. In pension systems funded by employee and employer contributions, that are in Bismarck's systems, the impact of the demographic factor on financial sustainability is smaller than in countries where pension systems are funded by accumulated taxes. The amount of pension costs is also affected by the diversity of the three pillars of the pension system. In the chapter, the authors will attempt to numerically, i.e. by applying an adequate analysis, to express the direct dependence of employment and population and pension fund. This is especially important and significant in smaller countries i.e. phenomenon in smaller economies, such as the economy of Serbia and similar countries of Serbia.

Is it necessary that employees work as long as it possible to make the pension system sustainable? On the other hand, is the extension of the working life of employees following the principles of sustainable development and protection of the social human being who deserved a pension after a certain number of life years? It is projected that by 2050, life expectancy in Europe will be extended by four years. This "extension" is "the result of" demographic trends since the last 50 years (in Europe) - it is evident the so-called demographic ageing (people are living longer). In other words, all Europe is getting older and the ratio of three workers per retiree will not be adequate in the EU. This will not cause the collapse of the pension systems, but only the necessity for reform implementation, which would be increasing the age of retirement, adequate to the formula indexation in 2020 and by using the Swiss formula (indexation) enabling the viability of the pension system and predictability pension increases. Private pension funds in most European countries represent additional revenue for public pensions, as recommendations for all countries.

However, European countries such as Slovakia, Hungary, Bulgaria, Croatia and Poland, have made a mistake in trying to replace the public pension system to private pensions. This proved to be a bad process (to what experts have warned) as the pensions become lower, so the countries lifted the obligation of private pension funds (Petrovic, 2010). Authors Altiparmakov and Matkovic also believe that to remain sustainable pension systems, it is necessary to increase the service life following the increase in life expectancy, in other words, that the „employee be employed" as long as it is possible (Altiparmakov, Matkovic, 2018). It is necessary to follow the trends of Western Europe, which means to achieve the sustainability of the pension system by reforming the first pension pillar and at the same time to stimulate voluntary pension funds. In other words, it will be necessary for all employees during their working life (which can) additional saving and to have an additional source of income, in addition to the public pension. In the case of Serbia, in the opinion of the author Arsic and colleagues, pension reform of 2014 increased the retirement age, especially for women.

Does this now mean that citizens have a greater incentive to work until regular age? It is believed that by 2032 the age of retirement for women and men to equalize (Arsic, Randjelovic, Altiparmakov, 2018). Based on the latest statistics, the ratio of workers to pensioners (specifically the example of Serbia) has improved slightly in recent years, amounting to more than 1.5 workers per pensioner. Thanks to the 2014 reform, there has also been an increase in the employment rate. "A member of the Fiscal Council of Serbia, Vuckovic (Vladimir), believes that a 10% increase in pensions for the Serbian state budget would mean an additional cost of 400 million euros.

Vuckovic believes that this increase could be implemented in several ways, but warns that it is quite reasonable to ask what is a priority at the moment for Serbian society. The last option is another fundamental reform of the pension system, in the sense that the mandatory payment of contributions go into private pension funds, but not limited to the state pension fund. Finally, when the effects on the income and expenditure side of Serbia are summed up, in an ideal scenario, money could be raised to increase pensions by ten per cent, but the question is whether this increase is a priority for Serbian society. The pension money supply, according to the value that is created in the country in the gross national income and by participation in the expenditure budget, in Serbia, for example, among the highest in Europe. However, the insufficient development of the economy and an insufficient number of employees does not allow higher spending on pensions, especially not immediately even higher percentage (Member of the Fiscal Council, 2017).

A THEORETICAL MODEL ON INCOME UNCERTAINTY

The economist who has incorporated a Theoretical model of income uncertainty was Hayne Leland. Many of his papers have found direct applications in asset management and corporate financial structure, such as portfolio insurance, option pricing with transaction costs, and valuation of risky corporate debt He has worked on introducing equity-sharing contracts in home purchase financing and structuring retirement funds to provide assured income over retirement years. A theoretical model of income uncertainty is based on two periods of consumption: the first period - before and others after retirement (Leland,1968). Analyzes are "cautious" individual savings accounts when they are in the second period of their retirement income uncertain. Individuals or households with a measure of caution and subjectively decide on the allocation of savings and their future income. It points to the uncertainty of savings and considers the certain period of correlation lifecycle uncertainty of pension income and the expected length of life. Life expectancy is divided into two periods: the period of employment, or full-service life, and the period after the end of useful life, the moment when person i.e. employee retired. Examining model assumed that (Santen, 2013):

- The per-period utility functionis of the Constant Absolute Risk Aversion;
- Presented by formula 1 (The choice of a CARA utility function is motivated by the possibility to obtain closed-form solutions, which is not possible with the class of Constant Relative Risk

Aversion (CRRA) utility functions. This choice prevents buffer-stock saving behaviour, which needs decreasing absolute risk aversion; see in Carroll, 1992):

$$U\left(c\right) = -\left(\frac{1}{\alpha}\right)\exp\left(\alpha c\right) \tag{1}$$

with the coefficient of absolute riskaversion α:

- Retirement is an exogenous variable, at age K;
- Income during working life;
- Y_τ is certain and varies by age τ;
- Retirement income Y_K is redistribution random variable with mean μ_{YK} and variation σ^2_{YK}, pension income after retirement is constant;
- The existential survival income denoted by a_τ is guaranteed until the moment of retirement, and from the moment of retirement the existence (length of survival) represents the probability until the period $\tau > K$;
- The highest age limit is indicated by L;
- The interest rate *r* is constant and equal to the rate of temporal preference ρ, and for notational convenience (Santen, 2013), defined R = 1+ r,and $\beta = (1+\rho)^{-1}$ as interest factor, respectively.

The problem that the younger population facing, is "how it will maximize the usefulness of the life cycle". This problem can be represented by formulas (1a and 1b):

$$\max_{c_t} -\frac{1}{\alpha}\sum_{\tau=t}^{K-1}\beta^{\tau-t}exp\left[-\alpha c_\tau\right] - \frac{1}{\alpha}E_t\sum_{\tau=K}^{L}\beta^{\tau-t}a_\tau exp\left[-\alpha c_\tau\right] \tag{1a}$$

$$s.t.\sum_{\tau=t}^{\mathrm{K}-1}R^{t-\tau}c_\tau + \sum_{\tau=K}^{L}R^{t-\tau}c_\tau = RA_{t-1} + \sum_{\tau=t}^{\mathrm{K}-1}R^{t-\tau}y_\tau + \sum_{\tau=K}^{L}R^{t-\tau}y_K \tag{1b}$$

where the: $\boldsymbol{c}_{\check{A}}$ is consumption in period τ, A_{t-1} is predetermined wealth, E_t is expectation operator conditional on information available in period τ. Author Santen explained and solved the problem of the two periods:

1. In a period in the retirement stage, when he calculated the values of future utility streams, which depends on wealth available at the beginning of retirement A_{K-1};
2. Then he considered a problem in the period of work activities and the calculated value of the living conditions of A_{K-1} that is available in the future demand.

He chooses A_{K-1} to maximize the usefulness of the life cycle. Current consumption was shown in the "closed" term ("closed-form expression") (formula 2):

$$c_t = \frac{RA_{t-1} + \sum_{\tau=t}^{K-1} R^{t-\tau} y_\tau + \sum_{\tau=K}^{L} R^{t-\tau} \mu_{yk}}{\sum_{\text{Ä}=t}^{L} R^{t-\text{Ä}}} - \frac{\sum_{\tau=K}^{L} R^{t-\tau} (\frac{1}{\alpha}\log(a_\tau) + \frac{1}{2}\alpha\sigma_{yk}^2)}{\sum_{\tau=t}^{L} R^{t-\tau}} \quad (2)$$

In this way, existing-present consumption is presented when future pension income is uncertain. In the first retirement period, it is certain to expect the present value of future cash flows (permanent) income. Consumption would be equal to permanent income, provided there is no uncertainty.

When uncertainty is present, consumption is equal to permanent income minus prudent savings, due to the length of uncertainty in pension income. If the probability of existence increases, $\left(a_\tau \uparrow\right)$, consumption decreases. He considers particularly interesting the strict relationship between spending and different pension benefits in an equivalent case at some uncertain time. The uncertainty of pension income affects the behavior of working individuals to spend less and save more. Also, consumption information based on annual savings can be obtained based on (formula 3):

$$s_t = \left(R-1\right)A_{t-1} + y_t - c_t$$

can be written as:

$$s_t = \frac{R^{t-L}}{\sum_{\tau=t}^{L} R^{t-\tau}} A_{t-1} \frac{\sum_{\tau=K}^{L} R^{t-\tau} y_t}{\sum_{\tau=t}^{L} R^{t-\tau}} - \frac{\sum_{\tau=K}^{L} R^{t-\tau} \mu_{yk}}{\sum_{\tau=t}^{L} R^{t-\tau}}$$

$$-\frac{\sum_{r=t+1}^{K-1} \Delta y_\tau \sum_{\rho=\tau}^{K-1} R^{t-\rho}}{\sum_{\tau=t}^{L} R^{t-\tau}} + \frac{\sum_{\tau=K}^{L} R^{t-\tau} \frac{1}{\alpha} \log\left(a_\tau\right)}{\sum_{\tau=t}^{L} R^{t-\tau}} + \frac{\sum_{\tau=K}^{L} R^{t-\tau} \frac{1}{2} \propto \sigma_{yK}^2}{\sum_{\tau=t}^{L} R^{t-\tau}} \quad (3)$$

where Δ is the differential operator. Previously accumulated assets have a negative impact on savings, but if the income of employees continues to be increased in age $\left(\Delta U_\tau > 0\right)$ current-present savings will be less. Santen explained that expected pension benefits should reduce savings, the effect of which refers to the section of period *1* and period *2*.

In today's modern conditions, it was discovered that there is a relationship between individuals who have economic resources and those who need them. During their lifecycle, individuals spend more than their income and do not have to cover consumption. It seems simple, but it has been found that financial resources are being created to shift between generations. Over time, such assets can be quantitatively matched linked to economic development in any society. In such conditions, macroeconomic theoretical models, such as Samuelson's overlapping generations model, have emerged.

Overlapping Generations Model

Paul Samuelson, (American economist who, as the first American, gets the Nobel i.e. Memorial Prize in the science of Economy) economic activity observed from the aspect of generation change, where generational transfer, are especially important (Samuelson, 1952). It is assumed that individuals are interested in equalizing spending given that they should retire. The transfer of money between generations at any given time is based on the impact of interest rates and savings (Samuelson, 1954). Many applications of the OLG model are known in the scientific literature and the impact of the demographic transition on the interest rate of return across a wide range of financial instruments has been studied (Merton, 1970). Possibilities of applying the model in households and PAYG pension systems were examined to evaluate the interaction between reforms of the pension system and private demand. In the economy of the United Kingdom has been found that in the pension system which is less"generous", the model is directly linked to an increased in the household demand, projecting an increase of 8.5% (Ratanabanchuen, 2013). If there is a demand for an increase in the minimum required retirement age, it is likely that the savings rate will decrease. This occurs because of the shorter period of saving the younger generation but also reduces the savings rate. Ratanbanchuen argued that reducing the level of "generosity" of the pension system may affect on increasing the well-being of the current middle-aged cohort but decreasing the well-being of the existing cohort of older people.

Application of the OLG Model in Australia

In Australia, the OLG model is incorporated in the pension system, which has two pillars. The first pillar is the public mandatory where the state guarantees pension benefits to individuals with low incomes. Superannuation`s second pillar is guaranteed and obliges employers to pay superannuation' contributions to each employee in the superannuation` fund. Applied the OLG model in Australia, has the characteristics of inter-temporal general equilibrium with the overlapping generations. Because of the projected demographic change and based on the estimated macroeconomic and fiscal implications, there is a reaction of the younger population in the form of savings, consumption, and supply in the labour market (Kudrna, Tran & Woodland, 2014). Model include population dynamics, the household sector, which includes overlapping generations with maximizing benefits sector productivity to maximize profit companies, the public sector, including foreign trade transactions.

The state budget allocations are made for the costs of certain age groups: for education, health, elderly care, pensions, family benefits, and others. According to Kudrna and colleagues, regarding the pension system OLG model includes two mandatory pension systems and policy fees. In the analysis, the population dynamics of the model is assumed: a)increasing the number of populations younger and the older generation in period t;b) the existence of the 101 generation (0 to 100 years, included the household of 21 years old and over (21 ... 100) because it is assumed that this age group is labour active and has the right to make economic decisions, where the a- is the size of the cohort age group at time *t*, P_t – size of the population which is the sum of all the cohorts in the period ***t*** (formula 4):

$$P_t = \sum_{a=0}^{100} N_{a,t} \tag{4}$$

$\mu_{a,t}$ – the share of the total population in any one moment is expressed as (formula 4a):

$$\mu_{a,t} = \frac{N_{a,t}}{P_t} \tag{4a}$$

In the analysis of population dynamics involved all relevant demographic parameters such as fertility, sex, mortality, migration, and others. The OLG model analyzed two pillars of pension systems (Kudrna, Tran& Woodland, 2014). Based on the fact of authors Kudrna and colleagues, households or overlapping generations were analyzed based on endogenous variables:*c* - consumption of households which decide the most optimal way, l– leisure of the age population (a = 21 ... 100).

Kudrna and colleagues represented population preferences by the inter-temporal utility function which is given for a generation of people who started working life at time *t* (formula 5):

$$U_t = \frac{1}{1-\frac{1}{\gamma}} \sum_{a=21}^{100} S_{a,i} \left(1+\beta\right)^{21-a} \left[\left(C_{a,i}\right)^{\left(1-\frac{1}{p}\right)} + \alpha_a \left(l_{a,i}\right)^{\left(1-\frac{1}{p}\right)} \right]^{\frac{1-1/\gamma}{1-1/p}} \tag{5}$$

i – is subscript and it is defined as i = a + t – 21. The parameters included in function are the inter-temporal substitution elasticity γ, the intra-temporal elasticity of substitutions ρ, the parameter of leisure distribution a_a, as well as the rate of time preference β. The term S_{ai} denotes unconditional survival probabilities. The expected lifetime utility function is maximized depending on a lifetime budget constraint and can be expressed as period by period asset accumulations (formula 6):

$$A_{a,t} - A_{a-1,t-1} = rA_{a-1,t-1} + \omega_t e_a \left(1 - l_{a,t}\right) + AP_{a,t} + SA_{60}$$

$$+SP_a + FB_{a,t} + B_t - T_{\left(Y_{a,t}\right)} - \left(1+\tau^c\right)_{C_{a,t}} \tag{6}$$

According to Kudrna and colleagues, expressed a left side of formula (6) denotes the household saving $A_{a,t} - A_{a-1,t-1}$, which equals the sum: interest income $rA_{a-1,t-1}$, labour earnings $\omega_t e_a \left(1 - l_{a,t}\right)$, age pension $AP_{a,t}$, superannuation payouts $SA_{60,t}$ and $SP_{a,t}$, family benefits $FB_{a,t}$, and receipts of inheritance B_t, minus the sum of income taxes $T_{\left(Y_{a,t}\right)}$ and consumption costs $\left(1+\tau^c\right)_{C_{a,t}}$. Labour earnings are the product of the supply of labour $1 - l_{a,t}$, and hourly wage $\omega_t e_a$, where ω_t is market wage rate and e_a representing the age-specific earnings ability. Preferably, the variable labour supply is non-negative, that is $1 - l_{a,t} \geq 0$, comprising a free time $l_{a,i}$, cannot have any value larger than the possible time available endowment and is normalized to one.

When $l_{a,t} = 1$, the household is not economically active and doesn`t work. The household tax rate on consumption is the rate τ^c and household pays the progressive income tax from their taxable income $Y_{a,t}$, including interest income, labour earnings, and the age pension.The Australian age pension $AP_{a,t}$ was means-tested, in such a way that pension is paid to age pension households (a$\geq$65), only if the following tested condition is satisfied, or based on the test (formula 7):

$$AP_{a,t} = \max\left\{\min\left\{p, p - \theta\left(y_{a,t} - IT\right)\right\}, 0\right\} \quad (7)$$

where:

p – the legally established maximum single rate of age pension
θ – the reduction of income rate
IT – the income threshold and assessable income is given by $y_{a,t} = rA_{a-1,t-1} + 0{,}5 \times \omega_t e_a \left(1 - l_{a,t}\right)$

Kudrna and colleagues presented the OLG model in the second pillar of the Australian pension system, which is known as the superannuation guarantee. It is completely private and fully-founded.

Kudrna and colleagues assumed that each producer pays contributions for employees age 21 to 60 years in households at the subsequent tax contribution rate $\left(1 - \tau^S\right)r$ from their labour income $\omega_t e_a \left(1 - l_{a,t}\right)$ to the superannuation fund. Contributions are accumulated in the superannuation assets $SA_{60,t}$ until age 60. Superannuation asset earns investment income at the after-tax interest rate $\left(1 - \tau^S\right)r$, in the period a £60 can be expressed as (formula 8):

$$SA_{a,t} = \left[1 + \left(1 - \tau^r\right)r\right]SA_{a-1,t-1} + \left[\left(1 - \tau^S\right)cr\right]\omega_t e_a \left(1 - l_{a,t}\right) \quad (8)$$

where: τ^r – the earnings tax rate, τ^S – contributory tax rate, cr – mandatory contribution rate. Kudrna and colleagues explained that it is assumed that the working active household age 60, and older, have paid the required contribute directly to their accumulation accounts, which are labeled as $SA_{a,t}$. Kudrma and colleagues concluded that the competitiveness of the macroeconomic model should have certain criteria, such: a) demand for the labour by the producer equals the labor supply i.e. working-active household, b) the market value of the share capital is equaled total amount of national and foreign financial resources (assets), c) supply of goods produced (GDP) equals the total amount (SUM) of household demands, firms for investment, demands government and foreigners, so the net trade equilibrium is established (import equals export).

EMPLOYMENT, POPULATION AND CIRCULAR ECONOMY - INTERRELATION

Improved data (The Aging Report, 2018) on employment results and employment rates, compared to base 2015, provide evidence that the EU is recovering from the crisis. On average at the EU level, current employment rates for the base year are 1.1. pp. larger than those projected three years ago.

By 2060, an employment rate of 0.8 pp. is also anticipated. In the EU, employment rates for the 20-64 age group are +1.1 pp higher than the base year 2015. in 2016 and are higher in the projected 2060 by +0.8 pp.

A higher increase in the employment rate compared to the base year (2015) at the EU level for the elderly (55-64) is +1.6 pp. in 2016 and in the projected 2060 it is an increase of +0.6 pp. For the Euro-zone (EU *) countries, the increase is even higher +1.7 pp. in 2060, as it is shown inTable 1.

Table 1. Labor force projections revisions: 2018 AR – 2015 (2016-2060)

	Employment Rate						Participation Rate						Unemployment Rate	
	(15-64)		(20-64)		(55-64)		(15-64)		(20-64)		(55-64)		(15-64)	
	2016	2060	2016	2060	2016	2060	2016	2060	2016	2060	2016	2060	2016	2060
EA	0.6	0.5	0.7	0.5	1.5	1.7	-0.1	0.6	-0.7	0.3	1.4	2.0	-0.9	0.6
EU*	1.0	0.7	1.1	0.8	1.6	0.6	0.1	0.7	0.2	0.7	1.4	0.8	-1.3	-0.1
EU 27	1.0	0.7	1.1	0.8	1.7	0.7	0.1	0.7	0.2	0.7	1.5	0.8	-1.2	-0.2

Source: (Commission services, EPS - The Aging Report 2018)

These increases are the result of the increased participation rates (0,9%) and reduced rates of unemployment (0,1) that lead to negative population-related effects (0,6%). According to The Aging Report, in this way, a large correlation is shown between employment/workforce and population.

The main cause of the financial crisis of the pension system in most countries has not adapted long-term trends such as longer life expectancy, an ageing population, the retirement age, the decline in fertility rates, inconsistency and immobility of the pension system in terms of changes in the parameters that have been designed in the past and which is not appropriate in the present (contribution rates, pension benefits, the unconformity with the increase in prices and wages, etc.) (Brunetti, Kisunko &Weder, 1999).

Factors such as the increasing life expectancy, a small number of employees, a growing number of pensioners, and increasing dependency rates, negatively affect the sustainability of the system.

In European countries, the crisis of pension systems is caused by limited resources in the public budget, an ageing population, and technological change. Financial issues unsustainability of the system is explained by inadequate long-term treatment in analyzing the long life of the pension system (http://documents.worldbank.org/curated/en/423111468766541642/Institutions-in-transition-reliability-of-rules-and-economic-performance-in-former-Socialist-countries).

The cause of the financial problems of unsustainability is caused by inappropriate change parameters in the long run. Table 2 present the pension parameters of a long term period. In the table, there are the parameters of the previous period and the parameters of the future period. The parameters of the con-

Table 2. Pension parameters of a long-term period

Previous Period	Future Period
lower age limit	greater age
less life expectancy	higher life expectancy
higher fertility rates	lower fertility rate
higher replacement rate	lower replacement rate
higher contribution rate	lower contribution rate

Source: (http//:www.nezavisnost.org/sindikat)

tribution rate and the age limit parameter from the previous period do not comply with the parameters such as "extended life expectancy", "replacement rate" and "fertility rate".

Addressing unsustainable fiscal deficit and GDP depends on the appropriate longterm concept of the pension system. The sectors and activities in circular economy EU that have potential impacts on employment and labor market, were selected with the criteria such: economic significance, circular economy policy importance and circular economy sector potential (Impacts of circular economy policies on the labour market, 2018). Based on the Impacts of circular economy policies on the labour market, the sectors which have the greatest importance and impact in a circular economy that increases employment and creates new jobs are: the waste management sector, the repair sector services and then manufacturing sectors. The results from the E3ME modelling of the sectors present combined scenarios in the circular economy and macro impacts for them.

In the report are presented the best impacts on GDP in the waste sectors, and additional labour demand to process recycled materials. The report shows positive trends in GDP and also in the production rate. The consequence of both combined scenarios is an increase inemployment, by almost 0,3% (around 650.000 do 700.000 jobs) in the EU.

Many other studies and literature review demonstrated the impacts of the circular economy at the national level into three categories: first - economic impacts (GDP growth, employment, investment, etc.); second - environmental impacts (use of resources, emissions reductions, pollution reduction, etc.) and third - social impacts (gender, social opportunities, and inequalities, etc.) (Rizos,Tuokko & Behrens, 2017:20).

SUSTAINABILITY OF PENSION SYSTEM – COMPARATIVE ANALYSIS

The primary and important goals in the international report and researching study were to benchmark each retirement income system using more than 4 indicators and highlighting some shortcomings in each system and to suggest possible areas of reform that would provide sustainability of pension system and adequate retirement benefits (Knox, D., 2019).

Table 3 presents the Melbourne Mercer Global Pension Grade Index in 2019. The general sustainability index (MMGPI) is the composite index, i.e. the average of the following indices: adequacy, sustainability, and integrity. With this index, the countries are divided by ranks i.e. categories (from A to E).

Countries that belong to the group "A" have the first class of a strong pension system. The values of one sub-index represent the weakness of pension systems (compare with other sub-indices). Future

Table 3. Melbourne Mercer Global Pension Grade Index (MMGPI), 2019

Grade	Index Value	Systems	Description
A	> 80	Netherlands, Denmark	A first class and robust retirement income system, sustainable with good benefits and a high level of integrity.
B+	75-80	AUSTRALIA	A system that has a good structure, with many good features, but has some areas for improvements that are different from A-grade system.
B	65-75	Chile, Finland, Sweden, Norway, Singapore, New Zealand, Canada, Ireland, Switzerland, Germany	
C+	60-65	UK, Hong Kong, SAR, USA, Malaysia, France	The system has some good features, but at the same time has great risks and disadvantages, without improving such characteristics and eliminating disadvantages, there are no conditions for efficiency and long-term stability of the system.
C	50-60	Peru, Colombia, Poland, Saudi Arabia, Brazil, Spain, Austira, Saouth Africa, Italy, Indonesia	
D	35-50	Korea, China, Japan, India, Mexico, Philippines, Turkey, Argentina, Thailand SERBIA*	The system that has some desirable characteristics, but significant disadvantages and failures, without improving conditions for efficiency and long-term sustainability system, can be questioned.
E	<35	Nil	A poor system that may be in the initial stages of development or inconsistent.

Source: (MMGPI,2019:23)
*Author`s assessment for Serbia, because there were not in research study 40 indicators for Serbia

directions for reform of the pension system are based on this index. So, it eliminates the weaknesses of the pension system.

Australia

Australia`s pension system is on the third place ranking and is among the best countries in the world, with 72,6 overall index value, i.e. points of possible 100 points and Sub-Index Values: Adequacy 63,4; Sustainability 73,8; Integrity 87,7 points. These values are among the best ranking countries in the world. According to Mercer`s study, Australia (the period in 2019) has some disadvantages, which need to do more work in encouraging individual contributions and Australia "needs better integration between the age pension and superannuation, which doesn`t currently provide enough incentive for individuals to contribute." Knox explained that the overall system needs to provide clear additional benefits from making extra contributions. Author Knox thinks that Australia is on the "cusp" of receiving the A-grade when retirement income for average earners would be improved followed by a life expectancy increasing when the asset test would be adjusted. The superannuation guarantee to 12 per cent from 9,5 per cent would improve the pension system. The government would examine three pension pillars, superannuation and voluntary savings, including home ownership, after reviewing retirement income in the previous period (Jones, S., 2019).The recommendations for improving sustainability are increasing household saving and reducing household debt, asset testing age pension for average income earners and increasing the net replacement rate (MMGPI, 2019).

Chile

According to the Overall Pension Index, (2015) pension system of Chile has values: 68,2 in 2014. i 69,1 in 2015. and in 2019. Overall Index Value in 2019. is 68,7, grade B, sub-index values are: adequacy 59,4, grade C, sustainability 71,7, grade B and integrity 79,2, grade B plus. The improvement in the general index and sub-categories was due to increased individual savings. To further improve the adequacy, sustainability, and integrity of the pension system, the following are proposed: 1. increasing contributions to the defined contribution pensionsystem to increase net replacement; 2. permanently increasing individual savings; 3. increasing retirement age and for men and women; 4. continuous monitoring of the sustainability of minimum pensions for the poorest pensioners and pension plans for all members.The Chilean pension system assesses that the pension system is improved, sustainable, has a good structure, with many good features, but some segments require improvements. Chile`s comparative advantages in achieving the reform of the system were: an increase in national income thanks to copper exports, a responsible government, political will, government commitment to the population, diversification of demographic macroeconomic and financial risks.

Serbia – Possible Modalities and Redefining the Existing Pension System

Positive messages based on the experience of Chilean reform are transparency, existence of adequate macroeconomic conditions, employment, financing of the public pension system with about 1/3 of the funds from the state budget, legislation protecting risk insurers, international approach to the supervision of the financial system, the existence of social pensions, political commitment to law-making and adequate social security strategies.

Adequacy of pension benefits is influenced by parameters such as indexation of pensions and raising the retirement age. Countries that have implemented a generous pension adjustment method have been categorized as countries with an adequate pension system, such as Australia and Chile. According to modelled ILO estimate, employment to population ratio, 15+, total (5) for Australia is the best ratio 61 PPS, for Chile is 58 PPS, and Serbia the worst ratio is 47 PPS. (https://data.worldbank.org.)

Unlike the generous indexation method, in other countries with an inadequate pension system, a less adequate method of adjusting pension benefits, which is below the level of financial sustainability, applies, such as Serbia.

FUTURE RESEARCH DIRECTIONS

According to The Global Competitive Index (2019), among the 20 best ranking countries is Australia, which has 16th rank/141, Chile 33rd/141, and Serbia 72nd/141. To restore the Serbian 9th pillar: financial system and stability based on agreement with the International Monetary Fund, Serbia should provide more domestic credits % GDP) for private sector, due to low value 43,3 and score 45,5, and 81 rank between 141 countries, develop financial market and market capitalization (% GDP), due value is 3,2, score is 35,9 and rank is 88. Financial stability has a score of 85,8 and ranks 83rd/141. The next pillar of reform involves strengthening doing business - 11th pillar: business dynamism (The Global Competitive Index, 2019). Staff noted that Serbia should strengthen institutions and improve the business environment and prevent migration of skilled labor and "drain brain" (Republic of Serbia, 2019). The

World Bank Data and report presents differences in combustible renewables and waste (solid biomass, gas, and liquid from biomass, animal products, industrial and municipal waste) (https://data.worldbank.org). Chile has the best value in terms of production combustibles and waste, 11,3 PPS in 2015, then Serbia 7,8 PPS in 2014, and Australia 3,3 PPS in 2015. " Renewable energy in the world is from solid biofuels and hydroelectricity and has been the driver of much of the growth in the global clean energy sector. It is the most economical means of improving energy and reducing greenhouse gas emissions" (https://data.worldbank.org).

The recommendations for Serbia in the coming period are that Serbia should ensure adequate financial and institutional resources for employment and social policies for young, women and long-term unemployed, improve the adequacy of social benefits for people below the poverty threshold and ensure consistent implementation of the labour and social welfare legislation throughout the country (Serbia 2019 Report, 2019). It is possible in a modern circular economy that involves the application of renewable energy and recycling and waste production.

CONCLUSION

Interconnection security and economic growth have been demonstrated, as through private pension funds encourages savings and loans for economic investments. Pension funds pay out benefits only after many years, so use long-term investments insured until the time of their retirement. In this way, the accumulated capital is used for investments, encouraging exports and economic growth, which has a positive impact on national competitiveness. Theoretically and empirically shown that countries with developed financial markets, long-term speaking, have a stable economy and dynamic growth. In developed countries, the insurance had a particular impact on economic growth. In contrast, countries that are in transition and less developed countries should encourage non-life insurance to a greater extent, because it has shown that it affects economic growth alike and in developed and developing countries.In countries in transition, such as the Republic of Serbia, there is an economic crisis, the collapse of a large number of companies in the privatization process and the process of integration and the European Union. Member States and the candidate countries should respect the directives and programs of the European Union in terms of economic restructuring, reforms of pension systems and social inclusion. In Serbia, there was a crisis in the pension system due to the rich of factors such as the high mortality rate, ageing population, the decline in fertility and birth rates, unemployment, inadequate economic structure, inadequate sustainability development, and circular economy, lack of competitiveness of the economy, foreign trade deficit, the deficit in the gross domestic product, as well as public debt.

Appropriate sustainable development and circular economy, economic policies, the choice of suitable foreign partners, the correct choice of greenfield foreign direct investment, would create the conditions for industrial development, increase exports, increase employment and an increase in GDP, which would have a positive impact on the rate increase in net earnings, adequacy of pension compensation and sustainability of the pension system. Establishing a sustainable pension system in Serbia is possible with the implementation of adequate reform. A reformed pension system would provide social and material security at the zero-pillar level formulated by the World Bank. This would primarily provide social pensions for the elderly population who did not qualify for retirement benefits and did not participate in the pension fund (absolute standard of living). To create appropriate conditions for the second pillar, according to the World Bank formulation, i.e. conditions of relative standard of living, corresponding to the public pension system in Serbia, it is necessary to take measures to restructure the economy primarily for the benefit of the ecological industry, as well as agriculture, because Serbia is predominantly an agricultural country.

Recommendations for a sustainable pension system are to create institutional conditions, financial resources and other macroeconomic conditions for employment, to provide adequate benefits for retirees and all the population below the poverty line. Assuming effective state action, the sustainability of the pension system would be achievable, by developing a circular economy, increasing employment and boosting exports. This would increase the competitiveness of the economy and the sustainability of Serbia's green development. Higher-level of national savings would influence to reduce pension costs in the state budget and would reduce the deficit in the pension fund and increase the pension benefits in Serbia. The authors conclude that the application of good practice examples of developed countries such as Australia, Chile, et al. possible in Serbia, provided that all three pillars of sustainability, respectively the economic, social and environmental component, are taken into account while leading the appropriate national macroeconomic policy at the highest level. The sustainability of the pension system, the sustainability of the circular economy, or macroeconomic stability in Serbia will depend on political decision-makers.

ACKNOWLEDGMENT

This research received no specific grant from any funding agency in the public, commercial, or not-for-profit sectors.

REFERENCES

Altiparmakov, N. & Matkovic, G. (2018). The development of private pensions in Serbia: caught between a generic blueprint and an unconducive local environment. Transfer: *European Review of Labor and Research, 24*, 57-71. 10.1177/1024258917746033

Arsic, M., Randjelovic, S. & Altiparmakov, N. (2018). Shadow Economy Trends in Serbia: 2012-2017. *Quarterly Monitor*, *52*(1-3), 51-58.

Bijlsma, M., Beonekamp, J., van Ewijk, C., & Haaijen, F. (2018). Funded Pensions and Economic Growth. *De Economist*, *166*(3). Retrieved from: https://pure.uva.nl/ws/files/28168930/10.1007_s10645_018_9325_z.pdf

Brunetti, A., Kisunko, G., & Weder, B. (1999). *Institutions in Transition, Reliability of Rules and Economic Performance in Former Socialist Countries*. Retrieved from: https://elibrary.worldbank.org/doi/abs/10.1596/1813-9450-1809

Carroll, C. D., Hall, R. E., & Zeldes, S. P. (1992). The buffer-stock theory of saving: Some macroeconomic evidence. *Brookings Papers on Economic Activity*, *1*(2), 61–156. doi:10.2307/2534582

Davis, P. E., & Hu, Y. W. (2004). *Handbook of Pensions and Retirement Income*. London: Brunel University.

Deaton, A. (2005). Franco Modigliani and the Life-cycle Theory of Consumption. *PSL Quarterly Review*, *5*(58), 233–234. doi:10.2139srn.686475

Dustin, D. W. (2019). *Understanding state pension challenges: a primer for Sheeos*. The State Higher Education Executive Officers Association. Retrieved from https://sheeo.org/wp-content/uploads/2019/09/SHEEO_UnderstandingStatePensionChallenges

Economic Performance in Former Socialist Countries. (n.d.). *Institutions in transition: reliability of rules and economic performance in former Socialist countries* (English). Retrieved from: http://documents.worldbank.org/curated/en/423111468766541642/Institutions-in-transition-reliability-of-rules-and-economic-performance-in-former-Socialist-countries

Holzmann, R., & Hinz, R. (Eds.). (2005). *Old-Age Income Support in the 21st Century: an international perspective on pension systems and reform*. Washington, DC: The World Bank. doi:10.1596/0-8213-6040-X

Impacts of circular economy policies on the labour market:Final report and Annexes. (2018). Brussels: European Commission (EC). Retrieved from: https://circulareconomy.europa.eu/platform/sites/default/files/ec_2018_-_impacts_of_circular_economy_policies_on_the_labour_market.pdf

Jones, S. (2019, Oct. 21). Australia ranks third in the world`s best pension systems. *Investment Magazine: Retirement*. Retrieved from: https://www.investmentmagazine.com.au/2019/10/australia-ranks-third-in-worlds-best-pension-systems/

Knox, D. (2019). *Melbourne Mercer Global Pension Index (MMGPI)*. Melbourne: Monash Centre for Financial Studies.

Kudrna, G., Tran, C., & Woodland, A. (2014). *The Dynamic Fiscal Effects of Demographic Shift: the case of Australia*. ANU Working Papers in Economics and Econometrics: Australian National University.

Leland, H. E. (1968). Saving and Uncertainty: The precautionary demand for saving. *The Quarterly Journal of Economics*, *3*(82), 465–473. doi:10.2307/1879518

Merton, R. C. (1970). *Analytical optimal control theory as applied to stochastic and non-stochastic economics*. Institute of Technology.

MMGP Index, . (2015). Melbourne: Mercer Company. Retrieved from https://www.mercer.com/content/dam/mercer/attachments/global/Retirement/Melbourne-Mercer-Global-Pension-Index-2015/Report.pdf

MMGP Index, . (2019). Melbourne: Mercer Company. Retrieved from https://info.mercer.com/rs/521-DEV-513/images/MMGPI%202019%20Full%20Report.pdf

Modigliani, F. (1985). *Life Cycle, Individual Thrift and the Wealth of Nations* Economic Sciences. Retrieved from https://www.nobelprize.org/nobel_prizes/economic-sciences/laureates/1985/modigliani-lecture.pdf

Petrovic, P. (2010). Economic crisis in Serbia. In V. Bartlet & V. Monastiriotis (Eds.), *South Eastern Europe after the Crisis*. Retrieved from http://www.lse.ac.uk/LSEE-Research-on-South-Eastern-Europe/Assets/Documents/Publications/Other/SEE-After-the-Crisis-Bartlett-Monastiriotis-eds.pdf

Ratanabanchuen, R. (2013). *Demographic Transition, Pension Schemes' Investment, and the Financial Market*. London: London School of Economics and Political Sciences.

Republic of Serbia. (2019). *IMF Country Report, No. 19/238.*Washington, DC: International Monetary Fund (IMF). Retrieved from: https://www.imf.org/en/Publications/CR/Issues/2019/07/22/Republic-of-Serbia-Staff-Report-for-the-2019-Article-IV-Consultation-and-Second-Review-under-48511

Rizos, V., Tuokko, K., & Behrens, A. (2017). The Circular Economy: A review of definitions, processes and impacts. CEE Research Report/8. Brussels: Energy Climate House.

Samuelson, P. A. (1952). Economic Theory and Mathematics – An Appraisal. *The American Economic Review*, *2*(42), 56–66.

Samuelson, P. A. (1954). The Pure Theory of Public Expenditure. *The Review of Economics and Statistics*, *36*(4), 387–389. doi:10.2307/1925895

Santen, P. C. V. (2013). *Precautionary Saving, Wealth Accumulation, and Pensions: an empirical Macroeconomic perspective*. Groningen: University of Groningen. Retrieved from https://www.netspar.nl/assets/uploads/001_PhD_Peter_van_Santen.pdf

Schwab, K. (Ed.). (2019). *The Global Competitiveness Report*. Geneva: World Economic Forum WEF. Retrieved from http://www3.weforum.org/docs/WEF_TheGlobalCompetitivenessReport2019.pdf

Serbia. (2019). *Report: Commission staff working document*. EC. Retrieved from: https://ec.europa.eu/neighbourhood-enlargement/sites/near/files/20190529-serbia-report.pdf

Serbian Pensioners' Union. (n.d.). Independence. *Retrieved from*.http://nezavisnost.org/sindikat-penzionera-srbije-nezavisnost-i-saveza-penzionera-srbije-potpisali-sporazum-o-saradnji/#

The Aging Report. (2018). *Underlying Assumptions & Projection methodologies*. European Economy. Institutional Paper, 065, November 2017. European Commission.

The International Bank for Reconstruction and Development, The World Bank. (1994). Averting the Old Age Crisis: policies to protect the old and promote growth. A World Bank Policy Research Report. New York: Oxford University Press.

Valdes-Prieto, S. (2006). A Market Method to Endow NDC Systems with Automatic Financial Stability. In R. Holzmann & E. Palmer (Eds.), *Pension Reform: Issues and prospects for Non-Financial Defined Contribution (NDC) Schemes* (pp. 149–150). Washington, DC: The World Bank.

World Bank Open Data. (n.d.). *Countries and Economies*. Retrieved from: https://data.worldbank.org

ADDITIONAL READING

Cesaratto, S. (2006). Transition to fully funded pension schemes: A non-orthodox criticism. *Cambridge Journal of Economics*, *1*(30), 33–48. doi:10.1093/cje/bei046

EMVCAPITAL. (2016). The Circular Economy Opportunity And Institutional Investors. Retrieved from:https://emvcapital.com/the-circular-economy-opportunity-and-institutional-investors/

Forbes (2019). Why Blackrock's New Circular Economy Fund is a Big Half-Step in the Right Direction. Retrieved from: https://www.forbes.com/sites/robkaplan/2019/10/14/why-blackrocks-new-circular-economy-fund-is-a-big-half-step-in-the-right-direction/#7a5eeb53182c

Harvey, D. (2010). *The Enigma of Capital*. London, England: Profile Books.

National Bank of Serbia - Insurance Supervision Department. (2019). *Voluntary Pension Funds Sector in* Serbia -Third Quarter Report. Retrieved from:https://www.nbs.rs/internet/english/62/62_2/vpf_III_19.pdf

Silk, L. (1976). *The Economists*. New York: Basic Books.

Sobel, R. (1980). *Worldly Economists*. New York: Free Press.

KEY TERMS AND DEFINITIONS

AR: Aging report.

CARA: Constant absolute risk aversion.

CRRA: Constant relative risk aversion.

EC: European Commission.

ILO: International Labour Organization.

IMF: International Monetary Fund.

MMGPI: Melbourne Mercer Global Pension Index.

OLG Model: Overlapping generations model.

PAYG: Pay as you go, requires individuals to fund their own retirement savings accounts with a portion of their earned income.

SILC: Survey on income and living conditions.

WEF: World Economic Forum.

Chapter 8
Implementation of Circular Practices in Small and Medium Enterprises in Developing Countries

Michael Torres-Franco
https://orcid.org/0000-0001-9891-5871
Universidad EAN, Colombia

Valentina Villamil
Universidad EAN, Colombia

ABSTRACT

New forms of production and consumption seek greater respect for the environment and the environment in which economic agents are. This has led to circular business practices becoming more important and generating benefits in the final product. This chapter will show the relationship between this practice and SMEs, the problems faced by these companies, and the benefits that this practice can generate for the growth and competitiveness of organizations. The chapter will show in its first part the evolution of the circular economy, and then explain the relationship between it and the SMEs, highlighting the problems and obstacles faced by these companies to implement best practices in production. Finally, recommendations are given to facilitate the implementation of this practice in companies.

INTRODUCTION

There is currently a great debate about the damage that for many years' humanity has done to the environment and the availability of resources; which are used without some measure and with the belief in their perpetual availability. This debate is given by the different information that shows the effects of climate change, the melting of polar ice caps, "continents" of garbage in the oceans, food waste in decomposition, industrial development in some nations and other actions that occur throughout the world.

DOI: 10.4018/978-1-7998-5116-5.ch008

Copyright © 2020, IGI Global. Copying or distributing in print or electronic forms without written permission of IGI Global is prohibited.

This undoubtedly has led businessmen, rulers and civil society in general to rethink the production and consumption model, seeking with these new paradigms that allow changing the situation and the problems that will be noticed for the future. The first major change that is intended is focused on production, so that it is cleaner, and the different goods produced can be reused; extending the life of products and reducing the effect of these on the environment. The other major change that is sought at the level of society is related to consumption. For years, a culture of consumption was fostered in which the production chain and the inputs used did not matter, if it was in the latest trend. Currently, it is responsible for responsible consumption, where consumers are demanding not only quality products but also being fair to their workers and the environment; in addition to this, consumers have been forcing companies to carry out practices focused on recycling or reuse of products.

These new trends in production and consumption should lead to thinking about how to take advantage of the changes so that small and medium-sized companies increase the opportunities to compete in the market and even reach new markets. Clearly the decision and the possibility of implementing new and better production practices will depend to a large extent on the capabilities and resources available to the company, for this reason the ways that allow the massification of these practices in all companies must be thought of and created and not reserve these developments for large companies with greater capital.

Probably in developed countries and specifically in big companies, the idea to implement circular practices is not difficult at all, these kind of companies have financial strength and they can generate process inside the company in order to guarantee the reuse or recycling or the remanufacturing of products or inputs used in the production; also they have the capacity to negotiate with suppliers in order to buy more and better inputs, with a better cost in the productive structure; aspect that has a huge importance in managerial decisions.

The problem is for the Small and Medium Enterprises (SME's), this kind of companies can be more that the 80% of the total number of companies in countries, even in some countries this category of company reach the 95% (in developing countries). There is huge number of small companies with short or limited resources that block the possibility to implement changes in production and in the stage after the client use. This is one problem, the other can be the degree of knowledge that owners have about this topic, probably is none, and obviously the need to change the production is not going to be in the agenda. A third problem can be faced, legislation in developing countries is still now in creation phase, so there is a lot of voids and lack of regulation that reduce the probability that producers implement this practice.

For those reasons, the purpose of this chapter is to show how circular economy has been developed in small and medium enterprises; from this, determine the ease or complexity that the implementation of circular practices can occur in this category of companies; showing the barriers that SMEs have and their degree of impact on the implementation of circular practices.

In order to do the above, the following research question has been established: *¿What are the barriers that avoid an adequate implementation of circular practices in small and medium enterprises?* with a special focus on developing countries. This problem question will allow, based on the determination of these barriers in the SMEs, to see not only the difficulties that these companies face, but also to generate possible proposals or strategies that allow them to solve this situation to achieve greater success to when implementing circular practices in production.

The formulation of the previous problem question leads to different hypotheses that allow further investigation and the chapter. As a first hypothesis was developed: H1: *Circular economy implementation in Small and Medium Enterprises has been complicated, especially in developing countries.* The second hypothesis was H2: *Circular economy implementation requires large investment, and sometimes Small and Medium Enterprises do not have financial capacity to perform it.*

As research objectives, the following were determined: (1) Define the circular economy, with special focus in SME's (after a previous definition and delimitation of this company category - SME, and a special focus in developing countries). (2) Stablish and explain barriers that companies must implement circular practices in the productive process. (3) Determine the process and strategies to implement circular practices in small and medium enterprises, guarantying quality and competitiveness in the whole stages of the productive process.

The chapter will be organized as follows: the first section will show the background of both the circular economy and the implementation of this practice in SMEs. The next section will show what are the problems and barriers that these companies face not only in the application of these practices both in production and in distribution and competition. At the end of this section the results of an investigation carried out in different establishments of the city of Bogotá (Colombia) on the degree of knowledge of the circular economy and its implementation in the operations of these companies will be shown, to better understand the perspective of these Businessmen about this practice. The third section will show the solutions and recommendations that can help to more easily implement these practices at the business level. Finally, it will show where we are going with the implementation of these practices in SME and the conclusions on this topic.

BACKGROUND OF THE CIRCULAR ECONOMY AND SMALL AND MEDIUM ENTERPRISES

Circular Economy, Definition and Evolution

The industrial revolution of the 18th century allowed to improve the production system prevailing up to that moment, and in addition to that it managed to allow the owners of the factors of production to see the form and the possibility of maximizing profits by implementing technological solutions in the production chain; this has been known as linear production and became the production model until the end of the 20th century.

This does not mean that there have been no significant developments in the production systems over the years, although this situation occurred, the motivation for this never ceased to be the maximization of profits; but the relationship between industrial production and the environment was never considered; which was generating systemic imbalances that gave birth to new forms of production during the last twenty years (Garbie, 2014). The linear production model is structured with a production sequence in which raw materials are extracted, transported, manufactured and processed in a wide range of products; which will be distributed to different consumers and will be consumed, generating different wastes that have effects on the environment.

The problem with this system is its undeniable effect on the environment and its poor sustainability, to the extent that production and consumption carried out irresponsibly leads to increased CO2 emissions, global warming, lack of raw materials, constant damage to natural resources (especially non-renewable) and air pollution from water sources (Geissdoerfer, Savaget, Bocken, & Hultink, 2017).

The effects derived from linear production and, in a certain way, from irresponsibility and lack of awareness regarding the environment led to new paradigms that allowed to maintain industrial production, the desire for greater utilities and at the same time the generation of responsible production with the environment (Ghisellini, Cialani, & Ulgiati, 2016). This gave way to the concept of "circular economy", which was gaining weight and acceptance over the years. This concept focuses on circularity in production, raw materials, inputs and energy use throughout the economic cycle (Masi, Kumar, Garza-Reyes, & Godsell, 2018). Bastein et al (2013) describe circular economy as an industrial economy, focused in showing the "restorative capacity of natural resources".

The circular economy is then based on moving from the concept of *cradle to grave* to *cradle to cradle*, which implies the generation of a *close loop system* that is based on recycling and reuse of products (Bocken N., De Pauw, Bakker, & Van der Grinten, 2016). Faced with this, Stahel (1981) stated that it was a *slow replacement system* that allowed to extend the life of the products. In this regard, Stahel (1994), McDonough and Braungart (2002) argue that two strategies must be established for the development of circular practices in industries; on the one hand the *slowing resource loops* (design of products with a longer life cycle) and the *closing resource loops* (close the distance between subsequent use and production, which generates a circular flow of resources). These strategies must be accompanied by a constant effort to reduce the resources used to produce.

One of the great advantages of the use of circular practices in production is that eventually a reduction in the use of energy, materials and environmental impact is achieved without restricting economic, social and technical progress; On the contrary, a greater potential for these can be achieved as products are maintained in the economy and reused, remanufactured or recycled in other activities (Lacy & Rutqvist, 2015).

Two graphs are shown below, taken form the Global Resource Outlook 2019 (Oberle, et al., 2019); the first one shows the projection of expenditure or use of natural resources, focused mainly on those that are not renewable. For its part, the second graph relates the level of income of the countries with the use or participation of natural resources in their foreign trade. These graphs allow us to see that the level of resource consumption increases exponentially every year and that middle-income countries are the ones that most pressure this resource consumption. Both graphs allow us to conclude that both production and consumption are being done irresponsibly, without taking into account that many of these resources are not renewable and will become scarce at any given time, hence the importance of thinking about practices that allow reducing use of resources and have cleaner production and consumption.

The economic development of nations leads to constant demand for natural resources and the creation of companies, which in their eagerness to achieve market shares undertake industrialization processes that sometimes do not consider the environmental damage that may arise. This same report shows how the plans implemented by manufacturing companies have led to reducing emissions, waste and even production costs. However, examples of developed countries such as the United States, the European Union and even China are seen; with large companies and supported by government policies for the development of circular practices (Oberle, et al., 2019). The examples or policies in developing countries are much scarcer or practically non-existent, which shows not only the deficiency or nonexistence of government policies but the weakness of the companies, which do not have the financial resources or knowledge to develop these practices.

It is worth considering not only what the circular economy is but those principles on which it is based, as expressed by the Ellen MacArthur Foundation; (i) preserve and strengthen natural capital through the control of finite resources and balance the flow of renewable resources. (ii) optimize the performance of resources through the circulation of products, components and materials as much as possible; and (iii) create effective systems that allow identifying and facing negative externalities (EMF, 2013). These

Figure 1. Extractions by major category. Million tons.
Source: International Resource Panel (Oberle, et al., 2019)

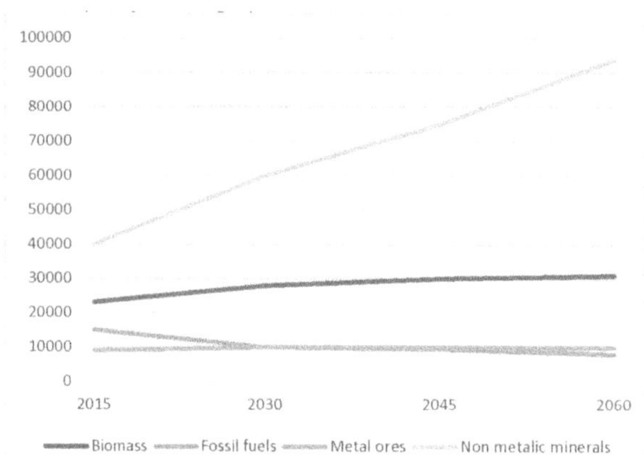

principles should allow both governments and companies to generate policies and strategies that lead to the development of circular practices in production; with a special focus on those companies that have less financial and human resources.

At present, there is a great consensus among developed countries, especially Europeans, among academics, businessmen and politicians regarding the importance of implementing a new model where the materials and energy used can be reintroduced to the economic system (Lehmann, De Leeuw, & Fehr, 2014). Circular economy will then focus on the handling of two different types of materials; those that can return to the biosphere as feedstock, and those technical materials that cannot be degraded or enter the atmosphere (Bicket, et al., 2014).

Up to this point a simple radiography of the circular economy and its main bases can be seen; but what is meant by small and medium business? And what are the limitations that these types of companies face? These points will be addressed in the next section with a special focus on the developing countries,

Figure 2. Deviation in economic activity and services. Towards sustainability vs. Historical trend. Tonnes per capita
Source: International Resource Panel (Oberle, et al., 2019)

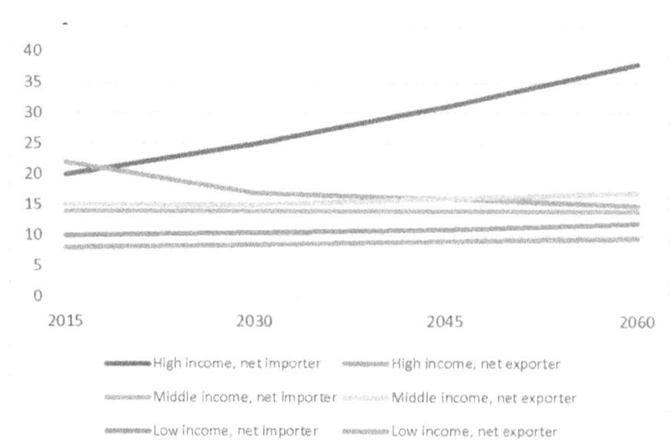

where these companies represent more than 90% of the total amount of companies and generate products and wastes that are not well treated.

Small and Medium Enterprises in Developing Countries

Although across countries the delimitations or ranges to be considered a company as small or large may be different, the OECD offers a general definition in this regard, saying that SMEs are independent non-subsidiary companies that employ a small number of workers, usually 250 workers, although in the United States there may be 500. Within this category of companies, we can talk about small companies that are those with a maximum of 50 employees and micro companies that can have 10 or even 5 employees (OECD, 2005).

The importance of SME's for a country will be that these types of companies are characterized by being or having started as family businesses, which in their evolution manage to include more people and reach all types of economic sectors or populations; and in remote places or rural areas they tend to be the livelihoods of families, helping to reduce unemployment rates and somehow improving economic and social development.

Within the delimitation mentioned above, financial resources are also considered, which will vary greatly depending on the country under analysis. Below are different countries with their categorizations on this type of companies. For the analysis of table 1 it should be considered that values shown were taken from different sources, each of them was calculated with an average exchange rate to try to level the existing disparities between countries and their respective exchange rates. These values reflect the size and economic structure of the different countries.

As can be seen in the previous table, the classification of this type of companies depends on each country, although there is some consensus or similarity between the countries regarding the number of employees to hire, in the financial aspect it is where more differences are presented, even though thc countries shown are of similar levels of development, they belong to the same region of the world (except for a couple of examples) and are classified as developing countries.

These differences are mainly due to the legal systems in each country, the size and needs of each economy; since the larger the economy of a nation, its companies will be larger and therefore have an even greater financial strength that leads to legislation changing in terms of requirements and requirements to be in determining group or business classification. It should also be borne in mind that the financial and operational capacities of these companies may be affected by the subsidies or incentives that governments grant; in developing countries, the ability to grant subsidies is lower than in developed economies, which leads to companies not having the same capabilities when compared to others of similar category but in different countries. This situation will also depend on the legal framework of the nations, since the granting of these grants may or may not be allowed due to legal issues.

Other investigations define SMEs as companies formally registered with government entities, pay taxes, allow employees to enter the labor market and join social security, develop the skills and abilities of employees, and allow investing capital in the development of the same (Gibson & Van der Vaart, 2008).

According to the statistics that OECD manages, 95% of companies and on average 65% of employment is generated by SME within the countries of this organization (OCDE, 2000). It highlights in that report the immense difficulties that these companies are facing for their consolidation in the market, as well as the urgency in the implementation of policies that allow this. This dynamic has not changed over

Table 1. Delimitation of SME according to the country or region (people and thousands of USD)

				Micro		Small		Medium	
	Employees	**Sales**	**Assets**	**Employees**	**VALUE**	**Employees**	**VALUE**	**Employees**	**VALUE**
Argentina		X			493,4		2.960,5		23.683,9
Bolivia	X	X	X	10	30	20	400	49	1.200
Brazil	X			19		99		199	
Chile	X	X		9	91	49	947,4	199	3.789,7
Colombia	X		X	10	108	50	1080	200	6480
Costa Rica	X	X	X	10	65,0	30	227,6	100	650,3
European Union	X	X	X	10	2.803,1	50	14.015,4	250	60.266
Guatemala	X			10		25		60	
India			X		34		680		1,3 mlls
Japan	X					20		300	
Mexico	X			10		50		250	
Peru	X	X		9	178,1	20	2.081,1	100	
Uruguay	X	X	X	4	0.02	19	0.05	99	0.35
Venezuela	X	X		10	230,8	50	2.564,6	100	6.411,5

Source: own elaboration based on United Nations ECLAC (CEPAL, 2009).

time and it is seen that both the importance and participation of SMEs in the economy and the different problems and obstacles they face for the development of their operations persist.

Beyond these figures, it is necessary to recognize and highlight the importance that these companies have for the business fabric of a nation and for its development. Many SMEs are created in cities, but in the same way in rural areas, allowing for greater development in these places; but in addition to this it allows to generate employment and to take advantage of the capacities of the population, as well as to develop them within the company and its workers (Tambunan, 2007). The development of SMEs allows greater economic and social growth, hence the importance of promoting them and allowing their endurance over time.

What can be concluded from the information shown above, in addition to the differences in conception that exist regarding SMEs, which is logical given the differences and sizes of the economies; is that these companies do not usually have a great financial strength, quite the contrary, they are quite sensitive to economic turbulence or the situations that may arise. This financial weakness attracts other complications for companies, not being able to make large investments that allow them to technify and improve processes or train their employees in the management of new technologies; this is a very big limitation for the implementation of circular practices in companies.

In the next section will be analyzed the barriers that SMEs face when implementing circular practices, some of these barriers could even be the explanation for many of these companies' problems and their low market survival rate; but as these are barriers, they can be understood as variables that would allow the development and implementation of circular practices in companies.

IMPLEMENTATION OF CIRCULAR PRACTICES IN SME'S

Barriers to Circular Economy Implementation on SME's

The circular economy is based on sustainability, as shown in previous sections; The idea of this is to be able to provide products, their parts and supplies with a new "life", thus achieving a lower impact on the environment and generating more sustainable products. In this section will be analyzed the main barriers faced by the circular practice in companies, mainly in those small companies that are in developing countries; but first those barriers that sustainability faces will be shown, since it is the base and the destination that is to be achieved with these circular practices in production.

The literature on sustainability and its application in small and medium enterprises has shown that there are both internal and external barriers to sustainability. Lewis et al (2015) show how communication and business relationships affect the implementation of sustainable practices. In addition to this barrier, they also found that the structure of the organization, the limited capacity for absorption, the lack of resources, legislation and knowledge on the impacts of sustainability; they become more barriers for SME.

On the other hand, Meath et al (2016) when studying both the barriers and the generators of barriers for SMEs, the result of the investigation showed the strong influence of the internal barriers in these companies, where lack of time, lease permits and acquired commitments hinder sustainable practices in these companies. Tsalis (2013), on the other hand, using statistical tools and a SWOT analysis of the opinions of managers and owners about sustainability in the SME, managed to identify barriers such as lack of financial resources and organizational structure.

Mbuyisa and Leonard (2015) found that one of the great barriers is the implementation of information, communication and technology (ICT) solutions, in addition to this the lack of financing, the lack of knowledge in the possibilities offered by the implementation of ICT solutions, the low qualification of the workforce and the low applicability of ICT solutions for SME end up creating a series of inflexibilities for these types of companies, which, although they focus on technological developments, are of concern as long as sustainability and circular practices strongly support this type of development.

Table 2 shows the different barriers to which an SME is exposed and that prevent it from implementing circular practices in its operational processes. As can be seen, these barriers cover different aspects that range from financial to the construction of a legal apparatus that supports and encourages the development of these practices.

These barriers can be synthesized into even simpler categories that allow understanding the main complications and obstacles that companies, especially SME's must face in the road to be "greener". Rizos et al (2015) established 7 barriers that group others together, including those mentioned in the previous table. These barriers are shown below.

Environmental Culture

Many of the SMEs in developing countries (without saying that this situation does not occur in developed countries) have a family organization and direction; in addition, the manager is often the same owner of the company, which positively or negatively affects the decisions and the way that are taken in the organization. Regarding the attitude they have towards green businesses, there is no clear trend regarding this, there are some that remain in the previous linear production trend and others that are

Table 2. Explanation of barriers to implement circular practices in SME's

Barriers	Explanation
Lack of industry incentives for 'greener' activities. **Lack of implementation of environmental management certifications and systems.**	These barriers refer to the lack of support by government entities to implement "green activities" and environmental management systems in the industry. Emphasizing that the lack of these aspects is considered as a significant obstacle in the case of developing countries.
Lack of environmental laws and regulations. **Lack of preferential tax policies for promoting the circular models.**	These barriers speak of the lack of regulations in the care of the environment and the lack of policies for the promotion of circular models. Being these considered as important factors of the social responsibility of the companies and facilitating the implementation of the circular economy in an effective way.
Lack of Management commitment and approach for CSCM adoption	This barrier is based on the lack of commitment that the administration of companies has to have an effective circular economy framework. The non-implementation of CSCM directly affects the circular model to be executed.
Lack of effective planning and management for CSCM concepts **Lack of middle and lower level managers' support and involvement in promoting 'greener' products.**	These barriers highlight the importance of the support of the administrators in the promotion of green products, additionally we have that the resources must be managed optimally, to reduce the environmental impact and in this way an effective CSCM model would be applied.
Lack of customer awareness and participation around CSC activities **Poor demand/ acceptance for environmentally superior technologies** **Lack of technology transfers** **Inadequacy in knowledge and awareness of organizational members about CSCM initiatives** **Lack of support and participation of stakeholders**	This group of barriers is made up of the technological aspects that are sought to be implemented in the corporation and how the lack of support can stall the innovation processes, causing the obstacles to the sustainable models that are to be promoted. In addition, the importance of technology transfer (developed country to developing country) is highlighted, to improve effectiveness towards CSC initiatives. In these processes, customers are a fundamental part since they are the ones who guide companies to make changes in their products. The lack of superior environmental technology is tight to the acceptance of circular models in the supply chain.
Lack of appropriate training and development programmers for SC members and HR **Lack of coordination and collaboration among SC members**	These barriers are born due to the lack of collaboration among all the members of the company's supply chain, adding the misinformation that each participant can have for the optimization of resources and the care of the environment. If the company does not have a coordination by all the members of the chain, the implementation of an adequate circular model can be stopped, considering an industrial context.
Lack of systematic information systems	This barrier refers to the lack of implementation of information systems obtains the development of circular models. When designing information systems, it is considered easier to maintain order in the organization by talking about superior ecological and financial means to plan and manage resources.
Lack of economic benefits in short run	This barrier addresses the short-term economic problems that companies pass through. This is because when companies focus on short-term environmental issues, there is a loss of value, leading to the creation of an initial internal barrier in any decision-making process, where as a result there is the obtaining of CSCM adoption.

Source: own elaboration based on Mangla, et al. (2018).

more receptive to this change in trend, the different authors suggest that the decision taken will depend a lot on the sector in which the company operates (Bradford & Fraser, 2007).

Financial Barriers

The first difficulty is in the costs of implementing and developing circular economy. This initial investment has longer periods of return on investment, which affects the cash flow of SMEs (Hollins, 2011). Other studies show that in many cases SMEs do not have sufficient resources to implement a recycling scheme and even, the waste collection and recycling process turns out to be less economical for these companies (Tura, et al., 2019). There are other indirect costs such as time and human resources necessary to develop these plans, which end up becoming critical aspects and major obstacles to the implementation of green practices (WRAP, 2011).

Different studies show that the smaller the company, the more difficult it is to access financing or government programs, mainly due to personnel limitations or even management restrictions (Hoevenagel, Brummelkamp, Peytcheva, & Van der Horst, 2007). On the other hand, when requesting financing with traditional banks, SMEs face difficulties with the presentation of guarantees required by these entities, since for the financial sector these companies are highly risky at the financial level (Muller & Tuncer, 2013).

Lack of Government Support and Effective Legislation

This is an aspect that affects SME's directly and strongly, since the legislation is usually created without distinguishing between small and large companies (Calogirou, et al., 2014), for this reason it is usually more complicated for small companies to comply with the legislation or obtaining funds or aid from the government (Rutherfoord, Blackburn, & Spence, 2000); this means that legal compliance, regardless of the issue at hand, is due more to a manager's commitment than to a true conviction on his part (Hillary, 2004).

Lack of Information

The lack of information or the lack of knowledge about what circular economy is, its benefits and its implementation help explain why many SMEs do not yet implement this practice. Different studies show that companies do not see the benefits of being more efficient in resource management and a strong belief that this management is expensive; which ultimately affects the implementation of circular practice (Radamaekers, Berg, & Asaad, 2011). In a survey of different establishments in the city of Bogotá (capital of Colombia) as part of a characterization of small and medium-sized companies, the companies surveyed showed little, practically no knowledge regarding this practice, and those who said they knew it, believed that high costs did not justify the development of circular practices. The above demonstrates how there is still a high ignorance regarding the circular economy and what it implies for organizations.

Administrative Burden

The administrative burden refers to the effects of the application of legislative measures by SMEs; These charges translate into money and time that companies lose or stop receiving. This is mainly due to the lack of knowledge of the companies that allows them to apply the regulatory changes; which leads to the hiring of consultants; this can be a significant cost for these companies, which are not able to deal with costs that negatively affect the company's profits (Oosterhuis, 2006).

Lack of Technical Skills

This is one of the most important and biggest barriers that SMEs face when implementing circular practices, which means that companies cannot take advantage of the opportunities and benefits of the green economy (Trianni & Cagno, 2012; Radamaekers, Berg, & Asaad, 2011). This barrier is understood as not having the technical capacity to identify, appropriate and implement advanced techniques or cutting-edge technology that allows reducing negative impacts on the environment and reducing costs. Entrepreneurs will prioritize the technology they already know and with which they are most familiar about the new one they don't know and that requires a certain level of technical skills and knowledge.

Lack of Support From the Supply and Demand Network

This last point refers to the lack of market support, focusing on the possible shortage of suppliers and the lack of interest in environmental issues by suppliers and consumers (Meqdadi, Johnsen, & Johnsen, 2012). In the case of consumers, usually other factors such as price are usually the most influential in the purchase decision, not environmental care by the company or the product (Wycherly, 1999). In the case of suppliers, many of these are reluctant to implement green practices in their production processes, since this increases their cost structure and therefore the final value of the input (Wooi & Sailani, 2009). This barrier becomes very important as it affects the supply chain of the product that is being offered to the final customer.

Process to Implement Circular Practices in SME´s

As mentioned in the previous section, the implementation of circular practices presents a series of barriers, but in turn these can become the necessary elements for the development of circular practices in SMEs. Faced with this, it is not possible to state with certainty what is required as the basis for the development of circular practices in companies, if the motivation and capabilities within the organization or the legal and governmental structure that creates the motivations for entrepreneurs to develop these practices. Each entrepreneur lives in a context and a reality different from that of the others; for this reason, making a statement in this regard is extremely risky by generalization. Something that can be said is that SME managers in developing countries are just turning and understanding the need to implement these practices in their production units, in order to access new consumers, a transit that is not being easy and that is being slow in a way.

Beyond what is stated in the previous paragraph, to guarantee the success of this process, companies must integrate circular practices from the earliest stages of the operation, which means that the product must be designed to meet this need, since if the product or service is being produced, the necessary changes will be larger and more expensive. Below are some strategies that allow companies to close or delay the cycle and generate greener products.

Design Strategies for Slowing Resource Loops

This strategy goes to the point of extending the time of use of products, which means less use of resources. In order to implement this strategy in the company, the way to create products with a longer life must be sought (this is achieved by products that generate more consumer confidence and have a design that allows this, basically physical durability) (Chapman, 2005; Bakker, Ariadne-Bakker, Den Hollander, Van Hinte, & Zijlstra, 2014) and extend the life of the product (through maintenance, repairs, improvements, standardization and compatibility and the possibility of reassembly) (Linton & Jayraman, 2005).

Design Long Life Products

This strategy implies that the products must be "loved" by consumers, a certain emotional link must be generated with the product to prevent it from being discarded after its first use. There must be in addition to the emotional design, a design for its durability in terms of the physical and the endurance that the product must have (Chapman, 2005). In addition to the above, there must be a reliability design that allows a long product life in terms of the operating capacity it can have without having load or energy failures (Moss, 1985).

Design for Product Life Extension

This strategy seeks to increase the time of use of the product through additional services such as reuse, maintenance, repair, technical improvement or combination of these practices (EFNMS, n.d.). Whether the product has these possibilities will depend on what the producer plans for this purpose and the capabilities he must print them to the final product (Linton & Jayraman, 2005). The producer must consider the possibility and ease of repairing the product, the ability to make expansions and modifications, that its parts have the possibility of being changed or used in another product (Bakker, Ariadne-Bakker, Den Hollander, Van Hinte, & Zijlstra, 2014; Crowther, 1999). Basically, the product must be thought of in order to increase the reuse rate and enters different cycles (biological and technological).

Design for Closing Resource Loops

This strategy is based on the spirit of Cradle to Cradle design; in which the materials used in production are part of a circular flow, relying on recycling to achieve it. The producer's effort lies in thinking of products with components that can fulfill this philosophy and have easy recycling.

Design for a Technological and Biological Cycle

In both cases the cycle is based on the possibility of reusing waste produced both in production and in the post-consumption phase of the products and ensure that the new product has the same properties as the initial one (Boulding, 2013). Products must be created with reusable components in the case of those that are part of a technological cycle, or with biodegradable materials in the case where the biological cycle leads to the biodegradation of the product and components (Hopewell, Dvorak, & Kosior, 2009).

Based on Bocket et al (2016) work, there are some other strategies that can help to develop and implement circular practices in companies depending on the business model, tool that will define the

Table 3. Business model strategies for slowing the loop

Business Model Strategies	Definition	Examples
Access and performance model	Providing the capability to satisfy user needs without needing to own physical products	Car sharing, launderettes, product leasing
Extending product value	Exploiting residual value of products or collection of products between distinct business entities	Clothing return initiatives, cash for products and reselling products
Classic long-life model	Business models focused on delivering long-product life, supported in design, durability and repair	White goods, luxury products
Encourage sufficiency	Solutions that seek to reduce end user consumption based on durability, upgradability, service, warranty and reparability	Premium, high service and quality brands, energy service companies
Extending resource value	Exploiting the residual value of resources	Interface, RecycleBank initiative
Industrial symbiosis	A process-oriented solution, concerned with using residual outputs	Kalundborg Eco-Industrial Park

Source: taken from Bocken et al (2016)

architecture of the enterprise and what will be done. Also, business model will help to create new products or new processes. The following table shows the strategies that can be implemented to slow the loops and reach circular practices in companies.

SOLUTIONS AND RECOMMENDATIONS

As it was shown throughout the chapter, circular economy and green practices have been changing the mentality of companies regarding traditional production patterns and their relationship with the environment. This change leads companies to look for strategies and get tools that allow them to generate more responsible products with the environment. This effort is associated with the realization of investments that allow changing traditional practices, which implies a disbursement of financial resources for companies, an aspect that in the case of SMEs is more limited and does not allow them to make the necessary investments; in addition to the fact that managers still have reservations about the importance and need to change production patterns.

To ensure that SMEs succeed with the implementation of circular practices, there must be a job on different fronts but that, when added, guarantees greater chances of success for companies. The first point to attack is the mentality of those who make the decisions and run the companies, there must be a real interest in improving production and marketing practices in companies. In addition to this there must be a legal framework that allows and facilitates the development of these circular practices through tax benefits and other incentives such as soft credit lines. The sum of these two efforts will create an incentive so that from the producer side there is a real interest in implementing circular practices in the company.

But the implementation of circular practices also starts from the demand side, since it is the consumers who must demand quality products and in this specific case, products that are friendly with the environment and that their components provide the possibility of recycling or to be used in other products. Through consumer demands, companies are implementing new and best practices at each stage of the supply chain.

As can be deduced from the previous paragraphs, the main obstacle to the implementation of circular practices is the stimulation of market agents; stimulation that comes partly from the government and partly from consumers, who ultimately have the capacity to influence and affect the decisions of producers.

SMEs in developing countries face not only internal competition, both from their peers and from large companies; but to the competition that comes from other countries, especially those developed countries where these companies have more capabilities and possibilities; for this reason, governments in developing countries must create legal strategies and tools that allow the creation of the necessary incentives, in addition to promoting such practices in companies and consumers; focusing on the benefits that this brings to the environment and its production units.

FUTURE RESEARCH DIRECTIONS

Circular economy is a trend that gives us both hope and fear at the same time, in recent years there has been talk about the implementation of a new sustainable and environmentally friendly economic system without negatively affecting production and production. profits of the company based on the reuse of products and the continuation of a cycle that was previously considered to end with the first use of the product.

This term is currently being used to change the mentality of entrepreneurs, since it is promoting better management of resources and thus achieving waste reduction so that companies become more socially responsible. However, as discussed throughout the chapter, there are still many limitations in its application, however, there are some countries that are already promoting the realization of this change.

One of these examples is Spain, currently small and medium-sized companies have the support of the COPADE Foundation (trade for development), which created a program that aims to introduce real and important changes in its internal structures and in this way, its policies are motivating companies to become part of sustainable development without affecting the sustainability and financial structure of companies (COPADE, 2019).

On the other hand, the president of the German Environment Agency (UBA), Maria Krautzberger, said that "*70% of raw materials consumed in Germany come from abroad, of which four fifths are not renewable. We must use our resources more carefully*" (Umweltbundesamt, 2020). This to give a mouthpiece to the proposed tax implementation to promote the use of the circular economy in the industry.

Some of the measures that are considered most important for a more efficient use of resources promoting the circular economy are the following:

- Value Added Tax (VAT) Reform: goods that make efficient use of resources should be subject to a 7% VAT. A VAT system that differentiates, based on environmental criteria, would be feasible;
- Mandatory environmental and social standards for resources throughout the entire product value chain. A standardized certification for resource efficient products;
- Ratios of recycled materials specific to products: The proportions of recycled material in the production of plastics should be established at European level in order to increase the use of secondary plastics;
- Rules to increase the minimum quota of recycled plastic in plastic bags and garbage cans;
- Introduce minimum information requirements: The EU Ecodesign Directive should be modified to include criteria related to material efficiency and product life. These criteria would comple-

ment the current labeling for energy consumption, making efficiency in the use of resources more transparent.

In terms of future and perspective to the circular economy, is possible to say that if society is part of a strategy that aims to promote awareness and importance of making a change in the habits of both consumers and in the structure of production. It is no secret to anyone that in recent years' society is inclined towards products that are friendly to the environment (biodegradable, use of less plastic, reusable packaging, among other features). In fact, in the textile industry this concept is being implemented a lot, now the garments are redesigned, this known as the ECODESIGN (European, 2020).

The renowned ZARA brand will distribute recycling bins throughout its stores, with the intention that the customer deposit, there, the clothes that he will no longer use (ZARA, 2020). Timberland is another example of the implementation of circular economy in the world of fashion, is recognized footwear brand manufactures shoe soles with dust from old tires and reuse plastic bottles (Timberland, 2020). H&M customers have the possibility to take their used clothes, of any brand, to be collected and recycled (H&M, 2020). This minimizes the generation of waste and the need to produce raw materials, causing a decrease in the impact that its production generates on the planet.

The implementation of this new system would bring several benefits as it has been tried to show in the previous sections, because many entrepreneurs are currently looking to invest in projects that have a more marked social responsibility, on the other hand, it would be demanded by the consumer, products with a high innovation and sustainability component. This allows all kinds of investments to be generated, which would boost the economy, mainly for developing countries.

A clear example of the benefits that would be obtained by the implementation of this system can be seen in Switzerland, since in that country they have invested in waste management plants to burn garbage in a safe way for the environment and also convert from heat resulting in energy which is used to heat homes.

In addition, it should be noted that Switzerland receives around 100 million euros yearly to process garbage from neighboring countries, and that excludes the free energy it enjoys as a byproduct of this service.

CONCLUSION

The green economy and circular practices are new trends that have emerged with the intention of diminishing the negative impact that linear production has brought over the years. Circular practice means that elements, parts and inputs used in production can be reused, remanufactured or reused; providing with this the possibility to "extend the life" of these products and reduce their impact on the environment.

Changing the structure or productive practices implies acquiring new technology or training workers, aspects that are feasible for large companies that have the resources, but that in the case of small and medium-sized companies is difficult to the extent that this category of companies does not have great resources, it is more complicated to access them and they do not have the necessary skills to implement these practices, which makes it even more impossible for these companies to improve their production methods but additionally they can compete against those who do have the abilities.

The chapter sought to provide a series of concepts and clarifications regarding what circular economy is and its relationship with small and medium enterprises, especially those that are domiciled in developing countries; since these companies have even more difficulties to progress and implement circular practices, and in addition to this they have a great reduction compared to small and medium enterprises in developed countries, which have greater resources or even legal devices that facilitate and favor the development of the companies.

Circular practices in companies are becoming stronger and becoming a source of competitiveness for those who manage to implement them, as well as improving their positioning in the mind of the consumer and increasing their presence in the market. There are many advantages that companies can obtain when implementing these practices in organizations, the effort is to understand the need to reach this point given the complexities facing the world now, derived from irresponsible production and constant damage to the environment ambient.

REFERENCES

Bakker, C., Ariadne-Bakker, C., Den Hollander, M., Van Hinte, E., & Zijlstra, Y. (2014). *Products That Last: Product Design for Circular Business Models*. Delft: TU Delft Library.

Bastein, T., Roelofs, E., Rietveld, E., & Hoogendoorn, A. (2013). Introduction. In T. Bastein, E. Roelofs, E. Rietveld, & A. Hoogendoorn (Eds.), *Opportunities for a Circular Economy in the Netherlands* (pp. 4-6). Delft: The Netherlands Organization for Applied Scientific Research-TNO. Retrieved from https://www.tno.nl/media/8551/tno-circular-economy-for-ienm.pdf

Bicket, M., Vanner, R., Guilcher, S., Tan, A., Hestin, M., Withana, S., & Watkins, E. (2014). *Scoping study to identify potential circular economy actions, priority sectors, material flows and value chains*. Brussels: European Commission. Retrieved from https://www.eesc.europa.eu/resources/docs/scoping-study.pdf

Bocken, N., De Pauw, I., Bakker, C., & Van der Grinten, B. (2016). Product design and business model strategies for a circular economy. *Journal of Industrial and Production Engineering*, *33*(5), 308–320. doi:10.1080/21681015.2016.1172124

Bocken, N. M., De Pauw, I., Bakker, C., & Van der Grinten, B. (2016). Product Design and Business Model Strategies for a Circular Economy. *Journal of Industrial and Production Engineering*, *33*(5), 308–326. doi:10.1080/21681015.2016.1172124

Boulding, K. E. (2013). The economics of the coming Spaceship Earth. In H. Jarrett (Ed.), *Environmental Quality in a Growing Economy* (pp. 3–14). New York: RFF Press. doi:10.4324/9781315064147

Bradford, J., & Fraser, E. (2007). Local authorities, climate change and small and medium enterprises: Identifying effective policy instruments to reduce energy use and carbon emissions. *Corporate Social Responsibility and Environmental Management*, *15*(3), 156–172. doi:10.1002/csr.151

Calogirou, C., Sorensen, S. Y., Larsen, P. B., Alexopoulou, S., Morgensen, J., & Papageorgiou, M. (2014). *SMEs and the environment in the European Union*. Copenhagen: Danish Technological Institute; DG Enterprise and Industry (EC).

CEPAL. (2009). *Manual de la Micro, Pequeña y Mediana Empresa.* Deutsche Gesellschaft. Retrieved from https://repositorio.cepal.org/bitstream/handle/11362/2022/1/Manual_Micro_Pequenha_Mediana_Empresa_es.pdf

Chapman, J. (2005). *Emotionally durable design: Objects, Experiences and Empathy*. London: Earthscan Publications Ltd.

COPADE. (2019). *Qué hacemos?* Retrieved February 14, 2020, from Pymes y ODS: https://copade.es/pymes-y-ods/

Crowther, P. (1999). *Design for Disassembly.* Environmental Design Guide.

EFNMS. (n.d.). *About Us*. Retrieved December 8, 2019, from The European Federation of National Maintenance Societies: www.efnms.org/What-EFNMS-stands-for/m1312/What-EFNMS-stands-for.html

EMF. (2013). *Towards the Circular Economy.* Cowes: Ellen MacArthur Foundation.

European, C. (2020). *Internal Market, Industry, Entrepreneurship and SMEs*. Retrieved from ECODESIGN: https://ec.europa.eu/growth/industry/sustainability/ecodesign_en

Garbie, I. H. (2014). An analytical technique to model and assess sustainable development index in manufacturing enterprises. *International Journal of Production Research*, *52*(16), 4876–4915. doi:10.1080/00207543.2014.893066

Geissdoerfer, M., Savaget, P., Bocken, N., & Hultink, E. J. (2017). The Circular Economy – A new sustainability paradigm? *Journal of Cleaner Production*, *143*(1), 757–768. doi:10.1016/j.jclepro.2016.12.048

Ghisellini, P., Cialani, C., & Ulgiati, S. (2016). A review on circular economy: The expected transition to a balanced interplay of environmental and economic systems. *Journal of Cleaner Production*, *114*(15), 11–32. doi:10.1016/j.jclepro.2015.09.007

Gibson, T., & Van der Vaart, H. J. (2008). *Defining SMEs: A Less Imperfect Way of Defining Small and Medium Enterprises in Developing Countries.* Washington, DC: Brookings Global Economy and Development. Retrieved from http://citeseerx.ist.psu.edu/viewdoc/download?doi=10.1.1.627.8740&rep=rep1&type=pdf

Hillary, R. (2004). Environmental management systems and the smaller enterprise. *Journal of Cleaner Production*, *12*(6), 561–569. doi:10.1016/j.jclepro.2003.08.006

H&M. (2020). *Garment Collecting*. Retrieved from Recycle at H&M: https://www2.hm.com/en_gb/ladies/shop-by-feature/16r-garment-collecting.html

Hoevenagel, R., Brummelkamp, G., Peytcheva, A., & Van der Horst, R. (2007). *Promoting Environmental Technologies in SMEs: Barriers and Measures*. Luxembourg: European Commission: Institute for Prospective Technological Studies.

Hollins, O. (2011). *The Further Benefits of Business Resource Efficiency*. London: Department for Environmental Food and Rural Affairs.

Hopewell, J., Dvorak, R., & Kosior, E. (2009). Plastics recycling: Challenges and opportunities. *Philosophical Transactions of the Royal Society of London. Series B, Biological Sciences*, *364*(1526), 2115–2126. doi:10.1098/rstb.2008.0311 PMID:19528059

Lacy, P., & Rutqvist, J. (2015). *Waste to Wealth: The Circular Economy Advantage*. London: Palgrave McMillan. doi:10.1057/9781137530707

Lehmann, M., De Leeuw, B., & Fehr, E. (2014). *Circular Economy: Improving the Management of Natural Resources*. Berne: Swiss Academy of Engineering Sciences. Retrieved from http://www.wrforum.org/wp-content/uploads/2015/04/a-_CircularEconomy_English.pdf

Lewis, K. V., Cassells, S., & Roxas, H. (2015). SMEs and the Potential for A Collaborative Path to Environmental Responsibility. *Business Strategy and the Environment*, *24*(8), 750–764. doi:10.1002/bse.1843

Linton, J., & Jayraman, V. (2005). A framework for identifying differences and similarities in the managerial competencies associated with different modes of product life extension. *International Journal of Production Research*, *43*(9), 1807–1829. doi:10.1080/13528160512331326440

Mangla, S. K., Luthtra, S., Mishra, N., Singh, A., Rana, N., Dora, M., & Dwivedi, Y. (2018). Barriers to effective circular supply chain management in a developing country context. *Production Planning and Control*, *29*(6), 551–569. doi:10.1080/09537287.2018.1449265

Masi, D., Kumar, V., Garza-Reyes, J. A., & Godsell, J. (2018). Towards a more circular economy: Exploring the awareness, practices, and barriers from a focal firm perspective. *Production, Planning & Control. The Management of Operations*, *29*(6), 539–550. doi:10.1080/09537287.2018.1449246

Mbuyisa, B., & Leonard, A. (2015). ICT adoption in SME's for the alleviation of poverty. In *International Association for Management of Technology Conference* (pp. 858-878). Pretoria: IAMOT 2015 Conference Proceedings. Retrieved from https://pdfs.semanticscholar.org/99a9/569c66efc2fee2c49e22a515b96df9680de0.pdf

McDonough, W., & Braungart, M. (2002). *Cradle to Cradle: Remaking the Way We Make Things*. New York: North Point Press.

Meath, C., Linnenluecke, M., & Griffiths, A. (2016). Barriers and motivators to the adoption of energy savings measures for small- and medium-sized enterprises (SMEs): The case of the ClimateSmart Business Cluster program. *Journal of Cleaner Production*, *112*(5), 3587–3604. doi:10.1016/j.jclepro.2015.08.085

Meqdadi, O., Johnsen, T., & Johnsen, R. (2012). The Role of SME Suppliers in Implementing Sustainability. *IPSERA 2012 Conference*. Napoli: IPSERA. Retrieved from https://hal-audencia.archives-ouvertes.fr/file/index/docid/824677/filename/The_Role_of_SME_Suppliers_in_Implementing_Sustainability.pdf

Moss, M. (1985). *Designing for Minimal Maintenance Expense: The Practical Application of Reliability and Maintainability*. New York: CRC Press.

Muller, S., & Tuncer, B. (2013). *Greening SMEs by Enabling Access to Finance. Strategies and Experiences from the Switch Assia Programme*. Wuppertal: SWITCH-Asia Network Facility.

Oberle, B., Bringezu, S., Hatfield-Dodds, S., Hellweg, S., Schandl, H., & Clement, J. (2019). *Global Resource Outlook 2019*. Paris: International Resource Panel.

OCDE. (2000). *Small and Medium sized enterprises: local strenght, global reach*. París: OCDE Observer.

OECD. (2005). *OECD SME and Entrepreneurship Outlook*. Paris: OECD Publishing; doi:10.1787/9789264009257-

Oosterhuis, F. (2006). *Ex-post estimates of costs to business of EU environmental legislation*. Amsterdam: European Commission, DG Environment.

Radamaekers, K., Berg, J., & Asaad, S. S. (2011). *Study on the Competitiveness of the European Companies and Resource Efficiency*. Rotterdam: ECORYS Research and Consulting, Tecnologisk Institut, Cambridge Econometrics.

Rizos, V., Behrens, A., Kafyeke, T., Hirschnitz-Garbers, M., & Ioannou, A. (2015). *The Circular Economy: Barriers and Opportunities for SMEs*. Brussels: CEPS Working Paper.

Rutherfoord, R., Blackburn, R., & Spence, L. (2000). Environmental Management and the Small Firm: An International Comparison. *International Journal of Entrepreneurial Behaviour & Research*, *6*(6), 310–326. doi:10.1108/13552550010362750

Stahel, W. (1981). The Product Life Factor. In S. Grinton (Ed.), *An Inquiry into the Nature of Sustainable Societies: The Role of the Private Sector* (pp. 72–96). Houston: HARC.

Stahel, W. (1994). The utilization focused service economy: Resource efficiency. In B. R. Allenby & D. J. Richards (Eds.), *The Greening of Industrial Ecosystems* (pp. 178–190). Washington: National Academy Press.

Tambunan, T. (2007). Transfer of Technology to and Technology Diffusion among Non-farm Small and Medium Enterprises in Indonesia. *Knowledge, Technology & Policy*, *20*(4), 243–258. doi:10.100712130-007-9031-7

Timberland. (2020). *Responsibility*. Retrieved from Materials Policy Staments-Recycling EOL: https://www.timberland.com/responsibility/product/materials-policy-statements/recycling-eol.html

Trianni, A., & Cagno, E. (2012). Dealing with barriers to energy efficiency and SMEs: Some empirical evidences. *Energy*, *37*(1), 494–504. doi:10.1016/j.energy.2011.11.005

Tsalis, T. A., Nikolaou, I. E., Grigoroudis, E., & Tsagarakis, K. P. (2013). A framework development to evaluate the needs of SMEs in order to adopt a sustainability-balanced scorecard. *Journal of Integrative Environmental Sciences*, *10*(3-4), 179–197. doi:10.1080/1943815X.2013.858751

Tura, N., Hanski, J., Ahola, T., Stahle, M., Piiparinen, S., & Valkokari, P. (2019). Unlocking circular business: A framework of barriers and drivers. *Journal of Cleaner Production*, *212*, 90–98. doi:10.1016/j.jclepro.2018.11.202

Umweltbundesamt. (2020). *Topics*. Retrieved from Economics-Consumption: https://www.umweltbundesamt.de/en/topics/economics-consumption

Wooi, G. C., & Sailani, S. (2009). Green Supply Chain Initiatives: Investigation on the Barriers in the Context of SMEs in Malaysia. *International Business Management*, *4*(1), 20–27. doi:10.3923/ibm.2010.20.27

WRAP. (2011). *Increasing SME Recycling*. Banbury: Waste & Resources Action Programme.

Wycherly, I. (1999). Greening supply chains: The case of the body shop international. *Business Strategy and the Environment, 8*(2), 120–127. doi:10.1002/(SICI)1099-0836(199903/04)8:2<120::AID-BSE188>3.0.CO;2-X

ZARA. (2020). *Sustainability Collection Program*. Retrieved from Clothing Collect: https://www.zara.com/uk/en/sustainability-collection-program-l1452.html

ADDITIONAL READING

Bakker, C., Ariadne-Bakker, C., Den Hollander, M., Van Hinte, E., & Zijlstra, Y. (2014). *Products That Last: Product Design for Circular Business Models*. Delft: TU Delft Library.

Bocken, N., De Pauw, I., Bakker, C., & Van der Grinten, B. (2016). Product design and business model strategies for a circular economy. *Journal of Industrial and Production Engineering, 33*(5), 308–320. doi:10.1080/21681015.2016.1172124

Geissdoerfer, M., Savaget, P., Bocken, N., & Hultink, E. J. (2017). The Circular Economy – A new sustainability paradigm? *Journal of Cleaner Production, 143*(1), 757–768. doi:10.1016/j.jclepro.2016.12.048

Ghisellini, P., Cialani, C., & Ulgiati, S. (2016). A review on circular economy: The expected transition to a balanced interplay of environmental and economic systems. *Journal of Cleaner Production, 114*(15), 11–32. doi:10.1016/j.jclepro.2015.09.007

Hoevenagel, R., Brummelkamp, G., Peytcheva, A., & Van der Horst, R. (2007). *Promoting Environmental Technologies in SMEs: Barriers and Measures*. Luxembourg: European Commission: Institute for Prospective Technological Studies.

Lacy, P., & Rutqvist, J. (2015). *Waste to Wealth: The Circular Economy Advantage*. London: Palgrave McMillan; doi:10.1057/9781137530707

McDonough, W., & Braungart, M. (2002). *Cradle to Cradle: Remaking the Way We Make Things*. New York: North Point Press.

Rizos, V., Behrens, A., Kafyeke, T., Hirschnitz-Garbers, M., & Ioannou, A. (2015). The Circular Economy: Barriers and Opportunities for SMEs. Brussels: CEPS Working Paper.

Tura, N., Hanski, J., Ahola, T., Stahle, M., Piiparinen, S., & Valkokari, P. (2019). Unlocking circular business: A framework of barriers and drivers. *Journal of Cleaner Production, 212*, 90–98. doi:10.1016/j.jclepro.2018.11.202

KEY TERMS AND DEFINITIONS

Barriers: Limitations or obstacles, which prevent the development of a specific activity.

Circular Economy: Strategy that aims to optimize resources and reduce waste.

Economic Cycle: Group of stages through which the economy passes, until reaching the final stage where the process begins again, it occurs both in periods of recession and in periods of expansion.

Governmental Policies: Activities that the state designs and manages, for the satisfaction of the needs of a society.

Recycle: Process by which waste passes to become raw materials or new products.

Remanufacture: Restoration process to convert one product into another, which meets the same functionality and quality as the original.

Resources: Available items that are used to meet a specific need, achieve a goal or establish a company.

Reuse: Action that allows to use again the goods or products that were already discarded and thus give them a new use, reducing the amount of waste generated.

Small and Medium Enterprises: Companies that have some occupational and financial limits, which are prefixed by the state or region. They are agents with specific logics, cultures, interests and entrepreneurial spirit.

APPENDIX

Company Cases of Circular Practices Implementation

Johnson Controls: This company designed a battery that is 99% recyclable. By encouraging consumers of conventional batteries to recycle, the company received enough material to prevent hundreds of millions of batteries from ending up in landfills and thereby reduce the amount of waste.

Aquazone: Finnish company who developed a method to recycle wastewater and convert it into fertilizers. Wastewater is treated biochemically, and solids, water and nutrients are separated. Water can be used for irrigation or can be recycled more in drinking water; the mud is rich in nutrients and can be used as an organic fertilizer.

DyeCoo: Has developed a fabric dyeing process that does not use water at all and does not contain chemicals other than dyes. It uses highly pressurized "supercritical" carbon dioxide, halfway between a liquid and a gas, which dissolves the dye and transports it deeply into the fabric. Carbon dioxide evaporates and, in turn, is recycled and used again. 98% of the dye is absorbed by the fabric, giving vibrant colors. And because the fabric does not need to dry, the process takes half the time, uses less energy and even costs less.

Close the Loop: This Australian company has spent more than a decade recovering value from old printer cartridges and soft plastics. Their innovation turns these materials into roads. The products are mixed with asphalt and recycled glass to produce a higher quality road surface that lasts up to 65% longer than traditional asphalt. On each kilometer of road laid, the equivalent of 530,000 plastic bags, 168,000 glass bottles and the residual toner of 12,500 printer cartridges are used.

Enerkem: With its technology, this company extracts carbon from garbage that cannot be recycled. It then takes five minutes to convert carbon into a gas that can be used to produce biofuels such as methanol and ethanol, as well as chemicals that can be used in thousands of everyday products.

Lehigh Technologies: The Atlanta company converts old tires and other rubber waste into something called micronized rubber powder, which can then be used in a wide variety of applications, from tires to plastics, asphalt and building materials. 500 million new tires have been manufactured with their products, which earned him the Circular Economy SME Award.

Looptworks: Reuse abandoned materials in "significant, durable and limited-edition products". By reusing the excess prior to the world's consumption, the Portland-based company says its goal is to rid the world of waste and inspire a generation to reduce its impact on the planet. The line includes jackets, hoodies, skirts, shirts and graphic shirts for men and women.

Levi Strauss: Levi's is working on some interesting short-term and long-term circular economy initiatives aimed at eliminating a part of this statistic. Each Levi's store accepts old clothing and shoes of any brand, which the company collects and reuses or recycles with its partner, I: CO. The collected clothing is transformed into elements such as insulation for buildings, cushioning material and new fibers for clothing. Eventually, the company hopes to recycle old Levi's jeans into new ones.

Method: The company adopts the principles of the circular economy using infinitely recyclable materials, the use of renewable energy and the certification of the cradle to the cradle. The products include concentrated detergent and its Ocean Plastic Bottle project, which uses plastic discarded from the sea to make its packaging.

Chapter 9
Circular Economy Experience:
A Russian Perspective

Elena Burdenko
https://orcid.org/0000-0001-5073-5062
Plekhanov Russian University of Economics, Russia

Elena Bykasova
https://orcid.org/0000-0001-8503-4645
The Kosygin State University of Russia, Russia

ABSTRACT

The chapter focuses on the historical aspect of economic development stages. It identifies agriculture-based, industrial, and post-industrial economies' characteristics. It is demonstrable that the problem of limited resources, the use of waste from consumption, and production has always existed. However, these problems were solved differently in different historical periods. The accumulated problems can be solved by the transition to a circular economy model. When studying the Russian experience in the transition to a circular economy model, the focus remains on Russian legislation. The example of Russian industrial enterprises shows the practical application of the circular economy principles. The research covers such enterprises as PJSC NK ROSNEFT (which includes PJSC ANK Bashneft, Bashneft-Ufaneftekhim, JSC Novokuibyshevsky Oil Refinery, and JSC Rospan International), PJSC TATNEFT, PJSC MMC Norilsk Nickel, PJSC Magnitogorsk Iron and Steel Works. The presentation is on strategies, policies, and programs aimed at ensuring industrial safety, labor protections, and the environment.

INTRODUCTION

The growth of population, which is accompanied by an increase in industrial production, has led to increased consumption of resources. The natural reserves on the planet are depleted. Intensive human economic activities lead to environmental pollution and climate change. The problems listed above make all the countries think about searching for solutions to them.

DOI: 10.4018/978-1-7998-5116-5.ch009

Copyright © 2020, IGI Global. Copying or distributing in print or electronic forms without written permission of IGI Global is prohibited.

The purpose of this chapter is to study the implementation of the circular economy principles in Russia. For a more complete understanding of the ongoing processes, it is necessary to pay attention to the historical aspect of economic development. All developed countries across the world went through the same stages in their economic development, thus, it is necessary to identify the differences between the stages of economic development. The transition to a circular economy model requires a serious review of existing business processes and the identification of business processes that are consistent with the circular economy model.

From our point of view, the introduction of the circular economy principles should be initiated by the government of the country, therefore, it is important to study the legislation that encourages enterprises to comply with industrial safety, environmental standards, the development and implementation of more efficient technologies. Enterprises that can have a negative impact on the environment include, first of all, mining enterprises, oil refineries, and metallurgical plants. Therefore, the chapter studies the use of business models corresponding to the circular economy in oil and gas companies, at metallurgical plants, and also in light industry. The following enterprises were selected as examples: PJSC NK ROSNEFT (consisting of PJSC ANK Bashneft, Bashneft-Ufaneftekhim, JSC Novokuibyshevsky Oil Refinery, JSC Rospan International), PJSC TATNEFT, PJSC MMC Norilsk Nickel, PJSC Magnitogorsk Iron and Steel Works. These enterprises use a systematic approach to ensure industrial safety, labor protection and reduce the negative impact on the environment. Russia houses 11 large vertically integrated oil producing companies as well as over 180 independent oil producing companies; 10 largest vertically integrated metallurgical companies and this is not an exhaustive list of industrial enterprises (Rosstat, 2019). We are limited by the volume of the chapter, therefore, we will not be able to consider all enterprises from different industries.

During the transition to a circular economy model, the role of manufacturing enterprises increases, thus, the application of business models in light industry enterprises was studied.

The data of the Federal State Statistics Service of Russia (Rosstat), as well as data from the reports published by the researched enterprises on official websites was used as a source of information.

BACKGROUND

Any production as consumption is associated with the use of resources and has an impact on the environment. K. Boulding tried reviewing the problem of a more efficient use of natural resources from the theoretical point of view, proposing circular economy. In the 70s of the twentieth century, this idea was supported by European countries. In 1972, Meadows et al. in their work The Limits to Growth, developed a model of world development provided that the existing population growth rates, industrial and agricultural production, irrational use of non-renewable natural resources, and environmental pollution stayed the same. The conclusions were sad: mankind was confidently heading for disaster, material growth cannot continue indefinitely on a physically finite planet. In further studies conducted in 1992 (20 years later) and 2002 (30 years later), these findings were confirmed with a slight adjustment of individual indicators.

In 2010, Ellen MacArthur established a foundation with a goal to popularize the ideas of a circular economy. The Foundation's initiatives are supported by the European Commission and in 2012 adopted the «MANIFESTO FOR A RESOURCE-EFFICIENT EUROPE», which decides on the transition to a resource-efficient, regenerative circular economy in the European Union. In 2014, the Ellen MacArthur

Foundation creates the Circular Economy 100 network, which unites 100 global corporations that implement and work on business models in line with the circular economy (Ellen MacArthur Foundation, 2019). The created network is aimed at the exchange of knowledge, the development of new approaches to solve existing problems and the training of all who wish to take advantage of the circular economy. The foundation grants scholarships to graduate students to study the circular economy and supports research on creating an effective business in the circular economy. The activities of the Ellen MacArthur Foundation have been recognized by the international community, it is supported by scientists, universities, global corporations, political figures, international organizations and famous cultural figures. Between 2012 and 2019, the Foundation published 25 studies and reports. Here are some of them: Completing the Picture: How the Circular Economy Tackles Climate Change (2019), Reuse – Rethinking Packaging (2019), Circular Economy in Cities (2019), Cities and Circular Economy for Food (2019), Artificial Intelligence and the Circular Economy (2019), Circular Consumer Electronics: An initial exploration (2018), The New Plastics Economy: Rethinking the future of plastics & catalysing action (2017) and others.

The problems of efficient and careful use of resources, energy efficiency, reduction of negative environmental impact and transition to a circular economy concern all countries across the world. Therefore, scientists from different countries conduct research on these problems. Let us review some of them, since only their listing will take up a lot of space.

Chertow (2007) conducted a study of industrial symbiosis and proposed to stimulate the identification and uncovering of symbiosis "kernels". In his article, he concludes that environmentally and economically viable symbiotic exchanges surround us, you just need to find them.

Preston (2012) in his article drew attention to the fact that the transition to a circular economy requires a fundamentally new model of industrial organization. He believes that environmental restrictions should be adopted at the global level, coordination of national policies will help create a level playing field in the main markets, reduce competitiveness problems and reduce the costs of implementing the concept of a circular economy.

Geissdoerfer & al. (2016) reviewed the literature to concretize the terms of "circular economy" and "sustainability". The study aims to introduce conceptual clarity of the terms used in research and practice.

Kirchherr & al. (2017) analyzed 114 definitions of a circular economy by 17 parameters. In their study, they conclude that the circular economy is a combination of actions aimed at reducing, reusing and recycling of resources. But, despite the fact that the main goal of the circular economy is economic prosperity and improving the quality of the environment, no mention is made of its impact on social justice and future generations.

In their study, Ritzén, & Sandström (2017) said that sustainable development requires breakthrough changes and radical innovations, therefore, a balance is needed between sustainability and business development amid a circular economy. The authors draw attention to the fact that the transition to a circular economy is hindered by financial, structural, operational, technological barriers.

A study by Korhonen & al. (2018) found that the content of the circular economy concept is superficial and disorganized. The authors propose a critical analysis of existing studies in order to identify global problems, which, once solved with the help of a circular economy, will help achieve sustainable development.

Prieto-Sandoval & al. (2016, 2018) based on a systematic review of the literature drafted a knowledge map of the circular economy, analyzed the basic concepts and principles, and also identified the determinants of the circular economy.

Liu & al. (2018) in their article conducted a study of the economic benefits brought by the circular economy to both developed countries and China. The authors draw attention to the fact that consumption in developed countries is higher than in developing countries; therefore, developed countries have more waste. To solve the problem, developed countries should reduce waste generation, help developing countries solve environmental problems by transferring advanced technologies of waste processing, and also introduce an extended producer responsibility system in developed and developing countries.

The problem of transition to a circular economy model is also relevant for Russian scientists. Among the Russian scientists studying the problems of the circular economy are Paramonova (2016), Vetrova & Richter (2017), Filchenkova (2019) and others.

The Historical Aspect of Economic Development Stages

The Russian economy, as well as the economy of developed countries, went through several stages in its development:

1. **Agriculture-based economy:** During this period, agriculture was the basis of the country's economy. Agricultural production is carried out by a separate family, mainly manual labor is used. This is the longest period in human economic activity. It can be considered that it began with a primitive communal system and lasted until the 18th century;
2. **Industrial economy:** The most important change is the transition from manual labor to machine production, which resulted in a sharp increase in labor productivity. It is characterized by the creation of large industrial enterprises: manufactories, factories, plants. The emergence of large joint-stock companies uniting the capital of entrepreneurs, not related to each other by kinship. The structure of the developed countries' economy is dominated by industry: mechanical engineering, mining, manufacturing, chemical industry, etc. The transition to an industrial economy started in the 18th century and was mostly spread in the 20th century;
3. **Post-industrial economy:** It is identified as a separate type of economy, but it is rather a transitional period from the industrial economy to a more perfect type. The new stage in the economic development appeared due to a change in the structure of the economy. An increase in the share of services in the GDP of developed countries, which in the second half of the 20th century was over 50% and reached 70-80% by 2018. Table 1 presents data on the GDP structure of the countries in the G7 group: Great Britain, Germany, Italy, Canada, USA, France, Japan. All sectors of the economy are united into 3 large groups: services, industry, and agriculture. For comparison with the G7 countries, data on the structure of the Russian economy are given.

The data in Table 1 shows that in the structure of developed countries, industry takes second place and its share in the country's GDP decreases and in 2017 amounts to 20-30%, while the share of agriculture is 1-2%. Moreover, the following changes can be identified:

- The role of science as a direct productive force is increasing. The volume of scientific knowledge and information that are the result of intellectual work is growing;
- Social and spiritual needs are crucial, i.e. needs in education, culture, creativity, healthy environment, etc.;

Table 1. GDP structure of G7 countries and Russia (2017)

Country	GDP Structure		
	Services %	Industry %	Agriculture %
Great Britain	78,4	21	0,6
Germany	78	20	2
Italy	73,9	24	2,1
Canada	70,2	28,1	1,7
USA	78	21	1
France	79,8	18,3	1,9
Japan	69,3	29,7	1
Russia	59,7	36,3	4

Source: Own elaboration

- An important role in the economy of the country and the world as a whole is now played by intellectual property while the role of tangible property decreases;
- Acceleration of scientific and technological progress leads to the appearance of new technologies, and, subsequently, professions, and requires a review of existing economic management methods.

Scientists all over the world tried to react to the changes that resulted in the emergence of various concepts of economic development: information economy, knowledge economy, network economy, circular economy, green economy and others.

Today, we can only single out the beginning of this stage which is the second half of the 20th century, but we cannot say for sure when this period will reach its greatest expansion and completion.

Table 2 presents a comparative description of the economic development stages.

All stages of the economic development of all countries in the world are united by two common problems – the limited resources and utilization of waste products, production and consumption waste. And at each stage, these problems were solved differently. In the agriculture-based economy, waste from agricultural production was either further recycled or disposed of under the influence of nature. This practice worsened the environmental situation, which led to deterioration in the quality of land, water sources, and epidemics. In the industrial economy, the volume of industrial goods production increases, synthetic, polymeric materials are developed, a large number of metals, various chemical elements are discovered, mined and used. Over the 20th century, the Earth population has grown 7 times, and life expectancy of people has increased. It all led to an increase in consumption. In the industrial economy, most of the waste from production and consumption was thrown away. Landfill sites for garbage collection appear in cities and their surroundings. Landfills poison not only land, water and air, but also occupy territory that could have been used. Post-industrial economy based on a circular economy model is meant to solve the problems accumulated during previous periods of human industrial and economic activity.

Table 2. Comparative characteristics of the economic development stages

N°	Characteristics	Agriculture-Based Economy	Industrial Economy	Post-Industrial Economy
1.	Domination period beginning end	5-6 thousand years BC XVII century	XVIII century XX century	Second half of XX century Not defined
2.	Dominating sector of economy	agriculture	industry	services
3.	Dominating type of property	tangible	tangible	intellectual (intangible)
4.	Form of doing business	family	joint-stock company	multinational company
5.	Type of production by volume of output	single-piece production	serial	mass made-to-order
6.	Type of labor	manual	machine	automated
7.	Key technology	plow, agricultural tools	steam engine, electric motor, internal combustion engine	information technology, digital technology, nanomaterials, bioengineering
8.	Consumption and production waste disposal model	natural	creation of landfills	secondary use for production and consumption

Source: Own elaboration

Business Models Used by Enterprises in a Circular Economy

A circular economy can be called a closed-loop economy. This model of the economy is based on the 3R principle: Reduce, Reuse and Recycle, which involves optimizing the production process, reusing or sharing goods, and recycling. Experts identify the following business models that are consistent with the concept of a circular economy:

1. *Circular value chains*, that is, a set of physical processes that convert raw materials, energy into finished products. Robert Ayres proposed industrial metabolism in the early 1990s. Such a model is characterized by a complete or almost complete internal cycle of materials;
2. *Recovery and recycling*. This model involves maintaining the product in good condition by repairing and replacing broken parts (blocks). Goods that can no longer be restored must be effectively processed into other types of goods;
3. *Increase in the product life cycle* suggests that in order to increase the useful life of the finished product already at the design stage, the following conditions must be met: ease of maintenance and repair; the possibility of modernization and adaptability; standardization and compatibility; ease of dismantling and reassembly. This business model can be used in the production of durable goods, various machines, equipment;
4. *Exchange and sharing* is meant to create information services through which people can exchange goods or share them;
5. *Use of goods as a service*. In this case, the manufacturer provides the goods to the buyer for temporary use. Therefore, the buyer pays only for the period of use, while ownership of the goods does not pass to the buyer. For example, as in case of car sharing.

Russian Approach to the Introduction of a Circular Economy

Russia is a large country with complex economy. This is due to both the diversity of climatic zones (from subtropics to the Arctic), and the variety of natural and biological resources located in the country.

To understand the responsibility for environmental damage, the classification of waste depending on their source is used. Waste is divided into 2 groups: from household consumption and from production (Figure 1).

Figure 1. Classification of waste by source
Source: Own elaboration

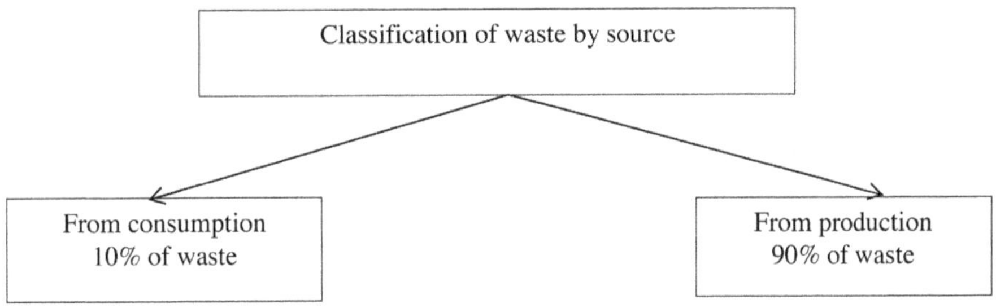

Waste generated from consumption by end consumers is called municipal solid waste (MSW). 55-60 million tons of MSW are generated annually in Russia, which makes up 10% of all waste. About 400 kilogram of waste per year accounts for 1 Russian resident. 90% of waste is generated in industry, the largest share of them is waste from mining and from manufacturing (Federal state statistics service of Russia, 2019).

In order to identify the degree of danger of the production process to the environment in Russia, the following criteria are applied:

1. Hazardous and harmful chemical compounds used at the enterprise;
2. The degree of exceeding the established limit standards;
3. Type of production process;
4. The activities of the enterprise connected with the use of atomic energy.

Hazardous substances and production processes that have a negative impact on the environment are divided into two large groups:

1. **Material:** They include chemical compounds that are classified by state of aggregation: solid, liquid, gaseous;
2. **Energetic:** This group includes: industrial noise, vibration, ultrasonic radiation, ionizing radiation, magnetic field, etc.

Moreover, when assigning an enterprise to a certain hazard class, the part of nature that is influenced by the production process is taken into account: land and mineral resources; water and groundwater; air; forests; solar energy, etc.

In 2002, the Law of the Russian Federation On Environmental Protection was adopted and in 2015, the Government of the Russian Federation approved the criteria based on which 4 hazard classes of the industrial activity danger to the environment were identified:

Class 1 – especially hazardous industries: This group includes enterprises that have the most negative impact on the environment, as they are associated with the generation and use of hazardous waste. For example, the extraction and processing of oil and gas, metallurgical complexes, pharmaceutical enterprises, the chemical industry, the manufacture of pesticides, the production of textiles, leather, leather products, etc. The state regularly monitors the production in this group of enterprises. An environmental audit is carried out at an enterprise to confirm compliance with established standards.

Class 2 – hazardous industries: This group includes enterprises that have a moderate impact on the environment. Waste from these enterprises is in the second hazard class. These enterprises comprise gas pipelines; oil pipelines; enterprises using nuclear fuel, nuclear facilities; complexes for the extraction and enrichment of uranium ore, etc.

Class 3 – low hazard production: This group includes enterprises that have an insignificant impact on the environment. The volume of emissions and the level of waste safety is minimal. Such enterprises include organizations that use special equipment to design new products, research, test new technologies.

Class 4 – safe production: The activities of enterprises assigned to class 4 are considered safe for the environment. Emissions are negligible and have little environmental impact. This group includes enterprises in the service sector, social and domestic activities, etc.

To carry out state environmental control over the production activities of the enterprise, the periodicity of a planned inspection has been developed and legislatively fixed, depending on the *category of risk* of environmental damage:

1. For the high-risk category, inspections are carried out once every 2 years;
2. For the significant risk category, inspections are carried out once every 3 years;
3. For the medium risk category, inspections are carried out once every 4 years;
4. For the moderate risk category, inspections are carried out once every 5 years;
5. For the low-risk category, no inspection is carried out.

State control is aimed at encouraging enterprises to comply with established environmental standards and develop more efficient technologies.

However, for the transition to a circular economy, it is necessary not only to take care of environmental protection, but also to introduce new technologies and business models that will maximize the use of resources and prevent the accumulation of waste.

Certain steps towards the transition to a circular economy have been taken since the late 1990s, when regulatory documents affecting environmental issues were drafted and adopted in Russia. They include the following laws:

- 1995-2000 On Environmental Protection, On Environmental Perspective, On Production and Consumption Wastes, On Air Protection and others;
- 2000-2009 On Land Management, On Energy Saving and Improving Efficiency and others.

In Russia, the transition to a circular economy was first announced in 2008 in the document "The Concept of Long-Term Socio-Economic Development of Russia until 2020". This document laid the foundation for the modernization of the Russian economy through innovative technologies with the introduction of closed-cycle production processes. From 2009 to 2019, the following documents were adopted aimed at introducing the principles of the circular economy in various sectors of Russia:

- In 2009, the "Energy Strategy of Russia for the Period up to 2030" was approved;
- In 2011, the "Strategy for Russia's Innovative Development 2020" was adopted;
- In 2012, the "Fundamentals of the State Policy in the Area of Environmental Development in the Russian Federation for the Period up to 2030" were adopted;
- In 2014, the "Forecast of the Scientific and Technical Development of Russia for the Period up to 2030" was adopted;
- In 2016, the "Strategy for the Development of the Mineral Resources Base of the Russian Federation up to 2030", the "Strategy for the Scientific and Technological Development of the Russian Federation" (until 2025) were approved;
- In 2017, the "Strategy for the Environmental Safety of Russia up to 2025" was adopted;
- In 2018, the "Strategy for the Development of the Mineral Resources Base of the Russian Federation up to 2035" was approved;
- In 2019, the "Strategy for the Scientific and Technological Development of the Russian Federation" (until 2030) was adopted.

The legislative documents of a general nature include environmental law: the Constitution of the Russian Federation, the Civil Code of the Russian Federation (Civil Code), the Code of Administrative Offenses (CAO RF), the Criminal Code of the Russian Federation (Criminal Code). They determine the environmental rights and obligations of citizens, as well as legal liability for violation of environmental legislation, compensation for damage to the environment, determine the amount of fines and criminalize ecologic violations.

To continue developing the regulatory framework for the transition and introduction of a circular economy in Russia, since 2020 the Government of Russia has been introducing a new environmental tax. Until 2020, in Russia, the Tax Code specified various individual fees for the use of wildlife and for the use of aquatic biological resources; water tax; tax on additional income from hydrocarbon production; mineral extraction tax, land tax. Environmental tax involves determining the tax base from various types of polluting factors:

1. The volume or mass of pollutants' emissions into the atmosphere from stationary sources;
2. Volume or mass of pollutants' discharges into water facilities that have entered the water facility as a result of the use of water;
3. The volume or mass of actually generated and disposed of production and consumption wastes minus the mass of wastes actually used or sent for processing;
4. For each stationary source actually used during the tax period, for each pollutant included in the list of pollutants.

In order to transfer the Russian economy to a circular model, the country takes measures to use the scientific and technological achievements as well as create safe environment. Figure 2 shows the main directions of state policy in this area.

Figure 2. The main directions of public policy to create a safe environment
Source: Own elaboration

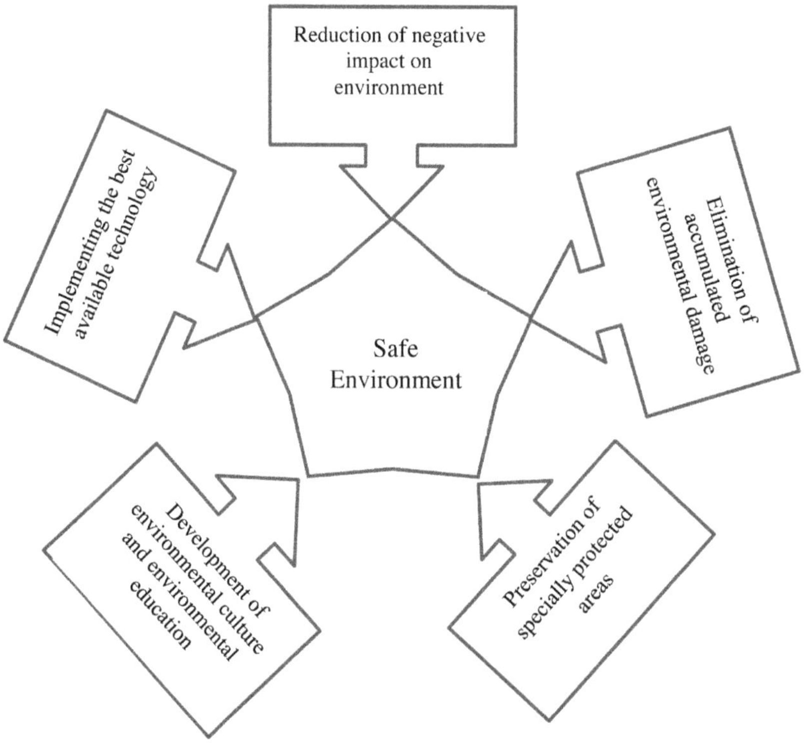

State policy aimed at reducing the negative impact of production processes and consumption is carried out in the following areas:

1. Reduction of negative impact on the environment;
2. Implementation of the best available achievements in production processes;
3. Elimination of accumulated environmental damage from previous periods of economic activity;
4. Development of environmental culture and environmental education among citizens of the country;
5. Carrying out activities aimed at the conservation of specially protected natural territories.

Let us study the examples of real enterprises where adopted strategies and concepts have influenced production processes.

Examples of Russian Enterprises Implementing Business Models of a Circular Economy

Enterprises that have particularly hazardous industries and are considered to be bearing high risk of environmental damage include oil producers, oil refineries, oil pipelines, gas producers, gas refineries, gas pipelines, metal mining, metallurgical plants, textile enterprises, tanneries, shoe factories, and others. Let us review some of them.

PJSC NK ROSNEFT

The enterprises included in the Public Joint-Stock Company ROSNEFT Oil Company (PJSC NK ROSNEFT) are the oldest Russian oil producing enterprises, where the production started at the end of the 19th century. In the Soviet period, exploration works were actively carried out and the deposits now used were discovered. In 1995, ROSNEFT Oil Company was transformed into an open joint stock company. In a short period, the company performed substantial work to consolidate oil-producing and oil-refining assets and increased the efficiency of corporate governance. Since 2006, the company's shares have been publicly traded on the London Stock Exchange. Today, NK ROSNEFT is a leader in the Russian oil industry and one of the largest oil corporations in the world.

The refinery and petrochemical block of the company includes 18 refineries located in different regions of Russia, Germany, Belarus, India. The company's network of gas stations covers 59 Russian regions. NK ROSNEFT conducts its production and financial and economic activities not only in Russia, but also in different countries of the world: Germany, India, China, Egypt, Venezuela, Iraq, Qatar, Indonesia, Vietnam, Brazil, Norway, the Republic of Cuba, Mozambique, Mongolia, Turkmenistan, Armenia, Belarus, Ukraine and others.

ROSNEFT has developed the ROSNEFT-2022 Strategy where special attention is paid to environmental protection; maintaining the health of the population living in the regions of the company's production activities; accident-free production activities; safe working conditions for employees. The company has developed and is implementing a "Policy in the field of industrial safety, labor protection and the environment", and for its implementation the Integrated Health, Safety, and Environment Management System was introduced in 2006 (ISU PBOTOS). Since 2010, ROSNEFT has been a member of the UN Global Compact, which declares ten principles in the field of human rights, labor relations, environmental protection, and the fight against corruption. These principles were integrated into the ROSNEFT-2022 Strategy and are used in the local regulatory acts of the company.

Figure 3 shows the elements that form the Integrated Health, Safety, and Environment Management System. This system complies with the requirements of ISO 14001 Environmental Management Systems. Requirements and application guidelines and OHSAS 18001 "Occupational safety and health management systems. Requirements". The compliance with the requirements of international standards are confirmed by certificates issued in 2018 to PJSC NK ROSNEFT in Moscow and in the companies of the group by business units: Exploration and Production, Oil Refining and Petrochemicals, Commerce and Logistics, Gas Business, Internal service (PJSC NK ROSNEFT, 2019).

Figure 3. The structure of the Integrated Health, Safety, and Environment Management System adopted by PJSC NK ROSNEFT
Source: Own elaboration

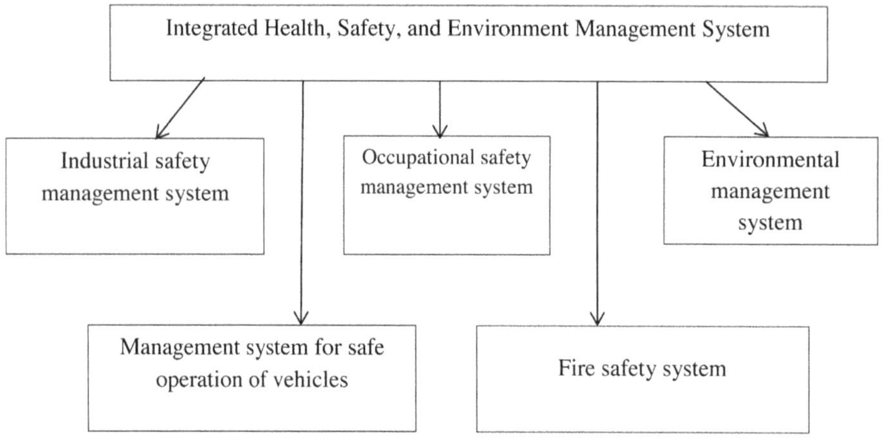

PJSC ANK Bashneft, Bashneft-Ufaneftekhim

In 2016, NK ROSNEFT acquired a controlling stake in the Bashkir oil company Bashneft. PJSC ANK Bashneft is the oldest enterprise in the oil industry of Russia. It has been mining since 1932. The company has more than 180 oil fields in commercial operation. The company produces and sells motor fuels of the highly environmental standard Euro-5 and Euro-6.

The reconstruction of a single complex of biological treatment facilities for PJSC ANK Bashneft, Bashneft-Ufaneftekhim was launched to take advantage of the circular economy.

The project cost in 2017 amounted to $ 49.3 million. The project implementation yielded the following positive results:

- Significantly improved quality of wastewater treatment;
- It became possible to reuse treated wastewater, which led to a 2.5-fold increase in the volume of supplied treated wastewater for technological needs;
- Water intake from a natural source of fresh water, the Belaya River, was minimized.

JSC Novokuibyshevsky Oil Refinery

Novokuibyshevsky refinery was commissioned in 1951. It is located in the Samara Region on the Volga River and has been part of the Samara Group of NK ROSNEFT Oil Refineries since 2007. For the first time in Russia, such products as jet fuel, oil for rocket carriers and cars, etc. were produced at this plant.

In order to use a business model that is consistent with the concept of a circular economy, the construction of a post-treatment unit for the existing treatment facilities of the hydrocracking complex at JSC Novokuibyshevsky Oil Refinery was started in 2018. The project cost in 2017 amounted to $106.17 million. Wastewater post-treatment is carried out using a membrane bioreactor. This technology has shown the best result compared to other technologies.

A positive outcome from the implementation of this project is expressed in the following:

- Reduction in the concentration of harmful substances in wastewater;
- Reduction in environmental charges and fines for pollutant discharges;
- Reduction in water consumption from a natural source by increasing the reuse of treated wastewater.

As part of the implementation of the ROSNEFT-2022 Strategy, the Digital Factory program is being implemented. One of the elements of the Digital Factory program is the use of ultra-precise accounting systems for the shipment of commercial products. Therefore, in 2019, JSC Novokuibyshevsky Oil Refinery introduced an ultra-precise system for measuring oil products at the river terminal on the Volga River.

The quality of all products produced at JSC Novokuibyshevsky Oil Refinery is guaranteed by the current quality management system and meets the requirements of ISO 9001: 2015.

JSC Rospan International

The joint-stock company Rospan International (JSC Rospan International) was established in 1994. In March 2013, it became a part of PJSC NK ROSNEFT. JSC Rospan International is located in Yamalo-Nenets Autonomous Okrug. The region belongs to the Far North regions, where more than half of the territory lies beyond the Arctic Circle, with the minimum temperature in winter dropping to – 70^0 C. Amid these difficult climatic conditions, the enterprise is conducting full-scale development of the East-Urengoysky and Novo-Urengoysky deposits, which include production, preparation, processing and transportation of produced raw natural gas.

To reduce the environmental impact, an integrated gas treatment unit was built in 2016-2018. The project cost in 2017 amounted to $3,534.3 million. The implementation of the project will lead to an increase in the quality of gas and condensate treatment, which will lead to a reduction in harmful emissions into the atmosphere.

PJSC TATNEFT

The company is one of the oldest in the Russian oil industry. Tatneft was officially established by a resolution of the USSR Council of Ministers in 1950. PJSC TATNEFT is one of the largest Russian oil companies. In terms of oil production, the company ranks 5th in Russia, and 32nd worldwide. PJSC TATNEFT is producing oil at 2 unique and 5 largest fields. The extracted oil is supplied both to the Russian market and to the markets of former Soviet republics and foreign countries. For oil refining, the company has an oil refining complex, which produces about 20 types of high-quality products: AI-92, AI-95, AI-98, TANECO-100 automobile gasoline; EURO-5 diesel fuel; aviation kerosene; high quality base oils; lubricants.

A large-scale environmental programs of Tatneft was first developed in 1990 and implemented in 1990-1995. After that, the second, third environmental programs were developed taking into account modern standards. In 2016, the company developed and approved the fourth “Environmental Program” and “Environmental Strategy” for the period 2016-2020 with a funding volume of more than $5800 million. As a result, the following environmental measures are carried out:

1. Improving the quality of well cementing;
2. Restoration of oil well tubings;
3. Tightening technological discipline;
4. Creation of mobile crews for servicing wells;
5. Establishment of environmental services;
6. Introduction of technology for trapping light fractions of hydrocarbons from reservoirs, which allowed reducing emissions of oil vapor to zero and restoring air purity in the region;
7. The use of anti-corrosion metal-reinforced plastic pipe for pipelines, which allowed reducing the number of accidents tenfold.

PJSC TATNEFT has a multi-level system of industrial environmental control, which allows obtaining objective information about the state of the environment. Air monitoring is carried out according to 33 indicators: hydrocarbon, hydrogen sulfide, nitrogen dioxide, carbon monoxide, etc. In order to verify compliance with the established standards for maximum permissible emissions of pollutants, more than 3000 analyzes are carried out annually.

To monitor the state of water resources, the company operates a local network of observation points, which consists of 491 observation points for surface water bodies (springs, rivers, reservoirs) and 1,419 observation points for underground water bodies (wells, artesian wells). Water control is carried out according to the indicators characteristic of oil production: chloride ion, sulfate ion, hardness, bicarbonates, calcium, the presence of oil and oil products, etc. Every year the company performs more than 100 thousand analyses of natural water.

Figure 4. The concentration of chloride ions in the main rivers (mg/l)
Source: In-house development based on company data (TATNEFT, 2019)

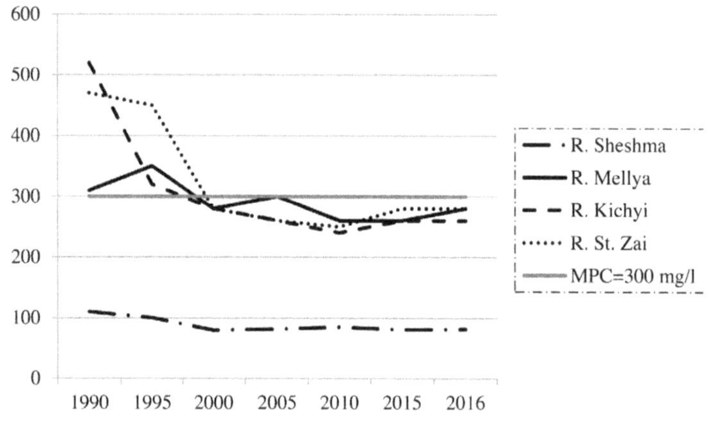

Figure 4 shows a decrease in the concentration of chloride ions in the main rivers from 1990 to 2016. Figure 5 demonstrates a decrease in the concentration of petroleum products in major rivers for the period from 1996 to 2016. As can be seen from Figures 4 and 5, a sharp decrease in pollutants occurred in 1999. In the years that followed, the number of pollutants did not exceed the maximum permissible standards. It was the result of regular environmental activities and constant monitoring.

Figure 5. The concentration of petroleum products in the main rivers (mg/l)
Source: In-house development based on company data (TATNEFT, 2019)

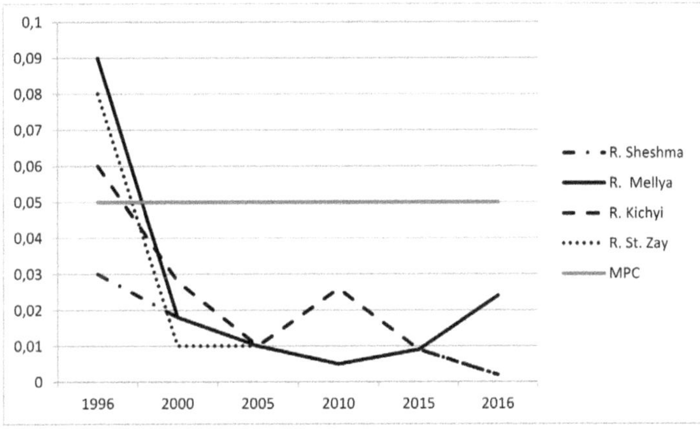

Conformity of PJSC TATNEFT production processes to ISO 14001: 2015 is confirmed by a certificate issued in December 2018.

PJSC MMC Norilsk Nickel

The first copper and nickel deposits on the Taimyr Peninsula were discovered back in the 17th century, however, the development of deposits became possible only in the 20th century. In 1935, the Council of People's Commissars of the USSR decided to build a mining and smelting plant in the Far North. Today, the company is the largest industrial enterprise in the Arctic zone of Russia. PJSC MMC Norilsk Nickel (the Norilsk Nickel Group of Companies) belongs to non-ferrous metallurgy enterprises and includes production plants located in Russia, Finland, Australia, and South Africa. The Nornickel Group of Companies occupies the following positions in the global market:

- 1st place in the production of palladium (39% of the market);
- 1st place in the refined nickel market (23% of the market);
- 4th place in the production of platinum (10% of the market);
- 4th place in the rhodium market (8%);
- 8th place in the production of cobalt (3% of the market);
- 11th place in copper production (2% of the market).

Apart from the metals listed above, the following products are produced: iridium, ruthenium, silver, gold, selenium, tellurium, sulfur, sodium sulfate, sodium chloride. The Group's products are delivered to 34 countries. The company's share in the industrial production of Russia in 2018 reached 11.4%, which corresponds to a share of 0.7% in the country's GDP.

Key divisions of the Norilsk Nickel Group are located in Russia. This is the Polar Division on the Taimyr Peninsula, which is the main enterprise for the city of Norilsk. The joining of enterprises is accounted for by the technological process, which includes the successive stages shown in Figure 6.

Figure 6. The technological process of PJSC MMC Norilsk Nickel
Source: In-house development based on company data (MMC Norilsk Nickel, 2019)

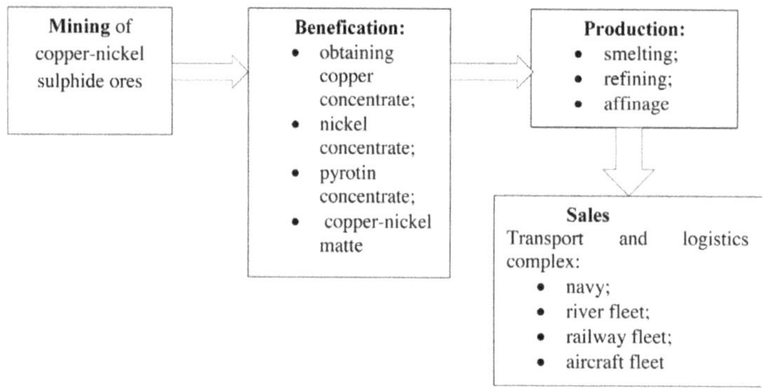

The Nornickel Group of Companies adheres to the Sustainable Development Goals adopted by the UN in 2015. To ensure sustainable development and the transition to a circular economy model, the Nornickel Group of Companies pursues a safety and labor protection policy and an environmental policy, which are included in the Corporate Social Responsibility Strategy. At the end of 2018, important non-financial results were:

1. Improving industrial safety and labor protection. The rate of injuries with loss of working time decreased by 48%;
2. More than 24,000 employees and members of their families have become participants in rehabilitation programs;
3. More than 18,000 employees have been insured under supplementary health insurance programs;
4. More than 87,000 employees underwent training, which included vocational training, retraining and advanced training;
5. In 2017, the enrichment facilities in the Polar Division were updated and the Nickel Plant was closed, which led to a decrease in the negative impact on the environment;
6. The share of multiple-reused and reused water reached 86%;
7. Local purifying facilities were built in Norilsk;
8. Implementation of a comprehensive program to reduce sulfur oxide emissions by 75% by 2023 in the Norilsk industrial region;
9. The share of waste reuse reached 70%;
10. Since 2011, a program has been carried out to relocate citizens from Norilsk and Dudinka to areas with a favorable climate in Russia. To implement the program, 533 apartments were bought in 2018, and in 2019 it is planned to buy 450 apartments.

For 2010 to 2018, the costs of PJSC MMC Norilsk Nickel for the improvement of social conditions amounted to $ 767.8 million. Since 2003, a land restoration program has been carried out, under which more than a million trees and bushes were planted over an area of about 100 hectares over 14 years.

The compliance of the production process in PJSC MMC Norilsk Nickel with ISO 9001: 2015 ISO 14001: 2015 is confirmed by a certificate issued in December 2017.

PJSC Magnitogorsk Iron and Steel Works

Magnitogorsk Iron and Steel Works was built on a unique iron ore deposit of Magnitnaya Mountain in the Southern Urals. In 1932, the first blast furnace was launched and the first cast iron was smelted. Magnitogorsk Iron and Steel Works is a global giant in steel production and belongs to the iron and steel industry. A large-scale reconstruction of the plant was started in 1997 and continues to this day. Worn out old equipment was replaced with new and more advanced, new technologies were introduced. As a result of technical re-equipment, the quality improved and the volume of smelted steel increased, while emissions of pollutants into the environment decreased.

Investments in the construction of environmental facilities from 2000 to 2018 increased 15 times and amounted to over $970 million. PJSC Magnitogorsk Iron and Steel Works developed and adopted the Clean City environmental program for the period until 2025. The Clean City environmental program sets the following targets for 2025:

1. Reduce emissions into the air by 24.5 thousand tons;
2. Reduce emissions of especially dangerous and dangerous substances (1-2 classes) by 10 times;
3. Reduce pollutant discharges by 35.7 thousand tons;
4. Annually process waste in production of at least 2.3 million tons;
5. Conduct annual land reclamation of depleted pits with an area of 20 thousand m^2;
6. Green the territory of Magnitogorsk and plant 11 thousand trees and bushes.

The Clean City ecological program is implemented in 4 directions (Figure 7):

1. Clean air;
2. Clean water;
3. Clean land;
4. Favorable environment.

Figure 7. The structure of the Clean City environmental program, conducted by PJSC Magnitogorsk Iron and Steel Works
Source: In-house development based on company data (PJSC Magnitogorsk Iron and Steel Works, 2019)

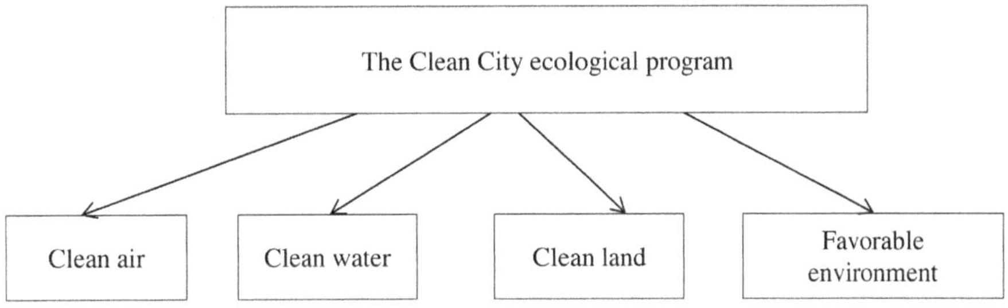

The current environmental measures have already yielded positive results. Let us study the positive outcomes in each of the areas in the environmental program.

Clean Air

The company implemented the following measures, which led to a reduction in atmospheric emissions:

- All open-hearth furnaces were decommissioned due to the construction of electric arc furnaces and with the transition to continuous steelmaking;
- Reconstruction of sulfur trapping plants of all sinter plants with a total capacity of 4.1 million m^3/h;
- Construction of aspiration systems for cast houses and sub-bunker rooms for blast furnaces with a total capacity of 7.2 million m^3/h;
- Reconstruction of a gas treatment plant of a two-shaft steelmaking unit with a fugitive emission capture system with a total capacity of 1.245 million m^3/h.

At present, PJSC Magnitogorsk Iron and Steel Works operates 274 gas treatment plants.

Figure 8. The dynamics of pollutant emissions into the atmosphere from 2000-2018 at PJSC Magnitogorsk Iron and Steel Works
Source: In-house development based on company data (PJSC Magnitogorsk Iron and Steel Works, 2019)

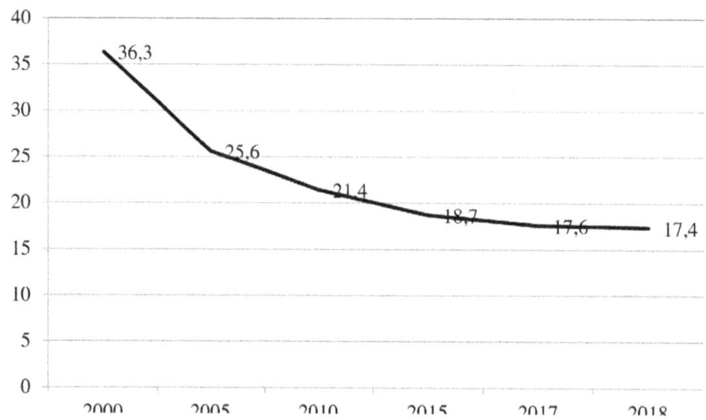

Figure 8 shows the change in pollutant emissions at Magnitogorsk Iron and Steel Works from 2000 to 2018. Over this period, gross emissions decreased by 1.6 times, and specific emissions decreased by 2.1 times.

In 2017, Magnitogorsk Iron and Steel Works reached the level of the best achieved technologies (BAT) of the world's leading steel companies in specific emissions of sulfur dioxide per 1 ton of steel (Figure 9).

Figure 9. Comparative data on specific emissions of sulfur dioxide (SO2) kg/ton of steel at the leading metallurgical plants in the world (2017)
Source: In-house development based on company data (PJSC Magnitogorsk Iron and Steel Works, 2019)

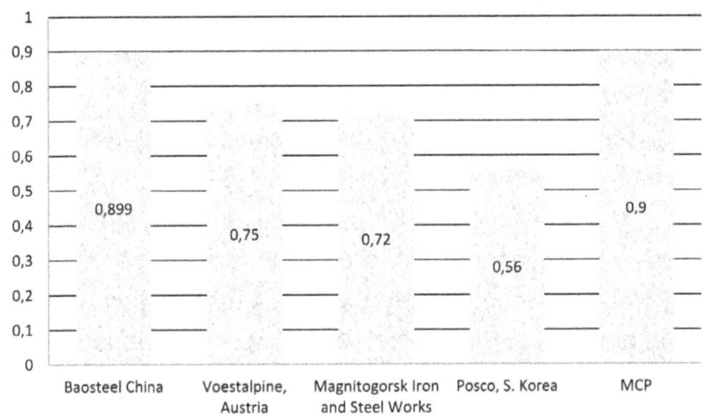

Clean Water

In 2018, a hydrotechnical structure, a dividing dam, was launched at Magnitogorsk Iron and Steel Works, and made it possible to switch to a closed circulating water supply system. This led to an 11-fold reduction in the volume of wastewater and a 7-fold reduction in the mass of pollutants (Figure 10).

Figure 10. Dynamics of reducing discharges to water bodies from Magnitogorsk Iron and Steel Works from 2000 to 2018
Source: In-house development based on company data (PJSC Magnitogorsk Iron and Steel Works, 2019)

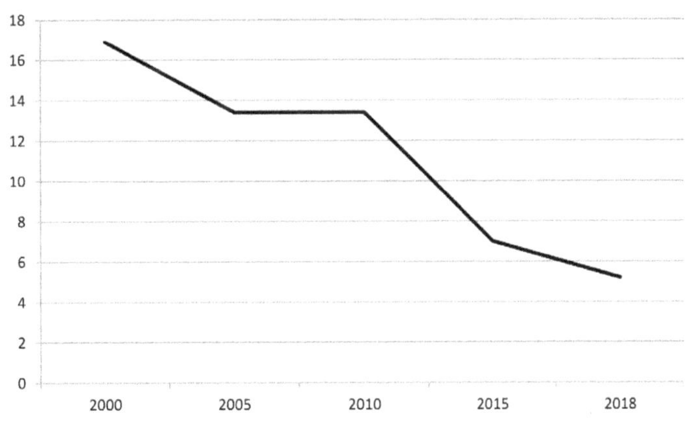

Today, 100% of industrial wastewater is used in the circulating water supply of technological units at Magnitogorsk Iron and Steel Works.

Clean Land

In the mining industry, the waste that is generated as a result of washing ore materials is called sludge. Modern technology allows the use of sludge, which was previously just dumped on a special territory. In 2013-2014, a plant for sludge dewatering was built at Magnitogorsk Iron and Steel Works. This allowed to dehydrate the entire volume of sludge and dispose of it in production. In 2017-2018, a complex was constructed at the plant to process more than 20 million tons of iron-containing waste accumulated in the sludge storage facility, which will allow annual processing of up to 2 million tons of industrial waste with the production of 500 thousand tons of concentrate with an iron content of up to 59%.

Slag is formed during the smelting of steel which is a by-product of metallurgical activity. Metallurgical slag is a complex system that includes both oxides of various metals and other impurities. The bulk of slag dumps at Magnitogorsk Iron and Steel Works was formed during the period from 1940 to 1990. Since 2000, the volume of slag dumps has ceased to increase and its annual processing has begun. Today, during production processes, 5.5 million tons of metallurgical slag is formed, which are completely disposed of. From 2000 to 2018, the volume of slag dumps decreased by 2.3 times. From 2012 to 2018, the first stage of biological land reclamation was completed and trees, bushes, perennial grasses were planted on an area of 154 thousand m^2.

Favorable Environment

Magnitogorsk Iron and Steel Works is a city-forming enterprise for the city of Magnitogorsk, so the Plant has developed a "Program for the greening of Magnitogorsk". The program was launched in 2017. It includes planting seedlings of trees and bushes in educational and social institutions, parks and gardens. During this time, more than 7,000 seedlings were planted.

The environmental safety of production processes at Magnitogorsk Iron and Steel Works is ensured not only by advanced technologies, but also modern management methods in environmental protection. The company has implemented an environmental management system in accordance with the requirements of ISO 14001. This is confirmed by a certificate issued to the company.

Moreover, an independent environmental assessment of Magnitogorsk Iron and Steel Works is carried out. The following organizations conducted an independent assessment in 2018: 1. Zhivaya Planeta television channel and the Modern Media Research Institute (MOMRI); 2. Rating of Interfax-Era energy rating agency; 3. Rating of the World Wide Fund for Nature (WWF).

Light Industry Enterprises

In the Russian economy, mining industry is of great importance, therefore, the Government pays special attention in the development strategy of the circular economy to such industries as oil and gas production, ferrous and non-ferrous metallurgy, mechanical engineering, chemical production, etc. However, manufacturing, including light industry, play an important role in the structure of the country's economy and is necessary in the transition to a circular economy model.

Light industry is the link between different sectors of the country's economy. Light industry enterprises use natural raw materials and materials produced in agriculture, as well as synthetic materials, fibers, fabrics produced from hydrocarbon raw materials from the oil refining industry. For the production of light industry goods, machine tools, machines, equipment, facilities, tools that are produced by the engineering industry are needed. Without light industry production, the normal functioning of power structures, industrial production, construction, agriculture, medicine and other sectors of the country's economy is impossible. The relationship of light industries with other industries is shown in Figure 11.

The statistics cited in the monograph "The Influence of Industrial Policy and Zoning on the Development of Light Industry in Russia" (Burdenko, 2015) shows that as of May 1, 2014, the number of light industry enterprises in Russia was around 991 enterprises, including 310 textile enterprises, 505 garment enterprises, 86 fur, leather, leather goods, etc. enterprises, 90 shoe enterprises. At the same time, in some central regions of Russia, light industry is a leading industry that provides employment and makes a significant contribution to total production. For example, in the Ivanovo region – 33.7%, in the Tver region – 6%, in the Kostroma and Rostov regions – 4.5%, in the Vladimir and Ryazan regions – about 3%. Given that in the modern weaving and clothing industry, textile waste makes up to 25% of the feedstock, and the residues from the manufacture of threads, yarn, fabrics constitute economic losses for the enterprise, it is beneficial to recycle such "waste". Depending on the structure and release of products, waste is divided into different groups. Some of these wastes are recycled, and some are disposed of.

There are two types of waste in light industry: waste generated during the manufacture of textiles and household waste. The Federal Waste Classifier defines the groups of light industry wastes:

- Waste from textile products;
- Waste from the production of clothing;
- Waste from the production of leather, leather products;
- Waste from textiles and textile products that have lost consumer properties;
- Leather products that have lost consumer properties.

The analysis of these textile industry wastes allows one to identify waste for secondary use and divide them into several groups, namely:

1. Production waste that is used in the same enterprises in which it is generated. These wastes are processed into main products without special equipment;
2. Production waste that cannot be recycled at the enterprise in which it is generated. These wastes are sent to specialized enterprises for processing. After various processes, such as grinding, cutting, sintering, etc., they are processed into simpler products. (For example, in wiping cloth, cotton wool, tow, etc.);
3. Production waste that cannot be recycled due to the lack of special technologies is used as a cleaning material and then taken out for burial;
4. Production wastes that are unsuitable for the production of textile products, but can be used in other sectors of the economy;

Table 3 shows the options for the use of textile waste, taking as an example cotton manufacture waste.

One of the types of cotton waste is linter, which contains up to 85% cellulose, and is used in the production of acetate silk, paper, plastics and other products. The ways of using spinning waste in the linen, wool industry are similar.

If we consider garment production, then waste is mainly used in the production itself. Let us study in table 4 how waste types are used in garment production.

Figure 11. The relationship of light industry with other sectors of the economy
Source: Own elaboration

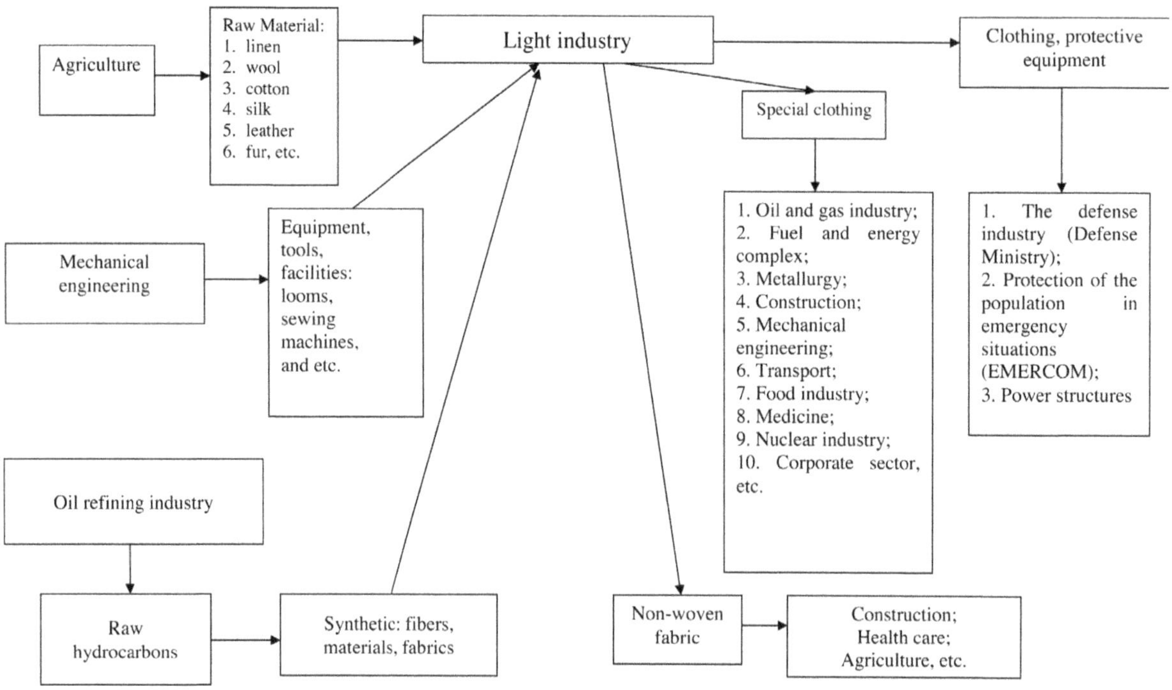

Table 3. Ways of using textile waste, taking cotton manufacture waste as an example

Name of Waste	Type of Waste	Ways of Recycling
Spinnable	Comber waste, roving waste, rings, ring waste	Yarn production
Cotton	Scutcher droppings, fly cotton, fly, etc.	Cotton wool production
Low grade	Dusthouse waste, motes and fly, second cut, dirty and weave sweeps	Production of furniture wool, plastics, roofing, roofing felt, etc.
Wiping	Halching, ends	In various sectors of the economy
Craft	Ends	Production of nets, grids, cords, etc.

Source: Own elaboration

Table 4. Ways of using garment industry waste

Name of Waste	Type of Waste	Ways of Recycling
End and fents	Cotton fabrics, silk fabrics, woolen fabrics, etc.	Headscarves, handkerchiefs, caps
Cabbages	Cotton fabrics, silk fabrics, woolen fabrics, rubberized silk, faux fur	Collars, cuffs for school uniforms; rugs, children's bags, children's fur coats, cut for toys, etc.
Fents and cabbages	Cotton fabrics, silk fabrics, woolen fabrics, etc.	Women's hats, dresses for dolls, covers, napkins, etc.

Source: Own elaboration

Thus, a significant part of the garment industry waste is sent back to production for the manufacture of consumer goods. Large waste is used for children's products: hats, toys, bags, clothes for dolls, etc. Smaller waste is sent as wiping materials, such as cuts for shoes, rollers, printed material, etc. Moreover, waste from the clothing and textile industries of small sizes can be processed into pulp, which can be used to produce yarn, technical wool, etc. Textile waste is also used for the manufacture of panels, felt, flooring, as additives in various types of plasters. Synthetic wastes of the textile industry is used to make various products in other industries, for example, in car decoration (interior upholstery, insulation, etc.).

In the shoe industry, large wastes of leather, textile, cardboard, rubber, etc. are used in its own production. Indoor shoes, insoles, cut watchbands, cases for glasses, etc. are made from waste. Table 5 lists the ways of using waste from the shoe industry.

Table 5. Ways of using shoe industry waste

Name of Waste	Type of Waste	Ways of Recycling
Leather ends	Natural or artificial leather, cardboard, rubber	Cuffs for various mechanisms, leather taps for shoes, etc.
Small rubber ends	Rubber	Heels, taps, handles, etc.
Rags	From leather cutting for upper shoes	Wallets, work gloves, belts for the clothing industry, shoes for dolls, sports slippers, rand for shoes, etc.
Rags	From cotton and cloth-woolen materials	Insoles, slippers for children, etc.
Small ends	Die cutting and felt	Insoles for women shoes
Sole rubber	Rubber	Rubber linings for shoes, gaskets, etc.
Faux fur	Fur	Carpets, rollers, stuffing mats, for toys

Source: Own elaboration

Summarizing the data on the types of waste from leather and fur industry, we can make a conclusion about their use in various industries:

- Food (gelatin, sausage casings, etc.);
- Agriculture (animal feed, fertilizer);
- Pharmaceutical (protein packaging for drugs);
- Medical (prostheses, surgical sutures);
- Textile (collagen threads, fibers, wool).

JSC Vtor-Kom

Joint Stock Company Vtor-Kom (JSC Vtor-Kom) was established in 1990 for the production of batting. However, in 1997, the company begins to accept secondary raw materials (various plastic bottles, cans) from other enterprises and individuals and use it in the production of non-woven materials for construction, oil and gas production, sewing and furniture enterprises.

Today, the company has organized in Chelyabinsk reception centers for secondary raw materials. The city has launched the "Veschevorot" project in which the unused things are sent to JSC Vtor-Kom. They accept the following types of secondary raw materials: paper, cardboard; plastic; rags; glass containers; aluminum cans. Paper and cardboard are used for the production of corrugated packaging. The collected rags are subjected to separation of fiber and used for the production of insulation. Synthetic fibers are made from assembled plastics. Glass containers are crushed and sent to glass plants. Every month, the company processes 4,500 tons of secondary raw materials (JSC Vtor-Kom, 2019).

Now, JSC Vtor-Kom is the only enterprise in the light industry in Russia using waste from production and consumption as resources for the manufacture of new products. An example of this enterprise shows the most comprehensive use of business models corresponding to the circular economy in light industry.

The circular economy, in essence as a waste-free technology, should be a practically almost closed system. However, even in natural ecosystems there is no absolute isolation, and in non-waste production, non-processed minimum, depending on the type of production and industry, can be allowed. In production, a certain cycle sometimes requires the consumption of resources outside a closed system, while the wear of materials and equipment also introduces a violation of non-waste technology into a closed cycle.

SOLUTIONS AND RECOMMENDATIONS

It is necessary to highlight the main directions in the transition to waste-free production in various industries:

1. Development of new technological processes, using a new type of equipment, which will maximally eliminate or reduce those stages of production that bring more waste;
2. Development and implementation of production systems for processing waste into secondary raw materials and secondary consumer goods;
3. Organization and development of regional and territorial clusters of enterprises, with the aim of joint processing of production waste;
4. Development of collaboration with retail chains for the collection of clothing, shoes, fabrics, etc. for recycling.

The phased transition to a fully circular economy consists of several stages: the transition from open production systems to semi-open systems with partial use of waste, and then to closed-loop systems with the complete processing of all waste.

The greatest benefits from switching to a circular economy model can be obtained if business models are introduced at all levels: municipal, regional, national and international.

FUTURE RESEARCH DIRECTIONS

This study focuses on the use of business models that are consistent with the concept of a circular economy at industrial enterprises. In the future, it would be possible to conduct a study of enterprises from other industries, as well as consider the problem of waste from domestic consumption.

In 2018, 38 billion 73 million tons of industrial and household waste were accumulated in Russia according to Russian statistics. In 2018, 2 billion 53.9 million tons of waste was disposed of for reuse. Only 4-5% of municipal solid waste is sent for processing and incineration, while the rest is disposed of in landfills. The area of landfill sites in Russia is increasing by 0.4 million hectares annually. (Rosstat, 2019).

CONCLUSION

According to the results of the study, we can say that the transition to a circular economy model gives mankind a chance to reduce not only the negative impact on the environment as a result of production activities and consumption, but also to eliminate the accumulated environmental damage from past stages of economic development. The principles of the circular economy have been most actively used in Russia since 2008, which is confirmed by the consistent development and adoption of legislation and strategies aimed at protecting the environment, specification of requirements for industrial enterprises, reduction of energy consumption, and the transition to a more efficient use of the mineral resource base.

Large vertically integrated companies in oil and gas production, metallurgy have a serious impact on the environment, but can also invest significant financial resources in research and development, the social sphere, and environmental measures.

As a result of the transition to a circular economy model, the level of useful use of waste from industry in Russia increased from 40% (2006) to 60% (2016). At enterprises extracting oil, gas, metals, the share of waste reuse is the highest and as a result of the use of modern equipment and technologies the negative impact on the environment is reduced. In general, waste from mining refers to hazard class 5, that is, these are natural materials that do not have a negative impact on the environment (Rosstat, 2019).

Among the manufacturing industries, the largest amount of waste falls on textile enterprises, however, most of it is returned to the production cycle. In light industry, enterprises mainly use the services of third-party specialized enterprises for the utilization of textile waste. In 2018, there were about 50-60 textile waste disposal enterprises in Russia, the largest number of them in Moscow and St. Petersburg. In terms of production volume, light industry enterprises are small and medium-sized businesses, for which it is difficult to find investments in the development and implementation of waste-free production within the concept of a circular economy. It is much cheaper not to recycle the waste, but to hand it over to specialized companies for recycling.

As long as the "fast fashion", focused on high energy costs, quick profits, with a large amount of primary and secondary waste, is relevant, it is rather difficult to stimulate light industry enterprises to intensively switch to the principles of a cyclical economy.

In recent years, terminals and points for the reception of clothes and shoes have been created in large cities in Russia in order to give "new life" to light industry products, distributing them to low-income families and homeless people. As part of the development of the circular economy concept, a fund for collecting clothes, "Vtoroye dykhaniye", was created in Russia. This organization sends things to charitable foundations in the country's regions, and textiles in poor condition is processed in the city of Kostroma.

ACKNOWLEDGMENT

The study was supported by Plekhanov Russian University of Economics. I want to express my gratitude for the help Agibalova Elena.

REFERENCES

Burdenko, E. V. (2015). *The Influence of Industrial Policy and Zoning on the Development of Light Industry in Russia*. Moscow: Pero.

Chertow, M. R. (2007, December). "Uncovering" industrial symbiosis. *Journal of Industrial Ecology*, *0*(0). doi:10.1162/jiec.0.1110

Ellen MacArthur Foundation. (2017). The New Plastics Economy: Rethinking the future of plastics & catalysing action. https://www.ellenmacarthurfoundation.org/publications/the-new-plastics-economy-rethinking-the-future-of-plastics-catalysing-action

Ellen MacArthur Foundation. (2018). Circular Consumer Electronics: An initial exploration. https://www.ellenmacarthurfoundation.org/publications/circular-consumer-electronics-an-initial-exploration

Ellen MacArthur Foundation. (2019). Artificial Intelligence and the Circular Economy. https://www.ellenmacarthurfoundation.org/publications/artificial-intelligence-and-the-circular-economy

Ellen MacArthur Foundation. (2019). Circular Economy in Cities. https://www.ellenmacarthurfoundation.org/publications/circular-economy-in-cities-project-guide

Ellen MacArthur Foundation. (2019). Cities and Circular Economy for Food. https://www.ellenmacarthurfoundation.org/publications/cities-and-circular-economy-for-food

Ellen MacArthur Foundation. (2019). Completing the Picture: How the Circular Economy Tackles Climate Change. https://www.ellenmacarthurfoundation.org/publications/completing-the-picture-climate-change

Ellen MacArthur Foundation. (2019). Reuse – Rethinking Packaging. https://www.ellenmacarthurfoundation.org/publications/reuse

Filchenkova, O. A. (2019). Transition of the Russian Federation to circular economy taking into account international experience. Actual questions of economy and management. https://moluch.ru/conf/econ/archive/329/14970

Geissdoerfer, M., Savaget, P., Bocken, N. M. P., & Hultink, E. J. (2017, February 1). The Circular Economy – A new sustainability paradigm? *Journal of Cleaner Production*. doi:10.1016/j.jclepro.2016.12.048

Kirchherr, J., Reike, D., & Hekkert, M. (2017). *Conceptualizing the circular economy: An analysis of 114 definitions*. Resources, Conservation and Recycling. Elsevier B.V.; doi:10.1016/j.resconrec.2017.09.005

Korhonen, J., Honkasalo, A., & Seppälä, J. (2018). Circular Economy: The Concept and its Limitations. *Ecological Economics*, *143*, 37–46. doi:10.1016/j.ecolecon.2017.06.041

Liu, Z., Adams, M., & Walker, T. R. (2018, September 1). Are exports of recyclables from developed to developing countries waste pollution transfer or part of the global circular economy? In *Resources*. Conservation and Recycling. Elsevier B.V.; doi:10.1016/j.resconrec.2018.04.005

Meadows, D. H., Meadows, D. L., & Randers, J. (1992). *Beyond the Limits (Post Mills)*. Chelsea Green Publishing Company.

Meadows, D. H., Meadows, D. L., Randers, J., Behrens, I. I. I., & William, W. (1972). *The Limits to Growth*. New York: Universe Books.

Paramonova, N. (2016). Cyclical economy on the threshold of Russia. Ecology and Law, 62.

Preston, F. (2012). A Global Redesign? Shaping the Circular Economy. Energy, Environment and Resource Governance, (March), 1–20. doi:10.1080/0034676042000253936

Prieto-Sandoval, V., Jaca, C., & Ormazabal, M. (2018). Towards a consensus on the circular economy. *Journal of Cleaner Production*, *179*, 605–615. doi:10.1016/j.jclepro.2017.12.224

Prieto-Sandoval, V., Jaca García, C., & Ormazabal Goenaga, M. (2016). Circular Economy : An economic and industrial model to achieve the sustainability of society. Proceedings of the 22nd Annual International Sustainable Development Research Society Conference. Rethinking Sustainability Models and Practices: Challenges for the New and Old World Contexts (vol. 2, pp. 504–520). Academic Press.

Rihter, P. K., & Vetrova, M. A. (2017). Making operational decisions in the transition to the principles of circular economy in the industries of the Russian Federation. Ecological and economic problems of development of regions and countries (sustainable development, management, environmental management) (pp. 229-234).

Ritzén, S., & Sandström, G. Ö. (2017). *Barriers to the Circular Economy - Integration of Perspectives and Domains. Procedia CIRP* (Vol. 64, pp. 7–12). Elsevier B.V.; doi:10.1016/j.procir.2017.03.005

KEY TERMS AND DEFINITIONS

Agriculture-Based Economy: The stage of the country's economic development when production is mainly carried out in agriculture.

Industrial Economy: The stage of the country's economic development when large industrial production prevails in the structure of the country's economy: mechanical engineering, mining, manufacturing, chemical industry, etc.

Light Industry: Includes a group of industries, such as textile, garment, knitting, footwear, fur, leather, and others.

Manufacturing Industry: A complex of industrial enterprises engaged in the processing and recycling of agricultural and industrial raw materials that are used to make new products. Manufacturing industry includes food, light, chemical, pharmaceutical industries, mechanical engineering, woodworking, pulp and paper, and others.

Mining Industry: A complex of industrial enterprises engaged in the extraction and primary processing of minerals from the Earth's interior. The mining industry includes enterprises that extract oil, gas, coal, metals, etc.

Non-Woven Material: Obtained without the use of weaving methods by combining fibers and threads with mechanical or physico-chemical methods. One of the oldest types of non-woven materials is felt, batting. Modern non-woven materials are polyester batting, spunbond, spunlace, isosoft, thinsulate.

Post-Industrial Economy: A transitional stage of the country's economic development from an industrial economy to a more advanced form.

Slag: A by-product that is formed in metallurgy during metal smelting. It is a frozen mass of various impurities and ash. Refers to the waste of metallurgical production.

Slag Dump: A place for storing slag.

Sludge: Dust and fine particles precipitated during ore washing, waste products.

Chapter 10
Sustainability and Justness for Transforming the Water Utility Companies' Business Models in the Circular Economy

Ninel Ivanova Nesheva-Kiosseva
https://orcid.org/0000-0001-7163-0200
New Bulgarian University, Bulgaria

ABSTRACT

The purpose of this chapter is to explore some of the problems of the transformation necessary to the business model of water and wastewater utility companies into a circular economy. This goal is accomplished by extending the understanding of the business model beyond the conventional understanding "within the framework of the corporation." This expansion of the scope of the water and wastewater utility companies' business model is justified by the fact that water, the source of their business, is a vital natural capital, and along with its economic value, water is a recognized human right. The study elaborates on the part of the business model related to the issues of fair treatment of society in its relations with business. The authors also explore the issue of value creation for stakeholders not only within a business but also through cooperation between water businesses and stakeholders.

BACKGROUND

The circular business model of water companies has not yet been fully developed as an archetype and in its specific application forms. Most of the known facts and results of creating circular business models for water companies are in practice and are strictly specific for company, region and business culture. (OECD, 2016; The International Water Association, 2018).

The issue justness as an element of the circular economy, which is a tool for sustainability, has also not been developed with regard to water companies. It is important to create an appropriate basic environment for a circular economy in the water sector.

DOI: 10.4018/978-1-7998-5116-5.ch010

Copyright © 2020, IGI Global. Copying or distributing in print or electronic forms without written permission of IGI Global is prohibited.

However, there are general theoretical and even concrete practical examples from other sectors that have taken the path of transformation to circularity, taking into account in business models a set of characteristics that incorporate different perceptions of equity in sustainable and circular business models.

In this chapter, we examine justness as arising from property rights and the distribution of value created through the transformation of property rights over water. We accept the hypothesis that well-defined treatment of water rights is the basis for sustainability in the water companies' circular business model.

It is our understanding that developing an archetype of a circular business model must be based on the particularities of each sector. The water sector is specific and important for the functioning of all other economic and social sectors, as well as for the life of the planet in general, since water is present in all production and life forms.

The subject of analysis in this chapter is water purification and its supply for the domestic, industrial and agricultural sectors, and does not cover other water industries.

Due to the influence of traditional historical and theoretical reasons, no clear property rights have been established in relation to water. The water companies, nor the society or the state neither owns water. The hypothesis of this study is that tradition can be reconsidered and such property rights established in relation to the needs of the circular economy in the WUC sector.

This will create the right business environment for a fair distribution of the value created by the circular water business.

The study addresses several issues that need to be investigated connectivity:

- The general layout of the business model;
- Circular economy itself and the business model of water companies in circular economy;
- Water in the circular economy as a human right and an economic resource;
- Questions on value and its distribution.

In order to propose a change in the structure of the business model of Water and Wastewater (sewer) Utility Companies, from linear to one compliant with the circular economy, the author puts forward the following issues:

1. The new elements that break the traditional business model, related to a new kind of close cooperation of companies with consumers, as stakeholders;
2. The problem of ownership of water resources in the circular economy in terms of property rights and the benefits of ownership. This is done from the standpoint of the neo-institutional paradigm and the concept of "property as a network of interests";
3. Redefining the assets of water companies;
4. The age-old problem of non-community involvement in operational and strategic water management, in conjunction with WSC, local and state government;
5. A fair distribution of all types of responsibilities but also of all types of benefits among all stakeholders in the management and use of water profits and risk. The symmetric responsibility of water companies and local communities for the pollution, recycling, conservation and adaptive use of water in the circular economy through fair cooperation in the context of property rights redefinition.

MAIN FOCUS OF THE CHAPTER

The main focus of this chapter is on building a hypothetical archetypal circular business model of water companies based on the idea of change in the approach to property rights and on that basis - on distributive justice. Defining the role of water in the business of water companies and redefining of property rights in relation to water in the conditions necessary for the realization of a circular economic system of fair cooperation between stakeholders and corporations.

ISSUES, CONTROVERSIES, PROBLEMS

The most controversial matter is that of property rights. So far, despite the obviousness of the unresolved issue of property rights over water, it has not found its solution. Although being acknowledged, and despite economic and anthropological studies proving the successful and fair management of water basised specific property rights of communities the property rights issue remains unresolved.

The other controversial matter is value distribution. Distribution is the rock of offence of economic theory. A dominant system has been formed historically empirically and theoretically. Distribution in this system is based primarily on state and private property rights. (There are also examples of private-public and public-private partnerships that do not always and not everywhere produce good results. Private-public partnerships, for example, in Bulgaria have undergone a full fiasco.) The effectiveness and efficiency of this dominant distribution nowadays is increasingly showing a high level of bankruptcy. The circular economy enables the distribution model to be changed.

INTRODUCTION

The idea of a circular economy dates to the time justified in the works of visionaries such as Kenneth Boulding (1966, pp. 1-3) Michael Braungart, William A. McDonoug, Katja Hansen and others, (Ellen Macarthur Foundation, n.d.), but it was not until the first decade of the twentieth century that it began to be seen as a serious tool for sustainable development.

In 2012, the United Nations accepted that "*successful implementation of policies requires establishing a planning framework for adaptive and integrated water resource management, under which appropriate pricing and multi-stakeholder participation are essential.*" (United Nations, 2012).

The European Commission adopted in December 2015 an Action Plan with 54 activities to create a circular economy. The objective of this plan and the establishment of a circular economy in the EU are to stimulate the additional creation of jobs, economic-and investment growth, and a carbon-neutral and competitive resource-efficient economy. (European Commission, 2015).

The Business Model a relatively new management tool - is entrusted with much of the hope of achieving sustainability and circularity in the economy.

The business model is a subject of considerable interest from academics and management. Peter Drucker first proposed the idea of business modeling, though he did not use the term. (Drucker, 1994)

The interest in this issue is so great that the Journal of Business models started to appear in 2015 (Journal of Bussiness Models, 2015). This interest and the increasing number of developments into the problems of business models is due to the certainty of opinion that the business model is nowadays a basic and even a major element of companies' competitiveness. (Casadesus-Masanell& Ricart, 2007; Zott & Amit, 2007).

The scientific definition of the Business Model phenomenon is manifold. The definitions of the business model relate primarily to how an entity manages its assets to generate cash flows.

Business models that have emerged in practice have their own theoretical typology. This typology is related to the definition of their functionality. In order to determine what type of business model an enterprise has; it is necessary to understand the goals of each business model and the activities undertaken to realize it.

The International Integrated Reporting Council gives a generalized assessment of what components are embedded in the content of the business model concept. According to this study 63% of the extensive scientific literature examined the business model is seen as the way the company makes money. For 56%, a key component of the business model is the company's inbound resources - resources, or "capital", according to IIRC terminology, the company relies on. (Under "capital" IIRC's concept of the six capitals emerges - financial, manufactured, social, human, intellectual and natural). In 56% of the studied sources, the business model refers to the activities of the enterprise, in 52% - the result of value creation); 48% - the strategy of the companies; 22% - the performance; 19% - value chain; 19% - an organizational system or "what the entity does, how it is structured or where it operates" (IIRC, 2013).

CIRCULAR ECONOMY AND CIRCULAR BUSINESS MODELS

Circular Business Models

The concept of 'development through sustainability' has emerged due to the problems of the current economic model based on consumption, the inevitable pollution from its growth, the growing population and the rapid depletion of non-renewable resources. A few theoretical tools and techniques have been developed - from investment management, new reporting tools, indicators, technological processes and so on to pave the way for 'development through sustainability'.

Circular economy has also emerged as a tool for implementing the concept of sustainable development, and has been defined as responsible use of resources to meet the needs of future generations.

The circular economy, as an alternative to the take-make-consume-dispose model, is characterized by several important topics - the elimination of external factors, waste without production, the maximum efficient use of resources. The circular economy has a very important characteristic - it is focused on the use of resources rather than consumption and this is a common and fundamental economic change. This requires a new fundamentally different business model by companies including WUC, in which consumers - water users - play a major role because they are part of the "cycle". For example, in TaKaDu's circular business model in Israel, 23% of wastewater is reused in agriculture due to consumer involvement. (Ben Gurion University of the Negev, Sapir Academic College & Jerusalem Institute for Policy Research, 2018, p. 21).

On the other hand, the concept of the business model, as stated, has traditionally been understood as the concept of profit. But innovative business models are increasingly being used to serve the concept of sustainability. Inevitably, they must also be consistent with the concept of the emerging idea of creating a circular economy.

Circular economy business models such as study, content and categorization are also subject to broad scientific interest. As a new field of research, interest in them is justified, but generalizations in the literature resulting from this interest in a logical and industry-specific practical applicability are difficult. This is the reason why Linder and Williander (2015) published the study "Circular Business Model Innovation: Inherent Uncertainties". A detailed categorization of the main characteristics of the traditional business model and the circular business model is made by Lewandowski (2016). Their diversity Lewandowski summarizes into the following categories of business activities - ReSOLVE framework (regenerate, share, optimize, loop, virtualize, exchange); ways of circular value creation; normative requirements for business models, and areas for integration. (Lewandowski, 2016, pp. 5-6).

The circular business model, as a strategic tool for sustainability, must meet the already set requirements for the extended functionality of the business model in a circular economy.

There is already considerable literature on the circular business model of companies and the management of circular companies. The problems with the creation and operation of circular business models are many and of a specific nature for each country, region and enterprise. Not all circular business models are innovative and they do not have to be innovative everywhere, because there is already experience in recycling, a Shared economy, tools that have long been used, such as material flow cost accounting, and more, applicable in building circular business models.

The definitions given to circular business models are also not straightforward, have different accents, and are evolving. They are developed from general perspectives, such as the first definition of the Ellen MacArthur Foundation Circular Business Model, as "*restorative or regenerative by intention and design*" (Ellen MacArthur Foundation, 2015).

There is and a view of circular business models as an "Economic System" (Mentink, 2014).

The definition of a circular business model can be:

A circular business model is how a company creates, captures, and delivers value with the value creation logic designed to improve resource efficiency through contributing to extending the useful life of products and parts (e.g., through long-life design, repair and remanufacturing) and closing material loops. (Nußholz, 2017)

or such:

Circular business models serve to reduce the extraction and use of natural resources and the generation of industrial and consumer wastes. They represent the key activities required to transition to a more resource efficient and circular economy. ... Circular business models use already existing materials and products as inputs and therefore their environmental footprint tends to be significantly smaller than that for traditional business models. (OECD, 2018)

Circular Business Model, Value and Sustainability

An important and unquestionable issue is the issue of value in the business model concept. Drucker first put it in 1994, followed by Amit and Zott (2001, 2002) and Magreta (2002) who raises the question of value provided to customers "*What is the underlying economic logic that explains how we can deliver value to customers at an appropriate cost?*"

Some of the accepted definitions of a business model today focus on proposing and creating value like this by Linder and Williander (2017) and Nußholz (2017).

Circular economy, as a tool for sustainability and circular business models have many identities with the concept of sustainability. They intersect with the problem of equity of interest in integrating non-economic aspects into development measurement, systemic changes and new design, as well as radical innovation changes, multidisciplinary research, the necessary cooperation and stakeholder cooperation, innovative business modeling as a key element of transformation from linear to circular economy. (Geissdoerfer, Savaget, Bocken & Hultink, 2017, p. 770).

"Accenture Strategy", a business, consulting firm, categorizes 5 circular business models: "Circular Supplies Resource Recovery, Product Life Extension, Sharing Platforms, and Product as a Service". Of interest is the latest "Product as a Service model", which has the meaning of "*Offer product access and retain ownership to internalize the benefits of circular resource productivity*." (Accenture, 2014).

The issue of achieving sustainability through the business model is its new function: Boons and Lüdeke-Freund (2013) identify four major parts of a common business model, each of which can be a source of greater sustainability. These include the provision of a value proposition with measurable and balanced environmental, social and economic value, and the use of a financial model that reflects the appropriate distribution of costs and benefits among the actors involved and must consider environmental and social impacts.

In the business models for "shared value", as well as in sustainability, the idea of justice emerges, such as the challenge to sustainable development, understood as "eco-justice" connected in some way or leading to social justice: as a concept and a challenge to the sustainable development of companies. (Schaltegger, 2013; Lüdeke-Freund, Massa, Bocken, Brent & Musango, 2014, pp. 20, 21, 55). On his part, Wells (2013) identifies six basic principles that underpin business models of sustainability: resource efficiency, social adequacy, localization and commitment, sustainability, ethics.

Practiced in lending to the poor, shared value business models also belong to circular business models. This is a business model that proposes to replace shareholders with stakeholders. Although used in microfinance, they have the overall philosophy of not being targeted solely in finance. (Yunus, Moingeon & Lehmann-Ortega, 2010, 308–325).

A circular economy is a tool for achieving sustainability and circular business models are subordinated to the concept of sustainability, including understood as economic, social and environmental sustainability:

All businesses must strive to become completely circular, designed to sustain products, components and material inputs and outputs at their highest utility and value at all times. A business model for sustainability helps describing, analyzing, managing, and communicating (i) a company's sustainable value proposition to its customers and all other stakeholders, (ii) how it creates and delivers this value, and (iii) how it captures economic value while maintaining or regenerating natural, social, and economic capital beyond its organizational boundaries. (Schaltegger, Lüdeke-Freund & Hansen, 2016)

In the business models for shared value, as well as in sustainability, the idea of justice emerges, such as the challenge to sustainable development, understood as 'eco-justice', linked to or leading to social justice: as a concept and challenge to sustainable development of the company. (Schaltegger, 2013).

Circular Business Models, CSR and Mixed Ownership

The issue of inequality (included in the obligations of the new sustainable and circular business models, underlined by a social component sought in the corporate social responsibility of companies and business models with corporate social responsibility. The authors of the article "Beyond CSR? Business, poverty and social justice: an introduction" (Newell & Frynas,2007) are trying to answer the question - is it possible for CSR to affect poverty through good business practices, including the use of a business model. They justify themselves with the concept of Prahaldand Stuart Hart, the key proponents of the idea, suggest that *"private firms can help reduce poverty, and make profits at the same time, by inventing new business models for providing products and services to the world's poor—the four billion people who live on less than $2000 a year"* and the book by Craig Wilson and Peter Wilson (2006) "Make Poverty Business: Increase Profits and Reduce Risks by Engaging with the Poor".

In the "Glossary of Business Models" we find such components of the business models of a sustainable and circular economy as *"No Frills - Minimum to deliver the core value proposition, where cost savings are shared with the customers; Open Business - Where collaboration with partners in the ecosystem becomes a central source of value creation; Differential Pricing - Charging more to those who can afford, and subsidizing those who cannot; Localization Favoring local and / or community-based production and consumption."* (Business and Sustainable Development Commission, 2016)

Successful circular economy business models, according to practitioners, will have the following characteristics:

- Closed Loop Partners
- Cost competitiveness
- Convenience
- Easy integration
- Measurable impact
- Health and safety standards (Croke, 2019)

Tonelli and Cristoni (2019), publish the book Management and the Circular Economy, which presents the logical and inevitable transition from Produce-Use-Dispose Model of the modern economy - to the circular model. The authors present as part of the strategic management of circular companies the circular business model.

Tonelli & Cristoni offer a common circular model that includes Servitization. Servitization word that comes from "*servitude*" - a restricted right to use someone else's property. The idea of introducing easement rights can also be used with the necessary modification to the specific meaning used by those authors in building the business model of water companies. (p. 90-113).

TRANSFORMATION OF WUC'S BUSINESS MODEL

WUC Circular Business Model Matrix

Water pollution, water scarcity, water availability, safety, quality and water management are an important and key issue in the context of a circular economy. According to the UN, water demand will exceed supply by 40 percent in 2030. (UN, 2016)

This is a huge risk to social sustainability. With a demand exceeding by 50% the supply, water prices will rise dramatically on equal other terms and will outweigh the ability of the greater part of the population and economic operators to pay an affordable price for water supply.

One of the key problems with the sustainability of the water sector is that in our time, consumers of water - for domestic, industrial and agricultural production - are completely separated from water management (including pricing). And this is a fact even when communities and nature are recognized as stakeholders.

How could external impacts such as water losses, water pollution and pollution due to water be eliminated if not all stakeholders' work for it? The answer to this question is also within the scope of the business model of water companies.

From the definitions and systematized business models of circular economy selected for the present sustainability study of circular business equity, it is important that the following groups of ideas exist in different texts without being unified and fully functionally clarified.

Water and Wastewater (sewer) utility companies are involved in the treatment of raw water and its supply, sewage collection, sewage treatment and sewage disposal. For the purposes of the study seeking to create a common archetypal business model of WUC, no specification is made as to whether they use groundwater and surface water or both. Catching, storage, water and sludge facilities, and their vast majority, are state or public and are maintained and funded by the public.

WUCs have their own opportunities to integrate into the circular economy by building a circular business model that is not only subject to their own goals of capturing value and profit, but also fairness and thus sustainability. Water in all three applications - for domestic use, as an energy source and logistics - functions as a carrier of chemicals, particles that represent a potential resource or pollutant. Therefore, water companies must participate in the circular water economy and they have a key place in it. What is the role of the water that is handled by WUC is clearly evident from the following quoted text: "*Water, with the energy it consumes and produces, and the materials it contains, has a critical role in transitioning to the circular economy. Water from industrial or domestic use contains energy, water, organics, phosphates, nitrogen, cellulose, rare earths, and other resources. Technologies are increasingly making resource recovery from wastewater commercially feasible, including biogas, fertilizer, paper, metals, plastics and, perhaps most importantly, it is a source of 'new' water. For the water sector, transitioning to a circular economy presents an opportunity to fast track achieving the sustainable development goals through accelerating and scaling-up recent scientific and technological advances that support greater efficiency in the sector.* (International Water Association, (2018).

The State of Raw Water in the WUC's Business

The place and role of raw water as a source of business for water suppliers remains uncertain from an economic and accounting point of view.

The raw water that WUCs purify and deliver to consumers is not reported and it does not appear in their financial statement. (Bloetscher, 2011)

As assets, WUCs show in their financial statements this: "*Asset: Infrastructure (e.g. buildings, treatment plants) and equipment (e.g. pumps, screens, treatment units, disinfection systems and control panels) controlled and operated by Irish water to deliver water and wastewater services. We divide these into Below Ground Assets such as pipework and valves and Above Ground Assets such as treatment plants.*" (Irish Water, 2015)

It is therefore clear that water does not belong to them. However, water is their only production output and source-business, and therefore their cash profits. Figure 1 presents a summary of the traditional business model of water companies. (WUCs have some differences in their business models that are negligible in the issues studied.)

Figure 1. Traditional business model of WUC
Source: The Author

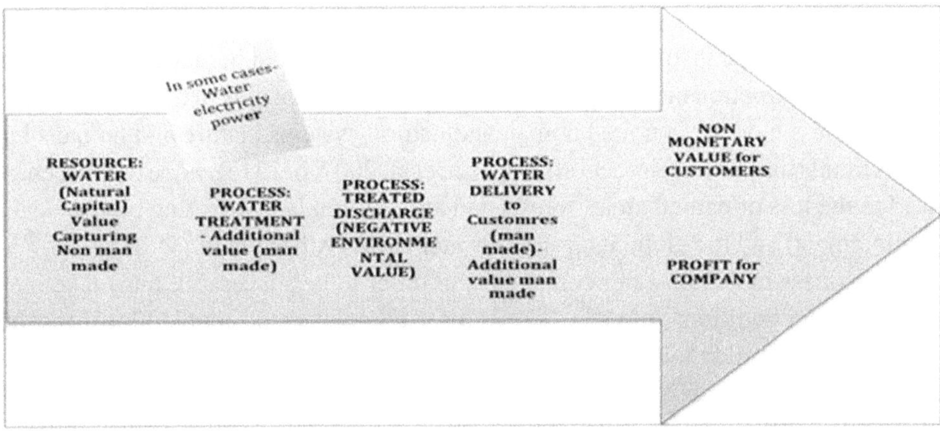

If the property rights to raw water are vague and unclear, then the benefits derived from doing business with it are unclear, and immanent injustice is rooted in the distribution of these benefits.

Ownership of an asset gives you the right to reap the benefits including monetary profit. This is not the case with water. The state (municipal) authorities have granted one property right belonging to the people to companies to make their business grow and to profit from it. Moreover, these companies are absolute monopolies - in fact, de jure monopolies, which are subject to regulation, which is obliged to provide them with revenue through pricing and to prevent them from going bankrupt. At the same time, water prices are rising steadily, exceeding tolerable thresholds for a large part of the population. According to a study by RobecoSAM "*Global average combined water tariffs rose 4.3% in 2014, following a 3.7% increase in 2013. Water tariffs have been outstripping inflation over the past years. In the US, the price of water and wastewater services increased by 7% in 2014, against 1.7% inflation*". (RobecoSAM, (2015). In the circular economy and in the circular business model, the end user is part of the system; he cannot be ignored by the system. (Antikainen& Valkokari, 2016)

The lack of clarity regarding water property rights and their use makes the additional beneficial properties and content of water in a circle unclear, since water contains many useful substances for further processing such as the mentioned organics, phosphorus, nitrogen, cellulose, bio-gas, fertilizer, paper, metals, plastics and, and is a source of 'new' water. Therefore, their ownership is dubious and questions the fairness of the benefits derived from these.

The sustainability of WUC's governance, economic and social performance can also be negative. Management weakness of organizations may stem from the discrepancy between reported and actual indicators. In a circular economy, the reported and real characteristics of the business model of companies are a management weakness. The review of traditional weaknesses, their identification and correction in the context of a circular economy is an issue that is relevant and worth discussing. The key issue here is that WUCs do not take into account in any way the incoming water resource, which is a natural capital.

This situation is a visible traditional flaw and can become a serious problem for the WUC circular business model, which circular business model requires not only production but also a social circle - stakeholder interaction. This could be corrected for the full and successful functioning of WUC's circular business models.

A group of scientists, including Nobel Prize winner in Economics Eleanor Ostrom raised the issue of complexity of coupled human and natural systems, including the interaction between social and natural sciences. (Liu *et al*, 2007)

This idea and the scientific justification of the authors for the related human and natural systems are quite relevant in the construction of the business model of water companies in the circular economy (and of any circular business model). In united human and natural systems, nature and humans interact and create feedback circuits that have reciprocal effects. (Liu et al, 2007. p. 1513). For example, changes in the land cover lead to the loss of natural areas, forests and agricultural land affecting biophysical processes such as water treatment) and the biotic integrity of water flow. (Alberti *et al.*, 2007).

The circular business model of water companies, in order to be successful, must take into account, unprecedented so far in traditional models, the need for complexity of coupled business, human and natural systems. To implement this model requires collective action and self-organization, which is determined by the expected benefits and expected costs. (Ostrom, 2009; Wagner, J., 2012).

In order for the circular business model of water companies to be successful what needs to be taken into account is the unprecedented, so far, in traditional models, the need for complexity of coupled business, human and natural systems. The implementation of this model requires collective action and self-organization, determined by the expected profits and expenses.

In the Integrated Reporting System <IR>, water is classified as "natural capital" (International Integrated Reporting Council (IIRC, 2017). Water is a global natural capital that is also defined as planetary climate system and hydrological system by European Environment Agency (EEA, 2019) and United Nations System of Environmental Economic Accounting (SEEA) (United Nations, 2012).

In Israel, for example, water is a public good that is legally recognized by the society. TaKaDu Water Company's circular business model is also recognized as the basis for ownership for sustainable revenues. (Ben Gurion University *at. al.*, p. 36)

Water is not only a global natural capital but also a local natural capital. The people in each location, whose life and livelihood depend on the presence, conservation and preservation) of water in it, as reasonable beings, are its owners. WUCs exist because of those peoples' vital needs and through water.

In most cases, as well as in cities, local communities do not exercise direct control over natural capital, including water, and this is done through their representative - the state and / or local authorities. Water collection is usually done through state or municipal dam owners who sell WUC water. However, supreme property rights belong to the community of people.

Water is a natural capital, not created by man. Like the air, it belongs to humanity and is a gift from Mother Nature to humans and all inhabitants of the earth. The entire planet participates in the global water cycle.

Non-clarification of property rights over water nowadays leads to unreporting, risks and instability for companies.

Raw water creates income and profits for the company, and it is a natural resource not created by man.

Therefore, water should be classified as a natural tangible nonfinancial capital asset for water companies. It is a gift from nature, part of the wealth of humanity and a human right (United Nations, 1992).

Water is excluded from the classification as an asset for two main reasons:

1. The tradition dating from Roman law and later from the Classical School of Economics;
2. The high transaction costs that were necessary to establish property rights to ever-moving water.

Today, we have both the theory and the science and technology that need to change this tradition, in order to achieve sustainability and justice in a circular economy. Artificial Intelligence and Big data are tools that can be adequately used to fairly apply the 4 points of the matrix to a different and adequate treatment of water in the business of water companies.

An Archetypal Business Model of WUC for a Circular Economy

Based on the existing scientific literature, the author propose to build the "Matrix of circular business model of WUC" for justness of property rights and fair distribution of value:

1. Justness of property rights:
    1.1. Servitization
    1.2. Exchange of shareholders with stakeholders.
2. Value. Linking the Circular Business Model to Value Creation and Value Form Questions:
    2.1. Value proposition
    2.2. Delivers of value
    2.3. Shared value
3. Circular Partnership:
    3.1. Closed Loop Partners
    3.2. Collaboration with partners is a central source of value creation
    3.3. Community-based production and consumption
4. Aimed at eliminating inequalities:
    4.1. Measurable impact
    4.2. Cost savings shared with customers
    4.3. Use of a financial model that reflects the appropriate distribution of costs and benefits among the actors involved and must consider environmental and social impacts.

These four groups of characteristics of the WUC circular business model raise the following questions:

1. How property issues need to be changed and arranged in a variety of ways in order for a circular business model to be successful;

2. What value, value to whom?

Assuming that humanity in the global sense and local communities - in the local aspect, is the owner and a-proprietor of water, and if we accept the authors' position that the circular (sustainable) business model needs a "matrix" and in particular a replacement to shareholders with stakeholders, Community-based production and consumption, shareholders of value, Shared value, Cost savings shared with the customers et cetera, it is fair to assume that WUCs receive profits from an asset other than theirs and a profit that they do not share with its owners. This is the reason for instability and inability to fully implement the circular model in the water sector.

Traditional and Circular/Justness WUC's Business Model

We will use two common traditional generalized business models: an empirical IIRC, created on the basis of a comprehensive study of the details used by companies in business models; and that of the "archetypal business models" of Weill, Malone, D'Urso, Herman and Woerner (2005, p.7), to describe changes in the business model of water companies in a circular economy that require circularity, sustainability and fairness.

Table 1. Five summarized categories of general characteristics of the WUC business model - water companies have a tight contour

General Model by IIRC		General Traditional Business Model of WUC
1	2	3
Organizational overview	What the entity does, How it is structured, Or Where it operates.	Water Utilities Absolute Natural Monopoly (Monopoly De Jure) in Local Areas
Business strategy	Key aspects of an organization's strategy	Investment Growth: physical assets, monetary profit, Customers (incomes, demography)
Value chain	Place in the value chain and dependencies on key inputs.	Non- monetary value of customers – delivery of water Key input is Raw Water Total dependence of Raw water
Financial performance	How the business model drives profitability or revenue generation. Profit and Revenue for Whom?	No single "financial model" Costs – (cost reduction)- no cost reduction Risk – (risk reduction)- growing risk for customers and company Sales - profit margin Reputation and brand value - with non transparent pricing growing the reputation cut down Attractiveness for HR- not clear Innovative capabilities- Artificial intelligence, Big Data at setera.
Value creation	How the organization's inputs, activities, and relationships lead to value and desired outcomes.	Raw water – not clear defined ownership Monetary profit for Company Non monetary value for Customers

Source: IIRC, (2013, p. 3) and the Author.

An empirical model of IIRC: The IIRC survey presents common features of traditional business models in 5 broad categories. In column 3, we present our estimation, ceteris paribus, in the WUC empirical business model of these 5 common and most used companies' categories.

In our opinion, the traditional business model of water companies is not circular. (Of course, we do not include water companies that have already made a transition to a certain extent to a circular business model like TaKaDu's.)

Weill, Malone, D'Urso, Herman and Woerner build four business model archetypes that can form the basis of water companies' circular business model. They distinguish between the archetypes of Creator, Distributor, Landlord and Broker.

What and whose rights are sold is what are important in defining this model based on the ownership of the asset. "The first, and most obvious kind of right a business can sell is the right of ownership of an asset. (Weill, *et al.*, 2005, p.7).

We accept that humanity, local communities involved in the management of water through their daily and economic activities have the rights of the landlord under servitude conditions - partial rights to use another person's property. Taking all this into consideration, we may say that humanity and local communities are "Landlord" and Nature is the "Creator".

The answer to the question "*What assets are involved*?" creates 16 detailed Business Model Archetypes.

Based on the archetypes of the circular business model created by Weill and colleagues (Weill *at al.* 2005, p. 33) we propose the following water company business model archetype in accordance with the content of the Circular Sustainability and Justness Matrix, given in *Table 2* and *Table 3*.

Table 2. A new archetypal business model for water companies designed for the conditions of the circular economy (italics- content from P. Weill's archetypal model, Malone, D'Urso, Herman and S. Woerner (2005), bold - originally made WUC archetype)

What rights are being sold?	How much does the business transform the asset?	
	Significant	**Limited**
Ownership of Asset with Supreme Property rights - Nature, Humanity	*Creator*- Nature	*Distributor*-WUC
Use of Asset - human and economical	*Landlord*-Nature, Easement Landlord – Humanity; Local Community	
Matching the buyer and seller-	*Broker*- WUC and have to add Local Community	

Source. Weill et al., (2005, p. 33) and the Author.

Value: What Value? Value for Whom?

In this part of the analysis we proceed from the predicates already substantiated in the above studies:

1. Collaboration with partners - a central source of value creation;
2. Community-based production and consumption;
3. Delivers of value, Shared value, Cost savings shared with the customers.

Table 3. New comprehensive archetypal business model of water companies designed for the conditions of the circular economy include assets (content from the archetypal model of P. Weill, Malone, D'Urso, Herman and S. Woerner (2005), bold - originally made WUC archetype. The circular business model of water companies has a solid outline)

Basic Business Model Archetype		**What Type of Asset/Capital is Involved?**				**Total by Asset Right**
		Financial	**Physical**	**Intangible**	**Human**	
What rights are being sold (swapped)*?*	*Creator (Ownership of asset with significant transformation)*	Investor-owner of financial capital: Individuals, corporate, state, municipal-local community	Nature (Raw water is Natural Capital)	-	-	Nature and Society
	Distributor (Ownership of asset with limited transformation)	WUC (Owner of equipment)	-	WUC (Patents)	-	WUC
	Landlord (Use of asset)	Investors	Nature-Humanity (under Servitization)	Intellectual (Owner of Intellectual property rights)	-	Investors Nature and Humanity
	Broker	Matching the buyer and seller	Matching the buyer and seller	Matching the buyer and seller	-	WUC and Local Community

Source. Weill et al., (2005, p. 33) and the Author.

There are many types of value in economic terminology. Whenever economists use the term "value", they put an adjective before it. There is no single theory of value. However, this term is used both in traditional business models and in innovative ones - sustainable and circular business models, without defining exactly what value and value for whom.

For example, Antikainen and Valkokari (2016) summarize that sustainable innovative circular business models create opportunities for "*benefits from the perspectives of society and the environment.*"

The archetype of these models according to Bocken, Short, Rana, & Evans (2014) is to "maximize material and energy efficiency; create value from waste; substitute with renewables and natural processes; deliver functionality rather than ownership; adopt a stewardship role; encourage sufficiency; repurpose the business for society/environment; and develop scale- up solutions (Bocken *et al.,* 2014).

In "Consumer Service Innovation in a Circular Economy", customer value in circular economy is reduced to a set of non-monetary "benefits" for which the poor consumer must make numerous "sacrifices", feeling less comfortable and at a higher price. (Antikainen& al. 2018)

According to Hsie, Nickerson & Zenger (2007), "*Value is created from the firm by a solution to a problem of a customer at a cost less than the value of the solved problem.*"

Water is a human right. Humanity as a whole and the local communities that run the water at their location have property rights over it, and if we adhere to the idea that a change in the recognition of their property in the name of justice is needed, then such an approach of imposing value in the circular model would only be for the benefit of the monopoly water companies and would not do well to the fair and equitable cooperation needed to realize the circular economy as a tool for sustainability.

Therefore, by creating a new system of taxes, fees and rents, the profit should be distributed and returned to the creator and owners of the capital. At present, for example, all environmental charges are calculated at the expense of consumers in their invoices for the delivery and treatment of water to consumers. They are appropriated by the water company. A water company that does not own water as an asset does not return these environmental taxes back to nature. Investing them for environmental aims and purposes is also unclear. The natural capital, property of nature - its creator, is not only not restored, but also exhausted. Water losses in the water system due to the inefficiency of the assets of the water companies are also calculated in the invoices of the consumers.

This situation is unfair to both nature and customers.

In this situation, Nature (The Landlord with supreme property rights) should receive a "natural rent", communities - a water rent from their participation in the circular economy in the conservation, management, conservation of water resources and nature as owners of common pool resources, water a company - profit from the efficiency of the use of its capital - tangible and intangible assets that are its property, financial capital suppliers — must receive dividends from the efficiency of the use of their financial capital.

The Circular Business Model Archetype for Justness and Sustainability of WUC - A business model that considers all non-financial and financial benefits for all stakeholders - Nature, humanity - local communities, water business.

SOLUTIONS AND RECOMMENDATIONS

Water, as recommended by International Integrated Reporting Council, should be accepted and treated as a natural capital that creates value for its owners and farmers. The distribution of the value created by water must rest on the principles of property rights recognized by humanity and local communities. In the circular economy, the linear production model is modified, the linear dependence of the trader - consumer - also.

In this chapter, we have theoretically explored the problems of transformation with a view to a fair distribution of value, not only as a non-monetary value.

Further research on this issue should concentrate on the financial part of the business model as well as the accounting treatment of the questions raised.

FUTURE RESEARCH DIRECTIONS

The future research directions of the problem under study for the circular business model of water companies should be directed towards the extension of the conceptual framework and testing of the presented theoretical model.

Apart from the theoretical model, the research should seek the practical engagement of companies, local communities and public government agencies.

Local community traditions in ownership, distribution and cooperation can show great diversity and resilience that need to be specifically examined, and the model has to be tested contextually.

The challenge of a fair circular business model for water companies is interdisciplinary in scientific and practical terms and requires the efforts of scientists and practitioners from diverse fields. It engages the expertise of business managers, entrepreneurs, economists; water engineers and geologists; accountants and Information technologies, and Artificial Intelligence specialists; lawyers, as well as local and state public administration.

Changing the Legal Framework - establishing mixed-type property rights to water and recognizing the different types of rents that result from them is the first step in the multi-layer test of the theoretical model. The fair accounting treatment of the created value from the natural capital - water, both monetary and non-monetary is the next step in this process. The formation of water partnerships between local communities and water providers will shape the specific concrete circular business models of water companies in the future.

CONCLUSION

The emerging wave of the New Economy creates empirically in practice and laboratory in scientists' offices, new (innovative) business models, including circular business models that are tools for achieving sustainability. Emerging business models in the circular economy are re defined-from theory to practice and from practice to theory. (OECD, 2000; Cohen, 2016).

The circular use of resources requires a change in the way in which value and profit are created and distributed - circular and equitable, based on the acceptance of water for a common pool resource, establishing a system of property rights on which the equitable distribution of created non-cash and monetary values).

The two main questions: "Value: what and for whom, and through what property rights is the distribution of value added?" concern water resources as natural capital and their circular use, due to the special role of water as a human right and an economic resource. They directly address the issue of equity, which has not yet been developed in the circular business modeling system.

The circular business model, as a necessity and a model of strategy and sustainability, must meet the requirements already set for the extended functionality of the business model.

Delaying the WUC from integrating them into the circular economy will lead to "management weakness" and hence to a lack of adaptability to new conditions and a lack of sustainability. Management weakness of organizations may stem from the discrepancy between reported and actual indicators. In a circular economy, the reported and real characteristics of the business model of companies are a management weakness. The review of traditional weaknesses, their identification and correction in the context of a circular economy is an issue that is relevant and worth discussing. The main issue here is that WUCs do not account for the incoming water resource, which is a natural capital.

Establishing a circular model in which common pool resource ownership is recognized, the role and stakeholder involvement will lead to:

1. Fairer pricing. Owners will have the responsibility to pay the necessary investments, from which they will receive part of the value added and in the form of monetary profit, which will engage them more with their part of water management - human management. They will no longer just be consumers, as already indicated in in several circular business models, but responsible owners;
2. The elimination of lack of transparency of water pricing characteristic of regulatory pricing;
3. Correction of the overcapitalization and monopoly profits of water monopolies;
4. The need for the set-up of new formal institutions to implement this model.

ACKNOWLEDGMENT

The author wishes to express her special gratitude to Professor Maria-Gabriella Baldarelli, PhD, Department of Management, Bologna University and Professor Mara Del Baldo PhD, Department of Economics, Society and Politics, University of Urbino "Carlo Bo" for their long-term support for her research. The author acknowledges the support she received from New Bulgarian University, through the opportunities that it provided for her scientific research. The author is very grateful to the Italian CSEAR for the opportunity to present some ideas of this study at the Seventh International Conference of the Italian CSEAR at the University of Urbino, Italy in September 2018.

REFERENCES

Accenture. (2014). Accenture Strategy Circular Advantage Innovative Business Models and Technologies to Create Value in a World without Limits to Growth, Accenture. Retrieved from https://www.accenture.com/%20t20150523T053139__w__/us-en/_acnmedia/Accenture/Conversion-Assets/Dot-Com/Documents/Global/PDF/Strategy_6/Accenture-Circular-Advantage-Innovative-Business-Models-Technologies-Value-Growth.pdf

Alberti, M., Booth, D., Hill, K., Coburn, B., Avolio, C., Coe, S., & Spirandelli, D. (2007). The impact of urban patterns on aquatic ecosystems: An empirical analysis in Puget lowland sub-basins. *Landscape and Urban Planning*, *80*(4), 346–341. doi:10.1016/j.landurbplan.2006.08.001

Amit, R., & Zott, C. (2002, Mar.). Creating Value Through Business Model Innovation. Spring Research Feature, 40–49.

Antikainen, M., & Valkokari, K. (2016). A Framework for Sustainable Circular Business Model Innovation. Technology Innovation Management Review, 6(7), 7. doi:10.22215/timreview/1000

Ben Gurion University of the Negev Sapir Academic College, & Jerusalem Institute for Policy Research. (2018). Israeli Water System: A Circular Economy Business Model Case, R2p the Route of Circular Economy. Retrieved from http://www.r2piproject.eu/wp-content/uploads/2019/05/Water-Case-Study.pdf

Bloetscher, F. (2011). *Utility Management for Water and Wastewater Operators*. Denver: American Water Works Association.

Bocken, N. M., Rana, P., & Short, S. W. (2015). Value mapping for sustainable business thinking. *Journal of Industrial and Production Engineering*, *32*(1), 67–81. doi:10.1080/21681015.2014.1000399

Boons, F., & Lüdeke-Freund, F. (2013). Business Models for Sustainable Innovation: State-of-the-Art and Steps Towards a Research Agenda. *Journal of Cleaner Production*, *45*, 9–19. doi:10.1016/j.jclepro.2012.07.007

Boulding, K. E. (1966). The Economics of the Coming Spaceship Earth. In Environmental Quality in a Growing Economy (pp. 3–11). Retrieved from http://arachnid.biosci.utexas.edu/

Business and Sustainable Development Commission. (2016). *Business Models. Exponentially more social, lean, integrated and circular*. London, UK: Volans.

Casadesus-Masanell, R., & Ricart, J. E. (2007). Competing Through Business Models. Working Paper 713, IESE Business School, Barcelona.

Cohen, M. J. (2016). *The Future of Consumer Society: Prospects for Sustainability in the New Economy*. Oxford University Press; doi:10.1093/acprof:oso/9780198768555.001.0001.

Croke, B. (2019). Key Ingredients for Scaling Circular Reuse Business Models. GreenBiz. Retrieved from https://www.greenbiz.com/article/key-ingredients-scaling-circular-reuse-business-models

Drucker, P. (1994). The Theory of the Business. Harvard Business Review Retrieved from https://hbr.org/1994/09/the-theory-of-the-business

Ellen MacArthur Foundation. (2013). Towards the Circular Economy: Economic and Business Rationale for an Accelerated Transition. Retrieved from https://www.ellenmacarthurfoundation.org/assets/downloads/publications/Ellen-MacArthur-Foundation-Towards-the-Circular-Economy-vol.1.pdf

Ellen MacArthur Foundation. (n.d.). Circular Economy Concept, Schools of Thought. Retrieved from https://www.ellenmacarthurfoundation.org/circular-economy/concept/schools-of-thought

European Commission. (2015). Communication from the Commission to the European Parliament, the Council, the European Economic and Social Committee and the Committee of the Regions, December 2. Retrieved December 11, 2019, from https://ec.europa.eu/transparency/regdoc/rep/1/2015/EN/1-2015-614-EN-F1-1.PDF

European Environment Agency (EEA). (2019). Water and marine environment. Retrieved December 16, 2019, from https://www.eea.europa.eu/themes/water

Geissdoerfer, M., Savaget, P., Bocken, N. M., & Hultink, E. J. (2017). The Circular Economy - A New Sustainability Paradigm? *Journal of Cleaner Production*, *143*, 770. doi:10.1016/j.jclepro.2016.12.048

Hsie, I., Nickerson, J., & Zenger, T. (2007). Opportunity Discovery, Problem Solving and a Theory of the Entrepreneurial Firm. *Journal of Management Studies*, *47*(7), 1255–1277. doi:10.1111/j.1467-6486.2007.00725.x

International Integrated Reporting Council. (2013). Business Model Background Paper for IR. International Integrated Reporting. Retrieved from https://integratedreporting.org/wp-content/uploads/2013/03/Business_Model.pdf

International Water Association. (2018). Wastewater Report 2018, The Water Reuse Opportunity. Retrieved from https://www.iwa-network.org/wp-content/uploads/2018/02/OFID-Wastewater-report-2018.pdf

Irish Water. (2015). Water Services Strategic Plan A. Plan for the Future of Water Services. Retrieved from https://www.water.ie/docs/WSSP_Final.pdf

Journal of Bussiness Models. (2015). Welcome to the journal of business models. Retrieved from http://journalofbusinessmodels.com/#about

Lewandowski, M. (2015). Designing the Business Models for Circular Economy - Towards the Conceptual Framework. MDPI Review, 3–5. Retrieved from https://www.mdpi.com

Linder, M., & Williander, M. (2017). Circular Business Model Innovation: Inherent Uncertainties. Business Strategy and the Environment. *Circular Business Model Innovation: Inherent Uncertainties, 26*(2), 182–186.

Liu, J., Dietz, T., Carpenter, S. R., Alberti, M., Moran, M., Pell, A. N., ... Taylor, W. W. (2007). Complexity of coupled human and natural systems. *Science, 317*(5844), 3165–3316. doi:10.1126/science.1144004 PubMed

Lüdeke-Freund, F., Massa, L., Bocken, N., Brent, A., & Musango, J. (2016). Business Models for Shared Value: Main Report. London, UK: The Economist.

Magretta, J. (2002). Why Business Models Matter. Harvard Business Review. Retrieved from https://hbr.org/2002/05/why-business-models-matter

Mentink, B. (2014). Circular Business Model Innovation: A Process Framework and a Tool for Business Model Innovation in a Circular Economy (Master's thesis). Leiden, The Netherlands: Delft University of Technology & Leiden University.

Newell, P., & Frynas, J. G. (2007). Beyond CSR? Business, poverty and social justice: An introduction. *Third World Quarterly, 28*(4), 670. doi:10.1080/01436590701336507

Nußholz, J. L. (2017). Circular business models: Defining a Concept and Framing an Emerging Research Field. *Sustainability, 9*(10), 12. doi:10.3390/su9101810

OECD. (2000). *A New Economy? The Changing Role of Innovation and Information Technology in Growth.* Paris: OECD Publishing.

OECD. (2016). Sustainable Business Models for Water Supply and Sanitation in Small Towns and Rural Settlements in Kazakhstan. OECD Studies on Water. doi:10.1787/9789264249400-en

OECD. (2018). *Business Models for Circular Economy - Opportunities and Challenges from a Policy Perspective.* Paris: OECD.

Ostrom, E. (2009, July 24). A general framework for analyzing sustainability of social ecological systems. *Science, 325*(5939), 419–422. doi:10.1126/science.1172133 PubMed

Robeco, S. A. M. (2015). Water: the Market of the future. Retrieved from https://www.google.com/search?q=RobecoSAM%2C+(2015)+Water%3A+the+market+of+the+future&rlz=1C5CHFA_enBG846BG846&oq=RobecoSAM%2C+(2015)+Water%3A+the+market+of+the+future&aqs=chrome.69i57.1720j0j9&sourceid=chrome&ie=UTF-8

Schaltegger, S. (2013). Sustainability management. In S. Idowu, N. Capaldi, L. Zu, & A. Das Gupta (Eds.), *Encyclopedia of corporate social responsibility* (pp. 2383–2388). Berlin: Springer; doi:10.1007/978-3-642-28036-8_741.

Schaltegger, S., Lüdeke-Freund, F., & Hansen, E. G. (2012). Business Cases for Sustainability: The Role of Business Model Innovation for Corporate Sustainability. *International Journal of Innovation and Sustainable Development, 6*(2), 6. doi:10.1504/IJISD.2012.046944

The International Water Association. (2018). Wastewater Report 2018. The Water Reuse Opportunity. Retrieved from https://www.iwa-network.org/wp-content/uploads/2018/02/OFID-Wastewater-report-2018.pdf

Tonelli, M., & Cristoni, N. (2018). Strategic Management and the Circular Economy. Project: Strategic Management and the Circular Economy, 90–113. doi:10.4324/9781315102641

United Nations. (1992). The Dublin Statement on Water and Sustainable Development. UN Documents Gathering a body of global agreements.

United Nations (UN). (2012). *Statistical Division & London Group on Environmental Accounting. Subgroup on Water Accounting. SEEA-Water System of Environmental-Economic Accounting for Water*. London: United Nations.

United Nations (UN). (2016, March 2). United Nations Environment Program. Retrieved December 16, 2019, from https://www.unenvironment.org/news-and-stories/press-release/half-world-face-severe-water-stress-2030-unless-water-use-decoupled

Wagner, J. (2012). Water and the Commons Imaginary. *Current Anthropology*, *53*(5), 621.

Weill, P., Malone, T. W., D'Urso, V. T., Herman, G., & Woerner, S. (2005). Do Some Business Models Reform Better Than Others? MIT Centre for Coordination, Science Working Paper, 226, 7.

Wells, P. (2013). *Business Models for Sustainability*. Cheltenham, UK: Edward Elgar; doi:10.4337/9781781001530.

Wilson, C., & Wilson, P. (2006). *Make poverty business: increase profits and reduce risks by engaging with the poor*. Greenleaf Publishing.

Yunus, M., Moingeon, B., & Lehmann-Ortega, L. (2010). Building social business models: Lessons from the Grameen experience. Long Range Planning International Journal of Strategic Management, 43(2-3), 10. doi:10.1016/j.lrp.2009.12.005

Zott, C., & Amit, R. (2007). Business Model Design and the Performance of Entrepreneurial Firms. *Organization Science*, *18*(2), 181–199. doi:10.1287/orsc.1060.0232

KEY TERMS AND DEFINITIONS

Integrated Reporting: A relatively new corporate reporting model that united in one report all statements and integrates their data with a strategic vision and focus on value creation and sustainability. There are three main components of Integrated reporting - value added, the business model, and the concept of the six capitals (financial, manufacturing, human, natural, social, human capital, and intellectual capital) is derived as a standalone value that is capable of creating value.

International Integrated Reporting Council (IIRC): International coalition whose mission is to create a new model of accounting for capital allocation.

Natural Capital: An economic category designates all things created by nature that are used as economic resources; one of the six capitals according to the IIRC concept. Water is one of the components of natural capital, without which life and economic activity are impossible. It's defined as capital because creates more value than its own value.

Value (in Accounting): In financial accounting, the monetary expression of the worth of something. In non-financial accounting defined as different tangible and intangible things depending on the satisfaction of stakeholders.

Value (in Economic Theory): The fundamental question of economic science, defined in a different way by different economic schools. In general, the basis of the value in economic theory is the quantitative ratio of goods in terms of free exchange between owners.

WUC: Water and wastewater (sewer) utility companies. The sole water providers and water purification services, "natural monopoly" in fact administrative monopoly/monopoly de jure, sole water providers.

WUC Circular Business Model Archetype for Justness and Sustainability: Business model set that considers all non-financial and financial benefits for all stakeholders – nature, humanity, local communities, and business.

Chapter 11
Circular Economy Model for the E-Waste Management Sector

Dileep Baburao Baragde
https://orcid.org/0000-0001-9112-5535
G. S. Moze College, India

Amit Uttam Jadhav
G. S. Moze College, India

ABSTRACT

The circular economy (CE) model has become highly relevant in recent years, with the electronics industry being one of the divisions that have thought about its application. Regardless of just a constrained measure of writing being accessible on waste electric and electronic equipment (e-waste), electronic waste or e-waste is a developing and quickly developing test for waste administration in the world. E-waste is a term for electronic items that have turned out to be undesirable, non-working, or outdated, and have basically come to the 'part of the arrangement', inside only a couple of brief years, given the quick innovative advances inside the business. E-waste is created from anything electronic —PCs, TVs, screens, PDAs, PDAs, VCRs, CD players, fax machines, printers, and coolers— and is commonly broken into two classes, information technology (IT) and consumer electronics (CE), on account of divergent systems and technologies required for recycling these products.

INTRODUCTION

The circular economy (CE) model has become highly relevant in recent years, with the electronics industry being one of the divisions that has thought about its application (Meloni, 2019) Regardless of just a constrained measure of writing being accessible on waste electric and electronic equipment (e-waste). Electronic waste or E-Waste is a developing and quickly developing test for waste administration in World. E-Waste, is a term for electronic items that have turned out to be undesirable, non-working or outdated, and have basically come to the 'part of the arrangement', inside only a couple of brief years, given the quick innovative advances inside the business. E-waste is created from anything electronic: PCs, TVs,

DOI: 10.4018/978-1-7998-5116-5.ch011

Copyright © 2020, IGI Global. Copying or distributing in print or electronic forms without written permission of IGI Global is prohibited.

screens, PDAs, PDAs, VCRs, CD players, fax machines, printers and coolers and is commonly broken into two classes, Information technology (IT) and Consumer electronics (CE) on account of divergent systems and technologies required for recycling these products.

E-Waste has both a positive and negative rescue esteem. Comprehensively, the IT class is described by positive rescue esteem where the segments can be destroyed and re-utilized and the CE classification is portrayed by negative rescue worth and comes up short on the monetary motivating force for reusing, where items are dumped back in the earth. With the IT part very much boosted and concentrated on the recuperation of base and valuable metals the CE segment, the treatment of coolers, LCD, CRTs and fluorescent lights remains to a great extent disregarded. In India the business overall is described by an enormous casual area that is utilized in the extraction of valuable metals in unsafe working conditions that post a noteworthy wellbeing hazard (Abhishek K, Awasthi, Xianlai, JinhuiLi 2016).

A circular economy approach relies on policy instruments that incentivize the manufacturers (producers) of electronics to take a life cycle approach to products past the factory gate, beyond the point of purchase and post the warranty period (Goel A, 2018). Globally systems to address the administration of E-Waste are introduced on the idea of the round economy. As indicated by the Ellen MacArthur Foundation the roundabout economy is restorative and regenerative by designs (EMAF, 2017). It involves a lifecycle and closed loop approach and encourages innovation at the design stage of products to minimize waste and the negative impacts of material used. A circular economy approach depends on arrangement instruments that boost the (makers) of hardware to adopt a real existence cycle strategy to items past the industrial facility entryway, past the purpose of procurement and post the guarantee time frame. A typical arrangement instrument applied is Extended Producer Responsibility (EPR) where makers pay for the expenses related with gathering, reusing and dependably arranging items toward the part of the arrangement. EPR urges structure development to make it simpler to reuse and discard items while limiting social and budgetary expenses to society as makers can coordinate the expenses related with reusing without bringing about any misfortune. Makers will regularly depend on a Producer Responsibility Organization (PRO) to gather and discard waste for their benefit. Electrical and electronic elements (e- elements) are characterized as any family unit or business thing with hardware, or electrical segments with force or battery supply (StEP, 2014). This incorporates items from essential kitchen machines to PCs to cellphones. Other than regular family use, e-items are additionally getting progressively incorporated in transport, vitality supply, wellbeing, and security frameworks, making them a significant piece of current society. These devices make lives increasingly helpful and work progressively productive. All things considered, all e-items accompany a future, and once they quit working or new innovation makes them out of date, they should be disposed of. Electronic waste (e-waste) is a term utilized for a wide range of e-elements, and their parts, that have been disposed of as waste without the goal of reuse (StEP, 2014). Around 50 million metric huge amounts of e-waste is created comprehensively every year, with a normal of in excess of 6 kg for each person (Baldé, Forti, Kuehr & Stegmann 2017). As anyone might expect, this dispersion is lopsided: more extravagant nations produce more. Norway, for instance, produces 28.5kg per individual every year, contrasted with a normal of under 2 kg in African nations. Frequently alluded to as the quickest developing strong waste stream, the development of e-waste isn't astounding given the rising interest and utilization of e-elements. The administration of e-waste, be that as it may, has demonstrated to be amazingly testing (Kiddeet, Naidu & Wong, 2013). Indeed, even industrialized countries with entrenched waste administration frameworks are battling with the intricate idea of e-waste. Furthermore, for less-created nations with practically no strategies or foundation, e-waste has added difficulties to the previously existing waste-administration emergency.

OBJECTIVES

This is done dependent on a far reaching understanding components connected to the e-squander issue and a viewpoint of the issue given potential situations. Given the flighty idea of innovative advancement, it is difficult to accurately measure the eventual fate of e-waste. Anyway dependent on the worldwide patterns of development and administrative activities, speculative projection can draw at smaller scale level. It is intended to be interesting activity for all entertainer in e-waste field including specialists, policymakers, representatives, e-waste supervisors, non-profit association and consistently stack holders of e-elements.

BACKGROUND

CE models for electronic items give components to broadening the life of the gear and afterward reusing and recuperating every material for reuse as an optional crude material in another framework. A several tools have been created to distinguish, break down, and assess these procedures in a framework (He, K., Sun, Z., Hu, Y. et al. 2017). Cellphone e-waste flows through a few procedures, and its materials can be utilized in various stages or mechanical procedures. It exhibits a similar examination of the strategy utilized in the exploration announced here and considers directed by Yu et al., Ghosh et al., Baldé et al., and Kumar et al., who assessed the procedures in electronic waste course, for example, the age of e-waste, fix, reusing, and the structure and stream of waste materials-utilizing their most elevated monetary incentive in the global market. The age of e-waste is straight forwardly identified with the Gross Domestic Product of a nation. The investigations of Yu et al., Baldé et al., and Kumar et al. indicated that the utilization of cellphone gear is somewhere in the range of 1 and 1.1 cellphones for each individual, and that as the GDP of a nation builds, the waste age increments at a comparable rate. Correspondingly, Baldé et al. connected the complete e-waste created in 50 nations with their GDPs and the measures of their populaces and affirmed that these three components are associated. Distributed CE models in the electronic items area have investigated the entertainers and situations engaged with electrical and electronic hardware stream. Various creators have assessed the reparability and reusing of gadgets to decide the plausibility of relocating toward a CE model. Dissecting the age, fix, the board, and reusing forms for electronic gear in a specific nation takes into account the assurance of its innovative capacities to empower a CE model. Most nations with rising economies have essential reusing forms, for example, manual partition of segments, squashing machines, metal separators, and compactors, and not very many recyclers recuperate important segments, for example, gold, copper, cobalt, and tin. Baldé et al. and Ghosh et al. dissected the electronic reusing industry and it's last preparing through physical, substance, as well as natural detachment to decide the innovative reusing level of a nation and build up whether it is conceivable to recuperate materials locally by methods for manual, mechanical, physical, synthetic, or potentially biotechnological forms. Their investigations indicated that developing nations don't have the end-preparing advancements to recuperate every one of the materials from printed circuit sheets (PCBs). StEP, UNU, and UNEP IETC have been working widely on e-waste issues and made an endeavor to investigate the eventual fate of the issue so as to start approach level dialogs on the difficulties and openings ahead. Having knowledge into the future will support policymakers and ventures, just as different partners, to settle on better key choices. Guaging is additionally vital versus vital ideas towards practical advancement, for example, round economy and the UN's Agenda 2030. We can't anticipate prompt accomplishment with these ideas without a functioning hunt arrangements. The entangled idea of generation, use, and transfer of hardware require noteworthy changes all together for the procedures to get practical. The earliest steps towards e-waste management came about in 1976 with the Resource Conservation and Recovery Act in the United States. While it became illegal to dump e-waste in the United States, it was the Basel Convention in 1989 which made ensured that laws and policies were adopted which would ensure safe disposal of e-waste anywhere in the world (J.A. Phillips 1998). This provided the platform for the recycling industry to prosper in a number of countries which has provided for resource recovery and mitigation of serious environmental hazards. Switzerland became the first country in 1991 to introduce a recycling system for refrigerators. Other items were gradually added to the system and by 2005 there was an established system for take back which was institutionalized by setting up of Producers Responsibility organizations (PROs).

Approaches to e-Waste

Since the 1990s, the discussion of e-waste has focused on actual and potential environmental damage, on major risks to human health, workers and communities, and on the flows of ewaste from developed to developing countries. Past policy recommendations have overwhelmingly focused on the introduction of environmental legislation and regulation. However, there is growing recognition of the key role of labour market policies and of enterprises, cooperatives, employers, workers and ministries of labour or employment in advancing decent work in the management of e-waste. There is also growing recognition that the prevailing linear model of "take, make, use and dispose" generates waste that could and should be reduced throughout the life cycle of electronic and electrical products. If such products are designed to last longer, and if more e-waste is recovered, reused and recycled throughout the life cycle, there will be less demand for virgin materials and less waste will be generated from the extraction of raw materials, packaging and transport (Figure 1).

Life cycle believing depends on the standards of pollution preservation where the environmental impact are decreased at the source, and of shutting the circle of materials and vitality. These standards have so far been actualized inside in the associations through cleaner creation, natural administration and eco-structure programs. Life cycle thinking grows the idea of contamination avoidance to incorporate the entire item life cycle and supportability. Source decrease in an item life cycle point of view is then proportionate to eco-design structure and what have been known as the "6 RE philosophy":

1. Re-think the product and its function. For instance, the product might be utilized more effectively, in this manner diminishing vitality use and other regular assets;
2. Re-duce energy and material consumption throughout a product's life cycle;
3. Re-place destructive substances with all the more naturally cordial other options;
4. Re-cycle. Select materials that can be reused, and fabricate the item to such an extent that it is dismantled simpler for reusing;
5. Re-use. Structure the item so parts can be reused;
6. Re-pair. Make the item simple to fix with the goal that the product doesn't yet should be supplanted.

In every life cycle organize there is the possibility to bring down asset utilization and improve the exhibition of items.

Figure 1. Life cycle
Source: Remmen (2003)

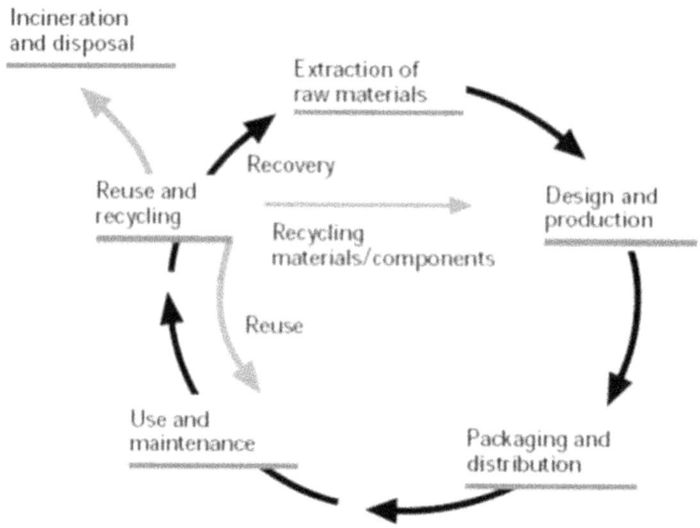

The EU implemented, in 2006, the WEEE Directive which aimed to set-up a system for product take back which would increase efficiency and move towards Circular Economy13. The RoHS directives also allowed for the reducing the use of hazardous substances which would make recycling safer for many of the end of life equipment. In the US, in 2004, the state of California introduced a waste recycling fee to cover the cost of recycling of monitors and televisions. The amount was adjusted to match the real cost of recycling later. Till date 18 such states have drafted rules for e-waste management. In Asia, many countries have drafted e-waste rules. India and China, which are among the largest producers of e-waste have implemented EPR within the ambit of the legislation. In India, targets have been given to producers, which keep increasing over a period of time, to collect end of life electronic and electrical products. The e-waste management rules, 2016, are a step in that direction in India which has led to PROs being set-up to manage targets for producers. E-waste the management framework in India have created throughout the years from various guidelines regarding the matter of waste. These incorporate the Hazardous Waste Management and Handling Rules, 2003, which highlighted some significant timetables characterized how perilous materials ought to be arranged which discovered relevance for e-waste since it was involved those metals and materials. E-waste was explicitly remembered for the waste and any individual who needed to process or reuse the equivalent needed to enroll with the Central Pollution Control Board. Considering the developing concern explicitly in e-waste, the Government upheld a few activities on the appraisal of the subject and concocted rules around the Environmentally Sound administration of e-waste in 2008 which prompted the appearance of the e-waste the board and taking care of rules, 2011. So as to guarantee that the system could be made progressively strong considering the expanding challenge of this quickly developing waste stream, the principles were modified to the present day e-waste the board rules, 2016. Expanded Producers Responsibility (EPR) was made a foundation of the principles.

DISCUSSION AND FINDINGS

Practically all e-waste contain some type of recyclable material, including plastic, glass, and metals; in any case, because of inappropriate transfer strategies and systems these materials can't be recovered for different purposes. On the off chance that e-waste is disassembled and handled in an unrefined way, its poisonous constituents can unleash destruction on the human body. Procedures, for example, disassembling parts, wet synthetic handling, and burning are utilized to arrange the waste and result in direct introduction and inward breathe of hurtful synthetic substances. Wellbeing hardware, for example, gloves and face veils are not generally utilized, and laborers frequently do not have the information and experience required to complete their employments appropriately. What's more, manual extraction of harmful metals prompts entering of risky material in the circulation system of the individual doing as such. The wellbeing risks extend from kidney and liver harm to neurological issue. Reusing of e-waste scrap is contaminating the water, soil, and the air. Consuming to recover metal from wires and links has prompted the outflow of brominated and chlorinated dioxins just as cancer-causing agents which contaminate the air and, in this manner, cause malignancy in people and creatures. Harmful synthetic compounds that have no monetary worth are just dumped during the reusing procedure. These poisonous synthetic substances filter into underground spring in this way debasing the neighborhood groundwater quality and rendering the water unfit for human utilization just as rural purposes. At the point when e-waste is dumped in landfills, the lead, mercury, cadmium, arsenic, and PCBs make the dirt dangerous and unfit for farming purposes. Extremely ongoing examinations on reusing of e-waste has pointed towards expanding groupings of PCBs, dioxins and furans, plasticizers, bisphenol-A (BPA), polycyclic sweet-smelling hydrocarbons (PAH), and substantial metals in the surface soil of the four metro urban communities of India, that is, New Delhi, Kolkata, Mumbai, and Chennai where e-waste is being prepared by the casual divisions (Chakraborty, M., VanKuren, N.W., Zhao, R., Zhang, X., Kalsow, S., Emerson, J.J. 2018). In those investigations, it has been seen that the locales occupied with metal recuperation forms are thc prime destinations for such diligent lethal substances. Concentrates from a similar gathering likewise revealed that the steady natural toxins delivered or discharged during the reusing procedure are getting away in the encompassing air because of their semi-unpredictable nature.

Findings in the UNU (United Nation University) report point to a clear, steady growth trend in e-waste, which is projected to continue at a rate of two million metric tons per year. This would mean almost 50 million metric tons by 2018. Of total e-waste, approximately one quarter – or 9.3 million metric tons is made up of personal digital devices such as computers, displays, smartphones and tablets and TVs. Household appliances as well as heating and cooling equipment account for the remainder.

E-waste statistics are not only relevant in terms of the environmental impact; there is also an important economic component to the debate. The total value of all raw materials present in waste is estimated at approximately 55 Billion Euros in 2016, which is more than the 2016 Gross Domestic Product of most countries in the world. The value of secondary raw materials after waste management is just a fraction of the value of its components or the price of used appliances. Circular economy models need to be adopted to encourage closing the loop of materials through better design of components, recycling, reusing, etc., while mitigating the environmental pollution. Therefore, the circular economy concept offers huge economic and employment opportunities for e-waste management; the presented 55 Billion Euros of secondary materials is an underestimate of those economic opportunities. This calls for the development of proper legislation to manage e-waste that is supported by data to show both the environmental and economic benefits the better management of e-waste.

Table 1. Electronic waste generated worldwide from 2010 to 2018 (in million metric tons)

Year	Million Metric Tons
2010	33.8
2011	35.8
2012	37.8
2013	39.8
2014	41.8
2015	43.8
2016	44.7
2017	47.8
2018	49.8

Source: Statista (2019).

Figure 2. Electronic waste generation
Source: Baldé, Forti, Kuehr, Stegmann, (2017)

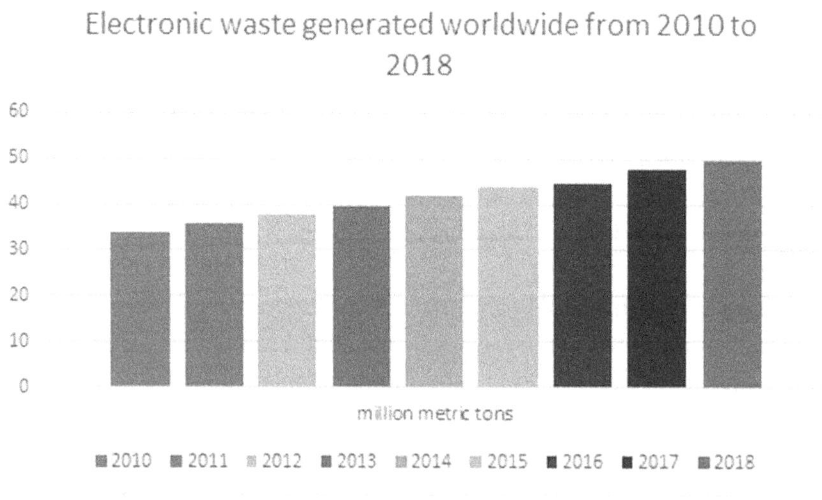

Electronic waste, or e-waste, refers to all items of electrical and electronic equipment (EEE) and its parts that have been discarded by its owner as waste without the intent of re-use (Step Initiative 2014). E-waste is also referred to as WEEE (Waste Electrical and Electronic Equipment), electronic waste or e-scrap in different regions and under different circumstances in the world. It includes a wide range of products – almost any household or business item with circuitry or electrical components with power or battery supply. In this methodology, defined by the Partnership on Measuring ICT for Development (Baldé et al., 2015a), the definition of e-waste is very broad. It covers six waste categories:

1. Temperature exchange equipment, more commonly referred to as cooling and freezing equipment. Typical equipment includes refrigerators, freezers, air conditioners, heat pumps;

Table 2. Equipment wise waste

Sr. No.	Equipment's	In Mt.
1	Small Equipment's	16.8
2	Large Equipment's	9.1
3	Temperature Exchange Equipment's	7.6
4	Screen	6.6
5	Small IT	3.9
6	Lamps	0.7
	Total	**44.7**

Figure 3. Global e-Waste generation
Source: Baldé, Forti, Kuehr, Stegmann, (2017)

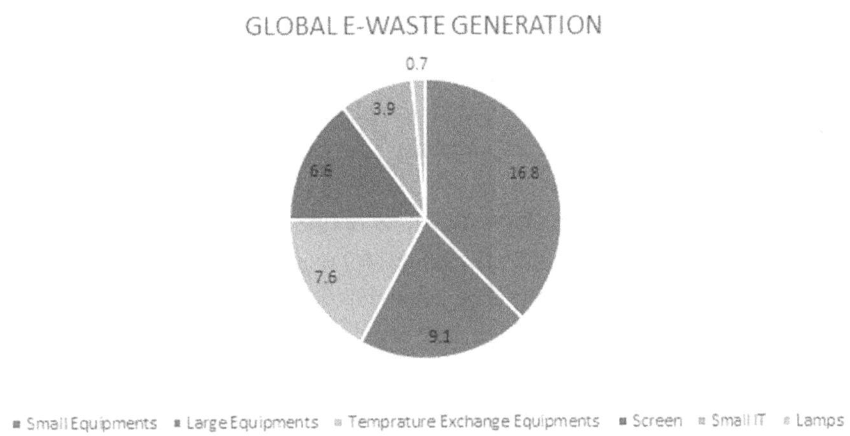

2. Screens, monitors. Typical equipment includes televisions, monitors, laptops, notebooks, and tablets;
3. Lamps. Typical equipment includes fluorescent lamps, high intensity discharge lamps, and LED lamps;
4. Large equipment. Typical equipment includes washing machines, clothes dryers, dish-washing machines, electric stoves, large printing machines, copying equipment, and photovoltaic panels;
5. Small equipment. Typical equipment includes vacuum cleaners, microwaves, ventilation equipment, toasters, electric kettles, electric shavers, scales, calculators, radio sets, video cameras, electrical and electronic toys, small electrical and electronic tools, small medical devices, small monitoring and control instruments;
6. Small IT and telecommunication equipment. Typical equipment includes mobile phones, Global Positioning Systems (GPS), pocket calculators, routers, personal computers, printers, telephones. Each product of the six e-waste categories has a different lifetime profile, which means that each category has different waste quantities, economic values, as well as potential environmental and health impacts, if recycled inappropriately. Consequently, the collection and logistical processes

and recycling technology differ for each category, in the same way as the consumers' attitudes when disposing of the electrical and electronic equipment also vary.

CHALLENGES

1. One of the fastest growing and most complex waste streams that severely impacts the environment and human health and is often traded illegally;
2. Lack of awareness and of sustainable disposal practices as well as e-waste management systems and infrastructure;
3. Low collection, reuse, refurbishing and recycling rates;
4. Informal management of e-waste and related health, labour & environmental challenges;
5. Loss of valuable resources - better e-waste management can generate sustainable enterprises and green jobs.

India positions 177 among 180 nations and is among the last five nations on the Environmental Performance Index 2018, according to a report discharged at the World Economic Forum 2018. This was connected to horrible showing in the earth wellbeing strategy and passing because of air contamination classifications. Likewise, India is positioned fifth on the planet among top e-waste creating nations after the USA, China, Japan, and Germany and reuses under 2 percent of the all-out e-waste it delivers yearly officially. Since 2018, India creates in excess of 2,000,000 tons of e-waste every year, and furthermore imports enormous measures of e-waste from different nations around the globe. Dumping in open dumpsites is a typical sight which offers ascend to issues, for example, groundwater sullying, unexpected frailty, and that's only the tip of the iceberg. The Associated Chambers of Commerce and Industry of India (ASSOCHAM) and KPMG study, Electronic Waste Management in India recognized that PC hardware represent right around 70 percent of e-waste, trailed by media transmission gear telephones (12 percent), electrical gear (8 percent), and medicinal hardware (7 percent) with staying from family unit e-waste. E-waste assortment, transportation, handling, and reusing is ruled by the casual division. The segment is all around arranged and unregulated. Frequently, every one of the materials and worth that could be possibly recouped isn't recuperated. What's more, there are not kidding issues in regards to spillages of poisons into the earth and laborers' security and wellbeing. Seelampur in Delhi is the biggest e-waste disassembling focus of India. Grown-ups just as youngsters go through 8–10 hours day by day removing reusable segments and valuable metals like copper, gold and different utilitarian parts from the gadgets. E-waste recyclers use procedures, for example, open cremation and corrosive siphoning. This circumstance could be improved by making mindfulness and improving the framework of reusing units alongside the pervasive approaches. Most of the e-waste gathered in India is overseen by a disorderly segment. Likewise, casual channels of reusing/reuse of hardware, for example, fix shops, utilized item sellers, online business entry merchants gather a noteworthy extent of the disposed of gadgets for reuse and cannibalization of parts and segments. A case in point could be a key job that can be played by the Ministry of Electronics and Information Technology in arrangement of indigenous innovation for reusing which can prompt compelling execution of the standards. This will probably help the distinctive Government of India missions which have entomb linkages and prod development. Besides, it won't just permit stricter consistence yet in addition lead to bring issues to light levels with regards to transfer of e-waste by customers. The resultant effect will prompt development of waste from the casual to the conventional area making it worthwhile to set-up reusing units in the nation. This is probably going to guarantee manageable practices which will prompt moderating ecological and wellbeing risks related with inappropriate reusing of e-waste.

OPPORTUNITIES

E-waste the executives rules, 2016, present an open door for not just gathering a few objectives under various missions as started by the Government of India yet in addition guaranteeing that asset productivity and circular economy can be worked at the core of approaches with regards to practical generation and utilization. This will take into account makers to consider plan of items which would be round in nature, take into consideration better transfer rehearses from shoppers and furthermore guarantee that reusing through best accessible innovations is advanced which will take into consideration age of business and opening new vistas for development. Tending to these difficulties can prompt coordination of partners in usage of the standards. This should happen not just for partner which have been referenced in the standards yet additionally at a between ecclesiastical level at the Government so as to guarantee that there is sufficient information which is made and tried at the ground level which can guarantee specialized usage of the guidelines. Although there are uncertainties about how future technology will evolve, the utilization of e-items and in this way the age of e-waste will more likely than not develop, in any event during the following scarcely any decades. It is particularly valid for quickly developing economies that are yet to be overflowed with the horde of e-elements that accompany monetary thriving. It implies more difficulties, just as circumstances, for all players in the worldwide e-waste field: makers, clients, e-waste authorities, recyclers, and strategy producers. Not with standing which bearing the future develops, guaranteeing a manageable creation and utilization framework for e-elements will require critical endeavors from all partners. With experiences into the future, makers most likely have the best chance to plan a future-evidence gadgets segment that is manageable monetarily just as earth. Other than assembling and reusing, creative organizations can likewise take advantage of the tremendous item and segment reuse potential. This can make neighborhood organizations and help nations, particularly those without any stores for essential assets or e-elements fabricating, to use the useful estimation of items for a more drawn out period, evading the import of new things. Numerous items running from family unit apparatuses (clothes washer and lighting hardware) to ICT gear (cell phones and PCs) can be offered as an assistance or rented as opposed to selling items. Such plans of action can give better chances to item lifetime expansion and smoother reclaim at the EoL. Practicing due tirelessness, organizations can limit the potential difficulties of basic assets and stricter legitimate prerequisites. Some enormous brands are hitting the cutoff points of plans of action that depend on offers of new items, while other people who organize item life span are picking up ubiquity. There is additionally interest for increasingly economical items, which can be ascribed to developing buyer mindfulness. Organizations will be in an ideal situation by proactively tending to clients' interest. There is additionally an open door for arrangement creators to encourage the change towards a progressively round framework. The EPR-based reclaim framework has been an important achievement in e-waste the board. How-ever, the present e-waste the board frameworks have not had the option to completely catch the practical and material estimation of EoL items. To a limited extent, this is additionally connected to an absence of motivating forces for entertainers in the worth chain, which could advance the most ideal EoL arrangements. So also, absence of coordinated effort among partners in the item lifecycle has been an issue with regards to executing 'plan for EoL' arrangements. Furthermore, at the essential level, absence of open mindfulness has likewise been an issue in e-waste the board, which might be tended to by arrangement level activities. Today, many creating nations need viable approaches and legitimate foundation for the administration of e-waste, yet in addition for different streams including city strong waste. This circumstance offers an extraordinary open door for nations in Asia, Africa, and South America where increasingly quick mechanical development is normal. Organizing casual reusing exercises can help make more secure workplace for waste laborers, less ecological effect, and an increasingly maintainable reusing industry. The exercises got the hang of during the most recent two decades from the European Union in creating and executing e-waste guidelines and setting up the board frameworks can be of an incentive in this procedure.

RECOMMENDATIONS

Limit Building Programs Including Awareness Programs for all Stakeholders and Actors. Waste transfer propensities and systems in India are totally different from a significant number of the created nations in the OECD. Waste in India has consistently been considered as an asset which there has been a monetary thought appended to the equivalent throughout the decades. This has been highlighted by an interest procedure which has been made by the casual part, which because of destitution and absence of monetary open doors has embraced waste assortment and the executives as its essential employment. The Ministry of Electronics and Information Technology has, considering the high stakes included, propelled a mindfulness activity in 2015. The activity titled 'Mindfulness Program on Environmental Hazards of Electronic Waste' looks to improve effort and promotion around the ecological and wellbeing perils of ill-advised transfer of e-waste in the nation. This is a multi-partner program which has been visualized to continue for a long time. The mindfulness program has been executed in a city each in 30 recognized states up until now. In future, urban areas in outstanding States/UTs would be secured. The various partners in the program where effort and promotion endeavors are being focused on are: Schools, Colleges, RWAs, Bulk Consumers, Dealers, Refurbishes, Informal Sector, and Manufacturers. The Ministry has been actualizing the program through industry affiliations, viz. MAIT, CEAMA, NASSCOM, PHDCCI, and so forth. Government is one of the biggest shopper in the gadgets and IT gear space. The National Institute of Electronics and Information Technology has been entrusted by the service to make mindfulness among various classes of government authorities so as to guarantee that e-waste is taken care of appropriately with the goal that administration divisions actualize the e-waste rules and discard their electronic waste through proper channels. Under the program, till December 2018, in around 600 Workshops and exercises sorted out in different urban areas, more than 3.00 lakhs members from School, universities, RWA, producer, casual administrators and so on and 6000 government authorities have so far taken an interest. The mass mindfulness among youth of the nation has likewise been made through film and in excess of 20 crore crowd has been shrouded in about 3000 film lobbies. The subtleties of the program and its effort can be seen on the committed site of the mindfulness program, www.greene.gov.in. The program in stage II has seen industry approached to add to the program in making mindfulness which is likewise part of their consistence necessity under broadened maker obligation as expressed in the e-waste the board rules, 2016.The program has been intended to guarantee that it is feasible just as prompts direct activity which takes into consideration e-waste to move into the proper chain for its naturally stable transfer. Exercises, workshops, combined with assortment drives take into consideration safe transfer of e-waste by partners. Moreover, mentors crosswise over urban communities are being outfitted with abilities to draw in with various partners so as to guarantee that exercises and workshops can be led to fabricate limits and make exceed on available resources for safe transfer of e-waste. These mentors can be received by makers, PROs, SPCBs as assets which can make mindfulness on e-waste transfer at a miniscule expense later on. Beneficial outcomes of mindfulness program can be seen with various partners. Teachers and understudies have driven the endeavors in directing exercises and workshops to upgrade the effort and construct further limits here. Subtleties of the equivalent can be gotten to from (see:www.greene.gov.in). The makers which have been ordered as a piece of consistence to embrace consciousness of partners have approached to join the program in the second stage in gigantic numbers through their PROs. Singular makers have likewise communicated enthusiasm for joining the program to improve mindfulness on safe e-waste transfer. This will prompt higher effort where close of a million people will be affected through this mindfulness and limit building exertion. The casual on-screen characters have additionally understood the significance of overseeing e-waste in an appropriate way through this backing exertion. Numerous in casual centers like Moradabad have communicated their positive aims towards formalizing with the goal that they don't work in conditions which are bad for wellbeing and condition. Many have given marked sworn statements proposing that they won't utilize techniques which are not condition well-disposed and won't utilize kids and pregnant ladies in such procedures. Limit working in the following stage ought to be viewed as an industry drove process as opposed to an administration drove one. Since mindfulness building is a consistence under the guidelines, it is significant that the administration utilize such projects to create foundations which can lead these endeavors and enhance too to guarantee that huge scale effect can be made. These establishments can be financed through various sources including people in general and the private division. For partners, who need to make mindfulness as a major aspect of consistence, a different body can be set-up which can oversee reserves implied for mindfulness and limit building. The foundations who might want to work around there can apply for awards which will enable the body to assess such proposition and pick the most ideal one. This will likewise take into consideration replication of most ideal endeavors since the learnings from various projects would be assessed by this body and picked as best practices.

RESEARCH AND DEVELOPMENT (R&D)

India has created rules and models for new item improvement in the hardware part. Any maker who wishes to present an item in the market needs to enroll with BIS under the Compulsory Registration Scheme (CRS) 28. Statement and testing of materials that are utilized in the items need to comply with Indian norms and at exactly that point the standard characteristic of the BIS is permitted to be utilized and item can be presented in the market. Essentially, there is a need to guarantee that a RE plot is concocted which envelops the utilization of auxiliary materials in items to guarantee that they are asset proficient and makers set roundabout economy standards in motion in the generation procedure. The plan ought to likewise address the advancement of R&D framework in the nation which gives practical reusing advances to WEEE and furthermore considers the fast innovative and material synthesis changes in the EEE. In spite of the fact that India isn't significantly fabricating items and segments in the nation so the use of Eco-Design or Design for Environment standards is hard to achieve through activities in India. Generally the segments utilized for gathering the last items are agreeable with the national and global guidelines or norms. Along these lines to upgrade RE, the plan can concentrate on reinforcing R&D progressions to make a stage for applied research toward this path. The utilization of auxiliary materials can be guided through an institutionalization of advances which are being utilized for extraction of the material during the reusing procedure. This will guarantee intentional accreditation by recyclers as the interest for auxiliary materials increments and will likewise give a fillip to the valuable metal reusing division in India, subsequently advancing the Make in India strategic. It will energize reuse and just as renovation, if benchmarks for utilization of optional materials are indicated. GHG outflows will diminish too since lesser materials will move into landfills and will be reused for industry attributable to request of auxiliary materials. Reuse and restoration will likewise profit the purchaser monetarily by diminishing the out of date quality pace of items and the age of WEEE.

CONCLUSION

The study archives worldwide accepted procedures and produce core values that can help build up a strong situation for e-waste the board; valuable for the business and the policymakers the investigation gives a depiction of the waste business with exceptional accentuation on e-waste condition and development potential. So as to push ahead, it is in this way significant that an activity plan be surrounded up by perceiving the key difficulties which exist in improving asset productivity in the e-waste part. The key difficulties which become known are: Estimating the quantum of e-waste produced in the nation which can help comprehend the size of the issue to evaluate framework required to fathom the equivalent. Gaps in Research and Development for innovation improvement on reusing and to address fast mechanical headway in EEE. Outreach and backing with all partners to guarantee that nature and wellbeing dangers are conveyed so transfer instruments can be formalized. Mapping of significant worth chains which will empower to get partners and draw explicit activity plans towards formalization. Capacity working of observing and execution offices at the state level with the goal that the standards are upheld crosswise over partners. Infrastructure for e-waste reusing in the nation which can upset development of e-waste in the casual area or push them to formalization. Product plan rules which can help make items and materials simpler to destroy and reuse accordingly improving asset effectiveness. Standards for reusing which will empower to guarantee that top tier advancements are utilized to relieve the natural and wellbeing effects of dangerous reusing, as in the casual part. The table underneath attempts to delineate these subtleties further regarding key partners who could be engaged with tending to these issues and the activity plan for every one of these offices. Between pastoral coordination will guarantee that asset proficiency and roundabout economy can be executed in the EEE part since this isn't only a checking issue. It is as a lot of a specialized issue similar to a waste issue which requires dealing with by explicit specialists and partners to such an extent that it tends to be tended to.

REFERENCES

Abhishek, Xianlai, & Li. (2016). *Environmental pollution of electronic waste recycling in India: A critical review.* Received 3 August 2015, Revised 19 November 2015, Accepted 19 November 2015, Available online 14 January 2016, https://www.sciencedirect.com/science/article/pii/S0269749115301871

Baldé, C., Forti, V., Kuehr, R., & Stegmann, P. (2017). *The Global E-waste Monitor 2017.* https://www.itu.int/en/ITU-D/Climate-Change/Documents/GEM%202017/Global-E-waste%20Monitor%202017%20.pdf

Banza Lubaba Nkulu, C., Casas, L., Haufroid, V., De Putter, T., Saenen, N. D., Kayembe-Kitenge, T., ... Nemery, B. (2018). Sustainability of artisanal mining of cobalt in DR Congo. *Nat Sustain, 1*(9), 495–504. doi:10.103841893-018-0139-4 PMID:30288453

Chakraborty, M., VanKuren, N. W., Zhao, R., Zhang, X., Kalsow, S., & Emerson, J. J. (2018). Hidden genetic variation shapes the structure of functional elements in Drosophila. *Nature Genetics, 50*(1), 20–25. doi:10.103841588-017-0010-y PMID:29255259

Cruz, S. E., Ojeda, S., Jáuregui, J., Velázquez, K., Santillán, N., García, R., ... Alcántara, C. (2017). E-Waste Supply Chain in Mexico: Challenges and Opportunities for Sustainable Management. *Sustainability, 9*(4), 503. doi:10.3390u9040503

Ellen MacArthur Foundation. (2017). *What is a circular economy? A framework for an economy that is restorative and regenerative by design.* Retrieved from https://www.ellenmacarthurfoundation.org/circular-economy/concept

European Parliament. Directive 2002/96/EU of the European Parliament and of the Council of 27 January 2003 on waste electrical and electronic equipment (WEEE). (Official Journal of the European Union, 2003).

Goel, A. (2018). *Circular Economy A business Imperative for India.* doi:10.13140/RG.2.2.29340.23689

Goodship, V., & Stevels, A. (2012). *Electronic and Optical Materials.* Woodhead Publishing Limited.

He, K., Sun, Z., Hu, Y., Zeng, X., Yu, Z., & Cheng, H. (2017). Comparison of soil heavy metal pollution caused by e-waste recycling activities and traditional industrial operations. *Environmental Science and Pollution Research International, 24*(10), 9387–9398. doi:10.100711356-017-8548-x PMID:28233211

Kiddee, P., Naidu, R., & Wong, M. (2013). Electronic waste management approaches: An overview. *Waste Management (New York, N.Y.), 33*(5), 1237–1250. doi:10.1016/j.wasman.2013.01.006 PMID:23402807

Korhonen, J., Honkasalo, A., & Seppälä, J. (2018). Circular Economy: The Concept and its Limitations. *Ecological Economics, 143*, 37–46. doi:10.1016/j.ecolecon.2017.06.041

Kyere, V. N., Greve, K., Atiemo, S. M., Amoako, D., Aboh, I. J. K., & Cheabu, B. S. (2018). Contamination and Health Risk Assessment of Exposure to Heavy Metals in Soils from Informal E-Waste Recycling Site in Ghana. *Emerging Science Journal, 2*(6), 428. doi:10.28991/esj-2018-01162

Meloni, M. (2019). *Green & Sustainable Electronics.* https://www.ewaste-expo.com/green-electronics/

Needhidasan, S., Samuel, M., & Chidambaram, R. (2014). Electronic waste - an emerging threat to the environment of urban India. *Journal of Environmental Health Science & Engineering*, *12*(1), 36. doi:10.1186/2052-336X-12-36 PMID:24444377

NITI Aayog. (n.d.). http://niti.gov.in/writereaddata/files/document_publication/Strategy%20Paper %20 on%20Resource%20Efficiency.pdf

Parajuly, K. (2017). *Circular Economy in E-Waste Management: Resource Recovery & Design For End-of-Life* (PhD thesis). University of Southern Denmark.

Parajuly, K., & Wenzel, H. (2017). Product Family Approach in E-Waste Management- A Conceptual Framework for Circular Economy. *Sustainability*, *9*(5), 768. doi:10.3390u9050768

Phillips, J. A. (1998). *National Renewable Energy Laboratory- Managing Americaís Solid Waste*. https:// www.csu.edu/cerc/researchreports/documents/ManagingAmericasSolidWaste1998.pdf

Puckett, J., Brandt, C., & Palmer, H. (2019). *Holes in the Circular Economy – WEEE Leakage from Europe*. Basel Action Network.

Riahi, K., van Vuuren, D. P., Kriegler, E., Edmonds, J., O'Neill, B. C., Fujimori, S., ... Tavoni, M. (2017). The Shared Socioeconomic Pathways and their energy, land use, and greenhouse gas emissions implications: An overview. *Global Environmental Change*, *42*, 153–168. doi:10.1016/j.gloenvcha.2016.05.009

StEP Initiative. (2014). *Solving the E-Waste Problem (StEP)*. White Paper.

UNEP. (2013). *Environmental Risks and Challenges of Anthropogenic Metals Flows and Cycles*. A Report of the Working Group on the Global Metal Flows to the International Resource Panel.

Wang, Z., Zhang, B., & Guan, D. (2016). Take responsibility for electronic-waste disposal. *Nature*, *536*(7614), 23–25. doi:10.1038/536023a PMID:27488785

World Economic Forum. (2014). *Towards Circular Economy: Accelerating the Scaleup across Global Supply Chains*. Published in collaboration with Ellen Mac- Arthur Foundation and McKinsey & Company. http://www3. weforum.org/docs/WEF_ENV_Towards CircularEconomy_Report_2014.pdf

Chapter 12
Development of Supply Chain Framework for the Circular Economy

Yanamandra Ramakrishna
https://orcid.org/0000-0001-9101-6072
School of Business, Skyline University College, UAE

ABSTRACT

The rapid pace at which technology has contributed several technological products and gadgets created a surplus in some areas and deficiencies in some areas of the modern world. For instance, there is a tremendous wastage of food in one country, excessive usage of electronic items in some other countries, and in many other countries, people starve for food and possession of basic electronic items. This situation has led to imbalance and wastage. In addition, sustained efforts to reuse/recycle the goods produced by different business organizations are inadequate. SCM plays a role in re-usability of goods and recycling of used goods. Organizations have to redesign their supply chains to achieve the objective of the circular economy, which propagates the concept of wealth out of waste by reusing/recycling the products. The research in the area of the role of the supply chain in the circular economy is just gaining its importance, and it is still in the nascent stage. Hence, this chapter highlights the significance of in circular economy by developing a framework that emphasizes its role.

INTRODUCTION

Industrial revolution and industrial development have contributed to the enormous progress and growth of humanity during the last several centuries. It has also led to unprecedented growth in technology and growth in products and services dependent on technology. While this growth enabled improvement in the overall quality of life of individuals, it also created several challenges to the humanity in terms of environmental pollution, biodegradation, deforestation, degeneration of natural resources of the plant, which resulted in social inequality (Liudmyla Deineko, Olena Tsyplitska & Oleksandr Deineko, 2019). At the same time, consumption levels have increased worldwide resulting into wastage of items and

DOI: 10.4018/978-1-7998-5116-5.ch012

Copyright © 2020, IGI Global. Copying or distributing in print or electronic forms without written permission of IGI Global is prohibited.

pollution to the environment. Implementation of strategies and practices of Supply Chain Management (SCM) by the business enterprises, like effective information sharing, matching of supply with demand, efficient inventory management throughout the chain and green practices have contributed to some extent a reduction in this wastage (Genovese, A., Acquaye, A.A., Figueroa, A. and Koh, S.L. 2017). SCM also has provided the enterprises with better decision-making ability and improved customer service by reducing the costs of operations (Junjun Liu, Yunting Feng, Qinghua Zhu, & Joseph Sarkis, 2018). However, at the same time, advancements in SCM related to other important aspects like reusability and recyclability of products, development of eco-friendly logistics and manufacturing systems, and usage of alternate environmentally friendly energy resources are yet to gain momentum (Roberta De Angelis, Mickey Howard & Joe Miemczyk, 2018). These advancements in SCM will shift the focus of SCM from a traditional one to a futuristic, sustainable and the one leading towards achieving the objectives of what is known as circular economy (Genovese, A., 2017).

Circular economy is an economic model, which provides economic growth with a focus on green development to transform the present mass consumption to what is known as responsible consumption, in which supply chain management plays a major role (Catherine Weetman, 2017). The supply chain in circular economy is also known as 'closed supply chain'. This type of economy is supposed to reduce the waste, improve reuse and recyclability. The circular economy has seen a significant increase in interest by the researchers and practitioners over the past few years and is continuing to gain steady momentum (Ellen MacArthur Foundation (EMF), 2019).

While traditional SCM has been defined by many authors from diverse perspectives (Sourabh Jain, 2018), for the purpose of this research, the definition of SCM as provided by Moh'd Anwer et al., (2017) is considered. It states that SCM is a process of coordination of the business functions across the businesses within the firm and across businesses within other firms in supply chain for providing and improving products and information flows from suppliers till end customers in order to enhance firm performance and satisfy customer needs, wants, and requests. Traditional SCM is also considered as an approach based on the linear flow of materials and fails to include both environmental aspects and management of the end-of-life phase of products (Sarkis, 1999). Thus, the concepts of reverse supply chains, closed supply chain, green and sustainable supply chains have emerged which have the ability to deal with the accumulation of waste and provide an appropriate methodology to minimize the waste (Johnsen, T., Howard, M., & Miemczyk, J., 2014; Junjun Liu et al., 2018) and contribute towards circular economy (Ellen MacArthur Foundation, 2019).

The weaknesses of traditional supply chains without much focus on reuse and reduce of waste also contributed to the growth of circular economy (Liudmyla Deineko et al., 2019). Increasing urbanization, rising inequality and political upheaval are also some other reasons. The traditional supply chain in many business enterprises works on the principle of profit maximization, leakage of value, excessive usage of raw material, and finally selling the products in high volumes (Catherine Weetman, 2017). This leads to the wastage of many natural resources like water, energy, land and finally causes harm to the environment. The linear operating models in economy and supply chain management also face challenges like expansion of middle class consumers, regulatory restrictions, and unprecedented competition. These challenges have become a threat to the sustainability of linear models in economy and supply chain management (Accenture, 2014; WEF *et al.*, 2014). It is accepted that if the practices and strategies of SCM at business enterprises are redesigned and focused, then SCM can play a significant role in contributing towards the achievement of the objectives of circular economy. But, neither the academic contribution in terms of adequate research nor the industry contribution in terms of appreciable practices has reached a commendable position (Sourabh Jain, 2018).

There exists a dearth of conceptual frameworks of supply chains practices to meet the objectives of circular economy (Lewandowski, M., 2016; Roberta De Angelis et al., 2018). This chapter addresses this research gap by developing a conceptual framework of supply chain management practices, which can achieve the objectives of circular economy, based on systematic literature review. The scope of this framework is limited to business enterprises and organizations in manufacturing sector. The above discussion leads to some important aspects related to traditional or linear supply chains, role of SCM strategies and practices in circular supply chain, which have the ability to achieve the objectives of circular economy. Thus, the objectives of this chapter are:

- To identify the need for circular economy;
- To analyze the weakness of linear supply chain;
- To identify the role of supply chain in circular economy;
- To establish a link between the practices of supply chain and objectives of circular economy;
- To develop a framework of supply chain practices to achieve the objectives of circular economy.

These objectives are achieved through a systematic literature review of articles published in leading peer-reviewed journals available in ProQuest and EBSCO. Based on the literature review, the research gaps are further established and a conceptual framework of supply chain is proposed.

BACKGROUND

Most of the business enterprises operate on an extraction-use-disposal approach, which is known as linear approach to resource utilization (Huysman et al., 2015). This linear approach results into excessive utilization of resources, increases harmful emissions, and accumulates waste. An immediate necessity for business enterprises to reduce waste and reverse the trend of excess utilization is to shift from this current linear approach to a circular approach by identifying alternative methods in which supply chains play a major role (Junjun Liu, et al., 2017; Sourabh Jain, 2018).

In the linear approach, the SCM consists of many diverse activities, which include sourcing, procurement, planning, manufacturing, distribution and logistics management through mutual collaboration, trust and coordination with the members of supply chain (Soosay et al., 2008). Due to the diverse nature of SCM, many authors proposed a variety of definitions for SCM, but there is no consensus on these definitions has yet been arrived (Feldmann & Muller, 2003). Most of SCM definitions are concentrated on three major focus areas: integrated logistics management, purchasing and supply management, and integrated SCM. It also includes a set of channel members, strategies and practices aimed at improving the long-term competitive performance of individual firms and their supply chains as a whole by integrating the internal functions within the firm and effectively linking them with the external operations of suppliers, manufacturers, distributors, customers and other channel members (Kim, 2006). However, this linear model of supply chain does not deal effectively with the accumulated waste at various channel members leading to imbalance in the ecology. Therefore, to effectively shift the focus from linear to circular economy, there is a need to develop robust frameworks related to supply chains and performance measures which facilitate the mapping of life-cycle impacts of resource production and consumption cycles in supply chains (Cucchiella et al., 2015; Huysman et al., 2015; Lewandowski, M., 2016). This transition from linear to circular faces many issues and challenges in its implementation (Geels et al., 2015).

Therefore, there is a need for all business organizations and enterprises to focus on redesigning their supply chain practices and strategies such that they contribute towards the achievement of the objectives of circular economy. With this background, and considering the need in the existing body of knowledge, this chapter focuses on developing a framework of supply chain practices for business organizations, which enables the achievement of objectives of circular economy and contributes to the growth of circular economy. To establish further the research gap identified above and to substantiate the need, a systematic literature review has been conducted as discussed in the next section of the chapter.

LITERATURE REVIEW

This literature review is conducted with the objectives of understanding the definitions of supply chain, evolution of supply chain, weaknesses of linear supply chain, evolution of circular economy and closed supply chain, dimensions of circular economy, objectives of circular economy, approaches and models of circular economy, challenges of implementation of circular supply chain and finally the role of supply chain in circular economy. In order to conduct the literature review, key words such as 'circular supply chains', 'circular economy', 'closed loop', 'sustainable supply chains', 'reverse logistics', 'green supply chain' and other combinations comprising similar terminology were used. In the later part of this literature review, supply chain management concepts are analyzed, definitions of supply chain management are discussed, practices related to supply chain are illustrated and finally the role of supply chain management practices in achieving the objectives of circular economy were highlighted. Based on this systematic literature review, a framework of supply chain practices towards the achievement of objectives of circular economy was developed.

Supply Chain Management

Increasing globalization, sourcing of raw materials and components from global suppliers, collaborations and strategic partnerships enabled the growth of supply chains and subsequently the concepts of SCM in the early 1980s (Roberta De Angelis, 2018). SCM encompasses all activities, which are involved in planning and management, sourcing and procurement, conversion and all logistics management activities as well as coordination and collaboration with channel partners (Soosay et al., 2008). SCM concept reflects the reality of SCM as a strategic, managerial philosophy, and practice containing all SC partners – from suppliers, manufacturers, to customers – achieving better performance, gaining competitive advantage, and increasing customer satisfaction.

Supply chain consists of several members like raw material manufacturers (suppliers), component and intermediate manufacturers, final product manufacturers, wholesalers and distributors, and finally towards the end of the chain are the retailers who provide the goods and services to the customers (Manikee Madhuri Sharma, 2013). These members of the chain perform several activities. SCM is the integration of all those activities associated with the flow and transformation of goods from the raw material stage, to the end user, as well as the associated information flows through improved inter-and intrafirm relationships to achieve sustainable competitive advantage (Ellinger, 2000). Similarly, another version of SCM is defined as a set of approaches and practices to effectively integrate suppliers, manufacturers, wholesalers, distributors, and customers for improving the long-term performance of the individual firms as well as supply chain as a whole in a cohesive and high-performing business model (Chopra & Meindle, 2004).

Circular Economy and Closed Loop Supply Chain

Supply chain management has evolved from linear model to sustainable supply chain to green supply chain to presently the closed loop or circular supply chain (Marco Antonio Ferreira, 2017; Catherine Weetman, 2017; Roberta De Angelis, 2018). Originally the traditional or linear supply chain was only focused on procuring and logistics management aspects (Cooper & Ellram, 1993) which was supported by the famous definition SCM as the management of upstream and downstream relationships with suppliers and customers to deliver superior customer value at less cost to the supply chain as a whole (Christopher, 1998). These concepts lead to the focus of SCM on cost and throughput as a linear model in which excessive usage of resources leads to wastage and creates imbalance in the environment.

A typical example of traditional, linear supply chains therefore is the fast-moving consumer goods (FMCG) sector, which focuses on high levels of efficiency, volume throughput and customer responsiveness (Holweg, 2005). The focus slowly shifted towards environment and adequate research was carried out in the area of Green Supply Chain Management (GSCM). The concept of green supply chain management (GSCM) integrates environmental dimensions in addition to the conventional dimensions in traditional supply chains (Dubey et al., 2017). In line with the emergence of GSCM concept, Sustainable Supply Chain Management (SSCM) has also gained its attention in academic and industrial world. Growth in the activities related to sustainability have compelled business organizations and enterprises to shift their focus on economic, environmental and social factors in supply chains (Morali and Searcy, 2013). This shift paved the way for the development of the concept of SSCM too which aims to reduce and minimize the flow of material across the supply chain and control the process of consumption, minimize the generation of waste and reduce the activities contributing to pollution (Sarkis et al., 2011; Genovese et al., 2017). GSCM and SSCM approaches of SCM have origins to the cradle-to-grave concept and have products going to the landfill, though at a delayed pace (Genovese et al., 2017).

Along with the growth of GSCM and SSCM approaches, the concept of circular economy also emerged as a solution to the issues related to waste and environmental imbalance which lead to the concept of Closed Supply Chain (CSC) also known as Circular Supply Chain (CSC) contributing to the closed economy (Roberta De Angelis, 2018). This type of economy is supposed to reduce the waste, improve reuse and recyclability. The circular economy has seen a significant increase in interest by the researchers and practitioners over the past few years and is continuing to gain steady momentum (Geng et al., 2013). Some authors also opined that green SCM and Sustainable SCM and Reverse SCM are part of CE (Junjun Liu et al., 2017).

Various definitions of circular economy and the practices contributing towards it were analyzed in this section of literature review.

A circular business model can be defined as the rationale of how an organization creates, delivers, and captures value with and within closed material loops (Mentink, 2014). It is considered as an economic model, which provides growth in the global economy focused on environment, and aims to reduce the existing excess consumption to responsible consumption in which supply chain management plays a major role. The chain of activities in circular economy move parallel to the chain of activities like plan, source, make, deliver, return. Therefore, at every stage of circular economy, the practices of supply chain are linked to the achievement of objectives of circular economy. A new value chain is created through this linkage which encourages reduce, reuse, recover and redesign concepts. It also results in development of durable products, which can be reused, repaired, recycled and remanufactured or used as inputs for production of new products (Catherine Weetman, 2017). CE requires efforts at different levels (micro, meso and macro) for effective implementation (Yuan et al., 2006; Geng et al., 2013).

In CE, businesses create new value from by-products and coproducts and look for ways to recover and reuse energy and water inputs. When supply chains become multi-dimensional, they implement new flows and formats, service networks, more touch points, recovery loops for products and materials – they are 'loopy' instead of leaky (Catherine Weetman, 2017). Though there are various objectives for circular economy, the major ones are renewable inputs, increasing the life cycle duration of usage of product and recovering and reusing the by-products and waste (Justenhoven et al., 2019). (Maria Antikainen & Katri Valkokari, 2016) developed a Framework for sustainable circular business model innovation. Liudmyla Deineko (2019) developed a mathematical model aimed at describing the peculiarities of a circular economy in the countries with low and high levels of industrial ecologization as well as understanding conditions for resource conservation during production processes.

Many authors are of the opinion that some of the objectives of circular economy are reducing the negative impact of existing supply and production practices on the environment, minimizing the utilization of natural resources and improving the overall efficiency of all economic activities (Valko, 2018; Liudmyla Deineko, 2019) These natural resources include water, energy, air and some mineral deposits. The existing economic model is known as linear one and is more focused towards producing in excess and contributing to the wastage (Junjun Liu, et al., 2017). In addition, the used products are thrown without any concern towards ecological balance instead of devising mechanisms for reusing them as input raw material for production of some other products. Thus, the circular economy contributes to sustainable economic development.

Sustainable procurement, eco-design, industrial and territorial ecology, economics of functionality (collaborative economy), responsible consumption, extending duration of use through repair, reuse and repurpose, and finally recycling are the major aspects of circular economy (Solarimpulse, 2019). Design for the future, incorporate digital technology, preserve and extend what is already made, prioritize regenerative resources, use waste as a resource, rethink the business model, and finally collaborate to create a joint value system are found to be the seven key elements of circular economy based on a systematic survey (Circle-Economy, 2019). Authors also analyzed that in circular economy, while the biological cycle focuses on natural systems to return the products, the technical cycle focuses on recreation of products by using the waste effectively as input (Valko, 2018; Liudmyla Deineko, 2019). Reintroduction of materials and resources into the cycle is usually considered to be more energy-effective and, as per (Ghisellini et al., 2016), results in less greenhouse gases than waste incineration (Liudmyla Deineko, 2019).

Ellen Mcarthur foundation (EMF) conducted several studies on circular economy and opined that it provides positive outcomes to the society by delinking the economic activity from the consumption of finite resources. It identified three principles as pillars for circular economy. These are, removal of waste and pollution, continuing the usage of materials and products and regeneration of natural systems (EMF, 2019). In addition, this economy is built on the premise that products can be made to be made again resulting into a resilient and environmentally sustainable economy. EMF also concluded that the dominant linear economic model is running out of road, with non-renewable natural resources dwindling and becoming more expensive. The need for a circular economy is evident given that a significant proportion of non-renewable resources is diminishing and natural resource price volatility is increasing (EMF, 2019).

To develop the circular economy, there is a need to rebuild and modernize the industrial sector. This requires redesigning the supply chain processes related to sourcing, procurement, production, delivery and distribution and reverse supply chain activities. Industrial enterprises should leave the traditional model of an "effective use of resources" and aspire for increasing the longevity and reusability of materials, products and assets (Deineko & Tsyplitska, 2018).

Being an innovative model, the circular economy promotes sustainability, provides greater opportunities, and improves the competitiveness globally. In order to achieve these positive outcomes, there is a need to build robust systems and processes in businesses across the world and it is found that majority of the existing businesses lack this (Maria Antikainen & Katri Valkokari, 2016). A system-wide innovation and development of disruptive business models is an immediate necessity to redesign the value chain towards this circular economy (Stahel, 2014). Current trends, such as increasing consumption, new generations of consumers, urbanization and employment, tightening legislation, and technological leaps, accelerate the transition to a circular economy (Maria Antikainen & Katri Valkokari, 2016).

Many authors proposed models related to the concept of circular economy and many schools of thought have contributed towards this concept. Most of these studies were focused on regenerative design (EMF, 2014), performance economy (EMF, 2014; Roberta De Angelis, 2018), Cradle-to-Cradle, Industrial Ecology, Biomimicry, Blue Economy, Permaculture, Natural Capitalism, Industrial Metabolism and Industrial Symbiosis (EMF, 2014) as means of achieving circular economy objectives. As proposed by Lewandowski, (2016), the principles of circular economy broadly are based on aspects like design out waste / design for reuse, build resilience through diversity, rely on energy from renewable sources, think in systems (Systems Thinking) and waste is food / think in cascades / share values. A framework titled as ReSOLVE (regenerate, share, optimize, loop, virtualize, exchange) was developed by The Ellen MacArthur Foundation (EMF), (2012). Catherine Weetman (2017) proposed five steps strategy for businesses to manage their supply chains in circular economy. These five are, prioritize, work with suppliers, use learnings, invest the learnings, and tell the story of success to suppliers and consumers. Based on the above discussion, four objectives of circular economy are considered for the purpose of present chapter. These are Reduce, Reuse, Recover and Redesign as proposed by Catherine Weetman, (2017) which are also more or less similar to the ones proposed by EMF (2012) and Roberta De Angelis, (2018).

Supply chain in circular economy consists of two loops. The first one is forward chain, which is concerned with the production and delivery of product to the customer. The second one is reverse chain, which is concerned with the recovery of the product for reentry into the forward chain for production and delivery of a new product (Wells & Seitz, 2005). This kind of economy opens up new options and opportunities. The service business has already been seen as a superior business model in many ways compared to selling products, and with the mindset of the circular economy, the potential is even larger. The transformation towards service businesses can be seen as one of the key solutions in accelerating a circular economy because companies could have incentives to create products that have a long service life, which are used intensively and which are cost- and material-effective (Tukker & Tischner, 2006).

A three-dimensional strategy for circular supply chain with business model, product design and supply chain management as the dimensions contributing to circular supply chain was developed by Sourabh Jain (2018). This model emphasized that decisions related to innovative business models at the strategic level and product design focusing on eco-friendly design at tactical level and effective supply chain management at the operational level are the key inputs for circular supply chain.

Sustainability issues on economic, environmental and social perspectives have drawn attention of environmentalists, ecologists and governments. In this context, circular economy provides an opportunity to transform waste into resources, reduction of production and consumption activities; and reduction of carbon footprints, all at the same time. Over the past decades, there is a growing interest in investigating supply chains that are circular or closed in nature (Agrawal et al., 2015; Ghisellini et al., 2016; Govindan et al., 2015). Recent developments in the areas of sustainability have led organizations to incorporate economic, environmental and social factors in the supply chain (Morali & Searcy, 2013). The new concept of circular economy is based on the cradle-to-cradle (C2C) approach and encompasses the reusability, remanufacturing and recycling such that, ideally, no material goes to the landfill.

Thierry et al. (1995) conceptualized the circular supply chain as an integrated supply chain model incorporating both forward and reverse aspects of supply chain. Circular supply chain focusses on end-of-life product management for reuse, repairing, re-assembly, remanufacturing, recycling and waste disposal (Govindan & Soleimani, 2017; Govindan et al., 2015; The Ellen MacArthur Foundation, 2012). There are two perspectives that have been adopted for defining a circular supply chain. According to the material perspective, the circular supply chain describes a supply chain in which materials are reused and recycled repeatedly at the end of their useful life and there are minimal material wastes throughout the supply chain (Genovese et al., 2017; Govindan & Soleimani, 2017). However, a few have adopted a broader perspective that goes beyond material recycling, and emphasize that that circular supply chain or C2C supply chain is part of production systems. In addition to closing material loop, the production system must generate no solid, liquid, and gaseous wastes, minimize use of toxic and hazardous chemicals, and run only on renewable energy (Ehrenfeld & Gertler, 1997; McDonough & Braungart, 2002). The major drivers for moving toward a circular supply chain are not only issues of material scarcity and concerns of several global resource and environmental problems (Rockstrom et al., 2009), but also inherent economic and business opportunities (The Ellen MacArthur Foundation, 2015b).

Measurement of performance of circular supply chain has been an important issue in the literature. Circular supply chains are measured with respect to resource consumption and environmental burden throughout the supply chain (Genovese et al., 2017). However, a successful shift to circular supply chain would require designing supply chain for reverse logistics. Businesses will have to design products that facilitate circularity of a supply chain rather than designing products that are hard to recycle or remanufacture (Govindan et al., 2015; Savaskan et al., 2004). Product redesign will improve re-manufacturability, reusability and recyclability (Ghisellini et al., 2016). According to Sourabh Jain (2018), circular supply chain can broadly be classified into upstream and downstream stages. Upstream stages include mining, material processing and product design stages and downstream part of supply chain includes the circular supply chain, which plays major role in closing loop of supply chain (Sourabh Jain, 2018). Circular supply chains incorporate sustainability, waste management and supply chain management (Sourabh Jain, 2018).

Supply chain cooperation can improve CE performance (Zhu, Geng & Lai, 2011). CE can be defined as an economic model wherein resourcing, purchasing, production, reprocessing is designed to consider environmental performance and human well-being (Murray et al., 2017). In addition to supply chain, it is also found that industrial ecology, industrial ecosystems, reverse logistics play a significant role in circular chain (Ghisellini et al., 2016). CE incorporates policies and strategies for more efficient energy, materials, and water consumption, limiting waste that flows into the environment (Geng et al., 2013; Junjun Liu, et al., 2017). The closed-loop economy is significant in implementing green initiatives. This type of a strategy involves product designing through artefact take-back and reverse logistics implemented in the supply chain components for waste reduction. Twelve steps are developed for the achievement of GSCM. These are, redesigning of the product, reconfiguration in manufacturing, shifting to green suppliers, shortening the distances, altering service level settlements, shrinkage in packaging, plan for inverse supply chain activity, consolidation of shipments, planning for shorter routes, coordination with partners and taking a holistic lifecycle view (Manikee Madhuri Sharma, 2013).

To effectively transition from linear economies to circular resource-efficient economies, robust indicators and frameworks, which facilitate the mapping of life-cycle impacts of resource production and consumption cycles in supply chains, are required (Cucchiella et al., 2015). Though the concept of circular economy has gained importance and become popular, there is still no consensus on what is included in it and precisely what it means (Circle-Economy, 2019).

FOCUS OF THE CHAPTER

The systematic review of literature reveals that there are many issues with the approach of linear supply chain management. In this approach, the manufacturing organizations produce very huge volumes without great concern about reusing and recycling of the produced goods (Holweg, 2011; Catherine Weetman, 2017; Ellen MacArthur Foundation, 2019; Liudmyla Deineko et al., 2019).

The emergence of usage of digital technologies in supply chain has reduced this excessive production to some extent due to the adoption of information sharing as one of the supply chain practices (Roberta De Angelis, 2018). However, still there is lot of effort to be carried out to reduce the overall waste produced in the linear supply chain (Huysman et al., 2015; Junjun Liu et al., 2018). This is one of the biggest issue for future supply chains, which are inclined towards circular supply chains. In addition, it is found that there is no consensus about circular supply chains among the authors and it is not yet established which practices of SCM are likely to contribute towards the achievement of objectives of circular economy (Maria Antikainen, 2017; Sourabh Jain, 2018; Circle-Economy, 2019). Therefore, there is an issue of non-availability of adequate academic literature in this area and this is one of the issues for the present chapter.

While the influence of SCM on reduction of overall costs of operations is well recognized and appreciated by majority of the authors (Zhu, Geng & Lai, 2011; Genovese et al., 2017), the controversy about the implementation of linear SCM is its inability to control the excess production which results into waste and lack of systematic mechanism to reuse and recycle the products (Ellen MacArthur Foundation, 2019). This created a controversy around the linear practices of supply chain and authors questioned its contribution towards sustainability, especially towards the environment (Holweg, 2011).

Challenges for Implementation of Circular Supply Chain

While many authors propose and recommend circular supply chains for achieving the circular economy concept, many other authors highlight the challenges faced by the business organizations and enterprises in its effective implementation (Cerasis, 2019). These issues revolve around technology, information sharing, problems related to suppliers, third-party logistics providers, distributors and supply chain awareness among the members of the chain (Cerasis, 2019). As product, recycling is generally not considered as contributing to the value adding process by many business organizations, implementation of circular supply chains through reverse logistics will be a challenging task in future (Guide et al., 2003). Also, lot of investment is required for these organizations towards resources, infrastructure, technology and integration of systems for implementing and creating awareness about circular supply chains (Loomba & Nakashima, 2012). Closed loop supply chains are not only challenging in their design and operation, but have important implications for the supply chain (Savaskan *et al.,* 2004). They must combine both traditional supply chain activity centered on efficient distribution, as well as reverse supply chain activity such as the returns process, product repair / refurbishment, testing and sorting, and remarketing (Guide *et al.,* 2003).

METHODOLOGY ADOPTED

A systematic literature review has been done to achieve the objectives of this paper. This review is done with multiple objectives of understanding the definitions of supply chain, evolution of supply chain, drawbacks of linear supply chain, evolution of circular economy and closed supply chain, dimensions of circular economy, objectives of circular economy, approaches and models of circular economy, and finally the role of supply chain in circular economy. The key words used for the purpose of this literature review are 'circular supply chains', 'circular economy', 'closed loop', 'sustainable supply chains', 'reverse logistics' and other combinations comprising similar terminology have been used. Articles published in leading online journal databases of ProQuest and EBSCO were reviewed. The research gaps were identified based on the literature review. An analysis of gaps in the existing research works was done to develop a framework of supply chain management practices, which can lead to the achievement of objectives of circular economy.

SOLUTIONS AND RECOMMENDATIONS

An analysis of research works from the literature review reveals that there is a gap as far as studies related to circular supply chains and on arrival of consensus about which practices of supply chain contribute towards the achievement of the objectives of circular economy (Roberta De Angelis et al., 2018). It also found that to shift effectively the focus from linear to circular economy, there is a need to develop robust frameworks related to supply chains and performance measures, which facilitate the mapping of life-cycle impacts of resource production and consumption cycles in supply chains (Cucchiella et al., 2015; Huysman et al., 2015).

Considering this need, the present research proposes a solution by developing a framework of supply chain practices for circular economy. This framework is developed based on the issues and challenges identified through the systematic literature review carried out in the previous sections of the chapter. The framework is discussed in the next section.

Framework of Supply Chain Practices in Circular Economy

The literature review reveals that supply chain management can play a major role in achieving the objectives of circular economy. The practices adopted in traditional supply chain management implementation have to be redesigned and refocused on the objectives of circular economy. Information technology and digital technologies can contribute significantly in this direction. Therefore, based on this discussion and the above literature review, a comprehensive framework is developed by linking SCM practices and objectives of circular economy.

Seven SCM practices identified by Moh'd Anwer Radwan Al-Shboul et al. (2017) are considered for the purpose of this study. These are, strategic supplier partnership (Li et al., 2006; Koh et al., 2007; Adebayo I. Toyin, 2012; Ramakrishna, Y. 2016), level of information sharing and quality of information sharing (Tan et al., 2002), customer relationship management (Tan et al. 2002; Murali Sambasivan, et al., 2008), internal lean practice (Cigolini et al., 2004; Burgess et al., 2006), postponement (Sanjay Jharkharia and Ravi Shankar 2004; Ferreira et al., 2015; Ramakrishna Yanamandra, 2018) and total quality management (Murali Sambasivan, et al,. 2008). All these practices are well established in the literature by various authors. The objectives of circular economy are considered as i) reduce, ii) reuse, iii) recover and iv) redesign for the purpose of developing the framework of supply chain practices in the present chapter based on the works of Catherine Weetman, (2017).

The seven practices mentioned above are dealt in a more a detailed manner in this section.

Strategic Supplier Partnership (SSP), the first of these practices is proposed as the long-term relationship between the organization and its suppliers by Li et al. (2006). It is identified as a critical component for an effective supplier partnership in supply chains (Arawati & Zafaran, 2008). The second of these practices, level of information sharing is defined as the extent to which critical and proprietary information is communicated to one's supply chain partner by Li et al. (2006). This view was supported by Zhou & Benton (2007) who proposed that information sharing enables the growth of effective strategic partnership in supply chains. Aspects such as timeliness, accuracy, adequacy and credibility of information exchanged are considered as components of quality of information sharing (Li et al., 2006). Organizations should have systems in place which can share quality information for smooth flow of activities across the supply chains (Li & Lin, 2006). Another important practice considered is CRM which is concerned with planning, implementing, and evaluating successful relationships between providers and recipients either upstream or downstream of supply chain (Lee et al., 2007). It is a practice which identifies the customer needs, interacts with the customers, providing information to the customers about their orders, inventory status and order status and updating about the delivery of products ordered by the customers (Lee et al., 2007). For an effective SCM, it is found that CRM is one of the key enablers (Tan et al. 2002; Lee et al., 2007; Murali Sambasivan, et al., 2008).

Practices related to internal lean management are considered as one of the most important ones for achieving the objectives of circular economy. Lean is an approach focused on identification and elimination of waste from all the processes of supply chain which create value and it uses a technique known as Value Stream Mapping (VSM) for this purpose (Boyle and Scherrer, 2009; Qrunfleh and Tarafdar, 2013). Lean approach reduces lead times, reduces costs and improves quality in supply chains (Cudney & Elrod, 2010; Garza-Reyes et al., 2012) and minimizes total waste in the upstream and downstream components of supply chains (Goldsby et al., 2013). Lean is found to eliminate all forms of waste in the internal processes of an organization and it is capable of producing more output with low utilization of resources (Lamming, 1996).

Product postponement or moving forward one or more operations or activities like making, sourcing and delivering to a much later in the supply chain is considered as another important supply chain practice (Li et al., 2006). The purpose of postponement is to reduce inventory at various stages of supply chain, based on a close monitoring of actual demand (Ferreira et al., 2015). The seventh practice is Total Quality Management (TQM), a popular approach for achieving overall quality in the organization by doing things right at the first time (Al-Khalifa & Aspinwall, 2000) through benchmarking, supplier relations, continuous improvement, customer satisfaction, empowerment and top management responsibility as the important elements of it (Garza-Reyes et al., 2011; Jraisat & Sawalha, 2013).

Thus, based on the above discussion, a framework by linking the SC practices and the achievement of objectives of circular economy is developed and presented in Figure 1.

Figure 1. A framework of supply chain practices for circular economy (developed by author)

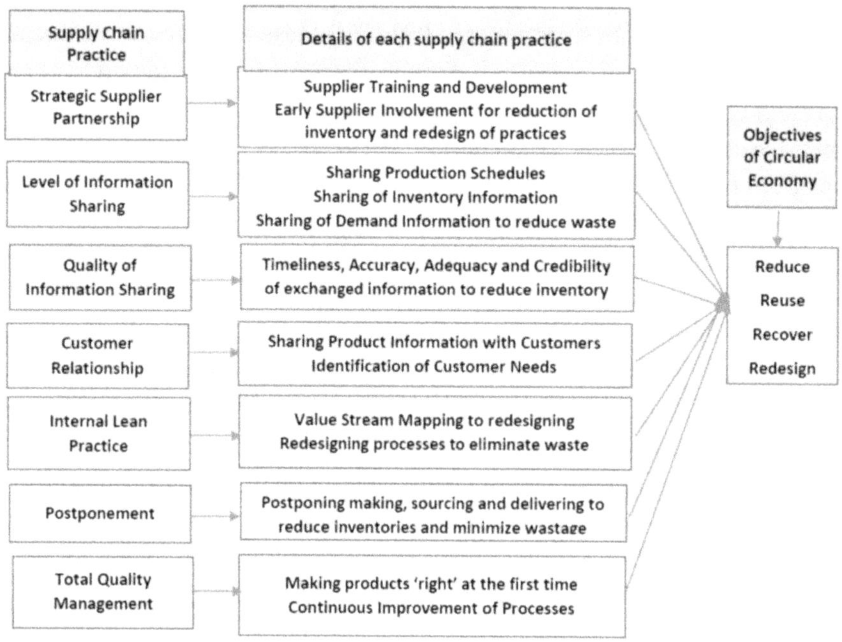

Discussion of Framework

The seven SCM practices adopted by a typical business organization / enterprise, also known as SCMPs are widely studied by the researchers as mentioned in the above sections. The details of these practices are mentioned in the framework which would enable the objectives of circular economy. The framework is discussed in the following section. Strategic supplier partnership is achieved through the practices like supplier training and development and early supplier involvement. These two practices enable reduction of raw material inventory and redesigning of supplier related processes for effective manufacturing of product. The second practice is related to level of information sharing in which sharing of production schedules by the manufacturer with the supplier, sharing of inventory information with the supplier and distributors, and sharing of demand information with the distributors enable the reduction of wastage and increase the accuracy of order and delivery management.

The third SCM practice focuses on quality of information provided. It emphasizes that timeliness, accuracy, adequacy and credibility are also very important rather than quantity of information. The fourth practice is about customer relationship management (CRM) which consists of practices like sharing of product information with customers by identifying their needs to reduce the wastage in the finished good inventory. Redesigning of processes using Value Stream Mapping (VSM) through internal lean practice is fifth SCM practice which will enable the achievement of minimization of waste in all processes. Postponement is the sixth SCM practice related to delaying the activities related to sourcing, making and delivering till reaching a minimum level of demand. This will enable the accumulation of inventory at all these stages and reduces the wastage of resources.

Implications of Framework

The above framework will enable the supply chain practitioners and researchers to focus on identifying the supply chain practices to achieve the objectives of circular economy. As emphasized by several authors, the concept of circular economy cannot be achieved by single firm or a single nation. Rather, it is achieved through a collective and system-wide initiative and committed effort by redesigning the existing systems and practices of supply chain at all levels of the chain with the mutual coordination of all members of the chain.

Therefore, this present study provides a highly useful contribution in the achievement of the objectives of circular economy through supply chain practices.

FUTURE RESEARCH DIRECTIONS

In order to shift from the existing linear supply chains to future-oriented circular supply chains which are supposed to contribute to the achievement of circular economy, there is an immediate need to create awareness among the managements of business organizations by developing supply chain frameworks (Cucchiella et al., 2015; Huysman et al., 2015; Lewandowski, M., 2016). There are very few studies covering in a more comprehensive manner, how a circular business model framework should look from a supply chain perspective (Lewandowski, M., 2016). Also, the existing frameworks have not focused approaches to circular economy, but not on practices related to supply chain which can contribute the achievement of the objectives of circular economy. Therefore, the present framework developed through this research contributes immensely to academicians and practitioners.

While it is generally accepted that conceptual frameworks provide basic platforms for visualizing the linkages of various aspects, it is necessary to test these frameworks in implementation. Therefore, the empirical validation of framework developed through this study would be the future topic for researchers. This framework can be validated across different industry sectors, including service sector for its viability, and for identifying issues and challenges in its implementation.

CONCLUSION

The outcome of this study brought out some interesting results about circular economy and the contribution of circular supply chain towards achieving the objectives of circular economy. The study was done with the objectives of identifying the need for circular economy, role of supply chain in circular economy, identify the SCM practices and establish a link between SCM and objectives of circular economy and finally to develop a framework of SC practices to achieve circular economy. The study brought the differences between linear economy and circular economy and the differences between linear supply chain and circular supply chain. It is concluded that linear supply chain focuses on excess production and leads to the accumulation of waste and results in ecological imbalance and social inequality (Sarkis, 1999). In addition, the weaknesses of linear supply chains were analyzed and it can be concluded that the focus on reuse and reduction of waste is absent in it and it operates on profit maximization as the final objectives (Catehrine Weetman, 2017). Inspite of several advancements in linear supply chains, the focus on reusability and recyclability of products, developing eco-friendly logistics and manufacturing systems, and usage of alternate environmentally friendly energy resources are yet to gain momentum (Roberta De Angelis, Mickey Howard & Joe Miemczyk, 2018).

In addition, though many researchers have highlighted the role of supply chain management in circular economy, there is no greater attention was paid to the identification and contribution of supply chain practices to meet the objectives of circular economy. The present study filled this gap and identified the practices, which would contribute to the achievement of objectives of circular economy.

Therefore, it can be concluded that seven practices of SCM strategic supplier partnership, level of information sharing, quality of information sharing, customer relationship, internal lean practice, postponement, and total quality management are the ones which contribute to the achievement of objectives of circular economy reduce, reuse, recover and redesign. These objectives are achieved through the sub-practices of each of the seven SCM practices as shown in Figure 1. The present framework also fills the gap in the existing frameworks and other schools of thought (Lewandowski, 2016) related to circular economy and supply chain management. The framework is highly useful to the academicians for further research and for industry practitioners for implementation to achieve the circular economy objectives.

REFERENCES

Accenture. (2014). Circular Advantage: Innovative Business Models and Technologies to Create Value in A World Without Limits to Growth. www.accenture.com

Agrawal, S., Singh, R. K., & Murtaza, Q. (2015). A literature review and perspectives in reverse logistics. *Resources, Conservation and Recycling*, *97*, 76–92. doi:10.1016/j.resconrec.2015.02.009

Al-Khalifa, K. N., & Aspinwall, E. M. (2000). The development of total quality management in Qatar. *The TQM Magazine*, *12*(3), 194–204. doi:10.1108/09544780010320250

Antikainen, M., & Valkokari, K. (2016). A Framework for Sustainable Circular Business Model Innovation, Technology Innovation. *Management Review*, *6*(7), 5–12.

Antonio Ferreira, M., Jose Chiappetta Jabbour, C., & Beatriz Lopes de Sousa Jabbour, A. (2017). Maturity levels of material cycles and waste management in a context of green supply chain management: An innovative framework and its application to Brazilian cases. *Journal of Material Cycles and Waste Management*, *19*(1), 516–525. doi:10.1007/s10163-015-0416-5

Arawati, A., & Zafaran, H. (2008). The strategic supplier partnership in a supply chain management with quality and business performance. *International Journal of Business and Management Science*, *1*(2), 129–145.

Boyle, T. A., & Scherrer, R. M. (2009). An empirical examination of the best practices to ensure manufacturing flexibility. *Journal of Manufacturing Technology Management*, *20*(3), 348–366. doi:10.1108/17410380910936792

Cerasis. (2019). Circular Supply Chain Vs. Linear Supply Chain: An Evolution. https://cerasis.com/circular-supply-chain/

Chopra, S., & Meindle, P. (2004). *Supply Chain Management: Strategy, Planning, and Operation*. Upper Saddle River, NJ: Prentice-Hall.

Christopher, M. (1998). *Logistics and Supply Chain Management: Strategies for Reducing Cost and Improving Service* (2nd ed.). Prentice Hall.

Cigolini, R., Cozzi, M., & Perona, M. (2004). A new framework for supply chain management: Conceptual model and empirical test. *International Journal of Operations & Production Management*, *24*(1), 7–41. doi:10.1108/01443570410510979

Circle-Economy. (2020). https://www.circle-economy.com/circular-economy/7-key-elements

Cooper, M. C., & Ellram, L. M. (1993). Characteristics of supply chain management and the implications for purchasing and logistics strategy. *International Journal of Logistics Management*, *4*(2), 13–24. doi:10.1108/09574099310804957

Cucchiella, F., D'Adamo, I., Koh, S. L., & Rosa, P. (2015). Recycling of WEEEs: An economic assessment of present and future e-waste streams. *Renewable & Sustainable Energy Reviews*, *51*, 263–272. doi:10.1016/j.rser.2015.06.010

Cudney, E., & Elrod, C. (2010). Incorporating Lean concepts into supply chain management. *International Journal of Six Sigma Competitive Advantage*, *6*(1/2), 12–30. doi:10.1504/IJSSCA.2010.034854

De Angelis, R., Howard, M., & Miemczyk, J. (2018). Supply chain management and the circular economy: Towards the circular supply chain. *Production Planning and Control*, *29*(6), 425–437. doi:10.1080/09537287.2018.1449244

Deineko, L., Tsyplitska, O., & Deineko, O. (2019). Opportunities and barriers of the Ukrainian industry transition to the circular economy. *Environment and Ecology*, *10*(1), 79–92. doi:10.21511/ee.10(1).2019.06

Deineko, L. V., & Tsyplitska, O. O. (2018). Circular economy as a route to industrial modernization: The European experience. *ECONOMICS: Time Realities*, *5*(39), 30–40. doi:10.5281/zenodo.2568944

Dubey, R., Gunasekaran, A., Papadopoulos, T., Childe, S. J., Shibin, K. T., & Wamba, S. F. (2017). Sustainable supply chain management: Framework and further research directions. *Journal of Cleaner Production*, *142*, 1119–1130. doi:10.1016/j.jclepro.2016.03.117

Ehrenfeld, J., & Gertler, N. (1997). Industrial ecology in practice: The evolution of Inter-dependence at Kalundborg. *Journal of Industrial Ecology*, *1*(1), 67–79. doi:10.1162/jiec.1997.1.1.67

Ellinger, A. (2000). Improving marketing/logistics cross-functional collaboration in the supply chain. *Industrial Marketing Management*, *29*(1), 85–96. doi:10.1016/S0019-8501(99)00114-5

EMF (Ellen MacArthur Foundation) and McKinsey & Co. (2019). Towards the Circular Economy: Economic and Business Rationale for an Accelerated Transition. Accessed on 15th January 2019 from https://www.ellenmacarthurfoundation.org/business/reports

Feldmann, M., & Muller, S. (2003). An incentive scheme for true information providing in supply chains. *Omega*, *31*(2), 63–73. doi:10.1016/S0305-0483(02)00096-8

Ferreira, K. A., Nogheira Tomas, R., & Alcantara, R. L. C. (2015). A theoretical framework for postponement concept in a supply chain, International Journal of Logistics Research and Appications: A Leading. *The Journal of Supply Chain Management*, *18*(1), 46–61.

Garza-Reyes, J. A., Parkar, H. S., Oraifige, I., Soriano-Meier, H., & Harmanto, D. (2012). An empirical exploratory study of the status of lean manufacturing in India. *International Journal of Business Excellence*, *5*(4), 395–412. doi:10.1504/IJBEX.2012.047906

Geels, F. W., McMeekin, A., Mylan, J., & Southerton, D. (2017). A critical appraisal of sustainable consumption and production research: The reformist, revolutionary and reconfiguration positions. *Global Environmental Change*, *34*, 1–12. doi:10.1016/j.gloenvcha.2015.04.013

Geng, Y., Sarkis, J., Ulgiati, S., & Zhang, P. (2013). Measuring China's circular economy. *Science*, *339*(6127), 1526–1527. doi:10.1126/science.1227059 PubMed

Genovese, A., Acquaye, A. A., Figueroa, A., & Koh, S. L. (2017). Sustainable supply chain management and the transition towards a circular economy: Evidence and some applications. *Omega*, *66*, 344–357. doi:10.1016/j.omega.2015.05.015

Ghisellini, P., Cialani, C., & Ulgiati, S. (2016). A review on circular economy: The expected transition to a balanced interplay of environmental and economic systems. *Journal of Cleaner Production*, *114*, 11–32. doi:10.1016/j.jclepro.2015.09.007

Goldsby, T. J., Michael Knemeyer, A., Miller, J. W., & Wallenburg, C. M. (2013). Measurement and moderation: Finding the boundary conditions in logistics and supply chain research. *Journal of Business Logistics*, *34*(2), 109–116. doi:10.1111/jbl.12013

Govindan, K., & Soleimani, H. (2017). A review of reverse logistics and closed-loop supply chains: A journal of cleaner production focus. *Journal of Cleaner Production*, *142*(Part 1), 371–384. doi:10.1016/j.jclepro.2016.03.126

Govindan, K., Soleimani, H., & Kannan, D. (2015). Reverse logistics and closed-loop supply chain: A comprehensive review to explore the future. *European Journal of Operational Research*, *240*(3), 603–626. doi:10.1016/j.ejor.2014.07.012

Guide, V. D. R., Harrison, T. P., & Van Wassenhove, L. N. (2003). The Challenge of Closed-Loop Supply Chains. *Interfaces*, *33*(6), 3–6. doi:10.1287/inte.33.6.3.25182

Holweg, M. (2005). The Three Dimensions of Responsiveness. *International Journal of Operations & Production Management*, *25*(7), 603–622. doi:10.1108/01443570510605063

Huysman, S., Debaveye, S., Schaubroeck, T., De Meester, S., Ardente, F., Mathieux, F., & Dewulf, J. (2015). The recyclability benefit rate of closed-loop and open-loop systems: A case study on plastic recycling in Flanders. *Resources, Conservation and Recycling*, *101*, 53–60. doi:10.1016/j.resconrec.2015.05.014

Jain, S., Jain, N. K., & Metri, B. (2018). Strategic framework towards measuring a circular supply chain management. Benchmarking, 25(8), 3238–3252. doi:10.1108/BIJ-11-2017-0304

Jharkharia, S., & Shankar, R. (2004). Supply Chain Management: Some insights from Indian Manufacturing Companies, Asian. *Academy of Management Journal*, *9*(1), 79–98.

Johnsen, T., Howard, M., & Miemczyk, J. (2014). Purchasing and Supply Chain Management: A Sustainability Perspective. Routledge.

Jraisat, L. E., & Sawalha, I. H. (2013). Quality control and supply chain management: A contextual perspective and a case study. *Supply Chain Management*, *18*(2), 194–207. doi:10.1108/13598541311318827

Justenhoven, P. (2019). The road to circularity: Why a circular economy is becoming the new normal. PricewaterhouseCoopers. Retrieved from https://www.pwc.de/de/nachhaltigkeit/pwc-circular-economy-study-2019.pdf

Kim, S. (2006). Effects of supply chain management practices, integration and competition on performance. *Supply Chain Management*, *11*(3), 241–248. doi:10.1108/13598540610662149

Koh, S. C. L., Sevkli, E., Zaim, S., Demirbag, M., & Tatoglu, E. (2007). The impact of supply chain management practices on performance of SMEs. *Industrial Management & Data Systems*, *107*(1), 103–124. doi:10.1108/02635570710719089

Lamming, R. (1996). Squaring lean supply with supply chain management. *International Journal of Operations & Production Management*, *16*(2), 183–196. doi:10.1108/01443579610109910

Lee, C., Kwon, I., & Severance, D. (2007). Relationship between supply chain performance and degree of linkage among supplier, internal integration, and customer. *Supply Chain Management*, *12*(6), 444–452. doi:10.1108/13598540710826371

Lewandowski, M. (2016). Designing the Business Models for Circular Economy. Towards the Conceptual Framework. *Sustainability*, *8*(43), 1–28. doi:10.3390/su8010043

Li, S., & Lin, B. (2006). Accessing information sharing and information quality in supply chain management. *Decision Support Systems*, *42*(3), 1641–1656. doi:10.1016/j.dss.2006.02.011

Li, S., Ragu-Nathan, B., Ragu-Nathan, T. S., & Rao, S. S. (2006). The impact of supply chain management practices on competitive advantage and organizational performance. *Omega*, *32*(2), 107–124. doi:10.1016/j.omega.2004.08.002

Liu, J., Feng, Y., Zhu, Q., & Sarkis, J. (2018). Green supply chain management and the circular Economy-Reviewing theory for advancement of both fields. *International Journal of Physical Distribution & Logistics Management*, *48*(8), 794–817. doi:10.1108/IJPDLM-01-2017-0049

Loomba, A. P., & Nakashima, K. (2012). Enhancing value in reverse supply chains by sorting before product recovery. *Production Planning and Control*, *23*(2-3), 205–215. doi:10.1080/09537287.2011.591652

Mattos, M. (2019). How a circular economy narrows, slows, intensifies and closes supply chain loops. MIT Supply Chain. https://medium.com/mitsupplychain/how-a-circular-economy-narrows-slows-intensifies-and-closes-supply-chain-loops-d85d9bab869

McDonough, W., & Braungart, M. (2002). *Cradle to Cradle: Remaking the Way We Make Things*. New York, NY: Farrar, Straus and Giroux.

Mentink, B. (2014). Circular Business Model Innovation: A Process Framework and a Tool for Business Model Innovation in a Circular Economy (Master's thesis). Delft University of Technology & Leiden University.

Moh'd, A. R. A.-S., Barber, K. D., Garza-Reyes, J. A., Kumar, V., & Reza Abdi, M. (2017). The effect of supply chain management practices on supply chain and manufacturing firms' performance. *Journal of Manufacturing Technology Management*, *28*(5), 577–609. doi:10.1108/JMTM-11-2016-0154

Morali, O., & Searcy, C. (2013). A review of sustainable supply chain management practices in Canada. *Journal of Business Ethics*, *117*(3), 635–658. doi:10.1007/s10551-012-1539-4

Qrunfleh, S., & Tarafdar, M. (2013). Lean and agile supply chain strategies and supply chain responsiveness: The role of strategic supplier partnership and postponement. *Supply Chain Management*, *18*(6), 571–582. doi:10.1108/SCM-01-2013-0015

Ramakrishna, Y. (2016). Supply Chain Management: Large vs. Small and Medium Enterprises (SMEs). In A. Dwivedi (Ed.), *Innovative Solutions for Implementing Global Supply Chains in Emerging Markets* (pp. 141–151). Hershey, PA: IGI Global; doi:10.4018/978-1-4666-9795-9.ch009.

Rockstrom, J., Steffen, W., Noone, K., Persson, A., Chapin, F. S. III, Lambin, E., ... Foley, J. (2009). Planetary boundaries: Exploring the safe operating space for humanity. *Ecology and Society*, *14*(2), 43–58. doi:10.5751/ES-03180-140232

Sambasivan, M., & Jacob, G. (2008). An Empirical Study on the Impact of Supply Chain Practices on Competitive Position of MNEs in Malaysia. *International Journal of Economics and Management*, *2*(2), 369–394.

Sarkis, J. (1999). *How green is the supply chain? Practice and research*. Graduate School of Management, Clark University.

Sarkis, J., Zhu, Q., & Lai, K. H. (2011). An organizational theoretic review of green supply chain management literature. *International Journal of Production Economics*, *130*(1), 1–15. doi:10.1016/j.ijpe.2010.11.010

Savaskan, R. C., Bhattacharya, S., & Van Wassenhove, L. N. (2004). Closed-loop supply chain models with product remanufacturing. *Management Science*, *50*(2), 239–252. doi:10.1287/mnsc.1030.0186

Sharma, M. M. (2013). A Study on the Concept of Green Supply Chain Management. *Journal of Supply Chain Management Systems*, *2*(1), 1–7.

Solarimpulse. (2019). Circular Economy – How to shape a sustainable future. https://solarimpulse.com/circular-economy-solutions

Soosay, C., Hyland, P., & Ferrer, M. (2008). Supply chain collaboration: Capabilities for continuous innovation. *Supply Chain Management*, *13*(2), 160–169. doi:10.1108/13598540810860994

Stahel, W. (2014). The Business Angle of a Circular Economy: Higher Competitiveness, Higher Resource Security and Material Efficiency. In *A New Dynamic: Effective Business in a Circular Economy*. Isle of Wight, UK: Ellen MacArthur Foundation.

Tan, K. C., Lyman, S. B., & Wisner, J. D. (2002). Supply chain management: A strategic perspective. *International Journal of Operations & Production Management*, *22*(6), 614–631. doi:10.1108/01443570210427659

Thierry, M., Salomon, M., Van Nunen, J., & Van Wassenhove, L. (1995). Strategic issues in product recovery management. *California Management Review*, *37*(2), 114–136. doi:10.2307/41165792

Toyin, A. I. (2012). Supply Chain Management (SCM) Practices in Nigeria Today: Impact on SCM Performance. *European Journal of Business and Social Sciences*, *1*(6), 107–115.

Tukker, A., & Tischner, U. (2006). Product-Services as a Research Field: Past, Present and Future Reflections from a Decade of Research. *Journal of Cleaner Production*, *14*(17), 1552–1556. doi:10.1016/j.jclepro.2006.01.022

Valko, D. V. (2018). Tsyrkuliarnaya ekonomika: teoreticheskaya model i effekty realizatsii [Circular economy: A theoretical model and implementation effects]. Natsionalnye interesy: prioritety ibezopasnost – National Interests. *Priorities and Security*, *14*(8), 1415–1429. doi:10.24891/ni.14.8.1415

Weetman, C. (2017). A Supply Chain Revolution: How the Circular Economy Unlocks New Value. https://www.koganpage.com/article/a-supply-chain-revolution-how-the-circular-economy-unlocks-new-value

WEF (World Economic Forum). EMF and McKinsey & Company. (2014). Towards the Circular Economy: Accelerating the scale-up across global supply chains. Retrieved from https://ellenmacarthurfoundation.org/business/reports

Wells, P., & Seitz, M. (2005). Business Models and Closed-Loop Supply Chains: A Typology. *Supply Chain Management*, *10*(4), 249–251. doi:10.1108/13598540510612712

Yanamandra, R. (2018). Development of an integrated healthcare supply chain model, Supply Chain Forum. *International Journal (Toronto, Ont.)*, *19*(2), 111–121. doi:10.1080/16258312.2018.1475823

Yuan, Z. W., Bi, J., & Moriguichi, Y. (2006). The circular economy – a new development strategy in China. *Journal of Industrial Ecology*, *10*(1/2), 4–8. doi:10.1162/108819806775545321

Zhou, H., & Benton, W. C. Jr. (2007). Supply chain practice and information sharing. *Journal of Operations Management*, *25*(6), 1348–1365. doi:10.1016/j.jom.2007.01.009

Zhu, Q., Geng, Y., & Lai, K. H. (2011). Environmental supply chain cooperation and its effect on the circular economy practice-performance relationship among Chinese manufacturers. *Journal of Industrial Ecology*, *15*(3), 405–419. doi:10.1111/j.1530-9290.2011.00329.x

KEY TERMS AND DEFINITIONS

Circular Economy: Circular economy is an economic model that provides economic growth with a focus on green development to transform the present mass consumption to what is known as responsible consumption, in which supply chain management plays a major role.

Closed Supply Chain: The supply chain in circular economy is also known as 'closed supply chain'. This type of economy is supposed to reduce the waste, improve reuse and recyclability. The circular economy has seen a significant increase in interest by the researchers and practitioners over the past few years and is continuing to gain steady momentum.

Green Supply Chain: The concept of green supply chain management (GSCM) integrates environmental dimensions in addition to the conventional dimensions in traditional supply chains.

Linear Economy: An economy based on 'take-make-dispose' is called as linear economy. The approach of linear economy involves the process of collection of raw material for transformation of them into finished goods and distribution until the customer until they are accumulated as waste. Volume of products manufactured is very high in this economy.

Linear Supply Chain: Linear supply chain is approach based on the linear flow of materials and fails to include both environmental aspects and management of the end-of-life phase of products.

Supply Chain Management: SCM encompasses all activities, which are involved in planning and management, sourcing and procurement, conversion and all logistics management activities as well as coordination and collaboration with channel partners.

Supply Chain Practices: Supply chain practices are defined as a multi-dimensional concept, including both sides of the SC (i.e., downstream and upstream). These are the actions and activities performed by organizations for implementing their supply chain processes and systems.

Sustainable Supply Chain: A Sustainable supply chain is a concept, which aims to reduce and minimize the flow of material across the supply chain and control the process of consumption, minimize the generation of waste and reduce the activities contributing to pollution.

Chapter 13
Circular Economy in Energizing Smart Cities

K. S. Sastry Musti
https://orcid.org/0000-0003-4384-7933
Namibia University of Science and Technology, Namibia

ABSTRACT

Principles of the circular economy are adopted in many fields to achieve sustainable ecosystems and to mitigate greenhouse gasses. Industry 4.0 technologies can significantly assist in applying circular economy principles to save energy and mitigate greenhouse gases to an extent. This chapter focuses on opportunities and challenges of adopting circular economy principles in the energy sector specifically in managing futuristic smart cities. Six major areas of energy conservation processes in smart cities are analyzed for this purpose. Given the interdisciplinary nature of the problem, an effective link is established between different areas such as circular economy, smart cities, Industry 4.0, and energy sector. Major energy conservation strategies such as demand-side management, waste to energy production, and recycling of apparatus are taken up. A novel, Industry 4.0-based information system for monitoring various energy-related processes in a smart city and a conceptual dashboard to visualize key indicators are proposed.

INTRODUCTION

The tenets of "circular economy" point to "circularity" feature in any ecosystem to reduce (or eliminate) waste and continuous use of resources. Many countries are now working towards using circular economy principles, processes and business models. There are several examples that have been presented by various authors over the years on the benefits of adopting the concepts of circular economy. Precious commodities such as water, energy etc., are taken up for efficient resource conservation. Manufacturing sectors like automobiles, batteries, construction and metal fabrication etc., have been also taken up to improve process efficiency. One of the good examples is producing energy from the waste. Municipal Solid Waste (MSW) Management is a widely discussed topic, related to energy, society, and environment, and thus has a lot of hygiene and economic implications (Singh, K, Kelly S and KS Sastry, Musti,

DOI: 10.4018/978-1-7998-5116-5.ch013

Copyright © 2020, IGI Global. Copying or distributing in print or electronic forms without written permission of IGI Global is prohibited.

2009). Thanks to the advances in technology; over the years, Waste-to-Energy (W2E) technologies have evolved to become more affordable and efficient. Besides the energy production, waste can be utilized to manufacture different products that can be used for long time. Hence, MSW is considered as a resource. Similarly, battery recycling is an excellent example for circular economy business model. Bloomberg estimates that globally Lithium-Ion battery sales for electrical vehicles and other storage purposes will reach 5 million tons by 2025 (Pagliaro, M, and Meneguzzo, F, (2019). Managing and disposing such large volumes of harmful waste is always a challenge. Technologies for recycle used batteries and other electronic equipment that have reached their end-of-life do exist and are continuously improving. Construction technologies specifically for roads and buildings are also changing and using waste and other materials along with conventional construction materials. Plastic blending with concrete for building construction and with tar for paving the roads are proven efficient, long lasting and environmental friendly; as the plastic, itself is not easily biodegradable and harmful to the environment. Lean manufacturing principles are actively being used to reduce the use of materials and resources such as water and energy. It is estimated that commercial opportunities in the implementation of circular economy may reach USD 4.5 trillion by the year 2030. This may also lead to 40% of S&P500 companies to go out of businesses in about 10 years' time, according to SAP (Coloumbus, 2016).

Electrical power is an essential commodity everywhere and expensive. Typically, the fossil fuels such as coal and gas are used in large quantities in energy production. The process of coal based energy production using fossil fuels is not only results in high volumes of greenhouse gas carbon dioxide and fly ash; and thus polluting the environment. Oil and gas are relatively cleaner forms of fuels, however are very expensive; and most countries have to import them from international markets. Renewable energy sources are now becoming the norm across the globe due to increased awareness of both economic and environmental impacts of using fossil fuels. Use of renewable energies, though is increasing; there are several challenges exist as on date. In any case, energy production is cost intensive, with or without the use of fossil fuels. The question is how well the energy sector can imbibe the core tenets of circular economy to reduce overall expenses and energy use. For applying circular economy principles, many parameters in the contemporary energy systems need to be monitored and measured. Some of such opportunities and challenges include - continuous monitoring of energy usage patterns of the customers, controlling (reducing) the energy usage during peak load conditions (just as the principle of postponing the usage), encouraging use of alternate forms of energies (such as solar water heaters, just as the principle of substitution) and many more.

While the opportunities in Recycling, Reducing and Reusing (3R) the infrastructure and resources are well understood and many industries across the globe are taking necessary actions to realize the benefits. However, it is important to understand the contemporary technological advances. With the advent of the fourth industrial revolution (aka industry 4.0), application of circular economy principles has also changed drastically. Internet of Things (IoT) and big data help significantly in data acquisition, information processing and apparatus control. Forbes estimates that around 10 billion Industrial Internet of Things (IIoT) devices will be online and they are likely to contribute a market value of USD 3.7 billion (Coloumbus, 2016). Similarly, it is estimated that market value for big data based analytics may exceed USD 200 billion (Press, 2017). However, such niche technologies do need relatively modern, smart infrastructure and economies. Smart cities are an excellent example, where such smart infrastructure can be seen in use right from the planning and developmental stages. The operating environment in smart cities with industry 4.0 will move common public forward into digital space, as a majority of the activities will be automated (BeSmartCity, 2019). At the same time, smart cities do need very high amounts of energy and water to operate and normally would cater to higher density of population per square kilometer. Hence, smart cities are the best candidates for considering the use of circular economy principles; due to the facts that they, use lot of energy, have niche technologies such industry 4.0 and produce lot of waste.

From the above it can be seen that indeed, there are different areas (renewable energy, smart cities, big data and industry 4.0) involved in the discussion. However, the literature so far explicitly did not focus on how industry 4.0 and big data can help in circular economy application specifically in energy sector. There is no explicit discussion on possibilities for energy sector in applying circular economy principles in smart cities. To address this gap, this chapter considers:

1. Typical futuristic smart cities as circular economies and thus focuses on applying circular economy principles particularly in the energy sector, in terms of resource utilization and waste mitigation aspects;
2. Illustration of various parallels that existing energy management practices and tenets of circular economy in managing the national level energy pools;
3. The treatment of six specific key areas in managing the energy context of smart cities.

Further, this chapter makes an attempt is made to propose a conceptual industry 4.0 based framework for managing the consumer demand (aka Demand Side Management –DSM) keeping the principles of circular economy. Overall content in this chapter is organized in various sections. A summary of the recent literature is provided first. In addition, the next section explains why energy sector and DSM for smart cities are good candidates for applying circular economy. Next section focuses on various recycling opportunities and ancillary services in energizing smart cities. Several authors point to lack of data and information in quantifying the benefits of circular economy. To address this issue, the next section presents a conceptual framework that functions with a cyber-physical system to process information related to various parameters that feed into application of circular economy principles. Lastly, a few opposing views and challenges in driving the circular economy forward are described.

LITERATURE REVIEW

Circular economy application to the topic of energy conversation in smart cities is wide and interdisciplinary area. This chapter takes up a systematic research methodology to provide clarity to the discussion. The research methodology includes – understanding the fact that various definitions do exist for circular economy and thus application of it depends on the context; identifying most recent and important publications that provide support to the present discussion; providing a background on energy sector and DSM; examining a few major areas of energy hungry processes within the smart cities; proposing a conceptual framework for monitoring circular economy indicators; and finally understanding the challenges in the overall process.

There are different definitions exist for Circular Economy, and so are the understanding and applying philosophies. Kirchherr et al (2017) provided an excellent analysis of about 114 different definitions that can be found in the literature for circular economy. The study suggested that circular economy is understood differently by different stakeholders based on the context; however a majority of the stakeholders do agree to accept 3R (reduce, reuse and recycle) as the core tenet of the circular economy. Interestingly,

Kirchherr et al (2017) points that the objectives of circular economy are economic prosperity and environmental quality. The study illustrates varying perceptions of stakeholders about circular economy. Naturally, there is an immediate need to raise the awareness on circular economy in general, among stakeholders. Following this need, Kirchherr et al (2019) highlighted the importance of educational and training needs about the same using a few case studies.

Given the complexity of circular economy framework, a few authors tried to explain various parameters associated with it. Moraga et al (2019) considered the explanation of circular economy indicators, specifically through a Life Cycle Thinking (LCT) approach. Both micro and macro indicators were considered and treated with proper classification. Murray et al (2017) pointed out the interdisciplinary nature of this circular economy. In the recent past, application of circular economy principles in different sectors has assumed a great interest. Given the huge financial implications and benefits, applying the three R principles (reduce, re-use, recycle) of circular economy in various fields; has started. Naturally, this in turn resulted in research investigations and publications in different directions such as renewable energies, industry 4.0, big data, recycling of batteries, recycling (or repurposing) EVs, DSM, smart cities etc. The research contributions in the recent years can be divided broadly into different areas as shown in Table 1.

Table 1. Areas of focus in applying circular economy

Area of Contribution	Author(s)
Circular Economy + Renewable Energies	Holmatov et al (2019), Charles et al (2019), Varma et al (2016)
Circular Economy + Industry 4.0	Manalavan et al (2019), Rajput et al (2019), Tseng et al (2018), Pagoropoulos et al (2017); Esposito M, (2017),
Circular Economy + Big Data	Gupta et al (2019), Pagliaro et al (2019), Rajput et al (2019), Tseng et al (2018)
Circular Economy + Recycling of Batteries	Charles et al (2019), Levanen et al (2018), Tran et al (2018), Velazquez et al (2019)
Circular Economy + DSM	Castro et al (2018)
Circular Economy + Supply Chain Management (SCM)	Manalavan et al (2019), Gupta et al (2019)
Circular Economy + Business Models	Levanen et al (2018), Ionescu et al (2017),
Circular Economy + Smart cities	Srivastav et al (2019), BeSmartCity (2019), Kumar (2020)

As seen in Table 1, it is clear that circular economy principles have been of significant interest to researchers in different areas, but mainly in energy. A few researchers (Srivastav et al (2019); Gupta et al (2019); Pagliaro et al (2019)) have indicated the need of niche technologies like industry 4.0, big data in managing the smart cities; while applying circular economy processes to manage the resources efficiently. However, no or little research suggests the presence of a strong link between DSM, smart cities and circular economy.

Varma et al (2016) studied existing energy resources and future estimations of energy demand for Indian context and proposed that circular economy principles need to be applied in energy management for achieving several benefits. Circularity in the energy sector can be achieved through addition of renewable energies, energy efficiency and ash management. Exhaustive studies undertaken by Charles et al (2019) concluded that extension of battery lives could reduce overall costs significantly; and thus recommends end-of-life treatment mechanisms for batteries. Charles et al (2019) further suggested that recycling the batteries would result in resource efficiency and a viable business model for circular economy within South Africa. For many years, the emphasis on energy capacity addition through renewable energies remained high. Solar and wind energies are leading in capacity addition in almost every country. Holmatov et al(2019) evaluated the impact of using land and water for growing different crops in circular fashion and suggested that using biomass to generate combined heat and power; leads to smaller amounts of water and land to produce same amount of crop. Such circular mechanisms also result in lower amounts of greenhouse gasses. Jin et al (2017) studied the synergies of energy and water usage/ conservation in China during 2007 to 2012 and suggested that savings in water consumptions benefit electrical power sector significantly. It can be seen that these studies are related to different countries and different aspects; yet point to the benefits of applying principles of circular economy.

Supply Chain Management (SCM) sector has great potential for the application of circular economy framework. Manavalan et al (2019) examined the case of processing industrial waste in production firms. The scenario of transforming the SCM processes from linear economy model to circular models. Three different production sites viz., a sugar factory, paper production factory and a recycling factory are considered to illustrate the impact of circular economy framework. Their study found that businesses would be sustainable and profitable if they adopt the circular economy framework through digital technologies of industry 4.0 standard.

Rajput et al (2019) explained the reasons behind linking industry 4.0 and circular economy principles from two different sides, enablers' and barriers sides. As many as six enablers and four challenges have been considered. The study also pointed to lack of information based on empirical data, just as pointed by Anna et al (2019). Gupta et al (2019) also worked on the application of circular economy in SCM from the perspective of the stakeholder for Indian context. Their study suggested adoption of circular economy would have positive impact for emerging economies. Just as other authors, their study pointed to lack of information based on datasets; and thus emphasized the importance of big data based analytics. A few countries have in fact developed industry 4.0 based modern infrastructures and are being benefitted from their initiatives. Esposito M, (2017) points that:

Cities such as Hong Kong have implemented IoT monitoring for preventative maintenance of transportation infrastructure, while Rio de Janeiro monitors traffic patterns and crime at its central operations center. Mexico City has installed fans in its buildings, which suck up local smog. In the waste management sector, San Francisco and London have installed solar-powered automated waste bins that alert local authorities to when they are full; creating ideal routes for trash collection and reducing operational costs by 70 percent.

Darla et al (2018) identified six different barriers (technological, regulatory, financial, managerial, performance indicators, consumer and social) in implementing the circular economy to contemporary society. However, lack information is the major source for these barriers. Studies that are more comprehensive are required to understand if these barriers can be overcome with help of big data analytics.

Ideally, application of circular economy should result in sustainable development, sustainable processes and environments. By definition, the term sustainability expects minimal adverse impact on economy, environment and society; as these are the three major pillars of any ecosystem. It is well established that renewable energies play significant role in reducing greenhouse gases, overall cost reduction and influencing the societies in positive manner. Traditional energies are slowly replaced by renewable energies. Energy and water are critical resources and indeed are key inputs to any society. Moreover, a lot of waste is produced by the modern societies and Municipal Solid Waste (MSW) is generally managed by the utility, just as energy and water. Traditionally state owned utilities manage energy, water and waste and consumers pay the associated charges.

In the changing times, many countries are trying to build smart cities and/or give a makeover to existing to convert them into smart. Essentially smart cities are supposed to meet a significant portion of total energy requirements on their own; manage waste; and conserve (and / or reuse, recycle) water all within themselves. Smart cities thus will have interesting proposition in the sense; a few residents may produce electrical power (using solar PV, with or without battery storage systems, biomass plant systems of their own), may produce clean water (through recycling, purifying systems of their own) and process some of the MSW. On the other hand, residents do consume electric power, other forms of energy (gas, thermal energy etc.) and of course water. In other words, different forms of energy are required for consumers. It is important to monitor both production and usage of these resources for billing/ crediting purposes.

Thus, smart cities essentially will have modern and sustainable infrastructure in - built environment, energy systems, transportation, bio-systems and local resource production. To manage such modern infrastructure, smart cities are expected to have effective waste collection/ treatment/ disposal; and/or effective resources monitoring/ management. In other words, smart cities are expected to self-sufficient in managing the vital resources such as energy, water and waste. Thus, smart cities are circular in nature and thus can be called circular cities. Typically, smart cities are expected to use fully automated systems to measure, monitor and control use of - water, electrical power, other forms of energy and waste. Hence, applying circular economy principles are integral for smart cities to estimate / quantify the financial and environmental impact of the eco-system. However, energy, water and waste management requirements of smart cities are very high for obvious reasons and hence they need to depend on public utility and other private players in the short term, though they are expected to be self-sufficient in the long term.

Energy Sector and DSM in the Context of Circular Economy

Circular economy is through a novel concept, actually its core principles are applied in energy sector for long. Not just smart cities, energy markets in a majority of the world, are very conscious of use of energy due to the enormous costs and resource requirements to produce energy; and then to distribute it to the consumers. In the past state utility used to have the monopoly where, all the energy resources, power transmission lines and other infrastructure exist under its control and are used to serve the consumers. It is in a way a linear economy model, where energy is generated, transmitted (transported) and sold to the consumers. However, that model has now changed and the monopoly of state utility has been reduced drastically. Independent power producers (IPPs) are given licenses by regulators to produce energy commercially. Consumer demand grows continuously and most developing countries (for example in Africa) even import power from neighboring countries.

This situation is a direct result of higher consumer demands, not having adequate energy resources and inability to add energy capacity etc. Figure 1 presents a schematic to illustrate such a condition. From the Figure 1 it can be seen that the consumer demand is met by three ways; energy imports from neighbors, utility's own generation and energy produced by IPPs. However, it should be noted that long-term energy imports could be very expensive as payments are made in foreign currency. Excessive dependency on external energy markets results in energy insecurity and thus long-term imports is not a sustainable

Figure 1. Schematic for a typical market driven energy pool
Source: Author

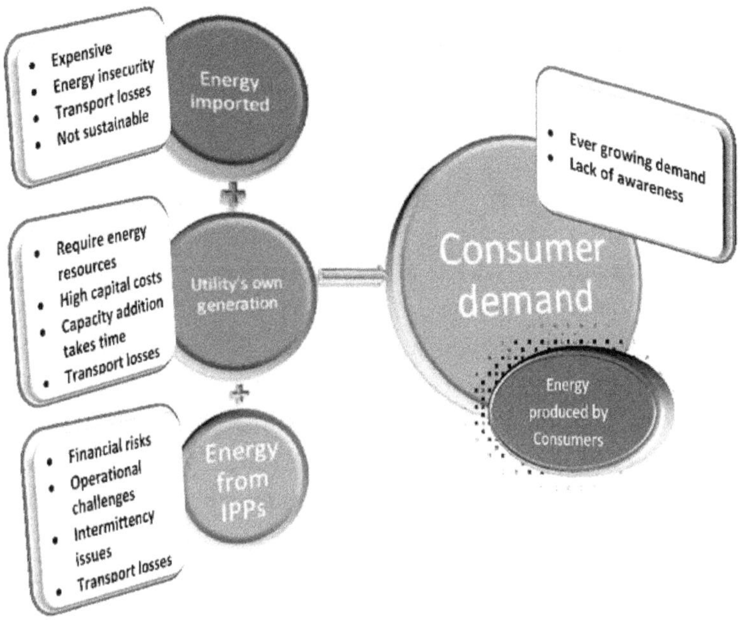

option. IPPs mostly are licensed to produce renewable energy and thus a welcoming aspect, as they do not necessarily pollute the environment. Though IPPs produce and contribute to the energy pool through Power Purchase Agreements (PPAs), they face numerous challenges due to technical, operational and other factors such as intermittency and climatic changes. Utility may want to expand the capacities of their existing generating plants; however, it requires a lot of in investment and time. Financial risks do exist due to various factors in energy markets, including varying costs of fossil fuel, random nature of renewable energy resources, logistics and dependencies in fuel transportation and even political and financial conditions of the state itself.

At the end, there will be significant gap between consumer demand and total available energy, and this gap needs to be managed by the utility with help of IIPs, stakeholders and even end consumers. Resource addition is very expensive due to higher capital costs. Interestingly, to supply 1 MW of electrical power to the end consumer, 1.5 to 1.8MW of generation (resource) is required.

In such a situation, DSM comes handy, as it is a well-known and widely practiced approach to influence energy consumption behavior of the consumers. End expectations and results of DSM are lower energy bills to the consumers, lower energy consumption across the system and use of alternative energy resources (such as consumers installing solar water heating systems) where electric power was used otherwise etc. Hence, DSM has a striking similarity to circular economy model. Use of alternative energy by consumers is nothing but substituting the electrical power with solar power and thus as good as one of the circular economy's business models 'dematerializing resources'. Then, circular economy suggests the regulations like 'polluter pays'. DSM also uses 'time-of-use (ToU)' tariffs where consumption of power during peak hours attracts higher charges. Interestingly, applying circular economy principles to national level energy pools may result in better solutions.

OPPORTUNITIES FOR CIRCULAR ECONOMY IN ENERGIZING SMART CITIES

Almost every country needs to spend significantly for meeting the energy needs and on top of that, many countries depend on energy imports from neighbors. Energy dependency is a major security threat for obvious reasons. At the same time fossil fuel, based energy production contributes to greenhouse gases. These circumstances naturally beg for energy conservation and efficiency in using. The following sections explain various opportunities for applying circular economy - specifically 3R principles; that exist in six different areas of energy sector in helping the societies in effective resource and material management.

DSM in Modern Era Practice and for Smart Cities

DSM in electrical power distribution systems has been the chief strategy for many utilities across the world. DSM empowers utility engineers to influence consumer behavior in energy consumption through numerous ways. For instance, Time of Use (ToU) tariff structure usually sets different rates for electricity during the day. Peak hours (typically during the noon) will have higher tariffs than the off-peak hours. With this, most cost conscious consumers switch off their appliances to the possible extent to save the costs. Interestingly, smart appliances (toasters, washing machines, refrigerators and room heaters etc) are already available in the markets and consumers can program their operational hours based on the ToU rates. Almost all such appliances can be controlled remotely through smartphones. However, it should be noted that most utilities apply ToU rates only to commercial and industrial consumers; and not to domestic consumers. However, it is expected that power distribution companies' in future smart cities may bring even domestic consumers also under the umbrella of ToU rates. For that matter, many utilities are now looking at dynamic pricing structures that allow utilities to determine the tariff based on real-time conditions of the season. Tariffs under dynamic pricing will be communicated to consumers electronically. For this all consumers must be on smart devices preferably; or at least literate; which is one of the characteristics of smart cities. Smart cities make living very comfortable, but the environment expects the residents to operate with a certain class of discipline in energy consumption, waste disposal and also in terms of awareness.

The major challenge for the utilities is shortage of energy resources to distribute power adequately to the consumers. Most developing countries are facing the challenge of every-increasing electrical power demand. In fact, utilities have more challenges too, besides the gap between generation and demand. A significant amount of efforts and investments are required to maintain the transmission and distribution lines every year. During the peak hours, the power transferred through the lines goes beyond the set limits and thus power lines are heated up. At the same time, overall power losses in the system also go up; and even the voltage may be low. Such situations need to be addressed in real-time to keep the power service within the specified standards. Especially the thermal stress on the power system is high during the peak hours and it may even result in failure of components. DSM comes handy, particularly, as it encourages consumers to produce their own electrical energy (usually solar energy) and thus many residents usually show interest in investing in rooftop solar panels and earn money through pumping the energy into the grid. This is facilitated either through net-metering concept where consumers pay or get paid based on the net energy consumed by them or sold to the utility. Importantly, solar energy is also available during the peak hours, due to the availability of sunshine. This leads to what is called peak clipping. Essentially, a portion of the peak energy can be avoided by different means: ToU (peak tariff during peak hours) and solar energy supplied by the consumers.

DSM also encourages consumers to install solar thermal (solar water heaters) systems for water heating and space heating purposes. Solar water heaters with storage facilities can save a lot of energy for the consumers and thus avoid the burden on utility as well. District water heating facilities in hotels, universities and factories are liberally assisted through UN funded programs. District water heating systems are ideally suited for people living in a closely buildup space, such as the smart cities. Under this concept, water is heated through a large-scale solar-thermal system, stored in large storage facilities and then circulated to residents. Obviously, district water heating facilities are managed centrally and offer reliable hot water supply. Scale, sophistication, measurement and control are the major differences between district water heating and a standalone rooftop water heater.

Besides encouraging consumers to opt for renewable energy production, DSM also uses an interesting mechanism called 'ripple control'. This is a typical way of controlling the energy consumption during a specific time of the day. Through this technique, utility can cut-off power to air-conditioners and/or electrical water heaters. In other words, utility can control specific consumer appliances for a specific duration in a given day. This methodology requires additional infrastructure (ripple control receiver at each consumer premises) and usually utility and consumers share the costs. Usually ripple control targets electric water heater segment and this in turn forces consumers to go for rooftop solar water heater. However, installing a solar water heater may not be a possibility for consumers who live in apartments due to lack of their own roof that can receive solar radiation. In such cases, consumers usually get up early and heat the water before the ripple control comes into effect. In a way, ripple control/ DSM significantly changes the consumer behavior as in this case, water heaters will be used when the energy is cheaper and /or utility can supply the energy without any issue. However, achieving ripple control is relatively difficult in normal communities, as this requires additional infrastructure and costs. However, in case of smart cities this becomes easier as a significant planning goes into the development and construction. Energy, Water and waste are the major items that receive a significant attention of the developers. In other words, smart city planners need to pay attention to DSM principles so that reliable electrical power supply is ensured. At the same time, DSM takes the problem/ burden of energy resource crunch to the consumers' doorstep and alters them to be aware of the collective responsibility in energy consumption. At the same time, utilities can implement 'load shedding' (another arm of DSM) in smart cities, as several additional features will be available to control the power apparatus and infrastructure. The problems of power thefts and non-payment of electricity bills are almost ruled out as most connections are serviced through pre-paid electronic meters and even caution deposits.

Peter Drucker's well-known quote says, "What gets measured gets managed." This suggests that effective management of any parameter requires proper tracking and measurement. For achieving good circular models to save energy over the time, appropriate models to quantify the various key parameters of the system are critical. Moraga et al (2019) presented a comprehensive framework for measuring CE parameters. Similarly, DSM processes rely on a sub-process 'measurement and verification' which ensures an accurate measurement of electrical energy consumed besides continuous monitoring and control. Localized 'control centers' (aka virtual power plants) are essential to monitor power flows, consumptions on continuous basis. For smart cities, such control centers are expected to monitor water, energies and even waste. The challenge is to accomplish the monitoring, measurement and control aspects at lower costs. Thankfully, Industrial Internet of Things (IIoT) - an integral part of fourth industrial revolution; offers cost effective solutions and strategies. Hence, it is possible to measure and control the vital resources in a smart fashion and the key CE parameters such as cost estimates, resource utilization, waste reduction etc., can be effectively determined.

Consumers producing their own energy and/or saving the energy costs (through rooftop solar systems and/ or solar water heaters) is nothing new. However, DSM changes the consumer behaviors in saving, post-phoning the energy consumption and re-using the energy etc. through its ToU tariff mechanisms. Due to the presence of ToU in place, consumers naturally research on their own on investing in such infrastructure to save money. Castro et al (2018) advocated on the link between renewable energies and circular economy principles and then favored the use of renewable energies. In fact, DSM forces the consumers to be aware of the varying tariff structures and then take actions accordingly.

Waste From Solar PV Industry

As the world is fast moving towards renewable energies, usage of solar Photovoltaic (PV) panels is on the exponential rise. Once reached their end-of life, solar PV panels contribute to a lot to waste production. Solar Power Europe indicates that overall capacity addition in solar PV segment has gone up by 45% in 2018 and by 58% in 2019. This capacity addition is in line with the EU projections to achieve renewable energy up to a third of the overall energy pool. This projection is to achieve low carbon, sustainable economy and efficient use of all available resources. Hence, the very renewable energy/ solar energy sector is directly pointing towards the same principles of circular economy. According to the current estimates, India alone accumulates around 200,000 tons of solar waste by 2030, with its present installed solar energy capacity. At the same time, a significant investment and planning is put in place for further enhancing the capacity addition, which means, that solar waste is going to increase by several folds.

At present solar PV, panels usually last up to 20 to 25 years from the point of installation. Of course, research into this area is undertaken in several directions, including enhancing the power per square inch (of the solar panel) and further enhancing the overall lifetime. However, a few, very recent researchers are suggesting that solar PV panels with short life span (typically 10-15 years) can further enhance solar PV energy sector. As part of the investigations, they have analyzed three different sites with different scales of solar energy installations; and then applied NREL benchmark parameters for financing and recycling. Their argument is that at present the industry standard expects the life span of the panels to be around 25 to 30 years; and that manufacturers are focusing on reducing overall solar energy price. In other words, their suggestion is that it will be profitable if manufacturers focus on cost per kilowatt and reduce the life span to 10-15 years. The concept of lower life span solar PV panels may produce cheaper energy and help the manufacturers as this situation leads to higher demand for their product. One important assumption here is that components such as supporting infrastructure, electrical component ratings and rakes to hold these panels should remain the same. In other words, the panels will become 'disposable' in future, if this suggestion becomes a reality. Naturally, this will result in creating huge amounts of waste, especially given the rise of solar energy capacity addition.

There are two important takeaways here. One is the ever-increasing solar waste across the globe and the other is the researchers advocating in favor of lower life span (disposable) panels. Both will potentially help recycling industry in the solar energy sector. At present, there are only a few companies that specialize in the solar panel recycling technologies. The PV cycle association collected and processed 30,000 tons of solar waste so far. Interestingly, specialists in solar energy recycling industry do not advocate on establishing recycling facilities locally and instead recommend that the waste be shipped to the existing facilities elsewhere. Transportation of bulk amounts of waste contributes to greenhouse gases and defeats the very merits of renewable energies. In fact, that at present, there is no adequate waste production, owing higher life span. PV solar panels - that have reached the end-of life, damaged during transportation or during installation, damaged due to bad weather and/or defective panels that no longer produce energy; need to be recycled. Currently there are no legislative frameworks on processing the waste locally in solar energy sector.

Opportunities in Repurposing Electrical Vehicles

As on today, the entire automobile industry is in general at the crossroads due to ongoing transition from conventional fossil-fuel powered vehicles to electric and/or hybrid vehicles. In the recent years, the growth of new range electric vehicles (EVs) is phenomenal and several hundreds of thousands of vehicles have been added to the roads across the globe. The biggest challenge that many nations are now battling with is the waste generated by condemned, outdated vehicles. Several firms that specialize in recycling of metal waste are busy with processing the waste generated by unused vehicles. The Grand View Research group suggested that the market size of global metal stamping industry is expected to reach nearly 300 billion USD by 2025. Several studies are now pointing towards the prospects of circular economy in automobile sector. Several opportunities for recycling exist in automobile sector that potentially can result in significant savings and creation of jobs. In addition to recycling, transforming a conventional fossil-fuel based vehicle into EV is a fast growing industry as well. A good number of companies that specialize in this segment are already operating. EVs are nothing but computers on wheels and hence transformation from legacy state to EV is fast becoming a well-organized industry. In addition, reusing the parts from disabled vehicles constitutes a significant reverse logistic industry by itself. 3D printing of some of the parts is also actively taken up in various parts of the world and thus reducing the burden of importing/ purchasing the parts. This means, automobile sector has many opportunities in reusing; local, low-cost manufacturing and other reverse logistics. Obviously, these opportunities and related actions closely agree with the principles of circular economy again. Ahmed et al (2019) suggested that ample synergies exist between circular economy principles and automobile recycling industry. Their study indicated two aspects - significant benefits in using repurposed galvanized sheet metal in building construction industry and savings for modern metal fabrication industries; once circular economy principles are adopted.

EVs require charging stations in strategic locations and this itself is a big logistical challenge for the global push towards EVs. Several countries though encouraging the manufacturing and use of EVs, realization of supporting infrastructure is increasingly becoming difficult. Smart cities due to their true definition can ideally support the incorporation of such infrastructure. Ideally, a separate DC grid for charging is better suited for charging stations and it is relatively easy in smart cities to accomplish the same. EVs can be better used and managed in a sophisticated environment like smart cities.

Recycling the Batteries

Energy storage in large groups of batteries is one of the major attraction in smart cities. This battery borne energy will come into service instantly when the main power goes off. Besides that, residents of smart cities are likely to use a vast number of batteries in various sizes and capacities. This results in significant amount of waste. Battery recycling is a big industry by itself. At present, several types of batteries with different functional properties are available in markets. Though the main purpose is to use the stored energy, batteries are used for different purposes including, storing the energy, power the electric vehicles and even serve as standby energy resources for homes and offices. Pagoropoulos et al

(2017) provided a few industry examples in their contribution to suggest that the reuse and the recycling of lithium batteries is an excellent choice for both battery and battery based electric vehicle manufacturers. Almost all types of batteries can be serviced after their end-of life, with the exception of a few; especially in small capacity segment. Various authors (Anna et al, 2019; Charles et al, 2019; Darla et al, 2018; Levanen et al, 2018; Tran et al, 2018 and Velazquez et al,2019) pointed to the fact that extension of end-of life results in excellent benefits, including reduction of greenhouse gases. However, such modern recycling technologies are not yet available and/or widely practiced in developing economies. Importance of recycling the lithium-ion type batteries is emphasized from the point of view of 'circular-energy systems'. Re-using the batteries is a major step in the transition to a low carbon energy system and thus follows circular economy principles.

Anna et al (2019) has taken up the case of reusing the batteries from electric vehicles and suggested that improvements in environmental sustainability can be achieved if proper circular economy strategies are used. Their study also pointed to the issue of 'measurement' and 'lack of data' of key parameters of energy model in evaluating the impact on environment. Hence, it is important to measure various energy parameters and process the gathered data into information. Such information can now be obtained with the deployment of IIoT devices and sensors. They are cheaper and easy to install. Which means, even the batteries need to be smart in nature. The very environment of the smart cities makes it possible to install sensors (or use modern batteries with sensors inside) thus making the monitoring of parameters easy. Planning of the futuristic smart cities should consider effective battery management and about the opportunities in recycling and/or reusing.

Heavy Oil Recycling and Heat Recovery

In addition to the above, other processes like 'heavy oil recycling' and 'heat recovery' are also related to energy industry. Oil is used as a coolant in power transformers and even automobiles. Over the years, the chemical and insulating properties of the oil are degraded due to thermal stress and hence the oil requires periodical replacement. However, heavy oils can be effectively recycled and is a well-known industry by itself. Similarly, air-conditioners extract a lot of heat from the buildings and push it out to the atmosphere. A good number of research studies indicate that the heat from air-conditioners can be extracted and reused as additional source energy for other purposes. Large-scale water heating systems such as 'district water heating systems' can effectively use this recovered heat energy. Smart cities are expected to use large-scale air conditioners or water chillers to cool the environment. Naturally, a lot of energy will be used and heat will be generated as well out of such large-scale cooling systems (Werner, 2017). Proper design keeping in view of energy (heat) recovery should be in place. Again, sensors and industry 4.0 systems should ensure continuous monitoring of the parameters and public disclosure of energy savings.

From the above, it can be noted that recycling industry in solar energy sector is open for research and business opportunities in several directions. In addition, smart cities can provide several opportunities for circular economy in managing the overall energy. A lot of data, monitoring and evaluation are required to assist various stakeholders such as the governments, investors, policy makers and even the consumers. It should be noted that circular economy strongly advocates on "reuse, repair, recycle, re-manufacture, and thus have continued ownership". Recycling the waste from solar energy sector is mandatory simply for managing the shear volumes of waste that is expected to be generated. Hence, this aspect alone establishes clear and strong link between the core principles of circular economy and renewable energies.

Conceptual Framework for Monitoring Key Indicators to Support Circular Economy

This study proposes for the first time, a conceptual framework for information visualization based on big data in line with industry 4.0 principles. The framework is based on IIoT sensors, cyber physical infrastructure, Enterprise Management Information System (EMIS) and big data that can usually exist in a typical futuristic smart city. Since the focus here is on the energy sector, let us consider a typical smart power system that supplies energy to a smart city; with IIoT apparatus to measure real time data and to control power apparatus; communication infrastructure, database servers, and an array of client computing devices. Usually such cyber-physical systems are managed by a comprehensive EMIS (Musti et al, 2020). Figure 2 shows a prototype for such an EMIS. The real-time data is stored in the servers and then processed to compute a wide-ranging parameters and to generate information. Since there can be several IIoT sensors and each sensor typically sends information for every 30 minutes or even 15 minutes based on the operating requirements. Within no time, the data fetched by various IIoT sensors will assume huge proportions and thus results in big data. To process large volumes of data, big data tools are needed to generate meaningful information. This information based on the big data analytics needs to be presented through interactive dashboards. Typical dashboards are very helpful in providing data and information through visualizations. Indeed, dashboards are the new paradigm to provide information using assorted visualizations (Musti, 2020).

A novel dashboard for indicating a few key parameters in the energy management of a typical smart city is shown in figure 3. These key parameters can contribute significantly to estimate circular economy indicators. Each tile in the dashboard takes the user to set of related information; where user can see the values, trends and other Meta data. For example, smart meters in the system provide data about the energy supplied by the utility.

This information can be obtained by clicking the first tile with the caption 'Energy Supplied by the utility'. User can obtain the nature of sources (such as a coal plant owned by public utility and/or a wind farm owned by an independent power producer etc) and amount of energies supplied each source over the time. Then, smart cities produce their own energy internally. IIoT sensors placed on solar panels, solar-water heaters etc, within the smart city send the data into the servers. Such information can be obtained by clicking the second tile with the caption 'Energy produced internally'. The tile with the caption 'Net energy savings' provides information on energy balance, or the difference between external and internal energies. The last tile in the first row provides information about the stored energy within the smart city. Such information is very valuable over the time especially for engineers in planning for either short term or long-term planning. Similarly, detailed information can be obtained related to energies involved in charging electric vehicles, municipal waste processing, heavy oil processing, recycling of batteries, solar waste management and management of automobiles. The data and information shown here is naturally representative of various operations in a smart city. For this to happen, IIoT devices need to be installed for monitoring every process element and to gather data. In other words, the infrastructure should be smart enough. For instance, IIoT sensors need to be placed in the heavy oil treatment plant processes; and thus making that plant as smart. Data measurement and processing is utmost essential to satisfy the criteria of circular economy principles. Without appropriate data and measurements, it is not possible to take decisions or/and quantify the benefits.

Figure 2. Conceptual schematic for a cyber-physical system for a typical smart city
Source: Musti et al (2020)

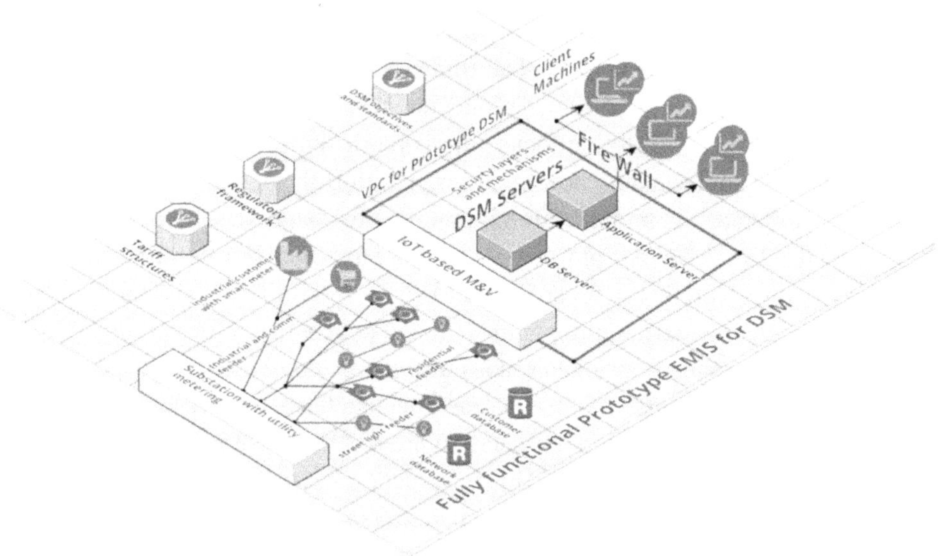

Importantly, the above information is only related a few key processes related to energy sector. From this information, the CE indicators can be estimated. Separate visualizations are required to provide insights into CE indicators and those visualizations are not illustrated here.

Opposing Views and Challenges for Circular Economy Adoption

Circular economy may look all good and positive, there do exist opposing views and criticisms. Reduced consumption may directly influence the manufacturing sector and thus might result in loss of jobs. Recycling the waste, in some cases may require more energy (and more costs) than the energy (financial benefit) that actually it produces. Recycled products may not have same quality and thus may not enjoy the consumer support. Awareness is also a major challenge; however, this can be minimized through proper training and education. Smart cities naturally require a significant number of IIoT devices to measure various aspects in real-time and transmit the data to the respective servers.

As the number of smart cities grows (even otherwise) the number of IIoT devices that operate online will grow into several billions. These devices need a lot of electrical energy and lot of communication bandwidth. Another challenge will be the possible e-waste that is generated out of non-functional or damaged devices. Data over the time becomes a precious commodity and an excellent resource for many purposes. However, ownership of data / information of cyber-physical systems is not well discussed and even legislative frameworks are not well defined as on date. Lastly, but not the least, cyber-security in IIoT device ecosystem can be difficult to deal with. For instance, a simple, unexpected cyber-attack can throw the life of a smart city out of gear and most of its services will go out of function; since it operates on digital platforms. Hence, modern societies need to find ways to combat these challenges. Naturally, these challenges pave the path for new range of jobs in Information processing, cyber-security, IT-infrastructure maintenance and real-time monitoring and control of cyber-physical systems.

Figure 3. A conceptual dashboard to display key energy parameters
Source: Author

Limitations of the Present Study

However, this chapter provides insights into six major areas of energy conservation in smart cities and the related opportunities for circular economy; there are several issues, (which are beyond the scope of this discussion) that need to examined. Those areas include – standardization of design and development of EMIS information systems; ownership and security issues related to data and information; rights of the residents in obtaining and further sharing the information; waste collection, processing and disposal processes; responsibilities of the residents and the state in periodical maintenance; linking various processes to circular economy indicators; etc. All such areas are heavily linked to niche technologies, circular economy and energy. Hence, energizing smart cities through circular economy principles, naturally offers many opportunities to the researchers. Lastly, this chapter provides a conceptual framework for a dashboard for visualizing circular economy parameters that are likely to be computed from various processes of a typical smart city. Hence, opportunities exist in further developing and implementing this framework.

CONCLUSION

From the above, it can be seen that circular economy has a lot of potential in the energy sector specifically in energizing the futuristic smart cities. This chapter establishes a strong relation between various areas - energy management, renewable energies, industry 4.0, smart cities and circular economy. A great deal of work needs to be done in modeling various sector parameters and then how they can be linked to circular economy indicators. However, lack of information is a challenge. To address this major challenge, a conceptual framework that consists of a cyber-physical system, EMIS and visualizations; is proposed.

REFERENCES

Anna, M., Guarino, F., Longo, S., Ferraro, M., & Cellura, M. (2019). Energy and environmental benefits of circular economy strategies: The case study of reusing used batteries from electric vehicles. *Journal of Energy Storage*, *25*. doi:10.1016/j.est.2019.100845

Bee Smart City. (2019). The Circular Economy: Vision, Problems and Smart City Solutions. Available online, https://hub.beesmart.city/strategy/the-circular-economy-and-smart-city-solutions

Castro, F., Colclough, S., Machado, B., & Andrade, J. (2018). European legislation and incentives programmes for Demand Side Management. *14th International Conference on Energy Storage*.

Chalkias, G. (2020). The digital circular economy. Available online, http://sharebox-project.eu/sharebox01/files/2019/06/PROSIN-A-digital-circular-economy-G.Chalkias.pdf

Charles, R. G., Davies, M. L., Douglas, P., Hallin, I. L., & Mabbett, I. (2019). Sustainable energy storage for solar home systems in rural Sub-Saharan Africa – A comparative examination of lifecycle aspects of battery technologies for circular economy, with emphasis on the South African context. *Energy*, *166*, 1207–1215. doi:10.1016/j.energy.2018.10.053

Coloumbus, L. (2016). Roundup Of Internet Of Things Forecasts And Market Estimates. Available online, https://www.forbes.com/sites/louiscolumbus/2016/11/27/roundup-of-internet-of-things-forecasts-and-market-estimates-2016/

Darla, G., Galvão, A., De Nadae, J., Honorato, D., Stief, P., Dantan, J., & Siadat, A. (2018). Circular Economy: Overview of Barriers. Procedia CIRP, 73, 79–85. doi:10.1016/j.procir.2018.04.011

Esposito, M. (2017). Where the circular economy meets the Internet of Things. Available online https://www.greenbiz.com/article/where-circular-economy-meets-internet-things

Gupta, S., Chen, H., Hazen, B. T., Kaur, S., & Santibañez Gonzalez, E. D. R. (2019). Circular economy and big data analytics: A stakeholder perspective. *Technological Forecasting and Social Change*, *144*, 466–474. doi:10.1016/j.techfore.2018.06.030

Holmatov, B., Hoekstra, A. Y., & Krol, M. S. (2019). Land, water and carbon footprints of circular bioenergy production systems. *Renewable & Sustainable Energy Reviews*, *111*, 224–235. doi:10.1016/j.rser.2019.04.085

Ionescu, C. A., Coman, M. D., Lixandru, M., & Groza, D. (2017). Business Model in Circular Economy, Valachain. *Journal of Economic Studies (Glasgow, Scotland)*, *8*(22), 101–108.

Jin, Y., Tang, X., Feng, C., & Höök, M. (2017). Energy and water conservation synergy in China: 2007 – 2012. *Resources, Conservation and Recycling*, *127*, 206–215. doi:10.1016/j.resconrec.2017.09.004

Kirchherr, J., & Piscicelli, L. (2019). Towards an Education for the Circular Economy (ECE): Five Teaching Principles and a Case Study. *Resources, Conservation and Recycling*, *150*, 104406. doi:10.1016/j.resconrec.2019.104406

Kirchherr, J., Reike, D., & Hekkert, M. (2017). Conceptualizing the circular economy: An analysis of 114 definitions. *Resources, Conservation and Recycling*, *127*, 221–232. doi:10.1016/j.resconrec.2017.09.005

Kumar, V. (2020). The Role of AI in Achieving a Circular Economy in Smart Cities. Available online, https://industrywired.com/the-role-of-ai-in-achieving-a-circular-economy-in-smart-cities/

Levänen, J., Lyytinen, T., & Gatica, S. (2018). Modelling the Interplay Between Institutions and Circular Economy Business Models: A Case Study of Battery Recycling in Finland and Chile. *Ecological Economics*, *154*, 373–382. doi:10.1016/j.ecolecon.2018.08.018

Manavalan, K., & Jayakrishna, K. (2019). An Analysis on Sustainable Supply Chain for Circular Economy, 16th Global Conference on Sustainable Manufacturing. Procedia Manufacturing, 477–484. DOI: 10.1016/j.promfg.2019.04.059

Moraga, G., Huysveld, S., Mathieux, F., Blengini, G. A., Alaerts, L., Van Acker, K., & Dewulf, J. (2019). Circular economy indicators: What do they measure? *Resources, Conservation and Recycling*, *146*, 452–461. doi:10.1016/j.resconrec.2019.03.045 PubMed

Murray, A., Skene, K., & Haynes, K. (2017). The Circular Economy: An Interdisciplinary Exploration of the Concept and Application in a Global Context. *Journal of Business Ethics*, *140*(3), 369–380. doi:10.1007/s10551-015-2693-2

Pagliaro, M., & Meneguzzo, F. (2019). Lithium battery reusing and recycling: A circular economy insight. *Heliyon (London)*, *5*(6), e01866. doi:10.1016/j.heliyon.2019.e01866 PubMed

Pagoropoulos, A., Pigosso, D. C. A., & McAloone, T. C. (2017). The Emergent Role of Digital Technologies in the Circular Economy: A Review. Procedia CIRP, 64, 19–24. doi:10.1016/j.procir.2017.02.047

Press, G. (2017). 6 Predictions For The $203 Billion Big Data Analytics Market. Available online, https://www.forbes.com/sites/gilpress/2017/01/20/6-predictions-for-the-203-billion-big-data-analytics-market/#645861502083, Forbes

Rajput, S., & Singh, S. P. (2019). Connecting circular economy and industry 4.0. *International Journal of Information Management*, *49*, 98–113. doi:10.1016/j.ijinfomgt.2019.03.002

Sastry Musti. (2020). Management Information Systems for Higher Education Institutions - Challenges and opportunities. In Successful Implementation of Quality Management Principles in Higher Education. Doi:10.4018/978-1-5225-9829-9.ch006

Sastry Musti, K. S. (2020). Industry 4.0-Based Enterprise Information System for Demand-Side Management and Energy Efficiency. In Novel Approaches to Information Systems Design. doi:10.4018/978-1-7998-2975-1.ch007

Singh, K., Kelly, S., & Sastry, K. S. (2009, October). Musti (2009), Municipal Solid Waste to Energy: Potential for Application in Trinidad and Tobago. *The Journal of the Association of Professional Engineers of Trinidad and Tobago*, *38*(1), 42–49.

Srivastav, P., & Goldstein, N. (2019). Circular Economy: Shaping the Next Wave of Smart Communities. Available online, https://guidehouse.com/-/media/www/site/insights/energy/2019/puf-smart-communities/puf-smart-communities-circular-economy.pdf

Tran, H. P., Schaubroeck, T., Swart, P., Six, L., Coonen, P., & Dewulf, J. (2018). Recycling portable alkaline/ZnC batteries for a circular economy: An assessment of natural resource consumption from a life cycle and criticality perspective. *Resources, Conservation and Recycling*, *135*, 265–278. doi:10.1016/j.resconrec.2017.08.018

Tseng, M. L., Tan, R. R., Chiu, A. S. F., Chien, C. F., & Kuo, T. C. (2018). Circular economy meets industry 4.0: Can big data drive industrial symbiosis? *Resources, Conservation and Recycling*, *131*, 146–147. doi:10.1016/j.resconrec.2017.12.028

Varma, R., Dahiya, R.P., & Susil, K. N. (2016). Circular Economy as Strategy for Sustainable Development in Electricity Sector in India. Global Journal of Business Excellence, 3-9(1), 23-36.

Velázquez Martínez, O., Van Den Boogaart, K. G., Lundström, M., Santasalo-Aarnio, A., Reuter, M., & Serna-Guerrero, R. (2019). Statistical entropy analysis as tool for circular economy: Proof of concept by optimizing a lithium-ion battery waste sieving system. *Journal of Cleaner Production*, *212*, 1568–1579. doi:10.1016/j.jclepro.2018.12.137

Werner, S. (2017). International review of district heating and cooling. *Energy*, *137*, 617–631. doi:10.1016/j.energy.2017.04.045

ADDITIONAL READING

Ebrahimi, K., Jones, G. F., & Fleischer, A. S. (2014). A review of data center cooling technology, operating conditions and the corresponding low-grade waste heat recovery opportunities. *Renewable & Sustainable Energy Reviews*, *31*, 622–638. doi:10.1016/j.rser.2013.12.007

García-Barragán, J. F., Eyckmans, J., & Rousseau, S. (2019). Defining and Measuring the Circular Economy: A Mathematical Approach. *Ecological Economics*, *157*, 369–372. doi:10.1016/j.ecolecon.2018.12.003

He, Z., Ding, T., Liu, Y., & Li, Z. (2018). Analysis of a district heating system using waste heat in a distributed cooling data center. *Applied Thermal Engineering*, *141*, 1131–1140. doi:10.1016/j.applthermaleng.2018.06.036

Kirchherr, J., Piscicelli, L., Bour, R., Huibrechtse-truijens, A., Hekkert, M., Kostense-smit, E., & Muller, J. (2018). Barriers to the Circular Economy: Evidence From the European Union (EU). *Ecological Economics*, *150*, 264–272. doi:10.1016/j.ecolecon.2018.04.028

Korhonen, J., Nuur, C., Feldmann, A., & Eshetu, S. (2018). Circular economy as an essentially contested concept. *Journal of Cleaner Production*, *175*, 544–552. doi:10.1016/j.jclepro.2017.12.111

Pauliuk, S. (2018). Critical appraisal of the circular economy standard BS 8001:2017 and a dashboard of quantitative system indicators for its implementation in organizations. *Resources, Conservation and Recycling*, *129*, 81–92. doi:10.1016/j.resconrec.2017.10.019

Wahlroos, M., Pärssinen, M., Rinne, S., Syri, S., & Manner, J. (2018). Future views on waste heat utilization – Case of data centers in Northern Europe. *Renewable & Sustainable Energy Reviews*, *82*, 1749–1764. doi:10.1016/j.rser.2017.10.058

KEY TERMS AND DEFINITIONS

Big Data: Is a field that deals with analysis, information extraction and visualization from very large data sets that are too complex to be processed by traditional systems.

Cyber Security: A software system to protect digital systems such as IIoT and network of computers, hardware, software and data from possible disruption, theft or damage.

Cyber-Physical System: An ecosystem where software, hardware and humans interact for a specific purpose and serve pre-defined purposes.

Enterprise Management Information System (EMIS): A large scale, industry grade digital platform that assists in processing data, information visualization, control physical and cyber processes and decision making in an organizational (such a smart city) context.

Industrial Internet of Things (IoT): It is same ecosystem as IoT that consists of interconnected sensors, data processing apparatus and communication infrastructure; that specifically meets the standards for industrial applications.

Industry 4.0: It is a part of the fourth industrial revolution that combines the modern concepts such as IoT, cloud computing, big data and Information systems.

Internet of Things (IoT): Is a system of sensors and computing devices that communicate wirelessly to transfer the data and information to central servers without human intervention.

Smart City: A modern form of urban area that operates more on digital platforms, uses niche technologies like IIoT and is driven by information provided by EMIS.

Section 2

Entrepreneurship and Economic Development in the Circular Economy

Chapter 14
Entrepreneurial Motivation to Participate in the Circular Economy

Colin David Reddy
https://orcid.org/0000-0002-6657-1071
University of Johannesburg, South Africa

ABSTRACT

Strong ecological values define the desire of individuals to exploit business opportunities in the circular economy. However, strong ecological values are unlikely to contribute to strong individual motivation when individuals sense that it is not feasible to exploit such opportunities. This chapter develops this argument conceptually using expectancy theory. Expectancy theory suggests that individuals derive their motivation from strong perceptions of both desirability and feasibility. Understanding an entrepreneur's motivation to participate in the circular economy is important for attempts at entrepreneurial development in this alternative economy. Policies as well as education and training programs must consider instilling the required ecological values in citizens as well as giving attention to technological, market, cultural, and regulatory constraints that render CE opportunities infeasible.

INTRODUCTION

Entrepreneurs participate in the circular economy (CE) when they have a strong motivation to do so. The CE involves private businesses minimizing their natural resource usage in service of the transition to a more sustainable world. Entrepreneurs require certain capabilities or must be able to access these capabilities within the economy. These capabilities are required to create a regenerative system where products, components and materials are maintained at their highest value for as long as possible and resources can be productively recovered and reintegrated in the economy. This can be achieved through long-lasting design, maintenance, repair, reuse, remanufacturing, refurbishing, and recycling.

With several simpler opportunities in the economy for entrepreneurs to exploit and earn a living, we need to understand an entrepreneur's motivation to exploit the often-difficult opportunities in the CE.

DOI: 10.4018/978-1-7998-5116-5.ch014

Copyright © 2020, IGI Global. Copying or distributing in print or electronic forms without written permission of IGI Global is prohibited.

The risks of a CE startup not becoming an established business are immense considering its technical complexity as well as the lethargic cultural and market dynamics that can constraint the profitability of a CE opportunity. To advance policies for entrepreneurship development within the CE, one needs to identify the components of motivation and understand how they interact with one another.

In any CE entrepreneurial development framework, policymakers will have to consider both whether the entrepreneurial population desire CE opportunities and whether they possess the confidence in their ability to exploit such opportunities. Because these ideas are available in the expectancy theory of motivation, this Chapter will use expectancy theory to develop a set of propositions about the entrepreneur's motivation to participate in the CE. The Chapter first provides a brief background to the literature available to understand entrepreneurial motivation for CE opportunities. It then looks into the notion of the motivation based on the values common to those entrepreneurs who exploit opportunities that can lead to a more sustainable world. Then it briefly describe expectancy theory and develops an argument for understanding a CE entrepreneur's motivation. It ends with a discussion of the implications for developing entrepreneurs to increase their participation in the CE.

BACKGROUND

We have little understanding about how desires and abilities interact to form the entrepreneur's motivation to participate in the CE. Thus far, motivation has been considered broadly in terms of sustainable entrepreneurship; and it is yet to be considered for specific CE opportunities (Bohnsack, & DiVito, 2018; Parrish, 2010; Schaltegger, & Wagner, 2011). However, CE entrepreneurship is a subset of sustainable entrepreneurship. Notably, it also shares characteristics of eco-preneurship and environmental entrepreneurship, which are all forms of sustainable entrepreneurship.

One has to bear in mind that entrepreneurs who exploit CE opportunities require specific knowledge because CE is an approach that focuses on increasing resource efficiency and resource productivity (D'Amato et al, 2017). This implies specific abilities amongst entrepreneurs or amongst the professionals employed by entrepreneurs. Yet research on entrepreneurial motivation in the sustainable economy has tended to focus on the desires or values of individuals (e.g. Kirkwood & Walton, 2010; York, O'Neil & Sarasvathy, 2016).

This research suggests that sustainable entrepreneurs share the economic desires of conventional entrepreneurs; but they have additional desires to preserve the environment: desires attributed to ecological values. Because meeting these desires serve the interests of people beyond the entrepreneur's immediate social circle, ecological values also have a strong altruistic content (Fauchart & Gruber, 2011). Often times sustainable entrepreneurs' ecological values serve as a stronger driver of their motivation than economic values; at other times, there can be a balanced blend of ecological and economic values; and yet other times a stronger economic than ecological values (York et al, 2016).

However, these values provide insights only about the entrepreneur's perceived desirability of CE opportunities. Particularly, considering the barriers to exploiting CE opportunities—technological, cultural, market and regulatory—entrepreneurs require strong perceptions of the feasibility of exploiting these opportunities. Thus strong perceptions of both desirability and feasibility are required to sustain a strong motivation to persist with the often difficult to exploit CE opportunities. This argument is derived from expectancy theory, which suggests that motivation develops through a cognitive process (Vroom, 1995). This process is fraught with doubt: doubt exists within entrepreneurs whether they can successfully exploit a CE opportunity--i.e. feasibility-- and whether performing successfully will fulfill their underlying needs--i.e. desirability—(McMullen & Shepherd, 2006).

THEORY DEVELOPMENT

Motivation and Values

There is a lasting tradition amongst motivation theories to look at the needs of humans and the process in which they stimulate their energy to sustain certain behaviour (Steers, Mowday & Shapiro, 2004). For example, Maslow (1970) proposed that though individuals possess relationship, esteem, and self-actualization needs, they are unlikely to seek such needs if they have not met their physiological and security needs. The materialistic needs prevalent in a business environment is akin to a need for financial security, and this might make it difficult for relationship-oriented and self-actualized entrepreneurs to implement their goals. Nevertheless, with the sustainability challenges facing the world, these higher order "humanistic values" can help entrepreneurs prosper their new firms (Parra, 2013: p16).

In a sense, sustainable entrepreneurs do possess affiliative, esteem, and self-actualization needs. This can be observed from their added ecological values compared to the largely material or economic values of conventional entrepreneurs (Cohen & Winn, 2007; Dean & McMullen, 2007; Lenox & York, 2012; York et al, 2016). This emerges from their desire to help stem an ecological crisis (Beveridge & Guy 2005; Bull, Cato, Arthur, Keenoy & Smith, 2008; Gibbs, 2009; Kirkwood and Walton 2010; Linnanen 2002; Schlange, 2006). This crisis is informed by the belief that the earth's resources are finite and inadequate to sustain human demand (Wackernagel, Monfreda & Deumling, 2002), which leads them to develop personal values "based on one's own moral obligation to protect the threatened environment" (Vollan, Prediger & Frölich, 2013: p3). Because such ecological values involve thinking about other life forms it also encompasses altruistic values (Fauchart & Gruber, 2011), which, perhaps, go some way to fulfilling affiliative, esteem, and self-actualization needs.

Nevertheless, sustainable entrepreneurs possess both ecological and economic values; but there is likely to be different strengths of coupling between these values (York et al, 2016). As a result, it is possible for some sustainable entrepreneurs to possess a stronger economic motivation and for others to regard economic and ecological values as complementary. For example, sustainable entrepreneurs such as Anita Roddick, the founder and former head of Body Shop, possess strong ecological values but still accompanied by a strong economic drive (Schaltegger, 2002).

Perhaps profits may serve, not so much for personal economic gain, but as financial resources for their new ventures (Shepherd & Patzelt, 2011). In addition, compared to entrepreneurs focused only on economic goals, they are more likely to form opportunity beliefs that preserve the natural environment and meet their economic goals (Patzelt & Shepherd, 2011).

Proposition 1: Both economic and ecological values will contribute to individual motivation to exploit CE opportunities.

Expectancy Theory: The Role of Perceived Feasibility

Current research around sustainable entrepreneurship has been limited by its focus on the content of motivation. This research attributes motivation mainly to the values of individuals. From the above review, one notes that sustainable entrepreneurs possess both economic and ecological values. Compared to entrepreneurs aspiring to meet their economic needs, CE entrepreneurs must possess additional knowledge and ability to exploit an opportunity that meets their ecological needs. Furthermore, the knowledge requirements to satisfy ecological needs might be higher than the requirements to meet economic needs (Shepherd & Patzelt, 2011: p154): "it not only requires knowledge of the industry and the market for economic gain but also knowledge, skills, and abilities to preserve the natural and/or social environment."

When not met, such additional knowledge requirements to meet ecological needs can reduce the perceived feasibility of a CE opportunity. With weak perceived feasibility, and despite strong perceived desirability, individuals are unlikely to sustain strong motivation to pursue a CE opportunity. Process theories of motivation have long suggested that individuals must perceive an opportunity to be both desirable and feasible for them to be motivated to act on an opportunity. In the process of developing strong motivation to act on an opportunity"

"...a belief is formed regarding a desired end state, but doubt exists regarding whether that desired end state is feasible (can be achieved in the manner envisioned) and desirable (whether its attainment will fulfill the motive for which it is being sought)" (McMullen & Shepherd, 2006: p141).

This thinking has its roots in expectancy theory (Vroom, 1995). It is a cognitive process theory of motivation that proposes that people go through a thought process identifying whether their efforts can lead to performance, whether their performance can lead to rewards and whether they indeed desire such rewards. Ultimately, they will be motivated to take action when they believe their decisions will lead to their desired outcomes. The belief that their efforts will result in performance has been referred to as expectancy; that performance will result in certain rewards has been referred to as instrumentality; that the outcomes are of personal value or importance is known as valence. The product of instrumentality and valence has been collapsed into a single component: perceived desirability (Segal, Borgia & Schoenfeld, 2005; Shapero, 1982). And entrepreneurship scholars have referred to expectancy as perceived feasibility, which corresponds with perceptions of personal self-efficacy (Fitzsimmons & Douglas, 2011): they are confident that they can complete the tasks required to launch and operate a successful firm (McGee, Peterson, Mueller & Sequeira, 2009).

CE requires the entrepreneur's long-term commitment; it is not a quick win (Kirchher et al, 2017). This is evidenced by the nature of barriers to exploit CE opportunities: cultural, market, regulatory and technological challenges (Kirchher et al, 2018). It is well known that cultural barriers take time to overcome. For many individuals, vying for economic prosperity, these barriers compromise the feasibility of an ongoing business. And expectancy theory suggests that without strong perceived feasibility, strong perceived desirability is unlikely to result in strong motivation to sustain any entrepreneurial persistence to form a successful business (Munoz, 2018; Smith & Woodworth, 2012).

Culturally, there is a general lack of lack of consumer and company interest and awareness to engage with CE. These interests also change quickly, limiting the life of a business model resting upon a CE product. Cultural barriers have the result of reducing the market demand for CE.

Market barriers include the higher price of recycled materials. Oftentimes, turning around recycled materials can be more expensive than the production of the original material (Preston, 2012). The investment cost of a CE initiative can also be prohibitive. Entrepreneurs require financial subsidies and actors in financial markets may not be familiar with CE (Linnanen, 2002).

Technologically, the tasks aimed at minimizing waste and making the most of materials are challenging. And apart from the ability to operate a business, the entrepreneur must "address production processes, products and the provision of services, but also redesign the patterns of consumption or lifestyles, as well as the institutions that underpin them" (Vezzoli, Ceschin, Diehl & Kohtala, 2015: p1). The entrepreneur needs to understand the material composition and its life cycle throughout the value chain (de los Rios, 2017; Ford & Despeisse, 2016). The entrepreneur also needs to identify and recognize the needs of all the stakeholders along the value chain (Evans, Gregory, Ryan, Bergendahl & Tan, 2009). They also need to realise the implications of redesigning products. Product innovations can take time to move from invention to commercialisation (Agarwal & Bayus, 2002). With new technologies, one also requires new capabilities and competencies: for example, the capability to work across the value chain instead of in a silo within one particular part of the value chain (Pheifer, 2017).

Entrepreneurs also face restrictive policy frameworks (Rizos, Behrens, Kafyeke, Hirschnitz-Garbers & Ioannou, 2015). Governments impose strict regulations on the waste management industry. Across nations, there can be contradictory regulations. Generally, it is difficult to integrate a value chain across borders. For example, if an entrepreneur locates a firm that can recycle a waste product, he/she may not be allowed to transport this waste across the border (Pheifer, 2017).

Proposition 2: Strong ecological values are unlikely to contribute to strong individual motivation to exploit CE opportunities when perceptions of the feasibility of exploiting such opportunities are weak.

IMPLICATIONS AND RECOMMENDATIONS

What does it take entrepreneurs to persist in the CE? This question can be answered by reviewing the research into entrepreneurial motivation. Current research tends to suggest, compared to conventional entrepreneurs, CE entrepreneurs derive their motivation from their ecological values more than their need for economic success. However, this Chapter has argued that despite strong ecological values, CE entrepreneurs are unlikely to sustain their motivation when they believe that they cannot exploit a CE opportunity in a feasible manner. This might stem, for example, from their lack of confidence in their knowledge and skills to reconfigure a production process to utilise recycled materials. In the end, without this confidence, albeit the strong desire to save the environment and make a profit, entrepreneurs are unlikely to persist with starting a firm.

This argument is derived from expectancy theory, which suggests that motivation develops through a cognitive process where people believe that they can accomplish performance goals from their efforts at work; and their accomplishments can bring rewards they value. However, this process is fraught with doubt: doubt whether it is feasible to perform certain tasks and doubt whether performing successfully will fulfill their underlying desires. In other words, for entrepreneurs to develop the motivation to pursue opportunities in the CE, they must perceive the CE opportunity to be both desirable and feasible.

Though research exists about entrepreneurial motivation in the broader sustainability context, scholars have yet to theorise about the entrepreneurial motivation in light of specific CE opportunities. This is important because CE opportunities are often technically complex and supply chain participants may be reluctant to make changes to their operations; besides the market may not readily adopt the solutions that new firms provide.

This Chapter provides two propositions to aid this research in the future. First, it proposes that underlying values contributing to entrepreneurial motivation in the CE will be no different to those identified for sustainable, ecological and environmental entrepreneurship. In other words, there ought to be significant overlap in values. Thus the current theories that ecological values and certain conventional entrepreneurial values such as economic success for example, (Kirkwood & Walton, 2010; Linnanen 2002; Schlange, 2006; York et al, 2016) can be applied to CE entrepreneurship.

However, this Chapter's second proposition suggests that theories about entrepreneurial motivation based solely on values will arrive at an incomplete explanation of motivation of entrepreneurs participating in the CE. Specifically, values will only have a strong influence on their motivation to exploit CE opportunities when entrepreneurs also perceive strong feasibility of exploiting the opportunity. When they possess strong ecological values, for instance, but cannot be certain that the CE opportunity is feasible, their motivation to exploit the CE opportunity is likely to remain weak. After all, CE entrepreneurship is a complex undertaking and is fraught with technological, cultural, market and regulatory hurdles.

The above argument builds on exploratory work confirming the importance of knowledge of sustainability issues to sustainable decision-making (Munoz, 2018). It also challenges and builds on the research of those who have focused on the values driven motivation of sustainable entrepreneurs (Kirkwood & Walton, 2010; Linnanen 2002; Schlange, 2006). Those who have attempted to test arguments about the impact of perceived feasibility have found little evidence of its importance to entrepreneurial intentions to exploit sustainability opportunities (Vuorio, Puumalainen, Fellnhofer, 2018). But the moderating effect of perceived feasibility is yet to be tested. This requires further research to model an interaction between perceived desirability and feasibility. Notably, the original expectancy theory proposes a multiplicative effect between components of motivation.

Practically, understanding entrepreneurs' motivation can help facilitate better education and training programs for these entrepreneurs. Expectancy theory helps us view participation in the circular economy because it helps scholars and policymakers look beyond the rewards that appeal to underlying individual values, to look also at capabilities and in particular the combined influence of capabilities and values.

Beginning with values, when education policymakers understand the appeal of ecological values to CE entrepreneurs they can ensure that education program designers inculcate these values in curricula. Business education, for example, can instil ecological values in young adults. This means demonstrating the value of altruism versus self-interest in attaining a successful business career. It helps to understand the sources of cultural hurdles to adopting ecological values. Strong ecological values appears to arise from the belief that humans are deeply connected to nature (Dunlap, 2008). This might be traced to religious teachings. For example, whereas Buddhism teaches that humans are equal to plant and animal life, Christianity teaches that humans have dominion over the earth. In addition, business education continues to rely on assumptions of entrepreneurs as economic maximizers. Thus, attention to the values component of motivation may compel us to build awareness amongst African entrepreneurs and business educators about pluralistic ways of thinking about business.

However, in light of the main proposition about the complementary interaction between desirability and feasibility perceptions, policymakers must enhance the perceived feasibility of CE opportunities in the minds of potential entrepreneurs. This will increase the confidence of entrepreneurs in their ability to start and operate a successful CE firm. Four types of barriers can hinder this confidence: consumer and company culture, regulatory, market and technology. Because these barriers are nested (Kircherr et al, 2018), tackling cultural barriers can help debottleneck constraints arising from the other three barriers because a nation's cultural norms tends to influence its design of formal regulations; regulations in turn influence market barriers; and this in turn influences technological barriers. Alternatively, when one can overcome technological barriers, one can still be constrained by economic and market limitations (De-Jesus & Mendoça, 2018).

Cultural barriers are likely to prevail within the supply and demand networks of the potential new firm. Within these networks, consumers and managers of existing firms might not currently engage in sustainable activities. Consumers may lack awareness of the benefits of sustainable products or they find the shift in lifestyle and behavior cumbersome and costly. Managers might be risk averse to the increased complexity introduced into the supply chain by a CE business model. Financial, logistical and legal aspects of the supply chain may change. For example, collaboration with new market players may be required and managers may be reluctant to spend time and money having to develop these networks (Rizos et al, 2015). As a result, they may not be open to the new ideas and changes introduced by the new firm (Agyemang *et al.*, 2018; Rizos et al, 2015). This lack of consumer and business manager interest can reduce sales of CE products and services, which can reduce an entrepreneur's perceived feasibility of a CE opportunity.

Just as education and training policy can embed ecological norms in tertiary business education for managers to recognize the importance of CE, more broadly, beginning with primary education, education institutions can influence consumer culture. Young students eventually become consumers when they develop the economic means to purchase products and services. The same youngsters may eventually occupy management roles and get to influence the purchasing decisions on behalf of business customers. Over the short term, however, current business leaders can "conduct workshops and training of their workers and suppliers to promote CE practices in their enterprise and supply chain" (Agyemang *et al.*, 2018: p27).

Government regulations can boost the feasibility of CE opportunities because it can serve as "a mandatory driver for many enterprises to implement CE practices" (Agyemang *et al;* 2018: p23). This can increase both the supply of input materials to CE firms as well as the demand for their products. Many governments have yet to develop a concrete and coherent legislative framework around greening their economy. Tax legislations, for example, will need to adapt to CE. For example, low taxes on virgin materials can thwart the demand for recycled materials by existing firms. Demand can also suffer with the lack of consumption taxes of polluting products because consumers face no pressure to change to green consumption behaviours. In addition, poor enforcement of environmental regulations can also thwart supply of input materials to CE firms because existing firms may not experience the pressure to redirect waste or byproducts for beneficiation. In this respect, government agencies involved in the CE must be resourced with both financial and technical capacity to enforce the law (Rizos et al, 2015).

Notably CE supply chains can traverse national borders. For example, if an entrepreneur locates a foreign firm that possesses the technology to recycle a waste product, regulations must permit transport of this waste across the border. This makes it important for governments to look at contradictory regulations across borders. For starters, national governments can begin to develop standard definitions and categories of waste. Note that educated individuals also occupy policy-making positions. Thus, the long-term benefit of an education system that promotes sustainability is also relevant to regulatory advances and enforcement.

One also needs to attend to the entrepreneur's perceived feasibility of CE opportunities arising from market barriers. To this extent, researchers have tended to categorize constraints in consumer markets as cultural barriers; but market barriers refer mainly to limitations CE entrepreneurs may experience in sourcing the necessary financial resources (Kirchoff et al, 2018). Startups appear to be more sensitive than large existing firms are to the costs arising from implementing a CE business model (Rizos et al, 2015). Turning around recycled materials can be more expensive than the production of virgin materials (Preston, 2012). Remanufacturing, for example, requires technically skilled engineers or technicians, whom many young firms cannot afford to remunerate. It is also the case that financiers may not be familiar with CE.

One can begin to look for solutions in both the private and public sectors. Private financiers can begin to look to current experience in funding innovative business models more generally. To this extent, they might look to venture capital funding models. Venture capitalists have established procedures to assess and manage the risks of innovative new firms. Notably governments can also introduce incentives to the financial markets to stimulate risk taking in new CE technologies. Increasingly, institutions will need to invite financiers, from China, for example, to establish how financiers in Africa can evaluate and manage risk of a CE opportunity. China appears to have begun the journey to CE some time ago.

Finally, the feasibility of exploiting a CE opportunity can be compromised by the technical difficulty of designing and operating a CE business model. For example, entrepreneurs may lack the confidence to pursue a CE opportunity if they or their potential employees do not possess the expertise to operate a new technology, to conduct a life cycle audit or to design the material composition of a new product. Thus, apart from the business training there needs to be training interventions around understanding of CE technologies. CE incubators, for example can train entrepreneurs on material composition, material lifecycles and value chains, including the stakeholder relationships within these value chains. For potential entrepreneurs to arrive at innovative designs, they must also be educated about the patterns of consumption or lifestyles in their societies.

FUTURE RESEARCH DIRECTIONS

Further research is required about the strength of coupling between ecological and economic values. Maslow's theory suggests that individuals need to meet their economic needs before meeting higher order needs. In less developed countries, for example, considering their pressures to survive economically, one expects economic needs to predominate over ecological needs. Accordingly, in less developed countries, one might expect the entrepreneurial motivation to pursue CE opportunities to arise primarily from economic needs. It will be useful to know whether coupling between ecological and economic values vary due to a country's economic development stage. Further research is also required about the reasons for lack of support for CE amongst existing firms and their managers because such leaders have the power to change organizational culture; and when unaware about CE, firms led by them will be slow to implement CE (Geng & Doberstein 2008).

CONCLUSION

Entrepreneurial motivation to seize opportunities in the CE relies on satisfying both economic needs and concerns about our ecology. However, such needs may have little impact on entrepreneurs' motivation to exploit a CE opportunity when they are not confident in their ability to ensure the feasibility of the opportunity. Apart from their own or their employees sound technological understanding of product and material lifecycles within existing supply chains, entrepreneurs confidence to operate a successful CE firm can be increased by a supportive cultural, regulatory and market environment. Currently, there exists little empirical evidence about how CE entrepreneurs engage in making sense of their business for themselves and for others and how they develop the motivation to reconcile being enterprising and ecologically aware. This Chapter has attempted to develop a conceptual view of the entrepreneurial motivation to pursue CE opportunities. What remains is to explore this empirically.

REFERENCES

Agarwal, R., & Bayus, B. L. (2002). The Market Evolution and Sales Takeoff of Product Innovations. *Management Science*, *48*(8), 1024–1041. doi:10.1287/mnsc.48.8.1024.167

Agyemang, M., Kusi-Sarpong, S., Khan, S., Mani, V., Rehman, S., & Kusi-Sarpong, H. (2019). Drivers and barriers to circular economy implementation. *Management Decision*. *57*, 971-994.

Beveridge, R., & Guy, S. (2005). The Rise of the Eco-preneur and the Messy World of Environmental Innovation. *Local Environment*, *10*(6), 665–676. doi:10.1080/13549830500321972

Bohnsack, R., & DiVito, L. (2018). Motivations and entrepreneurial orientation of sustainable entrepreneurs: an exploratory study of sustainable entrepreneurship archetypes in the fashion industry. In A. Lindgreen, C. Vallaster, F. Maon, S. Yousafzai, & B. P. Florencio (Eds.), *Sustainable Entrepreneurship: Discovering, Creating and Seizing Opportunities for Blended Value Generation* (pp. 24–37). Boca Raton, FL: Routledge. doi:10.4324/9781315611495-2

Bull, M., Cato, M. S., Arthur, L., Keenoy, T., & Smith, R. (2008). Entrepreneurial energy: Associative entrepreneurship in the renewable energy sector in Wales. *International Journal of Entrepreneurial Behaviour & Research*, *14*(5), 313–329. doi:10.1108/13552550810897678

Cohen, B., & Winn, M. I. (2007). Market imperfections, opportunity and sustainable entrepreneurship. *Journal of Business Venturing*, *22*(1), 29–49. doi:10.1016/j.jbusvent.2004.12.001

D'Amato, D., Korhonen, J., Toppinen, A., Droste, N., Allen, B., Kettunen, M., ... Matthies, B. D. (2017). Green, circular, bio economy: A comparative analysis of sustainability avenues. *Journal of Cleaner Production*, *168*, 716–734. doi:10.1016/j.jclepro.2017.09.053

De-Jesus, A., & Mendoça, S. (2018). Lost in Transition? Drivers and Barriers in the Eco-Innovation Road to the Circular Economy. *Ecological Economics*, *145*, 75–89. doi:10.1016/j.ecolecon.2017.08.001

De los Rios, R. I. C., & Charnley, F. J. S. (2017). Skills and capabilities for a sustainable and circular economy: The changing role of design. *Journal of Cleaner Production*, *160*, 109–122. doi:10.1016/j.jclepro.2016.10.130

Dean, T. J., & McMullen, J. S. (2007). Toward a theory of sustainable entrepreneurship: Reducing environmental degradation through entrepreneurial action. *Journal of Business Venturing*, *22*(1), 50–76. doi:10.1016/j.jbusvent.2005.09.003

Dunlap, R. E. (2008). The New Environmental Paradigm Scale: From Marginality to Worldwide Use. *The Journal of Environmental Education*, *40*(1), 1, 3–18. doi:10.3200/JOEE.40.1.3-18

Evans, S., Gregory, M., Ryan, C., Bergendahl, M. N., & Tan, A. (2009). *Towards a sustainable industrial system: With recommendations for education, research, industry and policy*. Cambridge: University of Cambridge.

Fauchart, E., & Gruber, M. (2011). Darwinians, Communitarians, and Missionaries: The Role of Founder Identity in Entrepreneurship. *Academy of Management Journal*, *54*(5), 935–958. doi:10.5465/amj.2009.0211

Fitzsimmons, J. R., & Douglas, E. J. (2011). Interaction between feasibility and desirability in the formation of entrepreneurial intentions. *Journal of Business Venturing*, *26*(4), 431–440. doi:10.1016/j.jbusvent.2010.01.001

Ford, S., & Despeisse, M. (2016). Additive manufacturing and sustainability: An exploratory study of the advantages and challenges. *Journal of Cleaner Production*, *137*, 1573–1587. doi:10.1016/j.jclepro.2016.04.150

Geng, Y., & Doberstein, B. (2008). Developing the circular economy in China: Challenges and opportunities for achieving'leapfrog development'. *International Journal of Sustainable Development and World Ecology*, *15*(3), 231–239. doi:10.3843/SusDev.15.3:6

Gibbs, D. (2006). Sustainability Entrepreneurs, Ecopreneurs and the Development of a Sustainable Economy. *Greener Management International*, *55*(55), 63–78. doi:10.9774/GLEAF.3062.2006.au.00007

Kirchherr, J., Piscicelli, L., Bour, R., Kostense-Smit, E., Muller, J., Huibrechtse-Truijens, A., & Hekkert, M. (2018). Barriers to the Circular Economy: Evidence From the European Union (EU). *Ecological Economics*, *150*, 264–272. doi:10.1016/j.ecolecon.2018.04.028

Kirchherr, J., Reike, D., & Hekkert, M. (2017). Conceptualizing the circular economy: An analysis of 114 definitions. *Resources, Conservation and Recycling*, *127*, 221–232. doi:10.1016/j.resconrec.2017.09.005

Kirkwood, J., & Walton, S. (2010). What motivates ecopreneurs to start businesses? *International Journal of Entrepreneurial Behaviour & Research*, *16*(3), 204–228. doi:10.1108/13552551011042799

Linnanen, L. (2002). An Insider's Experiences with Environmental Entrepreneurship. *Greener Management International*, *38*(38), 71–80. doi:10.9774/GLEAF.3062.2002.su.00008

Maslow, A. H. (1970). *Motivation and personality*. New York: Harper & Row.

McGee, J. E., Peterson, M., Mueller, S. L., & Sequeira, J. M. (2009). Entrepreneurial self-Efficacy: Refining the measure. *Entrepreneurship Theory and Practice*, *33*(4), 965–988. doi:10.1111/j.1540-6520.2009.00304.x

McMullen, J. S., & Shepherd, D. A. (2006). Entrepreneurial Action and the Role of Uncertainty in the Theory of the Entrepreneur. *Academy of Management Review*, *31*(1), 132–152. doi:10.5465/amr.2006.19379628

Muñoz, P. (2018). A cognitive map of sustainable decision-making in entrepreneurship: A configurational approach. *International Journal of Entrepreneurial Behaviour & Research*, *24*(3), 787–813. doi:10.1108/IJEBR-03-2017-0110

Parra, S. (2013). Exploring the incorporation of values for sustainable entrepreneurship teaching/learning. *Journal of Technology Management & Innovation*, *8*(1), 11–20. doi:10.4067/S0718-27242013000100002

Parrish, B. D. (2010). Sustainability-driven entrepreneurship: Principles of organization design. *Journal of Business Venturing*, *25*(5), 510–523. doi:10.1016/j.jbusvent.2009.05.005

Patzelt, H., & Shepherd, D. A. (2011). Recognizing opportunities for sustainable development. *Entrepreneurship Theory and Practice*, *35*(4), 631–652. doi:10.1111/j.1540-6520.2010.00386.x

Pheifer, A. G. (2017). *Barriers and Enablers to Circular Business Models*. Available at:https://www.circulairondernemen.nl/uploads/4f4995c266e00bee8fdb8fb34fbc5c15.pdf

Preston, F. (2012). *A global redesign? Shaping the circular economy*. London: Chatham House.

Rizos, V., Behrens, A., Kafyeke, T., Hirschnitz-Garbers, M., & Ioannou, A. (2015). *The circular economy: Barriers and opportunities for SMEs*. Brussels: CEPS.

Schaltegger, S. (2002). A Framework for Ecopreneurship. *Greener Management International*, *2002*(38), 45–58. doi:10.9774/GLEAF.3062.2002.su.00006

Schaltegger, S., & Wagner, M. (2011). Sustainable entrepreneurship and sustainability innovation: Categories and interactions. *Business Strategy and the Environment*, *20*(4), 222–237. doi:10.1002/bse.682

Schlange, L. (2006). *What drives sustainable entrepreneurs?* Paper presented at the Applied Business and Entrepreneurship Association International Conference, St. Gallen, Switzerland.

Segal, G., Borgia, D., & Schoenfeld, J. (2005). The motivation to become an entrepreneur. *International Journal of Entrepreneurial Behaviour & Research*, *11*(1), 42–57. doi:10.1108/13552550510580834

Shapero, A. (1982). *Social Dimensions of Entrepreneurship*. Englewood Cliffs, NJ: Prentice-Hall.

Shepherd, D. A., & Patzelt, H. (2011). The new field of sustainable entrepreneurship: Studying entrepreneurial action linking "what is to be sustained" with "what is to be developed". *Entrepreneurship Theory and Practice*, *35*(1), 137–163. doi:10.1111/j.1540-6520.2010.00426.x

Smith, I. H., & Woodworth, W. P. (2012). Developing Social Entrepreneurs and Social Innovators: A Social Identity and Self-Efficacy Approach. *Academy of Management Learning & Education*, *11*(3), 390–407. doi:10.5465/amle.2011.0016

Steers, R. M., Mowday, R. T., & Shapiro, D. L. (2004). The future of work motivation theory. *Academy of Management Review*, *29*(3), 379–387.

Vezzoli, C., Ceschin, F., Diehl, J. C., & Kohtala, C. (2015). New design challenges to widely implement 'Sustainable Product-Service Systems'. *Journal of Cleaner Production*, *97*, 1–12. doi:10.1016/j.jclepro.2015.02.061

Vollan, B., Prediger, S., & Frölich, M. (2013). Co-managing common-pool resources: Do formal rules have to be adapted to traditional ecological norms? *Ecological Economics*, *95*, 51–62. doi:10.1016/j.ecolecon.2013.08.010

Vroom, V. H. (1995). *Work and motivation*. San Francisco: Jossey-Bass Publishers.

Vuorio, A. M., Puumalainen, K., & Fellnhofer, K. (2018). Drivers of entrepreneurial intentions in sustainable entrepreneurship. *International Journal of Entrepreneurial Behaviour & Research*, *24*(2), 359–381. doi:10.1108/IJEBR-03-2016-0097

Wackernagel, M., Monfreda, C., & Deumling, D. (2002, Nov.). Ecological footprint of nations. *Redefining Progress. Sustainability Issue Brief.*

York, J. G., O'Neil, I., & Sarasvathy, S. D. (2016). Exploring Environmental Entrepreneurship: Identity Coupling, Venture Goals, and Stakeholder Incentives. *Journal of Management Studies*, *53*(5), 695–737. doi:10.1111/joms.12198

ADDITIONAL READING

Esposito, M., Tse, T., & Soufani, K. (2017). Is the circular economy a new fast-expanding market? *Thunderbird International Business Review*, *59*(1), 9–14. doi:10.1002/tie.21764

Esposito, M., Tse, T., & Soufani, K. (2018). Introducing a circular economy: New thinking with new managerial and policy implications. *California Management Review*, *60*(3), 5–19. doi:10.1177/0008125618764691

Gladwin, T. N., Kennelly, J. J., & Krause, T. S. (1995). Shifting paradigms for sustainable development: Implications for management theory and research. *Academy of Management Review*, *20*(4), 874–907. doi:10.5465/amr.1995.9512280024

Goyal, S., Esposito, M., & Kapoor, A. (2018). Circular economy business models in developing economies: Lessons from India on reduce, recycle, and reuse paradigms. *Thunderbird International Business Review*, *60*(5), 729–740. doi:10.1002/tie.21883

Hockerts, K., & Wüstenhagen, R. (2010). Greening Goliaths versus emerging Davids—Theorizing about the role of incumbents and new entrants in sustainable entrepreneurship. *Journal of Business Venturing*, *25*(5), 481–492. doi:10.1016/j.jbusvent.2009.07.005

Lieder, M., & Rashid, A. (2016). Towards circular economy implementation: A comprehensive review in context of manufacturing industry. *Journal of Cleaner Production*, *115*, 36–51. doi:10.1016/j.jclepro.2015.12.042

Ranta, V., Aarikka-Stenroos, L., Ritala, P., & Mäkinen, S. J. (2018). Exploring institutional drivers and barriers of the circular economy: A cross-regional comparison of China, the US, and Europe. *Resources, Conservation and Recycling*, *135*, 70–82. doi:10.1016/j.resconrec.2017.08.017

Renko, M., Kroeck, K. G., & Bullough, A. (2012). Expectancy theory and nascent entrepreneurship. *Small Business Economics*, *39*(3), 667–684. doi:10.100711187-011-9354-3

Spence, M., Ben, B. G. J., & Biwole, V. O. (2011). Sustainable Entrepreneurship: Is Entrepreneurial will enough? A North-South Comparison. *Journal of Business Ethics*, *99*(3), 335–367. doi:10.100710551-010-0656-1

KEY TERMS AND DEFINITIONS

Ecological Value: Value accorded to preservation of our ecosystem.

Economic Value: Value accorded to financial outcomes.

Ecosystem: The relationship between all living organisms, including humans, and their habitat (the environment). Thus, the ecosystem includes the environment, plants and animals (including humans).

Entrepreneurial Motivation: The drive of an entrepreneur that enables him/her to persist with the discovery, evaluation and exploitation of a future situation, which he/she perceives as desirable and feasible.

Entrepreneurial Self-Efficacy: An individual's belief in his/her capability to perform tasks and roles aimed at entrepreneurial outcomes.

Expectancy: The belief that if one works hard, one will be able to meet their performance targets. It is akin to self-efficacy.

Instrumentality: The belief that meeting one's performance targets can lead to a reward.

Motivation: While some define motivation in terms of its content such as needs or desires, this Chapter takes a process perspective and defines it as the process that initiates, guides, and maintains goal-oriented behaviours.

Perceived Desirability: The belief that the rewards associated with certain outcomes are personally attractive.

Perceived Feasibility: Similar to expectancy, this is the belief that one possesses the necessary skills and abilities required to be successful in a particular situation.

Valence: Used here in its psychological context and is similar to perceived desirability. It refers to the positive or negative value accorded to a reward.

Value: Similar to valence, this is used to reflect what is important to an individual.

Chapter 15
Application of Isenberg Model for Entrepreneurial Ecosystems as a Blueprint for Zimbabwe Socio-Economic Devolution

Takaruza Munyanyiwa
Apollos University, USA

ABSTRACT

Entrepreneurship plays a significant role in national economies around the world, including the Republic of Zimbabwe, which has largely focused on the socio-economic devolution program. The necessity for entrepreneurship and policymakers around the world currently is to advance the quality of the entrepreneurship outcomes rather than just increase the number of entrepreneurs. To strengthen the context of entrepreneurship and innovation, the authors suggested that governments need to move to what is called an entrepreneurial ecosystem approach. Isenberg's model for the entrepreneurial ecosystem is applied as a catalyst for building a robust entrepreneurial ecosystem under circular economies.

INTRODUCTION

This chapter presents stakeholder views and evaluation of devolution form of governance, entrepreneurial ecosystems models, opportunities, challenges, circular economy and application of the Isenberg's model to the Zimbabwean Devolution Model context. A review of the Zimbabwe Devolution Act (2013) key legislation objects, progress of implementation including the evolving policy framework, barriers and benefits is also presented. The data and information for this study were collected through an extensive literature review, interviewing of experts, and the author personal's experience. Key informants views and data were collected from government ministries, local authorities, community elders and business associations. The feedback and insights from stakeholders is supported by theory and existing literature on circular economy and entrepreneurial ecosystems.

DOI: 10.4018/978-1-7998-5116-5.ch015

Copyright © 2020, IGI Global. Copying or distributing in print or electronic forms without written permission of IGI Global is prohibited.

Objectives

- Review and evaluate Zimbabwe Devolution Act and progress of implementation;
- Presents Entrepreneurial Ecosystem models benefits and barriers;
- Discuss the application of the Isenberg Entrepreneurial Ecosystem Model;
- Discuss the theory of Circular Economy;
- Presents Models for successful implementation.

BACKGROUND

Zimbabwe is a unitary state with one source of state authority underpinned by a local government system decentralized to provide services to a heterogeneous citizenry in geographically defined and demarcated areas of jurisdiction. Prior to the promulgation in 2013 of a new Constitution, local government in Zimbabwe was a creature of statute, operating in a delegated capacity and largely dependent on central government. Local government functions, while defined in law, were open to central government variation and re-assignment to other national agencies.

Pre- and post-independence policy and structural developments have sustained centre-local relations that undermine the emergence of strong and devolved local governance. In the 1980s, associations of local authorities began to advocate for the 'constitutionalisation' of local government. A long and arduous process beginning in 1999 led to a referendum in 2000, at which point the draft Constitution was rejected. However, civil society groups and political parties re-initiated the process after a successful advocacy campaign in the post-2008 Government of National Unity (GNU) era.

The government set up the Parliamentary Constitution-making Committee (COPAC), with a mandate to produce a new Constitution. Through a series of debates and consultations, as well as a referendum in March 2013, the COPAC process culminated in the adoption of the 2013 Constitution, within which devolution is a key component and civic participation a cherished principle.

Local authorities were created through statutes or acts of parliament and therefore operate within the legislative framework enacted and promulgated by central government (legislature) as the primary legislative authority. Basically, there are two types of local authority in Zimbabwe: (i) Urban Councils and (ii) Rural District Councils. Local authorities are governed by the Urban Councils Act, the Rural District Councils Act and the Regional, Town and Country Planning Act. The three Acts form the principal legislative basis for the implementation of local government policy in Zimbabwe and establish the relationship between local authorities and central government. It is important to note that due to the doctrine of ultra vires, local authorities are not allowed to perform functions not specifically mentioned in the legislation.

Zimbabwe under its 2013 constitution created devolution under chapter 14 provinces sound framework for devolution. There are 92 local authorities in Zimbabwe; composed of 32 urban councils and 60 rural districts.

The urban councils are made up of the five city councils, 11 municipalities, 13 town councils and three local boards. Section 274(2) and 275(2)(b) provides that these councils will be managed by councilors elected by registered voters in the urban and rural areas concerned. The government of Zimbabwe anticipates that the devolution model of governance will help enhance socio-economic growth and bring political stability through the equitable distribution of wealth. The new constitution provides for increased budget support and 5% revenue retention by each region (Constitution of Zimbabwe, 2013). The new Constitution abolished the office of provincial governor, which was a presidential appointment and thus part of national government. Now, provincial and metropolitan councils will have elected chairs – and the councils will have more powers and some independence from central government the Constitution, all members of the national Parliament are now also members of the provincial or metropolitan council in which their constituency is based.

Specific laws are yet to en-acted so as transfer powers to provincial and local government level. Laws that govern public finance, natural resources, public tenders civil service employment, relationship and between the different tiers or layers of government so as to ensure that there is no conflict between government and local government nut rather complementarily subsist. Zimbabwe model envisages devolution with a unitary system as opposed to a federal system. The existing Urban Council Act, RDC Act and Traditional Leaders Act present a firm foundation for a robust devolution model that will drive prosperity.

Primarily objective of devolution is to include citizens in decision making through level government structures; service delivery is accessible, government is closer to the people, greater accountability, transparency, public finance management, effective and efficient revenue collection. Devolution address issues of uneven development, lack of citizen participation, deficiency bottom up development and absence of innovative service delivery. The new constitution has elevated the roles of provincial and district administrators from political administrative status to economic development oriented ones. These are expected to coordinate private players, state owned enterprises; spearhead development planning, promote investment and tourism development. They are also expected to be responsible for monitoring and evaluation of all programs and processes in their respective districts and provinces (ZIPARU, 2020).

Section 264 (2) of the Constitution outlines the specific goals and objectives of devolution in Zimbabwe. These are:

- To give powers of local governance to the people and enhance their participation in the exercise of the powers of the State and in making decisions affecting them; b) to promote democratic, effective, transparent, accountable and coherent government in Zimbabwe as a whole;
- To preserve and foster the peace, national unity and indivisibility in Zimbabwe; d) to recognize the right of communities to manage their own affairs and further their development;
- To ensure equitable sharing of national and local resources;
- To transfer responsibilities and resources from the national government in order to establish a sound financial base for each provincial and metropolitan council and local authority.

The Urban Councils Act and Rural District Council Act together provide a long list of permissible functions and of matters on which local authorities may enact their own by-laws. These include:

- Democratic representation of the service expectations of the local community;
- To govern defined areas with gazetted boundaries;
- Powers to make a budget;
- Powers to borrow money for capital developments;
- Provision of services and facilities that support production and expansion of private enterprise;
- Issue trading licenses and regulate trading activities within their areas of jurisdiction;
- Provision of safe water, roads and efficient telecommunication services in the local area;

- Provision and promotion of health, housing, education and recreational services to the local community;
- Regulation of private activities that affect community welfare and the health, safety and welfare of local people.

The key question that deserves further interrogation, is whether the different tiers of government have the institutional capacity to fully implement the devolution agenda; account for the funds disbursed to these lower levels of government; develop development programs; recruit and retain critical technical competencies and mobilize funding outside the allocations from Treasury. The other issue that deserves further reflection is the capacity of central government to monitor and evaluate use of resources within the devolved government structures. Some of the indentified capacities include hard infrastructure, human skills and competences; systems and procedures and hardware.

Case study lessons from Kenya, Uganda, South Africa and Swaziland) provide devolution reference points for Zimbabwe's program. Devolution has worked very well in Kenya with development being felt in different parts of the country. South African model has seen the devolution entities self-funding 85% of their costs thus dismissing the notion held that devolution is expensive. Devolution has worked well in Europe, Africa and Asia thus can work well in Zimbabwe. Examples in Europe include Netherlands, Spain, Denmark and Finland.

Presented below is an extract of the legislative devolution objects of Kenya and South Africa. Zimbabwean devolution objects share many similarities with the South Africa and Kenya.

Chapter 11 of the Constitution of Kenya establishes the Devolved Government. Unlike the Zimbabwean case, Chapter 11 divides the Kenyan administration into the National and County Governments. Section 174 of the Constitution of Kenya establishes the objects of Devolution in Kenya, as follows:

- To promote democratic and accountable exercise of power;
- To foster national unity by recognizing diversity;
- To give powers of self-governance to the people and enhance the participation of the people in the exercise of the powers of the State and in making decisions affecting them;
- To recognize the right of communities to manage their own affairs and to further their development;
- To protect and promote the interests and rights of minorities and marginalized communities;
- To promote social and economic development and the provision of proximate, easily accessible services throughout Kenya;
- To ensure equitable sharing of national and local resources throughout Kenya;
- To facilitate the decentralization of State organs, their functions and services, from the capital of Kenya; and
- To enhance checks and balances and the separation of powers.

Section 152 (1) of the Constitution of South Africa establishes the objects of local government/ devolution in South Africa, which include:

- To provide democratic and accountable government for local communities;
- To ensure the provision of services to communities in a sustainable manner;
- To promote social and economic development;
- To promote a safe and healthy;

- To encourage the involvement of communities and community organizations in the matters of local government.

METHODOLOGY

The methodology used to collect data, views and insights in this study included a review of the Zimbabwean devolution act framework; literature review and case study experiences from of other countries such as Kenya, South Africa and Uganda that have had successful devolution programs. Insights and views of purposively selected key informants and data from interviewee from government ministries (including justice, local government), local authority heads (Chief Executive Officers and Provincial Development Co-coordinators), Civil Society, academia involved in devolution programs were gathered. Data from key informants was collected using open ended questions that allowed respondents to express their insights and views. An extensive document reviews and analysis was done to identify the major capacity gaps; institutional and legislative reforms/gaps that can enhance/impede the implementation of devolution in Zimbabwe. The data collected was analyzed into thematic groups so as form opinions of the various views expressed by respondents and information from the various documents.

LITERATURE REVIEW

"The concept of devolution has evolved over time and in the process has undergone changes in terminology and meaning" (Jacobs and Chavhunduka 2003:2). In their paper presented at the 2012 International Conference on Public Administration, Mukonza and Chakauya (2012:101) define devolution as "a form of decentralization through which authority to formulate policies in selected areas of public policy is conferred to elected sub-national levels of government." Chigwenya (2010:2) defines devolution as the transfer of administrative and political powers from central government to lower tiers. According to Jacobs and Chavhunduka (2003:3), "compared to deconcentration and delegation, devolution can provide for better problem-solving capacity, which takes into account local knowledge and conditions." Many countries adopted either partial or full devolution of power in order to improve governance and promote economic growth. Similarly, intense debate on devolution is not unique to Zimbabwe. In Kenya there were heated debates before devolution found its way into Kenya's new Constitution. Many countries in Africa and even Europe have adopted devolution in order to improve the governance of local communities at the same time promoting local developmental initiatives. However, what is devolved and how it is devolved vary considerably depending on individual countries (Cascon-Pereirra *et al.* 2006:131). Hope (2000:520) points out that after they had gained independence, many African countries placed much emphasis on building nation-states which resulted in the emergence of highly centralized governments. The World Bank (2001) highlighted that the central government should have an oversight function which include the overall policy setting, setting of standards, and auditing while local governments should be involved with the provision of infrastructure and services. Experience from other countries has shown a number of key success and avoidable factors necessary for successful decentralization which include the following:

- Clear division of functions between local and central government;

- Adequate human and financial resources;
- Strong legal framework;
- Strong participation of citizens at local level;
- Clarity of roles and responsibilities for the many new structures created under devolution;
- Translation of information pertaining to devolution into other official national languages;
- Strong political will.

The key question that deserves further interrogation in devolution programs - is whether the different tiers of Anti-devolution proponents argue that devolution of power divides the people along tribal lines given that Zimbabwe's provinces are made up of homogenous societies. Those against devolution argue that the centralization of authority is ideal for Zimbabwe because not all regions have sufficient natural resources to sustain developmental initiatives. Given the challenge of unequal natural resources it can be argued that devolution of power perpetuates in-equality. Regional inequality is a potential source of conflict. Only central government can fairly distribute the scarce resources for the betterment of the entire country. From this premise it can be concluded that devolution does not foster national development. Instead it promotes individualistic tendencies at the expense of national cohesion. Regrettably regions endowed with natural resources may want to retain the resources for their exclusive use. Case study reviews and literature on devolution recommends a robust implantation model that brings together all stakeholder efforts. Thus, the need to develop a robust ecosystem model is required for a smooth implementation program that will yield the anticipated benefit of socio-economic growth. The Isenberg (2011) is such a model that aims at stimulating socio-economic growth.

Isenberg's Model of an Entrepreneurship Ecosystem

Isenberg model (2011) is viewed as a practical model for developing entrepreneurial ecosystems. In the case of Zimbabwe if adopted it can be applied in order to stimulate much needed socio-economic growth. The Isenberg framework (2011), suggests that the entrepreneurship ecosystem must include six key dimensions with twelve elements incorporated together. These are: policy (leadership, government); finance (financial capital); culture (success stories, societal norms); supports (infrastructure, support professions); human capital (labour, educational institutions); and markets (early customers, networks) (Isenberg, 2011). Isenberg also emphasize the point that each entrepreneurship ecosystem is unique. Although any society's entrepreneurship ecosystem can be described using the same six domains, each ecosystem is the result of the hundreds of elements interacting in highly complex and idiosyncratic ways. Isenberg gives the examples o such as:

- Israel's entrepreneurship ecosystem evolved in the 1970s with no natural resources, military necessity, and far from markets for its products;
- Ireland's ecosystem evolved in the 1980s in the context of free education, native English, foreign multinationals, and proximity to the European market;
- Taiwan's entrepreneurship ecosystem evolved in the 1990s in the context of a huge accrual of highly successful Taiwanese expatriates in the US. China's entrepreneurship ecosystem is evolving now in the context of diverse regional policies and a somewhat (some would argue, very) totalitarian political system.

Isenberg further postulates that entrepreneurship ecosystems become (relatively) self-sustaining. Emphasizing success does breed success by feeding back to enhance the six domains of the entrepreneurship ecosystem, that there is a tipping point at which government involvement can and should be significantly reduced; not eliminated, but reduced. Once the six domains are strong enough, they are mutually reinforcing, and public leaders do not have to invest quite so much to sustain them. In fact, it is critical that entrepreneurship programs are designed to be self-liquidating in order to focus on building sustainability into the environment.

Another particularly influential model of an ecosystem was designed by Erik Stam in 2015, and 2016. He argues that the key factors of an entrepreneurship ecosystem are framework conditions and system conditions respectively (Stam, 2015).

In addition to these factors, some researchers (e.g., Fellnhofer & Mueller, 2018; Kautonen; Krueger, 2017; Lehner & Harrer, 2019) consider government, media, and institutions as key actors. The framework consists of the presence of four key elements. These are physical infrastructure, formal institutions, demand for new products (goods & services), and an enabling culture. These elements are considered as the basic requirement of value creation in the Stam entrepreneurial ecosystem model. The second part of this framework "at the heart" is the systemic conditions which lead to entrepreneurial activities and these consist of the presence of six elements:- leadership, knowledge, entrepreneurship networks, finance, support services, and talent (Jansen, 2017). Therefore, these elements are essential to enhance the output of entrepreneurial activities. Further, (Jansen, 2017) highlights five steps of mapping a CE to include: research design, data collection, data analysis, data validation, from mapping to activity.

Entrepreneurship Ecosystem

Entrepreneurship as an engine of economic growth is related to a combination of several determinants such as education levels, business climate and legal and political conditions (Alvarez et al, 2014). Kaufmann (2015) six strategies for building sustainable entrepreneurial ecosystems as: listen to entrepreneurs, map the ecosystem, think big, start small, move fast, and avoid artificially segmenting your community or your strategies and Prepare to capitalize on crises. According to the systems approach by Acs (2014), entrepreneurship is an action undertaken and driven by agents on the basis of incentives. Second, the individual action is affected by an institutional framework for entrepreneurship. Third, entrepreneurship ecosystems are complex, multifaceted structures in which many elements interact to produce systems performance, thus, the system method needs to allow the constituent elements to interact.

Discussion of entrepreneurial ecosystems has largely focused on the essential ingredients, while largely ignoring the processes or "recipes" for their combination into a sustainable milieu with entrepreneurial vitality. The processes depend on the set of flows or relations within an entrepreneurial ecosystem, which change over time (Spigel, 2017a; Stam, 2007). Stam further postulated that systemic conditions are the heart of the ecosystem includes: networks of entrepreneurs, leadership, finance, and talent, knowledge, and support services. The presence of these elements and the interaction between them predominantly determine the success of the ecosystem" (Stam, 2015, p. 1766). Despite the local nature of entrepreneurship, entrepreneurial ecosystems are frequently identified at the national scale, following research on national innovation systems (Ács et al., 2014; Frenkel & Maital, 2014; Manimala & Wasdani, 2014; Voelker, 2012; WEF, 2013). Universities are perhaps the most frequently identified actor/institution in entrepreneurial ecosystems after entrepreneurs themselves, and a large subset of research focuses on universities as hubs of such ecosystems (Bramwell & Wolfe, 2008; Fernandez Fernandez, Blanco

Jimenez, & Cuadrado Roura, 2015; Fetters, Greene, Rice, & Butler, 2010; Kingma, 2014; O'Connor & Reed, 2015a; Rice, Fetters, & Greene, 2014; Schaeffer & Matt, 2016).

According to Funke (2015), an ecosystem can best be described through eleven basic building blocks that show the logic of how an ecosystem works. The eleven blocks cover the main areas of an ecosystem: Ideas and talents, Support and infrastructure, Startup community, Policy and finance, and Trends and markets. According to Gibb (2014), pathways for entrepreneurs entails teaching strategies and learning environments which offer targeted support for students and staff that aim at setting up a business. Higher education institutions can provide this support directly themselves or refer potential entrepreneurs to specialized start-up support services within the (local) entrepreneurship ecosystem.

The higher education institutions play an important role in the strengthening of the regional economy by triggering and coaching student/academic entrepreneurs and helping them connect with the growing network of incubators and accelerators.

In Belgium, the startup rate is very low (Calvino et al., 2015). The GEM (2013) report for Belgium and Flanders (Bosma et al., 2014) presents an overview of indicators for entrepreneurial activity and entrepreneurial attitudes and the growth aspirations of business owner-managers. Bosma et al. (2014). found that:

- The perceived skills and knowledge required to start a business are relatively low and the fear of failure associated with starting a business is relatively high;
- Belgian and Flemish adults believe entrepreneurship to be a good career choice but they do not attach high status to successful entrepreneurs;
- A high degree of entrepreneurial employee activity, i.e. entrepreneurship (conducting new entrepreneurial activities as an employee) rather than independent, early-stage entrepreneurial activity;
- The observed rate of early-stage entrepreneurial activity is rather low in international comparison.

The strategic model applied is that of a networked incubator (Hansen et al., 2000). This is a type of business incubator model, which is well suited to grow businesses. The networked incubator) has some features in common with other incubators such as fostering and promoting a spirit of entrepreneurship and offers economies of scale. Its unique feature is its ability to give startups preferential access to the platform and a network of key partners. Student entrepreneurship education is given a significant role in supporting the main goals of the Europe 2020 strategy. According to the European Union (2015), students participating in entrepreneurship education are more likely to start their own business and their companies tend to be more innovative and more successful than those led by persons without entrepreneurship education backgrounds. The entrepreneurial spirit of educational institutions can enhance student's start-up intentions (Iakovleva, 2015).

The entrepreneurship ecosystem is a highly complex multi-level construct. At the regional field level, it includes stakeholders, such as political decision makers, government agencies, universities and industry associations (Isenberg, 2011; World Economic Forum, 2014). At the firm level, the activities of new start-up and existing small or larger firms represent the engine to spur innovation-based regional economic development. According to Mokry (1988), local communities and individuals from communities help entrepreneurs in establishing their businesses, seeking a solution to their problem, locating resources, and preparing a team of dedicated persons for an enterprise. If society values entrepreneurs, then it will be a great support in the development of social systems that admire them (Vesper, 1983).

In the era of increasing attention to broader and more comprehensive approaches to entrepreneurship, the concept of entrepreneurship ecosystems has proven a promising field of research that helps capture interdependent entrepreneurial activities at various levels of analysis and involving a variety of quite heterogeneous stakeholders and actors. Obviously, related more comprehensive and broader causal models imply substantial theoretical and empirical challenges ((World Economic Forum, 2014).

The term entrepreneurial ecosystem was used by Prahalad (2005) and Cohen (2006) to describe conditions in which the individual, business, governments, civil society, and development partners come together regionally to support entrepreneurial activities with the objective to generate economic wealth and prosperity.

Entrepreneurship flourishes in ecosystems in which multiple stakeholders play key synergistic roles, which often requires multi-stakeholder collaboration (Van de Ven, 1993). Hence, the formation of entrepreneurship ecosystems implies that the involved stakeholders collaborate to create local conditions that foster entrepreneurial activities. This notion implies that all stakeholders and actors work together to support entrepreneurs to help them develop and grow new businesses.

Prior research indicates that the combinations observed differ across regions that have evolved organically for years depending on the social, economic, political, cultural, and geographic conditions (Cohen, 2006; Kshetri, 2014).In every economy entrepreneurship plays a significant role in forming opportunities, as well as finding a better outcome of new start-ups (Borissenko & Boschma, 2017; Nylund & Cohen, 2017). To achieve this goal and to strengthen the context of entrepreneurship and innovation (Acs *et al.*, 2017b; Stam, 2015) it is suggested that governments need to move to what is called an entrepreneurial ecosystem approach. Definition The Global Entrepreneurship Monitor defines entrepreneurship in its annual report (2014) as; any attempt will lead to create new business (Hart *et al.*, 2015), a phenomenon related to entrepreneurial activity (Pyper, 2016) whether it is a new business enterprise or an expansion of a current business, and regardless of whether it was created individually or by group of people.

However, the latest definition of an entrepreneurial ecosystem, presented by Spiegel in (2017) defines an entrepreneurial ecosystem as an interdependent group of local culture (actors), social networks, universities, sources of investment, economic policies (factors) coordinated in such a way as to create a good environment that enable productive entrepreneurship in a particular region (Spiegel, 2017). In recent years, many models have been created to gain better understanding of how to develop ecosystems for entrepreneurship but this current study has limited discussion to two of the most famous models; the Isenberg (2011), and Stam (2015) frameworks.

Also in order to assess the entrepreneurial ecosystem's performance the following indicators require monitoring: birth and death/survival rate of new businesses, entrepreneurial activity among the population, registration of new businesses, jobs created by new businesses, exports by new businesses, investments secured by new businesses, (loans and equity). In an entrepreneurial ecosystem the following actors are indentified: individuals, institutions and organizations circular economy system: Labour market, tax policies, Access to finance, labour laws and administration, business registration, quality of regulatory governance, land titles, access to commercial courts, private public partnership dialogue, market information, economic predictability and political situation.

According to Man and Lau (2000) the five entrepreneurial competencies describing the personality and behavioral traits of an entrepreneur were opportunity recognition, building relationship, analytical mindset, and innovative tendencies and operating ability. Other five traits centered on human functioning, strategic grounding, dedication and commitment, personal learning and personal strategic competencies (Man & Lau, 2000). Entrepreneurship is defined an entrepreneur to identify, explore and exploiting the process of value creation by venture formulation and leveraging resources through innovative tendencies which is directed by an individual or individuals, thus must be by taking cognizance of the opportunity and risk metrics to meet the investment needs of the market (Mistra & Zachary, 2015).

Van de Ven (1993) proposed four broad components on ecosystem (what he termed an infrastructure) for entrepreneurship building to include:

- Institutional arrangements that legitimate, regulate and incentive entrepreneurship;
- Public resources endowments of basic scientific knowledge, financing mechanisms and pools of competent labor;
- Market demand of informed consumers for the products and services offered by entrepreneurs and of course;
- Propriety business activities that private enterprises provide R&D manufacturing marketing and distribution (Van de Ven, 1993).

Further, Van de Ven unpacked Resource Endowments as including: physical infrastructure, demand, investments, talent, knowledge, leadership and finance. Informal arrangements: formal institutions, culture and networks. The following measurements are identified – formal institutions, physical infrastructure, demand, talent, knowledge, and leadership and entrepreneurship outputs:

- **Formal Institutions:** Reflect the rules of the game in society (North, 1990). For example, the quality and efficiency of formal institutions matter, level of corruption and the general regulatory framework within countries;
- **Physical Infrastructure:** Is a composite measure including highways, rail and airports potential accessibility and number of passengers (Dijkstra, 2013);
- **Demand:** Is measured by composite country disposable income per capita and two measures of potential market demand;
- **Knowledge:** Investments in new knowledge are an important source of entrepreneurial opportunities and if they lead to better solutions, they are also source prosperity;
- **Intermediate services:** Supply and accessibility of intermediate business services substantially lower barriers and increase the speed of new value creation;
- **Leadership:** Provide guidance for and direction of collective action;
- **Talent:** Human capital and more broadly talent for productive entrepreneurship and multifaceted and can be measured in many (Stam and Spigel, 2018) more generic (Unger et al., 2011);
- **Entrepreneurship outputs:** A healthy entrepreneurial ecosystem is said to produce entrepreneurship as an output and ultimately aggregate value as outcome.

Circular Economy (CE) Model

The World Economic Forum's (WEF, 2013) define CE as an industrial system that is restorative or regenerative by intention and design. It replaces the end-of-life concept with restoration, shifts towards the use of renewable energy, eliminates the use of toxic chemicals, which impair reuse and return to the biosphere, and aims for the elimination of waste through the superior design of materials, products, systems and business models.

Ellen McArthur Foundation (EMF), (2013) defined CE as looking beyond the current take-make-dispose extractive industrial model, a circular economy aims to redefine growth, focusing on positive society-wide benefits. It entails gradually decoupling economic activity from the consumption of finite resources and designing waste out of the system. Underpinned by a transition to renewable energy sources, the circular model builds economic, natural, and social capital. It is based on three principles: design out waste and pollution; keep products and materials in use; regenerate natural systems. The WEF (2013), Mckinsey Report (2018), and EMF (2013) identified the benefits of CE to include: *Fewer greenhouse gas emissions* that have a positive effect on the planet's ecosystems and to fight the excessive exploitation of natural resources when it comes to reducing greenhouse gases, a circular economy can be helpful: The reason being CE use renewable energy, promotes reusing, and dematerializing fewer materials and production processes are needed to provide good and functional products. Resides are seen as valuable and reused, energy efficient and nontoxic materials are preferred.

Healthy and resilient soils on the farming system ensure that important nutrients are returned to the soil through anaerobic processes or composting, which softens the exploitation of land and natural ecosystems. *Fewer negative externalities* such as land use, soil, water and air pollution are better managed, as well as the emission of toxic substances and climate change. Increased potential for economic growth driving increase in revenues from new circular activities, together with a cheaper production by getting products and materials more functional and easily disassembled and reused, has the power to increase GDP and therefore economic growth. Aaccording to a McKinsey report (2018) *More resources can be saved* compared with the raw material extraction that's common on the linear approach, the circular economy model has the potential to lead to a bigger (up to 70%) amount of material savings.

According to WEF (2013) CE stimulates employment growth with a new regulation (including taxation) and organization of the labor markets, can bring greater local employment in entry-level and semi-skilled jobs. Another study conducted by the EMF and McKinsey (2013) also concluded changes in employment growth attributed to a shift to a circular economy model. The study suggests that this new jobs will be created through increases in: recycling and repairing practices, where one could add new designers and mechanical engineers to make lasting and easily disassembled products and materials at the transformation/production stages; An increase in new businesses (and niches) due to innovation processes and new business models; and An increase in consumption and spending by lower prices. CE present new profit opportunities by lowering input costs and in some cases create entirely new profit streams.

Reduce volatility and safeguarded supplies raw materials used and instead, more recycled (or even reusable or easily transformed) inputs that have a higher share of labor costs would be used, leaving companies less dependent on the volatility of the price of raw materials. According EMF Report (2018) CE has the potential to create demand for new services and jobs opportunities such as collection and reverse logistics companies that support end of life products reintroduction into the system, product markets and parts components for manufacturing or production of new products. Getting to know clients better to foster business models where products are rented or leased by customers during different periods of time, depending on the type of products.

Barriers to the Implementation of a CE

According to (GEM, 2015) implementing a circular economic model would have several benefits for the environment, economy and businesses nevertheless, there are some reasons that explain why this model has been growing slowly because of barriers that have been categorized into economic and institutional.

Economic Barriers

- Social and environmental externalities are not considered in prices, privileging financial market signals instead of people and nature when economic decisions are made;
- Prices of raw materials are fickle and at low prices alternative, good quality secondary resources are not competitive;
- Circular economy business models are harder to develop, as most investors are still working under a linear economy logic and sometimes upfront investments are required;
- The demand for circular products and alternatives is still small; and
- There aren't still many qualified professionals with technical or 'information and communication technology' (ICT) knowledge.

Institutional Barriers

- The fact that our current economic system is geared towards the demand of the linear economy and not yet prepared to deal with circular economy entrepreneurs;
- New business models may be challenging to implement and develop because of laws and regulations that aren't prepared for this kind of innovations;
- Plenty of business rely on old and/or strong alliances, making it harder to create new alliances and therefore to close loops;
- Many companies still have goals and appraisal systems that focus on short-term value creation, whereas the circular economy model is a long-term value creation model; The GDP index doesn't consider social and environmental externalities, discouraging the creation of value in both these areas.

MAIN FOCUS OF THE CHAPTER

The main focus of this chapter highlights the devolution framework, arguments for and against devolution, entrepreneurial ecosystems model, Isenberg (2011) Model, and challenges facing Zimbabwe devolution program. Presentation of views and insight from key informants including empirical evidence and literature from case studies is presented to implement devolution. The recommended application of Isenberg's model is presented as pragmatic way to optimize the on the anticipated benefits of devolution.

ISSUES, CONTROVERSIES, PROBLEMS

This section presents stakeholder views and insights highlighting issues, controversies and problems hindering the smooth implantation of devolution program.

A stakeholder devolution meeting hosted by ZIPARU on 11-12 December 2019, in Harare highlighted the following as challenges impacting the smooth implementation of the devolution: lack of a clear framework, lack of political wills, by central government, authorities' resistance to relinquish power for fear of losing power to those in local government, some individuals in central government are slowing down the implementation of devolution. Lack of knowledge for the citizenry: Devolution is lacking in terms of publicity. It was noted that most citizens are not aware or knowledgeable of devolution. They need to be educated through awareness programs, mainly through the media. To provide wide coverage, all forms of media should be utilized. Different interests from key stakeholders: key stakeholder groups hold different interests and perspectives on the concept of devolution and its implementation. Some groups are concerned with power and authority issues whilst others believe that it is about natural and financial resources. Poor citizen engagement: Devolving power and authority involves the engagement of citizens or community residents in issues relating to the development of their areas. Citizen participation is central to the concept of devolution. Weak civil society: It was noted that our civil society is weak. Compromised people are taking leadership and consequently, citizens lose faith in Civil Society Organizations. CSOs are also not pushing hard enough for the implementation of devolution.

The workshop showed that devolution in Zimbabwe is a highly contested and complicated process. A clear framework, with clear timelines and benchmarks does not exist. This needs to be solved. In general, for devolution to become a reality there is significant need for citizen awareness and engagement, and also a convergence of ideas from the various key stakeholders to be involved in its implementation. There is no lead agency responsible for the implementation of devolution. The Ministry of Local Government and Public Works cannot be the only one that is talking about it. All Government ministries have functions and roles which have to be devolved to lower tiers of government, provincial or local, thus devolution is not a ministerial responsibility but a collective agenda which must be undertaken in a transparent and accountable manner.

Action Aid Report (2015) highlights some of issues which surround the smooth implementation of devolution to include: (a) Powers to execute are subject to other legislative framework; (b) Many of the functions are wholly or in part performed by government; (c) Some of the functions are performed subject to approval; (d) Many functions require a budget/funds and this restricted in many instances by central government; (e) Political landscape (political stability including decisions); (f) Main challenges facing local authorities: poor revenue collection mechanisms, rising poverty levels, adverse macro environment, dwindling public sector investment, payment of debts owed to departments by government.

Stakeholder Views Analysis

An analysis of views and insights of data collected from key informants that included government, local authorities, community leaders, private citizens, business and academics is presented in this section. Stakeholder relationships are very important in devolution model of governance. The selected key informants responded to the following questions: Do the proposed devolution objects adequately address all the key aspects necessarily for the smooth implantation of a vibrant model? What are the barriers to the smooth implementation of devolution program? What are perceived benefits of devolution? What is the role of private sector in the crafting and implementation of devolution?

The following was noted from Government, local authorities, community leaders respondents:

- That the Rural District Act (RDC) Act and Traditional Act and Urban Development ACT clearly stipulated the roles of various stakeholders within the implementation value chain;
- There is need for clarity in adequately articulating the following area: Funding, PSIP, Budget allocation, Role clarity of the key stakeholders that is Ministry, Local Authorities, Councilors and Publics;

- Barriers included –Inadequate funding, structural ambiguity, red tape, complicated reporting structure, need for role clarity to guide interaction among all stakeholders indentified as the Minister of Local Government, Minister of State, Council, private sector, District Councils, Village Heads, chiefs;
- Lack of transparency in the management and allocation of funds by central government. Lack of capacity to implement program including a standard implementation tool kit;
- The criteria for funds 5% revenue allocation based on population size was highlighted not to be favorable for marginalized societies that are low levels of development. For a district like Mbire is large in size but much marginalized in development. Thus, there was a need to relook at a favorable resource allocating index;
- Expanded use of the 5% disbursements towards water, roads, clinics, schools had empowered local authorities and pro development was a welcome development that would stimulate socio-economic growth;
- Localization of decisions via management committees and increased stakeholder participation thus empowered communities to ownership of their development programs;
- Devolution was viewed as a motivating, growth driver and increased internal drive, accountability, investment drive, infrastructure development, self-monitoring, prioritization, economic growth, ownership of process;
- The role of private sector is not clearly defined in the devolution model. There has not been any structured engagement between private sector and all other stakeholders. Private not involved in the crafting of the Act.

Private Sector and Academics and Special Interest Groups Perspectives

The following questions were asked to private sector, academics and special interest groups: What are the benefits of devolution? What are barriers to devolution? How much consultation was undertaken in crafting the proposed Act? What structural socio-economic aspects will require re-align in order to achieve desired goals? Responses are summarized below:

- The benefits of devolution were seen as pro development – distribution of power, stimulating development, innovation, promoting equity distribution of resources, 5% retention would stimulate growth of local economies, job creation, reduce red tape;
- Promotion of Public Private Partnerships (PPP) including regional investment platforms and business networking, incentives;
- Major barriers included the power of central government, minister powers to override, conflict with government priorities, politics, scarce resources, lack of clarity of the resource distribution model, diversity of regions including levels of development, poor communication, lack of infrastructure;
- Recommended socio-economic areas of realignment include role clarity and power rationalization, provision of adequate funding, relook at current retention model, development of a robust socio-economic tool kit (Isenberg Model). Increase stakeholder participation including marketing of the program.

Kenya Experience of devolution presents many lessons for unlocking the benefits of devolution model of governance. A study undertaken by the Kenya Institute of Economic Affairs highlighted similar perceived benefits of a implementing a devolution form of governance. The following challenges of devolution in Kenya were noted in the Kenya Institute Economic Affairs Report that:

- Devolution was characterized by interference from responsible institutions involved in devolution;
- Insufficient allocations and delayed disbursements of funds to counties;
- County governments have experienced delays in funds disbursement from the National government. This is evident in the Standard Media report (2017) on County funds is held up at the Treasury;
- Corruption mismanagement of funds is viewed as real in county governments as reported by Ethics and Anti-Corruption Commission (EACC 2014) during their 4th Governance Integrity and Investment Conference presentation in Mombasa;
- Lack of capacity to facilitate services delivery report by the Standard media (2016) revealed that there is lack of understanding of key issues around devolution that is generating a great deal of mistrust among stakeholders. The report further stated that some counties, for example contested the piecemeal transfer of functions arguing that all powers provided in Schedule Four of the Constitution be transferred at once. However, the reality is that many county governments lack the capacity to absorb all such powers within a short period.

FUTURE RESEARCH DIRECTIONS

More research is required in the area of developing entrepreneurship ecosystem focusing on developing countries. There is paucity of information in this area of study. Africa in particular presents a fertile study grounds for governance, socio economic and entrepreneurship studies.

SOLUTIONS AND RECOMMENDATIONS

The role of partners must be very clear with government central role and delegating the necessary powers or empower its arms to be able to undertake the work unhindered. Provision of adequate funding for projects, equitable distribution of resources, development of a robust resources allocation formula, an implementation tool kit based on Isenberg Model, capacity building, access to information, access to markets, promotion of innovation, increased stakeholder participation, rule of law, promotion of democratic principles, gender equity, upholding of the constitution.

The Isenberg Model as a framework will help with smooth deployment of a devolution program. The six dimensions of model ensures that all key aspects of considered in These are: policy (leadership, government); finance (financial capital); culture (success stories, societal norms); supports (infrastructure, support professions); human capital (labor, educational institutions); and markets (early customers, networks) (Isenberg, 2011). The issues identified in the literature review, in case studies for example Kenya; South Africa including Zimbabwe can be categorized into the Isenberg six domains. Thus, the Isenberg Model can be applied as one of the devolution deployment solutions for a successful devolution program. Table in Fig 1 presents a matrix demonstrating how the various issues, barriers and challenges can be taken care using the Isenberg Model (2011).

The OECD (2011) report recommend a number of variables that needed to be in place to in order to implement a successful entrepreneurship Ecosystem and these variables fit into the six domains of Isenberg (2011). Thus, the Isenberg model could provide a solution to dealing with issues of devolution governance and building a sustainable entrepreneurship ecosystem. The variables are presented below:

- An overall democratic society and governmental structure;
- Accessible and stable capital markets; private equity markets; low interest rates in debt markets;
- Tolerance for risk;
- Enforceable rule of law; effective court system;
- Reliable and fair intellectual property law;
- A culture that embraces and rewards successful individuals;
- Business entities that can be formed efficiently and cost-effectively, which limit personal liability (limited liability corporations, limited partnerships, etc.) and foster fair governance;
- Flexible labor and employment laws (which allow for hiring and firing) and reasonable enforcement of covenants not to compete;
- Strong educational systems and excellence in universities;
- Bankruptcy laws (which allow for failure without undue penalty or stigma);
- Technological resources and internet access that level the playing field, expedite start-ups, and open up access for smaller companies to global markets and trade;
- Access to mentors, coaches, professional advisors, mentoring programs, etc.;
- Research and development partnerships between government and private business as well as between universities and private business;
- Low tax and regulatory barriers;
- Vehicles such as mergers and acquisitions, initial public offerings, employee stock ownership plans, etc. that provide exit strategies for successful entrepreneurs;
- Estate planning and wealth transfer laws and systems that allow for wealth preservation, asset protection, succession planning, and management transition;
- Antitrust laws that encourage competitive but fair markets.

Legal variables which facilitate entrepreneurship and a growth oriented ecosystem:

- Court systems that allow for enforcement of contracts and obligations (including cost-effective alternative dispute resolution systems);
- Tax incentives;
- Encourage innovation and investment in smaller companies;
- Pension management rules that allow for risk capital;
- Intellectual property laws that protect the rights of innovative entrepreneurs and allow for licensing and franchising;
- Corporate governance that creates fiduciary duties for leaders and protects reasonable decision-making by the board without dilution of the rights of minority investors;
- Securities laws that ensure public and private offerings are made with full disclosure and decisions are made by informed investors;

Table 1. Matrix demonstrating issues, barriers and challenges using Isenberg Model

Dimension	Application
Finance	Provide adequate funding Re-align retention Model Promote FDI Efficient collection of taxes and levies Availability of finance Creative finance (JVs), Special Funds Property rights
Culture	Community participation Embrace diversity Equity promotion Demographics study Societal needs analysis
Supports	Infrastructure development –Roads, rail, air and water) Provide budget for capital projects Support professions Incentives schemes Legal framework Pro policy framework
Human Capital	Train skilled labor (TIVET) Strategic Alliances Capacity building in business skills Promote entrepreneurship impart ICT Skills including promoting Technology transfer Promote intra-regional skills mobility Promote sister city programs
Markets	Promote access to markets Promote access to information Access to technology – internet, mobile applications etc. Business network platforms including associations Contract production

Source: (Own, 2020)

- Bankruptcy processes that protect creditors and encourage risk-taking via orderly resolution of failures.

CONCLUSION

The chapter has presented the Zimbabwean devolution model, its challenges and advantages, case study experiences from Kenya, Uganda and South Africa, circular economy and recommended application of the Isenberg Model as blue print for successful implantation of Zimbabwe devolution program. Literature reviewed and perspectives gathered suggest that the benefits of devolution outweigh the costs. That implementation of devolution requires a fully integrated and coordinated stakeholder approach involving: public and private sector, communities, public and training institutions.

REFERENCES

Acs, Z. J., Estrin, S., Mickiewicz, T., & Szerb, L. (2017a). Institutions, entrepreneurship and growth: The role of national entrepreneurial ecosystems. *Small Business Economics*, (51), 501–514.

Acs, Z. J., Stam, E., Audretsch, D. B., & O'Connor, A. (2017b). The lineages of the entrepreneurial ecosystem approach. *Small Business Economics*, *49*(1), 1–10. doi:10.100711187-017-9864-8

Borissenko, J., and Boschma, R. (2017). *A critical review of entrepreneurial ecosystems research: towards a future research agenda*. Lund University, CIRCLE-Center for Innovation, Research and Competences in the Learning Economy.

Bosma, N., Holvoet, T., & Crijns, H. (2014). *Global Entrepreneurship Monitor 2013*. Report for Belgium & Flanders, Beleidsrapport STORE-B14-012.

Bosma, N., Sanders, M., & Stam, E. (2017). *Time series and panel data analysis of GEI and growth performance indicators*. Academic Press.

Bramwell, A., Nelles, J., & Wolfe, D. A. (2008). Knowledge, innovation and institutions: Global and local dimensions of the ICT cluster in Waterloo, Canada. *Regional Studies*, *42*(1), 101–116. doi:10.1080/00343400701543231

Bramwell, A., & Wolfe, D. A. (2008). Universities and regional economic development: The entrepreneurial University of Waterloo. *Research Policy*, *37*(8), 1175–1187. doi:10.1016/j.respol.2008.04.016

Bureau. (2015). *SME sector's growth in Oman*. Author.

Cannavacciuolo, L., Iandoli, L., Ponsiglione, C., & Zollo, G. (2017). *Learning by failure vs learning by habits*. Academic Press.

Clarke, R., Chandra, R., & Machado, M. (2016). SMEs and social capital: Exploring the Brazilian context. *European Business Review*, *28*(1), 2–20. doi:10.1108/EBR-03-2013-0065

Cohen, B., & Muñoz, P. (2015). Toward a theory of purpose-driven urban entrepreneurship. *Organization & Environment*, *28*(3), 264–285. doi:10.1177/1086026615600883

Creswell, J. w. (2009). *Research design: Qualitative, quantitative, and mixed methods approaches*. Sage Publications.

Curley, M., & Formica, P. (2013). *University Ecosystems Design Creative Spaces for Start-Up Experimentation*. Springer. https://www.springer.com/gp/book/9783319001784

De Vita, L., Mari, M., & Poggesi, S. (2014). Women entrepreneurs in and from developing countries: Evidences from the literature. *European Management Journal*, *32*(3), 451–460. doi:10.1016/j.emj.2013.07.009

Dell, S., & Sharma, Y. (2014). *Navigating the industry-academia partnership terrain*. http://www.universityworldnews.com/article.php?story=20141211194708818

Ethics and Anti-Corruption Commission (EACC). (2014). *4th Governance Integrity and Investment Conference: Combating Corruption, Unethical Conduct and Practices within the County Governments*. Available at www.icpsk.com

Fernandez Fernandez, M. T., Blanco Jimenez, F. J., & Cuadrado Roura, J. R. (2015). Business incubation: Innovative services in an entrepreneurship ecosystem. *Service Industries Journal*, *35*(14), 783–800. doi:10.1080/02642069.2015.1080243

Fetters, M. L., Greene, P., Rice, M. P., & Butler, J. S. (2010). *The development of university-based entrepreneurship ecosystems*. Cheltenham: Edward Elgar. doi:10.4337/9781849805896

Frenkel, A., & Maital, S. (2014). *Mapping national innovation ecosystems: Foundations for policy consensus*. Cheltenham: Edward Elgar. doi:10.4337/9781782546818

Funke, T. (2015). A Canvas that Describes Relationships within an Entrepreneurship Ecosystem. *Global Entrepreneurship Research Network*. http://gern.co/an-entrepreneurship-ecosystem-canvas-lessons-from-berlin/

Gibb, A. A. (2014). *The entrepreneurial higher education institution: a review of the concept and its relevance today*. https://heinnovate.eu/intranet/tef/downloads/HEInnovate_Analytical%20p aper.pdf

Hansen, M., Chesbrough, H., Nohria, N., & Sull, D. (2000). Networked incubators. Hothouses of the new economy. *Harvard Business Review*, *78*(5). https://www.ncbi.nlm.nih.gov/pubmed/11143156 PMID:11143156

Hart, M., Levie, J., Bonner, K., & Drews, C.-C. (2015). *Global Entrepreneurship Monitor United Kingdom 2014 Monitoring Report*. Academic Press.

Hope, R. K. (2014). *Devolved Government and Local Governance in Kenya*. Available at www.researchgate.net

Iakovleva, T. (2015). *Exploring the relationship between university context and entrepreneurial intentions*. Submitted paper.

Isenberg, D. (2011). *The entrepreneurship ecosystem strategy as a new paradigm for economic policy*. Academic Press.

Isenberg, D. (2014). *What an entrepreneurship ecosystem actually is*. https://hbr.org/2014/05/what-an-entrepreneurial-ecosystem-actually-is/

Isenberg, D. J. (2010, June). How to Start an Entrepreneurial Revolution. *Harvard Business Review*.

Jacobs, H.M., & Chavhunduka, C. (2003). *Devolution for Land Administration in Zimbabwe: opportunities and challenges*. Centre for Applied Social Sciences, University of Zimbabwe-Land Tenure Center, University of Wisconsin-Madison.

Kaufmann Foundation. (2015). *Six strategies for building an entrepreneurial ecosystem*. Retrieved from www.kaufmannfoundation.com

Kimenyi, S. M. (2013). *Devolution and Resources Sharing in Kenya*. Available at www.brookings.edu

Kingma, B. (2014). Creating a dynamic campus-community entrepreneurial ecosystem: Key characteristics of success. In A. C. Corbett, D. Siegel, & J. A. Katz (Eds.), Advances in entrepreneurship, firm emergence and growth (Vol. 16, pp. 97–114). Bingley: Emerald Group.

KIPPRA. (2018). An Assessment of Health Care Delivery in Kenya Under the Devolved System: Special Paper No 19. Available at www.kippra.or.ke

Krueger, N. F. (2017). Entrepreneurial intentions are dead: Long live entrepreneurial intentions. In M. Brännback & A. Carsrud (Eds.), *Revisiting the entrepreneurial mind. International studies in entrepreneurship* (Vol. 35). Cham: Springer. doi:10.1007/978-3-319-45544-0_2

Lehner, O. M., & Harrer, T. (2019). Crowd funding revisited: A neo-institutional field-perspective. *Venture Capital*, *21*(1), 75–96. doi:10.1080/13691066.2019.1560884

Manimala, M. J., & Wasdani, K. P. (2014). Emerging economies: Muddling through to development. In M. J. Manimala & K. P. Wasdani (Eds.), *Entrepreneurial ecosystem: Perspectives from emerging economies* (pp. 3–53). Berlin: Springer.

Mason, C., & Brown, R. (2014). Entrepreneurial ecosystems and growth oriented entrepreneurship. *Final Report to OECD, 30*(1), 77-102.

Nir, K. (2014). Developing successful entrepreneurial ecosystems: Lessons from a comparison of an Asian tiger and a Baltic tiger. *Baltic Journal of Management*, *9*(3), 330–356. doi:10.1108/BJM-09-2013-0146

Nylund, P. A., & Cohen, B. (2017). Collision density: Driving growth in urban entrepreneurial ecosystems. *The International Entrepreneurship and Management Journal*, *13*(3), 757–776. doi:10.100711365-016-0424-5

O'Connor, A., & Reed, G. (2015a). Promoting regional entrepreneurship ecosystems: The role of the university sector in Australia. In P. Davidsson (Ed.), *Conference Proceedings, Australian Centre for Entrepreneurship Research Exchange Conference 2015* (pp. 772–788). Adelaide: Queensland University of Technology.

Prahalad, C. K. (2005). The Fortune at the Bottom of the Pyramid: Eradicating Poverty through Profits. Wharton School Publishing.

Pyper, R. C. (2016). *An Entrepreneural Development Framework for SMEs in South Africa*. Nelson Mandela Metropolitan University.

Rahim, H. L., & Mohtar, S. (2015). Social entrepreneurship: A different perspective. *International Academic Research Journal of Business and Technology*, *1*(1), 9–15.

Schaeffer, V., & Matt, M. (2016). Development of academic entrepreneurship in a non-mature context: The role of the university as a hub-organization. *Entrepreneurship and Regional Development*, *28*(9-10), 724–745. doi:10.1080/08985626.2016.1247915

SID. (2011). *Devolution in Kenya's New Constitution*. Available at ww.sidnt.org

Spigel, B. (2017a). The relational organization of entrepreneurial ecosystems. *Entrepreneurship Theory and Practice*, *41*(1), 49–7. doi:10.1111/etap.12167

Stam, E. (2015). Entrepreneurial ecosystems and regional policy: A sympathetic critique. *European Planning Studies*, *23*(9), 1759–1769. doi:10.1080/09654313.2015.1061484

Stam, E., & Spiegel, B. (2016). *Entrepreneurial Ecosystems.* Utrecht School of Economic, Tjalling C. Koopmans Research Institute, Discussion paper Series 13-16, Utrecht, The Netherlands.

Suresh, J., & Ramraj, R. (2012). Entrepreneurial ecosystem: Case study on the influence of environmental factors on entrepreneurial success. *European Journal of Business and Management*, *4*(16), 1–2.

The Standard Media. (2016). *Devolution Still Facing Challenges*. Available at www.standardmedia.co.ke

The Standard Media. (2017). *County funds are held up at the Treasury*. Available at www.standardmedia.co.ke/business/article

The Standard Media. (2017). *How grand corruption in the counties undermines devolution*. Available at www.standardmedia.co.ke

Van de Ven, A. H. (1993). The development of an infrastructure for entrepreneurship. *Journal of Business Venturing*, *8*(3), 211–230. doi:10.1016/0883-9026(93)90028-4

Voelker, T. A. (2012). Entrepreneurial ecosystems: Evolutionary paths or differentiated systems? *Business Studies Journal*, *4*(2), 43–61.

World Economic Forum. (2014). *Entrepreneurial Ecosystems around the Globe and Early-Stage Company Growth Dynamics*. Geneva, Switzerland: Author.

ADDITIONAL READING

Åsterbro, T., & Bazzazian, N. (2011). Universities, entrepreneurship and local economic development. In M. Fritsch (Ed.), *Handbook of Research on Entrepreneurship and Regional Development* (pp. 252–333). Cheltenham: Edward Elgar. doi:10.4337/9780857936493.00013

Davidson, P. (1995). Culture, structure and regional levels of entrepreneurship. *Entrepreneurship and Regional Development*, *7*(1), 41–62. doi:10.1080/08985629500000003

Ebdrup, T. (2013). *Understanding business ecosystems*. FORA.

Feld, B. (2012). *Startup Communities: building an entrepreneurial ecosystem in your city*. Hoboken, NJ: Wiley. doi:10.1002/9781119204459

Harrison, R. T., Cooper, S. Y., & Mason, C. M. (2004). Entrepreneurial activity and the dynamics of technology-based cluster development: The case of Ottawa. *Urban Studies (Edinburgh, Scotland)*, *41*(5-6), 1045–1070. doi:10.1080/0042098041000l675841

Mason, G., Bishop, K., & Robinson, C. (2009). *Business Growth and Innovation; The Wider Impact of Rapidly Growing Firms in UK City-Regions*. London: NESTA. [http://www.niesr.ac.uk/pdf/ 190509_94959.pdf]

KEY TERMS AND DEFINITIONS

Barrier: A factor that impacts or hinders smooth implementation thus affecting performance towards desired objectives/goals.

Constitution: Set of laws governing a country.

Delegation: Sharing of power to others or empowering lower levels in an organization.

Devolution: Involves decentralization and delegation of power to lower levels of government.

Ecosystem: An environment made of interconnected stakeholders with same objectives.

Entrepreneurship Ecosystem: An environment made of stakeholders including activities that favor entrepreneurship.

Model: Type of system adopted in order to achieve desired results.

Power: Ability to influence others or having authority to take responsibility.

Stakeholder: An integral member of a system or group sharing same values working together.

Chapter 16
Industrialization in Tanzania: A Window of Entrepreneurial Opportunity

Nyanjige Mbembela Mayala
Moshi Co-Operative University, Tanzania

ABSTRACT

This chapter acknowledges the undeniable fact that the manufacturing sector plays a key role in the growth of any economy, and it is from this sector that Tanzania can catch up with the rest of the world. The stagnant contribution share of the manufacturing sector is linked with implementation lags on ambitious, uncoordinated plans and slow transforming economic structure, which is dominated by agriculture and competition from low priced manufactured import from Asian economies. Shifting the labor force from agriculture to manufacturing remains the best option for the country to enhance efforts towards industrialization, thus increasing the overall productivity. On the other hand, entrepreneurship and policies have a multifaceted nature and linkages with other areas, such as education and skills development, technology and innovation, finance and capacity building. Multiple new types of financial instruments can contribute to diversifying the financial solutions available to Tanzanian entrepreneurs in the process of industrialization.

INTRODUCTION

Different authors of economic development around the world have indicated that, industrialization has a vibrant role to play in that effect. Same argument of industrialization is said to be vital in supporting Tanzania to raise economic growth and development (URT, 2016). Productive expansion is the major purpose for making use of new technology to manufacturing and the most important source of technological innovation. It creates new skills and a work attitude, catalyses institutional change and fosters cutting-edge entrepreneurship. It serves as a means of modernizing the export structure and creating the base for sustained export growth, in conjunction with higher wages. Increased industrialization helps create the employment that poor economies like Tanzania need as they release surplus labour from agriculture by stimulating the improvement of modern services. For that reason, industrialization has long been, and stays, the most powerful engine of structural change and modernization. Indeed, developed world has

DOI: 10.4018/978-1-7998-5116-5.ch016

Copyright © 2020, IGI Global. Copying or distributing in print or electronic forms without written permission of IGI Global is prohibited.

undergone an extended period of industrialization before they reached levels of high income earnings and structural transformation of their economies that could support the development of modern services.

The chronic failure of Tanzanian industries to grow and compete has engendered deep pessimism about its prospects, especially as the context for industrialization is changing. International competition is intensifying with liberalization and globalization. Competition is taking new forms, driven through fast technical change and the emergence of international production networks, issues that require more advanced entry levels of competencies and abilities even for simple production are rising rapidly. Not only is industrialization in Tanzania becomes marginalized to the dynamics of the worldwide economic system, it indicates little signs of a dynamic technological response to the new demanding situations. This is despite the fact that access to world technology flows is now less difficult that is observed through capital and skills flowing throughout national boundaries more readily to tap local markets and to set up sites for global production.

It is not that the Tanzanian economic system isn't always open to Foreign Direct Investments (FDI) and technology inflows. The country has liberalized noticeably in current years. Even as the process continues to be incomplete, the actual problem appears to be that liberalization has now not inspired an aggressive response because of a loss of receptive capabilities. Few industries have upgraded their technologies or invested in advanced production technologies. There are few signs of technological processes in Tanzanian industries, even of absorbing new technology. Manufacturing sector is conspicuous by way of its structure of production that remains characterized by low value-added primary products. Global production chains and networks have largely bypassed Tanzania.

Tanzania's weak industrial performance appears to reflect deep problems in economic structure. If this is so, policymakers must address the underlying structural issues. Other countries have faced such problems in the recent past and overcome them to different degrees, some with dramatic success. There is no reason why Tanzania should not attempt to do the same; even modest success would be better than its current marginalization. The country must shed the growing pessimism regarding its ability to industrialize at all, and improve its investment climate. At the same time, it must simultaneously strive to overcome its structural problems, which are largely related to factor markets.

Structural problems in industrial development have a variety of causes. Some arise from past government policies that misdirected resource allocation, for instance into inefficient parastatal enterprises. Others arise from the market and institutional failures that characterize developing countries, like lack of skills or technical knowledge, entrepreneurial weaknesses, and widespread externalities. The institutions that help enterprises overcome these problems in advanced countries are absent in poor ones, and even when they exist in name, they are often ineffective, with low capabilities, poor motivation and very weak links with enterprises. Based on lessons drawn from implementation of Five Year Development Plan (FYDP 1) and The National Poverty Reduction Strategy II as well as lessons from successful comparable countries' industrialization experiences as well as assessment of Tanzania's comparative advantages; industrialization has been identified and brought forward as an intervention for economic growth and development. Industrialization that is envisaged in FYDP II focuses on realizing the country's aspirations, and is anchored on current and future drivers of the economy; fostering innovation and technological adaptation; and strategically repositioning the country to maximize gains on the global and regional economic dynamics. In addition, industrial sector is believed to be in line with realization of goals articulated in Tanzania Development Vision 2025, particularly that of propelling Tanzania to a semi-industrialized middle-income country by 2025. This criterion implies that the selected intervention should have large impact on set targets, especially on economic growth, employment creation through entrepreneurial opportunities, poverty reduction and national security. The Tanzania Long Term Perspective Plan, 2011/12- 2025/26 (LTPP), the key targets to be achieved by 2020 and 2025 respectively as stated in Table 1.

Table 1. Overall industrial sector performance targets

S/N	Indicators/Targets	2015	2020	2025
1	Real growth rate %	9.1	10.6	10.5
2	GDP share (Current prices) (%)	21.1	23.7	25.0
3	Share of total Exports (%)	27.1	27.5	31.1
4	Share of total employment (%)	8	12.5	20

Source: URT, 2018

NATURE OF TANZANIAN ECONOMY

The Tanzania's Manufacturing Sector

Even though industrialisation in Tanzania has become major and hot development agenda during fifth government presidency, the battle toward industrialisation has a long history. The country has been emphasizing on industrialisation since its independence in 1961; firstly 1961-1967, under mixed economic system when private sector led the economy, the country embraced industries passed from colonial power, in which mostly were industries producing consumer goods especially food, beverage, and textile products and value adding processing industries aiming to feed manufacturing industries in Europe.

Under the socialism era of 1967 to 1985 before structural change of the economy, the country aimed at establishing import substituting kind of manufacturing industries. During this time, given the slow performance and low capacity of private sector during early independence years, the government decided to jump in with all feet and take control of the economy by nationalizing all major means of production, all operations of private sector in manufacturing, banking services and other services were seized. During this time the country attained industrial development level that has not been experienced again in history. Number of industrial firms rose from 220 during independence to more than 2000 in 1970, with 7000 registered trademarks, accompanied with rapid growth of manufacturing value added with capacity of meeting 70 percent of domestic demand for consumer goods and increase in absolute and relative labour productivity. Some of the action taken by the government while exercising its power over the economy include, price control aimed at limiting monopoly power of local producers, stringent regulations to monitor capital account, and fixed exchange rate. Unfortunately, good intention of the government to have full control over the economy started to adversely affect economic performance.

The country started to experience negative macroeconomic performance and economic shocks from overvaluation of currency and forex shortage which hindered importation of industrial inputs. Together with oil crisis of 1973-74 and in 1978, extensive drought 1974-75 which eroded export of traditional cash crops such as sisal, cashew nuts, coffee and tea, a war with Uganda in 1979, high inflation of 30.2 percent in 1981and negative balance of payment, the economy was hit badly so was manufacturing sector. In the depth of crisis, negative real growth rate of economy was experienced in both 1981 and 1983, which necessitated the need for recovery programmes whereby efforts started with own recovery programmes. In 1981-82 a National Economic Survival Programme (NESP) was initiated with aim of resolving economic crisis using internal resources, and later 1982-83, in tackling the fiscal deficit problem, Structural Adjustment Programme (SAP) was implemented. However, none of these programmes were successful in reviving the economy.

Subsequently, the Structural Adjustment Programmes (SAP) and Economic Recovery Programmes (ERPs) under the supervision of Britton Wood institutions were implemented between 1986 and 1995. The programmes brought back the role of market in an economy by emphasizing on reduction of government control and involvement in investment and trading, and country's manufacturing sector was also reformed to allow private investors' involvement. However, given the pace of growth of manufacturing sector in most developing countries during the time, and global trade liberalization, competitiveness of local industries was too low leading to significantly loss of local industries against competitive low cost imports.

New Age of Industrialization

Industrialisation new era in Tanzania is discernable by establishment and implementation of Sustainable Industrial Development Policy 2020 (SIDP), with a goal of having an industrial sector geared toward human development and job creation, economic transformation for achieving sustainable economic growth, environmental sustainability and equitable development. The policy was to be implemented through three different phases; Phase I (1996-2000) a short term priority program focusing on rehabilitating and consolidating existing industries through capital financing and restructuring; Phase II (2000-2010) a medium term priority program aimed at having newly established intermediate goods and light capital goods and machinery industries, promote export manufacturing and taking into account emerging technological innovation to exploit country's natural resources; and Phase III (2010-2020) long term priority program aiming at consolidated industries came to exist in phase one and two, and provide major investment in basic capital goods.

Mostly, structural adjustment and other development agenda adopted after 1995 were not in vein in rectifying the poor economic performance of the economy. Macroeconomic stability started to be observed through decline of inflation rate from 27 percent to less than 5 percent in 2002, revenue authority was introduced to enhance revenue collection to tackle fiscal deficit, addressing tax evasion and exemption problem whereby government revenue rose from 11 percent of GDP in 1993 to 13 percent in 1996. Improvement was also observed in financial services through increased effectiveness and branch network, increased leading to private sector, and manufacturing sector experienced positive growth from increase of fish, minerals and other manufactured goods, and overall growth of economy increased from 3 percent in 1995 to 6 percent in 2002.

However, looking at Tanzania's manufacturing sector performance in comparison with other sectors in two decades, the sector has remained stagnant, in spite of various efforts and strategies proposed such as; adoption of development vision 2025 in 1999 focusing on industrial development, establishment of Export Processing Zones (EPZs) 2003, and introduction of Integrated Industrial Development Strategy (IIDS) in 2010. Generally sector's contribution to GDP has remained low, and currently statistics shows a decline. Does this stagnant and low contribution imply less importance of the sector towards growth of economy? Does the economy experience premature de-industrialization? Or, is the country failing in implementation of its industrial development policies and strategies?

INDUSTRIALIZATION ISSUES, CONTROVERSIES AND PROBLEMS IN TANZANIA

Industrialization has been strategically announced and being said to be among the key areas of the Tanzania's fifth phase of government. The plan is manifested and is seen in numerous spaces comprising the Second Five Years Development Plan and annual plans and budgets succeeding it. There have been some debates on this topical industrialization agenda in the country; this chapter is aimed at a contribution to that discussion. The discussion focuses on particular challenges that chiefs and titans the industry to face in the process of industrialization and its space. Furthermore, it is informed by the author's several studies including interviews with key private sector players, in-depth practical knowledge and experiences for that matter. The challenges are many, closely related and at time self-reinforcing. However, they all revolve around the axis of investment and business environment and climate, and are put in various broad categories as follows.

Sector Focus and Concentration

After decades of macro-economic stability policies, trade liberalization and regional integration, and despite improvements in the 2000s, the performance of Tanzania's manufacturing sector remains unimpressive. Tanzania lags behind regional role models both in terms of the quantity and quality of industrial goods produced and exported. It continues to rely heavily on an unproductive agricultural sector, the extractive sector and low value-added manufacturing. Manufacturing Value Added (MVA) in GDP in Tanzania increased to 2384031 TZS Million in the second quarter of 2019 from 2280570 TZS Million in the first quarter of 2019. GDP From Manufacturing in Tanzania averaged 1367086.95 TZS Million from 2005 until 2019, reaching an all-time high of 2647575 TZS Million in the fourth quarter of 2018 and a record low of 373896.38 TZS Million in the first quarter of 2005. MVA as a share of GDP has mostly stagnated at roughly 9.5 percent between 2000 and 2017, which is still below the average for the region, making Tanzania one of the least industrialized countries in the world.

Manufacturing value added is also highly concentrated in a few low-tech sectors, making Tanzania's industry vulnerable to international competition and limiting its ability to improve through learning and innovation. Food and beverages alone account for nearly half of total manufacturing value added, followed by non-metallic mineral products (11 percent), tobacco (7 percent) and textiles (5 percent). Industrial activity is largely concentrated in Dar es Salaam (more than half of all large manufacturing establishments are located there) and to a lesser extent in Arusha. The remaining 14 percent is spread out between Mwanza, Singida, Tanga, Kagera and Kilimanjaro (URT, 2018).

Employment

Manufacturing has also been unsuccessful to create formal jobs for Tanzanians, predominantly in the Small and Medium Enterprise (SME) sector. Manufacturing employment contributes less than 5 percent of the total labour force, with the biggest 40 manufacturing companies employing 36 percent of all manufacturing labour. This is equivalent to the employment generated by 24,000 micro enterprises. What is perhaps more worrying is the fact that only 11 percent of industrial employment has been generated by firms which began operations in 2005 or later. Clearly, new investments in manufacturing have not yet resulted in significantly more jobs. This may be attributable to the current focus on capital-intensive, resource-based sectors (e.g. extractive industries) at the expense of traditional labour-intensive manufacturing (e.g. textiles and clothing, etc.).

Labour Issues

Labour is among the key factors of production in virtually all sectors of the economy including the industrial and related ones such as agriculture. There are a number of labour-related challenges for entrepreneurs venturing in industrial investments and related investments in Tanzania. Challenges include inadequate skills and talents in the domestic labour market in general and for specific industrial projects in particular. Skills that are short labour supply relative to the domestic for the same include soft skills, such as trust, creativity, innovation, team spirit, communication, courage and many others along that line. There is also scarcity of hard skills especially for some particular industry experts. Other challenges have been related to workers disciplines and mentality as well as work and residence permits including their costs and time taken to be granted. There is also a mismatch between skills supply and demand in quantity and quality leading to low productivity.

Tax Issues

No one disputes the importance of paying taxes. However there are tax issues that stand to challenge those venturing into the industrial sector. They include predictability of fiscal regime, relatively high tax rates, multiplicity of tax rates, multiplicity of taxes and long-time taken for tax refunds. Un-refunded tax locked capital and related opportunity costs of not having the money at disposal for industrialization purpose. There is also cost related to human resource dedicated to making tax incentives refund follow-ups with the authorities. Other challenges in the tax space incentives misuse by some beneficiaries. For authorities, this is a wastage of tax revenues that is badly needed for provision of goods and services. For competing industries it constitutes unequal playing ground from competition perspective. Those misusing tax incentives will have lower costs and therefore become more cost competitive and therefore become more cost competitive than those not misusing the facility.

Furthermore, tax challenges for industrialists include tax avoidance, evasion and elicit financial flows, challenges related to the use of Electronic Fiscal Devices (EFDs); Skills Development Levy (SDL) which has been seen to be of relatively rates and its use in other areas than in developing skills in general and skills for industrialization in particular. There are also challenges related to taxing the informal sector. When it is not properly taxed it constitutes unfair competition to those in the formal industrial sector who are taxed. Others are challenges related to easy of paying taxes including estimation methods and inadequate one stop centre for paying taxes. There is also a challenge of availability and of long term access and structured finance for industrialization. The upfront 15 percent upfront payment of import duty on industrial sugar for example, is a specific challenge for industries using this production input. It is worth noting that, there have been many reforms to address some of the above challenges by the authorities including the Ministry of Finance and Planning through the Tanzania Revenue Authority (TRA).

Unfair Competition

In free market economy, competition is inevitable and actually healthy for consumers and producers in fair competition. However, in Tanzania is said to be unhealthy. Industrialization face challenges of unfair competition in various ways. These include via the route of cheap imported industrial good as well as elicit trades that bring counterfeits and sub-standard industrial goods in the market. When the initial position is not at level playing ground, the affected industrialists entrepreneurs may not be able to take off let alone growing and prospecting.

Regulations

Regulations have good aim of protecting both producers and consumers. In the context of market structure, regulations are good in terms of ensuring that no one abuses his or her market power. What becomes challenging in industrialization process in Tanzania includes multiple regulations some of which are contradicting each other. There has been also multiple and high regulatory fees, many regulators as well as lack of one stop centre for the said multiple regulatory authorities. All these inflate the cost of doing business and therefore leading to reduced industrial sector competitiveness. Of the key challenges related to regulations is predictability of regulatory frameworks. Investors wish to have long term and stable regulatory framework. The 2018 blueprint can partly deliver solutions by fixing what is broken in the regulations space. What are needed are smart regulations. These are the ones that avoid over regulations that can be counterproductive for investments and businesses. It constitutes bad investment and business climate.

Technology

Fragility and inefficiency have long characterized Tanzania's manufacturing sector. In previous times the problems were predominantly related to government failures in developing an economy on the basis of a centrally planned structure. In recent years the main problems have been related to adjusting not only the manufacturing sector but the whole Tanzanian economy to the fierce demands of globalization. The challenge has hence mainly been affiliated with creating an enabling environment for the productive sectors in the economy, most notably the manufacturing sector, in order to expand Tanzania's present low level of competitiveness. Tanzania's type of economy face a challenges related to availability and access to recent technology in general and for industrialization in particular. Challenging too, is upgrading of existing technologies to cope with todays' state of the art high and competitive technology.

Value Chain Issues

Most Tanzanians live in countryside areas and two-third of the labour force is involved in agriculture. For the manufacturing industry to assist as a catalyst for economic progress and poverty lessening, it has to be incorporated with the rest of the economy through forward and backward linkages. One such linkage is food supply from agriculture. The expected flourishing in the manufacturing industry will open up new market prospects for farmers to supply food items for high value buyers such as caterers, restaurants, supermarkets and processors. Nevertheless, to benefit from fast growing high-end food markets, farmers must have both the ability and the motivations to supply their produce at the desired quantity and quality. Currently significant portion of the new demand is already being filled by imported goods. There are generally disorganises supply and value chain linkages. This leads to challenges related to reliable supply of industrial factor inputs including raw materials as well as factor outputs. These include lack of adherence to agreed supply schedule in quality and quantity, agreed frequencies and time.

Corruption

Normally corruption increases the costs of doing business, presents non- level playing ground for example procurement, brings substandard good, in the industrial factor inputs and final output markets. Corruption remains a central and serious challenge for Tanzania, in terms of both good governance and for the entire social development. The levels of petty and grand corruption identified in international and domestic surveys continue to be of considerable concern and affect all sectors of the economy from public service delivery to natural resource exploitation, industrial production and business. The formal anti-corruption legislation and anti-corruption institutions in Tanzania are comparable to those of most other African countries. Hence, in principle, there should also be good possibilities to initiate a far more effective struggle against corruption, but this requires a combination of political commitment and increased engagement from the media, civil society and the parliament. There have been some positive developments in recent years, but key challenges remain in implementing and enforcing the legislation. Similarly, it is a great problem that very few of the corruption cases end up being prosecuted in the courts.

New major opportunities and initiatives are underway. Steps have been taken to implement legislation and to meet the standards promoted by organisations such as the Extractive Industries Transparency Initiative (EITI). This entails strengthening of domestic revenue and financial management, and positive developments within PFM reforms. Crucial, however, is a continued strengthening of the systems and mechanisms for openness, accountability and transparency in the public system.

WHY MANUFACTURING MATTERS FOR TANZANIA?

Manufacturing occurs at different levels of sophistication. Minimal processing of extraction resources or processing of goods using minimal technology is generally associated with a lower level of value addition. Therefore, it is desirable for Tanzania to engage in the production of resource based and low-technology sectors by adding high value and using more sophisticated technologies and specialized human resources to compete in a better position in the world market. In that sense, resource-based manufactures is an important industrial sector for Tanzania to maximize the rents of their natural resource exports. A sensible strategy for Tanzania in the long term could be to engage in more capital- and knowledge-intensive activities in medium- and high technology sectors.

Recent economic developments in East Asia certainly provide a solid argument for boosting manufacturing. Is this of any relevance to less advanced, agriculture based countries like Tanzania? A large body of empirical evidence suggests that manufacturing is important for growth and job creation:

1. First, evidence not only indicates that industrialization is linked to economic growth, but that manufacturing can also play a catalytic role in transforming the economic structure of agrarian societies;

2. Secondly, manufacturing accounts for the bulk of world exports (more than 75 percent in 2018), and is less exposed to external shocks, price fluctuations, climatic conditions and unfair competition policies. The price of manufactured goods tends to be more stable than that of commodities. Unfair competition policies have distorted prices around the world, limiting the potential for export growth in some commodities;
3. Third, manufacturing generates externalities in technology development, skill creation and learning that are crucial for competitiveness. For instance, manufacturing is the main vehicle for technology development and innovation, representing the hub of technological progress. Industry uses technology in many forms and at different levels to increase returns to investments by shifting from low to high productivity activities. Manufacturing also offers great potential for informal innovation activities such as ad hoc incremental improvements in products and processes;
4. Fourth, manufacturing has a 'pull effect' on other sectors of the economy. The development of the manufacturing sector stimulates demand for more and better services: banking, insurance, communication and transport;
5. Finally, the internationalization of production has spread the benefits of manufacturing. The geographical distribution of the activities of transformational corporations has benefited the manufacturing sector in the developing world more than other sectors of the economy. The trend towards the vertical disintegration of production activities in industrialized countries means that developing countries have higher chances of integrating into global value chains.

Entrepreneurship Nexus Industrialization in Tanzania

As it is for Tanzania, many African governments are implementing industrialisation, which calls for new economic strategies. At least 26 African countries have industrialization strategies in place by 2017. While past efforts to industrialise Africa were often unsuccessful, the current industrial revolution and global business environment offer new opportunities, along with challenges. Specifically for Tanzania, three strategies are indispensable for the country to industrialize: promote a competitive private sector, target economic sectors with high growth potential including non-manufacturing and better harness the potential of entrepreneurs. More developed regions have managed to shift their labour force from agriculture to manufacturing, thus increasing their overall productivity. Nevertheless, as in many other African countries, the extra labour force that emerges from the agricultural sector has been absorbed by low productivity sectors such as retail rather than being channelled in the manufacturing sector. Besides manufacturing, tradable services and farming activities such as horticulture and the agro-industry can enhance economic growth. Non-farm entrepreneurship can benefit rural households by diversifying their income sources and provide a steady source of income during difficult agricultural seasons.

The Tanzania governments' main objective is to create the conditions for the economy to return to a higher, more inclusive and sustainable growth path. To that end, Tanzania will need more and better jobs by offering mass employment opportunities that are relatively accessible to large population of unskilled workers. For that case, economic transformation will not be possible without a strong manufacturing sector in place. Industrialization is necessary to transform economy by reallocating resources from low-productivity sectors to higher ones. Only industrialization can bring about unconditional convergence with the more advanced economy. Industrialisation is a catalyst for job creation, higher productivity and innovation. The market has demand constraints but its growth provides opportunities for tradable manufactured goods, modern services and processed agricultural products. In turn, more exports can open the country to technology spill-overs from abroad. Industrialization can increase access to capital, technological innovation and learning. Among others, the following need to be seriously put in priority.

Industrialization Innovation Strategies

Twenty-first century industrialization strategies call for innovative approaches. Tanzania must harness new opportunities and challenges, which other countries did not have to face. These include i) the new industrial revolution enhancing automation in industrial production, ii) the changing economic environment characterised by the slow-down in global growth and by the end of the commodity super cycle), and iii) the rising labour costs in East Asia. Innovative approaches are also needed to take advantage of the latent comparative advantages in the geographic specificities the country have and unique cultural heritages. Simply replicating industrialisation strategies that have worked since the 1970s in North-East Asia will not suffice.

Manufacturing remains the central sector on which Tanzania's' industrialization policies can rest, however high-growth opportunities also exist in other sectors. For certain tradable services and farming activities such as horticulture and the agro-industry, production methods have become comparable to those of conventional manufacturing. These activities produce higher quantities of goods at lower marginal costs. These goods can then be exported, increasing competition and productivity. Investing all resources only in manufacturing may not always prove efficient, nor reflect the comparative advantages for the country. Different pathways to industrialization exist. Experience shows that the share of manufacturing in GDP does not necessarily grow with higher income levels. Other sectors can also significantly contribute to economic growth. The potential of non-manufacturing sectors for industrialization may become more and more important in the context of the Fourth Industrial Revolution, where robots tend to replace low-skilled workers in manufacturing activities. Innovative industrialization strategies could better target high-potential entrepreneurial activities to accelerate industrialization. Entrepreneurs play an essential role in bringing innovation to an economy, notably new technologies and production methods. High-potential entrepreneurs also experiment with new products in local markets. They offer fresh ideas and exchange information.

Industrialization strategies can serve as a platform to tap into the large continental base of entrepreneurs. Tanzania is a country with emerging relatively high proportion of entrepreneurs of working age to start their own business. These entrepreneurs are essential agents of industrialisation as they take on innovative yet risky activities which create jobs and demand for skilled workers. Firms with less than 5 years and fewer than twenty employees provide most of the new jobs in formal sector. While most entrepreneurs (55%) focus on low skill sectors such as retail trade, hotels and restaurants, efforts must be made to link young workers to sectors of high productivity potential such as manufacturing, tradable services and agribusiness.

Subsistence Entrepreneurship

Subsistence entrepreneurship may not be a first step towards transformational entrepreneurship for the vast majority engaged in subsistence enterprises. The implications of this could be pivotal for policy. For example, if the goal of policy is growth then identifying which of the subsistence entrepreneurs is able to transition to transformational entrepreneurship and focusing a policy on these individuals while supporting the existing transformational entrepreneurs may be the most efficient policy. As another example, improving access to capital may increases the profits of transformative entrepreneurs but not subsistence entrepreneurs, who may have low entrepreneurial ability or high opportunity cost of their own time and may not choose to make profitable investments that require additional time or attention to supervise. Similarly, if one's goal is poverty alleviation, it may not be possible to dramatically increase profits of purely subsistence entrepreneurs by providing money into their business. Instead, more impact may be possible by supporting growth policies that make jobs with better income paths available. The goal then is twofold. First, identify subsistence and transformational entrepreneurs. However, the distinction is surely not quite so severe, as it seems possible that some subsistence entrepreneurs could transition to transformational entrepreneurship. Identifying how this transition can be achieved provides the second goal.

Promoting Social and Economic Inclusion

There is increasing agreement that entrepreneurship is key to sustainable development and critical to poverty reduction, gender equality and environmental sustainability. Entrepreneurship policies have a multifaceted nature and linkages with other areas, such as education and skills development, technology and innovation, finance and capacity-building. To assist policymakers, UNCTAD developed the Entrepreneurship Policy Framework, which was launched during the thirteenth quadrennial conference of UNCTAD, held in Doha in 2012. Along with a growing recognition of the role of entrepreneurship in sustainable development, key trends include increased attention to a holistic approach to entrepreneurship policies and their implementation, the growth of women's entrepreneurship, and youth and social entrepreneurship.

The lack of decent jobs is matched with the on-going and pressing challenges of inequality elsewhere. Inequality has led to an overall loss in human development measured in terms of health, education, political participation and economic empowerment. Lowering inequality will increase the poverty- reducing power of economic growth so that the benefits accrue to a greater portion of the population. In addition, gender inequality is also negatively impacting industrialization. For example, in countries with high gender inequality, women have lower access to economic assets, workplace participation, entrepreneurship opportunities and benefits from natural resources and the environment.

Industrialization is an essential stepping stone for Tanzania's development. The country must develop its own policy mix based on its resources, development vision, technological capability and production systems. Industrialization will contribute to increased growth and will be key to the emergence of a middle class. A higher number of entrepreneurs are starting a new business in Africa than anywhere else in the developing world. Approximately 11% of working-age Africans starts a new venture to exploit a business opportunity. Thus, there is a good potential for entrepreneurship in Tanzania to build a solid and sustainable base for a diversified and inclusive industrialisation. At the same time, policies should acknowledge that different types of entrepreneurs will require customized policies. In Tanzania, self-employment constitutes the only alternative outside the agriculture sector.

Enabling Factors and Stumbling Blocks

Industrial policies have a role to play in promoting the structural transformation. Structural transformations, defined by structural reforms such as privatisations, reduction of customs barriers or fiscal policies, have the advantage of revealing comparative advantages by putting in place policies of accompaniment that create conditions conducive to the experimentation of new products and exports. These reforms should therefore foster intensive job growth, particularly in the formal sector, and are an essential vehicle for improving social indicators. Correspondingly, the analysis of industrial policies needs to focus on getting the policy process right, and these may vary depending on the circumstances and development objectives - for instance, industrial diversification, job creation, and reduction of income inequalities. Market forces and private entrepreneurship should drive industrialisation while governments perform a strategic and coordinating role in the productive sphere, beyond simply ensuring property rights, contract enforcement, and macroeconomic stability, notably through adequate public policies including active industrial policies.

Public Service Reforms

In an effort to sustaining the growing demand for democracy dividends, most African governments including Tanzania which have in recent years shifted devotion to the improvement of the public service. The marks are very noticeable, and the indication is overwhelming, that issues that had once been escaped in political circles (for example, issues of skills and knowledge, performance, and honesty of the public service) are now being deliberated within and across political parties. In consonance with the significant changes taking place in the broad governance sphere (mainly, the replacement of one-party rule with multi-party opposition) the career service is gradually being re-configured into a de-politicized and qualified institution. The public service reform programmes implemented in the last decade emphasize the significance that African leaders now attribute to the professionalism as well as the performance and productivity of the service. Taking their cues from the experience with the administrative reform initiatives of the early post-independence period (1960s and 1970s), and the negative impact of structural adjustment programmes on the public service, a growing number of countries embarked on "home-grown" reform initiatives as from the mid-1990s. To be specific in terms of making more radical improvements in the situation of human resources in the public service and to unlock its potential for supporting the implementation of NEPAD, Tanzania would do well to give serious consideration to investing in human resource capacities and improving labour relations.

Financing Strategies for Entrepreneurs

Multiple new types of financial instruments can contribute to diversifying the financial solutions available to Tanzanian entrepreneurs. These instruments include asset-based lending, various types of private equity funds and listings, and social investment funds. Other such investments are "profit with a purpose" funds, multiple types of debt instruments, microfinance for SMEs, crowd-funding, various solutions provided by development financial institutions, and philanthropic finance targeting SMEs and entrepreneurs. Asset-based lending such as factoring and leasing can bolster a firm's cash flow while removing the stringent requirements associated with traditional credit. Factoring refers to a firm selling its accounts receivable to a financial intermediary for immediate cash. Factoring can alleviate firms" problems with limited cash flow while doing away with collateral requirements. Burkina Faso as one of African countries has a successful programme that uses a mix of private capital and donor contributions. As for leasing, firms can acquire machinery and equipment without making large investments or providing collateral.

For SMEs in countries with deep capital markets, equity listings can constitute an alternative source of finance. Listing requirements are usually less stringent and costs are lower compared to those for larger companies. Tanzania has only one equity exchange for SMEs. The challenges with SME equity listings are information asymmetries for investors and a lack of know-how and expertise by entrepreneurs and managers. If enforced, the existing transparency requirements would address the first issue. The Dar es Salaam (DSE) equity exchanges solve the second by appointing advisors to guide SMEs through all the steps leading to the listing.

Providing capital directly to entrepreneurs increases their growth and creates more jobs. While it is almost impossible to identify which firms will grow quickly in the future, it is possible to identify those with a high potential for growth. Development partners can directly support entrepreneurs through co-financing and advisory services, entrepreneur's financial support as well as technical assistance in the form of coaching and mentoring. The initiative should involve partners from both public and private sectors. The potential for private investment in developing countries like Tanzania is substantial. Initiatives such as Boost Africa, jointly launched by the AfDB, the European Investment Bank and the European Commission, allow mobilizing private capital through initial public investments.

In addition, development partners provide financial assistance to governments and national development banks to on-lend to private companies. This can also generate considerable resources. For example, a study shows that USD 1.4 billion in financing from the Clean Technology Fund to the public sector has mobilized about USD 5 billion of private co-finance Other approaches include project preparation facilities and facilitation platforms. Project preparation facilities serve to design well-structured bankable projects. Project facilitation platforms match the interests of public and private financiers in carrying out joint projects. Examples include Grow Africa, an initiative of the African Union Commission, the New Partnership for Africa"s Development and the World Economic Forum. Grow Africa provides a platform for governments and companies to promote business models that engage smallholder farmers and facilitates value-chain linkages. It focuses specifically on women and youth. Prioritizing specific policy interventions depends on countries resources and capacities. The conditions differ between countries, based on their natural resources" endowment, their fragility and their income levels through:

- Effective use of natural resources by generating funds with the profits from natural resource extraction, transformation and export to promote entrepreneurship. Governments could also nurture financial sector improvement through laws and regulations. Donors could assist governments in managing the funds or in designing related regulations, as in the case of the multi-stakeholder Managing Natural Resource Wealth Trust Fund (IMF, 2016);
- It could be imperative for the country to search for private sector investment and donor assistance to build government capacity and engage with entrepreneurs. The government could also seek donor assistance to build government and private sector capacity and to develop financial markets through guarantees and funding. Where remittances are important, tailored regulation and policies could be developed in an attempt to tap their potential;
- Diversification of market environment with holistic financial sector laws and regulations as well as supervision that targets different agents and instruments. These could likewise mean request donor support to increase government and private sector capacity and market development, particularly through credit guarantees or by tapping domestic and international financial markets;
- Concentration on giving public servants the chance to participate in decisions which affect them and through measures that government is able in harnessing the talents of all its employees, wom-

en as well as men, including disadvantaged ethnic, religious and other groups. This is something that is indeed worth doing because human dignity is a noble objective in itself, but also because it is in this way that Tanzania will get the best return on the human capital in the public sector. The governments should make a voluntary, explicit, public and irrevocable commitment to a challenging programme of human resource reform. It should also follow a flexible and participatory approach to reform that focuses on enhancing the quality of the human capital rather than reducing the number of civil servants. Both politicians and senior officials should play a hands-on leadership role in improving human resource, seeing reform through to implementation by exercising transformational leadership skills;

- Conducting an explicit analysis of the views of stakeholders, capitalizing on their support where it exists, but also taking account of the opposition of others, whether by winning them over through dialogue, finding ways of circumventing their oppositions or modifying policies where stakeholder opposition cannot, or perhaps should not be overcome to support entrepreneurs in the industrialization process.

RECOMMENDATIONS

In an attempt to speed up industrial development of in the country, a number of efforts are needed to be made, including; creation of industrial development framework which will be a road map to be observed by any government that will be in power irrespective of time. It has been pointed out that one of failure of implementation of development policy is lack of implementation framework at early stage of policy inception. Coordination and harmonization of all sectoral development policies, since industrialization is possible only if interlink is made between sectors, such as having one ministry that is responsible of advocating, and overseeing implementation of development policies. This will allow easy monitoring and in time evaluation of policies' implementation and avoidance of having similar activities addressed by two different policies at different time intervals.

The best choice is to focus in one or two sectors in which the country can easily develop a comparative advantage. The current development in manufacturing sector is yet to bring significant job opportunities to Tanzanians because of focusing on capital-intensive resource- based industries such as extraction and construction industries at the expense of traditional labor intensive manufacturing industries like textile and clothing. Thus, given the current competitiveness of manufacturing sector globally, with an economy which is largely dependable on resource-based agricultural products with limited value addition, the focus may only be directed on agro-allied industries. The efforts should be on gaining competitiveness on adding value to agricultural products and establishment of textile and clothing industries which has advantage of reaching large part of population which are still in agriculture sector and with advantage of a country having largely potential arable agricultural land.

CONCLUSION

From the literature reviewed, interviews from manufacturing practitioners and review made on the economy, suffice it to say that Tanzania's manufacturing sector remain to be significant for the growth of economy notwithstanding her small share on GDP relative to other sectors. There is a potential for small and medium entrepreneurs if supported well to contribute much in the manufacturing sector. At the same time utilizing the labour force from the agricultural sector by creating more jobs will bring about inclusiveness in the process of industrialization in the country. However, the continuous low level share of the sector on GDP is associated with; implementation lags on ambitious plans with unrealistic goals, slow transforming economic structure which is dominated by agriculture, and competition from low priced manufactured imports from Asian economies.

REFERENCES

AfDB. (2012). *From billions to trillions: MDB contributions to financing development*. African Development Bank. http://pubdocs.worldbank.org/en/692914365543030711/dfi-ideaactionbooklet.pdf

AfDB. (2015). *The Role of Nascent Entrepreneurship in Driving Inclusive Economic Growth in North Africa*. Working Brief, North Africa Policy Series, African Development Bank. www.afdb.org/en/documents/document/north-africa-working-paper-the-role-of-nascententrepreneurship-indriving-inclusive-economic-growth-in-north-africa-90023/

African Development Bank. (1999). *African Development Report*. New York: Oxford University Press.

Balogun, M. J., & Mutahaba, G. (1999). Redynamising the African Civil Service for the Twentyfirst Century: Prospects for a Non-bureaucratic Structure. *Public Management Journal*, *51*(4), 520.

Balogun, M. J. (2002a). The Democratization and Development Agenda and the African Civil Service: Issues Resolved or Matters Arising. *International Review of Administrative Sciences*, *68*(4), 67–69. doi:10.1177/0020852302684003

Barzelay, M. (2001). *The New Public Management: Improving Research and Policy Dialogue*. Berkeley, CA: University of California Press.

Batley, R. (1999). The New Public Management in Developing Countries: Implications for Policy and Organizational Reform. *Journal of International Development*, *11*(5), 761–765. doi:10.1002/(SICI)1099-1328(199907/08)11:5<761::AID-JID616>3.0.CO;2-0

Boston, J. (2000). The challenge of evaluating systemic change: The case of public management reform. *International Public Management Journal*, *1*(3), 23–46. doi:10.1016/S1096-7494(00)00033-7

Caiden, G. E., & Sundaram, P. (2004). The specificity of public service reform. *Public Administration and Development*, *24*(5), 373–383. doi:10.1002/pad.329

Centre for Development and Enterprise. (2016). *An EPZ for the Nelson Mandela Bay Metro, Growth Series Report 7*. Retrieved from www.cde.org.za/wp-content/uploads/2016/04/7.EPZ.pdf

Clarke, J., & Wood, D. (2001). New public management and development: the case of public service reform in Tanzania and Uganda. In *The internationalization of public management: reinventing the third world state* (pp. 70–89). Cheltenham, UK: Edward Elgar. doi:10.4337/9781781952757.00011

Dodoo, R. (1996). The Core Elements of Civil Service Reform. *African Journal of Public Administration and Management*, *3*(2), 23–46.

Dwivedi, O. P. (2017). *Bureaucracy and the Alternatives in World Perspective*. London: Macmillan.

International Monetary Fund (IMF) & World Bank. (2000). *Zambia: preliminary document on the enhanced initiative for heavily indebted poor countries*. Washington, DC: IMF and World Bank.

Khaleghian, P., & Gupta, M. D. (2005). Public management and essential public health functions. *World Development*, *33I*(7), 1083–1099. doi:10.1016/j.worlddev.2005.04.001

Kirzner, I. M. (1997). Entrepreneurial Discovery and the Competitive Market Process: An Austrian Approach. *Journal of Economic Literature*, *35*(1), 60–85.

Lane, J. (2000). *New Public Management*. London: Routledge.

Larbi, G. A. (1999). *The New Public Management Approach and Crisis States*. UNRISD Discussion Paper 112. Geneva: United Nations Research Institute for Social Development.

Lienert, I., & Modi, J. (1997). *A decade of civil service reform in sub-Saharan Africa*. IMF Working Paper, WP/97/179. Washington, DC: International Monetary Fund.

Lin, J. Y., & Monga, C. (2013). *Comparative advantage: The silver bullet of industrial policy*. In J. E. S. Stiglitz & J. Y. Lin (Eds.), *The Industrial Policy Revolution I: The Role of Government Beyond Ideology* (pp. 19–38). London: Palgrave Macmillan.

Lindauer, D. L., & Nunberg, B. (1994). *Rehabilitating government: pay and employment reform in Africa*. Washington, DC: World Bank. doi:10.1596/0-8213-3000-4

Manning, N. (2001). The Legacy of New Public Management in developing countries. *International Review of Administrative Sciences*, *62*(2), 297–312. doi:10.1177/0020852301672009

McKenzie, D. (2015). *Identifying and spurring high-growth entrepreneurship: Experimental evidence from a business plan competition*. Policy Research Working Paper, No. 7391.

Minney, T. (2016). Exchanges give SMEs a helping hand. *African Banker Magazine*. Retrieved from www.africanbusinessmagazine.com/african-banker/exchanges-give-smeshelping-hand

Minogue, M., & McCourt, W. (2001). *Internationalization of Public Management*. Cheltenham, UK: Edward Elgar. doi:10.4337/9781781952757.00008

Minogue, M., Polidano, C., & Hulme, D. (Eds.). (1998). *Beyond the New Public Management: Changing Ideas and Practices in Governance*. Cheltenham, UK: Edward Elgar.

Nakusera, F., Kadhikwa, G., & Mushendami, P. (2008). *Enhancing the role of factoring and leasing companies in providing working capital to small and medium enterprises (SMEs) in Namibia*. BoN Occasional Paper, No. OP 3-2008, Research Department, Bank of Namibia.

Ntukamazina, D. A. (1996). Core Elements of Civil Service Reform. *Focus on Tanzania, AJPAM*, *5*(4), 6–10.

Pinkovskiy, M., & Xavier, S. (2009). *Parametric Estimations of the World Distribution of Income*. NBER Working Paper #15433.

Polidano, C., & Hulme, D. (1999). Public Management Reform in Developing Countries: Issues and Outcomes. *Public Management, 1*(1), 121–132. doi:10.1080/14719037800000007

Pollitt, C. (1990). *Managerialism and the Public Services: The Anglo-American Experience*. Oxford: Blackwell.

Sala-I-Martin, A., & Jay, K. (2010). Survival of private sector manufacturing establishments in Africa: The role of productivity and ownership. World Development, 37(3), 572-584.

Sindzingre, A. N. (2011). *The conditions for long-term growth in sub-Saharan Africa: China as a model, a constraint and an opportunity*. Cahiers du Centre Working Papers No. 9.

Stiglitz & J.Y. Lin. (2010). *The Industrial Policy Revolution I: The Role of Government beyond Ideology*. London: Palgrave Macmillan.

Woetzel, J. (2016). *Bridging Global Infrastructure Gaps*. McKinsey Global Institute. www.mckinsey.com/ind

World Economic Forum. (2010). *Global Competitiveness Report 2010-2011*. Geneva: WEF.

Yoshino, E. B. (2009). Clusters as a driving engine for FDI. *Economic Modelling, 26*(5), 934–945. doi:10.1016/j.econmod.2009.03.006

KEY TERMS AND DEFINITIONS

Entrepreneurship: Authors referring to the process of designing, launching and running a new business, which is often initially a small business. Entrepreneurship has also been described as the "capacity and willingness to develop, organize and manage a business venture along with any of its risks to make a profit" (McGhee, 2019).

Industrialization: Industrialization is a progressive transformation of an economic system from rudimentary productive methods to more complex manufacturing processes. It is a systematic change that aims to reshape the productive forces of a given country (Selden, 2016).

Chapter 17
Transitioning From Medium to Large Companies in the Circular Economy:
Key Factors for Colombian Companies

Rafael I. Perez-Uribe
https://orcid.org/0000-0001-9924-6657
Universidad EAN, Colombia

María Teresa Ramírez-Garzón
https://orcid.org/0000-0002-6319-3386
La Salle University, Colombia

Maria D.P. Ramirez-Salazar
https://orcid.org/0000-0002-9462-0897
Universidad EAN, Colombia

Carlos Salcedo-Perez
https://orcid.org/0000-0002-4433-5537
Universidad EAN, Colombia

ABSTRACT

In this chapter, some key factors of the companies were analyzed, which during the development of their activities marked positively or negatively their passage through different growth scenarios for the transition from a medium to a large company in a circular economy in Colombia. The methodology that served as the basis of analysis aimed at compiling the information in secondary sources of the growth data in the last five years (2014-2018) of 100 medium and large Colombians with more operational income. Focus explicitly was one those working with the concept of a circular economy, registered in public sources in Colombia, such as the superintendence of companies (Supersocieties) and EMIS database. After this analysis, the findings, conclusions, and steps of the analysis model were identified so that the transition

DOI: 10.4018/978-1-7998-5116-5.ch017

Copyright © 2020, IGI Global. Copying or distributing in print or electronic forms without written permission of IGI Global is prohibited.

between the different scenarios proposed would produce the expected results to the companies. The working hypothesis was that there are some key factors that allow a medium-sized company to become a large company in a circular economy.

INTRODUCTION

The difficulty to determine those factors and elements that condition or promote entrepreneurial growth increases when the perspective revolves around the different internal and external elements that could generate potential characteristics that promote such process and guarantee a sustainable expansion in the circular economy (Ruiz-Real, Uribe-Toril, De Pablo and Gázquez-Abad, 2018; Blázquez, Dorta and Verona, 2006).

Such reference seems obvious considering that expectations of managers and business owners about a circular economy are based on the analysis of the environment, looking for those external factors that condition the expansion as the best alternative to take advantage of the possibility to profit from a new segment or market. Besides, the business owner will tend to focus his/her internal efforts and economic resources on how to reach such market and how to face those external factors that condition his/her enterprise's growth, greatly strengthening internal areas such as marketing, sales and advertising, eventually leaving behind other processes that could be affected by such growth (Blázquez, *et al.,* 2006).

However, in recent years, new trends have emerged, whose analysis focus on the study of internal potentials that help explaining the position of the enterprise in a circular economy and how to make assertive use of the advantages that have been reached over time.

The objective of this chapter is to present some internal and external factors that promote the increase of sales of the most important Colombian enterprises in a lineal and circular economy; they will serve as reference to medium sized enterprises when becoming big enterprises (Mattos, Panzarin, Gomes & Ometto 2017; Montealegre and Calderón, 2007).

The methodology used was descriptive and the income data of the 100 medium and large Colombian companies with sustainable income in the last five years (2014-2018) were compiled. Data were taken from both companies in linear and circular economy, and twenty (20) of them, eight (8) with circular economy, were investigated, which were the factors by which they were stable in their sales in these years. Assuming that these are the factors that medium-sized companies must have to pass to large companies.

THEORETICAL FRAMEWORK

Circular Economy

In accordance with Bastante-Ceca, Fuentes-Bargues, Florin-Constantin, Iatu & Hufnagel, (2019) and The Ellen MacArthur Foundation (2013) the circular economy is based on the following principles: 1) the projection of products to generate zero waste, emphasizing on the optimization of products in their design to allow for their disassembly and reuse; 2) the projection of products at the moment of their design for reuse and 3) the use of renewable energy.

Geissdoerfer, Savaget, Bocken & Hultink (2016) define Circular Economy as a regenerative system in which resource input and waste, emission, and energy leakage are minimized by slowing, closing, and narrowing material and energy loops. This can be achieved through long-lasting design, maintenance, repair, reuse, remanufacturing, refurbishing, and recycling (Ellen MacArthur Foundation, 2015).

Ellen MacArthur Foundation (2017) states that "Industrial Investment in Europe is going through a long period of stagnation. Investments as a percentage of GDP are still well below the level seen before. In comparison, nominal levels of investment in the USA they were 16% higher than Europeans and Japanese investment levels 7% higher in 2015 versus 2008" (p.18).

For this foundation, the visible features of a circular economy are (pps. 20-27):

1. The circular economy offers a new, sizeable, and attractive area for industrial innovation and investment;
2. Nowadays, there is underinvestment in the circular economy, and there are several explanations for it: a) Generally, circular business models are different from linear business models; is not simply a matter of launching new products using a new technology to improve efficiency. It is almost always necessary to redefine roles throughout the value chain, both for suppliers and customers. Investing in the circular economy is different from another new investment in a particular area, such as clean technology. In the linear business model, it is a great step is to invest in new technologies, based on cost reduction, while investing in the circular economy model requires that enterprises think about the system as a whole. Although circular opportunities can use innovative technology, in many cases enterprises prefer to use technologies initially tested with additional technologies that have reached enough maturity, b) While for many enterprises the circular economy is attractive because of the forced intervention in their value chains, companies in a linear economy feel insecure when the transition to a circular economy could occur, c) Another barrier for enterprises to invest in circular economy, is government policies that instead of facilitating the from linear to circular, maintain complex policies that increase complexity and cost and therefore slow down progress towards circular models, c) In many cases, senior management lacks awareness of the costs and benefits of working in a circular business model; besides, there is a lack of skills and abilities necessary to implement circular business models, which further hinders the acceleration of the transition from linear to circular. However, the most important aspect is that companies can identify many circular opportunities with an underlying return, once the initial transition costs have been amortized;
3. Ten circular investment issues have been identified (Table 1).

MEDIUM AND BIG ENTERPRISES IN LATIN AMERICA AND COLOMBIA

Latin America

Micro, small and medium sized enterprises are an important component of Latin American industries due to their share of the total number of enterprises and jobs generation. However, their share of the GDP

Table 1. Description of next-wave circular economy investment themes

Next-Wave Circular Economy Investment Themes		Description
MOBILITY	Integrating mobility systems	Fully integration of public transportation systems with shared vehicles
	Designing and producing circular cars	Designing and producing zero emission cars with durable materials
	Remanufacturing car parts	Rollout remanufacturing of car parts at scale
FOOD	Deploying regenerative agricultural practices	Shifting towards an agricultural system that regenerates the soil and revitalizes ecosystems
	Closing nutrient loops	Scaling nutrient and energy recovery from various waste streams using anaerobic digestion or bio refineries
	Farming through indoor urban farms	Scaling hydroponic, aquaponic, and aeroponic farms in urban areas
	Developing next-wave protein sources	Developing new and efficient sources of protein from vegetables, bacteria, algae or insects
BUILT ENVIRONMENT	Designing and producing circular buildings	Design and produce multiuse highly modular and energy positive buildings made of durable non-toxic materials
	Closing building loops	Ramping up recycling and remanufacturing of building materials
	Developing circular cities	Integrating circularity into urban developments through innovative business models

Source. Ellen MacArthur Foundation (2017, p. 27)

of 25% is small in comparison to their numbers, opposite to the European Union where they account for 56% of the GDP on average (Correa *et al.,* 2018).

Micro, small and medium sized Latin American enterprises are characterized by their heterogeneous productive structure and products of low added value, generating a productivity gap and low share of exports when compared to their peers from the European Union. Such heterogeneity is one of the causes of the deep social inequality in Latin America, due to the differences in productivity from different industries and enterprises; this causes gaps in the capabilities, the adoption of new technologies, bargaining power, access to social media and in options of ascending mobility in the job, which in turn brings low competitiveness in such enterprises due to their low economic growth and reduced structural change (Correa, *et al.,* 2018, p. 10).

Regarding the formal sector of the economy in Latin America in 2016, 1.5% of it is composed by medium sized enterprises and 0.5% of it is composed by big enterprises. Most of them belong to the manufacturing industry and real estate activities, both for business and rent. In terms of jobs generation, the share of medium sized enterprises was 14% and 39% for big enterprises. Regarding sales or production, medium sized enterprises accounted for 12.6% and big enterprises accounted for 75.4% (Dini & Stumpo, 2019).

There are few cases of productive articulation both in networks and supply chain in Latin America, where the common situation is the market relation more than the cooperation between enterprises. Besides, Latin American countries have dependent economies, meaning that their accumulation process is determined by the role of big transnational corporations and the influx of foreign capital (Dini, *et al.,* 2019). Currently, in this globalized world, the rising presence of foreign enterprises occurs more because of a process of denationalization, concentration and economic concentration than for the creation of brand new enterprises (greenfield) and/or the development of new industrial sectors, this is the opposite to what used to happen in the 50's and 60's, decades in which big enterprises were considered as potential development agents since they were capable of investing important resources to modernize productive structures (Wainer, 2011, p. 102).

Regarding big enterprises, when it comes to the most developed environments, there is a high presence of technological enterprises, many of which started as startups or spin-offs from other big organizations, that could grow significantly. In Latin America, big enterprises have been increasingly working with startups during the last years; such growth has been occurring mainly in traditional activities based on natural resources, instead of growing based on activities related to technology, which require innovative efforts. Such technological efforts generally happen in headquarters or subsidiaries of transnational enterprises, and, in other cases, they come from external suppliers (Kantis, 2018).

Kantis (2018) states that in Latin America there are two big groups of countries that are different regarding the origin of their big enterprises. Countries such as Peru, Brazil and Ecuador compose the first group, characterized by the fact that over 60% are or local origin, and Argentina and Chile where over 50% of them are of local origin. The second group is composed by countries such as Colombia, Costa Rica, Mexico, Dominican Republic, Uruguay and Venezuela in which over 60% of their firms are or foreign origin.

Colombia

Micro, small and medium size enterprises account for over 40% of the Gross National Product, 96% of the enterprises, 9.8% of exports and generate over 17 million jobs, equivalent to 80% of all jobs in the country (Monterrosa, 2019; Padilla, 2018). Acccording to Dundon and Wilkinson (2009) cited by Pertuz, Leiva and Vega (2019) medium size enterprises are recognized for being an important source of job creation in a number of countries, contributing to the economic growth of such countries, therefore playing an important role in the economy.

Regarding the 1,000 biggest enterprises of the country in 2018, 80% of them reported profits, 78% registered an increase of sales, and 60% increased their net profits, while in 40% of them they decreased. In comparison to medium enterprises, big companies performed better that year since the former reported more losses, which means that they must work to strength certain topics related to financing, innovation and digital transformation, are the most important job generators (Correa, Leiva & Stumpo, 2018).

In terms of location, 78% of big enterprises are in the 3 most important regions of the country being them Bogota, Antioquia and the Western side of the country (Semana Review, 2018). According to Becerra (2019), on June 5th, 2019 the Ministry of Trade, Industry and Tourism of Colombia issued the Decree number 957, which will be in force starting December 2019 defining the new regulation to classify enterprises according to their size; before this Decree, the Law 905 issued in 2004 classified enterprises by size according to their number of workers, total assets expressed in current legal minimum monthly salaries and the value of their net sales yearly (Table 1).

The new classification of enterprises by size is based on the yearly income originated by their ordinary activities, expressed on Taxation Value Units and by the industry to which the enterprise belongs to whether it is manufacturing, service or trade (Ministerio de Comercio, Industria y Turismo, 2019) (Table 2).

Table 2. Clasification of Colombian enterprises by size according to Decree 957 issued in 2019

Size	Manufacturing	Service	Trade
Medium size	Those with income higher than 204,995 UVT (Taxation Value Unit) and lower than 1,736,565 UVT in one year.	Those with income higher than 131,951 UVT (Taxation Value Unit) and lower than 483,034 UVT in one year.	Those with income higher than 431,196 UVT (Taxation Value Unit) and lower than 2,160,692 UVT in one year.
Big	Those with income higher than 1,736,565 UVT (Taxation Value Unit) in one year	Those with income higher than 483,034 UVT (Taxation Value Unit) in one year.	Those with income higher than 2,160,692 UVT (Taxation Value Unit) in one year.

Source: The authors taking information from Decree 957 issued in 2019 by the Ministerio de Comercio Industria y Comercio (Colombian Ministry of Trade, Industry and Tourism)

Medium sized enterprises have certain characteristics both in Colombia and in the international field, which combined with the right strategy helps them reach their goals. According to Fernandez de Tejada and Saavedra-Robledo (2014) such characteristics are:

- Enterprises with higher flexibility, disposition to change and adaptation capacity. This is possible because of their flexible organizational structure, generic job positions and reduced command structure, which favors decision making and the efficiency of the organization. This is the opposite to what happens in big enterprises, where the organizational structure is bureaucratic and less flexible;
- Resource and capabilities adaptation and lower accumulation since there are no economies of scale and learning curves are flexible. Medium sized enterprises have the capability to easily adapt to changes in the environment;
- Higher disposition to take risk since their founding leaders have as characteristics their goal orientation, higher internal control and a high level of commitment towards their work and workers among others;
- People who work in medium sized enterprises have an entrepreneurial orientation and are more open to new ideas whether they are generated inside or outside the enterprise;
- Lack of differentiation or specialization in many areas of the organization; strict labor division is scarce as well as the functions developed. There is low horizontal differentiation, few hierarchical levels in their vertical structure, prioritizing lateral relations over norms as integration mechanism;
- Human resource is higher qualified, though not specialized, being qualified as workers, directors, business promoters and businesspeople.

Key Factors for Entrepreneurial Success in Circular Economy

González, Aponte & Salazar (2015), found that the processes in management of organizational learning center around induction and training related to job positions, and the solution of specific problems according to their operating activities. The prevailing learning methodologies are self-learning, experience sharing and team learning. Human resources are selected and hired based on their working competencies, and employees are evaluated based on management indicators; feedback and decisions are taken according to the results obtained in the evaluation.

Hernández-Villanueva & Mosquera-Rodas (2016) concluded that the organizational structure must be clearly defined and updated; they apply strategic planning, just in time and total quality management (to obtain quality certificates). The quality management system has allowed them being more competitive and has help them to upgrade technologies, therefore reducing labor and costs. In those who were working in a circular economy, they were concentrating on the 3R policy (reduce-reuse-recycle) based on waste hierarchy concept (where landfill and waste incineration are regarded as the least favorable options) is supplemented by product life expansion alternatives (repair-recovery-refurbishrepurpose-remanufacture).

Parra & Calderón (2013) emphasized on strategic positioning, finding that the process of training is part of a real policy of employees' training and development, as a contribution to the generation of competitiveness in the organizations. The former is evidenced by the integration existent between training policies, plans and programs, which are aligned with the strategic guiding of the enterprises analyzed; this is reflected in the productivity and quality of their products and services.

Another key factor around the word is the importance of the good name of the enterprise, this means the projected image. It has been proven that the consumer's perception about the product of an enterprise is an important factor; that is why enterprises spend a good share of their budget in advertising, which, according to empirical studies, impacts positively an enterprise's profits, market value and growth (Saionnz-Ochoa, 2001; Aaker, 1991).

Taweesak, King, Thabhatr, & King (2019) state that key factors for business success in circular economy are classified in four big areas: Strategy, clean Production, Technology and Entrepreneurship. [1] Strategy refers to making decisions that add value to the enterprise, establishing market objectives, establishing costs, operations management and having a different perspective of the business; [2] clean production refers to the Core Business, y which it is important to consider: that the production process must be modern and innovative; the knowledge about the customers' needs; and the networks available to make businesses; [3] technology refers to how to operate, which shows the importance of being aware of the changing environment of new technologies and their development and implementation inside the organization. [4] entrepreneurship refers to the dynamism and actions that lead to the creation of new products, market strategies, processes or business models in circular economy.

A number of experts on organizational culture, among them Pérez-Uribe (2012) and Basargekar, Iyer & Bhatia (2019), emphasize on the importance to build that distinctive factor that characterize them for having a friendship and trust environment, where impartiality, objectiveness, respect, collaboration and credibility become factors that are present in the daily activities of the enterprise. Great Place to Work is a worldwide recognized certification, which calculates scores for enterprises, obtaining a ranking of the best to work for every year.

The importance of social media for enterprises' success is no secret in this era of new technologies; among the most important benefits for business are the cost-benefit relation, since networks imply appreciable saving in marketing costs (Mukherjee & Hollenbaugh, 2019).

The Asociación de Jóvenes Emprendedores (Association of Young Entrepreneurs) (AJE, 2004) state that the main factors for entrepreneurial in a circular economy success are a good product or service, market knowledge, qualified human resources and the administration of a regenerative system in which resource input and waste, emission, and energy leakage are minimised by slowing, closing, and narrowing material and energy loops.

For Diaz-Cardiel (2012), the most important factor for business success is the constant surveillance of the economic situation of the countries where the enterprise operates and where it as its headquarters, this aimed at taking the best investment decisions and to make the necessary adjustments to operations.

The relevance of Internet is another factor every enterprise must consider (Latorre, 2018). This expert consultant as well as Saionz-Ochoa (2001) state the importance of reputation and the close relation between enterprises and the press, since the business success must be communicated.

Eco innovation is related to the need to use new consumption patterns, to manufacture fewer polluting products using environment friendly technologies. To start a path towards business sustainability is a big challenge for enterprises; those that have already started have realized the social, environmental and financial benefits, as well as the good reputation it comes with it (Solá, Farreny and Cormenzana, 2017).

The path towards reinvention or renovation is suggested by creating innovation-oriented cultures, meaning the singular way by which each enterprise is different from others and that encourages them to be creative, proactive and innovative (Collins and Porras, 2011; Chuang, Chun, Chien & Hsiung, 2019). It is here when those in the base of the organizational pyramid must be called to participated to listen to their ideas and to be participants of the changes generated inside their enterprises. A number of enterprises have been blind and do not foresee changes in technological and demographic trends. Hence, Oppenheimer (2009) insists not only on creating a culture but also on investing on education if a country wants to end poverty.

According to Kiernan (1996) and Geissdoerfer *et al.,* (2016), there are some commandments for XXI Century managers to be successful. Among those most important are: [1] being on a constant innovation environment within a circular economy philosophy, know itself and analyze the organization to find its most strategic assets to boost them; [2] being fast, not making an excessive number of diagnostics and studies to make a decision since the competition might make decisions faster and overtake the market; [3] Break barriers and change paradigms or modify the way of doing things, with more flexible schedules, inspirational compensations, and disruptive ways to develop products; [4] getting everybody to interiorize organizational learning, human talent is more important every time, so it is important to train it and improve its competences; a dynamic and innovative enterprise is one that is developing at the best its workers' potential; [5] to measure performance, since the operation of the enterprise needs to be measured; it is possible to find out mistakes, necessary investments and areas to improve based on good management indicators. A permanent and constructive measurement allows a continuous improvement.

Innovation is one of the factors that regularly repeats as a factor of business success in circular economy, even more when it is open collaborative innovation. More than ever, enterprises now are aware that they must reinvent themselves. In order to last and being successful, an enterprise must adopt innovation through the whole organization, in the reshape of the value chain, the products, the services, the market strategy, the structure, the advertisement, the customer relations, and any aspect related to the management of the enterprise in circular economy (Ellen Macarthur Foundation, 2017; Ramírez-Salazar, 2016; Ramírez-Salazar, 2015; Hanaysha, & Hilman, 2015; Dávila, Epstein & Shelton, 2008; Moraleda, 2004; Rodríguez - López,1999).

Important factors to take into consideration as key for business success, stating that the most important is being passionate for one's job. It is necessary to hire people who are committed to the organization; therefore, they will use their talent at their best and be happy at their jobs (OBS, 2019).

Besides, another necessary factor is persistence, the first time is not always the winning time, all entrepreneurs have had hard time, it is always necessary to persevere to reach goals and get products positioned in the mind of consumers. "Changing to a circular economy requires an integrated vision that focuses on long-term change or transition. Thus, the change to a circular economy will lead to new business models and value chains. Consequently, this affects the design, production, use, and disposal processes, as well as the collection of products and materials for reuse" (De Mattos and Meira de Albuquerque, 2018, p.1).

Customer-oriented service, service management, innovation of services and corporate social responsibility are the factors that drive customer satisfaction; service perceived quality and the organizations' reputation are the factors that make service enterprises successful, therefore that study becomes an important milestone for Chines enterprises to be always aware of the service provided (Zhang, Jin, Wang, Goh, & He, 2016).

Brand value is a determinant factor of business success (Saionnz-Ochoa, 2001). An enterprise whose brand is prestigious has an advantage over its competitors, its assets worth increases more, its products and services promotion is easier and therefore the customer loyalty increases, resulting in a profitable enterprise due to the permanent income coming from a successful operation (Hanaysha, & Hilman, 2015).

Managerial Skills and Cognitive Patterns of Entrepreneurs are a key factor for business success; according to Sánchez Garcia (2014), the growth of sales and size are caused by the entrepreneurs' motivations and objectives to expand their businesses or keep a size with which they feel comfortable. A good leader positions his/her enterprise in the position he/she wishes to. Examples of the former are found in family enterprises, which make up between 80 to 90% of all enterprises of the world, are an important component of GDP and contribute to the growth in the number of jobs in every country (Peterson-Whitorn, 2015; Serrano, Quezada & Márquez 2016).

Several activities of the best companies in the circular economy could be observed below (Table 3): 1) Disruptive innovation in their products according to market needs, 2) Development of clean processes taking into account the philosophy of the circular economy, 3) recovery of value in the inputs used, 4) No contamination of particles per million and decontamination of noise and 0 emissions in the use of engines, 5) use of recycled content and recyclable materials in their products, prolonging the life of the product through leasing and payment for use, and the introduction of return schemes in their supply chain, 6) Use of technologies that treat wastewater contaminated by industrial processes, not only turning them into clean water, but even producing biogas that can be used to generate clean energy, 7) Converting old tires and other rubber waste into something called micronized rubber powder, which can then be used in a wide variety of applications, from tires to plastics, asphalt and building material, 8) Smartphones and tablets have changed the way many people live and work, but their appetite for the last essential device has created a mountain of discarded devices. Develop reuse processes of the devices themselves and / or their components, 9) Management of recycling stations to divert recyclable material from a landfill, to save metric tons of carbon emissions, 10) Conversion and reuse of old materials into new products and sustainable applications and 11) Recycling and / or reuse of returnable packaging and reuse of product leftovers in new products.

HYPOTHESES

"There are some key factors that allow a medium-sized company to become a large company in a circular economy."

Table 3. The 11 most successful circulars enterprises of the world

Company Name	Description
Winnow	Winnow used to smart meters measuring electricity and water. But now British start-up Winnow has developed smart meters that analyse our trash. They are used in commercial kitchens to measure what food gets thrown away, and then identify ways to reduce waste. Up to a fifth of food purchased can be wasted in some kitchens, and Winnow has managed to cut that in half in hundreds of kitchens across 40 countries, saving its customers over $25 million each year in the process. That is the equivalent of preventing one meal from going to waste every seven seconds. This innovation earned Winnow the Circular Economy Tech Disruptor Award.
DyeCoo	The textiles industry uses vast quantities of water and chemicals and produces huge amounts of toxic waste, which is a major problem in countries like China, India, Bangladesh, Vietnam and Thailand. But Dutch company DyeCoo has developed a process of dyeing cloth that uses no water at all, and no chemicals other than the dyes themselves. It uses highly pressurised "supercritical" carbon dioxide, halfway between a liquid and a gas, that dissolves the dye and carries it deep into the fabric. The carbon dioxide then evaporates, and is in turn recycled and used again. 98% of the dye is absorbed by the cloth, giving vibrant colours. And because the cloth doesn't need to dry, the process takes half the time, uses less energy, and even costs less. The company already has partnerships with major brands like Nike and IKEA.
Close the Loop	This Australian company has spent more than a decade recovering value from old printer cartridges and soft plastics. Their new innovation turns these materials into roads. The products are mixed in with asphalt and recycled glass to produce a higher-quality road surface that lasts up to 65% longer than traditional asphalt. In every kilometre of road laid, the equivalent of 530,000 plastic bags, 168,000 glass bottles and the waste toner from 12,500 printer cartridges is used in the mix. So instead of ending up in landfill, all that waste is given a new life, getting us where we need to go.
Enerkem	Using trash to run your car may sound like something from Back to the Future, but Canadian firm Enerkem has turned it into reality. Their technology extracts the carbon from trash that can't be recycled. It then takes five minutes to turn the carbon into a gas that can be used to make biofuels like methanol and ethanol, as well as chemicals which can be used in thousands of everyday products. The city of Edmonton, for example, now reuses 90% of its waste, saving more than 100,000 metric tons of landfill every year.
Schneider Electric	French-based Schneider Electric, which specialises in energy management and automation, won the Award for the Circular Economy Multinational. Employing 142,000 people in more than 100 countries, it uses recycled content and recyclable materials in its products, prolongs product lifespan through leasing and pay-per-use, and has introduced take-back schemes into its supply chain. Circular activities now account for 12% of its revenues, and will save 100,000 metric tons of primary resources from 2018-2020.
Cambrian Innovation	This US firm's EcoVolt technology treats wastewater contaminated by industrial processes, not just turning it into clean water, but even producing biogas that can be used to generate clean energy. Cambrian Innovation has nine plants across the US, which have treated an estimated 300 million litres of wastewater.
Lehigh Technologies	This Atlanta firm turns old tyres and other rubber waste into something called micronized rubber powder, which can then be used in a wide variety of applications from tyres to plastics, asphalt and construction material. Five hundred million new tyres have been made using its products, earning it the Award for Circular Economy SME.
HYLA Mobile	Smartphones and tablets have changed the way many of us live and work, but our appetite for the latest must-have gadget has created a mountain of discarded devices. HYLA Mobile works with many of the world's leading manufacturers and service providers to repurpose and reuse either the devices themselves, or their components. It's estimated that more than 50 million devices have been reused, making $4 billion for their owners and stopping 6,500 tons of e-waste ending up in landfill.
TriCiclos	People's Choice Award winner TriCiclos began in Chile in 2009 with the stated aim of working towards a "world without waste". Since then it has built and operated the largest network of recycling stations in South America, diverting 33,000 metric tons of recyclable material from landfill and saving over 140,000 metric tons of carbon emissions.
Miniwiz	For the founder of Miniwiz, Arthur Huang, there is no such thing as trash. He is an evangelist for upcycling - turning old materials into something new. As he admits, this isn't a new idea - until the 20th century reusing whatever was lying around was the norm. But he is taking this principle to new levels, with the scientists and engineers in his Miniwiz Trash Lab inventing over 1,000 new sustainable materials and applications. The Trashpresso machine is the ultimate expression of sustainable upcycling. It is a mobile upcycling plant that can be transported in two shipping containers to its customers. Once there, it turns 50kg of plastic bottles an hour into a low-cost building material, using no water, and only solar power.
AB inBev	Proving that innovation in the circular economy isn't confined to small tech start-ups, the world's largest brewer wants 100% of its product to be in packaging that's returnable or made from majority-recycled content by 2025. Already nearly half of its drinks are sold in returnable glass bottles, and AB InBev is working with suppliers and customers to increase that. It has also launched a protein drink made from spent grains from the brewing process (which previously were only resold as animal feed).

Source. Adaptation of the authors of Thornton (2019).

METHODOLOGY

In order to identify key factors for success in circular economy for enterprises operating in Colombia, the authors gathered data from the 100 enterprises with the highest operating income in the 2014-2018 period. Such data was taken from the EMIS database. From such data, the authors selected enterprises with constant positive growth of income, especially those who were working in circular economy (Aes Chivor, Colgate Palmolive, Positiva Compania de Seguros S.A., Solla S.A., Nestle De Colombia S.A., Tecnoquimicas S.A., Colombina S.A., Cerro Matoso S.A.,) and researched about the factors that influenced such growth (Table 4).

FINDINGS

Common factors of success of these enterprises, both those who were working in a linear economy and those who were working in a circular economy (Table 4), that have allowed them to have a sustained increase in their income, have been based on four scenarios with a set of concrete activities:

Table 4. Twenty Colombian enterprises with constant income growth in the 2014-2018 period

Enterprises Name	Industry	Growth of Operating Income 2014-2018
Metrokia S.A.	Used Car Dealers; New Car Dealers; Automotive Repair and Maintenance; Automotive Parts, Accessories, and Tire Store; Motor Vehicle and Motor Vehicle Parts and Supplies Merchant Wholesalers.	27.84%
Distracom S.A.	General Freight Trucking; Gasoline Stations.	21.77%
Aes Chivor & Cia S C A E S P (Aes Chivor)	Electric Power Transmission, Control, and Distribution; Electric Power Generation.	20.16%
Colgate Palmolive Compañía	Internet Publishing and Broadcasting and Web Search Portals; Miscellaneous Nondurable Goods Merchant Wholesalers; Soap, Cleaning Compound, and Toilet Preparation Manufacturing.	19.79%
Cepsa Colombia S.A.	Natural Gas Extraction; Crude Petroleum Extraction	19.58%
Cbi Colombiana S.A.	Architectural, Engineering, and Related Services; Other Heavy and Civil Engineering Construction.	18.76%
Gunvor Colombia C I S.A.S.	Petroleum and Petroleum Products Merchant Wholesalers (except Bulk Stations and Terminals)	17.42%
Positiva Compania de Seguros S.A.	Direct Life Insurance Carriers	14.68%
Universidad Nacional De Colombia	Educational Services	14.66%
Entidad Promotora De Salud Famisanar S.A.S	Justice, Public Order, and Safety Activities	14.41%
Solla S.A.	Scientific and Technical Consulting Services; Animal Food Manufacturing; Farm Product Raw Material Merchant Wholesalers	13.08%
Nestle De Colombia S.A.	Soft Drink Manufacturing; Miscellaneous Food Manufacturing; Coffee and Tea Manufacturing; Dairy Product Manufacturing.	11.41%
Masser S.A.S.	Gasoline Stations	11.12%
Tecnoquimicas S.A.	Pharmaceutical Preparation Manufacturing; Drugs and Druggists' Sundries Merchant Wholesalers.	11.02%
Cooperativa Nacional De Droguistas Detallistas	Drugs and Druggists' Sundries Merchant Wholesalers.	9.52%
Colombina S.A.	Miscellaneous Food Manufacturing; Chocolate and Confectionery Manufacturing; Bakeries and Tortilla Manufacturing	9.13%
Entidad Promotora De Salud Sanitas S.A.S	Health Care and Social Assistance	8.41%
Banco Caja Social S.A.	Commercial Banking	8.10%
Cerro Matoso S A	Copper, Nickel, Lead, and Zinc Mining	8.09%
Almacenes La 14 S.A.	Pharmacies and Drug Stores; Grocery Stores	7.90%

Source. The authors based on data taken from EMIS (2019)

First Scenario

When demand exceeded installed and used capacity of the enterprise. That was the moment when the enterprise's production was insufficient to satisfy the quantities demanded by the market, creating a perfect time for growth or for a horizontal integration, searching for an opportunity with a higher Investment/Return on Investment rate in less time. Activities for this first scenario are:

- Development of a financial and logistic supporting plan until reaching production levels able to satisfy the demand. Once having a captive market, they have taking care of it, and in case expectations had not been fulfilled they have considered the possibility to explore the alternative of adopting a horizontal integration strategy in order to satisfy the demand in lesser time taking advantage of the installed capacity at a competitive cost;
- They have a competitive product, and have forecast its growth, not only to satisfy their current market, but also to evaluate the possibility to reach new markets. When their products have not been competitive in the market, they have work to innovate them to position their brand or they have evaluated to change drastically the essential product given the fact that the growth of the demand could have originated because of entry barriers in the market.

Second Scenario

To explore new markets: this opportunity occurs when the initial market demand is fully satisfied and the alternative to grow was to increase the initial market segmentation to a bigger one with common and more specific needs that allows the enterprise to select and gain this new market. The activities enterprises need to perform in this second scenarios are:

- To establish the new market: when getting into new market segments, specific about the opportunities available from current goods and services were conducted. Service models were changed in order to reach the new segment, evaluating if the enterprise was the market leader. Those who lead the market took advantage to evaluate a vertical integration;
- To develop competitiveness researches of the products that satisfy the market needs prone to reach, and they turn weaknesses into strengths of the product used to reach the new market.

Third Scenario

In this scenario, the enterprise identified an unsatisfied market; a new product could be used to reach this market, increasing the current and potential market. The activities to perform in this third scenario are: 1) Investing in research: defined when there is the possibility to invest in current markets in order to increase the market share and 2) Evaluating the market: the following questions were answer: is my current market fully satisfied with the good or service offered by my enterprise? Does the market have any other requirements regarding the good or service offered? Does the good or service offered covers all needs of the market or can the enterprise find new strategies to increase the market share either with a new product or in a new market?

Fourth Scenario

Some enterprises concentrated on an innovative product; this was an opportunity in which the product exceed the satisfaction of needs in an unexplored market with new goods or services. The activities to perform in this fourth scenario are:

- **Transition from linear economy to circular economy:** Senior management must consider that the change from a linear economy to a circular economy requires an integrated vision that focuses on long-term change or transition. Therefore, the change to a circular economy will lead to new business models and value chains. Consequently, this affects the design, production, use and disposal processes, as well as the collection of products and materials for reuse;
- **Clean Technology:** Enterprises evaluated the existence of technology suitable to produce goods and services; technology was implemented when available;
- **Innovation:** Enterprises research about the needs of the market, possible solutions to satisfy such needs and developed goods and services tailored to those needs;
- **Development of the strategic plan:** Enterprises develop a diagnostic of both the internal and external environments and developed a strategic plan consequently. Thus, they guarantee having a realistic analysis of the situation that allows the reformulation of forecasts and objectives to surpass the expectations of the market, product and investors, defining new mega goals from the vision and a detailed financial analysis that points out to an opportune and satisfactory return of investment. This includes the criteria that if production grows it is necessary to fulfill all legal requirements, to support the core business and to fulfill financial objectives;
- **Market study:** Enterprises develop international market researches aimed at increase the expected growth, being clear about the potential market and sales expectations, without forgetting the behavior of the current regional market;
- **Investment:** Enterprises perform an adequate study of the necessary amount to invest and its sources, being consistent with the risk to take according to the expectations that arise from the market study and strategic planning;
- **Financial Forecast:** Enterprises performed both an optimistic and pessimistic forecast to have a clear relation of time and fulfilment of goals in order to make decisions;
- **Human Talent:** Enterprises need to have qualified, competent, committed workers. Some of the people with the required competencies do not always come from inside the organization, so external human talent who can contribute from a similar experience is evaluated.

SOLUTIONS AND RECOMMENDATIONS

The suggested solutions and recommendations for senior management of medium-sized companies that want to jump to a large company, from a linear economy to a circular economy, are to develop each activity stated in the conclusions and prioritize them according to their sector and strategic direction: 1) Expand the value of resources, which is about collecting or obtaining materials and resources that are normally wasted, to transform them into new forms of value (value creation), 2) Formulate, implement and periodically evaluate a strategic address guided by principles and values of the circular economy, 3) Be vigilant to the changes in the external variables in what concerns the technological, social, political, legal, environmental, among other variables depending on each economic sector, 4) Adapt permanently and whenever the organizational structure is required adjusted to the strategies developed, always thinking about the aspects related to the circular economy, 5) A financial forecast that takes into consideration the required investment to implement the project from the transition from a linear to a circular economy, 6) The management of automation, the simplification of processes and the use of clean technology should be permanent policies of the companies, 7) The necessary conditions must be worked on so that all workers carry out their tasks in an innovative way and putting the philosophy of the circular economy into practice, 8) Development of customer service and after-sales processes that promote their loyalty towards the company's brands.

FUTURE RESEARCH DIRECTION

Develop a follow-up of research in the companies investigated, to the initiative launched by Colombian entrepreneurs that promotes the transition to the circular economy and will be unique in Latin America, stipulated in the framework of the 75 years of the National Association of Industrialists (ANDI)[1]. This is Vision 30/30, a packaging and packaging management project that aims to enable the country's productive sector to lead the necessary actions for regulatory compliance established in Resolution 1407 of 2018 of the Ministry of Environment (Ministerio de ambiente, 2018), which sets the commitments and goals for the use of containers and packaging placed on the market through any marketing channel (Revista Dinero, 2019).

"Vision 30/30 is the way in which we are preparing to create the conditions to improve the levels of use of packaging and packaging waste so that they do not affect the environment more", said Carlos Herrera, Vice President of Development Sustainable Andi. The project stipulates that, by 2030, companies in the country must comply with the use of 30% of the material used in packaging. To verify this compliance, the first measurement will be carried out with a cut-off as of December 31, 2021, at which time companies must show a 10% progress in this matter (Revista Dinero, 2019).

CONCLUSION

In general, the companies analyzed can be inferred that Medium sized enterprise have not identified the right moment to grow neither which factors to evaluate (demand, new markets, circular economy). Knowledge and implementation of these factors that guarantee a successful transition towards a big enterprise are empiric and undocumented.

Growth itself is not only the result of a decision, but also a consequence in an enterprise that is aligned to the market situation and internal results that merge to make that growth successful. Thus, it is possible to find: first, the moment of the enterprise for its innovation processes and financial capabilities; and second, the target market that can be reached with the product offered. This study describes the four ideal scenarios, however, it cannot be assured that they will occur exactly as described; besides, a mix scenario can occur, or the process might be unsuccessful due to unpredictable variables in the market behavior.

According to the theoretical review and findings in researched enterprises, it is stated that the key factors of success for the transition from a medium to a big sized enterprise in a circular economy in Colombia are:

- Value creation: This factor is aimed at reducing economic losses and structural waste, in terms of recycling of materials and energy based on waste (Mattos, *et al.,* 2017). Expand the value of resources, which is about collecting or obtaining materials and resources that are normally wasted, to transform them into new forms of value (Vanegas, *et al.,* 2018);
- An accurate strategic planning guided by principles and values of the circular economy, especially a commercial strategy is one of the main factors of success since a precise knowledge of the market and local cultures guides the enterprise to understand the real needs of each region and a tailored advertising for each market (Elston, 2002; García-García, 2004);
- The adequate identification of external factors that generate a direct impact to the grow of medium enterprises in a way that they can design strategies to mitigate the negative effects of such factors (Perez-Uribe, 2018) and a marketing research with a number of variables to identify in detail the market to reach, increasing the possibility to have an impact and to achieve the expected market share (Montoya, Montoya & Castellanos, 2010);
- An adequate organizational structure that includes the administrative and clean productive processes, aligned with the strategic management with which medium enterprises can guarantee a successful process of transition and growth and move from a linear economy to a circular economy (Genovese, Acquaye, Figueroa and Koh, 2017; Salazar, Guerrero, Machado & Cañedo, 2009; Jensen & Meckling, 1976);
- A financial forecast that takes into consideration the required investment to implement the project from the transition from a linear to a circular economy and the required labor from the starting moment until reaching breakeven point (De Abreu and Ceglia, 2018; Moscoso, Sepúlveda, García & Restrepo, 2012; Levine, 1997);
- In order to guarantee control of growth, it is necessary to constantly evaluate all internal processes of the organization, focusing on automation and process simplification. Thus, clean technology becomes a must (OECD, 2015);
- An Innovation-oriented culture that includes paradigm change and reinvention at every moment, according to the needs of the time; this way, enterprises evolve and become referents for their new goods and services (OBS Business School, 2019; Duréndez & Garcia, 2008);
- Customer service and after sales service that promotes customer loyalty are relevant factors that help enterprises to keep its stakeholders loyal to their brands (Saionnz-Ochoa, 2001);
- Organizational culture aimed at the generation of work with circular economy philosophy is an influential factor that helps the enterprise to be known for its service and shared vision, showing at all moments that it is the best place to work; this creates feelings of gratitude in the society towards those enterprises that have their workers happy, developing all their talent, having a positive impact in their families and communities (Oghazi and Mostaghel, 2018; Calderón, Naranjo & Álvarez, 2010; Mendoza & Ortiz, 2006; Jerez, 2001; Becker, Huselid, Pickus & Spratt, 1997; Barney, 1991);
- The research shows that clean production and sustainable servuction are not key factors of business success yet in all the companies investigated. However, more and more every time, customers want environment and society friendly enterprises; there are some cases of eco innovation and circular economy that are friendly with the planet, and therefore, these factors will be relevant in the future (Chavarro, *et al.,* 2017; Urquiola, Zulueta & Llano, 2017; Lieder and Rashid, 2016; Tovar, Perez-Uribe & Ocampo-Guzmán, 2015);

- Hypotheses are confirmed since the theoretical search did not find explicit information about key factors of success for a transition from a medium sized to a big enterprise in Colombia in circular economy. In Colombia, the first steps are being taken to enter the theme of the circular economy. This chapter pretends to be a concrete contribution to point out the factors that should be considered when making the transition from medium to large company from a linear economy to a circular economy.

REFERENCES

Aaker, D. A. (1991). *Managing Brand Equity*. New York, NY: Simon & Schuster.

AJE. (2004). *Análisis de los Factores que Contribuyen al Éxito de Proyectos Empresariales*. Retrieved from http://www.ajeimpulsa.es/documentos/banco_recursos/recurso_13.pdf

Barney, J. (1991). Firms Resources and Sustained Competitive Advantage. *Journal of Management, 17*(1), 99–120. doi:10.1177/014920639101700108

Basargekar, P., Iyer, R., & Bhatia, A. (2019). Assessing Employees' Perception Related to Entrepreneurial Climate in their Organization & its Impact on their Perception Related to Organization's Potential Success. *Journal of Asia Entrepreneurship and Sustainability, 15*(1), 3–66. doi:10.22622/jaes.2019.15-1.01

Bastante-Ceca, M.J., Fuentes-Bargues, J.L., Florin-Constantin, M., Iatu, C. & Hufnagel, L. (2019). *Introductory Chapter: The Need to Change the Paradigm - Sustainability and Development at the 21st Century*. Doi:10.5772/intechopen.90655

Becker, B. E., Huselid, M. A., Pickus, P. S., & Spratt, M. F. (1998). Los RH como fuente de valor para los accionistas: Investigación y recomendaciones. In D. Ulrich, M. R. Losey y G. Lake (Eds), El futuro de la dirección de recursos humanos (pp. 246-259). Barcelona: Gestión 2000.

Blázquez, S. F., Dorta, V. J. A., & Verona, M. M. C. (2006). Factores del crecimiento empresarial. Especial referencia a las pequeñas y medianas empresas. *INNOVAR. Revista de Ciencias Administrativas y Sociales, 16*(28), 43-56. Retrieved from: https://www.redalyc.org/pdf/818/81802804.pdf

Calderón Hernández, G., Naranjo Valencia, J. C., & Álvarez Giraldo, C. M. (2010). Gestión humana en la empresa colombiana: sus características, retos y aportes. Una aproximación a un sistema integral. *Cuadernos de Administración, 23*(41).

Chavarro, D., Vélez, M. I., Tovar, G., Montenegro, I., Hernández, A., & Olaya, A. (2017). Los objetivos de Desarrollo Sostenible en Colombia y el aporte de la ciencia, la tecnología y la innovación. Colciencias. *Documentos de trabajo No. 1*. Retrieved from: https://www.colciencias.gov.co/sites/default/files/objetivos_de_desarrollo_sostenible_en_colombia_y_el_aporte_de_la_ctei_2.pdf

Chesbrough, H. (2009). *Open Innovation, The New Imperative for Creating and Profiting from Technology*. Harvard Business School Press.

Chuang, L., Chung, Y., Chien, M., & Hsiung, P. (2019). Culture and Entrepreneurial Opportunity Recognition: Evidence from GEM and WVS. *Advances in Management & Applied Economics, 9*(4).

Correa, F., Leiva, V., & Stumpo, G. (2018). Mipymes y heterogeneidad estructural en América Latina. In M. Dini & G. Stumpo (Eds.), *MIPYMES en América Latina. Un frágil desempeño y nuevos desafíos para las políticas de fomento* (pp. 9–34). Santiago, Chile: United Nations.

Dávila, T., Epstein, M., & Shelton, R. (2008). *Making Innovation Work, How to Manage It, Measure It, and Profit from It*. Seventh Printing & Pearson Education.

De Abreu, M. C. S., & Ceglia, D. (2018). On the implementation of a circular economy: The role of institutional capacity-building through industrial symbiosis. *Resources, Conservation and Recycling*, *2018*(138), 99–109. doi:10.1016/j.resconrec.2018.07.001

De Mattos, C. A., & Meira de Albuquerque, T. L. (2018). Enabling Factors and Strategies for the Transition Toward a Circular Economy (CE). *Sustainability*, *2018*(10), 4628. doi:10.3390u10124628

Diaz-Cardiel, J. (2012). *Éxito con o sin crisis*. Lid Editorial Empresarial 2012. Retrieved from: https://books.google.com.co/books/about/%C3%89xito_con_o_sin_crisis.html?id=swdA6QEHmx0C&printsec=frontcover&source=kp_read_button&redir_esc=y#v=onepage&q&f=false

Dini, M., & Stumpo, G. (2019). Mipymes en América Latina: un frágil desempeño y nuevos desafíos para las políticas de fomento. Síntesis, Documentos de Proyectos (LC/TS.2019/20), Santiago, Economic Commission for Latin America and the Caribbean (ECLAC).

Duréndez, A., & Garcia, D. (2008). *Innovative Culture, Management Control Systems and Performance in Young SMEs*. Academic Press.

Ellen MacArthur Foundation. (2013). *Towards a Circular Economy: Business rationale for an accelerated transition*. Ellen MacArthur Foundation. Retrieved from https://www.ellenmacarthurfoundation.org/assets/downloads/publications/Ellen-MacArthur-Foundation-Towards-the-Circular-Economy-vol.1.pdf

Ellen MacArthur Foundation. (2015). *Towards a Circular Economy: Business rationale for an accelerated transition*. Ellen MacArthur Foundation. Retrieved from https://www.ellenmacarthurfoundation.org/assets/downloads/TCE_Ellen-MacArthur-Foundation_9-Dec-2015.pdf

Ellen Macarthur Foundation. (2017). *Achieving 'Growth Within'*. Retrieved from https://www.ellenmacarthurfoundation.org/assets/downloads/publications/Achieving-Growth-Within-20-01-17.pdf

Elston, J. A. (2002). *An Examination of the Relationship Between Firm Size, Growth, and Liquidity in the Neuer Markt*. Discussion paper 15/02, Economic Research Centre of the Deustche Bank. Retrieved from: https://www.bundesbank.de/Redaktion/EN/Downloads/Publications/Discussion_Paper_1/2002/2002_07_04_dkp_15.pdf?__blob=publicationFile

Fernández de Tejada, V., & Saavedra-Robledo, I. (2014). La gestión ética en las medianas empresas. *ResearchGate*. Retrieved from: https://www.researchgate.net/publication/28202482

García-García, J. (2004). *La Ley del Efecto Proporcional: una aplicación al estudio del crecimiento empresarial asturiano* (1993-1999). X Congresso Contabilidade, Estoril, Portugal.

Geissdoerfer, M. †, Savaget, P., Bocken, N. & Hultink, E.J. (2016). The Circular Economy – A new sustainability paradigm? *Journal of Cleaner Production*. doi:10.1016/j.jclepro.2016.12.048

Genovese, A., Acquaye, A. A., Figueroa, A., & Koh, S. L. (2017). Sustainable supply chain management and the transition towards a circular economy: Evidence and some applications. *Omega, 2017*(66), 344–357. doi:10.1016/j.omega.2015.05.015

González, J. J., Aponte, H. E., & Salazar, J. F. (2015). Medición del aprendizaje organizacional en las grandes y medianas empresas de Sogamoso, Colombia. *Cuadernos Latinoamericanos de Administración, 11*(20), 19-36. Retrieved from: https://www.redalyc.org/articulo.oa?id=409640743003

Hanaysha, J., & Hilman, H. (2015). Product Innovation as a Key Success Factor to Build Sustainable Brand Equity. *Management Science Letters, 5*(6), 567–576.

Hernández-Villanueva, C. A., & Mosquera-Rodas, J. J. (2016). Descripción de los modelos actuales de gestión gerencial, en las grandes empresas industriales de Pereira y Dosquebradas en el contexto actual de la economía periodo 2013 - 2014. *Sciences et Techniques (Paris), 21*(2), 122–127. Retrieved from https://search-ebscohost-com.hemeroteca.lasalle.edu.co/login.aspx?direct=true&AuthType=ip,url,uid&db=a9h&AN=122337584&lang=es&site=ehost-live

Jensen, M. C., & Meckling, W. H. (1976). Theory of the Firm: Managerial Behavior, Agency Costs and Ownership Structure. *Journal of Financial Economics, 3*(4), 305–360. doi:10.1016/0304-405X(76)90026-X

Jerez, P. (2001). *La gestión de recursos humanos y el aprendizaje organizativo: incidencia e implicaciones* (Unpublished PhD dissertation). Universidad de Almería, Departamento de Dirección y Gestión de Empresas, Almería, Spain.

Kantis, H. (2018). *¿Grandes empresas y Startups = nuevo modelo de innovación? Tendencias y desafíos del corporate venturing en América Latina*. Rafaela: Asociación Civil Red Pymes Mercosur. Retrieved from: https://www.researchgate.net/publication/327023031_Grandes_empresas_y_start_ups_nuevo_modelo_de_innovacion

Kiernan, M. (1999). *Los once mandamientos de la gerencia del siglo XXI.* Prentice Hall.

Latorre, M. (2018). *Historia de las Web, 1.0, 2.0, 3.0 y 4.0.* Universidad Marcelino Champagnat. Document. Retrieved from: umch. edu. pe/arch/hnomarino/74_Historia% 20de% 20la% 20Web. pdf

Levine, R. (1997). Desarrollo financiero y crecimiento económico: Enfoques y temario. *Journal of Economic Literature, 35*, 688–726.

Lieder, M., & Rashid, A. (2016). Towards circular economy implementation: A comprehensive review in context of manufacturing industry. *Journal of Cleaner Production, 2016*(115), 36–51. doi:10.1016/j.jclepro.2015.12.042

Mattos, D. R., Panzarin, S. J., Gomes, B. R. A., & Ometto, A. (2017). Trends in publications on the circular economy Tendências de publicações em economia circular.*Revista Espacios*. Vol. 38 (N° 58). *Year, 2017*, 20.

Mendoza Torres, M. R., & Ortiz Riaga, C. (2006). El Liderazgo Transformacional, Dimensiones e Impacto en la Cultura Organizacional y Eficacia de las Empresas. *Revista Facultad de Ciencias Económicas: Investigación y Reflexión, 14*(1), 118-134. Retrieved from: https://www.redalyc.org/pdf/909/90900107.pdf

Ministerio de ambiente. (2018). *Minambiente reglamenta la gestión de residuos de envases y empaques en Colombia.* Resolución 1407 de 2018. Retrieved from https://www.minambiente.gov.co/index.php/noticias-minambiente/4085-minambiente-reglamenta-la-gestion-de-residuos-de-envases-y-empaques-en-colombia

Ministerio de Comercio, Industria y Turismo. (2019). *Decreto 957 de 5 de junio de 2019.*

Montealegre, G. J. V., & Calderón, H. G. (2007). Relaciones entre actitud hacia el cambio y cultura organizacional. Estudio de caso en medianas y grandes empresas de confecciones de Ibagué. Rev. Innovar., 17(29).

Monterrosa, H. (2019). Mipymes representan 96% del tejido empresarial y aportan 40% al PIB. *La República.* Retrieved from: https://www.larepublica.co/economia/mipymes-representan-96-del-tejido-empresarial-y-aportan-40-al-pib-2903247

Montoya, R. A., Montoya, R. I., & Castellanos, O. (2010). Situación de la competitividad de las Pyme en Colombia: Elementos actuales y retos. *Agronomia Colombiana, 28*(1), 107–117.

Moraleda, A. (2004). La innovación, clave para la competitividad empresarial. *Universia Business Review*, (1): 128–136.

Moscoso Escobar, J., Sepúlveda Rivillas, C. I., García Cano, A., & Restrepo Londoño, A. L. (2012). Costo de capital en entornos económicos cambiantes: caso Valle de Aburra (Antioquia). *Rev.fac. cienc.econ, 20*(2). Retrieved from: http://www.scielo.org.co/scielo.php?script=sci_arttext&pid=S0121-68052012000200013

Mukherjee, D., & Hollenbaugh, E. (2019). Do Social Media Help in the Sustainability of Small Businesses? A Pedagogical Study Using Fictional Business Cases. *International Journal of Higher Education Management, 6*(1). Retrieved from https://ijhem.com/cdn/article_file/2019-08-07-22-50-06-PM.pdf

OBS Business School. (2019). *¿Cuáles son las claves del éxito empresarial?* Retrieved from: https://www.obs-edu.com/int/blog-project-management/herramientas-esenciales-de-un-project-manager/cuales-son-las-claves-del-exito-empresarial

OECD. (2015). *Colombia Políticas Prioritarias Para Un Desarrollo Inclusivo.* Serie "Mejores Políticas" January 2015. Retrieved from: https://www.oecd.org/about/publishing/colombia-politicas-prioritarias-para-un-desarrollo-inclusivo.pdf

Oghazi, P., & Mostaghel, R. (2018). Circular Business Model Challenges and Lessons Learned—An Industrial Perspective. *Sustainability, 2018*(10), 739. doi:10.3390u10030739

Oppenheimer, A. (2014). Crear o morir. La esperanza de Latinoamérica y los cinco secretos de la innovación. Academic Press.

Padilla, S. (2018). ¿Cuál es la mayor preocupación de las pymes? La competitividad. *El Espectador.* Retrieved from: https://www.elespectador.com/economia/cual-es-la-mayor-preocupacion-de-las-pymes-la-competitividad-articulo-740471

Parra, C., & Calderón, G. (2013). Formación y desempeño: un análisis de caso en empresas manufactureras grandes. *Pensamiento & Gestión*, (34), 137–160. Retrieved from https://search-ebscohost-com.hemeroteca.lasalle.edu.co/login.aspx?direct=true&AuthType=ip,url,uid&db=a9h&AN=91100294&lang=es&site=ehost-live

Pérez, A., Pertuz, V., Leiva, M., & Vega, A. (2019). Elementos estructurales y funcionales de los sistemas multiagente para la cooperación organizacional en medianas empresas. *Información Tecnológica*, *30*(4), 155–164. doi:10.4067/S0718-07642019000400155

Pérez-Uribe, R. (2018). *Gerencia Estratégica Corporativa*. Ediciones Ecoe Ltda. Available at: https://www.ecoeediciones.com/libros/libros-de-administracion-ecoe/gerencia-estrategica-corporativa/

Pérez-Uribe, R. I. (2012). *El ambiente laboral y su incidencia en el desempeño de las organizaciones: estudio en las mejores empresas para trabajar en Colombia*. Retrieved from: http://hdl.handle.net/10882/3203

Ramírez-Salazar, M. P. (2016). *Modelo De Innovación Abierta Colaborativa Para La Banca De Fomento: Caso Bancóldex* (PhD dissertation). Universidad EAN.

Ramírez-Salazar, M. P. (2015). La innovación abierta impulsa el desarrollo sostenible de las empresas. In *Gestión de la sostenibilidad en el marco de las organizaciones*. Bogotá, Colombia: Editorial EAN.

Revista Dinero. (2019). *Empresarios lanzan plan para consolidar la economía circular en el país*. Medio Ambiente. Retrieved from https://www.dinero.com/empresas/articulo/estrategia-de-los-empresarios-en-colombia-para-consolidar-la-economia-circular/275640

Rodríguez-López, N. (1999). *La innovación: clave del éxito empresarial*. Retrieved from: https://dialnet.unirioja.es/descarga/articulo/565208.pdf

Ruiz-Real, J. L., Uribe-Toril, J., De Pablo Valenciano, J., & Gázquez-Abad, J. C. (2018). Worldwide Research on Circular Economy and Environment: A Bibliometric Analysis. *International Journal of Environmental Research and Public Health*, *2018*(15), 2699. doi:10.3390/ijerph15122699 PMID:30501129

Saionz-Ochoa, A. (2001). *Análisis de los factores explicativos de éxito empresarial* (PhD dissertation). Universidad la Rioja. Retrieved from: https://dialnet.unirioja.es › descarga › tesis

Salazar Estrada, J. G., Guerrero Pupo, J. C., Machado Rodríguez, Y. B., & Cañedo Andalia, R. (2009). Clima y cultura organizacional: Dos componentes esenciales en la productividad laboral. *Acimed*, *20*(4), 67–75.

Sánchez García, J. C. (2014). Cognitive Scripts and Entrepreneurial Success. *Universitas Psychologica, 13*(1), 1–20. Retrieved from: https://bdbiblioteca.universidadean.edu.co:2111/10.11144/Javeriana.UPSY13-1.cses

Serrano Torres, G., Quezada Flores, D. L., & Márquez De, A. C. (2016). Investigación sobre Empresas Familiares exitosas en el Mundo [Research about Family Business More Successful of the World]. *Przedsiębiorczość i Zarządzanie, 435*. Retrieved from http://bdbiblioteca.universidadean.edu.co:2054/login.aspx?direct=true&db=edsbaz&AN=edsbaz.171486055&lang=es&site=eds-live&scope=site

Solà, J., Farreny, R., & Cormenzana, M. (2017). *La ecoinnovación como clave para el éxito empresarial Tendencias, beneficios y primeros pasos para ecoinnovar*. Editorial Libros de Cabecera.

Taweesak, R., King M., Thabhatr, A. & King M. (2019). Factors Affecting the Management Success, of Small and Medium Enterprises in the Electrical and Electronic Industry in Thailand. *Academy of Strategic Management Journal, 18*(2).

Thornton, A. (2019). *These 11 companies are leading the way to a circular economy.* Retrieved from https://www.weforum.org/agenda/2019/02/companies-leading-way-to-circular-economy/

Tovar Rojas, C. C., Perez-Uribe, R., & Ocampo-Guzmán, D. (2015). *MIIGO (Modelo de intervención e innovación de la gestión organizacional): Gestión de la producción de bienes y servicios (PBPS).* Universidad EAN. http://edicionesean.ean.edu.co/index.php/es/productos-de-investigacion1/colecciones/colecciones-digitales/miigo/44-miigo/443-miigo-gestion-de-produccion-de-bienes-y-prestacion-de-servicios-pbps

Urquiola, O., Zulueta, O. R., & Llano, R. (2017). La innovación para el desarrollo sostenible. Una experiencia en Cienfuegos, Cuba. *Universidad y Sociedad, 9*(1). Retrieved from: http://scielo.sld.cu/scielo.php?script=sci_arttext&pid=S2218-36202017000100015

Vanegas, P., Peeters, J. R., Cattrysse, D., Tecchio, P., Ardente, F., Mathieux, F., ... Duflou, J. R. (2018). Ease of disassembly of products to support circular economy strategies. *Resources, Conservation and Recycling, 2018*(135), 323–334. doi:10.1016/j.resconrec.2017.06.022 PMID:30078953

Wainer, A. (2011). Más allá del consejo monetario: grandes empresas. *Revista problemas del desarrollo, 164*(42), 98-126. Doi:10.22201/iiec.20078951e.2011.164.24490

Zhang, M., Jin, B., Wang, G. A., Goh, T. N., & He, Z. (2016). A Study of Key Success Factors of Service Enterprises in China. *Journal of Business Ethics, 134*(1), 1–14. doi:10.100710551-014-2074-2 PMID:30930508

KEY TERMS AND DEFINITIONS

Circular Economy: It is a strategy whose objective is to reduce the entrance of raw material as well as eliminating waste, closing the economic and ecologic flows of resources.

Key Factors for Success: They are the elements that allow an enterprise to reach its objectives, and that makes it different from its competitors, making it unique.

Servuction: It is the process of producing a service, which includes the organization of physical and human elements in the relation customer-business, necessary to provide a service and whose characteristics have been previously determined from design to the after-sale period.

Sustainable Development: It is development that satisfies the needs of the present without compromising the capacity of future generations to satisfy their own needs, guaranteeing balance between economic growth, the environment and social welfare.

ENDNOTE

1 The National Association of Entrepreneurs of Colombia (ANDI), is a non-profit union, which aims to disseminate and promote the political, economic and social principles of a healthy free enterprise system. It was founded on September 11, 1944 in Medellin and, since then, it is the most important business union in Colombia. It is made up of a significant percentage of companies belonging to various sectors of the Colombian economy.

Chapter 18
Youth Entrepreneurship in the Circular Economy

Idahosa Igbinakhase
https://orcid.org/0000-0003-4667-2809
University of KwaZulu-Natal, South Africa

ABSTRACT

The chapter focuses on the critical analysis of youth entrepreneurship in a circular economy. Youth entrepreneurs are important stakeholders in the circular economy operated in both developing and developed business environments. Youth entrepreneurial business activities include renewable energy, recycling, waste management, and organic food production. Youth entrepreneurial business activities are known to create both social and economic impacts in business environments despite the presence of several limiting issues and challenges that affect their overall potential as circular value creators in the circular economy. Some challenges experienced by youth entrepreneurs in a circular economy include waste prevention and lack of new and innovative circular technologies. In addition, key solutions to the challenges faced by youth entrepreneurs in a circular economy were discussed and analyzed.

INTRODUCTION

Several youths are involved in entrepreneurial activities in the different sectors of the economy both nationally and globally. According to Riahi (2010) youth entrepreneurship refer to individuals under 30 years of age involved in the "practical application of enterprising qualities, such as initiative, innovation, creativity, and risk-taking into the work environment (either in self-employment or employment in small start-up firms), using appropriate skills necessary for success in that environment and culture" (Chigunta, 2002, p.3). Existing studies on youth entrepreneurship have focused on youth entrepreneurial activities in other prevailing economic systems in diverse contexts (Brixiová, Ncube, & Bicaba, 2015; Dolan, & Rajak, 2016; Fatoki & Chindoga, 2011; Kojo Oseifuah, 2010), with few studies dedicated to the activities of youth entrepreneurship in a circular economy.

The circular economy presents vast opportunities for youth entrepreneurs to be involved in the creation of innovative products, services and business models that will bring positive impacts to the society and

DOI: 10.4018/978-1-7998-5116-5.ch018

Copyright © 2020, IGI Global. Copying or distributing in print or electronic forms without written permission of IGI Global is prohibited.

environment. The Circular economy is defined as an "industrial economy that is restorative or regenerative by intention and design" (Ellen MacArthur Foundation (EMF), 2013, p.14). Furthermore, Geissdoerfer, Savaget, Bocken, and Hultink (2017, p.762) defines the circular economy as "a regenerative system in which resource input and waste, emission, and energy leakages are minimised by slowing, closing, and narrowing material and energy loops". In addition, Geissdoerfer, Savaget, Bocken, and Hultink (2017) noted that the Circular economy can be achieved "...through long-lasting design, maintenance, repair, reuse, remanufacturing, refurbishing, and recycling" (p.762). Several countries such as China (Lieder & Rashid, 2016), Germany (Su et al., 2013) and Japan (METI, 2004) have made policy changes to incorporate the ideas and the key features of circular economies into their national and economic policies, and this has created an enabling environment for businesses to thrive in the different sectors of the economy. Key sectors of the economy with several opportunities for youth entrepreneurs to take advantage of include Waste management (Makropoulos et al, 2018), renewable energy (Gupta, 2003; Oluoko-Odingo & Mutisya, 2019), recycling (Winschiers-Theophilus et al, 2015), organic food (Dash, 2018) or eco-tourism (Choudhury, 2019).

In order to understand the activities of youth entrepreneurs in a circular economy establish the importance of youth entrepreneurship in a circular economy and identify the challenges of youth entrepreneurs in a circular economy, there is need for more studies to focus on youth entrepreneurship in a circular economy. This chapter attempts to fill this knowledge gap and provides current information and insights on youth entrepreneurship in a circular economy.

AIM

The aim of this book chapter is to present a critical analysis of youth entrepreneurship in a circular economy using case study analysis focusing on developing and developed business environments.

OBJECTIVES

The following are the objectives of the book chapter:

1. To examine the state of the art of youth entrepreneurship in a circular economy;
2. To identify evidence of the activities of youth entrepreneurs in a circular economy operating in developing and developed business environments; and
3. To analyze the case studies of youth entrepreneurs operating in circular economies present in both developing and developed business environments.

METHODOLOGY

The methodology utilized in this chapter is the Integrative Literature Review. According to Souza, Silva and Carvalho (2010) "an integrative review is the methodology that provides a synthesis of knowledge and applicability of results of significant studies to practice". Furthermore, Integrative literature reviews enable the incorporation of key studies (non-experimental and experimental) to provide an understanding of a research problem being investigated (Souza, Silva & Carvalho, 2010). In addition, integrative literature review is evidenced based.

Key steps involved in carrying out an integrative literature review include identifying the guiding question, searching the literature, data collection, critical analysis of the studies included, discussion of the result and presentation of the integrative review (Souza, Silva & Carvalho, 2010). Following this process allows for a scientific and rigorous synthesis of available information and investigations on a particular topic or area of inquiry. In addition, illustrative case studies (descriptive case studies) are utilized in this chapter to provide additional information on youth entrepreneurship in a circular economy.

CASE STUDIES OF YOUTH ENTREPRENEURSHIP IN A CIRCULAR ECONOMY

This section presents detailed information about youth entrepreneurship in a circular economy from two (2) business environments. In this section, illustrative case studies are used to describe the key features of youth entrepreneurship in a circular economy while providing useful insights on the impacts and challenges of the activities of youth entrepreneurs in different locations. Two (2) case studies selected for this book chapter are presented below.

CASE STUDY 1: YOUTH ENTREPRENEURS IN MATHARE'S INFORMAL WASTE ECONOMY (THIEME, 2010; 2013)

General Information

Country: Kenya
Sector: Informal Waste Management Sector
Focus: Waste Management Practices
Type of organisation: Self-employed youths (18-35 year old)

Characteristics

Background

Mathare is a settlement area in Kenya known as a district inhabited by very poor people. The Mathare Valley is located within an approximate distance of seven kilometres east of Nairobi's Central Business District and currently has over 300,000 residents (Thieme, 2013). According to Mathare Foundation (2020), the majority of the residents that live in Mathare live below the poverty index inn poor quality houses. In addition, Mathare does not have adequate sanitation, electricity, portable water and good access roads. Furthermore, the youths living in Mathare experience severe poverty and hardship and have been victims of several negative vices that include crime, gangs, drug abuse and prostitution (Mathare Foundation, 2020; Ombisa, 2017). In addition, Ombisa (2017) noted that poverty contributes to insecurity in slum settlements within Nairobi. In order to survive and realise their full potential, the youths living in Nairobi's largest and oldest informal settlements in Mathare have resorted to self-help to earn legitimate income. Focusing on the waste management sector, the youths in Matare are adopting waste management strategies and practices to earn a living in the informal waste management sector in Kenya. According to Thieme (2010), waste has become a source of income and has provided a sense of belonging to the youths residing in Mathare's slum settlements.

Objectives

The main objective of the youth entrepreneurs in Mathare is transform waste to wealth using several strategies and practices.

Details

According to Thieme (2013), youths in Mathare's informal settlements make use of unconventional strategies generate income in the informal waste economy.

Results

Youths in Mathare's slum settlement have been able to transform their lives by adding value in the recycling of re-usable garbage materials through the informal waste management economy.

Challenges

The slum settlements are often crime-ridden environments that make lives and properties highly insecure. In addition, there is lack of formal government support to assist youths involved in the waste recycling business. Furthermore, the business environment in the slum settlement is not conducive due to lack of basic amenities and other necessities that support business activities.

Conclusion

In the case of youth entrepreneurship in Mathare's informal waste economy, youth entrepreneurship in a circular economy serves as an escape out of poverty and the consequences of youth poverty for Mathare's youths. Furthermore, due to the informal nature of youth's activities in the Informal Waste Management Sector, youth entrepreneurs in Mathare encounter challenges such lack of basic infrastructure and the prevalence of crime.

CASE STUDY 2: ST KIZITO HIGH SCHOOL IN NAMUGONGO, KAMPALA (KAKEMBO, 2018)

General Information

Country: Uganda
Sector: Municipal Bio-Waste Sector (Waste Recycling to produce bio-fuels-biogas and briquettes)
Focus: Waste Management Practices
Type of organisation: High School Student Entrepreneurs

Characteristics

Background

St Kizito High School is located in Namugongo, Kampala, Uganda. Namugongo, which is located in central Uganda, is well known as a community that is surrounded by very green forest. Namugongo became very popular due to the activities of students of St Kizito High School who ventured into waste to wealth programme that has generated sustainable income for the students and the school. The High school students of St Kizito found ways of transforming waste products in their environment to useful items that have value within their immediate surroundings using different recycling methods. According to Kakembo (2018), high school students of St Kizito have carried out a complete chain of briquettes production and consumption.

Objectives

The main objective of the high school student entrepreneurs is to produce briquettes from municipal bio-waste and earn sustainable income.

Details

The high school students of St Kizito have the capacity of producing 20,000 kg of briquettes from municipal bio-waste, which are used to cook in three schools with a population of 2000 students (Kakembo, 2018). According to Kakembo (2018, p.146), "*bio-char and briquette-ash are used as organic fertilizers and biocide in vegetable gardens at the schools*".

Results

St Kizito's school project was successful and currently provides an average net profit of $3,000 based on an initial start-up cost of $12, 250 and with a payback period of 14.7 months.

Challenges

Waste recycling is still done at a small scale. The challenges to up-scaling recycling as noted by Kakembo (2018, p.147), include the following:

1. Poor quality plants and poor material choice and inexperienced contractors;
2. Heavy dependence of projects on donor subsidies and failing to survive beyond pilot phases;
3. Absence of entrepreneurial models to attract private capital and ignorance of about the business prospects of recycling;
4. Inadequate managerial and entrepreneurial skills;
5. Non-streamlined policies on recycling;
6. Cultural and socio-psycho sensitivities on consuming some products of recycling;
7. Absence of inter-sector linkages and partnerships on waste recycling;
8. Lack of start-up and scale-up capital for potential entrepreneurs.

Conclusion

In St Kizito high school's case study, youth entrepreneurship is practiced in an informal circular economy. The students of St Kizito have shown that youths can make important contributions to the circular economy by recycling waste and protect their environment despite challenges in Uganda's business environment.

ACTIVITIES OF YOUTH ENTREPRENEURSHIP IN A CIRCULAR ECONOMY

There are many business activities carried out by youth entrepreneurs in a circular economy in both developing and developed business environments. This is because the circular economy is more attractive to today's youth in terms of higher profitability and its environmental friendly impacts.

Some of the activities of youth entrepreneurs in a circular economy include the following:

- **Waste Management Business:** Waste management is an essential aspect of both human and business activities in any business environment and it involves actions taken to ensure that any waste (unwanted material or by-product) produced in any form is effectively disposed of. Therefore, waste management can be defined as the effective collection, transportation, treatment and disposal of waste materials in a safe manner and in line with national and international waste management regulations and practices (Pongracz & Pohjola, 2004). As a business activity, waste management involves the creation of companies that specializes in the collection and handling of waste materials (hazardous or non-hazardous or recyclable materials) for financial gains (Horvath, Mallinguh & Fogarassy, 2018; Michalec, Fodor, Hayes & Longhurst, 2018). Additionally, some examples of waste materials are animal wastes (Vodounnou, Kpogue, Tossavi, Mennsah, & Fiogbe, 2016), electronic wastes (Osibanjo, Nnorom, Adie, Ogundiran, & Adeyi, 2016) and radioactive wastes (Santana, 2016). Waste materials are to be handled properly to achieve the target economic and environmental benefits in a circular economy.
- **Renewable Energy Business:** The renewable energy industry is one of the key business activities in a circular economy that has witnessed active participation by youth entrepreneurs. Renewable energy can be defined as a natural source of energy that can be naturally replenished (Owusu & Asumadu-Sarkodie, 2016). Furthermore, Owusu and Asumadu-Sarkodie, 2016) affirms that renewable energy sources include solar energy, bio-energy, geothermal energy, hydropower, ocean and wind energy. Renewable energy sources have been certified as 'green' energy sources that can meet both current and future environmental and economic needs of both developing and developed economies in a responsible and sustainable manner if adopted globally.
- **Recycling Business:** Recycling business involves the creation of business activities that focus on the collection of waste for the purpose of reprocessing the waste material to increase its utility. Waste materials collected can be recycled, reused or resold to other future users (Ongondo & Williams, 2011). A major appeal for youths in the recycling business stems from the need to protect the environment (Garcia & Robertson, 2017) and effectively create an income stream from trash management. According to Geyer, Kuczenski, Zink and Henderson (2016), recycling is the process of recovering materials from waste and converting it into useful materials and products in an environmentally friendly manner. Currently, the separation of waste has become a well organized and coordinated activity, with several cities like Dhaka (a city in Bangladesh) providing

specific bins for specific waste materials to manage household waste (Ahsan & Zaman, 2014). This has made the residents of various cities to be an important stakeholder in the recycling value chain. The separation of waste materials in residential buildings, offices and other locations has led to improved recycling activities by recycling firms and entrepreneurs.

- **Material and Energy Efficiency:** Materials and energy efficiency is a vital aspect of a circular economy. The production of less new materials and energy resources is highly encouraged in a circular economy as it contributes positively to the protection and preservation of the environment. According to Allwood, Ashby, Gutowski and Worell (2013, p. 1), material efficiency refers to " the pursuit of the technical strategies, business models, consumer preferences and policy instruments that would lead to a substantial reduction in the production of high-volume energy intensive materials required to deliver human well-being". In its simplest form, material efficiency is the effective management of a production process with reduced reliance on newly extracted materials (Allwood et al. 2013). While energy efficiency refers to using minimal energy in the provision of services (Uyigue, Agho & Edevbaro, 2009). According to Allwood et al. (2013, p. 6), reducing the need for new materials will lead to "... reduced rates of extraction of natural resources, reduced energy demand, reductions in emissions and other environmental harms..." In order to attain material and energy efficiency, businesses set up by youths are among other businesses creating value through material and energy recycling.
- **Organic Food Production:** Organic food production is an environmentally friendly way of meeting a nation's food and nutrition needs in a circular economy. According to Niggli (2015), organic food production (often referred to as organic agriculture) "is a given set of farming practices that emphasise ecological sustainability" (p. 83). Furthermore, Niggli (2015) affirm that the major advantages of Organic food production include the biodiversity on organic farms, lower negative environmental impacts, stable soils which are less prone to erosion, carbon sequestration and less greenhouse gas emissions. As part of a circular economy, organic food production enables the circulation of key food production requirements that limits waste in the food production system. Also, organic food production plays an important role in a circular economy through the adoption of organic practices that include regenerative and sustainable farming (LaCanne & Lundgren, 2018), organic carbon and fertilizers (Borrello, Caracciolo, Lombardi, Pascucci, & Cembalo, 2017), and organic and biodynamic farming (McCarthy & Schurmann, 2018). These organic practices carried out by organic farmers in a circular economy have now become viable business options for youth entrepreneurs seeking income generation opportunities within the organic food production sector.

Importance and Impact of Youth Entrepreneurship in a Circular Economy

There are several positive consequences resulting from youth entrepreneurial activities in a circular economy. The following are some of the value created by youth entrepreneurs in a circular economy:

- **Economic Growth:** Youth entrepreneurs contribute to the economic growth of a nation through their green productive activities within a circular economy. According to Lacy and Rutquist (2016), young global leaders are making positive contributions to the economy through their waste to wealth initiatives;

- **Water Security:** According to the Centre for Mediterranean Integration (2017), youths have increasing benefit towards water security and water awareness. Water security refers to availability of sufficient amount of clean and usable water to meet the needs of a defined population within a given environment (Bakker, 2012). Due to the importance of water security for growth and development in the society, water awareness is an important social priority. The activity of youth entrepreneurs in alleviating this important social challenge will enable the society to handle both present and future water security challenge in a sustainable manner. Therefore, youths are important stakeholders in the water security goals of any society.
- **Reduction of Waste Material in the Environment:** Youth entrepreneurs' involvement in the circular economy has led to the reduction of waste materials in the environment. According to Mourad (2016), youth entrepreneurs can contribute to food waste reduction by becoming institutional entrepreneurs (Li, Feng & Jiang, 2006). Also, youth entrepreneurs have participated as informal entrepreneurs by engaging as waste pickers in the informal economy of some countries (Colette & Bisschop, 2017). Thus, youth entrepreneurs contribute to the reduction of waste materials in the environment through their involvement in recycling activities in their various environments.
- **Creation of Job Opportunities:** As more youth entrepreneurs participate in the circular economy through social and green enterprises, more jobs are created and added to the circular economy. According to Della Torre et al. (2020), the circular economy supports youth employment. In addition, Unay-Gailhard and Bojnec (2019) affirm that one of the impacts of a green economy is rural employment and this creates employment for youths in the agricultural sector. Furthermore, Ellis (2011) notes that youth entrepreneurship leads to poverty reduction and human capital development and there is need to maximise the impact of youth entrepreneurship support in different contexts. Therefore, youth entrepreneurship contributes to the creation of employment opportunities in the society and as a result assists in the alleviation poverty in the society.

Finally, youth entrepreneur's participation in the circular economy is of great importance to the society with various benefits for all stakeholders.

YOUTH ENTREPRENEURSHIP CHALLENGES IN CIRCULAR ECONOMY

There are many challenges affecting the activities of youth entrepreneurs in a circular economy. Some of these challenges are prevailing conditions experienced in a developing business environment. While a good number of challenges experienced by youth entrepreneurs in a circular economy are based on the nature of the circular economy or are circular economy challenges. Some of these challenges are discussed below:

- **Poor Waste Prevention:** Waste prevention is a major challenge associated with carrying out effective circular economy principles. According to Liu, Liang, Song and Li (2017) waste prevention and management is an important aspect of a circular economy and China has adopted the "reduce, reuse and recycle" waste prevention strategy. Despite the global adoption of this waste prevention strategy in a circular economy, waste prevention is still an issue in certain areas such as the food sector where key stakeholders are battling to reduce food waste and food loss (Vilarino,

Franco & Quarrington, 2017). Thus, poor waste prevention is a significant challenge that must be firmly addressed in a circular economy in order to effectively ensure the strict adherence to the circular economy vision and principles.

- **Lack of supportive policies:** Policy challenges are among significant barriers experienced in a circular economy by all stakeholders. According to Preston (2012), there is a need for policy makers to create enabling policies for proper transition from a linear economy to a circular economy in a timely manner in order to respond to pressing global challenges such as climate change (Tol, 2018) and other pressing global challenges. Also, evidence by Grant and Oteng-Ababio (2019) who investigated electronic -waste circuitry and value creation in Accra, Ghana revealed that government policies are unsuitable for the electronic-waste sector and upgrading e-waste activities as considerations are not given to informal activities and their contribution to the electronic –waste sector. Without the right supportive policies, youth entrepreneurs and other entrepreneurs will encounter difficulties in meeting their business and social goals. Therefore, creating supporting and suitable circular economy policies will boost stakeholders' participation in a circular economy and this will create more circular economic benefits in the business environment.
- **Lack of New and Innovative Circular Technologies:** Technologies are a critical component of a circular economy. There is an urgent need for new and innovative circular technologies to achieve the needed sustainable impact globally. According to Jawahir and Bradley (2016), the required technologies that are needed to create sustainable value for the circular economy are not given their due consideration. As a result, the required sustainable impacts expected from a circular economy are not being achieved. Furthermore, there is a need for new and innovative circular technologies such as the innovative new polymer recycling plant (designed and produced under the LIFE AGANFOILS project) (European Commission, 2019) and the innovate recycling process for thermoset polymer composites developed by Connora Technologies (Hayward, CA, USA) (La Rosa, Blanco, Banatao, Pastine, Bjorklund, & Cicala, 2018.Therefore, creating new and innovative circular technologies to meet growing circular technology demands in all industries and sectors within a circular economy will further advance the attainment of the circular economic objectives of any nation.
- **Lack of Public participation:** The circular economy requires stakeholders' cooperation and collective responsibility to be beneficial to all stakeholders. According to Zhihun and Nailing (2007), public participation in a circular economy is very vital and must be encouraged in order to extract useful opinions that are beneficial to all stakeholders. Examples of the expected and required public participation in a circular economy include the promotion of the circular economy (Guo, Geng, Sterr, Zhu, & Liu, 2017) and the implementation of the circular economy (Heshmati, 2017). Thus, active and constant participation by all stakeholders in a circular economy will contribute to the full transition to a circular economy in both developing and developed business environments and this will allow circular business models to thrive.
- **Lack of youth Awareness of Available Business opportunities in a Circular Economy:** A major challenge of some youths is the lack of awareness of the business opportunities that exist for their participation in a circular economy. According to Smol, Avdiushchenko, Kulczycka, and Nowaczek (2018), public awareness of circular economy is one of the reasons why the circular economy model is increasingly becoming relevant. However, Ezeudu and Ezeudu (2019), notes that insufficient expert knowledge and lack of information have hindered the implementation of circular economy principles in low and middle-income countries. Thus, there is a need for all

stakeholders, including youth entrepreneurs in low and middle-income countries to invest in practical training, seminars and workshops in key areas of the circular economy where there are business opportunities in order to benefit from the economy.

SOLUTIONS AND RECOMMENDATIONS

There are several possible practical solutions to the challenges experienced by youth entrepreneurs carrying out business activities in a circular economy. Some solutions and recommendations are suggested below:

1. Public Awareness: General awareness of the opportunities and benefits of a circular economy must always be made available for all stakeholders to benefit from it. Also, Seminars and workshops should be organized for youths in both developing and developed business environments on a regular basis to enable the full participation of youth entrepreneurs in the circular economy. According to Smol, Avdiushchenko, Kulczycka, and Nowaczek (2018), public awareness contributes positively to the circular economy model. Also, Liakos, Kumar, Pongsakornrungsilp, Garza-Reyes, Gupta and Pongsakornrungslip (2019) carried a study on understanding circular economy awareness and practices in manufacturing firms and found out that "with the growing emphasis on circular economy across the globe by governing bodies, firms are becoming aware of circular economy practices" (p. 563). Therefore, with the necessary public enlightenment campaigns about the impact of circular economy to livelihoods, environment and other important areas in the business environment, all stakeholders will receive the necessary information that will allow active participation in the circular economy.
2. There is a need for all stakeholders to be aware of their roles and responsibilities in a circular economy in order to achieve the public participation required to make a circular economy functional. Also, stakeholders must be aware of the dangers posed by failing in their responsibilities in a circular economy. Stakeholder participation is defined as "the inclusion of the various stakeholders that can affect, or are affected by the results of policy-making and decision making process" (Pisano, Lange, Lepuschitzand, & Berger, 2015, p. 5). According to Jakhar, Mangla, Luthra and Kusi-Sarpong (2019), stakeholders play an important role in a circular economy. Also, there are different forms of stakeholder participation and they include ad-hoc forms (e.g. public hearings, conferences and presentations), Institutional forms (e.g. dialogue, partnership, councils and committee) and hybrid forms (e.g. forums and workshops) (Pisano, Lange, Lepuschitzand, & Berger, 2015, p. 8).These stakeholders' forms of participation present tremendous opportunities for stakeholders to discuss their needs and ways of meeting their needs in a circular economy. Stakeholders' needs include increasing engagement, raising awareness, stakeholders' empowerment, coordinated advocacy and strengthening of governance, and these needs must be given priority attention in order to support stakeholders' participation and achieve collective sustainability goals in a circular economy (Pisano, Lange, Lepuschitzand, & Berger, 2015).
3. Circular Entrepreneurship Regulations and Supportive Policies: Regulatory stakeholders and government officials must ensure that quality supportive policies are made that ensure youth participation in a circular economy. Also, policies that enable a circular economy to thrive must be enacted on a continuous basis to protect all stakeholders in the circular economy. This view is supported by Rizos, Behrens, Drabik, Rinaldi and Tuokko (2018) who suggests that at the national level that a country

can "review the effectiveness of national waste management planning and adopt a set of policies (e.g., increased landfill taxes, investment in waste collection systems, development of recycling and reuse networks) to move up multiple levels in the waste hierarchy" (p.iii). The implementation of this suggestion will reduce regulatory challenges encountered by youth entrepreneurs in their quest to contribute and participate in the circular economy.

4. Waste Prevention: Waste prevention should be a duty for all stakeholders in a circular economy. Responsible production and responsible consumption by both businesses and the population should be encouraged to reduce product loss and wastage. According to Corvellec (2016), waste prevention is characterized by three actions and they are "raising awareness about the need to prevent waste, increasing material efficiency and developing sustainable consumption" (p. 1). Furthermore, Cristobal, Castellani, Manfredi and Sala (2018) investigated prioritizing and optimizing sustainable measures for food waste prevention and management, and revealed that "targets for food waste prevention must be set at the level of environmental impact" (p. 3). The cautious approach of target setting for food waste prevention in line with the resulting environmental impact can also be applied to other kinds of waste in order to achieve a specific waste prevention outcome desired by any industry based on the impact to the environment. Therefore, each stakeholder in the circular economy must take responsibility in disseminating important information necessary to prevent waste, encourage material and energy efficiency, and ensure responsible consumption in order for all stakeholders to benefit from the circular economy and protect the environment.
5. Innovative Circular Technologies: Efficient circular technologies should be invented and utilize in a timely manner to respond to current and future environmental threats, and stakeholders' needs. Also, ongoing research efforts for efficient circular technologies should be supported by the government while business must continue to invest in newer circular technological research that creates both national and global environmental impacts. Furthermore, Rizos et al. (2018) suggest that at the national level and with respect to digitalisation and emerging technologies, there is need to encourage the development of a working digital ecosystem with data generation capabilities for circular business models through:
   (a) Providing incentives for the creation of cross-industry collaboration platforms,
   (b) Assisting in the development of programmes and schemes that support business activities, and
   (c) Create laws and policies that govern data privacy and ownership (p.iii).

Implementing the suggestion by Rizos et al. (2018) on emerging circular technologies and digitalisation will boost rapid advancement in different industries in the circular economy.

FUTURE RESEARCH DIRECTIONS

Generating new information and increasing the understanding of youth entrepreneurship in a circular economy is an important task as the world gravitates towards sustainability and environmental protection and preservation. Evidence from existing studies have shown that youths are playing key roles in both formal (Dash, 2018; Mourad, 2016; Oluoko-Odingo &Mutisya, 2019) and informal (Coletto & Bisschop, 2017; Dolan & Rajak, 2016; Thieme, 2010; Thieme, 2013) circular economies.

Based on the existing literature on the subject and the coverage of this chapter, there is need for additional studies to be carried out to investigate youth entrepreneurship challenges and solutions to youth entrepreneurship challenges in a circular economy in both local (indigenous) and international environments and inn diverse sectors of the circular economy. In order to achieve these research goals, future studies can focus on youth entrepreneurship challenges in an informal circular economy in different rural environments. In addition, other studies can carry out comparative studies on the challenges experienced by youth entrepreneurs in both formal and informal circular economies in different research contexts.

CONCLUSION

The activities of youth entrepreneurs in a circular economy has seen an improvement of social, economic, environmental and other positive benefits in the business environment. Youth entrepreneurs have made business impacts in both formal and informal circular economies. While the regulated formal circular economy is more organized, the informal circular economy is less regulated and occurs in rural and poor countries. The overall goal of each business activity carried out by youth entrepreneurs and other entrepreneurs in the circular economy is to protect the environment, turn waste to wealth and ensure responsible natural resources use in addition to achieve their business goal(profit). Despite the good intentions of these entrepreneurs, certain barriers and challenges such as lack of public participation, lack of youth awareness of circular business opportunities, lack of innovative circular technologies, lack of supportive policies and poor waste prevention (from manufacturers and consumers) hinder the activities of youth entrepreneurs in the circular economy. In order to alleviate the challenges of the circular economy, solutions such as improved public awareness, increased investments in circular technologies, improved waste prevention attitudes and an increase in general awareness of the roles and responsibilities of all stakeholders were proffered as some of the very useful solutions.

REFERENCES

Bakker, K. (2012). Water security research challenges and opportunities. *Science*, *337*(6097), 914–915. doi:10.1126cience.1226337 PMID:22923564

Baporikar, N. (2014). Youth entrepreneurship in India scenario. *International Journal of Asian Business and Information Management*, *5*(2), 74–84. doi:10.4018/ijabim.2014040106

Baporikar, N. (2017). Cluster approach for entrepreneurship development in India. *International Journal of Asian Business and Information Management*, *8*(2), 46–61. doi:10.4018/IJABIM.2017040104

Baporikar, N. (2017). Critical review of Entrepreneurship in Oman. In P. Zgheib (Ed.), *Entrepreneurship and Business Innovation in the Middle East* (pp. 147–174). Hershey, PA: IGI Global. doi:10.4018/978-1-5225-2066-5.ch008

Baporikar, N. (2018). Current scenario of youth entrepreneurship in India. In M. Khosrow-Pour, D.B.A. (Ed.), Encyclopaedia of Information Science and Technology, Fourth Edition (pp. 2989-2997). Hershey, PA: IGI Global. doi:10.4018/978-1-5225-2255-3.ch261

Baporikar, N. (2019). Significance and role of Entrepreneurial University in Emerging Economies. *International Journal of Applied Management Sciences and Engineering*, *6*(1), 46–61. doi:10.4018/IJAMSE.2019010104

Brixiová, Z., Ncube, M., & Bicaba, Z. (2015). Skills and youth entrepreneurship in Africa: Analysis with evidence from Swaziland. *World Development*, *67*, 11–26. doi:10.1016/j.worlddev.2014.09.027

Centre For Mediterranean Integration (CMI). (2017). *Youth Innovation with wastewater for sustainable Mediterranean*. Available at https://www.cmimarseille.org

Chigunta, F. J. (2002). *Youth Entrepreneurship: Meeting the key policy challenges*. Education Development Centre.

Choudhury, A.S.B. (2019). *Eco-tourism: The mantra for sustainable rural livelihood*. Academic Press.

Coban, G. U., Akpinar, E., Kucukcankurtaran, E., Yildiz, E., & Ergin, O. (2011). Elementary school students water awareness. *International Research in Geographical and Environmental Education*, *20*(1), 65–83. doi:10.1080/10382046.2011.540103

Coletto, D., & Bisschop, L. (2017). Waste pickers in the informal economy of the Global South: Included or excluded? *The International Journal of Sociology and Social Policy*, *37*(5/6), 280–294. doi:10.1108/IJSSP-01-2016-0006

Dash, D. (2018). A review of Organic Farming as a potential sector for Agripreneurship development among tribal youths in India. *International Journal of Agriculture Environment and Biotechnology*, *11*(5), 761–767. doi:10.30954/0974-1712.10.2018.8

Dolan, C., & Rajak, D. (2016). Remaking Africa's informal economies: Youth, entrepreneurship and the promise of inclusion at the bottom of the pyramid. *The Journal of Development Studies*, *52*(4), 514–529. doi:10.1080/00220388.2015.1126249 PMID:28989182

Ellen MacAthur Foundation (EMF). (2014). Towards the Circular Economy, Vow 3. Isle of Wight. Author.

Ellis, K., & Williams, C. (2011). *Maximising the impact off youth entrepreneurship support in different contexts*. London: Overseas Development Institute.

Ezeudu, O. B., & Ezeudu, T. S. (2019). Implementation of circular economy principles in industrial solid waste management: Case studies from developing Economy (Nigeria). *Recycling*, *4*(4), 42. doi:10.3390/recycling4040042

Fatoki, O., & Chindoga, L. (2011). An investigation into the obstacles to youth entrepreneurship in South Africa. *International Business Research*, *4*(2), 161–169. doi:10.5539/ibr.v4n2p161

Geissdoerfer, M., Savaget, P., Bocken, N. M., & Hultink, E. J. (2017). The circular economy-A new sustainability paradigm? *Journal of Cleaner Production*, *143*, 757–768. doi:10.1016/j.jclepro.2016.12.048

Gough, K. V., & Langerang, T. (2016). *Introduction: Youth entrepreneurship in Sub-Saharan Africa. In young entrepreneurs in Sub-Saharan Africa*. Routledge. doi:10.4324/9781315730257

Green, F. (2013). *Youth entrepreneurship*. Background paper for the OECD centre for entrepreneurship, SMEs and local development.

Gupta, C. L. (2003). Role of renewable technologies in generating sustainable livelihoods. *Renewable & Sustainable Energy Reviews*, *7*(2), 155–174.

Jakhar, S. K., Mangla, S. K., Luthra, S., & Kusi-Sarpong, S. (2019). When Stakeholder pressure drives the circular economy. *Management Decision*, *57*(4), 904–920. doi:10.1108/MD-09-2018-0990

Jawahir, I. S., & Bradley, R. (2016). Technological elements of circular economy and the principles of 6R-based closed-loop material flow in sustainable manufacturing. *Procedia CIRP*, *40*(1), 103–108. doi:10.1016/j.procir.2016.01.067

Kakembo, F. (2019). University Education and Waste-to-Wealth Entrepreneurship for Youth Employment in Uganda. Universities, Entrepreneurship and Enterprise Development in Africa-Conference Proceedings 2018.

Kojo Oseifuah, E. (2010). Financial literacy and youth entrepreneurship in South Africa. *African Journal of Economic and Management Studies*, *1*(2), 164–182. doi:10.1108/20400701011073473

Lacy, P., & Rutquist, J. (2016). *Waste to wealth: The circular economy advantage*. Springer.

Li, D. D., Feng, J., & Jiang, H. (2006). Institutional entrepreneurs. *The American Economic Review*, *96*(2), 358–362. doi:10.1257/000282806777211775

Lieder, M., & Rashid, A. (2016). Towards a circular economy implementation: A comprehensive review in context of manufacturing industry. *Journal of Cleaner Production*, *115*, 36–51. doi:10.1016/j.jclepro.2015.12.042

Liu, L., Liang, Y., Song, Q., & Li, J. (2017). A review of waste prevention through 3R under the concept of circular economy in China. *Journal of Material Cycles and Waste Management*, *19*(4), 1314–1323. doi:10.100710163-017-0606-4

Makropoulos, C., Rozos, E., Tsoukalas, I., Plevri, A., ... Ripis, C. (2018). S.ewer-mi.ning: A water reuse option supporting circular economy, public service provision and entrepreneurship. *Journal of Environmental Management*, *216*, 285–298. doi:10.1016/j.jenvman.2017.07.026 PMID:28728973

METI. (2004). *Handbook on Resource Recycling Legislation and 3R initiatives*. Tokyo: Japanese Ministry of Economy, Trade and Industry.

Mourad, M. (2016). Recycling, recovering and preventing food waste: Competing solutions for food systems sustainability in the United States and France. *Journal of Cleaner Production*, *126*, 461–477. doi:10.1016/j.jclepro.2016.03.084

Oluoko-Odingo, A. A., & Mutisya, E. (2019). The enterprise of waste management among urban youth for sustainable development in Kenya. *Journal of Sustainability. Environment and Peace*, *1*(2), 45–51.

Ombisa, B. A. (2017). Poverty as a Driving Force to Insecurity in Slums within Nairobi. *Journal of Poverty. Investment and Development.*, *31*, 24–32.

Preston, F. (2012). *A global redesign? Shaping the circular economy*. London: Chatham House.

Rada, E.C. (2019). Special waste valorization and renewable energy generation under a circular economy: Which priorities? *WIT Transactions on Ecology and the Environment, 222*, 145-157.

Riahi, S. (2010). *Youth Entrepreneurship: Ottawa's portfolio in talent development*. Open Source Business Resource.

Smol, M., Avdiushchenko, A., Kulczycka, J., & Nowaczek, A. (2018). Public awareness of circular economy in Poland: Case of the Malopolska region. *Journal of Cleaner Production*, *197*, 1035–1045. doi:10.1016/j.jclepro.2018.06.100

Souza, M. T. D., Silva, M. D. D., & Carvalho, R. D. (2010). Integrative review: What is it? How to do it? *Einstein (Sao Paulo, Brazil)*, *8*(1), 102–106. doi:10.15901679-45082010rw1134 PMID:26761761

Su, B., Heshmati, A., Geng, Y., & Yu, X. (2013). A review of the circular economy in China: Moving from rhetoric to implementation. *Journal of Cleaner Production*, *42*, 215–227. doi:10.1016/j.jclepro.2012.11.020

Thieme, T. A. (2010). Youth, waste and work in Mathare: Whose business and whose politics? *Environment and Urbanization*, *22*(2), 333–352. doi:10.1177/0956247810379946

Thieme, T. A. (2013). The "hustle" amongst youth entrepreneurs in Mathare's informal waste economy. *Journal of Eastern African Studies: the Journal of the British Institute in Eastern Africa*, *7*(3), 389–412. doi:10.1080/17531055.2013.770678

Unay-Gailhard, I., & Bojnec, S. (2019). The impact of green economy measures on rural employment: Green jobs in farms. *Journal of Cleaner Production*, *208*, 541–551. doi:10.1016/j.jclepro.2018.10.160

Vilarino, M. V., Franco, C., & Quarrington, C. (2017). Food loss and waste reduction as an integral part of a circular economy. *Frontiers in Environmental Science*, *5*, 21. doi:10.3389/fenvs.2017.00021

Winschiers-Theophilus, H., Cabrero, D. G., Angula, S., Chivuno-Kuria, S., Mendonca, H., & Ngolo, R. (2015). A challenge base approach to promote entrepreneurship among youth in an informal settlement in Windhoek. *Proceedings of the SATN*.

Zhihun, F., & Nailing, Y. (2007). Putting a circular economy into practice in China. *Sustainability Science*, *2*(1), 95–101. doi:10.100711625-006-0018-1

ADDITIONAL READING

Dunmade, I. (2018). The pursuing of circular economy goal in Africa: An exploratory study on the activities of the African Union and its member states. *Journal of Popular Education in Africa*, *2*(2).

Gelbmann, U., & Hammerl, B. (2015). Integrative re-use systems as innovative business models for devising sustainable product-service-systems. *Journal of Cleaner Production*, *97*, 50–60. doi:10.1016/j.jclepro.2014.01.104

Hart, S. L. (2007). *Capitalism at crossroads: Aligning Business, Earth, and Humanity*. Pearson Prentice Hall.

Horvath, B., Mallinguh, E., & Fogarassy, C. (2018). Designing business solutions for plastic waste management to enhance circular transitions in Kenya. *Sustainability*, *10*(5), 1664. doi:10.3390u10051664

Kirchherr, J., Reike, D., & Hekkert, M. (2017). Conceptualizing the circular economy: An analysis of 114 definitions. *Resources, Conservation and Recycling*, *127*, 221–232. doi:10.1016/j.resconrec.2017.09.005

Lindner, J., & Cox, K. J. (1998). Youth entrepreneurship. *Journal of Extension*, *36*(5), 1–6.

Preston, F. (2012). *A global redesign? Shaping the circular economy*. London: Chattam House.

Schroeder, P., Anggraeni, K., & Weber, U. (2019). The relevance of circular economy practices to sustainable development goals. *Journal of Industrial Ecology*, *23*(1), 77–95. doi:10.1111/jiec.12732

KEY TERMS AND DEFINITIONS

Entrepreneurship: A business activity that leads to the creation of a company where the business owner takes full responsibility for the financial risk involved in running the business.

Environment: This refers to existing conditions in any geographical location.

Pollution: This is the introduction of harmful substances into the environment.

Recycle: A process of converting waste materials for reuse as new materials or products.

Regeneration: A process of renewal/rebirth.

Repair: An activity carried out to restore a faulty item to a functional state.

Reuse: A practice of continuous usage of an item for a particular or different purpose.

Waste Economy: An economy that operates based on waste.

Waste Management: This involves the identification, collection, transportation, and processing (disposal or recycling) of waste.

Youth: A young person, usually between 14 and 35 years old.

Chapter 19
Women's Power as Employees and Entrepreneurs in the Circular Economy:
A Comparative Analysis

Harold Andrew Patrick
CMS Business School, Jain University (Deemed), India

Ujjal Mukherjee
CMS Business School, Jain University (Deemed), India

ABSTRACT

This chapter measures optimism in terms of success factors and a lack of success factors. The purpose of this chapter is to study the personality and optimism level of women employees and women entrepreneurs in the circular economy. Responses from 121 women employees from five employment sectors and 103 women entrepreneurs from five different sectors were surveyed for the chapter. Results indicated there was a significant difference among women entrepreneurs and women employees in terms of group directedness, compliance, and self-confidence. The results of the chapter will have both theoretical and practical implications for the long-standing quest to discover the similarities and differences between women's entrepreneurial personality and women employees. The chapter will contribute to the entrepreneurship literature by testing the influence of personality traits on the optimism level of the entrepreneur and comparing the same with the employees.

INTRODUCTION

The notion surrounding the circular economy is that the organizations have a duty to help overcome the environmental and sustainable challenges faced by the society which not only comprises of the shareholders but, a variety of stakeholders. This notion has introduced a new arena which is away from the traditional make-use-dispose business model [EMF report 2013;2014]. According to Okorie (2018),

DOI: 10.4018/978-1-7998-5116-5.ch019

Copyright © 2020, IGI Global. Copying or distributing in print or electronic forms without written permission of IGI Global is prohibited.

circular economy (CE) is "an economic system that represents a change of paradigm in the way that human society is interrelated with nature and aims to prevent the depletion of resources, close energy and material loops, and facilitate sustainable development". Women workforce have a crucial role to play in the circular economy (Candice Stevens, 2010). This part of the workforce adds more than 20 percent in the country's economy (McKinsey Global Institute report 2017). They are occupying decision-making positions at offices, be it as entrepreneurs or as employees. This chapter compares the personality and optimism levels of women employees and women entrepreneurs and studies the influence of the personality on their level of optimism. To the best of researcher's knowledge, there is no study, which has tried to this difference between these two sections of the women workforce.

Several factors have created the need for the journey towards a more sustainable environment. It includes factors such as the economic challenges and the uncertainty in different industries (Sachs, 2015), the ever increasing population (Geissdoerfer., et al., 2017) and the diminution of the natural resources (Jackson, 2009; Meadows., et al., 2009). Banerjee and Duflo (2011) has underlined high unemployment and poor working conditions, as other challenges.

Power of these women decision-makers decides the level of impact of their decisions including, decisions pertaining to sustainability, on the stakeholders. Power is defined as "the ability of individuals to include or influence the beliefs or behavior of other persons or groups" (Koontz and Weihrich, 1988). Both personality (Al-Ghamdi, 1997) and psychological capacities such as optimism (Schaefer and Palanski, 2013) of individuals is found to influence the behavior of people in the surrounding. The current chapter considers personality and optimism levels of employees and entrepreneurs, as the sources of power. The current chapter helps to understand the underlying difference between personality and optimism level of woman entrepreneurs as compared to women employees.

Employees work within an established business organization with work processes. Entrepreneurs work in an unstructured setting where, they all primarily are responsible for the success or failure of a venture Studies indicate that the personality traits differ between employees and entrepreneurs (Zhao, H., & Seibert, S. E., 2006). Few studies in the past have suggested that neuroticism is reasonably low for entrepreneurs when judged against employees (Kerr et al., 2017; Rauch, 2014; Nanda & Sorensen, 2011). However, these studies have considered both the genders (male and female) in the sampling process. With the gender disparities that exist in India like, the existence of glass ceiling effect, wage gap and lack of women friendly policies (Fletcher et al; 2017), the results obtained from the current study might look different as compared to the results of studies which have considered the responses of both male and female entrepreneurs and employees. Hence, there is a need to study the variation that exists between women employees and women entrepreneurs.

While the personality traits are more or less stable over the years (Terracciano., et al., 2008), a psychological capacity such as optimism is malleable and may be improved with interventions (Luthans, Youssef, et al., 2007). The organizations, nowadays are increasing looking for employees who an intrapreneurs (Neessen, 2018). Studies over the years have revealed that the qualities of an entrepreneur are quite similar to intrapreneurs (Birkemalm & Sandra, 2018). Both are quite similar in terms of creativity, identification of opportunities etc. The organizations may use the entrepreneurial traits identified in this study to identify perspective Intrapreneurs.

This chapter also compares the malleable "optimism" level of women entrepreneurs with women employees, which will give directions to the training professionals in the companies on how to develop intrapreneurial behavior among the existing employee workforce. The current study also identifies the influence of personality on the optimism levels of employees and entrepreneurs. The results of which may be utilized by the practitioners to identify the kind of personality who will be more optimistic at work and develop a positive work environment.

LITERATURE REVIEW

Optimism

Tiger (1979) says optimism is a frame of mind or thoughts associated with a hope of societal or material expectations. Optimists stress positive aspects of circumstances, actions and events and believing in the finest possible results in the future world (Furnham, (1997). Optimists spot out high-quality events with permanence (happen again), occurrence (can expand to other potential events) and internality (can happen again). Bad events are, by disparity, regarded as transient, non-pervasive and due to reasons exterior to the self. Research suggest that people in general, are not only optimistic about their forthcoming events and competencies, but are also more realistic about the future of others (Sharot, (2011). Optimism has been found to positively influence goal setting and achievement of individuals (Lightsey, 1996).

Entrepreneurs are more likely to be optimistic than people with similar demographic, financial, and educational backgrounds (Puri and Robinson, 2013). A lot of other studies (Arabsheibani., et al., 2000; Dawson, de Meza, Henley, Arabsheibani, 2012; Fraser and Greene, 2006) in different contexts, have found similar results. Studies (de Meza and Southley, 1996; Gartner, 2005; Hmieleski and Baron, 2009) have suggested that the optimism levels among entrepreneurs were found to be extremely high.

Study conducted by Chen et al., (2017) revealed entrepreneurs with high levels of optimism, had significant higher social network size, social network heterogeneity, and better new venture performance (Cheng 2017). Chen et al., (2017) also proposed and found that entrepreneur's optimism indeed is contagious. In addition, certain characteristics like clarity of vision and leadership authenticity strengthen the contagiousness. Liang and Dunn (2007) suggested that more an entrepreneur is optimistic they were happy and contended with the way things were shaping up hoping that business is doing very well and will maximize their profits.

Research reveals that there is negative relationship between entrepreneurs' optimism and performance with regard to growth and revenues especially of new ventures. Hmieleski and Robert (2009) suggested that entrepreneurs' optimism level was negatively related to the performance of the new ventures and the negative relationship was the highest when there was non-stability in the work atmosphere with the experienced compared to none or less experienced entrepreneurs.

Several studies have been conducted on employees to understand the influence of optimism on their job performance (Makikangas, 2003), satisfaction with life (Jibeen, 2013), job satisfaction (Jung, 2015) and job stress (Tuten,2004). Jibeen (2013) in her studies revealed optimism moderated between neuroticism, distress; neuroticism, and satisfaction with life, among university employees. Tuten (2004) further established that optimists did perceive lower levels of job stress and lower work/no work conflict. Mäkikangas (2003) study revealed optimism levels among female employees moderated the relationship between their time pressure at work, job insecurity and organizational climate; and mental distress.

Bakker et al., (2008) proposed that job resources such as autonomy, supervisory coaching, performance feedback and personal resources such as optimism, self-efficacy, and self-esteem best predict work engagement. Bressler's (2006) study among United States army reserve soldiers indicated hope and optimism has an influence on effective commitment.

This study measures optimism in terms of success factors and lack of success factors. This is concerned with perception of causal thinking. It measures ones' attribution thinking- to what one attributes the success and failure to (internal or external, and the stable or variable factors).

Personality

In common speech, personality is usually referred to one's public image. Allport (1961) defined personality as "a dynamic organisation, inside the person, of psychophysical systems that create the person's characteristic patterns of behaviour, thoughts and feelings". This internal factor is considered more or less stable and it assures one's behavior is consistent over a period, but is different from the behavior of other people in same or similar contexts (Child, 1968).

One of the popular instruments to measure personality traits if "The Big Five", which is a five-dimensions hierarchical organization of personality traits. These five dimensions are Extraversion, Agreeableness, Conscientiousness, Neuroticism, and Openness to Experience (Soto, 2018). McCrae& John (1992) underlined the importance of this inventory, stating that it brings together a wide range of personality dimensions, which is easier to compare in different contexts and helps in creating a fundamental to develop causal relationship with other variables.

Openness to experience indicates an individuals' inquisitiveness for different experiences and discovering original thoughts. This means being creative, innovative, imaginative, reflective (Silvia et al., 2009). However, employees have limited access to experiment at the workplace, as they have to follow the guidelines laid in their place of work. On the contrary, employees are expected to be more experimental which may lead to business opportunities. Individuals who are high on agreeableness are characterized as easy going, non-manipulative, naive, sympathetic, and thoughtful and have high regard for constructive interpersonal relationships. Employees work atmosphere is different from entrepreneurs. They sometimes work with a large number of team members and superiors spread across the globe. Therefore, it is very essential to have good interpersonal relationship for job satisfaction and success. Contrastingly, majority of entrepreneurs work in smaller setups and, although good interpersonal relationship is necessary but not as important as employees are. Conscientiousness involves accomplishment drive and reliability (e.g., Mount & Barrick, 1995). Individuals having different levels of extraversion behave differently in in social engagement, assertiveness, and energy level (Soto, 2018). Individuals with higher levels of extraversion prefer socializing and are easy expression their emotions in front of others. Introvert individuals on the contrary, have difficulty in socializing and expressing their emotions in-group situations. Introverts might be considered as more reserved in terms of social and emotional dimensions. This is a required attribute among both employees and entrepreneurs. Entrepreneurs may be expected to be slightly more extravert, considering they have to attend frequent business related meetings.

Neuroticism (Soto, 2018) described as the emotional stability of individuals, measures the differences in the occurrence and magnitude of negative emotions. Individuals having high levels of neuroticism, experience anxiety, sadness and frequent mood swings as compared to individuals with lower levels of neuroticism. This is not a welcome attribute, both among employees and entrepreneurs. Considering that emotions have been found to be contagious, these negative emotions can pass through the workplace and may influence the work environment, and this is applicable even in challenging situations. Entrepreneurs' neuroticism might have far adverse effect as compared to employees, as entrepreneurs interacts with a wider audience.

Study by Zhao et al (2009) found that Big Five personality dimensions were found to influence two pillars of the entrepreneurial process: entrepreneurial intentions and entrepreneurial performance. Among entrepreneurs, it is found that extraversion is found to influence positive wellbeing (Diener and Lucas, 1999) and neuroticism has been found to develop negative well-being (Keyes et al., 2002). Vigor, one of the dimensions of work engagement is found to be higher among entrepreneurs having higher levels extraversion.

Several studies have also been done on employees to analyze the influence of personality on attrition and discipline (Conte., et al, 2017), task proficiency and work –role performance (Yeo., et al., 2012) job satisfaction, job stress, career path Linda., et al., 2011) etc. Studies by Yeo., et al., (2012) revealed openness to experience and agreeableness had opposing effects on individual proactivity – openness to experience positively influenced to individual proactivity, on the contrary, agreeableness has a negative influence. Conscientiousness is found to be a stronger predictor of an employee's task proficiency as compared to the other traits neuroticism and extraversion is found to negatively influence individual is task proficiency.

Conte et al (2017) study revealed that, the resilient class had significantly higher discipline ratings and significantly lower attrition. Objective career success of individuals is found to be positively influenced by their extraversion, agreeableness and conscientiousness and negatively by neuroticism (Dodangoda, 2016).

In terms of personality, study by Zhao & Seibert (2006) pointed towards significant differences between managers and entrepreneurs, particularly in their levels of conscientiousness, openness to experience, neuroticism and agreeableness. Entrepreneurs were found to possess higher levels of conscientiousness and openness to experience and lower on neuroticism and agreeableness. No difference was found for levels of extraversion.

The above studies indicate that personality traits have been significantly different among employees and entrepreneurs. Furthermore, none of the researches considered only women as their respondent. Therefore, it was worth researching, whether there is a difference in personality between women entrepreneurs and women employees.

Research Questions

- Do women employees and women entrepreneurs differ significantly on success / lack of success factors and big five personality traits?
- Is there an influence of personality on the level of optimism among the entrepreneurs and the employees?

Research Design

Sample of 121 women full time employees, having minimum 1-year work experience, from 5 employment sectors and 103 women entrepreneurs, having minimum 1-year experience, from 5 different sectors were surveyed. The sample was drawn from manufacturing, IT, IT services, trading and others. Women employees were drawn from executive, senior executive, assistant managers and manager level. Quota sampling technique was used for data collection.

Tools Employed: Two standardized tools were adopted:

Optimism was measured using the Attribution of success and failure inventory- ASUFA-G, developed by Pareek (2002). ASUFA (Attribution of Success and Failure) Inventory comprises of 32 pairs of factors leading to success or failure of a person. It produces the sketch of sample on internality and optimism. The origin of this inventory is based on Rotter's concept of locus of control, Weiner's theory of attribution and Seligman's studies of optimism. Following are the different dimensions measured by the instrument:

1. **Self-directedness:** It is defined as high personal internality. A self-directed person will exercise his or her choices in most contexts;
2. **Group-directedness:** It is defined as high collective internality, a group-directedness person will follow norms and work with his/her team to influence situation;
3. **Conformity:** It is defined as high personal externality. A conformist will be guided by the wishes of the significant persons;
4. **Fatalism:** It is defined as high non-person externality. A fatalist will attribute most outcomes to external forces and is not likely to exercise much effort to bring about change;
5. **Optimism:** It is defined as attributing failure and miseries to variable factors both internal and external;
6. **Pessimism:** It is defined as attributing success variable and miseries to stable factors (both internal and external);
7. **Hope:** It is defined as the ratio between attribution to variable and attribution to stable factors;
8. **Self-confidence:** It is defined as the ratio between internality and externality.

Donahue and Kentle (1991) developed big Five Personality tool. It measures the big five personality dimensions of personality: Neuroticism, Extraversion, and Openness to Experience, Agreeableness, and Conscientiousness. A 5-point Likert scale was used ranging from "Strongly Disagree" to "Strongly Agree":

- **Pilot Study:** To determine reliability the questionnaire was administered to 30 women employees and 30 women entrepreneurs. The Cronbach alpha for the ASUFA-G scale (0.76) and the Big Five Inventory (0.78) indicated that the tools were reliable;
- **Characteristics and distribution of the sample:** The sample was tested for normality of distribution using Shapiro Wilk Test. The Z values of skewness and kurtosis of the variables, lie between -1.96 and 1.96 which does not deviate grossly from the bell-shaped normal distribution, confirming that the data is normal and parametric tests can be applied;
- **Statistical technique:** The data collected was processed and analysed using Microsoft Excel 14.00 and SPSS version 19.0. The data was analysed using t-test and regression.

Respondent Profile

Majority of the respondents belong to the age group of 31-40 yrs. (39.50%) and were graduates (51.5%). More than half the number of respondent (52%) is having work experience of less than 5 years. Around 85% of the women employee were from the service sector whereas 69% of the entrepreneurs belonged to the manufacturing sector.

RESULTS AND ANALYSIS

Figure 1 and Figure 2I also indicate that women entrepreneurs scored higher on the four big five dimensions as compared to women employees. Women employees scored higher only in neuroticism. As Far as women entrepreneurs are concerned, the highest was willingness to try to new things and the ability to think outside the box. (Openness to experience) and the least being anxiety, sadness, worry, and low self-esteem (neuroticism). Women employees scored also highest in openness to experience (36.36) and least on neuroticism (22.53).

Figure 1. Indicating mean, standard deviation, and inter-correlations for women employees

	M	*SD*	*1*	*2*	*3*	*4*	*5*	*6*	*7*	*8*
1 .Self Directedness	60.58	8.00								
2 .Group Directedness	46.95	5.99								
3. Compliance	49.21	6.93								
4. Fatalism	43.18	7.08								
5. Optimism	58.00	7.50								
6. Pessimism	49.45	4.32								
7 .Self Confidence	55.64	6.16								
8 .Hope	57.47	5.92								
9. Extraversion	24.52	4.68	.074	-.005	.039	-.112	-.038	.114	.024	.067
10. Agreeableness	31.79	4.40	.134	-.073	-.032	-.056	.004	-.013	-.003	.081
11. Conscientiousness	32.57	5.39	.134	-.073	-.037	-.053	.237	-.133	-.189	0.08
12. Neuroticism	22.53	5.40	-.132	.142	.037	.067	.084	.066	.096	-.069
13. Openness to Exp.	*36.36*	*4.21*	*.072*	*.-.069*	*-.015*	*-.001*	*-.009*	*.052*	*.024*	*.030*

** Significant at the 0.05 level, ** Significant at the 0.01 level.*

Figure 2 and Figure 3 indicate that women entrepreneurs as compared to women employees, were higher at all four success factors, the ability to regulate and adapt behavior to the demands of a situation (self-directedness), hopefulness and confidence about the future or the success of something (optimism), a feeling of expectation and desire for a particular thing to happen. (Hope) and feeling of trust in one's abilities, qualities, and judgment (self-confidence). The highest being self-directedness and the least being self-confidence. When we compare the mean score of lack of success factors, group directedness (47.94), and pessimism (49.50) were higher for women entrepreneurs. However, compliance (50.02) and fatalism (43.80) for women employees scored higher than women entrepreneurs. The highest on lack of success was compliance by women employees and least on fatalism (42.56) by women entrepreneurs.

Figure 2 and Figure 3 indicates that there was no significant relationship between big five-personality trait and success and lack of success factors among women employees. However, among women entrepreneurs, there was a significant relationship between Big Five personality trait extraversion with success/lack of success factors self-directedness and conscientiousness (Figure 3). There was a significant relation between Big Five personality trait agreeableness with success factors optimism and hope, conscientiousness with success/lack of success factors such as self-directedness, optimism, self-confidence, hope and fatalism.

Figure 2. Indicating Means (M), Standard Deviation (SD), and inter-correlations for women entrepreneurs

	M	SD	1	2	3	4	5	6	7	8
1.Self Directedness	61.06	7.93								
2.Group Directedness	47.94	5.61								
3.Compliance	48.40	7.93								
4.Fatalism	42.56	7.57								
5.Optimism	58.28	8.43								
6.Pessimism	49.50	4.34								
7.Self Confidence	56.75	6.97								
8.Hope	57.78	6.62								
9.Extraversion	26.95	5.09	.269**	.235*	-.429	-.027	.118	-.077	.394**	.107
10.Agreeableness	31.96	4.00	.048	-.038	.149	-.189	.271**	-.178	.028	.243*
11.Conscientiousness	32.71	4.98	.281**	-.006	-.096	-.217*	.222*	-.068	.266**	.260**
12.Neuroticism	20.30	4.95	.076	.041	-.140	.049	-.185	.077	.090	-.196
13.Openness to Exp.	37.92	4.23	.093	-.141	-.079	.102	.094	.016	.008	.126

* Significant at the 0.05 level, ** Significant at the 0.01 level.

Hypothesis 1: There is no significant difference between success and lack of success factors across women employees and women entrepreneurs.

There is a significant difference among women entrepreneurs and women employees in terms of group directedness, compliance and self-confidence.

Compliance was found to be significantly higher among women entrepreneurs as compared to women employees whereas group directedness was found to be higher among women employees.

Hypothesis 2: There is no significant difference between big five personality traits across women employees and women entrepreneurs.

There is a significant difference among women entrepreneurs and women employees in terms of extraversion, neuroticism and openness to experience (refer Figure 4).

Extraversion and openness to experience were found to be higher among women entrepreneurs as compared to women employees whereas women employees were found to have higher levels of neuroticism.

Hypothesis 3: There is no significant influence of big five personality traits on success and lack of success factors among women entrepreneurs and women employees.

Among women entrepreneurs, lack of success factors is found to be influenced by extroversion and conscientiousness. It is also found that success factors of the women entrepreneurs are significantly influenced by the big five personality traits. Out of the five personality traits, extraversion and conscientiousness is found to influence positively the success factors (refer figure 5). Openness to experience is the only personality trait, which is found to significantly influence both the success factors as well as lack of success factors.

Among women employees, agreeableness and conscientiousness are found to influence the success factors.

Figure 3. Indicating difference between success/lack of success factors among women employees and women entrepreneurs

Success and lack of success attributes	Sample	Count	Mean	SD	F Score	Sig
Self-Directedness						
	Women Employees	121	60.09	8.08	0.732	0.393
	Women Entrepreneurs	103	61.06	7.93		
	Total	224	60.58	8.00		
Group Directedness						
	Women Employees	121	45.96	6.22	5.582	0.019
	Women Entrepreneurs	103	47.94	5.61		
	Total	224	46.95	5.99		
Compliance						
	Women Employees	121	50.02	5.69	2.772	0.097*
	Women Entrepreneurs	103	48.40	7.93		
	Total	224	49.21	6.93		
Fatalism						
	Women Employees	121	43.80	6.52	1.538	0.216
	Women Entrepreneurs	103	42.56	7.57		
	Total	224	43.18	7.08		
Optimism						
	Women Employees	121	57.72	6.47	0.280	0.597
	Women Entrepreneurs	103	58.28	8.43		
	Total	224	58.00	7.50		
Pessimism						
	Women Employees	121	49.39	4.33	0.032	0.859
	Women Entrepreneurs	103	49.50	4.34		
	Total	224	49.45	4.33		
Self-confidence						
	Women Employees	121	54.54	5.04	6.614	0.011*
	Women Entrepreneurs	103	56.75	6.97		
	Total	224	55.64	6.16		
Hope	Women Employees	121	57.16	5.14	0.566	0.457
	Women Entrepreneurs	103	57.78	6.62		
	Total	224	57.47	5.92		

** Significance level 0.01 *Significance level 0.05

DISCUSSION

As far as success factors or lack of success factors are concerned, this study revealed that there was a significant difference in compliance and group directedness among women employees and women entrepreneurs. It showed that compliance was higher among the women employees. It is very essential that employees who work in organizations that function in a stable environment, having employees from different demographic backgrounds and policies of varying complexity; to comply with the set rules and regulations of the organization. Group directedness was found to be higher among women entrepreneurs. Group- directedness is the ability to give credit or blame oneself for the results applicable to self or group (collective internal control). Cantillon (1934) suggested that, "an entrepreneur is someone who has the foresight and willingness to assume risk and take the requisite action to make a profit (or loss)". Therefore, ideally, it is expected the entrepreneur takes the credit or blames oneself for the results in the business.

Figure 4. Indicating difference in the big five personality traits across women employees and women entrepreneurs

Big Five attributes	Sample	Count	Mean	SD	F Score	Sig
Extraversion	Women Employees	121	24.52	4.68	12.34	0.001**
	Women Entrepreneurs	103	26.95	5.09		
	Total	224	25.74	5.03		
Agreeableness						
	Women Employees	121	31.79	4.40	0.08	0.77
	Women Entrepreneurs	103	31.96	4.00		
	Total	224	31.88	4.20		
Conscientiousness						
	Women Employees	121	32.57	5.39	0.03	0.84
	Women Entrepreneurs	103	32.71	4.98		
	Total	224	32.64	5.18		
Neuroticism						
	Women Employees	121	22.53	5.40	9.26	0.00**
	Women Entrepreneurs	103	20.30	4.95		
	Total	224	21.42	5.29		
Openness to Experience						
	Women Employees	121	36.36	4.21	6.83	0.01*
	Women Entrepreneurs	103	37.92	4.23		
	Total	224	37.14	4.28		

** Significance level 0.01 *Significance level 0.05

Figure 5. Indicating regression coefficient of lack of success factors and big five personality traits factors on women employees and entrepreneurs

	Lack of Success Factors				Success Factors			
	R^2	ΔR^2	β	S.E.	R^2	ΔR^2	β	S.E.
Women Entrepreneurs	0.15	0.15			0.19	0.15		
Extraversion			0.32**	-0.88			0.25*	0.76
Agreeableness			0 .49	-0.23			0.08**	1.16
Conscientiousness			0 .44**	-1.05			0.28	1.04
Neuroticism			0 .37	-0.42			0.03	0.88
Openness to experience			0.31*	-0.21			0.03**	0.81
Women Employees	0.02	0.02			0.01	0.04		
Openness to experience			0.31	0.31			0.81	0.23
Extraversion			0.43	0.27			0.90	0.15
Agreeableness			0.49	-0.25			1.04*	0.41
Conscientiousness			0.57	-0.06			1.20*	0.59
Neuroticism			0.46	0.48			.96	0.25

* Significant at the 0.05 level, ** Significant at the 0.01 level.

The results of the study indicated that women entrepreneurs are more assertive, dominant, energetic, active, talkative and enthusiastic (extraversion) as compared to women employees. Entrepreneurs must interact with diverse number of people have challenging roles to fulfill. For entrepreneurs in their day-to-day operations, they have to interact with people from various occupations, which require them to be energetic and have good interpersonal skills. This result contradicts with Zhao & Siebert's (2006) meta-analysis result where no significant difference was found between employees and entrepreneurs in terms of extraversion. However, the sample considered for Zhao & Siebert's chapter considered both male and female employees and entrepreneurs. Therefore, the results obtained from this chapter, is of great value as this considers only females as samples.

This study indicated that women entrepreneurs are more likely to be rationally inquisitive, inclined towards different knowledge and discover new thoughts (openness to experience) as compared to women employees. This is expected, as one of the most important resources in today's business in the dynamic environment is, information and the ability to accept and interpret the information to the advantage of the business. One can innovate and grow in the current scenario only when he/she is ready to discover new thoughts and explore fresh avenues. The results suggested that the employees have a comparatively lesser levels of achievement orientation as compared to entrepreneurs. However, these two sections of the workforce do not significantly differ in the levels of conscientiousness (Zhao & Siebert, 2006).

It indicated that the differences here were primarily due to the entrepreneurs having a higher achievement orientation as compared to managers (employees). Entrepreneurs and managers (employees) did not differ on other aspects of Conscientiousness such as dependability and organizational skills.

The results of the study indicated that women employees could exhibit higher levels of nervousness, unfriendliness, dejection, self-consciousness, spontaneity, and susceptibility (neuroticism) as compared to women entrepreneurs. The employees work in a dynamic environment, which produces a large amount of psychological stress. They have to spend more time at work and less time with family, more responsibility as there is large amount of financial stake taken up for the business venture, more insecurity with changing times and conditions of the economy which has a direct impact on their performance.

There was no significant influence of any of the Big Five personality traits on success/lack of success factors among women employees. However, among the women entrepreneurs, there was a significant influence of extraversion and conscientiousness on success factors. The results from this research is actually, in agreement with Leutner (2014) research chapter, which revealed that extraversion and agreeableness among entrepreneurs actually predict entrepreneurial outcomes. The chapter further, suggests that individuals with higher levels of extraversion is more likely to involve in a variety of entrepreneurial activities, such as planning start-up's, developing ventures which may help the society and behaving like an entrepreneur in the organization (intrapreneurial behavior). Individuals having high levels of conscientiousness are found to be achievement oriented and more dependable as compared to individuals possessing lower levels of conscientiousness. Zhao & Siebert 's (2006) meta-analysis study on identifying the predictor of job performance across contexts, identified that at work, individuals with higher conscientiousness levels tend to outperform individuals with lower levels of conscientiousness. The results in the current also indicates that the levels of conscientiousness and openness to experience is higher among the entrepreneurs.

Implications

The results of the present study have theoretical and practical implications in the quest to understand personality of an entrepreneur, particularly women entrepreneurs and; the factors, which may lead to their success in their entrepreneurial ventures. Majority of research working on the relationship between personality of individuals and their level of optimism have found significant relationship between Extraversion, Agreeableness, and Conscientiousness and optimism and these researches will generally conducted on students and employees (Costa & McCrae, 1992: Milligan,2003). The researchers did not come across any chapter which suggests the influence of personality of entrepreneurs specially women, on their level of optimism. The present study contributes to the entrepreneurship literature by testing the influence of personality traits on the optimism level of the entrepreneur and comparing the same with the employees.

In an article that appeared in the American Psychologist, Peterson (2000) referred to optimism as a ''Velcro construct, to which everything sticks for reasons that are not always obvious'' (p. 47). This means that "optimism" influences the behaviour of individuals for reasons which are sometimes visible and sometimes not. The chapter also identifies the personality traits of employees, which can help to increase the level of optimism among them.

To develop positive personality aspects among the women employees, short training courses can be designed to enhance the aspects of positive psychology. The training program should involve the participants to set goals, sub goals, and alternate goals, which can result in desirable results.

It is the responsibility of those in leadership roles to create a workplace climate, which fosters well-being and facilitates resilience, especially among the women employees. The leaders should help women employees find purpose in their work and personal life, which is the key to workplace optimism. Mental (cognitive) training programs can help the women employees develop extraversion, openness to experience and overcome signs of neuroticism. Line managers can help the women employees to set their own day-to-day schedules and then encourage them to follow the same which can help the employee to develop conscientiousness.

For the industry professionals, our results show that personality inventories may be considered as a tool to predict entrepreneurial behavior among employees and their levels of optimism at the workplace. Organizations promoting intrapreneurship can use the results of this chapter to identify women having the relevant personality. There is evidence in the literature, which suggests that organizations, which are able to identify, recruit and retain employees with entrepreneurial mindsets, have competitive advantage in the market (Lumpkin, 2007). A better understanding of employee personality dimensions would boost the strategic business planning activities, which ultimately leads to achieving business goals. Thus, Big Five inventories can not only help business professions in creating more value for the employees specially the women employees, but also in minimizing the risk of business failure.

Limitation and Direction for Future Research

Although the findings of this study are contributes to the development of theory, the study has some limitations that can be addressed for future research. The present study was cross-sectional in nature and inferences regarding causality cannot be claimed. Future studies should test the relationship between personality and optimism using other research designs like a longitudinal study. The responses on the instruments were self-reported; therefore, the relationships among the variables might have been inflated due to the common method variance. However, common method bias was somewhat controlled by ensuring the anonymity of respondents and confidentiality of the responses collected but the possibility of this error cannot be very erased. Future research can include mediators and moderators to develop further understanding of the relationship between personality of employees and entrepreneurs and their level of optimism. Variables such as motivation and justice perception can be considered as potential mediating and moderating variables. Nowadays, with workplace becoming more and more team oriented, it will be interesting for future researchers to consider the influence of personality of employees and entrepreneurs on their team's optimism.

REFERENCES

Abele, A. E., & Guido, H. E. (2007). Individual differences in optimism predict the recall of personally relevant information. *Personality and Individual Differences*, *43*(5), 1125–1135. doi:10.1016/j.paid.2007.03.005

Allport, G. W. (1961). *Pattern and Growth in Personality*. New York: Holt, Rinehart and Winston.

Allport, G. W., & Odbert, H. S. (1936). Trait-names: A psycho-lexical study. *Psychological Monographs*, *47*(1), 211–215. doi:10.1037/h0093360

Arabsheibani, G., de Meza, D., Maloney, J., & Pearson, B. (2000). And a vision appeared unto them of a great profit: Evidence of self–deception among the self–employed. *Economics Letters*, *67*(1), 35–41. doi:10.1016/S0165-1765(99)00242-6

Bakker, A. B., Schaufeli, W. B., Leiter, M. P., & Taris, T. W. (2008). Work engagement: An emerging concept in occupational health psychology. An International Journal of Work. *Health &Organisations.*, *22*(3), 187–200.

Banerjee, A., & Duflo, E. (2005). *Growth Theory through the Lens of Development Economics*. Massachusetts Institute of Technology.

Banerjee, A., & Duflo, E. (2011). *Poor Economics: A Radical Rethinking of the Way to Fight Global Poverty*. New York, NY, USA: Public Affairs.

Buchanan, G. M., & Seligman, M. E. P. (Eds.). (1995). *Explanatory style*. Hillsdale, NJ: Erlbaum.

Cattell, R. B. (1943). The description of personality: Basic traits resolved into clusters. *Journal of Abnormal and Social Psychology*, *38*(4), 476–506. doi:10.1037/h0054116

Census of India. (2011). Accessed from: http://censusindia.gov.in/

Centre for Women Business Research. (2011). Key4Women Confidence Index. Retrieved from:www.key.com

Chen, Y., Zhou, X., Yang, G., Bao, J., & Wang, G. (2017). Social networks as mediator in entrepreneurial optimism and new venture performance. *Social Behavior and Personality*, *45*(4), 551–562. doi:10.2224/sbp.5924

Child, I. L. (1968). Personality in Culture. In E. F. Borgatta & W. W. Lambert (Eds.), *Handbook of personality theory and research*. Chicago: Rand McNally.

Cole, A. H. (1946). An Approach to the Study of Entrepreneurship: A Tribute to Edwin F. Gay. *The Journal of Economic History*. doi:10.1017/S0022050700052876

Conte, J. M., Heffner, T. S., Roesch, S. C., & Aasen, B. (2017). A person-centric investigation of personality types, job performance, and attrition. *Personality and Individual Differences, 104*(January), 554–559. doi:10.1016/j.paid.2016.09.004

Dawson, C. J., Meza, D., Henley, A., & Arabsheibani, G. R. (2012). *Entrepreneurship: Cause or Consequence of Financial Optimism?* Rochester, NY: Social Science Research Network; Retrieved from http://chapters.ssrn.com/abstract=2157986

Daymard, A. (2015). Determinants of Female Entrepreneurship in India. Economics Department Working Chapters No. 1191. Organisation for Economic Co-operation and Development. https://www.oecd-ilibrary.org/economics/determinants-of-female-entrepreneurship-in-india_5js4rfh5gtbq-en

De Meza, D., & Southey, C. (1996). The Borrower's Curse: Optimism, Finance and Entrepreneurship. *Economic Journal (London), 106*(435), 375–386. doi:10.2307/2235253

Digman, J. M., & Takemoto-Chock, N. K. (1981). Factors in the natural language of personality: Reanalysis and comparison of six major studies. *Multivariate Behavioral Research, 16*(2), 149–170. doi:10.1207/s15327906mbr1602_2 PubMed

Dodangoda, H. C., & Arachchige, B. J. H. (2015). Impact of Personality on Career Success of the Employees in the Sri Lankan Banking Sector in Western Province. *Human Resource Management Journal, 3*(2). doi:10.31357/hrmj.v3i2.2863

EMF. (2013). *Towards the Circular Economy: Economic and Business Rationale for an Accelerated Transition*. Cowes, UK: Ellen MacArthur Foundation.

EMF. (2014). Towards the Circular Economy: Accelerating the Scale-Up across Global Supply Chains. Ellen MacArthur Foundation.

Fletcher, E.K., Pande. R., & Moore, C. T. (2017). Women and Work in India: Descriptive Evidence and a Review of Potential Policies. Accessed from: file:///C:/Users/UJJAL/Downloads/RWP18-004_Pande.pdf

Forbes, D. P. (2005). Are some entrepreneurs more overconfident than others? *Journal of Business Venturing, 20*(5), 623–640. doi:10.1016/j.jbusvent.2004.05.001

Fraser, S., & Greene, F. J. (2006). The Effects of Experience on Entrepreneurial Optimism and Uncertainty. *Economica., 73*(290), 169–192. doi:10.1111/j.1468-0335.2006.00488.x

Furnham, A. (1997). The half full or half empty glass, the views of the economic optimist vs. pessimist. *Human Relations, 50*(2), 197–209. doi:10.1177/001872679705000206

Gartner, W. B. (2005). America's manic entrepreneurs. *American Enterprise (Washington, D.C.), 16*(5), 18–21.

Geissdoerfer, M., Savaget, P., Bocken, N. M. P., & Hultink, E. J. (2017). The Circular Economy—A new sustainability paradigm? Journal of Cleaner Production, 2017(143), 757–768. doi:10.1016/j.jclepro.2016.12.048

George, L. G., Helson, R., & John, O. P. (2011). The "CEO" of women's work lives: How Big Five Conscientiousness, Extraversion, and Openness predict 50 years of work experiences in a changing sociocultural context. *Journal of Personality and Social Psychology, 101*(4), 812–830. doi:10.1037/a0024290 PubMed

Goldberg, L. R. (1981). Language and individual differences: The search for universals in personality lexicons. In L. Wheeler (Ed.), Vol. 2, pp. 141–165). Review of personality and social psychology Beverly Hills, CA: Sage.

Goyal, M., & Parkash, J. (2011). Women Entrepreneurship in India-problems and prospects. *International Journal of Multidisciplinary Research, 1*(5).

Hmieleski, K. M., & Baron, R. A. (2009). Entrepreneurs' Optimism and New Venture Performance: A Social Cognitive Perspective. *Academy of Management Journal, 52*(3), 473–488. doi:10.5465/amj.2009.41330755

Holland, J. L. (1997). *Making vocational choices: A theory of vocational personalities and work environments* (3rd ed.). Psychological Assessment Resources.

India's women are the secret to a potential economic boom. (2018). Accessed from: https://www.weforum.org/agenda/2018/07/india-could-boost-its-gdp-by-770-billion-by-just-treating-women-better

Jackson, T. (2009). *Prosperity without Growth: Economics for a Finite Planet*. London, UK: Earthscan; doi:10.4324/9781849774338.

Jibeen, T. (2014). Personality Traits and Subjective Well-Being: Moderating Role of Optimism in University Employees. *Social Indicators Research, 118*(1), 157–172. doi:10.1007/s11205-013-0416-6

Jung, H. S., & Yoon, H. H. (2015). The impact of employees' positive psychological capital on job satisfaction and organizational citizenship behaviors in the hotel. *International Journal of Contemporary Hospitality Management, 27*(6), 1135–1156. doi:10.1108/IJCHM-01-2014-0019

Khanka, S. S. (1998). Women entrepreneurship in India. *Journal of Assam University, 3*(1), 11–16.

Klages, L. (1926). *The science of character (Translated 1932)*. London: Allen and Unwin.

Klapper, L. F., & Parker, S. C. (2011). Gender and the Business Environment for New Firm Creation. *The World Bank Research Observer, 26*(2), 237–257. doi:10.1093/wbro/lkp032

Klein, W. M., & Radcliffe, N. M. (2002). Dispositional, unrealistic, and comparative optimism: Differential relations with the knowledge and processing of risk information and beliefs about personal risk. Personality and Social Psychology, 28(6), 836–846. doi:10.1177/0146167202289012

Leutner, F., & Premuzic, T. C. (2014). The relationship between the entrepreneurial personality and the Big Five personality traits. *Personality and Individual Differences, 63*(June), 58–63. doi:10.1016/j.paid.2014.01.042

Liang, C. K., & Dunn, P. (2007). Triggers of decisions to launch a new venture – is there any difference between pre-business and in-business entrepreneurs? *Academy of Entrepreneurship Journal, 13*(1), 79–95.

Lightsey, R. L. (1996). What leads to Wellness? The Role of Psychological Resource in well-being. *Journal of Counseling Psychology*, *24*, 658–735.

Lounsbury, J. W., & Gibson, L. W. (2006). *Personal style inventory: A Work-Based Personality Measurement System*. Knoxville, TN: Resource Associates.

Luthans, F., & Youssef, C. M. (2007). Emerging positive organizational behavior. *Journal of Management*, *33*(3), 321–349. doi:10.1177/0149206307300814

Mäkikangas, A., & Kinnunen, U. (2003, August). Psychosocial work stressors and well-being: Self-esteem and optimism as moderators in a one-year longitudinal sample. *Personality and Individual Differences*, *35*(3), 537–557. doi:10.1016/S0191-8869(02)00217-9

Meadows, D. H., Randers, J., & Meadows, D. L. (2009). *The Limits to Growth: The 30-Year Update*. London, UK: Routledge.

Nanda, R., & Sorensen, J. (2011). Workplace peers and entrepreneurship. *Management Science*, *56*(7), 1116–1126. doi:10.1287/mnsc.1100.1179

Neal, A., Yeo, G., Koy, A., & Xiao, T. (2012). Predicting the form and direction of work role performance from the Big 5 model of personality traits. *Journal of Organizational Behavior*, *33*(2), 175–192. doi:10.1002/job.742

Neessen, P., Caniëls, M., Vos, B., & De Jong, J. (2018). The intrapreneurial employee: Toward an integrated model of intrapreneurship and research agenda. *The International Entrepreneurship and Management Journal*. doi:10.100711365-018-0552-1

Neider, L. (1987). A preliminary investigation of female entrepreneurs in Florida. *Journal of Small Business Management*, *25*(3), 22–29.

Okorie, O., Salonitis, K., Charnley, F., Moreno, M., Turner, C., & Tiwari, A. (2018). Digitisation and the Circular Economy: A Review of Current Research and Future Trends. *Energies*, *3009*(11), •••. doi:10.3390/en11113009

Oldham, G., & Hackman, J. (1980). Work design in the organizational context. *Research in Organizational Behavior*, *2*, 247–278.

Pareek, U., & Purohit, S. (2002). *Training Instruments in HRD and OD* (3rd ed.). Tata McGraw Hill Education Private Limited.

Pauline, B., & Sandra, J. (2018). Entrepreneurs vs. Intrapreneurs A comparative study about motivation factors of entrepreneurs and intrapreneurs. Accessed from: http://www.diva-portal.org/smash/get/diva2:1224155/FULLTEXT01.pdf

Peterson, C. (2000). The future of optimism. *The American Psychologist*, *55*(1), 44–55. doi:10.1037/0003-066X.55.1.44 PubMed

Peterson, C. (2006). *A primer in positive psychology*. New York: Oxford University Press.

Puri, M., & Robinson, D. T. (2013). The Economic Psychology of Entrepreneurship and Family Business. *Journal of Economics & Management Strategy*, *22*(2), 423–444. doi:10.1111/jems.12013

Rauch, A. (2014). Predictions of entrepreneurial behavior: A personality approach. In E. Chell & M. Karatas-Ozkan (Eds.), *Handbook of Research on Small Business and Entrepreneurship* (pp. 165–183). London, UK: Edward Elgar; doi:10.4337/9781849809245.00018.

Sachs, J. (2015). *The Age of Sustainable Development*. New York, NY: Columbia University Press; doi:10.7312/sach17314.

Sari, P. K. (2019). Wellesley College William R. Kerr, HBS and NBER Tina Xu, Wellesley College November 2017. Personality Traits of Entrepreneurs: A Review of Recent Literature. Accessed from: https://www.hbs.edu/faculty/Publication%20Files/KKX-Personality-Review_RIS_5ea5da25-c8ab-41d2-90ee-e30b3d5b071c.pdf

Seligman, M. (1998). *Learned Optimism: How to Change your Mind and your Life*. Free Press.

Seligman, M. E. P., Abramson, L. Y., Semmel, A., & Baeyer, C. (1979). Depressive attributional style. *Journal of Abnormal Psychology*, *88*(3), 242–247. doi:10.1037/0021-843X.88.3.242 PubMed

Sharma, D. D., & Dhameja, S. K. (2002). *Indian Entrepreneurship; Theory and Practice*. Abhishek Publications.

Sharot, T. (2011). The optimism bias. *Current Biology*, *21*(23), R941–R945. doi:10.1016/j.cub.2011.10.030 PubMed

Silvia, P., Nusbaum, E., Christopher, M., & O'Connor, A. (2009). Openness to experience, plasticity, and creativity: Exploring lower-order, high-order, and interactive effects. *Journal of Research in Personality*, *43*(6), 1087–1090. doi:10.1016/j.jrp.2009.04.015

Singer, L., & Millage, P. (2013). The interaction of leadership and personality among Chinese and American nascent entrepreneurs. *Journal of Technology Management in China*, *8*(1), 44–54.

Soto, C. J. (2018). Big Five personality traits. In M. H. Bornstein, M. E. Arterberry, K. L. Fingerman, & J. E. Lansford (Eds.), *The SAGE encyclopedia of lifespan human development* (pp. 240–241). Thousand Oaks, CA: Sage; Available from https://www.researchgate.net/publication/324115204_Big_Five_personality_traits

Stevens, C. (2010). Are Women the Key to Sustainable Development? https://www.bu.edu/pardee/files/2010/04/UNsdkp003fsingle.pdf

Terracciano, A., McCrae, R. R., & Costa, P. (2008). Personality traits: Stability and change with age. *Geriatrics & Aging*, *11*, 474–478.

Tiger, L. (1979). *Optimism: The biology of hope*. New York: Simon and Schuster.

Tuten, L., & Neidermeyer, P. E. (2004). Performance, satisfaction and turnover in call centers: The effects of stress and optimism. *Journal of Business Research*, *57*(1), 26–34. doi:10.1016/S0148-2963(02)00281-3

Vaughan, S. C. (2000). *Half Empty, Half Full: Understanding the Psychological Roots of Optimism*. New York: Harcourt.

Weinstein, N. D. (1987). Unrealistic optimism about susceptibility to health problems: Conclusions from a community-wide sample. *Journal of Behavioral Medicine*, *10*(5), 481–500. doi:10.1007/BF00846146 PubMed

Weinstein, N. D. (1989). Optimistic biases about personal risks. *Science*, *246*(4935), 1232–1233. doi:10.1126/science.2686031 PubMed

Woodfield, R. (2000). *Women, Work and Computing*. Cambridge University Press; doi:10.1017/CBO9780511488948.

World Bank Report. (2012). Gender Equality and Development. Accessed from:https://siteresources.worldbank.org/INTWDR2012/Resources/7778105-1299699968583/7786210-1315936222006/Complete-Report.pdf

Ying, C., Xiaohu, Z., Guojun, Y., Jiani, B., & Guan, W. (2017). Social networks as mediator in entrepreneurial optimism and new venture performance. *Social Behavior and Personality*, *45*(4), 551–562. doi:10.2224/sbp.5924

Zhao, H., & Seibert, S. E. (2006). The Big Five personality dimensions and entrepreneurial status: A meta-analytical review. *The Journal of Applied Psychology*, *91*(2), 259–271. doi:10.1037/0021-9010.91.2.259 PubMed

Zhao, H., Seibert, S. E., & Lumpkin, G. T. (2010). The Relationship of Personality to Entrepreneurial Intentions and Performance: A Meta-Analytic Review. *Journal of Management*, *36*(2), 381–404. doi:10.1177/0149206309335187

Chapter 20
Viability of Entrepreneurship Education for Employability to Meet Industry 4.0 Challenges in the Circular Economy:
A Namibian Case

Wilfred Isak Aibs April
University of Namibia, Namibia

Ngepathimo Kadhila
University of Namibia, Namibia

ABSTRACT

Worldwide, a circular economy is seen as an innovative conduit for sustainable development. A body of knowledge exists in the literature in which scholars have outlined educational approaches and tools that can be used to accelerate the transition to a circular economy. This chapter contributes to this debate by arguing for the promotion of a circular economy through entrepreneurial education for sustainability as a graduate attribute. The chapter analyses the current state about circular entrepreneurial education in higher education institutions in Namibia as a case study, identifies the educational benefits of challenges to implementing circular entrepreneurial education, and makes suggestions for future development.

INTRODUCTION

The origins of the linear economy – the "take-make-use-dispose" model of consumption – date from the first, second and third industrial revolutions and the global economy developed around this model. Currently, sustainability is a hot topic globally as various social, economic and environmental factors mean that the linear economy is no longer sustainable. Therefore, a radical new model – the circular economy – is being advocated although it is not yet widely practised (Andrews, 2015). Many as a novel

DOI: 10.4018/978-1-7998-5116-5.ch020

Copyright © 2020, IGI Global. Copying or distributing in print or electronic forms without written permission of IGI Global is prohibited.

pathway to sustainable development see the circular economy concept. Numerous scholars have outlined educational approaches and tools that lecturers can use to accelerate the transition to a circular economy (Andrews, 2015; Kirchherr & Piscicelli, 2019; Mendoza, Schmid, & Azapagic, 2019). The circular economy entails reducing the consumption of raw materials, designing products in such a manner that they can easily be taken apart after use and reused (eco-design), prolonging the lifespan of products through maintenance and repair, using recyclables in products, and recovering raw materials from waste flow (Kirchherr & Piscicelli, 2019). The concept has become part of political, economic, social and environmental discourse around the world in recent years and a policy priority in many countries. The circular economy has been promoted from its previous status as a "well-intended" marginal model to a viable and essential alternative to current and predominant linear practice (Andrews, 2015).

In educational terms, the recognition that education, at all levels, can be a powerful tool for promoting sustainable development led to the idea of "education for sustainable development" (Mohamedbhai, 2015). According to Mohamedbhai (2015), in 2002, the United Nations declared 2005–2014 the Decade of Education for Sustainable Development, with the objective of integrating the principles and practices of sustainable development into all aspects of education and learning, with UNESCO being appointed as the lead implementing agency.

Nevertheless, how can sustainable development be achieved and what is the role of higher education in promoting it? In a world dominated by linear economic systems, the road to improving resource use is multifaceted. Various frameworks have been developed to guide organisations in embedding circular economy principles in their strategy and operational practice. Higher education institutions are strategic agents in supporting sustainable development through entrepreneurial education as one of the critical graduate attributes in the Fourth Industrial Revolution era, as they represent an area of particular interest for circular economy implementation owing to their socioeconomic relevance for the service sector and their influential role in supporting sustainable development in cities and regions worldwide (Mendoza et al., 2019). However, they also represent a source of environmental impact as a result of significant resource consumption and waste generation. As the engines driving skills and knowledge, higher education institutions play a primary role in making circular economy approaches reality and, as such, hold the potential for raising the bar on sustainable performance (Nunes et al., 2018). However, whilst public and private organisations are making progress in introducing sustainable practices, there is a lack of studies analysing the practical implementation of circular economy thinking through entrepreneurship education in the higher education sector (Mendoza et al., 2019).

Entrepreneurship plays a fundamental role in the economy and entrepreneurship education may help to achieve a circular economy, as it equips graduates with entrepreneurial skills that are geared to this (Mendoza et al., 2019). However, interest in entrepreneurship education is a relatively new concept in Europe and is certainly the case for Africa. Entrepreneurship in itself is a relatively young discipline; Shigeru Fijii, who started teaching the subject in 1938 at Kobe University in Japan (Dana, 1992), pioneered entrepreneurship in education. The reason why entrepreneurship is so important in the higher education space is that it is a dynamic process of vision, change and creation, which is valuable for both the employability of graduates and their self-employment in the future. The implementation of new ideas and creative solutions will require a certain application of energy and passion (Kuratko, 2003). Developing an inclination for entrepreneurship is not something, which happens by chance; one has to be intentional about it. It is envisaged that through entrepreneurial education students should be able to create products in the face of knowledge, which is already established, as well as challenge the status quo. In ensuring that the circular economy functions at its optimum, they must strive to be risk takers, pursuing opportunities that others may not be able to recognise or spot in normal circumstances (Nicolades, 2011). This however does not, imply that entrepreneurship can only be learnt in a formal setting; it is of course possible to gain entrepreneurial skills through informal training or in a setting, which is not strictly formal.

Against this background, most higher education institutions in Namibia are considering integrating mandatory entrepreneurship education in curricula and making it compulsory for all students. However, now theories specifically focused on entrepreneurship in the relatively new research area of the circular economy are lacking (Mendoza et al., 2019). This chapter seeks to determine the extent to which education providers are contributing to the circular economy. The focus of this chapter is on the promotion of circular entrepreneurial education that goes beyond merely promoting graduate employability and the role of higher education institutions in producing graduates with a circular entrepreneurship mindset who will create jobs in an environmentally sustainable manner by implementing circular economy business model innovations.

BACKGROUND

Worldwide, there is a greater sense of urgency regarding the implementation of a circular economy in all economic sectors to enhance resource efficiency. Countries have over time-experienced development in line with growth in industrialisation and globalisation, leading to a discussion as to whether this development is sustainable. Development practitioners have focused on sustainable development as an environmental concept, placing the emphasis on intergenerational equality in the future development of the world (Vitharana, 2015). For example, China has already taken some important steps such as passing a circular economy promotion law in 2009. This law was formulated for the purpose of facilitating a circular economy, raising resource utilisation rates, protecting and improving the environment and promoting sustainable development (Ghosh, 2019).

Namibia is faced with a multitude of challenges including the need for growing the national economy, which is currently in negative growth. This negative growth can be attributed to a number of critical factors including corruption, nepotism, favouritism and tribalism to name but a few. Accordingly, it is crucial that institutions of higher learning in Namibia such as the University of Namibia (UNAM), the Namibia University of Science and Technology (NUST) and the International University of Management (IUM) start with the promotion of entrepreneurial thinking and action as this will in essence contribute significantly to creating employment, which is essential for the masses of the unemployed in Namibia. In addition to these three main institutions of higher learning, there are also smaller institutions that offer courses in entrepreneurship. This is important given the fact that the unemployment rate in Namibia stands at 34%.

Although these efforts could be regarded as relatively small, they have recently begun to gain momentum. Thus, this chapter looks at entrepreneurial education as a viable option for employment or opening a business in the circular economy. The stance of this chapter is that in institutions of higher learning such as the University of Namibia, students have inherent untapped entrepreneurial potential and educators have to try and use all possible techniques or avenues of teaching and learning (e.g. blended learning) so that our graduates have the necessary skills when they enter the world of work and also to make a national impact. Furthermore, if Namibia is to be regarded as a circular economy. No skills or resources should go to waste and we should strive for sustainability in the education space. This implies that every student who undergoes our training should be able to plough back positively into the national economy. We will explore the background to this chapter in the next section.

This chapter explores the ways in which graduates can prepare for the world of work, as this has been actively promoted in Namibia over the past couple of years. The chapter focuses on the teaching of circular entrepreneurial skills. This chapter argues that through entrepreneurship in the Namibia economy a fresh competitiveness can be created in the marketplace, as entrepreneurs are individuals who identify opportunities and use them for their benefit and also to the benefit of those around them (Dana, 2012).

It is important to reiterate that Namibia is obliged to promote entrepreneurial thinking and action, as this will assist largely in creating employment and opportunities for the unemployed masses. As with many other nations around the globe it is important that Namibia become far more competitive in the market space. Entrepreneurs are essential in this regard, as they are able to spot the most needed opportunities. However, entrepreneurship in itself is not enough; there is thus a need to promote sustainable economic development through circular entrepreneurship, and higher education institutions have a role to play in achieving this goal. The stance of this chapter is that one should not only strive to prepare students to be employees but also to create employment for themselves and those around them. At the same time, graduates should not just create any employment but employment of an environmentally sustainable nature. Circular economy entrepreneurship education has the potential to achieve this goal. Higher education institutions in Namibia have introduced a number of programmes relating to entrepreneurial education that to date have not been fully implemented. Moreover, no reference is made to the circular economy discourse in those programmes, and thus there is still much work to be done. Most of the programmes comprise modules that students have to take as electives. Accordingly, higher education has overlooked the fact that the knowledge produced should also contribute to a better curriculum (Vitharana, 2015).

The main objective of this chapter is to demonstrate how circular entrepreneurial education can produce graduates who are ready for the world of work, whether employed or self-employed, in a manner that promotes sustainable development. In addition, the chapter seeks to demonstrate why it is not enough merely to offer entrepreneurship as a subject; the practical application of the subject is also crucial. Entrepreneurship education requires an understanding of the subject discipline and is essential for the performance of the organisation. It has to go beyond mere entrepreneurial skills to include the circular economy in line with the demands of the 21st century and the Fourth Industrial Revolution.

This chapter will also look at the skills required of graduates when entering employment or when becoming employers. In addition, issues such as efficacy beliefs will be examined, looking at a range of personal qualities and attributes that have a bearing on whether we produced graduates who are effective in the labour market. Issues such as "metacognition" which pertains to reflective practice as outlined by Schon (1983) and other scholars will be outlined. It is crucial that within the curriculum students be afforded an opportunity to reflect critique and practise the subject knowledge or content, as this had the potential to render them ready for the world of work upon graduation. If higher education institutions foster circular entrepreneurship education, graduates will be empowered to become savvy risk takers, implementers and innovators thus promoting the competitiveness of not only the institutions of higher learning but also businesses in Namibia. They in turn will be able to transform the economic landscape by creating and exploiting new opportunities in a sustainable manner.

The study on which this chapter is based comprised a case study design to assess the circular economy for sustainable development through entrepreneurship education in Namibia. A critical literature analysis was conducted and qualitative data collection involved the conducting of semi-structured interviews with academics from higher education institutions in Namibia.

CIRCULAR ECONOMY

According to Geissdoerfer, Savaget, Bocken, and Hultink (2017), the concept of a circular economy has been gaining momentum since the late 1970s, and has received increased attention in academic research in recent years. The circular economy is a system of production and consumption based on reusable and sustainable design. It seeks to eliminate waste from the current linear production system, also known as "take–make–waste" – where raw materials are extracted from the ground, and not long after are thrown away. A circular or closed loop system develops products and services in a way that is regenerative, restorative and reusable. This typically means using recycled materials and ensuring that at the end of a product's use, it can once again be recycled or happily decompose back to nature (Velenturf, Purnell, Macaskie, Mayes, & Sapsford, 2019). According to Velenturf et al. (2019), the main reason why there is a paradigm shift towards a circular economy is that natural resource exploitation is accelerating in the face of resource decline, while at the same time people are generating ever-growing fluxes of wastes and pollutants.

A circular economy differs from a linear economy in that in the latter products are made, for example mobile phones are used and when they break or there is a better model available, they are thrown away. At this point, all of the resources (i.e. energy, metal and water) used to make that phone are lost. For example, in Europe an average of 95% of a product's material and energy value is wasted in this way (Gower, Schroeder, Khinmaung-Moore, & Cook, 2016). The circular economy would address these challenges by eliminating waste and inefficiency at each stage of the product life cycle, from reducing the amount of time the product sits idle, to increasing the scope for reparability or re-manufacturing of the used components.

Globally, a growing number of innovative businesses have begun identifying viable opportunities for adopting sustainable business practices. This new forefront in corporate social responsibility is the circular business model, which unlike the current linear model, focuses on strategies for recycling and product life extension (Cooper, 2018). According to Cooper (2018), a circular economy business model is one in which users keep resources in use for as long as possible, extract the maximum value from them whilst in use, then recover and regenerate products and materials at the end their life. It is a more efficient and environmentally sound alternative to the traditional linear economy in which we make, use and dispose of resources. Examples of embracing the concept of circular economy vary from tyres to shoes to recycled batteries and turning wastewater into fertilisers.

Circular Entrepreneurship Theory

For the purpose of this chapter, a "circular entrepreneur" is defined as an agent who promotes change and exploits opportunities, with the purpose of doing business according to the principles of the circular economy concept. The concept of circular entrepreneurship has been developed with the purpose of stimulating research on this kind of entrepreneurial activity. Furthermore, the labelling of entrepreneurs who act outside the linear economy may interest researchers in the circular economy. Moreover, the theoretical distinction may help in understanding entrepreneurial activities and may assist in facilitating a transition Dana, 2012).

The circular entrepreneurship concept is derived from theory on sustainable, social and institutional entrepreneurship. In the current linear system, several different types of entrepreneur may be distinguished and this holds for the circular economic system. For the sake of furthering circular entrepreneurial theory, it is important to characterise the different types of circular entrepreneur. Accordingly, in this chapter it is argued that when sustainable, social and institutional entrepreneurs pursue their efforts according to the principles of circular economy, they are circular entrepreneurs. Circular entrepreneurship promotes both graduate employability and sustainable development. This implies that entrepreneurs will be able to implement circular economy business ventures that create jobs that preserve the environment. Therefore, this chapter argues that higher education institutions in Namibia have a role to play in producing circular entrepreneurs who will practise circular economy entrepreneurship to meet the demands for the 21st century and the Fourth Industrial Revolution by implementing circular economy business model innovations focusing on sustainable development.

State Entrepreneurial Education and the Circular Economy in Namibia

The thrust of this chapter is to establish whether entrepreneurial education is a viable option for a circular economy in Namibia and how this entrepreneurial behaviour and mind-set could be sustained in the long haul term the benefit of generations to come. If one explores the issue on a global scale in terms of macro-level private sector development, it is evident that the numerous United Nations goals can only be achieved through entrepreneurship. The country will need policies to this effect and access to markets must be provided. We argue that entrepreneurship can revitalise markets and, as new businesses are created, more jobs will be created in the Namibian economy, which will have a huge knock-on effect on the entire economy.

Looking into this from a social perspective, circular entrepreneurship has the ability to empower citizens, generate innovation and change stagnant mind-sets. These changes will create the potential to integrate successfully developing economies such as Namibia into the formal global economy. In order for this to happen, students in the current higher education system or space must be trained in such a way that they fully develop their employability skills in order to meet the ever-changing demands of the labour market (DIUS, 2008). Schumpeter (1947, 1949) was of the view that economic development is the fundamental basis for reinterpreting a vital process, which has in the past been crowded by neoclassical economic analysis with regard to static general equilibrium theory. In his analysis, he sees the entrepreneur as creating disequilibrium in order to profit from it. He maintained that invention and innovation should take central stage. The question now is, how easy can it be to teach an individual to become an entrepreneur and invent something that will lead to disequilibrium? Schumpeter's sentiments begs the question as to whether only ventures which generate profit can be regarded as entrepreneurial or is there perhaps a space for other arguments?

In contrast, Kirzner (1973, 1982) maintained that entrepreneurship might simply be able to identify an opportunity rather than creating one. In Kirzner's view, an entrepreneur is likely to benefit from education in general especially when they are given managerial training, without necessarily developing innovation skills. It is also important to understand that managerial skills are not the same as entrepreneurial skills. In the olden days, entrepreneurship was usually passed on from father to son. Associations known as "guilds" had complete control over entry to the various sectors in which economies were operating. Perfecting one's skills generally took long periods of training. These association expected everyone wishing to enter a particular craft or profession to undertake an apprenticeship during which a specific trade would be acquired or learnt. This type of training was usually related to personal or commercial relationships rather than a formal educational qualification that one is enrolled for. However, if we look at the Namibian education space today, vocational training is not regarded as a viable career option even though in Asian countries it has had fruitful results.

To foster circular entrepreneurial education, a number of organisations in Asia established networks, which were viewed as important mediums for establishing networks through which entrepreneurial knowledge, and skills could be transferred from entrepreneurs who were deemed successful to budding entrepreneurs. An informal vocational education system, which usually stemmed from ethnic networks, also provided mentors and on-the-job training. A number of research papers by Light (1972), studying Chinese entrepreneurs in New York, have indicated the significance of ethnic networks. Similar studies have been conducted in Italy and Canada, illustrating that networks have the ability to provide mentors and focused training and business ideas, market information and technical assistance. The invaluable contributions which networks can make to individuals should never be underestimated, for example sourcing, regulation, production, marketing, distribution logistics, customer service and even issues pertaining to taxation. According to Aldrich, Rosen, and Woodward (1987), the accessibility of networks is very important in predicting the creation of new ventures.

When addressing the issue of circular entrepreneurship education there is indeed an interrelationship between higher education, the labour market and sustainable development. It is from this vantage point that entrepreneurship education and its importance in terms of employability will be discussed. The way we teach entrepreneurship and understand it influence how we manage the employability of the graduates now and in the future. The current education in Namibia be it at a primary, secondary or tertiary level, does not give room to promote entrepreneurial thinking, creativity or innovation. The authors take this stance because although the government has invested heavily in education, investment does not correspond with the number of entrepreneurs, which the country is able to produce, and the unemployment levels in Namibia continue to rise.

There are a number of organisations in Namibia such as the Namibian Institute for Development Agency, the Namibia Chamber of Commerce and Industry (NCCI), and Small Medium Enterprises (SMEs) Compete, which provide entrepreneurial training for businesses. SME's Compete in Namibia specifically organises training for various small businesses from all corners of the country. There are number of non-governmental organisations in Namibia that provide training for entrepreneurs. Other noteworthy organisations in Namibia that provide training include the Konrad Adnenauer Stiftung, which believes that the development and drive of the entrepreneurial spirit can really help the society to achieve self-reliance and in turn lead to both the personal and entrepreneurial development of people. These organisations usually operate at a national level, but there are student organisations such as the Maltas Club Namibia, which was founded nine years ago, whose mission it is to foster entrepreneurial leadership among young people at institutions of higher learning. Higher education institutions in Namibia are encouraged to form partnerships with such organisations to promote circular entrepreneurship.

Teaching entrepreneurship is very different from teaching other courses in the social sciences. Entrepreneurship has a lot to do with practice. In entrepreneurship, students have to learn by doing. In addition, the discipline of entrepreneurship requires reflective praxis. Most of the dominant conversations about graduates are centred on the economic role that graduates can play and how they have to be prepared for jobs now and in the future.

This is certainly still the challenge institutions of higher learning are struggling with in Namibia – students look forward to getting a degree and finding employment in large corporations or any formal setting. They have no ambitious dreams and aspirations of a workspace, which can be innovative and creative in order to change history. Institutions of higher learning are thus faced with the challenge of striving to instil a greater entrepreneurial spirit in students. Currently, there is a move to advocate entrepreneurship through entrepreneur education in Namibia. However, there is no evidence yet that this has promoted circular entrepreneurial education, hence the need to do so. Circular entrepreneurial education must be spearheaded by local development needs and the role of education in changing lives must be clearly defined.

Circular entrepreneurship education should not just start at tertiary level but at the primary and secondary school, levels and the government should constantly strive to support such initiatives and promote holistic education at all levels, as this may result in great entrepreneurial ventures (Nieuwenhuizhen & Kroon, 2002). There are a number of reasons why higher education is so important in meeting the socioeconomic needs of a nation, while safeguarding social justice and democratic values. Universities or institutions of higher learning must serve as producers of knowledge and teach agents of change in society. It should be the raison d'etre of institutions of higher learning to promote research, knowledge and a highly skilled labour force if a nation wishes to compete in the international arena, which is highly diverse and yet dynamic. There is a huge demand for entrepreneurial education in Namibia, given its current challenges of corruption, nepotism and tribalism. This can bring about the necessary changes, as people will have a change of mind-set. This should not just be seen as a niche activity, but as an ongoing activity, which could result in both academics and students coming up with thought-provoking ideas.

According to Timmons and Spinelli (2004), entrepreneurial education has the potential to contribute to the creation of jobs as well as reduce poverty because people or communities will be able to sustain themselves. Since 1998, a number of institutions of higher learning in Namibia have seen entrepreneurship education as a viable option for promoting circular economy entrepreneurship. Upon its independence in 1990, Namibia had no formal entrepreneurship programmes in place. Since its inception in 1992, UNAM has only offered Entrepreneurship as a module. However, when we look at the school curriculum, which was formally introduced in 1998, there have been a number of changes. Although not offered as a formal programme, it is a course, which students in higher education institutions can choose as part of their curriculum. At UNAM and NUST, there are a number of diploma and degree programmes. However, many students who enrol for these programmes do not necessarily want to become entrepreneurs.

Another challenge is that universities do not teach students entrepreneurial skills, but rather managerial skills. When we refer to entrepreneurial skills, we are looking at the skills, which will really help students to succeed, regardless of the tall hierarchical structures in large organisations. These skills will enable students to rely on their own initiative and perform at their optimal level. The traditional schooling system has the potential to develop only the left hemisphere of the brain, while through the inculcation of entrepreneur skills the right hemisphere of the brain is improved (Dana, 2012).

Students studying business usually develop a cognitive understanding of concepts, especially when they are combined with traditional courses such as business and economics and this empowers them to develop managerial skills. However, it is important to reiterate that in order to develop entrepreneurs who will perform well in the circular economy, entrepreneurial skills that will enable them to make judgements and use their imaginations must be stressed. Dana (2012) linked courses such as accounting and logical thinking skills with the left hemisphere of the brain, while issues pertaining to creativity and judgement are associated with the right hemisphere of the brain.

Nicolaides (2011) work on experiential learning illustrates the role experience plays in the entire learning process. It is his assertion that concrete experience leads to effective observations and reflections, which are valuable for the learning process. In turn, these can be used to build abstract concepts, which lead to new scenarios, enabling learners to set more concrete ground for the basis of learning.

Nicolaides (2011) identified four categories, which clearly show the different aptitudes individuals have for different subjects. These are the *converger,* which has the dominant trait of being an abstract conceptualiser. This is usually someone who is not very emotional and prefers to deal with things rather than people. At the opposite end, the *diverger* is imaginative, emotional, and interested in working with people. Experience and reflective observation are their core strengths. The *assimilator* is someone who is focused on logic and precision and, finally, the *accommodator* is talented and is engaged in learning and in active experimentation, takes risk and does things according to the immediate circumstances.

In a study conducted by Ahmad (2012), graduates of McGill University were asked whether university training prepared them to be entrepreneurs. Twenty graduates responded that the MBA course was very helpful, while only 15 regarded the small business course as useful. The current methods used to judge entrepreneurial education have been deemed inappropriate because, while the present pedagogical approaches produce managers, to create the much-needed entrepreneurs, entrepreneurial skills should be developed to the fullest to compete in the international marketplace. Students are taught how to manage a business and not how to develop their own enterprises. Currently, the majority of the graduates from institutions of higher learning in Namibia are unemployed. This is because there have been many changes in organisations and the pace at which technology has changed, and graduates are required to respond to performance targets, thus the graduates of the late nineties are no longer an asset to employers.

Graduates are required to hit the ground running immediately they graduate and must demonstrate that they are willing and able to work. In this circular economy, waste of resources is not an option, as organisations cannot afford to retrain graduates who have been through the university system using government resources (such as loans or scholarships). Namibian companies are demanding that graduates exhibit more attributes that will make them successful once they are employed. For employers, having a degree is just a start but qualities such as friendliness, adaptability, flexibility and the willingness to learn are important. Graduates are expected to be good communicators and their interpersonal skills must be superb. Communication refers to writing, reading, verbal and listening skills, producing formal reports, bullet point summaries and effective email and telephone etiquette. Furthermore, graduates are expected to be able to engage with clients, persuade colleagues in teams and network within and outside the organisation, as it is important to understand that teamwork is not merely about taking a specific role on the team, but it is about taking different roles as the circumstances present themselves. Emotional and social intelligence are critical for 21st century graduates to succeed.

Teaching Circular Economy Through Entrepreneurship in the 21st Century

Entrepreneurial education can be viewed broadly in terms of the skills that can be taught in the educational system and the characteristics that can be engendered in individuals that will enable them to develop new and innovative plans (Ahmad, 2012). It is acknowledged in the literature that entrepreneurship knowledge and skills can be taught and developed provided the appropriate environment is present, and that education plays an important role in building entrepreneurial capacity (Ahmad, 2012). Ahmad suggests that there are three main objectives for introducing entrepreneurship education, namely, to develop a wide understanding of entrepreneurship, acquire an entrepreneurial mind-set, and know how to start and operate an enterprise effectively. This can provide students with an understanding of business – its purpose, its structure and its interrelationship with other segments of the economy and society. One of the ways of developing a culture of entrepreneurial thinking is by integrating entrepreneurship into educational systems. Some educators have proposed that introducing entrepreneurship into the school curriculum could serve the dual purpose of improving student performance outcomes and of exposing students to the concept of business ownership as an employment option after completing higher education. According to (Nicolaides, 2011), entrepreneurship gives students a new way of looking at the world, irrespective of whether or not they opt to develop their own enterprises. New business start-up activity is probably one of the most important social activities for countries around the world. The rise of new business significantly affects economies, creates jobs, and generally makes society more prosperous. Entrepreneurial education can have an impact on entrepreneurial personality traits as follows (Remeikiene, Startiene, & Dumciuviene, 2013):

- **Self-efficacy:** The power or capacity to produce a desired effect and is one of the key factors of the entrepreneurial intention;
- **Risk taking:** The tendency of an individual to take risks. Individuals who tolerate higher risk are more inclined to entrepreneurship while those who tolerate lower risk are less inclined;
- **Proactiveness or the propensity to act:** Is associated with entrepreneurial behavioural intentions;
- **Behavioural control:** Individuals' perceptions of how easily and successfully they could establish and run a business if they chose to start one;
- **Need for achievement:** One of the widespread indicators showing whether a person is inclined to entrepreneurship or not;
- **Internal locus of control:** Is associated with entrepreneurial success whereby the people who show strong self-control usually believe that the quality of life depends on their own actions, for example education, hard work and so forth.

According to Remeikiene et al. (2013), in practice most individuals start and develop a private business without proper education. Yet they are looking for a particular form of learning (university studies, different kinds of training, seminars) in order to acquire or improve business knowledge that can be helpful in finding more efficient business solutions and gaining confidence in personal abilities and decisions. Against this backdrop, entrepreneurship is now mainstream in the curricula of many higher education institutions around the world. However, there is little evidence of a focus of the circular economy in the teaching of entrepreneurship.

A circular economy is one that seeks to establish a system of consumption where materials continuously flow, being used and then reused, with as little waste and negative environmental impact as possible. Biological materials are returned to the environment and technological materials are utilised in a "make – use – repair/upgrade" cycle. Circular economics is seen as a break from our current linear economic system, where resources are used in a "make-consume-dispose" model with high waste and significant negative environmental impact. Circular economy seeks to make our societies less wasteful and more resourceful (Murray, 2019). As the Finnish Innovation Fund Sitra (n.d, 1) puts it:

In order to create a circular economy society, we need a new kind of expertise, co-operation between silos, development of the operating environment and a general change in attitudes and operating methods. Professionals, experts and decision-makers, both now and in the future, will play a decisive role in building a new future. Education plays an important role in developing experts.

Against the backdrop of Fourth Industrial Revolution, entrepreneurship is critical to unlocking job creation and fostering sustainable economic growth. Higher education in Namibia must therefore develop attributes that will equip graduates with awareness of the problems that the world faces and who are armed with ideas on how to tackle those (Nicolaides, 2011). Higher education is seen as the most effective tool when it comes to shaping the future by developing circular economy entrepreneurs and ensure sustainable entrepreneurship. For example, most higher education institutions during the Fourth Industrial Revolution are focusing on the provision of skills that would help to drive a rapidly growing economy and ultimately raise living standards. The challenges faced today are not simply supplying an industrialising economy with skilled labour, they are environmental – climate change, biodiversity collapse, plastic pollution (Murray, 2019). There have been a number of recent calls to introduce the teaching of entrepreneurship into the mainstream curriculum. If higher education institutions could focus on the teaching about the circular economy through entrepreneurship, this would help to equip graduates with entrepreneurial skills that would help them to create jobs related to environmental sustainability. Building a sustainable future and turning towards a circular economy signify a new type of thinking, and higher education plays a critical role in realising this goal. This could be achieved through circular economy strategies, such as circular product design, recycling and remanufacturing.

Benefits of Entrepreneurship Education in Circular Economy

Studying entrepreneurship benefits students and learners from different social and economic backgrounds because it teaches people to cultivate unique skills and think outside the box. Moreover, it creates opportunity, instils confidence, ensures social justice and stimulates the economy. Entrepreneurship students are more likely to launch businesses and have a greater intention to become entrepreneurs (Ahmad, 2012). Scholars argue that even if we cannot teach someone to be an entrepreneur, we can still teach the entrepreneurial skills needed to be successful (Ahmad, 2012; Nicolaides, 2011; Remeikiene et al., 2013). This highlights the need for entrepreneurship education to be introduced as a subject at all levels of education institutions in developing countries generally and Namibia in particular. Entrepreneurship education focuses on developing real-world skills that will help students to lead exceptional lives in a rapidly changing world. Entrepreneurship education teaches students crucial life skills, such as how to (Murray, 2019):

- Collaborate and work with a team;
- Speak in public and prepare an effective presentation;
- Collect and analyse data;
- Use social media as an advocacy tool;
- Solve real, complex problems that don't have a definitive answer; and
- Use curiosity and creativity to find an innovative approach to difficult problems.

Students learn to understand the product development cycle, come up with their own unique business proposals and establish their own business enterprises. Entrepreneurial education and training provides individuals with the ability to recognise commercial opportunities, as well as the self-esteem, knowledge and skills to act on them. It includes instruction in opportunity recognition, commercialising a concept, managing resources, and initiating a business venture. It also includes instruction in traditional business disciplines such as management, marketing, information systems and finance. Entrepreneurs or the move towards self-employment is, and will continue to become, an increasingly important element of economic growth and development (Govender, 2005).

In the Namibian context, it is important to consider how higher education institutions implement a curriculum that teaches students about the importance of sustainability within business. For instance, the circular economy is gaining momentum and attention within every industry and sector. By eliminating the traditional linear economy, the circular economy ultimately works to limit waste and maximise resources by implementing a closed-loop production process that is both restorative and regenerative. It is therefore important to shift from traditional entrepreneurial education towards circular entrepreneurial education to promote circular entrepreneurship. That way, entrepreneurship will help to promote graduate employability and at the same time promote sustainable economic development.

In addition, a circular economy has many benefits. For example, the more an industry reuses and recycles its waste and the closer it gets to the idea of circular economy, it will be more profitable while also less harmful to the environment. A circular economy would therefore be beneficial for societies not only in terms of conserving the environment but in terms of also minimising the exhaustive use of material, which is a potential competitive edge. This will also help with the elimination of waste from the value chain, which has the quantifiable benefit of reducing material cost (Remeikiene et al., 2013).

Progress and Challenges

Graduate employability is high on the agenda for many higher education institutions in the world for several reasons, including those related to government policy, employer demand and the shortage of skills in the workforce. For this reason, entrepreneurship education has expanded rapidly in higher education institutions around the world. This expansion has been driven by entrepreneurship's promise as a vehicle for promoting economic renewal and growth (Murray, 2019). A major premise underpinning the expansion of entrepreneurship education is that entrepreneurship can be learnt, can develop student entrepreneurial intentionality and ultimately facilitate business start-up (Remeikiene et al., 2013). The development of entrepreneurial intentions is increasingly being encouraged from the outset of higher education through to graduation, with the aim of stimulating entrepreneurial behaviour. The early development of entrepreneurial intentions is particularly important because it can lead to later persistence with the intention to start up a business (Crecu & Denes, 2017). Student participation in real-world projects and industry engagement through entrepreneurship, while completing academic qualifications, sets students apart when seeking graduate employment.

One way to identify opportunities for circular entrepreneurship in the Namibia is to be aware of the sustainability challenges that can inspire us to act. In this chapter, we present ways in which entrepreneurial education can result in graduate employability in Namibia. It is this chapter's assertion that there are specific skills and attributes that the Namibian graduate must embody. The chapter also argues that the various theories of learning will be essential when higher education institutions train graduates in entrepreneurial education. For Namibian graduates to be employable and hit the ground running as required by the market, we as institutions of higher learning must change the way we teach. Furthermore, national policies need to promote the circular economy, and students must be taught in such a way that they come up with genuine new ideas and develop entrepreneurial skills while in university. Curricula also need to be aligned with the needs of the labour market and students should be cognisant of their inherent capabilities and how they relate to the needs of employers and the world of work.

One of the challenges facing the entrepreneurial education sector is the gap between the rich and the poor. It is still the inherent deep-rooted belief that formal education is the only means by which citizens can reach their dreams and professional aspirations. However, this has not always been the case, as vocational education and training can also help the people in achieving their dreams and aspirations. Entrepreneurship should be a separate standalone subject and not be viewed as an integral part of business management or only as a field which is interdisciplinary. The manner in which the teaching of the subject is handled at universities or colleges should also change, by including lectures with guest speakers and experts from the industry. Other fundamental yet important changes or recommendations should be that the course content focus on the skills and knowledge of a particular entrepreneur that will make him/her successful.

It is of paramount importance that universities or colleges that are teaching entrepreneurship create environmental awareness of the various facets of entrepreneurship to support teaching and knowledge acquisition of the field. The learning should be seen as a lifelong endeavour in ensuring that there is sustenance in this new and dynamic century, where businesses are changing on a daily basis (Govender, 2005). Institutions of higher learning that are championing the teaching of entrepreneurship need to ask the critical question as to what the relationship is between the ever-changing workplace and the critical issues that employers are looking for in terms of the skills and capabilities that young people need to possess for success. It is critical that universities and colleges in Namibia, which are fostering entrepreneurial programmes to be supportive by making a deliberate effort to give students, more practical experience in sales and marketing in all fields of specialisation. They can thus use these skills whichever sector or career they intend to pursue in future. It is not an absolute guarantee that students will find appropriate employment once they finish their studies, but once they participate in projects and income-generating initiatives, they will be in a much better position to generate income for themselves while improving their personal and professional development at the same time.

If institutions of higher learning commit themselves to developing entrepreneurial hubs, students who are in their final year or have completed modules related to entrepreneurial studies will have an opportunity to develop their curriculum vitae by including the experiences they have developed by co-working with the entrepreneurship hub. At a macro level, entrepreneurial hubs at institutions of higher learning can alleviate poverty and unemployment as they equip students with the basic skills and instil a spirit of entrepreneurship which Namibia needs in this era (Govender, 2005).

Another suggestion is that higher education institutions should use reflective entrepreneurship practice so that it has a positive impact on the national economy of not only Namibia but also the continent of Africa. If people are equipped with skills and knowledge of entrepreneurship, there is a possibility that not only individual decisions will be impacted but also those of them around them. The places where young people are learning should be set up in such a manner that they are viewed as catalysts for entrepreneurial motivation and should be seen as a valuable alternative to working for an employer. When teaching and learning is taking place, the curiosity of those who take part in the learning process should be sparked, so that they too become aware of the opportunities.

Furthermore, higher education institutions should be seen as spaces where the mentality of teamwork is developed between students and academics with respect to things which are entrepreneurial. For this to materialise, a paradigm shift needs to take place, where team-based work is encouraged and the levels of management are fewer with minimum supervision. In encouraging learning in a circular economy, learning groups can also go a long way to sustaining a learning climate. These groups may constitute students learning from one another, with the guidance of the academic staff or facilitators to succeed in envisaged business ventures now and in the near future. One of the key implications is that it is not enough knowing that the students have developed entrepreneurial skills; we need to fully understand and follow up with employers upon graduation and see whether any significant strides have been made.

It is important to reiterate that our key emphasis will be on entrepreneurial education and how it can be a viable option for employability in the circular economy.

The chapter established that there are also no specific guidelines for sectors on how to implement a circular economy. Public awareness about a circular economy is still not sufficient. Furthermore, there are no regulations pertaining to the circular economy and its implementation. Finally, this research study had some limitations and challenges. When collecting the secondary data, documentation on the circular economy in Namibia was sparse. The concept of a circular economy is relatively new in Namibia and therefore there is little documented information about this concept in the Namibian context. Therefore, background information related to the circular economy was lacking and out of date. In fact, a comprehensive study regarding the circular economy in Namibia has never been done, which increased the importance of the thesis on which this chapter is based.

SOLUTIONS AND RECOMMENDATIONS

The vision of a circular economy is that key non-renewable resources should be used sustainably, and this involves different parts of the university working together with others in a symbiotic way. By reducing the level of material input needed in the production of products, the economy may save billions of dollars. Furthermore, deploying a circular economy design in technological products may result in securing access to better and cheaper products. Therefore, higher education institutions may play a critical role in the promotion of a circular economy through circular entrepreneur education. The key recommendations to higher education institutions and policy makers alike are as follows:

- Higher education institutions must use circular economy as a focus for teaching entrepreneurship to produce circular entrepreneurs who will not only create jobs but also at the same time develop businesses that focus on sustainable economic development;
- Higher education institutions must engage in partnerships with industries, which are already pursuing sustainability strategies to explore collaborative opportunities and exposure for students in the teaching of circular entrepreneurship;
- Circular entrepreneurship education requires higher education institutions to observe a shift in pedagogy. In traditional classrooms, each act of teaching focuses on a particular segment of the curriculum; each learning situation is controlled in such a way that students do not feel insecure while they learn;
- There is a need for curriculum reform to deal with concrete didactical and pedagogical issues: teaching and learning, involving subject content, didactics, pedagogical development and evaluation. Changes in pedagogy could include a greater use of various types of case studies, lectures by guest speakers, inviting entrepreneurs into the classroom, and business venture assignments with guidance and consultation with practising entrepreneurs, company visits, and computer simulations with new venture decision-making programs, interviews with entrepreneurs, student entrepreneurship clubs and hands-on experience of business start-up;
- National policies in Namibia should emphasise the development of circular entrepreneurship, which in turn should be reflected in the integration of circular entrepreneurship into curricula at the tertiary level;
- Policymakers should develop policies that focus on circular economy and sustainable development.

CONCLUSION AND FURTHER RESEARCH DIRECTIONS

This chapter observed that the fundamental challenges of the current economic arrangements in most countries worldwide, including Namibia, are based on the linear economy. It was established that the take–make–dispose construct is not suited to the current demands of the 21st century and Industry 4.0. The circular economy is therefore a viable option for sustainable development. This chapter explored the possibilities that exist to achieve circular economy in Namibia and elsewhere, through circular entrepreneurship education in terms of both promoting graduate employability and sustainable economic development. Firstly, entrepreneurship gives students a new way of looking at the universe, regardless of whether they are interested in pursuing an enterprising career or not. If entrepreneurship is based on circular economy principles, it will help to promote sustainable development. Given the current landscape and the challenges Namibian organisations are experiencing, starting one's own enterprise should be one of the most important activities. If young people are encouraged to start their own circular businesses the rise of new enterprises may indeed affect economies and generate jobs, which will in turn make society more prosperous and successful, while at the same time preserving the environment. For many economies around the globe, entrepreneurship is now vital for any economy. This chapter highlighted that a paradigm shift is required to change the way that entrepreneurship is viewed across different economies. This chapter, therefore, highlighted the essence of moving away from entrepreneurial education towards circular entrepreneurial education to advocate for sustainable economic development through the establishment of circular economy business ventures.

Finally, this study used Namibia as a case study. The study could have been more valuable if it had expanded the scope to include other countries especially in the Southern African Development Community (SADC) region. A more thorough, in-depth and broader study covering different countries is therefore suggested to increase the generalisability of the findings. This will help to establish how circular economy entrepreneur education could be integrated in the higher education curricula beyond Namibia to produce graduates who will become circular entrepreneurs to promote sustainable development.

REFERENCES

Ahmad, S. Z. (2012). The need for inclusion of entrepreneurship education in Malaysia lower and higher learning institutions. *Education + Training*, *55*(2), 191–203. doi:10.1108/00400911311304823

Aldrich, H. E., Rosen, B., & Woodward, W. (1987). *The impact of social networks on business: Foundlings and profit in a longitudinal study. In Frontiers of entrepreneurship research* (pp. 154–168). Wellesley, MA: Babson College.

Andrews, D. (2015). The circular economy, design thinking and education for sustainability. *Local Economy*, *30*(3), 305–315. doi:10.1177/0269094215578226

Cooper, R. (2018). *The growing trend of circular economy*. Retrieved from http://www.climateaction.org/climate-leader-papers/the-growing-trend-of-circular-economy

Dana, L. P. (1992, November). Entrepreneurial education in Europe. *Journal of Education for Business*, *68*(2), 74–78. doi:10.1080/08832323.1992.10117590

Finnish Innovation Fund Sitra. (n.d.). *Circular economy teaching for all levels of education.* Retrieved from https://www.sitra.fi/en/projects/circular-economy-teaching-levels-education/

Geissdoerfer, M., Savaget, P., Bocken, N., & Hultink, E. (2017). The circular economy: A new sustainability paradigm? *Journal of Cleaner Production, 143*, 757–768. doi:10.1016/j.jclepro.2016.12.048

Ghosh, A. (2019). *The circular economy is a golden opportunity: Don't let it go to waste.* Retrieved from https://www.weforum.org/agenda/2019/01/the-circular-economy-turns-waste-into-gold-so-lets-get-on-with-it/

Govender, K. K. (2005). *Executive Deans Message.* Partnership between Direct Selling Association and the University of Johannesburg.

Gower, R., Schroeder, P. M., Khinmaung-Moore, J., & Cook, P. (2016). *Virtuous circle: How the circular economy can create jobs and save lives in low and middle-income countries.* Retrieved from https://www.ids.ac.uk/publications/virtuous-circle-how-the-circular-economy-can-create-jobs-and-save-lives-in-low-and-middle-income-countries/

Grecu, V., & Denes, C. (2017). *Benefits of entrepreneurship education and training for engineering students.* Retrieved from https://www.researchgate.net/publication/319023075_Benefits_of_entrepreneurship_education_and_training_for_engineering_students

Kirchherr, J., & Piscicelli, L. (2019). *Towards an Education for the Circular Economy (ECE): Five teaching principles and a case study.* doi:10.1016/j.resconrec.2019.104406

Kirzner, I. M. (1973). *Competition and entrepreneurship.* Chicago, IL: University of Chicago.

Kirzner, I. M. (1982). *Method, process and Austrian economics.* Lexington, MA: Kolb Lexington Books.

Kuratko, D. F. (2003). Entrepreneurship education: Emerging trends and challenges for the 21st century. The Entrepreneurship Program, College of Business, Ball State University, Muncie, IN.

Light, I. (1972). *Ethnic enterprise in America: Business and welfare amongst Chinese, Japanese and Blacks.* Berkeley, CA: University of California.

Mendoza, J. M. F., Schmid, A. G., & Azapagic, A. (2019). Building a business case for implementation of circular economy in higher education institutions. *Journal of Cleaner Production, 220*, 553–567. doi:10.1016/j.jclepro.2019.02.045

Mohamedbhai, G. (2015). *What role for higher education in sustainable development?* World University News. Retrieved from https://www.universityworldnews.com/post.php?story=20150108194231213

Nicolades, A. (2011). Entrepreneurship: The role of higher education in South Africa. *Educational Research, 2*(4), 103–105.

Nieuwenhuizhen, C., & Kroon, J. (2002). Identification of entrepreneurial success factors to determine the content of entrepreneurship subjects. *South African Journal of Higher Education, 16*(3), 157–166.

Nunes, B. T., Pollard, S. J. T., Burgess, P., Ellis, G., De los Rios, T. C., & Charnley, F. (2018). Contributions to the circular economy: Professing the hidden curriculum. *Sustainability, 10*(8), 1–24. doi:10.3390u10082719

Remeikiene, R., Startiene, G., & Dumciuviene, D. (2013). *Explaining entrepreneurial intention of university students: The role of entrepreneurial education.* Paper presented at the International Conference on Knowledge Management, Innovation and Learning, Zadar, Croatia.

Schon, D. (1993). *The reflective practitioner: How professionals think in action.* New York: Basic Books.

Schumpeter, J. (1947). The creative response to economic history. *The Journal of Economic History, 7*(2), 149–159. doi:10.1017/S0022050700054279

Schumpeter, J. (1949). *Economic theory and entrepreneurial history: Change and the entrepreneur.* Cambridge, MA: Harvard University Press.

Timmons, J. A., & Spinelli, S. (2004). *New venture creation: Entrepreneurship for the 21st century.* Boston, MA: McGraw Hill Irwin.

Velenturf, A. P. M., Purnell, P., Macaskie, L. E., Mayes, W. M., & Sapsford, D. J. (2019). A new perspective on a global circular economy. In Resource recovery from wastes: Towards a circular economy (pp. 1–22). doi:10.1039/9781788016353-00001

ADDITIONAL READING

Basu, A., & Virick, M. (2008). *Assessing entrepreneurial intentions amongst students: a comparative study.* Paper presented at 12th Annual Meeting of the National Collegiate Inventors and Innovators Alliance. Dallas, TX.

Burnett, H. (2008). Designing and implementing an undergraduate course in entrepreneurship in Australia using experiential and problem-based learning techniques. *Training and Management Development Methods, 5*(22), 375–383.

Colette, H., Frances, H., & Hill, C. L. (2005). Entrepreneurship education and training: Can entrepreneurship be taught? Part I. *Education + Training, 47*(2), 98–111. doi:10.1108/00400910510586524

Kuratko, D. F. (2003). Entrepreneurship education: Emerging trends and challenges for the 21st century. The Entrepreneurship Program, College of Business, Ball State University, Muncie, IN.

Pomponi, F., & Moncaster, A. (2017). Circular economy for the built environment: A research framework. *Journal of Cleaner Production, 143*, 710–718. doi:10.1016/j.jclepro.2016.12.055

Schaltegger, S., & Wagner, M. (2011). Sustainable entrepreneurship and sustainability innovation: Categories and interactions. *Business Strategy and the Environment, 20*(4), 222–237. doi:10.1002/bse.682

Vitharana, A. D. (2015). The solid waste management for sustainable development: A case study of Hambantota municipal council area in Sri Lanka. *Sri Lanka Journal of Economic Research, 3*(1), 79–111.

KEY TERMS AND DEFINITIONS

Circular Economy: A systemic approach to economic development designed to benefit businesses, society and the environment for a regenerative economy.

Circular Entrepreneur: An agent that fosters the creation of a circular economy through innovative products, services and/or business models, who take risks and takes advantage of new opportunities to create positive changes.

Circular Entrepreneurship Education: Refers to entrepreneurship education that purposefully educates students in such a manner that stimulates them to implement circular economy business model innovations.

Entrepreneurship: The process through which an individual takes capital, labour and natural resources and combines them with the risk linked to the provision of goods and services.

Linear Economy: A linear economy traditionally follows the "take–make–dispose" step-by-step plan. This means that raw materials are collected and then transformed into products that are used until they are finally discarded as waste.

Sustainable Development: Development that meets the needs of the present without compromising the ability of future generations to meet their own needs.

Chapter 21
Design Thinking Perspective in Entrepreneurship Education

Mufaro Dzingirai
Midlands State University, Zimbabwe

ABSTRACT

To stimulate the exploitation of entrepreneurial opportunities in a circular economy, there is a growing need for educators, especially in the context of universities, to make a paradigm shift from conventional entrepreneurship teaching methodologies to design thinking. As such, the call for a design-based entrepreneurship curriculum has attracted the interests of scholars, researchers, educators, and policymakers in recent years. Unfortunately, little is known about how design thinking processes and tools are being incorporated into entrepreneurship education. Consequently, this chapter captures in detail the worldwide practices and controversies mainly associated with entrepreneurship education from a design thinking standpoint, reviews entrepreneurship education in relation to entrepreneurship development in a circular economy, captures perceptions of academics about design-based entrepreneurship education, proposes recommendations to policymakers and practitioners, and identifies research gaps for further studies.

INTRODUCTION

In recent years, entrepreneurship education as a phenomenon has become a central topic in the face of a complex, dynamic and chaotic environment. This has pressurized universities to be accountable for churning out entrepreneurial graduates who can increasingly seize entrepreneurial opportunities in a circular economy. Despite the fact that producing entrepreneurial graduates is now a strategic priority of many universities around the world, entrepreneurship education that is currently offered by many universities is being often criticized for being too managerial-oriented and rational (Daniel, 2016). With this in mind, it appears that design thinking can be a powerful tool for attaining business goals and exploiting untapped entrepreneurial opportunities. Worryingly, little is known about how we can learn from principles of design thinking so as to enrich entrepreneurship education scholarship (Huq & Gilbert, 2017).

The importance of entrepreneurship education has gained much prominence in the current stock of knowledge on entrepreneurship over the last two decades. With the adoption of entrepreneurship

DOI: 10.4018/978-1-7998-5116-5.ch021

Copyright © 2020, IGI Global. Copying or distributing in print or electronic forms without written permission of IGI Global is prohibited.

education, it is common knowledge that economic growth can be accelerated (McGuigan, 2016; Rauch & Hulsink, 2015). Despite the calls for entrepreneurship education in higher education, it is necessary to mention that the construct of entrepreneurship education has generated much scholarly debate when it comes to fostering entrepreneurial behavior. Within this context, entrepreneurship education that is currently offered by many universities is being often criticized for being too managerial-oriented and rational (Daniel, 2016; Pittaway & Edwards, 2012). As such, it appears that the incorporation of design thinking into the entrepreneurship curriculum is necessary for attaining business goals and exploiting untapped entrepreneurial opportunities in the current uncertain environment (Huber, Peisl, Gedeon, Brodie, & Sailer, 2016; Val et al., 2017). This means that a need emerges for a deeper understanding of the interaction between entrepreneurship education and design thinking principles in an attempt to advance the entrepreneurship scholarship. This is supported by the fact that the design thinking approach acknowledges the inherent intricacy of the 21st century and embraces the open-ended, ambiguous, wicked and open-ended problems associated with the current era (Conklin, 2005; Liedtka & Ogilvie, 2014; Stovang & Nielsen, 2015).

Given the popularity and importance of design thinking, it is not surprising to witness the widespread application of design thinking tenets and tools outside the context of the industry (Huq & Gilbert, 2017; Neck & Greene, 2011). This is in harmony with the view of Stewart (2011) who stressed that there is a paradigm shift from designing things that are material in nature to immaterial things like systems and services. With this in mind, several academics from the management field have suggested that the design thinking lens should receive much attention in the education and management practice (Brown, 2009; Liedtka & Ogilvie, 2014; Razzouk & Shute, 2012; Watson, 2015). In fact, with respect to entrepreneurship education, there is growing literature that views the design thinking approach as a valuable ingredient when it comes to curriculum development in an effort to stimulate creativity, innovation, collaboration and problem-solving in a rapidly-changing and complex environment.

It is imperative at this juncture to mention that different ways can be used by educators to teach entrepreneurship courses. More strikingly, a survey of entrepreneurship education literature revealed that “about”, “for”, and “through” are the main approaches linked to the teaching of entrepreneurship (Lackéus, 2015; Pittaway & Edwards, 2012). Nonetheless, most of the entrepreneurship education provided by institutions of higher education has been found to be based on “about” approach which has been linked to traditional pedagogy that does not promote problem-centered approach and active student engagement in learning activities and projects (Mwasalwiba, 2010; Stovang & Nielsen, 2015). In order to address the challenges associated with the traditional pedagogy of entrepreneurship, it appears as the right time for entrepreneurship educators to effectively and efficiently use the design thinking methodologies (Stovang & Nielsen, 2015). However, to the best knowledge of the author, little is known about the interaction between entrepreneurship education and design thinking principles at the university level especially in the context of developing countries.

In light of the above insightful discussion, there is an emerged need to conduct empirical research to cover this knowledge gap within the mainstream entrepreneurship literature. Notably, the current study employed an exploratory research design. The chapter’s main objectives are to capture how academics perceive entrepreneurship education from a design thinking perspective and capture the infrastructure support that is deemed necessary to effectively incorporate a design-thinking approach into entrepreneurship course. Admittedly, this research gathers empirical evidence to inform policymakers and practitioners.

BACKGROUND

There is a limited but burgeoning body of extant literature that apparently captures the role of higher education in providing entrepreneurship education. Undoubtedly, institutions of higher learning in both developing and developed countries are increasingly expected by educational stakeholders to be entrepreneurial institutions that are accountable for churning out knowledgeable and entrepreneurial graduates (Millican, 2014). In fact, it is widely recognized that universities should play a vital role in delivering entrepreneurship education with a focus on stimulating entrepreneurship development. With multiple existing streams of entrepreneurship inquiry, it is salient to observe that entrepreneurship education is not a new concept within the context of the higher education sector. In this regard, entrepreneurship education was firstly offered in American business schools in the 1940s. Specifically, Harvard Business School has managed to firstly offer entrepreneurship course in 1947 (Nabi, Linan, Fayolle, Krueger, & Walmsley, 2017) and the first entrepreneurship conference in America was hosted by Purdue University in 1970 (Nieuwenhuizen, Groenewald, Davids, van Rensburg, & Schachtebeck, 2016). From 1947 up to date, we have witnessed an exponential growth of entrepreneurship programs offered by institutions of higher learning globally (Nabi, Linan, Fayolle, Krueger, & Walmsley, 2017; Solomon, 2007). Entrepreneurship education in Germany was witnessed in 1998 and it was adopted by many institutions as a strategic approach to instill an entrepreneurial spirit in students. The entrepreneurship education programs in Germany are regarded as successful as they are achieving their intended goals (Brem & Licha, 2018; Mauchi et al., 2011). The entrepreneurship education wave in the higher education sector can be linked to the fact that many governments across the globe are promoting entrepreneurship in their laws and policies owing to its notable economic and social benefits (O'Connor, 2013).

India is widely recognized as one of the pioneering developing countries with respect to the provision of entrepreneurship education. In this respect, after independence, India managed to embrace entrepreneurship education as a strategic priority for encouraging the creation of Small to Medium Enterprises (SMEs) and promoting self-employment. Hence, financial institutions, as well as state governments, started to offer entrepreneurship education in India in the 1960s and 1970s (Rehman & Elahi, 2012). During the 1980s, there was also a general widespread acceptance of entrepreneurship education as evidenced by the adoption of entrepreneurship education by management and technology institutions in India. Specifically, the government of India managed to support entrepreneurship education initiatives through setting up incubation centers and Science and Technology Parks (STEPs) at few selected technical institutions. In the 1990s, India witnessed success stories of entrepreneurship education and widespread adoption of entrepreneurship education by various institutions like Non-Governmental Organisations (NGOs) and consultancy organizations. More strikingly, in 2012, a survey was carried out in India on entrepreneurship education. The results of the survey revealed that 44 500 students were enrolled in various entrepreneurship courses and the number of students was expected to reach 54 700 at the end of 2012 (Rehman & Elahi, 2012).

With respect to the South African context, entrepreneurship education has started to be offered in institutions of higher education in the early 1990s (Kroon & Meyer, 2001). With this observation in mind, Co & Mitchell, (2006) concluded that entrepreneurship education is at an infant stage within the South African context particularly in the institutions of higher learning. Nonetheless, it is impressive to note that many universities in South Africa like Cape Peninsula University of Technology, Nelson Mandela Metropolitan University, Durban Institute of Technology, North-West University, University of Pretoria, Tswane University of Technology, University of Stellenbosch, Rhodes University, University of Witswatersrand, University of Free State, University of South Africa, University of Western Cape and University of KwaZulu-Natal are offering entrepreneurship education. In spite of the adoption of entrepreneurship education, some scholars are very skeptical about the teaching methods of entrepreneurship education in these institutions in South Africa owing to the fact that the traditional classroom teaching methods are being practiced (Co & Mitchell, 2006).

In the case of Zimbabwe, following a 1999 Nziramasanga Commission, many institutions of higher learning like universities, colleges, and vocational institutes have managed to come up with entrepreneurship courses from 2000 onwards. The main purpose of embracing entrepreneurship education is to ensure that students from institutions of higher learning in Zimbabwe become entrepreneurial-minded so that they can establish their own new ventures and contribute immensely towards economic development and growth. Nevertheless, limited is known about how entrepreneurship courses can be taught so that more startups owned by graduates can be witnessed (Mauch et al., 2011). It seems to be apparent that entrepreneurship education among universities in Zimbabwe is at an infant stage. Admittedly, there is no doubt that the issues related to economic development, economic growth, poverty alleviation, drug abuse by youths, and graduate unemployment have apparently heightened the need for entrepreneurship education in Zimbabwe. More interestingly, the government of Zimbabwe is playing a great role in promoting entrepreneurship education in the higher education sector of Zimbabwe through the Ministry of Small to Medium Enterprises.

Going forward, various institutions of higher education in Zimbabwe like the University of Zimbabwe have introduced a non-compulsory entrepreneurship curriculum with a particular bias towards students in the faculty of commerce (Munyanyiwa, Svotwa, Rudumbu, & Mutsau, 2016). However, since 2011, Zimbabwean polytechnic students studying towards national certificate with Higher Education Examination Council (HEXCO) have had mandated to take a compulsory entrepreneurship course in an effort to unlock the entrepreneurial potential of students. The Ministry of Higher Education and Technology's 2010-15 Strategic Plan provides ample evidence of the entrepreneurship education drive in Zimbabwe as it apparently stipulates the urgent need for entrepreneurship education in the Zimbabwean technical and vocational institutions (Ministry of Higher Education, 2010). This positive development in terms of inculcating entrepreneurial spirit among polytechnic students can accelerate the entrepreneurship process in the Zimbabwean context. Nevertheless, Mauchi et al., (2011) found that teacher-centered approaches are mainly used to teach entrepreneurship at the university level in Zimbabwe.

Despite the fact that entrepreneurship education is not a new concept, it is evident in the available entrepreneurship literature that there is no standard definition of entrepreneurship education. In this respect, entrepreneurship education is a process whereby transformational education is provided to students from a learner-centered approach so that they can have a better understanding of their capacity to create, identify and exploit future opportunities for their satisfaction (Jones, 2011). While there is no one-size-fits-all definition of entrepreneurship education, it is clear, based on the above definition of entrepreneurship education that effective entrepreneurship education encompasses a learner-based approach that stimulates the transformation of mindset and behavior of students towards new venture creation through creation, identification, and exploitation of untapped opportunities. More interestingly, Fayolle, Gally, & Lassas-Clerc (2006) defined entrepreneurship education as a detailed pedagogical process or program aimed at developing entrepreneurial skills and attitudes of students. Put simply, it is common knowledge that entrepreneurship education can be defined as the study of the process of discovery and source of opportunities in a manner that leads to economic value (Shane & Venkataraman, 2000).

Based on the above definitions of entrepreneurship education, it is of great importance to mention that entrepreneurship education is a complex and relative concept that can mean differently to different stakeholders of the education sector such as students, educators, employers, and policymakers. Accordingly, entrepreneurship educators play a pivotal role as they are accountable for shaping the entrepreneurial attitudes, skills, and knowledge with the aim of producing entrepreneurial students who can solve the complex socio-economic problems (Huq & Gilbert, 2017).

More strikingly, it is deemed necessary to highlight that the current body of knowledge on entrepreneurship widely support the notion that the main thrust of delivering entrepreneurship education in higher education is to foster entrepreneurial skills, attitude, behavior, values, knowledge, intentions, and managerial attributes as well as idea generation (Fayolle, 2009; Jones & Matlay, 2011; Co & Mitchell, 2006). With this observation in mind, it is widely recognized that more support for entrepreneurship education has been witnessed in developed and developing nations over the past decade (Akhuemonkhan & Sofoluwe, 2013; McGuigan, 2016; Rauch & Hulsink, 2015; Storen, 2014). In fact, it appears that the rationale for such support is based on the fact that entrepreneurship education can lead to an exponential increase of successful entrepreneurs who can address the societal problems (Millán, Congregado, Román, van Praag, & van Stel, 2014; Roman & Maxim. 2017). In spite of a general consensus among scholars about the importance of entrepreneurship education, some scholars underscored that entrepreneurship education cannot lead to successful entrepreneurs (Nabi, Walmsley, Liñán, Akhtar, & Neame, 2018; Peterman & Kennedy, 2003).

The increase in the provision of entrepreneurship education in both developing and developed countries appears to be an apparent indication that many institutions of higher learning are starting to recognize the potential positive outcomes associated with delivering high-quality entrepreneurship education (Rideout & Gray, 2013). The potential benefits associated with effective entrepreneurship education such as enhancement of student's entrepreneurial knowledge, behavior and attitude, establishment of graduate start-ups, employment creation, and economic development and growth can be witnessed (Bosma, Acs, Autio, Coduras, & Levine, 2008; Greene & Saridakis, 2008; Rideout & Gray,2013). It is widely known that universities must play a leading role in inculcating a strong entrepreneurial culture and creating an entrepreneurial mindset among students. With this in mind, it is not surprising that the challenges and problems associated with a circular economy can be solved by the entrepreneurs.

In light of the above debate on the importance of entrepreneurship education in higher education, entrepreneurship education that is currently offered by many universities is being often criticized for being too managerial-oriented and rational. In fact, the traditional ways of teaching entrepreneurship in the context of universities seem to be ineffective to produce entrepreneurial graduates that can address wicked problems associated with the 21st century. Specifically, Fayolle & Gailly (2008) and Oosterbeek, Van Praag, & Ijsselstein (2010) accentuated that the traditional teaching methodologies are not effective in the 21st century given the complexities associated with the process of entrepreneurship. Consequently, many questions can be raised concerning the best methods to teach entrepreneurship. In this respect, it seems to be the right time to embrace the design thinking approach to teaching entrepreneurship. This could allow universities to churn out entrepreneurial students who are capable to address wicked problems and ill-defined problems using creative and innovative techniques. Unfortunately, our knowledge about designing thinking approach in relation to entrepreneurship education within the context of the institutions of higher education is limited (Huq & Gilbert, 2017). Additionally, there are also ongoing hot debates surrounding the applicability of the design thinking lens in the higher education sector (Von Kortzfleisch, Zerwas, & Mokanis, 2013).

It is imperative to note that there is a multiplicity of developments that led to the applicability of design thinking processes and methodologies in entrepreneurship pedagogy. Firstly, entrepreneurship context that is more associated with dynamism and uncertainty has pressurized various actors such as educators, policymakers, mentors, students and entrepreneurs to deviate from conventional analytic approaches like writing a business plan (Blank & Dorf, 2012; Stovang & Nielsen, 2015). Secondly, the emergence of the Lean Startup movement has managed to contextualize the tenets, processes, and methodologies of the design thinking approach into entrepreneurship courses (Ries, 2011). Thirdly, the recent paradigm shift in the available entrepreneurship literature towards acceptance of the idea that avenues of entrepreneurial opportunities can be created supports the call for utilization of designer's methodology by an entrepreneur (Sarooghi, Sunny, Hornsby, & Fernhaber, 2019). In spite of the fact these noticeable developments have apparently transformed the manner in which we perceive entrepreneurship education, empirical studies that examine the entrepreneurship education from design thinking standpoint is still scant. Consequently, it appears to be the most suitable time to probe how design thinking is being incorporated into entrepreneurship education within the higher education landscape.

Design Thinking and Entrepreneurship Education in Higher Education

It is generally agreed that design thinking is a new form of teaching entrepreneurship course that focuses more on the generation of new alternative solutions and development of creative ideas rather than focusing on available alternatives as well as picking up of existing alternatives. With this in mind, it is very important to note that there is a plethora of design thinking models in the extant literature. For the purpose of this study, the researcher adopted the model proposed by Brown (2008) that captures empathizing, defining, ideation, prototyping, and testing as five stages of design thinking approach. This approach has gained prominence in recent years as an efficient and effective method that advocates for action-oriented when it comes to tackling highly complex, chaotic and ambiguous situations and unmasking unanticipated wicked problems at a very early stage (Fixson & Rao, 2014). In this regard, several scholars documented that the design thinking approach can be appropriately applied to entrepreneurship education (Garbuio, Dong, Lin, Tschang, & Lovallo, 2018; Nielsen & Stovang, 2015). With the adoption of design thinking, entrepreneurship students are oriented to wicked and complex entrepreneurial problems and prepared to address these problems as graduates (Garbuio et al., 2018). Interestingly, Penaluna & Penaluna, (2019) underscored that entrepreneurship education from a design thinking standpoint allows instructors to apply entrepreneurship curriculum to other study programs outside business schools. To this end, design thinking seems to be a powerful teaching method of entrepreneurship course that arrest the weaknesses of traditional methods of teaching entrepreneurship education.

Design thinking as a notion can be traced back to architecture, industry and design fields. The design thinking movement started to gain popularity as a robust methodology to address complex societal problems in the late 1960s (Sarooghi, Sunny, Hornsby, & Fernhaber, 2019). To address the ineffectiveness of traditional teaching methods of entrepreneurship, it appears that the design thinking approach can be a powerful tool for teaching entrepreneurship education particularly in the landscape of higher education. This approach can allow the institutions of higher education to produce entrepreneurial students who can efficiently and effectively deal with ill-defined problems associated with 21st society. It is common knowledge that both designers and entrepreneurs have many aspects in common like problem-solving. This shows that entrepreneurs can think like designers (Neck & Greene, 2011). In fact, in recent years, the design thinking approach has gained prominence in the extant entrepreneurship education literature

(Lahn & Erikson, 2016). Nonetheless, not much is known about how academics perceive the design thinking approach as a teaching methodology.

It is imperative at this juncture to stress that design thinking as a concept has been defined in various ways in the extant literature. In academic circles, there is no consensus among scholars about what design thinking means since it is a multi-dimensional and complex construct (Liedtka, 2014; Von Thienen, Noweski, Meinel, & Rauth, 2011). According to Ilipinar, Montana, & Spender (2008), design thinking refers to a unique process of mind that is aimed at producing a new product, process, user experience, organic change or service. With a deeper knowledge of the design thinking lens, educators can create a conducive learning environment that supports learner-centeredness.

While there is a noticeable ongoing debate in the existing entrepreneurship literature pertaining to how an educator can best teach entrepreneurship with the confinement of higher education sector, designing thinking approach towards teaching entrepreneurship is gaining momentum as it emerges as a more effective methods to teach entrepreneurship (Huber, Peisl, Gedeon, Brodie, & Sailer, 2016). This is in harmony with the view of Stewart (2011) who echoed that the focus of the design thinking approach has made a significant paradigm shift from designing material things to intangible things like organizations, education, and systems. As such, this state of affairs heightens the need for educators to import the underlying principles of design thinking when delivering entrepreneurial education. Nonetheless, the unique context of the higher education sector must not be overlooked when applying designing thinking since the designing thinking approach is rooted in the industry.

The Need for Entrepreneurship Education in a Circular Economy

The scientific research that explored circular economy from an entrepreneurship development perspective is very scarce in the mainstream entrepreneurship literature. The recent research has applied the notion of Schumpeter's (1942) creative destruction to circular economy whereby the circular economy is recognized as a type of economy that is mainly associated with new opportunities that can be exploited by circular entrepreneurs (Cohen & Winn, 2007; Hall, Daneke, & Lenox, 2010; Lewandowski, 2015; Patzelt & Shepherd, 2011). In fact, these researchers explicitly expressed that entrepreneurship is a powerful tool that can be used in an effort to address market imperfections like social and environmental disruptions. Provided that scores of opportunities lie in the circular economy, it seems that there is a dire need to interrogate the role of entrepreneurship education in the circular economy and how best to teach entrepreneurship education in higher education in a manner that guarantees entrepreneurship development. Notably, circular economy refers to reduction of waste and protection of the environment in a sustainable way as well as rethinking the manner in which we produce, buy and work so as to create new jobs and generate untapped new opportunities (European Commission, 2015; Ghisellini, Cialani, & Ulgiati, 2016; Sauve, Bernard, & Sloan, 2015).

In a circular economy, entrepreneurs especially the young entrepreneurs must be well- furnished with entrepreneurial knowledge and skills so that they are in a better position to create, detect and exploit scores of opportunities that lie in a circular economy through relentless pursuit for innovations (Dean & McMullen, 2007; Senge & Carstedt, 2001). The author argues that how can entrepreneurs be taught effectively to think like designers when solving problems and how can they effectively make use of the designer's methodologies. In this regard, it is of great significance to observe that the market failures represent avenues of entrepreneurial opportunities that can be tapped into in a manner that ensures profitability and at the same time eliminating or reducing unfriendly environmental behaviors associated with the linear economy. This state of affairs necessitates a transformational process of how entrepreneurship content can be delivered especially at the university level. It is common knowledge that the universities are expected by the stakeholders to play a greater role when it comes to producing enterprising graduates. In fact, the power for change, creativity and innovation resides in the young entrepreneurs.

The paradigm shift from a linear economy (take-make-waste system) to a circular economy can be only successful provided that there is also a paradigm shift in a manner in which entrepreneurship is delivered in higher education. This transitional process to a circular economy calls for entrepreneurs who are well equipped with a wealth of entrepreneurial knowledge, experiences, and skills so that they can detect and utilize untapped avenues of opportunities in a manner that promotes sustainability communal and natural environment (Patzelt & Shepherd, 2011).

With the possession of entrepreneurial knowledge, it is very easy for entrepreneurs to recognize untapped opportunities that lie in a circular economy. Nonetheless, it seems to be appropriate to note that there is a growing trend concerning criticisms of the conventional approach (lecture and textbook) of teaching entrepreneurship especially in business schools (Carey & Matlay, 2010; Neck & Greene, 2011). In fact, the traditional way of teaching entrepreneurship can only expose students to a simplistic image of the realities of entrepreneurship especially when it comes to entrepreneurship in a circular economy. With all controversies that revolve around entrepreneurship education in mind, one may ask a question: How do academics perceive the design thinking approach as a teaching method for entrepreneurship course? In this regard, it is the aim of this empirical research to answer this thought-provoking question.

RESEARCH METHODOLOGY

Research Paradigm

Interpretivism paradigm was adopted as the most appropriate philosophical stance that underpinned the current study since this study is mainly based on qualitative methods. It is imperative to note that the interpretivism paradigm is mainly linked to qualitative methods especially when a phenomenon is studied in its unique context (Creswell, 2014; Hammersley, 2013; Saunders, Lewis, & Thornhill, 2012). The rationale for this interpretivism paradigm was based on its suitability for the development of a new, richer, deeper and more nuanced understanding of entrepreneurship education from multiple perspectives within the context of higher education. With this in mind, academicians from Centre for Entrepreneurship at Midlands State University were solicited to provide their views, experiences and opinions with respect to entrepreneurship education from a design thinking perspective.

Research Design

Exploratory research design underpinned the current study on entrepreneurship education from a design-thinking lens in higher education. Consistent with the tenets of exploratory design, a case study (Centre for Entrepreneurship) was embraced as a research strategy in this empirical work. Midlands State University through the Centre for Entrepreneurship was the first university in Zimbabwe to offer university-wide entrepreneurship module (ENT205 - Entrepreneurship 1) at the undergraduate level. This case appears to be an extreme case (Gerring, 2007) or paradigmatic (Flybierg, 2006; Palys, 2008) since Midlands State University is exemplary when it comes to delivery of university-wide entrepreneurship education.

Admittedly, a case study as a research strategy helped the researcher to have a deeper understanding of the phenomenon under investigation in real-life and this strategy is applicable to business, science and social work (Baxter & Jack, 2008; Yin, 2014). Indeed, a case study allows the researcher to embrace multiple sources of evidence which can enhance the validity and reliability of research findings (Hyett, Kenny, & Dickson-Swift, 2014).

Sampling Procedure

The author believed that it is more interesting to explore entrepreneurship education from a design thinking perspective with a particular focus on the university that has implemented a university-wide entrepreneurship curriculum. Eight lecturers from the Center for Entrepreneurship were meticulously chosen using a purposive sampling technique based on their extensive teaching experience and their distinctive ability to provide in-depth insights about the phenomenon under investigation (Creswell, 2014; Patton, 2015). Moreover, the issues surrounding the availability of participants, ability to communicate opinions and experiences in a reflective manner and willingness to participate were considered during the sample selection process. In the case of sample size for a qualitative study, Creswell (2013) echoed that data collection could end even at two participants.

Data Collection Techniques

Firstly, the author managed to undertake in-depth semi-structured personal interviews with academics from the Centre for Entrepreneurship. Secondly, primary data from focused observations were used to supplement data from personal interviews in an effort to enhance research validity and reliability. With respect to interviews, the author purposively conducted eight personal interviews. Generally, the interview session with each participant lasted about 30 minutes and all responses of the participants were audio-recorded. The collection of primary data took place during the August – November 2019 semester.

Data Analysis

Thematic analysis was deemed suitable in this study as it allows the researcher to capture themes that were linked to the issues under robust investigation since the emerged themes from the data set represented the patterns of responses (Braun & Clarke, 2012). To ensure methodological rigor, Braun & Clarke's (2006) six stages of thematic analysis were perfectly applied in this study in an attempt to efficiently and effectively explore entrepreneurship education from a design thinking standpoint at the university level.

RESULTS AND DISCUSSION

This part covers the key findings of the study. The collected data from the participants were subjected to thematic analysis. Notably, six overarching themes emerged from a meticulous thematic analysis of the data, namely, *Teaching methods, Design-thinking, Ideation, Prototype, failure,* and finally *Infrastructure support*. The following findings were in tandem with these emerged predominant themes.

Teaching Methods

When the researcher posed a question about how the respondents taught entrepreneurship course (ENT205-Entrepreneurship 1), the majority of the responses from interviewees were predominantly focused on a mixture of conventional and non-conventional teaching methods of entrepreneurship education. In this regard, some of the issues that were raised by interviewees are recorded below:

The teaching methods that I use when teaching my students are normally a lot of group discussions, group works, case studies, creation of business plans, lectures and to some extent role-playing. (R2)

I believe that teaching entrepreneurship must not be mainly based on traditional teaching methods, therefore, I use brainstorming sessions, business pitches, idea generation exercises and lectures. (R4)

My teaching methods are more practical so as to promote actioning of ideas, dreams, aspirations and hopes of my students. (R5)

The preceding quotes with respect to teaching methods apparently revealed that the interviewees had a deep appreciation of the urgent need for non-traditional teaching methods of entrepreneurship education. This is in line with the view of Daniel (2016) who stressed that entrepreneurship education should be based on non-traditional approaches owing to the fact that entrepreneurship education that is currently offered by many universities is being often criticized for being too managerial-oriented and rational. Nonetheless, it is evident the interviewees were also using some of the traditional methods of teaching entrepreneurship education.

Design Thinking

Analysis of data pertaining to the perceptions of design-based entrepreneurship education revealed that most of the interviewees were of the opinion that design thinking was ideal for teaching entrepreneurship. The participants were advocating for a paradigm shift from traditional teaching methods to design thinking. The quotes underneath shows the position of some of the participants:

In line with design thinking, I use brainstorming sessions whereby the students identify problems in their society and generate ideas about how can they solve such problems. (R1)

Design thinking is more of how to solve societal problems, as you know when we are designing our curriculum we capture issues that affect our society with the aim to produce innovative and creative students. (R7)

I think incorporating design thinking tenets in our entrepreneurship course is ideal. This can instill entrepreneurship spirit in our students because design thinking supports the idea of solving complex problems. (R3)

As illustrated in the above quotes, the respondents mainly highlighted their positive perceptions of designing thinking as a teaching method of entrepreneurship. As such, it appears that the incorporation of design thinking into the entrepreneurship curriculum is necessary for exploiting new untapped entrepreneurial opportunities in the current uncertain environment (Huber et al., 2016; Val et al., 2017). From the researcher's experience and observation, I noticed that learners could gain a better understanding when entrepreneurship course is taught based on a practical approach. However, a minority of the respondents indicated mixed feelings about the effectiveness of design thinking as a teaching approach in the Zimbabwean context. They were skeptical about the effectiveness of some elements of design thinking like prototyping and testing in light of the current economic turmoil in Zimbabwe.

Ideation

Ideation is one of the themes that frequently emerged from the collected data. With respect to how academics promote ideation, the respondents highlighted a variety of ideation techniques during the interview sessions. The majority of the respondents identified three ideation techniques, namely, brainstorming, sketching and mind mapping. The response from one of the interviewees is quoted as follows:

I normally use brainstorming and sketching to promote idea generation among my students. (R6)

As indicated in the above response, there is evidence that idea generation activities are encouraged among students through the usage of brainstorming sessions. However, the respondents also highlighted that they use business plans as a way to generate new ideas and solutions. Notably, the use of business plans is commonly linked to traditional business management and not unique to entrepreneurship (Pittaway & Edwards, 2012).

Prototype

Another key issue that emerged from data analysis was how lectures encouraged their students to come up with product or service prototypes. The majority of the participants indicated that they encourage the creation of product or service prototypes through the provision of the necessary information required for one to test his or her product prototype at Midlands State University Innovation Hub. For instance, the following quote captures the response of one of the interviewees:

Normally, in my class, I encourage the students to approach our innovation hub and other relevant authorities so that they can test their product prototypes. (R8)

Based on the preceding quote, students are motivated to come up with product prototypes. More interestingly, students were given necessary information concerning the roles of the innovation hub. This is supported by Wagener & Watch (2017) who underscored that innovation centers can be a physical manifestation of collaboration.

Failure

The interviewees were asked to provide their views on how they taught entrepreneurship students about business failure. The majority of the interviewees highlighted that they taught their entrepreneurship students to accept business failure as a business lesson. One of the interviewees presented an apparent picture of business failure as recorded below:

In business, one can win or lose, therefore, I usually teach my students that when you fail in business don't quit but learn from your failure as an entrepreneur and then redesign your business model. (R3)

As illustrated in the above response, entrepreneurs can encounter business failure given that the business environment is highly turbulent, dynamic and chaotic in nature. Consequently, entrepreneurs can learn from business failure and then adopts a new business model that can promote resuscitation of the business. Nonetheless, it worth noting that the interviewees were trying their level best to develop a culture of accepting failure as a learning process in business owing to the fact that entrepreneurship is about risk-taking. This is in line with the view of Minniti & Bygrave (2001) who echoed that entrepreneurial learning is centered on acquiring entrepreneurship skills and knowledge through experience from failure.

Infrastructure Support

The researcher posed a question to get a deeper understanding of the views of interviewees concerning the infrastructure support that is necessary for supporting an effective design-based entrepreneurship educational experience. Infrastructure support such as interactive whiteboards, monitors and displays, digital and physical design thinking tools, co-working spaces, big prototyping labs, accelerators and brainstorming labs were frequently highlighted by the majority of interviewees. In this respect, some of the issues raised by interviewees are captured in the following quotes:

Obviously, we need plenty of interactive whiteboards that allow learners to connect their devices to demonstrate their concepts. (R3)

Well, adequate interactive instructional technology like projectors must be provided to allow students to invite spontaneous feedback during brainstorming sessions. (R5)

As revealed in the above quotes, it is apparent that there is a need for infrastructure support that can ensure the effective use of design thinking as a teaching method of entrepreneurship education. This is in harmony with the view of Wagener & Watch (2017) who echoed that infrastructure support such as co-working spaces and accelerators are necessary for supporting design thinking methodologies.

SOLUTIONS AND RECOMMENDATIONS

Based on the findings of the current empirical study, there is ample evidence that the incorporation of design thinking processes and tools into entrepreneurship education is at the infant stage. Accordingly, the following recommendations are made based on the findings of this research:

- **Development of Design-Led Entrepreneurship Curriculum:** The Centre for Entrepreneurship should come up with a distinctive entrepreneurship curriculum that is based on design thinking tenets. The entrepreneurship curriculum must be focused on the integration of the Centre for

Entrepreneurship and Innovation Hub so that entrepreneurial students can be well-equipped with the issues related to the ideation, prototyping and testing;

- **Sharing of Success Stories of Entrepreneurship Education:** To sustain the momentum of entrepreneurship education, the management of institutions of higher education should encourage the sharing of success stories of entrepreneurship education;
- **Integrated Entrepreneurship Culture:** Top management of entrepreneurial universities should develop an integrated entrepreneurial culture among university elements. This could make an entrepreneurial university to be agile to changes in the operating environment;
- **Focusing on Interactive Teaching Methods:** Educators of entrepreneurship in higher education should embrace interactive teaching methods like simulation and role-playing in a manner that ensures that students can be equipped with problem-solving and analytical skills. Indeed, students should be exposed to community development and small business consulting activities and events so that they can be oriented to real-life complex problems and experiences of entrepreneurs;
- **Attending Design Thinking Conferences and Workshops:** Academicians in higher education institutions especially those in Centre for Entrepreneurship should continuously update themselves by constantly attending both local and international design thinking conferences, seminars and workshops. This could expose them to new teaching trends when it comes to entrepreneurship education;
- **Promotion of National Entrepreneurship Culture:** The government as a policymaker should promote entrepreneurship culture among its citizens. This can be done by creating a conducive entrepreneurial environment through the establishment of Technology Parks (TPs).

FUTURE RESEARCH DIRECTIONS

Further studies are required to enrich the entrepreneurship education scholarship. Given that this study only captures qualitative issues revolving around entrepreneurship education from the design thinking lens, future research should capture quantitative measures for generalizability purposes with regard to entrepreneurship education and design thinking in higher education. Admittedly, comparative studies related to entrepreneurship education and design thinking should be undertaken.

CONCLUSION

This chapter aims to make a significant contribution to the scant empirical research on entrepreneurship education from the design thinking lens. In this respect, the study intends to cover this research gap by developing insights into design-driven entrepreneurship education in the higher education sector. In this exploratory study, six overarching themes emerged from thematic analysis of data, namely, teaching methods, design thinking, ideation, prototype, failure and infrastructure support. Suggestions and recommendations were offered in this chapter. This empirical research unmasked some future research opportunities for researchers who have much interest in entrepreneurship education especially with a particular bias towards designing thinking. This research provides ample empirical evidence that allows policymakers and practitioners to make well-informed decisions when it comes to design-led entrepreneurship education. Particularly, the findings of this study can help top management of institutions of higher learning to appraise the teaching and assessment methodologies of entrepreneurship education from a design thinking perspective. Given the empirical evidence from this study, it is imperative to conclude that design thinking is a powerful teaching method of entrepreneurship as it allows students to actively learn about creation, identification and utilization of entrepreneurship opportunities in a circular economy, problem-solving, divergent and convergent thinking modes, creativity, failure, ideation, prototyping, testing and product-solution fit.

REFERENCES

Akhuemonkhan, I. A. R. L., & Sofoluwe, A. O. (2013). Entrepreneurship education and employment stimulation in Nigeria. *Journal of Studies in Social Sciences*, *3*(1), 55–79.

Baxter, P., & Jack, S. (2008). Qualitative case study methodology: Study design and implementation for novice researchers. *Qualitative Report*, *13*(4), 544–559.

Blank, S., & Dorf, B. (2012). *The start-up owner's manual: The step-by-step guide for building a great company*. Pescadero, CA: K&S Ranch Publishers.

Bosma, N., Acs, Z. J., Autio, E., Coduras, A., & Levine, J. (2008). *Global entrepreneurship report: 2008 executive report*. Wellesley, MA: Babson College.

Braun, V., & Clarke, V. (2006). Using thematic analysis in psychology. *Qualitative Research in Psychology*, *3*(2), 77–101. doi:10.1191/1478088706qp063oa

Braun, V., & Clarke, V. (2012). Thematic analysis. In H. Cooper (Ed.), *APA Handbook of research methods in psychology: Research design: Quantitative, Qualitative, Neuropsychological and Biological* (Vol. 2, pp. 57–71). Washington, DC: American Psychological Association. doi:10.1037/13620-004

Brem, A., & Licha, J. (2018). Entrepreneurship education in Europe - insights from Germany and Denmark. *International Journal of Entrepreneurship and Small Business*, *33*(1), 1–25. doi:10.1504/IJESB.2018.088641

Brown, T. (2008). Design thinking. *Harvard Business Review*, *86*(6), 84–92. PMID:18605031

Brown, T. (2009). *Change by design: How design thinking transforms organizations and inspires innovation*. New York, NY: Harper Collins.

Carey, C., & Matlay, H. (2010). Creative disciplines education: A model for assessing ideas in entrepreneurship education? *Education + Training*, *52*(8/9), 695–709. doi:10.1108/00400911011088999

Co, M., & Mitchell, B. (2006). Entrepreneurship education in South Africa: A nationwide survey. *Education + Training*, *48*(5), 348–359. doi:10.1108/00400910610677054

Cohen, B., & Winn, M. (2007). Market imperfections, opportunity, and sustainable entrepreneurship. *Journal of Business Venturing*, *22*(1), 29–49. doi:10.1016/j.jbusvent.2004.12.001

Conklin, J. (2005). *Dialogue mapping: Building shared understanding of wicked problems*. London, UK: Wiley.

Creswell, J. W. (2013). *Qualitative Inquiry and Research Design: Choosing among five approaches* (3rd ed.). Thousand Oaks, CA: Sage Publication.

Creswell, J. W. (2014). *Research design; Qualitative, quantitative and mixed-method approaches* (4th ed.). Thousand Oaks, CA: Sage Publication.

Daniel, A. D. (2016). Fostering an entrepreneurial mindset by using a design thinking approach in entrepreneurship education. *Industry and Higher Education*, *30*(3), 215–223. doi:10.1177/0950422216653195

Dean, T. J., & McMullen, J. S. (2007). Toward a theory of sustainable entrepreneurship: Reducing environmental degradation through entrepreneurial action. *Journal of Business Venturing*, *22*(1), 50–76. doi:10.1016/j.jbusvent.2005.09.003

European Commission. (2015). *Closing the loop: Commission adopts ambitious new circular economy: Package to boost competitiveness, create jobs and generate sustainable growth*. Retrieved November 10, 2019, from https://europa.eu/rapid/press-release_IP-15-6203_en.htm

Fayolle, A. (2009). *Entrepreneurship education in Europe: Trends and challenges. OECD LEED Programme. Universities, innovation and entrepreneurship: Good practice workshop*. Retrieved November 12, 2019, from http://www.oecd.org/dataoecd/11/36/43202553.pdf

Fayolle, A., & Gailly, B. (2008). From craft to science: Teaching models and learning processes in entrepreneurship education. *Journal of European Industrial Training*, *32*(7), 569–593. doi:10.1108/03090590810899838

Fayolle, A., Gally, B., & Lassas-Clerc, N. (2006). Assessing the impact of entrepreneurship education programs: A new methodology. *Journal of European Industrial Training*, *30*(9), 701–720. doi:10.1108/03090590610715022

Fixson, S. K., & Rao, J. (2014). Learning emergent strategies through design thinking. *Design Management Review*, *25*(1), 46–53. doi:10.1111/drev.10271

Garbuio, M., Dong, A., Lin, N., Tschang, T., & Lovallo, D. (2018). Demystifying the genius of entrepreneurship: How design cognition can help create the next generation of entrepreneurs. *Academy of Management Learning & Education*, *17*(1), 41–61. doi:10.5465/amle.2016.0040

Gerring, J. (2007). *Case study research: Principles and practices*. New York, NY: Cambridge University Press.

Ghisellini, P., Cialani, C., & Ulgiati, S. (2016). A review on circular economy: The expected transition to a balanced interplay of environmental and economic systems. *Journal of Cleaner Production*, *114*(7), 11–32. doi:10.1016/j.jclepro.2015.09.007

Greene, F. J., & Saridakis, G. (2008). The role of higher education skills and support in graduate self-employment. *Studies in Higher Education*, *33*(6), 653–672. doi:10.1080/03075070802457082

Hall, J. K., Daneke, G. A., & Lenox, M. J. (2010). Sustainable development and entrepreneurship: Past infrastructure contributions and future directions. *Journal of Business Venturing*, *25*(5), 439–448. doi:10.1016/j.jbusvent.2010.01.002

Hammersley, M. (2013). *What is qualitative research?* London, UK: Bloomsbury.

Huber, F., Peisl, T., Gedeon, S., Brodie, J., & Sailer, K. (2016). *Design thinking-based entrepreneurship education: How to incorporate design-thinking principles into an entrepreneurship course.* Paper presented at the 4th 3E Conference – ECSB Entrepreneurship Education Conference, Leeds, UK.

Huq, A., & Gilbert, D. (2017). All the world's a stage: Transforming entrepreneurship education through design thinking. *Education + Training*, *9*(2), 155–170. doi:10.1108/ET-12-2015-0111

Hyett, N., Kenny, A., & Dickson-Swift, V. (2014). Methodology or method? A critical review of qualitative case study reports. *International Journal of Qualitative Studies on Health and Well-being*, *9*(1), 10. doi:10.3402/qhw.v9.23606 PMID:24809980

Ilipinar, G., Montana, J., & Spender, J. C. (2008). *Design thinking in the postmodern organization.* Paper presented at the International Education 2008 Conference on Design thinking.

Jones, C. (2011). *Teaching entrepreneurship to undergraduates.* Cheltenham, UK: Edward Elgar Publishing Limited. doi:10.4337/9781781002001

Jones, C., & Matlay, H. (2011). Understanding the heterogeneity of entrepreneurship education: Going beyond Gartner. *Education + Training*, *53*(8/9), 692–703. doi:10.1108/00400911111185026

Kroon, J., & Meyer, S. (2001). The role of entrepreneurship education in career expectations of students. *South African Journal of Higher Education*, *15*(1), 47–53. doi:10.4314ajhe.v15i1.25379

Lackéus, M. (2015). *Entrepreneurship in Education: What, Why, When, How.* Paris: OECD.

Lahn, L. C., & Erikson, T. (2016). Entrepreneurship education by design. *Education + Training*, *58*(7/8), 684–699. doi:10.1108/ET-03-2016-0051

Lewandowski, M. (2015). Designing the business models for circular economy: Towards the conceptual framework. *Sustainability*, *8*(43), 1–28.

Liedtka, J. (2014). Perspective: Linking design thinking with innovation outcomes through cognitive bias reduction. *Journal of Product Innovation Management*, *32*(6), 925–938. doi:10.1111/jpim.12163

Liedtka, J., & Ogilvie, T. (2014). *Designing for growth. A design-thinking toolkit for managers.* New York, NY: Columbia University Press.

Mauchi, F. N., Karambakuwa, R. T., Gopo, R. N., Kosmas, N., Mangwende, S., & Gombarume, F. B. (2011). Entrepreneurship education lessons: A case of Zimbabwean tertiary education institutions. *Educational Research*, *2*(7), 1306–1311.

McGuigan, P. (2016). practicing what we preach: Entrepreneurship in entrepreneurship education. *Journal of Entrepreneurship Education*, *19*(1), 38–50.

Millán, J. M., Congregado, E., Román, C., van Praag, M., & van Stel, A. (2014). The value of an educated population for an individual's entrepreneurship success. *Journal of Business Venturing*, *29*(5), 612–632. doi:10.1016/j.jbusvent.2013.09.003

Millican, J. (2014). Higher education and student engagement: Implications for a new economic era. *Education + Training*, *56*(7), 635–649. doi:10.1108/ET-07-2014-0077

Ministry of Higher Education and Technology-Zimbabwe. (2010). *Strategic plan 2010–2015*. Harare: Government Printers.

Minniti, M., & Bygrave, W. (2001). A dynamic model of entrepreneurial learning. *Entrepreneurship Theory and Practice*, *25*(3), 5–16. doi:10.1177/104225870102500301

Munyanyiwa, T., Svotwa, D., Rudumbu, N., & Mutsau, M. (2016). A comparative study of entrepreneurship curriculum development and review at the University of Zimbabwe and Botho University. Botswana. *Journal of Education and Practice*, *7*(13), 63–72.

Mwasalwiba, E. S. (2010). Entrepreneurship education: A review of its objectives, teaching methods, and impact indicators. *Education + Training*, *52*(1), 20–47. doi:10.1108/00400911011017663

Nabi, G., Linan, F., Fayolle, A., Krueger, N., & Walmsley, A. (2017). The Impact of Entrepreneurship education in Higher Education: A systematic review and research agenda. *Academy of Management Learning & Education*, *16*(2), 277–299. doi:10.5465/amle.2015.0026

Nabi, G., Walmsley, A., Liñán, F., Akhtar, I., & Neame, C. (2018). Does entrepreneurship education in the first year of higher education develop entrepreneurial intentions? The role of Learning and Inspiration. *Studies in Higher Education*, *43*(3), 452–467. doi:10.1080/03075079.2016.1177716

Neck, H. M., & Greene, P. G. (2011). Entrepreneurship education: Known worlds and new frontiers. *Journal of Small Business Management*, *49*(1), 55–70. doi:10.1111/j.1540-627X.2010.00314.x

Nieuwenhuizen, C., Groenewald, D., Davids, J., vanRensburg, L. J., & Schachtebeck, C. (2016). Best practice in entrepreneurship education. *Problems and Perspectives in Management*, *14*(3/2), 528-536.

O'Connor, A. (2013). A Conceptual Framework for Entrepreneurship Education Policy: Meeting Government and Economic Purposes. *Journal of Business Venturing*, *28*(4), 246–563. doi:10.1016/j.jbusvent.2012.07.003

Oosterbeek, H., Van Praag, M., & Ijsselstein, A. (2010). The impact of entrepreneurship education on entrepreneurship skills and motivation. *European Economic Review*, *54*(3), 442–454. doi:10.1016/j.euroecorev.2009.08.002

Palys, T. (2008). Purposive sampling. In L. M. Given (Ed.), *The Sage Encyclopedia of Qualitative Research Methods* (pp. 697–698). Los Angeles, CA: Sage.

Patton, M. Q. (2015). *Qualitative research and evaluation methods: Integrating theory and practice* (4th ed.). Thousand Oaks, CA: Sage.

Patzelt, H., & Shepherd, D. A. (2011). Recognizing opportunities for sustainable development. *Entrepreneurship Theory and Practice*, *35*(4), 631–652. doi:10.1111/j.1540-6520.2010.00386.x

Penaluna, A., & Penaluna, K. (2019). I am a designer, get me out of here: Can entrepreneurial education advance through learning from design education. In A. Fayolle, D. Kariv., & H. Matlay (Eds.), The Role and Impact of Entrepreneurship Education – Methods, Teachers and Innovative Programmes. Cheltenham, UK: Edward Elgar Publishing.

Peterman, N. E., & Kennedy, J. (2003). Enterprise education: Influencing students' perceptions of entrepreneurship. *Entrepreneurship Theory and Practice*, *28*(2), 129–144. doi:10.1046/j.1540-6520.2003.00035.x

Pittaway, L., & Edwards, C. (2012). Assessment: Examining practice in entrepreneurship education. *Education + Training*, *54*(8/9), 778–800. doi:10.1108/00400911211274882

Rauch, A., & Hulsink, W. (2015). Putting entrepreneurship education where the intention to act lies: An investigation into the impact of entrepreneurship education on entrepreneurial behavior. *Academy of Management Learning & Education*, *14*(2), 187–204. doi:10.5465/amle.2012.0293

Razzouk, R., & Shute, V. (2012). What is design thinking and why is it important? *Review of Educational Research*, *82*(3), 330–348. doi:10.3102/0034654312457429

Rehman, A. U., & Elahi, Y. A. (2012). Entrepreneurship education in India – Scope, challenges and role of B-schools in promoting entrepreneurship education. *International Journal of Engineering and Management Research*, *2*(5), 5–14.

Rideout, E. C., & Gray, D. O. (2013). Does entrepreneurship education really work? A review and methodological critique of the empirical literature on the effects of university-based entrepreneurship education. *Journal of Small Business Management*, *51*(3), 329–351. doi:10.1111/jsbm.12021

Ries, E. (2011). *The lean start-up: How today's entrepreneurs use continuous innovation to create radically successful businesses*. New York, NY: Crown Books.

Roman, T., & Maxim, A. (2017). National culture and higher education as pre-determining factors of student entrepreneurship. *Studies in Higher Education*, *42*(6), 993–1014. doi:10.1080/03075079.2015.1074671

Sarooghi, H., Sunny, S., Hornsby, J., & Fernhaber, S. (2019). Design thinking and entrepreneurship education: Where are we, and what are the possibilities? *Journal of Small Business Management*, *57*(S1), 78–93. doi:10.1111/jsbm.12541

Saunders, M. N. K., Lewis, P., & Thornhill, A. (2012). *Research methods for business students* (6th ed.). Harlow, UK: Pearson Education Ltd.

Sauve, S., Bernard, S., & Sloan, P. (2015). Environmental sciences, sustainable development and circular economy: Alternative concepts for trans-disciplinary research. *Environmental Development*, *17*, 48–56. doi:10.1016/j.envdev.2015.09.002

Schumpeter, J. (1942). *Capitalism, Socialism, and Democracy*. New York, NY: Harper & Bros.

Senge, P., & Carstedt, G. (2001). Innovating our way to the next industrial revolution. *MIT Sloan Management Review*, *42*(2), 24–38.

Shane, S., & Venkataraman, S. (2000). The promise of entrepreneurship as a field of research. *Academy of Management Review, 25*(1), 217–226. doi:10.5465/amr.2000.2791611

Solomon, G. (2007). An examination of entrepreneurship education in the United States. *Journal of Small Business and Enterprise Development, 14*(2), 168–182. doi:10.1108/14626000710746637

Stewart, S. C. (2011). Interpreting design thinking. *Design Studies, 32*(6), 515–520. doi:10.1016/j.destud.2011.08.001

Storen, L. A. (2014). Entrepreneurship in higher education: Impacts on graduates entrepreneurial intentions, activity and learning outcome. *Education + Training, 56*(8/9), 795–813. doi:10.1108/ET-06-2014-0070

Stovang, P., & Nielsen, S. L. (2015). DesUni: University entrepreneurship education through design thinking. *Education + Training, 57*(8/9), 977–991. doi:10.1108/ET-09-2014-0121

Val, E., Gonzalez, I., Iriarte, I., Beitia, A., Lasa, G., & Elkoro, M. (2017). A design thinking approach to introduce entrepreneurship education in European school curricula. *The Design Journal, 20*(sup1), S754–S766.

Von Kortzfleisch, H. F. O., Zerwas, D., & Mokanis, I. (2013). Potentials of entrepreneurial design thinking for entrepreneurship education. *Social and Behavioural Sciences, 106*, 2080–2092. doi:10.1016/j.sbspro.2013.12.237

Von Thienen, J., Noweski, C., Meinel, C., & Rauth, I. (2011). The co-evolution of theory and practice in design thinking -or -"mind the oddness trap! In H. Plattner, C. Meinel, & L. J. Leifer (Eds.), *Design thinking: Understand -improve –apply* (pp. 81–99). Heidelberg: Springer. doi:10.1007/978-3-642-13757-0_5

Watson, A. D. (2015). Design Thinking for Life. *Art Education, 68*(3), 12–18. doi:10.1080/00043125.2015.11519317

ADDITIONAL READING

Brenner, W., Uebernickel, F., & Abrell, A. (2016). Design thinking as mindset, process, and toolbox. In W. Brenner & F. Uebernickel (Eds.), *Design Thinking for Innovation: Research and practice*. Cham: Springer. doi:10.1007/978-3-319-26100-3_1

Carlgren, L., Rauth, L., & Elmquist, M. (2016). Framing design thinking: The concept in idea and enactment. *Creativity and Innovation Management, 25*(1), 38–57. doi:10.1111/caim.12153

Dimov, D. (2016). Toward a design science of entrepreneurship. In J. Katz & A. C. Corbett (Eds.), *Models of start-up thinking and action: Theoretical, empirical and pedagogical approaches* (pp. 1–31). Bingley, UK: Emerald Group Publishing. doi:10.1108/S1074-754020160000018001

Glen, R., Suciu, C., & Baughn, C. (2014). The need for design thinking in business schools. *Academy of Management Learning & Education, 13*(4), 653–667. doi:10.5465/amle.2012.0308

Kickul, J., Gundry, L., Mitra, P., & Bercot, L. (2018). Designing with purpose: Advocating innovation, impact, sustainability, and scale in social entrepreneurship education. *Entrepreneurship Education and Pedagogy*, *1*(2), 205–221. doi:10.1177/2515127418772177

Micheli, P., Wilner, S. J., Bhatti, S. H., Mura, M., & Beverland, M. B. (2019). Doing design thinking: Conceptual review, synthesis, and research agenda. *Journal of Product Innovation Management*, *36*(2), 124–148. doi:10.1111/jpim.12466

Rasmussen, E. A., & Sorheim, R. (2006). Action-based entrepreneurship education. *Technovation*, *26*(2), 185–194. doi:10.1016/j.technovation.2005.06.012

Thrane, C., Blenker, P., Korsgaard, S., & Neergaard, H. (2016). The promise of entrepreneurship education: Reconceptualizing the individual–opportunity nexus as a conceptual framework for entrepreneurship education. *International Small Business Journal*, *34*(7), 905–924. doi:10.1177/0266242616638422

Wagner, J., & Watch, D. (2017). *Innovation spaces: The new design of work*. Washington, DC: Brookings Institution.

KEY TERMS AND DEFINITIONS

Circular Economy: Economic system based on a systemic approach to the elimination of waste and continuous utilization of scarce resources.

Circular Entrepreneur: An individual who takes risks and creates innovative products or services in a circular economy.

Entrepreneurial Culture: Refers to common beliefs, standards and practices related to innovation, creativity and risk affinity shared by a group of people with the aim to increase awareness and utilization of entrepreneurial opportunities.

Entrepreneurial University: This refers to any university that takes a leading role in creating and promoting an entrepreneurial mindsets, actions and entrepreneurial capital with the aim to augment competitiveness and stimulate economic development and growth.

Entrepreneurship Development: Process aimed at augmenting entrepreneurial acumen.

Entrepreneurship Education: Curriculum aimed at developing entrepreneurial knowledge, skills, attitudes, behavior, venture creation spirit and motivation in a manner that ensure entrepreneurial success.

Higher Education: Accredited tertiary education awarded by post-secondary education institutions.

Chapter 22
Critical Review of Entrepreneurship Development in Namibia

Sigried Shikokola
Ministry of Safety and Security, Namibia

ABSTRACT

With the appearance of entrepreneurship as a major economic force, the field of entrepreneurship education and training had gained legitimacy and had grown substantially. In Namibia, however, the trial of complete academic legitimacy for entrepreneurship development remains. Entrepreneurs and SMEs are considered as change agents in altering economies, and the implication of entrepreneurship and SME development is not often realized and normally ignored. Despite heightened awareness and interest by both scholars and practitioners, entrepreneurship development for entrepreneurs is still an emerging field of inquiry. Furthermore, limited research has so far been conducted on entrepreneurship development for entrepreneurs in the Namibian context. A review of the literature on entrepreneurship development revealed a critical review gap. Therefore, the chapter intends to review critically entrepreneurship development in Namibia and to suggest the way forward regarding entrepreneurship, youth, and entrepreneurs in order to fight poverty and unemployment.

INTRODUCTION

The prevailing perception in societies is that entrepreneurship is a fundamental skill that is acquired through lifelong learning to enhance human capital development in the form of competence and manpower, which is Namibia's most vital asset.

Entrepreneurship is learned and developed. Its core activities are innovation and creativity. Therefore, it is not limited to special individuals with certain personality traits rather, it is a combined effect of personality, environment, experience, acquired attitude and learning on the competitive behaviours required by the entrepreneur to drive the market process and create value (Stokes & Wilson, 2006).

DOI: 10.4018/978-1-7998-5116-5.ch022

Copyright © 2020, IGI Global. Copying or distributing in print or electronic forms without written permission of IGI Global is prohibited.

Hult et al. (2002) claimed that there are four culture-based factors of entrepreneurship; innovativeness; market orientation, and organisational learning collectively increase to an organisation's "cultural competitiveness." Cultural competitiveness is the degree to which an organisation is disposed to sense and fill gaps between what the market desires and what is currently unfilled (Hult et al., 2002).

Entrepreneurship, as originally conceived by Schumpeter (1934), is very important to economic development. Schumpeter made a difference between entrepreneurship as a function and the entrepreneur as a person. An entrepreneur can be anyone who creates an innovation—an independent businessperson, an employee or manager of a firm, and so on. Moreover, the range of innovations created by entrepreneurs is virtually unlimited, including the development of a new product or service, a new channel of distribution, or the reorganisation of an entire industry (Birkinshaw, 2000).

Entrepreneurship refers to the interruption of equilibrium in a firm (or economy) caused by the creation and application of new combinations of resources. As a function, entrepreneurship can happen both within and across organisations. Also, the degree of entrepreneurship varies across organisations. For example, an organisation that pursues a "prospector" strategy creates, on average, more resource combinations than a firm pursuing a "defender" strategy (Miles & Snow, 1978). Over time, an organisation cultivates an orientation towards entrepreneurship that changes embedded in its culture. Some organisations hold entrepreneurship more than others, and this affects their orientations toward other competitiveness factors such as innovativeness, customers and markets, and learning.

Innovativeness Innovation, the invention or adoption of something new or different, is conceptually quite close to entrepreneurship (the creation of a new combination of resources).the focus in our study is on "innovativeness," which is the organisation's cultural orientation (values and beliefs) towards innovation. Innovativeness can be famed from the capacity to innovate, which is the ability of the organisation to successfully develop or adopt new products and processes (Cohen & Levinthal, 1990). Innovativeness, when shared with other cultural competitiveness factors, can create a greater capacity to innovate that, in turn, leads to superior organisational performance.

Market Orientation a market-driven organisation is one that places a high implication on creating value for existing and prospective customers (Day, 1994). Firms with a market-oriented culture advance skills in market intelligence, and their strategies are receptive to information gleaned from customers and other external stakeholders. Those firms also improve the ability to coordinate internal processes so that they can act quickly and effectively (Day, 1994; Narver & Slater, 1990). A strong market orientation, when coupled with a culture that highlights entrepreneurship and innovativeness, promotes organisational learning (Slater & Narver, 1995). Even though numerous feasible market orientation frameworks exist (e.g., Deshpandé, Farley & Webster, 1993; Kohli & Jaworski, 1990), we embrace the conceptualisation of Narver and Slater (1990) because of its focus on organisational culture. Of particular importance in their framework is the influence on culture of customer orientation, competitor orientation, and inter-functional coordination.

These dimensions of a market orientation thus become part of an organisation's cultural competitiveness. Organisational Learning Knowledge, derived from learning, is potentially the most productive resource of an organisation and can be a key source of competitive advantage (Barney, 1991; Grant, 1996). An organisation's stock of knowledge is generated and extended through a learning process (Daft & Huber, 1987; Daft & Weick, 1984). A dynamic learning process in an organisation involves several major phases, each of which must be carefully designed and managed: information acquisition, interpretation, focused experimentation, diffusion of experience, and knowledge restructuring (Hanssen-Bauer & Snow, 1996).

To educate the new generation in entrepreneurship is a strategy for strengthening the individual's ability to exploit opportunities in life, both in business and industry thus preparing the ground for future economic growth and value creation in Namibia. The role of entrepreneurship as an engine of economic development was widely recognised by policy makers in most countries, including Namibia (Nieman, 1999). Evidence recommended, however, that its potential was far from having been fulfilled.

Therefore, the chapter indents to explore entrepreneurship development in Namibia and to suggest the way forward regarding entrepreneurship, youth and entrepreneurs in order to fight poverty and unemployment. This chapter adopts the qualitative research method, which entails the systematic collection and analysis of information on the subject matter. The author extracted the relevant information from scholarly works, government reports, journals, books, online materials and all the relevant materials with information regarding entrepreneurship development. The sourced pieces of information were systematically analysed using critical literature review on the basis of which findings and prescriptions were made.

LITERATURE REVIEW

The Role of Entrepreneurship

The role of entrepreneurship as an engine of economic development was widely recognised by policy makers in most countries, including Namibia (Nieman, 1999). Evidence recommended, however, that its potential was far from having been fulfilled. Much more coordinated training of entrepreneurs and SMME's is needed to allow for entrepreneurs to enter the SME sector without any hassles. Entrepreneurs in the country and especially in the SME sector relies too much on government for support and subsidies and therefore their full potential is yet to be researched. Namibia needs to nurture entrepreneurship, not only by creating the macroeconomic environment that allows entrepreneurship to thrive, but also by actively training and educating present and future entrepreneurs. The training and development of present day entrepreneurs is closely related to the small business environment and it is not based on the management of large companies (Nieman, 1999).

It is through proper and efficient training and development of entrepreneurs that entrepreneurial performance could be boosted (Wickham, 1998). The future entrepreneurs are expected to be more educated and technologically advanced individuals. Entrepreneurs in Windhoek city have been facing many problems in terms of attaining start-up capital and access to training facilities. They are opportunists who go in search of possible business ventures with the aim of growing it, making use of their own experience and resources.

Despite the fact that entrepreneurs and SMEs are considered as change agents in altering economies (Aidis, 2003a; Aidis, 2003b; Smallbone & Welter, 2009), the implication of entrepreneurship and SME development is not often realised and is normally ignored to a large extent. Instead, government and its policy makers rather directed their attention to the reshuffle and denationalisation of state owned enterprises. During that process, the government inclined to assign fewer resources and attention towards the development needs of entrepreneurs as well as to the encouragement of entrepreneurship.

With the appearance of entrepreneurship as a major economic force, the field of entrepreneurship education and training had gained legitimacy and had grown substantially (Kroon, 1997). In Namibia, however, the trial of complete academic legitimacy for entrepreneurship remains. According to Kroon (1997), entrepreneur education and/or development should be directed at formulating individuals to be agents of change for the future. Business and technical skills training at Namibian training institutions are readily available, while Entrepreneurial skills training are nonexistence. While it could be debated that some legitimacy had been reached in the current state of entrepreneurship education and training, there are critical needs that had been left unaddressed. The basis of that reasoning in the foregoing paragraph was that quite a number of Namibian training institutions claimed to be offering entrepreneurial training whereas it was merely business training (Ladzani, 1999).

Moreover, personal characteristics of the business owners may contribute to the growth and development of the firm, such as motivation, education, and ownership/management experience, number of founders, ethnicity, age and gender. Motivation can influence on the strategic choices made by the business owners (Storey, 1994). However, Woodward (2006) distinguishes "necessity" and "opportunity" entrepreneurs. Necessity entrepreneurs are those who decide to start-up in order to make a living as they don't find other opportunity choices for work. They are considered survival oriented entrepreneurs. On the other hand, opportunity entrepreneurs are those that are more closely to classical idea of Schumpeter entrepreneurs, characterised by inventiveness, vision and perception to discover opportunities in the market. They are considered growth-oriented entrepreneurs. Another personal characteristic, as described by Storey (1994), is education, where educated business owners usually establish a firm in the discipline they have been educated and use a number of skills for business management. The business owners, who have prior experience, are likely to observe better growth-related opportunities and avoid pitfalls. When there is more than one business owner, it leads to a diversity of experience, skills and resources which complement each other. Ethnicity is another factor which is connected to the socio-cultural attributes of the owners. Also, middle-aged owners have more potential to succeed because of the experience, credibility, energy and availability of resources (Storey, 1994).

Many of the small and upcoming as well as established entrepreneurs are urban based and largely focussed around Windhoek, Namibia's capital (LaRRI, 2002). However, many of their enterprises are also spread across regions in areas such as Oshakati, Ondangwa, Katima Mulilo, Rundu as well as Keetmanshoop and Luderitz in the south. However most Namibian entrepreneurs are opportunity entrepreneurs, most of them started up their businesses to make a living due to high rate of unemployment in the country, the country needs more of growth-oriented entrepreneurs in order to grab opportunities as they arise in the market in order for the country to even compete in international markets.

Entrepreneurship is seen as playing a pivotal role in developing the local economy, in addition to generating income once it is fully embraced. However, entrepreneurship not being embraced in Namibia remains a challenge. The country is faced with numerous challenges, such as youth unemployment and poverty. Entrepreneurship for any economy plays a crucial role in eradicating poverty; promote economic development, income-generating and improving people's standard of living. Furthermore other challenges for Namibia is the goal of getting more and more people involved in small and medium sized businesses. In business words, the change of mind set implies a full acceptance and incorporation (both at individual and business level) of the business concepts. It involves a paradigm shift of culture or attitude of taking up a job or small business activities for subsistence reasons towards taking ownership, exhibiting entrepreneurship behaviour and feeling challenged by goals that lay beyond the individual interest of earning some money for a living. For an entrepreneur this change of mind set means not just the mere acquisition of knowledge, skills and experience, but the ability to apply entrepreneurial characteristics which he/she might have acquired to a certain extent as well as the ability to develop the proper entrepreneurial competence (Mbaziira, S., & Oyedokun, C, 2007).

Various surveys, GEM (2002 & 2004); the European commission studies (2004) and Honig (1998) in Coleman (2004) positively indicate a clear and strong correlation between education and entrepreneurial success. People with secondary and a tertiary education are more likely to progress their businesses beyond the start-up phase, thereby enabled to create more jobs in the process. The entrepreneur's level of education therefore seems to impact on his/her success in growing the business and creating jobs. A survey study by Harris (2003) showed that entrepreneurship sector in Namibia does not attract people with tertiary education since they can enter directly into waged employment but those with secondary education; some have grade one to nine qualifications only. More entrepreneurial training is thus of necessity in schools.

Africa's economies face serious political and social challenges and statistics hide the real story. Colonisation is very much a contributing factor to our state of affairs: it has dispossessed and deprived indigenous people of resources and other means, and the rights to own and manage a business. It has also very strongly fostered passive customs and conformist practices which are contrary to creativity, innovation and risk-taking, and impede entrepreneurship. It is in the midst of all these obstacles that we as Africans have to find a way to bring about economic growth and prosperity to our people. Africa needs to overcome the legacy of colonization and adopt an attitude and behaviour that foster long-term, competitive entrepreneurship, based on initiative, innovation, knowledge and skills. This change needs to be inculcated at an early age of an individual in society. Therefore, entrepreneurial training is absolutely necessary at home, primary and secondary school levels, and in tertiary education. The concept of entrepreneurship is generally inherent in human and in our societies. African governments have tried to support entrepreneurship in many ways. In Namibia indigenous entrepreneurship had been characterised by many problems: marginalisation of entrepreneurs from mainstream commerce, lack of proficiency, competencies, expertise, training, lack of finance, and general support. These have resulted in badly costed goods and businesses, and survival strategies which tend to focus on limited sectors which require little capital investment (Tjivikua, T, 2002).

Entrepreneurship Development

An entrepreneur is a person who makes money by starting or running businesses which Involves taking financial risks and uncertainty by identifying opportunities and bringing in the necessary resources (labour, materials and other assets) to exploit on them (Samson et al., 2013). It is through this vibrant process, the entrepreneur acts to announce changes, innovation and a new order to create monetary and personal approval. This act of doing new things or doing things that are already being done in a new way is referred to as entrepreneurship (Ojo, 2009).

The development of entrepreneurship as a concept matches another concept called entrepreneurship development. Entrepreneurship development refers to the process of improving entrepreneurial skills and knowledge through organised training and institution - building programmes (Ojo, 2009). It aims to widen the base of entrepreneurs in order to secure the pace at which new projects are shaped which then accelerates employment generations and economic development. Afteb and Naveed (2013) defined it as innovation, creativity, leadership, income development or the start of a new business and are estimated to be a holistic approach to poverty alleviation, curbing unemployment and economic development (Ngugi et al., 2014).

Microfinance is described as a developmental tool for the poor people with innovative ideas on business but lack financial strengths to fully implement their business idea (Akingunola et al., 2013.

Microfinancing has been accredited throughout the globe for its positive properties on improving rural micro entrepreneurship development, especially in developed countries like China, Bangladesh, India and USA as stated by numerous authors (e.g. Biswas & Sengupta, 2009; Ferdousi, 2015; Ojo, 2009; Van Rooyen, Stewart, & De Wet, 2012 & Waithaka, Marangu & N'gondu, 2014). In Sub-Saharan Africa, the effect of microfinancing has been mostly recorded in countries such as Botswana, Kenya and Nigeria as presented by BIDPA (2011); Osunde et al. (2012) and Van Rooyen et al. (2012). Microfinancing has been encouraged extensively in Namibia through government Ministries, state-owned enterprises as well as by the private sector.

Microfinance is one of the largest development platforms worldwide presumed to empower rural poor households access to credit that helps households begin micro enterprises which would support them develop their livelihood (Omunjalu & Fondo, 2014). It is achievement importance as a tool that is extensively used for poverty alleviation, empower disadvantaged population groups allowing them to engage in economic activities, create employment, be self-reliant and improve their household income as well as create wealth (Osunde & Mayowa, 2012; Singh, 2009). This view appears to be reinforced by Ngugi & Kerongi (2014) when they claimed that: accessing microfinance is the main key for micro enterprises to succeed in building productive capacity, competition, jobs creation and power to poverty alleviation. It also upsurges dynamic resources for rural families and their housing conditions which results in economic security.

The overall success of microfinancing, however, does not depend only on instant alleviation of poverty, but also on long-term sustainability. Long-term sustainability is said to depend on accrual of assets, amended revenues and employment creation (Ferdousi, 2015; Ngugi et al., 2014). A study conducted by Afrin, Islam and Ahmed (2008) showed that microfinance is a solid tool to alleviate poverty through the social and economic empowerment of rural and disadvantaged women. Nonetheless, sign for the positive claims surrounding microfinance is being tested because Augsburg, De Haas, Harmgart and Mehgir (2014) demand the ability of microfinance to moderate poverty because their involvement only detected increased levels of business activity and more self-employment which, did not translate into increased business profits or increased household income.

Micro enterprises are however believed to encourage economies of most African countries because they are a major cause of entrepreneurial skills, innovation and economic development (Asa & Prasad, 2014). They make a substantial contribution in the transition of agriculture-led economies into industrial ones, furnishing simple opportunities for handling activities that can produce sustainable sources of revenue and enhance the development process (Kambwale, Chisoro & Karodia, 2015). They also have been the means through which enhanced growth and rapid industrialisation have been attained. This can be accomplished by creating opportunities for processing activities which can produce a sustainable source of revenue and enhance the development process (Kongolo, 2010). Despite this, micro enterprises are tested with various restrictions (including lack of finances) to develop entrepreneurship (Ojo, 2009). Thus, promoting entrepreneurship is an important goal of most countries by finding different ways to support and improve entrepreneurship and microenterprise development (Mwobobia, 2012). However, all these can only be accomplished if there are suitable tools (like microfinance) that can have measurable impact on local economies in terms of job creation and serve as a vital compound for increased prosperity and economic development.

Micro entrepreneurship ached greatly when Namibia skilled integrated planning under South African rule because colonial economic policies were biased towards larger businesses only (Jauch, 2010; Nuyoma, 2010), up to 1990 when it attained majority rule.

Soon after independence, the government developed policies and legislative instruments such as the Decentralisation policy and the Decentralisation Allowing Act of 2000 to facilitate decentralisation, as well as Micro, Small and Medium Enterprises (MSMEs) policy to generate an empowering business environment for the MSMEs. MoITSD (2015) defined a micro enterprise as a business that employs up to 10 people and has an annual turnover of not more than N$300 000. Micro enterprises are the drivers of growth, innovation, development and job creation in an emerging economy. By nature, they are flexible enterprises and as such they are at the vanguard of technological innovation. Micro enterprising is a very important aspect in Namibia as it is stated in Vision 2030 that SMEs are embattled to contribute over 30% to the Gross National Product (GNP), and it is because of this immense expected contribution that the role of SMEs is highly recognised (Asa et al., 2014; Kambwale et al., 2015). Ramsden (2010, p. 6) stated that over the past five years, SMEs have subsidised approximately 12 percent to the Gross Domestic Product (GDP) and have promised about 20 percent of the work force during the same period.

It has been discussed that Namibian rural people are economically active, but lack access to financial assistance (Kambwale et al., 2015). This is even worse as they lack collateral security, thus, often lost out in obtaining capital to recognise their businesses' potential (Aftab & Naveed, 2013). The Namibia Chamber of Commerce and Industry (NCCI) and Institute for Public Policy Research (IPPR) (2012) exposed that an ordinary rural person in Namibia is not able to produce collateral security as required by the commercial institutions. This inability to access financial assistance brought about by lack of collateral, twisted a great setback to micro entrepreneurship development (Samson, Olubunmi & Olusegun, 2013).

Due to these rural challenges, the Namibian government through its Line Ministries including the Ministry of Urban and Rural Development (MURD) distinguish the significance of rural development in its efforts to fight poverty through establishment of financial assistances to maintenance rural projects (Ramsden, 2010). Thus, the Ministry of Urban and Rural Development provides funds from the Government's capital to finance rural projects through the Regional Councils. The purpose is to diminish financial constraints by making funds available to those who want to grow their businesses first into micro then small, medium until they develop into major industries (MRLGHD, 2012)

The main problem for successful entrepreneurship development is finance; finance is the heart and backbone of projected project, without capital or enough funds one cannot move forward. Most entrepreneurs are unable to achieve their targets due to financial issues. Financial matters play a vital role

Figure 1. Finance as the main constraint factor

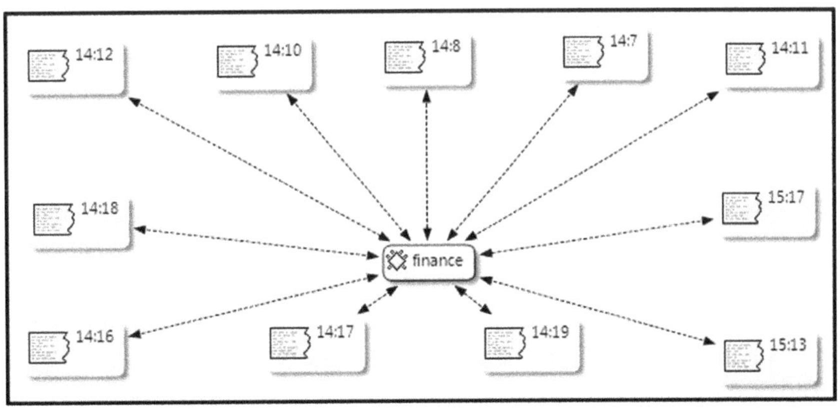

for every organisation but small firms find it way difficult than large firms because they hardly have financial collateral or security for financial institutions to offer financial help to them.

Moreover, according to Hashi and Krasniqi (2010), the Schumpeterian entrepreneurs are still responsible to make organisational changes, by bringing new products, or making changes in the existing ones, as well as by using new methods to decrease costs and ensure higher productivity regardless of financial issues. Entrepreneurs are flexible to adapt to business environment changes in order to meet market needs. Business environment changes may include changes in regulations, taste, demand, and technology. It should be highlighted that entrepreneurial activities should be developed in the long term to ensure firm growth.

Several entrepreneurs are under international competition pressure and growing necessities from key clients and key suppliers (Yeoh, 2009). Generally, less prepared in financial, technological and human resources than big enterprises, SMEs however have rewards in terms of suppleness, reaction time, and innovation capability that make them central actors in the new economy (Raymond, 2000). In this complicated trade atmosphere, entrepreneurs must hold development so as to stay competitive and hence endure, grow, and flourish (Skandalakis & Nelder, 2001). This development can be accomplished in three ways. One way is by innovating, which means to create new products for current and possible consumers (Roper & Love, 2002). Another way is to shape up new markets for their products- that is- to grow from a neighbourhood or regional market to a national or international market (Levrato, 2002). This indicates cooperation and partnerships with clients, suppliers, distributors, competitors and other organisations such as consulting firms and research centres (Gulati, 1998; Smedlund, 2007; Evanschitsky, et al., 2007), as well as umbrella organisations such as Chambers of Commerce and specific associations for specific trades and branches. In this paper, we have named these three approaches as „strategic development".

Berte, et al. (2010), while conflicting in the context of small technology-based firms, state that to support their growth and diversification, these firms must choose a development plan that takes into account the product, market, expected firm size, know-how and organisational structure as preferred strategies which will influence the direction and the market placement of the firm. Entrepreneurs, which are defined by degree technology-dependent therefore, have to pay attention to their strategic development (Beaver, 2007; Megicks, 2007) in terms of their markets, products and also networks. The fact that entrepreneurs occasionally devote suitable time to this issue has been well documented (Heriot & Loughman, 2009). In small firms, deep-seated decisions and choices in terms of strategic development are taken by their owner-managers (Kotey & Meredith, 1997). It therefore stands to reason that owner-managers" knowledge and skills as well as their entrepreneurial orientation (EO) will impact these choices and the enterprise.

Scholars such as Ansoff (1957) concluded early on that entrepreneurs can develop their business processes along two axes- that is- markets and products. Augmenting sales of existing products to existing markets (market penetration), realising new markets for existing products (market development), producing new products for existing markets (product development), and building new products for new markets (diversification) represent four fundamental internal growth strategies for these organisations. Lately however, with the arrival of globalisation, and with new information and communication technologies, some entrepreneurs, and high growth firms in particular, have been found to grow along a third axis- that is- in terms of networks that link them with clients, suppliers, and other business partners in joint relationships (Morgan and Hunt, 1999). Every axis of development has been subjected to experimental investigations with a mission of understanding two basic questions. The first demand is concerned with understanding the nature of the development activities themselves, be they associated with expanding markets, innovating or partnering. The other demand relates to the environmental, organisational and individual elements or experiences of these activities. Researchers (Koufteros et al., 2002; Simon et al., 2002; van Dijk et al., 1997) have considered the product novelty process in particular, including its entrepreneurial and internal perspective within entrepreneurs. The participation of owner-managers and their firms in different types of social or commercial networks has been deliberated as to its nature, background and consequences (e.g. Ebers and Jarillo, 1998; Freel, 2000; Hakansson and Schakenraad, 1994), as well as the result of networks upon innovation activities of SMEs (e.g. Hanna & Walsh, 2002; Lee & Jang, 1998).

Network Development Collaboration is vibrant for resource-poor entrepreneurs to achieve development. Networks help entrepreneurs attain economies of scale. They can bring new value-added products to market fast and can market more efficiently than an individual. For example, speciality food producers and organic meat producers can work cooperatively to market their wares, buy refrigerated trucks or storage, or create training modules. They can therefore uphold their flexibility but still share financial, human and relational capital with others so as to reduce the risks connected with the new global business environment. Networking might make an entrepreneur more dynamic by boosting its supply chain management (Raymond, 1997) and its customer relationship management (Kalwani & Narayandas, 1995). According to Goleman (2002), partnership agreements allow organisations to benefit from market opportunities and respond to customer needs in collaboration, allowing them to more efficiently and effectively do so than they possibly will separately.

Gulati (1998) describes network development or strategic partnering as collaboration and partnerships with customers, suppliers, distributors, competitors and other organisations such as consulting firms and research centres. Moreover, Goleman (2002) argues that network development means the following: increasing risk and imagining others to perform in mutual best interests; seeking a tactical fit among partners so that goals contest and action plans show synergy; finding complementary skills, competences and resources in partners; and sharing fortunate or confidential information. According to Wincent and Westerberg (2005), small firms need to succeed social and professional networks with other actors and are therefore no longer considered as individual and self-fulfilling units that do not involve other actors to be competitive. Rather the individual firm can be seen as an "organiser" that interacts with other actors in order to be able to carry out a strategy and build competitive advantage that is far beyond the scope of the single firm. All collaborating partners can focus on their core business and by interlinking these, competitive advantage can be accomplished. Having a capability to know about and make use of other firm's resources seems to be a valuable asset in the harsh competitive landscape of today's business environment (Wincent & Westerberg, 2005; Smedlund, 2007). The literature suggests the benefits of networking for small firms such as right to use technical or commercial resources (Hoang and Antoncic, 2003; Baum et al, 2000), enlightening organisational learning (Kale et al, 2002; Oliver, 2001) and innovation (Pittaway et al, 2004; Powell et al, 1996). In the introductory phases of a small firm's life, it needs access to more external information and guidance. This dependence persists also after the introductory phases. Access to external knowledge could result into better presentation. Entrepreneurs may as well use their network as a foundation for "idea generation and gather information to identify entrepreneurial opportunities" (Hoang and Antoncic, 2003).

A crucial but less appreciated advantage of networking establishes itself in the form of social standing and respect. When an entrepreneur joins a network, they stand for that network. This is then of support to them in getting noticed and recognised easily within their respective industry. However, it is imperative to select the correct partners because an unknown firm will not add much value to the firm's standing. This gain of legitimacy exists even when the network fails to achieve its core objectives (Stuart, 2000;

Bradley et al, 2006; Baum and Oliver, 1991). Strategic partnering recovers a firm's aptitude to learn and realise competitive advantage. However, learning from networking is not easy. Moreover, inferred knowledge is a hefty part of learning which cannot be readily transferred (Oliver, 2001). Therefore, entrepreneurs have to be talented enough to categorise and use outside knowledge for learning, which strongly relates with the theory of "absorptive capability" i.e. a firm's ability and capacity to identify and make use of outside knowledge for commercial accomplishment (Cohen and Levinthal, 1990). Oliver (2001) states that learning from networking is not linear throughout the life cycle of entrepreneurs. Enterprises change their way of learning from networking based on their experience and desires. Experience grew from networking can aid an entrepreneur in making the best from their networks (Anand and Khanna, 2000). The "locus of innovation" is no longer within individual firms but in their network (Powell et al., 1996). This relays back to the logic of learning from networking. When entrepreneurs work in collaboration, new ideas surface because each entrepreneur brings their distinctive ability to the network. The probability of success with innovation is also likely to increase, when it is developed in a network, as it inclines to be more technologically and economically feasible (Pittaway et al., 2004). The trial that remains for entrepreneur/managers is how to create and manage the network to appreciate the benefits offered (Trim, et al., 2008).

Network Capability

Walter et al. (2006) define networking capability as a firm's "ability to develop and make use of inter-organisational relationships to advance contact to a variety of resources held by other actors". Kale et al. (2002) note that it is not sufficient to build networks – it is also crucial for entrepreneurs to accomplish network success. Managing networks is not straightforward. An entrepreneur has to put some hard work in evolving trust with partners, sharing resources and working closely for efficiency. Or else, inter-organisational ties - also termed as "inter organisational learning linkages" (Cohen & Levinthal, 1990) - would just lead to loss of hard work and resources (Gulati et al., 2000). entrepreneurs with high networking capability should not only be able to spot strategic partners but also sustain close relations (Walter et al., 2006). According to Walter et al. (2006), networking capability is a concept consisting of four elements, i.e. coordination, relationship skills, partner knowledge, and internal communication. All these elements are different but would often appear interrelated. For instance, when entrepreneurs have good relationship skills they would be able to have access to external knowledge, which in turn makes possible for them to develop their partner knowledge. An entrepreneur's coordination activity can help them in synchronising with different external partners and achieving mutual advantages. But just establishing relation with a firm is not sufficient, since interpersonal skills i.e. ability to maintain a healthy relationship, is also of the essence. An important characteristic of relationship skills is linked to individuals because firms do not have relations but rather individuals/employees who cultivate these relationships. Hence, entrepreneurs need to be vigilant while allocating responsibility to individuals for managing such relations. Entrepreneurs should also focus on accepting their partners and improving partner knowledge. Partner knowledge is an essential component of networking capability. This type of partner knowledge can lead to unwavering and long-term relationships between different actors because they would understand each other's needs and wants better. Furthermore, successful internal communication is the lifeblood of all organisations. Above all, from a relationship viewpoint, it is important that internally, everyone in the organisation speaks the same language. This can only be achievable when everyone is regularly updated about information of their partners, such as a change in agreements (Walter et al., 2006). Entrepreneurs with high networking capability will be able to discover potential partners, establish relationships, and use and share each other's resources and competences. Anand and Khanna (2000) state that not all inter-firms relations are advantageous, since some relations can be complicated to manage and complex in nature. Therefore, entrepreneurs need to advantageously position themselves in a network because this endows them with the capability to successfully search for selective strategic partners (Hagedoorn et al, 2006). Entrepreneurs also need to be careful when selecting partners for two reasons: first, some partners can bring very important knowledge and information which fosters the learning process (Lorenzoni and Lipparini, 1999); second, collaborating with highly credible partners adds value to an entrepreneur's standing in form of authenticity (Stuart, 2000). The aptitude to build and handle a partnership is important in all industries; many scholars believe that networking can boost a firm"s ability to be innovative (Pittaway et al, 2004; Powell et al, 1996).

Owner-Manager's Education and Experience

Entrepreneurs are considered to be organic to the extent that their strategy, organisation and culture are personified by their owner-managers. The principal goals and features of owner-managers are therefore vital in establishing the firm's level of innovation and orientation towards product uniqueness and technological superiority (Miller, 1993). Studies have exposed that the formerly acquired knowledge and experience of entrepreneurs/managers influence their managerial conduct (Thong, 1999). A main constituent in the small firm"s learning experience is the owner-manager's individual learning (Riemenschneider & Mykytyn, 2000). Domain-specific knowledge which comes with experience as well as more general knowledge obtained from higher education would consequently influence the entrepreneur's awareness of the various strategic development practices to be integrated and integrated by the organisation.

Entrepreneurial Orientation (EO)

Business conventions and practices which have been accepted for many years are no longer effective (Vargha and Pettigrew, 2001; Haynes, Becherer and Helms, 1998). This unpredictability is typical of hostile environments that require an entrepreneurial orientation to negotiate successfully (Covin and Slevin, 1989). It is often stated that innovation is one characteristic that differentiates entrepreneurial businesses from those that are not (Carland et al., 1984). Miller (1983) and Covin and Slevin (1989) define entrepreneurial orientation as the extent to which small business owners will be inclined to develop innovative products, undertake moderate risk and be proactively orientated towards competitors. Furthermore, Schumpeter (1934) states that taking risks is essential to the ownership of a business. This view was supported by the research of Brockhaus (1980) who recommended that risk-taking could be used as a characteristic to distinguish between entrepreneurs and non-entrepreneurs. Covin and Slevin (1989) claimed that entrepreneurial conduct entails taking more risks than non-entrepreneurial behaviour. In other words, the concept of risk can be viewed as existing in a continuum with non-entrepreneurial businesses embracing moderate or low risk, and entrepreneurial firms taking higher degrees of risk. In addition to innovation and the taking of risks, entrepreneurial orientation includes the degree to which managers embrace change (Covin & Slevin, 1989; Miller, 1983; Miller & Friesen, 1983). This view was supported by Hills and LaForge (1992) who, in a review of the entrepreneurship literature, concluded that entrepreneurship requires the creation of new entities, innovation, uniqueness and growth. Many authors have assessed entrepreneurial orientation by appraising firm tendencies in terms of proactiveness, innovativeness, and risk taking (Wiklund, 1999; Wincent and Westerberg, 2005). Innovativeness refers to a firm's readiness to support new ideas, creativity and experimentation, which will result in changing the firm's traditional business practices. Proactiveness refers to a firm's ability to be geared up for any unanticipated situation and acting at an early stage. This may assist a firm to transform threats into opportunities. Finally, risk-taking refers to a firm's inclination to take bold actions, which may cause considerable losses. It also means that a firm might venture into investments where outcomes are unknown but promising (Lumpkin and Dess, 1996).

According to Okorie (2018), circular economy (CE) is "an economic system that represents a change of paradigm in the way that human society is interrelated with nature and aims to prevent the depletion of resources, close energy and material loops, and facilitates sustainable development".

According to the author's understanding, circular economy (CE) is about private businesses diminishing their natural resource practice in service of the evolution to a more sustainable world. With several simpler opportunities in the economy for entrepreneurs to exploit and earn a living, however current entrepreneurs might find it difficult to exploit the opportunities in the CE. The risks of a CE start-up not becoming an established business are immense considering its technical complexity as well as the lethargic cultural and market dynamics that can constraint the profitability of a CE opportunity. To advance policies for entrepreneurship development within the CE, our entrepreneurs need to be empowered, motivated and schooled about CE as it might be hard for them to survive.

Solutions and Recommendations

In that case it is about time Namibian youth take a bold step to get involved in entrepreneurial activities, the most neglected area in Namibia is agriculture and manufacturing, we are rich in natural resources but mostly we export our raw materials to other countries and import finished products at a very high price, while we could export finished products. There is a lack of land distribution in our country, and if sold, plots are sold at high prices, making it hard for people to afford land either farming. Food production is lacking in Namibia and youth need to come together, collaborate, work together, combine their knowledge and skills to take up that gap in our country, this could be an opportunity that would create jobs, provide food to the community, contribute to the GDP and I will improve people's standards of living. Entrepreneurs/managers need to enrol for management courses; most entrepreneurs do not have tertiary education which could be a contributing factor to the slow entrepreneurship development in our country.

The government and private entity can join forces to help the entrepreneurs in the following recommendations:

- The Government of the Republic of Namibia should consider establishing business incubator facilities, whereby SME owners are nurtured for future growth through innovation and entrepreneurship activity developments. Incubator facilities generally enable firms that lack the management, technical and financial ability to survive on their own. This may be a perfect opportunity to monitor the progress of SMEs and help where it becomes necessary;
- Entrepreneurial education must be imposed on both secondary education and tertiary level curriculums; whereby young citizens of the country are instructed about the basics on entrepreneurship. If they eventually choose to become owners of their businesses, they have a clear understanding of what entrepreneurship entails;

- Mentorship: Create and build associations among existing businesses and SME owners in order to expand the ability of the business to meet the rising demands;
- Ensure funding and assistance to SME owners to invest into innovation activities and thereby creates innovation culture in their organisations;
- Establish linkages with researchers and academia to promote creativity and innovation.

CONCLUSION

Namibia is a developing country with a small population, rich in natural resources but, lack brilliant entrepreneurs to grab opportunities in the market, however the future looks promising, if correct measures are put in place to empower our youth to take entrepreneurship seriously and for them to partake more into entrepreneurship activities. However with technology comes change, and our entrepreneurs need to be motivated, empowered and schooled in order to get familiar with Circular Economy as well, for that reason, future researchers should research on how entrepreneurs in Namibia can be empowered and motivated to exploit the opportunities in the CE.

REFERENCES

Aidis, R. (2003a). *Entrepreneurship and Economic Transition.* Tinbergen Institute discussion paper, 2003 – 0151/2.

Aidis, R. (2003b). *By law and by custom: Factors affecting small and medium-sized enterprises during the transition in Lithuania.* Amsterdam: Thelda Thesis.

Akingunola, R. O., Adekunle, O. A., Adegbesan, K. J., & Aninkan, O. O. (2013). Microfinance banks and entrepreneurship development in Nigeria: A case of Ogun State. *European Journal of Business and Management, 5*(28), 100–110.

Ansoff, H. (1957). Strategies for diversification. *Harvard Business Review, 35*, 113–124.

Asa, R. A., & Prasad, N. S. (2014). Analysis on the factors that determine sustainable growth of small firms in Namibia. *International Journal of Management Science and Business Administration, 1*(1), 5–11. doi:10.18775/ijmsba.1849-5664-5419.2014.11.1001

Augsburg, B., De Haas, R., Harmgart, H., & Mehgir, C. (2012). *Microfinance at the margin: experimental evidence from Bosnia and Herzegovina.* European Bank for Reconstruction and Development. Working Paper no.146.

Beaver, G. (2007). *The strategy pay-off for smaller enterprises.* Academic Press.

Berte, E., Rodrigues, L. C., & Ameida, M. I. (2010). *The Lessons Learned from the Unique Characteristics of Small technology-based Firms.* Academic Press.

Biswas, T., & Sengupta, P. P. (2009). Role of microfinance in promoting microentrepreneurship: The Indian experience. *International Journal of College Science in India, 3*(2), 73–90.

Brockhaus, R. (1980). Risk taking propensity of entrepreneurs. *Academy of Management Journal*, *23*(3), 509–520.

Carland, J. H., Hoy, F., Boulton, W. R., & Carland, J. A. C. (1984). Differentiating entrepreneurs from small business owners: A conceptualization. *Academy of Management Review*, *9*(2), 349–354. doi:10.5465/amr.1984.4277721

Cohen, W., & Levinthal, D. A. (1990). Absorptive Capacity: A New Perspective on Learning and Innovation. *Administrative Science Quarterly*, *35*(1), 128–152. doi:10.2307/2393553

Covin, J., & Slevin, D. P. (1989). Strategic management of small firms in hostile and benign environments. *Strategic Management Journal*, *10*(1), 75–87. doi:10.1002mj.4250100107

Covin, J. G., & Miles, M. P. (1999). Corporate Entrepreneurship and the Pursuit of Competitive Advantage. *Entrepreneurship Theory and Practice*, *23*(3), 47–63. doi:10.1177/104225879902300304

Day, G. S. (1994). The Capabilities of Market Driven Organisations. *Journal of Marketing*, *58*(4), 37–52. doi:10.1177/002224299405800404

Efron, B. a. (1993). *An introduction to the boostrap: Monographs on Statistics and Applied Probability*. New York: Chapman & Hall. doi:10.1007/978-1-4899-4541-9

European Commission Studies. (2004). *Final report of the expert group education for entrepreneurship*. Brussels: Enterprise Directorate General. Available at: http://europa.eu.int/comm/enterprise/entrepreneurship/support-measusures/index.htm

Ferdousi, F. (2015). Impact of microfinance on sustainable entrepreneurship development. *Development Studies Research*, *2*(1), 51–56. doi:10.1080/21665095.2015.1058718

GEM2002. (2004). *Global entrepreneurship monitor*. South African Report.

Goleman, D. (2002). *Business: The ultimate resource*. London: Bloomsbury Publishing Plc.

Gulani, M. G., & Usman, A. (2012). Financing Small and Medium Scale Enterprises (SMEs): A Challenge for Entrepreneurial Development in Gombe State. *Asian Journal of Business and Management Sciences*, *2*(9), 17–23.

Gulati, R. (1998). Alliances and networks. *Strategic Management Journal*, *19*(4), 293–317. doi:10.1002/(SICI)1097-0266(199804)19:4<293::AID-SMJ982>3.0.CO;2-M

Gulati, R. N. (2000). Strategic networks". *Management Journal*, *21*, 203–216.

Harris, A. (2003). Opportunities and constraints for indigenous entrepreneurs in SME development and growth in foreign markets. SME development and growth in foreign markets: The involvement of Indigenous Entrepreneur. Workshop 3(2); Center for Entrepreneurship Development, Windhoek. Polytechnic of Namibia.

Hashi, I., & Krasniqi, B. (2010). Entrepreneurship and SME growth: Evidence from advanced and laggard transition economies. *International Journal of Entrepreneurial Behaviour & Research*, *17*(5), 456–487. doi:10.1108/13552551111158817

Heriot, K. C., & Loughman, T. P. (2009). *Resolving the Planning Conundrum in New Venture Creation: An adaptation of Mintzberg's formation perspective*. Academic Press.

Hills, G., & Laforge, R. W. (1992). Research at the marketing interface to advance entrepreneurship theory. *Entrepreneurship Theory and Practice*, *16*(3), 33–59. doi:10.1177/104225879201600303

Hoang, H., & Antoncic, B. (2003). Network-based research in entrepreneurship: A critical review. *Journal of Business Venturing*, *18*(2), 165–187. doi:10.1016/S0883-9026(02)00081-2

Jauch, H., & Sakaria, I. (2009). *Chinese investments in Namibia: A labour perspective*. Windhoek, Namibia.

Kale, P. D., Dyer, J. H., & Singh, H. (2002). Alliance capability, stock market response, and long-term alliance success: The role of the alliance function. *Strategic Management Journal*, *23*(8), 747–767. doi:10.1002mj.248

Kalwani, M., & Narayandas, N. (1995, January). Long-term manufacturer-supplier relationships: Do they pay off for supplier firms? *Journal of Marketing*, *59*(1), 1–16. doi:10.1177/002224299505900101

Kambwale, J. N., Chisoro, C., & Karodia, A. M. (2015). Investigation into the causes of Small and medium enterprise failures in Windhoek, Namibia. *Arabian Journal of Business and Management Review*, *4*(7), 80–109. doi:10.12816/0019074

Kotey, B. A. (1997, April). Relationships among owner/manager personal values, business strategies, and enterprise performance. *Journal of Small Business Management*, 37–64.

Koufteros, X. V., Vonderembse, M. A., & Doll, W. J. (2002). Integrated product developement practices and competitive capabilities: The effects of uncertainty, equivocality, and platform strategy. *Journal of Operations Management*, *20*(4), 331–355. doi:10.1016/S0272-6963(02)00018-9

Kroon, J. (1997). *Entrepreneurship education in South Africa*. Retrieved June 29, 2009 https://www.ask.com/web?qsrc=2417&o=10181&l=dir&q=+entrepreneurship+education+in+south+africa+a+life+long+process%2C+10th+annual+conference+of+the+Southern+African +entrepreneurship+and+small+business+association+%2C+Victoria+falls%2C+Kroon%2CJ

Ladzani. M.W. (1999). *Small Business development in South Africa under the majority rule*. Pretoria: Van Shaik Books.

LaRRI, (2002). *The Small and Micro Enterprise (SME) Sector in Namibia: Conditions of Employment and Income*. Report by LaRRI for the Joint Consultative Committee.

Levrato, N. (2002). *Diversité des mondes de production et des voies d'accession à la rentabilté des petites entreprises: une analyse par les cartes auto-organisatrices*. 6e Congrès international francophone sur la PME, Octobre. HEC-Montréal.

Lorenzoni, G., & Lipparini, A. (1999). The leveraging of interfirm relationships as a distinctive organizational capability: A longitudinal study. *Strategic Management Journal*, *20*(4), 317–338. doi:10.1002/(SICI)1097-0266(199904)20:4<317::AID-SMJ28>3.0.CO;2-3

Lumpkin, G. a. (1996). Clarifying the entrepreneurial orientation construct and linking it to performance. *Academy of Management Journal*, *21*, 135–172.

Marwa, N. (2014). Micro, Small and Medium Enterprises' external financing challenges: The role of formal financial institutions and development finance intervention in Tanzania. *International Journal of Trade, Economics and Finance, 5*(3), 230-234. doi: .2014.V5.376 doi:10.7763/IJTEF

Mbaziira, S., & Oyedokun, C. (2007). *Advancing entrepreneurship education in Namibia: A practical approach*. Academic Press.

Miller, D. (1993). The architecture of simplicity. *Academy of Management Review, 18*(1), 116–13. doi:10.5465/amr.1993.3997509

Ministry of Industrialisation, Trade and SME Development. (2015). *National Policy on Micro, Small and Medium Enterprises in Namibia (Zero draft)*. Windhoek, Namibia: Author.

Ministry of Regional and Local Government, Housing and Rural Development. (2012). National Rural Development Policy. Windhoek, Namibia: Author.

Ministry of Urban and Rural Development. (2011-2015). *Annual Progress Review and Planning Reports*. Windhoek, Namibia: Author.

Morgan, R., & Hunt, S. (1999). Relationship-based competitive advantage: The role of relationship marketing in marketing strategy. *Journal of Business Research, 46*(3), 281–290. doi:10.1016/S0148-2963(98)00035-6

Mwobobia, F. M. (2012). The challenges facing small-scale women entrepreneurs: A case of Kenya. *International Journal of Business Administration, 3*(2), 112–121. doi:10.5430/ijba.v3n2p112

Ngugi, W. V., & Kerongi, F. (2014). Effects of micro-financing on growth of small and micro enterprises in Mombasa County. *International Journal of Scientific and Engineering Research, 2*(4), 138–142.

Nieman, G. (1999). *Training entrepreneurs and small business enterprises in South Africa*. University of Pretoria.

Ojo, O. (2009). Impact of microfinance on entrepreneurial development: The case of Nigeria. *Proceedings of the International Conference on Economics and Administration*. Retrieved from http://conference.faa.ro

Oliver, A. (2001). Strategic alliances and the learning life-cycle of biotechonology firms. *Organization Studies, 22*(3), 467–489. doi:10.1177/0170840601223004

Omunjalu, B. S., & Fondo, F. (2014). The role of microfinance empowerment of the youth: A case of Mombasa County. *Journal of Business and Management, 16*(5), 26–32.

Pittaway, L. R., Robertson, M., Munir, K., Denyer, D., & Neely, A. (2004). Networking and innovation: A systematic review of evidence. *International Journal of Management Reviews, 5*(3-4), 137–168. doi:10.1111/j.1460-8545.2004.00101.x

Powell, W. K.-D., Koput, K. W., & Smith-Doerr, L. (1996). Interorganizational Collaboration and the Locus of Innovation: Networks of Learning in Biotechnology. *Administrative Science Quarterly, 41*(1), 116–145. doi:10.2307/2393988

Ramsden, N. (2010). *The role of SMEs in employment creation and economic growth: lessons from other countries*. Paper presented at the Bank of Namibia 12th Annual Symposium, Windhoek, Namibia.

Raymond, L., & Blili, S. (1997). Adopting EDI in a network enterprise: The case of subcontracting SMEs. *European Journal of Purchasing and Supply Management*, *3*(3), 165–175. doi:10.1016/S0969-7012(97)00008-7

Riemenschneider, C., & Mykytyn, P. P. Jr. (2000). What small business executives have learned about managing information technology. *Information & Management*, *37*(5), 257–269. doi:10.1016/S0378-7206(99)00052-X

Roper, S. (2002). Product innovation and small business growth: A comparison of the strategies of German, U.K. and Irish companies. *Research Policy*, *31*, 1087–1102. doi:10.1016/S0048-7333(01)00175-5

Samson, A. Y., Olubunmi, A. B., & Olusegun, A. A. (2013). Microfinance bank as a catalyst for entrepreneurship development in Nigeria: Evidence from Ogun State. *International Journal of Business and Social Science*, *4*(12), 100–110.

Schumpeter, J. (1934). *The Theory of Economic Development: An Enquiry into Profits, Capital, Credit, Interest, and the Business Cycle*. Cambridge: Harvard University Press.

Skandalakis, A. A. (2001). Benchmarking as a diagnostic process to increase the competitiveness of Small and medium-sized Manufacturing Enterprises. *International Journal of Business Performance Management, 3*(2-4), 261-275.

Stokes, D., & Wilson, N. (2006). *Small business management and entrepreneurship*. London: Thomson Learning.

Storey, D. (1994). *Understanding the small business sector*. London, UK: Routledge.

Stuart, T. (2000). Interorganizational Alliances and The Performance of Firms: A Study of Growth and Innovation Rates in a High-Technology Industry. *Strategic Management Journal*, *21*(8), 791–811. doi:10.1002/1097-0266(200008)21:8<791::AID-SMJ121>3.0.CO;2-K

Thong, J. (1999). An integrated model of information systems in small business. *Journal of Management Information Systems*, *15*(4), 187–214. doi:10.1080/07421222.1999.11518227

Tjivikua, T. (2002). *Welcome message from the Rector of the Polytechnic of Namibia: The role of academic institutions in entrepreneurship*. Academic Press.

Trim, P. R., & Lee, Y.-I. (2008). *A Strategic Approach to sustainable partnership development*. Academic Press.

Van Rooyen, C., Stewart, R., & De Wet, T. (2012). The impact of microfinance in sub Saharan Africa: A systematic review of the evidence. *World Development*, *40*(11), 2249–2262. doi:10.1016/j.worlddev.2012.03.012

Vargha, R. a. (2001). *Internet Issues for Small ansd Medium-sized Australian Business. Australian and New Zealand Marketing Academy (ANZMAC) conference. Auckland: Massey University.*

Wickham, P. A. (1998). *Strategic entrepreneurship: a decision-making approach to new venture creation and management*. London: Pitman.

Wiklund, J. (1999). The sustainability of the entrepreneurial orientation-performance relationship. *Entrepreneurship Theory and Practice*, *24*(1), 37–49. doi:10.1177/104225879902400103

Wincent, J., & Westerberg, M. (2005). Personal traits of CEOs, inter-firm networking and entrepreneurship in their firms: Investigating strategic SME network participants. *Journal of Developmental Entrepreneurship*, *10*(03), 271–284. doi:10.1142/S1084946705000215

Yeoh, P.-L. (2009). Realised and potential absorptive Capacity: Understanding their antecedents and Performance in the Sourcing Context. *Journal of Marketing Theory and Practice*, *17*(1), 21–36. doi:10.2753/MTP1069-6679170102

Chapter 23
Entrepreneurship Development Interventions as a Pragmatic Approach to Political and Economic Restructuring in Nigeria

Lukman Raimi
https://orcid.org/0000-0002-5329-8715
American University of Nigeria, Nigeria

Hassan Yusuf
https://orcid.org/0000-0001-7307-3313
American University of Nigeria, Nigeria

ABSTRACT

This study discusses the imperative of entrepreneurship development interventions as pragmatic responses to political and economic restructuring in Nigeria. The qualitative research method, which entails a systematic collection of information extracted from government documents and scholarly articles, was adopted. The extracted information was critically reviewed and synthesized using content analysis. The chapter found that political and economic structures in Nigeria are largely ineffective and require urgent restructuring. For political restructuring, there is a need for constitutional amendments, while for economic restructuring, the establishment of industrial clusters to reinvigorate entrepreneurship development interventions is imperative. The study concludes with policy implications and suggestions for further research.

DOI: 10.4018/978-1-7998-5116-5.ch023

Copyright © 2020, IGI Global. Copying or distributing in print or electronic forms without written permission of IGI Global is prohibited.

INTRODUCTION

The most critical barriers hindering Nigeria's search for peace, national unity and sustainable progression towards a circular economy are the dysfunctional political and economic structures, which have continued to reinvent themselves as bad governance, political corruption, violent ethno-political agitations, resource dependency curse and endemic underdevelopment. The global community focuses a circular economy - a contemporary attempt to rethink development in a manner that integrates economic activity, social concerns and environmental wellness. Specifically, Murray, Skene and Haynes (2017, p. 369) define circular economy as "an economic model wherein planning, resourcing, procurement, production and reprocessing are designed and managed, as both process and output, to maximize ecosystem functioning and human well-being". The economic growth of China and a number of Westerns countries is linked to the acceptance, exploration and implementation of the ideals of a circular economy (Ellen MacArthur Foundation 2012; Preston 2012). Particularly, the two successive 'Five Year Plans' of the Chinese government is driven by the model of circular economy (Zhijun & Nailing 2007). The circular economy is a sustainable economic model that offers a new chance of innovation and integration between natural ecosystems, corporate businesses, people's daily lives, and waste management in a complex the ecosystem (Ghosh, 2020).

Furthermore, a circular economy thematically is framed to address three dimensions of sustainability – Economic, Social and Environmental often called Sustainable Triangle (ST) or Sustainable Development Triangle (SDT) in the development literature (Munasinghe, 1994; Munasinghe, 2012). Unfortunately, the thoughts of the Nigerian government and the various ethnic nationalities in Nigeria are far from the ideals of circular economy, rather, they have continued to nurture mutual distrust and suspicious among themselves with little consideration for social, economic and environmental sustainability. The spirit of cooperation, solidarity, patriotism and national unity that drive a circular economy is very weak or even non-existence, as evident by the unending incidences of fighting and killing over land resources in Benue, Adamawa, Zamfara, Plateau and other parts of Nigeria. The three dominant ethnic groups view and judge one another from the prism of ethnicity - firstly as Yoruba, Igbo and Hausa-Fulani before recognising their Nigerian citizenship. Consequently, the national identity question (NIQ) needs to be addressed because it embeds in the nation's polity political contestations and unhealthy rivalry among the ethnic nationalities. For long scholars, academics and policy analysts have warned that, the recurring national identity question needs to be addressed through restructuring of the present federal structure, which suddenly reinvent itself into a unitary structure (Osaghae, 1990; Naanen, 1995; Sagay, 2008).

Similarly, political leaders, politicians and academics have always cautioned that Nigeria's current federal structure is an anomaly, hence needs to be redefined, refocused and restructured in line with the true ethos of federalism. The beneficiaries of the status quo (members of the National Assembly, Ministers, Governors and those holding political offices) have always ignored the clarion calls for political and economic restructurings. Several attempts had been made in the past with empty promises from the regimes in power. The 2014 Constitution Conference was the best attempt at restructuring, but the timing, membership composition, acceptability of the resolutions by some elements and lack of political will by President Goodluck Jonathan's government to get the constitutional amendments implemented before handing over to another regime were major shortcomings of the 2014 restructuring process. The manifestations of failure to restructure have reared their ugly heads in the forms of bad governance, institutional corruption, unending violent agitations, rising poverty, growing unemployment, endemic religio-ethnic wars, weak governmental institutions, bloody electoral process, marginalisation, nepotism and other socio-economic and political ills.

Conceptually, restructuring is a development-oriented term that signals the need for a steady or revolutionary change(s) in the socio-economic and political pulses of a nation. The sluggish socio-economic and political performances experienced by some developed and emerging economies few years back were rejuvenated through a restructuring strategy. A good example of a restructured economy is France whose recession-ridden economy in early 1980s manifested problems of unemployment, inadequate social security and balance of payments deficits. France's restructuring yielded positive result, as it paved the way for a dynamic industrial sector with accompanying substantial rise in earnings and living standards of the citizens (Tuppen, 1988). Besides, the former Union of Soviet Socialist Republic (USSR) was restructured in 1991 by Mikhail Gorbachev leveraging Glasnost and Perestroika – a political restructuring that was premised on more openness and structural reform of communist political structures (Cygan, 2002). Canada is another classic example, whose economy was restructured through a neo-conservative agenda of deregulation, privatization and liberalisation that paid off in several respects (Campbell, 1993).

With reference to Nigeria, the term restructuring became a sing-song of a sort with new dimensions and colourations. According to El-Rufai (2017), the general disaffection experienced by Nigerians in the polity precipitated the call for restructuring. Specifically, he asserted that for a variety of reasons and motives individuals and groups call for political, constitutional, and fiscal reform using different but related words such as restructuring, true federalism, devolution, resource control, regionalism and self-determination. Some analysts preferred the word economic diversification, having reasoned that reliance on oil wealth, a phenomenon of a mono-economy is the bane of Nigeria's moribund economy. The Nigerian economy depends on the oil sector as a major source of foreign exchange earnings, without which the Federal, State and Local Governments cannot survive. Unfortunately, the huge foreign exchange revenues generated for over four decades from oil exploration, exploitation and exportation were mismanaged, stolen and wasted by corrupt political officeholders at the three levels of government. With crash in oil prices at the international level, the nation's economy lay prostrate in the face of self-inflicted Economic Recession – a phenomenon of short period of economic downturn in a country that leads to fall real GDP, income, employment, manufacturing and retail sales (Raimi, Fadipe and Ogunjirin, 2017).

The call for restructuring by many politicians subsequently awaken the consciousness of Nigerians to the foundational problems of the present federal structure. It also precipitated the resurgence of ethic agitations - seeking self-help, self-relevance and self-determination. In the Southeast, the Biafra agenda was resurrected - a cause championed by the Indigenous People of Biafra (IPOB) under the leadership of Nnamdi Kanu. In addition, a non-violent element with less political visibility in the South-West called for the creation of Oduduwa republic from Nigeria. The Yoruba Summit purportedly representing the Yoruba interests met in early September 2017, to discuss restructuring and the position of the South-West. In its communique, the Yoruba Summit observed that Nigeria was dangerously edging towards the precipice that should be quickly averted through restructuring. It stressed that there is an urgent need to transit from a unitary constitution to a federal constitution as obtained in the 1960 and 1963 (Ajayi, Akinrefon & Yakubu, 2017).

The political parties and the 8th National Assembly have made restructuring a front-burner issue at different political circles. The media is also not left out in the restructuring debates. Ironically, those passionately calling for economic, political and constitutional restructuring now were personalities that had many opportunities to redress the diverse problems facing the nation when they occupied positions of authority. Why were they unable to restructure Nigeria until now? How sincere are the calls for restructuring? Are the proponents of restructuring agitating for self-fish ends, considering the new realities threatening Nigeria's corporate existence? What are the elements of sustainable political and economic restructurings? These issues require in-depth analysis.

The purpose of this paper discusses the significance of entrepreneurship development interventions (through the establishment of industrial clusters in the six geo-political zones) as pragmatic responses to political and economic restructuring debates. There are five parts to this paper. The first part is the introduction, which discusses background to restructuring debates in Nigeria including the methods and approach adopted. Second part focuses on the history of Nigeria with special reference to the contradictions that trailed the creation of 36 weak federating states. The third part discusses the need for political restructuring. The fourth part looks at economic restructuring with a proposal for adoption of industrial clusters as a pragmatic response to sustainable entrepreneurship development across the six geopolitical zones in Nigeria. The final part of the paper concludes with policy implications and suggestion for further research.

METHODS AND ANALYSIS

This chapter adopts the qualitative research method, which entails the systematic collection and analysis of information on the subject matter. Specifically, the authors extracted the relevant information from scholarly works, government reports and online materials. The sourced pieces of information were systematically analysed using critical literature review based on which findings and prescriptions were made. Operationally, the critical literature review is a systematic and objective analysis and evaluation of series of research materials on a specific subject matter using appropriate language which gives new insights, richer findings and enriched understanding about the subject of inquiry (*Saunders and Rojon 2011;* Saunders, Lewis and Thornhill, 2012). To ensure some degree of objectivity in the selection of scholarly works, a sample of 30 Nigerian scholarly works were purposively selected, analysed and evaluated based on which findings and prescriptions were made on Nigeria's political and economic restructurings.

Background: Evolution of State and Governance Contradiction

The socio-economic and political problems of Nigeria have their roots in the history and evolution of the country. Historians reported that, the name Nigeria was formed from merger of two words, 'Niger' and 'Area' (Omoruyi, 2002; Helly & Callaway, 2004). There is a consensus that the country after sustained agitations gained political independence on October 1, 1960 with pomp and pageantry, driven by high hope and tall vision that the country would swiftly become an industrial giant and a worthy economic reference point for other third-world nations (TWNs) in the Sub-Saharan Africa (Raimi, Patel, Yekini, & Fadipe, 2014b). From independence till date, the country is immersed in an unending political and economic controversies that have continued to threaten its nationhood. Analysts asserted that Nigeria as a federation was hurried put together by the colonialists without constructive engagement with the legitimate representatives of the dominant ethnic nationalities on structures, nature of constitution and the desirable political frameworks that suite Nigeria. The unending agitations, discontent and factional tendencies are resultant effects of absence of robust consensus on governance issues. Mallam Nasir El-Rufai, describing the nation as "a Federation without Federalism", aptly captured this reality. At present,

Nigeria has a population of 174.5 million (CIA Factbook, 2013). It is strategically located in western Africa on the Gulf of Guinea with a total land area of 923,768 km^2.

Nigeria operates a federal system of government in theory, with constitutionally defined degree of autonomy and fiscal responsibilities, which recognized 36 states, a federal capital territory and 774 local governments majorly funded with resources from oil revenues (The World Bank, 2002). The reality is that the 36 states in the six geographical zones have not been meeting their statutory responsibilities to the citizens because there is a great deal of variation in their capacity for governance and access to economic resources. The structural problem that had engendered the legacy of stagnation and decay in the country is linked to how states were created by successive governments (Barkan, Gboyega & Stevens, 2001).

At present, many of the states are not economically viable – they cannot fulfil their financial obligations to civil servants and contractors handling their capital projects, and they lack the capacity to respond to emergencies arising from natural disasters and insurgencies. They always look forward to bailout and support interventions from the Federal government, at the slightest opportunity. The recent example is the bailout provided to several states because of their inability to pay workers' salaries and fund critical developmental projects. States' financial crisis is linked to lack of entrepreneurial governance, blurred managerial vision, shortsightedness in planning, endemic political corruption, mismanagement, ineffective leadership and weak fund generation capacity (Edogbanya & Sule, 2013).

Retrospectively, the 36 autonomous states in Nigeria were created by successive administration to score cheap political points without due regards for their economic viability, financial sustainability and human resources potentials. Apart from political and administration considerations that ought to be carefully examined in determining the viability of state creation, the financial consideration linked to abundance of economic resources is also a major consideration that must ascertained before pronouncing a certain geo-political entity as a state. Unfortunately, approval of a state status in Nigeria was premised largely on the presumption that the oil revenue would flowing endlessly. The financial considerations such as revenue base, size and major sources of revenue, ability of the area to execute development projects and availability of human resources have not been properly considered. This neglect largely left many states in Nigeria unviable and unsustainable.

The inability of successive and present leadership to lift the nation beyond the precarious state of insecurity, where the polity stinks leaves room for serious concern. Despite the numerous resources Nigeria is endowed with, it could not rival several developing countries that it started the journey of nationhood together with such as Ghana, Malaysia, and United Arab Emirate. The major cause of Nigeria's endless journey is absence of true federalism and associated principles.

Federalism is a type of governmental structure where there exists sharing of power between the federal government and constituent units otherwise called states in Nigeria. The federating units agree on the areas of jurisdiction/autonomy/resources that each will concede to the federal government, not an imposition by the federal as it is practised currently in Nigeria. Issues are well discussed and debated before final ratification. The constitution under federalism is usual written to specify the jurisdiction of the federating units (federal, states and local governments) with nomenclatures like exclusive list, concurrent list and residual list. There are two main models of federalism in the political or governance literature, namely: Dual Federalism and Cooperative Federalism (Hills, 1998). Nigeria's adoption of the two models had far-reaching socio-economic and political consequences on the sustainable growth and development in the country.

With regard to dual federalism, it was the model of federal system chosen by the founding father of Nigeria, at the dawn of independence. Its adoption was predicated on the fear of strong central government.

The dual federalism (regional governments) agreed upon, allowed for strong regional government (west, east and north) and weak federal government. It also allowed for control over resources at the various regions. Dual federalism gave more responsibilities to the regions then, relative to federal government.

More importantly, the dual model provided for larger share of the revenue to the regions than the federal government because of larger responsibilities given to the regional governments/regions. Dual model of Federalism was driven by the principle of separation of powers; and checks and balances. This is the type of federalism that many Nigerians are agitating. Alas! The Constitution of Federal Republic of Nigeria would have to be amended for this tall dream to be realised. Under the Dual federalism model, the regions compete with one another in the areas of industrial development, educational system, infrastructural facilities, tax system collection and other forms of revenue mechanisms. The positive deliverables are too numerous to list.

Cooperative federalism on the other hand describes a broader sharing of authority between the federating units (federal government and regional governments). It is a model of federalism that we are currently operating. Its adoption some decades ago was predicated on the need to save the nation from precipices of civil wars and disintegration, specifically Biafran war and Western region upheavals. This model as currently being practised, allows for strong federal government and weak state governments (which currently stood at thirty-six with federal capital). These states as earlier discussed are weak and unsustainable. Little delay in the release of their monthly allocations causes instability and inability to meet financial obligations. Structurally, economic resources within this model of Federalism tilt revenue allocations and appropriation in favour of the federal government, contrary to the tenets of federalism (Salami, 2011). Cooperative federalism also gives more responsibilities to the federal government and provides larger share of the revenue to the federal government as defined in the Exclusive Legislative List. After the civil war and takeover of control by successive military regimes, Nigeria's federalism shifted to this model "unknowingly" and without mutual agreement among Nigerians or the political elites representing the ethnic nationalities in the three known regions –North, East and West. Nigeria operated has been operating this model for long.

The violent and non-violent agitations and the recent calls for restructuring are signs of discontent and disaffection with the present model of federalism. There is therefore a strong need for political, constitutional and economic restructuring with a view to deepening the governance structure of Nigeria.

RESTRUCTURING DEBATES: POLITICAL AND ECONOMIC PERSPECTIVES

The restructuring debates in Nigeria have political and economic perspectives. The section discusses these two critical angles to the debates.

Political Restructuring

Nigeria's political landscape needs fundamental restructuring that would institute true federalism and its enduring principles. Specifically, the country requires a constitution and political structures that are people-centred and people-oriented. In other words, a constitution and political structures that allow power and resources to be divided and appropriated between the federal and the states without rifts and acrimonies. The present constitution is far from these ideals.

The history of political restructuring including agitations for constitutional amendments is traced to the weak political structures contained in the 1946 Richard's constitution and other constitutions (except the 1960 and 1963 constitutions) that were forced on Nigeria by the military governments without exhaustive consultations. Consequently, the political structures that emerged from the weak constitutions failed to redress critical issues such as resource control, ethno-tribal and regional discrimination, and citizen rights (Nwafor-Orizu, Chinyere & Tochukwu, 2018; Sagay, 2008).

The agitation on political restructuring worsened with the advent of ethnic politics in Nigeria that subsequently polarized the country along north and south divide with the southerners assuming the role of protagonists and the northerners being tagged the antagonists of political restructuring (Dickson & Asua, 2016; Yaqub, 2016). Attempts described as corrective and curative restructuring measures were made in the past by different political regimes in Nigeria through emphasis on issues of intergovernmental relations between the federal and subnational governments, resource control and allocation, revenue allocation, efficiency and functionality of the constitution, inequality of states and autonomy local governments amongst others. Unfortunately, the historical conflict of interest of policymakers undermined the intention to redress the faulty political structures (Nwafor-Orizu et al., 2018).

Political restructuring based on constitutional amendments would engender pluralist democracy, equitable revenue sharing formula, competition among the states, state police, and rule of law, independent judiciary and protection of minority rights. The present federalism favoured arbitrariness, rent-seeking, self-seeking, monopoly of resources by powerful centre, funding of non-viable states created for political reasons, nepotism, unequal opportunities and institutional corruption. These are negative fall-outs of over concentration of power with the federal government. Lending credence to the foregoing, the legal luminary, Sagay (2008) asserted that, the 1960 and 1963 Constitutions reflected true Federalism, while other constitutions thereafter were selectively put together without exhaustive consensus-building. From 1950 to 1959, a period of 10 years, there were consensus building and negotiations among the major stakeholders. The engagement process culminated into the 1960 Constitution. It could therefore be stated boldly that, apart from minor, non-structural modifications, it represented the most legitimate Constitution, as its development engaged and attracted inputs from different nationalities in Nigeria.

Apart from the above, the constitutional restructuring is expected to focus on political inclusiveness, electoral process, political representation, sharing of offices, citizens; right, protection of lives and properties, and building of critical political infrastructure. Political restructuring is delicate and should not be rushed. Rather, a four-phase approach is prescribed. In the first phase of four years, the Federal Government through the instrumentality of the law should allow state police, greater control of the education, health and transportation systems, and the generation and distribution of power by the states. In the second phase, there is a need to free the local government from the apron strings of the states by granting them autonomy. This should be followed with an upward review of the revenue-sharing formula to 65 per cent in favour of the states. The exclusive list should be drastically reduced while increasing the concurrent list. The third phase should be the time to stop federal ownership of inter-state roads and the federal character principle. Full resource control should be the last item on the agenda when it is clear that there is maturity and level-headedness on the part of the administrators of the states (Abdur Raheem, 2017).

Furthermore, the proposed political restructuring should extend to fight against financial and political corruption in all segments of the society. The concept of corruption has not been able to attract a universally definition, as it has diverse contexts, connotations and typologies based on the actors involved, the initiators, the beneficiaries, the scope level, the sophistication and the spread. However, Rosenbloom and Gong, (2013) defined corruption as clandestine and illegal individual conduct of embezzling public money or a one-on-one illicit exchange between two parties for preferential treatment in exchange for goods or services, which extends to a betrayal of the public trust for reasons of private interest.

Nigeria has consistently been ranked as one of the most corrupt countries in the world because of the lack of probity and accountability in the handing and utilisation of public resources. Each time the Corruption Perception Index report of the Transparency International is released, it normally generates public debates that centred on: Why is there an increase in the rate of corruption in Nigeria? In Nigeria, the level of corruption is responsible for the comatose state of power sector, transport sector, health sector, education sector and communications sector (Nwankwo, 2014). Even one of the anti-graft agency noted that corruption is a canker worm that has hampered development in all sectors of the Nigeria economy (EFCC, 2005).

In 2019, Nigeria ranked by the Transparency International as the 146 least corrupt nation out of 180 countries, while for 2018, 2017, 2016, 2015, 2014, 2013, 2011 and 2010, the country was ranked 144, 148, 136, 136, 136, 144, 139, 143 and 134 respectively (Trading Economics, 2020). The implication of the low ranking from 2010-2019 is that the anti-corruption policies have been very ineffective, and the anti-graft agencies such as EFCC, ICPC, Code of Conduct Bureau have had their activities compromised.

Some of the past efforts of the government at stemming corruption include Murtala Mohammed's attack of corrupt practices among public officers in Nigeria. Buhari-Idiagbon's prosecution of notorious and corrupt politicians that served in the previous administration; Abacha's fight against financial crimes in all strata of the nation's life; Musa Bamaiyi's arrest of bank, business executives and practitioners of advanced fraudsters; and the establishment of Economic and Financial Crimes Commission (EFCC) and Independent Corrupt Practices & Other Related Offences Commission (ICPC) as anti-graft agencies to fight corruption in the country (Raimi, Suara & Fadipe, 2013). Political restructuring targeted at corruption is imperative because Nigeria inherited operational base and social superstructures of post-colonial politics and public life that are too weak to combat corruption and corrupt practices.

Economic Restructuring

Nigeria's present economic structure is defective, unfair, unequitable and unsustainable because it is built of resource-dependency or rentier state structure. The Nigerian economy is largely dependent on the oil sector for its foreign exchange earnings – an indication that the oil is the driver of the nation's economy, while the non-oil sector only complements (Raimi, 2015). The oil revenue that accrued to the country led to appreciable growth in the gross domestic product (Oil GDP) at different periods, but there was no real economic development because of the rentier political economy. Adibe, Nwagwu and Albert (2018) recounted that the phenomenon of rentier state structure encourages political patronage, settlement of militant, award of contracts without consideration for organisational competencies of the companies and entrenchment of culture of laziness/entitlement among the states and citizens. Unfortunately, the humongous wealth that accrued to the nation from oil exploitation could therefore not translate into sustainable economic development due to institutional corruption, oil theft, profligacy and bad governance leading to mismanagement of oil resources with impunity by the political elites (Watts, 2009; McLoughlin & Bouchat, 2013). There is a need to return to the days of health rivalry for wealth creation amongst the federating units in Nigeria.

Moreover, before independence and few years after independence, Nigeria survived as an agrarian economy making fortunes from agriculture, mining and other real sectors of the economy. The discovery oil and the resultant wealth arising from cruel oil became a curse rather than a blessing to Nigeria. Igbuzor (2006) noted with nostalgia that Nigeria was once rated among the 50 affluent economies in the early 1970s, but the country suddenly fell from the development ladder to become one of the 25 poorest economies in early 2000s. Until date, the nation's economy depends heavily on revenues from oil resources, at the expense of other critical sectors such as solid minerals, services, manufacturing, tourism and agriculture that should have been well developed to complement the revenue base of the economy (Raimi, Patel, Yekini & Fadipe, 2014). The real solution that could put a check to the weak foundation of the Nigeria economy is to embrace economic restructuring by deploying wealth accumulated from oil into critical sectors of the economy through massive investment. Nigeria's developmental challenges and poverty issues fuelling violent agitations and other political crises are self-inflicted.

Attempts have been made by the by the Federal Government through a number of public-sector entrepreneurship development interventions (EDIs) with the intention of promoting agricultural, industrial and overall economic development in the country. Some of the past EDIs include: the National Development Plans (NDPs), the Structural Adjustment Programme (SAP), the National Economy Reconstruction Fund (NERFUND); the People's Bank, Community Banking Models, the Bank of Industry (BOI), the National Economic Empowerment and Development Strategy, the Microfinance Institutions (MFIs), the Small and Medium Enterprises Development Agency of Nigeria (SMEDAN), the Small and Medium Enterprises Equity Investment Scheme (SMEEIS), the National Poverty Eradication Programme (NAPEP), the Millennium Development Goals (MDGs). The 7- Point Agenda, Vision 20:2020 Economic Blueprints, Economic Transformation Agenda, the N200 Billion Small and Medium Scale Enterprises Guarantee Scheme (SMECGS), the N200 Million Film Fund, the N100 billion Cotton, Textile and Garment (CTGF), the Youth Enterprise with Innovation in Nigeria (You Win), the Subsidy Reinvestment & Empowerment Programme (Sure Programme (SURE-P) (Njoku, Ihugba & Odii, A. 2014; Oghojafor, Okonji, Olayemi, & Okolie, 2011; Raimi, Patel, Yekini, & Fadipe, 2014b). Unfortunately, these EDIs have consistently failed to stimulate employment generation, poverty reduction and accelerated economic growth and development in Nigeria because they were development paradigms hinged heavily on foreign financing/external loans from developed countries and international monetary institutions (Ajayi & Oke, 2012; Raimi et al., 2014b).

As a departure from the past, the EDI proposed by this paper is the development of industrial clusters across the six-geopolitical zones based on the types of natural resource endowment in different locations in Nigeria. Industrial clusters would provide sound industrial and technological progress across Nigeria. It is better than the previous Adhoc efforts, because it is more sustainable and functionally does not create a dependency culture - a critical factor for failures of economic policies in Nigeria (Raimi et al., 2014b).

Economic restructuring is therefore structurally and functionally a gradual long-term process. Focusing industrial clusters to drive economic restructuring in Nigeria is practically and logically the best way to restructure the bartered economy learning from the experiences and technological progress of America, Europe and emerging economies like Brazil, Russia, India and China where industrial clusters were vigorously promoted by both public and private sectors (Raimi et al, 2016). Industrial clusters have been recognised worldwide as a desirable and worthwhile industrial strategy with inherent competitive advantages otherwise called agglomeration economies (Raimi, Fadipe & Ogunjirin, 2017). View differently, industrial clusters accommodated businesses that are interdependent, specialized suppliers, service providers, and other organisations operating in the same geographical area for mutually beneficial cooperation and collaboration with one another (Boja, 2011; Martin & Sunley, 2003).

Across the continents, clusters represent an industrial strategy that is critical in the development process because companies operating within industrial clusters source their raw material, components and value-added services cheaper and promptly from other companies in what could be described a symbiotic relationship (Raimi et al, 2017). Some model clusters across the globe include the wine clusters in California, textiles industry in northern Italy, shipbuilding clusters in Glasgow in Scotland, steel clusters in Pittsburgh in Pennsylvania, USA, car manufacturing clusters in Detroit, Michigan USA (Kuah, 2002; Mueller, Sumner & Lapsley, 2006).

The six-geopolitical zones in Nigeria are blessed with abundant natural resources, which if well harnessed and developed could be bases of clusters development. The understanding of clusters extends to knowledge-based institutions and financial institutions that cluster together in a particular location training, research and consulting services in various disciplines to the society (Raimi et al, 2016).

The economic opportunities of clusters include employment and increase in income generation for all players in the clusters including the government (Oyeyinka, 2017). Besides, industrial clusters stimulate competitiveness as they increase the productivity of all collaborating businesses operating in the clusters. Thirdly, industrial clusters encourage the development of innovative products and novel services. Finally, industrial clusters stimulate emergence of new businesses often called spin-off and embedment of technological improvements of both process and products in places where clusters are allowed to flourish (Amobi, 2006; Raimi et al, 2017).

Furthermore, industrial clusters foster specialisation among collaborating companies of different sizes and strengths operating within a particular industry. Clusters afford different companies the opportunities of exploiting their specialties thereby fostering innovation, emergence of new business or spin-offs and embedment of technological improvements of both process and products. Moreover, the 36 states in Nigeria seeking to operate industrial clusters have to situate strategically their natural resources with the types of industrial clusters that fit their states.

Endowed Resources and Proposed Clusters for the Six Geo-Political Zones in Nigeria

The South-West geographical zone of Nigeria often called Yoruba-speaking states could explore the industrial clusters in the Table 1.

The Southeast geographical zone of Nigeria often called Igbos or Ibo-speaking states should leverage industrial clusters listed in Table 2.

The South-South zone of Nigeria should focus at least five major industrial clusters in Table 3.

The Northeast zone of Nigeria should create at least six major industrial clusters as presented in Table 4.

The North-Central zone of Nigeria should create six major clusters in this zone shown in Table 5.

North-Central zone of Nigeria should create six major clusters in this zone presented in Table 6.

PRACTICAL IMPLICATIONS

The managerial and policy implications of this chapter leveraging critical literature review are diverse. First, the weak political structure and poor performance of the economy affirmed the presumption that existing political and economic structures need to be restructured. Specifically, the country's political structure should be re-modelled along true federalism in order to accommodate all ethno-regional

Table 1. Industrial clusters in the south-west of Nigeria

SN	States	Resource Endowment	Cluster Type
1.	Lagos	Water Resources, Agricultural Resources Bitumen, Beach, Clay & Glass-sand, colonial relics and recently oil	Fish production cluster Crops & Food production cluster Manufacturing/Services Cluster Ecotourism services Cluster Pleasure Tourism Cluster
2.	Osun	Solid Minerals such as Columbite, Gold, Granite, Talc, Tantalite, Tourmaline, Agricultural Resources, Natural Ecosystem, Traditional Festivals	1
3.	Ogun	Solid Minerals - Bitumen, Clay, Feldspar, Gemstone, Kaolin, Limestone, Phosphate, Rocks, Agricultural Resources, Natural Ecosystem, Traditional Festivals	1
4.	Oyo	Aqua Marine, Clay, Arable land, Dolomite, Gemstone, Gold, Kaolin, Marble, Silimonite, Talc, Tantalite, Cassiterite, Ancient monuments and Traditional Festivals	1
5.	Ondo	Water resources, Bitumen, Clay, Coal, Dimension Stones, Feldspar, Gemstone, Glass-Sand, Granite, Gypsium, Kaolin, Limestone & Oil/Gas	1
6.	Ekiti	Water Resources, Land Resources, Feldspar, Granite, Kaolin, Syenite, Tatium, Traditional Festivals	1

Source: Content Analysis of States' Endowment (Raimi, Fadipe & Ogunjirin, 2017)

Table 2. Industrial clusters in the southeast of Nigeria

SN	States	Resource Endowment	Cluster Type
1.	Imo	Water Resources, Arable land, Gypsium, Lead, Zinc, Lignite, Limestone, Marcasite, Oil/Gas, Phosphate, Salt, Ancient Shrines and Festivals	Fish production Cluster Mineral Mining Clusters Manufacturing Clusters Petro-Chemical Cluster Wood and Furniture Cluster Pleasure Tourism Cluster
2.	Eboyin	Water Resources, Oil, Arable Land, Forest Resources, Natural Ecosystem, Gold, Lead/ Zinc, Salt	1
3.	Anambra	Water Resources, Arable Land, Clay, Glass Sand, Gypsium, Iron-ore, Lead/Zinc, Lignite, Limestone, Phosphate, Salt, Ancient Shrines and Festivals	1
4.	Enugu	Water Resources, Arable Land, Solid Minerals such Coal, Lead, Zinc, Limestone, Ancient Shrines and Festivals	1
5.	Abia	Water Resources, Forest Resources, Gold, Lead, Zinc, Limestone, Oil/Gas, Salt, Ancient Shrines and Festivals	1

Source: Content Analysis of States' Endowment (Raimi, Fadipe & Ogunjirin, 2017)

Table 3. Industrial clusters in southern Nigeria

SN	States	Resource Endowment	Cluster Type
1.	Rivers	Water Resources, Forest Resources, Clay, Glass-Sand, Lignite, Marble, Oil/Gas and Ancient monuments	Fish production cluster Petro-Chemical Cluster Manufacturing Cluster Wood production and Furniture Cluster Pleasure Tourism Cluster
2.	Cross River	Water Resources, Forest, Barite, Lead/Zinc, Lignite, Limestone, Manganese, Oil/Gas, Salt, Uranium, Traditional Festivals	1
3.	Delta	Clay, Glass-sand, Gypsium, Iron-ore, Kaolin, Lignite, Marble & Oil/Gas, Water Resources and Forest Resources.	1
4	Edo	Water Resources, Forest Resources, Bitumen, Clay Dolomite, Oil, Phosphate, Glass-sand, Gold, Gypsium, Iron-ore, Lignite, Limestone, Marble, and Ancient monuments	1
5.	Bayelsa	Water Resources, Glay, Gypsium, Lead/Zinc, Lignite, Limestone, Maganese, Oil, Uranium	1
6.	Akwa-Ibom	Water Resources, Forest Resources, Clay, Lead, Zinc, Lignite, Limestone, Oil/Gas, Salt, Uranium	1

Source: Content Analysis of States' Endowment (Raimi, Fadipe & Ogunjirin, 2017)

Table 4. Industrial clusters in the north-east Nigeria

SN	States	Resource Endowment	Cluster Type
1.	Adamawa	Bentonite, Gypsium, Kaolin & Magnesite, Land Resources, Animal resources, Traditional Festivals	Meat, Dairy and Leather Production Clusters Food production cluster Manufacturing Cluster Mineral Mining Clusters Pleasure Tourism Cluster
2.	Bauchi	Gold, Cassiterite (tine ore), Columbite, Gypsium, Wolfram, Coal, Limestone, Lignite, Iron-ore & Clay, Animal Resources, Land Traditional Festivals	1
3.	Bornu	Bentonite, Clay, Diatomite, Gypsium, Hydro-carbon, Kaolin & Limestone, Animal Resources, Land Resources, Traditional Festivals	1
4	Gombe	Animal Resources, Agricultural Resources Land Resources, Gemstone & Gypsium, Traditional Festivals	1
5.	Taraba	Lead/Zinc, Animal Resources, Land Resources, Traditional Festivals	1
6.	Yobe	Soda Ash & Tintomite, Animal Resources Agricultural Resources, Land Resources, Solid Minerals, Traditional Festivals	1

Source: Content Analysis of States' Endowment (Raimi, Fadipe & Ogunjirin, 2017)

Table 5. Industrial clusters in the north-central of Nigeria

SN	States	Resource Type	Cluster Type
1.	Benue	Water Resources, Agricultural Resources Barite, Clay, Coal, Gemstone, Gypsium, Iron-Ore, Lead/Zinc, Limestone, Marble & Salt; Traditional Festivals	Meat, Dairy and Leather Production Clusters Crops production cluster Manufacturing Cluster Mineral Mining Clusters Salt Manufacturing Clusters Pleasure Tourism Cluster
2.	Kogi	Agricultural Resources, Cole, Dolomite, Feldspar, Gypsium, Iron-ore, Kaolin, Marble, Talc, Tantalite Natural Ecosystem, Traditional Festivals	1
3.	Kwara	Agricultural Resources, Cassiterite, Columbite, Feldspar, Gold, Iron-ore, Marble, Mica, Tantalite, Animal resources, Traditional Festivals	1
4	Nasarawa	Agricultural Resources Amethyst (Topaz Garnet), Barytex, Clay, Barite, Cassirite, Coal, Chalcopyrite, Talc, Columbite, Coking Dolomite, Marble, Feldspar, Galena, Iron-ore, Limstone, Mica, Salt, Sapphire, Tantalite, Tourmaline Quartz, Zireon	1
5.	Niger	Agricultural Resources, Gold, Lead/Zinc & Talc, Natural Water, Traditional Festivals	1
6.	Plateau	Barite, Bauxite, Coal, Betonite, Bismuth, Cassiterite, Clay, Tin, Kaolin, Emeral, Salt, Fluoride, Gemstone, Granite, Iron-ore,Lead, Zinc, Marble, Molybdenite, Columbite, Phrochlore, Tantalite; Tin Wolfram Agricultural Resources	1
7.	FCT	Agricultural Resources Cassiterite, Clay, Dolomite, Gold, Lead/Zinc, Marble & Tantalite, Natural Ecosystem	1

Source: Content Analysis of States' Endowment (Raimi, Fadipe & Ogunjirin, 2017)

interests and agitations for a true federal structure. The manifestations of failure to restructure are bad governance, institutional corruption, unending violent agitations, rising poverty, growing unemployment, endemic religio-ethnic wars, weak governmental institutions, bloody electoral process, marginalisation, nepotism and other socio-economic and political ills. The starting point is to start from where the 2014 constitutional conference stopped. The present administration should choose the right timing for this expedient issue. The membership composition should be adequate and representative cutting across the six geopolitical zones, religions and other critical divides. When the timing for political and economic restructuring is right, and representations of all critical stakeholders are perceived to be balanced, then acceptability of the final resolutions and outcomes of the restructuring will be very easy.

The implication of economic restructuring is that the executive and national assembly need to co-operate and forge alliance to tackle headlong the perpetual dependence on oil as the mainstay of the Nigerian economy. Similarly, there is a need to develop the agriculture, industrial, tourism, service, and construction sectors in the six geo-political zones leveraging the cluster strategy. Oil-driven economic structure has proven to be non-beneficial, as it encourages laziness, dependency and lack of competition among the states. Related to the above is the need to come up with a sustainable circular economy with a collaborative synergy from critical stakeholders in the nation's developmental process. The circular

Table 6. Industrial clusters in the north-west of Nigeria

SN	States	Resource Type	Cluster Type
1.	Jigawa	Water Resources Agricultural Resources Butyles Traditional Festivals	Meat, Dairy and Leather Production Clusters Mineral Mining Clusters Crops & Food Production and Agro-allied clusters Ecotourism services Cluster Pleasure Tourism Cluster Manufacturing/Services Cluster
2.	Kaduna	Amethyst, Aqua Marine, Asbestos, Clay, Flosper, Gemstone, Gold, Ruby Graphite, Kaolin, Mica, Hyanite, Rock Crystal, Sapphire, Sihnite, Superntinite, Tentalime, Topaz, Tourmaline Agricultural Resources Traditional Festivals	1
3.	Kano	Gassiterite, Copper, Gemstone, Glass-sand, Lead/Zinc, Pyrochinre, Tantalite, Agricultural Resources Natural Ecosystem Traditional Festivals	1
4	Katsina	Kaolin, Marble, Salt, Agricultural Resources Natural Ecosystem Traditional Festivals	1
5.	Kebbi	Gold, Agricultural Resources, Natural Ecosystem Traditional Festivals	1
6.	Sokoto	Clay, Flakes, Gold, Salt, Granite, Gypsium, Kaolin, Laterite, Potash, Limestone, Phosphate, Silica Sand, Agricultural Resources, Traditional Festivals	1
7.	Zamfara	Coal, Cotton, Gold, Agricultural Resources Natural Ecosystem Traditional Festivals	1

Source: Content Analysis of States' Endowment (Raimi, Fadipe & Ogunjirin, 2017)

economy unlike previous approach to development is sustainable and unlikely to generate a dependency culture, a critical factor for policy failure in Nigeria. A circular economy would help to alleviate poverty, provide employment opportunities for the hopeless and hapless members of the public especially the able-bodied youth who are easy recruits for people with diabolical agenda. The stolen but recovered billions of naira should be utilised for building infrastructural facilities across the six-geopolitical zones in the country. Finally, the three levels of government need to create enabling environment for attracting foreign direct investment (FDI) for agricultural, commercial and industrial development of clusters in Nigeria; this should be complemented with the promotion of entrepreneurship development at individual, group and institutional levels.

FUTURE RESEARCH DIRECTIONS

The issue of economic political restructurings in Nigeria requires detailed rigorous conceptual, theoretical and empirical research. Therefore, further research direction should focus on failure of previous economic and political reform policies in Nigeria. Another area of further research is the rationale for lack of continuity in policy implementation as well as reasons for non-implementation of previous constitutional amendments.

CONCLUSION

This chapter sets out to contribute to the restructuring debate in Nigeria by discussing the significance of entrepreneurship development interventions (through the establishment of industrial clusters) as pragmatic responses to political and economic restructurings in Nigeria. The chapter discussed both the political and economic perspectives of restructuring. It proposes constitutional amendments with focus on political inclusiveness, resource control, electoral process, political representation and building of enduring political infrastructure for political restructuring. For economic restructuring, the establishment of industrial clusters as entrepreneurship development interventions across the six geo-political zones for sustainable development was articulated. The chapter concludes with policy implications and suggestions for further research.

REFERENCES

AbdurRaheem, L. (2017). *State of the Nation Address: Why think of restructuring at this time? – TMC.* Available: http://therenaissanceng.com/feed-items/state-of-the-nation-address-why-think-of-restructuring-at-this-time-tmc

Adibe, R., Nwagwu, E., & Albert, O. (2018). Rentierism and security privatisation in the Nigerian petroleum industry: Assessment of oil pipeline surveillance and protection contracts. *Review of African Political Economy, 45*(156), 345–353. doi:10.1080/03056244.2017.1391771

Ajayi, L. B., & Oke, M. O. (2012). Effect of External Debt on Economic Growth and Development of Nigeria. *International Journal of Business and Social Science, 3*(12), 297-304.

Ajayi, O., Akinrefon, D., & Yakubu, D. (2017). *Yoruba demands return to regionalism, restructuring.* Available:https://www.vanguardngr.com/2017/09/yoruba-demands-return-regionalism-restructuring/

Amobi, I. C. (2006). *Unleashing of Industrial Clusters for Growth and Prosperity in South East Nigeria.* Lead Presentation at the *Enugu Forum Seminar.*

Barkan, J. D., Gboyega, A., & Stevens, M. (2001). *State and local governance in Nigeria. Public Sector and Capacity Building Program, Africa Region.* The World Bank.

Boja, C. (2011). Clusters Models, Factors and Characteristics. *International Journal of Economic Practices and Theories, 1*(1), 1-43.

Campbell, B. (1993). Restructuring the economy: Canada into the free trade era. In The political economy of North American free trade (pp. 89-104). Palgrave Macmillan UK.

Central Intelligence Agency Factbook. (2013). *Country Socio-economic data*. The online Factbook.

Cygan, A. (2002). The White Paper on European Governance–Have Glasnost and Perestroika Finally Arrived to the European Union? *The Modern Law Review*, *65*(2), 229–240. doi:10.1111/1468-2230.00376

Dickson, M., & Asua, S. A. (2016). The Politics of Resource Control in Nigeria: Agitation and Innovation. *International Journal of Politics and Good Governance.*, *7*(2), 1–13.

Edogbanya, A., & Sule, M. J. A. G. (2013). Revenue Generation: It's Impact on Government Developmental Effort (A Study of Selected Local Council in Kogi East Senatorial District). *GJMBR-A: Administration and Management*, *13*(4), 13–25.

EFCC. (2005). *Effect of Corruption on Nigeria's Economy*. Abuja: Nigeria EFFC Information Communication Technology Department.

El-RufaiN. (2007). *A Federation Without Federalism*. Available: http://saharareporters.com/2012/04/06/federation-without-federalism-nasir-ahmad-el-rufai

Ellen Macarthur Foundation. (2012). Towards the Circular Economy Vol.1: Economic and business rationale for a Circular Economy. Ellen Macarthur Foundation.

Federal Ministry of Youth and Sports. (2013). *Nigeria Natural Resources*. Available: http://youthdevelopment.gov.ng/index.php/nigeria/2013-12-19-03-40-31/natural-resources

Ghosh, S. K. (Ed.). (2020). *Circular Economy: Global Perspective*. Springer. doi:10.1007/978-981-15-1052-6

Hills, R. M. (1998). The Political Economy of Cooperative Federalism: Why State Autonomy Makes Sense and "Dual Sovereignty" Doesn't. *Michigan Law Review*, *96*(4), 813–944.

Igbuzor, O. (2006) *The millennium development goals: can Nigeria meet the goals in 2015?* Presentation at the Symposium of The Institute Of Chartered Accountants Of Nigeria (ICAN), Abuja, Nigeria.

Kuah, A. T. (2002). Cluster Theory and Practice: Advantages for the small business locating in a vibrant cluster. *Journal of Research in Marketing and Entrepreneurship*, *4*(3), 206–228.

Martin, R., & Sunley, P. (2003). Deconstructing clusters: Chaotic concept or policy panacea? *Journal of Economic Geography*, *3*(1), 5–35. doi:10.1093/jeg/3.1.5

Mueller, R. A., Sumner, D. A., & Lapsley, J. (2006). *Clusters of grapes and wine*. In *Third International Wine Business Research Conference*, Montpellier, France.

Munasinghe, M. (1994). Sustainomics: a transdisciplinary framework for sustainable development. *Proc. 50th Anniversary Sessions of the Sri Lanka Assoc. for the Adv. of Science (SLAAS)*.

Munasinghe, M. (2012). *Sustainable Development Triangle (SDT)*. Available: http://www.eoearth.org/view/article/156365/

Murray, A., Skene, K., & Haynes, K. (2017). The circular economy: An interdisciplinary exploration of the concept and application in a global context. *Journal of Business Ethics*, *140*(3), 369–380. doi:10.100710551-015-2693-2

Naanen, B. (1995). Oil-producing minorities and the restructuring of Nigerian federalism: The case of the Ogoni people. *The Journal of Commonwealth & Comparative Politics*, *33*(1), 46–78.

Nwafor-Orizu, I., Chinyere, O. M., & Tochukwu, E. K. (2018). Political Restructuring in Nigeria: The Need, Challenges and Prospects. *International Journal of Public Policy & Governance*, *5*(1), 28-53.

Nwankwo, O. F. (2014). Impact of corruption on economic growth in Nigeria. *Mediterranean Journal of Social Sciences*, *5*(6), 41. doi:10.5901/mjss.2014.v5n6p41

Oyeyinka, O. (2017). Living Standards and Industrial Clusters in Nigeria. In Industrial Clusters, Institutions and Poverty in Nigeria (pp. 57-99). Springer International Publishing.

Preston, F. (2012). A Global Redesign: Shaping the Circular Economy. London: Chatham House: The Royal Institute of International Affairs.

Raimi, L. (2015). *Entrepreneurship Development through Corporate Social Responsibility – A Study of the Nigerian Telecommunication Industry* (Unpublished PhD. Thesis). Leicester Business School, De Montfort University, Leicester, UK.

Raimi, L., Fadipe, A. O., & Ogunjirin, O. D. (2017). Potential Roles of Industrial Clusters in Economic Diversification in Nigeria. International Journal of Development Strategies in Humanities. *Management and Social Sciences*, *7*(2), 50–68.

Raimi, L., Patel, A., Yekini, K., & Fadipe, A. O. (2014). Spatio-Temporal Audit of Nigeria's Industrial Policies and Entrepreneurship Development Interventions from 1946 to 2013. *International Journal of Humanities and Social Science*, *4*(1), 294–309.

Raimi, L., Peluola, S. B., & Shokunbi, M. O. (2016). Prospects and challenges of managing clusters as entrepreneurship development interventions for sustainable development in Nigeria: a discourse analysis. In *Managing Knowledge and Innovation for Business Sustainability in Africa*. Palgrave MacMillan.

Raimi, L., Suara, I. B., & Fadipe, A. O. (2013). Role of Economic and Financial Crimes Commission (EFCC) and Independent Corrupt Practices & Other Related Offences Commission (ICPC) at Ensuring Accountability and Corporate Governance in Nigeria. *Journal of Business Administration and Education*, *3*(2), 105–122.

Rosenbloom, D. H., & Gong, T. (2013). Coproducing "clean" collaborative governance: Examples from the United States and China. *Public Performance & Management Review*, *36*(4), 544–561. doi:10.2753/PMR1530-9576360403

Sagay, I. (2008). *Nigeria: Federalism, the constitution and resource control.* Available: http://www.nigerdeltapeoplesworldcongress.org/articles/nigeria_federalism_.pdf

Salami, A. (2011). Taxation, revenue allocation and fiscal federalism in Nigeria: Issues, challenges and policy options. *Economic Annals*, *56*(189), 27-51.

Saunders, M., Lewis, P., & Thornhill, A. (2012). Research Methods for Business Students. Pearson Education Limited.

Saunders, M. N., & Rojon, C. (2011). On the attributes of a critical literature review. *Coaching (Abingdon, UK)*, *4*(2), 156–162. doi:10.1080/17521882.2011.596485

Tuppen, J. (1988). Restructuring the Economy. In France under Recession, 1981–86 (pp. 90-162). Palgrave Macmillan UK. doi:10.1007/978-1-349-08274-2_3

World Bank. (2002). *Nigeria State and Local Governance in Nigeria*. AFTPR, Africa Region Report of The World Bank, No.24477-UNI.

World Bank. (2017). *Nigeria Economic Update: Beyond Oil, Key Drivers for Sustainable Growth*. Available: https://www.worldbank.org/en/country/nigeria/publication/nigeria-economic-update-beyond-oil-key-drivers-for-sustainable-growth

Yaqub, N. (2016). What is Restructuring in the Era of Change in Nigerian Politics. In *IASTEM International Conference* (pp. 5-18). Dammian, Saudi Arabia: Academic Press.

Zhijun, F., & Nailing, Y. (2007). Putting a circular economy into practice in China. *Sustainability Science*, *2*(1), 95–101. doi:10.100711625-006-0018-1

ADDITIONAL READING

Raimi, L., Peluola, S. B., & Shokunbi, M. O. (2016). Prospects and challenges of managing clusters as entrepreneurship development interventions for sustainable development in Nigeria: a discourse analysis. In A. Ahmed (Ed.), *Managing Knowledge and Innovation for Business Sustainability in Africa* (pp. 69–81). Palgrave MacMillan.

KEY TERMS AND DEFINITIONS

Economic Restructurings: This is defined as a structural shift of the Nigerian economy from a mono-economy dependent on oil revenue to a diversified economy with multiple incomes from the manufacturing, agricultural and service sectors.

Entrepreneurship Development Interventions: These are intervention programs designed by government and industrial associates to promote the growth and development of micro, small and medium enterprises in the agricultural, industrial and commercial sectors of the Nigerian economy.

Political Restructuring: This is defined as a transition from a lopsided federal political structure to a true federalism charcterised by political inclusiveness, people-oriented constitutional amendments, resource control, electoral process, political representation, sharing of offices, citizens; right, protection of lives and properties, and building of enduring political infrastructure.

Chapter 24
Inclusive Markets and Enterprise Growth Through Public–Private Partnerships for Local Economic Development

Isaac Okoth Randa
Namibia University of Science and Technology, Namibia

ABSTRACT

Collaborative partnerships have become a source of hope in tackling complicated and complex societal issues such as underdevelopment facing many local authorities. Through public-private partnership (PPPs), remove interventions between the government, private organizations, and civil society, obstacles impeding business growth in these localities can be removed successfully. Whereas donor agencies and governments in developing countries increasingly propagate local economic development (LED), there are limited cases of LED success. Using an exploratory descriptive case study research design, this chapter explores the reasons why inclusive markets and enterprises' development are unsuccessful in Oshakati and Luderitz and why local authorities aimed at identifying suitable recommendations for improvement. The study concludes that entrepreneurs in Oshakati and Luderitz are unable to diversify and grow their business ideas to achieve inclusive markets due to lack of institutional support, access to finance, innovation, necessary expertise, and other necessary business support services.

INTRODUCTION

Contemporary global thinking on development appears to emphasise place and locality driven initiatives. In an environment characterised by reduced central government involvement and control of development processes; Local economic development (LED) represents a move towards a more decentralised, bottom-up approach to economic development. LED originated as an alternative development paradigm dating back to the 1960s (Rodriguez-Pose & Tijmstra, 2007) in the high-income countries of the west. It is an intervention in which local governments, community-based organisations and the private sector form

DOI: 10.4018/978-1-7998-5116-5.ch024

Copyright © 2020, IGI Global. Copying or distributing in print or electronic forms without written permission of IGI Global is prohibited.

partnerships for managing existing resources to create jobs and stimulate the economy of a well-defined region (Fiseha & Oyelana, 2015). Recently LED initiatives have received much attention in developing countries including sub-Sahara Africa underpinned by significant social and economic challenges. These challenges include the failure of traditional top-down development paradigms in addressing local problems, slow economic growth and increasing poverty, changes in national and international economy, failed structural adjustment programmes, and inability of states to effectively intervene at the local level among others (Mensah et.al., 2013). LED implies the replacement of traditional development approaches by new and modern development thinking that tend to adopt more strategic and contingency-based approaches to development (Tulder & Rosa, 2011).

Literature points out linkages between LED and entrepreneurship. For example, Helmsing (2003) argues that in sub-Saharan Africa, three new generations of LED strategies are identifiable: community economy, enterprise and locality development. New enterprises contribute to economic development in a number of ways: as a channel for converting innovative ideas into economic opportunities, revival of social and productive networks' competitiveness, source of new employment, and productivity enhancement (Kantis, Ishida & Komori, 2002). Whereas various definitions exist for entrepreneurship, recently Schumpeterian concept of entrepreneurship appears popular: the entrepreneur as an innovator and source of disequilibrium (Fischer & Nijkamp, 2009). Also, the Organisation of Economic Cooperation and Development ([OECD], 1998) positions entrepreneurship as an essential change agent especially in market driven economies. By fuelling the drive for new economic and technological opportunities for efficient and effective use of resources, entrepreneurship promotes growth through the generation, dissemination and application of innovative ideas which link knowledge capital to economic growth – arguably the missing link in the endogenous growth models (Acs, et al., 2004). This broad conceptualisation of entrepreneurship arguably is central in understanding the contribution of entrepreneurship for circular economy and LED (Fischer & Nijkamp, 2009).

According to Heshmati (2015), the importance of entrepreneurship and sustainability for social-economic development is well recognized. Circular economy (CE) underpinned by theories of cleaner production (CP), industrial ecology, and ecological modernisation is a sustainable development strategy currently embraced to tackle urgent problems of environmental degradation and resource scarcity. CE represents a reaction against the traditional linear production and consumption patterns ('take-make-dispose') which are currently constrained by resources availability and environmental conservation concerns. International organizations including the United Nations (UN), the Organisation for Economic Co-operation and Development (OECD) and the World Economic Forum (WEF) increasingly call for a new development paradigm. Paradigms that prioritises pathways for poverty reduction and improved standards of living, while promoting resource efficiency and easing pressure on natural resources and the environment (Preston, Lehne, & Wellesley, 2019). From the concept of entrepreneurship involving uncertainty-bearing, innovation, opportunity-seeking, management and enterprising (Iversen, et al., 2007); the concept of a circular economy could be the main source of competitiveness for future business organizations and LED activities. Successful implementation of circular economy demands innovation featuring new product and process design which are central to entrepreneurship.

According to UNDP (2007), overcoming barriers that prevent markets from operating more inclusively include strategies not only for promoting entrepreneurship, enterprise development and investment promotion, but also for creating sustainable market infrastructure and services. These strategies support equitable and transparent rules and institutions for effective market operations. As markets are prone to a number of well-documented sources of market failures (Jackson & Jabbie, 2019), inclusive market approach to development recognises that markets on their own cannot allocate resources efficiently and equitably. Markets especially in developing countries may fail the poor, for example markets in poor rural areas may be non-existent or too thin, the costs and risks of participation may be too high or social and economic barriers may effectively exclude the marginalised. Extending this line of argument, most research focussing on the effects of entrepreneurship on economic growth tend to emphasise its linkages with innovation, competition, productivity, job generation, agents of change etc. However, mechanisms like public-private partnerships that create an environment for successful entrepreneurial activity thereby contributing to local economic growth (Bell, 2015; Dwight, 2017) have not received much attention in Namibia.

According to Geiseb (2008), there is a plethora of evidence in support of formal LED approaches to development in Namibia. For example, LED white paper drives Regional and Local Economic Development in Namibia. The paper outlines LED as a strategic process by which actors within urban and rural areas work collectively with the public, business and non-government sectors to create better conditions for economic growth, employment generation and community wealth creation in order to enhance the quality of life for the community (MRLGHRD, 2011). However, in practice there is scant knowledge of what LED involves in terms of processes, structures and resources needs in the Namibian context. This notwithstanding, the most recent estimates from the Labour Force Survey (LFS) in Namibia bears testimony as youth unemployment rate range from 37.8% to 41.7% for the youth population (Namibia Statistics Agency, 2015). Unfortunately, there are no known LED networks in Namibia mainly because there is limited funding from local authorities despite their keenness to initiate LED processes. The priorities currently dominating on the local authorities' agenda include addressing service needs of marginalised urbanites and infrastructure development for achieving reliable and quality municipal services (Geiseb, 2008). In Sub-Saharan Africa, the main challenge of LED has been that most municipalities lack adequate and implementable economic growth strategies for addressing unemployment and poverty (Sekhampu, 2010). These incidences remain damaging to establishment of meaningful LED efforts in Namibia and the rest of Sub-Saharan Africa.

According to World Economic Forum (2016), measures such as strong macroeconomic conditions and well-developed support infrastructure provide conducive business environment for enterprises growth and development. In Namibia business enterprises ranked the following challenges in descending order of importance: access to finance; inadequately educated workforce; inefficient government bureaucracy; poor work ethics; corruption; inflation; lack of innovation; high level taxation; restrictive labour laws; insufficient infrastructure; unstable government policies; instability of the state and poor public health (World Economic Forum, 2016). Additionally, the Namibian Business and Investment Climate Survey ([NamBIC], 2014) indicates the need for a conducive business and investment climate that potentially benefits both domestic and foreign investors. Also, there is need to complement it by using effective enterprise development strategies to help facilitate business networks, entrepreneurial skills and inclusive growth. Besides, Popa (2012) posits that the status of Small and Medium Enterprises (SMEs) in Namibia exposes them to a number of vulnerabilities, which need urgent attention to reduce such risks. These shortcomings with the current practice of LED in Namibia arguably require the creation of Public Private Partnerships (PPPs) to enhance the processes for reforming governance and the business climate at the local level, (Centre for international private enterprise [CIPE], 2015).

This chapter represents an attempt to investigate and shed light on local entrepreneurship development strategies through Public-Private Partnerships (PPPs) as a network interventional mechanism and therefore a tool for engendering LED in Oshakati and Luderitz Municipalities in Namibia. More specifically, the chapter has two objectives:

1. Assess institutional factors hindering the growth and development of PPP initiatives and thereby limiting the achievement of sustainable and inclusive markets for enterprises' development in Oshakati and Lüderitz;
2. Suggest possible strategic policy interventions suitable for promoting the development of PPPs for more sustainable and inclusive markets for enterprises' development in Oshakati and Lüderitz.

LITERATURE REVIEW

Recently scholars recognise development as increasingly complex and non-linear processes, involving multiple actors, potential power struggles and behavioural change (Ruffer et al., 2018a). Market systems approaches to development involves partnering with a range of public and private sector institutions that depends on the market system in the delivery, sustainability and use of business development services as an instrument for engendering LED. Often, the type of partnership depends on the type of system-level changes required and inherent constraints being addressed (Burjorjee & Scola, 2015). Lea and Dercon (2012) in reacting to the question "how can firms be encouraged to invest in expanding their production"; produced a broad range of responses relating to factors that encourage or inhibit business investments and therefore business expansion. For example, with reference to the overall business, environment factors may include general government failure, the costs of doing business, etc., as well as particular features of enterprises and their limitations. Further, it would most likely include references to aspects of the market environment in which these businesses operate such as lack of availability of finance, consumer awareness, a poor regulatory environment, or problems relating to high distribution costs arising from infrastructure deficiencies. Central to the implementation of initiatives for inclusive markets for LED is the need for partnership between the stakeholders. But partnerships require governance mechanisms, which comprise processes by which: collective problems get defined and analysed; goals and solutions formulated and assessed; and action strategies coordinated (Voss and Kemp, 2006). Therefore, entrepreneurship is not only concerned with new value creation, but also a systemic socio-economic change.

Globally, entrepreneurship represents an instrument for bottom-up, low cost-high impact approach to development. Arguably, not only is it capable of addressing individual-level needs that relate to income and employment, but also it requires minimal infrastructure and resources (Desai, 2009). According to the United Nations Conference on Trade and Development ([UNCTAD], 2014) entrepreneurship plays a critical role in sustainable development and poverty eradication. It stimulates economic growth through job creation; establishment of formal businesses; create opportunities for and empower disadvantaged groups such as youth and women. Entrepreneurship strengthens local productive capacity by developing linkages with multinational corporations and thus indirectly maximizes the impact of foreign investment. Besides, according to McKague, Wheeler and Karnani (2015) through the process of social transformation and entrepreneurship; private sector-led, market-based economies are relatively successful in mobilizing human energy and capital for productive purposes. Similarly, according to the United Nations Development Programmes ([UNDP], 2007) private sector development (PSD) strategy, also called Promoting Inclusive Market Development, a generic framework for all of UNDP's PSD interventions; entrepreneurship is one of the five strategic pillars mentioned. These pillars include policy and institutional infrastructure development, facilitation of pro-poor value chains, supporting pro-poor goods and services, development of entrepreneurship initiatives, and corporate social responsibility (CSR) (UNDP, 2007). Broadly defined, inclusive markets result in expanded choices and opportunities for the poor and produce outcomes that benefit the poor in several capacities. For example, the poor can participate in such markets as entrepreneurs, employees and consumers. For entrepreneurs, beneficial outcomes are identifiable in terms of either increased returns on goods sold, improved access to labour markets or increased opportunities for decent work. Similarly, for the poor as consumers, benefits accrue in terms of increased choice and affordability for essential goods and services, including access to financial services that arguably help in reducing risks and vulnerability (UNDP, 2007). Therefore, entrepreneurship development is not only central to major global development initiatives but also as a strategy for LED as well as an instrument for achievement of Sustainable Development Goals (SDG's).

Enterprise and Entrepreneurship Growth Theories

There is evidence that early-stage opportunity based SMEs potentially drive economic growth in terms of increased GDP and employment, particularly in countries with an emerging private sector (Cook & Olafsen, 2016). Enterprise growth is a term used in describing a development process of enterprises from small to large and weak to strong in terms of market share, sales volume, profits or employment etc. In addition, enterprise growth may represent technological innovation which includes mature production technology, optimal efficiency of investments and output, and organizational innovation etc. (Mao, 2009). Brock and Evans in Le (2009) provide a comprehensive review of three models of firm growth that are relevant for understanding growth in small firms. These models include the stochastic model, the human capital model and the learning model. Arguably, these three models seem to capture essential elements embedded in other SMEs growth models.

First, classical and neoclassical economics based on an extensive econometric work featuring both large and small firms and suggest that firm size, most often measured by employment growth, appear to follow a random walk and provides the foundation for stochastic growth model (Geroski, 2002). However, the stochastic model according to scholars like O'Farrell and Hitchens (1988) is that it does not have a dominant theory of firm growth, and therefore does not provide a good framework for examining a firm's growth.

Second, the human capital model assumes individual entrepreneurs have certain business or managerial abilities, which influence their success in business. Subsequently, the size distribution of firms arguably relates to relative endowment of entrepreneurial talents and skills of owners and employees (Le, 2009). The human capital model follows the tradition of firm growth effect model discussed by Penrose (1995) containing two different strands of arguments. One is the 'resource push' argument which sees firms as a bundle of resources bound together by a set of administrative skills or capabilities which are used to deploy these resources as effectively as possible. The other is the managerial limits to growth hypothesis (Geroski, 2002), which postulates that there are limits to the expansion that existing managers can achieve, and limits to the management capacity due to constraints to the expansion of the number of managers.

Finally, the learning model assumes that managerial abilities vary between entrepreneurs. However, the business owner does not explicitly know the level of such abilities ex ante when a new business is established. Additionally, firms have other sources of efficiencies, which are not directly observable. The implication is that a firm can only learn its true efficiency gradually after the firm enters into production (Le, 2009). This model has important implications and indicates that both firm age and size are crucial determinants of firm dynamics. It predicts an inverse relationship between firm failure and growth rates of firms to their age and size (Liedholm & Mead, 1999). Thus, the learning model attempts to synthesize key elements of the human capital and the stochastic models.

The three models of firm growth discussed above appear to capture different elements and determinants of growth for small firms in other models. For example, another framework, Geroski (1999) depicts four categories of firm growth theories: optimum firm size, stage theories of growth, models with Penrose effects, and organizational capabilities to explain the determinants of a firm's growth. Similarly, Barringer et al. (2005) analysed determinants of firm growth and grouped them into four explanatory factors: founder characteristics, firm attributes, business practices and human resource management practices. More recently Gupta, Guha, and Krishnaswami (2013), identify four theoretical perspectives of enterprise growth: the resource-based perspective, the motivation perspective, the strategic adaptation perspective and the resources configuration perspective. The following section considers some major theoretical perspectives relating to the entrepreneurship growth.

Entrepreneurship Growth

Literature sometimes conceptualises the creation of enterprises and entrepreneurship to mean the same thing. However, Cuervo, Ribeiro, and Roig (2007) draws a line between these concepts, entrepreneurship is a phenomenon whereby individual entrepreneurs detect or create business opportunities that they then exploit through the establishment of small and medium-sized firms. According to Carton et al. in Gupta, Guha, and Krishnaswami (2013) and Van Aardt et al. (2008), entrepreneurship is all about the identification of an opportunity, creating, building and expanding an organization or enterprise, and pursuing new ventures to exploit an opportunity in the marketplace for long-term growth. Recently policymakers around the globe have emphasised the importance of Entrepreneurship. Plethora of recent entrepreneurial initiatives focused on start-up competitions, one-stop shops for business registration, and programs for business incubation and operationalisation is evidence (Cook & Olafsen, 2016). However, a majority of newly created enterprises fail. Furthermore, among the few that succeed, only a small subset constitute "high-growth" firms that are able to grow within short time-frames, and have the potential to create increased values in the form of employment and incomes (Cook & Olafsen, 2016). Arguably, these firms appear to play a central role in stimulating innovation and therefore national competitiveness.

Discussions linking innovation and economic growth places entrepreneurship at the centre of the development process. These discussions acknowledge that entrepreneurship and innovation occur within appropriate supportive institutional context (Tan, 2011). Acs et al. (2004) and Braunerhjelm, et al., (2015), recognise entrepreneurship as the missing link in the literature connecting innovation and business growth. Innovation explains the processes of knowledge accumulation, its diffusion and conversion into economically relevant knowledge. Innovation therefore complements the endogenous economic growth models by establishing a process through which investment in Research and Development (R&D) leads to economic growth. Accordingly, it suggests that entrepreneurship facilitates the spill-over of knowledge in the form of new firm establishment and therefore a catalyst for economic growth and development (Randa, 2018). Scholars exploring determinants of entrepreneurship have put several theories forward. These theories seem to have their roots in either economics, psychology, sociology, anthropology, or management (Simpeh, 2011).

Economic Entrepreneurship Theories

Economic entrepreneurship theories deeply rooted in classical and neoclassical theories of economics and the Austrian market process (AMP), tend to explore determinants of entrepreneurship from economic factors that enhance entrepreneurial behaviour (Simpeh, 2011). For example, the AMP, influenced by Schumpeter (1934) concentrated more on human actions in the context of an economy of knowledge. Schumpeter argued that enterprises create something new which result in new processes that are signals for the transformation of market economy. The AMP supersedes earlier conceptualisation of entrepreneurship by the classical and neoclassical frameworks that failed to explain the entrepreneurship process; these earlier schools argued for perfect competition, carried closed-system assumptions, traced observable factual data for analysis, and inferred repeatable observation-based principles as indicators for entrepreneurial activities. Also, whereas the AMP is central in understanding the advent of knowledge economy, Acs and Audretsch (1988), it however rejects Schumpeterian argument that economies of scale are necessary for innovation.

Psychological Entrepreneurship Theories

Psychological theories of entrepreneurship tend to emphasise the role of personal characteristics in defining entrepreneurship. For example, the need for achievement and control are important in explaining the individual entrepreneurial motives. Besides, other more recent personality traits include risk taking, innovativeness, and tolerance for ambiguity have also been associated with entrepreneurial inclination (Nkansah, 2011). Some common personality characteristics or behaviours associated with entrepreneurs are that they tend to be more opportunity driven, demonstrate high level of creativity and innovation, and show high level of management skills and business expertise. According to Mohar, Singh and Kishore (2007), risk taking and innovativeness, need for achievement, and tolerance for ambiguity have positive and significant influence on entrepreneurial disposition. Generally, the need to achieve, excel and control drive entrepreneurs.

Sociological Entrepreneurship Theory

In the case of sociological theories of entrepreneurship, the locus and level of analysis is traditionally the society (Landstrom, 1998). For some people, their sociological background is often the decisive factor that motivate them to become entrepreneurs. Marginalized or minority groups of people often may go against all odds, obstacles and strive for success, urged on by their disadvantaged background to break through and serve as an example for generations to come. Similarly, the social context also called population ecology. The idea is that environmental factors play an important role in the success and survival of businesses. For example, the political system, government legislation, customers' base, employees and competition are some of the environmental factors that may have an impact on survival of new ventures (Nkansah, 2011).

Anthropological Entrepreneurship Theory

Anthropology is the study of the origin, development, customs, and beliefs of a community. It involves the study of the culture of the people in the community. Anthropological theory of entrepreneurship suggests that social and cultural contexts play a major role in successful venture creation, growth and survival. Besides, certain cultural practices lead to certain entrepreneurial attitudes such as innovation that also lead to venture creation and behaviour change. According to Baskerville (2003), often Individual ethnicity affects their entrepreneurial attitude and behaviour premised on certain ethnic aspirations, social, economic, ecological, and political complexities for individual personalities (Mitchell et al., 2002a).

Opportunity–Based Entrepreneurship Theory

The opportunity-based theory of entrepreneurship underpinned with innovation bestows existing resources with new wealth-producing capacity, provides a broad conceptual framework for entrepreneurship research. According to Drucker (1985), entrepreneurs do not cause change but exploit opportunities that change brings for example changes in technology, consumer preferences, environment etc. He further argues that entrepreneurs always search for change, responds and exploits it. What is apparent in Drucker's opportunity conceptualisation of entrepreneurs is that they are people with an eye more for identifying possibilities created by change rather than problems associated with such changes.

Resource-Based Entrepreneurship Theories

Resource-Based of entrepreneurship suggests that access to resources improves the individual's ability to discover and act upon entrepreneurial opportunities. Therefore, access to resources by individuals is an important predictor of opportunity based entrepreneurship and new venture growth (Alvarez & Busenitz, 2001). Financial, social and human capital represents three classes of theories under the resource-based entrepreneurship theories (Nkansah, 2011).

According to financial capital/liquidity theory, people with access to financial capital are more able to acquire other resources to effectively exploit entrepreneurial opportunities, and set up firms to do so (Clausen, 2006). In addition, whereas founders' access to capital is an important predictor of new venture creation and growth, it is not necessarily an important factor for starting a new venture (Hurst & Lusardi, 2004).

Similarly, literature on social capital or social network theory shows that individuals with stronger social ties to resource providers often facilitate the acquisition of such resources and thereby enhance the probability of opportunity exploitation (Aldrich & Zimmers, 1986). Similarly other researchers also suggest that new venture founders require access to entrepreneurs within their social network, as this competency represents a kind of cultural capital that nascent ventures can draw upon in order to detect and exploit opportunities (Gartner et al, 2004; Kim, Aldrich & Keister, 2003).

Human capital theory of entrepreneurship rests on two factors namely, level of education and experience (Becker, 1975). Arguably, the knowledge gained from education and experience represents an entrepreneurship resource central in articulating differences in opportunity discovery and exploitation that differs across individuals (Gartner et al, 2004).

Public Private Partnerships (PPPs) Perspectives

According to Carrol and Steane (2000), PPPs are formalized co-operative ventures that involve at least one private and the public actor as partners and both partners recognise that they have benefits and obligations arising from this agreement. Such benefits and obligations may encompass two-way communication, long term commitment, joint decision making, financial transparency, reciprocal accountability, willingness to negotiate, working relationship and trust (Lister, 2000; Bovaird, 2004). PPPs represent expressions of alternative governance modalities to hierarchies and markets. The design of partnerships depend on their purposes, Brinkerhoff & Brinkerhoff (2011) proposed a purpose-based framework for classifying and defining partnerships. These purposes include among others: policy, service delivery, infrastructure, capacity building, and economic development.

As a response to unilateral approaches to dealing with societal issues, PPPs have received wide support from many sectors of the society including the public sector, private companies, and local communities and are anticipated to remain a relevant policy intervention for years to come in tackling complicated and complex societal issues (Keast, Mandell, Brown, & Woolcock, 2004; Staedtler, 2016). Arguably, the essence of entering into public-private partnerships by government institutions and business owners is the opportunity to merge multi-sector capacities and joint management of economic and social changes (Grossman, 2012). World over, governments tend to collaborate with private business owners to enhance quality of service delivery to the communities (Babatunde, Opawole, & Akinsiku, 2012). There are several possibilities and perspectives in describing the functioning of PPPs ranging from institutional, resources dependency, stakeholder, and interdependency theories each explaining an aspect of PPPs operation.

Institutional Theory

The institutional theory depends on hypothesised institutional infrastructure through which dependence, normative and cognitive mechanisms exert their influence on partnerships. Institutions are social constructions and normative patterns of behaviour and regulations that shape organisational activities and entrepreneurial agency, as opposed to constrained institutional legacies (Greve & Rao, 2012). This theory is rooted on the impact of organisational design on existing systems of human activity, particularly on public and private interactions, which constitute a core area of this study.

Inclusive institutions encourage participation of the majority of people in economic activities through efficient use of skills and talent. Barriers to entry into an industry and organisations' failure to protect their property rights restrict free functioning of markets. However, organisations owned by political figures tend to override institutions and extract resources from the environment by charging uncompetitive monopoly prices which discourages the formation of effective inclusive markets (Acemoglu, Liabson & List, 2015).

Resource Dependency Theory

Resource dependence theory suggests that no matter how self-sufficient in resources organisations are, how well institutional arrangements organisations have made, and how much authoritative power organisations possess; they still will depend on other individuals or organisations for certain essential resources, Pfeffer and Salancik (2003). The competition for scarce resources is likely to be the cause of institutional change (Sherer & Lee, 2002). There are different strategies used in managing resource dependence. Governments often rely on outsourcing public services such as garbage collection, correctional facilities, education, and health care from private organisations as instruments. This often creates quasi-markets for these services. Governments establish quasi markets to attract social service providers but retain regulation of these providers in order to meet social goals. The private providers engage in stiff competition to receive state funding so that they can roll out the social services. The controlling state agency meanwhile regulates entry of suppliers (Coupet, 2017). The persistence of quasi-markets is due to the fact that firms to whom economic activities are contracted often form dependencies on both government revenues and policies that allow them to access markets for public services and government contracts. Governments often constrain profit maximising behaviour by threatening funding reduction and other forms of policy shocks, which may derail survival and profitability of these organisations (Coupet, 2017) from using these dependency relationships. Such scenarios work against the formation of inclusive markets and therefore is relevant for this study.

Interdependence Theory

When two or more organisations equally depend on each other, there is mutuality of dependence. The opposite is true when there is differential power (non-mutual dependence). If an organisation A is more dependent on an organisation B, then organisation B holds more power to control organisation A. The more dependent partner often experiences threats, coercion and possible abandonment while the less dependent runs the show by controlling resources and taking key decisions (Murray, Holmes, & Collins, 2006).

The interdependence of organisations determines resource complementarities, positive externalities and public-private collaborations (Kivleniece & Quelin, 2012). In addition, all social interactions have distinct forms of interdependence, with each having unique effects on behaviour. Unfortunately, the nature of interdependence and the psychological mechanisms that enable people to detect and respond in accordance with this nature of interaction is unknown. In this study, interdependency theory can help highlight power dynamics between all actors in PPP interaction.

Stakeholder Theory

This theory is associated with the promotion of ethical, efficient, practical and effective way of managing highly turbulent and complex business environments (Freeman, Harrison & Wicks, 2007). Stakeholders are organisations, groups or individuals that have interest in the activities of a specific organisation upon whom the organisation depends for its goal attainment (Freeman, et al., 2007). In a business context stakeholders include suppliers, employees, government agencies, investors, and customers.

The stakeholder theory advocates for proper management of stakeholders by attending to their wellbeing and exercise of fairness (Harrison, Bosse & Phillips, 2010). Scholars classify stakeholders into primary and secondary or internal and external categories. The government, customers, investors and shareholders are the primary stakeholders (i.e., essential for the organisation's survival) while trade unions and the media form the secondary category of stakeholders (i.e., not essential for the organisation's survival) (Helmig, Spraul & Ingenhoff, 2016). Progressive enterprise development is dependent on the creation of strategic partnerships. Therefore, contemporary institutions invest in caring for the interests of their stakeholders by developing them in line with the organisation's developmental philosophy (Frynas & Stephens, 2015).

Modes of Network Governance

Networks are mechanisms for governing partnerships, categorised as brokered on one extreme and unbrokered on the other. Within the brokered-unbrokered divide, networks can also be participant or externally governed leading to three popular modes of network governance: Participant-Governed, Lead Organization–Governed, and Network Administrative Organization (NAO) networks (Provan & Kenis, 2008). The successful adoption of a particular form of network governance depends on four key structural and relational contingencies: trust, number of participants, goal consensus, and the nature of the task or network level competency.

Arguably trust a key element of network governance becomes less densely distributed within the network as the number of participants increases, similarly network goal consensus declines, and the need for network-level competencies increases, suggesting the need for brokered forms of network governance, like lead organization and Network Administrator Organisation (NAO), as more likely to become more effective than shared-governance networks. Figure 1 shows the specific relationships within network organisations.

Figure 1. Specific relationships within network organisations
Source: Adapted from Provan & Kenis, (2008)

Governance Forms	Trust	Number of Participants	Goal Consensus	Need for Network-Level Competencies
Shared governance	High Density	Few	High	Low
Lead Organisation	Low density, highly centralized	Moderate number	Moderately low	Moderate
Network Administrative Organisation	Moderate density, NAO monitored by members	Moderate to many	Moderately high	High

Public-Private Partnerships Best Practices for LED

PPPs manifests in market economy in three aspects: provides a framework of participants' equity in accessing public services offered by private organisations; autonomy of partners to enter into a PPP contracts of their choice, and ensures that organisations have freedom to choose an appropriate method to achieve the goals of the partnership (Vecchio, 2015). Taking part in a PPP is always not mandatory, meaning there are chances that both sides can change their objectives and rationale for the collaboration (Goldstein & Mele, 2016). Trust as a factor in PPPs plays a significant role. In partnerships, the partners do not only have to deal with the uncertainty of their respective environment but also with the uncertainty of others' environments (Krishnan, Geyskens, & Steenkamp, 2016). Thus, successful partnership agreements crucially require trust.

Other factors that are necessary for the success of PPPs are the presence of legislation, an institutional framework that governs PPP, transparency, adequate financing, political will and capacity development of public servants for effective project implementation (Sanusi, 2012; Ameyan & Chan, 2015). According to Ismail & Haris (2014), in Malaysia five critical success factors for PPPs include good economic policy, sound governance, presence of financial market, commitment by both private and public sectors, and favourable legal framework. Whereas, a study in Indonesia found five key success factors to include strong political support, irrevocable contracts, well defined coordination mechanisms, a sound legal system and sensible risk sharing arrangements (Wibowo & Alfen, 2014). Regardless of the presence of critical success factors, PPPs still experience challenges during their implementation and operations. Mittal and Kalampukah (2009) identified some of these challenges as communication barriers among partners, resource commitment difficulty, power imbalances, diverse partner organisation goals and partner organisations' conflicts of interest.

STUDY THEORETICAL FRAMEWORK/ CONCEPTUAL FRAMEWORK

The theoretical framework of this study is based on the Organisation for Economic Co-operation and Development ([OECD], 2012) framework for inclusive markets development and other theories pertinent to the objectives of the study. Figure 2 articulates the conceptual framework of the study.

Figure 2. Conceptual framework
Source: Adapted from Organisation for Economic Co-operation and Development (OECD), (2012)

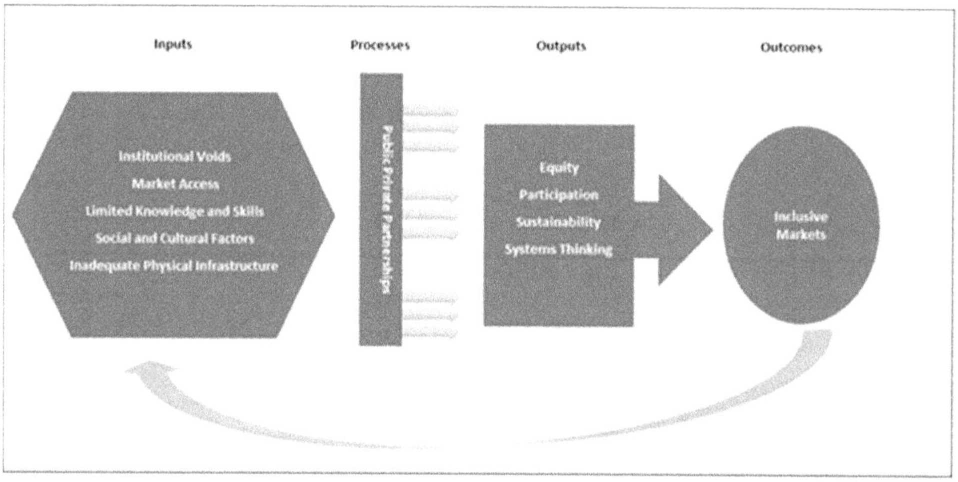

The framework recognises institutional voids' key role in shaping the behaviour of actors, entrepreneurs and organisations in developing market economies. The institutional voids are associated with weak government institutions, poor regulatory environments and lack of distribution networks. Inadequate markets arise from lack of clearly defined communication channels and marketing, geographic dispersion and lack of access to information technology to address problems of inadequate markets. Market advocates for community empowerment and development use social capital as knowledge bridges (Ansari, Munir & Gregg, 2012). In this framework, key barriers to attainment of inclusive and effective markets include resource limitations such as scarcity of human capital due to low skills development and low education levels, affordability and cost constraints for organisations in overcoming lack of social, human and financial capital, prompting the need for better ideas and improvement in production innovation (Bradley, 2012). The diversity of preferences emanates from cultural and social factors, which result in heterogeneous attitudes, consumption patterns and behaviours. Often solutions come in the form of educational initiatives for sustainable market development (Viswanathan, Yassine, & Clarke, 2011).

Additionally, the United Nations Development Programme (UNDP) has identified the following factors that hinder inclusive markets from developing (UNDP, 2008): Limited market information for organisations to assess market viability before entering; ineffective regulatory environment reflecting entrenched bureaucratic institutional structures; inadequate critical physical infrastructure leading to high transaction costs of doing business; limited knowledge and skills crucial for the poor to be included in markets either as employees, consumers and producers; and restricted access to financial products and services

The World Vision Australia Policy Paper (2018), also highlights the following factors as important to inclusive market development: equal opportunity for all segments of society; ensuring participation of all marginalised groups; ensuring sustainability of individual market actors in the market system; systems thinking involving all market actors as part of unified and interacting adaptive market system; and farmer-focused facilitation.

Methodology

Since this study seeks to investigate and interpret reality of the world and participants' understanding of interactions between inclusive markets determinants and LED within a particular context (Honebein, 1996), an interpretivist research philosophical with its subjectivist ontology was appropriate. This approach enabled the researcher to rely on a much narrower field study aimed at acquiring deeper knowledge and understanding of subjects' motives in doing certain things (Ghauri & Grønhaug, 2010). Further being a qualitative study focusing on a few selected cases, the case study research design using deductive-inductive approach is appropriate.

The study was conducted in three locations Oshakati, a northern economic hub of Namibia and Luderitz, a small southern fishing and harbour town in Namibia, as well as in Windhoek, the capital City of Namibia. The study uses purposive non-probability sampling strategies designed to enhance the understanding of selected individual's experiences on the subject. As such knowledgeable respondents, who for the purpose of this study were the actors from public, private sectors and the civil society, were selected to provide insights into the research issues. Semi-structured interviews and focus groups were used with the respondents based on their likely ability to contribute to the practical understanding on the PPPs. The study targeted twenty (20) respondents selected from the actors from the following institutions: a Deputy Director responsible for LED and staff members in the LED Division at Ministry of Urban and Rural Development, an Advocacy Manager at the Chamber of Commerce and Industry (NCCI), as well as branch chairpersons of local branches of the identified towns and CEOs and LED officers of Local Authority Councils of Lüderitz and Oshakati. Civil society and community members were also interviewed. The sample was constituted as follows: Namibia Chamber of Commerce and Industry 3, Oshakati Town Council 4, Lüderitz Town Council 4, Ministry of Urban and Rural Development (MURD) 3, civil society 3, and community leaders 3.

Using interviews and focus group discussions as data collection tools allowed for asking non-structured questions to small samples and exploring individual experiences or opinions regarding the research phenomenon. The interviews and focus group discussions were recorded on permission from respondents and later transcribed. Transcription allowed the researcher to check for accuracies in the wording of the statements from the transcribed notes. Deductive themes from secondary sources were identified appriori including institutional voids, market access, resource limitations and diverse preferences as input variables. The outcome variable was the development of inclusive markets and enterprises development. Besides, interventional variables were equity, participation, sustainability and systems thinking. Also adopting the 8 steps of Creswell (2003) for qualitative data analysis, research themes were also generated from the focus group discussions and interviews. In order to achieve internal validity, the study adopted appropriate mechanisms, such as pilot testing, triangulation, member checking, saturation and reflexivity for dependability and trustworthiness.

This study encountered limitations too linked to the small sample size. Although these limitations were overcome by the study design to ensure validity and reliability of results, additionally thorough and in-depth analysis of cases were conducted. The period for the research was two (2) months and the theoretical coverage included topics on LED, PPPs, Inclusive markets, Circular Economy and Enterprise Development.

FINDINGS AND DISCUSSIONS

This section discusses data collected from respondents guided by two research objectives, the conceptual framework as well as the literature underpinning the study. The first objective is to assess institutional factors hindering the growth and development of PPP initiatives and thereby limiting the achievement of circular and inclusive markets for enterprises' development in Oshakati and Lüderitz. Second objective is to suggest possible strategic interventions for promoting the development of PPPs for more circular and inclusive markets for enterprises' development in Oshakati and Lüderitz.

Firstly, themes were derived from the research objectives and extant literature and subsequently themes were also derived from data for comparison. The themes identified include successes of enterprise development, PPPs success factors, business support interventions, best practices for market accessibility, strategies for accessing local markets, challenges of public private partnerships, challenges for accessing finances, factors hindering inclusive markets' development, strategies for inclusive growth, incentives for enterprise development and acceleration of pro poor growth strategies.

Successes of Enterprise Development in Oshakati and Lüderitz

The researcher enquired whether LED initiatives aimed at achieving enterprise development and market access were successful in Oshakati and Lüderitz. A majority of participants interviewed, 18 out of 20 indicated that achieving enterprise development and market access in these local authorities for the poor is still a long way to go. The respondents indicated that in order to improve the success-rate for enterprise development and market access, there needs to be an environment where the poor can earn a decent livelihood, especially in sectors that provide new opportunities for the poor to participate and benefit from new market opportunities. To improve success, the forms of business activities need to be expanded and diversified. Dwight (2017) argues that inclusive development is likely to lead simultaneously to enterprise development (ED) as individuals or organisations that have an interest in the results of the enterprise activity are often also responsible for funding and promoting the enterprise development activity. Similarly, another intervention that enables market access is PPPs acting both as knowledge and social bridges to otherwise previously isolated communities (Dwight, 2017).

Respondents also mentioned the need for capacity development and training for aspirant poor entrepreneurs on issues like marketing, product packaging, costing and pricing as possible solutions to achieve enterprise development and inclusive markets for the poor. These findings are supported by Ansari, Munir and Gregg (2012) who argue that inadequate markets are the result from lack of clear communication channels and marketing, geographic dispersions and lack of access to information technology to address the problem of inadequate markets. Other solutions are in the form of educational initiatives for sustainable market development (Viswanathan, Yassine, & Clarke, 2011). Respondents also suggested need for encouraging entrepreneurs to embrace innovation and aggressive marketing strategies. These findings aligns to Bradley (2012), who argues that enterprise development improves through product innovation, coupled with better ideas for overcoming lack of financial, social and human capital deficiencies.

Existing Business Support Interventions

The second field question aimed at evaluating the respondents' opinion regarding existing pro-poor business support interventions that are effective for the success of enterprise development. The majority of respondents argued microfinance support was most likely to enhance the success of enterprise development for the poor with 10 participants. However, there is debate in the literature on whether microfinance support is the best solution for enterprise development (Hurst & Lusardi, 2004).

Other participants felt social entrepreneurship (SE) which combines traditional entrepreneurship and social service models aimed at changing the society can provide better support. They argue these new business models create opportunities for higher profits and business growth, which are precursors to the alleviation of poverty and exclusion (Thompson & MacMillan, 2010).

Finally, other respondents felt these inclusive business models have the potential for providing the low segment of the population opportunities that enables them to be part of mainstream economic activities for reducing poverty while sustaining a viable level of profitability. The inclusive business model considers poverty as an opportunity and advocates for incorporating the usually neglected and disadvantaged groups into mainstream business activities (Golja & Pozega, 2012). Additionally, respondents noted that business advisory services like mentorship, participation and training opportunities are other interventions required for effective enterprise development for the poor. This agrees with Goldmark (1996), who suggests that business development services include training, technology transfer, marketing assistance, business advice, mentoring, and information sharing aimed at helping small and micro-entrepreneurs improve their businesses performance.

PPPs Success Factors in Oshakati and Lüderitz

The third field question intended to identify the success factors of PPPs in the context of LED in these localities. All respondents indicated that establishment of appropriate legal and regulatory frameworks is particularly important for PPPs as large-scale investments are often required to set up and manage market infrastructure. Respondents argue investments at the local level by the private sector can only be successful with appropriate support of parallel investments in utilities infrastructure by the local authorities. These include developed connecting roads, affordable electricity, supply of clean water, sewage provision and efficient waste management. Successful PPPs harness the core strengths of all partners to increase overall outcomes and efficiency. Certain key factors are necessary for PPP to be successful for example legislation and enforcement, institutional framework that governs PPP, transparency and accountability, political will and capacity development of public servants for effective project implementation (Sanusi, 2012). Respondents also suggested the playing field needs levelling by dropping legal barriers that prevent potential partners from entry into a PPP arrangement. This ensures fair and equal access to relevant information. Moreover, all potential PPP bidders should have access to the same information about the project and comply with the same minimum requirements to avoid collusion, this agrees with the Malaysian experience (Ismail & Haris, 2014).

Challenges of Public Private Partnerships

Another question attempted to identify challenges and barriers affecting the implementation of effective Public Private Partnerships for inclusive markets in Oshakati and Lüderitz. The interviewees indicated that there are inadequate funding provision from the private sector, stringent conditions from external partnerships and lack of trust between the partners. Other challenges identified by the respondents include lack of commitment by either of the partners, lack of understanding of the PPP concept, inadequate stakeholder consultations, and inadequate socio-economic controls, lack of environmental and financial assessments. These factors resemble those cited by Mittal and Kalampukah (2009) who observed that challenges such as conflict of interest between partner organisations, diversity of underlying goals among partner organisations, power imbalance, communication barriers among partner organisations, and difficulty in resource commitment are some hindrances.

Similarly, a question was asked to determine challenges enterprises face in accessing finances. The respondents indicated that finances affect upcoming businesses as most upcoming entrepreneurs have good business ideas, but cannot kick start due to access to finances. Without finances, entrepreneurs are unable to diversify their business ideas and expand. Respondents pointed out that small enterprise owners in Oshakati and Lüderitz are constrained by a lot of paper work to be submitted to financing institutions albeit their low level of education, besides lack of collateral as most of them are not registered and do not own assets such as land and fixed properties that can serve as securities when accessing loans. Hansohm and Matsaert (2013) and Ogbokor and Ngeendepi (2011), support these assertions by arguing that some of the key reasons why SMEs fail to access loans is due to gaps in the financial system such as collateral requirements, lack of financial management skills, high administrative costs, financial illiteracy and other financial complexities.

Best Practices for Market Accessibility

The researcher asked about the best practices in fostering market accessibility for the excluded poor. Most respondents indicated that participation is key a factor to attaining market accessibility for the excluded poor. Besides, The World Vision Australia Policy Paper (2018) highlights factors that are important for inclusive market development. These include equity, participation, sustainability, and systems thinking amongst others. Moreover, the respondents are of the opinion that informal traders be integrated into the mainstream tourism industry in the case of Luderitz whereby craft sellers take turns and sell their crafts inside ships and hotels. In the case of Oshakati, open markets be made accessible and well positioned to the buying public instead of being hidden as they are now.

The researcher also enquired about strategies needed to assist Namibian enterprises to access the local market. Respondents indicated that strategies such as infant industry protection policies, market segmentation where only local businesses should be allowed to engage in informal and small business spaces should be employed. Other suggestions include improving conditions for competitiveness, reducing the administrative and regulatory burden on enterprises and embracing the culture of supporting local businesses. In addition, the development of linkages between the producers and market owners for improved market access. Ensuring the provision of Micro Small and Medium Enterprises (MSME) policy for shelf space for local products in local markets requires enforcement. Branding and marketing of products especially local products should also be encouraged.

Joint work between small and bigger businesses to create necessary synergies and value addition of the raw materials was also put forward as a possible strategy. In this regard, the focus group suggested that Namibia Trade Forum, a trade agency under The Ministry of Industrialization, Trade and SME Development (MITSMED) to speed up the formalization of the Namibia Retail Charter that will assist local entrepreneurs to access shelf space of big retail outlets. According to National Planning Commission ([NPC], 2017) strategies such as accelerating MSME's development through the provision of government services in order to support and promote new enterprises and existing MSMEs is advocated.

Factors Hindering Inclusive Markets

A question determining the establishment of institutional factors that hinder inclusive markets from developing was asked. The respondents noted that internal capacity, including number of staff members and skills in local authorities were mentioned. Customs and traditions that exclude women from doing business hinder inclusive markets from developing. Johnson (2004) supports these assertions by arguing that gender discrimination prevents inclusive market access such as financial services, constrained by legal institutions of property rights and prevailing social norms. Other hindering factors identified by respondents include, lack of support and coordination, lack of policies promoting inclusivity, strategies and plans aimed at achieving inclusive markets. Barriers to entry into an industry and organisations' failure to protect their property rights can restrict free functioning of markets. The customs, beliefs and norms of the organisation also shape the institutional arrangements and ways of participating and interacting in the market-based activities (Banerjee & Duflo, 2011; Acemoglu, Liabson & List, 2015).

Focus group discussions pointed out that there are sectors in the economy for instance tourism dominated by previously advantaged groups hence it becomes difficult to penetrate if one was previously disadvantaged. Other factors include political connections; respondents argued that only well-connected individuals get Government tenders and fishing quotas at the expense of the less connected majority. This agrees with the United Nations Development Programme ([UNDP], 2008), factors such as lack of comprehensive data about markets, physical infrastructure, inadequate critical infrastructure such as dams, irrigation, water, logistics, sanitation and electricity supply; lack of adequate skills and knowledge; lack of good education or access to information, lack of access to credit facilities, lack of businesses protection through insurance policies, as well as lack of transactional banking services.

Another question was asked to determine measures that can be implemented to give market access so that the excluded poor are able to participate fully in economic life and engage in markets as either workers, consumers, and / or business owners. Respondents noted that introduction of business funding for start-ups in the form of business grants targeting those with the most innovative ideas was necessary. This echoes Sánchez, Ricart, and Rodríguez (2006) argument that low-income segments of the society were traditionally ignored from inclusive markets and certain foreign markets. However, meaningful poverty alleviation is determined among others by involving a productive and diversified private sector. Sánchez *et al.* (2006), further argues that African businesses require the creation of more inclusive business models which incorporate the low-income segment of the population as retailers, suppliers, consumer, employees, distributors, service providers and so on.

Focus group discussions suggested the establishment of one-stop shops for easy registration and incubation centers for business support services to small and emerging enterprises. Also availing of trading space/open markets by local authorities is another intervention. There needs to be an intervention from both the central and local governments to promote economic fairness by combating inequities through regulation, taxation and grants so that the less fortunate can fully participate in the markets. This agrees with Metcalf *et al.*, (2003) argument that the organisation's competitive advantage is determined not only by internal efficiency, but also the efficiency in the prevailing markets for capital, labour and products/services. Also ensuring participation of rural dwellers and allowing them to utilise effectively resources in remote areas require access to a range of enabling services and conditions (Temu, 1999).

Incentives for Entrepreneurship Development

Finally, the researcher wanted to determine the availability of incentives for entrepreneurship development in Oshakati and Lüderitz local authorities as poverty alleviation strategies. The respondents stated the provision of open markets, industrial stalls, and business parks at reduced rentals, marketing incentives to local entrepreneurs to sell their goods, entrepreneurship programmes with access to training and funding of innovative ideas. Other incentives include subsidised land for business purposes, local authorities acting as business facilitators between markets and producers, preferential procurement by local authorities, provision of training by SME compete and Peace Corps volunteers. To alleviate poverty, municipalities need to introduce the provision of credit facilities for income generation projects such as tea stalls, small-scale agriculture, breeding small livestock, tuck-shops, transport vans, handcraft and others. In addition, local authorities tend to rely on either direct or indirect policy interventions to support marginalised entrepreneurs. Indirect support for job creation manifests through zoning changes, local information base, periodic market facilitation, capacity development via vocational training and skills training via workshops (Gibson, 2007). These among others are strategies that respondents felt are required for a meaningful engagement of the micro-entrepreneurs in economic activities.

RECOMMENDATIONS

The study recommends the introduction of business funding for start-ups in the form of grants for businesses with the most innovative ideas and potential to succeed. Similarly, respondents noted that provision of training in the areas of financial, marketing and business management; consumer education through information sharing sessions and established business networks should be utilised. Further, in Namibia like the rest of African, businesses require the creation of more inclusive business models which incorporate the low-income segments of the population either as retailers, suppliers, consumer, employees, distributors, service providers and so on. Inclusive growth requires bridging inequalities of market access, which currently remains a significant challenge in these localities.

In addition, focus group discussions suggested the establishment of a one-stop point for easy business registration and incubation centres for business support services to the poor. There needs to be an intervention from both the central and local governments to promote economic fairness by combating inequities through appropriate regulations, taxation and grants so that the less fortunate can fully participate in the markets system.

The study further recommends the provision of open markets, industrial stalls, and business parks at reduced rentals, marketing incentives to local entrepreneurs to sell their goods, entrepreneurship programmes with access to training and funding opportunities for innovative ideas. Other incentives include subsidised land for business purposes, local authorities acting as facilitators between markets and producers, preferential procurement by local authorities to prefer local companies, provision of training by SME compete, Peace Corps volunteers, and business support services such as training on how to register a business. In addition, to alleviate poverty, municipalities need to introduce the provision of credit facilities for income generation projects such as tea stalls, small-scale agriculture, breeding small livestock, tuck-shops, transport vans, handcraft and others.

There is need for establishing regional coordinating bodies for entrepreneurship development offering both direct and indirect entrepreneurial support. This is to support existing forms of policy intervention including the development of a local information base, marketing support and promotion, zoning changes, entrepreneurship labs, assistance for the development of appropriate vocational training and facilitation of periodic markets. Moreover, local job creation initiatives in poor communities, focusing on improving the skills base of community members are other potential interventions for the creation of inclusive markets (Gibson, 2007).

Further Research and Implications for Practice

This study potentially influences the target communities of practice as they can benefit by looking at how manufacturing and export promotion spearheaded by the central government can benefit MSME's in opening new markets in the circular economy through value chain promotion linking local producers to global markets networks and vice-versa. Product innovation or product upgradation by local producers through packaging and marketing of the products can also enhance the possibility of finding new markets for the economically excluded segments of the society. Further, Public Private Partnerships specifically aimed at development can be beneficially established to champion the course of the marginalised through inclusive markets and therefore enterprise development.

Possible areas for future research could explore how national conditions such as history and politics affect the application of public private partnerships in the context of LED. Another area that deserves investigation is the relationship between the informal economy and SMEs financing strategies available. Finally, another study could look into how local conditions such as customs and traditions exclude women from participating in markets on an equal footing with their male counterparts.

CONCLUSION

This study concludes that entrepreneurs in Oshakati and Lüderitz are unable to diversify their businesses majorly due to lack of ideas, access to finance, and business support and development services. A business without finances cannot implement innovative ideas. Hindrances in accessing credit include high interest for loan repayment to commercial banks, personal insurance requirements, loan processing fees, traveling costs, negotiation and legal fees (Hansohm & Matsaert, 2013). The other major challenge for small enterprises in accessing credit from funding institutions is the lack of collateral. Besides, the absence of transactional banking services also expose them to expensive and insecure financing.

Factors hindering inclusive markets from evolving include lack of innovation and skills coupled with insufficient resources to grow and diversify businesses. Also constraints such as high rates and taxes, inadequate capacity to digitalise their businesses to gain a competitive edge and lack of access to capital markets, inadequate marketing strategies, lack of trust from customers and business development support for emerging businesses, harsh rules and regulations and lack of human and financial resources. Besides, there are customs and traditions that exclude women and youth from doing business, all these hinder inclusive markets from developing.

From a macro-perspective, hindrances include lack of institutional support and coordination mechanisms, inadequate policies, strategies and plans aimed at achieving inclusive markets and therefore LED. Also of significance are the excessive bureaucratic institutional structures that discriminate instead of facilitating business which create red tape and slow decision-making, for example processing of business licences, registrations and others.

Further, lack of critical physical infrastructure adds to high transaction costs of doing business, which includes dams, irrigation, water, logistics, sanitation and electricity supply these limit business expansion and growth. Also inadequate skills and knowledge crucial for the poor to be included in markets as either employees, consumers or producers. Besides, most small business owners lack protection of their businesses as well as income in the event of illness, theft or drought through insurance policies.

REFERENCES

Acemoglu, D., Liabson, D., & List, J. (2015). Why Isn't the Whole World Developed? In Macroeconomics. Pearson.

Acs, Z. J., & Audretsch, D. B. (1988). Innovation in large and small firms: An empirical analysis. *The American Economic Review*, *78*, 678–690.

Acs, Z. J., Audretsch, D. B., Braunerhjelm, P., & Carlsson, B. (2004). *The missing link: The knowledge filter and endogenous growth (discussion paper)*. Stockholm: Center for Business and Policy Studies.

Aldrich, H.E., & Zimmer. (1986). Entrepreneurship through Social Networks. In *The Art and Science of Entrepreneurship*. New York: Ballinger.

Alvarez, S. A., & Busenitz, L. W. (2001). The entrepreneurship of resource-based theory. *Journal of Management*, *27*(6), 755–775. doi:10.1177/014920630102700609

Ameyan, E. E., & Chan, A. P. C. (2015). Implementing PPP Water Supply Projects in Ghana. *African Journal of Applied Research*, *1*(1), 453–469.

Ansari, S., Munir, K., & Gregg, T. (2012). Impact at the Bottom of the Pyramid: The Role of Social Capital in Capability Development and Community Empowerment. *Journal of Management Studies*, *49*(4), 813–842. doi:10.1111/j.1467-6486.2012.01042.x

Babatunde, S. O., Opawole, A., & Akinsiku, O. E. (2012). Critical success factors in public-private partnership (PPP) on infrastructure delivery in Nigeria. *Journal of Facilities Management*, *10*(3), 212–225. doi:10.1108/14725961211246018

Banerjee, A. V., & Duflo, E. (2011). *Poor economics: A radical rethinking of the way to fight global poverty*. New York: Public Affairs.

Barringer, B. R., Jones, F. F., & Neubaum, D. O. (2005). A quantitative content analysis of the characteristics of rapid-growth firms and their founders. *Journal of Business Venturing*, *20*(5), 663–687. doi:10.1016/j.jbusvent.2004.03.004

Baskerville, R. F. (2003). Hofstede Never Studied Culture. *Accounting, Organizations and Society*, *28*(1), 1–14. doi:10.1016/S0361-3682(01)00048-4

Becker. (1975). *Human Capital*. Chicago, IL: Chicago University Press.

Bennett, C. J. (1991). What is policy convergence and what causes it? *British Journal of Political Science*, *21*(2), 215–233. doi:10.1017/S0007123400006116

Bovaird, T. (2004). Public-private partnerships: From contested concepts to prevalent practice. *International Review of Administrative Sciences*, *70*(2), 199–215. doi:10.1177/0020852304044250

Bradley, S. W., McMullen, J. S., Artz, K., & Simiyu, E. M. (2012). Capital is not enough: Innovation in developing economies. *Journal of Management Studies*, *49*(4), 684–717. doi:10.1111/j.1467-6486.2012.01043.x

Braunerhjelm, P., Acs, Z., Audretsch, D. B., & Carlsson, B. (2015). *The missing link: knowledge diffusion and entrepreneurship in endogenous growth*. Edward Elgar Publishing.

Brinkerhoff, D. W., & Brinkerhoff, J. M. (2011). Public–private partnerships: Perspectives on purposes, publicness, and good governance. *Public Administration and Development*, *31*(1), 2–14. doi:10.1002/pad.584

Burjorjee, D. M., & Scola, B. (2015). *A Market Systems Approach to Financial Inclusion*. Washington, DC: Consultative Group to Assist the Poor.

Carroll, P., & Steane, P. (2000). *Public-Private Partnerships. Theory and Practice in International Perspective*. London: Routledge.

CIPE. (2015). *Public-Private Dialogue: The Key to Good Governance and Development*. Washington, DC: Centre for International Private Enterprise.

Clausen, T. H. (2006). *Who identifies and Exploits entrepreneurial opportunities*. Retrieved from www.ccsr.ac.uk

Cook, P., & Olafsen, E. (2016). *Growth Entrepreneurship in Developing Countries: A Preliminary Literature Review*. Washington, DC: World Bank.

Coupet, J. (2017). Strings attached? Linking Historically Black Colleges and Universities public revenue sources with efficiency. *Journal of Higher Education Policy and Management*, *39*(1), 40–57. doi:10.1080/1360080X.2016.1254427

Creswell, J. (2003). *Research Design: Qualitative, Quantitative and Mixed Methods Approaches* (2nd ed.). Thousand Oaks, CA: SAGE Publications.

Cuervo, Á., Ribeiro, D., & Roig, S. (2007). Entrepreneurship: concepts, theory and perspective. Introduction. In *Entrepreneurship* (pp. 1–20). Berlin: Springer. doi:10.1007/978-3-540-48543-8_1

de Bell, L. (2015). Promoting Entrepreneurship and Innovation in Africa. In J. Kettunen, U. Hyrkkänen, & A. Lehto (Eds.), *Applied Research and Professional Education* (pp. 78–89). Turku: University of Applied Sciences.

Desai, S. (2009). *Measuring Entrepreneurship in Developing Countries.* UNU-WIDER Research Paper, No. 2009/10, United Nations University, World Institute for Development Economics Research.

Drucker, P. F. (1985). *Innovation and Entrepreneurship*. New York: Harper & Row Publishers.

Dwight, C. (2017). *Definition of Enterprise Development*. Retrieved from https://bizfluent.com/facts-7152868-definition-enterprise-development.html

Fischer, M. M., & Nijkamp, P. (2009). *Entrepreneurship and regional development* (No. 0035). Academic Press.

Fiseha, G. G., & Oyelana, A. A. (2015). An assessment of the roles of small and medium enterprises (SMEs) in the local economic development (LED). *The South African Journal of Economics*, *6*(3), 280–290.

Freeman, R. E., Harrison, J. S., & Wicks, A. C. (2007). *Managing for stakeholders: Survival, Reputation and Success*. New Haven: Yale University Press.

Frynas, J. G., & Stephens, S. (2015). Political Corporate Social Responsibility: Reviewing theories and setting new agendas. *International Journal of Management Reviews*, *17*(4), 483–509. doi:10.1111/ijmr.12049

Gartner, W. B., Shaver, K. G., Carter, N. M., & Reynolds, P. D. (2004). *Handbook of entrepreneurial dynamics*. Thousand Oaks, CA: Sage Publications.

Geiseb, S. (2008). *LEDNA LED Stocktaking Survey Report on the State of LED for Namibia*. Windhoek: GTZ/PEG.

Geroski, P. (1999). *The growth of firms in theory and practice*. Center for Economic Research Policy, Working Paper No. 2092.

Ghauri, P. N., & Grønhaug, K. (2010). *Research Methods in Business Studies. Financial Times.* New York: Prentice Hall.

Gibson, S. W. (2007). *Micro-franchising Creating Wealth at the Bottom of the Pyramid*. Cheltenham: Edward Elgar.

Goldmark, L. (1996). *Business Development Services: A Framework for Analysis*. Unpublished Manuscript, No. MIC -101, Inter-American Development Bank.

Goldstein, B. T., & Mele, C. (2016). Governance within public-private partnerships and the politics of urban development. *Space and Polity*, *20*(2), 194–211. doi:10.1080/13562576.2016.1157968

Golja, T., & Pozega, S. (2012). Inclusive Business – What Is It All About? Managing Inclusive Companies. *International Review of Management and Marketing*, *1*(2), 22–42.

Greve, H. R., & Rao, H. (2012). Echoes of the Past: Organisational Founding as Sources of an Institutional Legacy of Mutualism. *American Journal of Sociology, 118*(3), 635–675. doi:10.1086/667721

Grossman, S. A. (2012). Public-Private Partnerships: Introduction: The Emerging Role of Partnership Governance. *Public Performance & Management Review, 35*(4), 575–577. doi:10.2753/PMR1530-9576350400

Gupta, P. D., Guha, S., & Krishnaswami, S. S. (2013). Firm growth and its determinants. *Journal of Innovation and Entrepreneurship, 2*(1), 15. doi:10.1186/2192-5372-2-15

Hansohm, D., & Matsaert, F. (2013). *Credit Delivery Systems for SMEs in Namibia.* Windhoek: Frederich Ebert Stiftung.

Harrison, J. S., Bosse, D. A., & Phillips, R. A. (2010). Managing for stakeholders, stakeholder utility functions, and competitive advantage. *Strategic Management Journal, 31*(1), 58–74. doi:10.1002mj.801

Helmig, B., Spraul, K., & Ingenhoff, D. (2016). Under Positive Pressure How Stakeholder Pressure Affects Corporate Social Responsibility Implementation. *Business & Society, 55*(2), 151–187. doi:10.1177/0007650313477841

Helmsing, A. H. J. (2003). Local economic development: New generations of actors, policies and instruments for Africa. *Public Administration and Development: The International Journal of Management Research and Practice, 23*(1), 67–76. doi:10.1002/pad.260

Heshmati, A. (2015). *A Review of the Circular Economy and its Implementation.* IZA Discussion Papers, No. 9611. Institute for the Study of Labour (IZA), Bonn. https://www. econstor. eu/bitstream/10419/130297/1/dp9611

Honebein, P. C. (1996). *Constructivist learning environments: case studies in instructional design.* Educational Technology Publications.

Hurst, E., & Lusardi, A. (2004). Liquidity constraints, household wealth, and entrepreneurship. *Journal of Political Economy, 112*(2), 319–347. doi:10.1086/381478

Ismail, S., & Haris, F. A. (2014). Constraints in implementing public private partnership (PPP) in Malaysia. *Built Environment Project and Asset Management, 4*(3), 238–250. doi:10.1108/BEPAM-10-2013-0049

Iversen, J., Jørgensen, R., & Malchow-Møller, N. (2007). Defining and measuring entrepreneurship. *Foundations and Trends® in Entrepreneurship, 4*(1), 1-63.

Jackson, E. A., & Jabbie, M. (2019). Understanding market failure in the developing country context. In *Decent Work and Economic Growth: Encyclopedia of Sustainable Development Goals* (pp. 1–10). Cham: Springer Nature Switzerland. doi:10.1007/978-3-319-71058-7_44-1

Johnson, S. (2004). Gender norms in financial markets: Evidence from Kenya. *World Development, 32*(8), 1355–1374. doi:10.1016/j.worlddev.2004.03.003

Kantis, H., Ishida, M., & Komori, M. (2002). Entrepreneurship in emerging economies: The creation and development of new firms in Latin America and East Asia (No. 34958). Washington, DC: Inter-American Development Bank.

Keast, R., Mandell, M. P., Brown, K., & Woolcock, G. (2004). Network structures: Working differently and changing expectations. *Public Administration Review*, *64*(3), 363–371. doi:10.1111/j.1540-6210.2004.00380.x

Kim, P., Aldrich, H. E., & Keister, L. A. (2003). *The Impact of financial, human and cultural capital on becoming a Nascent Entrepreneur*. Working paper.

Kivleniece, I., & Quelin, B. V. (2012). Public-Private Ties? A Private Actor's Perspective. *Academy of Management Review*, *37*(2), 272–299. doi:10.5465/amr.2011.0004

Krishnan, R., Geyskens, I., & Steenkamp, J. E. M. (2016). The effectiveness of contractual and trust-based Governance. *Strategic Management Journal*, *37*(12), 2521–2542. doi:10.1002mj.2469

Landstrom, H. (1998). *The Roots of Entrepreneurship Research*. Conference proceedings, Lyon, France.

Le, V. (2009, September). Small Firm Growth Theory and Models: A Review. In *22nd SEAANZ Annual Conference*. Massey University.

Lea, N., & Dercon, S. (2012). *Refreshing DFID's Approach to Growth*. Working Paper, London: DFID.

Liedholm, C., & Mead, D. C. (1999). *Small Enterprises and Economic Development: The Dynamics of Micro and Small Enterprises*. London: Routledge.

Lister, S. (2000). Power in partnership: An analysis of NGOs relationship with its partners. *Journal of International Development*, *12*(2), 227–239. doi:10.1002/(SICI)1099-1328(200003)12:2<227::AID-JID637>3.0.CO;2-U

Mao, H. (2009). Review on enterprise growth theories. *International Journal of Business and Management*, *4*(8), 20–23. doi:10.5539/ijbm.v4n8p20

McKague, K., Wheeler, D., & Karnani, A. (2015). An integrated approach to poverty alleviation: roles of the private sector, government and civil society. In *The business of social and environmental innovation* (pp. 129–145). Cham: Springer. doi:10.1007/978-3-319-04051-6_7

Mensah, J. K., Domfeh, K. A., Ahenkan, A., & Bawole, J. N. (2013). Policy and institutional perspectives on local economic development in Africa: The Ghanaian perspective. *Journal of African Studies and Development*, *5*(7), 163–170.

Metcalfe, J. S., Ramlogan, R., & Uyarra, E. (2003). Economic Development and the Competitive Process. *Conferência Internacional Sobre Sistemas De Inovação E Estratégias De Desenvolvimento Para O Terceiro Milênio*, 1-31.

Mitchell, R. K., Smith, J. B., Morse, E. A., Seawright, K. W., Peredo, A. M., & McKenzie, B. (2002). Are entrepreneurial cognitions universal? Assessing entrepreneurial cognitions across cultures. *Entrepreneurship Theory and Practice*, *26*(4), 9–32. doi:10.1177/104225870202600402

Mittal, A., & Kalampukah, P. K. (2009). *Partnership Challenges in Achieving Common Goals - A Study of Public Private Partnership in E-Governance Projects* (Unpublished M.Sc. Thesis). Umea School of Business.

Mohar, Y. M. S., Singh, J., & Kishore, K. (2007). Relationship Between psychological characteristics and entrepreneurial inclination: A Case Study of Students at Tun Abdul Razak University. *Journal of Asia Entrepreneurship and Sustainability*, 3(2), 1-10.

MRLGHRD. (2011). *Regional and Local Economic Development: White paper*. Windhoek: Ministry of Regional and Local Government, Housing and Rural Development.

Murray, S. L., Holmes, J. G., & Collins, N. L. (2006). Optimizing assurance: The risk regulation system in relationships. *Psychological Bulletin, 132*(5), 641–666. doi:10.1037/0033-2909.132.5.641 PMID:16910746

Namibia Business and Investment Climate Survey (NamBIC). (2014). *NCCI, IPPR, Namibia Manufacturers Association*. Windhoek: NMA.

Namibia Statistics Agency. (2015). *Analysis of Youth Employment and Unemployment in Namibia 2012-2013*. Windhoek, Namibia: Namibia Statistics Agency.

OECD. (2012). *Social Protection, Poverty Reduction and Pro-poor Growth: A Policy Guidance Note*. Paris: OECD.

Ogbokor, A. C., & Ngeendepi, E. J. (2010). *Investigation the challenges faced by SMEs in Namibia*. Retrieved from http://ir.polytechnic.edu.na

Organisation for Economic Cooperation and Development. (1998). *Fostering entrepreneurship*. Paris: OECD.

Pfeffer, J., & Salancik, G. R. (2003). *The external control of organisations: A resource dependence perspective*. Stanford: Stanford University Press.

Popa, D. (2012). Competitiveness of Romanian Small and Medium-Sized Enterprises in European Union. *Journal of Knowledge Management. Economics and Information Technology*, 2(2), 1–11.

Preston, F., Lehne, J., & Wellesley, L. (2019). *An Inclusive Circular Economy: Priorities for Developing Countries*. London: The Royal Institute of International Affairs.

Provan, K. G., & Kenis, P. (2008). Modes of network governance: Structure, management, and effectiveness. *Journal of Public Administration: Research and Theory, 18*(2), 229–252. doi:10.1093/jopart/mum015

Randa, I. O. (2018). Leveraging Knowledge Management for Value Creation in Service-Oriented Organisations of Namibia. In *Global Practices in Knowledge Management for Societal and Organizational Development* (pp. 145–167). IGI Global. doi:10.4018/978-1-5225-3009-1.ch007

Rodríguez-Pose, A., & Tijmstra, S. A. (2007). Local economic development in sub-Saharan Africa. *Environment and Planning. C, Government & Policy, 25*(4), 516–536. doi:10.1068/c5p

Ruffer, T., Bailey, H., Dahlgren, S., Spaven, P., & Winters, M. (2018a). *Evaluation of the market systems development approach: Lessons for expanded use and adaptive management at Sida*. Stockholm: Sida.

Sanusi, L. S. (2012). The role of development finance institution in Infrastructure development: What Nigeria can learn from BNDES and the Indian Infrastructure finance company. *3rd ICRC PPP Stakeholders Forum.*

Schumpeter, J. A. (1934). *The Theory of Economic Development*. Cambridge, MA: Harvard University Press.

Sekhampu, T. J. (2010). *An investigation into the economic sustainability of Kwakwatsi* (Unpublished PhD thesis). NWU.

Sherer, P. D., & Lee, K. (2002). Institutional Change in Large Law Firms: A Resource Dependency and Institutional Perspective. *Academy of Management Journal*, *45*(1), 102–119.

Simpeh, K. N. (2011). Entrepreneurship theories and Empirical research: A Summary Review of the Literature. *European Journal of Business and Management*, *3*(6), 1–8.

Staedtler, L. (2016). Scrutinizing public-private partnerships for development: Towards a broad evaluation conception. *Journal of Business Ethics*, *135*(1), 71–86. doi:10.100710551-015-2730-1

Tan, J. (2011). Conceptualising entrepreneurship, innovation and late industrialisation: The state creation of entrepreneurs in Malaysia. *International Journal of Management Concepts and Philosophy*, *5*(2), 138–158. doi:10.1504/IJMCP.2011.041519

Temu, A. E. (1999). The Kilimanjaro Cooperative Bank: A potentially sustainable rural financial institutional model for sub-Saharan Africa, *African Review of Money, Finance and Banking*. *Supplement for the Savings and Development Journal*, *1*(2), 45–77.

Thompson, J. D., & MacMillan, I. C. (2010). Business Models: Creating New Markets and Societal Wealth. *Long Range Planning*, *43*(2-3), 291–307. doi:10.1016/j.lrp.2009.11.002

Tulder, R., & Rosa, A. (2011). *Inclusive business through partnerships, Special Contribution to Fourth High Level Forum on Aid Effectiveness*. The Partnerships Resource Centre.

UNDP. (2007). *UNDP Private Sector Strategy, Promoting Inclusive Market Development*. Washington, DC: United Nations.

United Nations Conference on Trade and Development. (2014). *Entrepreneurship for development, Report of the Secretary*. Washington, DC: United Nation General Assembly.

United Nations Development Programme (UNDP). (2008). *Creating Value for All: Strategies for doing Business with the Poor*. New York: UNDP.

Van Aardt, I., Van Aardt, C., Bezuidenhout, S & Mumba, M. (2008). *Entrepreneurship and New Venture Management* (3rd ed.). Oxford University Press.

Vecchio, V., Caselli, S., & Corbetta, G. (2015). *Public-Private Partnerships for Infrastructure and Business Development: Principles, Practices, and Perspectives*. Palgrave Macmillan.

Viswanathan, M., Yassine, A., & Clarke, J. (2011). Sustainable Product and Market Development for Subsistence Marketplaces: Creating Educational Initiatives in Radically Different Contexts. *Journal of Product Innovation Management*, *28*(4), 558–569. doi:10.1111/j.1540-5885.2011.00825.x

Voss, J. P., & Kemp, R. (2006). Sustainability and reflexive governance: An introduction. In J. P. Voss, D. Bauknecht & R. Kemp (Eds.), Reflexive governance for sustainable development (pp. 3-28). Cheltenham: Edward Elgar.

Wibowo, A., & Alfen, H. W. (2014). Identifying macro-environmental critical success factors and key areas for improvement to promote public-private partnerships in infrastructure. *Engineering, Construction, and Architectural Management*, *21*(4), 383–402. doi:10.1108/ECAM-08-2013-0078

World Economic Forum. (2016). *The Global Competitiveness Report 2016–2017: Full Data Edition*. World Economic Forum.

World Vision Australia Policy Paper. (2018). *Inclusive Market Systems Development—Sustainable growth for everyone*. Sydney: World Vision Australia.

Chapter 25
Knowledge Management for Entrepreneurship Development in the Circular Economy

Mukund Deshpande
Independent Researcher, India

ABSTRACT

Entrepreneurship development is continuously tied to boosting the economy of the individuals, society, and the nation. Amongst a variety of approaches devised for economic development by scientists, researchers, and economists, a novel tool of the circular economy has emerged to help industries generate dual benefits. The ability to revamp the economy and reduce awful environmental impact are its objectives. Further revelation is about the knowledge of traditional, recycling, and circular economies and useful strategies for developing entrepreneurship in a circular economy. The findings further revealed essential links to build processes and measures to manage the knowledge for circular economy development. The chapter has revealed a three-pronged approach as important to the development of entrepreneurship in a circular economy. In that context, economics, regulations, and technology are the three important dimensions found essential to developing entrepreneurship.

INTRODUCTION

Public viewpoints undoubtedly indicate Entrepreneurship as the "capacity and willingness to develop, organize and manage" a business venture along with any of its risks to make a profit that leads to empowerment. That is a process of strengthening individuals, organizations and communities so they get more control over their own situations and environments. In the context of circular economy, it is considered as (WEF, 2019) an industrial system that is restorative or regenerative by intention and design. It replaces the end-of-life concept with restoration, shifts towards the use of renewable energy, eliminates the use of toxic chemicals, which impair reuse and return to the biosphere, and aims for the elimination of waste through the superior design of materials, products, systems and business models. Quality entrepreneurship is also believed to be a crucial factor in combating poverty and inequality in

DOI: 10.4018/978-1-7998-5116-5.ch025

Copyright © 2020, IGI Global. Copying or distributing in print or electronic forms without written permission of IGI Global is prohibited.

society. Often said is the other fact that, peaceful environment promotes national development (Clark, 2013) and highly educated people more often have a peaceful attitude in life than their lower counterparts (Komatsu, 2017). Maintaining harmony (Narendran, 2012) and perpetually pursuing to enhance Circular Economy (Berger & Fisher, 2013) is the attitude exhibited by highly educated class of people. Entrepreneurship for Circular Economy Development fosters focused knowledge of subject matter and Individuals look for its utility at work-place.

Significance of Knowledge Development

Quality Entrepreneurship calls for knowledge of the subject and that of managing the operations. In view of this backdrop aspirants need gaining and adding knowledge continuously. Therefore, developing knowledge has significance, priority and value. Known is that fact that age limit does not exist for making entry into the domain of entrepreneurship. In family owned businesses, the new comer is often exposed to the business situation through family members. Therefore, knowledge gain is rapid and sure. Many more adults and youngsters choose to enter business of some kind with a view to brighten career, gain social respect and enhance earning capability. Majority of first time entrepreneurs, despite having good educational background, remain incompetent to manage the business due to lack of particular skills, exposure and handling experience. This is often the experience with technical people who have the mastery over technology but the marketing, administrative and financial management. Furthermore, good general knowledge leads to success in business has proven (Brian, 2015) as an invalid proverb. Researchers have further exposed that operating the business rightly and effectively required knowledge (Aytekin, 2019) in the specific domain, practical experience and luck. As Entrepreneurs in the recycling economy are in infant stage, having good knowledge in them on recycling economy is therefore a remote probability. Moreover, new knowledge keeps continuously developed and added but that takes time to reach the entrepreneurs rapidly. Updating of the knowledge is essential to know emerging trends, make changes within and to survive in competition and make growth. Responsibility therefore lies with the entrepreneurs to devise a system of knowledge management. Business Link UK (2009) reports that all businesses have access to an extensive pool of knowledge-whether this is their understanding of customers' needs and the business environment or the skills and experience of staff. The way a business gathers and shares information and exploits this knowledge is the chief motive to develop the enterprise successfully. This doesn't just apply to huge multinational companies. Knowledge management can benefit everyone from a local newsstand to a manufacturing firm. Stockholders' report (2018) states that the transition from linear to circular" is an EU Horizon 2020 project that aims to enable companies and their value chains to transition towards more viable, sustainable and compete economic models. Researchers have usefully exposed Entrepreneurship for Circular Economy Development stating it as neither a purely public nor a purely private good but as a benefit that combines features of both. A new bimodal view of Entrepreneurship for Circular Economy Development is becoming increasingly important at the start of the 21st Century.

Cesar (2016) has cited that, most literature on knowledge management (KM) focuses on large firms, the domain in which KM was originally developed, and most KM literature on entrepreneurship focuses on entrepreneurial activities in post-revenue firms. The domain of the start-up, however, is traditionally very different from these, characterized by a lack of tangible assets and validated value proposition. The authors review the literature on KM and entrepreneurship with a particular focus on young micro-enterprises that have yet to cross the "valley of death" stage of maturation. Using the Dynamic

Knowledge Creation Process as a guide, they elaborate on the challenges facing the implementation of KM in start-ups, and on the subsequent opportunities for start-up growth. Finally, the authors reflect upon research questions that may engage future researchers in proposing strategies that better integrate KM as a discipline into the fabric of entrepreneurship and the start-up domain. This chapter initiates with the management of knowledge and how one can best harness and exploit information and create a knowledge strategy for the circular economy.

Underestimating the Importance of Strategic Planning

Business can face competition from many areas. Business Owners need to have a clear understanding of the Industry, its direction, various market segments and the niche that can represent profitable opportunity. The business must understand all aspects of competition and its offering must score over other alternatives for the Target Segment. Many business owners fail to do this hard work.

Baporikar & Deshpande (2009) have revealed variety of entrepreneurial weaknesses as follows.

Lack of Financial Analysis and System of Review

Business Owners tend to do many things. Financial Analysis and a regular system of review happens to be one of the most neglected areas. Importance of Systems and Processes keeps increasing with business growth.

Lack of Expertise in Critical Areas (And Not Seeking Outside Help)

No individual, however capable, can have expertise in all areas. To compete effectively, business, on the other hand, needs expertise in Marketing, Selling, Finance, Purchasing, Production, Hiring, Motivating and Managing. Business Owners, unfortunately, fail to recognize the need for outside help.

BACKGROUND

Entrepreneurship has a natural tendency to spread amongst aspirants owing to its inherent characteristics like freedom of work, enhancement of career and monetary benefits. Continuous research in this area is adding valuable facets resulting into long lasting entrepreneurship. New approaches, alternatives and options to entrepreneurship have been devised (Awasthi, 1991) and are continually emerging. People are known to be the real strength of the nation whilst entrepreneurs the actual wealth. Maintaining sound economy and making it enhance is the proficiency of the government. The administration has strongly been spreading out privatization in the country for national economy to spin through private entrepreneurship. Consequently, entrepreneurs are the big drivers of economic growth, innovation, regional development and job creation. A strong and vibrant entrepreneurship provides a sturdy foundation to increase economy, standards of living and reduce poverty. Making right choice for business is elegance, whilst leading the enterprise to sustenance, growth and global recognition is talent. Most of the Governments implement favourable policy to cheering prospective entrepreneurs to speed up the economy. Large numbers of SMEs, for example, therefore established to perform not only supporting role to the majors but also became a smart model of extra ordinary growth of entrepreneurship, local population, the nation through its expansion worldwide.

Entrepreneurs are always inquisitive about new business opportunities to create first time appearance (Baporikar & Deshpande, 2009) in a particular sector or field. Establishing the foundation and making the business sustainable are their priorities. Truth as well prevails that entrepreneurs keep away from making entry into a business of competition. Conversely, they find it a threat in making ingress into an unidentified business line. Launching businesses, therefore with knowledge and calculated risk is their inclination (Brown, 2013). Three major areas viz. Circular Economy, Knowledge Management and Entrepreneurship Development are therefore considered for understanding the background. Circular Economy is the upcoming tool (WEF, 2018) which manufacturing industries aspire to adopt in revamping their economy (UNIDO, 2019) and reducing dreadful environmental impact since that is the need of the time. Tim J. (1993) initiated interesting discussion on economy building approach through "Clean Production Strategies' to developing preventive environmental management in the Industrial Economy. Economy building through traditional approach (Kimberly, 2019), cites making and selling a value added commodity to make profit, is already known from olden times. As such, entrepreneurs always look for better approaches in doing business. They always lay emphasis on new avenues (SEF, 2012) that emerge through research. Another view of selecting the approach to economy building is by reducing the cost (Scuderi, 2012) and environmental pollution. Further approach to building economy is to search for projects with low investment and high returns. Emerging industrial revolution offers enormous opportunities for economic growth (UNCTAD, 2018) and sustainable development with potential benefits on a scale that is difficult to imagine. In view of this background, entrepreneurs need to make a balancing study of all business parameters, since they form basis to the launching new business or adding new lines in existing set-up. In all these circumstances, knowledge in depth forms the only criteria to undertake a start-up. In knowledge management (Harvey & Knight, 1996) also there are multiple routes available and entrepreneurs always think of setting an effective system of managing the knowledge.

Knowledge Management

Girard & Ors, (2015) have highlighted a multidisciplinary approach to achieving organisational objectives by making the best use of knowledge. An organisation is an integration of various units and to achieve their objectives, knowledge should be managed effectively (KM) by creating, sharing, and using. Each unit in the structure of organisation is made to receive relevant information which is then classified, organized, and converted into knowledge that is shared to make it effective for use within the firm. An integrated approach in knowledge management is thus essential.

Shih, (2018) has stated that Knowledge Management (KM) relates to even the most basic work processes of firms. Few terms e.g. work characteristics; work design, work outcomes and work behavior are often used in the context of knowledge management. Work design plays a major activity in managing knowledge. Literature has further revealed that even with regard to the existence and importance of the interaction between work characteristics and work outcomes, only the knowledge characteristics of work design had a significant effect on both dimensions of work behavior. It is also found that while many of the attributes were significantly correlated with employees' innovative idea generation, functional and motivational attributes appeared to be the most important. Many authors have proposed KM capabilities as important activities that help firms continuously improve their environments because of the great emphasis on green product development in competitive and sustainable markets. Some referred to KM as the creation, storage and utilization of routines. Therefore, these KM approaches raise concerns about the creation, storage, dissemination, and application of firm knowledge within supply chain networks.

Entrepreneurship Development

Diverse instruments (Baporikar & Deshpande, 2011) have been in vogue and recognized to be conventional approaches to entrepreneurship. Fairly impressive instruments are available for the growth of entrepreneurship but many of them are unilateral as they can tackle just one or the other situation. Although their utility toward entrepreneurship development cannot be ignored, they lack in their competitiveness and effectiveness. As such entrepreneurship development has its own significance. At the firm level, competitiveness is the ability to sell products or services at a profit over a sustained period of time in comparison to competitors. A firm should have a competitive edge in marketing successfully with other firms. As a result, entrepreneurship should be based on an instrument that is able to sell a broad-range of goods and services in international markets and attract efficiency-seeking investment from abroad.

Yetisen & Ors (2015), have stated that Entrepreneurship is the process of designing, launching and running a new business. The people who initiate with small beginning and create these businesses are called entrepreneurs. Analysis of this definition reveals that designing is the basis and that makes use of various tools like approach, alternatives and options based on the philosophy of the Entrepreneur. Philosophy is a thought process and obtaining knowledge for business development is therefore a prime move while managing it is the subsequent.

Organization excellence has at all times aroused curiosity and has been a most wanted area of dialogue for entrepreneurs (Baporikar & Deshpande, 2011). The diligent fostering of a candid habit of mind even in trifles is a matter of high moment both to character and opinions. This realism speaks of human behaviour that is only accountable for the betterment of the entrepreneurship. Whilst technology endeavours to bring in precious techniques based on functional logic for proactively conducting business, excellence is only attainable in the course of good behavioural practices. Striving hard to develop sustainable grounds has been the skill of entrepreneurship. Therefore, every entrepreneur sees that he makes appropriate choices among the solutions available to him and those are favourable to him and do not generate adverse reactions.

The behaviour of entrepreneurs is strongly affected by intentions (Krueger & Carsrud, 1993; Bird, 1988). The firm's strategic behaviour and subsequent growth is understandable in the light of its growth intention. Therefore, firm growth is based not merely on chance, but on the management's conscious decision making and choice. Naturally, the firm can grow even though it is not the management's aim, but in such a case the growth is not planned and so may include more risks. Planning therefore helps in managing growth and that is the essence of implementing entrepreneurship.

Circular Economy

Strubei (2015) states that because a new kind of economy is taking root, called the circular economy, that's capturing the attention of change-makers around the world. It offers a way of growing the economies and businesses while facing up to the resource shortages and environmental degradation that threaten human communities. It presents a generational opportunity for creative thinking and action by entrepreneurs and consumers everywhere. Renault and H & M, for example, have shown that recycling and remanufacture improve not only resource sustainability but also revenues, profits, and customer loyalty. Green companies are pioneering ambitious circular models, and myriad startups from all sectors are entering the scene. Meanwhile, Governments are joining the movement, too, in both developed and developing countries. What the burgeoning circular economy needs, in addition to new technologies and large-scale collaboration, are innovative business models that create value for all stakeholders. So far, large companies have led the way through intelligent intrapreneurship.

Gawel (2019) has reported that, the trends in circular economy are clear. Movement has taken towards an economy of disposability where the valuable resources extracted are going to waste and causing harm to people and planet. The challenges presented by single-use plastics are now well known, with an estimated truckload being dumped into the ocean every minute: ae for about 25% of food made for human consumption goes waste; and over the past 15 years, clothing production has doubled, yet consumers wear their clothes for half as long, to highlight just a few examples.

The extraction and processing of the natural resources that flow quickly through our economies contributes to half of global greenhouse gas emissions. At the same time, the embedded value of these resources is immense. An estimated $ 62.5 billion annually is locked up in e-waste in the form of gold, platinum and other valuable materials and that's three times more than the annual output of the world's silver mines and more than the GDP of most countries.

Geissdorfer (2017) states that a circular economy is an economic system aimed at eliminating waste and the continual use of resources. Circular systems employ reuse, sharing, repair, refurbishment, remanufacturing and recycling to create a close-loop system, minimising the use of resource inputs and the creation of waste, pollution and carbon emissions. Analysis of the above definition clearly reveals that waste generated in any manufacturing process could be reused to generate inputs or new products which could be sold to create income. Amalgamation of manufacturing and recycling processes form circulation.

Industry and Administration

Razorpay (2017) has gainfully stated that every entrepreneur essentially requires knowledge of policies, laws and operations involved in the business that is chosen as career. Entrepreneurs need opting for education, training or guidance of the administrative requirements to make the business viable, dependable and sustainable. In view of this backdrop, study of the policies of the Government in Circular economy seeks prime attention of the entrepreneurs.

Circular economy concept has emerged from the origin of earning profit by recycling the waste. In this backdrop, making safe disposal of the waste is the task of Industry (Sambyal, 2018) to protect land, ground and surface water and air while controlling the waste is that of administration. Statutory bodies have framed policies and regulations for waste management to maintain environmental balance. For that reason it is a joint working approach.WBCSD (2019) reported policy enablers to accelerate circular economy. They are "Incentive Mechanisms"; "Partnership and collaboration"; Aligning Circular economies in main stream policies and Traceable actions and Targets. CSR Europe (2018) has reported that, there are many enablers supporting the circular transformation of the private sector such as the commitment of the statutory control board wherein senior-level management has been set accountable for supporting recycling and circular processes. The responsibility on leakage and spillover effects of international corporations on local supply chains during procurement has been assigned. The statutory bodies have also devised quality standards for recycled products. In addition, to promote innovation on recycling and circulation processes, funding provisions have also been made.

ISSUES, CONTROVERSIES AND PROBLEMS

Stakeholders have reported challenges, issues and controversies in circular economy. They are dependable to impede the development process particularly during implementation. Equally so, literature has reported (BBS, 2019 and Ritzen, 2017) multiple challenges while adopting circular economy and their understanding is as a result vital:

1. Difficulty in understanding the correlations between circular economy practices, some enabling factors and their adoption;
2. Adoption of circular economy practices is negatively correlated to the perception of sustainability as a cost;
3. Lack of regulatory coordination;
4. About the enabling factors, instead, the implementation of circular economy practices is facilitated by a support process in finding raw materials with low environmental impact;
5. Barriers to a transition to Circular Economy are financial, structural, operational, attitudinal and technological. They are also, a need to increase integration between a number of different perspectives and domains in industry.

MAIN FOCUS OF THE CHAPTER

This chapter focuses mainly on the understanding about circular economy and approaches to addressing the challenges through knowledge management so that aspirants will find them motivating to initiating their entrepreneurship development, based on review of literature. Typically a lesson is prepared to search answers from literature to the questions with following objectives:

1. To understand relationship between entrepreneurship and economy;
2. To understand traditional and circular economy;
3. To know what challenges are faced for managing knowledge in circular economy;
4. To distinguish between Recycling & Circular Process;
5. To address the aforesaid challenges in CE;
6. To understand what knowledge is required in CE;
7. To understand how to manage the knowledge;
8. To know how is entrepreneurship developed in circular economy.

SOLUTIONS AND RECOMMENDATIONS

Entrepreneurship and Economy

These two terms are well known and they express their direct relationship between each other as, entrepreneurship leads to action (Dhaliwal, 2016) and economy is the effect. Literature has further exposed (Caoile, 2016) that economy building, at all times relies upon the philosophy of the entrepreneur. Running the business on profit is the main objective of a firm or enterprise and as such the entrepreneur applies its philosophy to generate it. Researchers have frequently exposed that the economy of an enterprise relies on the common principle that, (Phansalkar, 2015) "Money Saved is Money Earned". In that context, familiar observation is that the entrepreneurs create savings by two traditional approaches viz. by controlling the expenses over the revenue or increasing the revenue over expenses. Entrepreneurs' view of creating savings is for gaining sustainability and growth of the enterprise. Although entrepreneurs are aware of this reality, new avenues of generating revenue and reducing the cost of processing keep evolving through research and they look for new knowledge of them. The birth of circular economy has come up as a boon to increasing revenue and helping maintain the environmental balance. Literature (Rangappa, 2018) cites following simple equations to understand economy clearly:

Higher Income - Lower Expenditure = Savings

Income = Selling Price (Qty of business)

Expenditure = Purchase Price (Qty of materials)

Analysis of above equations makes important revelations that in order to build savings income should be higher than the expenditure and further finding is that the circular economy is a function of factors like resources, processing and reprocessing, products and the scale of operations. By analogy inference could be (Bioregional, 2017) drawn to identify the technical, commercial and financial/economic enablers of (Garmulewicz & Ors, 2018) circular economy. Technical enablers include measures on quantity, quality, processes and yields while economic enablers include capital cost, operating expenses, revenue and profitability. The commercial enablers mean the size of market, competition and prices of materials. In addition to these enablers there is a next category of regulatory enablers which indicate the dimensions designed by the statutory bodies in controlling environmental impact. Antikainen & Ors, (2018) have reported digitalisation enablers for circular economy. They can help closing the material loops by providing accurate information on the availability, location and condition of products. Managing knowledge on these enablers is another requisite for developing entrepreneurship.

Traditional Economy and Recycling Economy

Szaky (2019) has stated that the revenue model of traditional economy relies on a straight-line route, also named as linear route, of earning revenue by converting materials into new products. This creates a value addition while the recycling economy follows a reverse route of earning revenue (Mateusz, 2015) by converting waste into useful products thereby creating new revenue for the enterprise and reducing the waste to minimum for maintaining environmental regulations. Following are those simple equations (Rongbing, 2012) reported in literature (Seiford & Ors, 2001) to understand the grounds for recycling:

Input + Process = Desired Output + Recyclable Waste + discard able waste

Product is always the desired output and the one of major interest to the manufacturing firm. Making the process generate better yield and quality of the product is the further objective. Frequent occurrence is that, the desired output is in majority of cases associated with creation of undesired output that is considered as waste. Regulations laid down by statutory bodies reveal that the discard able output must match the standard on quantity and quality of waste. Qualities are specified in the standard for safe discharge and firms have to abide by the rules prescribed. For meeting difficult standards, the manufacturing firm needs to repeat process of development of treating that waste and making it suitable for discharge. This treatment may call for additional cost that may have to be borne and firms therefore keep evaluating the economics and searching processes that generate margin of profit as well as meet the standards of discharge. In dealing with the subject of waste treatment therefore, following equations, to building economy from waste, emerge for appropriate action:

Generation of new inputs for use within or products for sale = Economy Building

Distinction Between Recycling and Circular Processes

Zhou (2018) has suggested that with more funding and product stewardship, the recycling crisis could turn into an opportunity. Recycling is a linear process in which the waste from a manufacturing industry is treated independently in another industry while circular process is one in which the waste from manufacture is treated in the same industry forming a closed loop system (Geissdoerfer & Ors, 2017). Legge & Klett, (2018) have also described the recycling and circular processes giving configurations to understand the process clearly. More particularly in a circular process, both the linear and reverse processes are jointly conducted.

Example on Recycling Process: Linear Route:

Recyclable Waste+ Process=New inputs or Product

Example on Circular Process: Linear and reverse routes forming Closed Loop System:

Input+ Process=Desired Output+ Recyclable Waste

Recyclable Waste+ Process=New Input or Product+ Discard able waste

Addressing the Challenges

1. Difficulty in understanding the correlations between circular economy practices, some enabling factors and their adoption.

Circular Economy is the outcome of philosophy employed (Geisendorf & Ors, 2017) to treating and reducing the waste to earning income. Process of recycling generates new products for sale and so added revenue for the enterprise. Manufacturing programs, essentially engage three factors such as inputs, process and outputs (Landy & Ors., 2008). Each such a factor has its own characteristic (Redman & Ors., 2013) like quality, quantity, state, source and price. Studies on the utility of inputs (raw materials), their adaptability to convert them into products, operational convenience, environmental norms and costing are conducted to arrive at the economics in treating the wastes. Repeated experimentation (Dahlstrand & Ors, 2017) by processing intended materials and verifying results facilitates confirmation of process and economics. As a result, knowledge on dimensions enables understanding the economy through a correlation, Input + Process = output that is further extended to Input+ Process=Output+ waste and Waste+ Process= New Products. Therefore, these factors are expediently adaptable in designing waste treatment and understanding the straight and reverse line economics. Industry and administration jointly work for waste management. Like enablers have been evolved by Industry, the administration has as well worked out few enablers such as incentive mechanisms; partnership and collaboration to boost circular economy initiative. Administration has designed a policy to providing monetary incentives to the industry to make the waste management more attractive to the industries. The ground for this incentive is to reduce environmental impact of bad emissions while reducing the quantity of waste. Administration has floated few schemes and every industry in waste management sphere has the option to adopt them. In few areas of waste management, the administration is offering partnership or collaboration with the industry where the volume of waste is huge and heavy investment may be necessary.

2. Adoption of circular economy practices is negatively correlated to the perception of sustainability as a cost

Researchers have exposed (Bandera, 2017) that for resolving various issues, challenges and problems in connection with the circular economy, knowledge alone is responsible to change the biased (Zhang & Ors., 2015) mindset of Entrepreneurs. The issue of sustainability at additional cost, raised by few stakeholders, rests on the fear of adding economical, environmental and social cost to the ongoing costs of manufacturing. Geissdoerfer & Ors (2017), report that there are at least eight different relationship types between sustainability and they need to be followed to adapt circular economy. Proponents of the circular economy suggest that a sustainable world does not mean a drop in the quality of life for consumers, and can be achieved without loss of revenue or extra costs for manufacturers. Firms mistakenly believe circular economy gives rise to additional costs without gaining compensation thereby leading to financial loss. Truth sustains that adopting CE incurs cost (Bowdish, 2019) nevertheless much higher is the revenue generated. In resolving this mind set of the entrepreneurs, multiple examples have been cited to prove the view, of loss making, as incorrect. Researchers' reports have shown that, recycling of waste is undertaken to generating new revenue. In that context, Riel (2018) has categorically stated that circular economy unlocks new revenue streams. She further explains that as circular economy initiatives take hold, it is important that companies understand the financial benefits of embracing these new business models, including the opportunity for new revenue streams, reduced costs, more efficient supply chains and improved business intelligence. Initiating this view will turn adoption of circular economy practices for profit. Sustainable development requires disruptive changes and radical innovations, and the capability to deliver this in relation to adapt to a sustainable development is needed in mature large industrial companies. Since no one can stop the volume of waste overnight, (Lemille, 2019) investments in the recycling industry are needed.

Lack of Regulatory Coordination

Firms run their businesses by following rules and regulations, laws and policies of the regulatory body of a nation. In manufacturing segment, for instance, regulations are, as a matter of course, deployed more particularly on the discharge of waste from the industries while the control vests on the quality and quantity (EPA, 2018) of the output. Regulations are inapplicable on the inputs while control is laid on the processes which emit out hazardous gases or leakages. In view of this reality, firms have the liberty to alter their inputs and processes. Therefore, majority of the firms introduced philosophy of circular economy without waiting for new regulations to be introduced. They accepted that, recycling saves energy, (EPA, 2018) helps keep materials out of landfills and incinerators, and provides raw materials for the production of new products. BSI (2017) has now come up with strategies and launched for implementing the principles of the circular economy in organizations. The standard tries to align the far-reaching ambitions of the CE with established business routines at the organizational level. Stefan (2017) also reports that the standard contains a comprehensive list of CE terms and definitions, a set of general CE principles, a flexible management framework for implementing CE strategies in organizations, and a detailed description of economic, environmental, design, marketing, and legal issues related to the CE.

Technopolis Group (2016), for example, has usefully cited multiple considerations to resolve the issue of barriers for circular economy such as market prices, dominance of existing technologies, consumer demands and prohibitive business models. They further state that when revising the existing legislation, it is important to consider potential uncertainties for stakeholders involved because continuity and predictability in legislations are very important; and potential conflicts between legislations to avoid hampering investments in capacity and technology development. The nomenclature of circular economy has been coined by the circular route it follows to generate income by the process of recycling of the waste. Continuous data mining is crucial to understand emerging theories to improving economy of the enterprise. Amongst various initiatives reported by researchers to improve economics of the firm, circular economy has come out as the prominent drive for manufacturing firms. Therefore, arranging knowledge in that domain helps in treating waste, raise revenue and / or reduce cost. Literature has exposed (Garfield, 2018) multiple approaches to managing the knowledge on circular economy. Initiatives include framing the objectives, mining right information and classifying it and drawing inferences to convert it into knowledge. Authentic sources of information are the further requirement. Organizing the information is the subsequent action based on the dimensions of economy and issues to be addressed and approaches searched and selected. Amongst various approaches searched only the befitting ones are selected and finalized to turn them into knowledge. Thus knowledge gains value and useful to bring in competitiveness in the business resources, process, products, people, places and promotion through costing balance. Processing step consists of using the resources, data and tools to reviewing its prospects of its application or usefulness. Receiving the information through technology tools, like the ICT, is the preference of entrepreneurs since it offers facility of large volumes, ability to classify as per objective with pace and accuracy. However, Technology alone isn't the answer to sharing knowledge as it has to be effectively managed using proper channels. Thus common choice of strategy is to appoint a senior manager, a professional, as knowledge champion for the business.

The knowledge for Circular Economy Development on the other hand is a set of dimensions that are useful to generate revenue from linear and reverse routes. In the backdrop of this chapter, dimensions of circular economy are nothing but the technology, regulations and economics. Searching information on these dimensions is a continuous exercise as rising developments create new knowledge that brings new approaches, alternatives and options to regulations at the work-place. Knowledge of these dimensions to capture timely changes in the environment is a hard task for many entrepreneurs or individuals. Designing the dimensions is another challenge for the individuals since they need to generate capabilities to address all issues. Observation, of the literature, reveals that majority of the entrepreneurs are inquisitive about designing the quality of knowledge management. As such quality of knowledge management for Development through circular economy essentially calls for inclusion of knowledge, skills & capabilities development, and better known as culture of Entrepreneurship for Circular Economy Development. Robust quality measures applied in the Entrepreneurship for Circular Economy Development system produce hands of good personal behaviour, skills and capabilities. Quality entrepreneurship is to attaining "publicly accepted standards (Borgue & Hall, 2003) of accountability and integrity" and as such, it is an essential attribute of the Entrepreneurship for Circular Economy Development system.

3. The views that, circular economy is facilitated by a support process in finding raw materials with low environmental impact

Many stakeholders debate the above issues. Realism is that, the waste produced in manufacturing can be recycled to generate either raw materials for reuse or new products for sale. For hazardous waste stringent regulations are prescribed and only then firms need to search raw materials with low environmental impact. In that case, new raw materials to avoid processes creating pollution and minimizing waste would be used. The other route suggests developing processes without making any changes in raw materials but conducting changes in the treatment of waste. Therefore for adapting circular economy, firms prefer second route over the first. Rigorous analysis of the undesired waste (generated in any manufacturing process) and identification of its contents (Pongracz & Ors, 2018) is conducted to verify if they are usable (Recyclable) in some way. Decision is then made to dispose of the unusable. Chen & Ors, (2019) cited the driving mechanism on research on waste separation behaviour. The other challenge of enabling factors has also been resolved. In that, Jenson J.P. & Ors. (2017) have cited adaptable approaches to circular economy giving a gist of enabling processes. According to them industry 4.0 sets new requirements for becoming a sustainable manufacturer where data management, the Internet of Things and extended product service systems are tightly linked with traditional manufacturing processes.

4. Barriers to a transition to Circular Economy are financial, structural, operational, attitudinal and technological.

Amongst the various barriers pointed out by stakeholders, repealing financial profitability is the major ground in not adapting CE initiatives. This negative philosophy or mindset of the entrepreneurs came up owing to the belief of additional investment and the probability of loss. On this ground alone entrepreneurs reject such proposals on CE. However, this view could be corrected or modified if entrepreneurs set a proper knowledge management system on waste processing through repeated research for cost reduction and revenue enhancement. They are also, as analyzed in relation to innovation management, characterized by a need to increase integration between a number of different perspectives and domains in industry.

Structural barriers of CE have been reported stating that they arise due to absence of information exchange and unclear responsibility distribution. This issue is prominently related to the knowledge management and therefore firms need to adopt a proper system of information gathering, organization and distribution with fixation of accountability. Struebi (2015) has suggested that substantive collaborations across sectors and industries are essential. For social entrepreneurs, this means linking up with next-generation technologists, forging partnerships with other companies up and down the supply chain, and listening closely to all stakeholders. In many cases, it will mean all of the above.

Firms which create production without CE need very low infrastructure and so no supply chain or additional cost. However for adopting CE, they need additional infrastructure to recycle the waste and further engage supply chain to manage increased resources. This view of stakeholders could be corrected by knowledge which shows that the additional cost can be recovered by earning added revenue. Therefore circular economy is considered as the most powerful tool. It is also beneficial in shaping sustainable infrastructure as the world's population grows, writes built environment expert Toyne, (2019). Attitudinal barriers have also been reported by few other stakeholders wherein the firms have been observed going on negative perception of sustainability and concerned more about risk aversion. Sustainability is actuality the stability gained on economical, environmental and social grounds. The action plan to remedy this barrier is to prove the perception otherwise through means of knowledge in every aspect of sustainability. Therefore continuous source of right information and case studies which provide successful evidence needs to be brought in place by the firm to change the biased attitude. Technological barriers relate to raw materials, process and output design and their integration. Although researchers essentially lay emphasis on developing processes without waste generation, majority of the processes invariably produce output along with undesired waste. Therefore, probability of total elimination of waste is rare and so circular economy will continue to run for ever. Kaplan (2015) reports that the cities essentially pay to send waste to landfills, however if they send this waste to a recycling facility it costs nothing

To Understand What Knowledge is Required in CE

Circular economy is an upcoming field and to boost entrepreneurship engaging proper knowledge on technology, regulations and economics, is essential to introduce sustainability in business. This is as such a three prong approach in knowledge management to entrepreneurship development.

Technology

It means logical applications of the techniques and includes scientific processes used (Naude & Szirmai, 2013) for manufacturing certain products. Techniques are evolved by applying logic based on the principles and considerations in the fields of science, humanity and commerce. In the context of circular economy it is the process of manufacturing and waste treatment.

Regulations

It means and includes rules, policies or legal acts pertaining to processes and disposable waste that are formulated by a statutory body. Rules / Regulations (Álvare, Amorós, Urbano, 2014) are framed to control the environmental nuisance.

Economics

It means the knowledge, understanding and capability to make assessment on costing, revenue and profitability (Price, 2015) of a process that is computed by examining the capital requirement to treat the waste and returns obtainable there from.

Majority of the entrepreneurs being studious, evade going unplanned due to probability of high risk in the business while they prefer opting a business with calculated risk since that is more practical to reality. More so as the information and estimates are drawn from market prices and thus practically create new venture to gain profit. They also create a prototype model of treating the waste to ascertain the quality of products and to find if processing conditions create no impact on environment.

Managing the Knowledge

1. Create a Knowledge Strategy for the Business.

Requirements to creating knowledge management include taking a strategic approach to discovering, collating and sharing it. This is done via a knowledge strategy (Mohajan, 2019), a set of written guidelines to be applied across the business. If the strategy is to be effective, one must make sure the senior managers are committed to it and are fully aware of the benefits it can bring. Discuss with them the best ways of collecting and using knowledge. Deciding to appoint a senior manager as knowledge champion for the business is a good practice followed. This strategy leads to make knowledge central to the business.

2. Designing the knowledge management strategy.

Dunham (2018) has described methodology of designing an effective knowledge management strategy for the organization. Considering how effective the business currently is at using its knowledge. Analyse the internal processes for gathering and sharing information and find if there are successful ways of generating ideas and do staff have a good grasp of what is happening. Mohapatra (2016), has also described that knowledge management, acquisition and distribution is a continuing process, so that it becomes central to the business strategy. Identifying the value of knowledge to the business is the subsequent step. Think of ways one could exploit the knowledge for financial gain - perhaps by gaining a larger market share, developing new products, or selling or licensing the protected intellectual property to others. Earning through waste recycle leads to circular economy. Ensure this fits in with the overall business plan. After designing the model for knowledge management, verification of its effectiveness is the next step to implementation. While quality is the end result, the process of attaining good quality is the prime focus of this chapter. Management is an approach to designing, monitoring and controlling key performance indicators (Poleski, 2016). Monitoring process key indicators is convenient and reliance is placed on their design. Bear minimum key performance indicators in numbers are simple to remember, easy to operate and quick to comply with, thus leading to a Knowledge Strategy of quality measurement. Knowledge is all about adding value into the process steps while eliminating inefficient steps. Knowledge Management helps doing more with less (FMEA, 2018) while doing it better. Knowledge Strategies carry reputation owing to their value addition into the process steps to reach the goal within minimum work flow paths and therefore accrue benefits of zero waste, recycle efficiency & cost effectiveness & revenue generation. (Helveting, 2018). Knowledge management is an offshoot of knowledge creating principles. Companies develop strategies to reduce their business operations to only those essential ones to produce quality goods and services. Although four dimensions of quality in Entrepreneurship for Circular Economy Development such as behaviour, knowledge, skills and capability are previously recognized, their application is a challenge for many Entrepreneurs for Circular Economy Development and that is the focus of this study. This chapter will throw light on the opinions of experts in the line to reveal the excellence of Knowledge Strategy for Circular Economy Development.

Entrepreneurship Development in Circular Economy

Three entrepreneurial attitudes have been revealed by researchers. They say that entrepreneurs come from political, economical, social or technological background therefore their attitude towards the industry varies according to their motivation and that only operates the enterprise. In view of this reality, entrepreneur's philosophy is highly accountable to prepare business models that could yield good results. References show that philosophy is highly experimental in running a business. Research findings (Baporikar & Deshpande, 2009) also indicated that a business operation successfully emerged with analytical, organizational and judgemental attitudes of the entrepreneurs. The businessman visualises the opportunities offered by the situation and studies them in depth one by one and risks involved with regulations that need to be complied with. The entrepreneur makes plans, draws out process flows for organising resources to make the entry and also studies its impact on survival and growth of the enterprise. This leads to organisational approach for the enterprise. This attitude of the entrepreneur looks into the utility, flexibility, viability, and competitiveness of the approach that call for matching the type, size and value of their resources with their capability that makes up the judgement for making choice of the approach.

Le Roux and Ors (2014) have revealed three dimensions of entrepreneurial orientation (EO), namely the pro-activeness, risk-taking and competitive aggressiveness as essential for entrepreneurship development. Although these dimensions are a general requirement for any entrepreneurship, specific enablers relating to circular economy are technology, recycling, regulations and economics.

Marenelli (2014) reported that in the past few years, circular economy has gained attention of the society and industry. This is due to the fact of the world facing the challenge of balancing the economic growth with the use and availability of natural resources. Royal Philips embraced the circular economy concept and started its journey to integrate this new business model in its business processes. Six key areas for integration were identified including the sales model, product design & material composition, IT & data Management, supply loops, strategic sourcing for own operations and HR & incentives. There is a call on the European policy makers to create the right conditions for the circular economy. When implementing a new business model the company is interested to measure the success.

Heshmati (2015) has reported that entrepreneurship is the process of starting a business or organization. The development process has many dimensions such as management, social, political, knowledge, technology, legal, financial, manpower and economics. Each of these can be seen as a challenge; entrepreneurs also face many barriers. A number of public measures like establishing business incubators and science parks are aimed at supporting entrepreneurship and their operations, survival and success. Few stakeholders have suggested using a corporate social responsibility-based approach. Sustainable entrepreneurs are expected to have a clear vision of the direction including sustainable development that balances social, economic and environmental impacts. These act as catalysts for transitioning from a current linear economy to a sustainable economy and as such entrepreneurs face various forms of risks, challenges and barriers. Stakeholder further maintains that beyond entrepreneurial will, socio-cultural conditions and institutional realities could affect CE adoption practices by SMEs. Other stakeholders focus on the types of sustainable entrepreneurship and conditions for sustainable innovations. Their focus is on the administration of technical challenges to the management of opportunities. They see management as a challenge to comply with regulations and tight regulatory frameworks and requirements for business. Business leaders play a role in creating market innovations and in their promotion and implementation.

FUTURE RESEARCH DIRECTIONS

In order to facilitate the advancement of circular economy, additional research to identifying various enablers, their utility and applications are essentially the need of future research. Further research is suggested to identifying additional dimensions of entrepreneurship particularly in circular economy.

CONCLUSION

Literature review has exposed that to developing entrepreneurship in circular economy the aspirant will need knowledge of technology, regulation and economics. Further revelation is that the knowledge could be managed using strategies of receiving information, organising and sharing as well as continuously researching the information with regard to organizational success. The chapter has also disclosed that to implementing knowledge strategy in circular economy an appointment of an official in an organizational structure is essential.

REFERENCES

3e.eu. (2019). *Flexible Adaptable Buildings Serve Circular Economy.* http://www.3e.eu

Alexandre, L. (2019). *For a true circular economy, we must redefine waste.* https://www.weforum.org

Álvare, C., Amorós, J. E., & Urbano, D. (2014). Regulations and Entrepreneurship: Evidence from Developed and Developing Countries. Innovar, 24.

Antikainen, M., Uusitalo, T., & Kivikytö-Reponen, P. (2018). Digitalisation as an Enabler of Circular Economy. *Digitalisation as an Enabler of Procedia CIRP*, *73*, 45–49. doi:10.1016/j.procir.2018.04.027

Antonia, G. (2019). *Innovation and entrepreneurship can cut waste and deliver the circular economy.* https://www.weforum.org

Aytekin, T. (2019). *Why More Knowledge Won't Make You More Successful.* https://www.entrepreneur.com

Baporikar, N., & Deshpande, M. (2009). Designing Policies for Business. In *Fourth Annual International Conferenceon Public Policy and Management*. Indian Institute of Management, Bangalore.

BBS. (2019). *Small and Medium Enterprises Facing the Challenge of Circular Economy.* https://www.bbs.unibo.eu

Bioregional. (2017). *Four Key Enablers That Will Speed Up Circular Economy.* https://www.bioregional.com

Blackburn, R. (2008). Small Business and Entrepreneurship. Academic Press.

Bowman, E. (2011). *Entrepreneur Training Manual, Third Edition: Certified Entrepreneur Workbook.* Guanzi Institute Press.

Brian, T. (2015). *The Basics of Business Success.* https://www.entrepreneur.com

Brown, P. B. (2013). *Entrepreneurs Are Calculated Risk Takers*. https://www.forbes.com

Bruder, J. (2013). *The Psychological Price Of Entrepreneurship Inc*. Academic Press.

BSI. (2017). *Developing BS 8001- A World First*. The British Standards Institution.

Cesar, B. (2017, December). Knowledge Management and the Entrepreneur. *International Journal of Innovation Studies.*, *1*(3), 163–174. doi:10.1016/j.ijis.2017.10.005

Dahlstrand, Asa, Lindholm, & Ors. (2017). *Entrepreneurial Experimentation: A Key Function in Entrepreneurial Systems of Innovation*. Research Institute of Industrial Economics. IFN Working Paper No. 1154.

Dana, Leo, & Paul. (2010). Nunavik, Arctic Quebec: Where Co-operatives Supplement Entrepreneurship. *Global Business and Economics Review*, *12*(1/2), 42–71.

Deakins, D., & Freel, M. S. (2009). *Entrepreneurial activity, the economy and the importance of small firms. Entrepreneurship and small firms*. McGraw-Hill Education.

Dinesh, A. (1991). *Approaches to Entrepreneurship Development. A Trend Analysis. ILO/INTERMAN Entrepreneurship Semina*. Ahmedabad: Entrepreneurship Development Institute of India. https://www.ediindia.org

Duening, T. N., Hisrich, R. A., & Lechter, M. A. (2009). *Technology Entrepreneurship: Creating, Capturing, and Protecting Value*. Academic Press.

Elise, D. (2018). *How to Design an Effective Knowledge Management Strategy for Your Organization*. https://www.e-nor.com

EPA. (2018). *Managing-and-Reducing-Wastes-Guide-Commercial-Buildings*. https://www.epa.gov

Europe, C. S. R. (2018). *Circular economy: What are the enablers and barriers?* https://www.csreurope.org

Foo, M. D. (2011). Emotions and entrepreneurial opportunity evaluation. *Entrepreneurship Theory and Practice*, *35*(2), 375–393. doi:10.1111/j.1540-6520.2009.00357.x

Garmulewicz, A., & Ors. (2018). *Disruptive Technology as an Enabler of the Circular Economy: What Potential Does 3D Printing Hold?* https://journals.sagepub.com

Geissdoerfer, M., Savaget, P., Bocken, N. M. P., & Hultink, E. J. (2017). The Circular Economy A new sustainability paradigm. *Journal of Cleaner Production*, *143*, 757–768. doi:10.1016/j.jclepro.2016.12.048

Girard, J. P., & Girard, J. L. (2015). Defining Knowledge Management: Toward an Applied Compendium. *Online Journal of Applied Knowledge Management*, *3*(1), 14.

Halloran, J. W. (2014). *Your Small Business Adventure: Finding Your Niche and Growing a Successful Business*. ALA/Huron Street Press.

Harvey, L., & Knight, P. (1996). *Transforming higher education*. Bristol, PA: Society for Research into Higher Education: Open University Press.

Heshmati, A. (2015). *A Review of the Circular Economy and its Implementation*. http://ftp.iza.org

Jenson, J.P., & Ors. (2017). *Enabling Circular Economy through Product Stewardship*. https://www.sciencedirect.com

Karthik, R. (2018). *Business Economy*. https://www.moneycontrol.com

Kimberly, A. (2019). *Traditional Economy With Its Characteristics, Pros, Cons, and Examples*. https://www.thebalance.com

Landy, F. J., & Conte, J. M. (2009). *Work in the 21st Century: An Introduction to Industrial and Organizational Psychology*. John Wiley & Sons.

Lawrence, B. (2019). *Trash to Treasure*. https://www.uschamberfoundation.org

Legge, S., & Klett, T. C. (2018). *How To Build Business In Circular Economy*. https://www.weforum.org

Leitão, J., & Baptista, R. (2009). *Public Policies for Fostering Entrepreneurship: A European Perspective*. Springer Science Business Media.

Lowe & Marriott. (2006). *Enterprise: Entrepreneurship and Innovation: Concepts, Contexts and Commercialization*. Butterworth-Heinemann.

Lundstrom, A., & Stevenson, L. A. (2005). *Entrepreneurship Policy: Theory and Practice*. Springer.

Marenelli, T. (2014). *Integration of circular economy in business*. https://www.researchgate.net

Mateusz, L. (2015). *Designing the Business Models for Circular Economy*. https://www.mdpi.com

Miller, K. (2005). *Communication theories: perspectives, processes, and contexts* (2nd ed.). New York, NY: McGraw-Hill.

Minniti, M., & Moren, L. (2010). Entrepreneurial types and economic growth. *Journal of Business Venturing*, *25*(3), 305–314. doi:10.1016/j.jbusvent.2008.10.002

Mohajan, H. K. (2019). *Knowledge Sharing among Employees in Organizations*. https://mpra.ub.uni-muenchen.de

Mohapatra, S. (2016). *Designing Knowledge Management Strategy*. https://www.researchgate.net

Naaman, Z. (2018). *Rethinking Recycling. Could a Circular Economy Solve a Problem?* https://www.theguardian.com

Nanayakkara, S. (2013). *How Can We Promote More Entrepreneurial Environment Together*. https://blogs.worldbank.org

Naude, W., & Szirmai, A. (2013). *Technical Innovation Entrepreneurship and Development*. https://www.europeanbusinessreview.com

Patrick, C. (2016). *Entrepreneurship Philosophy Defined*. https://business.inquirer.net

Patrick, S. (2015). *For Entrepreneurs, Circular Economy Offers a Massive Opportunity*. https://www.huffpost.com

Price, R. W. (2015). *How Does Economics Connect To Entrepreneurship?* https://news.gcase.org

Razorpay. (2017). *Legal Basics That Every Indian Start up Should Know*. https://razorpay.com/blog

Rea, C., & Volland, N. (2015). *The Business of Culture: Cultural Entrepreneurs in China and Southeast Asia, 1900-65*. UBC Press.

Redman, T. C. (2013). *Data Driven: Profiting from Your Most Important Business Asset*. Harvard Business Press.

Riel, A. (2018). *How Circular Economy Unlocks Revenue Streams*. https://www.greenbiz.com

Rob, K. (2015). *The Reign of Recycling is not Over*. http://greatforest.com

Roux, Ingrid, Le, & Or. (2014). Dimensions of Entrepreneurial Orientation & SME performance in Emerging Economies. *Development Southern Africa, 31*(4).

Pauliuk, S. (2017). Critical Appraisal of the Circular Economy standard BS 8001:2017 And a Dashboard of Quantitative System Indicators for its Implementation in Organizations. *Resources, Conservation and Recycling, 129*, 81-92.

Sambyal, S. S. (2018). *Government Notifies New Solid Waste management Rules*. https://www.downtoearth.org.in

Scheufele, D., & Moy, P. (2000). Twenty-five years of the spiral of silence: A conceptual review and empirical outlook. *International Journal of Public Opinion Research, 12*(1), 3–28. doi:10.1093/ijpor/12.1.3

Scuderi, R. (2012). *Ten Simple Ways to Cut Business Costs*. https://www.americanexpress.com

SEF. (2012). *Swedish Entrepreneurship Forum*. The Evolving Domain of Entrepreneurship Research. https://entreprenorskapsforum.se

Seiford, L. M., & Ors. (2001). *Modeling Undesirable Factors in Efficiency Evaluation*. http://www.deafrontier.net

Shane, S., & Nicolaou, N. (2013). The genetics of entrepreneurial performance. *International Small Business Journal, 31*(5), 473–495. doi:10.1177/0266242613485767

Shane, S., & Venkataraman, S. (2000). The Promise of Entrepreneurship as A Field of Research. *Academy of Management Review, 25*(1), 217–226. doi:10.5465/amr.2000.2791611

Shih, D. H. (2018). *A Strategic Knowledge Management Approach to Circular Agribusiness*. https://www.mdpi.com

Sofia, R. (2017). Barriers to the Circular Economy – integration of perspectives and domains. The 9th CIRP IPSS Conference: Circular Perspectives on Product/Service-Systems. *Procedia CIRP, 64*, 7–12. doi:10.1016/j.procir.2017.03.005

Stan, G. (2018). *10 Types of Knowledge Management Strategies*. https://medium.com

Szaky, T. (2019). Processes and Ethical Challenges. *Journal of Business Venturing, 24*(5). https://www.huffpost.com

Technopolis Group. (2016). *Regulatory Barriers for the Circular Economy.* https://www.technopolis-group.com

Tim, J. (1993). *Clean Production Strategies Developing Preventive Environmental Management in the Industrial Economy*. CRC Press.

Toyne, P. (2019). *How can the circular economy make infrastructure more sustainable?* https://www.eco-business.com

UNCTAD. (2018). *World Investment Report*. https://unctad.org

UNIDO. (2019). *Circular Economy*. https://www.unido.org

Viren, P. (2015). *Money Saved is Money Earned*. http://www.marketexpress.in

WBCSD. (2019). *Policy Enablers to accelerate the circular economy*. https://docs.wbcsd.org

Yetisen, A. K., Volpatti, L. R., Coskun, A. F., Cho, S., Kamrani, E., Butt, H., ... Yun, S. H. (2015). Entrepreneurship. *Lab on a Chip*, *15*(18), 3638–3660. doi:10.1039/C5LC00577A PMID:26245815

Zhang, S. X., & Cueto, J. (2015). The Study of Bias in Entrepreneurship. *Entrepreneurship Theory and Practice*, *41*(3), 419–454. doi:10.1111/etap.12212

KEY TERMS AND DEFINITIONS

Circular Economy: It is defined as a process of gaining monetary benefit by converting resources in manufacturing industry in linear direction and treating the waste produced therein in reverse direction forming a circulatory process.

Entrepreneurship Development: It is defined as a process of training or preparing an aspirant to adding skills, capacities and abilities in handling risk in a particular business or situation.

Knowledge Management: It is defined as a process of seeking informative material content by planning, organising, and verifying and is the one which could be converted into useful knowledge using intelligence and philosophy by a qualified person.

Section 3

Managing in the Circular Economy

Chapter 26
Sustainable Entrepreneurship and Management Skills at a Crossroad in the Circular Economy

Booysen Sabeho Tubulingane
University of Giessen, Germany & UNICAF, Cyprus & Namibia University of Science and Technology, Namibia

ABSTRACT

Entrepreneurship is the process of starting a business, a start-up company, or an organization. Before a person is capable of starting a business, there are entrepreneurship and business management skills that need to be acquired. Business management skills involve planning, decision making, leadership, marketing, selling, financial management, project management, delegation, time management, problem-solving, and networking. Entrepreneurship skills enable an entrepreneur to be self-efficacy, innovative, taking control of business activities, articulating a need for achievement, and able to take risks. Thus, this chapter provides a desktop literature analysis of the relationship between entrepreneurship and management skills within a circular economy. The chapter further examines problems and solutions to sustainable entrepreneurship. There is a need for a study to investigate how innovative sustainable business models can be both fully profitable and sustainably oriented.

INTRODUCTION

Entrepreneurship involves the presence of an opportunity and enterprising individuals who can see business opportunities and such individuals are capable enough to respond to it irrespective of the existing resources (Feit & Pisapia, 2014). Additionally, an entrepreneur is a person who can spot and pursue opportunities without regard to existing resources. Similarly, Heshmati (2015) defines entrepreneurship as a process of starting a business, a start-up company or an organisation. Moreover, an entrepreneur develops a business plan, acquires required resources, and is fully responsible for the business outcomes.

DOI: 10.4018/978-1-7998-5116-5.ch026

Copyright © 2020, IGI Global. Copying or distributing in print or electronic forms without written permission of IGI Global is prohibited.

There are basic management skills needed to be an effective and efficient entrepreneur. According to the Small Business Development Corporation (2019:1), the following management skills are required to run a successful business; "financial management, marketing, sales and customer service, communication and negotiation, leadership, project management and planning, delegation and time management, problem solving, and networking". Lahti, Parida, and Wuncent (2018:1) argue that the idea behind the circular economy is that "companies have a responsibility to uphold the environmental and sustainable values of society and must respond to a broad set of stakeholders rather than just their closest shareholders. This idea has resulted in research into ways management can expand and rethink the traditional make-use-dispose business model". The make-use-dispose business model is based on a linear economy, which is detrimental to the environment and cannot sustainably supply the growing population of our planet with essential services (Sariatli, 2017). Also, the linear economy is profit oriented, however it can lead to strained profitability in the long run as raw materials become scarce. Hence, this chapter intends to investigate how businesses are participating in the circular economy. The investigation is essential because the circular economy has achieved a broad appeal from business leaders, policy-makers and academics (Behrens, Drabik, Kranendijk, Rinaldi, Rizos, Stuchtey & Tuokko, 2018). Additionally, the economic benefits arising from using less energy and material inputs and the new emerging business models have fuelled business interest in the circular economy worldwide. Entrepreneurship businesses have been the leading contributors to many national economies, for instance a study by Farayibi (2017) confirms the roles of entrepreneurship as one of the key drivers of economic growth in Nigeria. As revealed by Heshmati (2015), entrepreneurship cannot be successful without business leaders who possess appropriate level of business management skills. Thus, the study will analyse entrepreneurship and management skills within a circular economy.

There is a need to find an alternative to the traditional linear model of business growth, thus the circular economy has emerged as a replacement of the linear economic business model (Wautelet, 2018). According to Grigorescu, Mocanu and Zamfir (2017), circular economy practices at the company level can involve targeting waste reduction while maintaining the value of products and resources in the system for the achievement of entrepreneurial sustainability. Wautelet (2018) also established that the circular economy has been receiving increasing attention in the academia fraternity in which scholars have shared different views on what a circular economy entails. This is evident in current literature on the circular economy. The circular economy has been highly linked to fields of natural resource management and economics. For example, a study by Laubscher and Marinelli (2014) established that circular economy has gained prominence in society and in business (industry) because the world is faced with the challenge of balancing economic growth with the use and availability of natural resources. It must be noted that sustainable businesses have a great probability of being more successful as time passes, and for continuously succeeding not only for months or years, but also for generations (Huang, Plas & Salam, 2016). According to the SB Insight (2019:1), circular business processes can be based on seven steps of the circular product value chain as follows:

1. Raw materials should be carefully chosen as the need to be regenerative by nature, keeping their value for as long as possible;
2. Product design should be designed in order to save the maximum amount of resources and energy used, designing out waste is key;
3. The production and manufacturing of products should be made with maximal energy efficiency and all energy sources should be renewable;

4. Distribution processes refer to e.g. logistics and transportation. Using logistics as an example, actors can create incentives to participate in the circular economy by offering for example pre-paid shipping labels, smart packaging, and innovative take-back mechanisms;
5. Use and reuse of products, this stage refers to the consumption phase of products, including; using, reusing, repairing and sharing principles;
6. Collection processes are vital in order to prepare for recycling and take advantage of existing resources. The collection phase consists of more than solely providing consumers with containers for separating their plastics from their glass waste. It also means finding innovative methods to get people to collect their recyclable waste and provide it to the right actor for recycling. The goal is a stricter separation of waste streams at the source instead of after the collection;
7. Recycling is the most outer loop in a circular economy. It is preferably the last action, when other options are closed in order to retain the resource and its value through reuse, reparation or remanufacturing.

Drivers of the circular economy transition are namely, environmental sustainability, competitiveness, investment, digitalisation and security of supply of resources (Kranendijk & Stuchtey, 2018). This entails that the circular economy is based on the reuse, reduction and recycling of materials used to produce the businesses' products using less or renewable energy sources such as solar power. Furthermore, in order for the circular economy to succeed, the end-users (customers) need to actively participate in the process, for example, customers might be requested to return empty bottles for recycling purposes after consuming products preserved in bottles.

Research Objectives and Methodology

A study by Boufaden (2018) analysed the role of entrepreneurship in economic growth through the concept of entrepreneurial capital where factors stimulating entrepreneurial opportunities were uncovered. However, such factors were not discussed in the context of a linear or circular economic model. Similarly, Laubscher and Marinelli (2014) established that the circular economy concept is a new business model which can integrate key areas such as the sales model, product design, supply loops, strategic sourcing for own operations and human resources and incentives. Very little emphasis has been placed on the role of business management skills in relation to entrepreneurship within the context of a circular economy. Thus, the main objective of this chapter is to analyse how the evolution of entrepreneur management skills has not evolved to meet the needs of a circular economy. This will be achieved by looking at entrepreneur management skills from global perspectives. Specific research objectives are as follows:

- To link the entrepreneur and management skills to their business practices which uphold the environmental and sustainable values of society;
- To analyse the relationship between sustainable business practices, entrepreneurship, and business management skills;
- To examine sustainable entrepreneurship and its challenges.

A desktop study method will be used for collecting secondary data to find out how entrepreneurship and management skills are incorporated to achieve sustainable business practices in a circular economy. The researcher opted for a desk study approach in order to take advantage of the high quality of published literature in the area of circular economy, entrepreneurship and business management. A desk study method involves secondary data analysis, which offers methodological benefits geared towards generating new knowledge by analysing existing published information (Johnston, 2014).

ENTREPRENEURSHIP AND BUSINESS MANAGEMENT

Business Management Skills

Management skills are regarded as one of the key factors for entrepreneurs to succeed in their businesses (Agbim, 2013). Furthermore, entrepreneurial success is positively associated with skills for planning and budgeting for a marketing strategy that provides an attractive range of products and/or services. Entrepreneurs need business skills to detect changes in the market environment quickly; skills for assessing sales problems as a way of maintaining good customer relations are also required. Moreover, entrepreneurs also need business, management expertise skills to attract and retain competent employees. Business management skills involve planning, decision-making, motivating, marketing, finance and selling (Cooney, 2012). The required business skills ensure proficiency in the performance of a task due to human capital investments (entrepreneurial education, work, industry and entrepreneurship experiences) (Kele, Kerrin & Mamabolo, 2017).

Entrepreneurship Skills

A person who has entrepreneurship skills is usually disciplined, inclined to take innovative risks, change oriented and steady when doing business (Cooney, 2012). Business management is about better planning, implementation, control and managing risks (Mwakio, 2018). Some 'typical' characteristics of an entrepreneur consist of core values, problem-solving skills, flexibility, ability to lead a team, analysing competition and being confident. According to Kerr, Kerr and Xu (2017), entrepreneurs are usually self-efficate, innovative, take control of business activities, and articulate a need for achievement and have a risk attitude. Correspondingly, the Standing Committee for Economic and Commercial Cooperation of the Organization of the Islamic Cooperation (COMCEC) (2016:1) identified the following qualities of entrepreneurs:

- Ability to identify and invest in business opportunities;
- Enjoy being independent; they like doing things their own way;
- Have an appetite for hard work, persistence and a culture of high performance and good leadership;
- Have self-confidence, must demonstrate extreme self-confidence in order to cope with all the risks of operating their own businesses;
- Disciplined and resist the temptation to do what is unimportant or the easiest but have the ability to think through what is the most essential;
- Good at making judgements as they have the ability to think quickly and make wise decisions;
- Select experts rather than friends and relatives to assist them at the time of need. Have the ability to accept change, entrepreneur in many cases; changes their business plans in order to help their businesses grow. Entrepreneurs look at many solutions to their problems than exploring only one solution;

- Able to cope with business stress by focusing on the result and not the process of getting there;
- Have the profit margin in sight and know that their business' success is measured by profits;
- Take decisions under uncertainty and thus they are willing to take risks, but never gamble with the results. Choose moderate calculated risks rather than play wild gamble to have a reasonable chance to succeed;
- Believe in their own ability to control the consequences of their endeavour by influencing their socio-economic environment rather than leave everything to luck;
- Constantly put their efforts in introducing new products, new methods of production, opening new markets and reorganising the enterprise;
- Have ability to mobilise resources; and to arrange all the inputs to obtain the product.

Entrepreneurial skills had a significant impact on the growth of Small and Medium Enterprises (SMEs) in Nigeria and the UK (United Kingdom) (Omolara, 2018). However, the respondents in Nigeria and the UK agreed that creative thinking, problem solving, and communication skills are critical for business success in terms of increasing sales and competitive advantage. Nigerian respondents strongly agreed that a high level of creative thinking with a bit of problem solving and communication skills results in the growth and success of SMEs. Some of the UK entrepreneurs who argued that both the high level of creative thinking and problem solving reported the opposite that communication skills are critical to SMEs' success and growth.

ENTREPRENEURSHIP AND BUSINESS MANAGEMENT SKILLS RELATIONSHIP

According to Kele et al. (2017), globally, business management skills are one of the essential requirements for entrepreneurs to succeed in businesses. Other required business skills include financial management, human resource management, leadership and marketing. According to Lowden (2007), there are four areas an entrepreneur needs to develop to become successful in business, namely, good planning, organising, leading and controlling of business processes. Similarly, de Wild (2014) states that, entrepreneurs use business management skills such as planning, organising, leading teams and controlling business activities. Business management ensures that all operational activities needed to provide goods or services to the customers are conducted efficiently and effectively to create a high profit margin. In other words, business management is a process that is used by entrepreneurs to accomplish business goals (Bohoris & Vorria, 2007). Business management as a process ensures the achievements of the desired business goals through the key functions of planning and budgeting, organising and staffing, problem solving and controlling. However, modern entrepreneurs need new business management skills in order to strategise globally (Passari, 2019). New business management skills based on sustainable business practices enable entrepreneurs to formulate more efficient production methods. Additionally, new business management skills aid entrepreneurs to improve the quality of products produced. Entrepreneurs will have a faster response time to changing market conditions, thus becoming more competitive (Passari, 2019).

According to Almeida and Sousa (2014), entrepreneurs need both personal skills (reasoning, social and relational skills, technical skills and management) as well as business skills (strategy that the company will adopt, products/services to be sold, the corporate image, management systems: human resource management, financial management and marketing). Entrepreneurs must know their business environment and the market they want to target for them to be successful in their businesses (de Wild,

2014). Additionally, entrepreneurs must know the suppliers of the inputs or raw materials they require; they must conduct a competitiveness analysis, and they need to segment potential target customers for their goods or services. In addition, entrepreneurs need to know the rules and laws governing their potential target market, and the infrastructure and support services available in the market. In essence, entrepreneurs need to conduct market research studies before implementing their business plans to increase the chances of succeeding in their businesses. Examining the marketplace environment is one of the functions, which creates profit opportunities that provide the potential growth, and financial viability of the business (Liraz, 2013).

According to Fakhrisadat, Narges and Zahra (2014), the managerial skills of entrepreneurship have a positive and significant impact on business success. Furthermore, the skill of venture launch was identified to have the highest impact while the skill of negotiation was rated to have the lowest impact on business success. Moreover, skills in management, decision making, control, planning, finance and accounting, human relations, and growth management also impact the success of the business.

ENTREPRENEURSHIP, BUSINESS MANAGEMENT SKILLS AND SUSTAINABLE BUSINESS PRACTICES

A country can have a high economic growth based on the linear business economic development model; however, linear business economic models are being clouded by increasing environmental damage and resource scarcity (Manimala & Prasad, 2018). Furthermore, a high rate of environment damages and resource scarcity is usually experienced when operating in a linear economy; consequently, policy makers and businesses around the world are increasingly looking towards the circular economy business model. Moreover, circular economic models aim to enable an effective flow of materials, energy, labour and information so that natural and social capital can be rebuilt. Thus, circular economic models encourage sustainable business practices such as recycling, reuse and reduce materials needed to achieve end products/services of a business. According to Hahn, Ince and Spieth (2018), entrepreneurs can become sustainable by relying on innovative approaches and business models to build a commercial logic for achieving social or ecological goals. The following are the drivers for sustainable business practices as adopted from Scottish Enterprise (2019):

- Cost savings (using less material and energy means reduced costs and less exposure to volatile raw material prices);
- Customer demand/loyalty/trust (many consumers now alter their buying habits for environmental benefit);
- Regulations (increase in government regulation, standards, green taxes and incentives);
- Supply chain (pressure from suppliers to improve efficiency and become more sustainable);
- Employee recruitment, retention and motivation (many employees demonstrate greater commitment when they work for environmentally responsible firms);
- Innovation (going green requires a commitment to innovation, which can increase profits);
- Moral issues (many companies adopt a sustainability position because of the moral imperative to tackle environmental issues).

According to de Wild (2014), entrepreneurs' first interest should be the needs and preferences of the people they want to sell their goods or services to. Customers want sustainable products (products that can be recycled or reused); this is because close to 50 percent of the customers globally, are willing to pay more for sustainable products (Connors & Sweeney, 2019). For instance, Patagonia Company developed:

Woolyester, a material that blends wool, polyester and nylon to use approximately 50 percent of waste materials. The reason for this eco-friendly trend? It is what consumers want. Nearly 70 percent of CGS survey respondents said that sustainability is at least "somewhat important" to them when making a purchase and 47 percent would pay more for a sustainable product. (p. 1)

The demand for sustainable business practices does not only end with customers (at individual level) but has become a critical factor in selecting suppliers of big firms. For instance, any supplier that provides a product or service to Vodafone is screened for potential social, ethical and environmental risks, as defined by the Code of Ethical Purchasing (Vodafone Group Plc, 2018). Additionally, new suppliers are selected based on the supplier's production scale, the countries in which the activity takes place and the nature of the activity the supplier is engaged in. This is because some countries do operate based on a circular economy, thus such companies from those countries will be disadvantaged when applying to be a supplier for firms like Vodafone.

Globally, leading companies are recognising the growing demand for sustainability as a key driver for strategic products, services and business model innovation (Delloitte, 2012). In addition, businesses that view such a change as an opportunity and develop sustainable products and services are likely to command a higher market share than their competitors and to continue to operate efficiently as well as effectively in the changing world. Similarly, the Scottish Enterprise (2019) recognised that the advantages of adopting a sustainable business model stem from connecting to increasingly eco-conscious customers and to differentiating one's business from one's competitors. In addition, company employees are more likely to be motivated when they work for a company, which emphasises sustainable business practices. It was established by the Scottish Enterprise (2019) that companies, which do not adopt sustainable business practices, could leave their businesses exposed to volatile fuel prices, disruptions to the supply of raw materials and increased competition from competitors who are taking advantage of new sustainable business practices to expand their market share.

According to Delloitte (2012) in a study entitled 'sustainability for customer business companies':

The transition to more sustainable patterns of production and personal consumption is not optional. Government understands this and will regulate and tax accordingly to shape customer and business behaviours. Leading businesses recognise this as an opportunity and want to be part of the solution rather than to be part of the problem, as more and more customers look to buy smart and will increasingly establish new norms for socially accepted behaviours. (p.1)

Using the same line of thought, Best, Cramer, Olson and Park (2017), affirm that businesses that succeed in the future will be those that figure out how to harness these emerging innovations to address real human needs, placing sustainability at the heart of the business strategy. A list of possible entrepreneurial success criteria as adopted from Fakhrisadat et al. (2014) is as follows:

1. **Portability:** High yields, good profit margin;
2. **Growth:** Growth in the number of employees, sales, market share and/or distribution;
3. **Innovation:** Introduction of new products or production methods;
4. **Firm survival/continuity:** Enables generational transfer or can be sold with a profit;
5. **Contributing back to society:** Socially conscious, sustainable production methods;
6. **Personal satisfaction:** Through attaining important things in life, such as autonomy, challenge, security, power, creativity, etc.;
7. **Satisfied stakeholders:** Satisfied and engaged employees, satisfied customers;
8. **Good balance between work and private life:** Positive mutual influence between work and private life, allows time for yourself, family, and friends;
9. **Public recognition:** Good reputation, prize-winners;
10. **Utility or usefulness:** Organization fulfils a need in society; it provides an important service or product (p.45).

Researchers such as Fakhrisadat et al. (2014) have affirmed the demand for sustainable business practices as an ingredient to entrepreneurial success. At the same time, there are implications for businesses to adhere to sustainable business practices. According to Best et al. (2017), businesses now are required to implement business models, which deliver value for consumers consistent with environmental limits. One way companies can achieve sustainable business practices, is by producing sustainable products and services. However, according to Schaltegger and Wagner (2011) some of the sustainable products and services produced may have a limited effect and success if market conditions are very unfavourable. Thus, entrepreneurial activities aiming at sustainable development have to consider market issues and focus on influencing market conditions in order for the business to become a success.

SUSTAINABLE ENTREPRENEURSHIP CONTROVERSIES

Currently, it is difficult to conduct empirical comparative studies on the characteristics of entrepreneurship from country to country as researchers and practitioners use entrepreneurship and self-employment in different contexts with divergent understanding and definitions (Skrzek-Lubasińska & Szaban, 2018). For instance, Kuehl (as cited in Schaltegger & Wagner, 2011:1) note that various researchers define entrepreneurship differently as follows:

- Many authors concentrate on the process of a start-up company (e.g. Bennett as cited in Schaltegger & Wagner, 2011). In this view entrepreneurs are actors opening a new company and entrepreneurship is the process of creating and establishing a new company or organization;
- Another aspect of entrepreneurship is the striving for growth (Kyrö, Gartner, as cited in Schaltegger & Wagner, 2011). Entrepreneurs are viewed as actors enlarging companies and expanding businesses;
- Entrepreneurship has also been interpreted as a social movement (social entrepreneurship) or another kind of environmental grass-root or social concern movement (Pastakia, Mair & Marti, as cited in Schaltegger & Wagner, 2011). In this perspective entrepreneurs are actors changing existing consumption and production patterns on the basis of individual initiatives;

- Entrepreneurs are sometimes distinguished from traditional companies by their capability to innovate and to create competitive advantage (Risker, Schumpeter, Staber, Wiklund as cited in Schaltegger & Wagner, 2011). Entrepreneurship links inventions with market success;
- Finally entrepreneurship is characterised by the personal characteristics of a leader like ambition, leadership, team building personal involvement and commitment (Keogh & Polonsky, 1998).

According to Kele et al. (2017), many researchers do not clearly define or have conflicting definitions of the required entrepreneurial business management skills to establish successful businesses. This is because of the differing existing market conditions across countries where entrepreneurs operate. For instance, Bansal, Garg and Sharma (2019) argue that:

In developing countries where resources are scarce and banks and financial institutions are reluctant to lend financial support to SMEs, the governments have an even larger role to play by providing sources of financing for SME development. While lack of resources is considered the major barrier or hindrance to responsible business practices in SMEs, resource-poor entrepreneurs are looking for innovative business models in order to sustain themselves. (p.1)

Based on the above statement from Bansal et al. (2019), it can be concluded that entrepreneurs in developed countries are likely to easily have access to resources (business loans) compared to entrepreneurs in developing countries. Entrepreneurs in developing countries are likely to experience challenges to access business loans. Thus, the resource mobilization skill is not highly needed for entrepreneurs in such developed countries while in developing countries resource mobilisation is a critical skill needed for entrepreneurs to succeed in their businesses. Thus, when defining entrepreneurship skills needed in developed countries resource mobilisation is likely to be disregarded while in developing countries, it is likely to be one of the critical skills an entrepreneur needs to possess.

Heshmati (2015) established that businesses, which operate, based on sustainable business practices have a high environmental and social performance but low market share, while businesses, which operate within a linear economic model, have a low environmental and social performance but high market share. This indicates that governments of many countries in the world are likely to promote businesses operating on linear economic models as in many cases their main aim is to solve the unemployment problem in order to win votes/confidence from the masses. This is because entrepreneurship acts as a cure for unemployment and growth problems that are caused by the recent global economic crisis (Aúkun & Yıldırım, 2011). This is based on the logic that, the higher the profit the business makes the higher the chances to expand such a business resulting in many employment opportunities.

Sustainable business practices are likely to experience resistance from entrepreneurs as such business models are likely to lead to reduction in the entrepreneurs' profit margins. This is because sustainable business practices enable a company to have a system of interconnected business activities that are oriented towards resolving social and environmental issues, than focusing on profit generation (Baumgartner, Dentchev, Dieleman, Johannsdottis, Jonker, Nyberg, Rauter, Rosano, Snihur, Tang, & van Hoof, 2016). However, in future, the decision of a company to get involved in sustainability innovation will be triggered by a number of factors, which can relate for instance to changes or application of regulations and laws. For example, the Environmental Protection Agency (EPA) found that many Volkswagen (VW) cars being sold in the United State of America (USA) had a "defeat device" or software in diesel engines that could detect when they were being tested for pollution (British Broadcasting Corporation [BBC],

2015). The device was programmed to change the car engine performance accordingly in order to deliver results, which indicate that the car engine does not cause pollution above the legal allowed pollution level.

Contrary to the above statements, Arabska and Terziev (2017) established that entrepreneurs who start social enterprises (based on sustainable business practices) may derive less than half their income through commercial activity while mature social enterprises aim to generate close to 100% of their income from commercial activity. Furthermore, entrepreneurs who are engaged in social enterprises are likely to benefit from support networks and greater economies of scale. This is because, once a lot of people are involved with social enterprises, there are opportunities for inter-trading, partnership working and consortia bids for public procurement contracts, leading to further growth.

According to Geels (as cited in Hörisch, 2015: p.287) "the empirical domains where sustainability transitions are most needed are characterised by large firms. This poses the question of whether entrepreneurship and start-ups are, in turn, unimportant for sustainability transitions". This is likely because large firms operates on a large economic business scale compared to SMEs which are run by start-up entrepreneurs with a very small market share which requires small scale business operations. Correspondingly, to Grigorescu et al. (2017), most of the researchers, who study sustainability entrepreneurship address large and industrial companies as agents to implement sustainability, and in doing so, they sometimes overlook SMEs. In many cases, such researchers believe that SMEs are generally one-step behind in their implementation of environmental measures.

SUSTAINABLE ENTREPRENEURSHIP AND ITS CHALLENGES

Many entrepreneurs (with start-up businesses) do not seek the managerial skills and knowledge needed for successful management of their small enterprises (Mokroš & Papulová, 2007). This is due to the high self-confidence of some entrepreneurs, that they believe more in their ability rather than hiring somebody else or paying attention to educating themselves to gain the needed knowledge and managerial skills. Amaia, Aparicio and Iturralde (2019) established that entrepreneurial education programs could help people to improve their attitudes, overall entrepreneurial activity and motivation when conducting businesses. However, entrepreneurship courses in universities in Turkey and South Africa are not sufficient to provide entrepreneurship and business management skills that are required for creating entrepreneurs that can contribute to economic growth and employment (Aúkun & Yıldırım, 2011; Kele et al., 2017). According to Kele et al. (2017), after receiving entrepreneurship education, students still need practical (on the job training) exposure to financial management, human resource management, leadership, personality, marketing, technical and business management skills. A similar study done in Poland by Staniewski and Szopiński (2015) revealed that Polish university students exhibit a strong interest in establishing their own businesses. However, student business successes could be increased if institutions financing and supporting business activities promote entrepreneurial behaviour and cooperate more closely with universities, which naturally foster entrepreneurship and innovation.

There might be a need for the involvement of the industry (successful entrepreneurs) to mentor new entrepreneurs in order to lessen the time needed for new entrepreneurs to succeed in their businesses. This is in line with a study by Sousa (2018), in which entrepreneurship, management and successful entrepreneurs identified leadership skills as a key element to potentiate the entrepreneurial capacity of the students when leading their teams. According to Heshmati (2015), socio-cultural conditions and institutional realities affect the adoption of sustainable business practices by entrepreneurs. Moreover, many entrepreneurs have limited management and leadership skills to comply with regulations and tight regulatory frameworks and requirements for businesses, which operate, based on sustainable business practices. Zamfir, Mocanu and Grigorescu (2017) conclude that such entrepreneurs who operate based on sustainable business practices use circular economy practices, which fall under the framework of entrepreneurial sustainability.

According to the Scottish Enterprise (2019) and Hörisch (2015), globally, most businesses are not keen to operate on a sustainable business model because such models encourage reduction in the use of raw materials while in many cases profits are made by increasing the consumption of goods and services. This is because economic growth correlates with growth of energy and material throughput (Johanisova et al. as cited in Hörisch, 2015). Also, companies usually get short term pressures from investors to maximise profits at the expense of sustainability as in most cases such companies face organisational challenges of integrating environmental performance into the economic business logic (Scottish Enterprise, 2019; Schaltegger & Wagner, 2011). Sustainable entrepreneurs place profit generation in a secondary role of importance, for the benefit of employers, the community, and nature (Grigorescu et al., 2017). As such, sustainable entrepreneurs (Grigorescu et al., 2017) prioritise social and environmental benefits. On the other hand, the Scottish Enterprise (2019) observed that many businesses provide low purchase prices, which are attractive to consumers, and this may be at the expense of sustainable design and product quality. This is because sustainable products and services are usually produced at a high cost while the benefits to consumers of the improved product design are not appealing to customers as in many cases the price dictates. Additionally, sustainable entrepreneurs mostly follow a de-growth business logic in the sense that they limit the market effect of their own venture (Hörisch, 2015). Sustainable entrepreneurs usually target small markets because they are required to reduce the energy or use renewable energy and materials to achieve their sales targets (Hörisch, 2015). By doing so, they support the provisioning of sustainable products and services to local communities, resulting in pollution reduction.

Circular economic business models have become a basic national policy in many countries. This is done in order to resolve effectively the dilemma between economic growth and resource shortages or environmental degradation (Hong, Liang & Zhao, 2018). Even though many international communities such as the World Commission on Environment and Development (WCED) have actively promoted the development of circular economic business models; and many countries around the world have passed laws and regulations promoting sustainable practices, numerous environmental problems remain unsolved, such as climate change or resource scarcity (Hong et al., 2018; Hörisch, 2015). These environmental challenges hinder current generations, particularly in the developing countries, from achieving their goals.

SOLUTIONS AND RECOMMENDATIONS

There is a need to embrace the circular economy concept in order to integrate the new business model in entrepreneurship business processes (Laubscher & Marinelli, 2014). In addition, the circular economy business model can be integrated in six key areas, namely, the business sales model, product design and material composition, information technology and data management, supply loops, strategic sourcing for own operations and human resources and incentives. Additionally, the circular business model needs to encourage sustainable entrepreneurship business management processes. In order to promote sustainable business practices further it is imperative to improve the current and develop new regulations, environmental, health awareness, and various sustainable innovation policy and incentive programs for businesses, which operate, based on the circular economic principles (Heshmati, 2015; Hörisch, 2015). Many countries like Sweden for a long time successfully introduced various incentive programs for the implementation of sustainable business models (Heshmati, 2015). Correspondingly, Daalderop (2016:1) discovered that "the circular entrepreneurship is purposefully educating the masses and stimulating action; thereby influencing the cognitive and normative institutions. The circular entrepreneurship mainly uses regulative institutions that are set-up to mitigate the externalised costs of the linear economy".

Challenging the problem of resource shortage and environmental pollution, the idea of circular economic business models has attracted widespread attention as the demand for sustainable products and services continues to increase (Hong et al., 2018). To address these problems, several industrial companies and entrepreneurs have incorporated sustainable business practices in their operations or designs. The European Union countries are already promoting the circular economy since they intend to become a recycling society to bring about many changes and provide new opportunities to potential entrepreneurs (Dahl, Hughes, Husgafvel, Kanerva, & Linkosalmi, 2018). Thus, there is a need for sustainable entrepreneurs to apply sustainable business practices by generating new products, services, techniques and organisational modes that substantially reduce environmental impacts and increase the quality of life (Schaltegger & Wagner, 2011). This is because sustainable entrepreneurs destroy existing conservative production methods, products, market structures and consumption patterns, and replace them with superior environmental and social products and services (Schaltegger & Wagner, 2011). Hörisch (2015) who asserts that there is a need for a sustainable product development policy, which promotes production of sustainable products and services, corroborates this. The produced products/services need to have an integrated product policy for the life cycle management of good and services to ensure continuation of supply.

FUTURE TRENDS

According to Laubscher and Marinelli (2014), there is a call on the European policy makers to create the right conditions for the circular economy. This is because the circular economy is a sustainable development strategy that has been proposed to tackle urgent problems of environmental degradation and resource scarcity; as the circular economy 3R principles are to reduce, reuse and recycle materials (Heshmati, 2015). Premised on the analysed literature, it can be concluded that a circular economy business model has potential to establish successful businesses with societal and environmental benefits likely exceeding linear business models.

Entrepreneurship has been promoted as a vehicle for growth and poverty alleviation in Africa as entrepreneurship has gained wide acceptance from experts and policy makers in many African countries (Economic Commission for Africa, 2019). This has culminated in changes in the role of the Non-Governmental Organizations (NGOs) and People's Organizations (Pos). Their roles are slowly shifting from the relief types of activities to more complicated entrepreneurship development oriented actions, since the need to equip entrepreneurs with income, generating business skills has become very crucial (Economic Commission for Africa, 2019). Thus, there is increasing support from donor organisations, as well as bilateral and multilateral aid organisations engaged in poverty alleviation by investing in entrepreneur development.

FURTHER AREAS OF RESEARCH

Having only business management and entrepreneurship skills is not enough to achieve business success, thus there is a need for studies geared towards intergrating leadership, management and entrepreneurship in order to realise business successes (Dayi & Esmer, 2016; Sousa, 2018). According to Dayi and Esmer (2016), entrepreneurial leadership is a new and modern type of leadership that is a combination of leadership and entrepreneurship. Entrepreneurial leadership involves creating new products, new processes and expansion opportunities in existing businesses, thus contributing to the change of current services and policies implemented by civil society organisations and governments.

There is a need for a study to explore how entrepreneurs can be both profit and sustainable oriented. This recommended study is in line with a discovery by Baumgartner et al. (2016:1), which established that "it is not yet well researched or understood how alternative, often new, creative or innovative sustainable business models function and how their application in the real world evolve to create value without predominantly generating only profit in their ventures". Similarly, Hahn et al. (2018) highlight that there are few researches which explore sustainable business models with regard to their ability to successfully operate on commercial markets as a prerequisite of achieving social and ecological goals.

Adopted from Baumgartner et al. (2016:1), there is a need for a study to investigate and recommend the intended roles of governments in stimulating and/or controlling sustainable business models. To be successful, this agenda hinges on sustainable business practices, without inhibiting the development of entrepreneurship across countries. Success because of government policies has already been recorded, for instance, China's Industrial Park Recycling Transformation (IPRT) policies, and projects revealed successful practices (Yun Hu, Ke, Lee, Li, Luo & Wen, 2018). Success was reported in areas such as water resource conversion, recycling projects, energy saving projects, pollution prevention projects, platform construction projects, and infrastructure construction sharing projects (Yun et al., 2018). However, the policies experienced challenges as deficiencies were recorded in industrial development, management, policy-making, and information sharing. Government policies' intervention to implement sustainable business practices need be accompanied by staff development trainings to upgrade entrepreneurship, and business management skills of entrepreneurs in order for businesses to become sustainable.

CONCLUSION

Business management skills such as planning, controlling business processes, decision-making, leadership, marketing, finance and selling are pre-requests to entrepreneurship skills for start-up business success. In order to succeed in sustainable entrepreneurship, business skills should be integrated into entrepreneurship skills. An entrepreneur needs self-efficacy, innovativeness to take control of the business activities, articulate a need for achievement and be able take calculated risks while applying business management skills. Thus, an entrepreneur's success is highly dependent on his/her business management skills and knowledge.

Entrepreneurship education at universities is inadequate as it fails to provide all the required entrepreneurship and business management skills for graduates to succeed in their start-up businesses. University graduates are in dire need of practical exposure to entrepreneurship, business management processes and mentorship from experienced entrepreneurs in order to be successful in their businesses.

There is a need to establish business incubators for new entrepreneurs for them to be trained in business management in order to maximise entrepreneurship successes.

Few people are likely to engage in sustainable entrepreneurship because it is not profit oriented, but social and ecologically oriented. Notably, the priority for sustainable entrepreneurs is to solve social and environment problems instead of generating profit. Sustainable business practices can have a great impact and influence on maximising social and ecological benefits from business only when large firms are encouraged to use regulations and laws at a global level. For instance, the United Nations can compel all member countries to enforce sustainable business practices in support of establishing a global circular economic business model.

REFERENCES

Agbim, C. K. (2013). The Relative Contribution of Management Skills to Entrepreneurial Success: A Survey of Small and Medium Enterprises (SMEs) in the Trade Sector. *IOSR Journal of Business and Management, 7*(1). Retrieved November 17, 2019 from http://www.iosrjournals.org/iosr-jbm/papers/Vol7-issue1/B0710816.pdf?id=5304

Almeida, D. M., & Sousa, J. M. (2014). *Entrepreneurial Skills Development*. Retrieved November 16, 2019 from https://www.researchgate.net/publication/268816221_Entrepreneurial_Skills_Development

Amaia, M., Aparicio, G., & Iturralde, T. (2019). Conceptual structure and perspectives on entrepreneurship education research: A bibliometric review. *European Research on Management and Business Economics, 25*(3), 105–113. doi:10.1016/j.iedeen.2019.04.003

Arabska, E., & Terziev, V. (2017). Social Enterprises: A Sustainable Business Model. *The British Journal for the Philosophy of Science*, 1113–1126. https://ssrn.com/abstract=3142935

Aúkun, B., & Yıldırım, N. (2011). Insights on Entrepreneurship Education in Public Universities in Turkey: Creating Entrepreneurs Or Not? *Procedia: Social and Behavioral Sciences, 24*, 663–676. doi:10.1016/j.sbspro.2011.09.050

Bansal, S., Garg, I., & Sharma, D. G. (2019). Social Entrepreneurship as a Path for Social Change and Driver of Sustainable Development: A Systematic Review and Research Agenda. *Sustainability, 11*(4), 1091. doi:10.3390u11041091

Baumgartner, R., Dentchev, N., Dieleman, H., Johannsdottis, L., Jonker, L., Nyberg, T., ... van Hoof, B. (2016). Embracing the variety of sustainable business models: Social entrepreneurship, corporate intrapreneurship, creativity, innovation, and other approaches to sustainability challenges. *Journal of Cleaner Production, 113*, 1–4. doi:10.1016/j.jclepro.2015.10.130

Behrens, A., Drabik, E., Kranendijk, S., Rinaldi, D., Rizos, V., Stuchtey, M., & Tuokko, K. (2018). *Markets, Processes and Enabling Policies The Role of Business in the Circular Economy*. Retrieved November 17, 2019 from https://www.researchgate.net/publication/324013764_The_Role_of_Business_in_the_Circular_Economy_Markets_Processes_and_Enabling_Policies

Best, E., Cramer, A., Olson, E., & Park, J. (2017). *The Future of Sustainable Business: New Agenda, New Approach, New Advocacy*. Retrieved December 18, 2019 from https://www.bsr.org/reports/BSR_The_Future_Sustainable_Business.pdf

Bohoris, A. G., & Vorria, E. P. (2007). *Leadership vs Management a Business Excellence / Performance Management view*. Retrieved January 21, 2020 from https://www.ep.liu.se/ecp/026/076/ecp0726076.pdf

Boufaden, N. (2018). *Entrepreneurship and Business Growth Affiliation*. Retrieved January 19, 2020 from https://www.researchgate.net/publication/326479296_Entrepreneurship_and_Business_Growth

British Broadcasting Corporation (BBC). (2015). *Volkswagen: The scandal explained*. Retrieved December 5, 2019 from https://www.bbc.com/news/business-34324772

Connors, K., & Sweeney, S. (2019). *CGS Survey Reveals Sustainability Is Driving Demand and Customer Loyalty: Consumer expectations are high for eco-friendly products, especially with Gen Z buyers*. Retrieved November 30, 2019 from https://www.globenewswire.com/news-release/2019/01/10/1686144/0/en/CGS-Survey-Reveals-Sustainability-Is-Driving-Demand-and-Customer-Loyalty.html

Cooney, M. T. (2012). *Entrepreneurship Skills for Growth-Orientated Businesses*. Retrieved November 10, 2019 from http://www.oecd.org/cfe/leed/cooney_entrepreneurship_skills_HGF.pdf

Daalderop, T. (2016). *Circular Entrepreneurship, the case of Urban Agriculture in the Circular Economy*. Retrieved January 26, 2020 from https://edepot.wur.nl/385546

Dahl, O., Hughes, M., Husgafvel, R., Kanerva, J., & Linkosalmi, L. (2018). Forest sector circular economy development in Finland: A regional study on sustainability driven competitive advantage and an assessment of the potential for cascading recovered solid wood. *Journal of Cleaner Production*, *181*, 483–497. doi:10.1016/j.jclepro.2017.12.176

Dayi, F., & Esmer, Y. (2016). Entrepreneurial Leadership: A Theoretical Framework. *Proceedings of the 25th International Academic Conference in Paris on 06-09 September 2016*. Retrieved November 28, 2019 from https://www.researchgate.net/publication/323365395_ENTREPRENEURIAL_LEADERSHIP_A_THEORETICAL_FRAMEWORK

de Wild, D. (2014). *Business Skills Training Course for Beneficiaries of Microeconomic Initiatives*. Retrieved November 12, 2019 from https://shop.icrc.org/icrc/pdf/view/id/1909

Deloitte. (2012). *Sustainability for customer business companies: A story of growth*. Retrieved January 8, 2020 from https://www2.deloitte.com/content/dam/Deloitte/global/Documents/Consumer-Business/dttl_cb_Sustainability_Global%20CB%20POV.pdf

Economic Commission for Africa. (2019). *Small Business Management: A Training Manual*. Retrieved November 24, 2019 from https://repository.uneca.org/bitstream/handle/10855/572/Bib-9145.pdf;jsessionid=CF0E6728F6A1DD5249BFF70459CE31EB?sequence=1

Fakhrisadat, N., Narges, I., & Zahra, A. (2014). Explaining the Role of Managerial Skills of Entrepreneurship in Business Success. *International Journal of Management Sciences*, *4*(1), 42–52. https://www.researchgate.net/publication/313824665_Explaining_the_Role_of_Managerial_Skills_of_Entrepreneurship_in_Business_Success

Farayibi, A. O. (2017). Entrepreneurship as a Driver of Economic Growth: Evidence from Enterprise Development in Nigeria. *SSRN Electronic Journal*. Retrieved November 19, 2019 from https://www.researchgate.net/publication/309374424_Entrepreneurship_as_a_Driver_of_Economic_Growth_Evidence_from_Enterprise_Development_in_Nigeria_Entrepreneurship_as_a_Driver_of_Economic_Growth_Evidence_from_Enterprise_Development_in_Nigeria

Feit, K., & Pisapia, J. (2014). Entrepreneurial Leadership at a Crossroads. *Management and Organization*. Retrieved December 31, 2019 from http://www.untag-smd.ac.id/files/Perpustakaan_Digital_1/ENTREPRENEURSHIP%20Crossroads%20of%20entrepreneurship.pdf

Grigorescu, A., Mocanu, C., & Zamfir, A. (2017). Circular Economy and Decision Models among European SMEs. *Sustainability*, *9*(9), 1–15. doi:10.3390u9091507

Hahn, R., Ince, I., & Spieth, P. (2018). Business model design in sustainable entrepreneurship: Illuminating the commercial logic of hybrid businesses. *Journal of Cleaner Production*, *176*, 439–451. doi:10.1016/j.jclepro.2017.12.167

Heshmati, A. (2015). *A Review of the Circular Economy and its Implementation*. Retrieved November 27, 2019 from http://ftp.iza.org/dp9611.pdf

Hong, C., Liang, W., & Zhao, G. (2018). Performance assessment of circular economy for phosphorus chemical ðrms based on VIKOR-QUALIFLEX method. *Journal of Cleaner Production*, *196*, 1365-1378. doi:10.1016/j.jclepro.2018.06.147

Hörisch, J. (2015). The Role of Sustainable Entrepreneurship in Sustainability Transitions: A Conceptual Synthesis against the Background of the Multi-Level Perspective. *Administrative Sciences*, *5*(4), 286–300. doi:10.3390/admsci5040286

Hu, Y. Y., Ke, S., Lee, C.J.K., Li, H., Luo E., & Wen, Z. (2018). Approaches and policies for promoting industrial park recycling transformation (IPRT) in China: Practices and lessons. *Journal of Cleaner Production*, *172*, 1370-1380. Retrieved October 16, 2019 from www.elsevier.com/locate/jclepro

Huang, B., Plas, L., & Salam, N. (2016). *Exploring Prospective Entrepreneurial Engagement and Stakeholders' Involvement in the Circular Economy: An Empirical Study on the Concept of Växjö Reuse Village*. Retrieved November 29, 2019 from https://pdfs.semanticscholar.org/689b/41720bbe6beff5e7cdf7778a4a98b5110fae.pdf

Insight, S. B. (2019). *The Nordic Market for Circular Economy: Attitudes, Behaviours & Business Opportunities*. Retrieved October 23, 2019 from https://www.nordea.com/Images/37-308788/Circular%20Economy%2019_small.pdf

Johnston, M. P. (2014). Secondary Data Analysis: A Method of which the Time Has Come. *Qualitative and Quantitative Methods in Libraries*, *3*, 619–626.

Kele, T., Kerrin, M., & Mamabolo, M. A. (2017). Entrepreneurship management skills requirements in an emerging economy: A South African outlook. *The Southern African Journal of Entrepreneurship and Small Business Management*, *9*(1), 2071-3185. Retrieved November 16, 2019 from https://www.researchgate.net/publication/317127302_Entrepreneurship_management_skills_requirements_in_an_emerging_economy_A_South_African_outlook

Keogh, P., & Polonsky, M. J. (1998). Environmental commitment: A basis for environmental entrepreneurship. *Journal of Organizational Change Management*, *11*(1), 38–49. doi:10.1108/09534819810369563

Kerr, P. S., Kerr, R. W., & Xu, T. (2017). *Personality Traits of Entrepreneurs: A Review of Recent Literature*. Retrieved December 10, 2019 from https://www.hbs.edu/faculty/publication%20files/18-047_b0074a64-5428-479b-8c83-16f2a0e97eb6.pdf

Kranendijk, S., & Stuchtey, M. R. (2018). *The Role of Business in the Circular Economy Markets, Processes and Enabling Policies Report of a CEPS Task Force*. Retrieved November 2, 2019 from https://circulareconomy.europa.eu/platform/sites/default/files/rolebusinesscirculareconomytfr.pdf

Lahti, T., Parida, V., & Wuncent, J. (2018). A Definition and Theoretical Review of the Circular Economy, Value Creation, and Sustainable Business Models: Where Are We Now and Where Should Research Move in the Future? *Sustainability*, *10*(8), 2799. doi:10.3390u10082799

Laubscher, M., & Marinelli, T. (2014). *Integration of Circular Economy in Business*. Retrieved November 7, 2019 from https://www.researchgate.net/publication/270207909_Integration_of_Circular_Economy_in_Business

Liraz, M. (2013). *How to Improve Your Leadership and Management Skills Effective Strategies for Business Managers*. Retrieved November 3, 2019 from http://www.liraz.com/leadership-and-management-skills.pdf

Lowden, J. S. (2007). *Managerial Skills for the Entrepreneur*. Retrieved December 7, 2019 from https://pdfs.semanticscholar.org/649b/9b7ef100768078739d96873eee6027b8546d.pdf

Mair, J., & Seelos, C. (2005). Social entrepreneurship: Creating new business models to serve the poor. *Business Horizons*, *48*(3), 241–246. doi:10.1016/j.bushor.2004.11.006

Manimala, J. M., & Prasad, A. (2018). *Circular Social Innovation: A New Paradigm for India's Sustainable Development*. Retrieved November 30, 2019 from https://www.springerprofessional.de/en/circular-social-innovation-a-new-paradigm-for-india-s-sustainabl/15733952

Mokroš, M., & Papulová, Z. (2007). *Importance of Managerial Skills and Knowledge in Management for Small Entrepreneurs*. Retrieved October 25, 2019 from https://www.g-casa.com/PDF/Papulova-Mokros.pdf

Mwakio, E. M. (2018). *Business skills and entrepreneurship development training and planning manual for Potato producer cooperatives and youth groups*. Retrieved October 26, 2019 from https://cgspace.cgiar.org/bitstream/handle/10568/99165/avcd_cip_manual.pdf?sequence=1&isAllowed=y

Omolara, A. E. (2018). *Entrepreneurial skills and growth of Small and Medium Enterprise (SMEs): A comparative analysis of Nigerian entrepreneurs and Minority entrepreneurs in the UK*. Retrieved October 17, 2019 from https://mpra.ub.uni-muenchen.de/86751/1/MPRA_paper_86751.pdf

Passari, C. E. (2019). *The Business of Globalization and the Globalization of Business*. Retrieved November 15, 2019 from https://journals.lib.unb.ca/index.php/JCIM/article/view/5666/10661

Sariatli, F. (2017). Linear Economy versus Circular Economy: A Comparative and Analyzer Study for Optimization of Economy for Sustainability. *Visegrad Journal on Bioeconomy and Sustainable Development*, 31-34. Retrieved November 12, 2019 from https://www.researchgate.net/publication/318183876_Linear_Economy_Versus_Circular_Economy_A_Comparative_and_Analyzer_Study_for_Optimization_of_Economy_for_Sustainability

Schaltegger, S., & Wagner, M. (2011). Sustainable entrepreneurship and sustainability innovation: categories and interactions. *Business Strategy and the Environment*. Retrieved October 19, 2019 from https://www.academia.edu/10906857/Sustainable_entrepreneurship_and_sustainability_innovation_categories_and_interactions

Scottish Enterprise. (2019). *Sustainable Business Models*. Retrieved October 21, 2019 from https://ecoknights.org.my/images/doc/Sustainable-Business-Models.pdf

Skrzek-Lubasińska, M., & Szaban, J. (2018). Self-Employment and Entrepreneurship: A Theoretical Approach. *Journal of Management and Business Administration. Central Europe*, *26*(2), 89–120. https://content.sciendo.com/view/journals/jmbace/26/2/article-p89.xml

Small Business Development Corporation. (2019). *Essential business skills*. Retrieved 12 September, 2019 from https://www.smallbusiness.wa.gov.au/business-advice/starting-your-business/business-skills

Sousa, J. M. (2018). Entrepreneurship Skills Development in Higher Education Courses for Teams Leaders. *Administrative Sciences*, *8*(18), 18. doi:10.3390/admsci8020018

Standing Committee for Economic and Commercial Cooperation of the Organization of the Islamic Cooperation (COMCEC). (2016). *Training Manual on Entrepreneurship and Management of Small Business for Women*. Retrieved October 30, 2019 from http://www.comcec.org/pcm/wp-content/uploads/2018/02/2016-GMBPOVER-206.pdf

Staniewski, M. W., & Szopiński, T. (2015) Student readiness to start their own business. *Economic Research-Ekonomska Istraživanja*, *28*(1), 608-619. Retrieved October 25, 2019 from https://www.tandfonline.com/doi/abs/10.1080/1331677X.2015.1085809?needAccess=true#aHR0cHM6Ly93d3cudGFuZGZvbmxpbmUuY29tL2RvaS9wZGYvMTAuMTA4MC8xMzMxNjc3WC4yMDE1LjEwODU4MDk/bmVlZEFjY2Vzcz10cnVlQEBAMA

Vodafone Group Plc. (2018). *Sustainable Business Report 2018*. Retrieved November 28, 2019 from https://www.vodafone.com/content/dam/vodcom/sustainability/pdfs/sustainablebusiness2018.pdf

Wautelet, T. (2018). *The Concept of Circular Economy: its Origins and its Evolution*. Retrieved October 29, 2019 from https://www.researchgate.net/publication/322555840_The_Concept_of_Circular_Economy_its_Origins_and_its_Evolution

ADDITIONAL READING

Daiva, B., & Rima, T. (2016). Sustainable Development: The Circular Economy Indicators' Selection Model. *Journal of Security & Sustainability Issues*, *6*(2), 315–323. doi:10.9770/jssi.2016.6.2(10)

Lewandowski, M. (2016). Designing the Business Models for Circular Economy: Towards the Conceptual Framework. *Sustainability*, *8*(1), 1–28. doi:10.3390u8010043

Najmaei, A. (2016). Sustainable Entrepreneurship: Business Success through Sustainability. *International Journal of Sustainable Entrepreneurship and Corporate Social Responsibility*, *1*(1), 46–47. https://www.researchgate.net/publication/312129989_Book_Review_Sustainable_Entrepreneurship_Business_Success_Through_Sustainability

Schaper, M. (Ed.). (2016). *Making Ecopreneurs: Developing Sustainable Entrepreneurship* (2nd ed.). London: Routledge Taylor and Francis Group. doi:10.4324/9781315593302

United Nation. (2017). *Promoting Entrepreneurship for Sustainable Development: A Selection of Business Cases from the Empretec Network*. Retrieved December 18, 2019 from https://unctad.org/en/PublicationsLibrary/diaeed2017d6_en.pdf

Zamfir, A. M., Mocanu, C., & Grigorescu, A. (2017). Circular Economy and Decision Models among European SMEs. *Sustainability*, *9*(9), 1507. doi:10.3390u9091507

KEY TERMS AND DEFINITIONS

Business Management Skills: Business management skills involve planning, decision making, motivating, marketing selling, financial management, customer service, communication and negotiation, leadership, project management, delegation, time management, problem solving, and networking.

Circular Economic Model: Is a business model which is not profit oriented but promotes the sustainable use of environmental and social resources.

Entrepreneurship: It is a process undertake by an individual or a group of people to start a successful business.

Linear Economic Model: Is a business model which is profit oriented and does not re-introduce raw materials back into the business products and services production process, resulting in environmental and social damages.

Raw Materials: Items used to produce a business product.

Social Entrepreneurship (SE): Business created to address social and environmental problems.

Sustainable Business Model: Is a business model based on sustainable business practices such as recycling, reuse and reduce materials needed to achieve end products/services of a business.

Chapter 27
Knowledge Management for the Circular Economy

Sulaiman Olusegun Atiku
https://orcid.org/0000-0001-9364-3774
Namibia University of Science and Technology, Namibia

ABSTRACT

The place of knowledge management in ensuring effective transition into a circular economy by developing a circular business model as an alternative to the conventional linear economic model is under-investigated. Knowledge coordination, creation, and dissemination capability of a firm are important in developing the green industry and offering new job opportunities. This chapter adopted a literature review approach to establish the link between knowledge management and transition into a circular economy. Findings show that the firm's eco-innovation process depends largely on strategic knowledge management. Therefore, systems understanding and self-motivated creativity are essential professional knowledge levels in developing circular business models for sustainability. Hence, firms need to enhance the knowledge-based for continuous business process improvement, eco-efficiency, and eco-innovation.

INTRODUCTION

There is a massive sensitization intimating the need for circularity and sustainability by major players in the global business environment. The ongoing sensitization came as a way of providing solutions to environmental problems such as biodiversity loss, water, air, and soil pollution, resource depletion, and excessive land use are increasingly jeopardising the earth's life-support systems (Geissdoerfer, Savaget, Bocken, & Hultink, 2017). The provision of information on circular economy through knowledge creation and application is necessary in developing professionals and organisational process for sustainable development. Knowledge sharing through data or information is also important for individual and organisational development. Therefore, management of such an important aspect of individual and organisational development could be regarded as an effort in the right direction.

Knowledge management can be referred to as a fundamental driver of eco-innovative performance in a circular economy. A circular economy is an alternative economic system that encourages reuse,

DOI: 10.4018/978-1-7998-5116-5.ch027

Copyright © 2020, IGI Global. Copying or distributing in print or electronic forms without written permission of IGI Global is prohibited.

sharing, repair, refurbishment, remanufacturing and recycling to create a closed system with the aim of minimising resource input and reduction of waste, pollution and emissions (Geissdoerfer et al., 2017). In a nutshell, such an economy promotes reduce, reuse and recycle (3R) policies (Geissdoerfer et al., 2017; Mohajan, 2019). Evidently, an effective knowledge management has been described as a critical ingredient for organisation seeking sustainable competitive advantage (Omotayo, 2015). For example, there is need for adequate investment and the will to promote eco-efficiency and eco-innovation (Fields & Atiku, 2017) for organisations to implement reuse and recycling applications (Mohajan, 2019) necessary to become resource-efficient (Tukker, 2015).

The chapter seeks to establish the interplay between knowledge management and circularity by showcasing the levels of professional knowledge required in advancing the circular business models for sustainability. This chapter provides insights on the place of professional knowledge (know-why and care-why) at various levels in an organisation for eco-efficiency and eco-innovation, leading to sustainable competitive advantage. This chapter positions that effective knowledge management could be used as a basis to promote green consciousness for individuals, and eco-innovation in creating green industries and jobs by investors or companies in the 21st century. This chapter is structured to provide the background of circular economy, and the challenges of different companies in adopting sustainable business practices. The methodology adopted to examine the place of knowledge management in promoting effective transition into a circular economy was also emphasised accordingly.

BACKGROUND

The term circular economy is a sustainable economic model developed as an alternative to the conventional linear economic model. The conventional economic model of produce-consume-waste posed a serious challenge to sustainable development. The circular economy as an alternative economic model has a long origin that could be traced back to the 1970s (Allwood, 2014). Specifically, Stahel and Reday introduced some of the features of circular economy in 1976 based on their focus on industrial economics (Geissdoerfer et al., 2017). The authors in their focus on industrial economics came up with the concept ‘a loop economy’ in their explanation of workplace strategies for resource-efficiency, job opportunities, and dematerialisation of the industrial economy. Circular economy became more pronounced as a concept in China in 1998 (Qi, et al., 2016).

Recently, circular economy has received many attention from policymakers, researchers and practitioners world-wide as a way of promoting sustainable development goals (Niero & Hauschild, 2017). For example, the European Commission’s action plan for circular economy aims at developing a sustainable, low carbon emission, resource-efficient and competitive European economy (European Commission, 2015). The reason is that the traditional linear production and consumption systems is detrimental to the environmental and social aspect of sustainability. Therefore, circular economy is regarded as a sustainable approach, which requires a transformation of both production and consumption systems (De los Rios, & Charnley, 2017). Circular economy is an alternative economic model that supports the implementation of resource-efficiency, reuse and recycling policies to promote sustainable development. Theoretically, some of the pertinent influences on circular economy are cradle to cradle, looped and performance economy, regenerative design, industrial ecology, biomimicry and blue economy (Ellen MacArthur Foundation, 2017). Some of these schools of thought focus on minimising waste and resource extradition (European Commission, 2015), economic growth potential (Ellen MacArthur Foundation, 2017), while others concentrate on environmental sustainability (Zink & Geyer, 2017).

The Cradle to Cradle was developed by Braunqart and McDonough in the 1990s as a design and/or concept, which stands for eco-innovation, quality and good design to describe healthier and potentially infinite use of materials in cycles (McDonough & Braungart, 2010). The first step in studying or implementing Cradle to Cradle is to consider its core principles, which are; waste, use current solar income, and celebrate diversity (Mulhall & Braungart, 2010). Accordingly, the first principle holds that waste is equal to food in the sense that everything is a nutrient for something else. The second (use current solar income) principle is based on the premise that energy can be renewed as it is being used. The third (celebrate diversity) principle supports species, cultural and innovation diversity. Evidently, cradle to cradle principles support two types of metabolisms (nutrient cycles) in the production and consumption systems (McDonough & Braungart, 2010; Mulhall & Braungart, 2010). The metabolisms for products or processes are biological (biosphere) and technical (technosphere) metabolisms or cycles. In the biological circle, which is products for consumption; materials are returned to the biosphere in form of manure from which new material are created. The technical circle is a domain of products for service in which the materials that are not consumed in the production process can be reprocessed or ingested into a new product line. The implementation of cradle to cradle design or proposition will support circularity and sustainability. Knowledge management in industries on circular economy is lacking, therefore, effective knowledge management is necessary for attainment of sustainable development goals.

The notion that economies and industrial society as a whole has transformed into information-based or knowledge-intensive industry overtaking the manufacturing industry as the main wealth creator could be traced back to the mid-1970s (Hislop, Bosua, & Helms, 2013; Spender, 2015). By implication, knowledge is now an essential commodity for growth and development. And then the emergence of knowledge-based global economy occasioned by information and communication technologies, and knowledge-intensive services (Hislop, Bosua, & Helms, 2013). This laid a solid foundation for effective management of knowledge in organisations.

Knowledge management in the context of circular economy for sustainable development could be referred to as an integral part of organisational learning and development. A fundamental part in knowledge management is accessibility of data and/or provision of essential information to the stakeholders within an organisation or transfer of credible information between groups or organisations (Paulin & Suneson, 2015). For example, knowledge sharing on 3R policies of circular economy should be adequately communicated in various industries. Similarly, a range of in-depth information on material composition to gain better insights about social behaviour is also necessary in promoting circularity (De los Rios & Charnley, 2017). Therefore, organisations operating in emerging economies need to consider putting policies in place for effective knowledge sharing in the areas of circularity and sustainability. The next section presents the challenges of different companies in the circular economy.

Challenges of Different Companies in the Circular Economy

Despites the economic, social and environmental imperatives of circular economy as advocated in global business environment by key policymakers, practitioners and researchers; companies operating in different sectors across the globe are confronted with some challenges hindering effective implementation of 3R policies. The following challenges are accounted for by the Circular Academy (2019), as factors hindering the smooth compliance to 3R policies of circular economy in companies:

- The first challenge confronting companies in implementing the policies of circular economy relates to achievability and desirability. Some companies are faced with the problem of attaining one hundred percent level of compliance. The question is how long can materials be reused and/or products be remanufactured, and how long can the loop be closed without ejecting waste? Finding answers to such questions without compromising quality and incurring higher cost of production is one of the biggest challenges of manufacturing companies (Circular Academy, 2019). For example, paper recycling is limited to a certain number of cycles. Moreover, the circular economy requires more energy for recycling or remanufacturing compared to the linear business model, thereby making provision for more waste;
- Besides the issues pertaining to one hundred percent achievability is the pressure to justify its desirability for business. Arguably, an attempt to reach a one hundred percent recyclability rate (Lewandowski, 2016) might be counterproductive (Circular Academy, 2019). For example, the price of recovery in most cases remains higher than the value of materials recovered along the process. Oghazi and Mostaghel (2018) put it that due to the required major upfront investments in circular business model, recycled materials are usually more expensive than in the linear business models;
- Another concern in the implementation process is that social sustainability is lacking in the core framework of circular economy. This implies that circular economy framework is deeply rooted in business and environmental sustainability, the description of social aspect of sustainability seems missing in the model. For example, the framework lacks fulfilment of human needs. Hence, there is need for "ethical circular economy training" to avoid the possibility of over-reliance on technology and recycled materials leaving out human sustainability (Khalamayzer, 2017; Lewandowski, 2016). This is one of the gaps that effective knowledge management for circular economy needs to fill;
- Organisational barriers such as cost of restructuring and the risks involved, as well as resistant to change among the stakeholders profiting from the linear business model are issues surrounding adoption of circular economy in companies (Oghazi & Mostaghel, 2018). These challenges might rule out the anticipated benefits of circular economy for companies and the environment;
- Lack of clear guidelines and standardisation (Circular Academy, 2019) for transition from linear business model to a circular business model (Oghazi & Mostaghel, 2018). This shows there is absence of supporting regulations in the midst of complexities associated with circularity. This chapter holds that there is need for effective knowledge management in order to promote business and environmental sustainability through circular business models. The next section explains the methodology adopted in this chapter to provide insights on the place of knowledge management in ensuring effective transition into a circular economy.

METHODOLOGY

This chapter adopted a literature-based methodology by examining the 'textual data", and showing the place of knowledge management in ensuring effective transition into a circular economy. A critical examination of literature was engaged in tracing the background of circular economy, and showcasing the challenges of different companies in implementing 3R policies. This approach provides understanding on the link between knowledge management and circular economy through the levels of professional knowledge that are essential in developing circular business models. The next section presents analysis on knowledge management, levels of professional knowledge, and knowledge management as a strategy for the circular economy.

KNOWLEDGE MANAGEMENT

Knowledge management is considered as the most basic work processes of companies (Shih et al 2018). Knowledge management is also described as an effective intervention by organisations for sustainable competitive advantage (Tseng, 2010). Duhon (1998) cited in Shih et al (2018) defines knowledge management as an integrated approach to identify, capture, evaluate, retrieve, and share all information, and this information can take the form of databases, documents, policies, procedures, or formerly uncaptured expertise and experience among individual workers. Similarly, knowledge management is "the deliberate and systematic coordination of an organisation's people technology, processes, and organisational structure in order to add value through reuse and innovation" (Dalkir, 2011, p. 4). This definition informs that knowledge management processes are important for business process improvement and development of circular business models.

In the context of eco-innovation for economic, social, and environmental sustainability, knowledge management capability of an organisation is an important activity that supports collective green intelligence and eco-efficiency required in developing green products and services in competitive and sustainable markets (Fields & Atiku, 2017). Therefore, knowledge coordination capability of an organisation is essential for continuous business process improvement (Atiku & Fields, 2018), pro-environmental behaviour, and sustainability (Atiku, 2019). Hence, organisations need to build structure and culture that support knowledge sharing within a system and/or knowledge transfer between groups for sustainable competitive advantage. There are two basic types of knowledge (i.e. explicit and tacit), which must be adequately coordinated within an organisation. For innovative performance in a circular economy, there is need for effective coordination of explicit and tacit knowledge in organisational design and work processes.

Explicit knowledge refers to information or learning content that has been recorded in many forms, namely; words, audio and video recordings, or graphs for easy retrieval, dissemination, and critical analysis of conceptual or operational frameworks for updates to meet the environmental needs (Dalkir, 2013). Explicit knowledge of various kinds are easily accessible in print (text-books, encyclopaedia, and subject specific magazines, among others) as well as electronic learning platforms. The knowledge coordination is the ability to create systems within an organisational structure for effective transmission of information for the purpose of improving employees and organisational capability. It includes ability to organise, systematise and translate a vision into a mission statement, as well as operational guidelines. Explicit knowledge enables the ability to disseminate, reproduce, access, and reapply information throughout the organisation in order to teach (Dalkir, 2013) or facilitate training and development programmes. For example, an explicit knowledge on circular economy built into work processes (Shih et al 2018) could promote employee green behaviour, and pro-environmental behaviour at organisational level (Atiku, 2019).

Tacit knowledge on the other hand can be described as the technical know-how, skills, dynamic capabilities and experiences developed on the job (Dalkir, 2011; Dalkir, 2013). Such experiential knowledge or capabilities are domicile in individual job holders, and are not readily access to others. Organisations should create a platform for effective transfer of technical know-how through job-sited management development. For example, through coaching and mentoring a technical know-how in specific role within an organisation may be codified or transferred from a superior officer to subordinates. This arrangement is essential for effective succession in case of resignation, sudden death or early retirement in organisations.

Levels of Professional Knowledge

The success of an organisation in recent times lies with professional intellect and system capabilities towards innovative performance rather than its physical capital (Atiku & Fields, 2018). Accordingly, the ability to manage professional intellect in promoting collective green intelligence, and developing eco-friendly products and services through process improvement and ensure talent retention are some of the requirements for sustained competitive advantage. Hence, the recent demand for sustainable business solutions by policy makers has created the need to manage professional intellect for sustainable economy. Quinn, Anderson, and Finkelstein (1998) cited in Nomura (2008), categorised professional knowledge into four levels, which are cognitive knowledge (know-what); advanced skills (know-how); systems understanding (know-why); and self-motivated creativity (care-why):

- Cognitive knowledge (know-what) could be described as the expertise in specific discipline that professionals have achieved through extensive training and certification (Nomura, 2008). This is important, but has no influence on business performance;
- Advanced skills (know-how) is the ability to translate explicit knowledge into work related outcomes (Jamal & Tilchin, 2016). It has to do with the ability to apply discipline-based rules or principles in providing solutions to complex business problems;
- Systems understanding (know-why) on the other hand can be referred to as in-depth understanding of network of cause-and-effect relationships or principles underlying a specialisation or practice (Quinn, Anderson, & Finkelstein, 1998; cited in Nomura, 2008). System understanding allows professionals to act beyond their day-to-day job responsibilities to application of the systems understanding in solving complex business problems and add value to innovative performance of an organization;
- Lastly, self-motivated creativity (care-why) has to do with self-efficacy, which is the will and desire for success. For example, a well-motivated and creative teams will make tremendous contribution towards continuous process improvement required for development of sustainable business models (Jamal & Tilchin, 2016). Therefore, systems understanding and self-motivated creativity knowledge levels are important in developing the critical thinking (Jamal & Tilchin, 2016) required for eco-innovation.

Knowledge Management as a Business Strategy

The place of knowledge management in promoting eco-efficiency and eco-innovation across the industries cannot be overemphasised in the circular economy. A knowledge management strategy that promotes eco-efficiency and eco-innovation could be regarded as a business strategy for sustainability. Eco-efficiency can be described as the ratio of value (economic value) a company adds to the waste it generates in the production process (Derwall, Guenster, Bauer, & Koedijk, 2005; Ehrenfeld, 2005). Basically, eco-efficiency is a ratio of some measures of economic value added to some measures of environmental impact (Ehrenfeld, 2005). The higher the value added, the more efficient is the use of environmental services. Eco-efficiency can be regarded as a useful tool for strategists and policy makers in the circular economy.

Eco-innovation from a policy maker's point of view is any form of innovation aiming at significant and demonstrable progress towards sustainable development goals, by reducing the environmental impact or achieving a more efficient and responsible use of natural resources (European Commission, 2013). Accordingly, eco-innovation refers to all forms of innovation (technological and non-technological) that create business opportunities and benefit the environment by preventing or reducing their impact, or by optimising the use of resources. Similarly, Eco-Innovation Observatory (2013) referred to eco-innovation as an introduction of any new or improved product (good or service), process, organisational change or marketing solution that reduces the use of natural resources (including materials, energy, water and land) and decreases the release of harmful substances across the whole life-cycle.

Companies are currently driven by environmental and social concerns, as such corporate strategies are formulated towards rethinking and/or redesigning business models to reduce costs and improve customers' experience (Eco-Innovation Observatory, 2013). Hence, alignment of knowledge management strategies with the corporate and environmental management strategy (Prieto-Sandoval, Jaca, Santos, Baumgartner, & Ormazabal, 2019) is fundamental in developing sustainable business models. For example, an integrated knowledge management strategy will enhance activities of the research and development unit (Díaz-García, González-Moreno, & Sáez-Martínez, 2015) towards inventing green products and services for sustainability. The next section provides discussions on the circular business models.

CIRCULAR BUSINESS MODELS

Circular business model is a sustainable business model developed in response to the global decline in resources or raw-materials, and to address the environmental issues. The focus of circular business model is centred on economic and environmental benefits. Circular business models represent solutions to move towards zero waste, reducing environmental impacts and increasing economic profit (Oghazi & Mostaghel, 2018). A point of concern in practice is the extent to which zero waste is achievable in the production and consumption systems. Perhaps, decrease in waste may be more appropriate in the context of a circular business model in practice. The Organisation for Economic Co-operation and Development (OECD, 2018) in its capacity as a custodian of better policies for better lives referred to circular business models as fundamentally different ways of producing and consuming goods and services. Accordingly, the circular business model is an initiative to promote a more resource efficient production and consumption systems; thereby reducing the environmental impact of human and economic activities. However, an in-depth understanding on design of sustainable business models is necessary to enhance the application of circular economy at organisational level (Lewandowski, 2016). This chapter offers explanation on the several circular business models that are essential in promoting sustainability. The five circular business models are circular supplies, resource recovery, product life extension, sharing platforms, and product as a service (Accenture, 2014).

Circular Supplies

The circular supplies is a sustainable economic model which relies on supply of renewable, recyclable and/or biodegradable material inputs in sustainable production and consumption systems (Accenture,

2014). This is an alternative model to the linear economic model, which seeks to eliminate waste by ensuring that the waste at a particular stage becomes a source of supply for remanufacturing in the flow of input and output circles. The rationale behind circular supplies business model is to provide solutions to the issues of resource depletion across the global and add value to the organisation.

Resource Recovery

Resource recovery is a circular business model targeted at recovering useful resources out of disposed products or by-products. This model enables companies to bring material wastage or leakage into minimal level, culminating into resource efficiency and circularity. In practice, it recovers embedded value at the end of one product lifecycle to feed into another by transforming waste into value through innovative recycling and upcycling services (Accenture, 2014). For instance, creating more than one product use lifecycles requires manufacturers to invest in innovative ways of using resources and materials for a long period. Accenture positions that solutions to the global paucity of resources range from industrial symbiosis to integrated closed loops recycling and Cradle-to-Cradle designs, where disposed products can be reprocessed into a new product. Statistically, the amount of recycled products in the global supply of industrial metals ranged between 15 and 35 percent in the last four decades (OECD, 2018).

Resource recovery as a circular business model is rooted in the traditional recycling market leveraging on technological innovations and its know-how to recover almost any type of resource output at a level of value equivalent to, or even above, that of the initial investment. For example, resource recovery business model is more pronounced in the manufacturing industry, particularly in the steel sector (OECD, 2018). Hence, recycling is a necessity in promoting reuse to attain high level of resource efficiency with the aim of reducing the environmental impact of human and industrial activities.

Product Life Extension

The term product life or lifetime is "the duration of the period that starts at the moment a product is released for use after manufacture and ends at the moment a product becomes obsolete beyond recovery at product level" (Den Hollander, Bakker, & Hultink, 2017, p. 519). Accordingly, products can have one or more use lifecycles, but only one lifetime. A shorter product lifetime which is inherent in the linear economic model is causing environmental degradation and paucity of natural resources (Word Bank, 2018). Hence, product life extension was developed as a responsive business model to overcome the environmental issues across the global (Ertz, Leblanc-Proulx, Sarigöllü, & Morin, 2019b).

Product life extension provides an opportunity to expand the lifecycle of goods and assets for the manufacturers. This business model allows companies to invest in the innovative ways of expanding the product lifecycles for economic, social and environmental sustainability. This model gives room for repairs, upgrades, refurbishment, remanufacture and reuse of products or components to ensure that they last longer or slowing the resource loops (Bocken, De Pauw, Bakker, & van der Grinten, 2016); thereby minimising the adverse effects of industrial activities on the environment (Accenture, 2014; Ertz, Leblanc-Proulx, Sarigöllü, & Morin, 2019a). In the context of product life extension, the goal of a manufacturer is to extend its product lifetime as long as possible. Such manufacturers need to understand the effective product life extension strategies for sustainable development. Product life extension strategies are sets of plans or approaches to extend the durability of products, slow the flow of constituent materials through the economy, and reduce the rate of resource extraction and waste generation (OECD, 2018; World

Bank, 2019). In the automobile industry, a car is a good example of a product that has been designed for durability, maintenance, and reparability. The components have more than one use lifecycles, providing opportunity for resource recovery and recycling.

Sharing Platforms

Sharing platforms is a circular business model that supports improved utilisation rate of products through an integrated platform for communal access to products by users (individuals or organisations) (Accenture, 2014). In other words, it is a service compensation model in which access to underutilised assets is being offered to other users by the owner (Circular Economy Practitioner Guide, 2018). Accordingly, the number of users of assets in a sharing platform is much greater, justifying the name of this change in behaviour as "collaborative consumption". For example, sharing platforms include; vehicle ride sharing, short-term accommodation rentals, available labour and expertise, tools and equipment, excess food supplies. This business model assists companies in attaining the highest level optimal utilisation of products or assets for the owners and other users. Arguably, over reliance on sharing platforms as a business model may add to the challenges of traditional manufacturer of the products or assets being shared (Accenture, 2014). For example, demand for such products may be forced to dwindle, resulting into an adverse effect on the sales revenue of the traditional manufacturers.

Product as a Service

The product as a service became prominent based on the need for innovative ways to close customer loops and providing additional services. Product as a service business model is an innovative circular business that enables companies or manufacturers to shift away from selling ownership of products to selling service or usage to customers (Accenture, 2014). Accordingly, it offers product access to customers, but affords companies the opportunity to retain ownership of their products. The companies or manufacturers provide for the maintenance of such products as the owners, as well as providing benefits to the customers. The customers pay for the utility derived from such products. Therefore, companies are encouraged to produce sustainable products in order to reduce waste generation (OECD, 2018; World Bank, 2019).

This business model makes resource recovery much easier for recycling, refurbishing and remanufacturing when companies retain the ownership of their products (Bocken, De Pauw, Bakker, & van der Grinten, 2016). In a nutshell, product as a service is an alternative business model to the conventional "buy and own" business model. Customers only pay for the service derived from the usage of such products, while companies retain the ownership of their products.

By extension product as a service is a sustainable model that gives room for resource recovery, and product remanufacturing in a circular economy. For example, a remanufactured part in Renault's remanufacturing process resulted into a high level of efficiency; which indicates 80% less energy, 88% less water, 92% fewer chemical products, and generates 70% less waste during production comparing to new parts (Perella, 2014). These statistics indicate that recycling or remanufacturing in the automotive industry is very efficient and would be of great benefits to other companies in the industry if embraced accordingly. The next section presents the benefits of circular economy.

BENEFITS OF CIRCULAR ECONOMY

A circular economy is beneficial to both internal and external stakeholders of an organisation. The internal stakeholders that benefit from responsible business solutions include employees, managers, board of directors and shareholders (Laurenti, Martin, & Stenmarck, 2018). Accordingly, the external stakeholders are customers, regulators and suppliers, and the society at large. Therefore, the circular business models analysed above are fundamental for effective transition into a circular economy, and are beneficial to different stakeholders in the following areas.

Creation of Green Industries and Jobs

Development of circular business model and effective transition to a circular economy creates an opportunity for investments in green industries for investors who are interested in producing goods and services that are eco-friendly (Edwards, Sutton-Grier, & Coyle, 2013). It creates job opportunities for individuals who are interested in working on projects that require high level of green creativity and innovation (stimulating eco-innovation); essential for sustainable development (Global Environment Facility, 2019). Apart from creating investment and job opportunities for investors and job seekers respectively, it offers opportunity for customers who prefer to patronise green industries for products and services that are eco-friendly.

Reduced Importation of Raw Materials

Another benefit of the circular business models has to do with reduced dependence on the importation of raw materials (Haas, Krausmann, Wiedenhofer, & Heinz, 2015; MacArthur, 2013). The circular economy offers opportunity to reconfigure the product lifecycles. For example, the product life extension, resource recovery and product as a service are circular business models (Accenture, 2014) that afford manufacturers the opportunity to overcome the issue of overdependence on importation of raw materials. The policies of circular economy are reduce, reuse and recycle afford the opportunity to overcome the global issues of paucity of raw materials and resource depletion (Geissdoerfer et al., 2017; Mohajan, 2019). Therefore, the manufacturers are able to minimise the cost of production, which will ultimately result to reduction in price of goods and services. Hence, reduced dependence on importation of raw materials are beneficial to manufacturers, customers, and the environment by reducing carbon emission with less importation of raw materials.

Avoidance of Environmental Damage Caused by Resource Extraction

Transition into circular economy through circular business model helps in reducing the environmental damage as a result of resource extraction (Lèbre, Corder, & Golev, 2017a). Resource extraction impact on the environment. For example, soil degradation, water shortages, biodiversity loss, damage to ecosystem functions and global warming exacerbation (Zhao et al. 2019) is avoidable in a circular economy. The benefits include reducing pressure on the environment, and improving the security of supply of raw-materials. Avoidance of environmental damage through resource extraction is an effort to ensure social and environmental sustainability (Tayebi-Khorami, Edraki, Corder, & Golev, 2019), which is beneficial to all stakeholders.

Less Pollution Entering the Earth's Life Support Systems

The pollution entering the earth's life support systems can be reduced by adopting the circular business models. For example, a circular economy would minimise the ill effects of pollution, through such measures as redesigning products to cut waste and make products last longer, encouraging recycling and reuse; using plastic wastes as a resource (Global Environment Facility, 2019). A circular economy is beneficial in managing waste generation and industrial pollution for a safer human health and the environment. Therefore, the journey towards a pollution free world is attainable through circular business models that promote sustainable use of plastics, reuse, recycle, and reduce waste (United Nations Environment Programme, 2017). Also, knowledge sharing on the impact of human activities or consumption and disposal of wastes in developed and developing countries will go a long way in reducing the level of pollution entering the earth's life support systems.

Waste Management

A circular business model is effective in managing the entire waste cycle; from waste prevention, reuse and recycling to resource recovery and disposal (Lèbre, Corder, & Golev, 2017b). These tasks include collection, transport, sorting and treatment of waste. The circular business models emphasise the importance of closed loop systems in order to reduce the need for extraction and processing of new resources (Tayebi-Khorami et al., 2019). For example, adopting a circular business model affords the opportunity to reduce the liability and increase the value of mining waste. Waste management in a circular economy involves planning for the future application of resource recovery, as well as devising plans towards extending the life of materials, products or services. Therefore, stakeholders' sensitisation for effective waste management is necessary in reducing the impacts of consumer and industrial waste on the environment (Laurenti et al., 2018).

KNOWLEDGE MANAGEMENT AND CIRCULAR ECONOMY

There are sufficient literature on knowledge management (Dalkir, 2011; 2013; Jamal & Tilchin, 2016; Nomura, 2008; Paulin & Suneson, 2015), as well the conceptualisation and development of circular business models (Accenture, 2014; Allwood, 2014; De los Rios, & Charnley, 2017; Ellen MacArthur Foundation, 2017; European Commission, 2015; Geissdoerfer et al., 2017; McDonough & Braungart, 2010; Mulhall & Braungart, 2010; Niero & Hauschild, 2017; Zink & Geyer, 2017). The link between knowledge management and innovation has been extensively researched across the globe (Donate & de Pablo; 2015; Fields & Atiku, 2017; Omotayo, 2015; Tseng, 2010). The results signified a positive relationship between knowledge management and innovative performance. There are limited studies showcasing the interplay between knowledge management and circular economy (i.e. development of circular business models or transition into a circular economy). This chapter seeks to fill this gap by establishing the influence of strategic knowledge management on the circular economy.

The connection between strategic knowledge management and development of a circular business model was established by Shih et al (2018). The authors put it that knowledge management cycles are the most important aspects of strategic knowledge management to drive eco-innovation in a circular economy. Strategic knowledge management could be referred to as an alignment of knowledge management plans, cycles, and practices with green initiatives, as well as the sustainable development goals (Prieto-Sandoval et al., 2019). The Global Environment Facility (2019) suggests that knowledge management is essential in creating new green industries and jobs for sustainable development. A company's innovation process depend largely on strategic knowledge management (Gloet & Terziovski, 2004 cited in Shih et al., 2018), especially the professional knowledge levels; know-why and care-why (Jamal & Tilchin, 2016). Jamal and Tilchin (2016) claim that systems understanding (know-why), and self-motivated creativity (care-why) are important in advancing the critical thinking by professionals for eco-innovation in a circular economy.

Furthermore, empirical evidence confirms that a company's strategic knowledge management capability is linked with its innovative performance (Lopes, Scavarda, Hofmeister, Thomé, & Vaccaro, 2017). Accordingly, companies can leverage on knowledge management as a strategy that promotes eco-innovation for sustainable competitive advantage in a circular economy. Similarly, companies could make significant contribution to sustainable development goals by innovating and developing technology to advance business projects, introducing products and services that are eco-friendly into the market with efficiency and sustainability as guiding principles (Lainez, González, Aguilar, & Vela, 2018). Having established the link between knowledge management and eco-efficiency/eco-innovation through investment in research and innovation, emerging economies could emulate the guidelines provided by the European Commission for economic transformation and waste management. The next section presents the recommendations required in transforming the global economy into a circular economy in line with the United Nations Sustainable Development Goals.

RECOMMENDATIONS

The environmental issues confronting most of the developed, developing and underdeveloped countries are resource depletion, extinction of animal and plant species, and pollution emerging from consumer and industrial wastes. A policy maker at global level (United Nations) in an effort to resolve the global challenges has mandated the member states to strive towards accomplishing the sustainable development goals. The holistic approach of solving environmental problems across the global is by transforming the global economy into a circular economy. Therefore, companies operating in different countries have roles to play in developing a knowledge-based for sustainable development and effective transition into a circular economy. Based on literature review on the link between knowledge management and circular economy, this chapter offers the following recommendations:

- It was established that knowledge management cycles or practices are the most important aspects of strategic knowledge management to drive eco-innovation (Shih et al., 2018), therefore companies need to enhance the knowledge-based for continuous business process improvement. This is fundamental in creating green industries, and developing new jobs to promote green consciousness, as well as pro-environmental behavior;
- The most important professional knowledge levels in developing circular business models are systems understanding, and self-motivated creativity (Jamal & Tilchin, 2016). Therefore, the Human Resources in collaboration with Research and Development/Innovation could develop and communicate a culture that embrace knowledge sharing and transfer on systems understanding, and self-motivated creativity to promote critical thinking by professionals for eco-innovation

in a circular economy. Organisational learning culture might be useful in ensuring transfer of tacit knowledge within the system;

- The issue of paucity of resources could be overcome by developing a knowledge-based for resource recovery in different industries and effective stakeholders' sensitisation in order to reduce the waste generation or pollution from the production and consumption systems. For example, manufacturing companies in the emerging and developing countries might consider product as a service business model as a resource recovery, thereby reducing the impacts of consumer and industrial waste on the environment;
- A sustainable business model developed by an entrepreneur to reduce households' use of water is "DryBath", a product which is estimated to saves 40 litres of water per user (Perella, 2016). Accordingly, "DryBath" is being pushed as a complete hygiene solution with new features such as biodegradable wipes. This business model is targeted at reducing the global usage of water at household level. This product will reduce the issue of global paucity of water if used once or twice a week by individuals;
- The mode of operations and production systems varies from one sector to another. Hence, there is no one-size-fits-all approach in a circular economy. Therefore, there is need for the management in different industries to develop a knowledge-based system in promoting eco-efficiency and eco-innovation in each industry. This is crucial in ensuring active participation in the transformation agenda for effective transition into a circular economy at company, sectoral, national, regional and global levels;
- Finally, there is need for information dissemination on the benefits of circular economy at organisational level for employees and managers to have a pledge and join the organisation in its commitment to reuse, recycle and reduce carbon footprint.

FUTURE AREAS OF RESEARCH

The chapter embarked on a literature review approach to unveil the place of knowledge management practices in developing circular business models and effective transition into a circular economy. This chapter holds that systems understanding, and self-motivated creativity are essential professional knowledge domains in promoting eco-innovation for sustainability. However, there is need for empirical studies to establish the relationship between knowledge management process and transition into a circular economy in selected emerging economies.

Future research could be structured to showcase the challenges of different industries in developing circular business models empirically. For example, an empirical evidence on the influence of knowledge management process and responsible business solutions in the oil and gas, and mining industries could be considered as a future area of research. It could be structured along a mixed methods approach to showcase the level of significance of results, and at the same time provide an in-depth information and analysis of participants' point of view on the subject.

CONCLUSION

This chapter examined the place of knowledge management in developing circular business models with the aid of literature review approach. The background of circular economy was provided, as well as the challenges of different companies in implementing the policies of circular economy. This chapter also provides efforts of policy makers in transforming the global economy into a circular economy by providing the guidelines for sustainable developments. In spites of the desirability of sustainability, the challenges of different companies include attainment of one hundred percent compliance, the extent to which the loops can be closed without ejecting waste, and stakeholders resistant to change based on perceived disruption.

This chapter concludes that knowledge management is instrumental in developing circular business models. The systems understanding and self-motivated creativity are essential professional knowledge levels in developing circular business models for sustainability. The circular business models presented in this chapter are circular supplies, resource recovery, product-life extension, sharing platforms, and product as a service. These circular business models are beneficial to the stakeholders, as well as the environment. Therefore, knowledge management cycles are important in driving eco-innovations for the circular economy.

REFERENCES

Accenture (2014). *Circular advantage: Innovative business models and technologies to create value in a world without limits to growth.* Retrieved 5 October, 2019 from file:///C:/Users/satiku/Downloads/978-87-93435-86-5.pdf

Allwood, J. M. (2014). Squaring the circular economy: the role of recycling within a hierarchy of material management strategies. In *Handbook of recycling* (pp. 445–477). Elsevier. doi:10.1016/B978-0-12-396459-5.00030-1

Atiku, S. O. (2019). Institutionalizing Social Responsibility through Workplace Green Behaviour. In *Contemporary Multicultural Orientations and Practices for Global Leadership* (pp. 183–199). Hershey, PA: IGI Global. doi:10.4018/978-1-5225-6286-3.ch010

Atiku, S. O., & Fields, Z. (2018). Organisational Learning Dimensions and Talent Retention Strategies for the Service Industries. In N. Baporikar (Ed.), Global Practices in Knowledge Management for Societal and Organizational Development (pp. 358-381). IGI Global. doi:10.4018/978-1-5225-3009-1.ch017

Bocken, N. M., De Pauw, I., Bakker, C., & van der Grinten, B. (2016). Product design and business model strategies for a circular economy. *Journal of Industrial and Production Engineering*, *33*(5), 308–320. doi:10.1080/21681015.2016.1172124

Circular Academy. (2019). *Circular Academy: Critics and challenges.* Retrieved 3 October, 2019 from http://www.circular.academy/circular-economy-critics-and-challenges

Circular Economy Practitioner Guide. (2018). *Sharing Platforms.* Retrieved 7 November, 2019 from https://www.ceguide.org/Strategies-and-examples/Sell/Sharing-platforms

Dalkir, K. (2011). *Knowledge Management in Theory and Practice*. Cambridge, MA: Massachusetts Institute of Technology.

Dalkir, K. (2013). *Knowledge Management in Theory and Practice*. Routledge. doi:10.4324/9780080547367

De los Rios, I. C., & Charnley, F. J. (2017). Skills and capabilities for a sustainable and circular economy: The changing role of design. *Journal of Cleaner Production*, *160*, 109–122. doi:10.1016/j.jclepro.2016.10.130

Den Hollander, M. C., Bakker, C. A., & Hultink, E. J. (2017). Product design in a circular economy: Development of a typology of key concepts and terms. *Journal of Industrial Ecology*, *21*(3), 517–525. doi:10.1111/jiec.12610

Derwall, J., Guenster, N., Bauer, R., & Koedijk, K. (2005). The eco-efficiency premium puzzle. *Financial Analysts Journal*, *61*(2), 51–63. doi:10.2469/faj.v61.n2.2716

Díaz-García, C., González-Moreno, Á., & Sáez-Martínez, F. J. (2015). Eco-innovation: Insights from a literature review. *Innovation*, *17*(1), 6–23. doi:10.1080/14479338.2015.1011060

Donate, M. J., & de Pablo, J. D. S. (2015). The role of knowledge-oriented leadership in knowledge management practices and innovation. *Journal of Business Research*, *68*(2), 360–370. doi:10.1016/j.jbusres.2014.06.022

Eco-Innovation Observatory. (2013). *Europe in transition. Paving the way to a green economy through eco-innovation. Eco-innovation Observatory Annual Report 2012. Funded by the European Commission*. Brussels: DG Environment.

Edwards, P. E. T., Sutton-Grier, A. E., & Coyle, G. E. (2013). Investing in nature: Restoring coastal habitat blue infrastructure and green job creation. *Marine Policy*, *38*, 65–71. doi:10.1016/j.marpol.2012.05.020

Ehrenfeld, J. R. (2005). Eco-efficiency. *Journal of Industrial Ecology*, *9*(4), 6–8. doi:10.1162/108819805775248070

Ellen MacArthur Foundation. (2017). *Schools of thought*. Retrieved 2 October, 2019 from https://www.ellenmacarthurfoundation.org/publications

Ertz, M., Leblanc-Proulx, S., Sarigöllü, E., & Morin, V. (2019a). Made to break? A taxonomy of business models on product lifetime extension. *Journal of Cleaner Production*, *234*, 867–880. doi:10.1016/j.jclepro.2019.06.264

Ertz, M., Leblanc-Proulx, S., Sarigöllü, E., & Morin, V. (2019b). Advancing quantitative rigor in the circular economy literature: New methodology for product lifetime extension business models. *Resources, Conservation and Recycling*, *150*, 104437. doi:10.1016/j.resconrec.2019.104437

European Commission. (2013). *Eco-innovation the key to Europe's future competitiveness*. Retrieved 15 November, 2019 from https://ec.europa.eu/environment/pubs/pdf/factsheets/ecoinnovation/en.pdf

European Commission. (2015). Closing the loop-An EU action plan for the Circular Economy. *Communication from the Commission to the European Parliament, the Council, the European Economic and Social Committee and the Committee of the Regions COM, 614*(2).

Fields, Z., & Atiku, S. O. (2017). Collective Green Creativity and Eco-Innovation as key drivers of Sustainable Business Solutions in Organisations. In *Collective Creativity for Responsible and Sustainable Business Practice* (pp. 1–25). Hershey, PA: IGI Global. doi:10.4018/978-1-5225-1823-5.ch001

Geissdoerfer, M., Savaget, P., Bocken, N. M., & Hultink, E. J. (2017). The Circular Economy–A new sustainability paradigm? *Journal of Cleaner Production*, *143*, 757–768. doi:10.1016/j.jclepro.2016.12.048

Global Environment Facility. (2019). *The circular economy: Tackling plastic pollution*. Retrieved 2 December, 2019 from https://www.thegef.org/news/circular-economy-tackling-plastic-pollution

Haas, W., Krausmann, F., Wiedenhofer, D., & Heinz, M. (2015). How circular is the global economy? An assessment of material flows, waste production, and recycling in the European Union and the world in 2005. *Journal of Industrial Ecology*, *19*(5), 765–777. doi:10.1111/jiec.12244

Hislop, D., Bosua, R., & Helms, R. (2013). *Knowledge management in organizations: A critical introduction*. Oxford University Press.

Jamal, A. H., & Tilchin, O. (2016). Teachers' Accountability for Adaptive Project-Based Learning. *American Journal of Educational Research*, *4*(5), 420–426.

Khalamayzer, A. (2017). *Five challenges to scaling the circular economy*. Retrieved 3 October, 2019 from https://www.greenbiz.com/article/5-challenges-scaling-circular-economy

Lainez, M., González, J. M., Aguilar, A., & Vela, C. (2018). Spanish strategy on bioeconomy: Towards a knowledge based sustainable innovation. *New Biotechnology*, *40*, 87–95. doi:10.1016/j.nbt.2017.05.006 PMID:28552816

Laurenti, R., Martin, M., & Stenmarck, Å. (2018). Developing adequate communication of waste footprints of products for a circular economy—A stakeholder consultation. *Resources*, *7*(4), 78–91. doi:10.3390/resources7040078

Lèbre, É., Corder, G., & Golev, A. (2017a). The role of the mining industry in a circular economy: A framework for resource management at the mine site level. *Journal of Industrial Ecology*, *21*(3), 662–672. doi:10.1111/jiec.12596

Lèbre, É., Corder, G. D., & Golev, A. (2017b). Sustainable practices in the management of mining waste: A focus on the mineral resource. *Minerals Engineering*, *107*, 34–42. doi:10.1016/j.mineng.2016.12.004

Lewandowski, M. (2016). Designing the business models for circular economy—Towards the conceptual framework. *Sustainability*, *8*(1), 43. doi:10.3390u8010043

Lopes, C. M., Scavarda, A., Hofmeister, L. F., Thomé, A. M. T., & Vaccaro, G. L. R. (2017). An analysis of the interplay between organizational sustainability, knowledge management, and open innovation. *Journal of Cleaner Production*, *142*, 476–488. doi:10.1016/j.jclepro.2016.10.083

MacArthur, E. (2013). Towards the circular economy. *Journal of Industrial Ecology*, *2*, 23–44.

McDonough, W., & Braungart, M. (2010). *Cradle to cradle: Remaking the way we make things*. North Point Press.

Mohajan, H. K. (2019). Knowledge sharing among employees in organizations. *Journal of Economic Development. Environment and People*, *8*(1), 52–61. doi:10.26458/jedep.v8i1.612

Mulhall, D., & Braungart, M. (2010). Cradle to cradle criteria for the built environment. *EKONOMIAZ. Revista vasca de Economía, 75*(04), 182-193.

Niero, M., & Hauschild, M. Z. (2017). Closing the loop for packaging: Finding a framework to operationalize Circular Economy strategies. *Procedia CIRP*, *61*, 685–690. doi:10.1016/j.procir.2016.11.209

Nomura, H. (2008). Developing the "why" facet of medical professionalism. *The Kaohsiung Journal of Medical Sciences*, *24*(1), 31–34. doi:10.1016/S1607-551X(08)70070-6 PMID:18218567

OECD. (2018). *Business models for the circular economy: Opportunities and challenges from a policy perspective.* Retrieved 3 October, 2019 from https://www.oecd.org/environment/waste/policy-highlights-business-models-for-the-circular-economy.pdf

Oghazi, P., & Mostaghel, R. (2018). Circular business model challenges and lessons learned—An industrial perspective. *Sustainability*, *10*(3), 739. doi:10.3390u10030739

Omotayo, F. O. (2015). Knowledge management as an important tool in organisational management: A Review of Literature. *Library Philosophy and Practice*, *1*, 1–23.

Paulin, D., & Suneson, K. (2015). Knowledge transfer, knowledge sharing and knowledge barriers–three blurry terms in KM. *Leading Issues in Knowledge Management*, *2*(2), 73.

Perella, M. (2014, March 14). Renault, JLR, Nissan and Toyota drive car industry towards sustainability. *The Guardian*. Retrieved 10 February, 2020 from https://www.theguardian.com/sustainable-business/renault-jaguar-nissan-toyota-sustainability-circular-economy

Perella, M. (2016, April 28). Baths to washing machines: Welcome to the (almost) waterless home of the future. *The Guardian*. Retrieved 10 February, 2020 from https://www.theguardian.com/sustainable-business/2016/apr/28/baths-washing-machines-drybath-almost-waterless-home-of-the-future

Prieto-Sandoval, V., Jaca, C., Santos, J., Baumgartner, R. J., & Ormazabal, M. (2019). Key strategies, resources, and capabilities for implementing circular economy in industrial small and medium enterprises. *Corporate Social Responsibility and Environmental Management*, csr.1761. doi:10.1002/csr.1761

Qi, J., Zhao, J., Li, W., Peng, X., Wu, B., & Wang, H. (2016). Origin and background of circular economy development. In *Development of Circular Economy in China* (pp. 1–19). Singapore: Springer. doi:10.1007/978-981-10-2466-5_1

Shih, D. H., Lu, C. M., Lee, C. H., Parng, Y. J., Wu, K. J., & Tseng, M. L. (2018). A Strategic Knowledge Management Approach to Circular Agribusiness. *Sustainability*, *10*(7), 2389. doi:10.3390u10072389

Spender, J. C. (2015). Knowledge management: Origins, history, and development. In *Advances in Knowledge Management* (pp. 3–23). Cham: Springer.

Tayebi-Khorami, M., Edraki, M., Corder, G., & Golev, A. (2019). Re-Thinking Mining Waste through an Integrative Approach Led by Circular Economy Aspirations. *Minerals (Basel)*, *9*(5), 286–298. doi:10.3390/min9050286

Tseng, M. L. (2010). Using linguistic preferences and grey relational analysis to evaluate the environmental knowledge management capacity. *Expert Systems with Applications*, *37*(1), 70–81. doi:10.1016/j.eswa.2009.05.020

Tukker, A. (2015). Product services for a resource-efficient and circular economy–a review. *Journal of Cleaner Production*, *97*, 76–91. doi:10.1016/j.jclepro.2013.11.049

United Nations Environment Programme. (2017). *The role of Circular Economy in the transition "Towards a Pollution-Free Planet"*. Retrieved 2 December, 2019 from web.unep.org/environmentassembly/role-circular-economy-transition-towards-pollution-free-planet-1

World Bank. (2019). *Solid waste management*. Retrieved 7 November, 2019 from https://www.worldbank.org/en/topic/urbandevelopment/brief/solid-waste-management

Zhao, S., Wang, H. M., Chen, W. Q., Yang, D., Liu, J. R., & Shi, F. (2019). Environmental impacts of domestic resource extraction in China. *Ecosystem Health and Sustainability*, *5*(1), 67–78. doi:10.1080/20964129.2019.1577703

KEY TERMS AND DEFINITIONS

Circular Business Model: A sustainable business model developed in response to the global decline in resources or raw-materials, and to address the environmental issues. It is an alternative to linear economic model to promote a more resource efficient production and consumption systems; thereby reducing the environmental impact of human and economic activities.

Eco-Efficiency: A process of reducing ecological damage and at the same time maximizing the efficiency of company's production process utilising less water, material, and energy while recycling.

Green Industries: A more sustainable pathway for growth, by providing adequate investments for sustainable business solutions and implementing public policy initiatives that encourage environmentally responsible private investments.

Product as a Service: A sustainable business model that enables companies or manufacturers to shift away from selling ownership of their products to customers, to quantifying and selling the utility derived from their products to customers.

Resource Recovery: Is a sustainable business model that requires manufacturers to invest in innovative ways of using resources and materials for a long period, thereby creating more than one product use lifecycles.

Self-Motivated Creativity: The critical level of professional knowledge that promotes critical thinking by professionals for eco-innovation in a circular economy.

System Understanding: An application of the systems understanding in solving complex business problems and add value to innovative performance of an organisation.

Chapter 28
Creativity and Innovation for Entrepreneurs in the Circular Economy

Vannie Naidoo
University of KwaZulu-Natal, South Africa

ABSTRACT

SMEs uplift a country's economic wellbeing by creating jobs and alleviating poverty. Since poverty and job creation are so important to economies worldwide, policies and legislation have to be developed and implemented that encourage SME growth in world markets. It, however, does not stop there; SMEs have to use tools to strengthen their business operations. This is where the aspect of innovation and creativity is crucial. The researcher is of the opinion that many other theorists share, that is, SMEs cannot grow or sustain themselves without creativity and innovation.

INTRODUCTION

SMEs are fast becoming major players in the economy. They stimulate employment and growth and are instrumental in job creation within the world's economies. SMEs contribute substantially to a country's GDP. SME owners are vital social transformation agents who actively participate in the economy by selling their goods or services in a dynamic business environment. Due to the 4th industrial revolution the playing field for entrepreneurs has become more complex through globalization and the rapidly changing technological environment. SME owners have to constantly keep abreast of the changes in the technological environment. In order for SMEs to grow, develop and sustain themselves in the turbulent technological era entrepreneurs need to focus on creativity and innovation to remain competitive in their respective business sectors. This chapter will focus on SMEs that are registered business entities both in urban and rural South Africa. The aim of this chapter is to explore pivotal themes that relate to creativity and innovation for entrepreneurs' in a circular economy.

In the discussion that follows a background into the economic implications of SMEs in South Africa is explored.

DOI: 10.4018/978-1-7998-5116-5.ch028

Copyright © 2020, IGI Global. Copying or distributing in print or electronic forms without written permission of IGI Global is prohibited.

BACKGROUND INTO ECONOMIC IMPLICATIONS OF SMES IN SOUTH AFRICA

The discussion will explore the economic relevance of SMEs in the South African economy. The South African economy is made up of large businesses and small and medium term businesses. SMEs within South Africa and the world at large have a direct impact on the economy. According to Statistics South Africa (Stats SA, 2015), the SMME sector currently contributes approximately 42% of South Africa's gross domestic product (GDP) and accounts for 60% employment, as well as provides an incubator and breeding ground for entrepreneurship and innovation. According to The World Bank (2010) they have introduced a pro-SME policy and this is based on three fundamental pillars. Firstly, SMEs have benefits to the economy such as efficiency, innovation and productivity growth; this is due to the enhanced competition and entrepreneurship that the SME sector brings with it. Secondly, SMEs are more productive than larger companies, despite this fact, the financial market and other institutional failure obstruct SME development.

South Africa has urban and rural SMEs. The statistics above relate to all SMEs that are registered business entities in South Africa. The statistics above clearly articulate the importance of SMEs in South Africa as they drive economic growth, and stimulate employment. The researcher would like to add that the government of South Africa believes in transforming both rural and urban SMEs landscape in South Africa. According to SEDA (2007) South Africa is equally promoting the growth and development of rural small businesses. Bates et al. (2005) argues that there are various government-initiated structures that contribute to the development and promotion of SMEs. Some of these structures are SEDA, Khula Enterprise Finance and the Umsobomvu Youth Fund to name but a few.

There are many challenges that are faced by SMEs in South Africa, but despite these constraints, SMEs which are growing have become successful and have been seen to be making a vital contribution to the government's policy objectives of poverty alleviation, employment creation and the promotion of economic growth (Rogerson, 2008). Research evidence by Hein (2010) further shows that rural SMEs have great potential and value in creating employment, achieving equitable income distribution, alleviating poverty, building a local technological base, promoting participation of vulnerable groups, providing training ground for entrepreneurial and managerial skills and providing opportunities for use of own capital resources.

A challenge that globalization has created is in regards to the economies of scales and research and development. These two factors are of utmost importance in order for a firm to be competitive in the global economy. It may seem as though SMEs are at a great disadvantage for both of these instruments of competitiveness, and many experts have predicted the demise of SME competitiveness as globalization increases as the years go by (Organisation for Economic Co-operation and Development, 2000).

Economist (2012) indicates that SMEs in South Africa, much like the rest of the world, are exposed to systemic factors. These systemic factors include contractual and informational frameworks and macroeconomic environment, social factors such as crime, corruption and ethics, technology and the regulatory environment. High interest rates, low growth rates (which results in low consumption), high inflation rates and declining exchange rates are but a few macros economic factors that are currently affecting the South African economic environmental climate. General investor confidence and consumer consumption have both decreased, resulting in firms getting reduced sales. In additional to this, the current South African unemployment rate is at an all-time high. These abovementioned macro environmental factors will adversely affect sales, revenues, market potential and any expansion plans of new and existing SMEs (Economist, 2012).

The discussion that follows will highlight entrepreneurs in a circular economy.

ENTREPREURS IN A CICULAR ECONOMY

Before the researcher embarks on the discussion on the impact and influence of the circular economy on entrepreneurs and SMEs, it is best to first unpack and conceptualize the circular economy.

The circular economy is understood as "an economic system that represents a change of paradigm in the way that human society is interrelated with nature and aims to prevent the depletion of resources, close energy and materials loops, and facilitate sustainable development through its implementation at the micro (enterprises and consumers) and macro (city, regions and governments) levels. Attaining this circular model requires cyclical and regenerative environmental innovations in the way society legislates, produces and consumes" (Prieto-Sandoval et al.:2018). Ellen MacArthur Foundation (2015) proposes a more comprehensive definition that includes environmental and economic advantages, according to which the circular economy is "an industrial economy that is restorative or regenerative by intention and design".

Su et al. (2013) suggests that the economic circular model has three dimensions that reach three distinct but interlinked systemic levels. These dimensions are economic, social and the environment. the economic dimension expresses the contribution of the circular economic model to the increase of the national and regional competitiveness, the environmental dimension envisages the reconfiguration of the industrial platforms in an ecological way, while the social dimension is correlated with the contribution of the circular economic model to the reduction of unemployment problems and improving the quality of life in general. According to the European Commission, (2014, 2015a) they posit that in the process of achieving a European circular economy, SMEs and social enterprises had been acknowledged as particularly important, particularly in terms of their contribution to activities such as recycling, repair and innovation.

Prieto-Sandoval, Jaca, & Ormazabal (2017) argues that the circular economy can be understood through five main fields of action: take, make, distribute, use and recover. These five fields will be discussed in detail below:

- **Take:** This term refers to the way in which industries take resources and energy from the environment. In the circular economy paradigm, companies should try to be more efficient and responsible about their use of biological and technical resources. This means they should select the suppliers and the materials they use according to environmental criteria that reduce the impact on nature (Prieto-Sandoval, Jaca, & Ormazabal,2017);
- **Make:** As soon as resources are obtained, they become part of the process that produces goods and services. In this field of action, those processes can be carried out in a sustainable way with ecological innovations (eco-innovations) and the best technological practices (Carrillo-Hermosilla, Del Río, & Könnölä, 2010);
- **Distribution:** This phase is associated with the way in which a product or service is delivered to the customer. Companies must ensure the efficiency and traceability of the product's distribution in order to reduce environmental impact. For example, companies can optimize transport routes or packaging (Zhang, Li, Zhao, & Mu, 2010);

- **Use:** As soon as consumers or other companies purchase goods and services, the CE proposes reducing the environmental impact associated with the use of the product (Stahel, 2016);
- **Recover:** In the CE, eco-innovation processes are boosted to recover the waste, materials and energy that remain in used products at the end of their lifecycle (Park, Sarkis, & Wu, 2010).

A new theme has emerged in the field of business in recent years that encompasses the sustainable entrepreneur. These SME owners' business practices are guided by his/her worldviews on being responsible towards the environment. Many of the business opportunities that he/she might pursue is aimed towards sustaining the environment. The entrepreneur's creativity and innovation are strongly rooted in his/her pursuit of sustaining the environment. Common innovation practices entrepreneurs' have embarked on in recent years have been for example; developing solo powered energy mechanisms, recycling of waste and using them to make products, developing devices to extract water from sea water and becoming organic farmers. Berent-Braun, Uhlaner, Jeurissen, & deWit (2010) argue that an operational definition of sustainability entrepreneurship refers to a firm that is developing any kind of environmentally friendly activities. Masurel (2007) describes the sustainable entrepreneur as one focused at the same time on people, the planet, and profit.

O'Neill, Hershauer & Golder (2006) argue that in a rapidly changing global environment, the free-market economy affects nature, and nature's change affects the life of people and communities, and the lives of those socially and economically disadvantaged most of all. McDonald & Oates (2003) adds that sustainability entrepreneurship is promoted as a solution both to environmental changes but also to negative social changes. It is recognized that the choices of firms and people on production and consumption styles are all vital for sustainable development and consumers need to embrace CE. As a result, many papers have analyzed the profiles of the so-called green consumers and their behavior regarding household waste reduction, reuse, recycling, green purchasing and focusing on different parts of the world.

SMEs encounter barriers to operating in a circular economy. One of the major carriers sustainable entrepreneurs face is not understanding what sustainability entails and not understanding technologies, which are pivotal to assisting entrepreneurs in creativity and innovation of sustainable goods and services. The green market segment is also not easy for entrepreneurs to understand, as they might not share the green customers' attitudes and values towards environmentalism and sustainability. According to Ritzén and Sandström (2017) they classify the barriers encountered in the process of implementation of the circular economy's principles, as follows: financial (turnover), structural (lack of information, unclear distribution of responsibilities), operational, (infrastructure), attitudinal (risk aversion, perceptions related to the sustainability of actions) and technological.

SMALL BUSINESSES IN SOUTH AFRICA AND EXAMPLES OF WHAT THEY ARE DOING

There are various forms of SMEs that are registered in rural and urban South Africa. Small medium enterprises may take the form of a legal structure that is legislated by South African government. In South Africa, some forms of small and medium enterprises are namely; sole proprietorship, partnership, close corporation or companies.

In South African rural and urban areas a SME that is really doing well are funeral parlours. Since crime is high in South Africa, coupled by AIDS and road accidents funeral small business owners in this sector are doing very well despite the poor economic conditions in the South African economy. Small business owners are involved in the food and catering industry. In rural are urban areas there are a lot of taverns and restaurants that sell traditional and fast foods.

Another area where small businesses are doing very well is in the beauty industry. Many small business people are involved in hair salons, make-up, waxing, nail and the cosmetic sector. Since the new millennials love beauty, they spend a lot of money to look good.

In up- market suburbs, getting rid of taking care of gardens and getting rid of garden refuse is often problematic. There has been a rise in small business owners in the garden refuse removal and garden services sector.

Crime is also a major problem experienced in South Africa. This has resulted in an increase in the number of security companies that have opened up in South Africa. These small businesses look after private residents in urban areas. They also install alarms and security systems.

Fintech is an innovative start-up that offers electronic fund transfer (EFT) processing system that automates EFT transactions and allows users to make instant, secure payments. The i-Pay already operates in South African and Nigeria. Organico was launched by Annabel Biggar-David a small businesswoman to offer safe, and holistic and natural health solutions. She launched her online store, which is the supplier of South Africa's largest organic store, Faithful to Nature. VoiceMap is another small business doing interesting innovative things in the tourism industry. This product is a walking tour app. It provides locations on GPS and an audio of interesting local stories and experiences of the location to tourists.

UNPACKING THE CONCEPTS OF CREATIVITY IN SMES

According to Tarik (2006), the concept creativity is defined as the ability to produce original, novel, and unexpected work with high quality expertise, and unusual ability in solving problems, and suggesting solutions in a particular field.

Torrance (1969) argues that creativity is:

- The capacity to detect gaps;
- Propose various solutions to problem solving;
- Producing novel ideas;
- Alternatively, recombining ideas (relationships between ideas).

In the section two models of creativity will be discussed, namely the Componential model of creativity and the Team Creativity Model (TCM). In 1983 the componential model of creativity was developed. The theory suggests that creativity is based on three components that are "domain-relevant skills, creativity relevant skills, and task motivation" (Amabile, 1983). The theory further asserted that the process of creativity is in the following sequence: "problem or task representation, preparation, response generation, response validation, and outcome evaluation". Zhang & Gheibi (2015) argue that intrinsic motivation drives creativity by influencing individuals to execute creative activities. Amabile (1997) further posits that the theory dwells on the individual (or small group) creativity. According to the theory, there are three main parts of creativity namely; expertise, creative-thinking skill, and intrinsic task motivation. They drive the level of creativity. Expertise comprises the capacity to have accurate knowledge, technical Creative thinking can include the ability to explore new strategies of perceiving and solving problems mostly backed by perseverance, tolerance, and risk taking. The third component suggests that someone who is intrinsically stimulated to carry out a particular task can reveal creativity.

Lombardo and Roddy (2010) indicates that the Team Creativity Model (TCM) was employed to explain the constructs that affect team creativity. They began by introducing the nucleus of their research, which was how individual creativity of one team member could be enhanced to influence the entire team. Every member was encouraged to make input without thinking that his or her ideas were silly or less useful. The study posits that when team productivity is seen as a whole rather than an individual input, it empowers members to have a sense of responsibility and achievement, which in turn triggers more efforts that are creative. Newell, Scarborough, Robertson & Swan (2002) indicates that cross-functional team working within organizations is often portrayed as the key to creativity and success of organizations. There is ample evidence from psychological research on team working of how diverse range of individuals can create, through synergy, ideas which go beyond what any single individual could have produced on their own.

Andriopoulos (2003) argues that the following conditions should be included within an organisations work environment to foster creativity namely:

Proposition 1: Conducive working environment.
Proposition 2: Align employee creativity with organisational goals.
Proposition 3: Directed expression and self-fulfilment for employees.

Amabile (2013) affirms that many techniques can be used to stimulate a creative work environment such as the creation of work teams that are collaborative, diversely skilled and idea-focused; the creation of incentives that recognise creative work; and through creating norms for actively sharing ideas across the organisation. On the other hand, political problems within the firm, excessive time pressures and harshly criticising new ideas can block creativity. Mumford (2000) argues that organisations should consider multiple interventions that take into account the individual, the group, the organisation and the strategic environment when selecting interventions intended to enhance creativity. Zhou and George (2001) show that the information and skills of co-workers generates feedback, new information and the elaboration of unusual ideas thus enhancing creativity. Adams (2006) argues that environments or efforts that encourage individuals to generate new variations and new combinations of ideas can enhance the creative mind. Adams (2006) further posits that brainstorming is one of the most popular techniques used to induce creativity. Johansson (2004), amongst others, argues that group brainstorming can be particularly effective when individuals are allowed 15–20 minutes to think individually and write their ideas on an anonymous piece of paper, which is then handed to a facilitator. All ideas can then be discussed openly with a view to considering whether each one could be feasible rather than seeking to criticise or find the reasons why it would not work.

In order for creativity to be successful within an SME, the owner needs to nurture an environment that is conducive to creativity. Doran & Ryan (2017) indicates that the working environment has a significant impact on creativity and innovation activities within a business. Incentives like reward and recognition schemes, training, and the creation of platforms to freely share knowledge and discuss ideas characterise effective working environments among SMEs and subsequently yield substantial creativity and innovation. Klijn & Tomic (2010) add that favourable relationships among employees and between owners/managers and their employees create effective working environments that ultimately affects employee motivation and creativity.

Klijn & Tomic (2010) add that creativity is driven by numerous factors. They include availability of resources, and effective policies. SME management must therefore foster an environment of trust and cooperation with their employees, who can integrate their knowledge with opportunities in order to develop innovative products for the customers in the market. This would in turn, guarantee SME survival and future sustainability within its' respective business sector. Ismail, Abdelrahman, & Majid (2018) indicate that training among SME's is also crucial in acquiring creativity-relevant skills that foster creative solutions. Through training, employees get an opportunity to integrate the existing understanding and new knowledge.Poon, Mohamad, & Yusoff, (2018) are of the opinion that an employee's capacity to utilize effectively organizational resources influences creativity among SMEs. They add that SME owners' need to empower effectively their employees to utilize the firm's resources and exploit various business opportunities. They can achieve this by encouraging and nurturing their workforce through training.

UNPACKING INNOVATION IN SMEs

In order to gain an understanding of how innovation influences SMEs, it is first imperative that we look at the diffusion of innovation theory. Roger (2003) argues that the theory provides details about the mechanisms and rate at which new ideas, practices and technology is spread into a social system. The theory confirms that the adoption of new technologies is associated with "five attributes of innovations: relative advantage, compatibility, complexity, trialability, and observability". Roger (2003) further adds that an innovation is "an idea, practice, or object that is perceived as new by an individual or other unit of adoption".

SMEs are on the rise in South Africa. In order to grow and sustain themselves they must use technology to operate their businesses more efficiently and effectively. A way forward to improve SME efficiency which can also make these businesses become more productive which will translate into improving their competitive advantage in the market place. According to Fulton & Hon (2009) to accomplish this would require innovation from SMMEs regarding production practices and usually require technology implementation in the form of advanced manufacturing techniques. This applies specifically to manufacturing SMMEs but may be extended to any SMME (service or production) which may improve the efficiency of their operations with greater use of technology. Nicolescu & Nicolescu (2012) indicates that largely, SMEs tend to make frequent innovations in product development, and in process innovation. Bozkurt & Kalkan (2014) add that SMEs also execute marketing innovations by designing and implementing enhanced promotion, product, and pricing techniques. They also execute marketing innovations by designing and implementing enhanced promotion.

Bozkurt & Kalkan (2014) argue that there are several challenges affecting the innovation practices in SMEs. They include:

- The lack of high skilled and experienced staff in innovation;
- The failure to integrate SME sections through effective communications;
- The volatility in the market;
- Failure to access government support, and the support from research and academic institutions.

SME owners can learn a lot about innovation from other SME in the same industry. Therefore, it is important for a SME owner to build good networks within the industry, government and research institutions and universities. Szłapka, Stachowiak, Batz, & Fertsch (2017) posit that innovation can be enhanced through cooperation among SMEs from various industries. Through cooperation, SMEs access knowledge on innovation opportunities, and matters pertaining to industrial property protection. Bozkurt & Kalkan (2014) argue that apart from collaborating with other SMEs, an SME owner can also collaborate with other entities particularly in research and development. In this regard, SMEs need to improve their communication processes and structures, and enhance their relations with key innovation stakeholders in order to facilitate innovation activities. Thrikawala (2011) is of the opinion that SME networks can also be established with close individuals such as family members, and friends. Through these social relationships, they are likely to access valuable business information. The same information can also be accessed through trade fairs and exhibitions, and workshops.

SMEs play a very important role in the progression of both historically and in the present for developing nations. This is so because the SME sector contributes significantly to the spurring of innovation and thus contributing to economic growth (Kim, 2011). However, it is also important to bear in mind that many SMEs fail because they do not adopt new technologies. New technologies are pivotal for sustainable entrepreneurs' to understand and implement, since they can be instrumental in the spurring of innovative new sustainable products and green products that are safe and environmentally friendly to the planet. According to Ngwenyama and Morawczynski (2009), the following are categories of barriers that prevent SMEs from adopting and advancing its technological capacity:

- Lack of knowledge about the strategic use of technology;
- Lack of necessary skills-base;
- Perceived high setup cost;
- Ever-changing technological environment;
- Geographical factors.

Within South Africa, it is important to note that government has committed to SME innovation. The National Advanced Manufacturing Technology Strategy (NAMTS) was established with the goal of stimulating technological upgrading in industry and to facilitate the flow of technological resources and building of an environment, which is conducive to innovation. The resources required for such an environment include skilled work force, technology infrastructure and funding which form the approach for the support provision of the NAMTS [RSA (2002)].

Further goals of the NAMTS include:

- Ensuring that technology resources are better developed, focused and utilized;
- Developing the capacity of the manufacturing sector to master advanced technology to become more innovative, flexible and customer oriented;
- Facilitating the move from raw material-intensive manufactured goods towards progressively more knowledge-intensive goods and services RSA (2002).

CHALLENGES AFFECTING THE INNOVATION PRACTICES IN SMES

The major challenges that impact on SME's are namely: the failure to integrate SME sections through effective communications; lack of risk taking by entrepreneurs; lack of training and development for staff within the SME, volatility in the market, failure by the SME owner to motivate his/her staff and failure to access government support. These challenges will now be discussed in detail.

The Failure to Integrate SME Sections Through Effective Communications

SMEs need to improve their communication processes and structures, and enhance their relations with key innovation stakeholders in order to facilitate innovation activities (Bozkurt & Kalkan, 2014). Supyuenyong, Islam, & Kulkarni (2007) suggests that the commitment of SME owners/managers in creating working environments that promote knowledge sharing among employees and its utilization is a major strategy that enhances knowledge management initiatives and practices in SMEs. Such commitment is likely to reduce costs related to acquisition of knowledge from the external business environment. Wincent & Westerberg (2005) posit that the influence of owner /manager's personality in establishing and maintaining business networks is significant. Ultimately, these networks fuel entrepreneurial spirit in SMEs.

Lack of Risk Taking by Entrepreneurs

According to Lawal, Adegbuyi, Iyiola, Ayoade, & Taiwo (2018) risk taking can drive SME competitiveness. Smit & Watkins (2012) argue that the enterprise risk management approaches need to be adopted by SMEs in order to manage risks, and operation and production costs, and integrate risk practices in their strategic objectives. These approaches enable SMEs to make self-risk assessment. Additionally, such approaches are likely to enable SMEs to prioritize risks according to the SME's specific needs and resources. Nanthuru, Pingfeng, Guihua, & Mkonya (2018) indicate that the risk management capabilities in SMEs should be built through frequent risk trainings, and capacity building programs. It is important to note that collaborations with research institutions and universities can also assist entrepreneurs in learning and managing their business risk.

Failure to Adapt Technology

Another area of challenge that can hinder a SMEs innovation and creativity. According to Dangayach & Deshmukh (2004), greater use technology will improve the competitive position of the business and may allow it to gain a competitive advantage. The benefits associated with employment of advanced production techniques or methods include reduced unit cost of production, increased return on equity, inventory or resource savings, increased flexibility and improved quality of production.

Volatility in the Market

The major challenge facing SMEs is to devise and implement strategies that will manage the dynamics in markets and adjust their product development activities in order to influence SME sustainable growth. Innovative marketing strategies that enable SME's to translate their markets, carryout a competitor diagnosis, and enhance product development initiatives are required. These strategies should also enable SME's to integrate the market needs with the development and management of distribution networks, and the communication of products to potential and existing customers, (Tripathi & Siddiqui, 2012). van Scheers & Makhitha, (2016) adds that in this regard, strategic marketing should be adopted by SMEs in order to influence their current and future positions in dynamic markets.

Lack of Training

In order for employees to be innovative and creative, they need to provide training. Many SME owners do not invest in training their staff and this can be a major challenge for the SMEs future sustainability. Ogunyomi & Bruning (2016) argues that within Africa, SMEs engage in training to improve their competitive edge and chances of survival. Ramukumba (2014) has a different view and states that South African SMEs acknowledge training as a means of staying relevant and profitable. McLean (2005) suggests that elements of an organisational culture that support creativity and innovation may be enhanced through training and development. SMEs are generally hesitant to provide funds for employee training and development (Mazzarol, 2003). Lipman (2013) argues that in order to retain the high-quality employees that the owners/managers have hired, it is fundamental to have training and development, because it helps to build loyalty. Sarvadi (2005) indicates that training and development should be viewed as an investment and not an expense, because it is essential and not optional for the success of the business.

Failure to Motivate Staff

SME owners fail to motivate their staff and this could influence innovation and creativity within the firm. Ames (1992) argues that motivation is the reason individuals behave in a particular manner in a certain situation. Motivation exists as part of one's goal structures, one's beliefs about what is important, and it determines whether one will engage in any given pursuit. Laffont and Martimort (2002) are of the opinion that Incentives are commonly used in business to motivate employees and to align their wants with the needs of the employer. Dewhurst et al. (2009) adds that in a survey conducted by MacKinsey Quarterly, it was found that praise is the best incentive as it makes employees feel like the firm appreciates them. Other incentives valued by employees are leadership attention (for example, one-on-one conversations), and a chance to lead projects or task forces.

A Lack of Understanding of the Circular Economy

If the entrepreneurs fail to understand the circular economy and its implications on SMEs, then they will fail to contribute towards its goals and objectives of sustaining the environment. Entrepreneurs' lack of understanding of the dynamics of circular economics can hinder them from being involved in innovative business practices and product developments that can sustain the planet.

The Entrepreneurs Fail to Understand the Attitudes and Values of the Green Market Segment

If the sustainable entrepreneurs does not understand the green market segment then he/she will not be in a position to respond to the green consumers' demands and they would fail to be innovative and develop goods and services that protect the environment and sustain the planet. The green market segment is a very lucrative segment of the market, and being innovative in this aspect of market development can yield high profits for a business.

Failure to Access Government Support

In order for SME's to grow and sustain themselves, they need the support of governments and NGO's. This is often not easy. Kesper (2002) observes that awareness of the existence of SMME support initiatives, among new and existing SMMEs, is very low. He adds that both the high opportunity costs, associated with owner-managers spending time accessing support, and the cumbersome application processes for accessing support, are often unclear and plagued with bureaucratic 'red tape'. Berry et al (2002) further note that the inability of support institutions to raise awareness of their existence and purpose is one of the main factors contributing to poor implementation of SMME policy measures. As identified by Courseault Trumbach, Payne and Kongthon (2006), it is important that SMEs engage government for their support regarding technology initiatives and networks in order to reach strategic business goals. Morrison (2006) argues that innovation relies heavily on research and development; this is especially true for SMEs in the manufacturing sector. If SMEs cannot carry out extensive R&D, they are at great risk of falling behind competitors in innovation and technology. On average, countries that are developed spend approximately 3% of the overall GDP on research and development initiatives. Some developing countries such as China, India and Brazil have in recent years built up their research and development expenditure to the levels of most developed countries.

FUTURE AREAS OF INTEREST

For future interest, it is important for studies to be conducted on SMEs in developing countries to establish their relationship with adopting new technologies. Barriers for SMEs in innovation and creativity in both developing and undeveloped countries is another area that has a severe knowledge gap. Lastly, how SMEs respond to the 4th industrial revolution challenges is another area of research that can add to the body of knowledge on SMEs.

CONCLUSION

Technology is here to stay. It is also constantly changing. The circular economy places a lot of pressure on the entrepreneurs' and SMEs to adapt to technology. Since the only way forward for the human race is to protect the environment, SMEs have to embrace circular economic principles in their business. To raise to the challenge of technology and its' rapidly changing dynamics, entrepreneurs in their respective SMEs need to train themselves and their staff in order to keep abreast of technological changes. Owners and managers in SMEs need to create a culture and environment in their business that fosters creativity and innovation. Staff have to change with the times and respond to change in a positive manner. This is the only way for a small business to remain current and survive.

REFERENCES

Adams, K. (2006). *The sources of innovation and creativity*. Paper Commissioned by the National Center on Education and the Economy for the New Commission on the Skills of the American Workforce.

Amabile, T. M. (1983). The Social Psychology of Creativity: A Componential Conceptualization. *Journal of Personality and Social Psychology*, *45*(2), 357–376. doi:10.1037/0022-3514.45.2.357

Amabile, T. M. (1997). Motivating Creativity in Organizations: On Doing What You Love and Loving What You Do. *California Management Review*, *40*(1), 39–58. doi:10.2307/41165921

Amabile, T. M. (2013). *Componential Theory of Creativity. Encyclopedia of Management Theory*. London: Sage Publications.

Ames, C. (1992). Classrooms: Goals, structures, and student motivation. *Journal of Educational Psychology*, *84*(3), 261–271. doi:10.1037/0022-0663.84.3.261

Andriopoulos, C. (2003). Determinants of organisational creativity: A literature review. *Management Decision*, *39*(10), 834–841. doi:10.1108/00251740110402328

Bates, B., Botha, M., Botha, S., Goodman, S., Ladzani, W., DeVries, C., ... Southey, L. (2005). *Business management: fresh perspectives*. Cape Town: Maskew.MillerLongman.

Berent-Braun, M. M., Uhlaner, L. M., Jeurissen, R. J. M., & deWit, G. (2010). Family ownership,innovation and other context variables as determinants of sustainability entrepreneurship in SMEs: An empirical research study. *SCALES Sci. Anal. Entrep. SMEs*. Available at:http://citeseerx.ist.psu.edu/viewdoc/download?doi=10.1.1.471.1649&rep=rep1&type=pdf Aaccessed on 13 Oct 2019.

Berry, A., von Blottnitz, M., Cassim, R., Kesper, A., Rajaratnam, B., & Ernst van Seventer, D. (2002). *The Economics of SMMEs in South Africa*. Trade and Industrial Policy Strategies. Available at: https://www.tips.org.za/node/204

Bozkurt, Ö. C., & Kalkan, A. (2014). Business Strategies of SME's, Innovation Types and Factors Influencing Their Innovation: Burdur Model. *Ege Academic Review*, *14*(2), 189–198.

Courseault-Trumbach, C., Payne, D., & Kongthon, A. (2006). Technology mining for small firms: Knowledge Prospecting for competitive Advantage. *Technological Forecasting and Social Change*, *1*(1), 937–949.

Crampton, N. (2020). *Watch List: 50 Top SA Small Businesses To Watch*. Entrepreneur South Africa. Entrepreneur Media, Inc.

Dangayach, G., & Deshmukh, S. (2004). Advanced manufacturing technology implementation: Evidence from Indian small and medium enterprises (SMEs). *Journal of Manufacturing Technology Management*, *16*(5), 16–26.

Dewhurst, M., Guthridge, M., & Mohr, E. (2009). Motivating people: Getting beyond money. *The McKinsey Quarterly*, *145*(1), 45–56.

Doran, J., & Ryan, G. (2017). The Role of Stimulating Employees' Creativity and Idea Generation in Encouraging Innovation Behaviour in Irish Firms. *Irish Journal of Management, 36*(1), 32–48. doi:10.1515/ijm-2017-0005

Economist, T. (2012, July). South Africa in recession. Repo rate down. *The Economist*.

Ellen MacArthur Foundation. (2015). *Towards the Circular Economy: Economic and Business Rationale for an Accelerated Transition, Isle of Wight*. Available on: https://www.ellenmacarthurfoundation.org/assets/downloads/TCE_Ellen-MacArthur-Foundation_9-Dec-2015.pdf

Fulton, M., & Hon, H. (2009). Managing advanced manufacturing technology (AMT) implementation in manufacturing SME. *International Journal of Productivity and Performance Management, 59*(4), 12–22.

Hein, A. M. (2010). *A Critical Analysis of Local Government Support in the Promotion of Small Enterprises*. Cape Town: Cape Peninsula University of Technology.

Ismail, A. I., Abdelrahman, S. E., & Majid, A. H. A. (2018). Closing Strategic Human Resource Management Research Lacunas with Mediating Role of Employee Creativity. *Academy of Strategic Management Journal, 17*(1), 1–18.

Johansson, F. (2004). *The Medici Effect: Breakthrough Insights at the Intersection of Ideas, Concepts, and Cultures*. Boston: Harvard Business Press.

Kesper, A. (2002). *Tracing trajectories of successful manufacturing SMMEs in South Africa* (PhD thesis). University of the Witwatersrand, Johannesburg, South Africa.

Klijn, M., & Tomic, W. (2010). A Review of Creativity within Organizations from a Psychological Perspective. *Journal of Management Development, 29*(4), 322–343. doi:10.1108/02621711011039141

Laffont, J. L., & Martimort, D. (2002). *The Theory of Incentives: The Principal-Agent Model*. Princeton, NJ: Princeton University Press. doi:10.1515/9781400829453

Lawal, F. A., Adegbuyi, O. A., Iyiola, O. O., Ayoade, O. E., & Taiwo, A. A. (2018). Nexus between Informal Networks and Risk-taking: Implications for Improving the Performance of Small and Medium Enterprises (SMEs) in Nigeria. *Academy of Strategic Management Journal, 17*(2), 1–13.

Lipman, V. (2013). *Why employee development is important, neglected and can cost you talent*. Available at: https://www.forbes.com/sites/victorlipman/2013/01/29/why-development-planning-is-important-neglected-and-cancost-you-young-talent/

Lombardo, B. J., & Roddy, D. J. (2010). Cultivating organizational creativity in an age of complexity. In *IBM 2010 Global Chief Human Resource Officer Study*. Armonk: IBM Institute for Business Value.

Masurel, E. (2007). Why SMEs invest in environmentalmeasures: Sustainability evidence fromsmall andmedium—Sized printing firms. *Business Strategy and the Environment, 16*(1), 190–201. doi:10.1002/bse.478

Mazzarol, T. (2003). A model of small business HR growth management. *International Journal of Entrepreneurial Behaviour & Research, 9*(1), 24–49. doi:10.1108/13552550310461036

McDonald & Oates. (2003). Reasons for non-participation in a curbside recycling scheme. *Resources, Conservation and Recycling*, *39*(1), 369–385.

McLean, L. (2005). Organizational culture's influence on creativity and innovation: A review of the literature and implications for human resource development. *Advances in Developing Human Resources*, *7*(2), 226–246. doi:10.1177/1523422305274528

Morrison, J. (2006). *International Business Environment: Global and Local Marketplaces in a changing world*. New York: Palgrave MacMillan. doi:10.1007/978-0-230-20957-2

Mumford, M. D. (2000). Managing creative people: Strategies and tactics for innovation. *Human Resource Management Review*, *10*(3), 313–351. doi:10.1016/S1053-4822(99)00043-1

Nanthuru, S. B., Pingfeng, L., Guihua, N., & Mkonya, V. L. (2018). An Assessment of Risk Management Practices of SME Taxpayers in Malawi and their Impact on Tax Compliance. *International Journal of Management Science and Business Administration*, *4*(4), 7–17. doi:10.18775/ijmsba.1849-5664-5419.2014.44.1001

Newell, S., Scarborough, H., Robertson, M., & Swan, J. (2002). *Managing Knowledge Work* (1st ed.). New York: Palgrave Macmillan.

Ngwenyama, O., & Morawczynski, O. (2009). Factors Affecting ICT Expansion in Emerging Economies: An Analysis of ICT Infrastructure Expansion in Five Latin American Countries. *Information Technology for Development*, *15*(4), 237–258. doi:10.1002/itdj.20128

Nicolescu, L., & Nicolescu, C. (2012). Innovation in SMEs – Findings from Romania. *Economia e Sociologia*, *5*(2a), 71–85.

O'Neill, G. D., Hershauer, J. C., & Golder, J. S. (2006). The cultural context of sustainability entrepreneurship. *Greener Manag. Inst.*, *55*(1), 33–46. doi:10.9774/GLEAF.3062.2006.au.00005

Ogunyomi, P., & Bruning, N. S. (2016). Human resource management and organizational performance of small and medium enterprises (SMEs) in Nigeria. *International Journal of Human Resource Management*, *27*(6), 612–634. doi:10.1080/09585192.2015.1033640

Organisation for Economic Co-operation and Development. (2000). *Enhancing the competitiveness of SMEs in the global economy: Strategies and policies*. OECD.

Poon, W. C., Mohamad, O., & Yusoff, W. F. (2018). Examining the Antecedents of Ambidextrous behaviours in Promoting Creativity among SMEs in Malaysia. *Global Business Review*, *21*(3), 1–1. doi:10.1177/0972150918779267

Ramukumba, T. (2014). Overcoming SMEs challenges through critical success factors: A case of SMEs in the Western Cape Province, South Africa. *Economic and Business Review for Central and South-Eastern Europe*, *16*(1), 19–38.

Republic of South Africa (RSA). (2002). *Advanced Manufacturing Technology Strategy*. Cape Town: Department of Science and Technology.

Rogers, E. M. (2003). *Diffusion of Innovations* (5th ed.). New York: Free Press.

Rogerson, C. A. (2008). Tracking SMME development in South Africa: issues of finance, training and regulatory environment. *Urban Forum, 1*(1), 61-81.

Sarvadi, P. (2005). *The importance of employee development*. Available at: https://www.entrepreneur.com/article/77678

Small Enterprise Development Agency (SEDA). (2007). Available at: www.seda.co.za

Smit, Y., & Watkins, J. A. (2012). A Literature Review of Small and Medium Enterprises (SME) Risk Management Practices in South Africa. *African Journal of Business Management*, *6*(21), 6324–6330.

Statistics South Africa. (2015). *Quarter 2. Quarterly Labour Force Survey, Pretoria*. Available at: Http://Www.Statssa.Gov.Za/Default.Asp

Szłapka, J. O., Stachowiak, A., Batz, A., & Fertsch, P. M. (2017). The Level of Innovation in SMEs, the Determinants of Innovation and their Contribution to Development of Value Chains. *Procedia Manufacturing*, *11*, 2203–2210. doi:10.1016/j.promfg.2017.07.367

Tarik, B. (2006). Dynamics of 'technological creativity' as a decision in knowledge creation process. *Proceedings of the PICMET'06 Conference: Technology Management for the Global Future*.

The South African Reserve Bank. (2015). *The role of small business in the economy*. Author.

Torrance, E. P. (1969). *Creativity*. Sioux Falls: Adapt Press.

Tripathi, S. N., & Siddiqui, M. H. (2012). Marketing of SME Products: A 'Relationship' Approach. *ASCI Journal of Management*, *41*(2), 76–106.

van Scheers, L., & Makhitha, K. M. (2016). Are Small and Medium Enterprises (SMEs) Planning for Strategic Marketing in South Africa? *Foundations of Management*, *8*(1), 243–250. doi:10.1515/fman-2016-0019

World Bank. (2010). *World Development Indicator Database*. Available at: http://worldbank.org/wbsite/external/datastatistics

Zhang, P., & Gheibi, S. (2015). From Intrinsic Motivation to Employee Creativity: The Role of Knowledge Integration and Team Psychological Safety. *European Scientific Journal*, *11*(11), 380–392.

Zhou, J., & George, J. M. (2001). When job dissatisfaction leads to creativity: Encouraging the expression of voice. *Academy of Management Journal*, *44*(4), 682–696.

KEY TERMS AND DEFINITIONS

Circular Economy: An economic system aimed at eliminating wastage by continually using same resource.

Creativity: It refers to a person using his/her original thoughts to invent something or create something for the marketplace.

Entrepreneurs: An entrepreneur is a person who takes risks in order to create a new lucrative business opportunity to make profits.

Innovation: It can refer to the creation of a new product or service that is more efficient and effect.

SMEs: This refers to small and medium-sized businesses.

Chapter 29 Leadership to Cultivate the Circular Economy

Damini Saini
https://orcid.org/0000-0001-5734-5067
Indian Institute of Management, Raipur, India

Juhi Agarwal
https://orcid.org/0000-0001-9768-440X
Techno Institute of Higher Studies, Lucknow, India

ABSTRACT

A business meets the need of the present world and the environment without compromising the requirement of the current scenario, that is, sustainability of the resources. Everyone affects the sustainability of the marketplace and the Earth in some way or another. Sustainable development within a business is able to create value for customers, investors, and the environment. This naturally involves taking a long-term perspective and balancing economic, environmental, and social impacts of business. In today's business environment, it is highly important that organizations develop and adhere to the appropriate policies and systems that create a sustainable future for the world. The purpose of this chapter is to highlight the circular economy and the critical role leadership will play in it. The authors describe the circular economy and its major concepts and approaches along with its background. Further, the major challenges and encounters of leadership in a circular economy are also discussed.

INTRODUCTION

The world population is standing at around 7.5 billion as of April 2019, according to recent statistics, out of which, India alone is contributing approximately 17.9% in the total population. Together, we have reached at an alarming situation where the bearing capacity of our planet has jeopardized to the extent that if immediate panacea is not looked out, the reverberations will be unendurable. The rate of consumption is far beyond the regenerating capacity of the planet. The continuous increase in the physiological needs of the humans has put the business organizations under immense pressure to provide them with their

DOI: 10.4018/978-1-7998-5116-5.ch029

Copyright © 2020, IGI Global. Copying or distributing in print or electronic forms without written permission of IGI Global is prohibited.

necessities at the right time and right place. The notion of take-make-consume-waste, as followed by the majority of people, is one of the main reasons behind the destructive use of the limited resources. The Millennium Ecosystem Assessment 2005, as given by the Ellen MacArthur Foundation (2013), says that fifteen out of the recognized twenty-four ecosystem services (i.e. processes of nature that support human wellbeing) are used in an unsustainable manner and are being depleted. Thus, continuous measures at global, institutional and individual level have to be taken up for the sustainability so as to ensure that there are no pernicious consequences in near future. This realization has led to the emergence of the concepts like Circular Economy,sustainable development, resource planning and management, triple bottom line, Reuse-Reduce-Recycle and many more,keeping aside the old school of thought, like Linear Economy. Where Linear Economy works on the simple principle of gratification of needs, Circular Economy takes into consideration the environmental sustainability as well.

Circular economy is the major focus of this chapter. The chapter will be talking about the how the leadership impact upon circular economy. We will try to focus sustainability first which is again a very popular and important expression these days. Then we will relate it with economy and will move forward to linear and circular economy. Finally, we will discuss that how leadership can be helpful in establishing circular economy in countries.

Sustainability

The word sustainability is derived from the Latin *sustinere* (*tenere*, to hold; *sus*, up). Various dictionaries postulatevarious different meanings for *sustain*, the main ones being to "maintain", "support", or "endure".

Sustainability serves as a preservative material which preserves the pleasant and delicious recipe of economic jam all around economic enterprises in its profitable state for both producer as well as consumers. Containers play an important role in keeping them quite in act and fresh fit to consume to fixing any date of expiry on the product. So we can say that ethics and sustainability can be seldom the two sides of current coin.

Corporate sustainability is a business approach that creates long-term consumer and employee value by not only creating a "green" strategy aimed towards the natural environment, but taking into thought every dimension of the surrounding of business as how a business operates in the social, cultural, and economic environment. Corporate sustainability also express approaches to build a company that cultivatespermanence through transparency and proper employee development.

The term 'sustainable development' was coined by the 1987 report 'Our Common Future' by the World Commission of Environment and Development (WCED) (Redclift, 1989, p.365 ff.; Palmer, 1992, p.1011 ff.).

The growing concern for environment, resources and social equity in the 1980s led to the emergence of the concept of sustainable development (Hunter, 1997; Mowforth& Munt, 2009), which was defined as 'development that meets the needs of the present without comprising the ability of future generations to meet their own needs' (WCED, 1987: 43) by the 'Brundtland Report'.

It is a constant horizontal graph line of output must be maintained at all cost. The concept of sustainability had been in the all the field of human activities since time. Immemorial in the field of health, wealth, name, fame, sovereignty, command, kingdom, sports and lastly in spiritual achievement as well. The champions in the above field tried their level best to standard and their level forever. Its common when the aims and targets are high, simply achieving is not enough. achievement is only the starting for output for which so mush labor, planning has been put in the crop is ready for harvesting. the desired fruit is here, but n the field of economy it must be kept constant. Since the acceleration of communication technology, the thinkers and the scholars of economic development are constantly searching and researching the ways, means methods through collecting data's, graph by visiting personally so that they might be able to evolve such methods techniques to maintain the most valuable achievement in entering the hundred percent efficiency zone of quality and quantity of the economic activity. The effort or consciousness to maintain the level of efficiency has been named as stability in social development. It can also be called sustainability.

Sustainability is basically the capacity to endure. For human being sustainability is the long-term maintenance of responsibilities in the fields of all economic activities. This also covers the environmental, economic and social dimension and covers larger area of leadership or stewardship, the responsible management of resources available for economic purposes. Since 1980's sustainability has been used more in the sense of human sustainability on the globe and this sense has been used in most widely quoted definition of sustainable and sustainable development. At 2005 world summit it was observed that At the 2005 World Summit on Social Development it was noted that this requires the reconciliation of environmental, social equity and economic demands - the "three pillars" of sustainability, and business comes under these three spheres of life that is how itis also connect with sustainability.

Sustainability, in layman terms, refers to the generic development, but not at the cost of others. Others could be any living or non-livingconstituent of the planet. With the devastating state of the environment, either because of the overutilization or wastage of resources, the term sustainability came into existence, but it is no less than just a buzzword. Business organizations, general public, universal platforms are endlessly working on adoption of the measures for sustainable development but the term is not well elaborated and understood by many. Some understand Sustainability as reduction in the over exploitation of limited resources for the sake of future generations, whereas some take it as reducing and eliminating the over pollutants.

According to Harwood (1990), "it is a system that can evolve indefinitely toward greater human utility, greater efficiency of resource use, and a balance with the environment which is favorable to humans and most other species." According to Pearce, Makandia and Barbier (1989) – "it involves devising the economic and social system, which ensures that these goals are sustained, i.e., that real income rise, that educational standards increase, that the health of the nation improves, that the general quality of life is advanced."

In the year 1987, the United Nations Brundtland Commission defined sustainability as "meeting the needs of the present without compromising the ability of future generations to meet their own needs." Sustainability Development Goals have been adopted by the UN in the year 2015 so as to eradicate the evils of destruction like poverty, degradation of planet, inequality, lack of educational facilities and many more to make this world a peaceful and prosperous place by the year 2030.

Linear Economy

According to the Ellen MacArthur Foundation (2013), "the currently prevailing economic design has its roots in the historically uneven distribution of wealth by geographic region." This unevenness is the mother of most of the problems prevailing. Some has it in abundance and thus take undue advantage of this natural favor and some are completely deprived off it and thus their thrust to acquire it may lead to severe repercussions.

Linear Economy works on the traditional outlay of take-make-use-throw, where the resources are first extracted from the system; they are then molded so as to sell them to the prospective buyers, and thus the liability of using and disposing ultimately lies with the buyer. Companies make profits by fulfilling the demands of the prospective consumers and completely ignore the ill effects that follow like over exploitation of the scarce resources, wastage, over consumption and many more. Henceforth, in this economic system perspective, value creation depends on the large-scale manufacturing and selling. In the process of human need satisfaction and value creation, many million tons of energy and resources are wasted either as being an outcome of production process or after the ultimate consumption by the end users, leading to deterioration of the planet and environment as a whole. Manufacturing and consumption will be leading towards non-transformable waste. The global economy is deeply embedded in this vicious circle. Linear Economy now seems to be a noxious cocktail of damaging consequences, leading to social injustice, inequalities, depletion and extinction of our natural resources and worsening the situation by risking and effecting climate and environment, which is an utmost necessity for human survival.

Circular Economy

A 'circular economy' (CE) is an approach that would transform the function of resources in the economy. Waste from factories would become a valuable input to another process – and products could be repaired, reused or upgraded instead of thrown away (Preston, 2012).

The concept of the Circular Economy has become popular since the late 1970s (EMF, 2013b). Several authors, like Andersen (2007), Ghisellini,Cialani and Ulgiati(2016), and Su,Heshmati, Geng and Yu(2013) helped to develop the concept of circular economy to Pearce and Turner (1989). With the description of how natural resources influence the economy by providing inputs for production and consumption as well as serving as a sink for outputs in the form of waste, they investigated the linear and open-ended characteristics of contemporary economic systems. (Martin, Paulo, Bocken&Hultink, 2016). Circular economy involveremodelling industrial systems along lines of ecosystems, recognizing the efficiency of resource cycling in the natural environment.

The term Circular Economy was introduced by Pearce and Turner (1989), although the concept has its hold since the 1960s. The term is defined as "a guiding principle for development that encompasses three aims which must be accomplished simultaneously: Environmental quality, economic prosperity and social equity" (Taylor, 2016; Fulton, 2012; Elkington, 1997; WCED, 1987).

We define the Circular Economy as a regenerative system in which resource input and waste, emission, and energy leakage are minimised by slowing, closing, and narrowing material and energy loops. This can be achieved through long-lasting design, maintenance, repair, reuse, remanufacturing, refurbishing, and recycling. Otherwise the meaning of circular economy will be changed to the different sectors. It can be good for some, but on the other side for some it might mean having to battle for survival.

Circular economy, thus, concentrates on the notion of reuse, reduce, and recycle of the resources and adopting innovating measures to minimize the wastage rather than simply dumping the resources used, thereby ensuring sustainability with profitability. To make it a success, innovative business models are required so as to eradicate the loopholes of the existing economic system, and move forward with the mechanisms to shape and redesign the waste and pollutants, production systems and preserving the natural environment. This type of economy necessitates the detachment of the economy from the use of limited resources and couple up with the usage of renewable resources so as to design out waste from the system. It is fostered by the use of these non- conventional sources thereby building and nurturing social, economic environment altogether.

Leadership

Leadership refers to the process of influencing others towards a common goal as directed by the leader. It can be defined as a social, interactional process of uplifting and empowering others for those evolutionary changes that are more advisable.

Peter F. Drucker (1996) explains leadership as "The only definition of a leader is someone who has followers." Warren Bennis stated that "Leadership is the capacity to translate vision into reality." He further explored that "Leadership is a function of knowing yourself, having a vision that is well communicated, building trust among colleagues, and taking effective action to realize your own leadership potential". According to Rauch and Behling (1984), – "It is defined as the process of influencing the activities of an organized group towards goal achievement." Here as Hemphill and Coons (1957) explains leadership as "the behavior of an individual when he is directing the activities of a group towards a shared goal."

Leading is an art of directing people to act in a way that common objectives are achieved. When we talk of it in business organizations, it can be understood as directing the employees towards the accomplishment of the organizational goals along with the individual objectives. It is an inspirational act to motivate and direct others to behave and perform in a certain pre-decided manner.Leadership cannot be confined to something that comes with position; it can be present at different levels of management. Many presume leadership to be the trait of Top Management of an organization, which is creating an illusion for the ones who have this as inherited trait but are not at any specified position.

They are the ones having a vision, and it takes time to implement. They are not in the present, they dive with their skills and mindset into the future. One of the prominent futurechallenges is of the sustainable development. And thus, it requires leaders to base their work on environment, innovation and fulfillment of human aspirations and needs. Leaders build trustsand confidence among its followers and take advantage of the good coordination, connectivity and intelligence of team members. Leaders do not get influenced with present profits,but by an amazing, sustainable, innovative way of changing an aspect of life or of doing business or anything that is unique and makes a difference. Leaders invest most often in people, helping them to feel proud of being the member of the team and getting their support in reaching the target, sometimes even by exceeding their performance levels, bylearning new things, and having a creative approach and ultimately by having effective communication.

Relevance of Circular Economy

With the continuous degradation in the quality of life because of the unsustainable factors, it is a prerequisite to adopt a different approach so as to jump out of the vicious circle of the traditional theory of make-use-dispose. The new approach will create awareness and keep the utility of resources high which in turn will lead to sustainability, through innovative leadership style and efficient management. The inner loops of re-use reduce and recycle complements the whole phenomenon of circular economy. Some of the major precedence that it provides constitutes of:

- Regeneration of the system;
- Elongating the life span of goods and services;

- Optimizing the production and supply chains;
- Technological advancements;
- Resource efficiency along with societal welfare;
- Delivery system shift to virtual platforms;
- Positive impact on the economic growth;
- Natural environment protection and conservation;
- Expansion and growth opportunities for the corporate and business houses;
- Elevating the standards of living for the individuals.

It is utmost clear that circular Economy is relatively new in its conceptualisation and implementation, there may also be further add-ons and limitations inherent in its appropriation and application.

Relevance of Leadership in Circular Economy

The roles and responsibilities of the leaders and the top-level managements of organizations in creating a space for circular economy and sustainability in their already existing cycles is very crucial. Henceforth, this related concept of sustainability and circular economy is of great deal for creating an ethical culture for the overall development.

Major system changes in the organizations are not easy to implement as employees refrain themselves from accepting them either because of the fear of employment loss, or the inability to adjust in the new working culture. Shifting towards the circular economy often faces such barriers, even though it is an altogether developing approach, because of the narrow mindedness of the stakeholders. Hence, it is of utmost importance that the leaders take up the front seat and handle the state of affairs. Business leaders have the responsibility to foster collaboration and direct the organization towards a sustainability approach and configure new agendas and policies for the same.

With the changing requirements of the humans and the already depleted resource bank of the planet, it is quite evident that the society is compelled to shift towards the circular economy. The ongoing situations be it Amazon Fire or uneven climatic conditions or overproduction and exploitation of the resources and wastage, are an alarming situation that we need to alter our practices and move towards a sustainable approach. It is not only impacting the economy but the environment at large.

One aspect here is to know and be aware about what has to be transformed and the other is to analyze how to overcome the resistance to change in the whole new process. In order to understand and make through this potential, effective leadership is required across all the facets of the organization that anything and everything that we extract and utilize from the planet need not to be disposed of, rather it has to be restored back in the process. This drastic change cannot be implemented overnight, it requires purposeful and transformational leadership to combat the situation (Geng, Sarkis, & Ulgiati, 2016).

Business Leaders need to adopt a collaborative approach to manifest this circular goal. It is a prerequisite to create such a corporate working environment, at a global level, that regardless of the place of origin or country, the main objective is clinched. This can only be embraces with the presence of good leaders who have the required skills to direct this journey towards a success. As a leader, they have to understand the changing requirements of the people, needs and requirements of the stakeholders as well as the concern towards the environment and society.

Policy-makers should focus on accelerating transition to a CE in a timescale consistent with the response to climate change, water scarcity and other global challenges. Smart regulation can reward private-sector leadership and align incentives along the supply chain – for example, to deliver a step-change in remanufacturing rates (Preston, 2012).

Collaborative leadership involves the employees as well, understanding their part of contribution to the whole process as well as working in group culture, catering to the requirements of a larger geographical distribution at once. In this form of leadership, the leaders do not adopt authoritative but participatory leadership style so as to keep the whole system in touch. This often leads to:

- Providing a sense of empowerment to the stakeholders, so as to inculcate them completely in the process;
- Networking and inter-connectivity of the stakeholders across the globe;
- Participation leading to closer look at what the work groups are leading to;
- Immediate resolution to the conflicts and resistance among people.

Industry bodies can play a key role in facilitating dialogue between leaders on a CE and other companies that stand to gain from making the transition (Preston, 2012).

Value based leadership can also give the positive outcomes as it involves the amalgamation of the personal beliefs of the stakeholders along with the organizational values and thereby striking a balance between the two so as to sustain any change.

This change can only be catalyzed at such a large scale if the multiple players of research field and business communities, across the globe, come together and identify the gaps and devise the strategy for the obstacles undisputedly. In addition to the collaborative style, many other different styles of leadership can be practiced by the business leaders as per the need and environment of that place.

As a leader, one needs to understand that since the human footprint on the environment is heavily increasing, so does the responsibility towards sustaining it and at the same time the barriers restricting it. The role of effecting leadership thus emerges as of utmost importance to direct the whole situation in a right manner and at right time. According to Wallici(2017)The leader can take various steps so as to take circular economy on a right platform, like:

- Realizing the importance and benefit of shifting from a linear economy to a circular one and make the people understand it as well in due time so as to limit the undue exploitation of resources on the verge of extinction;
- Committing towards the circular supply chain, and inducing changes in all the other facets of the business process;
- Standardizing the materials that are used in the industries so that recycling and reusing cannot be limited and product improvements can be made across sectors;
- Aligning the circular concept with every part and process of the business so as to implement it in an effective and efficient way;
- Limiting to the methodologies and changes prescribed under the jurisdiction and aligning with the laws and rules formulated at the global level.

There are numerous examples from round the world to add to the same.

France has seen leadership initiatives from the NGO sector with organisations like l'instituteconomiecirculaire campaigning and organising events and initiatives. French companies like SNCF, Orange France, Capenergies and La Poste have partnered with a French Business School in a

Research Chair researching the circular economy. In the Netherlands, a similar impetus is being developed with the NGO 'Circle Economy' working to the same ends in partnership with public and private enterprises. There are similar initiatives are developing in many other European countries also, as interest grows. (Murray, Skene&Haynes, 2017).

Carrez, D., and Van Leeuwen, P. (2015). Stated that EU governments and Members of the European Parliament (MEPs) will have to decide on how to go about legislating on this one: as a team deploying a vision for Europe, or as the sum of national interests? The circular economy is an opportunity to lead Europe and its citizens into the economic model of the 21st century. A Circular economy vision for a competitive Europehighlighteda few very important key benefits for Europefor example GDP increase, development path, Co^2 emission reduction and positive employment. All of these can be converted into reality but only with the effective political leadership wit interest in this matter.

Discussing effective leadership Bejjani (2019) stated that in the Atlantic, Costa Rica is emerging to be a global leader in initiatives circulating conservation of the resources, while, California and its groundbreaking laws towards limiting greenhouse gas emissions is becoming exemplar for other legislatures to follow the same. The United Arab Emirates (UAE) became the first government to sign the initiative of guaranteeing to make investmentin the development of circular supply chains, in the world. With this stratagem, it has showcased the world that visionary leadership is required from government, people, society, business, individuals, to succeed in every facet of life.There are other nations as well who have willingly committed themselves towards attaining a sustainable future with their distinctive leadership strategies. Countries like Denmark, Norway and many more are heavily investing in renewable energy projects, recycling measures, so as to ensure improved future. There are many global business houses like Tata, Dell, PepsiCo, etc, who are continuously evolving in terms of adopting sustainable measures as a result of the guidance and leadership they are receiving from the top management and owners (Bejjani, 2019).

The circular economy offers a transformational agenda that aims to redesign global production and consumption systems. Many of the ideas are decades old, but a combi- nation of environmental and resource price pressures, technological advancements and changes in consumer demand is finally building momentum. Both the private sector and governments increasingly recognize that future competitiveness will depend on leadership in resource-related innovation.

Visionary and transformational leadership will definitely mark its success in the long run and ultimately create the difference in this world (Epure & Bucea-Manea-Ţoniş, 2017). Having high emotional intelligence, the leaders do understand people effectively and patiently drive themtowards transforming problems and risks present in opportunities and challenges respectively. Leaders work according to their own visions, and have a clear picture of what the final target is, they know how to formulate strategies, knows how to effectively communicate the goals to the teammates and how to get them involved, and keep them motivated and inspired by their project. As a consequence, every new situation needs a leader to direct it in the right direction.

CHALLENGES AND OPPORTUNITIES IN CIRCULAR ECONOMY

There are various challenges imposed by different sections of the society while implementing the phenomenon of circular economy discarding the linear one. Some of them might be:

- **Effectuation and worthiness:** It cannot be validated that all the materials can be recycled at 100% again and again in the process. There are certain constraints which clamp down the process of recycling at a later stage. Henceforth the execution is quite grueling. Alternately, the overall cost and expenditure can be detrimental. In many instances, the cost of material after recycling may be less than that of the expenses put in while recycling;
- **Lack of judicious guidelines:** The framework of circular economy does not provide standardized norms and implementation measures, as the cycle differs with the product differentials, thereby making it a complicated set of actions to be undertaken. The same measures cannot be applied to sectors non-identical sectors across the globe;
- **Socio-environmental sustainability:** Circular Economy somewhere lacks the social as well as environmental sustainability agendas, as it is deeply rooted in the business tactics and henceforth strives to achieve them equally;
- **Training and Development:** It requires high cost of investment in training and development of the employees so as to enhance their aptitude and knowledge bank in alignment with the objectives of Circular Economy.

There are numerous other challenges like standardization, evaluation, implementation problems and challenges associated with the approving and adopting the circular economy measures. Nevertheless, with great challenges come great opportunities. The ongoing consequences of the already depleted resource bank have created ample opportunities for taking up the measures for ensuring sustainability. For example:

- **Economic and industrial resumption:** Circular Economy transition requires change in the capital investments, assets management, human resource policies, henceforth overall strategic change, giving the industry and the economy a new boost to refrain from all the shortcomings and renew its work policies and measures;
- **Pertinent timeframe:** With the diminishing resource bank of the planet, considerations towards this deficiency has been highlighted throughout and the public is outraged for a change, henceforth paving the way to shift towards the Circular approach;
- **Employment generation:** The changing model of circular economy is carving out employment opportunities as well for the people as it involves creation of multiple circular loops in the economy and adding up steps in the procedures of production and waste management;
- **Capacity to innovate:** It created window for innovation backed by researches from the academia and corporate and new learning so as to arrogate creative measures and implement them effectively and efficiently.

Analysis of Adoption of Circular Economy in Other Countries

Different models, ideas and programs are being initiated in world's economy time and again, which are helpful in serving the humanity in terms of creating the values in management and meeting and overcoming the sustainability challenges. Although, a single country cannot achieve it, efforts from round the world is required. The need to move from extracting and using economy to restoring and recycling economy is welcomed by the global leaders and henceforth various nations like China, Europe, Germany, Netherlands and many more are redirecting their economy towards these required circular economy plans.

Looking at the European point of view, the concept of circular economy was leaded by the European Union (EU). It has been a long time since its inception, it can be observed that the member countries are also preparing their strategic moves towards the adoption of circular economy, be it Italy, France, Dutch, Finland and many more. They are still on the preparation and planning phase of policy making so as to enhance the resource efficiency, leading the way ahead for others to adopt the similar.

Germany on the other hand, is escalating towards the implementation of circular economy with the prime focus towards waste management and recycling with the enactments like German Closed Cycle Management Act, National Waste Prevention Programme and many more, as they are high on industrial economy and their cycle of manufacture-using-disposing-recycling is crucial, because of the limited availability of the resources.

In China, the circular economy framework was adopted because of the resource scarcity and environment issues that the country was facing, and since then it is being implemented in the different sectors of the country successfully so as to optimally utilize the resources and energy in the whole process. Be it the Cleaner Production Promotion Law, Circular Economy Promotion Law (2009) or the adoption of Triple R (reuse, reduce, recycle), or inculcating circular economy provisions in their 11th and 12th Five Year Plans, they are continually evolving new policies and frameworks for economical and natural conservation.

In countries like France and Netherlands, the concepts of public-private partnerships are being idealized for the execution of circular economy, with the alliance of Ngo sectors. Similar initiatives are taken up by many other European Countries as well, because of the growing need and curiosity towards it.

The leading advocate of Circular Economy is the Ellen MacArthur Foundation of UK, which keep on bringing up the issue through its reports year after year. In its report of 2014, it stated that the inputs used in the process of manufacturing should be categorized according to their potential of being recycled and redesigned, using specific examples which can be implemented by the global organizations. Various other countries are still lacking the clear vision towards the conceptualization of Circular Economy as it is hard for them to keep up with these high order issues.

CONCLUSION AND RECOMMENDATIONS

We began this chapter by identifying the necessity for a new economy, that is called as circular economy, which is successfully growing in few parts of the world. Chapter already talked about the meaning and understanding of circular economy. We believed this new way of envisioning economy would serve as a remedy and help in creating a sustainable future that every nation is looking forward to. The work contributes to the contemporary debate on the contribution of leadership in developing circular economy. Circular economy is the valuation of resources in a circular loop system with the object to allow for use of natural resources while shredding pollutants or avoiding resource constraints and henceforth sustaining the socio-economic and environmental growth. Transitioning towards a circular economy requires lot of time, effort and energy as it inculcates catering to all the hiccups and acquiring numerous opportunities in the way. This has to be implemented at the individual, regional, and global level so as to make it a great success. It has been discussed in the chapter that moving towards circular economy is a boon for the planet if implemented in an appropriate manner. Various countries have already started working towards it and now it is spreading its roots all over the globe. It has been observed that circular economy can lead us towards social, economic, as well as natural conservation and development. As we move forward, the corporate momentum clearly specifies that the opportunities are only going to expand in favor of circular economy in near future. Circular economy measures are often present with the developing and underdeveloped nations, but are not mainstreamed because of the existence of uneven economic growth and lack of financial backup. Corporate houses, academic and research personnel, together with the government and political support, needs to capture the concept altogether to attain sustainability. Different leaders from public-private-not for profit sector can catalyze innovative and creative measures of circular economy towards new processes, products, policy frameworks.

REFERENCES

Andersen, M. S. (2007). An introductory note on the environmental economics of the circular economy. *Sustainability Science*, *2*(1), 133–140. doi:10.100711625-006-0013-6

Bejjani, A. (2019). Here's how the business can make the circular economy a reality. *Circular economy*. Accessed on 23 Feb 2020 https://www.weforum.org/agenda/2019/12/circular-economy-business-environment/

Bennis, W. G., & Thomas, R. J. (2002). *Geeks and Geezers: How era, values, and defining moments shape leaders*. Boston, MA: Harvard Business School Press.

Carrez, D., & Van Leeuwen, P. (2015). Bioeconomy: Circular by nature. *The European Files*, *38*, 34–35.

Drucker, P. F. (1996). Your leadership is unique. *Leadership*, *17*(4), 54.

Elkington. (1997). *Cannibals with Forks: Triple Bottom Line of 21st Century Business*. Capstone Publishing.

Epure, M., & Bucea-Manea-Țoniș, R. (2017). Branding and Leadership in the context of Circular Economy. *Procedia of Economics and Business Administration*, 163-172.

Fulton, S. C. (2012). Twenty years after the rio earth summit: What is the agenda for the 2012 United Nations Conference on Sustainable Development? *Proceedings of the Annual Meeting American Society of International Law*, 91-94.

Geissdoerfer, M., Savaget, P., Bocken, N. M., & Hultink, E. J. (2017). The Circular Economy–A new sustainability paradigm? *Journal of Cleaner Production*, *143*, 757–768.

Geng, Y., Sarkis, J., & Ulgiati, S. (2016). Sustainability, well-being, and the circular economy in China and worldwide. *Science*, *6278*(Supplement), 73–76.

Ghisellini, P., Cialani, C., & Ulgiati, S. (2016). A review on circular economy: The expected transition to a balanced interplay of environmental and economic systems. *Journal of Cleaner Production*, *114*, 11–32. doi:10.1016/j.jclepro.2015.09.007

Harwood, R. R. (1990). A history of sustainable agriculture. *Sustainable agricultural Systems*, 3-19.

Hemphill, J. K., & Coons, A. E. (1957). Leader behavior: Its description and measurement. *Administrative Science Quarterly*, 6–38.

Hunter, C. (1997). Sustainable tourism as an adaptive paradigm. *Annals of Tourism Research, 24*(4), 850–867. doi:10.1016/S0160-7383(97)00036-4

MacArthur, E. (2013). *Towards the circular economy, economic and business rationale for an accelerated transition*. Cowes, UK: Ellen MacArthur Foundation.

Mowforth, M., & Munt, I. (2009). *Tourism and sustainability: Development. Globalisation and New Tourism in the Third World* (3rd ed.). London: Routledge.

Murray, A., Skene, K., & Haynes, K. (2017). The circular economy: An interdisciplinary exploration of the concept and application in a global context. *Journal of Business Ethics, 140*(3), 369–380. doi:10.100710551-015-2693-2

Our Common Future. (2013b). *World Commission on Environment and Development. (1987). Oxford University Press*. Oxford: EMF.

Palmer, G. (1992). New ways to make international environmental law. *The American Journal of International Law, 86*(2), 259–283. doi:10.2307/2203234

Pearce, D. W., Markandya, A., & Barbier, E. B. (1989). Blueprint for a Green Economy. *Earthscan, London, UK., 1989*, 1–47.

Pearce, D. W., & Turner, R. K. (1990). *Economics of natural resources and the environment*. Baltimore: The John Hopkis University Press.

Preston, F. (2012). *A global redesign?: Shaping the circular economy*. London: Chatham House.

Rauch, C. F., Jr., & Behling, O. (1984). Functionalism: Basis for an alternate approach to the study of leadership. In Leaders and managers (pp. 45-62). Pergamon.

Redclift, M. (1989). The environmental consequences of Latin America's agricultural development: Some thoughts on the Brundtland Commission report. *World Development, 17*(3), 365–377. doi:10.1016/0305-750X(89)90210-6

Standing Committee of the National People's Congress. (2009). China Circular Economy Promotion Law of the People's Republic of China.

Su, B., Heshmati, A., Geng, Y., & Yu, X. (2013). A review of the circular economy in China: Moving from rhetoric to implementation. *Journal of Cleaner Production, 42*, 215–227. doi:10.1016/j.jclepro.2012.11.020

Taylor, S.J. (2016). *A Review of Sustainable Development Principles*. Academic Press.

Walicki, J. (2017). 5 Things Leaders Can Do to Create a Truly Circular Economy. World Economic Forum Annual Meeting 2017. Accessed on 23feb2020

WCED. ((1987). *Report of the World Commission on Environment and Development: Our Common Future*. WCED.

Chapter 30
Measuring Infopreneurial Intentions of Library and Information Science Graduating Students

Gratitude Chiwara-Ndoro
National University of Science and Technology, Zimbabwe

Peterson Dewah
https://orcid.org/0000-0002-3856-7921
National University of Science and Technology, Zimbabwe & University of KwaZulu-Natal, South Africa

ABSTRACT

The purpose of the study anchoring this chapter was to measure the extent to which the students from the Department of Library and Information Science had intentions to venture into infopreneurship after graduating with their Bachelor of Science Honours Degree in Library and Information Science. Using a mixed-method design, data were collected from a population of 45 students through questionnaires and semi-structured interviews. Findings revealed that the majority (25) students intended to pursue infopreneurship as information consultants, information brokers, researchers, information literacy assistants, writers, and proofreaders. The study concluded that infopreneurship could be a panacea to the unemployed information science graduates in Zimbabwe. Since the field of infopreneurship is unique and under-researched, the study recommends the creation of a community of practice of infopreneurs who research, share ideas, collaborate, and make the field of infopreneurship robust and efficient in creating employment opportunities for information science graduates.

DOI: 10.4018/978-1-7998-5116-5.ch030

Copyright © 2020, IGI Global. Copying or distributing in print or electronic forms without written permission of IGI Global is prohibited.

INTRODUCTION

Entrepreneurship development in higher education equips students with knowledge and skills to venture into businesses that create employment and contribute to the economic growth of a country. With the broadness of entrepreneurship bearing in mind the discipline specific competencies of university students, Infopreneurship has been deemed a panacea for the unemployment situation being faced by Information Science graduates. This is because infopreneurship encourages the leveraging of familiar capacities in information science to create individual business ventures (information-based entrepreneurship). With the unemployment rate steadily rising in Zimbabwe, this study aimed at measuring the extent at which the part 4 final year students from the department of Library and Information Science had intentions to venture into infopreneurship after graduating with their Bachelor of Science Honours Degree in Library and Information Science. The infopreneurship module was introduced at the National University of Science Technology in 2011 (Dewah and Mutula, 2016), but for Records and Archives Management (RAM) students. The 2018- 2019 part 4 final year LIS class was the pioneer group to enrol in this specialised field of infopreneurship hence the researchers' desire to measure if the students had infopreneurial intentions upon completion of this new module borrowed from the sister department, Records and Archives Management. Ivwurie and Ocholla (2016) observed that in South Africa and Nigeria, the graduates who had intentions and ultimately the behaviour to engage in infopreneurship were from the Computer Science department compared to the Information and Communication Science departments like Library and Information Science. David and Dube's (2014) study focused on the infopreneurial behaviour of people who had graduated from National University of Science and Technology [NUST] and their findings indicated positive infopreneurial initiatives, which were however discouraged by the lack of business and technical skills to translate the initiatives into real businesses. The few studies on infopreneurship that were identified (David and Dube, 2014; Dewah and Mutula, 2016; Iwurie and Ocholla, 2016) did not address the aspect of infopreneurial intentions by students. The present study addressed this gap by empirically examining students' views.

The chapter is organised in to four sections. The background section covers the entrepreneurship and infopreneurship development in students. Entrepreneurship in information studies is contextualised followed by the theoretical framework. The statement of the problem is explained and evidence is adduced. The methodology used to carry out the study processes is described and justified while the findings are presented first quantitative and then qualitative results in that order. Discussion of the findings follow before the chapter concludes with recommendations and areas for further research.

BACKGROUND

Universities and colleges, in various countries, across the globe have introduced entrepreneurial courses in their curriculum as a response to the increasing demand and to the request to promote careers in entrepreneurship (Postigo and Tamborini, 2002). Coduras, Urbano, Rojas and Martinez (2008) commends the significance of the university's support to the entrepreneurial activities. Kazmi and Nabradi (2017: 149) opine that "studies on entrepreneurship education focus on measuring the effectiveness of entrepreneurship education programmes in tertiary education only". It is important to note that some of the intentions to starting a business maybe induced by aspects in which the students can plan on or exercise self-control on. Xie (2014) has attributed traits, cognitive, environmental and demographic factors. The ultimate goal of infopreneurship is to create graduates who are self-motivated, confident and innovative to take opportunities and chances to engage in their own infopreneurial businesses.

Khan (2013) is of the view that business ventures contribute towards the generation of employment. After completing their Infopreneurship module, the part four final year Library and Information Science (LIS) students at the National University of Science and Technology are expected to venture into their own businesses. This study therefore sought to establish if the students had intentions to venture into infopreneurship after graduating. These unclear intentions may be attributed to the uniqueness of infopreneurship as a self –administered information business with the fundamentals of librarianship like managing information in libraries and information centres. Traditional library and information science modules describe the different parameters to librarianship. The students completed courses in Marketing, Human Resources Management, Comparative Librarianship and Knowledge Management. These courses supplement the traditional librarianship courses in Information retrieval, indexing and abstracting, cataloguing, organization of knowledge and database management. On the other hand, infopreneurship describes and encourages the use of all the skills acquired from the mentioned modules in starting one's own business venture.

Engaging in a self- administered business may be attributed to factors such as unemployment or menial jobs which retard professional growth, flexibility in the operating hours, desire for money, the need to use specific skills to the fullest and the preference to work independently (Xie, 2014; Ivwurie and Ocholla, 2016). Infopreneurial ventures may also be attributed to the willingness of people to pay for information services, weaknesses of the information service providers in providing specialised information, tailor made to user preferences and even motivation from the infopreneurs who are doing very well in the industry (David and Dube, 2014; Ivwurie and Ocholla, 2016; Dewah and Mutula, 2016; Ocholla, 1999; 1998). One can venture into information systems consultancy, bibliographic management consultancy, information digitisation consultancy, research consultancy, database management consultancy and even knowledge management consultancy. Ramugondo (2010) notes that infopreneurship fares well with the popularisation of information brokers, researchers, information advisors with activities in Compilation of directories, Publishing, Translation services, Information repackaging, Writing, editing and proof reading, Collection management, Records management, Cataloguing and research.

The objectives of this chapter are the following:

1. Find out the attitude of part 4 final year LIS students towards establishing an infopreneurial business after graduating with the BSc Hon. in LIS;
2. Establish how subjective norms influence infopreneurial intentions of the final year LIS students;
3. Identify the perceived behavioural control factors on intentions towards infopreneurial business of the final year LIS students;
4. Identify if the students' enrolment in the infopreneurship course influence their infopreneurial intentions;
5. Determine if the final year part 4 LIS students do possess infopreneurial qualities.

THE THEORY OF PLANNED BEHAVIOUR

The study draws from Ajzen's (1988) Theory of Planned Behaviour. The theory proposes that attitude, subjective norms and perceived behavioural control constructs influence intentions. Intentions are therefore precursors of behaviour. Figure 1 is how the theory explains that the stronger the intention, the more likely behaviour is to be performed.

Figure 1. Schematic presentation of the theory of planned behaviour
Source: Adapted from Ajzen (1988)

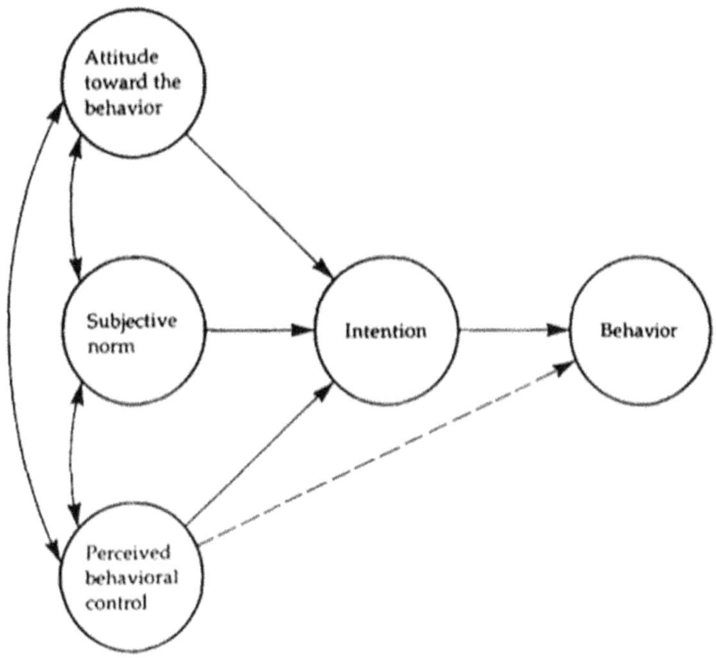

Lowe and Marriott (2006) describes the 'support environment' as comprising of family members, advisors and friends, the 'micro environment' comprising of competitors while the 'macro environment' comprising of the social, economic, legal, political and environmental factors. Though this theory has been refined, expanded and modified it has remained popular and has been applied in a number of studies. For instance, Kautonen, Van Gelderen, and Fink (2013) acknowledge the relevance and robustness of the theory of planned behavior as a framework for the prediction of new venture intentions and the subsequent behaviors.

Issues, Controversies, Problems

There is increasing evidence that job opportunities are limited in today's competitive job environment Keat, Selvarajah, Chr and Meyer (2011) and Zimbabwe is in a situation where job posts are frozen and unemployment is rampant. The Dean of students at the University of Zimbabwe, David Sithole, remarked that, 'our industries are either downsizing or shutting down completely. For our university graduates, there is nowhere to go' (Moyo, 2016). Noko and Ngulube (2015) conducted a tracer study of records and archives management graduates between 2008 and 2012 in Zimbabwe and found that 33% of RAM graduates were unemployed. The number may have increased significantly by now considering the time that has since passed yet the economy is not performing. Newsday (2016) reported on graduate employment uptake in Zimbabwe. Over 100 000 jobs have been lost since 2013. It also reported that 60% of the companies that were operating in 2010 have since shut down. Contrary to this situation, the statistics from the Zimbabwe Ministry of Higher and Tertiary Education acknowledges approximately 30,000 students to graduate from higher and tertiary education every year (Moyo, 2016). On the 3 December 2017 reality check on the British Broadcasting Corporation, the International Labour Organisation opined that 'the challenge for Zimbabwe is not the quantum of employment but the quality of employment'. This implies that the economic situation in Zimbabwe is bad to the extent that university graduates are engaging in menial jobs because the ones which suit their qualifications are not available.

It is also important to note that starting an infopreneurship business is not without its challenges and risks. Boehle (2018) describes the glamour in calling yourself the CEO after starting your own business but however, acknowledges the challenges involved. Abdullahi (2015) warns that any business venture is prone to risks. Cowdrey (2012) thinks that when starting a business venture, individuals are overzealous to get cards printed Managing Director whilst it is the result that should speak not the self-appointed title. In Xie's (2014) view in line with the cognitive approach, attitude is not stable for it is bound to change with time and situation through the human-environment interactions. Attitude as a component of the cognitive approach has been deemed a better indicator for entrepreneurial behaviour than personal traits or demographic variables (McCline et al., 2000). However, Xie (2014) argues on the lack of rationality in human beings hence the existence of biases in decision making. In the research conducted by Xie (2014) on why some people choose to start their own businesses, it emerged that cognitive biases were at play. The current study sought to find out the attitude of graduating LIS students on infopreneurial venture intentions.

Literature on infopreneurship available is mostly in line with student's perceptions of infopreneurial education (Dewah and Mutula, 2016), the status and development of infopreneurship (Ivwurie and Ocholla, 2016), infopreneurial behaviour among university graduates (David and Dube, 2014), the changing role of an info- entrepreneur (Bates, 2005). Very little has been done on the successful infopreneurial ventures in developing countries. To the best knowledge of the researchers no study has been conducted on infopreneurial intentions on students.

The Department of Library and Information Science at NUST revised its curriculum and introduced infopreneurship, a module that is taught in sister department of Records and Archives Management. The Infopreneurship course is unique in the Faculty of Communication and Information Science (Dewah and Mutula, 2016) since most of the Library and Information Science modules describe the different parameters to librarianship such as cataloguing, information retrieval, marketing, knowledge management, comparative librarianship, web designing and content management. On the other hand, infopreneurship encourages the use of all the knowledge and skills acquired from the different modules in creating an individual business venture. The module is however without doubt, indispensable where the economic situation fails to create immediate employment opportunities for the Library and Information Science students. As a pioneer group, the unclear infopreneurial intentions of the part 4 final year LIS students upon the completion of an infopreneurship module motivated the researchers to ask the question, 'Do LIS students have intentions to establish infopreneurial business after completing their BSc Hon. LIS degree?' given the efforts from the department in accommodating this unique but indispensable module to leverage on the information skills possessed by Library and Information Science students in a country where unemployment level is exceptionally high. The purpose of the study was to measure the infopreneurial intentions of the part 4 final year LIS students of the 2018/ 2019 academic year.

Figure 2. Choice of venture

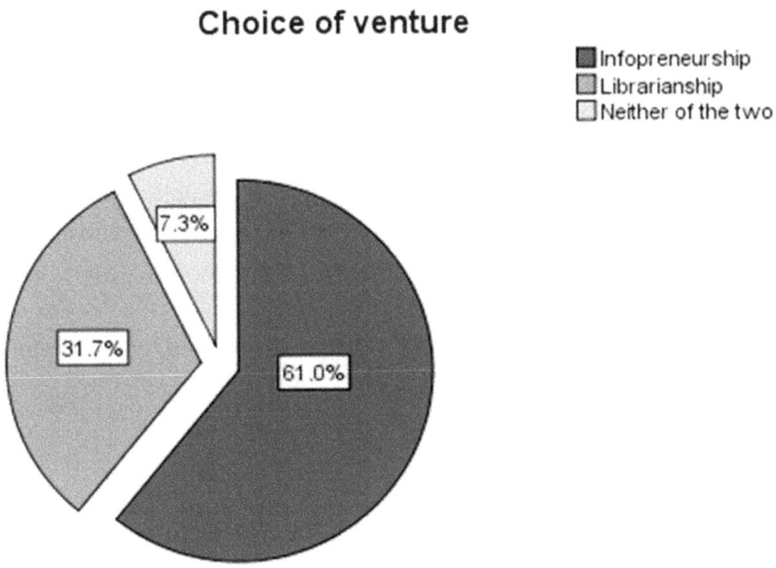

Methodology

Using a mixed methods design, data were collected from a population of 45 students through a survey. Semi-structured face to face interviews were conducted on a sample of 12 students who were coded P1-12 for participant 1-12. The researchers administered 45 questionnaires and 41 were filled and returned giving a response rate of 86.7%. Prior to administration and collection of data the instruments were tested through pilot study and some lecturers assisted with comments to ensure that reliability and validity concerns of the instruments are addressed. The study sought to measure the infopreneurial intentions of the part 4 final year (graduating) LIS class because it is the pioneer group to enrol in infopreneurship education. The study employed a sequential explanatory strategy as described by Terrell (2012) with the collection and analysis of quantitative data first, followed by the collection and analysis of qualitative data where there is the 'quan' and 'qual' or QUAN and QUAL to emphasize primacy for quantitative and qualitative research respectively (Bian,2018; Morse, 1991). When following a sequential explanatory strategy, it is imperative to ensure an integration of quantitative findings and qualitative findings (Guetterman, 2017). The integrated results and discussions are presented in the next section.

RESULTS AND DISCUSSIONS

This section presents the findings of the study based on the objectives of the research.

Attitude of Graduating LIS Students on Infopreneurship

The graduating LIS students were asked questions on whether they had intentions to venture into either infopreneurship or librarianship after graduating with their BSc Hon.in LIS. Figure 2 shows the result.

From the findings, it emerged that majority 25 (61%) of the students want to venture into infopreneurship. On the other hand, 13 (31.7%) students intend to pursue librarianship while very few students, 3(7.3%), are neither willing to venture in librarianship nor infopreneurship. The choice of infopreneurship at the expense of librarianship may be attributed to the scarcity of library and information science jobs in the information industry. The encouraging perceived behavioural explained the majority's (25:61%) infopreneurial intentions. This result is consistent with Ajzen's (1991) view that the performance of a behavior is collated to the confidence of the individual in his or her ability to performing a behavior.

During interviews students were asked about their views on infopreneurship and whether they would consider taking infopreneurship ventures. One interviewee revealed that:

Infopreneurship is a lucrative business worth venturing into, considering the digitisation of information resources and services. [P1]

Another interviewee said:

Without networks, you can't be recognised, hence getting employed by well established brands first and working your way up is better. After I have created a name for myself in the field,that is when I can consider independent infopreneurial ventures. [P3]

Students were asked to show if they would benefit from infopreneurship and the following were responses from two interviewees:

It is an ideal business because one is made to leverage on the information skills that they already have hence we can be information hubs and address information needs for different societies who suffer information gaps because of poor information skills. [P7]

Infopreneurship is a favourable venture for we can be able to make information available to research institutions like universities at any time because of our competency in information retrieval. [P3]

Based on the findings from the study that quite a number of students based their immediate infopreneurial intents on the need to secure employment, it supports literature on push factors where one engages into a business venture because of uncomfortable circumstances which are not related to their infopreneurial characteristic (Amit and Muller, 2013).

An analysis on whether the interesting or uninteresting nature of infopreneurship contributed to the choice of venture is shown in Table 1.

Table 1 shows the relationship between attitude and infopreneurial intentions. From the analysis, all the 25 students who chose infopreneurship as a venture to pursue do acknowledge that it is an interesting venture. This confirms Ivwurie and Ocholla's (2016) assertion who describe infopreneurship as an alternative sector of employment to information providers that is valuable to explore, understand and exploit. It is not surprising to note that students want to explore and exploit the available opportunities. There are 9 students who think infopreneurship is an interesting venture but are however opting for librarianship. This fear to embark on an individual venture though an infopreneurial venture might be interesting or afraid of challenges (Boehle, 2018) involved and risks associated with new business (Abdullahi, 2015). Those who thought infopreneurship is not an interesting venture were only 3 and this

*Table 1. Choice of venture * interesting cross tabulation*

Count					
		Interesting			Total
		Yes	No	Not Sure	
Pursue	Librarianship	9	2	2	13
	Infopreneurship	25	0	0	25
	Neither of the two	0	1	2	3
Total		34	3	4	41

justifies their choices of ventures where the 2 are opting for librarianship where the other one neither of the two. All the 25 students who opted for infopreneurship had positive attitude towards the venture.

This contradicts Emad and Siddig's (2018) study that disagree on the influence of attitude towards entrepreneurial intentions. This contradiction may be attributed to the assumption that the population studied by Emad and Siddig (2018) did not have enough time to reflect on the favourable or unfavourable nature of a business venture hence their study not realising the influence of attitude towards entrepreneurial intentions. In the case of the LIS part 4 final year students, the students managed to identify and reflect on the attractiveness of infopreneurship hence the subsequent positive intents. This justifies Ajzen's (2002) opinion that, attitude can be ascribed to the magnitude at which one has advantageous or unbeneficial evaluation of a particular venture in question.

The above results were tested using the chi-square under which the hypotheses were as follows:

H_0: There is no association between choice of venture and attitude.
H_1: There is association between the choice of venture and attitude.

The results of the chi-square tests are as shown in Table 2.

Table 2. Chi-square tests

	Value	Df	Asymptotic Significance (2-Sided)
Pearson Chi-Square	22.242[a]	4	.000
Likelihood Ratio	21.626	4	.000
Linear-by-Linear Association	.521	1	.471
N of Valid Cases	41		

Decision

The null hypothesis is rejected since the p-value is less than 0.05, thus there is a statistically significant association between the choice of venture and attitude of the respondent towards infopreneurship.

The rare findings of the students who had neither librarianship nor infopreneurial intents were mainly on the basis that they do not want a formal librarianship job nor infopreneurship. Instead, they want entrepreneurship where they can sell anything not just limited to information products and services.

Participants were asked: "Do you have past experiences in operating a business? What type of business did you operate? What therefore do you think about starting an infopreneurship business after graduating?" and the following most prominent and significant views pertaining to attitude on infopreneurial ventures from two participants:

I used to sell sweets and chocolates to my class mates. From this experience, I have good marketing skills which I could use to encourage people to consider my infopreneurship services. [P2]

I have experience in family business where my father is an entrepreneur. I have learnt a lot from his business and am sure I can manage infopreneurship also with him as a mentor. [P9]

The positive intents were also based on the nature of infopreneurship being a business where one could use the skills they already have and can just create their own jobs from the already existing knowledge. In this case, one is his or her own boss and this conforms to a study by Mirjam van Praag and Versloot (2008) that business people or entrepreneurs are more satisfied than employees are. Furthermore, using the skills one already has means no training is needed for the venture.

Influence of Subjective Norms on Infopreneurship Intentions

The other objective of the study was to establish how subjective norms influence infopreneurial intentions of the LIS part 4 final year students. Respondents were asked to choose from a given list their sources of pressure and advice in line with intentions to venture into infopreneurship business. Figure 3 shows the results.

Figure 3. Sources of advice in line with intentions to venture into infopreneurship business

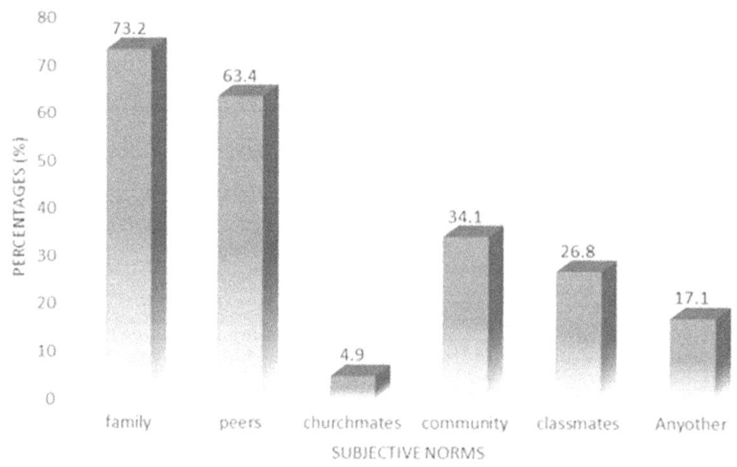

While a number of students acknowledged subjective norms as huge contributors to their infopreneurial intentions, it emerged that 30 (73.2%) respondents would consider pressure and advice from the family on decisions to venture into infopreneurship confirming Palacio et. al's (2018) in- group collectivism as pride and loyalty to family and close friends where one happens to be a member. This might have been attributed to the fact that these students are still the responsibility of their families hence they consider family input most. Quite a number, 26 (63.4%), of students acknowledged peers as subjective norms. This may mean that the majority of the students believe in the credibility of the advice from peers. Regarding business intentions, Xie (2014) is of the view that traits, the cognitive factors, environmental and demographic factors are strong influences to intentions on business ventures. However, Forbes (1999) posits that business journeys are usually generated under uncertainty, hence cognitive factors like perception and interpretation of limited information can contribute in decision making towards the creation of new ventures. Advice and pressure from church mates was acknowledged by only 2 (4.9%) students. This may be attributed to the lack of close relationships between the students and their church mates for the students to take advice from them or it may mean the majority of the students are not regular attendants of church. Another 34.1% rely on the advice from the community for decision making on infopreneurial ventures. Naushad et al. (2018) opine that successful entrepreneurial ventures are considered an offshoot of entrepreneurial intent. Only 11 (26.8%) students succumb to pressure from classmates on the decision to engage or not engage in infopreneurship business. This might be attributed to lack of trust on the credibility of the advice from a fellow classmate since one might argue that a classmate is by no means an expert to help in decision making. Krueger (2000) opined that perceived feasibility and desirability had positive impact on individuals' intention to start a new business. Only 7 (17.1%) students show that they get their advice and pressure from other sources which they did not specify. From the analysis it can be noted that church mates, classmates and community are not much relied upon by the students on advice and pressure to perform or not perform a behaviour whilst family, peers and the community constitute the highest subjective norms towards infopreneurial intentions. That is why Cowdrey (2012) thinks that it is the family and friends that are the first to believe in one's vision and those are the same people who offer support. Hence taking advice from them especially when they are convinced on the achievability of your dream both financially and physically is crucial since most of the support comes from them (Cowdrey,2012).

During the interview students were asked about how often they relied on other people's suggestions for decision making. A follow up question required them to identify those people who influenced their decision making. To this question one student said:

Very often! My family influence the choices that I make. Being here at school is because of them. Considering their opinions in the decisions that I need to make is the least I could do to acknowledge the crucial roles they have been playing in my life. [P4]

Another question was, "If you were to start an infopreneurial business, whom would you approach for advice and why?"

Another student responded:

If possible, I would approach that visiting infopreneur who presented to us that day for he is already in the infopreneurship business. [P8]

Another student said:

I would approach our lecturer for he seems quite versed in the field of infopreneurship. [P12]

Responding to the same question another student said:

As an aspiring infopreneur I would use the internet to research on successful infopreneurs and if possible try to reach out to them so that they could offer advice in line with infopreneurial ventures. [P10]

From all the interviewees, no one said that they are independent on decision-making; they acknowledged that knowledge had no harm hence there is need to take advice especially when it is coming from authentic sources and close people. Significant responses are listed below.

Participants were asked during the interview: After the presentation by the visiting infopreneur on 22 October 2018, did his own personal successes in infopreneurship motivate you to consider pursuing infopreneurship?

The visiting infopreneur motivated me for it is always good to see someone who is already in the field that you would want to venture in, you therefore have a better standing for you know what to expect thanks to him. [P5]

The infopreneur referred to is an information consultant for records and information management who is faring very well in the field of infopreneurship:

That infopreneur who presented to us that day has been quite influential with regard to my infopreneurial intents because it is always good to see someone who is pursuing the venture in person where they share the challenges they encounter and how they still managed to succeed. He also motivated me to see that from our own Zimbabwean qualifications we are being recognised internationally from the contracts he mentioned that he has in different countries for information and records management consultancy services. [P3]

On subjective norms, the study at hand yields similar results to Emad and Siddig's (2018) study that subjective norms are strong predictors of student's intentions to start a business. Family and peers were a huge source of pressure and advice.

Perceived Behavioural Control Factors Towards Infopreneurial Business

One of the objectives of the study was to identify the perceived behavioural control factors on the LIS part 4 final year student's intentions towards infopreneurial business. The literature consulted (Ivwurie and Ocholla, 2016; Kazmi and Nabradi, 2017) acknowledged experience as a huge contributor to perceived ease of a venture. The findings of the study revealed that 31 students had business experience whilst the remaining 10 did not have.

Respondents were asked to mention the type of business that they ventured in to. The results indicate that quite a number of students, 19 (46.3%), had ventured into family business followed by sole trading 15 (36.6%) and partnership 7 (17.1%). Figure 4 shows the types of business ventured into by the respondents who acknowledged business experience.

Figure 4. Types of business ventured into by the respondents who acknowledged business experience

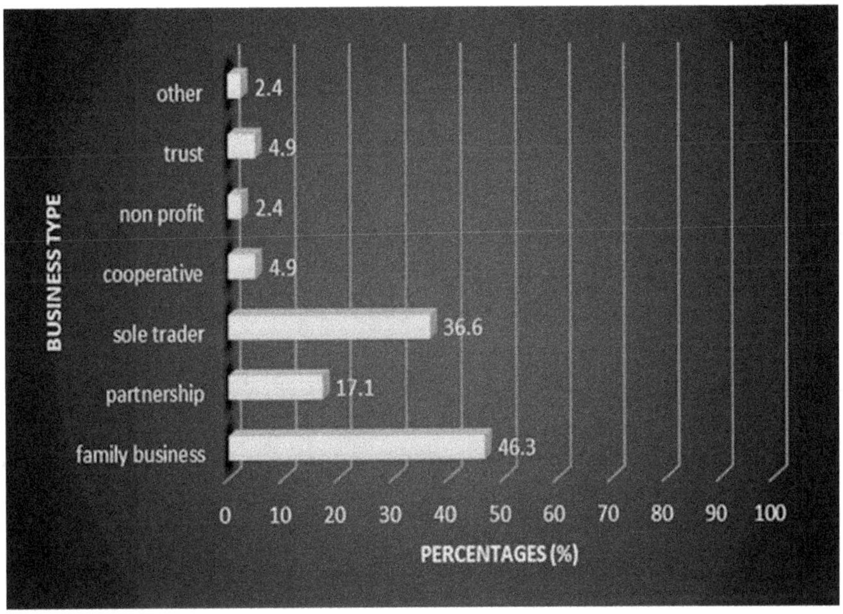

Results of the analysis seem to suggest that the popularity of family business may mean the students are still young to start and fund for their own businesses. According to Delmar and Davidsson (2000), entrepreneurial experience has been found to have positive impact on venture creation. However, Xie (2014) gives a contradicting remark that many people who venture into entrepreneurship do not have any entrepreneurial experience. The popularity of family business at the expense of other business types might also be attributed to the lack of exposure, which aids participation in other businesses like partnership and cooperatives. The popularity of sole trading amongst 15 (36.6%) students may be attributed to the need to make extra pocket money to cater for different needs at university. Non-profit business has been the lowest with 1 (2.4%) student. This may be attributed to the enormous demands in money and time that students meet at university discouraging them to participate in charity work. Lack of experience amongst the majority of students on trusts 2 (4.9%), cooperatives 2 (4.9%) and other business types 1 (2.4%) maybe attributed to lack of exposure and the poor economy which resulted in many of the cooperatives going out business for students to participate in them.

Table 3 presents an analysis of the relationship that exists between the perceived behavioural control of the infopreneurial venture and the choice of venture, which was opted for by the students.

From the 25 students opting for infopreneurship, it emerged that 10 agree on the easiness of the venture while 7 disagree and 8 are not sure. Those in disagreement may be intimidated by starting a new venture like infopreneurship confirming what Mueller and Thomas' (2001) observation that individuals who doubt their ability to influence the outcome, are not likely to risk their own money to create a new business. Meanwhile, 4 students who are opting for librarianship agree that infopreneurship is an easy

*Table 3. Choice of venture * easy venture cross tabulation*

Count					
		Easy Venture			Total
		Agree	Disagree	Not Sure	
Pursue	Librarianship	4	4	5	13
	Infopreneurship	10	7	8	25
	neither of the two	0	1	2	3
Total		14	12	15	41

venture. This may mean that they are optimistic of getting librarianship jobs after graduating hence not motivated to pursue the easy infopreneurial venture.

The above results were tested using the chi-square under which the hypotheses were as follows:

H_0: There is no association between choice of venture and the perceived behavioural control of the infopreneurial venture.

H_1: There is association between the choice of venture and perceived behavioural control of the infopreneurial venture.

The results of the test are shown in Table 4.

Table 4. Chi-square tests

	Value	Df	Asymptotic Significance (2-Sided)
Pearson Chi-Square	2.258[a]	4	.689
Likelihood Ratio	3.129	4	.536
Linear-by-Linear Association	.158	1	.691
N of Valid Cases	41		

Decision

The p-value is greater than 0.05 which means there is no a statistically significant relationship between the perceived behavior of control of the venture and the choice of venture.

Students were asked to rate themselves on a scale of 1 to 10 on their confidence level that if they are to pursue infopreneurship they might succeed or fail as another way of determining their perceived behavioural control.

The results in Table 5 were obtained.

The analysis did not use the mean because it is affected by extreme values or outliers. In terms of the central tendency, the median and the mode were used. Using these ratings, the mode and the median

Table 5. Behavioural control

N		Valid	41
		Missing	0
Mean			6.46
Median			7.00
Mode			7
Std. Deviation			1.583
Variance			2.505
Range			7
Minimum			2
Maximum			9
Percentiles	25		5.50
	50		7.00
	75		7.00

tells us that the majority of the students rated themselves at 7. This means that the students are quite confident that they will succeed if they are to venture into infopreneurship business. This may be attributed to the fact that students will be using the skills they already have hence infopreneurial ventures may not be that difficult.

The majority of interviewees responded positively towards perceived infopreneurial behavioural control explaining the rating at 7 of perceived behavioural control on the quantitative findings. The students acknowledged the leveraging on familiar skills in infopreneurship. These skills include web designing skills, research skills and information literacy skills hence deeming the venture quite easier. However, there were quite significant exceptions towards the easiness of the venture.

Significant verbatim are listed below:

1. With the knowledge that you acquired in infopreneurship education, do you think you can be able to venture into infopreneurship business after completing your degree?

Dealing with human beings has never been easy so it won't start with infopreneurship. But with my marketing experience, I may be able to sail through this business venture.

2. How confident are you with the knowledge that you acquired from infopreneurship education towards starting your own infopreneurial business?

I am quite confident with the infopreneurial knowledge that I have, yes there are areas which might need more detail but as an aspiring infopreneur, I can do further research on my own.

Influence of Enrolling for Infopreneurship Course on Intentions

Another objective of the study was to establish if the students' enrolment in the infopreneurship course influenced their infopreneurial intentions. Results from the survey are shown in Table 6. The results show that 22 students who have infopreneurial intentions were motivated by the infopreneurial course while only three of those with infopreneurial intents were not motivated by the infopreneurial education. Ten students were motivated by infopreneurial education but opted for librarianship. This may be attributed to other reasons like subjective norms, which may hinder infopreneurial intents though infopreneurial education had played its part. In total only 7 students were not motivated by the course as shown in Table 6.

*Table 6. Choice of venture * motivation1 cross tabulation*

		Count		
		Motivated by Infopreneurial Education		**Total**
		Yes	**No**	
Pursue	Librarian	10	3	13
	Infopreneurship	22	3	25
	neither of the two	2	1	3
Total		34	7	41

In a study on introducing entrepreneurship into non- business disciplines, Hynes (1996) describes education as a precondition required for training since it offers basic skills and abilities. The possible reason behind the fact that most of the students (34) were motivated by the course may be attributed to students envisioning and discovering great opportunities in infopreneurship. Hynes' (1996) study on entrepreneurial education describes the output of entrepreneurial education as personal with attributes such as confidence, personal development and clearer personal and career objectives.

The above results were tested using the chi-square under which the hypotheses were as follows:

H_0: There is no association between choice of venture and infopreneurship education.
H_1: There is an association between choice of venture and infopreneurship education.

The results are as shown in Table7.

Table 7. Chi-square tests

	Value	Df	Asymptotic Significance (2-Sided)
Pearson Chi-Square	1.346[a]	2	.510
Likelihood Ratio	1.267	2	.531
Linear-by-Linear Association	.044	1	.835
N of Valid Cases	41		

Decision

There is no relationship which is statistically significant between the two since the p-value is greater than 0.05

The students were also asked if they would recommend infopreneurial education to other departments (Publishing Studies, Journalism, and Media Studies) in the Faculty of Communication and Information Science and the results are presented in Figure 5.

Figure 5. Recommending infopreneurship to publishing, journalism and media studies departments

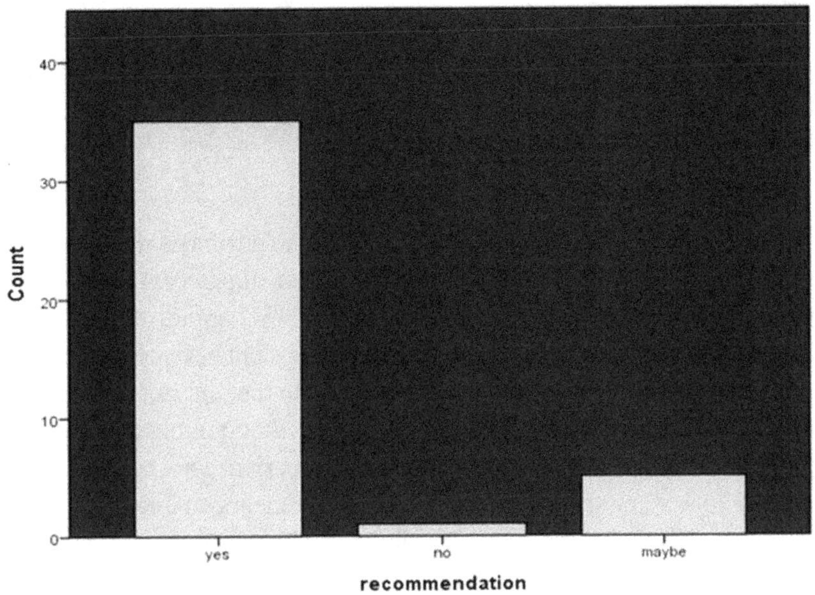

The majority of the students 35 (85%) recommended infopreneurship education to other students in the FCIS. Only 1 (2.4%) is in disagreement. The positive results may be attributed to the faith that the LIS part 4 final year students have in infopreneurship that it could also be used at the advantage of the Journalism and Media Studies students as well as the Publishing Studies students. Matlay (2008) and Storen (2014) agree that intentions can be inspired by education together with the support needed for the success of a business venture.

Students were asked on what would motivate them to venture into infopreneurship. Motivators are close influence to attitude and some encompass subjective norms. The results from the survey on the motivational factors among students on starting an infopreneurial business are shown in Figure 6.

From the analysis, it can be observed that opportunities motivated 22 (53.7%) students, access to financial resources motivated 18 (43.9%) students thus confirming Carter and Allen (1997) who have attributed the access to financial resources as a motivating factor to business ventures like infopreneurship. Their observation concluded that the access to finance and any other financial aspects of a business had a huge contribution on business ventures rather than choice or intention (Carter and Allen, 1997). Students were equally motivated by unemployment 18 (43.9%) and the love for money 16 (39%) to start

Figure 6. Motivators to infopreneurship business

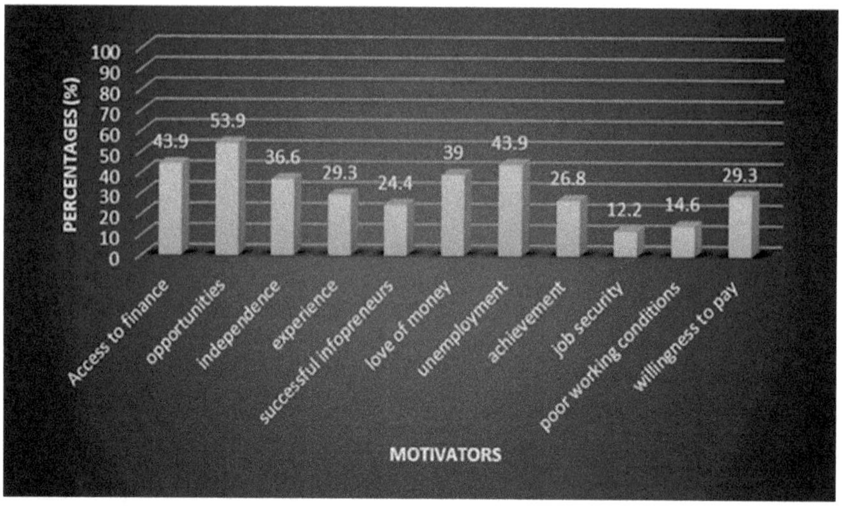

their business. This is consistent with Ocholla (1999; 1998) who attributes the interest in self –employment and increase in unemployment as motivating factors. A small percentage of students, 12 (29.3%), are motivated by their past business experience. Timmons (1994) argues that most of the successful entrepreneurs do not only possess certain personal characteristics but have usually served an apprenticeship within a framework of a small business, hence giving them the relevant experience in the business environment. This could mean that the businesses they ventured into in the past were not successful or they have not yet ventured into business hence past business experience not being the greatest motivator. A few students 10 (24.4%) were motivated by successful infopreneurs on intentions to venture into infopreneurship. The lowest proportion of the population indicated that they are motivated by the job security 5 (12.2%). This is consistent with Stefanovic et.al (2010) who described greater business achievement, independence, job security as well as intrinsic factors as motivating factors which might encourage the pursuing of a business venture. The reason for such a small result might be because the students do not have a sound employment experience for them to comprehend what job security really entails. Next to job security in terms of the lowest motivators to infopreneurial ventures are poor working conditions 6 (14.6%). Very few people are motivated with the poor working conditions. This could be attributed to the fact that most of the students have not yet been employed hence they do not have experience in good or poor working conditions. The few who are motivated many come from the parallel class for it is a class that accommodates a number of students who go to work hence may be the respondents that acknowledged poor working conditions.

Only 12 (29.3%) acknowledged the willingness of people to pay for information services as a motivator to their infopreneurial intentions a finding consistent with Ocholla (1999; 1998) and Coulson –Thomas' (2000) studies.

From the interviews it emerged, that one student had bad experiences on attachment where bosses would for example ask her to make tea for them. This alone made the student have a negative attitude on being under someone hence the choice for infopreneurship where one is his or her own boss. Unemployment was a significant motivator where students acknowledged the scarcity of librarianship jobs.

Other significant views can be found below.

During the interview, students were asked about the greatest motivating factor or reason for pursuing infopreneurship. Two students responded as follows:

I would want to get a time table of my own. I wouldn't want to beg anyone for leave days. [P5]

This confirms what Ivwurie and Ocholla (2016), Dewah and Mutula (2016) have found in their studies.

The economy is a bit shaky, there are no job opportunities in the market but with infopreneurship, one may become successful in this shaking economy for it is a matter of who you know and who you network with. [P6]

Interviewees were asked to indicate if there was anyone who inspired them to engage in to infopreneurial business. To this, one student responded:

Our very own Strive Masiiwa, the Econet boss, who is faring very well in the information and communication sector motivated me to consider infopreneurship. [P7]

Infopreneurial Qualities in the LIS Graduating Students

For a person intending to venture in to the business of infopreneurship, they must possess infopreneurial qualities in order to succeed. Mazubane (2009) is of the view that individuals in entrepreneurship process optimise market opportunities through creative actions and differentiated applications in production and management systems. Students were then asked to indicate those qualities, which they thought they possess. Figure 7 shows the infopreneurial qualities in the part 4 final year LIS students.

The results indicate that majority of the students do possess all the infopreneurial qualities and as such may lead to infopreneurial success. The most popular qualities in the students are being risk takers

Figure 7. Infopreneurial qualities in the part 4 final year LIS students

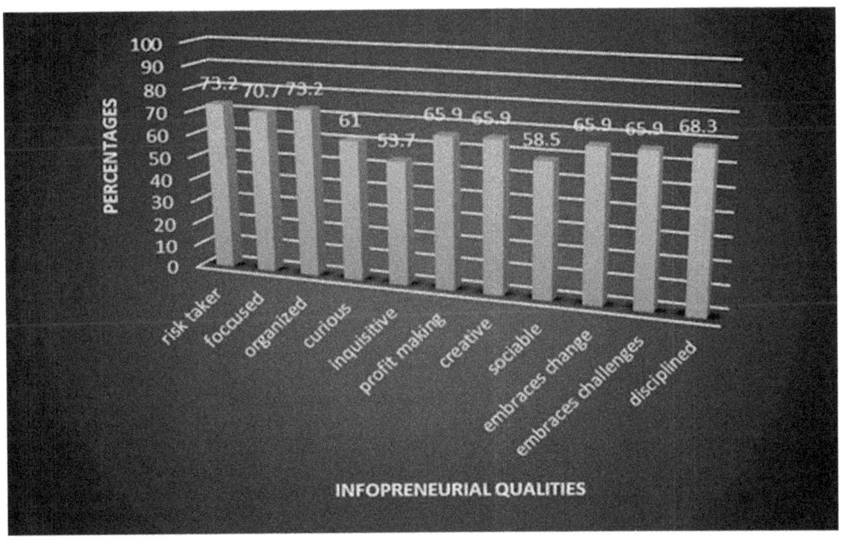

30 (73.2%) students. Blawatt (1998) attributes risk-taking, creativity, innovation and market niching as examples of infopreneurial qualities. The other popular ones were being organised 30 (73.2%) students, their need to make profit 27 (65.9%) students, creativity 27 (65.9%) students, and disciplined 28 (68.3%) students. The fact that the students who embrace change and those who embrace challenges are both at 27 (65.9%) maybe attributed to the knowledge and understanding by the students that change brings forth challenges therefore, they cannot be treated in different respects. Only 22 (53.7%) are inquisitive which is the lowest quality possessed by the students. This may be attributed to the students' understanding that posing too many questions is irritative hence the perceived annoying nature of someone who can be deemed inquisitive. Anthony (2018) supports this by acknowledging that through interactions with your clients or potential clients either face to face or them reading about your work, you make an impact on people because they are highly receptive either with the social skills that you possess face to face or in writing. Rugge and Glossbrenner (1997) believe infopreneurship is a venture that is undertaken by self-employed individuals who possess specialised skills that addresses various information needs of people where accessing the necessary information supports and justifies monetary charges for a profit.

Infopreneurial Education on Infopreneurial Intentions

All the 12 interviewees acknowledged the importance of infopreneurial education to the LIS students. This is in line with Skrob (2009) who thinks that the easiness of an infopreneurial venture that Infopreneurship could leverage on could be what an information professional knows best. The other interviewee acknowledged that the knowledge was basic, but claimed that as aspiring infopreneurs, we are able to do further research on our own pertaining to infopreneurial ventures because we have a good research background. Others however had suggestions on the inclusion of areas in the module like business management and risk management. Some of the responses are presented below.

Interviewees were asked what they thought about infopreneurship education to Library and Information Science students:

It has been fundamental for not every one of us is going to get a job after graduating. However, there is need to add in detail, areas to do with funding for a business, inflation challenges and liquidity crises. [P1]

Shar and Tripsas' (2007) view that the possession of technical knowledge qualifications has a direct contribution to the growth of a new business.

Interviewees were also asked about which other topics could have been covered in the infopreneurship course:

Business Management and Risk Management are degrees that are done for four years at NUST by the students from the Faculty of Commerce. The business information we got from the course was a bit too basic to sustain us in this business world where competition is stiff. [P6]

This is consistent with Blenker and Christensen (2010) on variety of roles and didactical approaches when teaching entrepreneurship.

Studies by Matlay (2008) and Storen (2014) concluded that intentions could be inspired by education together with the support needed for the success of a business venture.

The females constitute 31 (75.6%) of the total population of this research while males are only 10 (24.4%). This means that there are more females than males in the LIS department. However, the number of males could have been greater than the discovered and this could be because of the other males' constituting part of the 4 students who were unavailable to participate in the survey as shown in Table 8.

*Table 8. Choice of venture * gender cross tabulation*

Count				
		Gender		Total
		Male	Female	
Choice of venture	Librarianship	5	8	13
	Infopreneurship	5	20	25
	Neither of the two	0	3	3
Total		10	31	41

From the analysis, it emerged that the male students who participated in the survey were balanced between the two ventures that is librarianship and infopreneurship. What was quite significant was how the majority of the females opted for infopreneurship at the expense of librarianship given the common norm that women are not usually risk takers as they attribute their success to hard work rather than taking smart risks (Cheng, 2018). The female students demonstrated a very high risk-taking propensity by choosing infopreneurship at the expense of librarianship. To support this, from a population of 31 females, 22 are risk takers whilst only 9 are not. This supports Maxfield, Shapiro, Gupta and Hass' (2010) argument that labelling females as risk adverse really limits women from the benefits they could gain from risk taking like the positive benefits of infopreneurial ventures. The female students are therefore not limited by the norms hence can benefit from infopreneurial ventures.

Solutions and Recommendations

The chapter is based on the study that aimed at measuring the infopreneurial intentions of the part 4 final year LIS students of the 2018/ 2019 academic year. It can be concluded that the majority of the students have favourable attitude towards infopreneurial venture intentions. The intentions to start infopreneurship business have proven greater than the intentions to venture into librarianship. In support of the argument by Ajzen (1992), the results revealed that entities such as family, peers and successful business personnel were the major subjective norms that influenced the student's infopreneurial intentions while classmates, community the church did not contribute much on infopreneurial intentions. From the research findings, it can be concluded that the Theory of Planned Behavior's perceived behavioral control determines infopreneurial intentions. The encouraging perceived behavioral control was attributed to the fact that students will be leveraging on the skills that they already possess, past business experience so, the venture may be deemed easier. Enrolment in infopreneurship indeed influenced the infopreneurial intentions of the students to venture in to information consultancy, broker, information literacy training and research as a result of infopreneurship education. Above half of the students possessed nearly all the infopreneurial qualities. Students also acknowledged the perceived easiness on infopreneurship, which ultimately influenced their infopreneurial intentions.

Regarding implications for research, the present study makes several contributions to the infopreneurship education literature. In light of the findings the study recommends business collaborations and partnerships between the LIS students and the students in other departments like Computer Science and Business Administration. For 'the synergistic and skilful combining of different disciplines can achieve insight beyond current boarders hence generating novel solutions to complex problems' (Knapp et al, 2015).

In terms of implications for practice, with the positive embracing of Infopreneurship education by the graduating LIS students, the study recommends the extension of Infopreneurship education to the sister departments in the faculty of Communication and Information Science. This study also recommends the inclusion of topics in business and risk management to equip fully students with knowledge and skills that aid the success and competitiveness of infopreneurial ventures. The students from these two departments are in the faculty of Communication and Information Science hence can be able to leverage on the specialised information skills they have and create employment opportunities for themselves in an economy where unemployment is a serious challenge. The study also recommends a tracer study of infopreneurial behaviour to check if the graduating students of the 2018/2019 academic year have used the knowledge from infopreneurship in their careers. With the encouraging infopreneurial intentions yielded by the study, the university policy should accommodate or squeeze in the provision of grants to students with innovative ideas pertaining to starting businesses. This avoids innovative ideas going down to waste especially with the economic situation of the country where low bank loan supply results in financial constraints, which impede firm creation (Bermejo et al., 2018).

From the encouraging infopreneurial intentions, the study recommends the creation of a community of practice, which comprises of infopreneurs who share ideas and collaborate in making infopreneurship a success.

Future Research Directions

The study was confined to the LIS Final Year students (did not include RAM final year students yet they were taking the same course at the same time) and thus it cannot be generalized to all departments in the faculty. The study also recommends research on Library and Information Science literature being taught to the students, its compliance with this evolving era. This can also be used to predict the usefulness of the skills possessed in creating individual ventures in infopreneurship. The study also recommends a study involving the four departments in the Faculty of Communication and Information Science on entrepreneurship and infopreneurship.

CONCLUSION

This study aimed to find out if the graduating class of 2018/2019 had intentions to venture into infopreneurship since it was the first LIS class to enrol in the course and the intentions of this group were unclear after having completed an infopreneurship module at NUST. The study employed a mixed methods design. The study concluded that the majority of the graduating LIS students have favourable attitude towards starting infopreneurship business than the intentions to venture into librarianship. This has been attributed to the nature of the Zimbabwean economy where there are few jobs to cater for each graduate from the department of Library and Information Science. Those who weighed the nature of infopreneurship and preferred librarianship instead were on the basis that there is need to first work for an established brand in librarianship to create a name for themselves then later pursue infopreneurship. Enrolment in infopreneurship indeed influenced the infopreneurial intentions of the graduating LIS students. Students could leverage on the skills they acquired to create their own independent jobs instead of embracing common norms that librarianship students are limited to libraries, archives and other information centres, working as librarians and information officers.

The constructs of the Theory of Planned Behaviour that is attitude, subjective norms and perceived behavioural control greatly illustrated the roots behind the infopreneurial intentions of the graduating LIS students. Entities such as family, peers and successful business personnel were the major subjective norms that influenced the student's infopreneurial intentions while classmates, community and the church did not contribute much on infopreneurial intentions.

REFERENCES

Abdullah, F. (2015). *Prospects and challenges of Entrepreneurship and Librarianship in Nigeria*. Paper Presented at the 2nd Conference of Certified Librarians' of Nigeria at National Space Research Development Agency (NASRDA), Abuja, Nigeria.

Ajzen, I. (1985). From intentions to actions: A theory of planned behaviour. In J. Kuhland & J. Beckman (Eds.), *Action-Control: From cognitions to behaviour* (pp. 11–39). Heidelberg: Springer. doi:10.1007/978-3-642-69746-3_2

Ajzen, I. (2002). Perceived behavioural control, self-efficacy, locus of control and the theory of planned behaviour. *Journal of Applied Social Psychology*, *32*(4), 665–683. doi:10.1111/j.1559-1816.2002.tb00236.x

Ajzen, I., Ellen, P. S., & Madden, T. J. (1992). A comparison of the theory of planned behaviour and the theory of reasoned action. *Journal of Society for Personality and Social Psychology*, *18*(1), 3–9. doi:10.1177/0146167292181001

Amit, R., & Muller, E. (2013). 'Push' and 'Pull' Entrepreneurship. *Journal of Small Business and Entrepreneurship*, *12*(4), 64–80. doi:10.1080/08276331.1995.10600505

Bermejo, V. J., Ferreira, M. A., Zambrana, R., & Wolfenzon, D. (2018). *Entrepreneurship and economic conditions: Evidence from regional windfall gains*. Retrieved April 1, 2019, from www.madbarworkshop.com

Bian, H. (2018). *Mixed methods research*. Retrieved December 23, 2018, from http://core.ecu.edu/StatisticsResearch

Blenker, P., & Christensen, P. R. (2010). Hunting the entrepreneurial expertise: entrepreneurs in education. In A. Fayolle (Ed.), Handbook of Research in Entrepreneurship Education, (vol. 3, pp. 43-53). International Perspectives, Edward Elgar Publishing Limited. doi:10.4337/9781849806688.00010

Calisto-Palacio, M., Batista-Canino, R.M., & Zuniga-Collazos, A. (2017). *The relationship between culture and entrepreneurship: From Cultural Dimensions of Globe Project*. Academic Press.

Cheng, M. (2018). *Want to nature the women on your team? Help them take risks (and fail sometimes).* Retrieved March 29, 2019, from https://www.inc.com

Coduras, A., Urbano, D., Rojas, Á., & Martinez, S. (2008). The Relationship Between University Support to Entrepreneurship with Entrepreneurial Activity in Spain: A Gem Data Based Analysis. *International Advances in Economic Research, 14*(4), 395–406. Retrieved January 12 2019. doi:10.100711294-008-9173-8

Cowdrey, R. (2012). *Creating an entrepreneurial mindset: Failure is an option.* Retrieved January 10, 2019, from www.bookboon.com

David, R., & Dube, A. (2014). Infopreneurial Behaviour among University Graduates in the Information Science Faculty of a University in Zimbabwe. *Infopreneurship Journal, 1*(2), 1–8.

Dewah, P., & Mutula, S. (2016). Students' perceptions of the infopreneurship education in the Department of Records and Archives Management at the National University of Science and Technology. *South African Journal of Information Management, 18*(1), 1–8. doi:10.4102ajim.v18i1.717

Emad, A. E., & Siddig, B. I. (2018). *Determinants of entrepreneurial intentions using the Theory of Planned Behaviour.* Retrieved March 31, 2019, from www.researchgate.net

Guetterman, T.C. (2017). Designing a rigorous mixed methods research study. *Journal of Qualitative Research, 18*(1), 1–16.

Ivwurie, O. M., & Ocholla, D. N. (2016). The status and development of infopreneurship in Nigeria and South Africa. *Education for Information, 32*(4), 323–342. doi:10.3233/EFI-160980

Johnson, B. R., & Onwuegbuzie, A. (2004). Mixed Methods Research: A Research Paradigm Whose Time Has Come. *Educational Researcher, 33*(7), 14–26. doi:10.3102/0013189X033007014

Kautonen, T., Van Gelderen, M., & Fink, M. (2013). Robustness of the theory of planned behavior in predicting entrepreneurial intentions and actions. *Entrepreneurship Theory and Practice, 39*(3), 1–20.

Kazmi, S.Z.A., & Nabradi, A. (2017). New venture creations- The influence of entrepreneurship education on student's behaviour (A literature review-based study). *A Journal of Applied Studies in Agribusiness and Commerce, 11*(1-2), 147–154.

Keat, O.Y., Selvarajah, C., & Meyer, D. (2011). Inclination towards entrepreneurship among university students: An empirical study of Malaysian university students. *International Journal of Business and Social Science, 2*(4).

Khan, M. R. (2013). Mapping entrepreneurship ecosystem of Saudi Arabia. *World Journal of Entrepreneurship, Management and Sustainable Development, 9*(1), 28–54. doi:10.1108/20425961311315700

Knapp, B., Bardenet, R., & Deane, C. M. (2015). Ten simple rules for a successful cross-disciplinary collaboration. *PLoS Computational Biology, 11*(4), e1004214. doi:10.1371/journal.pcbi.1004214 PMID:25928184

Lowe, R., & Marriott, S. (2006). *Enterprise: Entrepreneurship and Innovation: Concepts, Contexts and Commercialization.* Oxford: Butterworth-Heinemann.

Matlay, H. (2008). The impact of entrepreneurship education on entrepreneurial outcomes. *Journal of Small Business and Enterprise Development, 15*(2), 382–396. doi:10.1108/14626000810871745

Maxfield, S., Shapiro, M., Gupta, V., & Hass, S. (2010). Gender and risk: Women, risk taking and risk aversion. *Gender in Management, 25*(7), 586–604. doi:10.1108/17542411011081383

Mirjam van Praag, C., & Versloot, P. H. (2008). The economic benefits and costs of entrepreneurship: A review of the research. *Small Business Economics, 29*(4), 351–383. doi:10.1561/0300000012

Morse, J. M. (1991). Approaches to qualitative-quantitative methodological triangulation. *Nursing Research, 40*(2), 120–123. doi:10.1097/00006199-199103000-00014 PMID:2003072

Moyo, J. (2016). *Unemployment: Graduates living in poverty.* Retrieved November 21, 2018, from https://www.dandc.ou

Mueller, S. L., & Thomas, A. S. (2001). Culture and entrepreneurial potential: A nine country study of locus of control and innovativeness. *Journal of Business Venturing, 16*(1), 51–75. doi:10.1016/S0883-9026(99)00039-7

Newsday. (2016). *From varsity to the streets: cry the Zimbabwean graduate.* Retrieved November 21, 2018, from www.newsday.co.zw

Noko, P., & Ngulube, P. (2015). A vital feedback loop in educating and training archival professionals: A tracer study of records and archives management graduates in Zimbabwe. *Information Development, 31*(3), 270–283. doi:10.1177/0266666913510308

Ocholla, D. (1998). Information consultancy and brokerage in Botswana. *Journal of Information Science, 24*(2), 83–95. doi:10.1177/016555159802400203

Ocholla, D. (1999). Information intermediaries in the next millennium: An agenda for action for the development of information consultancy and brokerage in Africa. *Library Management, 20*(2), 105–114. doi:10.1108/01435129910251584

Postigo, S., & Tamborini, F. (2002). Entrepreneurship education in Argentina: The case of San Andres University. *International Entrepreneurship Education and Training Conference, IntEnt02*, Kuala Lumpur, Malaysia.

Ramugondo, L. S. (2010). *An Exploratory study of infopreneurship as a job option for Library and Information Science students: A literature review.* Paper presented at the 11th DIS Annual Conference 2010, University of Zululand.

Rugge, S., & Glossbrenner, A. (1997). *The information brokers handbook* (3rd ed.). New York: McGraw Hill.

Shar, S. K., & Tripsas, M. (2007). The accidental entrepreneur: The emergent and collective process of user entrepreneurship. *Strategic Entrepreneurship Journal, 1*(12), 123–140.

Skrob, R. (2009). *Beneðt of infopreneurship.* Retrieved December12, 2018, from www.info-marketing.org

Stefanovic, I., Prokic, S., & Rankovic, L. (2010). *Motivational and success factors for entrepreneurs: the evidence from a developing country.* Academic Press.

Storen, L. A. (2014). Entrepreneurship in higher education: Impacts on graduates' entrepreneurial intentions, activity and learning outcome. *Education + Training*, *56*(8/9), 795–813. doi:10.1108/ET-06-2014-0070

Terrell, S. R. (2012). Mixed-Methods Research Methodologies. *Qualitative Report*, *17*(1), 254–280. http://www.nova.edu/ssss/QR/QR17-1/terrell.pdf

Xie, C. (2014). Why Do Some People Choose to Become Entrepreneurs? An Integrative Approach. *Journal of Management Policy and Practice*, *15*(1), 25–38.

ADDITIONAL READING

Mirjam van Praag, C., & Versloot, P. H. (2008). The economic benefits and costs of entrepreneurship: A review of the research. *Small Business Economics*, *29*(4), 351–383. Retrieved April 1, 2019. doi:10.1561/0300000012

Patel, N. (2016). How The Best Entrepreneurs Stay Organised? Retrieved February 4, 2019, from www.forbes.com

Wennekers, S., Van Stel, A., Thurick, R., & Reynolds, P. (2005). Nascent Entrepreneurship and the Level of Economic Development. *Small Business Economics*, *24*(3), 293–309. doi:10.100711187-005-1994-8

KEY TERMS AND DEFINITIONS

Behaviour: Can be understood as a state of engagement.

Entrepreneurship: The capacity and willingness to develop, organise and manage a business venture along with any of its risks in order to make a profit (Business Dictionary, 2018).

Graduating Students: Are Part 4 final year students who on successful completion of their fourth year academic year can be awarded with a first degree.

Infopreneurship: Is the act or practice of self-employed individuals who have acquired specialised skills that addresses people's information needs by accessing necessary information that supports the demand and justifies charging fees for a profit (Kody, 2011).

Compilation of References

3e.eu. (2019). *Flexible Adaptable Buildings Serve Circular Economy.* http://www.3e.eu

Aaker, D. A. (1991). *Managing Brand Equity.* New York, NY: Simon & Schuster.

Abdullah, F. (2015). *Prospects and challenges of Entrepreneurship and Librarianship in Nigeria.* Paper Presented at the 2nd Conference of Certified Librarians' of Nigeria at National Space Research Development Agency (NASRDA), Abuja, Nigeria.

AbdurRaheem, L. (2017). *State of the Nation Address: Why think of restructuring at this time? – TMC.* Available: http://therenaissanceng.com/feed-items/state-of-the-nation-address-why-think-of-restructuring-at-this-time-tmc

Abele, A. E., & Guido, H. E. (2007). Individual differences in optimism predict the recall of personally relevant information. *Personality and Individual Differences, 43*(5), 1125–1135. doi:10.1016/j.paid.2007.03.005

Abhishek, Xianlai, & Li. (2016). *Environmental pollution of electronic waste recycling in India: A critical review.* Received 3 August 2015, Revised 19 November 2015, Accepted 19 November 2015, Available online 14 January 2016, https://www.sciencedirect.com/science/article/pii/S0269749115301871

Accenture (2014). *Circular advantage: Innovative business models and technologies to create value in a world without limits to growth.* Retrieved 5 October, 2019 from file:///C:/Users/satiku/Downloads/978-87-93435-86-5.pdf

Accenture. (2014). Accenture Strategy Circular Advantage Innovative Business Models and Technologies to Create Value in a World without Limits to Growth, Accenture. Retrieved from https://www.accenture.com/%20t20150523T053139__w__/us-en/_acnmedia/Accenture/Conversion-Assets/DotCom/Documents/Global/PDF/Strategy_6/Accenture-Circular-Advantage-Innovative-Business-Models-Technologies-Value-Growth.pdf

Accenture. (2014). Circular Advantage: Innovative Business Models and Technologies to Create Value in A World Without Limits to Growth. www.accenture.com

Acemoglu, D., Liabson, D., & List, J. (2015). Why Isn't the Whole World Developed? In Macroeconomics. Pearson.

Acs, Z. J., & Audretsch, D. B. (1988). Innovation in large and small firms: An empirical analysis. *The American Economic Review, 78*, 678–690.

Acs, Z. J., Audretsch, D. B., Braunerhjelm, P., & Carlsson, B. (2004). *The missing link: The knowledge filter and endogenous growth (discussion paper).* Stockholm: Center for Business and Policy Studies.

Acs, Z. J., Estrin, S., Mickiewicz, T., & Szerb, L. (2017a). Institutions, entrepreneurship and growth: The role of national entrepreneurial ecosystems. *Small Business Economics*, (51), 501–514.

Acs, Z. J., Stam, E., Audretsch, D. B., & O'Connor, A. (2017b). The lineages of the entrepreneurial ecosystem approach. *Small Business Economics, 49*(1), 1–10. doi:10.100711187-017-9864-8

Adams, K. (2006). *The sources of innovation and creativity*. Paper Commissioned by the National Center on Education and the Economy for the New Commission on the Skills of the American Workforce.

Adamson, G. (2003). *Industrial strength design how brooks stevens shaped your world*. Cambridge: The MIT Press.

Adibe, R., Nwagwu, E., & Albert, O. (2018). Rentierism and security privatisation in the Nigerian petroleum industry: Assessment of oil pipeline surveillance and protection contracts. *Review of African Political Economy*, *45*(156), 345–353. doi:10.1080/03056244.2017.1391771

AENOR. (2016). Hacia el residuo cero [Towards the Zero Waste]. In Revista La Norma y la Certificación. AENOR.

AfDB. (2012). *From billions to trillions: MDB contributions to financing development*. African Development Bank. http://pubdocs.worldbank.org/en/692914365543030 71/dfi-ideaactionbooklet.pdf

AfDB. (2015). *The Role of Nascent Entrepreneurship in Driving Inclusive Economic Growth in North Africa*. Working Brief, North Africa Policy Series, African Development Bank. www.afdb.org/en/documents/document/north-africa-working-paper-the-role-of-nascententrepreneurship-indriving-inclusive-economic-growth-in-north-africa-90023/

African Development Bank. (1999). *African Development Report*. New York: Oxford University Press.

Agarwal, R., & Bayus, B. L. (2002). The Market Evolution and Sales Takeoff of Product Innovations. *Management Science*, *48*(8), 1024–1041. doi:10.1287/mnsc.48.8.1024.167

Agbim, C. K. (2013). The Relative Contribution of Management Skills to Entrepreneurial Success: A Survey of Small and Medium Enterprises (SMEs) in the Trade Sector. *IOSR Journal of Business and Management*, *7*(1). Retrieved November 17, 2019 from http://www.iosrjournals.org/iosr-jbm/papers/Vol7-issue1/B0710816.pdf?id=5304

Agrawal, S., Singh, R. K., & Murtaza, Q. (2015). A literature review and perspectives in reverse logistics. *Resources, Conservation and Recycling*, *97*, 76–92. doi:10.1016/j.resconrec.2015.02.009

Agyemang, M., Kusi-Sarpong, S., Khan, S., Mani, V., Rehman, S., & Kusi-Sarpong, H. (2019). Drivers and barriers to circular economy implementation. *Management Decision*. *57*, 971-994.

Ahamed, Z., Inohara, T., & Kamoshida, A. (2013). The servitization of manufacturing: An empirical case study of IBM corporation. *International Journal of Business Administration*, *4*(2), 18. doi:10.5430/ijba.v4n2p18

Åhlström, P., & Nordin, F. (2006). Problems of establishing service supply relationships: Evidence from a high-tech manufacturing company. *Journal of Purchasing and Supply Management*, *12*(2), 75–89. doi:10.1016/j.pursup.2006.05.002

Ahmad, S. Z. (2012). The need for inclusion of entrepreneurship education in Malaysia lower and higher learning institutions. *Education + Training*, *55*(2), 191–203. doi:10.1108/00400911311304823

Aidis, R. (2003a). *Entrepreneurship and Economic Transition*. Tinbergen Institute discussion paper, 2003 – 0151/2.

Aidis, R. (2003b). *By law and by custom: Factors affecting small and medium-sized enterprises during the transition in Lithuania*. Amsterdam: Thelda Thesis.

Ajayi, L. B., & Oke, M. O. (2012). Effect of External Debt on Economic Growth and Development of Nigeria. *International Journal of Business and Social Science, 3*(12), 297-304.

Ajayi, O., Akinrefon, D., & Yakubu, D. (2017). *Yoruba demands return to regionalism, restructuring*. Available:https://www.vanguardngr.com/2017/09/yoruba-demands-return-regionalism-restructuring/

AJE. (2004). *Análisis de los Factores que Contribuyen al Éxito de Proyectos Empresariales*. Retrieved from http://www.ajeimpulsa.es/documentos/banco_recursos/recurso_13.pdf

Ajzen, I. (1985). From intentions to actions: A theory of planned behaviour. In J. Kuhland & J. Beckman (Eds.), *Action-Control: From cognitions to behaviour* (pp. 11–39). Heidelberg: Springer. doi:10.1007/978-3-642-69746-3_2

Ajzen, I. (2002). Perceived behavioural control, self-efficacy, locus of control and the theory of planned behaviour. *Journal of Applied Social Psychology*, *32*(4), 665–683. doi:10.1111/j.1559-1816.2002.tb00236.x

Ajzen, I., Ellen, P. S., & Madden, T. J. (1992). A comparison of the theory of planned behaviour and the theory of reasoned action. *Journal of Society for Personality and Social Psychology*, *18*(1), 3–9. doi:10.1177/0146167292181001

Akhuemonkhan, I. A. R. L., & Sofoluwe, A. O. (2013). Entrepreneurship education and employment stimulation in Nigeria. *Journal of Studies in Social Sciences*, *3*(1), 55–79.

Akingunola, R. O., Adekunle, O. A., Adegbesan, K. J., & Aninkan, O. O. (2013). Microfinance banks and entrepreneurship development in Nigeria: A case of Ogun State. *European Journal of Business and Management*, *5*(28), 100–110.

Alberti, M., Booth, D., Hill, K., Coburn, B., Avolio, C., Coe, S., & Spirandelli, D. (2007). The impact of urban patterns on aquatic ecosystems: An empirical analysis in Puget lowland sub-basins. *Landscape and Urban Planning*, *80*(4), 346–341. doi:10.1016/j.landurbplan.2006.08.001

Albert, M. (2019). Sustainable frugal innovation - The connection between frugal innovation and sustainability. *Journal of Cleaner Production*, *237*, 117747. doi:10.1016/j.jclepro.2019.117747

Aldrich, H.E., & Zimmer. (1986). Entrepreneurship through Social Networks. In *The Art and Science of Entrepreneurship*. New York: Ballinger.

Aldrich, H. E., Rosen, B., & Woodward, W. (1987). *The impact of social networks on business: Foundlings and profit in a longitudinal study. In Frontiers of entrepreneurship research* (pp. 154–168). Wellesley, MA: Babson College.

Alexandre, L. (2019). *For a true circular economy, we must redefine waste*. https://www.weforum.org

Alhawari, S., Karadsheh, L, Nehari Talet, A., & Mansour, E. (2011). *Knowledge-Based Risk Management framework for Information Technology project*. Academic Press.

Alhawari, S., Karadsheh, L., Talet, A. N., & Mansour, E. (2012). Knowledge-based risk management framework for information technology project. *International Journal of Information Management*, *32*(1), 50–65. doi:10.1016/j.ijinfomgt.2011.07.002

Al-Khalifa, K. N., & Aspinwall, E. M. (2000). The development of total quality management in Qatar. *The TQM Magazine*, *12*(3), 194–204. doi:10.1108/09544780010320250

Allport, G. W. (1961). *Pattern and Growth in Personality*. New York: Holt, Rinehart and Winston.

Allport, G. W., & Odbert, H. S. (1936). Trait-names: A psycho-lexical study. *Psychological Monographs*, *47*(1), 211–215. doi:10.1037/h0093360

Allwood, J. M. (2014). Squaring the circular economy: the role of recycling within a hierarchy of material management strategies. In *Handbook of recycling* (pp. 445–477). Elsevier. doi:10.1016/B978-0-12-396459-5.00030-1

Almeida, D. M., & Sousa, J. M. (2014). *Entrepreneurial Skills Development*. Retrieved November 16, 2019 from https://www.researchgate.net/publication/268816221_Entrepreneurial_Skills_Development

Alston, K. (2008). Cradle to Cradle design initiatives: Lessons and opportunities for prevention through design (PtD). *Journal of Safety Research*, *39*(2), 135–136. doi:10.1016/j.jsr.2008.02.017 PubMed

Altiparmakov, N. & Matkovic, G. (2018). The development of private pensions in Serbia: caught between a generic blueprint and an unconducive local environment. Transfer: *European Review of Labor and Research, 24*, 57-71. 10.1177/1024258917746033

Álvare, C., Amorós, J. E., & Urbano, D. (2014). Regulations and Entrepreneurship: Evidence from Developed and Developing Countries. Innovar, 24.

Alvarez, S. A., & Busenitz, L. W. (2001). The entrepreneurship of resource-based theory. *Journal of Management, 27*(6), 755–775. doi:10.1177/014920630102700609

Alvial Muñoz, A. (2015). *Economía Azul: Una revisión en el marco de nuevas tendencias en Economía.* Obtenido de Bioeconomía Argentina: http://www.bioeconomia.mincyt.gob.ar/wp-content/uploads/2014/12/1.-Econom%C3%ADa-azul-A.-Alvial.pdf

Amabile, T. M. (1983). The Social Psychology of Creativity: A Componential Conceptualization. *Journal of Personality and Social Psychology, 45*(2), 357–376. doi:10.1037/0022-3514.45.2.357

Amabile, T. M. (1997). Motivating Creativity in Organizations: On Doing What You Love and Loving What You Do. *California Management Review, 40*(1), 39–58. doi:10.2307/41165921

Amabile, T. M. (2013). *Componential Theory of Creativity. Encyclopedia of Management Theory*. London: Sage Publications.

Amaia, M., Aparicio, G., & Iturralde, T. (2019). Conceptual structure and perspectives on entrepreneurship education research: A bibliometric review. *European Research on Management and Business Economics, 25*(3), 105–113. doi:10.1016/j.iedeen.2019.04.003

Ames, C. (1992). Classrooms: Goals, structures, and student motivation. *Journal of Educational Psychology, 84*(3), 261–271. doi:10.1037/0022-0663.84.3.261

Ameyan, E. E., & Chan, A. P. C. (2015). Implementing PPP Water Supply Projects in Ghana. *African Journal of Applied Research, 1*(1), 453–469.

Amit, R., & Zott, C. (2002, Mar.). Creating Value Through Business Model Innovation. Spring Research Feature, 40–49.

Amit, R., & Muller, E. (2013). 'Push' and 'Pull' Entrepreneurship. *Journal of Small Business and Entrepreneurship, 12*(4), 64–80. doi:10.1080/08276331.1995.10600505

Amobi, I. C. (2006). *Unleashing of Industrial Clusters for Growth and Prosperity in South East Nigeria*. Lead Presentation at the *Enugu Forum Seminar*.

Amuda, O., Adebisi, S., Jimoda, L., & Alade, A. (2014). Challenges and possible panacea to the municipal solid wastes management in Nigeria. *Journal of Sustainable Development Studies, 6*(1), 64–70.

Andersen, M. S. (2007). An introductory note on the environmental economics of the circular economy. *Sustainability Science, 2*(1), 133–140. doi:10.100711625-006-0013-6

Andrews, D. (2015). The circular economy, design thinking and education for sustainability. *Local Economy, 30*(3), 305–315. doi:10.1177/0269094215578226

Andriopoulos, C. (2003). Determinants of organisational creativity: A literature review. *Management Decision, 39*(10), 834–841. doi:10.1108/00251740110402328

Anna, M., Guarino, F., Longo, S., Ferraro, M., & Cellura, M. (2019). Energy and environmental benefits of circular economy strategies: The case study of reusing used batteries from electric vehicles. *Journal of Energy Storage, 25*. doi:10.1016/j.est.2019.100845

Annarelli, A., Battistella, C., & Nonino, F. (2016). Product service system: A conceptual framework from a systematic review. *Journal of Cleaner Production, 139*, 1011–1032. doi:10.1016/j.jclepro.2016.08.061

Ansari, S., Munir, K., & Gregg, T. (2012). Impact at the Bottom of the Pyramid: The Role of Social Capital in Capability Development and Community Empowerment. *Journal of Management Studies, 49*(4), 813–842. doi:10.1111/j.1467-6486.2012.01042.x

Ansoff, H. (1957). Strategies for diversification. *Harvard Business Review, 35*, 113–124.

Antikainen, M., & Valkokari, K. (2016). A Framework for Sustainable Circular Business Model Innovation. Technology Innovation Management Review, 6(7), 7. doi:10.22215/timreview/1000

Antikainen, M., & Valkokari, K. (2016). A framework for sustainable circular business model innovation. *Technology Innovation Management Review, 6*(7).

Antikainen, M., Uusitalo, T., & Kivikytö-Reponen, P. (2018). Digitalisation as an Enabler of Circular Economy. *Digitalisation as an Enabler of Procedia CIRP, 73*, 45–49. doi:10.1016/j.procir.2018.04.027

Antikainen, M., & Valkokari, K. (2016). A Framework for Sustainable Circular Business Model Innovation, *Technology Innovation. Management Review, 5*, 1–8.

Antikainen, M., & Valkokari, K. (2016). A Framework for Sustainable Circular Business Model Innovation, Technology Innovation. *Management Review, 6*(7), 5–12.

Antikainen, R., Lazarevic, D., & Seppälä, J. (2018). Circular economy: origins and future orientations. In H. Lehmann (Ed.), *Factor X: challenges, implementation strategies and examples for a sustainable use of natural resources* (pp. 115–129). Cham, Switzerland: Springer International Publishing; doi:10.1007/978-3-319-50079-9_7.

Antonia, G. (2019). *Innovation and entrepreneurship can cut waste and deliver the circular economy.* https://www.weforum.org

Antonio Ferreira, M., Jose Chiappetta Jabbour, C., & Beatriz Lopes de Sousa Jabbour, A. (2017). Maturity levels of material cycles and waste management in a context of green supply chain management: An innovative framework and its application to Brazilian cases. *Journal of Material Cycles and Waste Management, 19*(1), 516–525. doi:10.1007/s10163-015-0416-5

Arabsheibani, G., de Meza, D., Maloney, J., & Pearson, B. (2000). And a vision appeared unto them of a great profit: Evidence of self–deception among the self–employed. *Economics Letters, 67*(1), 35–41. doi:10.1016/S0165-1765(99)00242-6

Arabska, E., & Terziev, V. (2017). Social Enterprises: A Sustainable Business Model. *The British Journal for the Philosophy of Science*, 1113–1126. https://ssrn.com/abstract=3142935

Aragón-Correa, J. A. (2019). *What is a Circular Economy: Why is industrial symbiosis the best approach to a circular economy?* Retrieved on 28th July 2019 from https://blogs.ugr.es/empresas-con-futuro/en/what-is-a-circular-economy-why-is-industrial-symbiosis-the-best-approach-to-a-circular-economy/

Arawati, A., & Zafaran, H. (2008). The strategic supplier partnership in a supply chain management with quality and business performance. *International Journal of Business and Management Science, 1*(2), 129–145.

Arsic, M., Randjelovic, S. & Altiparmakov, N. (2018). Shadow Economy Trends in Serbia: 2012-2017. *Quarterly Monitor, 52*(1-3), 51-58.

Arthur D. Little (ADL) Group. (2015). *How Leading Companies Are Using Sustainability-Driven Innovation to Win Tomorrow's Customers?* Innovation High Ground Report.

Asa, R. A., & Prasad, N. S. (2014). Analysis on the factors that determine sustainable growth of small firms in Namibia. *International Journal of Management Science and Business Administration, 1*(1), 5–11. doi:10.18775/ijmsba.1849-5664-5419.2014.11.1001

Atiku, S. O., & Fields, Z. (2018). Organisational Learning Dimensions and Talent Retention Strategies for the Service Industries. In N. Baporikar (Ed.), Global Practices in Knowledge Management for Societal and Organizational Development (pp. 358-381). IGI Global. doi:10.4018/978-1-5225-3009-1.ch017

Atiku, S. O. (2019). Institutionalizing Social Responsibility through Workplace Green Behaviour. In *Contemporary Multicultural Orientations and Practices for Global Leadership* (pp. 183–199). Hershey, PA: IGI Global. doi:10.4018/978-1-5225-6286-3.ch010

Augsburg, B., De Haas, R., Harmgart, H., & Mehgir, C. (2012). *Microfinance at the margin: experimental evidence from Bosnia and Herzegovina.* European Bank for Reconstruction and Development. Working Paper no.146.

Auinger, A., Nedbal, D., & Hochmeier, A. (2013). An Enterprise 2.0 project management approach to facilitate participation, transparency, and communication. *International Journal of Information Systems and Project Management, 1*(2), 43–60.

Aúkun, B., & Yıldırım, N. (2011). Insights on Entrepreneurship Education in Public Universities in Turkey: Creating Entrepreneurs Or Not? *Procedia: Social and Behavioral Sciences, 24*, 663–676. doi:10.1016/j.sbspro.2011.09.050

Avlonitis, V., Frandsen, T., Hsuan, J., & Karlsson, C. (2014). Driving competitiveness through servitization. A guide for practitioners. Academic Press.

Aytekin, T. (2019). *Why More Knowledge Won't Make You More Successful.* https://www.entrepreneur.com

Baas, L. (2011). Planning and Uncovering Industrial Symbiosis: Comparing the Rotterdam and Östergötland Regions. *Business Strategy and the Environment, 20*(7), 428–440. doi:10.1002/bse.735

Babatunde, S. O., Opawole, A., & Akinsiku, O. E. (2012). Critical success factors in public-private partnership (PPP) on infrastructure delivery in Nigeria. *Journal of Facilities Management, 10*(3), 212–225. doi:10.1108/14725961211246018

Baines, T. S., Lightfoot, H. W., Benedettini, O., & Kay, J. M. (2009). The servitization of manufacturing: A review of literature and reflection on future challenges. *Journal of Manufacturing Technology Management, 20*(5), 547–567. doi:10.1108/17410380910960984

Baines, T., & Lightfoot, H. (2013). *Made to Serve. How manufacturers can compete through servitization and product-service systems.* New York, NY: Jhon Wiley & Sons.

Baines, T., Lightfoot, H., Steve, E., Neely, A., Greenough, R., Peppard, J., ... Walton, I. (2007). State-of-the-art in product service-systems. Journal of Engineering Manufacture. *Proceedings of the Institution of Mechanical Engineers. Part B, Journal of Engineering Manufacture, 221*(10), 1543–1553. doi:10.1243/09544054JEM858

Bakker, A. B., Schaufeli, W. B., Leiter, M. P., & Taris, T. W. (2008). Work engagement: An emerging concept in occupational health psychology. An International Journal of Work. *Health &Organisations., 22*(3), 187–200.

Bakker, C., Ariadne-Bakker, C., Den Hollander, M., Van Hinte, E., & Zijlstra, Y. (2014). *Products That Last: Product Design for Circular Business Models.* Delft: TU Delft Library.

Bakker, C., Wever, R., Teoh, C., & De Clercq, S. (2010, March). Designing Cradle-to-Cradle products: A reality check. *International Journal of Sustainable Engineering*, *3*(1), 2–8. doi:10.1080/19397030903395166

Bakker, K. (2012). Water security research challenges and opportunities. *Science*, *337*(6097), 914–915. doi:10.1126cience.1226337 PMID:22923564

Balboa, C. H., & Domínguez Somonte, M. (2014). *Economía circular como marco para el ecodiseño: el modelo ECO-3.* Obtenido de Universidad Nacional de Educación a Distancia: https://www2.uned.es/egi/publicaciones/articulos/Economia_circular_como_marco_para_el_ecodiseno_el_modelo_ECO-3.pdf

Baldé, C., Forti, V., Kuehr, R., & Stegmann, P. (2017). *The Global E-waste Monitor 2017.* https://www.itu.int/en/ITU-D/Climate-Change/Documents/GEM%202017/Global-E-waste%20Monitor%202017%20.pdf

Ballie, J., & Woods, M. (2018). Circular by Design: A Model for Engaging Fashion/Textile SMEs with Strategies for Designed Reuse. In Unmaking Waste in Production and Consumption: Towards the Circular Economy, (pp. 103-121). Emerald Publishing Limited. Doi:10.1108/978-1-78714-619-820181010

Balogun, M. J. (2002a). The Democratization and Development Agenda and the African Civil Service: Issues Resolved or Matters Arising. *International Review of Administrative Sciences*, *68*(4), 67–69. doi:10.1177/0020852302684003

Balogun, M. J., & Mutahaba, G. (1999). Redynamising the African Civil Service for the Twentyfirst Century: Prospects for a Non-bureaucratic Structure. *Public Management Journal*, *51*(4), 520.

Banerjee, A. V., & Duflo, E. (2011). *Poor economics: A radical rethinking of the way to fight global poverty.* New York: Public Affairs.

Banerjee, A., & Duflo, E. (2005). *Growth Theory through the Lens of Development Economics.* Massachusetts Institute of Technology.

Banerjee, A., & Duflo, E. (2011). *Poor Economics: A Radical Rethinking of the Way to Fight Global Poverty.* New York, NY, USA: Public Affairs.

Bannerman, P. L. (2008). Risk and risk management in software projects: A reassessment. *Journal of Systems and Software*, *81*(12), 2118–2133. doi:10.1016/j.jss.2008.03.059

Bansal, S., Garg, I., & Sharma, D. G. (2019). Social Entrepreneurship as a Path for Social Change and Driver of Sustainable Development: A Systematic Review and Research Agenda. *Sustainability*, *11*(4), 1091. doi:10.3390u11041091

Banza Lubaba Nkulu, C., Casas, L., Haufroid, V., De Putter, T., Saenen, N. D., Kayembe-Kitenge, T., ... Nemery, B. (2018). Sustainability of artisanal mining of cobalt in DR Congo. *Nat Sustain*, *1*(9), 495–504. doi:10.103841893-018-0139-4 PMID:30288453

Baporikar, N. (2018). Current scenario of youth entrepreneurship in India. In M. Khosrow-Pour, D.B.A. (Ed.), Encyclopaedia of Information Science and Technology, Fourth Edition (pp. 2989-2997). Hershey, PA: IGI Global. doi:10.4018/978-1-5225-2255-3.ch261

Baporikar, N., & Deshpande, M. (2009). Designing Policies for Business. In *Fourth Annual International Conferenceon Public Policy and Management*. Indian Institute of Management, Bangalore.

Baporikar, N. (2014). Youth entrepreneurship in India scenario. *International Journal of Asian Business and Information Management*, *5*(2), 74–84. doi:10.4018/ijabim.2014040106

Baporikar, N. (2017). Cluster approach for entrepreneurship development in India. *International Journal of Asian Business and Information Management*, *8*(2), 46–61. doi:10.4018/IJABIM.2017040104

Baporikar, N. (2017). Critical review of Entrepreneurship in Oman. In P. Zgheib (Ed.), *Entrepreneurship and Business Innovation in the Middle East* (pp. 147–174). Hershey, PA: IGI Global. doi:10.4018/978-1-5225-2066-5.ch008

Baporikar, N. (2019). Significance and role of Entrepreneurial University in Emerging Economies. *International Journal of Applied Management Sciences and Engineering*, *6*(1), 46–61. doi:10.4018/IJAMSE.2019010104

Barbier, E. B. (2003). The role of natural resources in economic development. *Australian Economic Papers*, *42*(2), 253–272. doi:10.1111/1467-8454.00198

Bărbulescu, O., & Constantin, P. S. (2019). Sustainable Growth Approaches: Quadruple Helix Approach for Turning Brasov into a Startup City. *Sustainability*, *11*(21), 6154. doi:10.3390u11216154

Barkan, J. D., Gboyega, A., & Stevens, M. (2001). *State and local governance in Nigeria. Public Sector and Capacity Building Program, Africa Region*. The World Bank.

Barney, J. (1991). Firms Resources and Sustained Competitive Advantage. *Journal of Management*, *17*(1), 99–120. doi:10.1177/014920639101700108

Barringer, B. R., Jones, F. F., & Neubaum, D. O. (2005). A quantitative content analysis of the characteristics of rapid-growth firms and their founders. *Journal of Business Venturing*, *20*(5), 663–687. doi:10.1016/j.jbusvent.2004.03.004

Barry, J. (2010). Towards a model of green political economy: From ecological modernisation to economic security. In Global Ecological Politics (Advances in Ecopolitics, Vol. 5) (pp. 109-128). Emerald. Doi:10.1108/S2041-806X(2010)0000005010

Barzelay, M. (2001). *The New Public Management: Improving Research and Policy Dialogue*. Berkeley, CA: University of California Press.

Basargekar, P., Iyer, R., & Bhatia, A. (2019). Assessing Employees' Perception Related to Entrepreneurial Climate in their Organization & its Impact on their Perception Related to Organization's Potential Success. *Journal of Asia Entrepreneurship and Sustainability*, *15*(1), 3–66. doi:10.22622/jaes.2019.15-1.01

Bascavusoglu-Moreau, E., & Tether, B. (2010). *Servitization, Survival and productivity*. Paper presented at the DRUID conference. Copenhagen Business School.

Baskerville, R. F. (2003). Hofstede Never Studied Culture. *Accounting, Organizations and Society*, *28*(1), 1–14. doi:10.1016/S0361-3682(01)00048-4

Bastante-Ceca, M.J., Fuentes-Bargues, J.L., Florin-Constantin, M., Iatu, C. & Hufnagel, L. (2019). *Introductory Chapter: The Need to Change the Paradigm - Sustainability and Development at the 21st Century*. Doi:10.5772/intechopen.90655

Bastein, T., Roelofs, E., Rietveld, E., & Hoogendoorn, A. (2013). Introduction. In T. Bastein, E. Roelofs, E. Rietveld, & A. Hoogendoorn (Eds.), *Opportunities for a Circular Economy in the Netherlands* (pp. 4-6). Delft: The Netherlands Organization for Applied Scientific Research-TNO. Retrieved from https://www.tno.nl/media/8551/tno-circular-economy-for-ienm.pdf

Bates, B., Botha, M., Botha, S., Goodman, S., Ladzani, W., DeVries, C., ... Southey, L. (2005). *Business management: fresh perspectives*. Cape Town: Maskew.MillerLongman.

Batley, R. (1999). The New Public Management in Developing Countries: Implications for Policy and Organizational Reform. *Journal of International Development*, *11*(5), 761–765. doi:10.1002/(SICI)1099-1328(199907/08)11:5<761::AID-JID616>3.0.CO;2-0

Bauman, Z. (2015). *Özgürlük*. İstanbul: Ayrıntı Yayınevi.

Baxter, P., & Jack, S. (2008). Qualitative case study methodology: Study design and implementation for novice researchers. *Qualitative Report, 13*(4), 544–559.

BBS. (2019). *Small and Medium Enterprises Facing the Challenge of Circular Economy*. https://www.bbs.unibo.eu

Beaver, G. (2007). *The strategy pay-off for smaller enterprises*. Academic Press.

Becker, B. E., Huselid, M. A., Pickus, P. S., & Spratt, M. F. (1998). Los RH como fuente de valor para los accionistas: Investigación y recomendaciones. In D. Ulrich, M. R. Losey y G. Lake (Eds), El futuro de la dirección de recursos humanos (pp. 246-259). Barcelona: Gestión 2000.

Becker. (1975). *Human Capital*. Chicago, IL: Chicago University Press.

Bee Smart City. (2019). The Circular Economy: Vision, Problems and Smart City Solutions. Available online, https://hub.beesmart.city/strategy/the-circular-economy-and-smart-city-solutions

Behrens, A., Drabik, E., Kranendijk, S., Rinaldi, D., Rizos, V., Stuchtey, M., & Tuokko, K. (2018). *Markets, Processes and Enabling Policies The Role of Business in the Circular Economy*. Retrieved November 17, 2019 from https://www.researchgate.net/publication/324013764_The_Role_of_Business_in_the_Circular_Economy_Markets_Processes_and_Enabling_Policies

Bejjani, A. (2019). Here's how the business can make the circular economy a reality. *Circular economy*. Accessed on 23 Feb 2020 https://www.weforum.org/agenda/2019/12/circular-economy-business-environment/

Ben Gurion University of the Negev Sapir Academic College, & Jerusalem Institute for Policy Research. (2018). Israeli Water System: A Circular Economy Business Model Case, R2p the Route of Circular Economy. Retrieved from http://www.r2piproject.eu/wp-content/uploads/2019/05/Water-Case-Study.pdf

Benkler, Y. (2002). Coase's Penguin, or, Linux and "The Nature of the Firm,". *The Yale Law Journal, 112*(3), 369–446. doi:10.2307/1562247

Bennett, C. J. (1991). What is policy convergence and what causes it? *British Journal of Political Science, 21*(2), 215–233. doi:10.1017/S0007123400006116

Bennis, W. G., & Thomas, R. J. (2002). *Geeks and Geezers: How era, values, and defining moments shape leaders*. Boston, MA: Harvard Business School Press.

Berent-Braun, M. M., Uhlaner, L. M., Jeurissen, R. J. M., & deWit, G. (2010). Family ownership,innovation and other context variables as determinants of sustainability entrepreneurship in SMEs: An empirical research study. *SCALES Sci. Anal. Entrep. SMEs*. Available at:http://citeseerx.ist.psu.edu/viewdoc/download?doi=10.1.1.471.1649&rep=rep1&type=pdf Aaccessed on 13 Oct 2019.

Berkhout, F. (1996). Life cycle assesment and innovation in large firms. *Business Strategy and the Environment, 5*(3), 145–155. doi:10.1002/(SICI)1099-0836(199609)5:3<145::AID-BSE65>3.0.CO;2-P

Bermejo, V. J., Ferreira, M. A., Zambrana, R., & Wolfenzon, D. (2018). *Entrepreneurship and economic conditions: Evidence from regional windfall gains*. Retrieved April 1, 2019, from www.madbarworkshop.com

Berry, A., von Blottnitz, M., Cassim, R., Kesper, A., Rajaratnam, B., & Ernst van Seventer, D. (2002). *The Economics of SMMEs in South Africa*. Trade and Industrial Policy Strategies. Available at: https://www.tips.org.za/node/204

Berte, E., Rodrigues, L. C., & Ameida, M. I. (2010). *The Lessons Learned from the Unique Characteristics of Small technology-based Firms*. Academic Press.

Best, E., Cramer, A., Olson, E., & Park, J. (2017). *The Future of Sustainable Business: New Agenda, New Approach, New Advocacy*. Retrieved December 18, 2019 from https://www.bsr.org/reports/BSR_The_Future_Sustainable_Business.pdf

Beveridge, R., & Guy, S. (2005). The Rise of the Eco-preneur and the Messy World of Environmental Innovation. *Local Environment, 10*(6), 665–676. doi:10.1080/13549830500321972

Bian, H. (2018). *Mixed methods research*. Retrieved December 23, 2018, from http://core.ecu.edu/StatisticsResearch

Bıçakcıoğlu, N., Theoharakis, V., & Tanyeri, M. (2019). Green business strategy and export performance: An examination of boundary conditions from an emerging economy. *International Marketing Review, 37*(1), 56–75. doi:10.1108/IMR-11-2018-0317

Bicket, M., Vanner, R., Guilcher, S., Tan, A., Hestin, M., Withana, S., & Watkins, E. (2014). *Scoping study to identify potential circular economy actions, priority sectors, material flows and value chains*. Brussels: European Commission. Retrieved from https://www.eesc.europa.eu/resources/docs/scoping-study.pdf

Bijlsma, M., Beonekamp, J., van Ewijk, C., & Haaijen, F. (2018). Funded Pensions and Economic Growth. *De Economist, 166*(3). Retrieved from: https://pure.uva.nl/ws/files/28168930/10.1007_s10645_018_9325_z.pdf

Bioregional. (2017). *Four Key Enablers That Will Speed Up Circular Economy*. https://www.bioregional.com

Biswas, T., & Sengupta, P. P. (2009). Role of microfinance in promoting microentrepreneurship: The Indian experience. *International Journal of College Science in India, 3*(2), 73–90.

Bjørn, A., & Strandesen, M. (2011). The Cradle to Cradle concept - is it always sustainable? Paper presented at the meeting of the The Life Cycle Management (LCM) conference: Towards Life Cycle Sustainability Management, Berlin, Germany.

Blackburn, R. (2008). Small Business and Entrepreneurship. Academic Press.

Blank, S., & Dorf, B. (2012). *The start-up owner's manual: The step-by-step guide for building a great company*. Pescadero, CA: K&S Ranch Publishers.

Blázquez, S. F., Dorta, V. J. A., & Verona, M. M. C. (2006). Factores del crecimiento empresarial. Especial referencia a las pequeñas y medianas empresas. *INNOVAR. Revista de Ciencias Administrativas y Sociales, 16*(28), 43-56. Retrieved from: https://www.redalyc.org/pdf/818/81802804.pdf

Blenker, P., & Christensen, P. R. (2010). Hunting the entrepreneurial expertise: entrepreneurs in education. In A. Fayolle (Ed.), Handbook of Research in Entrepreneurship Education, (vol. 3, pp. 43-53). International Perspectives, Edward Elgar Publishing Limited. doi:10.4337/9781849806688.00010

Bloetscher, F. (2011). *Utility Management for Water and Wastewater Operators*. Denver: American Water Works Association.

Blomsma, F., & Brennan, G. (2017). The Emergence of Circular Economy: A New Framing Around Prolonging Resource Productivity. *Journal of Industrial Ecology, 21*(3), 603–614. doi:10.1111/jiec.12603

Bocken, N. M. P., Short, S. W., Rana, P., & Evan, S. (2014). A literature and practice review to develop sustainable business model archetypes. *Journal of Cleaner Production, 65*, 42–56. doi:10.1016/j.jclepro.2013.11.039

Bocken, N. M., Rana, P., & Short, S. W. (2015). Value mapping for sustainable business thinking. *Journal of Industrial and Production Engineering, 32*(1), 67–81. doi:10.1080/21681015.2014.1000399

Bocken, N., De Pauw, I., Bakker, C., & Van der Grinten, B. (2016). Product design and business model strategies for a circular economy. *Journal of Industrial and Production Engineering, 33*(5), 308–320. doi:10.1080/21681015.2016.1172124

Boehm, B. W. (1991). Software risk management: Principles and practices. *IEEE Software*, *8*(1), 32–41. doi:10.1109/52.62930

Bohnsack, R., & DiVito, L. (2018). Motivations and entrepreneurial orientation of sustainable entrepreneurs: an exploratory study of sustainable entrepreneurship archetypes in the fashion industry. In A. Lindgreen, C. Vallaster, F. Maon, S. Yousafzai, & B. P. Florencio (Eds.), *Sustainable Entrepreneurship: Discovering, Creating and Seizing Opportunities for Blended Value Generation* (pp. 24–37). Boca Raton, FL: Routledge. doi:10.4324/9781315611495-2

Bohoris, A. G., & Vorria, E. P. (2007). *Leadership vs Management a Business Excellence / Performance Management view*. Retrieved January 21, 2020 from https://www.ep.liu.se/ecp/026/076/ecp0726076.pdf

Boja, C. (2011). Clusters Models, Factors and Characteristics. *International Journal of Economic Practices and Theories, 1*(1), 1-43.

Bonanno, S., Amato, F., Silluzio, C., Trimarchi, E. G., Matarazzo, A., & Bentivegna, G. (2018). Smart and circular economy applied to a Sicilian company as a sewage treatment model. *Procedia Environmental Science. Engineering and Management*, *5*(1), 21–28.

Bonime-Blanc, A., & Ponzi, L. J. (2016). *Understanding Reputation Risk the Qualitative and Quantitative Imperative*. GEC Risk Advisory LLC & ReputationInc.

Boons, F., & Lüdeke-Freund, F. (2013). Business Models for Sustainable Innovation: State-of-the-Art and Steps Towards a Research Agenda. *Journal of Cleaner Production*, *45*, 9–19. doi:10.1016/j.jclepro.2012.07.007

Borissenko, J., and Boschma, R. (2017). *A critical review of entrepreneurial ecosystems research: towards a future research agenda*. Lund University, CIRCLE-Center for Innovation, Research and Competences in the Learning Economy.

Bosma, N., Holvoet, T., & Crijns, H. (2014). *Global Entrepreneurship Monitor 2013*. Report for Belgium & Flanders, Beleidsrapport STORE-B14-012.

Bosma, N., Sanders, M., & Stam, E. (2017). *Time series and panel data analysis of GEI and growth performance indicators*. Academic Press.

Bosma, N., Acs, Z. J., Autio, E., Coduras, A., & Levine, J. (2008). *Global entrepreneurship report: 2008 executive report*. Wellesley, MA: Babson College.

Boston, J. (2000). The challenge of evaluating systemic change: The case of public management reform. *International Public Management Journal*, *1*(3), 23–46. doi:10.1016/S1096-7494(00)00033-7

Boufaden, N. (2018). *Entrepreneurship and Business Growth Affiliation*. Retrieved January 19, 2020 from https://www.researchgate.net/publication/326479296_Entrepreneurship_and_Business_Growth

Boulding, K. E. (1966). The Economics of the Coming Spaceship Earth. In Environmental Quality in a Growing Economy (pp. 3–11). Retrieved from http://arachnid.biosci.utexas.edu/

Boulding, K. E. (1965). *The Economies of the Coming Spaceship Earth*. Boulder, CO: The University of Colorado at Boulder Libraries.

Boulding, K. E. (2013). The economics of the coming Spaceship Earth. In H. Jarrett (Ed.), *Environmental Quality in a Growing Economy* (pp. 3–14). New York: RFF Press. doi:10.4324/9781315064147

Bovaird, T. (2004). Public-private partnerships: From contested concepts to prevalent practice. *International Review of Administrative Sciences*, *70*(2), 199–215. doi:10.1177/0020852304044250

Bowman, E. (2011). *Entrepreneur Training Manual, Third Edition: Certified Entrepreneur Workbook*. Guanzi Institute Press.

Boyle, T. A., & Scherrer, R. M. (2009). An empirical examination of the best practices to ensure manufacturing flexibility. *Journal of Manufacturing Technology Management*, *20*(3), 348–366. doi:10.1108/17410380910936792

Bozkurt, Ö. C., & Kalkan, A. (2014). Business Strategies of SME's, Innovation Types and Factors Influencing Their Innovation: Burdur Model. *Ege Academic Review*, *14*(2), 189–198.

Bradford, J., & Fraser, E. (2007). Local authorities, climate change and small and medium enterprises: Identifying effective policy instruments to reduce energy use and carbon emissions. *Corporate Social Responsibility and Environmental Management*, *15*(3), 156–172. doi:10.1002/csr.151

Bradley, S. W., McMullen, J. S., Artz, K., & Simiyu, E. M. (2012). Capital is not enough: Innovation in developing economies. *Journal of Management Studies*, *49*(4), 684–717. doi:10.1111/j.1467-6486.2012.01043.x

Bramwell, A., Nelles, J., & Wolfe, D. A. (2008). Knowledge, innovation and institutions: Global and local dimensions of the ICT cluster in Waterloo, Canada. *Regional Studies*, *42*(1), 101–116. doi:10.1080/00343400701543231

Bramwell, A., & Wolfe, D. A. (2008). Universities and regional economic development: The entrepreneurial University of Waterloo. *Research Policy*, *37*(8), 1175–1187. doi:10.1016/j.respol.2008.04.016

Braunerhjelm, P., Acs, Z., Audretsch, D. B., & Carlsson, B. (2015). *The missing link: knowledge diffusion and entrepreneurship in endogenous growth*. Edward Elgar Publishing.

Braungart, M. (2009). Criticism on Cradle to Cradle? Right on schedule. https://www.duurzaamgebouwd.nl/artikel/20090320-criticism-on-cradle-to-cradle-right-on-schedule-says-michael-braungart

Braungart, M., McDonough, W., & Bollinger, A. (2007). Cradle-to-Cradle design: Creating healthy emissions - a strategy for eco-effective product and system design. *Journal of Cleaner Production*, *15*(13-14), 1337–1348. doi:10.1016/j.jclepro.2006.08.003

Braun, V., & Clarke, V. (2006). Using thematic analysis in psychology. *Qualitative Research in Psychology*, *3*(2), 77–101. doi:10.1191/1478088706qp063oa

Braun, V., & Clarke, V. (2012). Thematic analysis. In H. Cooper (Ed.), *APA Handbook of research methods in psychology: Research design: Quantitative, Qualitative, Neuropsychological and Biological* (Vol. 2, pp. 57–71). Washington, DC: American Psychological Association. doi:10.1037/13620-004

Brears, R. (2018). *The circular economy. in: natural resource management and the circular economy*. Cham: Palgrave Studies in Natural Resource Management. Palgrave Macmillan; doi:10.1007/978-3-319-71888-0.

Brears, R. C. (2018). *Natural Resource Management and the Circular Economy*. London, UK: Palgrave Macmillan. doi:10.1007/978-3-319-71888-0

Brem, A., & Licha, J. (2018). Entrepreneurship education in Europe - insights from Germany and Denmark. *International Journal of Entrepreneurship and Small Business*, *33*(1), 1–25. doi:10.1504/IJESB.2018.088641

Bresson, M., & Gallon, V. (2008). Kiehl's Experiments New Green Cosmetic Concepts. Retrieved at 28.10.2019, from https://www.premiumbeautynews.com/en/Kiehl-s-experiments-new-green,367

Brian, T. (2015). *The Basics of Business Success*. https://www.entrepreneur.com

Brinkerhoff, D. W., & Brinkerhoff, J. M. (2011). Public–private partnerships: Perspectives on purposes, publicness, and good governance. *Public Administration and Development*, *31*(1), 2–14. doi:10.1002/pad.584

British Broadcasting Corporation (BBC). (2015). *Volkswagen: The scandal explained*. Retrieved December 5, 2019 from https://www.bbc.com/news/business-34324772

Brixiová, Z., Ncube, M., & Bicaba, Z. (2015). Skills and youth entrepreneurship in Africa: Analysis with evidence from Swaziland. *World Development*, *67*, 11–26. doi:10.1016/j.worlddev.2014.09.027

Brockhaus, R. (1980). Risk taking propensity of entrepreneurs. *Academy of Management Journal*, *23*(3), 509–520.

Brown, P. B. (2013). *Entrepreneurs Are Calculated Risk Takers*. https://www.forbes.com

Brown, T. (2008). Design thinking. *Harvard Business Review*, *86*(6), 84–92. PMID:18605031

Brown, T. (2009). *Change by design: How design thinking transforms organizations and inspires innovation*. New York, NY: Harper Collins.

Bruder, J. (2013). *The Psychological Price Of Entrepreneurship Inc*. Academic Press.

Brundtland, G. H. (1987). *Our Common Future*. Obtenido de UN: http://www.un-documents.net/our-common-future.pdf

Brunetti, A., Kisunko, G., & Weder, B. (1999). *Institutions in Transition, Reliability of Rules and Economic Performance in Former Socialist Countries*. Retrieved from: https://elibrary.worldbank.org/doi/abs/10.1596/1813-9450-1809

BSI Group. (2017). *Resource Management and the Circular Economy*. Available at bsigroup.com

BSI. (2017). *Developing BS 8001- A World First*. The British Standards Institution.

Buchanan, G. M., & Seligman, M. E. P. (Eds.). (1995). *Explanatory style*. Hillsdale, NJ: Erlbaum.

Bull, M. (2008). Challenging tensions: Critical, theoretical and empirical perspectives on social enterprise. *International Journal of Entrepreneurial Behaviour & Research*, *14*(5), 268–275. doi:10.1108/13552550810897641

Bull, M., Cato, M. S., Arthur, L., Keenoy, T., & Smith, R. (2008). Entrepreneurial energy: Associative entrepreneurship in the renewable energy sector in Wales. *International Journal of Entrepreneurial Behaviour & Research*, *14*(5), 313–329. doi:10.1108/13552550810897678

Bulow, J. (1986). An economic theory of planned obsolescence. *The Quarterly Journal of Economics*, *101*(4), 729–749. doi:10.2307/1884176

Burdenko, E. V. (2015). *The Influence of Industrial Policy and Zoning on the Development of Light Industry in Russia*. Moscow: Pero.

Bureau. (2015). *SME sector's growth in Oman*. Author.

Burjorjee, D. M., & Scola, B. (2015). *A Market Systems Approach to Financial Inclusion*. Washington, DC: Consultative Group to Assist the Poor.

Business and Sustainable Development Commission. (2016). *Business Models. Exponentially more social, lean, integrated and circular*. London, UK: Volans.

Caceido García, C. L. (2017). *Economía circular y su papel en el diseño e innovación sustentable*. Obtenido de Libros Editorial UNIMAR: http://ojseditorialumariana.com/index.php/libroseditorialunimar/article/view/1154

Caiden, G. E., & Sundaram, P. (2004). The specificity of public service reform. *Public Administration and Development*, *24*(5), 373–383. doi:10.1002/pad.329

Cainelli, G., D'Amato, A., & Mazzanti, M. (2020). Resource-efficient eco-innovations for a circular economy: Evidence from EU firms. *Research Policy*, *49*(1), 103827. doi:10.1016/j.respol.2019.103827

Calderón Hernández, G., Naranjo Valencia, J. C., & Álvarez Giraldo, C. M. (2010). Gestión humana en la empresa colombiana: sus características, retos y aportes. Una aproximación a un sistema integral. *Cuadernos de Administración, 23*(41).

Calisto-Palacio, M., Batista-Canino, R.M., & Zuniga-Collazos, A. (2017). *The relationship between culture and entrepreneurship: From Cultural Dimensions of Globe Project.* Academic Press.

Calogirou, C., Sorensen, S. Y., Larsen, P. B., Alexopoulou, S., Morgensen, J., & Papageorgiou, M. (2014). *SMEs and the environment in the European Union.* Copenhagen: Danish Technological Institute; DG Enterprise and Industry (EC).

Campbell, B. (1993). Restructuring the economy: Canada into the free trade era. In The political economy of North American free trade (pp. 89-104). Palgrave Macmillan UK.

Cannavacciuolo, L., Iandoli, L., Ponsiglione, C., & Zollo, G. (2017). *Learning by failure vs learning by habits.* Academic Press.

Carey, C., & Matlay, H. (2010). Creative disciplines education: A model for assessing ideas in entrepreneurship education? *Education + Training, 52*(8/9), 695–709. doi:10.1108/00400911011088999

Carland, J. H., Hoy, F., Boulton, W. R., & Carland, J. A. C. (1984). Differentiating entrepreneurs from small business owners: A conceptualization. *Academy of Management Review, 9*(2), 349–354. doi:10.5465/amr.1984.4277721

Carrez, D., & Van Leeuwen, P. (2015). Bioeconomy: Circular by nature. *The European Files, 38*, 34–35.

Carrillo-Hermosilla, J., Del Río, P., & Könnölä, T. (2010). Diversity of Eco-innovations: Reflections from Selected Case Studies. *Journal of Cleaner Production, 18*(10-11), 1073–1083. doi:10.1016/j.jclepro.2010.02.014

Carroll, C. D., Hall, R. E., & Zeldes, S. P. (1992). The buffer-stock theory of saving: Some macroeconomic evidence. *Brookings Papers on Economic Activity, 1*(2), 61–156. doi:10.2307/2534582

Carroll, P., & Steane, P. (2000). *Public-Private Partnerships. Theory and Practice in International Perspective.* London: Routledge.

Casadesus-Masanell, R., & Ricart, J. E. (2007). Competing Through Business Models. Working Paper 713, IESE Business School, Barcelona.

Castro, F., Colclough, S., Machado, B., & Andrade, J. (2018). European legislation and incentives programmes for Demand Side Management. *14th International Conference on Energy Storage.*

Cattell, R. B. (1943). The description of personality: Basic traits resolved into clusters. *Journal of Abnormal and Social Psychology, 38*(4), 476–506. doi:10.1037/h0054116

Cearley, D., & Burke, B. (2018). *Top 10 Strategic Technology Trends for 2019.* Gartner.

Census of India. (2011). Accessed from: http://censusindia.gov.in/

Central Intelligence Agency Factbook. (2013). *Country Socio-economic data.* The online Factbook.

Centre for Development and Enterprise. (2016). *An EPZ for the Nelson Mandela Bay Metro, Growth Series Report 7.* Retrieved from www.cde.org.za/wp-content/uploads/2016/04/7.EPZ.pdf

Centre For Mediterranean Integration (CMI). (2017). *Youth Innovation with wastewater for sustainable Mediterranean.* Available at https://www.cmimarseille.org

Centre for Women Business Research. (2011). Key4Women Confidence Index. Retrieved from:www.key.com

CEPAL. (2009). *Manual de la Micro, Pequeña y Mediana Empresa.* Deutsche Gesellschaft. Retrieved from https://repositorio.cepal.org/bitstream/handle/11362/2022/1/Manual_Micro_Pequenha_Mediana_Empresa_es.pdf

Cerasis. (2019). Circular Supply Chain Vs. Linear Supply Chain: An Evolution. https://cerasis.com/circular-supply-chain/

Cesar, B. (2017, December). Knowledge Management and the Entrepreneur. *International Journal of Innovation Studies.*, *1*(3), 163–174. doi:10.1016/j.ijis.2017.10.005

Cezarino, L., Liboni, L., Oliveira Stefanelli, N., Oliveira, B., & Stocco, L. (2019). Diving into emerging economies bottleneck: Industry 4.0 and implications for circular economy. *Management Decision*, MD-10-2018-1084. doi:10.1108/MD-10-2018-1084

Chakraborty, M., VanKuren, N. W., Zhao, R., Zhang, X., Kalsow, S., & Emerson, J. J. (2018). Hidden genetic variation shapes the structure of functional elements in Drosophila. *Nature Genetics*, *50*(1), 20–25. doi:10.103841588-017-0010-y PMID:29255259

Chalkias, G. (2020). The digital circular economy. Available online, http://sharebox-project.eu/sharebox01/files/2019/06/PROSIN-A-digital-circular-economy-G.Chalkias.pdf

Chapman, J. (2005). *Emotionally durable design: Objects, Experiences and Empathy*. London: Earthscan Publications Ltd.

Charles, R. G., Davies, M. L., Douglas, P., Hallin, I. L., & Mabbett, I. (2019). Sustainable energy storage for solar home systems in rural Sub-Saharan Africa – A comparative examination of lifecycle aspects of battery technologies for circular economy, with emphasis on the South African context. *Energy*, *166*, 1207–1215. doi:10.1016/j.energy.2018.10.053

Chavarro, D., Vélez, M. I., Tovar, G., Montenegro, I., Hernández, A., & Olaya, A. (2017). Los objetivos de Desarrollo Sostenible en Colombia y el aporte de la ciencia, la tecnología y la innovación. Colciencias. *Documentos de trabajo No. 1*. Retrieved from: https://www.colciencias.gov.co/sites/default/files/objetivos_de_desarrollo_sostenible_en_colombia_y_el_aporte_de_la_ctei_2.pdf

Cheng, M. (2018). *Want to nature the women on your team? Help them take risks (and fail sometimes).* Retrieved March 29, 2019, from https://www.inc.com

Chen, Q. (2009, August). Evaluate the effectiveness of the natural cosmetic product compared to chemical-based products. *International Journal of Chemistry*, *1*(2), 57–59. doi:10.5539/ijc.v1n2p57

Chen, Y., Zhou, X., Yang, G., Bao, J., & Wang, G. (2017). Social networks as mediator in entrepreneurial optimism and new venture performance. *Social Behavior and Personality*, *45*(4), 551–562. doi:10.2224/sbp.5924

Chertow, M. R. (2007). "Uncovering" Industrial Symbiosis. *Journal of Industrial Ecology*, *11*(1), 11–30. doi:10.1162/jiec.2007.1110

Chertow, M. R. (2007, December). "Uncovering" industrial symbiosis. *Journal of Industrial Ecology*, *0*(0). doi:10.1162/jiec.0.1110

Chesbrough, H. (2009). *Open Innovation, The New Imperative for Creating and Profiting from Technology*. Harvard Business School Press.

Chigunta, F. J. (2002). *Youth Entrepreneurship: Meeting the key policy challenges*. Education Development Centre.

Child, I. L. (1968). Personality in Culture. In E. F. Borgatta & W. W. Lambert (Eds.), *Handbook of personality theory and research*. Chicago: Rand McNally.

Choi, D. Y., & Gray, E. R. (2008). The venture development processes of "sustainable" entrepreneurs. *Management Research News*, *31*(8), 558–569. doi:10.1108/01409170810892127

Chopra, S., & Meindle, P. (2004). *Supply Chain Management: Strategy, Planning, and Operation*. Upper Saddle River, NJ: Prentice-Hall.

Choudhury, A.S.B. (2019). *Eco-tourism: The mantra for sustainable rural livelihood*. Academic Press.

Christopher, M. (1998). *Logistics and Supply Chain Management: Strategies for Reducing Cost and Improving Service* (2nd ed.). Prentice Hall.

Chuang, L., Chung, Y., Chien, M., & Hsiung, P. (2019). Culture and Entrepreneurial Opportunity Recognition: Evidence from GEM and WVS. *Advances in Management & Applied Economics, 9*(4).

Čiegis, R., & Štreimikienė, D. (2005). Integration of Sustainable Development Indicators into Sustainable Development Programmes. *The Engineering Economist*, *2*(42), 7–13.

Cigolini, R., Cozzi, M., & Perona, M. (2004). A new framework for supply chain management: Conceptual model and empirical test. *International Journal of Operations & Production Management*, *24*(1), 7–41. doi:10.1108/01443570410510979

CIPE. (2015). *Public-Private Dialogue: The Key to Good Governance and Development*. Washington, DC: Centre for International Private Enterprise.

Circle-Economy. (2020). https://www.circle-economy.com/circular-economy/7-key-elements

Circular Academy. (2019). *Circular Academy: Critics and challenges*. Retrieved 3 October, 2019 from http://www.circular.academy/circular-economy-critics-and-challenges

Circular Economy Practitioner Guide. (2018). *Sharing Platforms*. Retrieved 7 November, 2019 from https://www.ceguide.org/Strategies-and-examples/Sell/Sharing-platforms

Clarke, J., & Wood, D. (2001). New public management and development: the case of public service reform in Tanzania and Uganda. In *The internationalization of public management: reinventing the third world state* (pp. 70–89). Cheltenham, UK: Edward Elgar. doi:10.4337/9781781952757.00011

Clarke, R., Chandra, R., & Machado, M. (2016). SMEs and social capital: Exploring the Brazilian context. *European Business Review*, *28*(1), 2–20. doi:10.1108/EBR-03-2013-0065

Clausen, T. H. (2006). *Who identifies and Exploits entrepreneurial opportunities*. Retrieved from www.ccsr.ac.uk

Coban, G. U., Akpinar, E., Kucukcankurtaran, E., Yildiz, E., & Ergin, O. (2011). Elementary school students water awareness. *International Research in Geographical and Environmental Education*, *20*(1), 65–83. doi:10.1080/10382046.2011.540103

Coduras, A., Urbano, D., Rojas, Á., & Martinez, S. (2008). The Relationship Between University Support to Entrepreneurship with Entrepreneurial Activity in Spain: A Gem Data Based Analysis. *International Advances in Economic Research*, *14*(4), 395–406. Retrieved January122019. doi:10.100711294-008-9173-8

Cohen, B. (2006). Sustainable valley entrepreneurial ecosystems. *Business Strategy and the Environment*, *15*(1), 1–14. doi:10.1002/bse.428

Cohen, B., & Muñoz, P. (2015). Toward a theory of purpose-driven urban entrepreneurship. *Organization & Environment*, *28*(3), 264–285. doi:10.1177/1086026615600883

Cohen, B., & Winn, M. I. (2007). Market imperfections, opportunity and sustainable entrepreneurship. *Journal of Business Venturing*, *22*(1), 29–49. doi:10.1016/j.jbusvent.2004.12.001

Cohen, M. J. (2016). *The Future of Consumer Society: Prospects for Sustainability in the New Economy*. Oxford University Press; doi:10.1093/acprof:oso/9780198768555.001.0001.

Cohen-Rosenthal, E. (2000). A Walk of the Human Side of Industrial Ecology. *The American Behavioral Scientist*, *44*(2), 245–264. doi:10.1177/00027642000044002007

Cohen, W., & Levinthal, D. A. (1990). Absorptive Capacity: A New Perspective on Learning and Innovation. *Administrative Science Quarterly*, *35*(1), 128–152. doi:10.2307/2393553

Cole, A. H. (1946). An Approach to the Study of Entrepreneurship: A Tribute to Edwin F. Gay. *The Journal of Economic History*. doi:10.1017/S0022050700052876

Coletto, D., & Bisschop, L. (2017). Waste pickers in the informal economy of the Global South: Included or excluded? *The International Journal of Sociology and Social Policy*, *37*(5/6), 280–294. doi:10.1108/IJSSP-01-2016-0006

Coloumbus, L. (2016). Roundup Of Internet Of Things Forecasts And Market Estimates. Available online, https://www.forbes.com/sites/louiscolumbus/2016/11/27/roundup-of-internet-of-things-forecasts-and-market-estimates-2016/

Co, M., & Mitchell, B. (2006). Entrepreneurship education in South Africa: A nationwide survey. *Education + Training*, *48*(5), 348–359. doi:10.1108/00400910610677054

Conceição, O., Dieguez, T., & Duarte, M. (2019). A Multivariate Approach to Entrepreneurial Intentions. In J. Machado, F. Soares, & G. Veiga (Eds.), *Innovation, Engineering and Entrepreneurship. HELIX 2018. Lecture Notes in Electrical Engineering* (Vol. 505). Cham: Springer.

Conklin, J. (2005). *Dialogue mapping: Building shared understanding of wicked problems*. London, UK: Wiley.

Connors, K., & Sweeney, S. (2019). *CGS Survey Reveals Sustainability Is Driving Demand and Customer Loyalty: Consumer expectations are high for eco-friendly products, especially with Gen Z buyers*. Retrieved November 30, 2019 from https://www.globenewswire.com/news-release/2019/01/10/1686144/0/en/CGS-Survey-Reveals-Sustainability-Is-Driving-Demand-and-Customer-Loyalty.html

Constanza, R., Alperovitz, G., Daly, H. E., Farley, J. Franco, C., Jackson, T., … Victor, P. (2012). Building a Sustainable and Desirable Economy-in-Nature. New York: United Nations Division for Sustainable Development.

Consumer Reports News. (2008). Toy trend: organic and natural toys. Retrieved at 27.10.2019, from https://www.consumerreports.org/cro/news/2008/12/toy-trend-organic-and-natural-toys/index.htm

Conte, J. M., Heffner, T. S., Roesch, S. C., & Aasen, B. (2017). A person-centric investigation of personality types, job performance, and attrition. *Personality and Individual Differences*, *104*(January), 554–559. doi:10.1016/j.paid.2016.09.004

Cook, P., & Olafsen, E. (2016). *Growth Entrepreneurship in Developing Countries: A Preliminary Literature Review*. Washington, DC: World Bank.

Cooney, M. T. (2012). *Entrepreneurship Skills for Growth-Orientated Businesses*. Retrieved November 10, 2019 from http://www.oecd.org/cfe/leed/cooney_entrepreneurship_skills_HGF.pdf

Cooper, R. (2018). *The growing trend of circular economy*. Retrieved from http://www.climateaction.org/climate-leader-papers/the-growing-trend-of-circular-economy

Cooper, T. (1999, January). Creating an economic infrastructure for sustainable product design. The Journal of Sustainable Product Design, (8), 7 - 17.

Cooper, M. C., & Ellram, L. M. (1993). Characteristics of supply chain management and the implications for purchasing and logistics strategy. *International Journal of Logistics Management*, *4*(2), 13–24. doi:10.1108/09574099310804957

Cooper, T. (2004). Inadequate life? Evidence of consumer attitudes to product obsolescence. *Journal of Consumer Policy*, *27*(4), 421–449. doi:10.1007/s10603-004-2284-6

COPADE. (2019). *Qué hacemos?* Retrieved February 14, 2020, from Pymes y ODS: https://copade.es/pymes-y-ods/

Cornescu, V., & Adam, R. (2013). Considerations regarding the role of indicators used in the analysis and assessment of sustainable development in the E.U. *Procedia Economics and Finance*, *8*, 10–16. doi:10.1016/S2212-5671(14)00056-2

Correa, F., Leiva, V., & Stumpo, G. (2018). Mipymes y heterogeneidad estructural en América Latina. In M. Dini & G. Stumpo (Eds.), *MIPYMES en América Latina. Un frágil desempeño y nuevos desafíos para las políticas de fomento* (pp. 9–34). Santiago, Chile: United Nations.

COSO. (2004a). *Enterprise risk management –integrated framework. Executive summary & framework.* Committee of Sponsoring Organizations of the Treadway Commission.

COSO. (2004b). *Enterprise risk management –integrated framework. Application techniques. Executive summary & framework.* Committee of Sponsoring Organizations of the Treadway Commission.

Coupet, J. (2017). Strings attached? Linking Historically Black Colleges and Universities public revenue sources with efficiency. *Journal of Higher Education Policy and Management*, *39*(1), 40–57. doi:10.1080/1360080X.2016.1254427

Courseault-Trumbach, C., Payne, D., & Kongthon, A. (2006). Technology mining for small firms: Knowledge Prospecting for competitive Advantage. *Technological Forecasting and Social Change*, *1*(1), 937–949.

Covin, J. G., & Miles, M. P. (1999). Corporate Entrepreneurship and the Pursuit of Competitive Advantage. *Entrepreneurship Theory and Practice*, *23*(3), 47–63. doi:10.1177/104225879902300304

Covin, J., & Slevin, D. P. (1989). Strategic management of small firms in hostile and benign environments. *Strategic Management Journal*, *10*(1), 75–87. doi:10.1002mj.4250100107

Cowdrey, R. (2012). *Creating an entrepreneurial mindset: Failure is an option.* Retrieved January 10, 2019, from www.bookboon.com

Cradle to Cradle Products Innovation Institute. (2019). What is Cradle to Cradle certified™? Retrieved at 28.10.2019, from https://www.c2ccertified.org/get-certified/product-certification

Crampton, N. (2020). *Watch List: 50 Top SA Small Businesses To Watch.* Entrepreneur South Africa. Entrepreneur Media, Inc.

Creswell, J. (2003). *Research Design: Qualitative, Quantitative and Mixed Methods Approaches* (2nd ed.). Thousand Oaks, CA: SAGE Publications.

Creswell, J. w. (2009). *Research design: Qualitative, quantitative, and mixed methods approaches.* Sage Publications.

Creswell, J. W. (2013). *Qualitative Inquiry and Research Design: Choosing among five approaches* (3rd ed.). Thousand Oaks, CA: Sage Publication.

Creswell, J. W. (2014). *Research design; Qualitative, quantitative and mixed-method approaches* (4th ed.). Thousand Oaks, CA: Sage Publication.

Croke, B. (2019). Key Ingredients for Scaling Circular Reuse Business Models. GreenBiz. Retrieved from https://www.greenbiz.com/article/key-ingredients-scaling-circular-reuse-business-models

Crowther, P. (1999). *Design for Disassembly.* Environmental Design Guide.

Cruz, S. E., Ojeda, S., Jáuregui, J., Velázquez, K., Santillán, N., García, R., ... Alcántara, C. (2017). E-Waste Supply Chain in Mexico: Challenges and Opportunities for Sustainable Management. *Sustainability*, *9*(4), 503. doi:10.3390u9040503

Cucchiella, F., D'Adamo, I., Koh, S. L., & Rosa, P. (2015). Recycling of WEEEs: An economic assessment of present and future e-waste streams. *Renewable & Sustainable Energy Reviews*, *51*, 263–272. doi:10.1016/j.rser.2015.06.010

Cudney, E., & Elrod, C. (2010). Incorporating Lean concepts into supply chain management. *International Journal of Six Sigma Competitive Advantage*, *6*(1/2), 12–30. doi:10.1504/IJSSCA.2010.034854

Cuervo, Á., Ribeiro, D., & Roig, S. (2007). Entrepreneurship: concepts, theory and perspective. Introduction. In *Entrepreneurship* (pp. 1–20). Berlin: Springer. doi:10.1007/978-3-540-48543-8_1

Cui, J. (2014). Sustainable Utilization of Tourism Resources in the Concept of Circular Economy Analysis. *Proceedings of International Symposium - Management, Innovation & Development (MID2014)*, 73-76.

Curley, M., & Formica, P. (2013). *University Ecosystems Design Creative Spaces for Start-Up Experimentation.* Springer. https://www.springer.com/gp/book/9783319001784

Cygan, A. (2002). The White Paper on European Governance–Have Glasnost and Perestroika Finally Arrived to the European Union? *The Modern Law Review*, *65*(2), 229–240. doi:10.1111/1468-2230.00376

D'Amato, D., Droste, N., Allen, B., Kettunen, M., Laehtinen, K., Korhonen, J., ... Toppinen, A. (2017). Green, circular, bio-economy: A comparative analysis of sustainability avenues. *Journal of Cleaner Production*, *168*, 716–734. doi:10.1016/j.jclepro.2017.09.053

Daalderop, T. (2016). *Circular Entrepreneurship, the case of Urban Agriculture in the Circular Economy*. Retrieved January 26, 2020 from https://edepot.wur.nl/385546

Daddi, T., & Iraldo, F. (2015). The Effectiveness of Cluster Approach to Improve Environmental Corporate Performance in an Industrial District of SMEs: A Case Study. *International Journal of Sustainable Development and World Ecology*, *23*, 1–11.

Daddi, T., Nucci, B., & Iraldo, F. (2017). Using Life Cycle Assessment (LCA) to measure the environmental benefits of industrial symbiosis in an industrial cluster of SMEs. *Journal of Cleaner Production*, *147*, 157–164. doi:10.1016/j.jclepro.2017.01.090

Dahl, O., Hughes, M., Husgafvel, R., Kanerva, J., & Linkosalmi, L. (2018). Forest sector circular economy development in Finland: A regional study on sustainability driven competitive advantage and an assessment of the potential for cascading recovered solid wood. *Journal of Cleaner Production*, *181*, 483–497. doi:10.1016/j.jclepro.2017.12.176

Dahlstrand, Asa, Lindholm, & Ors. (2017). *Entrepreneurial Experimentation: A Key Function in Entrepreneurial Systems of Innovation*. Research Institute of Industrial Economics. IFN Working Paper No. 1154.

Dalkir, K. (2011). *Knowledge Management in Theory and Practice*. Cambridge, MA: Massachusetts Institute of Technology.

Damodaran, A. (2007). *Strategic risk taking: a framework for risk management*. Pearson Prentice Hall.

Dana, Leo, & Paul. (2010). Nunavik, Arctic Quebec: Where Co-operatives Supplement Entrepreneurship. *Global Business and Economics Review*, *12*(1/2), 42–71.

Dana, L. P. (1992, November). Entrepreneurial education in Europe. *Journal of Education for Business*, *68*(2), 74–78. doi:10.1080/08832323.1992.10117590

Danciu, V. (2013). The sustainable company: New challenges and strategies for more sustainability. *Theoretical and Applied Economics*, *9*(586), 7–26.

Dangayach, G., & Deshmukh, S. (2004). Advanced manufacturing technology implementation: Evidence from Indian small and medium enterprises (SMEs). *Journal of Manufacturing Technology Management*, *16*(5), 16–26.

Daniel, A. D. (2016). Fostering an entrepreneurial mindset by using a design thinking approach in entrepreneurship education. *Industry and Higher Education*, *30*(3), 215–223. doi:10.1177/0950422216653195

Dannoritzer, C. (Director) (2010). The light bulb conspiracy: The untold story of planned obsolescence (Documentary).

Darla, G., Galvão, A., De Nadae, J., Honorato, D., Stief, P., Dantan, J., & Siadat, A. (2018). Circular Economy: Overview of Barriers. Procedia CIRP, 73, 79–85. doi:10.1016/j.procir.2018.04.011

Dash, D. (2018). A review of Organic Farming as a potential sector for Agripreneurship development among tribal youths in India. *International Journal of Agriculture Environment and Biotechnology*, *11*(5), 761–767. doi:10.30954/0974-1712.10.2018.8

Datschefski, E. (1999, January). Cyclic, solar, safe - biodesign's solution requirements for sustainability. The Journal of Sustainable Product Design, 42 - 52.

David, R., & Dube, A. (2014). Infopreneurial Behaviour among University Graduates in the Information Science Faculty of a University in Zimbabwe. *Infopreneurship Journal*, *1*(2), 1–8.

Dávila, T., Epstein, M., & Shelton, R. (2008). *Making Innovation Work, How to Manage It, Measure It, and Profit from It*. Seventh Printing & Pearson Education.

Davis, P. E., & Hu, Y. W. (2004). *Handbook of Pensions and Retirement Income*. London: Brunel University.

Dawson, C. J., Meza, D., Henley, A., & Arabsheibani, G. R. (2012). *Entrepreneurship: Cause or Consequence of Financial Optimism?* Rochester, NY: Social Science Research Network; Retrieved from http://chapters.ssrn.com/abstract=2157986

Day, G. S. (1994). The Capabilities of Market Driven Organisations. *Journal of Marketing*, *58*(4), 37–52. doi:10.1177/002224299405800404

Dayi, F., & Esmer, Y. (2016). Entrepreneurial Leadership: A Theoretical Framework. *Proceedings of the 25th International Academic Conference in Paris on 06-09 September 2016*. Retrieved November 28, 2019 from https://www.researchgate.net/publication/323365395_ENTREPRENEURIAL_LEADERSHIP_A_THEORETICAL_FRAMEWORK

Daymard, A. (2015). Determinants of Female Entrepreneurship in India. Economics Department Working Chapters No. 1191. Organisation for Economic Co-operation and Development. https://www.oecd-ilibrary.org/economics/determinants-of-female-entrepreneurship-in-india_5js4rfh5gtbq-en

De Abreu, M. C. S., & Ceglia, D. (2018). On the implementation of a circular economy: The role of institutional capacity-building through industrial symbiosis. *Resources, Conservation and Recycling*, *2018*(138), 99–109. doi:10.1016/j.resconrec.2018.07.001

De Angelis, R., Howard, M., & Miemczyk, J. (2018). Supply chain management and the circular economy: Towards the circular supply chain. *Production Planning and Control*, *29*(6), 425–437. doi:10.1080/09537287.2018.1449244

de Bell, L. (2015). Promoting Entrepreneurship and Innovation in Africa. In J. Kettunen, U. Hyrkkänen, & A. Lehto (Eds.), *Applied Research and Professional Education* (pp. 78–89). Turku: University of Applied Sciences.

De los Rios, R. I. C., & Charnley, F. J. S. (2017). Skills and capabilities for a sustainable and circular economy: The changing role of design. *Journal of Cleaner Production*, *160*, 109–122. doi:10.1016/j.jclepro.2016.10.130

De Meza, D., & Southey, C. (1996). The Borrower's Curse: Optimism, Finance and Entrepreneurship. *Economic Journal (London)*, *106*(435), 375–386. doi:10.2307/2235253

De Pauw, I., Kandachar, P., Karana, E., Peck, D., & Wever, R. (2010). Nature inspired design: strategies towards sustainability. Paper presented at the meeting of the Knowledge Collaboration & Learning for Sustainable Innovation ERSCP-EMSU Conference, Delft, The Netherlands.

De Vita, L., Mari, M., & Poggesi, S. (2014). Women entrepreneurs in and from developing countries: Evidences from the literature. *European Management Journal*, *32*(3), 451–460. doi:10.1016/j.emj.2013.07.009

de Wild, D. (2014). *Business Skills Training Course for Beneficiaries of Microeconomic Initiatives*. Retrieved November 12, 2019 from https://shop.icrc.org/icrc/pdf/view/id/1909

Deakins, D., & Freel, M. S. (2009). *Entrepreneurial activity, the economy and the importance of small firms. Entrepreneurship and small firms*. McGraw-Hill Education.

Dean, T. J., & McMullen, J. S. (2007). Toward a theory of sustainable entrepreneurship: Reducing environmental degradation through entrepreneurial action. *Journal of Business Venturing*, *22*(1), 50–76. doi:10.1016/j.jbusvent.2005.09.003

Deaton, A. (2005). Franco Modigliani and the Life-cycle Theory of Consumption. *PSL Quarterly Review*, *5*(58), 233–234. doi:10.2139srn.686475

Deineko, L. V., & Tsyplitska, O. O. (2018). Circular economy as a route to industrial modernization: The European experience. *ECONOMICS: Time Realities*, *5*(39), 30–40. doi:10.5281/zenodo.2568944

Deineko, L., Tsyplitska, O., & Deineko, O. (2019). Opportunities and barriers of the Ukrainian industry transition to the circular economy. *Environment and Ecology*, *10*(1), 79–92. doi:10.21511/ee.10(1).2019.06

De-Jesus, A., & Mendoça, S. (2018). Lost in Transition? Drivers and Barriers in the Eco-Innovation Road to the Circular Economy. *Ecological Economics*, *145*, 75–89. doi:10.1016/j.ecolecon.2017.08.001

Del Río, P., Carrillo-Hermosilla, J., Könnölä, T., & Bleda, M. (2016). Resources, capabilities, and competences for eco-innovation. *Technological and Economic Development of Economy*, *22*(2), 274–292. doi:10.3846/20294913.2015.1070301

Dell, S., & Sharma, Y. (2014). *Navigating the industry-academia partnership terrain*. http://www.universityworldnews.com/article.php?story=20141211194708818

DeLoach, J. (2016). *Reimagining Risk*. Corporate Compliance Insights.

Deloitte. (2012). *Sustainability for customer business companies: A story of growth*. Retrieved January 8, 2020 from https://www2.deloitte.com/content/dam/Deloitte/global/Documents/Consumer-Business/dttl_cb_Sustainability_Global%20CB%20POV.pdf

Den Hollander, M. C., Bakker, C. A., & Hultink, E. J. (2017). Product design in a circular economy: Development of a typology of key concepts and terms. *Journal of Industrial Ecology*, *21*(3), 517–525. doi:10.1111/jiec.12610

Dentchev, N., Baumgartner, R., Dieleman, H., Jóhannsdóttir, L., Jonker, J., Nyberg, T., ... Van Hoof, B. (2016). Embracing the variety of sustainable business models: Social entrepreneurship, corporate intrapreneurship, creativity, innovation, and other approaches to sustainability challenges. *Journal of Cleaner Production*, *113*, 1–4. doi:10.1016/j.jclepro.2015.10.130

Derwall, J., Guenster, N., Bauer, R., & Koedijk, K. (2005). The eco-efficiency premium puzzle. *Financial Analysts Journal*, *61*(2), 51–63. doi:10.2469/faj.v61.n2.2716

Desai, S. (2009). *Measuring Entrepreneurship in Developing Countries*. UNU-WIDER Research Paper, No. 2009/10, United Nations University, World Institute for Development Economics Research.

Deselnicu, D. C., Militaru, G., Deselnicu, V., Zainescu, G., & Albu, L. (2018). Towards a Circular Economy - A Zero Waste Programme for Europe. *Proceedings of the 7th International Conference on Advanced Materials and Systems*, 563-568. 10.24264/icams-2018.XI.4

Desmet, S., Van Dierdonck, R., & Van Looy, B. (2003). Servitization: or why services management is relevant for manufacturing environments. In B. Van Looy, P. Gemmel, & R. Van Dierdonck (Eds.), *Services Management: An Integrated Approach* (pp. 40–51). Harlow: Pearson Education.

Deutz, P., & Gibbs, D. (2008). Industrial Ecology and Regional Development: Eco-Industrial Development as Cluster Policy. *Regional Studies*, *42*(10), 1313–1328. doi:10.1080/00343400802195121

Devrim, Ö. (2014). Tarihsel süreç içinde C2C'nin izini sürmek. Retrieved at 28.10.2019, from https://trendyazilari.blogspot.com/2014/06/tarihsel-sureci-icinde-cradle-to-cradle.html

Dewah, P., & Mutula, S. (2016). Students' perceptions of the infopreneurship education in the Department of Records and Archives Management at the National University of Science and Technology. *South African Journal of Information Management*, *18*(1), 1–8. doi:10.4102ajim.v18i1.717

Dewhurst, M., Guthridge, M., & Mohr, E. (2009). Motivating people: Getting beyond money. *The McKinsey Quarterly*, *145*(1), 45–56.

Diacono, S. (2017). *Navigating the circular economy for entrepreneurial opportunities* (Master Dissertation). L'Universitàta Malta. Accessed on 18 September 2019. https://www.um.edu.mt/library/oar/handle/123456789/27819

Diaz-Cardiel, J. (2012). *Éxito con o sin crisis*. Lid Editorial Empresarial 2012. Retrieved from: https://books.google.com.co/books/about/%C3%89xito_con_o_sin_crisis.html?id=swdA6QEHmx0C&printsec=frontcover&source=kp_read_button&redir_esc=y#v=onepage&q&f=false

Díaz-García, C., González-Moreno, Á., & Sáez-Martínez, F. J. (2015). Eco-innovation: Insights from a literature review. *Innovation*, *17*(1), 6–23. doi:10.1080/14479338.2015.1011060

Dickson, M., & Asua, S. A. (2016). The Politics of Resource Control in Nigeria: Agitation and Innovation. *International Journal of Politics and Good Governance.*, *7*(2), 1–13.

Dieguez, T. (2017). Empowering Hub. In N. Baporikar (Ed.), Handbook of Knowledge Integration Strategies for Entrepreneurship and Sustainability (pp. 256–284). Academic Press.

Dieguez, T., Porfirio, J. A., & Amador, F. (2012). Institutions and the Emerging Challenges of Sustainable Development: The Case of Automotive Suppliers Industry. *ICERI2012 Proceedings*.

Dieguez, T. (2018). Sustainable Development: A controversial concept. *International Journal of Modern Research in Engineering & Management*, *1*(7), 15–21.

Digman, J. M., & Takemoto-Chock, N. K. (1981). Factors in the natural language of personality: Reanalysis and comparison of six major studies. *Multivariate Behavioral Research*, *16*(2), 149–170. doi:10.1207/s15327906mbr1602_2 PubMed

Dijk, S., Tenpierik, M., & den Dobbelsteen, A. (2014). Continuing the building's cycles: A literature review and analysis of current systems theories in comparison with the theory of Cradle to Cradle. *Resources, Conservation and Recycling*, (82): 21–34. doi:10.1016/j.resconrec.2013.10.007

Dinesh, A. (1991). *Approaches to Entrepreneurship Development. A Trend Analysis. ILO/INTERMAN Entrepreneurship Semina*. Ahmedabad: Entrepreneurship Development Institute of India. https://www.ediindia.org

Dinges, V., Urmetzer, F., Martinez, V., Zaki, M., & Neely, A. (2015). *The future of servitization: Technologies that will make a difference*. Working Paper. Cambridge University.

Dini, M., & Stumpo, G. (2019). Mipymes en América Latina: un frágil desempeño y nuevos desafíos para las políticas de fomento. Síntesis, Documentos de Proyectos (LC/TS.2019/20), Santiago, Economic Commission for Latin America and the Caribbean (ECLAC).

Dodangoda, H. C., & Arachchige, B. J. H. (2015). Impact of Personality on Career Success of the Employees in the Sri Lankan Banking Sector in Western Province. *Human Resource Management Journal*, *3*(2). doi:10.31357/hrmj.v3i2.2863

Dodoo, R. (1996). The Core Elements of Civil Service Reform. *African Journal of Public Administration and Management*, *3*(2), 23–46.

Doğa Sektörel Yayın Grubu. (2016). 2. Sanayi devrimi: "beşikten beşiğe" tasarım. Retrieved at 08.10.2019, from https://www.termodinamik.info/guncel/2-sanayi-devrimi-besikten-besige-tasarim

Dolan, C., & Rajak, D. (2016). Remaking Africa's informal economies: Youth, entrepreneurship and the promise of inclusion at the bottom of the pyramid. *The Journal of Development Studies*, *52*(4), 514–529. doi:10.1080/00220388.2015.1126249 PMID:28989182

Domenget, B.-E. (2019). *Top Trends in Hospitality for 2019*. Sommet Education. Retrieved on 28th July 2019 from http://www.sommet-education.com/wp-content/uploads/Sommet-Education-Top-Hospitality-Trends-2019.pdf

Donate, M. J., & de Pablo, J. D. S. (2015). The role of knowledge-oriented leadership in knowledge management practices and innovation. *Journal of Business Research*, *68*(2), 360–370. doi:10.1016/j.jbusres.2014.06.022

Dong, S., Li, Y., Li, Z., Li, F., Cheng, H., Yang, Y., . . . Bazarzhapov, T. (2018). Ecological environment risks and green development modes of China-Mongolia-Russia economic corridor. *IOP Conference Series: Earth and Environmental Science*, *190*(1), art. no. 012053. 10.1088/1755-1315/190/1/012053

Dong, Q. (2018). Study on the development strategy of tourism circular economy based on renewable energy technology. *Journal of Advanced Oxidation Technologies*, *21*(2), 201809023.

Doran, J., & Ryan, G. (2017). The Role of Stimulating Employees' Creativity and Idea Generation in Encouraging Innovation Behaviour in Irish Firms. *Irish Journal of Management*, *36*(1), 32–48. doi:10.1515/ijm-2017-0005

Drucker, P. (1994). The Theory of the Business. Harvard Business Review Retrieved from https://hbr.org/1994/09/the-theory-of-the-business

Drucker, P. F. (1985). *Innovation and Entrepreneurship*. New York: Harper & Row Publishers.

Drucker, P. F. (1996). Your leadership is unique. *Leadership*, *17*(4), 54.

Dubey, R., Gunasekaran, A., Papadopoulos, T., Childe, S. J., Shibin, K. T., & Wamba, S. F. (2017). Sustainable supply chain management: Framework and further research directions. *Journal of Cleaner Production*, *142*, 1119–1130. doi:10.1016/j.jclepro.2016.03.117

Duening, T. N., Hisrich, R. A., & Lechter, M. A. (2009). *Technology Entrepreneurship: Creating, Capturing, and Protecting Value*. Academic Press.

Dunlap, R. E. (2008). The New Environmental Paradigm Scale: From Marginality to Worldwide Use. *The Journal of Environmental Education*, *40*(1), 1, 3–18. doi:10.3200/JOEE.40.1.3-18

DuPont, U. S. A. (2018). Innovation starts here. Retrieved at 05.03.2018 from Https://www.dupont.com/corporatefunctions/our-company/dupont-history.html

Duréndez, A., & Garcia, D. (2008). *Innovative Culture, Management Control Systems and Performance in Young SMEs*. Academic Press.

Durugbo, C., Bankole, O., Erkoyuncu, J. A., Tiwari, A., Alcock, J. R., Roy, R., & Shehab, E. (2010). Product-Service Systems across Industry Sectors: Future Research Needs and Challenges. *CIRP IPS2 Conference 2010*.

Duska, R. (1997). The Why's of business revisited. *Journal of Business Ethics*, *16*(12/13), 1401–1409. doi:10.1023/A:1005731008313

Dustin, D. W. (2019). *Understanding state pension challenges: a primer for Sheeos*. The State Higher Education Executive Officers Association. Retrieved from https://sheeo.org/wp-content/uploads/2019/09/SHEEO_UnderstandingStatePensionChallenges

Dwight, C. (2017). *Definition of Enterprise Development*. Retrieved from https://bizfluent.com/facts-7152868-definition-enterprise-development.html

Dwivedi, O. P. (2017). *Bureaucracy and the Alternatives in World Perspective*. London: Macmillan.

Eco-Innovation Observatory. (2013). *Europe in transition. Paving the way to a green economy through eco-innovation. Eco-innovation Observatory Annual Report 2012. Funded by the European Commission*. Brussels: DG Environment.

Ecointeligencia. (2017). *¿En qué consiste la Economía del Rendimiento?* Recuperado el Mayo de 2019, de Ecointeligencia: https://www.ecointeligencia.com/2017/01/economia-rendimiento/

Ecología, U. N. A. M. (2015). *Fundación UNAM*. Obtenido de UNAM: http://www.fundacionunam.org.mx/ecologia/sostenibilidad-vs-sustentabilidad/

Economic Commission for Africa. (2019). *Small Business Management: A Training Manual*. Retrieved November 24, 2019 from https://repository.uneca.org/bitstream/handle/10855/572/Bib-9145.pdf;jsessionid=CF0E6728F6A1DD5249BFF70459CE31EB?sequence=1

Economic Performance in Former Socialist Countries. (n.d.). *Institutions in transition: reliability of rules and economic performance in former Socialist countries* (English). Retrieved from: http://documents.worldbank.org/curated/en/423111468766541642/Institutions-in-transition-reliability-of-rules-and-economic-performance-in-former-Socialist-countries

Economist, T. (2012, July). South Africa in recession. Repo rate down. *The Economist*.

Edogbanya, A., & Sule, M. J. A. G. (2013). Revenue Generation: It's Impact on Government Developmental Effort (A Study of Selected Local Council in Kogi East Senatorial District). *GJMBR-A: Administration and Management*, *13*(4), 13–25.

Edwards, P. E. T., Sutton-Grier, A. E., & Coyle, G. E. (2013). Investing in nature: Restoring coastal habitat blue infrastructure and green job creation. *Marine Policy*, *38*, 65–71. doi:10.1016/j.marpol.2012.05.020

EFCC. (2005). *Effect of Corruption on Nigeria's Economy*. Abuja: Nigeria EFFC Information Communication Technology Department.

EFNMS. (n.d.). *About Us*. Retrieved December 8, 2019, from The European Federation of National Maintenance Societies: www.efnms.org/What-EFNMS-stands-for/m13l2/What-EFNMS-stands-for.html

Efron, B. a. (1993). *An introduction to the boostrap: Monographs on Statistics and Applied Probability*. New York: Chapman & Hall. doi:10.1007/978-1-4899-4541-9

Ehrenfeld, J. R. (2005). Eco-efficiency. *Journal of Industrial Ecology*, *9*(4), 6–8. doi:10.1162/108819805775248070

Ehrenfeld, J., & Gertler, N. (1997). Industrial ecology in practice: The evolution of Inter-dependence at Kalundborg. *Journal of Industrial Ecology*, *1*(1), 67–79. doi:10.1162/jiec.1997.1.1.67

Elgin, D. (1993). Voluntary Simplicity. In Sustainable Development or collapse, regeneration and transformation? From Noha's Ark to the Titanic and Back Again. Palacky University.

Elise, D. (2018). *How to Design an Effective Knowledge Management Strategy for Your Organization.* https://www.e-nor.com

Elkington. (1997). *Cannibals with Forks: Triple Bottom Line of 21st Century Business.* Capstone Publishing.

Elkington, J. (1997). *Cannibals with Forks: The Triple Bottom Line of 21st Century Business.* Oxford, UK: Capstone.

Ellen Mac Arthur Foundation. (2015a). *Delivering the circular economy: a toolkit for policymakers.* Author.

Ellen Macarthur Foundation (2013). Towards the circular economy. Economic and business rationale for an accelerated transition. *Rethink the Future, 1.*

Ellen Macarthur Foundation (EMF). (2013). *Towards the Circular Economy: Economic and business rationale for an accelerated transition.* Cowes, UK: Ellen Macarthur Foundation.

Ellen Macarthur Foundation (EMF). (2015). *Towards the Circular Economy: Business Rationale for an Accelerated Transition.* Cowes, UK: Ellen Macarthur Foundation.

Ellen Macarthur Foundation. (2012). Towards the Circular Economy Vol.1: Economic and business rationale for a Circular Economy. Ellen Macarthur Foundation.

Ellen MacArthur Foundation. (2013). *Towards a Circular Economy: Business rationale for an accelerated transition.* Ellen MacArthur Foundation. Retrieved from https://www.ellenmacarthurfoundation.org/assets/downloads/publications/Ellen-MacArthur-Foundation-Towards-the-Circular-Economy-vol.1.pdf

Ellen MacArthur Foundation. (2013). *Towards the circular economy. Economic and Business rationale for an accelerated transition.* Author.

Ellen MacArthur Foundation. (2013). Towards the Circular Economy: Economic and Business Rationale for an Accelerated Transition. Retrieved from https://www.ellenmacarthurfoundation.org/assets/downloads/publications/Ellen-MacArthur-Foundation-Towards-the-Circular-Economy-vol.1.pdf

Ellen MacArthur Foundation. (2015). *Towards a Circular Economy: Business rationale for an accelerated transition.* Ellen MacArthur Foundation. Retrieved from https://www.ellenmacarthurfoundation.org/assets/downloads/TCE_Ellen-MacArthur-Foundation_9-Dec-2015.pdf

Ellen MacArthur Foundation. (2015). *Towards the Circular Economy: Economic and Business Rationale for an Accelerated Transition, Isle of Wight.* Available on: https://www.ellenmacarthurfoundation.org/assets/downloads/TCE_Ellen-MacArthur-Foundation_9-Dec-2015.pdf

Ellen MacArthur Foundation. (2015b). *Towards a circular economy: Business rationale for an accelerated transition.* Author.

Ellen Macarthur Foundation. (2017). *Achieving 'Growth Within'.* Retrieved from https://www.ellenmacarthurfoundation.org/assets/downloads/publications/Achieving-Growth-Within-20-01-17.pdf

Ellen MacArthur Foundation. (2017). *Schools of thought.* Retrieved 2 October, 2019 from https://www.ellenmacarthurfoundation.org/publications

Ellen MacArthur Foundation. (2017). The New Plastics Economy: Rethinking the future of plastics & catalysing action. https://www.ellenmacarthurfoundation.org/publications/the-new-plastics-economy-rethinking-the-future-of-plastics-catalysing-action

Ellen MacArthur Foundation. (2017). *What is a circular economy? A framework for an economy that is restorative and regenerative by design*. Retrieved from https://www.ellenmacarthurfoundation.org/circular-economy/concept

Ellen MacArthur Foundation. (2018). Circular Consumer Electronics: An initial exploration. https://www.ellenmacarthurfoundation.org/publications/circular-consumer-electronics-an-initial-exploration

Ellen MacArthur Foundation. (2019). Artificial Intelligence and the Circular Economy. https://www.ellenmacarthurfoundation.org/publications/artificial-intelligence-and-the-circular-economy

Ellen MacArthur Foundation. (2019). Circular Economy in Cities. https://www.ellenmacarthurfoundation.org/publications/circular-economy-in-cities-project-guide

Ellen MacArthur Foundation. (2019). Cities and Circular Economy for Food. https://www.ellenmacarthurfoundation.org/publications/cities-and-circular-economy-for-food

Ellen MacArthur Foundation. (2019). Completing the Picture: How the Circular Economy Tackles Climate Change. https://www.ellenmacarthurfoundation.org/publications/completing-the-picture-climate-change

Ellen MacArthur Foundation. (2019). Reuse – Rethinking Packaging. https://www.ellenmacarthurfoundation.org/publications/reuse

Ellen MacArthur Foundation. (2019a). *Economía Circular: Concepto*. Recuperado el 10 de Mayo de 2019, de Ellen MacArthur Foundation: https://www.ellenmacarthurfoundation.org/es/economia-circular/concepto

Ellen MacArthur Foundation. (2019b). *Economía Circular: Escuelas de pensamiento*. Recuperado el 16 de Mayo de 2019, de Ellen MacArthur Foundation: https://www.ellenmacarthurfoundation.org/es/economia-circular/escuelas-de-pensamiento

Ellen MacArthur Foundation. (n.d.). Circular Economy Concept, Schools of Thought. Retrieved from https://www.ellenmacarthurfoundation.org/circular-economy/concept/schools-of-thought

Ellen MacAthur Foundation (EMF). (2014). Towards the Circular Economy, Vow 3. Isle of Wight. Author.

Ellinger, A. (2000). Improving marketing/logistics cross-functional collaboration in the supply chain. *Industrial Marketing Management*, *29*(1), 85–96. doi:10.1016/S0019-8501(99)00114-5

Ellis, K., & Williams, C. (2011). *Maximising the impact off youth entrepreneurship support in different contexts*. London: Overseas Development Institute.

El-RufaiN. (2007). *A Federation Without Federalism*. Available: http://saharareporters.com/2012/04/06/federation-without-federalism-nasir-ahmad-el-rufai

Elston, J. A. (2002). *An Examination of the Relationship Between Firm Size, Growth, and Liquidity in the Neuer Markt*. Discussion paper 15/02, Economic Research Centre of the Deustche Bank. Retrieved from: https://www.bundesbank.de/Redaktion/EN/Downloads/Publications/Discussion_Paper_1/2002/2002_07_04_dkp_15.pdf?__blob=publicationFile

Emad, A. E., & Siddig, B. I. (2018). *Determinants of entrepreneurial intentions using the Theory of Planned Behaviour*. Retrieved March 31, 2019, from www.researchgate.net

EMF (Ellen MacArthur Foundation) and McKinsey & Co. (2019). Towards the Circular Economy: Economic and Business Rationale for an Accelerated Transition. Accessed on 15th January 2019 from https://www.ellenmacarthurfoundation.org/business/reports

EMF. (2013). *Towards the Circular Economy.* Cowes: Ellen MacArthur Foundation.

EMF. (2013). *Towards the Circular Economy: Economic and Business Rationale for an Accelerated Transition.* Cowes, UK: Ellen MacArthur Foundation.

EMF. (2014). Towards the Circular Economy: Accelerating the Scale-Up across Global Supply Chains. Ellen MacArthur Foundation.

EPA. (2018). *Managing-and-Reducing-Wastes-Guide-Commercial-Buildings.* https://www.epa.gov

EPEA GmbH – Part of Drees & Sommer. (2002). Cradle to Cradle: remaking the way we make things. Retrieved at 28.10.2019 from https://epea-hamburg.com/cradle-to-cradle-remaking-the-way-we-make-things/

Epure, M., & Bucea-Manea-Țoniş, R. (2017). Branding and Leadership in the context of Circular Economy. *Procedia of Economics and Business Administration*, 163-172.

Erkoyuncu, J. A., Roy, R., Shehab, E., & Wardle, P. (2009). Uncertainty challenges in service cost estimation for products-service systems in the aerospace and defence industries. *Proceedings of the 1st CIRP IPS2 Conference*, 200-206.

Erten, D. (2018). Beşikten beşiğe atık. Yeşil Bina, (48), 20 - 23. Retrieved from http://www.yesilbinadergisi.com/edergi/21/48/index.html

Ertz, M., Leblanc-Proulx, S., Sarigöllü, E., & Morin, V. (2019a). Made to break? A taxonomy of business models on product lifetime extension. *Journal of Cleaner Production*, *234*, 867–880. doi:10.1016/j.jclepro.2019.06.264

Ertz, M., Leblanc-Proulx, S., Sarigöllü, E., & Morin, V. (2019b). Advancing quantitative rigor in the circular economy literature: New methodology for product lifetime extension business models. *Resources, Conservation and Recycling*, *150*, 104437. doi:10.1016/j.resconrec.2019.104437

Espaliat, M. (2017). *Economía circular y sostenibilidad: nuevos enfoques para la creación de valor*. CreateSpace Independent Publishing Platform.

Esposito, M. (2017). Where the circular economy meets the Internet of Things. Available online https://www.greenbiz.com/article/where-circular-economy-meets-internet-things

Estarrona, U. M., Seneviratne, D., Villarejo, R. and Galar, D. (2019). The New Asset Management: Implications of Servitization in Circular Economy. *Journal of Industrial Engineering and Management Science*, 109-120.

Ethics and Anti-Corruption Commission (EACC). (2014). *4th Governance Integrity and Investment Conference: Combating Corruption, Unethical Conduct and Practices within the County Governments.* Available at www.icpsk.com

EU Commission. (2017a). *History and idea behind the EMAS Awards.* Available at ec.europa.eu

EU Commission, . (2017b). *COM(2017) 355 Final Report.* Brussels, Belgium: EU Commission.

Europe, C. S. R. (2018). *Circular economy: What are the enablers and barriers?* https://www.csreurope.org

European Commission Studies. (2004). *Final report of the expert group education for entrepreneurship.* Brussels: Enterprise Directorate General. Available at: http://europa.eu.int/comm/enterprise/entrepreneurship/support-measusures/index.htm

European Commission. (2013). *Eco-innovation the key to Europe's future competitiveness*. Retrieved 15 November, 2019 from https://ec.europa.eu/environment/pubs/pdf/factsheets/ecoinnovation/en.pdf

European Commission. (2014). *The Circular Economy. Connecting, creating, and conserving value*. Author.

European Commission. (2015). Circular economy. Retrieved at 19.08.2019 from https://ec.europa.eu/growth/industry/sustainability/circular-economy_en

European Commission. (2015). *Closing the loop: Commission adopts ambitious new circular economy: Package to boost competitiveness, create jobs and generate sustainable growth*. Retrieved November 10, 2019, from https://europa.eu/rapid/press-release_IP-15-6203_en.htm

European Commission. (2015). Closing the loop-An EU action plan for the Circular Economy. *Communication from the Commission to the European Parliament, the Council, the European Economic and Social Committee and the Committee of the Regions COM, 614*(2).

European Commission. (2015). Communication from the Commission to the European Parliament, the Council, the European Economic and Social Committee and the Committee of the Regions, December 2. Retrieved December 11, 2019, from https://ec.europa.eu/transparency/regdoc/rep/1/2015/EN/1-2015-614-EN-F1-1.PDF

European Commission. (2016). *Open Innovation, Open Science, Open to the World: A vision for Europe*. Directorate-General for Research and Innovation.

European Commission. (2019). *Report from the Commission to the European Parliament, the Council, the European Economic and Social Committee and the Committee of the Regions on the implementation of the Circular Economy Action Plan*. Author.

European Environment Agency (EEA). (2019). Water and marine environment. Retrieved December 16, 2019, from https://www.eea.europa.eu/themes/water

European Environment Agency. (2016). *Circular economy in Europe: developing the knowledge base*. Luxembourg: Publications Office of the European Union.

European Parliament. (2006). *A Longer Lifetime for Products: Benefits for Consumers and Companies*. Brussels, Belgium: Directorate-General for Internal Policies.

European Parliament. Directive 2002/96/EU of the European Parliament and of the Council of 27 January 2003 on waste electrical and electronic equipment (WEEE). (Official Journal of the European Union, 2003).

European, C. (2020). *Internal Market, Industry, Entrepreneurship and SMEs*. Retrieved from ECODESIGN: https://ec.europa.eu/growth/industry/sustainability/ecodesign_en

Evans, S., Gregory, M., Ryan, C., Bergendahl, M. N., & Tan, A. (2009). *Towards a sustainable industrial system: With recommendations for education, research, industry and policy*. Cambridge: University of Cambridge.

Ezeudu, O. B., & Ezeudu, T. S. (2019). Implementation of circular economy principles in industrial solid waste management: Case studies from developing Economy (Nigeria). *Recycling*, *4*(4), 42. doi:10.3390/recycling4040042

Fabricius, G., & Büttgen, M. (2015). Project managers' overconfidence: How is risk reflected in anticipated project success? *Business Research*, *8*(2), 239–263. doi:10.100740685-015-0022-3

Fakhrisadat, N., Narges, I., & Zahra, A. (2014). Explaining the Role of Managerial Skills of Entrepreneurship in Business Success. *International Journal of Management Sciences*, *4*(1), 42–52. https://www.researchgate.net/publication/313824665_Explaining_the_Role_of_Managerial_Skills_of_Entrepreneurship_in_Business_Success

Fan, Y. (2008). Research on the development of tourism circular economy in Henan province. In H. Zhang, R. M. Zhao, & Z. Q. Xie (Eds.), Industry Cluster and Meta-Studies (pp. 550–554). Academic Press.

Fang, X., & Zhang, X. (2010). On tourism environment protection for world cultural heritage sites in China. *2010 International Conference on Management and Service Science (MASS 2010)*, art. no. 5578038. 10.1109/ICMSS.2010.5578038

FAO (Food and Agriculture Organization of the United Nations). (2017). Pulp and Paper Capacities. UN Publications.

Farayibi, A. O. (2017). Entrepreneurship as a Driver of Economic Growth: Evidence from Enterprise Development in Nigeria. *SSRN Electronic Journal*. Retrieved November 19, 2019 from https://www.researchgate.net/publication/309374424_Entrepreneurship_as_a_Driver_of_Economic_Growth_Evidence_from_Enterprise_Development_in_Nigeria_Entrepreneurship_as_a_Driver_of_Economic_Growth_Evidence_from_Enterprise_Development_in_Nigeria

Fatemi, A., & Luft, C. (2002). Corporate risk management: Costs and benefits. *Global Finance Journal*, *13*(1), 29–38. doi:10.1016/S1044-0283(02)00037-6

Fatoki, O., & Chindoga, L. (2011). An investigation into the obstacles to youth entrepreneurship in South Africa. *International Business Research*, *4*(2), 161–169. doi:10.5539/ibr.v4n2p161

Fauchart, E., & Gruber, M. (2011). Darwinians, Communitarians, and Missionaries: The Role of Founder Identity in Entrepreneurship. *Academy of Management Journal*, *54*(5), 935–958. doi:10.5465/amj.2009.0211

Fayolle, A. (2009). *Entrepreneurship education in Europe: Trends and challenges. OECD LEED Programme. Universities, innovation and entrepreneurship: Good practice workshop*. Retrieved November 12, 2019, from http://www.oecd.org/dataoecd/11/36/43202553.pdf

Fayolle, A., & Gailly, B. (2008). From craft to science: Teaching models and learning processes in entrepreneurship education. *Journal of European Industrial Training*, *32*(7), 569–593. doi:10.1108/03090590810899838

Fayolle, A., Gally, B., & Lassas-Clerc, N. (2006). Assessing the impact of entrepreneurship education programs: A new methodology. *Journal of European Industrial Training*, *30*(9), 701–720. doi:10.1108/03090590610715022

Federal Ministry of Youth and Sports. (2013). *Nigeria Natural Resources*. Available: http://youthdevelopment.gov.ng/index.php/nigeria/2013-12-19-03-40-31/natural-resources

Feit, K., & Pisapia, J. (2014). Entrepreneurial Leadership at a Crossroads. *Management and Organization*. Retrieved December 31, 2019 from http://www.untag-smd.ac.id/files/Perpustakaan_Digital_1/ENTREPRENEURSHIP%20Crossroads%20of%20entrepreneurship.pdf

Feldmann, M., & Muller, S. (2003). An incentive scheme for true information providing in supply chains. *Omega*, *31*(2), 63–73. doi:10.1016/S0305-0483(02)00096-8

Ferdousi, F. (2015). Impact of microfinance on sustainable entrepreneurship development. *Development Studies Research*, *2*(1), 51–56. doi:10.1080/21665095.2015.1058718

Fernández de Tejada, V., & Saavedra-Robledo, I. (2014). La gestión ética en las medianas empresas. *ResearchGate*. Retrieved from: https://www.researchgate.net/publication/28202482

Fernandez Fernandez, M. T., Blanco Jimenez, F. J., & Cuadrado Roura, J. R. (2015). Business incubation: Innovative services in an entrepreneurship ecosystem. *Service Industries Journal*, *35*(14), 783–800. doi:10.1080/02642069.2015.1080243

Ferreira, F. N. H., Proença, J. F., Spencer, R., & Cova, B. (2013). The transition from products to solutions: External business model fit and dynamics. *Industrial Marketing Management*, *42*(7), 1093–1101. doi:10.1016/j.indmarman.2013.07.010

Ferreira, K. A., Nogheira Tomas, R., & Alcantara, R. L. C. (2015). A theoretical framework for postponement concept in a supply chain, International Journal of Logistics Research and Appications: A Leading. *The Journal of Supply Chain Management*, *18*(1), 46–61.

Fetters, M. L., Greene, P., Rice, M. P., & Butler, J. S. (2010). *The development of university-based entrepreneurship ecosystems*. Cheltenham: Edward Elgar. doi:10.4337/9781849805896

Fields, Z., & Atiku, S. O. (2017). Collective Green Creativity and Eco-Innovation as key drivers of Sustainable Business Solutions in Organisations. In *Collective Creativity for Responsible and Sustainable Business Practice* (pp. 1–25). Hershey, PA: IGI Global. doi:10.4018/978-1-5225-1823-5.ch001

Filchenkova, O. A. (2019). Transition of the Russian Federation to circular economy taking into account international experience. Actual questions of economy and management. https://moluch.ru/conf/econ/archive/329/14970

Finnish Innovation Fund Sitra. (n.d.). *Circular economy teaching for all levels of education*. Retrieved from https://www.sitra.fi/en/projects/circular-economy-teaching-levels-education/

Firstbrook, P., Reed, B., Olyaei, S., Sadowski, G., Mahdi, D., Bhajanka, P., Perkin, E. (2019). *Top Security and Risk Management Trends*. Gartner.

Fischer, M. M., & Nijkamp, P. (2009). *Entrepreneurship and regional development* (No. 0035). Academic Press.

Fiseha, G. G., & Oyelana, A. A. (2015). An assessment of the roles of small and medium enterprises (SMEs) in the local economic development (LED). *The South African Journal of Economics*, *6*(3), 280–290.

Fitzsimmons, J. R., & Douglas, E. J. (2011). Interaction between feasibility and desirability in the formation of entrepreneurial intentions. *Journal of Business Venturing*, *26*(4), 431–440. doi:10.1016/j.jbusvent.2010.01.001

Fixson, S. K., & Rao, J. (2014). Learning emergent strategies through design thinking. *Design Management Review*, *25*(1), 46–53. doi:10.1111/drev.10271

Flash Eurobarometer. (2010). *Entrepreneurship in the EU and beyond 2010*. The Gallup Organization.

Fletcher, E.K., Pande. R., & Moore, C. T. (2017). Women and Work in India: Descriptive Evidence and a Review of Potential Policies. Accessed from: file:///C:/Users/UJJAL/Downloads/RWP18-004_Pande.pdf

Foo, M. D. (2011). Emotions and entrepreneurial opportunity evaluation. *Entrepreneurship Theory and Practice*, *35*(2), 375–393. doi:10.1111/j.1540-6520.2009.00357.x

Forbes, D. P. (2005). Are some entrepreneurs more overconfident than others? *Journal of Business Venturing*, *20*(5), 623–640. doi:10.1016/j.jbusvent.2004.05.001

Ford, S., & Despeisse, M. (2016). Additive manufacturing and sustainability: An exploratory study of the advantages and challenges. *Journal of Cleaner Production*, *137*, 1573–1587. doi:10.1016/j.jclepro.2016.04.150

Fraser, S., & Greene, F. J. (2006). The Effects of Experience on Entrepreneurial Optimism and Uncertainty. *Economica.*, *73*(290), 169–192. doi:10.1111/j.1468-0335.2006.00488.x

Freeman, R. E., Harrison, J. S., & Wicks, A. C. (2007). *Managing for stakeholders: Survival, Reputation and Success*. New Haven: Yale University Press.

Frenkel, A., & Maital, S. (2014). *Mapping national innovation ecosystems: Foundations for policy consensus*. Cheltenham: Edward Elgar. doi:10.4337/9781782546818

Fromm, E. (2004). *Çağdaş Toplumların Geleceği*. İstanbul: Arıtan Yayınevi.

Frosch, R. A., & Gallopoulos, N. E. (1989). Strategies for Manufacturing—Wastes from one industrial process can serve as the raw material for another, thereby reducing the impact on the environment. *Scientific American*, *261*(3), 144–152. doi:10.1038cientificamerican0989-144

Frynas, J. G., & Stephens, S. (2015). Political Corporate Social Responsibility: Reviewing theories and setting new agendas. *International Journal of Management Reviews*, *17*(4), 483–509. doi:10.1111/ijmr.12049

Fulton, S. C. (2012). Twenty years after the rio earth summit: What is the agenda for the 2012 United Nations Conference on Sustainable Development? *Proceedings of the Annual Meeting American Society of International Law*, 91-94.

Fulton, M., & Hon, H. (2009). Managing advanced manufacturing technology (AMT) implementation in manufacturing SME. *International Journal of Productivity and Performance Management*, *59*(4), 12–22.

Funke, T. (2015). A Canvas that Describes Relationships within an Entrepreneurship Ecosystem. *Global Entrepreneurship Research Network*. http://gern.co/an-entrepreneurship-ecosystem-canvas-lessons-from-berlin/

Furnham, A. (1997). The half full or half empty glass, the views of the economic optimist vs. pessimist. *Human Relations*, *50*(2), 197–209. doi:10.1177/001872679705000206

Gapp, R., & Fisher, R. (2007). Developing an intrapreneur-led three-phase model of innovation. *International Journal of Entrepreneurial Behaviour & Research*, *13*(6), 330–348. doi:10.1108/13552550710829151

Garbie, I. H. (2014). An analytical technique to model and assess sustainable development index in manufacturing enterprises. *International Journal of Production Research*, *52*(16), 4876–4915. doi:10.1080/00207543.2014.893066

Garbuio, M., Dong, A., Lin, N., Tschang, T., & Lovallo, D. (2018). Demystifying the genius of entrepreneurship: How design cognition can help create the next generation of entrepreneurs. *Academy of Management Learning & Education*, *17*(1), 41–61. doi:10.5465/amle.2016.0040

Garcés-Ayerbe, C., Rivera-Torres, P., Suárez-Perales, I., & Leyva-de la Hiz, D. (2019). Is It Possible to Change from a Linear to a Circular Economy? An Overview of Opportunities and Barriers for European Small and Medium-Sized Enterprise Companies. *International Journal of Environmental Research and Public Health*, *16*(5), 85. doi:10.3390/ijerph16050851 PMID:30857193

Garcés-Ayerbe, C., Rivera-Torres, P., Suárez-Perales, I., & Leyva-de la Hiz, D. (2019). Is it possible to change from a linear to a circular economy? An overview of opportunities and barriers for European small and medium-sized enterprise companies. *International Journal of Environmental Research and Public Health*, *16*(851), 1–15. doi:10.3390/ijerph16050851 PubMed

García-García, J. (2004). *La Ley del Efecto Proporcional: una aplicación al estudio del crecimiento empresarial asturiano* (1993-1999). X Congresso Contabilidade, Estoril, Portugal.

Garmulewicz, A., & Ors. (2018). *Disruptive Technology as an Enabler of the Circular Economy: What Potential Does 3D Printing Hold?* https://journals.sagepub.com

Gartner, W. B. (2005). America's manic entrepreneurs. *American Enterprise (Washington, D.C.)*, *16*(5), 18–21.

Gartner, W. B., Shaver, K. G., Carter, N. M., & Reynolds, P. D. (2004). *Handbook of entrepreneurial dynamics*. Thousand Oaks, CA: Sage Publications.

Garza-Reyes, J. A., Parkar, H. S., Oraifige, I., Soriano-Meier, H., & Harmanto, D. (2012). An empirical exploratory study of the status of lean manufacturing in India. *International Journal of Business Excellence*, *5*(4), 395–412. doi:10.1504/IJBEX.2012.047906

Gebauer, H., Fleisch, E., & Friedli, T. (2005). Overcoming the service paradox in manufacturing companies. *European Management Journal*, *23*(1), 14–26. doi:10.1016/j.emj.2004.12.006

Gebauer, H., Gustafsson, A., & Vittel, L. (2011). Competitive advantage through service differentiation by manufacturing companies. *Journal of Business Research*, *64*(12), 1270–1280. doi:10.1016/j.jbusres.2011.01.015

Geels, F. W., McMeekin, A., Mylan, J., & Southerton, D. (2017). A critical appraisal of sustainable consumption and production research: The reformist, revolutionary and reconfiguration positions. *Global Environmental Change*, *34*, 1–12. doi:10.1016/j.gloenvcha.2015.04.013

Geiseb, S. (2008). *LEDNA LED Stocktaking Survey Report on the State of LED for Namibia*. Windhoek: GTZ/PEG.

Geissdoerfer, M., Savaget, P., Bocken, N. M. P., & Hultink, E. J. (2017). The Circular Economy—A new sustainability paradigm? Journal of Cleaner Production, 2017(143), 757–768. doi:10.1016/j.jclepro.2016.12.048

Geissdoerfer, M., Savaget, P., Bocken, N. M. P., & Hultink, E. J. (2017a). The Circular Economy - A new sustainability paradigm? *Journal of Cleaner Production*, *143*, 757–768. doi:10.1016/j.jclepro.2016.12.048

Geissdoerfer, M., Savaget, P., Bocken, N. M., & Hultink, E. J. (2017). The Circular Economy - A New Sustainability Paradigm? *Journal of Cleaner Production*, *143*, 770. doi:10.1016/j.jclepro.2016.12.048

Geissdoerfer, M., Savaget, P., Bocken, N. M., & Hultink, E. J. (2017). The Circular Economy–A new sustainability paradigm? *Journal of Cleaner Production*, *143*, 757–768.

Geissdoerfer, M., Vladimirova, D., & Evans, S. (2018). Sustainable business model innovation: A review. *Journal of Cleaner Production*, *198*, 401–416. doi:10.1016/j.jclepro.2018.06.240

GEM. (2017). *Women's entrepreneurship report*. Global Entrepreneurship Monitor.

GEM2002. (2004). *Global entrepreneurship monitor*. South African Report.

Geng, Y., & Doberstein, B. (2008). Developing the circular economy in China: Challenges and opportunities for achieving'leapfrog development'. *International Journal of Sustainable Development and World Ecology*, *15*(3), 231–239. doi:10.3843/SusDev.15.3:6

Geng, Y., Sarkis, J., & Ulgiati, S. (2016). Sustainability, well-being, and the circular economy in China and worldwide. *Science*, *6278*(Supplement), 73–76.

Geng, Y., Sarkis, J., Ulgiati, S., & Zhang, P. (2013). Measuring China's circular economy. *Science*, *339*(6127), 1526–1527. doi:10.1126/science.1227059 PubMed

Genovese, A., Acquaye, A. A., Figueroa, A., & Koh, S. L. (2017). Sustainable supply chain management and the transition towards a circular economy: Evidence and some applications. *Omega*, *66*, 344–357. doi:10.1016/j.omega.2015.05.015

George, D. A., Lin, B. C. A., & Chen, Y. (2015). A circular economy model of economic growth. *Environmental Modelling & Software*, *73*, 60–63. doi:10.1016/j.envsoft.2015.06.014

George, L. G., Helson, R., & John, O. P. (2011). The "CEO" of women's work lives: How Big Five Conscientiousness, Extraversion, and Openness predict 50 years of work experiences in a changing sociocultural context. *Journal of Personality and Social Psychology*, *101*(4), 812–830. doi:10.1037/a0024290 PubMed

Gerlach, J., Richter, N., & Richter, U. J. (2016). Mobility indicators put to test – German strategy for sustainable development needs to be revised. *Transportation Research Procedia*, *14*, 973–982. doi:10.1016/j.trpro.2016.05.077

Geroski, P. (1999). *The growth of firms in theory and practice*. Center for Economic Research Policy, Working Paper No. 2092.

Gerring, J. (2007). *Case study research: Principles and practices*. New York, NY: Cambridge University Press.

Ghauri, P. N., & Grønhaug, K. (2010). *Research Methods in Business Studies. Financial Times*. New York: Prentice Hall.

Ghisellini, P., Cialani, C., & Ulgiati, S. (2016). A review on circular economy: The expected transition to a balanced interplay of environmental and economic systems. *Journal of Cleaner Production*, *114*, 11–32. doi:10.1016/j.jclepro.2015.09.007

Ghosh, A. (2019). *The circular economy is a golden opportunity: Don't let it go to waste*. Retrieved from https://www.weforum.org/agenda/2019/01/the-circular-economy-turns-waste-into-gold-so-lets-get-on-with-it/

Ghosh, S. K. (Ed.). (2020). *Circular Economy: Global Perspective*. Springer. doi:10.1007/978-981-15-1052-6

Gibb, A. A. (2014). *The entrepreneurial higher education institution: a review of the concept and its relevance today*. https://heinnovate.eu/intranet/tef/downloads/HEInnovate_Analytical%20p aper.pdf

Gibbs, D. (2006). Sustainability Entrepreneurs, Ecopreneurs and the Development of a Sustainable Economy. *Greener Management International*, *55*(55), 63–78. doi:10.9774/GLEAF.3062.2006.au.00007

Gibbs, D., & Deutz, P. (2007). Reflections on implementing industrial ecology through eco-industrial park development. *Journal of Cleaner Production*, *15*(17), 1683–1695. doi:10.1016/j.jclepro.2007.02.003

Gibson, T., & Van der Vaart, H. J. (2008). *Defining SMEs: A Less Imperfect Way of Defining Small and Medium Enterprises in Developing Countries*. Washington, DC: Brookings Global Economy and Development. Retrieved from http://citeseerx.ist.psu.edu/viewdoc/download?doi=10.1.1.627.8740&rep=rep1&type=pdf

Gibson, S. W. (2007). *Micro-franchising Creating Wealth at the Bottom of the Pyramid*. Cheltenham: Edward Elgar.

Girard, J. P., & Girard, J. L. (2015). Defining Knowledge Management: Toward an Applied Compendium. *Online Journal of Applied Knowledge Management*, *3*(1), 14.

Girard, L. F., & Nocca, F. (2017). From linear to circular tourism. *Aestimum (Firenze)*, *70*, 51–74.

Giurea, R., Ioan, A. M., Ragazzi, M., & Cioca, L.-I. (2017). Focusing agro-tourism structures for environmental optimization. *Quality - Access to Success*, *18*(1), 115–120.

Gleason Espíndola, J., Cordova, F., & Casiano Flores, C. (2018). The importance of urban rainwater harvesting in circular economy: The case of Guadalajara city. *Management Research Review*, *41*(5), 533–553. doi:10.1108/MRR-02-2018-0064

Gliedt, T., & Parker, P. (2007). Green community entrepreneurship: Creative destruction in the social economy. *International Journal of Social Economics*, *34*(8), 538–553. doi:10.1108/03068290710763053

Global Environment Facility. (2019). *The circular economy: Tackling plastic pollution*. Retrieved 2 December, 2019 from https://www.thegef.org/news/circular-economy-tackling-plastic-pollution

Godelnik, R., & van der Meer, J. (2019). Sustainable Business Models in an Entrepreneurial Environment. In A. Aagaard (Ed.), *Sustainable Business Models* (pp. 239–276). Cham, Germany: Palgrave Macmillan. doi:10.1007/978-3-319-93275-0_9

Goedkoop, M. J., van Halen, C. J. G., te Riele, H. R. M., & Rommens, P. J. M. (1999). *Product Service System, Ecological and Economic Basic*. The Report No. 1999/36 Submitted to Ministerje van Volkshuisvesting, Ruimtelijke Ordening en Milieubeheer, Hague.

Goel, A. (2018). *Circular Economy A business Imperative for India*. doi:10.13140/RG.2.2.29340.23689

Goh, J., & Yoon-Chung, C. (2018). Towards a closed-loop system for the steel industry. *Asian Steel Watch*, *6*, 84–85.

Goldberg, L. R. (1981). Language and individual differences: The search for universals in personality lexicons. In L. Wheeler (Ed.), Vol. 2, pp. 141–165). Review of personality and social psychology Beverly Hills, CA: Sage.

Goldmark, L. (1996). *Business Development Services: A Framework for Analysis*. Unpublished Manuscript, No. MIC -101, Inter-American Development Bank.

Goldsby, T. J., Michael Knemeyer, A., Miller, J. W., & Wallenburg, C. M. (2013). Measurement and moderation: Finding the boundary conditions in logistics and supply chain research. *Journal of Business Logistics*, *34*(2), 109–116. doi:10.1111/jbl.12013

Goldstein, B. T., & Mele, C. (2016). Governance within public-private partnerships and the politics of urban development. *Space and Polity*, *20*(2), 194–211. doi:10.1080/13562576.2016.1157968

Goleman, D. (2002). *Business: The ultimate resource*. London: Bloomsbury Publishing Plc.

Golja, T., & Pozega, S. (2012). Inclusive Business – What Is It All About? Managing Inclusive Companies. *International Review of Management and Marketing*, *1*(2), 22–42.

González, J. J., Aponte, H. E., & Salazar, J. F. (2015). Medición del aprendizaje organizacional en las grandes y medianas empresas de Sogamoso, Colombia. *Cuadernos Latinoamericanos de Administración*, *11*(20), 19-36. Retrieved from: https://www.redalyc.org/articulo.oa?id=409640743003

Goodpaster, K. E., & Matthews, J. B. Jr. (1982). Can a Corporation Have a Conscience? *Harvard Business Review*, *60*, 132–141.

Goodship, V., & Stevels, A. (2012). *Electronic and Optical Materials*. Woodhead Publishing Limited.

Gough, K. V., & Langerang, T. (2016). *Introduction: Youth entrepreneurship in Sub-Saharan Africa. In young entrepreneurs in Sub-Saharan Africa*. Routledge. doi:10.4324/9781315730257

Govender, K. K. (2005). *Executive Deans Message*. Partnership between Direct Selling Association and the University of Johannesburg.

Govindan, K., & Soleimani, H. (2017). A review of reverse logistics and closed-loop supply chains: A journal of cleaner production focus. *Journal of Cleaner Production*, *142*(Part 1), 371–384. doi:10.1016/j.jclepro.2016.03.126

Govindan, K., Soleimani, H., & Kannan, D. (2015). Reverse logistics and closed-loop supply chain: A comprehensive review to explore the future. *European Journal of Operational Research*, *240*(3), 603–626. doi:10.1016/j.ejor.2014.07.012

Gower, R., Schroeder, P. M., Khinmaung-Moore, J., & Cook, P. (2016). *Virtuous circle: How the circular economy can create jobs and save lives in low and middle-income countries*. Retrieved from https://www.ids.ac.uk/publications/virtuous-circle-how-the-circular-economy-can-create-jobs-and-save-lives-in-low-and-middle-income-countries/

Goyal, M., & Parkash, J. (2011). Women Entrepreneurship in India-problems and prospects. *International Journal of Multidisciplinary Research*, *1*(5).

Graedel, T. (2000). The Evolution of Industrial Ecology. *Environmental Science & Technology*, *34*(1), 28A–31A. doi:10.1021/es003039c PMID:21657590

Grecu, V., & Denes, C. (2017). *Benefits of entrepreneurship education and training for engineering students*. Retrieved from https://www.researchgate.net/publication/319023075_Benefits_of_entrepreneurship_education_and_training_for_engineering_students

Green, F. (2013). *Youth entrepreneurship*. Background paper for the OECD centre for entrepreneurship, SMEs and local development.

Green, D., & McCann, J. (2011). Benchmarking a leadership model for the green economy. *Benchmarking: An International Journal*, *18*(3), 445–465. doi:10.1108/14635771111137804

Greene, F. J., & Saridakis, G. (2008). The role of higher education skills and support in graduate self-employment. *Studies in Higher Education*, *33*(6), 653–672. doi:10.1080/03075070802457082

Greve, H. R., & Rao, H. (2012). Echoes of the Past: Organisational Founding as Sources of an Institutional Legacy of Mutualism. *American Journal of Sociology*, *118*(3), 635–675. doi:10.1086/667721

Grigorescu, A., Mocanu, C., & Zamfir, A. (2017). Circular Economy and Decision Models among European SMEs. *Sustainability*, *9*(9), 1–15. doi:10.3390u9091507

Gro Harlem Brundtland. (1987). *Our Common Future*. Obtenido de UN Documents: http://www.un-documents.net/our-common-future.pdf

Grossman, S. A. (2012). Public-Private Partnerships: Introduction: The Emerging Role of Partnership Governance. *Public Performance & Management Review*, *35*(4), 575–577. doi:10.2753/PMR1530-9576350400

Grown, H. (n.d.). *Diseño Regenerativo*. Recuperado el Mayo de 2019, de Heaven Grown: http://heavengrown.com/arquitectura-regenerativa/

Guetterman, T.C. (2017). Designing a rigorous mixed methods research study. *Journal of Qualitative Research*, *18*(1), 1–16.

Guide, V. D. R., Harrison, T. P., & Van Wassenhove, L. N. (2003). The Challenge of Closed-Loop Supply Chains. *Interfaces*, *33*(6), 3–6. doi:10.1287/inte.33.6.3.25182

Gulani, M. G., & Usman, A. (2012). Financing Small and Medium Scale Enterprises (SMEs): A Challenge for Entrepreneurial Development in Gombe State. *Asian Journal of Business and Management Sciences*, *2*(9), 17–23.

Gulati, R. (1998). Alliances and networks. *Strategic Management Journal*, *19*(4), 293–317. doi:10.1002/(SICI)1097-0266(199804)19:4<293::AID-SMJ982>3.0.CO;2-M

Gulati, R. N. (2000). Strategic networks". *Management Journal*, *21*, 203–216.

Guldmann, E., & Huulgaard, R. D. (2020). Barriers to circular business model innovation: A multiple-case study. *Journal of Cleaner Production*, *243*, 118160. doi:10.1016/j.jclepro.2019.118160

Guo, P. (2011). Information Management System with the Application to Tourism Management in the Period of Circular Economy. *International Conference on Energy, Environment and Development (ICEED2010)*, *5*, 1525-1529.

Gupta, P. D., Guha, S., & Krishnaswami, S. S. (2013). Firm growth and its determinants. *Journal of Innovation and Entrepreneurship*, *2*(1), 15. doi:10.1186/2192-5372-2-15

Gupta, C. L. (2003). Role of renewable technologies in generating sustainable livelihoods. *Renewable & Sustainable Energy Reviews*, *7*(2), 155–174.

Gupta, S. (2008). The purpose of business: profit maximization versus corporate citizens. *Proceedings of the Academy of Business Economics*, P1 - P2.

Gupta, S., Chen, H., Hazen, B. T., Kaur, S., & Santibañez Gonzalez, E. D. R. (2019). Circular economy and big data analytics: A stakeholder perspective. *Technological Forecasting and Social Change*, *144*, 466–474. doi:10.1016/j.techfore.2018.06.030

H&M. (2020). *Garment Collecting*. Retrieved from Recycle at H&M: https://www2.hm.com/en_gb/ladies/shop-by-feature/16r-garment-collecting.html

Haas, W., Krausmann, F., Wiedenhofer, D., & Heinz, M. (2015). How circular is the global economy? An assessment of material flows, waste production, and recycling in the European Union and the world in 2005. *Journal of Industrial Ecology*, *19*(5), 765–777. doi:10.1111/jiec.12244

Hadjichambis, A., Paraskeva-Hadjichambi, D., Ioannou, H., Georgiou, Y., & Manoli, C. (2015). Integrating sustainable consumption into environmental education: A case study on environmental representations, decision making and intention to act. *International Journal of Environmental and Science Education*, *10*(1), 67–86. doi:10.12973/ijese.2015.231a

Hahn, R., Ince, I., & Spieth, P. (2018). Business model design in sustainable entrepreneurship: Illuminating the commercial logic of hybrid businesses. *Journal of Cleaner Production*, *176*, 439–451. doi:10.1016/j.jclepro.2017.12.167

Haldar, S. (2019). Green entrepreneurship in the renewable energy sector – a case study of Gujarat. *Journal of Science and Technology Policy Management*, *10*(1), 234–250. doi:10.1108/JSTPM-12-2017-0070

Halden, R. (2010, January). Plastics and health risks. *Annual Review of Public Health*, *31*(1), 179–194. doi:10.1146/annurev.publhealth.012809.103714 PubMed

Hall, J. K., Daneke, G. A., & Lenox, M. J. (2010). Sustainable development and entrepreneurship: Past infrastructure contributions and future directions. *Journal of Business Venturing*, *25*(5), 439–448. doi:10.1016/j.jbusvent.2010.01.002

Halloran, J. W. (2014). *Your Small Business Adventure: Finding Your Niche and Growing a Successful Business*. ALA/Huron Street Press.

Hamari, J., Sjöklint, M., & Ukkonen, A. (2016). The Sharing Economy: Why People Participate in Collaborative Consumption. *Journal of the Association for Information Science and Technology*, *67*(9), 2047–2059. doi:10.1002/asi.23552

Hammersley, M. (2013). *What is qualitative research?* London, UK: Bloomsbury.

Hanaysha, J., & Hilman, H. (2015). Product Innovation as a Key Success Factor to Build Sustainable Brand Equity. *Management Science Letters*, *5*(6), 567–576.

Han, L., Pan, Z., & Yan, Q. (2010). Analysis of the Construction of Hainan International Tourism Island Based on Circular Economy. *Proceedings of 2010 International Symposium on Tourism Resources and Management*, 77-82.

Hansen, M., Chesbrough, H., Nohria, N., & Sull, D. (2000). Networked incubators. Hothouses of the new economy. *Harvard Business Review*, *78*(5). https://www.ncbi.nlm.nih.gov/pubmed/11143156 PMID:11143156

Hansohm, D., & Matsaert, F. (2013). *Credit Delivery Systems for SMEs in Namibia*. Windhoek: Frederich Ebert Stiftung.

Harris, A. (2003). Opportunities and constraints for indigenous entrepreneurs in SME development and growth in foreign markets. SME development and growth in foreign markets: The involvement of Indigenous Entrepreneur. Workshop 3(2); Center for Entrepreneurship Development, Windhoek. Polytechnic of Namibia.

Harrison, J. S., Bosse, D. A., & Phillips, R. A. (2010). Managing for stakeholders, stakeholder utility functions, and competitive advantage. *Strategic Management Journal*, *31*(1), 58–74. doi:10.1002mj.801

Hart, M., Levie, J., Bonner, K., & Drews, C.-C. (2015). *Global Entrepreneurship Monitor United Kingdom 2014 Monitoring Report*. Academic Press.

Harvey, L., & Knight, P. (1996). *Transforming higher education*. Bristol, PA: Society for Research into Higher Education: Open University Press.

Harwood, R. R. (1990). A history of sustainable agriculture. *Sustainable agricultural Systems*, 3-19.

Hashi, I., & Krasniqi, B. (2010). Entrepreneurship and SME growth: Evidence from advanced and laggard transition economies. *International Journal of Entrepreneurial Behaviour & Research*, *17*(5), 456–487. doi:10.1108/13552551111158817

Hawken, P., Lovins, A., & Lovins, L. (2000). *Natural Capitalism: Creating the Next Industrial Revolution.* Obtenido de Research Gate: https://www.researchgate.net/publication/265074221_Natural_Capitalism

Hein, A. M. (2010). *A Critical Analysis of Local Government Support in the Promotion of Small Enterprises.* Cape Town: Cape Peninsula University of Technology.

He, K., Sun, Z., Hu, Y., Zeng, X., Yu, Z., & Cheng, H. (2017). Comparison of soil heavy metal pollution caused by e-waste recycling activities and traditional industrial operations. *Environmental Science and Pollution Research International*, *24*(10), 9387–9398. doi:10.100711356-017-8548-x PMID:28233211

Helmig, B., Spraul, K., & Ingenhoff, D. (2016). Under Positive Pressure How Stakeholder Pressure Affects Corporate Social Responsibility Implementation. *Business & Society*, *55*(2), 151–187. doi:10.1177/0007650313477841

Helmsing, A. H. J. (2003). Local economic development: New generations of actors, policies and instruments for Africa. *Public Administration and Development: The International Journal of Management Research and Practice*, *23*(1), 67–76. doi:10.1002/pad.260

Hemphill, J. K., & Coons, A. E. (1957). Leader behavior: Its description and measurement. *Administrative Science Quarterly*, 6–38.

Hens, L., Block, C., Cabello-Eras, J. J., Sagastume-Gutierez, A., Garcia-Lorenzo, D., Chamorro, C., ... Vandecasteele, C. (2018). On the evolution of Cleaner Production as a concept and a practice. *Journal of Cleaner Production*, *172*, 3323–3333. doi:10.1016/j.jclepro.2017.11.082

Heriot, K. C., & Loughman, T. P. (2009). *Resolving the Planning Conundrum in New Venture Creation: An adaptation of Mintzberg's formation perspective*. Academic Press.

Hernández, N., Yelandy, M., & Cuza, L. (2013). Modelos causales para la Gestión de Riesgos. *Revista Cubana de Ciencias Informáticas*, *7*(4).

Hernandez, R. J. (2019). Sustainable Product-Service Systems and Circular Economies. *Sustainability*, *11*(19), 5383. doi:10.3390u11195383

Hernández-Villanueva, C. A., & Mosquera-Rodas, J. J. (2016). Descripción de los modelos actuales de gestión gerencial, en las grandes empresas industriales de Pereira y Dosquebradas en el contexto actual de la economía periodo 2013 - 2014. *Sciences et Techniques (Paris)*, *21*(2), 122–127. Retrieved from https://search-ebscohost-com.hemeroteca.lasalle.edu.co/login.aspx?direct=true&AuthType=ip,url,uid&db=a9h&AN=122337584&lang=es&site=ehost-live

Heshmati, A. (2015). *A Review of the Circular Economy and its Implementation.* http://ftp.iza.org

Heshmati, A. (2015). *A Review of the Circular Economy and its Implementation.* IZA Discussion Papers, No. 9611. Institute for the Study of Labour (IZA), Bonn. https://www. econstor. eu/bitstream/10419/130297/1/dp9611

Heshmati, A. (2015). *A Review of the Circular Economy and its Implementation.* Retrieved November 27, 2019 from http://ftp.iza.org/dp9611.pdf

Hillary, R. (2004). Environmental management systems and the smaller enterprise. *Journal of Cleaner Production*, *12*(6), 561–569. doi:10.1016/j.jclepro.2003.08.006

Hills, G., & Laforge, R. W. (1992). Research at the marketing interface to advance entrepreneurship theory. *Entrepreneurship Theory and Practice*, *16*(3), 33–59. doi:10.1177/104225879201600303

Hills, R. M. (1998). The Political Economy of Cooperative Federalism: Why State Autonomy Makes Sense and "Dual Sovereignty" Doesn't. *Michigan Law Review*, *96*(4), 813–944.

Hindle, T. (2008). *Guide to management ideas and gurus*. Exmouth House.

Hislop, D., Bosua, R., & Helms, R. (2013). *Knowledge management in organizations: A critical introduction*. Oxford University Press.

Hmieleski, K. M., & Baron, R. A. (2009). Entrepreneurs' Optimism and New Venture Performance: A Social Cognitive Perspective. *Academy of Management Journal*, *52*(3), 473–488. doi:10.5465/amj.2009.41330755

Hoang, H., & Antoncic, B. (2003). Network-based research in entrepreneurship: A critical review. *Journal of Business Venturing*, *18*(2), 165–187. doi:10.1016/S0883-9026(02)00081-2

Hobson, K. (2015). Closing the loop or squaring the circle? Locating generative spaces for the circular economy. *Progress in Human Geography*, 40.

Hoevenagel, R., Brummelkamp, G., Peytcheva, A., & Van der Horst, R. (2007). *Promoting Environmental Technologies in SMEs: Barriers and Measures*. Luxembourg: European Commission: Institute for Prospective Technological Studies.

Holland, J. L. (1997). *Making vocational choices: A theory of vocational personalities and work environments* (3rd ed.). Psychological Assessment Resources.

Hollins, O. (2011). *The Further Benefits of Business Resource Efficiency*. London: Department for Environmental Food and Rural Affairs.

Holmatov, B., Hoekstra, A. Y., & Krol, M. S. (2019). Land, water and carbon footprints of circular bioenergy production systems. *Renewable & Sustainable Energy Reviews*, *111*, 224–235. doi:10.1016/j.rser.2019.04.085

Holweg, M. (2005). The Three Dimensions of Responsiveness. *International Journal of Operations & Production Management*, *25*(7), 603–622. doi:10.1108/01443570510605063

Holzmann, R., & Hinz, R. (Eds.). (2005). *Old-Age Income Support in the 21st Century: an international perspective on pension systems and reform*. Washington, DC: The World Bank. doi:10.1596/0-8213-6040-X

Honebein, P. C. (1996). *Constructivist learning environments: case studies in instructional design*. Educational Technology Publications.

Hong, C., Liang, W., & Zhao, G. (2018). Performance assessment of circular economy for phosphorus chemical ðrms based on VIKOR-QUALIFLEX method. *Journal of Cleaner Production*, *196*, 1365-1378. doi:10.1016/j.jclepro.2018.06.147

Hope, R. K. (2014). *Devolved Government and Local Governance in Kenya*. Available at www.researchgate.net

Hopewell, J., Dvorak, R., & Kosior, E. (2009). Plastics recycling: Challenges and opportunities. *Philosophical Transactions of the Royal Society of London. Series B, Biological Sciences*, *364*(1526), 2115–2126. doi:10.1098/rstb.2008.0311 PMID:19528059

Hörisch, J. (2015). The Role of Sustainable Entrepreneurship in Sustainability Transitions: A Conceptual Synthesis against the Background of the Multi-Level Perspective. *Administrative Sciences*, *5*(4), 286–300. doi:10.3390/admsci5040286

Hoyt, R. E., & Liebenberg, A. P. (2011). The value of enterprise risk management. *The Journal of Risk and Insurance*, *78*(4), 795–822. doi:10.1111/j.1539-6975.2011.01413.x

Hsie, I., Nickerson, J., & Zenger, T. (2007). Opportunity Discovery, Problem Solving and a Theory of the Entrepreneurial Firm. *Journal of Management Studies*, *47*(7), 1255–1277. doi:10.1111/j.1467-6486.2007.00725.x

Hu, Y. Y., Ke, S., Lee, C.J.K., Li, H., Luo E., & Wen, Z. (2018). Approaches and policies for promoting industrial park recycling transformation (IPRT) in China: Practices and lessons. *Journal of Cleaner Production*, *172*, 1370-1380. Retrieved October 16, 2019 from www.elsevier.com/locate/jclepro

Huang, B., Plas, L., & Salam, N. (2016). *Exploring Prospective Entrepreneurial Engagement and Stakeholders' Involvement in the Circular Economy: An Empirical Study on the Concept of Växjö Reuse Village*. Retrieved November 29, 2019 from https://pdfs.semanticscholar.org/689b/41720bbe6beff5e7cdf7778a4a98b5110fae.pdf

Huber, F., Peisl, T., Gedeon, S., Brodie, J., & Sailer, K. (2016). *Design thinking-based entrepreneurship education: How to incorporate design-thinking principles into an entrepreneurship course*. Paper presented at the 4th 3E Conference – ECSB Entrepreneurship Education Conference, Leeds, UK.

Hunter, C. (1997). Sustainable tourism as an adaptive paradigm. *Annals of Tourism Research*, *24*(4), 850–867. doi:10.1016/S0160-7383(97)00036-4

Huq, A., & Gilbert, D. (2017). All the world's a stage: Transforming entrepreneurship education through design thinking. *Education + Training*, *9*(2), 155–170. doi:10.1108/ET-12-2015-0111

Hurst, E., & Lusardi, A. (2004). Liquidity constraints, household wealth, and entrepreneurship. *Journal of Political Economy*, *112*(2), 319–347. doi:10.1086/381478

Huthala, A. (2015, November). Circular economy: a commentary from the perspectives of the natural and social sciences. EASAC (European Academies Science Advisory Council), 1 - 18. Retrieved from https://www.easac.eu/fileadmin/PDF_s/reports_statements/EASAC_Circular_Economy_Web.pdf

Huysman, S., Debaveye, S., Schaubroeck, T., De Meester, S., Ardente, F., Mathieux, F., & Dewulf, J. (2015). The recyclability benefit rate of closed-loop and open-loop systems: A case study on plastic recycling in Flanders. *Resources, Conservation and Recycling*, *101*, 53–60. doi:10.1016/j.resconrec.2015.05.014

Hyett, N., Kenny, A., & Dickson-Swift, V. (2014). Methodology or method? A critical review of qualitative case study reports. *International Journal of Qualitative Studies on Health and Well-being*, *9*(1), 10. doi:10.3402/qhw.v9.23606 PMID:24809980

Iakovleva, T. (2015). *Exploring the relationship between university context and entrepreneurial intentions*. Submitted paper.

Igbuzor, O. (2006) *The millennium development goals: can Nigeria meet the goals in 2015?* Presentation at the Symposium of The Institute Of Chartered Accountants Of Nigeria (ICAN), Abuja, Nigeria.

Ilipinar, G., Montana, J., & Spender, J. C. (2008). *Design thinking in the postmodern organization*. Paper presented at the International Education 2008 Conference on Design thinking.

Imboden, A. (2019). *Top Trends in Hospitality for 2019*. Sommet Education. Retrieved on 28th July 2019 from http://www.sommet-education.com/wp-content/uploads/Sommet-Education-Top-Hospitality-Trends-2019.pdf

Immacolata, V. (2018). Agriculture, Rural Tourism and Circular Paradigm. *Quality - Access to Success*, *19*(1), 556–562.

Impacts of circular economy policies on the labour market:Final report and Annexes. (2018). Brussels: European Commission (EC). Retrieved from: https://circulareconomy.europa.eu/platform/sites/default/files/ec_2018_-_impacts_of_circular_economy_policies_on_the_labour_market.pdf

India's women are the secret to a potential economic boom. (2018). Accessed from: https://www.weforum.org/agenda/2018/07/india-could-boost-its-gdp-by-770-billion-by-just-treating-women-better

Insight, S. B. (2019). *The Nordic Market for Circular Economy: Attitudes, Behaviours & Business Opportunities.* Retrieved October 23, 2019 from https://www.nordea.com/Images/37-308788/Circular%20Economy%2019_small.pdf

International Integrated Reporting Council. (2013). Business Model Background Paper for IR. International Integrated Reporting. Retrieved from https://integratedreporting.org/wp-content/uploads/2013/03/Business_Model.pdf

International Monetary Fund (IMF) & World Bank. (2000). *Zambia: preliminary document on the enhanced initiative for heavily indebted poor countries.* Washington, DC: IMF and World Bank.

International Water Association. (2018). Wastewater Report 2018, The Water Reuse Opportunity. Retrieved from https://www.iwa-network.org/wp-content/uploads/2018/02/OFID-Wastewater-report-2018.pdf

Ionescu, C. A., Coman, M. D., Lixandru, M., & Groza, D. (2017). Business Model in Circular Economy, Valachain. *Journal of Economic Studies (Glasgow, Scotland)*, *8*(22), 101–108.

Irish Water. (2015). Water Services Strategic Plan A. Plan for the Future of Water Services. Retrieved from https://www.water.ie/docs/WSSP_Final.pdf

Isenberg, D. (2014). *What an entrepreneurship ecosystem actually is.* https://hbr.org/2014/05/what-an-entrepreneurial-ecosystem-actually-is/

Isenberg, D. (2011). *The entrepreneurship ecosystem strategy as a new paradigm for economic policy.* Academic Press.

Isenberg, D. J. (2010, June). How to Start an Entrepreneurial Revolution. *Harvard Business Review.*

Ismail, A. I., Abdelrahman, S. E., & Majid, A. H. A. (2018). Closing Strategic Human Resource Management Research Lacunas with Mediating Role of Employee Creativity. *Academy of Strategic Management Journal*, *17*(1), 1–18.

Ismail, S., & Haris, F. A. (2014). Constraints in implementing public private partnership (PPP) in Malaysia. *Built Environment Project and Asset Management*, *4*(3), 238–250. doi:10.1108/BEPAM-10-2013-0049

Iversen, J., Jørgensen, R., & Malchow-Møller, N. (2007). Defining and measuring entrepreneurship. *Foundations and Trends® in Entrepreneurship, 4*(1), 1-63.

Ivwurie, O. M., & Ocholla, D. N. (2016). The status and development of infopreneurship in Nigeria and South Africa. *Education for Information*, *32*(4), 323–342. doi:10.3233/EFI-160980

Jackson, T. (2009). Prosperity without growth? The transition to a sustainable economy. Sustainable Development Commission.

Jackson, E. A., & Jabbie, M. (2019). Understanding market failure in the developing country context. In *Decent Work and Economic Growth: Encyclopedia of Sustainable Development Goals* (pp. 1–10). Cham: Springer Nature Switzerland. doi:10.1007/978-3-319-71058-7_44-1

Jackson, T. (2009). *Prosperity without Growth: Economics for a Finite Planet.* London, UK: Earthscan; doi:10.4324/9781849774338.

Jacobs, H.M., & Chavhunduka, C. (2003). *Devolution for Land Administration in Zimbabwe: opportunities and challenges.* Centre for Applied Social Sciences, University of Zimbabwe-Land Tenure Center, University of Wisconsin-Madison.

Jain, S., Jain, N. K., & Metri, B. (2018). Strategic framework towards measuring a circular supply chain management. Benchmarking, 25(8), 3238–3252. doi:10.1108/BIJ-11-2017-0304

Jakhar, S. K., Mangla, S. K., Luthra, S., & Kusi-Sarpong, S. (2019). When Stakeholder pressure drives the circular economy. *Management Decision*, *57*(4), 904–920. doi:10.1108/MD-09-2018-0990

Jamal, A. H., & Tilchin, O. (2016). Teachers' Accountability for Adaptive Project-Based Learning. *American Journal of Educational Research*, *4*(5), 420–426.

Jauch, H., & Sakaria, I. (2009). *Chinese investments in Namibia: A labour perspective*. Windhoek, Namibia.

Jawahir, I., & Bradley, R. (2016). Technological elements of circular economy and the principles of 6R-based closed-loop material flow in sustainable manufacturing. Procedia CIRP, 40, 103–108. doi:10.1016/j.procir.2016.01.067

Jawahir, I. S., & Bradley, R. (2016). Technological elements of circular economy and the principles of 6R-based closed-loop material flow in sustainable manufacturing. *Procedia CIRP*, *40*(1), 103–108. doi:10.1016/j.procir.2016.01.067

Jensen, M. C., & Meckling, W. H. (1976). Theory of the Firm: Managerial Behavior, Agency Costs and Ownership Structure. *Journal of Financial Economics*, *3*(4), 305–360. doi:10.1016/0304-405X(76)90026-X

Jenson, J.P., & Ors. (2017). *Enabling Circular Economy through Product Stewardship*. https://www.sciencedirect.com

Jerez, P. (2001). *La gestión de recursos humanos y el aprendizaje organizativo: incidencia e implicaciones* (Unpublished PhD dissertation). Universidad de Almería, Departamento de Dirección y Gestión de Empresas, Almería, Spain.

Jharkharia, S., & Shankar, R. (2004). Supply Chain Management: Some insights from Indian Manufacturing Companies, Asian. *Academy of Management Journal*, *9*(1), 79–98.

Jia, Z., Qin, A., & Jia, H. (2012). Research on the Development of Leisure Agriculture Tourism in Yi County Based on Circular Economy. In M. Kuek, Z.Q. Xie, & R. Zhao (Eds.), *Proceedings of the Third International Symposium - Industrial Engineering and Management*, (pp. 125-129). Academic Press.

Jibeen, T. (2014). Personality Traits and Subjective Well-Being: Moderating Role of Optimism in University Employees. *Social Indicators Research*, *118*(1), 157–172. doi:10.1007/s11205-013-0416-6

Jin, Y., Tang, X., Feng, C., & Höök, M. (2017). Energy and water conservation synergy in China: 2007 – 2012. *Resources, Conservation and Recycling*, *127*, 206–215. doi:10.1016/j.resconrec.2017.09.004

Johansson, F. (2004). *The Medici Effect: Breakthrough Insights at the Intersection of Ideas, Concepts, and Cultures*. Boston: Harvard Business Press.

Johnsen, T., Howard, M., & Miemczyk, J. (2014). Purchasing and Supply Chain Management: A Sustainability Perspective. Routledge.

Johnson, B. R., & Onwuegbuzie, A. (2004). Mixed Methods Research: A Research Paradigm Whose Time Has Come. *Educational Researcher*, *33*(7), 14–26. doi:10.3102/0013189X033007014

Johnson, S. (2004). Gender norms in financial markets: Evidence from Kenya. *World Development*, *32*(8), 1355–1374. doi:10.1016/j.worlddev.2004.03.003

Johnston, M. P. (2014). Secondary Data Analysis: A Method of which the Time Has Come. *Qualitative and Quantitative Methods in Libraries*, *3*, 619–626.

Jones, S. (2019, Oct. 21). Australia ranks third in the world`s best pension systems. *Investment Magazine: Retirement*. Retrieved from: https://www.investmentmagazine.com.au/2019/10/australia-ranks-third-in-worlds-best-pension-systems/

Jones, C. (2011). *Teaching entrepreneurship to undergraduates*. Cheltenham, UK: Edward Elgar Publishing Limited. doi:10.4337/9781781002001

Jones, C., & Matlay, H. (2011). Understanding the heterogeneity of entrepreneurship education: Going beyond Gartner. *Education + Training*, *53*(8/9), 692–703. doi:10.1108/00400911111185026

Jones, P., & Wynn, M. (2019). The circular economy, natural capital and resilience in tourism and hospitality. *International Journal of Contemporary Hospitality Management*, *31*(6), 2544–2563. doi:10.1108/IJCHM-05-2018-0370

Jorna, R. (2006). *Sustainable Innovation - the Organisational, Human and Knowledge Dimension*. Sheffield: Greenleaf.

Journal of Bussiness Models. (2015). Welcome to the journal of business models. Retrieved from http://journalofbusinessmodels.com/#about

Jraisat, L. E., & Sawalha, I. H. (2013). Quality control and supply chain management: A contextual perspective and a case study. *Supply Chain Management*, *18*(2), 194–207. doi:10.1108/13598541311318827

Jung, H. S., & Yoon, H. H. (2015). The impact of employees' positive psychological capital on job satisfaction and organizational citizenship behaviors in the hotel. *International Journal of Contemporary Hospitality Management*, *27*(6), 1135–1156. doi:10.1108/IJCHM-01-2014-0019

Justenhoven, P. (2019). The road to circularity: Why a circular economy is becoming the new normal. PricewaterhouseCoopers. Retrieved from https://www.pwc.de/de/nachhaltigkeit/pwc-circular-economy-study-2019.pdf

Kahriman Öztürk, D., Olgan, R., & Güler, T. (2012, Autumn). Preschool children's ideas on sustainable development: How preschool children perceive three pillars of sustainability with the regard to 7R. *Educational Sciences: Theory and Practice*, ▪▪▪, 2987–2995.

Kakembo, F. (2019). University Education and Waste-to-Wealth Entrepreneurship for Youth Employment in Uganda. Universities, Entrepreneurship and Enterprise Development in Africa-Conference Proceedings 2018.

Kale, P. D., Dyer, J. H., & Singh, H. (2002). Alliance capability, stock market response, and long-term alliance success: The role of the alliance function. *Strategic Management Journal*, *23*(8), 747–767. doi:10.1002mj.248

Kalwani, M., & Narayandas, N. (1995, January). Long-term manufacturer-supplier relationships: Do they pay off for supplier firms? *Journal of Marketing*, *59*(1), 1–16. doi:10.1177/002224299505900101

Kambwale, J. N., Chisoro, C., & Karodia, A. M. (2015). Investigation into the causes of Small and medium enterprise failures in Windhoek, Namibia. *Arabian Journal of Business and Management Review*, *4*(7), 80–109. doi:10.12816/0019074

Kantis, H. (2018). *¿Grandes empresas y Startups = nuevo modelo de innovación? Tendencias y desafíos del corporate venturing en América Latina*. Rafaela: Asociación Civil Red Pymes Mercosur. Retrieved from: https://www.researchgate.net/publication/327023031_Grandes_empresas_y_start_ups_nuevo_modelo_de_innovacion

Kantis, H., Ishida, M., & Komori, M. (2002). Entrepreneurship in emerging economies: The creation and development of new firms in Latin America and East Asia (No. 34958). Washington, DC: Inter-American Development Bank.

Karaca, B. (2018). Sürüdürülebilir mobilya üretiminde tasarım bilinci üzerine bir araştırma (Unpublished Master's Thesis). Ankara: Başkent University Social Sciences Institute.

Karthik, R. (2018). *Business Economy*. https://www.moneycontrol.com

Kasperson, R. E., Renn, O., Slovic, P., Brown, H. S., Emel, J., Goble, R., ... Ratick, S. (1988). The social amplification of risk: A conceptual framework. *Risk Analysis*, *8*(2), 177–187. doi:10.1111/j.1539-6924.1988.tb01168.x

Kaufmann Foundation. (2015). *Six strategies for building an entrepreneurial ecosystem*. Retrieved from www.kaufmannfoundation.com

Kautonen, T., Van Gelderen, M., & Fink, M. (2013). Robustness of the theory of planned behavior in predicting entrepreneurial intentions and actions. *Entrepreneurship Theory and Practice*, *39*(3), 1–20.

Kavinski, H., De Souza-Lima, J. E., Maciel-Lima, S. M., & Floriani, D. (2010). La apropiación del discurso de la sustentabilidad por las organizaciones empresariales brasileñas. *Cultura y Representaciones Sociales*, *4*(8), 34–69.

Kazmi, S.Z.A., & Nabradi, A. (2017). New venture creations- The influence of entrepreneurship education on student's behaviour (A literature review-based study). *A Journal of Applied Studies in Agribusiness and Commerce*, *11*(1-2), 147–154.

Keast, R., Mandell, M. P., Brown, K., & Woolcock, G. (2004). Network structures: Working differently and changing expectations. *Public Administration Review*, *64*(3), 363–371. doi:10.1111/j.1540-6210.2004.00380.x

Keat, O.Y., Selvarajah, C., & Meyer, D. (2011). Inclination towards entrepreneurship among university students: An empirical study of Malaysian university students. *International Journal of Business and Social Science*, *2*(4).

Kele, T., Kerrin, M., & Mamabolo, M. A. (2017). Entrepreneurship management skills requirements in an emerging economy: A South African outlook. *The Southern African Journal of Entrepreneurship and Small Business Management*, *9*(1), 2071-3185. Retrieved November 16, 2019 from https://www.researchgate.net/publication/317127302_Entrepreneurship_management_skills_requirements_in_an_emerging_economy_A_South_African_outlook

Kemp, R., & Pearson, P. (2007). *Final report MEI project about measuring eco-innovation*. UM-MERIT, United Nations University, and Maastricht University.

Keogh, P., & Polonsky, M. J. (1998). Environmental commitment: A basis for environmental entrepreneurship. *Journal of Organizational Change Management*, *11*(1), 38–49. doi:10.1108/09534819810369563

Kerr, P. S., Kerr, R. W., & Xu, T. (2017). *Personality Traits of Entrepreneurs: A Review of Recent Literature*. Retrieved December 10, 2019 from https://www.hbs.edu/faculty/publication%20files/18-047_b0074a64-5428-479b-8c83-16f2a0e97eb6.pdf

Kesper, A. (2002). *Tracing trajectories of successful manufacturing SMMEs in South Africa* (PhD thesis). University of the Witwatersrand, Johannesburg, South Africa.

Khalamayzer, A. (2017). *Five challenges to scaling the circular economy*. Retrieved 3 October, 2019 from https://www.greenbiz.com/article/5-challenges-scaling-circular-economy

Khaleghian, P., & Gupta, M. D. (2005). Public management and essential public health functions. *World Development*, *33I*(7), 1083–1099. doi:10.1016/j.worlddev.2005.04.001

Khanka, S. S. (1998). Women entrepreneurship in India. *Journal of Assam University*, *3*(1), 11–16.

Khan, M. R. (2013). Mapping entrepreneurship ecosystem of Saudi Arabia. *World Journal of Entrepreneurship, Management and Sustainable Development*, *9*(1), 28–54. doi:10.1108/20425961311315700

Kharas, K. (2017). *The unprecedented expansion of the global middle class: An update*. Global Economy and Development Working Paper, 100. Washington, DC: The Brookings Institution.

Kiddee, P., Naidu, R., & Wong, M. (2013). Electronic waste management approaches: An overview. *Waste Management (New York, N.Y.)*, *33*(5), 1237–1250. doi:10.1016/j.wasman.2013.01.006 PMID:23402807

Kiernan, M. (1999). *Los once mandamientos de la gerencia del siglo XXI*. Prentice Hall.

Kim, P., Aldrich, H. E., & Keister, L. A. (2003). *The Impact of financial, human and cultural capital on becoming a Nascent Entrepreneur*. Working paper.

Kimberly, A. (2019). *Traditional Economy With Its Characteristics, Pros, Cons, and Examples*. https://www.thebalance.com

Kimenyi, S. M. (2013). *Devolution and Resources Sharing in Kenya*. Available at www.brookings.edu

Kim, S. (2006). Effects of supply chain management practices, integration and competition on performance. *Supply Chain Management*, *11*(3), 241–248. doi:10.1108/13598540610662149

Kingma, B. (2014). Creating a dynamic campus-community entrepreneurial ecosystem: Key characteristics of success. In A. C. Corbett, D. Siegel, & J. A. Katz (Eds.), Advances in entrepreneurship, firm emergence and growth (Vol. 16, pp. 97–114). Bingley: Emerald Group.

Kinnunen, R., & Turunen, T. (2012). Identifying Servitization Capabilities of Manufacturers: A Conceptual Model. *The Journal of Applied Management and Entrepreneurship*, *17*(3), 55–78.

KIPPRA. (2018). An Assessment of Health Care Delivery in Kenya Under the Devolved System: Special Paper No 19. Available at www.kippra.or.ke

Kirchherr, J., & Piscicelli, L. (2019). *Towards an Education for the Circular Economy (ECE): Five teaching principles and a case study*. doi:10.1016/j.resconrec.2019.104406

Kirchherr, J., & Piscicelli, L. (2019). Towards an Education for the Circular Economy (ECE): Five Teaching Principles and a Case Study. *Resources, Conservation and Recycling*, *150*, 104406. doi:10.1016/j.resconrec.2019.104406

Kirchherr, J., Piscicelli, L., Bour, R., Kostense-Smit, E., Muller, J., Huibrechtse-Truijens, A., & Hekkert, M. (2018). Barriers to the Circular Economy: Evidence From the European Union (EU). *Ecological Economics*, *150*, 264–272. doi:10.1016/j.ecolecon.2018.04.028

Kirchherr, J., Reike, D., & Hekkert, M. (2017). Conceptualizing the circular economy: An analysis of 114 definitions. *Resources, Conservation and Recycling*, *127*, 221–232. doi:10.1016/j.resconrec.2017.09.005

Kirchherr, J., Reike, D., & Hekkert, M. (2017). *Conceptualizing the circular economy: An analysis of 114 definitions*. Resources, Conservation and Recycling. Elsevier B.V.; doi:10.1016/j.resconrec.2017.09.005

Kirkwood, J., & Walton, S. (2010). What motivates ecopreneurs to start businesses? *International Journal of Entrepreneurial Behaviour & Research*, *16*(3), 204–228. doi:10.1108/13552551011042799

Kirzner, I. M. (1973). *Competition and entrepreneurship*. Chicago, IL: University of Chicago.

Kirzner, I. M. (1982). *Method, process and Austrian economics*. Lexington, MA: Kolb Lexington Books.

Kirzner, I. M. (1997). Entrepreneurial Discovery and the Competitive Market Process: An Austrian Approach. *Journal of Economic Literature*, *35*(1), 60–85.

Kivleniece, I., & Quelin, B. V. (2012). Public-Private Ties? A Private Actor's Perspective. *Academy of Management Review*, *37*(2), 272–299. doi:10.5465/amr.2011.0004

Klages, L. (1926). *The science of character (Translated 1932)*. London: Allen and Unwin.

Klapper, L. F., & Parker, S. C. (2011). Gender and the Business Environment for New Firm Creation. *The World Bank Research Observer*, *26*(2), 237–257. doi:10.1093/wbro/lkp032

Klein, W. M., & Radcliffe, N. M. (2002). Dispositional, unrealistic, and comparative optimism: Differential relations with the knowledge and processing of risk information and beliefs about personal risk. Personality and Social Psychology, 28(6), 836–846. doi:10.1177/0146167202289012

Klijn, M., & Tomic, W. (2010). A Review of Creativity within Organizations from a Psychological Perspective. *Journal of Management Development*, *29*(4), 322–343. doi:10.1108/02621711011039141

Klingenberg, B., & Kochanowski, S. (2015). Hiring for the green economy: Employer perspectives on sustainability in the business curriculum. *Journal of Management Development*, *34*(8), 987–1003. doi:10.1108/JMD-06-2014-0058

Knapp, B., Bardenet, R., & Deane, C. M. (2015). Ten simple rules for a successful cross-disciplinary collaboration. *PLoS Computational Biology*, *11*(4), e1004214. doi:10.1371/journal.pcbi.1004214 PMID:25928184

Knox, D. (2019). *Melbourne Mercer Global Pension Index (MMGPI)*. Melbourne: Monash Centre for Financial Studies.

Koç, Z., & Ekşi Akbulut, D. (2017). Ekolojik tasarım kapsamında dünyada ve Türkiye'de toprak yapı standart ve yönetmeliklerinin değerlendirilmesi. *MEGARON*, *12*(4), 647–657. doi:10.5505/megaron.2017.48615

Koh, S. C. L., Sevkli, E., Zaim, S., Demirbag, M., & Tatoglu, E. (2007). The impact of supply chain management practices on performance of SMEs. *Industrial Management & Data Systems*, *107*(1), 103–124. doi:10.1108/02635570710719089

Kojo Oseifuah, E. (2010). Financial literacy and youth entrepreneurship in South Africa. *African Journal of Economic and Management Studies*, *1*(2), 164–182. doi:10.1108/20400701011073473

Kopnina, H. (2019). Green-washing or best case practices? Using circular economy and Cradle to Cradle case studies in business education. *Journal of Cleaner Production*, *219*, 613–621. doi:10.1016/j.jclepro.2019.02.005

Koren, Y. (2010). The global manufacturing revolution: product-process-business ıntegration and reconfigurable systems. Wiley. doi:10.1002/9780470618813

Korhonen, J., Honkasalo, A., & Seppälä, J. (2018). Circular Economy: The Concept and its Limitations. *Ecological Economics*, *143*, 37–46. doi:10.1016/j.ecolecon.2017.06.041

Korhonen, J., Nuur, C., Feldmann, A., & Eshetu-Birkie, S. (2018). Circular economy as an essentially contested concept. *Journal of Cleaner Production*, *2018*(175), 544–552. doi:10.1016/j.jclepro.2017.12.111

Kortmann, S., & Piller, F. T. (2016). Open Business Models and Closed-Loop Value Chains: Redefining the Firm-Consumer Relationship. *California Management Review*, *58*(3), 88–108. doi:10.1525/cmr.2016.58.3.88

Kotey, B. A. (1997, April). Relationships among owner/manager personal values, business strategies, and enterprise performance. *Journal of Small Business Management*, 37–64.

Koufteros, X. V., Vonderembse, M. A., & Doll, W. J. (2002). Integrated product developement practices and competitive capabilities: The effects of uncertainty, equivocality, and platform strategy. *Journal of Operations Management*, *20*(4), 331–355. doi:10.1016/S0272-6963(02)00018-9

Kranendijk, S., & Stuchtey, M. R. (2018). *The Role of Business in the Circular Economy Markets, Processes and Enabling Policies Report of a CEPS Task Force*. Retrieved November 2, 2019 from https://circulareconomy.europa.eu/platform/sites/default/files/rolebusinesscirculareconomytfr.pdf

Krishnan, R., Geyskens, I., & Steenkamp, J. E. M. (2016). The effectiveness of contractual and trust-based Governance. *Strategic Management Journal*, *37*(12), 2521–2542. doi:10.1002mj.2469

Kristensen, H. S., & Mosgaard, M. A. (2020). A review of micro-level indicators for a circular economy – moving away from the three dimensions of sustainability? *Journal of Cleaner Production*, *243*, 118531. doi:10.1016/j.jclepro.2019.118531

Kroon, J. (1997). *Entrepreneurship education in South Africa*. Retrieved June 29, 2009 https://www.ask.com/web?qsrc=2417&o=10181&l=dir&q=+entrepreneurship+education+in+south+africa+a+life+long+process%2C+10th+annual+conference+of+the+Southern+African +entrepreneurship+and+small+business+association+%2C+Victoria+falls%2C+Kroon%2CJ

Kroon, J., & Meyer, S. (2001). The role of entrepreneurship education in career expectations of students. *South African Journal of Higher Education*, *15*(1), 47–53. doi:10.4314ajhe.v15i1.25379

Krueger, N. F. (2017). Entrepreneurial intentions are dead: Long live entrepreneurial intentions. In M. Brännback & A. Carsrud (Eds.), *Revisiting the entrepreneurial mind. International studies in entrepreneurship* (Vol. 35). Cham: Springer. doi:10.1007/978-3-319-45544-0_2

Kuah, A. T. (2002). Cluster Theory and Practice: Advantages for the small business locating in a vibrant cluster. *Journal of Research in Marketing and Entrepreneurship*, *4*(3), 206–228.

Kuckertz, A., & Wagner, M. (2010). The influence of sustainability orientation on entrepreneurial intentions - Investigating the role of business experience. *Journal of Business Venturing*, *25*(5), 524–539. doi:10.1016/j.jbusvent.2009.09.001

Kudrna, G., Tran, C., & Woodland, A. (2014). *The Dynamic Fiscal Effects of Demographic Shift: the case of Australia*. ANU Working Papers in Economics and Econometrics: Australian National University.

Kumar, N., & Puranam, P. (2012). Frugal engineering: an emerging innovation paradigm. *Ivey Business Journal, 76*(2). Retrieved from https://iveybusinessjournal.com/publication/frugal-engineering-an-emerging-innovation-paradigm/

Kumar, V. (2020). The Role of AI in Achieving a Circular Economy in Smart Cities. Available online, https://industrywired.com/the-role-of-ai-in-achieving-a-circular-economy-in-smart-cities/

Kumar, S., & Putman, V. (2008). Cradle to Cradle: Reverse logistics strategies and opportunities across three industry sectors. *International Journal of Production Economics*, *115*(2), 305–315. doi:10.1016/j.ijpe.2007.11.015

Kumar, V., Sezersan, I., Garza-Reyes, J., Gonzalez, E., & AL-Shboul, M. A. (2019). Circular economy in the manufacturing sector: Benefits, opportunities and barriers. *Management Decision*, *57*(4), 1067–1086. doi:10.1108/MD-09-2018-1070

Kumlien, S. (2010). From Here to Returnity - A Small Scale Effort for Big Scale Change. Design, 90 - 94.

Kuratko, D. F. (2003). Entrepreneurship education: Emerging trends and challenges for the 21st century. The Entrepreneurship Program, College of Business, Ball State University, Muncie, IN.

Kyere, V. N., Greve, K., Atiemo, S. M., Amoako, D., Aboh, I. J. K., & Cheabu, B. S. (2018). Contamination and Health Risk Assessment of Exposure to Heavy Metals in Soils from Informal E-Waste Recycling Site in Ghana. *Emerging Science Journal*, *2*(6), 428. doi:10.28991/esj-2018-01162

L'Oréal. (2018). *L'Oréal Annual Report, 2018*. Author.

Lackéus, M. (2015). *Entrepreneurship in Education: What, Why, When, How*. Paris: OECD.

Lacy, P., & Rutquist, J. (2016). *Waste to wealth: The circular economy advantage*. Springer.

Lacy, P., & Rutqvist, J. (2015). *Waste to Wealth: The Circular Economy Advantage*. London: Palgrave McMillan. doi:10.1057/9781137530707

Ladzani. M.W. (1999). *Small Business development in South Africa under the majority rule*. Pretoria: Van Shaik Books.

Laffont, J. L., & Martimort, D. (2002). *The Theory of Incentives: The Principal-Agent Model*. Princeton, NJ: Princeton University Press. doi:10.1515/9781400829453

Lahn, L. C., & Erikson, T. (2016). Entrepreneurship education by design. *Education + Training*, *58*(7/8), 684–699. doi:10.1108/ET-03-2016-0051

Lahti, T., Parida, V., & Wuncent, J. (2018). A Definition and Theoretical Review of the Circular Economy, Value Creation, and Sustainable Business Models: Where Are We Now and Where Should Research Move in the Future? *Sustainability*, *10*(8), 2799. doi:10.3390u10082799

Lainez, M., González, J. M., Aguilar, A., & Vela, C. (2018). Spanish strategy on bioeconomy: Towards a knowledge based sustainable innovation. *New Biotechnology*, *40*, 87–95. doi:10.1016/j.nbt.2017.05.006 PMID:28552816

Lamming, R. (1996). Squaring lean supply with supply chain management. *International Journal of Operations & Production Management*, *16*(2), 183–196. doi:10.1108/01443579610109910

Landstrom, H. (1998). *The Roots of Entrepreneurship Research*. Conference proceedings, Lyon, France.

Landy, F. J., & Conte, J. M. (2009). *Work in the 21st Century: An Introduction to Industrial and Organizational Psychology*. John Wiley & Sons.

Lane, J. (2000). *New Public Management*. London: Routledge.

Larbi, G. A. (1999). *The New Public Management Approach and Crisis States*. UNRISD Discussion Paper 112. Geneva: United Nations Research Institute for Social Development.

LaRRI, (2002). *The Small and Micro Enterprise (SME) Sector in Namibia: Conditions of Employment and Income*. Report by LaRRI for the Joint Consultative Committee.

Latorre, M. (2018). *Historia de las Web, 1.0, 2.0, 3.0 y 4.0*. Universidad Marcelino Champagnat. Document. Retrieved from: umch. edu. pe/arch/hnomarino/74_Historia% 20de% 20la% 20Web. pdf

Laubscher, M., & Marinelli, T. (2014). *Integration of Circular Economy in Business*. Retrieved November 7, 2019 from https://www.researchgate.net/publication/270207909_Integration_of_Circular_Economy_in_Business

Laurenti, R., Martin, M., & Stenmarck, Å. (2018). Developing adequate communication of waste footprints of products for a circular economy—A stakeholder consultation. *Resources*, *7*(4), 78–91. doi:10.3390/resources7040078

Lavalle, S., Lesser, E., Shockley, R., Hopkins, M. S., & Kruschwitz, N. (2011). Big Data, Analytics and the Path From Insights to Value. *MIT Sloan Management Review*, *52*(2), 21–32.

Lawal, F. A., Adegbuyi, O. A., Iyiola, O. O., Ayoade, O. E., & Taiwo, A. A. (2018). Nexus between Informal Networks and Risk-taking: Implications for Improving the Performance of Small and Medium Enterprises (SMEs) in Nigeria. *Academy of Strategic Management Journal*, *17*(2), 1–13.

Lawrence, B. (2019). *Trash to Treasure*. https://www.uschamberfoundation.org

Lea, N., & Dercon, S. (2012). *Refreshing DFID's Approach to Growth*. Working Paper, London: DFID.

Lèbre, É., Corder, G. D., & Golev, A. (2017b). Sustainable practices in the management of mining waste: A focus on the mineral resource. *Minerals Engineering*, *107*, 34–42. doi:10.1016/j.mineng.2016.12.004

Lèbre, É., Corder, G., & Golev, A. (2017a). The role of the mining industry in a circular economy: A framework for resource management at the mine site level. *Journal of Industrial Ecology*, *21*(3), 662–672. doi:10.1111/jiec.12596

Lee, C., Kwon, I., & Severance, D. (2007). Relationship between supply chain performance and degree of linkage among supplier, internal integration, and customer. *Supply Chain Management*, *12*(6), 444–452. doi:10.1108/13598540710826371

Legge, S., & Klett, T. C. (2018). *How To Build Business In Circular Economy*. https://www.weforum.org

Lehmann, M., De Leeuw, B., & Fehr, E. (2014). *Circular Economy: Improving the Management of Natural Resources.* Berne: Swiss Academy of Engineering Sciences. Retrieved from http://www.wrforum.org/wp-content/uploads/2015/04/a-_CircularEconomy_English.pdf

Lehner, O. M., & Harrer, T. (2019). Crowd funding revisited: A neo-institutional field-perspective. *Venture Capital, 21*(1), 75–96. doi:10.1080/13691066.2019.1560884

Leitão, J., & Baptista, R. (2009). *Public Policies for Fostering Entrepreneurship: A European Perspective.* Springer Science Business Media.

Leland, H. E. (1968). Saving and Uncertainty: The precautionary demand for saving. *The Quarterly Journal of Economics, 3*(82), 465–473. doi:10.2307/1879518

Leonard, A. (2010). *The story of stuff: How our obsession with stuff is trashing the planet, our communities, and our health - and a vision for change.* New York: Free Press.

Leutner, F., & Premuzic, T. C. (2014). The relationship between the entrepreneurial personality and the Big Five personality traits. *Personality and Individual Differences, 63*(June), 58–63. doi:10.1016/j.paid.2014.01.042

Le, V. (2009, September). Small Firm Growth Theory and Models: A Review. In *22nd SEAANZ Annual Conference.* Massey University.

Levänen, J., Lyytinen, T., & Gatica, S. (2018). Modelling the Interplay Between Institutions and Circular Economy Business Models: A Case Study of Battery Recycling in Finland and Chile. *Ecological Economics, 154*, 373–382. doi:10.1016/j.ecolecon.2018.08.018

Levine, R. (1997). Desarrollo financiero y crecimiento económico: Enfoques y temario. *Journal of Economic Literature, 35*, 688–726.

Levrato, N. (2002). *Diversité des mondes de production et des voies d'accession à la rentabilté des petites entreprises: une analyse par les cartes auto-organisatrices.* 6e Congrès international francophone sur la PME, Octobre. HEC-Montréal.

Lewandowski, M. (2015). Designing the Business Models for Circular Economy - Towards the Conceptual Framework. MDPI Review, 3–5. Retrieved from https://www.mdpi.com

Lewandowski, M. (2015). Designing the business models for circular economy: Towards the conceptual framework. *Sustainability, 8*(43), 1–28.

Lewandowski, M. (2016). Designing the Business Models for Circular Economy. Towards the Conceptual Framework. *Sustainability, 8*(43), 1–28. doi:10.3390/su8010043

Lewandowski, M. (2016). Designing the Business Models for Circular Economy-Towards the Conceptual Framework. *Sustainability, 8*(1), 43. doi:10.3390u8010043

Lewis, M., Portioli Staudacher, A., & Slack, N. (2004). *Beyond products and services: Opportunities and threats in servitization.* Paper presented at IMS Intl. Forum, Italy.

Lewis, K. V., Cassells, S., & Roxas, H. (2015). SMEs and the Potential for A Collaborative Path to Environmental Responsibility. *Business Strategy and the Environment, 24*(8), 750–764. doi:10.1002/bse.1843

Liakos, N., Kumar, V., Pongsakornrungsilp, S., Garza-Reyes, J., Gupta, B., & Pongsakornrungsilp, P. (2019). Understanding circular economy awareness and practices in manufacturing firms. *Journal of Enterprise Information Management, 32*(4), 563–584. doi:10.1108/JEIM-02-2019-0058

Liang, C. K., & Dunn, P. (2007). Triggers of decisions to launch a new venture – is there any difference between pre-business and in-business entrepreneurs? *Academy of Entrepreneurship Journal*, *13*(1), 79–95.

Li, D. D., Feng, J., & Jiang, H. (2006). Institutional entrepreneurs. *The American Economic Review*, *96*(2), 358–362. doi:10.1257/000282806777211775

Lieder, M., & Rashid, A. (2016). Towards circular economy implementation: A comprehensive review in the context of the manufacturing industry. *Journal of Cleaner Production*, *115*, 36–51. doi:10.1016/j.jclepro.2015.12.042

Liedholm, C., & Mead, D. C. (1999). *Small Enterprises and Economic Development: The Dynamics of Micro and Small Enterprises*. London: Routledge.

Liedtka, J. (2014). Perspective: Linking design thinking with innovation outcomes through cognitive bias reduction. *Journal of Product Innovation Management*, *32*(6), 925–938. doi:10.1111/jpim.12163

Liedtka, J., & Ogilvie, T. (2014). *Designing for growth. A design-thinking toolkit for managers*. New York, NY: Columbia University Press.

Lienert, I., & Modi, J. (1997). *A decade of civil service reform in sub-Saharan Africa*. IMF Working Paper, WP/97/179. Washington, DC: International Monetary Fund.

Light, I. (1972). *Ethnic enterprise in America: Business and welfare amongst Chinese, Japanese and Blacks*. Berkeley, CA: University of California.

Lightsey, R. L. (1996). What leads to Wellness? The Role of Psychological Resource in well-being. *Journal of Counseling Psychology*, *24*, 658–735.

Lindauer, D. L., & Nunberg, B. (1994). *Rehabilitating government: pay and employment reform in Africa*. Washington, DC: World Bank. doi:10.1596/0-8213-3000-4

Linder, M., & Williander, M. (2015). Circular Business Model Innovation: Inherent Uncertainties. *Business Strategy and the Environment*, *26*(2), 182–196. doi:10.1002/bse.1906

Linder, M., & Williander, M. (2017). Circular Business Model Innovation: Inherent Uncertainties. Business Strategy and the Environment. *Circular Business Model Innovation: Inherent Uncertainties*, *26*(2), 182–186.

Lin, J. Y., & Monga, C. (2013). *Comparative advantage: The silver bullet of industrial policy.* In J. E. S. Stiglitz & J. Y. Lin (Eds.), *The Industrial Policy Revolution I: The Role of Government Beyond Ideology* (pp. 19–38). London: Palgrave Macmillan.

Linnanen, L. (2002). An Insider's Experiences with Environmental Entrepreneurship. *Greener Management International*, *38*(38), 71–80. doi:10.9774/GLEAF.3062.2002.su.00008

Linton, J., & Jayraman, V. (2005). A framework for identifying differences and similarities in the managerial competencies associated with different modes of product life extension. *International Journal of Production Research*, *43*(9), 1807–1829. doi:10.1080/1352816051233132644O

Lipman, V. (2013). *Why employee development is important, neglected and can cost you talent*. Available at: https://www.forbes.com/sites/victorlipman/2013/01/29/why-development-planning-is-important-neglected-and-cancost-you-young-talent/

Liraz, M. (2013). *How to Improve Your Leadership and Management Skills Effective Strategies for Business Managers.* Retrieved November 3, 2019 from http://www.liraz.com/leadership-and-management-skills.pdf

Li, S., & Lin, B. (2006). Accessing information sharing and information quality in supply chain management. *Decision Support Systems*, *42*(3), 1641–1656. doi:10.1016/j.dss.2006.02.011

Li, S., Ragu-Nathan, B., Ragu-Nathan, T. S., & Rao, S. S. (2006). The impact of supply chain management practices on competitive advantage and organizational performance. *Omega*, *32*(2), 107–124. doi:10.1016/j.omega.2004.08.002

Lister, S. (2000). Power in partnership: An analysis of NGOs relationship with its partners. *Journal of International Development*, *12*(2), 227–239. doi:10.1002/(SICI)1099-1328(200003)12:2<227::AID-JID637>3.0.CO;2-U

Littig, B., & Grießler, E. (2005). Social sustainability: A catchword between political pragmatism and social theory. *International Journal of Sustainable Development*, *8*(1/2), 65–79. doi:10.1504/IJSD.2005.007375

Liu, F. L. (2014). Green management of tourist attractions region under the background of circular economy. *Advanced Materials Research*, *989*(994), 989–994, 5592–5595. doi:10.4028/www.scientific.net/AMR.989-994.5592

Liu, J. (2014). Developing circular economy and protecting the ecological environment of scenic spot. *Manufacture Engineering and Environment Engineering, 84, 1369-1374.*

Liu, J., Dietz, T., Carpenter, S. R., Alberti, M., Moran, M., Pell, A. N., ... Taylor, W. W. (2007). Complexity of coupled human and natural systems. *Science*, *317*(5844), 3165–3316. doi:10.1126/science.1144004 PubMed

Liu, J., Feng, Y., Zhu, Q., & Sarkis, J. (2018). Green supply chain management and the circular Economy-Reviewing theory for advancement of both fields. *International Journal of Physical Distribution & Logistics Management*, *48*(8), 794–817. doi:10.1108/IJPDLM-01-2017-0049

Liu, L., & Liang, M. (2011). A reception model of rural low-carbon tourism based on circular economy - Take Cuandixia Village as an example. *Proceedings of the Fifth International Symposium on Green Hospitality and Tourism Management*, 96-104.

Liu, L., Liang, Y., Song, Q., & Li, J. (2017). A review of waste prevention through 3R under the concept of circular economy in China. *Journal of Material Cycles and Waste Management*, *19*(4), 1314–1323. doi:10.100710163-017-0606-4

Liu, Y., & Bai, Y. (2014). An exploration of firms' awareness and behavior of developing circular economy: An empirical research in China. *Resources, Conservation and Recycling*, *87*, 145–152. doi:10.1016/j.resconrec.2014.04.002

Liu, Z., Adams, M., & Walker, T. R. (2018, September 1). Are exports of recyclables from developed to developing countries waste pollution transfer or part of the global circular economy? In *Resources*. Conservation and Recycling. Elsevier B.V.; doi:10.1016/j.resconrec.2018.04.005

Li, X., Deng, B., & Ye, H. (2011). The Research Based on the 3-R Principle of Agro-circular Economy Model-The Erhai Lake Basin as an Example. *2010 International Conference on Energy, Environment and Development*, *5*, 1399-1404.

Lombardo, B. J., & Roddy, D. J. (2010). Cultivating organizational creativity in an age of complexity. In *IBM 2010 Global Chief Human Resource Officer Study*. Armonk: IBM Institute for Business Value.

Loomba, A. P., & Nakashima, K. (2012). Enhancing value in reverse supply chains by sorting before product recovery. *Production Planning and Control*, *23*(2-3), 205–215. doi:10.1080/09537287.2011.591652

Lopes, C. M., Scavarda, A., Hofmeister, L. F., Thomé, A. M. T., & Vaccaro, G. L. R. (2017). An analysis of the interplay between organizational sustainability, knowledge management, and open innovation. *Journal of Cleaner Production*, *142*, 476–488. doi:10.1016/j.jclepro.2016.10.083

Lorenzoni, G., & Lipparini, A. (1999). The leveraging of interfirm relationships as a distinctive organizational capability: A longitudinal study. *Strategic Management Journal*, *20*(4), 317–338. doi:10.1002/(SICI)1097-0266(199904)20:4<317::AID-SMJ28>3.0.CO;2-3

Lounsbury, J. W., & Gibson, L. W. (2006). *Personal style inventory: A Work-Based Personality Measurement System*. Knoxville, TN: Resource Associates.

Lovins, L. H. (2008). Chapter three: rethinking production. in the world watch institute. In State of The World: Innovations for A Sustainable Economy (pp. 32–44). The Worldwatch Institute.

Lowden, J. S. (2007). *Managerial Skills for the Entrepreneur*. Retrieved December 7, 2019 from https://pdfs.semanticscholar.org/649b/9b7ef100768078739d96873eee6027b8546d.pdf

Lowe & Marriott. (2006). *Enterprise: Entrepreneurship and Innovation: Concepts, Contexts and Commercialization*. Butterworth-Heinemann.

Lowe, R., & Marriott, S. (2006). *Enterprise: Entrepreneurship and Innovation: Concepts, Contexts and Commercialization*. Oxford: Butterworth-Heinemann.

Lüdeke-Freund, F., Massa, L., Bocken, N., Brent, A., & Musango, J. (2016). Business Models for Shared Value: Main Report. London, UK: The Economist.

Lumpkin, G. a. (1996). Clarifying the entrepreneurial orientation construct and linking it to performance. *Academy of Management Journal*, *21*, 135–172.

Lundstrom, A., & Stevenson, L. A. (2005). *Entrepreneurship Policy: Theory and Practice*. Springer.

Luthans, F., & Youssef, C. M. (2007). Emerging positive organizational behavior. *Journal of Management*, *33*(3), 321–349. doi:10.1177/0149206307300814

Lütjen, H., Tietze, F., & Schultz, C. (2017). Service transitions of product-centric firms: An explorative study of service transition stages and barriers in Germany's energy market. *International Journal of Production Economics*, *192*, 106–119. doi:10.1016/j.ijpe.2017.03.021

Lu, Y. (2012). Study on the Development Plan of the Lanzhou Tourism Industry in Line with Circular Economy. *Proceedings of the 7th Euro-Asia Conference on Environment and CSR: Tourism, MICE, Hospitality Management and Education Session*, 100-105.

Lu, Y., & Hu, X. X. (2014). A path study on the tourism circular economic development of Shandong province. *Advanced Materials Research*, *962-965*, 2234–2239. doi:10.4028/www.scientific.net/AMR.962-965.2234

MacArthur, E. (2013). *Towards the circular economy, economic and business rationale for an accelerated transition*. Cowes, UK: Ellen MacArthur Foundation.

MacArthur, E. (2013). Towards the circular economy. *Journal of Industrial Ecology*.

Magretta, J. (2002). Why Business Models Matter. Harvard Business Review. Retrieved from https://hbr.org/2002/05/why-business-models-matter

Mair, J., & Seelos, C. (2005). Social entrepreneurship: Creating new business models to serve the poor. *Business Horizons*, *48*(3), 241–246. doi:10.1016/j.bushor.2004.11.006

Mäkikangas, A., & Kinnunen, U. (2003, August). Psychosocial work stressors and well-being: Self-esteem and optimism as moderators in a one-year longitudinal sample. *Personality and Individual Differences*, *35*(3), 537–557. doi:10.1016/S0191-8869(02)00217-9

Makropoulos, C., Rozos, E., Tsoukalas, I., Plevri, A., ... Ripis, C. (2018). S.ewer-mi.ning: A water reuse option supporting circular economy, public service provision and entrepreneurship. *Journal of Environmental Management, 216*, 285–298. doi:10.1016/j.jenvman.2017.07.026 PMID:28728973

Malik, M. F., Zaman, M., & Buckby, S. (2020). Enterprise risk management and firm performance: Role of the risk committee. *Journal of Contemporary Accounting & Economics, 16*(1), 100178. doi:10.1016/j.jcae.2019.100178

Manavalan, K., & Jayakrishna, K. (2019). An Analysis on Sustainable Supply Chain for Circular Economy, 16th Global Conference on Sustainable Manufacturing. Procedia Manufacturing, 477–484. DOI: 10.1016/j.promfg.2019.04.059

Mangla, S. K., Luthtra, S., Mishra, N., Singh, A., Rana, N., Dora, M., & Dwivedi, Y. (2018). Barriers to effective circular supply chain management in a developing country context. *Production Planning and Control, 29*(6), 551–569. doi:10.1080/09537287.2018.1449265

Manimala, J. M., & Prasad, A. (2018). *Circular Social Innovation: A New Paradigm for India's Sustainable Development.* Retrieved November 30, 2019 from https://www.springerprofessional.de/en/circular-social-innovation-a-new-paradigm-for-india-s-sustainabl/15733952

Manimala, M. J., & Wasdani, K. P. (2014). Emerging economies: Muddling through to development. In M. J. Manimala & K. P. Wasdani (Eds.), *Entrepreneurial ecosystem: Perspectives from emerging economies* (pp. 3–53). Berlin: Springer.

Mann, R. (2008). Kiehl's unveils new eco-effective body cleanser, created in partnership with Brad Pitt. Retrieved at 29.10.2019, from https://www.moodiedavittreport.com/kiehls-unveils-new-eco-effective-body-cleanser-created-in-partnership-with-brad-pitt-180908/

Manning, N. (2001). The Legacy of New Public Management in developing countries. *International Review of Administrative Sciences, 62*(2), 297–312. doi:10.1177/0020852301672009

Manzini, E., & Vezzoli, C. (2003). A strategic design approach to develop sustainable product service systems: Examples taken from the 'environmentally friendly innovation' Italian prize. *Journal of Cleaner Production, 11*(8), 851–857. doi:10.1016/S0959-6526(02)00153-1

Mao, H. (2009). Review on enterprise growth theories. *International Journal of Business and Management, 4*(8), 20–23. doi:10.5539/ijbm.v4n8p20

Marenelli, T. (2014). *Integration of circular economy in business.* https://www.researchgate.net

Marmier, F., Gourc, D., & Laarz, F. (2013). A risk oriented model to assess strategic decisions in new product development projects. *Decision Support Systems, 56*, 74–82. doi:10.1016/j.dss.2013.05.002

Martin, R., & Sunley, P. (2003). Deconstructing clusters: Chaotic concept or policy panacea? *Journal of Economic Geography, 3*(1), 5–35. doi:10.1093/jeg/3.1.5

Marwa, N. (2014). Micro, Small and Medium Enterprises' external financing challenges: The role of formal financial institutions and development finance intervention in Tanzania. *International Journal of Trade, Economics and Finance, 5*(3), 230-234. doi: .2014.V5.376 doi:10.7763/IJTEF

Masi, D., Kumar, V., Garza-Reyes, J. A., & Godsell, J. (2018). Towards a more circular economy: Exploring the awareness, practices, and barriers from a focal firm perspective. *Production, Planning & Control. The Management of Operations, 29*(6), 539–550. doi:10.1080/09537287.2018.1449246

Maslow, A. H. (1970). *Motivation and personality.* New York: Harper & Row.

Mason, C., & Brown, R. (2014). Entrepreneurial ecosystems and growth oriented entrepreneurship. *Final Report to OECD, 30*(1), 77-102.

Massingham, P. (2010). Knowledge risk management: A framework. *Journal of Knowledge Management, 14*(3), 464–485. doi:10.1108/13673271011050166

Masurel, E. (2007). Why SMEs invest in environmentalmeasures: Sustainability evidence fromsmall andmedium—Sized printing firms. *Business Strategy and the Environment, 16*(1), 190–201. doi:10.1002/bse.478

Mateusz, L. (2015). *Designing the Business Models for Circular Economy*. https://www.mdpi.com

Matlay, H. (2008). The impact of entrepreneurship education on entrepreneurial outcomes. *Journal of Small Business and Enterprise Development, 15*(2), 382–396. doi:10.1108/14626000810871745

Mattos, M. (2019). How a circular economy narrows, slows, intensifies and closes supply chain loops. MIT Supply Chain. https://medium.com/mitsupplychain/how-a-circular-economy-narrows-slows-intensifies-and-closes-supply-chain-loops-d85d9bab869

Mattos, C. A., & Albuquerque, T. L. (2018). Enabling Factors and Strategies for the Transition Toward a Circular Economy (CE). *Sustainability, 10*(12), 4628. doi:10.3390u10124628

Mattos, D. R., Panzarin, S. J., Gomes, B. R. A., & Ometto, A. (2017). Trends in publications on the circular economy Tendências de publicações em economia circular.*Revista Espacios*. Vol. 38 (Nº 58). *Year, 2017*, 20.

Mauchi, F. N., Karambakuwa, R. T., Gopo, R. N., Kosmas, N., Mangwende, S., & Gombarume, F. B. (2011). Entrepreneurship education lessons: A case of Zimbabwean tertiary education institutions. *Educational Research, 2*(7), 1306–1311.

Ma, X., Li, S., Ai, Q., & Chen, K. (2016). Research on Renewable Energy Systems Used in Tourism Circular Economy. *Proceedings of the 28th Chinese Control and Decision Conference (2016 CCDC)*, 6203-6206. 10.1109/CCDC.2016.7532113

Maxfield, S., Shapiro, M., Gupta, V., & Hass, S. (2010). Gender and risk: Women, risk taking and risk aversion. *Gender in Management, 25*(7), 586–604. doi:10.1108/17542411011081383

Maycroft, N. (2009). Consumption, planned obsolescence and waste. Working Paper. (Unpublished).

Mazzarol, T. (2003). A model of small business HR growth management. *International Journal of Entrepreneurial Behaviour & Research, 9*(1), 24–49. doi:10.1108/13552550310461036

Mbaziira, S., & Oyedokun, C. (2007). *Advancing entrepreneurship education in Namibia: A practical approach*. Academic Press.

Mbuyisa, B., & Leonard, A. (2015). ICT adoption in SME's for the alleviation of poverty. In *International Association for Management of Technology Conference* (pp. 858-878). Pretoria: IAMOT 2015 Conference Proceedings. Retrieved from https://pdfs.semanticscholar.org/99a9/569c66efc2fee2c49e22a515b96df9680de0.pdf

McDonald & Oates. (2003). Reasons for non-participation in a curbside recycling scheme. *Resources, Conservation and Recycling, 39*(1), 369–385.

McDonough, W., & Braungart, M. (2010). *Cradle to cradle: Remaking the way we make things*. North Point Press.

McDonough, W., Braungart, M., & Bollinger, A. (2007). *Cradle-to-cradle design: creating healthy emissions – a strategy for eco-effective product and system design.* Obtenido de Science Direct: https://www.sciencedirect.com/science/article/pii/S0959652606002587

McDonough, W., & Braungart, M. (2002). *Cradle to cradle. Remaking the way we make things*. New York: North Point Press.

McDonough, W., & Braungart, M. (2002). *Cradle to Cradle: remaking the way we make things*. New York: North Point Press.

McDonough, W., & Braungart, M. (2002). *Cradle to Cradle: Remaking the Way We Make Things*. New York: North Point Press.

McDonough, W., & Braungart, M. (2002). *Remaking the way we make things: Cradle to cradle*. New York: North Point Press.

McDonough, W., Braungart, M., Anastas, P. T., & Zimmerman, J. B. (2003). Peer-Reviewed: Applying the Principles of Green Engineering to Cradle-to-Cradle Design. *Environmental Science & Technology*, *37*(23), 434–441. doi:10.1021/es0326322

McGee, J. E., Peterson, M., Mueller, S. L., & Sequeira, J. M. (2009). Entrepreneurial self-Efficacy: Refining the measure. *Entrepreneurship Theory and Practice*, *33*(4), 965–988. doi:10.1111/j.1540-6520.2009.00304.x

McGuigan, P. (2016). practicing what we preach: Entrepreneurship in entrepreneurship education. *Journal of Entrepreneurship Education*, *19*(1), 38–50.

McKague, K., Wheeler, D., & Karnani, A. (2015). An integrated approach to poverty alleviation: roles of the private sector, government and civil society. In *The business of social and environmental innovation* (pp. 129–145). Cham: Springer. doi:10.1007/978-3-319-04051-6_7

McKenzie, D. (2015). *Identifying and spurring high-growth entrepreneurship: Experimental evidence from a business plan competition.* Policy Research Working Paper, No. 7391.

McLean, L. (2005). Organizational culture's influence on creativity and innovation: A review of the literature and implications for human resource development. *Advances in Developing Human Resources*, *7*(2), 226–246. doi:10.1177/1523422305274528

McMullen, J. S., & Shepherd, D. A. (2006). Entrepreneurial Action and the Role of Uncertainty in the Theory of the Entrepreneur. *Academy of Management Review*, *31*(1), 132–152. doi:10.5465/amr.2006.19379628

Meadows, D. H., Meadows, D. L., & Randers, J. (1992). *Beyond the Limits (Post Mills)*. Chelsea Green Publishing Company.

Meadows, D. H., Meadows, D. L., Randers, J., Behrens, I. I. I., & William, W. (1972). *The Limits to Growth*. New York: Universe Books.

Meadows, D. H., Randers, J., & Meadows, D. L. (2009). *The Limits to Growth: The 30-Year Update*. London, UK: Routledge.

Meadows, D., Donatella Meadows, J., Randers, W., & Behrens, W. III. (1972). *The Limits to Growth—A Report for the Club of Rome's Project on the Predicament of Mankind*. Universe Books.

Meath, C., Linnenluecke, M., & Griffiths, A. (2016). Barriers and motivators to the adoption of energy savings measures for small- and medium-sized enterprises (SMEs): The case of the ClimateSmart Business Cluster program. *Journal of Cleaner Production*, *112*(5), 3587–3604. doi:10.1016/j.jclepro.2015.08.085

Mejía Dugand, S. (2010). *La Ecología Industrial*. Obtenido de El Colombiano: https://www.elcolombiano.com/historico/la_ecologia_industrial-HEEC_101107

Meloni, M. (2019). *Green & Sustainable Electronics*. https://www.ewaste-expo.com/green-electronics/

Mendoza Torres, M. R., & Ortiz Riaga, C. (2006). El Liderazgo Transformacional, Dimensiones e Impacto en la Cultura Organizacional y Eficacia de las Empresas. *Revista Facultad de Ciencias Económicas: Investigación y Reflexión*, *14*(1), 118-134. Retrieved from: https://www.redalyc.org/pdf/909/90900107.pdf

Mendoza, J. M. F., Schmid, A. G., & Azapagic, A. (2019). Building a business case for implementation of circular economy in higher education institutions. *Journal of Cleaner Production*, *220*, 553–567. doi:10.1016/j.jclepro.2019.02.045

Mensah, J. K., Domfeh, K. A., Ahenkan, A., & Bawole, J. N. (2013). Policy and institutional perspectives on local economic development in Africa: The Ghanaian perspective. *Journal of African Studies and Development*, *5*(7), 163–170.

Mentink, B. (2014). Circular Business Model Innovation: A Process Framework and a Tool for Business Model Innovation in a Circular Economy (Master's thesis). Delft University of Technology & Leiden University.

Mentink, B. (2014). Circular Business Model Innovation: A Process Framework and a Tool for Business Model Innovation in a Circular Economy (Master's thesis). Leiden, The Netherlands: Delft University of Technology & Leiden University.

Meqdadi, O., Johnsen, T., & Johnsen, R. (2012). The Role of SME Suppliers in Implementing Sustainability. *IPSERA 2012 Conference*. Napoli: IPSERA. Retrieved from https://hal-audencia.archives-ouvertes.fr/file/index/docid/824677/filename/The_Role_of_SME_Suppliers_in_Implementing_Sustainability.pdf

Merton, R. C. (1970). *Analytical optimal control theory as applied to stochastic and non-stochastic economics*. Institute of Technology.

Metcalfe, J. S., Ramlogan, R., & Uyarra, E. (2003). Economic Development and the Competitive Process. *Conferência Internacional Sobre Sistemas De Inovação E Estratégias De Desenvolvimento Para O Terceiro Milênio*, 1-31.

METI. (2004). *Handbook on Resource Recycling Legislation and 3R initiatives*. Tokyo: Japanese Ministry of Economy, Trade and Industry.

Michelini, G., Moraes, R. N., Cunha, R. N., Costa, J. M., & Ometto, A. R. (2017). From Linear to Circular Economy: PSS Conducting the Transition. *Procedia CIRP*, *64*(C), 2–6. doi:10.1016/j.procir.2017.03.012

Millán, J. M., Congregado, E., Román, C., van Praag, M., & van Stel, A. (2014). The value of an educated population for an individual's entrepreneurship success. *Journal of Business Venturing*, *29*(5), 612–632. doi:10.1016/j.jbusvent.2013.09.003

Miller, D. (1993). The architecture of simplicity. *Academy of Management Review*, *18*(1), 116–13. doi:10.5465/amr.1993.3997509

Miller, K. (2005). *Communication theories: perspectives, processes, and contexts* (2nd ed.). New York, NY: McGraw-Hill.

Miller, K. D. (1992). A framework for integrated risk management in international business. *Journal of International Business Studies*, *23*(2), 311–331. doi:10.1057/palgrave.jibs.8490270

Millican, J. (2014). Higher education and student engagement: Implications for a new economic era. *Education + Training*, *56*(7), 635–649. doi:10.1108/ET-07-2014-0077

Ministerio de ambiente. (2018). *Minambiente reglamenta la gestión de residuos de envases y empaques en Colombia*. Resolución 1407 de 2018. Retrieved from https://www.minambiente.gov.co/index.php/noticias-minambiente/4085-minambiente-reglamenta-la-gestion-de-residuos-de-envases-y-empaques-en-colombia

Ministerio de Comercio, Industria y Turismo. (2019). *Decreto 957 de 5 de junio de 2019*.

Ministry of Higher Education and Technology-Zimbabwe. (2010). *Strategic plan 2010–2015*. Harare: Government Printers.

Ministry of Industrialisation, Trade and SME Development. (2015). *National Policy on Micro, Small and Medium Enterprises in Namibia (Zero draft).* Windhoek, Namibia: Author.

Ministry of Regional and Local Government, Housing and Rural Development. (2012). National Rural Development Policy. Windhoek, Namibia: Author.

Ministry of Urban and Rural Development. (2011-2015). *Annual Progress Review and Planning Reports.* Windhoek, Namibia: Author.

Minney, T. (2016). Exchanges give SMEs a helping hand. *African Banker Magazine.* Retrieved from www.africanbusinessmagazine.com/african-banker/exchanges-give-smeshelping-hand

Minniti, M., & Bygrave, W. (2001). A dynamic model of entrepreneurial learning. *Entrepreneurship Theory and Practice, 25*(3), 5–16. doi:10.1177/104225870102500301

Minniti, M., & Moren, L. (2010). Entrepreneurial types and economic growth. *Journal of Business Venturing, 25*(3), 305–314. doi:10.1016/j.jbusvent.2008.10.002

Minogue, M., & McCourt, W. (2001). *Internationalization of Public Management.* Cheltenham, UK: Edward Elgar. doi:10.4337/9781781952757.00008

Minogue, M., Polidano, C., & Hulme, D. (Eds.). (1998). *Beyond the New Public Management: Changing Ideas and Practices in Governance.* Cheltenham, UK: Edward Elgar.

Mirjam van Praag, C., & Versloot, P. H. (2008). The economic benefits and costs of entrepreneurship: A review of the research. *Small Business Economics, 29*(4), 351–383. doi:10.1561/0300000012

Missé, A., Moreno, J. A., Vázquez Oteo, O., Escorsa, P., & Casado Cañeque, F. (2015). *Responsabilidad Social de la Empresa: ¿RSE o RIP?* Obtenido de jstor: http://www.jstor.org/stable/26360524

Mitchell, R. K., Smith, J. B., Morse, E. A., Seawright, K. W., Peredo, A. M., & McKenzie, B. (2002). Are entrepreneurial cognitions universal? Assessing entrepreneurial cognitions across cultures. *Entrepreneurship Theory and Practice, 26*(4), 9–32. doi:10.1177/104225870202600402

Mittal, A., & Kalampukah, P. K. (2009). *Partnership Challenges in Achieving Common Goals - A Study of Public Private Partnership in E-Governance Projects* (Unpublished M.Sc. Thesis). Umea School of Business.

MMGP Index, . (2015). Melbourne: Mercer Company. Retrieved from https://www.mercer.com/content/dam/mercer/attachments/global/Retirement/Melbourne-Mercer-Global-Pension-Index-2015/Report.pdf

MMGP Index, . (2019). Melbourne: Mercer Company. Retrieved from https://info.mercer.com/rs/521-DEV-513/images/MMGPI%202019%20Full%20Report.pdf

Modigliani, F. (1985). *Life Cycle, Individual Thrift and the Wealth of Nations* Economic Sciences. Retrieved from https://www.nobelprize.org/nobel_prizes/economic-sciences/laureates/1985/modigliani-lecture.pdf

Moh'd, A. R. A.-S., Barber, K. D., Garza-Reyes, J. A., Kumar, V., & Reza Abdi, M. (2017). The effect of supply chain management practices on supply chain and manufacturing firms' performance. *Journal of Manufacturing Technology Management, 28*(5), 577–609. doi:10.1108/JMTM-11-2016-0154

Mohajan, H. K. (2019). *Knowledge Sharing among Employees in Organizations.* https://mpra.ub.uni-muenchen.de

Mohajan, H. K. (2019). Knowledge sharing among employees in organizations. *Journal of Economic Development. Environment and People, 8*(1), 52–61. doi:10.26458/jedep.v8i1.612

Mohamedbhai, G. (2015). *What role for higher education in sustainable development?* World University News. Retrieved from https://www.universityworldnews.com/post.php?story=20150108194231213

Mohapatra, S. (2016). *Designing Knowledge Management Strategy*. https://www.researchgate.net

Mohar, Y. M. S., Singh, J., & Kishore, K. (2007). Relationship Between psychological characteristics and entrepreneurial inclination: A Case Study of Students at Tun Abdul Razak University. *Journal of Asia Entrepreneurship and Sustainability*, 3(2), 1-10.

Mokroš, M., & Papulová, Z. (2007). *Importance of Managerial Skills and Knowledge in Management for Small Entrepreneurs*. Retrieved October 25, 2019 from https://www.g-casa.com/PDF/Papulova-Mokros.pdf

Moncada Niño, Á. F., & Oviedo Franco, M. L. (2013). Las TIC como fuente de ventaja competitiva en las PYMES. *Sotavento M.B.A., 21*, 126-134. Recuperado el Mayo de 2019, de Universidad Externado de Colombia: https://revistas.uexternado.edu.co/index.php/sotavento/article/view/3441/3128

Montealegre, G. J. V., & Calderón, H. G. (2007). Relaciones entre actitud hacia el cambio y cultura organizacional. Estudio de caso en medianas y grandes empresas de confecciones de Ibagué. Rev. Innovar., 17(29).

Monterrosa, H. (2019). Mipymes representan 96% del tejido empresarial y aportan 40% al PIB. *La República*. Retrieved from: https://www.larepublica.co/economia/mipymes-representan-96-del-tejido-empresarial-y-aportan-40-al-pib-2903247

Mont, O. (2002). Clarifying the concept of product–service system. *Journal of Cleaner Production*, *10*(3), 237–245. doi:10.1016/S0959-6526(01)00039-7

Montoya, R. A., Montoya, R. I., & Castellanos, O. (2010). Situación de la competitividad de las Pyme en Colombia: Elementos actuales y retos. *Agronomia Colombiana*, *28*(1), 107–117.

Moraga, G., Huysveld, S., Mathieux, F., Blengini, G. A., Alaerts, L., Van Acker, K., & Dewulf, J. (2019). Circular economy indicators: What do they measure? *Resources, Conservation and Recycling*, *146*, 452–461. doi:10.1016/j.resconrec.2019.03.045 PubMed

Moraleda, A. (2004). La innovación, clave para la competitividad empresarial. *Universia Business Review*, (1): 128–136.

Morali, O., & Searcy, C. (2013). A review of sustainable supply chain management practices in Canada. *Journal of Business Ethics*, *117*(3), 635–658. doi:10.1007/s10551-012-1539-4

Morelli, N. (2006). Developing new product service systems (PSS): Methodologies and operational tools. *Journal of Cleaner Production*, *14*(17), 1495–1501. doi:10.1016/j.jclepro.2006.01.023

Morgan, R., & Hunt, S. (1999). Relationship-based competitive advantage: The role of relationship marketing in marketing strategy. *Journal of Business Research*, *46*(3), 281–290. doi:10.1016/S0148-2963(98)00035-6

Morlet, A., Blériot, J., Opsomer, R., Linder, M., Henggeler, A., Bluhm, A., & Carrera, A. (2016). *Intelligent Assets: Unlocking the Circular Economy Potential*. Ellen MacArthur Foundation.

Morrison, J. (2006). *International Business Environment: Global and Local Marketplaces in a changing world*. New York: Palgrave MacMillan. doi:10.1007/978-0-230-20957-2

Morse, J. M. (1991). Approaches to qualitative-quantitative methodological triangulation. *Nursing Research*, *40*(2), 120–123. doi:10.1097/00006199-199103000-00014 PMID:2003072

Moscoso Escobar, J., Sepúlveda Rivillas, C. I., García Cano, A., & Restrepo Londoño, A. L. (2012). Costo de capital en entornos económicos cambiantes: caso Valle de Aburra (Antioquia). *Rev.fac.cienc.econ*, *20*(2). Retrieved from: http://www.scielo.org.co/scielo.php?script=sci_arttext&pid=S0121-68052012000200013

Moss, M. (1985). *Designing for Minimal Maintenance Expense: The Practical Application of Reliability and Maintainability*. New York: CRC Press.

Mourad, M. (2016). Recycling, recovering and preventing food waste: Competing solutions for food systems sustainability in the United States and France. *Journal of Cleaner Production*, *126*, 461–477. doi:10.1016/j.jclepro.2016.03.084

Mowforth, M., & Munt, I. (2009). *Tourism and sustainability: Development. Globalisation and New Tourism in the Third World* (3rd ed.). London: Routledge.

Moyano, V., & Paniagua, S. (2018). Citizens and the Circular Economy, Current situation and prospects for the future. Creafutur. ESADE Business School. Cataluña.

Moyo, J. (2016). *Unemployment: Graduates living in poverty*. Retrieved November 21, 2018, from https://www.dandc.ou

MRLGHRD. (2011). *Regional and Local Economic Development: White paper*. Windhoek: Ministry of Regional and Local Government, Housing and Rural Development.

Mueller, R. A., Sumner, D. A., & Lapsley, J. (2006). *Clusters of grapes and wine*. In *Third International Wine Business Research Conference*, Montpellier, France.

Mueller, S. L., & Thomas, A. S. (2001). Culture and entrepreneurial potential: A nine country study of locus of control and innovativeness. *Journal of Business Venturing*, *16*(1), 51–75. doi:10.1016/S0883-9026(99)00039-7

Mukherjee, D., & Hollenbaugh, E. (2019). Do Social Media Help in the Sustainability of Small Businesses? A Pedagogical Study Using Fictional Business Cases. *International Journal of Higher Education Management, 6*(1). Retrieved from https://ijhem.com/cdn/article_file/2019-08-07-22-50-06-PM.pdf

Mulhall, D., & Braungart, M. (2010). Cradle to cradle criteria for the built environment. *EKONOMIAZ. Revista vasca de Economía, 75*(04), 182-193.

Muller, S., & Tuncer, B. (2013). *Greening SMEs by Enabling Access to Finance. Strategies and Experiences from the Switch Assia Programme*. Wuppertal: SWITCH-Asia Network Facility.

Mumford, M. D. (2000). Managing creative people: Strategies and tactics for innovation. *Human Resource Management Review*, *10*(3), 313–351. doi:10.1016/S1053-4822(99)00043-1

Munasinghe, M. (1994). Sustainomics: a transdisciplinary framework for sustainable development. *Proc. 50th Anniversary Sessions of the Sri Lanka Assoc. for the Adv. of Science (SLAAS).*

Munasinghe, M. (2012). *Sustainable Development Triangle (SDT)*. Available: http://www.eoearth.org/view/article/156365/

Muñoz, P. (2018). A cognitive map of sustainable decision-making in entrepreneurship: A configurational approach. *International Journal of Entrepreneurial Behaviour & Research*, *24*(3), 787–813. doi:10.1108/IJEBR-03-2017-0110

Munoz, P., & Dimov, D. (2015). The call of the whole in understanding the development of sustainable ventures. *Journal of Business Venturing*, *30*(4), 632–654. doi:10.1016/j.jbusvent.2014.07.012

Munyanyiwa, T., Svotwa, D., Rudumbu, N., & Mutsau, M. (2016). A comparative study of entrepreneurship curriculum development and review at the University of Zimbabwe and Botho University. Botswana. *Journal of Education and Practice*, *7*(13), 63–72.

Murray, A., Skene, K., & Haynes, K. (2017). The circular economy: An interdisciplinary exploration of the concept and application in a global context. *Journal of Business Ethics*, *140*(3), 369–380. doi:10.100710551-015-2693-2

Murray, A., Skene, K., & Haynes, K. (2017). The Circular Economy: An Interdisciplinary Exploration of the Concept and Application in a Global Context. *Journal of Business Ethics*, *140*(3), 369–380. doi:10.1007/s10551-015-2693-2

Murray, S. L., Holmes, J. G., & Collins, N. L. (2006). Optimizing assurance: The risk regulation system in relationships. *Psychological Bulletin*, *132*(5), 641–666. doi:10.1037/0033-2909.132.5.641 PMID:16910746

Mwakio, E. M. (2018). *Business skills and entrepreneurship development training and planning manual for Potato producer cooperatives and youth groups*. Retrieved October 26, 2019 from https://cgspace.cgiar.org/bitstream/handle/10568/99165/avcd_cip_manual.pdf?sequence=1&isAllowed=y

Mwasalwiba, E. S. (2010). Entrepreneurship education: A review of its objectives, teaching methods, and impact indicators. *Education + Training*, *52*(1), 20–47. doi:10.1108/00400911011017663

Mwobobia, F. M. (2012). The challenges facing small-scale women entrepreneurs: A case of Kenya. *International Journal of Business Administration*, *3*(2), 112–121. doi:10.5430/ijba.v3n2p112

Naaman, Z. (2018). *Rethinking Recycling. Could a Circular Economy Solve a Problem?* https://www.theguardian.com

Naanen, B. (1995). Oil-producing minorities and the restructuring of Nigerian federalism: The case of the Ogoni people. *The Journal of Commonwealth & Comparative Politics*, *33*(1), 46–78.

Nabi, G., Linan, F., Fayolle, A., Krueger, N., & Walmsley, A. (2017). The Impact of Entrepreneurship education in Higher Education: A systematic review and research agenda. *Academy of Management Learning & Education*, *16*(2), 277–299. doi:10.5465/amle.2015.0026

Nabi, G., Walmsley, A., Liñán, F., Akhtar, I., & Neame, C. (2018). Does entrepreneurship education in the first year of higher education develop entrepreneurial intentions? The role of Learning and Inspiration. *Studies in Higher Education*, *43*(3), 452–467. doi:10.1080/03075079.2016.1177716

Nakusera, F., Kadhikwa, G., & Mushendami, P. (2008). *Enhancing the role of factoring and leasing companies in providing working capital to small and medium enterprises (SMEs) in Namibia*. BoN Occasional Paper, No. OP 3-2008, Research Department, Bank of Namibia.

Namibia Business and Investment Climate Survey (NamBIC). (2014). *NCCI, IPPR, Namibia Manufacturers Association*. Windhoek: NMA.

Namibia Statistics Agency. (2015). *Analysis of Youth Employment and Unemployment in Namibia 2012-2013*. Windhoek, Namibia: Namibia Statistics Agency.

Nanayakkara, S. (2013). *How Can We Promote More Entrepreneurial Environment Together*. https://blogs.worldbank.org

Nanda, R., & Sorensen, J. (2011). Workplace peers and entrepreneurship. *Management Science*, *56*(7), 1116–1126. doi:10.1287/mnsc.1100.1179

Nanthuru, S. B., Pingfeng, L., Guihua, N., & Mkonya, V. L. (2018). An Assessment of Risk Management Practices of SME Taxpayers in Malawi and their Impact on Tax Compliance. *International Journal of Management Science and Business Administration*, *4*(4), 7–17. doi:10.18775/ijmsba.1849-5664-5419.2014.44.1001

Naude, W., & Szirmai, A. (2013). *Technical Innovation Entrepreneurship and Development*. https://www.european-businessreview.com

Naydenov, K. (2018). Circular tourism as a key for eco-innovations in circular economy based on sustainable development. *International Multidisciplinary Scientific GeoConference Surveying Geology and Mining Ecology Management*, *18*(5.3), 135-142.

Neal, A., Yeo, G., Koy, A., & Xiao, T. (2012). Predicting the form and direction of work role performance from the Big 5 model of personality traits. *Journal of Organizational Behavior*, *33*(2), 175–192. doi:10.1002/job.742

Neck, H. M., & Greene, P. G. (2011). Entrepreneurship education: Known worlds and new frontiers. *Journal of Small Business Management*, *49*(1), 55–70. doi:10.1111/j.1540-627X.2010.00314.x

Needhidasan, S., Samuel, M., & Chidambaram, R. (2014). Electronic waste - an emerging threat to the environment of urban India. *Journal of Environmental Health Science & Engineering*, *12*(1), 36. doi:10.1186/2052-336X-12-36 PMID:24444377

Neely, A. (2008). Exploring the Financial Consequences of the Servitization of Manufacturing. *Operations Management Research*, *1*(2), 1–50. doi:10.100712063-009-0015-5

Neessen, P., Caniëls, M., Vos, B., & De Jong, J. (2018). The intrapreneurial employee: Toward an integrated model of intrapreneurship and research agenda. *The International Entrepreneurship and Management Journal*. doi:10.100711365-018-0552-1

Neider, L. (1987). A preliminary investigation of female entrepreneurs in Florida. *Journal of Small Business Management*, *25*(3), 22–29.

Nejeala, J. (2011). Planned obsolescence understanding the reality of durable goods obsolescence and consumers disposal behavior (Unpublished doctoral dissertation). University of Economics in Prague, Faculty of Business Administration International Business and Management, Czech Republic.

Newell, P., & Frynas, J. G. (2007). Beyond CSR? Business, poverty and social justice: An introduction. *Third World Quarterly*, *28*(4), 670. doi:10.1080/01436590701336507

Newell, S., Scarborough, H., Robertson, M., & Swan, J. (2002). *Managing Knowledge Work* (1st ed.). New York: Palgrave Macmillan.

Newsday. (2016). *From varsity to the streets: cry the Zimbabwean graduate*. Retrieved November 21, 2018, from www.newsday.co.zw

Ngugi, W. V., & Kerongi, F. (2014). Effects of micro-financing on growth of small and micro enterprises in Mombasa County. *International Journal of Scientific and Engineering Research*, *2*(4), 138–142.

Ngwenyama, O., & Morawczynski, O. (2009). Factors Affecting ICT Expansion in Emerging Economies: An Analysis of ICT Infrastructure Expansion in Five Latin American Countries. *Information Technology for Development*, *15*(4), 237–258. doi:10.1002/itdj.20128

Nicolades, A. (2011). Entrepreneurship: The role of higher education in South Africa. *Educational Research*, *2*(4), 103–105.

Nicolescu, L., & Nicolescu, C. (2012). Innovation in SMEs – Findings from Romania. *Economia e Sociologia*, *5*(2a), 71–85.

Nidumolu,, R., Pralahad, K. C., & Rangaswami, M. R. (2009, Sept.). Why Sustainability Is Now the Key Driver of Innovation. *The Magazine*.

Nieman, G. (1999). *Training entrepreneurs and small business enterprises in South Africa*. University of Pretoria.

Niero, M., & Hauschild, M. Z. (2017). Closing the loop for packaging: Finding a framework to operationalize Circular Economy strategies. *Procedia CIRP*, *61*, 685–690. doi:10.1016/j.procir.2016.11.209

Nieuwenhuizen, C., Groenewald, D., Davids, J., vanRensburg, L. J., & Schachtebeck, C. (2016). Best practice in entrepreneurship education. *Problems and Perspectives in Management*, *14*(3/2), 528-536.

Nieuwenhuizhen, C., & Kroon, J. (2002). Identification of entrepreneurial success factors to determine the content of entrepreneurship subjects. *South African Journal of Higher Education*, *16*(3), 157–166.

Niinimäki, K. (2013). *Sustainable fashion: new approaches*. Helsinki, Finland: Aalto University Publication Series.

Nijaki, L. (2014). Why sustainability is not a stool or pretzel, but a Mobius strip. *Open Citizenship*, *5*(1), 100–104.

Nir, K. (2014). Developing successful entrepreneurial ecosystems: Lessons from a comparison of an Asian tiger and a Baltic tiger. *Baltic Journal of Management*, *9*(3), 330–356. doi:10.1108/BJM-09-2013-0146

NITI Aayog. (n.d.). http://niti.gov.in/writereaddata/files/document_publication/Strategy%20Paper %20on%20Resource%20 Efficiency.pdf

Nocco, B. W., & Stulz, R. M. (2006). Enterprise risk management: Theory and practice. *Journal of Applied Corporate Finance*, *18*(4), 8–20. doi:10.1111/j.1745-6622.2006.00106.x

Noko, P., & Ngulube, P. (2015). A vital feedback loop in educating and training archival professionals: A tracer study of records and archives management graduates in Zimbabwe. *Information Development*, *31*(3), 270–283. doi:10.1177/0266666913510308

Nomura, H. (2008). Developing the "why" facet of medical professionalism. *The Kaohsiung Journal of Medical Sciences*, *24*(1), 31–34. doi:10.1016/S1607-551X(08)70070-6 PMID:18218567

Norwegian Ministry of the Environment. (1994). *Oslo Roundtable on Sustainable Production and Consumption*. Oslo, Norway: Norwegian Ministry of the Environment.

Ntukamazina, D. A. (1996). Core Elements of Civil Service Reform. *Focus on Tanzania, AJPAM*, *5*(4), 6–10.

Nunes, B. T., Pollard, S. J. T., Burgess, P., Ellis, G., De los Rios, T. C., & Charnley, F. (2018). Contributions to the circular economy: Professing the hidden curriculum. *Sustainability*, *10*(8), 1–24. doi:10.3390u10082719

Nußholz, J. L. (2017). Circular business models: Defining a Concept and Framing an Emerging Research Field. *Sustainability*, *9*(10), 12. doi:10.3390/su9101810

Nwafor-Orizu, I., Chinyere, O. M., & Tochukwu, E. K. (2018). Political Restructuring in Nigeria: The Need, Challenges and Prospects. *International Journal of Public Policy & Governance, 5*(1), 28-53.

Nwankwo, O. F. (2014). Impact of corruption on economic growth in Nigeria. *Mediterranean Journal of Social Sciences*, *5*(6), 41. doi:10.5901/mjss.2014.v5n6p41

Nylund, P. A., & Cohen, B. (2017). Collision density: Driving growth in urban entrepreneurial ecosystems. *The International Entrepreneurship and Management Journal*, *13*(3), 757–776. doi:10.100711365-016-0424-5

O'Connor, A. (2013). A Conceptual Framework for Entrepreneurship Education Policy: Meeting Government and Economic Purposes. *Journal of Business Venturing*, *28*(4), 246–563. doi:10.1016/j.jbusvent.2012.07.003

O'Connor, A., & Reed, G. (2015a). Promoting regional entrepreneurship ecosystems: The role of the university sector in Australia. In P. Davidsson (Ed.), *Conference Proceedings, Australian Centre for Entrepreneurship Research Exchange Conference 2015* (pp. 772–788). Adelaide: Queensland University of Technology.

O'Neill, G. D., Hershauer, J. C., & Golder, J. S. (2006). The cultural context of sustainability entrepreneurship. *Greener Manag. Inst.*, *55*(1), 33–46. doi:10.9774/GLEAF.3062.2006.au.00005

Oberle, B., Bringezu, S., Hatfield-Dodds, S., Hellweg, S., Schandl, H., & Clement, J. (2019). *Global Resource Outlook 2019*. Paris: International Resource Panel.

OBS Business School. (2019). *¿Cuáles son las claves del éxito empresarial?* Retrieved from: https://www.obs-edu.com/int/blog-project-management/herramientas-esenciales-de-un-project-manager/cuales-son-las-claves-del-exito-empresarial

OCDE. (2000). *Small and Medium sized enterprises: local strenght, global reach.* París: OCDE Observer.

Ocholla, D. (1998). Information consultancy and brokerage in Botswana. *Journal of Information Science*, *24*(2), 83–95. doi:10.1177/016555159802400203

Ocholla, D. (1999). Information intermediaries in the next millennium: An agenda for action for the development of information consultancy and brokerage in Africa. *Library Management*, *20*(2), 105–114. doi:10.1108/01435129910251584

OECD. (2000). *A New Economy? The Changing Role of Innovation and Information Technology in Growth.* Paris: OECD Publishing.

OECD. (2005). *OECD SME and Entrepreneurship Outlook.* Paris: OECD Publishing; doi:10.1787/9789264009257-

OECD. (2012). *Social Protection, Poverty Reduction and Pro-poor Growth: A Policy Guidance Note.* Paris: OECD.

OECD. (2015). *Colombia Políticas Prioritarias Para Un Desarrollo Inclusivo.* Serie "Mejores Políticas" January 2015. Retrieved from: https://www.oecd.org/about/publishing/colombia-politicas-prioritarias-para-un-desarrollo-inclusivo.pdf

OECD. (2015). Material resources, productivity and the environment. *OECD Green Growth Studies.* Available: http://www.oecd.org/env/waste/material-resources-productivity-and-the-environment-9789264190504-en.htm

OECD. (2016). Sustainable Business Models for Water Supply and Sanitation in Small Towns and Rural Settlements in Kazakhstan. OECD Studies on Water. doi:10.1787/9789264249400-en

OECD. (2018). *Business Models for Circular Economy - Opportunities and Challenges from a Policy Perspective.* Paris: OECD.

OECD. (2018). *Business models for the circular economy: Opportunities and challenges from a policy perspective.* Retrieved 3 October, 2019 from https://www.oecd.org/environment/waste/policy-highlights-business-models-for-the-circular-economy.pdf

Ogbokor, A. C., & Ngeendepi, E. J. (2010). *Investigation the challenges faced by SMEs in Namibia.* Retrieved from http://ir.polytechnic.edu.na

Oghazi, P., & Mostaghel, R. (2018). Circular Business Model Challenges and Lessons Learned—An Industrial Perspective. *Sustainability*, *2018*(10), 739. doi:10.3390u10030739

Ogunyomi, P., & Bruning, N. S. (2016). Human resource management and organizational performance of small and medium enterprises (SMEs) in Nigeria. *International Journal of Human Resource Management*, *27*(6), 612–634. doi:10.1080/09585192.2015.1033640

Ojo, O. (2009). Impact of microfinance on entrepreneurial development: The case of Nigeria. *Proceedings of the International Conference on Economics and Administration.* Retrieved from http://conference.faa.ro

Okorie, O., Salonitis, K., Charnley, F., Moreno, M., Turner, C., & Tiwari, A. (2018). Digitisation and the Circular Economy: A Review of Current Research and Future Trends. *Energies*, *3009*(11), •••. doi:10.3390/en11113009

Olalla, B., San José, C., & Mata, M. (2012). Factor humano: un elemento clave en la búsqueda de la eficiencia de los proyectos. In *VII Congreso Nacional VISION12.* Madrid: itSMF Spain.

Olalla, B., & Mata, M. (2016). *Value Creation in a Network Economy. In Handbook of Research on Social Entrepreneurship and Solidarity Economics* (pp. 93–110). IGI Global. https://www.igi-global.com/book/handbook-research-social-entrepreneurship-solidarity/142130

Oldham, G., & Hackman, J. (1980). Work design in the organizational context. *Research in Organizational Behavior*, *2*, 247–278.

Oliver, C. (1998). *Sustainable Competitive Advantage: Combining Institutional and Resource-Based Views*. Recuperado el Mayo de 2019, de Strategic Management Journal: http://www.jstor.org/stable/3088134

Oliver, A. (2001). Strategic alliances and the learning life-cycle of biotechonology firms. *Organization Studies*, *22*(3), 467–489. doi:10.1177/0170840601223004

Oluoko-Odingo, A. A., & Mutisya, E. (2019). The enterprise of waste management among urban youth for sustainable development in Kenya. *Journal of Sustainability. Environment and Peace*, *1*(2), 45–51.

Ombisa, B. A. (2017). Poverty as a Driving Force to Insecurity in Slums within Nairobi. *Journal of Poverty. Investment and Development.*, *31*, 24–32.

Omolara, A. E. (2018). *Entrepreneurial skills and growth of Small and Medium Enterprise (SMEs): A comparative analysis of Nigerian entrepreneurs and Minority entrepreneurs in the UK*. Retrieved October 17, 2019 from https://mpra.ub.uni-muenchen.de/86751/1/MPRA_paper_86751.pdf

Omotayo, F. O. (2015). Knowledge management as an important tool in organisational management: A Review of Literature. *Library Philosophy and Practice*, *1*, 1–23.

Omunjalu, B. S., & Fondo, F. (2014). The role of microfinance empowerment of the youth: A case of Mombasa County. *Journal of Business and Management*, *16*(5), 26–32.

Önder, H. (2018, July). Sürdürülebilir kalkınma anlayışında yeni bir kavram: döngüsel ekonomi. Dumlupınar Üniversitesi Sosyal Bilimler Dergisi, (57), 196 - 204.

Oosterbeek, H., Van Praag, M., & Ijsselstein, A. (2010). The impact of entrepreneurship education on entrepreneurship skills and motivation. *European Economic Review*, *54*(3), 442–454. doi:10.1016/j.euroecorev.2009.08.002

Oosterhuis, F. (2006). *Ex-post estimates of costs to business of EU environmental legislation*. Amsterdam: European Commission, DG Environment.

Oppenheimer, A. (2014). Crear o morir. La esperanza de Latinoamérica y los cinco secretos de la innovación. Academic Press.

Opresnik, D., & Taisch, M. (2015). The value of Big Data in servitization. *International Journal of Production Economics*, *165*, 174–184. doi:10.1016/j.ijpe.2014.12.036

Organisation for Economic Cooperation and Development. (1998). *Fostering entrepreneurship*. Paris: OECD.

Organisation for Economic Co-operation and Development. (2000). *Enhancing the competitiveness of SMEs in the global economy: Strategies and policies*. OECD.

Ostrom, E. (2009, July 24). A general framework for analyzing sustainability of social ecological systems. *Science*, *325*(5939), 419–422. doi:10.1126/science.1172133 PubMed

Our Common Future. (2013b). *World Commission on Environment and Development. (1987). Oxford University Press*. Oxford: EMF.

Oyeyinka, O. (2017). Living Standards and Industrial Clusters in Nigeria. In Industrial Clusters, Institutions and Poverty in Nigeria (pp. 57-99). Springer International Publishing.

Özkan, A., Günkaya, Z., Özdemir, A., & Banar, M. (2018). Sanayide temiz üretim ve döngüsel ekonomiye geçişte enüstriyel simbiyoz yaklaşımı: Bir değerlendirme. Anadolu Üniversitesi Bilim ve Teknoloji Dergisi B - Teorik Bilimler, 6(1), 84 - 97. doi:10.20290/aubtdb.332377

Özsoy, T. (2018). Endüstriyel ekolojiyi anlamak adına endüstriyel ortakyaşarlık örneklerinin incelenmesi. Artıbilim. *Adana Bilim ve Teknoloji Üniversitesi Sosyal Bilimler Dergisi*, *1*(2), 22–34.

Paape, L., & Speklè, R. F. (2012). The adoption and design of enterprise risk management practices: An empirical study. *European Accounting Review*, *21*(3), 533–564. doi:10.1080/09638180.2012.661937

Packard, V. (1960). *The waste makers*. London: Penguin Books.

Padilla, S. (2018). ¿Cuál es la mayor preocupación de las pymes? La competitividad. *El Espectador*. Retrieved from: https://www.elespectador.com/economia/cual-es-la-mayor-preocupacion-de-las-pymes-la-competitividad-articulo-740471

Pagán, J. I., López, I., Tenza-Abril, A. J., Aragonés, L., & Villacampa, Y. (2018). Urban growth and beach nourishment: Experiences on the coast of Alicante, Spain. *WIT Transactions on the Built Environment*, *179*, 93–102. doi:10.2495/UG180091

PAGEV. (2015). *Döngüsel ekonomi: Avrupa'da stratejik kaynak politikasının baş faktörü*. Türk Plastik Sanayicileri Araştırma, Geliştirme ve Eğitim Vakfı.

Pagliaro, M., & Meneguzzo, F. (2019). Lithium battery reusing and recycling: A circular economy insight. *Heliyon (London)*, *5*(6), e01866. doi:10.1016/j.heliyon.2019.e01866 PubMed

Pagoropoulos, A., Pigosso, D. C. A., & McAloone, T. C. (2017). The Emergent Role of Digital Technologies in the Circular Economy: A Review. Procedia CIRP, 64, 19–24. doi:10.1016/j.procir.2017.02.047

Palma, P. J., & Cunha, M. P. (2006). New challenges in entrepreneurship: Introduction to the special issue. *Comportamento Organizacional e Gestão*, *12*(1), 3–6.

Palmer, G. (1992). New ways to make international environmental law. *The American Journal of International Law*, *86*(2), 259–283. doi:10.2307/2203234

Palys, T. (2008). Purposive sampling. In L. M. Given (Ed.), *The Sage Encyclopedia of Qualitative Research Methods* (pp. 697–698). Los Angeles, CA: Sage.

Pamfilie, R., Firoiu, D., Croitoru, A.-G., & Ionescu, G. H. I. (2018). Circular Economy - A New Direction for the Sustainability of the Hotel Industry in Romania? *Amfiteatru Economic*, *20*(48), 388–404. doi:10.24818/EA/2018/48/388

Pan, S.-Y., Gao, M., Kim, H., Shah, K. J., Pei, S.-L., & Chiang, P.-C. (2018). Advances and challenges in sustainable tourism toward a green economy. *The Science of the Total Environment*, *635*, 452–469. doi:10.1016/j.scitotenv.2018.04.134 PMID:29677671

Parajuly, K. (2017). *Circular Economy in E-Waste Management: Resource Recovery & Design For End-of-Life* (PhD thesis). University of Southern Denmark.

Parajuly, K., & Wenzel, H. (2017). Product Family Approach in E-Waste Management- A Conceptual Framework for Circular Economy. *Sustainability*, *9*(5), 768. doi:10.3390u9050768

Paramonova, N. (2016). Cyclical economy on the threshold of Russia. Ecology and Law, 62.

Pareek, U., & Purohit, S. (2002). *Training Instruments in HRD and OD* (3rd ed.). Tata McGraw Hill Education Private Limited.

Parida, V., Sjödin, D. R., Wincent, J., & Kohtamäki, M. (2014). Mastering the transition to product-service provision: Insights into business models, Learning activities, and capabilities. *Research Technology Management*, *57*, 44–52.

Park, J., Sarkis, J., & Wu, Z. (2010). Creating an integrated business and environmental value within the context of China's circular economy and ecological modernization. *Journal of Cleaner Production*, *18*(15), 1494–1501. doi:10.1016/j.jclepro.2010.06.001

Parra, C., & Calderón, G. (2013). Formación y desempeño: un análisis de caso en empresas manufactureras grandes. *Pensamiento & Gestión*, (34), 137–160. Retrieved from https://search-ebscohost-com.hemeroteca.lasalle.edu.co/login.aspx?direct=true&AuthType=ip,url,uid&db=a9h&AN=91100294&lang=es&site=ehost-live

Parra, S. (2013). Exploring the incorporation of values for sustainable entrepreneurship teaching/learning. *Journal of Technology Management & Innovation*, *8*(1), 11–20. doi:10.4067/S0718-27242013000100002

Parrish, B. D. (2010). Sustainability-driven entrepreneurship: Principles of organization design. *Journal of Business Venturing*, *25*(5), 510–523. doi:10.1016/j.jbusvent.2009.05.005

Passari, C. E. (2019). *The Business of Globalization and the Globalization of Business*. Retrieved November 15, 2019 from https://journals.lib.unb.ca/index.php/JCIM/article/view/5666/10661

Patrick, C. (2016). *Entrepreneurship Philosophy Defined*. https://business.inquirer.net

Patrick, S. (2015). *For Entrepreneurs, Circular Economy Offers a Massive Opportunity*. https://www.huffpost.com

Patti, S. (2017). Circular economy and sharing consumption: Attitudes towards low-carbon tourism. *Economics and Policy of Energy and the Environment*, *2017*(1), 219–234. doi:10.3280/EFE2017-001011

Patton, M. Q. (2015). *Qualitative research and evaluation methods: Integrating theory and practice* (4th ed.). Thousand Oaks, CA: Sage.

Patzelt, H., & Shepherd, D. A. (2011). Recognizing opportunities for sustainable development. *Entrepreneurship Theory and Practice*, *35*(4), 631–652. doi:10.1111/j.1540-6520.2010.00386.x

Paulauskas, S. (2018). Blue Growth Circular Innovation. *Transnav-International Journal on Marine Navigation and Safety of Sea Transportation*, *12*(4), 813–818. doi:10.12716/1001.12.04.21

Pauli, G. (2010). *The Blue Economy—10 Years, 100 Innovations, 100 Million Jobs*. Brookline, MA: Paradigm Publications.

Paulin, D., & Suneson, K. (2015). Knowledge transfer, knowledge sharing and knowledge barriers–three blurry terms in KM. *Leading Issues in Knowledge Management*, *2*(2), 73.

Pauline, B., & Sandra, J. (2018). Entrepreneurs vs. Intrapreneurs A comparative study about motivation factors of entrepreneurs and intrapreneurs. Accessed from: http://www.diva-portal.org/smash/get/diva2:1224155/FULLTEXT01.pdf

Pauliuk, S. (2017). Critical Appraisal of the Circular Economy standard BS 8001:2017 And a Dashboard of Quantitative System Indicators for its Implementation in Organizations. *Resources, Conservation and Recycling, 129*, 81-92.

Paulsen, J. (2001, April). Life cycle assesment for building products: the significance of the usage phase (Unpublished doctoral dissertation). Kungliga Tekniska Höghskolan.

Pearce, D. W., Barbier, E. B., Markandya, A., & Barbier, E. (1989). *Blueprint for a Green Economy*. London, UK: Earthscan.

Pearce, D. W., Markandya, A., & Barbier, E. B. (1989). Blueprint for a Green Economy. *Earthscan, London, UK., 1989*, 1–47.

Pearce, D. W., & Turner, R. K. (1990). *Economics of natural resources and the environment*. Baltimore: The John Hopkis University Press.

Penaluna, A., & Penaluna, K. (2019). I am a designer, get me out of here: Can entrepreneurial education advance through learning from design education. In A. Fayolle, D. Kariv., & H. Matlay (Eds.), The Role and Impact of Entrepreneurship Education – Methods, Teachers and Innovative Programmes. Cheltenham, UK: Edward Elgar Publishing.

Perella, M. (2014, March 14). Renault, JLR, Nissan and Toyota drive car industry towards sustainability. *The Guardian*. Retrieved 10 February, 2020 from https://www.theguardian.com/sustainable-business/renault-jaguar-nissan-toyota-sustainability-circular-economy

Perella, M. (2016, April 28). Baths to washing machines: Welcome to the (almost) waterless home of the future. *The Guardian*. Retrieved 10 February, 2020 from https://www.theguardian.com/sustainable-business/2016/apr/28/baths-washing-machines-drybath-almost-waterless-home-of-the-future

Pérez, A., Pertuz, V., Leiva, M., & Vega, A. (2019). Elementos estructurales y funcionales de los sistemas multiagente para la cooperación organizacional en medianas empresas. *Información Tecnológica*, *30*(4), 155–164. doi:10.4067/S0718-07642019000400155

Pérez-Uribe, R. (2018). *Gerencia Estratégica Corporativa*. Ediciones Ecoe Ltda. Available at: https://www.ecoeediciones.com/libros/libros-de-administracion-ecoe/gerencia-estrategica-corporativa/

Pérez-Uribe, R. I. (2012). *El ambiente laboral y su incidencia en el desempeño de las organizaciones: estudio en las mejores empresas para trabajar en Colombia*. Retrieved from: http://hdl.handle.net/10882/3203

Peterman, N. E., & Kennedy, J. (2003). Enterprise education: Influencing students' perceptions of entrepreneurship. *Entrepreneurship Theory and Practice*, *28*(2), 129–144. doi:10.1046/j.1540-6520.2003.00035.x

Peterson, C. (2000). The future of optimism. *The American Psychologist*, *55*(1), 44–55. doi:10.1037/0003-066X.55.1.44 PubMed

Peterson, C. (2006). *A primer in positive psychology*. New York: Oxford University Press.

Petrovic, P. (2010). Economic crisis in Serbia. In V. Bartlet & V. Monastiriotis (Eds.), *South Eastern Europe after the Crisis*. Retrieved from http://www.lse.ac.uk/LSEE-Research-on-South-Eastern-Europe/Assets/Documents/Publications/Other/SEE-After-the-Crisis-Bartlett-Monastiriotis-eds.pdf

Pfeffer, J., & Salancik, G. R. (2003). *The external control of organisations: A resource dependence perspective*. Stanford: Stanford University Press.

Pheifer, A. G. (2017). *Barriers and Enablers to Circular Business Models*. Available at:https://www.circulaironderne-men.nl/uploads/4f4995c266e00bee8fdb8fb34fbc5c15.pdf

Phillips, J. A. (1998). *National Renewable Energy Laboratory- Managing Americaís Solid Waste*. https://www.csu.edu/cerc/researchreports/documents/ManagingAmericasSolidWaste1998.pdf

Pimchangthong, D., & Boonjing, V. (2017). Effects of Risk Management Practice on the Success of IT Project. *Procedia Engineering*, *182*, 579–586. doi:10.1016/j.proeng.2017.03.158

Pinchot, G. (1988). *Intrapreneuring*. Wiesbaden: Gabler. doi:10.1007/978-3-322-94468-9

Pinkovskiy, M., & Xavier, S. (2009). *Parametric Estimations of the World Distribution of Income*. NBER Working Paper #15433.

Pittaway, L. R., Robertson, M., Munir, K., Denyer, D., & Neely, A. (2004). Networking and innovation: A systematic review of evidence. *International Journal of Management Reviews*, *5*(3-4), 137–168. doi:10.1111/j.1460-8545.2004.00101.x

Pittaway, L., & Edwards, C. (2012). Assessment: Examining practice in entrepreneurship education. *Education + Training*, *54*(8/9), 778–800. doi:10.1108/00400911211274882

Plastics Europe. (2016). *World Plastics Production 1950–2015*. Available at https://committee.iso.org/files/live/sites/tc61/files/The%20Plastic%20Industry%20Berlin%20Aug%202016%20-%20Copy.pdf

Plummer, D., Brethenoux, E., Lu, C. K., Andrews, W., Runyon, B., Lovelock, J. D., ... Tirosh, A. (2018). *Top Strategic Predictions for 2019 and Beyond: Practicality Exists Within Instability*. Gartner.

Polidano, C., & Hulme, D. (1999). Public Management Reform in Developing Countries: Issues and Outcomes. *Public Management*, *1*(1), 121–132. doi:10.1080/14719037800000007

Pollitt, C. (1990). *Managerialism and the Public Services: The Anglo-American Experience*. Oxford: Blackwell.

Poon, W. C., Mohamad, O., & Yusoff, W. F. (2018). Examining the Antecedents of Ambidextrous behaviours in Promoting Creativity among SMEs in Malaysia. *Global Business Review*, *21*(3), 1–1. doi:10.1177/0972150918779267

Popa, D. (2012). Competitiveness of Romanian Small and Medium-Sized Enterprises in European Union. *Journal of Knowledge Management. Economics and Information Technology*, *2*(2), 1–11.

Popkova, E., Bogoviz, A., & Ragulina, J. (2018). Technological Parks, "Green Economy," and Sustainable Development in Russia. In Exploring the Future of Russia's Economy and Markets (pp. 143-159). Emerald. Doi:10.1108/978-1-78769-397-520181008

Porter, M. (1996). *¿Qué es la estrategia?* Recuperado el Mayo de 2019, de Harvard Business Review: https://s3.amazonaws.com/academia.edu.documents/37851742/4_Que_es_Estrategia.pdf?AWSAccessKeyId=AKIAIWOWYYGZ2Y53UL3A&Expires=1558381861&Signature=132Q27yedrcb1MADZWvjsnckcC8%3D&response-content-disposition=inline%3B%20filename%3DQue_es_la_estrategia.pdf

Porter, M. (2015). *Ventaja Competitiva: Creación y sostenimiento de un desempeño superior.* Recuperado el Mayo de 2019, de Grupo Editorial Patria: https://books.google.com.mx/books?hl=es&lr=&id=wV4JDAAAQBAJ&oi=fnd&pg=PT3&dq=que+es+ventaja+competitiva&ots=mwvClbT58A&sig=O2eioD4ADfMxwU5PBfOy20qH-SA#v=onepage&q=que%20es%20ventaja%20competitiva&f=false

Porter, M. E., & Kramer, M. R. (2011). How to reinvent capitalism and unleash a wave of innovation and growth? *Harvard Business Review*, *89*, 62–77.

Postigo, S., & Tamborini, F. (2002). Entrepreneurship education in Argentina: The case of San Andres University. *International Entrepreneurship Education and Training Conference, IntEnt02*, Kuala Lumpur, Malaysia.

Potting, J., Hekkert, M., Worrell, E., & Hanemaaijer, A. (2017). *Circular economy: measuring innovation in the product chain*. The Hague: PBL Netherlands Environmental Assessment Agency.

Powell, W. K.-D., Koput, K. W., & Smith-Doerr, L. (1996). Interorganizational Collaboration and the Locus of Innovation: Networks of Learning in Biotechnology. *Administrative Science Quarterly*, *41*(1), 116–145. doi:10.2307/2393988

Prahalad, C. K. (2005). The Fortune at the Bottom of the Pyramid: Eradicating Poverty through Profits. Wharton School Publishing.

Prahalad, C. K., & Hammond, A. (2002). Serving the world's poor, profitably. *Harvard Business Review, 80*(9), 48–57. PMID:12227146

Press, G. (2017). 6 Predictions For The $203 Billion Big Data Analytics Market. Available online, https://www.forbes.com/sites/gilpress/2017/01/20/6-predictions-for-the-203-billion-big-data-analytics-market/#645861502083, Forbes

Preston, F. (2012). A Global Redesign: Shaping the Circular Economy. London: Chatham House: The Royal Institute of International Affairs.

Preston, F. (2012). A Global Redesign? Shaping the Circular Economy. Energy, Environment and Resource Governance, (March), 1–20. doi:10.1080/0034676042000253936

Preston, F. (2012). *A global redesign? Shaping the circular economy*. London: Chatham House.

Preston, F. (2012). *A global redesign?: Shaping the circular economy*. London: Chatham House.

Price, R. W. (2015). *How Does Economics Connect To Entrepreneurship?* https://news.gcase.org

Prieto-Sandoval, V., Jaca García, C., & Ormazabal Goenaga, M. (2016). Circular Economy : An economic and industrial model to achieve the sustainability of society. Proceedings of the 22nd Annual International Sustainable Development Research Society Conference. Rethinking Sustainability Models and Practices: Challenges for the New and Old World Contexts (vol. 2, pp. 504–520). Academic Press.

Prieto-Sandoval, V., Jaca García, C., & Ormazabal Goenaga, M. (2016). Circular Economy: An economic and industrial model to achieve the sustainability of society. In *Proceedings of the 22nd Annual International Sustainable Development Research Society Conference. Rethinking Sustainability Models and Practices: Challenges for the New and Old World Contexts*. ISDRS.

Prieto-Sandoval, V., Jaca, C., & Ormazabal, M. (2018). Towards a consensus on the circular economy. *Journal of Cleaner Production, 179*, 605–615. doi:10.1016/j.jclepro.2017.12.224

Prieto-Sandoval, V., Jaca, C., Santos, J., Baumgartner, R. J., & Ormazabal, M. (2019). Key strategies, resources, and capabilities for implementing circular economy in industrial small and medium enterprises. *Corporate Social Responsibility and Environmental Management, 26*(6), 1473–1484. doi:10.1002/csr.1761

Prieto-Sandoval, V., Ormazabal, M., Jaca, C., & Viles, E. (2018). Key elements in assessing circular economy implementation in small and medium-sized enterprises. *Business Strategy and the Environment, 27*(8), 1525–1534. doi:10.1002/bse.2210

Project Management Institute. (2004). *A guide to the project management body of knowledge: PMBOK guide*. Project Management Institute.

Provan, K. G., & Kenis, P. (2008). Modes of network governance: Structure, management, and effectiveness. *Journal of Public Administration: Research and Theory, 18*(2), 229–252. doi:10.1093/jopart/mum015

Public Law. (1965). Solid waste disposal act. As Amended Through P.L. 115–232, Enacted August 13, 2018.

Puckett, J., Brandt, C., & Palmer, H. (2019). *Holes in the Circular Economy – WEEE Leakage from Europe*. Basel Action Network.

Puentes-Poyatos, R., Yebra-Rodríguez, Á., & Guerrero, F. (2016). *Responsabilidad Social Corporativa: El compromiso de la Universidad con los ciudadanos*. Obtenido de Revista de Antropología Experimental: http://revistaselectronicas.ujaen.es/index.php/rae

Puri, M., & Robinson, D. T. (2013). The Economic Psychology of Entrepreneurship and Family Business. *Journal of Economics & Management Strategy*, *22*(2), 423–444. doi:10.1111/jems.12013

Pyper, R. C. (2016). *An Entrepreneural Development Framework for SMEs in South Africa*. Nelson Mandela Metropolitan University.

Qi, J., Zhao, J., Li, W., Peng, X., Wu, B., & Wang, H. (2016). Origin and background of circular economy development. In *Development of Circular Economy in China* (pp. 1–19). Singapore: Springer. doi:10.1007/978-981-10-2466-5_1

Qrunfleh, S., & Tarafdar, M. (2013). Lean and agile supply chain strategies and supply chain responsiveness: The role of strategic supplier partnership and postponement. *Supply Chain Management*, *18*(6), 571–582. doi:10.1108/SCM-01-2013-0015

Rada, E., Ragazzi, M., Torretta, V., Castagna, G., Adami, L., & Cioca, L. (2018). Circular economy and waste to energy. Technologies and Materials for Renewable Energy, Environment and Sustainability, 1 - 6. doi:10.1063/1.5039237

Rada, E.C. (2019). Special waste valorization and renewable energy generation under a circular economy: Which priorities? *WIT Transactions on Ecology and the Environment, 222*, 145-157.

Radamaekers, K., Berg, J., & Asaad, S. S. (2011). *Study on the Competitiveness of the European Companies and Resource Efficiency*. Rotterdam: ECORYS Research and Consulting, Tecnologisk Institut, Cambridge Econometrics.

RAE. (2017). *Real Academia Española*. Obtenido de DLE: http://dle.rae.es/?w=diccionario

Rahim, H. L., & Mohtar, S. (2015). Social entrepreneurship: A different perspective. *International Academic Research Journal of Business and Technology*, *1*(1), 9–15.

Raimi, L. (2015). *Entrepreneurship Development through Corporate Social Responsibility – A Study of the Nigerian Telecommunication Industry* (Unpublished PhD. Thesis). Leicester Business School, De Montfort University, Leicester, UK.

Raimi, L., Fadipe, A. O., & Ogunjirin, O. D. (2017). Potential Roles of Industrial Clusters in Economic Diversification in Nigeria. International Journal of Development Strategies in Humanities. *Management and Social Sciences*, *7*(2), 50–68.

Raimi, L., Patel, A., Yekini, K., & Fadipe, A. O. (2014). Spatio-Temporal Audit of Nigeria's Industrial Policies and Entrepreneurship Development Interventions from 1946 to 2013. *International Journal of Humanities and Social Science*, *4*(1), 294–309.

Raimi, L., Peluola, S. B., & Shokunbi, M. O. (2016). Prospects and challenges of managing clusters as entrepreneurship development interventions for sustainable development in Nigeria: a discourse analysis. In *Managing Knowledge and Innovation for Business Sustainability in Africa*. Palgrave MacMillan.

Raimi, L., Suara, I. B., & Fadipe, A. O. (2013). Role of Economic and Financial Crimes Commission (EFCC) and Independent Corrupt Practices & Other Related Offences Commission (ICPC) at Ensuring Accountability and Corporate Governance in Nigeria. *Journal of Business Administration and Education*, *3*(2), 105–122.

Rajput, S., & Singh, S. P. (2019). Connecting circular economy and industry 4.0. *International Journal of Information Management*, *49*, 98–113. doi:10.1016/j.ijinfomgt.2019.03.002

Rakitovac, K. A. (2016). The Transition towards Responsible Tourism. *Political Sciences, Law, Finance, Economics and Tourism Conference Proceedings*, *4*, 889-896.

Ramakrishna, Y. (2016). Supply Chain Management: Large vs. Small and Medium Enterprises (SMEs). In A. Dwivedi (Ed.), *Innovative Solutions for Implementing Global Supply Chains in Emerging Markets* (pp. 141–151). Hershey, PA: IGI Global; doi:10.4018/978-1-4666-9795-9.ch009.

Ramírez-Salazar, M. P. (2016). *Modelo De Innovación Abierta Colaborativa Para La Banca De Fomento: Caso Bancóldex* (PhD dissertation). Universidad EAN.

Ramírez-Salazar, M. P. (2015). La innovación abierta impulsa el desarrollo sostenible de las empresas. In *Gestión de la sostenibilidad en el marco de las organizaciones*. Bogotá, Colombia: Editorial EAN.

Ramsden, N. (2010). *The role of SMEs in employment creation and economic growth: lessons from other countries*. Paper presented at the Bank of Namibia 12th Annual Symposium, Windhoek, Namibia.

Ramugondo, L. S. (2010). *An Exploratory study of infopreneurship as a job option for Library and Information Science students: A literature review*. Paper presented at the 11th DIS Annual Conference 2010, University of Zululand.

Ramukumba, T. (2014). Overcoming SMEs challenges through critical success factors: A case of SMEs in the Western Cape Province, South Africa. *Economic and Business Review for Central and South-Eastern Europe*, *16*(1), 19–38.

Randa, I. O. (2018). Leveraging Knowledge Management for Value Creation in Service-Oriented Organisations of Namibia. In *Global Practices in Knowledge Management for Societal and Organizational Development* (pp. 145–167). IGI Global. doi:10.4018/978-1-5225-3009-1.ch007

Ratanabanchuen, R. (2013). *Demographic Transition, Pension Schemes' Investment, and the Financial Market*. London: London School of Economics and Political Sciences.

Rauch, C. F., Jr., & Behling, O. (1984). Functionalism: Basis for an alternate approach to the study of leadership. In Leaders and managers (pp. 45-62). Pergamon.

Rauch, A. (2014). Predictions of entrepreneurial behavior: A personality approach. In E. Chell & M. Karatas-Ozkan (Eds.), *Handbook of Research on Small Business and Entrepreneurship* (pp. 165–183). London, UK: Edward Elgar; do i:10.4337/9781849809245.00018.

Rauch, A., & Hulsink, W. (2015). Putting entrepreneurship education where the intention to act lies: An investigation into the impact of entrepreneurship education on entrepreneurial behavior. *Academy of Management Learning & Education*, *14*(2), 187–204. doi:10.5465/amle.2012.0293

Raymond, L., & Blili, S. (1997). Adopting EDI in a network enterprise: The case of subcontracting SMEs. *European Journal of Purchasing and Supply Management*, *3*(3), 165–175. doi:10.1016/S0969-7012(97)00008-7

Razorpay. (2017). *Legal Basics That Every Indian Start up Should Know*. https://razorpay.com/blog

Raz, T., & Michael, E. (2001). Use and benefits of tools for project risk management. *International Journal of Project Management*, *19*(1), 9–17. doi:10.1016/S0263-7863(99)00036-8

Raz, T., Shenhar, A. J., & Dvir, D. (2002). Risk management, project success, and technological uncertainty. *R & D Management*, *32*(2), 101–109. doi:10.1111/1467-9310.00243

Razzouk, R., & Shute, V. (2012). What is design thinking and why is it important? *Review of Educational Research*, *82*(3), 330–348. doi:10.3102/0034654312457429

Rea, C., & Volland, N. (2015). *The Business of Culture: Cultural Entrepreneurs in China and Southeast Asia, 1900-65*. UBC Press.

Redclift, M. (1989). The environmental consequences of Latin America's agricultural development: Some thoughts on the Brundtland Commission report. *World Development*, *17*(3), 365–377. doi:10.1016/0305-750X(89)90210-6

Redman, T. C. (2013). *Data Driven: Profiting from Your Most Important Business Asset*. Harvard Business Press.

Reh, L. (2013). Process engineering in circular economy: Invited review. *Particuology*, *11*(2), 119–133. doi:10.1016/j.partic.2012.11.001

Rehman, A. U., & Elahi, Y. A. (2012). Entrepreneurship education in India – Scope, challenges and role of B-schools in promoting entrepreneurship education. *International Journal of Engineering and Management Research*, *2*(5), 5–14.

Reijnders, L. (2008). Are emissions or wastes consisting of biological nutrients good or healthy? *Journal of Cleaner Production*, *16*(10), 1138–1141. doi:10.1016/j.jclepro.2008.02.003

Reike, D., Vermeulen, W. J., & Witjes, S. (2018). The circular economy: New or refurbished as CE 3.0?—Exploring controversies in the conceptualization of the circular economy through a focus on history and resource value retention options. *Resources, Conservation and Recycling*, *135*, 246–264. doi:10.1016/j.resconrec.2017.08.027

Reim, W., Parida, V., & Örtqvist, D. (2015). Product–Service Systems (PSS) business models and tactics–A systematic literature review. *Journal of Cleaner Production*, *97*, 61–75. doi:10.1016/j.jclepro.2014.07.003

Remeikiene, R., Startiene, G., & Dumciuviene, D. (2013). *Explaining entrepreneurial intention of university students: The role of entrepreneurial education.* Paper presented at the International Conference on Knowledge Management, Innovation and Learning, Zadar, Croatia.

Republic of Serbia. (2019). *IMF Country Report, No. 19/238.*Washington, DC: International Monetary Fund (IMF). Retrieved from: https://www.imf.org/en/Publications/CR/Issues/2019/07/22/Republic-of-Serbia-Staff-Report-for-the-2019-Article-IV-Consultation-and-Second-Review-under-48511

Republic of South Africa (RSA). (2002). *Advanced Manufacturing Technology Strategy.* Cape Town: Department of Science and Technology.

Research and Degrowth. (2012). *Definition of degrowth. Research and Degrowth.* Available on https://degrowth.org/

Revista Dinero. (2019). *Empresarios lanzan plan para consolidar la economía circular en el país.* Medio Ambiente. Retrieved from https://www.dinero.com/empresas/articulo/estrategia-de-los-empresarios-en-colombia-para-consolidar-la-economia-circular/275640

Riahi, K., van Vuuren, D. P., Kriegler, E., Edmonds, J., O'Neill, B. C., Fujimori, S., ... Tavoni, M. (2017). The Shared Socioeconomic Pathways and their energy, land use, and greenhouse gas emissions implications: An overview. *Global Environmental Change*, *42*, 153–168. doi:10.1016/j.gloenvcha.2016.05.009

Riahi, S. (2010). *Youth Entrepreneurship: Ottawa's portfolio in talent development.* Open Source Business Resource.

Rideout, E. C., & Gray, D. O. (2013). Does entrepreneurship education really work? A review and methodological critique of the empirical literature on the effects of university-based entrepreneurship education. *Journal of Small Business Management*, *51*(3), 329–351. doi:10.1111/jsbm.12021

Ridley-Duff, R. (2008). Social enterprise as a socially rational business. *International Journal of Entrepreneurial Behaviour & Research*, *14*(5), 291–312. doi:10.1108/13552550810897669

Riel, A. (2018). *How Circular Economy Unlocks Revenue Streams.* https://www.greenbiz.com

Riemenschneider, C., & Mykytyn, P. P. Jr. (2000). What small business executives have learned about managing information technology. *Information & Management*, *37*(5), 257–269. doi:10.1016/S0378-7206(99)00052-X

Ries, E. (2011). *The lean start-up: How today's entrepreneurs use continuous innovation to create radically successful businesses.* New York, NY: Crown Books.

Rihter, P. K., & Vetrova, M. A. (2017). Making operational decisions in the transition to the principles of circular economy in the industries of the Russian Federation. Ecological and economic problems of development of regions and countries (sustainable development, management, environmental management) (pp. 229-234).

Ritzén, S., & Sandström, G. Ö. (2017). Barriers to the Circular Economy–integration of perspectives and domains. *Procedia CIRP*, *64*, 7–12. doi:10.1016/j.procir.2017.03.005

Rizos, V., Behrens, A., Kafyeke, T., Hirschnitz-Garbers, M., & Ioannou, A. (2015). *The Circular Economy: Barriers and Opportunities for SMEs*. Brussels: CEPS Working Paper.

Rizos, V., Tuokko, K., & Behrens, A. (2017). The Circular Economy: A review of definitions, processes and impacts. CEE Research Report/8. Brussels: Energy Climate House.

Rizos, V., Behrens, A., Kafyeke, T., Hirschnitz-Garbers, M., & Ioannou, A. (2015). *The circular economy: Barriers and opportunities for SMEs*. Brussels: CEPS.

Rizos, V., Behrens, A., van der Gaast, W., Hofman, E., Ioannou, A., Kafyeke, T., ... Topi, C. (2016). Implementation of Circular Economy Business Models by Small and Medium-Sized Enterprises (SMEs): Barriers and Enablers. *Sustainability*, *8*(11), 1–18. doi:10.3390u8111212

Rob, K. (2015). *The Reign of Recycling is not Over*. http://greatforest.com

Robeco, S. A. M. (2015). Water: the Market of the future. Retrieved from https://www.google.com/search?q=RobecoSAM%2C+(2015)+Water%3A+the+market+of+the+future&rlz=1C5CHFA_enBG846BG846&oq=RobecoSAM%2C+(2015)+Water%3A+the+market+of+the+future&aqs=chrome.69i57.1720j0j9&sourceid=chrome&ie=UTF-8

Rockstrom, J., Steffen, W., Noone, K., Persson, A., Chapin, F. S. III, Lambin, E., ... Foley, J. (2009). Planetary boundaries: Exploring the safe operating space for humanity. *Ecology and Society*, *14*(2), 43–58. doi:10.5751/ES-03180-140232

Rodríguez-López, N. (1999). *La innovación: clave del éxito empresarial*. Retrieved from: https://dialnet.unirioja.es/descarga/articulo/565208.pdf

Rodríguez-Pose, A., & Tijmstra, S. A. (2007). Local economic development in sub-Saharan Africa. *Environment and Planning. C, Government & Policy*, *25*(4), 516–536. doi:10.1068/c5p

Rogers, E. M. (2003). *Diffusion of Innovations* (5th ed.). New York: Free Press.

Rogerson, C. A. (2008). Tracking SMME development in South Africa: issues of finance, training and regulatory environment. *Urban Forum*, *1*(1), 61-81.

Roman, T., & Maxim, A. (2017). National culture and higher education as pre-determining factors of student entrepreneurship. *Studies in Higher Education*, *42*(6), 993–1014. doi:10.1080/03075079.2015.1074671

Romeiro, A. R. (2012). Sustainable development: An ecological economics perspective. *Estudos Avançados*, *26*, 74.

Roper, S. (2002). Product innovation and small business growth: A comparison of the strategies of German, U.K. and Irish companies. *Research Policy*, *31*, 1087–1102. doi:10.1016/S0048-7333(01)00175-5

Rosenberg, E., Lotz-Sisitka, H., & Ramsarup, P. (2018). The green economy learning assessment South Africa: Lessons for higher education, skills and work-based learning. *Higher Education. Skills and Work-Based Learning*, *8*(3), 243–258. doi:10.1108/HESWBL-03-2018-0041

Rosenbloom, D. H., & Gong, T. (2013). Coproducing "clean" collaborative governance: Examples from the United States and China. *Public Performance & Management Review*, *36*(4), 544–561. doi:10.2753/PMR1530-9576360403

Roux, Ingrid, Le, & Or. (2014). Dimensions of Entrepreneurial Orientation & SME performance in Emerging Economies. *Development Southern Africa, 31*(4).

Ruffer, T., Bailey, H., Dahlgren, S., Spaven, P., & Winters, M. (2018a). *Evaluation of the market systems development approach: Lessons for expanded use and adaptive management at Sida.* Stockholm: Sida.

Rugge, S., & Glossbrenner, A. (1997). *The information brokers handbook* (3rd ed.). New York: McGraw Hill.

Ruiz-Real, J. L., Uribe-Toril, J., De Pablo Valenciano, J., & Gázquez-Abad, J. C. (2018). Worldwide Research on Circular Economy and Environment: A Bibliometric Analysis. *International Journal of Environmental Research and Public Health, 2018*(15), 2699. doi:10.3390/ijerph15122699 PMID:30501129

Rutherfoord, R., Blackburn, R., & Spence, L. (2000). Environmental Management and the Small Firm: An International Comparison. *International Journal of Entrepreneurial Behaviour & Research, 6*(6), 310–326. doi:10.1108/13552550010362750

Saavedra García, M. L., & Saavedra García, M. E. (2014). La PYME como generadora de empleo en México. *Revista Clío América*, 153-172.

Sachs, J. (2015). *The Age of Sustainable Development.* New York, NY: Columbia University Press; doi:10.7312/sach17314.

Sagay, I. (2008). *Nigeria: Federalism, the constitution and resource control.* Available: http://www.nigerdeltapeoplesworldcongress.org/articles/nigeria_federalism_.pdf

Şahin, Y., & Odabaşı, S. (2018). Sürdürülebilir kalkınmada moda tasarımcısının rolüne yönelik alanyazın incelemesi. *Uluslararası Yönetim İktisat ve İşletme Dergisi, 14*(2), 413–425. doi:10.17130/ijmeb.2018239940

Saionz-Ochoa, A. (2001). *Análisis de los factores explicativos de éxito empresarial* (PhD dissertation). Universidad la Rioja. Retrieved from: https://dialnet.unirioja.es › descarga › tesis

Saiz-Álvarez, J. M. (Ed.). (2019). Handbook of Research on Digital Marketing Innovations in Social Entrepreneurship and Solidarity Economics. Hershey, PA: Information Science Reference (IGI Global). doi:10.4018/978-1-5225-8939-6

Saklı, A. R. (2007). Kapitalist Gelişim Surecinde Fordizm ve Post - Fordizm. Retrieved at 15.11.2018 from http://2015.ses.org.tr/wp-content/uploads/fordizmpostfordizm.pdf

Sala-I-Martin, A., & Jay, K. (2010). Survival of private sector manufacturing establishments in Africa: The role of productivity and ownership. World Development, 37(3), 572-584.

Salami, A. (2011). Taxation, revenue allocation and fiscal federalism in Nigeria: Issues, challenges and policy options. *Economic Annals, 56*(189), 27-51.

Salazar Estrada, J. G., Guerrero Pupo, J. C., Machado Rodríguez, Y. B., & Cañedo Andalia, R. (2009). Clima y cultura organizacional: Dos componentes esenciales en la productividad laboral. *Acimed, 20*(4), 67–75.

Sambasivan, M., & Jacob, G. (2008). An Empirical Study on the Impact of Supply Chain Practices on Competitive Position of MNEs in Malaysia. *International Journal of Economics and Management, 2*(2), 369–394.

Sambyal, S. S. (2018). *Government Notifies New Solid Waste management Rules.* https://www.downtoearth.org.in

Samson, A. Y., Olubunmi, A. B., & Olusegun, A. A. (2013). Microfinance bank as a catalyst for entrepreneurship development in Nigeria: Evidence from Ogun State. *International Journal of Business and Social Science, 4*(12), 100–110.

Samuelson, P. A. (1952). Economic Theory and Mathematics – An Appraisal. *The American Economic Review, 2*(42), 56–66.

Samuelson, P. A. (1954). The Pure Theory of Public Expenditure. *The Review of Economics and Statistics, 36*(4), 387–389. doi:10.2307/1925895

Sánchez García, J. C. (2014). Cognitive Scripts and Entrepreneurial Success. *Universitas Psychologica, 13*(1), 1–20. Retrieved from: https://bdbiblioteca.universidadean.edu.co:2111/10.11144/Javeriana.UPSY13-1.cses

Santen, P. C. V. (2013). *Precautionary Saving, Wealth Accumulation, and Pensions: an empirical Macroeconomic perspective*. Groningen: University of Groningen. Retrieved from https://www.netspar.nl/assets/uploads/001_PhD_Peter_van_Santen.pdf

Sanusi, L. S. (2012). The role of development finance institution in Infrastructure development: What Nigeria can learn from BNDES and the Indian Infrastructure finance company. *3rd ICRC PPP Stakeholders Forum.*

Sapmaz Veral, E. (2018). Döngüsel ekonomiye geçiş doğrultusunda yeni trendler ve AB üye ülkelerinin stratejileri. Ankara Avrupa Çalışmaları Dergisi, 17(2), 463–488. doi:10.32450/aacd.511998

Sapmaz Veral, E. (2019, March). An evaluation on the circular economy model and the loops design in the context of waste management. Avrupa Bilim ve Teknoloji Dergisi, (15), 18 - 27. doi:10.31590/ejosat.479333

Sari, P. K. (2019). Wellesley College William R. Kerr, HBS and NBER Tina Xu, Wellesley College November 2017. Personality Traits of Entrepreneurs: A Review of Recent Literature. Accessed from: https://www.hbs.edu/faculty/Publication%20Files/KKX-Personality-Review_RIS_5ea5da25-c8ab-41d2-90ee-e30b3d5b071c.pdf

Sariatli, F. (2017). Linear Economy versus Circular Economy: A Comparative and Analyzer Study for Optimization of Economy for Sustainability. *Visegrad Journal on Bioeconomy and Sustainable Development*, 31-34. Retrieved November 12, 2019 from https://www.researchgate.net/publication/318183876_Linear_Economy_Versus_Circular_Economy_A_Comparative_and_Analyzer_Study_for_Optimization_of_Economy_for_Sustainability

Sarkis, J. (1999). *How green is the supply chain? Practice and research*. Graduate School of Management, Clark University.

Sarkis, J., Zhu, Q., & Lai, K. H. (2011). An organizational theoretic review of green supply chain management literature. *International Journal of Production Economics*, *130*(1), 1–15. doi:10.1016/j.ijpe.2010.11.010

Sarooghi, H., Sunny, S., Hornsby, J., & Fernhaber, S. (2019). Design thinking and entrepreneurship education: Where are we, and what are the possibilities? *Journal of Small Business Management*, *57*(S1), 78–93. doi:10.1111/jsbm.12541

Sarvadi, P. (2005). *The importance of employee development*. Available at: https://www.entrepreneur.com/article/77678

Sastry Musti, K. S. (2020). Industry 4.0-Based Enterprise Information System for Demand-Side Management and Energy Efficiency. In Novel Approaches to Information Systems Design. doi:10.4018/978-1-7998-2975-1.ch007

Sastry Musti. (2020). Management Information Systems for Higher Education Institutions - Challenges and opportunities. In Successful Implementation of Quality Management Principles in Higher Education. Doi:10.4018/978-1-5225-9829-9.ch006

Satyro, W. C. A., Sacomano, J. B. A., Contador, J. C. A., Cardoso, A. A., & Silva, E. P. (2017, May). Planned obsolescence and sustainability. Paper presented at the meeting of the 6th International Workshop Advances in Cleaner Production, Academic Work, São Paulo, Brazil.

Saunders, M., Lewis, P., & Thornhill, A. (2012). Research Methods for Business Students. Pearson Education Limited.

Saunders, M. N. K., Lewis, P., & Thornhill, A. (2012). *Research methods for business students* (6th ed.). Harlow, UK: Pearson Education Ltd.

Saunders, M. N., & Rojon, C. (2011). On the attributes of a critical literature review. *Coaching (Abingdon, UK), 4*(2), 156–162. doi:10.1080/17521882.2011.596485

Sauve, S., Bernard, S., & Sloan, P. (2015). Environmental sciences, sustainable development and circular economy: Alternative concepts for trans-disciplinary research. *Environmental Development, 17*, 48–56. doi:10.1016/j.envdev.2015.09.002

Savaskan, R. C., Bhattacharya, S., & Van Wassenhove, L. N. (2004). Closed-loop supply chain models with product remanufacturing. *Management Science, 50*(2), 239–252. doi:10.1287/mnsc.1030.0186

Sbicca, J. (2019). Urban Agriculture, Revalorization, and Green Gentrification in Denver, Colorado. *The Politics of Land*, 149-170. Doi:10.1108/S0895-993520190000026011

Schaeffer, V., & Matt, M. (2016). Development of academic entrepreneurship in a non-mature context: The role of the university as a hub-organization. *Entrepreneurship and Regional Development, 28*(9-10), 724–745. doi:10.1080/08985626.2016.1247915

Schaltegger, S., & Wagner, M. (2011). Sustainable entrepreneurship and sustainability innovation: categories and interactions. *Business Strategy and the Environment.* Retrieved October 19, 2019 from https://www.academia.edu/10906857/Sustainable_entrepreneurship_and_sustainability_innovation_categories_and_interactions

Schaltegger, S. (1997). Economics of life cycle assessment: Inefficiency of present approach. *Business Strategy and the Environment, 6*(1), 1–8. doi:10.1002/(SICI)1099-0836(199702)6:1<1::AID-BSE84>3.0.CO;2-D

Schaltegger, S. (2002). A Framework for Ecopreneurship. *Greener Management International, 2002*(38), 45–58. doi:10.9774/GLEAF.3062.2002.su.00006

Schaltegger, S. (2013). Sustainability management. In S. Idowu, N. Capaldi, L. Zu, & A. Das Gupta (Eds.), *Encyclopedia of corporate social responsibility* (pp. 2383–2388). Berlin: Springer; doi:10.1007/978-3-642-28036-8_741.

Schaltegger, S., Lüdeke-Freund, F., & Hansen, E. G. (2012). Business Cases for Sustainability: The Role of Business Model Innovation for Corporate Sustainability. *International Journal of Innovation and Sustainable Development, 6*(2), 6. doi:10.1504/IJISD.2012.046944

Schaltegger, S., & Wagner, M. (2011). Sustainable entrepreneurship and sustainability innovation: Categories and interactions. *Business Strategy and the Environment, 20*(4), 222–237. doi:10.1002/bse.682

Scheepens, A. E., Vogtlander, J. G., & Brezet, J. C. (2016). Two life cycle assessment (LCA) based methods to analyse and design complex (regional) circular economy systems. Case: Making water tourism more sustainable. *Journal of Cleaner Production, 114*, 257–268. doi:10.1016/j.jclepro.2015.05.075

Scheufele, D., & Moy, P. (2000). Twenty-five years of the spiral of silence: A conceptual review and empirical outlook. *International Journal of Public Opinion Research, 12*(1), 3–28. doi:10.1093/ijpor/12.1.3

Schlange, L. (2006). *What drives sustainable entrepreneurs?* Paper presented at the Applied Business and Entrepreneurship Association International Conference, St. Gallen, Switzerland.

Schmenner, R. W. (2009). Manufacturing, service, and their integration: Some history and theory. *International Journal of Operations & Production Management, 29*(5), 431–443. doi:10.1108/01443570910953577

Schneider, F., & Williams, C. C. (2013). The Shadow Economy. The Institute of Economic Affairs, IEA. doi:10.1017/CBO9781139542289

Scholtz, T. (2019). *Shift From Managing Risk and Security to Enabling Value Creation: The SRM Leaders' New Imperative.* Gartner.

Schon, D. (1993). *The reflective practitioner: How professionals think in action.* New York: Basic Books.

Schumpeter, J. (1934). *The Theory of Economic Development: An Enquiry into Profits, Capital, Credit, Interest, and the Business Cycle*. Cambridge: Harvard University Press.

Schumpeter, J. (1942). *Capitalism, Socialism, and Democracy*. New York, NY: Harper & Bros.

Schumpeter, J. (1947). The creative response to economic history. *The Journal of Economic History*, *7*(2), 149–159. doi:10.1017/S0022050700054279

Schumpeter, J. (1949). *Economic theory and entrepreneurial history: Change and the entrepreneur*. Cambridge, MA: Harvard University Press.

Schumpeter, J. A. (1934). *The Theory of Economic Development*. Cambridge, MA: Harvard University Press.

Schüritz, R. M., Seebacher, S., Satzger, G., & Schwarz, L. (2017). Datatization as the Next Frontier of Servitization - Understanding the Challenges for Transforming Organizations. *ICIS 2017 Proceedings*.

Schwab, K. (Ed.). (2019). *The Global Competitiveness Report*. Geneva: World Economic Forum WEF. Retrieved from http://www3.weforum.org/docs/WEF_TheGlobalCompetitivenessReport2019.pdf

Scientific Applications International Corporation (SAIC). (2006). *Life-cycle assessment: principles and practice*. Cincinnati: National Risk Management Research Laboratory, Office of Research and Development, US Environmental Protection Agency.

Scottish Enterprise. (2019). *Sustainable Business Models*. Retrieved October 21, 2019 from https://ecoknights.org.my/images/doc/Sustainable-Business-Models.pdf

Scuderi, R. (2012). *Ten Simple Ways to Cut Business Costs*. https://www.americanexpress.com

Secretaria Internacional de la Carta de la Tierra. (2019). *La Carta de la Tierra*. Obtenido de http://cartadelatierra.org/descubra/la-carta-de-la-tierra/

SEF. (2012). *Swedish Entrepreneurship Forum*. The Evolving Domain of Entrepreneurship Research. https://entreprenorskapsforum.se

Segal, G., Borgia, D., & Schoenfeld, J. (2005). The motivation to become an entrepreneur. *International Journal of Entrepreneurial Behaviour & Research*, *11*(1), 42–57. doi:10.1108/13552550510580834

Seiford, L. M., & Ors. (2001). *Modeling Undesirable Factors in Efficiency Evaluation*. http://www.deafrontier.net

Sekhampu, T. J. (2010). *An investigation into the economic sustainability of Kwakwatsi* (Unpublished PhD thesis). NWU.

Seligman, M. (1998). *Learned Optimism: How to Change your Mind and your Life*. Free Press.

Seligman, M. E. P., Abramson, L. Y., Semmel, A., & Baeyer, C. (1979). Depressive attributional style. *Journal of Abnormal Psychology*, *88*(3), 242–247. doi:10.1037/0021-843X.88.3.242 PubMed

Senge, P., & Carstedt, G. (2001). Innovating our way to the next industrial revolution. *MIT Sloan Management Review*, *42*(2), 24–38.

Serbia. (2019). *Report: Commission staff working document*. EC. Retrieved from: https://ec.europa.eu/neighbourhood-enlargement/sites/near/files/20190529-serbia-report.pdf

Serbian Pensioners' Union. (n.d.). Independence. *Retrieved from*.http://nezavisnost.org/sindikat-penzionera-srbije-nezavisnost-i-saveza-penzionera-srbije-potpisali-sporazum-o-saradnji/#

Serrano Torres, G., Quezada Flores, D. L., & Márquez De, A. C. (2016). Investigación sobre Empresas Familiares exitosas en el Mundo [Research about Family Business More Successful of the World]. *Przedsiębiorczość i Zarządzanie, 435*. Retrieved from http://bdbiblioteca.universidadean.edu.co:2054/login.aspx?direct=true&db=edsbaz&AN=edsbaz.171486055&lang=es&site=eds-live&scope=site

Shane, S., & Nicolaou, N. (2013). The genetics of entrepreneurial performance. *International Small Business Journal, 31*(5), 473–495. doi:10.1177/0266242613485767

Shane, S., & Venkataraman, S. (2000). The promise of entrepreneurship as a field of research. *Academy of Management Review, 25*(1), 217–226. doi:10.5465/amr.2000.2791611

Shao, J. (2019). Sustainable consumption in China: New trends and research interests. *Business Strategy and the Environment, 28*(8), 1507–1517. doi:10.1002/bse.2327

Shao, J. (2019). Sustainable consumption in China: New trends and research. *Business Strategy and the Environment, 28*(8), 1–11. doi:10.1002/bse.2327

Shapero, A. (1982). *Social Dimensions of Entrepreneurship*. Englewood Cliffs, NJ: Prentice-Hall.

Sharma, D. D., & Dhameja, S. K. (2002). *Indian Entrepreneurship; Theory and Practice*. Abhishek Publications.

Sharma, M. M. (2013). A Study on the Concept of Green Supply Chain Management. *Journal of Supply Chain Management Systems, 2*(1), 1–7.

Sharot, T. (2011). The optimism bias. *Current Biology, 21*(23), R941–R945. doi:10.1016/j.cub.2011.10.030 PubMed

Shar, S. K., & Tripsas, M. (2007). The accidental entrepreneur: The emergent and collective process of user entrepreneurship. *Strategic Entrepreneurship Journal, 1*(12), 123–140.

Shepherd, D. A., & Patzelt, H. (2011). The New Field of Sustainable Entrepreneurship: Studying Entrepreneurial Action Linking "What Is to Be Sustained" With "What Is to Be Developed". *Entrepreneurship Theory and Practice, 35*(1), 137–163. doi:10.1111/j.1540-6520.2010.00426.x

Sherburne, A. (2009). Achieving sustainable textiles: a designer's perspective. Sustainable Textiles, 3–32. doi:10.1533/9781845696948.1.3

Sherer, P. D., & Lee, K. (2002). Institutional Change in Large Law Firms: A Resource Dependency and Institutional Perspective. *Academy of Management Journal, 45*(1), 102–119.

Shi, C., & Zhang, G. (2013). The ecological construction of scenic spots. *BioTechnology: An Indian Journal, 8*(9), 1306–1310.

Shih, D. H. (2018). *A Strategic Knowledge Management Approach to Circular Agribusiness*. https://www.mdpi.com

Shih, D. H., Lu, C. M., Lee, C. H., Parng, Y. J., Wu, K. J., & Tseng, M. L. (2018). A Strategic Knowledge Management Approach to Circular Agribusiness. *Sustainability, 10*(7), 2389. doi:10.3390u10072389

Shimova, O. (2019). Belarus on the Way to Sustainable Development: Circular Economy and Green Technologies. In Modeling Economic Growth in Contemporary Belarus (Entrepreneurship and Global Economic Growth) (pp. 89-106). Emerald. Doi:10.1108/978-1-83867-695-720191007

Short, S. W., Bocken, N. M. P., Barlow, C. Y., & Chertow, M. R. (2014). From Refining Sugar to Growing Tomatoes. Industrial Ecology and Business Model Evolution. *Journal of Industrial Ecology, 18*(5), 603–618. doi:10.1111/jiec.12171

Shurrab, J., Hussain, M., & Khan, M. (2019). Green and sustainable practices in the construction industry: A confirmatory factor analysis approach. *Engineering, Construction, and Architectural Management*, *26*(6), 1063–1086. doi:10.1108/ECAM-02-2018-0056

SID. (2011). *Devolution in Kenya's New Constitution*. Available at ww.sidnt.org

Sienou, A., Lamine, E., & Pingaud, H. (2008). A Method for Integrated Management of Process-risk. Université de Toulouse-Mines d'Albi, Centre de Génie Industriel Campus Jarlard Route de Teillet.

Sihvonen, S., & Ritola, T. (2015). Conceptualizing ReX for aggregating end-of-life strategies in product development. *Procedia CIRP*, *29*, 639–644. doi:10.1016/j.procir.2015.01.026

Silvia, P., Nusbaum, E., Christopher, M., & O'Connor, A. (2009). Openness to experience, plasticity, and creativity: Exploring lower-order, high-order, and interactive effects. *Journal of Research in Personality*, *43*(6), 1087–1090. doi:10.1016/j.jrp.2009.04.015

Simpeh, K. N. (2011). Entrepreneurship theories and Empirical research: A Summary Review of the Literature. *European Journal of Business and Management*, *3*(6), 1–8.

Sindzingre, A. N. (2011). *The conditions for long-term growth in sub-Saharan Africa: China as a model, a constraint and an opportunity*. Cahiers du Centre Working Papers No. 9.

Singer, L., & Millage, P. (2013). The interaction of leadership and personality among Chinese and American nascent entrepreneurs. *Journal of Technology Management in China*, *8*(1), 44–54.

Singh, K., Kelly, S., & Sastry, K. S. (2009, October). Musti (2009), Municipal Solid Waste to Energy: Potential for Application in Trinidad and Tobago. *The Journal of the Association of Professional Engineers of Trinidad and Tobago*, *38*(1), 42–49.

SITRA. (2018). *Circular Economy for Sustainable Development*. Reports of the Finnish Environment Institute, 26/2018.

Sivam, A., Dieguez, T., Ferreira, L. P., & Silva, F. J. G. (2019). Key settings for successful Open Innovation Arena. *Journal of Computational Design and Engineering*, *6*(4), 507–515. doi:10.1016/j.jcde.2019.03.005

Skandalakis, A. A. (2001). Benchmarking as a diagnostic process to increase the competitiveness of Small and medium-sized Manufacturing Enterprises. *International Journal of Business Performance Management, 3*(2-4), 261-275.

Skrob, R. (2009). *Beneðt of infopreneurship*. Retrieved December12, 2018, from www.info-marketing.org

Skrzek-Lubasińska, M., & Szaban, J. (2018). Self-Employment and Entrepreneurship: A Theoretical Approach. *Journal of Management and Business Administration. Central Europe*, *26*(2), 89–120. https://content.sciendo.com/view/journals/jmbace/26/2/article-p89.xml

Slack, N. (2005). Operations strategy: Will it ever realize its potential? *Gestão & Produção*, *12*(3), 323–332. doi:10.1590/S0104-530X2005000300004

Slade, G. (2006). *Make to break technology and obsolescence in America*. Harvard University Press.

Small Business Development Corporation. (2019). *Essential business skills*. Retrieved 12 September, 2019 from https://www.smallbusiness.wa.gov.au/business-advice/starting-your-business/business-skills

Small Enterprise Development Agency (SEDA). (2007). Available at: www.seda.co.za

Smeels, E., & Stevels, A. (2003). Influencing product lifetime through productdesign. Proceedings Of Ecodesign 2003.

Smith, I. H., & Woodworth, W. P. (2012). Developing Social Entrepreneurs and Social Innovators: A Social Identity and Self-Efficacy Approach. *Academy of Management Learning & Education, 11*(3), 390–407. doi:10.5465/amle.2011.0016

Smit, Y., & Watkins, J. A. (2012). A Literature Review of Small and Medium Enterprises (SME) Risk Management Practices in South Africa. *African Journal of Business Management, 6*(21), 6324–6330.

Smol, M., Avdiushchenko, A., Kulczycka, J., & Nowaczek, A. (2018). Public awareness of circular economy in Poland: Case of the Malopolska region. *Journal of Cleaner Production, 197*, 1035–1045. doi:10.1016/j.jclepro.2018.06.100

Solà, J., Farreny, R., & Cormenzana, M. (2017). *La ecoinnovación como clave para el éxito empresarial Tendencias, beneficios y primeros pasos para ecoinnovar*. Editorial Libros de Cabecera.

Solarimpulse. (2019). Circular Economy – How to shape a sustainable future. https://solarimpulse.com/circular-economy-solutions

Solczak, R. (2013). Planned obsolescence: A question of consumerism and production of waste. Centria University of Applied Aciences, Ylivieska Unit, Degree Programme.

Solomon, G. (2007). An examination of entrepreneurship education in the United States. *Journal of Small Business and Enterprise Development, 14*(2), 168–182. doi:10.1108/14626000710746637

Song, X. (2013). Analysis of Green Hotel Marketing Management under the Background of Circular Economy. Advances in Energy Science and Technology, 291-294, 1478-1481. doi:10.4028/www.scientific.net/AMM.291-294.1478

Soosay, C., Hyland, P., & Ferrer, M. (2008). Supply chain collaboration: Capabilities for continuous innovation. *Supply Chain Management, 13*(2), 160–169. doi:10.1108/13598540810860994

Soto, C. J. (2018). Big Five personality traits. In M. H. Bornstein, M. E. Arterberry, K. L. Fingerman, & J. E. Lansford (Eds.), *The SAGE encyclopedia of lifespan human development* (pp. 240–241). Thousand Oaks, CA: Sage; Available from https://www.researchgate.net/publication/324115204_Big_Five_personality_traits

Sousa, J. M. (2018). Entrepreneurship Skills Development in Higher Education Courses for Teams Leaders. *Administrative Sciences, 8*(18), 18. doi:10.3390/admsci8020018

Souza, M. T. D., Silva, M. D. D., & Carvalho, R. D. (2010). Integrative review: What is it? How to do it? *Einstein (Sao Paulo, Brazil), 8*(1), 102–106. doi:10.15901679-45082010rw1134 PMID:26761761

Spender, J. C. (2015). Knowledge management: Origins, history, and development. In *Advances in Knowledge Management* (pp. 3–23). Cham: Springer.

Spigel, B. (2017a). The relational organization of entrepreneurial ecosystems. *Entrepreneurship Theory and Practice, 41*(1), 49–7. doi:10.1111/etap.12167

Spring, M., & Araujo, L. (2017). Product biographies in Servitization and the circular economy. *Industrial Marketing Management, 60*, 126–137. doi:10.1016/j.indmarman.2016.07.001

Srivastav, P., & Goldstein, N. (2019). Circular Economy: Shaping the Next Wave of Smart Communities. Available online, https://guidehouse.com/-/media/www/site/insights/energy/2019/puf-smart-communities/puf-smart-communities-circular-economy.pdf

Staedtler, L. (2016). Scrutinizing public-private partnerships for development: Towards a broad evaluation conception. *Journal of Business Ethics, 135*(1), 71–86. doi:10.100710551-015-2730-1

Stahel, W. R. (1998). From Products to Services. Selling Performance Instead of Goods. Geneva: Institute for Prospective Technological Studies (ITPS).

Stahel, W. R. (2016, March 23). The circular economy. Retrieved at 26.10.2019, from https://www.nature.com/news/the-circular-economy-1.19594#b2

Stahel, W. (1981). The Product Life Factor. In S. Grinton (Ed.), *An Inquiry into the Nature of Sustainable Societies: The Role of the Private Sector* (pp. 72–96). Houston: HARC.

Stahel, W. (1994). The utilization focused service economy: Resource efficiency. In B. R. Allenby & D. J. Richards (Eds.), *The Greening of Industrial Ecosystems* (pp. 178–190). Washington: National Academy Press.

Stahel, W. (2014). The Business Angle of a Circular Economy: Higher Competitiveness, Higher Resource Security and Material Efficiency. In *A New Dynamic: Effective Business in a Circular Economy*. Isle of Wight, UK: Ellen MacArthur Foundation.

Stahel, W. R. (2016). Circular Economy. *Nature*, *531*(7595), 6–9. doi:10.1038/531435a PMID:27008952

Stam, E., & Spiegel, B. (2016). *Entrepreneurial Ecosystems*. Utrecht School of Economic, Tjalling C. Koopmans Research Institute, Discussion paper Series 13-16, Utrecht, The Netherlands.

Stam, E. (2015). Entrepreneurial ecosystems and regional policy: A sympathetic critique. *European Planning Studies*, *23*(9), 1759–1769. doi:10.1080/09654313.2015.1061484

Stan, G. (2018). *10 Types of Knowledge Management Strategies*. https://medium.com

Standing Committee for Economic and Commercial Cooperation of the Organization of the Islamic Cooperation (COMCEC). (2016). *Training Manual on Entrepreneurship and Management of Small Business for Women*. Retrieved October 30, 2019 from http://www.comcec.org/pcm/wp-content/uploads/2018/02/2016-GMBPOVER-206.pdf

Standing Committee of the National People's Congress. (2009). China Circular Economy Promotion Law of the People's Republic of China.

Staniewski, M. W., & Szopiński, T. (2015) Student readiness to start their own business. *Economic Research-Ekonomska Istraživanja*, *28*(1), 608-619. Retrieved October 25, 2019 from https://www.tandfonline.com/doi/abs/10.1080/1331677X.2015.1085809?needAccess=true#aHR0cHM6Ly93d3cudGFuZGZvbmxpbmUuY29tL2RvaS9wZGYvMTAuMTA4MC8xMzMxNjc3WC4yMDE1LjEwODU4MDk/bmVlZEFjY2Vzcz10cnVlQEBAMA

Statistics South Africa. (2015). *Quarter 2. Quarterly Labour Force Survey, Pretoria*. Available at: Http://Www.Statssa.Gov.Za/Default.Asp

Steers, R. M., Mowday, R. T., & Shapiro, D. L. (2004). The future of work motivation theory. *Academy of Management Review*, *29*(3), 379–387.

Stefanovic, I., Prokic, S., & Rankovic, L. (2010). *Motivational and success factors for entrepreneurs: the evidence from a developing country*. Academic Press.

Steffen, W., Richardson, K., & Rockström, J., & Cornell. (2015). Planetary boundaries: Guiding human development on a changing planet. *Science*, *347*(6223). doi:10.1126cience.1259855

StEP Initiative. (2014). *Solving the E-Waste Problem (StEP)*. White Paper.

Stevens, C. (2010). Are Women the Key to Sustainable Development? https://www.bu.edu/pardee/files/2010/04/UNsdkp003fsingle.pdf

Stewart, S. C. (2011). Interpreting design thinking. *Design Studies*, *32*(6), 515–520. doi:10.1016/j.destud.2011.08.001

Stiglitz & J.Y. Lin. (2010). *The Industrial Policy Revolution I: The Role of Government beyond Ideology*. London: Palgrave Macmillan.

Stokes, D., & Wilson, N. (2006). *Small business management and entrepreneurship*. London: Thomson Learning.

Stoneburner, G., Goguen, A. Y., & Feringa, A. (2002). *Risk management guide for information technology systems*. National Institute of Standards and Technology.

Storen, L. A. (2014). Entrepreneurship in higher education: Impacts on graduates entrepreneurial intentions, activity and learning outcome. *Education + Training*, *56*(8/9), 795–813. doi:10.1108/ET-06-2014-0070

Storey, D. (1994). *Understanding the small business sector*. London, UK: Routledge.

Stovang, P., & Nielsen, S. L. (2015). DesUni: University entrepreneurship education through design thinking. *Education + Training*, *57*(8/9), 977–991. doi:10.1108/ET-09-2014-0121

Stuart, T. (2000). Interorganizational Alliances and The Performance of Firms: A Study of Growth and Innovation Rates in a High-Technology Industry. *Strategic Management Journal*, *21*(8), 791–811. doi:10.1002/1097-0266(200008)21:8<791::AID-SMJ121>3.0.CO;2-K

Stulz, R. M. (1996). Rethinking risk management. *Journal of Applied Corporate Finance*, *9*(3), 8–25. doi:10.1111/j.1745-6622.1996.tb00295.x

Su, B., Heshmati, A., Geng, Y., & Yu, X. (2013). A review of the circular economy in China: Moving from rhetoric to implementation. *Journal of Cleaner Production*, *42*, 215–227. doi:10.1016/j.jclepro.2012.11.020

Suğur, N. (2015). Endüstri Sosyolojisi. In V. Bozkurt & N. Suğur (Eds.), *Yeni Yönetim Metotları* (pp. 36–66). Eskişehir: Anadolu Üniversitesi Yayınları.

Suresh, J., & Ramraj, R. (2012). Entrepreneurial ecosystem: Case study on the influence of environmental factors on entrepreneurial success. *European Journal of Business and Management*, *4*(16), 1–2.

Szaky, T. (2019). Processes and Ethical Challenges. *Journal of Business Venturing, 24*(5). https://www.huffpost.com

Szłapka, J. O., Stachowiak, A., Batz, A., & Fertsch, P. M. (2017). The Level of Innovation in SMEs, the Determinants of Innovation and their Contribution to Development of Value Chains. *Procedia Manufacturing*, *11*, 2203–2210. doi:10.1016/j.promfg.2017.07.367

Takacs, F., Frankenberger, K., & Stechow, R. (2020). *Circular Ecosystems: Business Model Innovation for the Circular Economy*. Institute of Management & Strategy, University of St. Gallen.

Tambunan, T. (2007). Transfer of Technology to and Technology Diffusion among Non-farm Small and Medium Enterprises in Indonesia. *Knowledge, Technology & Policy*, *20*(4), 243–258. doi:10.100712130-007-9031-7

Tang, O., & Musa, S. N. (2011). Identifying risk issues and research advancements in supply chain risk management. *International Journal of Production Economics*, *133*(1), 25–34. doi:10.1016/j.ijpe.2010.06.013

Tangüler, M., Gürsel, P., & Meral, Ç. (2015). Türkiye'de uçucu küllü betonlar için yaşam döngüsü analizi. Paper presented at the meeting of the 9. Ulusal Beton Kongresi, Antalya: TMMOB İnşaat Mühendisleri Odası.

Tan, J. (2011). Conceptualising entrepreneurship, innovation and late industrialisation: The state creation of entrepreneurs in Malaysia. *International Journal of Management Concepts and Philosophy*, *5*(2), 138–158. doi:10.1504/IJMCP.2011.041519

Tan, K. C., Lyman, S. B., & Wisner, J. D. (2002). Supply chain management: A strategic perspective. *International Journal of Operations & Production Management*, *22*(6), 614–631. doi:10.1108/01443570210427659

Tarik, B. (2006). Dynamics of 'technological creativity' as a decision in knowledge creation process. *Proceedings of the PICMET'06 Conference: Technology Management for the Global Future.*

Taweesak, R., King M., Thabhatr, A. & King M. (2019). Factors Affecting the Management Success, of Small and Medium Enterprises in the Electrical and Electronic Industry in Thailand. *Academy of Strategic Management Journal*, *18*(2).

Tayebi-Khorami, M., Edraki, M., Corder, G., & Golev, A. (2019). Re-Thinking Mining Waste through an Integrative Approach Led by Circular Economy Aspirations. *Minerals (Basel)*, *9*(5), 286–298. doi:10.3390/min9050286

Taylor, S.J. (2016). *A Review of Sustainable Development Principles.* Academic Press.

Taylor, P. R. (1974). *The Kroll Institute for Extractive Metallurgy.* Golden, CO: KIEM.

Technopolis Group. (2016). *Regulatory Barriers for the Circular Economy.* https://www.technopolis-group.com

Temu, A. E. (1999). The Kilimanjaro Cooperative Bank: A potentially sustainable rural financial institutional model for sub-Saharan Africa, *African Review of Money, Finance and Banking. Supplement for the Savings and Development Journal*, *1*(2), 45–77.

Ten Brink, P., Kettunen, M., & Watkins, E. (2017). *Expert Group on Green and Circular Economy in the Outermost Regions: Final Report. For DG Regional and Urban Policy, European Commission.* Retrieved on 28th July 2019 from https://ec.europa.eu/regional_policy/sources/policy/themes/outermost-regions/pdf/green_circ_econ_report_en.pdf

Terracciano, A., McCrae, R. R., & Costa, P. (2008). Personality traits: Stability and change with age. *Geriatrics & Aging*, *11*, 474–478.

Terrell, S. R. (2012). Mixed-Methods Research Methodologies. *Qualitative Report*, *17*(1), 254–280. http://www.nova.edu/ssss/QR/QR17-1/terrell.pdf

The Aging Report. (2018). *Underlying Assumptions & Projection methodologies.* European Economy. Institutional Paper, 065, November 2017. European Commission.

The Horinko Group. (2016). *The future of RCRA — making the business case.* Washington, DC: The Horinko Group.

The International Bank for Reconstruction and Development, The World Bank. (1994). Averting the Old Age Crisis: policies to protect the old and promote growth. A World Bank Policy Research Report. New York: Oxford University Press.

The International Water Association. (2018). Wastewater Report 2018. The Water Reuse Opportunity. Retrieved from https://www.iwa-network.org/wp-content/uploads/2018/02/OFID-Wastewater-report-2018.pdf

The South African Reserve Bank. (2015). *The role of small business in the economy.* Author.

The Standard Media. (2016). *Devolution Still Facing Challenges.* Available at www.standardmedia.co.ke

The Standard Media. (2017). *County funds are held up at the Treasury.* Available at www.standardmedia.co.ke/business/article

The Standard Media. (2017). *How grand corruption in the counties undermines devolution.* Available at www.standardmedia.co.ke

The World Bank. (2017). Trends in Solid Waste Management. Retrieved at 07.10.2019, from http://datatopics.worldbank.org/what-a-waste/trends_in_solid_waste_management.html

Thieme, T. A. (2010). Youth, waste and work in Mathare: Whose business and whose politics? *Environment and Urbanization, 22*(2), 333–352. doi:10.1177/0956247810379946

Thieme, T. A. (2013). The "hustle" amongst youth entrepreneurs in Mathare's informal waste economy. *Journal of Eastern African Studies: the Journal of the British Institute in Eastern Africa, 7*(3), 389–412. doi:10.1080/17531055.2013.770678

Thierry, M., Salomon, M., Van Nunen, J., & Van Wassenhove, L. (1995). Strategic issues in product recovery management. *California Management Review, 37*(2), 114–136. doi:10.2307/41165792

Thompson, J. D., & MacMillan, I. C. (2010). Business Models: Creating New Markets and Societal Wealth. *Long Range Planning, 43*(2-3), 291–307. doi:10.1016/j.lrp.2009.11.002

Thong, J. (1999). An integrated model of information systems in small business. *Journal of Management Information Systems, 15*(4), 187–214. doi:10.1080/07421222.1999.11518227

Thornton, A. (2019). *These 11 companies are leading the way to a circular economy.* Retrieved from https://www.weforum.org/agenda/2019/02/companies-leading-way-to-circular-economy/

Tibbs, H. (2006). The Value Loop – A New Framework for Business Thinking. In *The International Handbook on Environmental Technology Management.* Cheltenham, UK: Edward Elgar.

Tiger, L. (1979). *Optimism: The biology of hope.* New York: Simon and Schuster.

Timberland. (2020). *Responsibility.* Retrieved from Materials Policy Staments-Recycling EOL: https://www.timberland.com/responsibility/product/materials-policy-statements/recycling-eol.html

Tim, J. (1993). *Clean Production Strategies Developing Preventive Environmental Management in the Industrial Economy.* CRC Press.

Timmons, J. A., & Spinelli, S. (2004). *New venture creation: Entrepreneurship for the 21st century.* Boston, MA: McGraw Hill Irwin.

Timmons, J., & Spinelli, S. (2009). *New Venture Creation: Entrepreneurship for the 21st Century* (8th ed.). McGraw-Hill.

Tjivikua, T. (2002). *Welcome message from the Rector of the Polytechnic of Namibia: The role of academic institutions in entrepreneurship.* Academic Press.

Tonelli, M., & Cristoni, N. (2018). Strategic Management and the Circular Economy. Project: Strategic Management and the Circular Economy, 90–113. doi:10.4324/9781315102641

Topoyan, M. (2005). Yeniden üretim sistemleri için sürdürülebilir ürün tasarımlarının oluşturulması. Paper presented at the meeting of the V. Ulusal Üretim Araştırmaları Sempozyumu, İstanbul Ticaret Üniversitesi, İstanbul.

Torrance, E. P. (1969). *Creativity.* Sioux Falls: Adapt Press.

Tóth, G. (2019). Circular Economy and its Comparison with 14 Other Business Sustainability Movements. *Resources, 8*, 159. doi:10.3390/resources8040159

Tovar Rojas, C. C., Perez-Uribe, R., & Ocampo-Guzmán, D. (2015). *MIIGO (Modelo de intervención e innovación de la gestión organizacional): Gestión de la producción de bienes y servicios (PBPS).* Universidad EAN. http://edicionesean.ean.edu.co/index.php/es/productos-de-investigacion1/colecciones/colecciones-digitales/miigo/44-miigo/443-miigo-gestion-de-produccion-de-bienes-y-prestacion-de-servicios-pbps

Toyin, A. I. (2012). Supply Chain Management (SCM) Practices in Nigeria Today: Impact on SCM Performance. *European Journal of Business and Social Sciences, 1*(6), 107–115.

Toyne, P. (2019). *How can the circular economy make infrastructure more sustainable?* https://www.eco-business.com

Tran, H. P., Schaubroeck, T., Swart, P., Six, L., Coonen, P., & Dewulf, J. (2018). Recycling portable alkaline/ZnC batteries for a circular economy: An assessment of natural resource consumption from a life cycle and criticality perspective. *Resources, Conservation and Recycling*, *135*, 265–278. doi:10.1016/j.resconrec.2017.08.018

Trianni, A., & Cagno, E. (2012). Dealing with barriers to energy efficiency and SMEs: Some empirical evidences. *Energy*, *37*(1), 494–504. doi:10.1016/j.energy.2011.11.005

Trim, P. R., & Lee, Y.-I. (2008). *A Strategic Approach to sustainable partnership development*. Academic Press.

Tripathi, S. N., & Siddiqui, M. H. (2012). Marketing of SME Products: A 'Relationship' Approach. *ASCI Journal of Management*, *41*(2), 76–106.

Tsalis, T. A., Nikolaou, I. E., Grigoroudis, E., & Tsagarakis, K. P. (2013). A framework development to evaluate the needs of SMEs in order to adopt a sustainability-balanced scorecard. *Journal of Integrative Environmental Sciences*, *10*(3-4), 179–197. doi:10.1080/1943815X.2013.858751

Tseng, M. L. (2010). Using linguistic preferences and grey relational analysis to evaluate the environmental knowledge management capacity. *Expert Systems with Applications*, *37*(1), 70–81. doi:10.1016/j.eswa.2009.05.020

Tseng, M. L., Tan, R. R., Chiu, A. S. F., Chien, C. F., & Kuo, T. C. (2018). Circular economy meets industry 4.0: Can big data drive industrial symbiosis? *Resources, Conservation and Recycling*, *131*, 146–147. doi:10.1016/j.resconrec.2017.12.028

Tseng, M.-L., Chiu, A. S. F., Liu, G., & Jantaralolica, T. (2020). The circular economy enables sustainable consumption and production in the multi-level supply chain system. *Resources, Conservation and Recycling*, *154*, 104601. doi:10.1016/j.resconrec.2019.104601

Tseng, M.-L., Tan, R., Chiu, A., Chien, C.-F., & Kuo, T. (2018). Circular economy meets industry 4.0: Can big data drive industrial symbiosis. *Resources, Conservation and Recycling*, *131*, 146–147. doi:10.1016/j.resconrec.2017.12.028

Tukker, A. (2015). Product services for a resource-efficient and circular economy – A review. *Journal of Cleaner Production*, *97*, 76–91. doi:10.1016/j.jclepro.2013.11.049

Tukker, A., & Tischner, U. (2006). Product-Services as a Research Field: Past, Present and Future Reflections from a Decade of Research. *Journal of Cleaner Production*, *14*(17), 1552–1556. doi:10.1016/j.jclepro.2006.01.022

Tulder, R., & Rosa, A. (2011). *Inclusive business through partnerships, Special Contribution to Fourth High Level Forum on Aid Effectiveness*. The Partnerships Resource Centre.

Tuppen, J. (1988). Restructuring the Economy. In France under Recession, 1981–86 (pp. 90-162). Palgrave Macmillan UK. doi:10.1007/978-1-349-08274-2_3

Tura, N., Hanski, J., Ahola, T., Stahle, M., Piiparinen, S., & Valkokari, P. (2019). Unlocking circular business: A framework of barriers and drivers. *Journal of Cleaner Production*, *212*, 90–98. doi:10.1016/j.jclepro.2018.11.202

Türk Standardları Enstitüsü. (2018). *Döngüsel ekonomi*. Ankara: TSE Basın Yayın Müdürlüğü.

Tuten, L., & Neidermeyer, P. E. (2004). Performance, satisfaction and turnover in call centers: The effects of stress and optimism. *Journal of Business Research*, *57*(1), 26–34. doi:10.1016/S0148-2963(02)00281-3

UANL. (2013). *El desarrollo sustentable en México*. Obtenido de Sustentabilidad: http://sds.uanl.mx/el-desarrollo-sustentable-en-mexico-3/

Umweltbundesamt. (2020). *Topics*. Retrieved from Economics-Consumption: https://www.umweltbundesamt.de/en/topics/economics-consumption

Ünal, E., Urbinati, A., & Chiaroni, D. (2018). Managerial practices for designing circular economy business models. *Journal of Manufacturing Technology Management*. doi:10.1108/JMTM-02-2018-0061

UNAM. (2015). *Ecología UNAM*. Obtenido de Fundación UNAM: http://www.fundacionunam.org.mx/ecologia/sostenibilidad-vs-sustentabilidad/

Unay-Gailhard, I., & Bojnec, S. (2019). The impact of green economy measures on rural employment: Green jobs in farms. *Journal of Cleaner Production*, *208*, 541–551. doi:10.1016/j.jclepro.2018.10.160

UNCTAD. (2018). *Achieving the Sustainable Development Goals in the Least Developed Countries — A Compendium of Policy Options*. New York: United Nations.

UNCTAD. (2018). *Policy Brief, 61*. Author.

UNCTAD. (2018). *World Investment Report*. https://unctad.org

UNDP. (2007). *UNDP Private Sector Strategy, Promoting Inclusive Market Development*. Washington, DC: United Nations.

UNEP. (2013). *Environmental Risks and Challenges of Anthropogenic Metals Flows and Cycles*. A Report of the Working Group on the Global Metal Flows to the International Resource Panel.

UNEP-UNIDO. (1992). *Resource Efficient and Cleaner Production (RECP)*. Available online: https://www.unido.org/our-focus/safeguarding-environment/resource-efficient-and-low-carbonindustrial-production/resource-efficient-and-cleaner-production-recp

UNIDO. (2019). *Circular Economy*. https://www.unido.org

United Nations (UN). (2012). *Statistical Division & London Group on Environmental Accounting. Subgroup on Water Accounting. SEEA-Water System of Environmental-Economic Accounting for Water*. London: United Nations.

United Nations (UN). (2016, March 2). United Nations Environment Program. Retrieved December 16, 2019, from https://www.unenvironment.org/news-and-stories/press-release/half-world-face-severe-water-stress-2030-unless-water-use-decoupled

United Nations Conference on Trade and Development. (2014). *Entrepreneurship for development, Report of the Secretary*. Washington, DC: United Nation General Assembly.

United Nations Development Programme (UNDP). (2008). *Creating Value for All: Strategies for doing Business with the Poor*. New York: UNDP.

United Nations Environment Programme (UNEP). (2015). *Sustainable Consumption and Production Global edition*. UNEP.

United Nations Environment Programme. (2017). *The role of Circular Economy in the transition "Towards a Pollution-Free Planet"*. Retrieved 2 December, 2019 from web.unep.org/environmentassembly/role-circular-economy-transition-towards-pollution-free-planet-1

United Nations. (1992). The Dublin Statement on Water and Sustainable Development. UN Documents Gathering a body of global agreements.

United Nations. (2017). *World Population Prospects: The 2017 Revision, Key Findings and Advance Tables*. Working Paper No. ESA/P/WP/248. Department of Economic and Social Affairs - Population Division.

United States of America Energy Information Administration. (2016). *International Energy Outlook*. Washington, DC: Author.

Urquiola, O., Zulueta, O. R., & Llano, R. (2017). La innovación para el desarrollo sostenible. Una experiencia en Cienfuegos, Cuba. *Universidad y Sociedad*, *9*(1). Retrieved from: http://scielo.sld.cu/scielo.php?script=sci_arttext&pid=S2218-36202017000100015

US Senate. (1970). Federal Low-Emission Vehicle Procurement Act: Joint Hearings Before the Subcommittee on Energy, Natural Resources, and the Environment. *Proceedings of the Ninety-first Congress*.

Val, E., Gonzalez, I., Iriarte, I., Beitia, A., Lasa, G., & Elkoro, M. (2017). A design thinking approach to introduce entrepreneurship education in European school curricula. *The Design Journal, 20*(sup1), S754–S766.

Valant, J. (2006). Planned obsolescence: Exploring the issue. EPRS | European Parliamentary Research Service, PE 581.999.

Valdes-Prieto, S. (2006). A Market Method to Endow NDC Systems with Automatic Financial Stability. In R. Holzmann & E. Palmer (Eds.), *Pension Reform: Issues and prospects for Non-Financial Defined Contribution (NDC) Schemes* (pp. 149–150). Washington, DC: The World Bank.

Valko, D. V. (2018). Tsyrkuliarnaya ekonomika: teoreticheskaya model i effekty realizatsii [Circular economy: A theoretical model and implementation effects]. Natsionalnye interesy: prioritety ibezopasnost – National Interests. *Priorities and Security*, *14*(8), 1415–1429. doi:10.24891/ni.14.8.1415

Van Aardt, I., Van Aardt, C., Bezuidenhout, S & Mumba, M. (2008). *Entrepreneurship and New Venture Management* (3rd ed.). Oxford University Press.

Van de Ven, A. H. (1993). The development of an infrastructure for entrepreneurship. *Journal of Business Venturing*, *8*(3), 211–230. doi:10.1016/0883-9026(93)90028-4

Van der Wiel, A., Bossink, B., & Masurel, E. (2012). Reverse logistics for waste reduction in cradle-to-cradle oriented firms: Waste management strategies in the Dutch metal industry. *International Journal of Technology Management*, *60*(1/2), 96–113. doi:10.1504/IJTM.2012.049108

Van Rooyen, C., Stewart, R., & De Wet, T. (2012). The impact of microfinance in sub Saharan Africa: A systematic review of the evidence. *World Development*, *40*(11), 2249–2262. doi:10.1016/j.worlddev.2012.03.012

van Scheers, L., & Makhitha, K. M. (2016). Are Small and Medium Enterprises (SMEs) Planning for Strategic Marketing in South Africa? *Foundations of Management*, *8*(1), 243–250. doi:10.1515/fman-2016-0019

Vandermerwe, S., & Rada, J. (1988). Servitization of business: Adding value by adding services. *European Management Journal*, *6*(4), 314–324. doi:10.1016/0263-2373(88)90033-3

Vanegas, P., Peeters, J. R., Cattrysse, D., Tecchio, P., Ardente, F., Mathieux, F., ... Duflou, J. R. (2018). Ease of disassembly of products to support circular economy strategies. *Resources, Conservation and Recycling*, *2018*(135), 323–334. doi:10.1016/j.resconrec.2017.06.022 PMID:30078953

Vargas-Sánchez, A. (2018). The unavoidable disruption of the circular economy in tourism. *Worldwide Hospitality and Tourism Themes*, *10*(6), 652–661. doi:10.1108/WHATT-08-2018-0056

Vargha, R. a. (2001). *Internet Issues for Small ansd Medium-sized Australian Business. Australian and New Zealand Marketing Academy (ANZMAC) conference. Auckland: Massey University.*

Varma, R., Dahiya, R.P., & Susil, K. N. (2016). Circular Economy as Strategy for Sustainable Development in Electricity Sector in India. Global Journal of Business Excellence, 3-9(1), 23-36.

Vaughan, S. C. (2000). *Half Empty, Half Full: Understanding the Psychological Roots of Optimism.* New York: Harcourt.

Vecchio, V., Caselli, S., & Corbetta, G. (2015). *Public-Private Partnerships for Infrastructure and Business Development: Principles, Practices, and Perspectives.* Palgrave Macmillan.

Velázquez Martínez, O., Van Den Boogaart, K. G., Lundström, M., Santasalo-Aarnio, A., Reuter, M., & Serna-Guerrero, R. (2019). Statistical entropy analysis as tool for circular economy: Proof of concept by optimizing a lithium-ion battery waste sieving system. *Journal of Cleaner Production, 212*, 1568–1579. doi:10.1016/j.jclepro.2018.12.137

Velenturf, A. P. M., Purnell, P., Macaskie, L. E., Mayes, W. M., & Sapsford, D. J. (2019). A new perspective on a global circular economy. In Resource recovery from wastes: Towards a circular economy (pp. 1–22). doi:10.1039/9781788016353-00001

Vence, X., & Pereira, A. (2019). Eco-innovation and Circular Business Models as Drivers for a Circular Economy. *Contaduría y Administración, 64*(1), 1-19.

Vezzoli, C., Ceschin, F., Diehl, J. C., & Kohtala, C. (2015). New design challenges to widely implement 'Sustainable Product-Service Systems'. *Journal of Cleaner Production, 97*, 1–12. doi:10.1016/j.jclepro.2015.02.061

Vigon, B. W. (1994). *Life-Cycle Assessment: Inventory Guidelines and Principles.* Boca Raton, FL: CRC Press.

Vilarino, M. V., Franco, C., & Quarrington, C. (2017). Food loss and waste reduction as an integral part of a circular economy. *Frontiers in Environmental Science, 5*, 21. doi:10.3389/fenvs.2017.00021

Viren, P. (2015). *Money Saved is Money Earned.* http://www.marketexpress.in

Viswanathan, M., Yassine, A., & Clarke, J. (2011). Sustainable Product and Market Development for Subsistence Marketplaces: Creating Educational Initiatives in Radically Different Contexts. *Journal of Product Innovation Management, 28*(4), 558–569. doi:10.1111/j.1540-5885.2011.00825.x

Vodafone Group Plc. (2018). *Sustainable Business Report 2018.* Retrieved November 28, 2019 from https://www.vodafone.com/content/dam/vodcom/sustainability/pdfs/sustainablebusiness2018.pdf

Voelker, T. A. (2012). Entrepreneurial ecosystems: Evolutionary paths or differentiated systems? *Business Studies Journal, 4*(2), 43–61.

Vollan, B., Prediger, S., & Frölich, M. (2013). Co-managing common-pool resources: Do formal rules have to be adapted to traditional ecological norms? *Ecological Economics, 95*, 51–62. doi:10.1016/j.ecolecon.2013.08.010

Von Kortzfleisch, H. F. O., Zerwas, D., & Mokanis, I. (2013). Potentials of entrepreneurial design thinking for entrepreneurship education. *Social and Behavioural Sciences, 106*, 2080–2092. doi:10.1016/j.sbspro.2013.12.237

Von Thienen, J., Noweski, C., Meinel, C., & Rauth, I. (2011). The co-evolution of theory and practice in design thinking -or -"mind the oddness trap! In H. Plattner, C. Meinel, & L. J. Leifer (Eds.), *Design thinking: Understand -improve –apply* (pp. 81–99). Heidelberg: Springer. doi:10.1007/978-3-642-13757-0_5

Voss, J. P., & Kemp, R. (2006). Sustainability and reflexive governance: An introduction. In J. P. Voss, D. Bauknecht & R. Kemp (Eds.), Reflexive governance for sustainable development (pp. 3-28). Cheltenham: Edward Elgar.

Vroom, V. H. (1995). *Work and motivation.* San Francisco: Jossey-Bass Publishers.

Vuorio, A. M., Puumalainen, K., & Fellnhofer, K. (2018). Drivers of entrepreneurial intentions in sustainable entrepreneurship. *International Journal of Entrepreneurial Behaviour & Research, 24*(2), 359–381. doi:10.1108/IJEBR-03-2016-0097

Wackernagel, M., Monfreda, C., & Deumling, D. (2002, Nov.). Ecological footprint of nations. *Redefining Progress. Sustainability Issue Brief.*

Wagner, J. (2012). Water and the Commons Imaginary. *Current Anthropology*, *53*(5), 621.

Wainer, A. (2011). Más allá del consejo monetario: grandes empresas. *Revista problemas del desarrollo, 164*(42), 98-126. Doi:10.22201/iiec.20078951e.2011.164.24490

Walicki, J. (2017). 5 Things Leaders Can Do to Create a Truly Circular Economy. World Economic Forum Annual Meeting 2017. Accessed on 23feb2020

Walters, D. (2009, Nov.). Understand the value chain network, understand te market, understand the industry and understand the customer. *Journal of Transport and Supply Chain Management.*

Wang, J., Lin, W., & Huang, Y. H. (2010). A performance-oriented risk management framework for innovative R&D projects. *Technovation*, *30*(11-12), 601–611. doi:10.1016/j.technovation.2010.07.003

Wang, Z., Zhang, B., & Guan, D. (2016). Take responsibility for electronic-waste disposal. *Nature*, *536*(7614), 23–25. doi:10.1038/536023a PMID:27488785

Warren, L. W. (2013, August). Community economic shortcomings: The three legged stool of sustainability. Practicing Democracy, 29 - 31.

Watson, A. D. (2015). Design Thinking for Life. *Art Education*, *68*(3), 12–18. doi:10.1080/00043125.2015.11519317

Wautelet, T. (2018). *The Concept of Circular Economy: its Origins and its Evolution.* Retrieved October 29, 2019 from https://www.researchgate.net/publication/322555840_The_Concept_of_Circular_Economy_its_Origins_and_its_Evolution

WBCSD. (2019). *Policy Enablers to accelerate the circular economy.* https://docs.wbcsd.org

WCED. ((1987). *Report of the World Commission on Environment and Development: Our Common Future.* WCED.

Weetman, C. (2017). A Supply Chain Revolution: How the Circular Economy Unlocks New Value. https://www.koganpage.com/article/a-supply-chain-revolution-how-the-circular-economy-unlocks-new-value

WEF (World Economic Forum). EMF and McKinsey & Company. (2014). Towards the Circular Economy: Accelerating the scale-up across global supply chains. Retrieved from https://ellenmacarthurfoundation.org/business/reports

Weidinger, C., Fischler, F., & Schmidpeter, R. (2013). *Sustainable Entrepreneurship: Business Success through Sustainability.* Springer Berlin Heidelberg.

Weill, P., Malone, T. W., D'Urso, V. T., Herman, G., & Woerner, S. (2005). Do Some Business Models Reform Better Than Others? MIT Centre for Coordination, Science Working Paper, 226, 7.

Weinstein, N. D. (1987). Unrealistic optimism about susceptibility to health problems: Conclusions from a community-wide sample. *Journal of Behavioral Medicine*, *10*(5), 481–500. doi:10.1007/BF00846146 PubMed

Weinstein, N. D. (1989). Optimistic biases about personal risks. *Science*, *246*(4935), 1232–1233. doi:10.1126/science.2686031 PubMed

Wellesley, L., Preston, F., & Lehne, J. (2019). *An Inclusive Circular Economy: Priorities for Developing Countries.* London, UK: Chatham House. The Royal Institute for International Affairs.

Wells, P. (2013). *Business Models for Sustainability.* Cheltenham, UK: Edward Elgar; doi:10.4337/9781781001530.

Wells, P., & Seitz, M. (2005). Business Models and Closed-Loop Supply Chains: A Typology. *Supply Chain Management, 10*(4), 249–251. doi:10.1108/13598540510612712

Werner, S. (2017). International review of district heating and cooling. *Energy, 137*, 617–631. doi:10.1016/j.energy.2017.04.045

Weterings, R., Bastein, T., Tukker, A., Rademaker, M., & de Ridder, M. (2013). *Resources for our Future: Key issues and best practices in Resource Efficiency*. Amsterdam University Press.

Wibowo, A., & Alfen, H. W. (2014). Identifying macro-environmental critical success factors and key areas for improvement to promote public-private partnerships in infrastructure. *Engineering, Construction, and Architectural Management, 21*(4), 383–402. doi:10.1108/ECAM-08-2013-0078

Wickham, P. A. (1998). *Strategic entrepreneurship: a decision-making approach to new venture creation and management*. London: Pitman.

Wieland, A., & Marcus, C. (2012). Dealing with supply chain risks: Linking risk management practices and strategies to performance. *International Journal of Physical Distribution & Logistics Management, 42*(10), 887–905. doi:10.1108/09600031211281411

Wiklund, J. (1999). The sustainability of the entrepreneurial orientation-performance relationship. *Entrepreneurship Theory and Practice, 24*(1), 37–49. doi:10.1177/104225879902400103

Wiklund, J., Nikolaev, B., Shir, M., & Bradley, S. (2019). Conquering Relevance: *Entrepreneurship Research's Grand Challenge. Journal of Business Venturing, 34*, 579–588. doi:10.1016/j.jbusvent.2019.01.002

Willard, B. (2012). *The new sustainability advantage: seven business case benefits of a triple bottom line*. New Society Publishers.

Wilson, D., & Rogero, A. (2015). Chapter 2: Background, definitions, concepts and indicators. In D. Wilson (Ed.), Global Waste Management Outlook (pp. 19 - 39). UNEP (United Nations Environment Programme).

Wilson, C., & Wilson, P. (2006). *Make poverty business: increase profits and reduce risks by engaging with the poor*. Greenleaf Publishing.

Wincent, J., & Westerberg, M. (2005). Personal traits of CEOs, inter-firm networking and entrepreneurship in their firms: Investigating strategic SME network participants. *Journal of Developmental Entrepreneurship, 10*(03), 271–284. doi:10.1142/S1084946705000215

Winschiers-Theophilus, H., Cabrero, D. G., Angula, S., Chivuno-Kuria, S., Mendonca, H., & Ngolo, R. (2015). A challenge base approach to promote entrepreneurship among youth in an informal settlement in Windhoek. *Proceedings of the SATN.*

Witty, R., & Jaggers, M. (2018). *Organizational Resilience is More Than Just the Latest trend*. Gartner.

Woetzel, J. (2016). *Bridging Global Infrastructure Gaps*. McKinsey Global Institute. www.mckinsey.com/ind

Woodfield, R. (2000). *Women, Work and Computing*. Cambridge University Press; doi:10.1017/CBO9780511488948.

Wooi, G. C., & Sailani, S. (2009). Green Supply Chain Initiatives: Investigation on the Barriers in the Context of SMEs in Malaysia. *International Business Management, 4*(1), 20–27. doi:10.3923/ibm.2010.20.27

World Aluminum. (2016). *Primary aluminum production database*. Author.

World Bank Open Data. (n.d.). *Countries and Economies*. Retrieved from: https://data.worldbank.org

World Bank Report. (2012). Gender Equality and Development. Accessed from:https://siteresources.worldbank.org/INTWDR2012/Resources/7778105-1299699968583/7786210-1315936222006/Complete-Report.pdf

World Bank. (2002). *Nigeria State and Local Governance in Nigeria*. AFTPR, Africa Region Report of The World Bank, No.24477-UNI.

World Bank. (2010). *World Development Indicator Database*. Available at: http://worldbank.org/wbsite/external/data-statistics

World Bank. (2012). *What A Waste: A Global Review of Solid Waste Management*. Washington, DC: Author.

World Bank. (2017). *Nigeria Economic Update: Beyond Oil, Key Drivers for Sustainable Growth*. Available: https://www.worldbank.org/en/country/nigeria/publication/nigeria-economic-update-beyond-oil-key-drivers-for-sustainable-growth

World Bank. (2019). *Solid waste management*. Retrieved 7 November, 2019 from https://www.worldbank.org/en/topic/urbandevelopment/brief/solid-waste-management

World Commission on Environment and Development. (1987). *Our common future*. Oxford University Press.

World Economic Forum. (2010). *Global Competitiveness Report 2010-2011*. Geneva: WEF.

World Economic Forum. (2014). *Entrepreneurial Ecosystems around the Globe and Early-Stage Company Growth Dynamics*. Geneva, Switzerland: Author.

World Economic Forum. (2014). *Towards Circular Economy: Accelerating the Scaleup across Global Supply Chains*. Published in collaboration with Ellen Mac- Arthur Foundation and McKinsey & Company. http://www3. weforum.org/docs/WEF_ENV_Towards CircularEconomy_Report_2014.pdf

World Economic Forum. (2016). From linear to circular – Accelerating a proven concept. Retrieved at Dec 21, 2016. from: http://reports.weforum.org/towardthe-circular-economy-accelerating-the-scale-up-across-global-supply-chains/fromlinear-to-circular-accelerating-a-proven-concept/

World Economic Forum. (2016). *The Global Competitiveness Report 2016–2017: Full Data Edition*. World Economic Forum.

World Vision Australia Policy Paper. (2018). *Inclusive Market Systems Development—Sustainable growth for everyone*. Sydney: World Vision Australia.

WRAP. (2011). *Increasing SME Recycling*. Banbury: Waste & Resources Action Programme.

WRAP. (2019). *WRAP and the circular economy*. Available on http://www.wrap.org.uk/about-us/about/wrap-and-circular-economy

Wycherly, I. (1999). Greening supply chains: The case of the body shop international. *Business Strategy and the Environment*, *8*(2), 120–127. doi:10.1002/(SICI)1099-0836(199903/04)8:2<120::AID-BSE188>3.0.CO;2-X

Xie, C. (2014). Why Do Some People Choose to Become Entrepreneurs? An Integrative Approach. *Journal of Management Policy and Practice*, *15*(1), 25–38.

Xu, F. (2012). The Studies of the Concept Plan of the Fengcheng Industrial Park towards the Circular Economy. In Z. H. Zhang & Y. J. Li (Eds.), *Architecture and Urban Development* (Vol. 598, pp. 220–223). doi:10.4028/www.scientific.net/AMR.598.220

Yanamandra, R. (2018). Development of an integrated healthcare supply chain model, Supply Chain Forum. *International Journal (Toronto, Ont.)*, *19*(2), 111–121. doi:10.1080/16258312.2018.1475823

Yang, Q., Zhou, J., & Xu, K. (2014, April). A 3R implementation framework to enable circular consumption in community. *International Journal of Environmental Sciences and Development*, *5*(2), 217–222. doi:10.7763/IJESD.2014.V5.481

Yanıklar, C. (2006). *Tüketimin Sosyolojisi*. İstanbul: Birey Yayıncılık.

Yaqub, N. (2016). What is Restructuring in the Era of Change in Nigerian Politics. In *IASTEM International Conference* (pp. 5-18). Dammian, Saudi Arabia: Academic Press.

Yeoh, P.-L. (2009). Realised and potential absorptive Capacity: Understanding their antecedents and Performance in the Sourcing Context. *Journal of Marketing Theory and Practice*, *17*(1), 21–36. doi:10.2753/MTP1069-6679170102

Yetisen, A. K., Volpatti, L. R., Coskun, A. F., Cho, S., Kamrani, E., Butt, H., ... Yun, S. H. (2015). Entrepreneurship. *Lab on a Chip*, *15*(18), 3638–3660. doi:10.1039/C5LC00577A PMID:26245815

Yıldırım, L. (2017, December). Geri dönüşüm/ileri dönüşüm/tekrar kullanım kapsamında ikinci el giysiler ve sürdürülebilirlik. *SDÜ ART-E Güzel Sanatlar Fakültesi Sanat Dergisi*, *10*(20), 484–503. doi:10.21602duarte.305698

Yong, R. (2007). The circular economy in China. *Journal of Material Cycles and Waste Management*, *9*(2), 121–129. doi:10.1007/s10163-007-0183-z

York, J. G., O'Neil, I., & Sarasvathy, S. D. (2016). Exploring Environmental Entrepreneurship: Identity Coupling, Venture Goals, and Stakeholder Incentives. *Journal of Management Studies*, *53*(5), 695–737. doi:10.1111/joms.12198

Yoshino, E. B. (2009). Clusters as a driving engine for FDI. *Economic Modelling*, *26*(5), 934–945. doi:10.1016/j.econmod.2009.03.006

Yuan, Q., & Xue, X. (2009). The Eco-industrial System Study of Circular Small Town. *Proceedings of the 2009 IEEE 16th International Conference on Industrial Engineering and Engineering Management*, 1-2, 1636-1639. 10.1109/ICIEEM.2009.5344355

Yuan, Z. W., Bi, J., & Moriguichi, Y. (2006). The circular economy – a new development strategy in China. *Journal of Industrial Ecology*, *10*(1/2), 4–8. doi:10.1162/108819806775545321

Yu, C., Davis, C., & Dijkema, D. P. J. (2014). Understanding the Evolution of Industrial Symbiosis Research. *Journal of Industrial Ecology*, *18*(2), 280–293. doi:10.1111/jiec.12073

Yunus, M., Moingeon, B., & Lehmann-Ortega, L. (2010). Building social business models: Lessons from the Grameen experience. Long Range Planning International Journal of Strategic Management, 43(2-3), 10. doi:10.1016/j.lrp.2009.12.005

ZARA. (2020). *Sustainability Collection Program*. Retrieved from Clothing Collect: https://www.zara.com/uk/en/sustainability-collection-program-l1452.html

Zech, T. (2018). Better than recycling. Retrieved at 07.10.2019, from https://www.deutschland.de/en/topic/environment/cradle-to-cradle-rather-than-recycling-these-are-the-advantages

Zeeuw van der Laan, A., & Aurisicchio, M. (2009). Designing product-service systems to close resource loops: Circular design guidelines. *Procedia CIRP*, *2019*(80), 631–636.

Zhang, A., Venkatesh, V. G., Liu, Y., Wan, M., Qu, T., & Huisingh, D. (2019). Barriers to smart waste management for a circular economy in China. *Journal of Cleaner Production*, *240*, 118198. doi:10.1016/j.jclepro.2019.118198

Zhang, M., Jin, B., Wang, G. A., Goh, T. N., & He, Z. (2016). A Study of Key Success Factors of Service Enterprises in China. *Journal of Business Ethics*, *134*(1), 1–14. doi:10.100710551-014-2074-2 PMID:30930508

Zhang, P., & Gheibi, S. (2015). From Intrinsic Motivation to Employee Creativity: The Role of Knowledge Integration and Team Psychological Safety. *European Scientific Journal*, *11*(11), 380–392.

Zhang, Q. (2016). Discussion on Significance of Forestry Tourism Circular Economy's Development. *3rd International Conference on Management Innovation and Business Innovation (ICMIBI 2016)*, *58*, 358-361.

Zhang, S. X., & Cueto, J. (2015). The Study of Bias in Entrepreneurship. *Entrepreneurship Theory and Practice*, *41*(3), 419–454. doi:10.1111/etap.12212

Zhang, Y. (2014). Circular economy perspective research Wanlu lake Eco-tourism Industry Gathering Area for innovation and development. *Advanced Materials Research*, *962-965*, 2301–2309. doi:10.4028/www.scientific.net/AMR.962-965.2301

Zhang, Y., & Tian, L. (2014). The sustainable development of circular economy under the perspective of ecological tourism. *Advanced Materials Research*, *1010-1012*, 2090–2093. doi:10.4028/www.scientific.net/AMR.1010-1012.2090

Zhao, A. (2016). Research on Circular Economy as Well as Energy Saving and Emission Reduction of Liaoning Rural Tourism. *International Conference on Material, Energy and Environment Engineering (ICM3E 2016)*, 129-133.

Zhao, F. (2005). Exploring the synergy between entrepreneurship and innovation. *International Journal of Entrepreneurial Behaviour & Research*, *11*(1), 25–41. doi:10.1108/13552550510580825

Zhao, H., & Seibert, S. E. (2006). The Big Five personality dimensions and entrepreneurial status: A meta-analytical review. *The Journal of Applied Psychology*, *91*(2), 259–271. doi:10.1037/0021-9010.91.2.259 PubMed

Zhao, H., Seibert, S. E., & Lumpkin, G. T. (2010). The Relationship of Personality to Entrepreneurial Intentions and Performance: A Meta-Analytic Review. *Journal of Management*, *36*(2), 381–404. doi:10.1177/0149206309335187

Zhao, P. (2015). Low Carbon Tourism and Strategies of Carbon Emission Reduction. *2nd International Symposium on Engineering Technology, Education and Management (ISETEM 2015)*, 391-399.

Zhao, S., Wang, H. M., Chen, W. Q., Yang, D., Liu, J. R., & Shi, F. (2019). Environmental impacts of domestic resource extraction in China. *Ecosystem Health and Sustainability*, *5*(1), 67–78. doi:10.1080/20964129.2019.1577703

Zhihun, F., & Nailing, Y. (2007). Putting a circular economy into practice in China. *Sustainability Science*, *2*(1), 95–101. doi:10.100711625-006-0018-1

Zhou, R., Ai, H., & Shi, K. (2012). Security system of Sustainable Tourism Development in Shandong Province based on Circular Economy. Natural Resources and Sustainable Development II, 524-527, 3245. doi:10.4028/www.scientific.net/AMR.524-527.3245

Zhou, H., & Benton, W. C. Jr. (2007). Supply chain practice and information sharing. *Journal of Operations Management*, *25*(6), 1348–1365. doi:10.1016/j.jom.2007.01.009

Zhou, J., & George, J. M. (2001). When job dissatisfaction leads to creativity: Encouraging the expression of voice. *Academy of Management Journal*, *44*(4), 682–696.

Zhu, Z., Li, M., & Ma, C. (2013). Explore and analyse development model of eco-agricultural tourism based on circular economy. In Environmental Protection and Resources Exploitation, 807-809, 902. doi:10.4028/www.scientific.net/AMR.807-809.902

Zhu, Q., Geng, Y., & Lai, K. H. (2011). Environmental supply chain cooperation and its effect on the circular economy practice-performance relationship among Chinese manufacturers. *Journal of Industrial Ecology*, *15*(3), 405–419. doi:10.1111/j.1530-9290.2011.00329.x

Zott, C., & Amit, R. (2007). Business Model Design and the Performance of Entrepreneurial Firms. *Organization Science, 18*(2), 181–199. doi:10.1287/orsc.1060.0232

Zsolnai, L. (2002). Green business or community economy? *International Journal of Social Economics, 29*(8), 652–662. doi:10.1108/03068290210434198

About the Contributors

Neeta Baporikar is currently Professor (Management) at Harold Pupkewitz Graduate School of Business (HP-GSB), Namibia University of Science and Technology, Namibia. Prior to this, she was Head-Scientific Research, with Ministry of Higher Education CAS-Salalah, Sultanate of Oman, Professor (Strategic Management and Entrepreneurship) at IIIT Pune and BITS India. With more than a decade of experience in the industry, consultancy, and training, she made a lateral switch to research and academics in 1995. Prof Baporikar holds D.Sc. (Management Studies) USA, Ph.D. in Management, University of Pune INDIA with MBA (Distinction) and Law (Hons.) degrees. Apart from this, she is also an external reviewer, Oman Academic Accreditation Authority, Accredited Management Teacher, Qualified Trainer, Doctoral Guide and Board Member of Academics and Advisory Committee in accredited B-Schools. She has to her credit many conferred doctorates, is international and editorial advisory board member and reviewer for Emerald, IGI, Inderscience refereed journals, published numerous refereed research papers, and authored books in the area of entrepreneurship, strategy, management, and higher education.

* * *

Juhi Agarwal is working as an Assistant Professor in Techno Institute of Higher Studies, an affiliated college of Lucknow University. She holds her MBA Degree (2019) from Institute of Management Science, Lucknow University with specialization in Human Resources and Industrial Relations, and has completed her internship project with Tata Consultancy Services, Lucknow (June 2018-August 2018), and Bachelor Degree (2016) from National Post Graduate College, Lucknow University. She has qualified for UGC-NET in December 2018. Her scholarly interest is in the areas of Corporate Social Responsibility, Leadership, Motivation, Talent Management, Labour Welfare, etc.

Wilfred Isak April is a generation Y scholar in Southern Africa: Namibia. He holds a PhD in Entrepreneurship from New Zealand. In addition he holds a Master of Commerce degree in collaboration with the European Business School (Germany) from the University of Stellenbosch in South Africa. Will also holds double Honors in Human Resource Development and Industrial Psychology from the University of Stellenbosch. He also holds a bachelor of Business Administration Degree from the University of Namibia. Will publish in numerous academic Journals and such as the International Journal of Small Business and Entrepreneurship, World Review of Entrepreneurship and INTECH Publishers to name a few. He is the founder of MALTAS CLUB NAMIBIA, which grooms young leaders from all universities to realize their full potential. Currently Will is pursuing a Masters of Law (LLM) Intellectual Property at Turino University (Italy) in collaboration with the World Intellectual Property Organization (WIPO).

He is an academic at the University of Namibia. Dr. April is an Alumnus of the U.S. International Visitors Leadership Program (IVLP) Exchange program and participated in the Entrepreneurship and Small Business Development program in 2014.

Sulaiman Olusegun Atiku is a Senior Lecturer (Human Resources) at Harold Pupkewitz Graduate School of Business (HP-GSB), Namibia University of Science and Technology, Namibia. He is a pragmatic researcher specializing in Strategic Human Resource Management. His current research area of interest includes; Human Capital Formation for the Fourth Industrial Revolution, and Advanced Green Human Resource Management Practices. He has over 11 years' experience in Higher Education. A native of Lagos, Sulaiman graduated from the University of KwaZulu-Natal with a PhD degree in Human Resource Management. His Master of Science degree was awarded in Human Resources and Industrial Relations at Lagos State University, Nigeria. His Bachelor of Science (Honours) degree was also awarded at Lagos State University in the field of Industrial Relations and Personnel Management. He has lectured several courses in his field home/abroad and published many scholarly articles in international journals. He is a member of International Labour and Employment Relations Association (ILERA), Nigerian Institute of Management (NIM), and Institute of People Management (IPM) South Africa.

Mladenka Balaban, PhD, works at the Faculty of Economics, Independent University of Banja Luka, as an associate professor. She worked at the Belgrade Banking Academy - Faculty of Banking, Insurance and Finance, as an associate professor. The Faculty of Economics in Belgrade, majoring in Banking, Finance and Insurance, finished with an average grade of 8.62 and a grade of 10 in the graduation exam. She defended her master's thesis on "The role of money market in the financial system" at the Faculty of Economics in Belgrade in 2004, and defended her doctoral dissertation entitled "The place and role of insurance companies in the financial market in Serbia" in 2007. at the Faculty of Management, Karic Brothers University. She was employed by the CIP Institute of Transportation as a research associate from 1996-2001. years. At CIP, she has worked on numerous investment appraisal and enterprise valuation projects. From 2001-2003. She worked at Europe Insurance as the Head of Planning and Analysis, and from 2003-2005. in the position of CFO. From 2005-2009. She worked as Executive Director of Finance at BK University. In 2004, and a PhD thesis entitled "The Place and Role of Insurance Companies at she defended her financial market in Serbia in 2007 at the Faculty of Management, University of the Brothers Karic ". She was employed by the CIP Institute of Transportation as a research associate from 1996-2001. years. At CIP, she has worked on numerous investment appraisal and enterprise valuation projects. From 2001-2003. She worked at Europe Insurance as the Head of Planning and Analysis, and from 2003-2005. in the position of CFO. From 2005-2009. she worked as Executive Director for finance of the University of BK.

Dileep Baragde is currently Head of Department/Professor (Computer/Management) at the G.S. Moze College, affiliated to Savitribai Phule Pune University, India. With more than a 10 Years of experience in teaching. Dr. Baragde holds PhD in Management, Savitribai Phule Pune University INDIA with MBA (Computer Management) and MSc (Computer Science) degrees. Apart from this, he is also Reviewer for international journals, several written research papers and authored Chapters in books in the area of Information Technology, Business Innovation, Entrepreneurship, Management and Higher Education.

Elena Bykasova works in JSC" MPO CLASSIC " Deputy General Director for Economics and Finance. Since 2007 he has been engaged in scientific activities, publishes scientific articles, participates in scientific conferences. From 2007 to 2019 she worked at the Department of "Audit and controlling" in RSU. A. N. Kosygina (Technologies. Design. Art) senior teacher. Since 2019, he has been working as a teacher at the Institute of Additional Education of the Moscow Financial and Legal Academy. E. V. bykasova-consultant on taxes and fees of the II category, member of the Chamber of tax consultants, member of the Institute of professional accountants and auditors of Russia.

Gratitude Chiwara-Ndoro is an MSc Library and Information Science student in the Department of Library and Information Science at the National University of Science and Technology in Zimbabwe. Her research interests are in library studies and information management.

Mukund Deshpande has an Engineering background and served in corporate firms for long time. After realising the importance of managing the business affairs, he decided and switched over to management field and then obtained Ph.D. in management. He has been practicising as an independent researcher after serving in reputed academic institutions. He is also rendering professional consultancy services in management for small and medium enterprises.

Peterson Dewah is a Lecturer in the Department of Records and Archives Management at National University of Science and Technology. He is also an Honorary Lecturer in the School of Social Sciences (Information Studies) at the University of KwaZulu-Natal, South Africa. He holds a PhD in Knowledge Management from the University of Fort Hare. His research interests are in infopreneurship and entrepreneurship education, records/archives management, knowledge management and ethics in information management. Contact: National University of Science and Technology, Private Bag AC939, Ascot, Bulawayo, Zimbabwe. Email: peterson.dewah@nust.ac.zw

Teresa Dieguez is a Doctor on Economics, MBA on Prospective and Organizational Strategy, Master on Innovation and Technological Transfer, Specialist on Strategy and Entrepreneurship, PhD Student on Social Development and Sustainability.

Gordana Djukic, PhD, defended her doctoral dissertation entitled "The Importance of Reforming the Pension Insurance System in Serbia to Overcome the Problem of its Sustainability" at the Faculty of Management Zajecar, Megatrend University Belgrade. She is employed at the Faculty of Economics in Belgrade and works as a research associate.

Mufaro Dzingirai is a PhD candidate in Business Management at Midlands State University and a teaching assistant at the Centre for Entrepreneurship, Midlands State University. He received his Master of Commerce in Strategic Management and Corporate Governance degree from Midlands State University in 2016. He was hired as a teacher by the Ministry of Education from 2014 to 2016. In 2013, he received the MSU Book Prize. His research interests include Higher Education, Strategy, Management, and Entrepreneurship.

Idahosa Igbinakhase PhD, is an Assistant Chief Education Officer (Federal Ministry of Education, Nigeria). His research interests include family entrepreneurship, technology management, strategic management, resource management and sustainable development. He is very passionate about management research and strongly believes that sound management practices holds the key to a sustainable society.

Biljana Ilic, PhD, was born on 10/01/1970, in Zajecar, Serbia. She graduated on Business Higher School of Belgrade University, in 1996. She continued further education on the Faculty of Management Zajecar, Megatrend University of Belgrade, in 2007. She Graduated on the Faculty of Management in Zajecar, in 2009. She received the degree of Master of Academic Studies in Management on the same faculty, defended master thesis with mark 10.00, and acquired the title of master manager. She defended her doctoral thesis titled "Strategic directions of regional economic and environmental development of the tourist potential of Gamzigrad Spa", in April 2016, mark 10.00. She was elected as assistant professor at the Faculty of Management in Zajecar on July 2016.

Amit Jadhav is currently Head of Department/Professor (Economics) at the G.S. Moze College, affiliated to Savitribai Phule Pune University, India. With more than a 10 Years of experience in teaching. Dr. Jadhav holds PhD in Economics, Savitribai Phule Pune University INDIA with MA (Economics) degrees and MPhil (Economics) from YCMOU.

Ngepathimo Kadhila holds a Bachelor of Education and Master of Education (Curriculum, Instructional and Assessment Studies) from the University of Namibia; Postgraduate Diploma in Higher Education (for Academic Developers) from Rhodes University in South Africa; and PhD in Higher Education Studies (with the focus on Quality Assurance) from the University of the Free State in South Africa. He currently serves as Quality Assurance Director at the University of Namibia. His research work lies in the areas of academic development, curriculum development, teaching and learning in higher education, assessment in higher education, and quality assurance in higher education.

Ezgi Karataş Yücel has an undergraduate degree from Hacettepe University Department of Business Administration (2008). Her master degree is from Dokuz Eylül University English Business Management MA (2011) with her thesis on "Hedonic Consumption: Confirmation of the Scale and Analyzing the Effects of Demographic Factors: An Application in Izmir by Using LISREL" and Ph.D. degree is from Dokuz Eylül University Business Administration with a thesis on "The Effect of Gender Roles on Decision-Making Styles: An Application on High Involvement Products". Her research areas are consumer behavior, marketing research, retailing, consumer psychology. She is married and has a daughter whose name is Eylül.

Jorge López-Lemus is a research professor in the Department of Multidisciplinary Studies, University of Guanajuato.

Montserrat Mata Fernández has a degree in Computer Science with a Master in Business Management and several certifications as PMP Certification and ITIL v3 Foundation among others. Collaborator in articles and papers. Wide experience as Project Manager, dealing with national and international projects.

Nyanjige Mbembela Mayala holds a PhD in Business Management from Moshi Co-operative University (MoCU), a Master in Business Administration and a Bachelor of Commerce and Management (Marketing) from the University of Dar es Salaam. Currently she works as a Lecture and Head of

Department of Management at MoCU. Prior to that, she served as a Branch Manager for Barclays Bank (T) and worked in a number of water development projects in Africa under the Water Utility Partnership Africa (WUP-Africa).

Ujjal Mukherjee is an MBA (HR), PGDHRM, qualified UGC- NET, FDP (IIM-A), Ph.D. (HR). He has a total work experience of over 20 years including15 years in post-graduate management teaching. His research areas include entrepreneurship, high-performance work system, creativity, and happiness.

Takaruza Munyanyiwa holds a Doctor of Management in Organizational Leadership. Adjunct Professor Apollos University, Midlands State University Part-Time Faculty, Bindura University of Science Education Part -Time Faculty. Research interests include Education, Entrepreneurship, Tourism, Management.

K. S. Sastry Musti has obtained his BTech in Electrical Engineering from JNTU, Kakinada, MTech and PhD from NIT, Warangal., India. He is currently with Namibia University of Science and Technology as Associate Professor with the Department of Electrical and Computer Engineering. He has more than 30 years of professional experience in both academia and industry. His research interests are in the extended areas of Engineering Education, Power Systems, Software Engineering and Systems and Information Systems. Professor Sastry is a senior member IEEE, USA and a Life member IE, India.

Vannie Naidoo is a full time staff member at the University of KwaZulu-Natal, South Africa, in the Faculty of Management and Law. Her field of teaching is in management, corporate strategy, project management and entrepreneurship. The research areas pursued by Dr Naidoo are in the areas of management, marketing, service marketing, entrepreneurship and social media and e-learning or learning with new technologies. She has presented papers at international conferences throughout the world and has written on various issues in management and marketing in journal articles and books.

Ninel Nesheva-Kiosseva received her Master Degree and PhD in University of National and World Economy, Sofia, Bulgaria. Her habilitation is held at the Higher Attestation Commission to the Council of Ministers of Bulgaria. She has published books in finance, environmental and social accounting, economic theory and history. Teaches at the New Bulgarian University, Sofia.

Beatriz Olalla-Caballero has a PhD in Computer Science, Information Technologies and Knowledge Society, Pontifical University of Salamanca, Spain. MSc in Quality Engineer, American Society for Quality. BSc in Telecommunication Engineer, University of Valladolid (Spain). Project Management Professional and ITIL Expert. Several years working in Information Technologies services and Quality and Project Management. Author of papers and articles about quality, projects and Information Technologies.

Pınar Özkan is Assistant Professor of Marketing at Business Department of Dokuz Eylül University. She holds a PhD degree from the same university. Her areas of research are relationship marketing, key account management and service marketing.

Harold Andrew Patrick is a qualified Industrial and organizational Psychologist with over 29 years of Postgraduate teaching, corporate training and research experience. Presently Professor and Dean, CMS

Business School, Jain (Deemed-to-be University). Former Senior Manager – Leadership and Organization Development, Infosys Leadership Institute, Infosys Limited. Professor and Head - Organizational Behaviour and Human Resource Management area, Christ (Deemed-to-be University). His interest lies in Human Behaviour and its application at the work place and has trained extensively in these areas with working managers, faculty members, Christian leaders, educational leaders, business graduate and working students. Elected member of the Society for Industrial and Organizational Psychology (SIOP), USA.

Rafael Pérez-Uribe has a PhD in Managerial Sciences, Nebrija University. Diploma of Advanced Studies in Applied Economics, Nebrija University. Master in Management of Organizations, EAN University. Maître es Sciences, University of Quebec a Chicoutimi. Specialist in Evaluation y Creation of Managerial Indicators for Tertiary Education, Business Administration School. Graduate studies as Kenkyusei (Assigned researcher) in Total Quality Control and Quality Circles, Fukushima University, Japan. Business Administrator, Jorge Tadeo Lozano University. Director of the research group in Management of Large, Medium and Small companies (G3pymes) and Professor assigned at the Research and Knowledge Management Division EAN University.

Lukman Raimi is an Assistant Professor of Entrepreneurship at the American University of Nigeria. Previously, he was a Principal Lecturer/Coordinator of Training & Part-Time Programme at the Centre for Entrepreneurship Development (CED), Yaba College of Technology, Lagos. His research interests include: Entrepreneurship, Development Economics, Corporate Social Responsibility, General Management and Human Resources Management. Raimi is an alumnus of both Cumberland Lodge, Windsor, United Kingdom and Entrepreneurship Development Institute (EDI), Ahmedabad, India. He had undergone special training in Enterprise Education for Employability facilitated by the Oxford Brookes University and the Pan African University Nigeria under the British Council's sponsorship. University Degree: Ph.D., De Montfort University, Leicester (UK); M.Sc., Industrial Relations & Personnel Management, University of Lagos (Nigeria); M.Sc.., Economics, University of Lagos (Nigeria); B.Sc., Economics, Obafemi Awolowo University (Nigeria); and Certificate; Small Business Promotion, Entrepreneurship Development Institute (India).

Maria Ramirez has a Ph.D. in Management at Universidad EAN. Ph.D. in Entrepreneurial Sciences at Universidad Nebrija- España. Master in Business Management at Universidad de Quebec, Universidad EAN. Graduate degree in Management Indicators to Evaluate Higher Education Institutions) at Universidad EAN. BA in Business Administration at Universidad EAN. BA in Education at Universidad Pedagógica Nacional.

Maria Teresa Ramirez-Garzon has a PhD in Management from Celaya University (Mexico), Master´s degree in Teaching from La Salle University, specialist in Human Resources Management and Business Administrator from EAN University, with wide experience in teaching and research, both nationwide and internationally. Experience as researcher and co-researcher in subjects such as competitiveness and organizational management in SMEs and as consultant in subjects related to organizational management in private and public companies. Publication of articles and chapters in books on the areas of research.

Isaac Randa is senior faculty in the area of Accounting and Finance at HP-GSB, Namibia University of Science and Technology, Namibia. With experience of more than a decade at university level of graduate and postgraduate teaching, Dr. Randa is also a qualified Insurance Professional .

Damini Saini is associated with IIM Raipur as an Assistant Professor. Prior to this she has worked at Institute of Management Sciences in University of Lucknow. Where she was a key member of library and research committee. Damini has received her PhD degree from Faculty of Management Studies (FMS), University of Delhi in HRM (OB). She holds her MBA and Graduation Degree from IET Lucknow and Lucknow University respectively and passed UGC–NET and has also been awarded UGC's Junior and Senior Research Fellowship. Damini has been awarded for the Best research paper award twice, at International Conference on, Vedic Foundations of Indian Management, organized by VFIM(2013) and PRMEs International Conference "Responsible Management Education, Training and Practice"(2015). Her scholarly interests are leadership and ethics, values and spiritual foundations for developing leadership etc. Damini has contributed to nationally and internationally acclaimed journals and conferences.

Jose Manuel Saiz-Alvarez has a Ph.D. in Economics and Business Administration from the Autonomous University of Madrid (Spain) and a Ph.D. in Sociology from the Pontifical University of Salamanca (Spain). He was a GIEE faculty-researcher at EGADE Business School-Tecnologico de Monterrey, Mexico, and he is now a Visiting Professor at The Catholic University of Santiago de Guayaquil (Ecuador), and Autonomous University of Manizales (Colombia). He is a member of the National System of Researchers of the National Council for Science and Technology (CONACYT) in Mexico, a regular member of the Mexican Academy of Sciences and an international researcher of the 'Enzo Faletto 'Center for Studies and Research at University of Santiago de Chile. He is accredited by the National Agency for the Evaluation of Quality and Accreditation (Spain). He is a member of dozens of Scientific Committees in highly-reputed international journals and has been the supervisor of 74 Ph.D. thesis. He is in the 'Who's Who in the World' from 2011.

Carlos Salcedo-Perez has a PhD in Entrepreneurial Sciences, Universidad Antonio de Nebrija, Madrid, Spain. Master of Sciences in Economic Development, University of Southern Mississippi, Hattiesburg, Mississippi. Bachelor of Sciences in Business Administration, University of Southern Mississippi, Hattiesburg, Mississippi.

Signed Shikokola is an MBA graduate and working in the department of finance at the Ministry of Safety and Security, Namibia.

Michael Torres Franco is Mg in Analysis of Political, Economical and International Affairs. Bachelor Degree in International Trade. Former public and private advisor in development affairs. Director of the International business program at EAN University, professor of international trade, internationalization, logistics and international physical distribution.

Booysen Sabeho Tubulingane is an Institutional Statistician at the Namibia University of Science and Technology (NUST) and is currently a PhD candidate at University of Giessen (German)/UNICAF University. His interests include but not limited to business management, institutional and spatial science researches. Booysen Sabeho Tubulingane has a Masters of Arts in Geography from the University of Namibia.

José G. Vargas-Hernández, M.B.A., Ph.D., Member of the National System of Researchers of Mexico and a research professor at University Center for Economic and Managerial Sciences, University of Guadalajara. Professor Vargas-Hernández has a Ph. D. in Public Administration and a Ph.D. in Organizational Economics. He has undertaken studies in Organisational Behaviour and has a Master of Business Administration, published four books and more than 200 papers in international journals and reviews (some translated to English, French, German, Portuguese, Farsi, Chinese, etc.) and more than 300 essays in national journals and reviews. He has obtained several international Awards and recognition.

Alfonso Vargas-Sánchez is Full Professor at the University of Huelva (Spain), in its Management and Marketing Department. Editor of "Enlightening Tourism. A Pathmaking Journal".

Valentina Villamil is a young researcher at Faculty of Management, Finances and Economic Sciences at EAN University.

Hassan Yusuf holds a doctorate degree (PhD) in Strategic Management from Usman Danfodiyo University, Sokoto, Nigeria, a master's degree (Master of Business Administration) from Bayero University, Kano, Nigeria, and a Bachelor's Degree (B.Sc.) in Business Administration from Ahmadu Bello University, Zaria, Nigeria. Before joining AUN, Dr. Hassan lectured in the Department of Marketing, Federal Polytechnic, Bida, Nigeria. He is a full member of the Institute of Strategic Management, Nigeria (ISMN), and an Associate Member, National Institute of Marketing of Nigeria (NIMN). While his research interests are Strategic Management, Marketing Management and Entrepreneurship. He is currently the Chair of Entrepreneurship.

Index

D

E

F

G

R

S

T

V

W

Y

Purchase Print, E-Book, or Print + E-Book

IGI Global's reference books are available in three unique pricing formats: Print Only, E-Book Only, or Print + E-Book.

Shipping fees may apply.

www.igi-global.com

Recommended Reference Books

ISBN: 978-1-5225-6201-6
© 2019; 341 pp.
List Price: $345

ISBN: 978-1-5225-7262-6
© 2019; 360 pp.
List Price: $215

ISBN: 978-1-5225-8003-4
© 2019; 216 pp.
List Price: $205

ISBN: 978-1-5225-5763-0
© 2019; 304 pp.
List Price: $205

ISBN: 978-1-5225-6980-0
© 2019; 325 pp.
List Price: $235

ISBN: 978-1-5225-7808-6
© 2019; 397 pp.
List Price: $215

Do you want to stay current on the latest research trends, product announcements, news and special offers?

Join IGI Global's mailing list today and start enjoying exclusive perks sent only to IGI Global members.

Add your name to the list at **www.igi-global.com/newsletters.**

Publisher of Peer-Reviewed, Timely, and Innovative Academic Research

IGI Global
DISSEMINATOR OF KNOWLEDGE

www.igi-global.com Sign up at www.igi-global.com/newsletters facebook.com/igiglobal twitter.com/igiglobal linkedin.com/igiglobal

Ensure Quality Research is Introduced to the Academic Community

Become an IGI Global Reviewer for Authored Book Projects

The overall success of an authored book project is dependent on quality and timely reviews.

In this competitive age of scholarly publishing, constructive and timely feedback significantly expedites the turnaround time of manuscripts from submission to acceptance, allowing the publication and discovery of forward-thinking research at a much more expeditious rate. Several IGI Global authored book projects are currently seeking highly-qualified experts in the field to fill vacancies on their respective editorial review boards:

Applications and Inquiries may be sent to:
development@igi-global.com

Applicants must have a doctorate (or an equivalent degree) as well as publishing and reviewing experience. Reviewers are asked to complete the open-ended evaluation questions with as much detail as possible in a timely, collegial, and constructive manner. All reviewers' tenures run for one-year terms on the editorial review boards and are expected to complete at least three reviews per term. Upon successful completion of this term, reviewers can be considered for an additional term.

If you have a colleague that may be interested in this opportunity,
we encourage you to share this information with them.

eContent Pro International
PARTNERING
IGI Global

IGI Global Proudly Partners With eContent Pro International

Receive a 25% Discount on all Editorial Services

Editorial Services

IGI Global expects all final manuscripts submitted for publication to be in their final form. This means they must be reviewed, revised, and professionally copy edited prior to their final submission. Not only does this support with accelerating the publication process, but it also ensures that the highest quality scholarly work can be disseminated.

English Language Copy Editing

Let eContent Pro International's expert copy editors perform edits on your manuscript to resolve spelling, punctuaion, grammar, syntax, flow, formatting issues and more.

Scientific and Scholarly Editing

Allow colleagues in your research area to examine the content of your manuscript and provide you with valuable feedback and suggestions before submission.

Figure, Table, Chart & Equation Conversions

Do you have poor quality figures? Do you need visual elements in your manuscript created or converted? A design expert can help!

Translation

Need your documjent translated into English? eContent Pro International's expert translators are fluent in English and more than 40 different languages.

Hear What Your Colleagues are Saying About Editorial Services Supported by IGI Global

"The service was very fast, very thorough, and very helpful in ensuring our chapter meets the criteria and requirements of the book's editors. I was quite impressed and happy with your service."

– Prof. Tom Brinthaupt,
Middle Tennessee State University, USA

"I found the work actually spectacular. The editing, formatting, and other checks were very thorough. The turnaround time was great as well. I will definitely use eContent Pro in the future."

– Nickanor Amwata, Lecturer,
University of Kurdistan Hawler, Iraq

"I was impressed that it was done timely, and wherever the content was not clear for the reader, the paper was improved with better readability for the audience."

– Prof. James Chilembwe,
Mzuzu University, Malawi

Email: customerservice@econtentpro.com **www.igi-global.com/editorial-service-partners**

IGI Global
DISSEMINATOR OF KNOWLEDGE
www.igi-global.com

Celebrating Over 30 Years of Scholarly Knowledge Creation & Dissemination

InfoSci®-Books

A Database of Over 5,300+ Reference Books Containing Over 100,000+ Chapters Focusing on Emerging Research

GAIN ACCESS TO **THOUSANDS** OF REFERENCE BOOKS AT **A FRACTION** OF THEIR INDIVIDUAL LIST **PRICE**.

InfoSci®-Books Database

The **InfoSci®-Books** database is a collection of over 5,300+ IGI Global single and multi-volume reference books, handbooks of research, and encyclopedias, encompassing groundbreaking research from prominent experts worldwide that span over 350+ topics in 11 core subject areas including business, computer science, education, science and engineering, social sciences and more.

Open Access Fee Waiver (Offset Model) Initiative

For any library that invests in IGI Global's InfoSci-Journals and/or InfoSci-Books databases, IGI Global will match the library's investment with a fund of equal value to go toward **subsidizing the OA article processing charges (APCs) for their students, faculty, and staff** at that institution when their work is submitted and accepted under OA into an IGI Global journal.*

INFOSCI® PLATFORM FEATURES

- No DRM
- No Set-Up or Maintenance Fees
- A Guarantee of No More Than a 5% Annual Increase
- Full-Text HTML and PDF Viewing Options
- Downloadable MARC Records
- Unlimited Simultaneous Access
- COUNTER 5 Compliant Reports
- Formatted Citations With Ability to Export to RefWorks and EasyBib
- No Embargo of Content (Research is Available Months in Advance of the Print Release)

**The fund will be offered on an annual basis and expire at the end of the subscription period. The fund would renew as the subscription is renewed for each year thereafter. The open access fees will be waived after the student, faculty, or staff's paper has been vetted and accepted into an IGI Global journal and the fund can only be used toward publishing OA in an IGI Global journal. Libraries in developing countries will have the match on their investment doubled.*

To Learn More or To Purchase This Database:
www.igi-global.com/infosci-books
eresources@igi-global.com • Toll Free: 1-866-342-6657 ext. 100 • Phone: 717-533-8845 x100

IGI Global
DISSEMINATOR OF KNOWLEDGE
www.igi-global.com

IGI Global
DISSEMINATOR OF KNOWLEDGE
www.igi-global.com

Publisher of Peer-Reviewed, Timely, and Innovative Academic Research Since 1988

IGI Global's Transformative Open Access (OA) Model: How to Turn Your University Library's Database Acquisitions Into a Source of OA Funding

In response to the OA movement and well in advance of Plan S, IGI Global, early last year, unveiled their OA Fee Waiver (Offset Model) Initiative.

Under this initiative, librarians who invest in IGI Global's InfoSci-Books (5,300+ reference books) and/or InfoSci-Journals (185+ scholarly journals) databases will be able to subsidize their patron's OA article processing charges (APC) when their work is submitted and accepted (after the peer review process) into an IGI Global journal.*

How Does it Work?

1. When a library subscribes or perpetually purchases IGI Global's InfoSci-Databases including InfoSci-Books (5,300+ e-books), InfoSci-Journals (185+ e-journals), and/or their discipline/subject-focused subsets, IGI Global will match the library's investment with a fund of equal value to go toward subsidizing the OA article processing charges (APCs) for their patrons.

   Researchers: Be sure to recommend the InfoSci-Books and InfoSci-Journals to take advantage of this initiative.
2. When a student, faculty, or staff member submits a paper and it is accepted (following the peer review) into one of IGI Global's 185+ scholarly journals, the author will have the option to have their paper published under a traditional publishing model or as OA.
3. When the author chooses to have their paper published under OA, IGI Global will notify them of the OA Fee Waiver (Offset Model) Initiative. If the author decides they would like to take advantage of this initiative, IGI Global will deduct the US$ 1,500 APC from the created fund.
4. This fund will be offered on an annual basis and will renew as the subscription is renewed for each year thereafter. IGI Global will manage the fund and award the APC waivers unless the librarian has a preference as to how the funds should be managed.

Hear From the Experts on This Initiative:

"I'm very happy to have been able to make one of my recent research contributions, 'Visualizing the Social Media Conversations of a National Information Technology Professional Association' featured in the *International Journal of Human Capital and Information Technology Professionals*, freely available along with having access to the valuable resources found within IGI Global's InfoSci-Journals database."

– **Prof. Stuart Palmer**,
Deakin University, Australia

For More Information, Visit: www.igi-global.com/publish/contributor-resources/open-access or contact IGI Global's Database Team at eresources@igi-global.com.

Are You Ready to Publish Your Research?

IGI Global
DISSEMINATOR OF KNOWLEDGE

IGI Global offers book authorship and editorship opportunities across 11 subject areas, including business, computer science, education, science and engineering, social sciences, and more!

Benefits of Publishing with IGI Global:

- Free one-on-one editorial and promotional support.
- Expedited publishing timelines that can take your book from start to finish in less than one (1) year.
- Choose from a variety of formats including: Edited and Authored References, Handbooks of Research, Encyclopedias, and Research Insights.
- Utilize IGI Global's eEditorial Discovery® submission system in support of conducting the submission and blind review process.
- IGI Global maintains a strict adherence to ethical practices due in part to our full membership with the Committee on Publication Ethics (COPE).
- Indexing potential in prestigious indices such as Scopus®, Web of Science™, PsycINFO®, and ERIC – Education Resources Information Center.
- Ability to connect your ORCID iD to your IGI Global publications.
- Earn royalties on your publication as well as receive complimentary copies and exclusive discounts.

Get Started Today by Contacting the Acquisitions Department at:

acquisition@igi-global.com

www.igi-global.com/infosci-ondemand

InfoSci®-OnDemand

Continuously updated with new material on a weekly basis, InfoSci®-OnDemand offers the ability to search through thousands of quality full-text research papers. Users can narrow each search by identifying key topic areas of interest, then display a complete listing of relevant papers, and purchase materials specific to their research needs.

Comprehensive Service

- Over 125,000+ journal articles, book chapters, and case studies.
- All content is downloadable in PDF and HTML format and can be stored locally for future use.

No Subscription Fees

- One time fee of **$37.50** per PDF download.

Instant Access

- Receive a download link immediately after order completion!

"It really provides an excellent entry into the research literature of the field. It presents a manageable number of highly relevant sources on topics of interest to a wide range of researchers. The sources are scholarly, but also accessible to 'practitioners'."

- Lisa Stimatz, MLS, University of North Carolina at Chapel Hill, USA

"It is an excellent and well designed database which will facilitate research, publication, and teaching. It is a very useful tool to have."

- George Ditsa, PhD, University of Wollongong, Australia

"I have accessed the database and find it to be a valuable tool to the IT/IS community. I found valuable articles meeting my search criteria 95% of the time."

- Prof. Lynda Louis, Xavier University of Louisiana, USA

Recommended for use by researchers who wish to immediately download PDFs of individual chapters or articles.

www.igi-global.com/e-resources/infosci-ondemand

IGI Global
DISSEMINATOR OF KNOWLEDGE
www.igi-global.com

www.ingramcontent.com/pod-product-compliance
Lightning Source LLC
LaVergne TN
LVHW080617300926
849162LV00005B/1186